THE
HarperCollins
STUDY BIBLE

THE
HarperCollins
STUDY BIBLE

New Revised Standard Version

With the
APOCRYPHAL/DEUTEROCANONICAL BOOKS

General Editor
Wayne A. Meeks

Associate Editors
Jouette M. Bassler
Werner E. Lemke
Susan Niditch
Eileen M. Schuller

WITH THE SOCIETY OF
BIBLICAL LITERATURE

HarperCollins*Publishers*

CONTENTS

CONTENTS

NAMES AND ORDER OF
THE BOOKS OF THE OLD
AND NEW TESTAMENTS
WITH THE APOCRYPHAL/
DEUTEROCANONICAL BOOKS

The Old Testament with the
Apocryphal/Deuterocanonical Books

The Hebrew Scriptures

Genesis	3	Psalms	797
Exodus	77	Proverbs	938
Leviticus	151	Ecclesiastes	986
Numbers	198	Song of Solomon	1000
Deuteronomy	266	Isaiah	1011
Joshua	326	Jeremiah	1110
Judges	367	Lamentations	1208
Ruth	408	Ezekiel	1222
1 Samuel		Daniel	1302
(1 Kingdoms in Greek)	416	Hosea	1329
2 Samuel		Joel	1347
(2 Kingdoms in Greek)	466	Amos	1355
1 Kings		Obadiah	1370
(3 Kingdoms in Greek)	509	Jonah	1374
2 Kings		Micah	1379
(4 Kingdoms in Greek)	559	Nahum	1391
1 Chronicles		Habakkuk	1396
(1 Paralipomenon in Greek)	605	Zephaniah	1402
2 Chronicles		Haggai	1408
(2 Paralipomenon in Greek)	647	Zechariah	1412
Ezra	699	Malachi	1428
Nehemiah			
(2 Esdras in Greek)	717		
Esther	736		
Job	749		

The Apocryphal/Deuterocanonical Books

The Apocryphal/Deuterocanonical Books are listed here in four groupings, as follows:
(a) Books and Additions to Esther and Daniel that are in the Roman Catholic, Greek, and Slavonic Bibles

(b) Books in the Greek and Slavonic Bibles; not in the Roman Catholic Canon

(c) In the Slavonic Bible and in the Latin Vulgate Appendix

(d) In an Appendix to the Greek Bible

The New Testament

ALPHABETICAL LIST OF THE BOOKS OF THE NEW REVISED STANDARD VERSION

(Including the Apocryphal/ Deuterocanonical Books)

EDITORIAL BOARD

CONTRIBUTORS

Contributors have written the introductions and annotations to the books that follow their names.

James S. Ackerman, Th.D.
Professor of Religious Studies
Indiana University
Bloomington, Indiana
Jonah

Harold W. Attridge, Ph.D.
Dean of the College of Arts and Letters
University of Notre Dame
Notre Dame, Indiana
Hebrews

David E. Aune, Ph.D.
Professor of New Testament and Christian
   Origins
Loyola University of Chicago
Chicago, Illinois
Revelation

David L. Balch, Ph.D.
Professor of New Testament
Brite Divinity School
Texas Christian University
Fort Worth, Texas
1 Peter

Jouette M. Bassler, Ph.D.
Professor of New Testament
Perkins School of Theology
Southern Methodist University
Dallas, Texas
2 Thessalonians, 1, 2 Timothy, Titus

Richard J. Bauckham, Ph.D.
Professor of New Testament Studies
St Mary's College
University of St Andrews
St Andrews, Scotland
2 Peter, Jude

Adele Berlin, Ph.D.
Professor of Hebrew
University of Maryland
College Park, Maryland
Ruth

C. Clifton Black, Ph.D.
Associate Professor of New Testament
Perkins School of Theology
Southern Methodist University
Dallas, Texas
Mark

Robert G. Boling, Ph.D.
Professor of Old Testament
McCormick Theological Seminary
Chicago, Illinois
Joshua, Judges

Roger S. Boraas, Ph.D.
Professor of Religion
Upsala College
East Orange, New Jersey
Consultant for Maps

Claudia V. Camp, Ph.D.
Associate Professor of Religion
Texas Christian University
Fort Worth, Texas
Proverbs

Richard J. Clifford, Ph.D.
Professor of Old Testament
Weston School of Theology
Cambridge, Massachusetts
Letter of Jeremiah

David J. A. Clines, M.A.
Professor of Biblical Studies
University of Sheffield
Sheffield, England
Ezra, Nehemiah, 1 Esdras

John J. Collins, Ph.D.
Professor of Old Testament
The Divinity School
University of Chicago
Chicago, Illinois
3 Maccabees

Toni Craven, Ph.D.
Professor of Hebrew Bible
Brite Divinity School
Texas Christian University
Fort Worth, Texas
Judith

James L. Crenshaw, Ph.D.
The Robert L. Flowers Professor of Old
  Testament
The Divinity School
Duke University
Durham, North Carolina
Job

Dennis C. Duling, Ph.D.
Professor of Religious Studies
Canisius College
Buffalo, New York
Matthew

John T. Fitzgerald, Ph.D.
Associate Professor of New Testament
University of Miami
Coral Gables, Florida
2 Corinthians

Carole R. Fontaine, Ph.D.
Professor of Old Testament
Andover-Newton Theological School
Newton Centre, Massachusetts
Proverbs

Michael V. Fox, Ph.D.
Weinstein-Bascom Professor in Jewish
  Studies
University of Wisconsin
Madison, Wisconsin
Song of Solomon

Victor Paul Furnish, Ph.D.
University Distinguished Professor of New
  Testament
Perkins School of Theology
Southern Methodist University
Dallas, Texas
1 Corinthians

Beverly Roberts Gaventa, Ph.D.
Associate Professor of New Testament
Princeton Theological Seminary
Princeton, New Jersey
Acts

Edward L. Greenstein, Ph.D.
Professor of Bible
Jewish Theological Seminary of America
New York, New York
Exodus

Jo Ann Hackett, Ph.D.
Professor of Biblical Hebrew
Harvard University
Cambridge, Massachusetts
Numbers

Daniel J. Harrington, Ph.D.
Professor of New Testament
Weston School of Theology
Cambridge, Massachusetts
1, 2 Maccabees

Richard B. Hays, Ph.D.
Associate Professor of New Testament
The Divinity School
Duke University
Durham, North Carolina
Galatians

Richard A. Henshaw, Ph.D.
Professor of Old Testament Interpretation
Colgate Rochester Divinity School/Bexley
  Hall/Crozer Theological Seminary
Rochester, New York
Joel, Obadiah

Ronald F. Hock, Ph.D.
Associate Professor of Religion
University of Southern California
Los Angeles, California
Philippians, Philemon

W. Lee Humphreys, Ph.D.
Professor of Religious Studies
University of Tennessee
Knoxville, Tennessee
Esther, Esther with the Additions

Leander E. Keck, Ph.D.
Winkley Professor of Biblical Theology
The Divinity School
Yale University
New Haven, Connecticut
Romans

Philip J. King, S.T.D.
Professor of Biblical Studies
Boston College
Chestnut Hill, Massachusetts
Micah

Ralph W. Klein, Th.D.
Dean and Professor of Old Testament
Lutheran School of Theology at Chicago
Chicago, Illinois
1, 2 Chronicles

Edgar M. Krentz, Ph.D.
Professor of New Testament
Lutheran School of Theology at Chicago
Chicago, Illinois
1 Thessalonians

Sophie Laws, B.Litt., M.A. Oxon.
Professor of History and Religion
Regent's College
London, England
James

Werner E. Lemke, Th.D.
Professor of Old Testament Interpretation
Colgate Rochester Divinity School/Bexley
    Hall/Crozer Theological Seminary
Rochester, New York
Lamentations

S. Dean McBride, Jr., Ph.D.
Professor of Old Testament Interpretation
Union Theological Seminary in Virginia
Richmond, Virginia
Deuteronomy

P. Kyle McCarter, Jr., Ph.D.
William Foxwell Albright Professor of
    Biblical and Ancient Near Eastern
    Studies
Johns Hopkins University
Baltimore, Maryland
1, 2 Samuel

Burton Mack, Ph.D.
Professor of New Testament
School of Theology at Claremont
Claremont, California
Sirach

James Luther Mays, Ph.D.
Cyrus McCormick Professor Emeritus of
    Hebrew and the Old Testament
Union Theological Seminary in Virginia
Richmond, Virginia
Hosea

Jacob Milgrom, D.H.L.
Professor Emeritus of the Hebrew Bible
University of California at Berkeley
Berkeley, California
Leviticus

Patrick D. Miller, Ph.D.
Charles T. Haley Professor of Old
    Testament Theology
Princeton Theological Seminary
Princeton, New Jersey
Psalms

Pamela J. Milne, Ph.D.
Associate Professor of Religious Studies
University of Windsor
Windsor, Ontario, Canada
Daniel

Carol A. Newsom, Ph.D.
Associate Professor of Old Testament
Candler School of Theology
Emory University
Atlanta, Georgia
Baruch

George W. E. Nickelsburg, Th.D.
Professor of New Testament and Early
    Judaism
University of Iowa
Iowa City, Iowa
Tobit

Leo G. Perdue, Ph.D.
Dean and Professor of Hebrew Bible
Brite Divinity School
Texas Christian University
Fort Worth, Texas
Jeremiah

David L. Petersen, Ph.D.
Professor of Old Testament
Iliff School of Theology
Denver, Colorado
Ezekiel

David K Rensberger, Ph.D.
Associate Professor of New Testament
Interdenominational Theological Center
Atlanta, Georgia
John, 1, 2, 3 John

Kent Harold Richards, Ph.D.
Professor of Old Testament
Iliff School of Theology
Denver, Colorado
Nahum, Habakkuk, Zephaniah

J. J. M. Roberts, Ph.D.
William Henry Green Professor of Old
    Testament Literature
Princeton Theological Seminary
Princeton, New Jersey
Isaiah

Joel W. Rosenberg, Ph.D.
Associate Professor of Hebrew Literature
    and Judaic Studies
Tufts University
Medford, Massachusetts
Genesis

J. Paul Sampley, Ph.D.
Professor of New Testament
School of Theology
Boston University
Boston, Massachusetts
Ephesians, Colossians

James A. Sanders, Ph.D.
Professor of Biblical Studies
School of Theology at Claremont
Claremont, California
Prayer of Manasseh, Psalm 151

Michael E. Stone, Ph.D., D. Litt.
Professor of Armenian Studies
Hebrew University of Jerusalem
Jerusalem, Israel
2 Esdras

David L. Tiede, Ph.D.
President and Professor of New Testament
Luther Northwestern Theological
    Seminary
St. Paul, Minnesota
Luke

Thomas H. Tobin, Ph.D.
Associate Professor of Theology
Loyola University of Chicago
Chicago, Illinois
4 Maccabees

W. Sibley Towner, Ph.D.
The Reverend Archibald McFadyen
    Professor of Biblical Interpretation
Union Theological Seminary in Virginia
Richmond, Virginia
Haggai, Zechariah, Malachi

Gene M. Tucker, Ph.D.
Professor of Old Testament
Candler School of Theology
Emory University
Atlanta, Georgia
Amos

Raymond C. Van Leeuwen, Ph.D.
Professor of Old Testament
Calvin Theological Seminary
Grand Rapids, Michigan
Ecclesiastes

Lawrence Wills, Th.D.
Assistant Professor of New Testament
Harvard Divinity School
Harvard University
Cambridge, Massachusetts
*Prayer of Azariah and the Song of the Three
    Jews, Susanna, Bel and the Dragon*

Robert R. Wilson, Ph.D.
Professor of Old Testament and Hoober
    Professor of Religious Studies
Yale University
New Haven, Connecticut
1, 2 Kings

David Winston, Ph.D.
Professor of Hellenistic and Judaic Studies
Graduate Theological Union
Berkeley, California
Wisdom of Solomon

INTRODUCTION

TO THE

HARPER COLLINS STUDY BIBLE

By Wayne A. Meeks

THE BIBLE IS THE MOST FAMILIAR BOOK in the English-speaking world; certainly it is the one most often published and most widely owned. Yet many a serious reader has found it one of the strangest of books. This paradox arises from factors in the book's history as well as from dimensions of our own history that have shaped the expectations with which we begin to read.

Enabling the Reader to Read

The most elementary of the obstacles standing in the way of reading the Bible is that its component parts were originally written in languages most of us do not know. Reading must therefore begin with a translation. The New Revised Standard Version stands in a tradition, many centuries old, of translating the Bible so that ordinary people can understand it when it is read aloud in worship gatherings or when they study it for themselves. More immediately, the NRSV stands in a direct succession from the King James Version of 1611 (as Professor Metzger explains in the Translation Committee's preface, pp. xxv–xxx). The NRSV is one among a large number of recent translations of the whole or parts of the Bible that together give to the present generation of English readers an unprecedented variety of fresh renderings of the original languages. All these are informed by significant advances in historical, archaeological, and linguistic knowledge that have occurred in recent decades.

The NRSV is selected for this *HarperCollins Study Bible* for several reasons, of which two are most significant. First, the declared intention of the Translation Committee to produce a translation "as literal as possible" makes this version well adapted for *study*. For example, careful reading is enhanced when we can observe such things as the recurrence of certain key words; if these are rendered into our language with some consistency, the task is obviously easier. Second, the NRSV was designed to be as *inclusive* as possible, in two different senses. It includes the most complete range of biblical books representing the several differing canons of scripture (about which more will be said below) than any other English version. In addition, it avoids language that might inappropriately suggest limits of gender.

Yet even the most excellent translation from the Hebrew, Aramaic, and Greek texts cannot by itself completely remove the strangeness that many modern readers sense when they encounter the Bible. It is, after all, an ancient book. Indeed, it is a collection—no, several collections—of books that were formed and written in cultures distant from our own not only in time and space but also in character. Indeed, what is required of us as readers is rather to enter, through these texts, into another world of meaning. Only when we have sensed the peculiarity and integrity of that other world can we build a bridge of understanding between it and our own. The introductions and notes accompanying the text in the *HarperCollins Study Bible* are designed to provide readers with information that will make it easier to use this excellent translation for the deeper kind of translation readers must make for themselves: the actual encounter with the multiple worlds of meaning that these texts can reveal.

With the aim of removing as many obstacles as possible between readers and the text, the notes in this volume provide several kinds of information. First, they point to characteristics of the language that are significant for meaning. These include the biblical writers' choice of words, the formal patterns of speech, the styles and genres of ancient literature that appear in the texts, and the rhetorical strategies—familiar to ancient readers but foreign to us—adopted by the writers. Second, the notes contain facts about historical events alluded to in the texts or underlying their message. Many of these facts have come to light through modern archaeological discoveries and the analysis of ancient inscriptions and other material evidence. Comparisons and contrasts between the biblical writings and other writings from around the same time and from the same part of the world also help to place them in their historical context. Third, the notes call attention to echoes between different texts of scripture. Sometimes these are direct quotations or paraphrases of earlier texts by later ones. At other times, they represent parallel formulations of common traditions or retellings of familiar stories in new settings. Fourth, the notes sometimes illuminate ambiguities in the text, multiple possibilities that the original languages leave open but that cannot be directly expressed by a single English translation.

One Book or Many?

Anyone who looks carefully at the Bible will be struck by the immense variety of its contents. Here we have prose and poetry, expansive narratives and short stories, legal codes embedded in historical reports, hymns and prayers, quoted archival documents, quasi-mythic accounts of things that happened "in the beginning" or in God's court in heaven, collections of proverbs, maxims, aphorisms, and riddles, letters to various groups, and reports of mysterious revelations interpreted by heavenly figures. This variety accounts for some of the richness that generations of readers have found within its pages, but it also causes much of the puzzlement even the most devoted readers often feel. How did it come about that so many different kinds of writing have been brought together into one book?

This is a question that has preoccupied many modern scholars. They have sought to answer it by investigating the history of the Bible itself. The very word

"Bible" is derived from a plural Greek word, *ta biblia*, "the little scrolls." A Christian term, the latter refers to the separate rolls of leather or papyrus on which the sacred writings, like other literary works in antiquity, were ordinarily written. The physical limits of the roll meant that many rolls were required for the writings that had come to be held sacred in the Jewish and Christian communities. Sometimes a long document had to be divided into two scrolls, like the books of Samuel and Kings, or the Gospel of Luke and the Acts of the Apostles. As early as the second century, Christians began to use instead the relatively new form of the codex, very much like our modern books. This made it possible actually to put all the sacred writings into one large manuscript—but the name *ta biblia* somehow stuck.

The individual books that make up our Bible were written over a period of more than a thousand years. During that time the people of Israel underwent many changes, even deep transformations, in their national life and culture. Their patterns of government, their cultic and legal organization, and their relationships to neighboring peoples and to the great empires of the ancient Mesopotamian and Mediterranean regions all changed. Those changes go far to account for the variety we see in content, language, and style of the biblical books.

Critical Study of the Old Testament

Several major narrative complexes within the Bible extend across several books. These have been the focus of especially intense research in the attempt to understand how these books came to have the form in which we know them. The first of these complexes is the Pentateuch (so called from a Greek word meaning "Five Scrolls"): Genesis, Exodus, Leviticus, Numbers, and Deuteronomy. These five books constitute the Torah (Hebrew for "teaching") in the Hebrew scriptures. Some scholars have preferred to speak of a Tetrateuch ("Four Scrolls"), taking Deuteronomy to be the foundation and introduction for the second great narrative. That second narrative, comprising the books of Joshua, Judges, Samuel, and Kings, is called the "Deuteronomistic History" because its understanding of the Mosaic covenant and Israel's obligations under it are those expounded in Deuteronomy. The history of Israel's national life down to the Babylonian exile is explained and judged according to the degree to which each generation, particularly the monarchs of Israel and of the divided kingdoms of Israel and Judah, abided by the laws of Deuteronomy.

The third major composition presents the same history related in the Deuteronomistic account, though from a quite different point of view, and extends it to include the restoration of Israel as a subject people under the Persian Empire. This composition comprises the books of 1 and 2 Chronicles, Ezra, and Nehemiah. Its unknown author is often called "the Chronicler," though we cannot be certain that a single person was responsible for the composition.

In addition to the three major narrative complexes, some scholars have isolated smaller compositions, such as the cycle of Joseph stories (Gen 37–50) and the narrative of the succession to David's throne (2 Sam 9–1 Kings 2), that may

[margin annotations: Pentateuch or Law; Deuteronomistic History]

have existed on their own before being woven into the larger narratives.

The history of the biblical writings is further complicated by the fact that some of these books speak of still earlier times, before any of them were written. What were the sources for the pictures of the ancient days that these writers passed on? Some of the writings refer explicitly to other books or archives; others show less direct evidence of predecessors who told or sang the stories and codes and prayers that are now included in the larger literary frameworks.

In the eighteenth and nineteenth centuries, scholars began by trying to detect in the existing narratives differences in style, language, or ideas that might indicate "seams" in the text, where older documents had been inserted or where two older versions of one story or two different sets of similar rules had been joined together. The most famous and controversial of the hypotheses that emerged was a reconstruction of four extended sources that, its advocates proposed, had been brought together over a period of centuries and through several distinct stages of editing or "redaction" to produce the Pentateuch (or, in other versions of the theory, the Tetrateuch, Genesis–Numbers, or the Hexateuch, Genesis–Joshua). Beginning with the observations that some passages used almost exclusively the name represented by the Hebrew letters *YHWH* to speak of God, while others used mostly a common Semitic word for a divine being, but in its plural form, *'Elohim*, these scholars guessed that these passages had originally belonged to separate documents. These hypothetical documents, which also differed in other characteristics of both style and content, were accordingly labeled "J" for "Yahwist" (because *j* in German and neo-Latin is pronounced like the Hebrew *y*) and "E" for "Elohist." A later source, called "D" by the scholars, was identified with an early version of the book of Deuteronomy. The fourth and latest document, thought to serve as the framework for the final stage of editing the whole Pentateuch, was intensely concerned with cultic matters, especially rules for priests and the temple, so it was called "P" for "priestly."

This "Documentary Hypothesis," first associated especially with the name of the German Protestant scholar Julius Wellhausen, came to dominate much of Old Testament scholarship in Europe, Britain, and America in the early twentieth century. In some circles great ingenuity was exercised in trying to assign each verse, or even parts of verses, to one or another of the hypothetical sources or to the "redactors" who put them together. The very complexity of the results aroused skepticism in other quarters, and many scholars came to feel that the documentary analysts were not taking sufficient account of two other factors affecting the formation of the biblical books. The first was the importance of oral transmission and memory in ancient societies. The other was the stylistic conventions and inventions of ancient writers, which were in many ways quite different from the expectations of modern print-based intellectual culture.

The response to the first of these concerns was the attempt to investigate characteristics of oral folklore that might be comparable to the lore of ancient Israel lying behind the written documents we possess. By studying the particular patterns of speech often repeated in various texts and by comparing these with similar patterns found in neighboring cultures, "form critics" undertook to discover the typical settings in the life of the community in which each "form" or pattern was characteristically used. By further analyzing variations in that form in other texts, they tried further to reconstruct a "history of forms" or "history of traditions." For example, one might seek to show how a maxim or a style of address first used in village courts under local elders could later have affected central legal codes and, again, how it might have become a metaphor in prophetic speech to describe God's "case" against the whole people.

Some of the "form critics" were satisfied to describe small, individual units of tradition they thought were eventually embedded in the literary compositions of the Bible. Others, however, were interested in the process of oral composition as seen, for example, in the sagas of the Old Norse and Icelandic peoples or in the lengthy tales sung by skilled reciters in some parts of the modern Balkans and Africa. For some, it seemed plausible that the supposed "documents" of the Pentateuch had been rather the orally transmitted traditions of different groups within the people Israel. There also seemed no good reason to suppose that the oral culture of such groups would have disappeared once their traditions were put into writing. Oral recitation would have continued to affect the way writers remembered and copied documents.

Furthermore, many readers felt that the attempts to distinguish separate sources and the early, analytic kind of form criticism tended to dissolve the larger units of the text into unrelated fragments. They sensed that these results obscured the unique literary qualities of the final compositions, for some of these qualities are produced by the interplay between just those "doublets" and dissonant elements that had set the critics looking for earlier sources or embedded forms. Both within the guild of biblical scholars and from literary critics outside it, there has come in recent decades a new attention to the rhetorical and literary qualities of the biblical books and larger compositions as we have received them.

Critical Study of the New Testament

The New Testament contains no narrative of the length and scope of those of the Old Testament, but the four Gospels and the Acts of the Apostles present problems that are in some ways analogous to the OT compositions. The methods by which scholars have tried to solve them have been, in part, similar. Scholars of the nineteenth century attempted to solve the "synoptic problem"—why Matthew, Mark, and Luke are in some places similar to the point of identical wording, while in other respects they differ substantially—by discovering what sources each Gospel writer used. The hypothesis that emerged as the dominant explanation was called the "Two-Source Hypothesis." According to it, Matthew and Luke independently used the earlier Gospel of Mark, keeping almost entirely to its narrative outline but adjusting its style to their own somewhat more literary tastes and adding to it large blocks of material they had from other sources.

Among these other sources was one that they had in common (the second of the "two sources"), from which they drew the sayings of Jesus that were not found in Mark. Conventionally, this hypothetical second source has been called "Q," presumably from the German word *Quelle*, "source."

The Two-Source Hypothesis is still taken as the working hypothesis by most critical scholars of the NT, though everyone acknowledges that it does not explain all the peculiarities of the relationships among the first three Gospels. Attempts to revive earlier hypotheses, such as the proposal that Matthew wrote first, Luke adapted Matthew's Gospel, and Mark excerpted rather idiosyncratically from both, have not won wide acceptance. Also unconvincing have been the many attempts to fine-tune the Two-Source Hypothesis by adding yet other hypothetical sources. The remaining problems with the hypothesis are better solved by considering the impact of oral tradition, on the one hand, and the skill and freedom of the Gospels' writers, on the other.

Form criticism, too, was employed by students of the NT in attempts to reconstruct the process by which the stories about Jesus and the sayings attributed to him were shaped, transmitted, and modified by their uses in the life of the early Christian communities. Applied to the Letters of the NT, similar techniques isolated some passages that seemed to be excerpts from liturgical poetry or from simple creeds or confessional formulas.

In NT scholarship, too, there have been reactions against what many have come to see as an overemphasis on the hypothetical prehistory of writings to the neglect of the rhetorical and literary qualities of the books as we have them. Many recent commentators have emphasized the role of the Gospel writers as authors, fully in command of whatever sources they used and creating from them coherent literary wholes. Others have warned against forcing these ancient writings into modern categories by imposing on them literary theories derived from the study of the modern novel or modern poetry. At the same time, extensive study of ancient genres of writing and patterns of rhetoric have provided sturdier models with which to compare the biblical documents.

Biblical Scholarship Today

The issues mentioned in this brief survey are only examples of the issues raised in the several phases of modern critical study of the Bible. Historical and literary studies have affected our understanding of the other parts of the Bible as well, raising analogous problems. Some of the issues are discussed in the introductions and notes to individual books.

The present moment in scholarly investigation of the Bible is a time when many different methods are in use. That diversity of method is reflected to some extent in the notes in this study Bible. The scholar chosen to annotate each book is an expert on that particular document and may emphasize the results of one or another method that seems most useful in understanding that book. Characteristic of the best scholarship is a healthy degree of self-criticism and skepticism about any rigid hypotheses. All of our annotators, even when they differ from one another on theoretical matters, have in common a primary focus on the text. Their notes are designed to help readers make sense of that text, in its parts and as a whole.

Some questions raised by material in the Bible, however, cannot be answered on the basis of our present knowledge. For example, despite the impressive results and continuing discoveries of archaeology in the Middle East, some places mentioned in the Bible cannot be located with certainty on a modern map. Some discrepancies in chronology cannot be resolved. In a few instances where experts differ on such matters, we have allowed inconsistencies between one scholar's notes and another's to stand, as a reminder that our knowledge of the ancient world remains imperfect.

Bibles and Their Communities

Despite the Bible's diversity, most readers do feel that *as a whole* it somehow makes sense. There is an odd concentricity about its diverse stories and its various genres. The tensions within it are held within some common framework. In some more than trivial way, "the Bible" is one book.

Yet our perception of the Bible's unity may obscure a complicated reality. If one asks a reader exactly what gives the Bible its oneness and wholeness, the answer will depend in part on the religious community to which that reader belongs. Our notes try to come to terms with the fact that we have, so to speak, at least two Bibles between the same covers: a Jewish Bible and a Christian Bible. This is not a superficial difference. It is not merely that the Christian Bible adds a New Testament and therefore calls the Jewish scriptures "the Old Testament." The Jewish scriptures are not the same as the Old Testament. The order is different (see the table on p. xxxvii). The text has been transmitted by different means and with different approaches to establishing authoritative readings. For example, the Bible of most of the early Christians was the Septuagint. Even the list of books included has differed.

More important than these external differences, however, is the different sense of the whole that is engendered when, on the one hand, we read the Torah, the Prophets, and the Writings of the Hebrew Bible as complete in themselves, the foundation of the life of Israel through the ages, or when, on the other hand, we read them as open toward a future that was "fulfilled" in the events of the NT and still awaits an "end." In the latter case, the Christian Bible presents us with a single narrative line that unites all the diverse episodes and different kinds of writing into a sweeping epic, almost a giant novel claiming to embrace the entire story of humanity. It begins "in the beginning," treats of God's electing a special people, recounts their disobedience, punishment, and hope, declares the story's climax in the appearance of God's Son, and looks to a final "coming."

When read independently of the Christian additions and Christian habits of reading, the unity of the Hebrew scriptures looks quite different. They do not have a single plot or a single center, but many. The many voices that speak are not united in a single hope, nor do they point to a single future. Their unity lies rather in a continuous counterpoint. The multiple plots of the narratives move forward with odd echoes of the past, repetitions and rehearsals, reminders and foreshadowings. The wisdom gathered and cultivated by professional elites and servants of kings rubs against the sensibilities of peasants. Codes from the time when "there was no king in Israel" stand beside laws of monarchy and laws of a temple state. Prophets name the injustice done to the common poor by petty local tyrants and perceive in the march of great empires the chastening hand of God. The people Israel sings in the manifold occasions of its national and cultic life, and it sings the complaints, fears, and hopes of its individuals. All this variety, and more, is woven together by complex threads, but its rhythms are quite different from the dominant pulse of the Christian Bible.

The overall arrangement of the NRSV is that of Protestant Bibles, because that is the arrangement that has dominated the public use of the Bible in English-speaking countries since the seventeenth century. However, the NRSV has included the books that are variously called apocryphal or deuterocanonical and are found in the Bible used by one or more of the Roman Catholic, Greek, and Slavonic churches. In this respect the NRSV is the most inclusive English version now commonly available. (For the several canons, see the tables on pp. xxxvii–xl, as well as the introductions to the books of the Apocrypha.) Readers thus have in hand not merely *two* Bibles, the Jewish and the Christian, but *several* Bibles that have spoken and continue to speak to historically diverse Jewish and Christian communities.

The Society of Biblical Literature

The editors and annotators who have worked together to produce the *Harper Collins Study Bible* themselves exemplify the diversity of confessional traditions for which the Bible is foundational. What unites them, however, is the tradition of historical, critical, and open scholarship that has been fostered for more than a century by the Society of Biblical Literature, the sponsor of the present project.

The Society of Biblical Literature and Exegesis was founded in 1880 and is one of the oldest learned societies in the United States. Its purpose is to stimulate the critical investigation of classical biblical literatures, together with other related literatures, by the exchange of scholarly research both in published form and in public forum. It has at present over 5,500 members from more than 80 countries.

The *HarperCollins Study Bible* is one of a series of publishing projects undertaken by the SBL in conjunction with HarperCollins. Others include *Harper's Bible Dictionary*, *Harper's Bible Commentary*, and *Harper's Bible Pronunciation Guide*. Users of the *HarperCollins Study Bible* who wish to pursue their studies further will find more detailed information on many biblical topics in the articles of those companion volumes. All of these joint projects represent the commitment of the Society to share the results of scholarly research with a wide public who are interested in the Bible and the religious traditions associated with it.

TO THE READER

This preface is addressed to you by the Committee of translators, who wish to explain, as briefly as possible, the origin and character of our work. The publication of our revision is yet another step in the long, continual process of making the Bible available in the form of the English language that is most widely current in our day. To summarize in a single sentence: the New Revised Standard Version of the Bible is an authorized revision of the Revised Standard Version, published in 1952, which was a revision of the American Standard Version, published in 1901, which, in turn, embodied earlier revisions of the King James Version, published in 1611.

In the course of time, the King James Version came to be regarded as "the Authorized Version." With good reason it has been termed "the noblest monument of English prose," and it has entered, as no other book has, into the making of the personal character and the public institutions of the English-speaking peoples. We owe to it an incalculable debt.

Yet the King James Version has serious defects. By the middle of the nineteenth century, the development of biblical studies and the discovery of many biblical manuscripts more ancient than those on which the King James Version was based made it apparent that these defects were so many as to call for revision. The task was begun, by authority of the Church of England, in 1870. The (British) Revised Version of the Bible was published in 1881–1885; and the American Standard Version, its variant embodying the preferences of the American scholars associated with the work, was published, as was mentioned above, in 1901. In 1928 the copyright of the latter was acquired by the International Council of Religious Education and thus passed into the ownership of the churches of the United States and Canada that were associated in this Council through their boards of education and publication.

The Council appointed a committee of scholars to have charge of the text of the American Standard Version and to undertake inquiry concerning the need for further revision. After studying the questions whether or not revision should be undertaken, and if so, what its nature and extent should be, in 1937 the Council authorized a revision. The scholars who served as members of the Committee worked in two sections, one dealing with the Old Testament and one with the New Testament. In 1946 the Revised Standard Version of the New Testament was published. The publication of the Revised Standard Version of the Bible, containing the Old and New Testaments, took place on September 30, 1952. A translation of the Apocryphal/Deuterocanonical Books of the Old Testament followed in 1957. In 1977 this collection was issued in an expanded edition, containing three additional texts received by Eastern Orthodox communions (3 and 4 Maccabees and Psalm 151). Thereafter the Revised Standard Version gained the distinction of being officially authorized for use by all major Christian churches: Protestant, Anglican, Roman Catholic, and Eastern Orthodox.

The Revised Standard Version Bible Committee is a continuing body, comprising about thirty members, both men and women. Ecumenical in representation, it includes scholars affiliated with various Protestant denominations, as well as several Roman Catholic members, an Eastern Orthodox member, and a Jewish member who serves in the Old Testament section. For a period of time the Committee included several members from Canada and from England.

Because no translation of the Bible is perfect or is acceptable to all groups of readers, and because discoveries of older manuscripts and further investigation of linguistic features of the text continue to become available, renderings of the Bible have proliferated. During the years following the publication of the Revised Standard Version, twenty-six other English translations and revisions of the Bible were produced by committees and by individual scholars—not to mention twenty-five other translations and revisions of the New Testament alone. One of the latter was the second edition of the rsv New Testament, issued in 1971, twenty-five years after its initial publication.

Following the publication of the rsv Old Testament in 1952, significant advances were made in the discovery and interpretation of documents in Semitic languages related to Hebrew. In addition to the information that had become available in the late 1940s from the Dead Sea texts of Isaiah and Habakkuk, subsequent acquisitions from the same area brought to light many other early copies of all the books of the Hebrew Scriptures (except Esther), though most of these copies are fragmentary. During the same period early Greek manuscript copies of books of the New Testament also became available.

In order to take these discoveries into account, along with recent studies of documents in Semitic languages related to Hebrew, in 1974 the Policies Committee of the Revised Standard Version, which is a standing committee of the National Council of the Churches of Christ in the U.S.A., authorized the preparation of a revision of the entire rsv Bible.

For the Old Testament the Committee has made use of the *Biblia Hebraica Stuttgartensia* (1977; ed. sec. emendata, 1983). This is an edition of the Hebrew and Aramaic text as current early in the Christian era and fixed by Jewish scholars (the "Masoretes") of the sixth to the ninth centuries. The vowel signs, which were added by the Masoretes, are accepted in the main, but where a more probable and convincing reading can be obtained by assuming different vowels, this has been done. No notes are given in such cases, because the vowel points are less ancient and reliable than the consonants. When an alternative reading given by the Masoretes is translated in a footnote, this is identified by the words "Another reading is."

Departures from the consonantal text of the best manuscripts have been made only where it seems clear that errors in copying had been made before the text was standardized. Most of the corrections adopted are based on the ancient versions (translations into Greek, Aramaic, Syriac, and Latin), which were made prior to the time of the work of the Masoretes and which therefore may reflect earlier forms of the Hebrew text. In such instances a footnote specifies the version or versions from which the correction has been derived and also gives a translation of the Masoretic Text. Where

it was deemed appropriate to do so, information is supplied in footnotes from sub-
sidiary Jewish traditions concerning other textual readings (the *Tiqqune Sopherim*,
"emendations of the scribes"). These are identified in the footnotes as "Ancient Heb
tradition."

Occasionally it is evident that the text has suffered in transmission and that none of
the versions provides a satisfactory restoration. Here we can only follow the best judgment of competent scholars as to the most probable reconstruction of the original text.
Such reconstructions are indicated in footnotes by the abbreviation Cn ("Correction"),
and a translation of the Masoretic Text is added.

For the Apocryphal/Deuterocanonical Books of the Old Testament the Committee
has made use of a number of texts. For most of these books the basic Greek text from
which the present translation was made is the edition of the Septuagint prepared by
Alfred Rahlfs and published by the Württemberg Bible Society (Stuttgart, 1935). For
several of the books the more recently published individual volumes of the Göttingen
Septuagint project were utilized. For the book of Tobit it was decided to follow the
form of the Greek text found in codex Sinaiticus (supported as it is by evidence from
Qumran); where this text is defective, it was supplemented and corrected by other
Greek manuscripts. For the three Additions to Daniel (namely, Susanna, the Prayer of
Azariah and the Song of the Three Jews, and Bel and the Dragon) the Committee
continued to use the Greek version attributed to Theodotion (the so-called
"Theodotion-Daniel"). In translating Ecclesiasticus (Sirach), while constant reference
was made to the Hebrew fragments of a large portion of this book (those discovered
at Qumran and Masada as well as those recovered from the Cairo Geniza), the Committee generally followed the Greek text (including verse numbers) published by Joseph Ziegler in the Göttingen Septuagint (1965). But in many places the Committee
has translated the Hebrew text when this provides a reading that is clearly superior to
the Greek; the Syriac and Latin versions were also consulted throughout and occasionally adopted. The basic text adopted in rendering 2 Esdras is the Latin version given
in *Biblia Sacra*, edited by Robert Weber (Stuttgart, 1971). This was supplemented by
consulting the Latin text as edited by R. L. Bensly (1895) and by Bruno Violet (1910),
as well as by taking into account the several Oriental versions of 2 Esdras, namely, the
Syriac, Ethiopic, Arabic (two forms, referred to as Arabic 1 and Arabic 2), Armenian,
and Georgian versions. Finally, since the Additions to the Book of Esther are disjointed
and quite unintelligible as they stand in most editions of the Apocrypha, we have
provided them with their original context by translating the whole of the Greek version of Esther from Robert Hanhart's Göttingen edition (1983).

For the New Testament the Committee has based its work on the most recent edition
of *The Greek New Testament*, prepared by an interconfessional and international committee and published by the United Bible Societies (1966; 3d ed. corrected, 1983;
information concerning changes to be introduced into the critical apparatus of the
forthcoming 4th edition was available to the Committee). As in that edition, double
brackets are used to enclose a few passages that are generally regarded to be later
additions to the text, but that we have retained because of their evident antiquity and

their importance in the textual tradition. Only in very rare instances have we replaced the text or the punctuation of the Bible Societies' edition by an alternative that seemed to us to be superior. Here and there in the footnotes the phrase, "Other ancient authorities read," identifies alternative readings preserved by Greek manuscripts and early versions. In both Testaments, alternative renderings of the text are indicated by the word "Or."

As for the style of English adopted for the present revision, among the mandates given to the Committee in 1980 by the Division of Education and Ministry of the National Council of Churches of Christ (which now holds the copyright of the RSV Bible) was the directive to continue in the tradition of the King James Bible, but to introduce such changes as are warranted on the basis of accuracy, clarity, euphony, and current English usage. Within the constraints set by the original texts and by the mandates of the Division, the Committee has followed the maxim, "As literal as possible, as free as necessary." As a consequence, the New Revised Standard Version (NRSV) remains essentially a literal translation. Paraphrastic renderings have been adopted only sparingly, and then chiefly to compensate for a deficiency in the English language—the lack of a common-gender third-person singular pronoun.

During the almost half a century since the publication of the RSV, many in the churches have become sensitive to the danger of linguistic sexism arising from the inherent bias of the English language toward the masculine gender, a bias that in the case of the Bible has often restricted or obscured the meaning of the original text. The mandates from the Division specified that, in references to men and women, masculine-oriented language should be eliminated as far as this can be done without altering passages that reflect the historical situation of ancient patriarchal culture. As can be appreciated, more than once the Committee found that the several mandates stood in tension and even in conflict. The various concerns had to be balanced case by case in order to provide a faithful and acceptable rendering without using contrived English. Only very occasionally has the pronoun "he" or "him" been retained in passages where the reference may have been to a woman as well as to a man, for example, in several legal texts in Leviticus and Deuteronomy. In such instances of formal, legal language, the options of either putting the passage in the plural or of introducing additional nouns to avoid masculine pronouns in English seemed to the Committee to obscure the historic structure and literary character of the original. In the vast majority of cases, however, inclusiveness has been attained by simple rephrasing or by introducing plural forms when this does not distort the meaning of the passage. Of course, in narrative and in parable no attempt was made to generalize the sex of individual persons.

Another aspect of style will be detected by readers who compare the more stately English rendering of the Old Testament with the less formal rendering adopted for the New Testament. For example, the traditional distinction between *shall* and *will* in English has been retained in the Old Testament as appropriate in rendering a document that embodies what may be termed the classic form of Hebrew, while in the New Testament the abandonment of such distinctions in the usage of the future tense in English reflects the more colloquial nature of the koine Greek used by most New Testament authors except when they are quoting the Old Testament.

Careful readers will notice that here and there in the Old Testament the word LORD (or in certain cases GOD) is printed in capital letters. This represents the traditional manner in English versions of rendering the Divine Name, the "Tetragrammaton" (see the text notes on Exodus 3.14, 15), following the precedent of the ancient Greek and Latin translators and the long-established practice in the reading of the Hebrew Scriptures in the synagogue. While it is almost if not quite certain that the Name was originally pronounced "Yahweh," this pronunciation was not indicated when the Masoretes added vowel sounds to the consonantal Hebrew text. To the four consonants YHWH of the Name, which had come to be regarded as too sacred to be pronounced, they attached vowel signs indicating that in its place should be read the Hebrew word *Adonai* meaning "Lord" (or *Elohim* meaning "God"). Ancient Greek translators employed the word *Kyrios* ("Lord") for the Name. The Vulgate likewise used the Latin word *Dominus* ("Lord"). The form "Jehovah" is of late medieval origin; it is a combination of the consonants of the Divine Name and the vowels attached to it by the Masoretes but belonging to an entirely different word. Although the American Standard Version (1901) had used "Jehovah" to render the Tetragrammaton (the sound of Y being represented by J and the sound of W by V, as in Latin), for two reasons the Committees that produced the RSV and the NRSV returned to the more familiar usage of the King James Version. (1) The word "Jehovah" does not accurately represent any form of the Name ever used in Hebrew. (2) The use of any proper name for the one and only God, as though there were other gods from whom the true God had to be distinguished, began to be discontinued in Judaism before the Christian era and is inappropriate for the universal faith of the Christian Church.

It will be seen that in the Psalms and in other prayers addressed to God the archaic second-person singular pronouns (*thee, thou, thine*) and verb forms (*art, hast, hadst*) are no longer used. Although some readers may regret this change, it should be pointed out that in the original languages neither the Old Testament nor the New makes any linguistic distinction between addressing a human being and addressing the Deity. Furthermore, in the tradition of the King James Version one will not expect to find the use of capital letters for pronouns that refer to the Deity — such capitalization is an unnecessary innovation that has only recently been introduced into a few English translations of the Bible. Finally, we have left to the discretion of the licensed publishers such matters as section headings, cross-references, and clues to the pronunciation of proper names.

This new version seeks to preserve all that is best in the English Bible as it has been known and used through the years. It is intended for use in public reading and congregational worship, as well as in private study, instruction, and meditation. We have resisted the temptation to introduce terms and phrases that merely reflect current moods, and have tried to put the message of the Scriptures in simple, enduring words and expressions that are worthy to stand in the great tradition of the King James Bible and its predecessors.

In traditional Judaism and Christianity, the Bible has been more than a historical document to be preserved or a classic of literature to be cherished and admired; it is recognized as the unique record of God's dealings with people over the ages. The Old Testament sets forth the call of a special people to enter into covenant relation with the God of justice and steadfast love and to bring God's law to the nations. The New Testament records the life and work of Jesus Christ, the one in whom "the Word became flesh," as well as describes the rise and spread of the early Christian Church. The Bible carries its full message, not to those who regard it simply as a noble literary heritage of the past or who wish to use it to enhance political purposes and advance otherwise desirable goals, but to all persons and communities who read it so that they may discern and understand what God is saying to them. That message must not be disguised in phrases that are no longer clear, or hidden under words that have changed or lost their meaning; it must be presented in language that is direct and plain and meaningful to people today. It is the hope and prayer of the translators that this version of the Bible may continue to hold a large place in congregational life and to speak to all readers, young and old alike, helping them to understand and believe and respond to its message.

For the Committee,

BRUCE M. METZGER

ABBREVIATIONS

The following abbreviations are used for the books of the Bible:

Old Testament

Gen	Genesis	2 Chr	2 Chronicles	Dan	Daniel
Ex	Exodus	Ezra	Ezra	Hos	Hosea
Lev	Leviticus	Neh	Nehemiah	Joel	Joel
Num	Numbers	Esth	Esther	Am	Amos
Deut	Deuteronomy	Job	Job	Ob	Obadiah
Josh	Joshua	Ps	Psalms	Jon	Jonah
Judg	Judges	Prov	Proverbs	Mic	Micah
Ruth	Ruth	Eccl	Ecclesiastes	Nah	Nahum
1 Sam	1 Samuel	Song	Song of Solomon	Hab	Habakkuk
2 Sam	2 Samuel	Isa	Isaiah	Zeph	Zephaniah
1 Kings	1 Kings	Jer	Jeremiah	Hag	Haggai
2 Kings	2 Kings	Lam	Lamentations	Zech	Zechariah
1 Chr	1 Chronicles	Ezek	Ezekiel	Mal	Malachi

Apocryphal/Deuterocanonical Books

Tob	Tobit	Pr Azar	Prayer of Azariah and
Jdt	Judith		the Song of the Three Jews
Add Esth	Additions to Esther	Sus	Susanna
Wis	Wisdom	Bel	Bel and the Dragon
Sir	Sirach (Ecclesiasticus)	1 Macc	1 Maccabees
Bar	Baruch	2 Macc	2 Maccabees
1 Esd	1 Esdras	3 Macc	3 Maccabees
2 Esd	2 Esdras	4 Macc	4 Maccabees
Let Jer	Letter of Jeremiah	Pr Man	Prayer of Manasseh

New Testament

Mt	Matthew	Eph	Ephesians	Heb	Hebrews
Mk	Mark	Phil	Philippians	Jas	James
Lk	Luke	Col	Colossians	1 Pet	1 Peter
Jn	John	1 Thess	1 Thessalonians	2 Pet	2 Peter
Acts	Acts of the Apostles	2 Thess	2 Thessalonians	1 Jn	1 John
Rom	Romans	1 Tim	1 Timothy	2 Jn	2 John
1 Cor	1 Corinthians	2 Tim	2 Timothy	3 Jn	3 John
2 Cor	2 Corinthians	Titus	Titus	Jude	Jude
Gal	Galatians	Philem	Philemon	Rev	Revelation

In the text notes to the books of the Old Testament the following abbreviations are used:

Ant.	Josephus, *Antiquities of the Jews*
Aram	Aramaic
Ch, chs	Chapter, chapters
Cn	Correction; made where the text has suffered in transmission and the versions provide no satisfactory restoration but where the Standard Bible Committee agrees with the judgment of competent scholars as to the most probable reconstruction of the original text.
Gk	Septuagint, Greek version of the Old Testament
Heb	Hebrew of the consonantal Masoretic Text of the Old Testament
Josephus	Flavius Josephus (Jewish historian, about 37 to about 95 C.E.)
Macc.	The book(s) of the Maccabees
Ms(s)	Manuscript(s)
MT	The Hebrew of the pointed Masoretic Text of the Old Testament
OL	Old Latin
Q Ms(s)	Manuscript(s) found at Qumran by the Dead Sea
Sam	Samaritan Hebrew text of the Old Testament
Syr	Syriac Version of the Old Testament
Syr H	Syriac Version of Origen's Hexapla
Tg	Targum
Vg	Vulgate, Latin Version of the Old Testament

Abbreviations used in the study notes:

ch(s).	chapter(s)
v(v).	verse(s)
OT	Old Testament
NT	New Testament
B.C.E.	Before the Common Era
C.E.	Common Era

LIST OF ILLUSTRATIONS, MAPS, AND TABLES

COLOR MAPS SECTION AT THE END OF THIS VOLUME

NAMES A
BOOKS (
IN SEVER

Je

Jewish Bibles include the books of
editions present the twenty-four boo
the following order:

TORAH	PROPH
Genesis	Joshua
Exodus	Judges
Leviticus	Samue
Numbers	Kings
Deuteronomy	Isaiah
	Jerem
	Ezeki(
	The

eas in New Testament Tir

: the Time of the New

dan

h can be known—but from their assemblage in a unified
tes that follow presuppose most of the customary source
practical purposes, as preliterary traditions.

sense of the Genesis traditions reveals subtle design in the
ok's stories and cycles. The most common arrangement of
in complex symmetries, revealing parallel relationships be-
motifs. The Garden story, for example (2.4–3.24), manifests
the main part of which is shown in the accompanying table,
the Garden Story." It begins with a headnote on the gener-
:s in the eating of the fruit (3.6), and ends with the birth of
ine generation (4.1). Within this larger symmetry is a smaller
able, "A Subsymmetry in the Garden Story," a postmortem
n event (3.11–19a). Through these symmetries, the story's

ETRY OF THE GARDEN STORY (GENESIS 2.4–4.1)

: "These are the generations . . ." (2.4)
economy: ". . . no one to till the ground" (2.5–6)
an beings given life, installed in Garden (2.7–17)
n prefers human companionship over beasts (2.18–22)
lan calls his companion "Woman" (2.23)
Etiological summary: "Therefore a man leaves . . ." (2.24)
G   Human couple "naked and . . . not ashamed" (2.25)
H   Serpent promises "eyes will be opened" (3.1–5)
I   Transgression (3.6)
H' The couple's "eyes are opened" (3.7a)
G' They experience shame (3.7b–10)
Etiological summary: "For . . . you are dust . . ." (3.19b)
Man calls his companion "Eve" ("Life-bearer") (3.20)
an and woman wear skins of beasts (3.21)
hans expelled from Garden, denied immortality (3.22–24)
economy begins (implied; see subsymmetry and 3.23b)
a child completes one generation (4.1)

METRY IN THE GARDEN STORY (GENESIS 3.11–19A)

iod questions man; man points to woman (3.11–12)
God questions woman; woman points to serpent (3.13)
Z   [Serpent is silent]
Z' God passes judgment on serpent (3.14–15)
God passes judgment on woman (3.16)
God passes judgment on man (3.17–19a)

underlying thematic contrasts (Garden/field, immortality/mortality, nakedness/ clothing, nature/culture, innocence/knowledge, etc.) are deepened to comment upon one another—and the entire complex causal scheme is centered on the fateful human choice made in Gen 3.6.

A similar symmetrical pattern can be shown to operate in story cycles. The Abraham cycle, for example, begins and ends with a genealogical framework (11.10–32; 25.1–18) and culminates in the story of the expulsion and rescue of Hagar (16.1–16; see the table, "The Abraham Cycle," at Gen 11). Two episodes lie largely outside this scheme: the second expulsion of Hagar, with the endangering and rescue of Ishmael (21.8–21), and the endangering and rescue of Isaac (22.1–19). But both episodes are virtually identical in structure to the one that stands at the center (X) of the symmetry, and both deepen the cycle's main preoccupation: the question of a child to succeed Abraham and the consequent rivalry between Sarah and Hagar. Thus, even the departures from symmetry supply a dynamic development to the overall framework, and so participate in it.

In short, virtually no detail of Genesis is casual or arbitrary; every variant tradition is permitted its unique voice and function amid the whole. The book's narratives and movements are bound by a systematic use of key words—where helpful the notes highlight the Hebrew wordplay punctuating each story—and the overall history is presented through the experience of paradigmatic households. Domestic relations—spouse and spouse, parent and child, sibling and sibling, householder and servant—form the core of the book's preoccupations, and these are carefully framed by a history of journeys and settlements, conflicts and treaties, and human and divine encounters. All the relevant themes and polarities of Israel's later history are present here—Genesis is the Hebrew Bible in miniature.   *Joel W. Rosenberg*

Six Days of Creation and the Sabbath

1 In the beginning when God created[a] the heavens and the earth,
[2] the earth was a formless void and darkness covered the face of the deep, while a
wind from God[b] swept over the face of
the waters. [3] Then God said, "Let there be
light"; and there was light. [4] And God saw
that the light was good; and God separated the light from the darkness. [5] God
called the light Day, and the darkness he
called Night. And there was evening and
there was morning, the first day.

[6] And God said, "Let there be a dome
in the midst of the waters, and let it separate the waters from the waters." [7] So God
made the dome and separated the waters
that were under the dome from the waters that were above the dome. And it was
so. [8] God called the dome Sky. And there
was evening and there was morning, the
second day.

[9] And God said, "Let the waters under the sky be gathered together into one
place, and let the dry land appear." And it
was so. [10] God called the dry land Earth,
and the waters that were gathered together he called Seas. And God saw that it
was good. [11] Then God said, "Let the
earth put forth vegetation: plants yielding
seed, and fruit trees of every kind on
earth that bear fruit with the seed in it."
And it was so. [12] The earth brought forth
vegetation: plants yielding seed of every
kind, and trees of every kind bearing fruit
with the seed in it. And God saw that it
was good. [13] And there was evening and
there was morning, the third day.

14 And God said, "Let there be lights
in the dome of the sky to separate the day
from the night; and let them be for signs
and for seasons and for days and years,
[15] and let them be lights in the dome of
the sky to give light upon the earth." And
it was so. [16] God made the two great lights
—the greater light to rule the day and the
lesser light to rule the night—and the
stars. [17] God set them in the dome of the
sky to give light upon the earth, [18] to rule
over the day and over the night, and to
separate the light from the darkness. And
God saw that it was good. [19] And there
was evening and there was morning, the
fourth day.

a Or *when God began to create* or *In the beginning God
created*   b Or *while the spirit of God* or *while a
mighty wind*

1.1–11.32 The primordial history recounts
the earliest generations of the world and humankind as background for the call of Abram in
12.1. Although human events are viewed
pessimistically—through its misdeeds humankind
repeatedly brings God's curse upon itself and all
life—the hope for a divinely blessed flourishing
of life never truly dies, and God does not abandon
the world.

1.1–2.3 The creation story serves as a preface
not just to Genesis but to the entire Hebrew Bible.
Recounting the origin of the cosmos and its glorious centerpiece, earth, it shows God masterfully
orchestrating the events of creation. Each phase
follows more or less the same basic pattern established on day one: divine command, result, divine
approval, enumeration of the day. But the effect
is anything but monotonous. Like a musical
theme with variations, the story shows the world
gradually becoming more mobile and complex,
until, by the sixth day, it is ready for self-
perpetuation through procreation. **1.1** *In the beginning when God created*, lit. "In the beginning of
God's creating" or "When God first created." Cf.
the dependent clause introducing the Babylonian
creation story, *Enuma Elish*: "When on high the
heavens had not been named . . . ." **1.2** *A formless
void*, Hebrew *tohu wabohu*, in effect "formlessness

and normlessness," the primordial chaos. Divine
mastery of the primordial deep, a motif common
in ancient creation myths, is drawn in more detail
in Isa 40.12; Ps 33.6–7; Job 38.8–11. **1.3** Sun
and stars do not yet exist, only undifferentiated
light. Cf. 1.14–19. **1.4** *Good* suggests both "acceptable, viable" (cf. Isa 41.7) and "intrinsically
good." The purpose of every creation is good and
for the benefit of all. **1.5** *God called.* The temporal and physical frameworks of the cosmos
(night/day, sky/earth, ocean/land) are named by
God; their inhabitants, by human beings; cf.
2.19–20. *Evening . . . morning.* The Israelite calendar, accordingly, reckons dates from sunset to
sunset. **1.5, 8** *The first day . . . the second day*, lit.
"one day . . . a second day." Similarly, "a third
day" (v. 13), etc. **1.6–8** The story depicts a flat
earth and curved celestial dome surrounded
above and below by primordial waters. The universe is conceived from the vantage point of
earth, its center. **1.11, 20, 24, 26** Remarkably,
the story's order of life-forms resembles that of
our modern theory of evolution: vegetation,
swarming creatures, fish, birds, animals (mam-
mals), and human beings. **1.14–19** *Lights.* The
undifferentiated primordial light is now parceled
into the heavenly orbs, by whose movements time

20 And God said, "Let the waters bring forth swarms of living creatures, and let birds fly above the earth across the dome of the sky." 21 So God created the great sea monsters and every living creature that moves, of every kind, with which the waters swarm, and every winged bird of every kind. And God saw that it was good. 22 God blessed them, saying, "Be fruitful and multiply and fill the waters in the seas, and let birds multiply on the earth." 23 And there was evening and there was morning, the fifth day.

24 And God said, "Let the earth bring forth living creatures of every kind: cattle and creeping things and wild animals of the earth of every kind." And it was so. 25 God made the wild animals of the earth of every kind, and the cattle of every kind, and everything that creeps upon the ground of every kind. And God saw that it was good.

26 Then God said, "Let us make humankind[c] in our image, according to our likeness; and let them have dominion over the fish of the sea, and over the birds of the air, and over the cattle, and over all the wild animals of the earth,[d] and over every creeping thing that creeps upon the earth."

27 So God created humankind[c] in
    his image,
  in the image of God he created
    them;[e]
  male and female he created
    them.

28 God blessed them, and God said to them, "Be fruitful and multiply, and fill the earth and subdue it; and have dominion over the fish of the sea and over the birds of the air and over every living thing that moves upon the earth." 29 God said, "See, I have given you every plant yielding seed that is upon the face of all the earth, and every tree with seed in its fruit; you shall have them for food. 30 And to every beast of the earth, and to every bird of the air, and to everything that creeps on the earth, everything that has the breath of life, I have given every green plant for food." And it was so. 31 God saw everything that he had made, and indeed, it was very good. And there was evening and there was morning, the sixth day.

2 Thus the heavens and the earth were finished, and all their multitude. 2 And on the seventh day God finished the work that he had done, and he rested on the seventh day from all the work that he had done. 3 So God blessed the seventh day and hallowed it, because on it God rested from all the work that he had done in creation.

4 These are the generations of the heavens and the earth when they were created.

The Garden of Eden

In the day that the LORD God made the earth and the heavens, 5 when no plant of the field was yet in the earth and no herb

c Heb *adam*   d Syr: Heb *and over all the earth*
e Heb *him*

---

is measured. **1.21** *Created*, Hebrew *bara'*, a verb whose sole subject is God, here takes only three objects: the universe as a whole (1.1); sea monsters, masters of the waters (1.21); and human beings, masters of land (1.27). **1.26–27** *Let us*. The plural form does not indicate multiple gods, but God and the retinue of the divine court. *In our image*. Paradoxically, the human image resembles imageless divinity in some respect—perhaps speech, reason, or morality. But biblical narrative was not hesitant to depict divine manifestation in human form. Cf. 18.1–2; 32.22–32; Ex 15.3; 24.10; Dan 7.9. *Male and female*. Both man and woman are created in the image of God, who is beyond gender or comprises both. **2.1–3** The true culmination of creation is the sabbath on the seventh day. God's cessation from labor is the paradigm of sabbath rest in the human household; cf. Ex 20.8–11.
2.4–3.24 The garden of Eden story recounts

the beginning of human life and culture as well as the first human transgression and its punishment. In presenting our present reality as an "exile" from a prior perfection, it portrays allegorically the origin of the awareness, in every lifetime, of life's difficulties and the need for human interdependence. By the end of the story (3.24), the groundwork for civilized life has been laid. **2.4** This verse—rendered in some translations as a single, whole sentence—forms a symmetry (*heavens/earth*, *earth/heavens*), marking the transition between the creation and garden of Eden stories. *These are the generations* (in the variant translations "These are the descendants," "This is the story") introduces the story as it introduces that of Noah (6.9), the post-flood era (10.1), Abraham (11.27), Isaac's household (25.19), and Jacob's household (37.2). See also 5.1; 11.10; 25.12; 36.1, 9; Num 3.1. **2.5–7** The creation of human beings (see 1.26–28) is described a second time,

of the field had yet sprung up—for the LORD God had not caused it to rain upon the earth, and there was no one to till the ground; 6 but a stream would rise from the earth, and water the whole face of the ground— 7 then the LORD God formed man from the dust of the ground,*f* and breathed into his nostrils the breath of life; and the man became a living being. 8 And the LORD God planted a garden in Eden, in the east; and there he put the man whom he had formed. 9 Out of the ground the LORD God made to grow every tree that is pleasant to the sight and good for food, the tree of life also in the midst of the garden, and the tree of the knowledge of good and evil.

10 A river flows out of Eden to water the garden, and from there it divides and becomes four branches. 11 The name of the first is Pishon; it is the one that flows around the whole land of Havilah, where there is gold; 12 and the gold of that land is good; bdellium and onyx stone are there. 13 The name of the second river is Gihon; it is the one that flows around the whole land of Cush. 14 The name of the third river is Tigris, which flows east of Assyria. And the fourth river is the Euphrates.

15 The LORD God took the man and put him in the garden of Eden to till it and keep it. 16 And the LORD God commanded the man, "You may freely eat of every tree of the garden; 17 but of the tree of the knowledge of good and evil you

shall not eat, for in the day that you eat of it you shall die."

18 Then the LORD God said, "It is not good that the man should be alone; I will make him a helper as his partner." 19 So out of the ground the LORD God formed every animal of the field and every bird of the air, and brought them to the man to see what he would call them; and whatever the man called every living creature, that was its name. 20 The man gave names to all cattle, and to the birds of the air, and to every animal of the field; but for the man*g* there was not found a helper as his partner. 21 So the LORD God caused a deep sleep to fall upon the man, and he slept; then he took one of his ribs and closed up its place with flesh. 22 And the rib that the LORD God had taken from the man he made into a woman and brought her to the man. 23 Then the man said,

"This at last is bone of my bones
    and flesh of my flesh;
  this one shall be called Woman,*h*
    for out of Man*i* this one was
        taken."

24 Therefore a man leaves his father and his mother and clings to his wife, and they become one flesh. 25 And the man and his wife were both naked, and were not ashamed.

f Or *formed a man* (Heb *adam*) *of dust from the ground* (Heb *adamah*)   *g* Or *for Adam*
h Heb *ishshah*   *i* Heb *ish*

---

now in more detail and from the human perspective. **2.5** The absence of vegetation and of humankind as tillers of the soil anticipates the sending forth of human beings to till the earth; see 3.23. **2.6** Eden is watered by a continuous flow from underground instead of by rain, which comes and goes capriciously; cf. 3.17–19. **2.8** The name *Eden* may mean "pleasure, delight." It corresponds to no known geographical site. **2.9** *The tree of life* is mentioned again only in 3.22, 24. *The tree of the knowledge of good and evil* anticipates the events of ch. 3. **2.10–14** The four rivers (only Tigris and Euphrates correspond to known ones) suggest the whole of the eventual settled world, with Eden at its center. *Havilah* is sometimes identified with the Arabian Peninsula and *Cush* with the Horn of Africa. **2.12** *Gold ... bdellium and onyx.* Cf. the mineral wealth and gems of the "Eden" in Ezek 28.13. **2.15** The human being will have labor, but none as demanding as that of the tiller of soil.

2.16–17 Cf. 1.29–30. **2.18–22** The creation of woman is also the origin of human society. Human beings require the company of their own species (see v. 20). **2.20** *But for the man ... was not found,* lit. "but for 'Adam' was not found." In Hebrew, male and female of a species are designated by masculine and feminine forms of the same word—except for "Adam." No creature born of earth (*'adamah*) is yet a fitting partner. *Helper* does not indicate a servant relation but a true partnership. Similarly, the making of woman from the man's rib suggests their equality and kinship, not her subordination (see 2.18). **2.23** The man expresses his partnership to the woman by renaming himself—'*adam* (human being) becomes '*ish* (man), partner to '*ishshah* (woman). '*Ish* is used only thrice more in the story: 2.24; 3.6; 3.16. **2.24** This adage justifies the later human institution of marriage by showing its origins with the first human couple. *One flesh,* in mutual loyalty, in sexual union, and in their offspring.

Expulsion from the Garden 'J'

3 Now the serpent was more crafty than any other wild animal that the LORD God had made. He said to the woman, "Did God say, 'You shall not eat from any tree in the garden'?" 2 The woman said to the serpent, "We may eat of the fruit of the trees in the garden; 3 but God said, 'You shall not eat of the fruit of the tree that is in the middle of the garden, nor shall you touch it, or you shall die.'" 4 But the serpent said to the woman, "You will not die; 5 for God knows that when you eat of it your eyes will be opened, and you will be like God,ʲ knowing good and evil." 6 So when the woman saw that the tree was good for food, and that it was a delight to the eyes, and that the tree was to be desired to make one wise, she took of its fruit and ate; and she also gave some to her husband, who was with her, and he ate. 7 Then the eyes of both were opened, and they knew that they were naked; and they sewed fig leaves together and made loincloths for themselves.

8 They heard the sound of the LORD God walking in the garden at the time of the evening breeze, and the man and his wife hid themselves from the presence of the LORD God among the trees of the garden. 9 But the LORD God called to the man, and said to him, "Where are you?" 10 He said, "I heard the sound of you in the garden, and I was afraid, because I was naked; and I hid myself." 11 He said, "Who told you that you were naked? Have you eaten from the tree of which I commanded you not to eat?" 12 The man said, "The woman whom you gave to be with me, she gave me fruit from the tree, and I ate." 13 Then the LORD God said to the woman, "What is this that you have done?" The woman said, "The serpent tricked me, and I ate." 14 The LORD God said to the serpent,

"Because you have done this,
    cursed are you among all
        animals
    and among all wild creatures;
upon your belly you shall go,
    and dust you shall eat
    all the days of your life.
15 I will put enmity between you
        and the woman,
    and between your offspring
        and hers;
    he will strike your head,
        and you will strike his heel."
16 To the woman he said,
"I will greatly increase your pangs
        in childbearing;
    in pain you shall bring forth
        children,
    yet your desire shall be for your
        husband,
    and he shall rule over you."
17 And to the manᵏ he said,

j Or *gods*   *k* Or *to Adam*

3.1–24 Ch. 3 continues the narrative, describing how the Garden was lost through human disobedience. **3.1** The *serpent* is reminiscent of the snake who steals from Gilgamesh a plant conferring immortality in the Mesopotamian epic (*Epic of Gilgamesh* 11.287–89). *More crafty*, in Hebrew a wordplay on "naked" in 2.25. *Wild animal*, or "beast of the field"; cf. the term's first use in 2.19–20. *Any tree*, or "every tree"; the serpent's ambiguity may be deliberate. **3.3** *Nor shall you touch it.* The woman possibly exaggerates or misconstrues the divine command of 2.16–17. Cf. Deut 4.2. **3.4–5** The serpent does not lie, but tailors the truth to incite envy. *Knowing good and evil.* See note on 3.22. **3.6** *The woman saw.* The eyes often lead one astray; cf. 12.14–15; Num 15.39; Judg 14.1; 2 Sam 11.2. *Desired to make one wise,* or simply "desirable to contemplate." *She took . . . and ate, and . . . gave . . . and he ate,* the story's central event. Both woman and man participate. No seduction is involved. **3.8** God appears physically close to earthly beings; cf. Ex 33.19–23. **3.9–11** God knows of the couple's whereabouts and deeds but asks in order to elicit confession. **3.11–19** God interrogates the man, who blames the woman, who blames the serpent. God's judgments are pronounced in the reverse order. These verses provide causal explanations (etiologies) for present-day historical realities: agriculture, prepared food, childbearing, the conjugal family. **3.12** *The woman whom you gave.* The man shifts the blame to his Creator as well. **3.13** *Tricked me,* Hebrew *hissi'ani,* a play on the serpent's hiss. **3.14** *Upon your belly* suggests that the serpent's posture was once upright. **3.15** *Enmity* perhaps suggests humanity's sad alienation not just from serpents but from all animals; see note on 3.21. **3.16** Woman's historical subordination to man is a consequence of human events, not an ideal in its own right. Responsibilities of procreation will compromise the autonomy of both sexes. **3.17–19** Humans will become tillers of the soil, a major step in human evolution but one beset with difficulty and hard work.

"Because you have listened to the
    voice of your wife,
and have eaten of the tree
about which I commanded you,
    'You shall not eat of it,'
cursed is the ground because
    of you;
in toil you shall eat of it all the
    days of your life;
18 thorns and thistles it shall bring
    forth for you;
and you shall eat the plants of
    the field.
19 By the sweat of your face
    you shall eat bread
until you return to the ground,
    for out of it you were taken;
you are dust,
    and to dust you shall return."

20 The man named his wife Eve,*l* because she was the mother of all living. 21 And the LORD God made garments of skins for the man*m* and for his wife, and clothed them.

22 Then the LORD God said, "See, the man has become like one of us, knowing good and evil; and now, he might reach out his hand and take also from the tree of life, and eat, and live forever"— 23 therefore the LORD God sent him forth from the garden of Eden, to till the ground from which he was taken. 24 He drove out the man; and at the east of the garden of Eden he placed the cherubim, and a sword flaming and turning to guard the way to the tree of life.

Cain Murders Abel

4 Now the man knew his wife Eve, and she conceived and bore Cain, saying, "I have produced*n* a man with the help of the LORD." 2 Next she bore his brother Abel. Now Abel was a keeper of sheep, and Cain a tiller of the ground. 3 In the course of time Cain brought to the LORD an offering of the fruit of the ground, 4 and Abel for his part brought of the firstlings of his flock, their fat portions. And the LORD had regard for Abel and his offering, 5 but for Cain and his offering he had no regard. So Cain was very angry, and his countenance fell. 6 The LORD said to Cain, "Why are you angry, and why has your countenance fallen? 7 If you do well, will you not be accepted? And if you do not do well, sin is lurking at the door; its desire is for you, but you must master it."

8 Cain said to his brother Abel, "Let us go out to the field."*o* And when they were in the field, Cain rose up against his brother Abel, and killed him. 9 Then the

l In Heb *Eve* resembles the word for *living*
m Or *for Adam*   *n* The verb in Heb resembles the word for *Cain*   *o* Sam Gk Syr Compare Vg: MT lacks *Let us go out to the field*

Unlike fruit, *bread* requires many steps and much human cooperation in its preparation. *Until you return . . . to dust you shall return*, the first clear indication of human mortality. **3.20** *Eve*, Hebrew for "Life-bearer." This second naming of woman (cf. 2.23) reflects the couple's new role as procreators. **3.21** *Garments of skins* perhaps suggests the new alienation between humans and animals; cf. 3.15; *Epic of Gilgamesh* 1.4.24–25. **3.22** *Like one of us.* See note on 1.26–27. *Knowing good and evil* can suggest "everything, all extremes," as well as knowledge of sex, mortality, and moral distinctions; cf. 2 Sam 14.17, 20; 1 Kings 3.9. Instead of the eternal life conferred by *the tree of life*, humans must settle for the collective immortality of generational succession—the human family tree. **3.23** *To till the ground from which he was taken*, and to which he will return; cf. 3.19b. **3.24** *Cherubim*, angelic guardians fearsome in appearance, wield *a sword flaming and turning* to prevent the couple from returning to Eden.

4.1–16 The story of Cain and Abel recounts the world's first human death, indeed, its first murder. In punishment, Cain is banished. A wanderer, he comes to build a city. Other inhabitants of the world seem to arise from nowhere in particular (see note on 5.4). **4.1** *The man knew his wife*, i.e., sexually. *Knew* presupposes "knowledge of good and evil" already described (3.22). *And bore*, in Hebrew a wordplay on "generations" in 2.4—the turning of one generation is now complete. *Cain*, in Hebrew folk etymology "Acquisition, Production." Biblical naming of children or places typically involves puns on key events. **4.2** *Abel*, in Hebrew folk etymology "Emptiness, Futility," the perfect counterpart of "Acquisition" (see note on 4.1). Biblical brother pairs are typically opposed in temperament, way of life, and destiny (see esp. 25.19–28). **4.2–5** The historical opposition of shepherds and farmers is told here. God favors the shepherd, but the choice comes to grief in any case. Unequal favor of one's children is often a source of strife; cf. 9.20–27; 21.10–21; 25.28; 27.1–40; 37.1–36. **4.6–7** The text is uncertain or elliptical. *Will you not be accepted*, lit. "[There is] uplifting, favor" (cf. Num 6.26). Cain is told that all depends on righteousness. **4.9** *Where is your brother Abel?* See note on

LORD said to Cain, "Where is your brother Abel?" He said, "I do not know; am I my brother's keeper?" 10 And the LORD said, "What have you done? Listen; your brother's blood is crying out to me from the ground! 11 And now you are cursed from the ground, which has opened its mouth to receive your brother's blood from your hand. 12 When you till the ground, it will no longer yield to you its strength; you will be a fugitive and a wanderer on the earth." 13 Cain said to the LORD, "My punishment is greater than I can bear! 14 Today you have driven me away from the soil, and I shall be hidden from your face; I shall be a fugitive and a wanderer on the earth, and anyone who meets me may kill me." 15 Then the LORD said to him, "Not so!p Whoever kills Cain will suffer a sevenfold vengeance." And the LORD put a mark on Cain, so that no one who came upon him would kill him. 16 Then Cain went away from the presence of the LORD, and settled in the land of Nod,q east of Eden. *Punish*

Beginnings of Civilization

17 Cain knew his wife, and she conceived and bore Enoch; and he built a city, and named it Enoch after his son Enoch. 18 To Enoch was born Irad; and Irad was the father of Mehujael, and Mehujael the father of Methushael, and Methushael the father of Lamech. 19 Lamech took two wives; the name of the one was Adah, and the name of the other Zillah. 20 Adah bore Jabal; he was the ancestor of those who live in tents and have livestock. 21 His brother's name was Jubal; he was the ancestor of all those who play the lyre

and pipe. 22 Zillah bore Tubal-cain, who made all kinds of bronze and iron tools. The sister of Tubal-cain was Naamah.

23 Lamech said to his wives:

"Adah and Zillah, hear my voice;
    you wives of Lamech, listen to
        what I say:
I have killed a man for
        wounding me,
    a young man for striking me.
24 If Cain is avenged sevenfold,
        truly Lamech
            seventy-sevenfold."

25 Adam knew his wife again, and she bore a son and named him Seth, for she said, "God has appointedr for me another child instead of Abel, because Cain killed him." 26 To Seth also a son was born, and he named him Enosh. At that time people began to invoke the name of the LORD.

From Adam to Noah

5 This is the list of the descendants of Adam. When God created humankind,s he made themt in the likeness of God. 2 Male and female he created them, and he blessed them and named them "Humankind"s when they were created.

3 When Adam had lived one hundred thirty years, he became the father of a son in his likeness, according to his image, and named him Seth. 4 The days of Adam after he became the father of Seth were

p Gk Syr Vg: Heb *Therefore*   q *That is Wandering*   r The verb in Heb resembles the word for *Seth*   s Heb *adam*   t Heb *him*

3.9–11. **4.11–12** The ground is again cursed for a human action; cf. 3.17. As *a fugitive and a wanderer*, Cain will enjoy no citizens' rights, at least in his initial homeland. **4.13–16** In antiquity, certain criminals were offered limited asylum when uncontrolled reprisals posed a greater social danger than the criminals themselves; cf. 4.23–24; Num 35.9–16; Deut 4.41–43; 2 Sam 14.1–24.

4.17–26 The line of Cain and the birth of Seth, third son of Adam and Eve. Most names from the Cainite genealogy have Sethite counterparts in 5.1–32 (e.g., Irad, Jared; Methushael, Methuselah; Naamah, Noah). The Cainites' stock-breeding and artisan trades were vital to the rise of cities. **4.23–24** Lamech's boastful song typi-

fies the world's multiplication of violence, despite God's effort in 4.15 to restrain blood vengeance. **4.26** *People began to invoke.* The worship of YHWH ("LORD"), by this account, long anticipates Israelite religion. The divine name means lit. "He-[who]-brings-into-being."

5.1–32 The Sethite genealogy seemingly ignores the line of Cain but duplicates most of its names; see note on 4.17–26. From Adam to Noah are ten generations. The average life span grows progressively shorter as we approach the present. **5.1** *List,* lit. "book," an originally independent scroll or source. **5.4** *And he had other sons and daughters.* This repeated formula stands as explanation for the world's growing population.

eight hundred years; and he had other sons and daughters. ⁵Thus all the days that Adam lived were nine hundred thirty years; and he died.

6 When Seth had lived one hundred five years, he became the father of Enosh. ⁷Seth lived after the birth of Enosh eight hundred seven years, and had other sons and daughters. ⁸Thus all the days of Seth were nine hundred twelve years; and he died.

9 When Enosh had lived ninety years, he became the father of Kenan. ¹⁰Enosh lived after the birth of Kenan eight hundred fifteen years, and had other sons and daughters. ¹¹Thus all the days of Enosh were nine hundred five years; and he died.

12 When Kenan had lived seventy years, he became the father of Mahalalel. ¹³Kenan lived after the birth of Mahalalel eight hundred and forty years, and had other sons and daughters. ¹⁴Thus all the days of Kenan were nine hundred and ten years; and he died.

15 When Mahalalel had lived sixty-five years, he became the father of Jared. ¹⁶Mahalalel lived after the birth of Jared eight hundred thirty years, and had other sons and daughters. ¹⁷Thus all the days of Mahalalel were eight hundred ninety-five years; and he died.

18 When Jared had lived one hundred sixty-two years he became the father of Enoch. ¹⁹Jared lived after the birth of Enoch eight hundred years, and had other sons and daughters. ²⁰Thus all the days of Jared were nine hundred sixty-two years; and he died.

21 When Enoch had lived sixty-five years, he became the father of Methuselah. ²²Enoch walked with God after the birth of Methuselah three hundred years, and had other sons and daughters. ²³Thus all the days of Enoch were three hundred sixty-five years. ²⁴Enoch walked

with God; then he was no more, because God took him.

25 When Methuselah had lived one hundred eighty-seven years, he became the father of Lamech. ²⁶Methuselah lived after the birth of Lamech seven hundred eighty-two years, and had other sons and daughters. ²⁷Thus all the days of Methuselah were nine hundred sixty-nine years; and he died.

28 When Lamech had lived one hundred eighty-two years, he became the father of a son; ²⁹he named him Noah, saying, "Out of the ground that the LORD has cursed this one shall bring us relief from our work and from the toil of our hands." ³⁰Lamech lived after the birth of Noah five hundred ninety-five years, and had other sons and daughters. ³¹Thus all the days of Lamech were seven hundred seventy-seven years; and he died.

32 After Noah was five hundred years old, Noah became the father of Shem, Ham, and Japheth.

The Wickedness of Humankind

6 When people began to multiply on the face of the ground, and daughters were born to them, ²the sons of God saw that they were fair; and they took wives for themselves of all that they chose. ³Then the LORD said, "My spirit shall not abide[u] in mortals forever, for they are flesh; their days shall be one hundred twenty years." ⁴The Nephilim were on the earth in those days—and also afterward—when the sons of God went in to the daughters of humans, who bore children to them. These were the heroes that were of old, warriors of renown.

5 The LORD saw that the wickedness of humankind was great in the earth, and that every inclination of the thoughts of their hearts was only evil continually.

---

u Meaning of Heb uncertain

5.6 *Enosh*, like "Adam," means "human being." As Adam's son is Cain (Kayin), Enosh's is Kenan (5.9). Enosh possibly begins the original genealogy used by the biblical author. **5.24** *He was no more because God took him*, an atypical wording suggesting something other than physical death; cf. Elijah in 2 Kings 2.11. **5.27** *Methuselah* is the Bible's longest-lived person; a proverbial symbol of longevity. **5.29** *Out of the ground that the LORD has cursed*. Cf. 3.17–19; 4.11–12.

6.2, 4 The *sons of God*—explained in later

eras as renegade angels—resemble many figures of ancient mythology who recognize no border between heaven and earth. The term is perhaps synonymous with *Nephilim* (v. 4), a word possibly related to the Hebrew root "to fall." These are called *heroes . . . of old, warriors of renown* with some irony—their legacy is now faint, nearly forgotten. **6.3** The fixing of a life span at *one hundred twenty years*, the age of Moses at his death, is only a moderate exaggeration of the normal, appropriate to a heroic era. God shortens human life out

the waters were dried up from the earth; and Noah removed the covering of the ark, and looked, and saw that the face of the ground was drying. 14 In the second month, on the twenty-seventh day of the month, the earth was dry. 15 Then God said to Noah, 16 "Go out of the ark, you and your wife, and your sons and your sons' wives with you. 17 Bring out with you every living thing that is with you of all flesh — birds and animals and every creeping thing that creeps on the earth — so that they may abound on the earth, and be fruitful and multiply on the earth." 18 So Noah went out with his sons and his wife and his sons' wives. 19 And every animal, every creeping thing, and every bird, everything that moves on the earth, went out of the ark by families.

God's Resolve Not to Destroy

20 Then Noah built an altar to the LORD, and took of every clean animal and of every clean bird, and offered burnt offerings on the altar. 21 And when the LORD smelled the pleasing odor, the LORD said in his heart, "I will never again curse the ground because of humankind, for the inclination of the human heart is evil from youth; nor will I ever again destroy every living creature as I have done.

22   As long as the earth endures,
      seedtime and harvest, cold and
        heat,

      summer and winter, day and
        night,
      shall not cease."

The Covenant with Noah

9 God blessed Noah and his sons, and said to them, "Be fruitful and multiply, and fill the earth. 2 The fear and dread of you shall rest on every animal of the earth, and on every bird of the air, on everything that creeps on the ground, and on all the fish of the sea; into your hand they are delivered. 3 Every moving thing that lives shall be food for you; and just as I gave you the green plants, I give you everything. 4 Only, you shall not eat flesh with its life, that is, its blood. 5 For your own lifeblood I will surely require a reckoning: from every animal I will require it and from human beings, each one for the blood of another, I will require a reckoning for human life.

6   Whoever sheds the blood of a
      human,
      by a human shall that person's
        blood be shed;
    for in his own image
      God made humankind.

7 And you, be fruitful and multiply, abound on the earth and multiply in it." 8 Then God said to Noah and to his sons with him, 9 "As for me, I am establishing my covenant with you and your descendants after you, 10 and with every living creature that is with you, the birds,

---

return, because it found a place to nest. **8.13** *Removed the covering*, opened the cover of the hatch, from which one peers forth. **8.15–19** The command to leave the ark parallels the one to enter it in 7.1–5. **8.17** *Be fruitful and multiply* recalls 1.28. **8.19** *By families*. All species exhibit domestic habits.

8.20–22 Noah's first act upon dry land, the building of an altar, and the divine resolve not to send another flood. **8.20** *Noah built an altar*. On sacrifice after the flood, cf. *Epic of Gilgamesh* 11.156–58. **8.21** *The pleasing odor*. Cf. *Epic of Gilgamesh* 11.159–61; Ex 29.18, 25, 41; Lev 1.9. *Said in his heart*, i.e., to himself. *I will never again curse the ground because of humankind*. Cf. 3.17–19; 4.11–12; 5.29. *For the inclination*, "although the inclination." *Nor will I . . . destroy*. God may punish individuals and communities but will not destroy the world. **8.22** The rhythms suggest an ancient verse or proverb.

9.1–17 The Noahide covenant is the precursor to the Sinai covenant; cf. the blessing of hu-

mankind in 1.28–30. **9.1** *Be fruitful and multiply*. Cf. 1.28. **9.2–3** *The fear and dread of you*, as users of animals for food, labor, and hides. *Into your hand they are delivered*. Humans have the power of life and death over animals and they are to use it wisely. *Every moving thing that lives*, all animal life. These words — like the story itself — continue the preoccupation with relations between humans and animals begun in 1.28–30; 2.18–20; 3.1–6, 13–15, 21; 4.7, 20. **9.4** Cf. Deut 12.23. Blood is the repository of life; it must be drained from every animal killed for food. Israelite law prohibited animal flesh torn in the field by beasts (see Ex 22.31 [v. 30 in Hebrew]). **9.5** *For your own lifeblood . . . a reckoning*. All taking of human life is subject to the rule of law. *From every animal*. Even animals were punished for homicide; see Ex 21.28–32. *And from human beings*. Cf. Ex 21.12–14. **9.6** *Whoever sheds . . . blood be shed*. In Hebrew the couplet is symmetrical: (a) Shedder (b) of blood (c) of a human parallels (c′) by a human (b′) his blood (a′) shall be shed. **9.8** *Cove-*

the domestic animals, and every animal of the earth with you, as many as came out of the ark.ˣ 11 I establish my covenant with you, that never again shall all flesh be cut off by the waters of a flood, and never again shall there be a flood to destroy the earth." 12 God said, "This is the sign of the covenant that I make between me and you and every living creature that is with you, for all future generations: 13 I have set my bow in the clouds, and it shall be a sign of the covenant between me and the earth. 14 When I bring clouds over the earth and the bow is seen in the clouds, 15 I will remember my covenant that is between me and you and every living creature of all flesh; and the waters shall never again become a flood to destroy all flesh. 16 When the bow is in the clouds, I will see it and remember the everlasting covenant between God and every living creature of all flesh that is on the earth." 17 God said to Noah, "This is the sign of the covenant that I have established between me and all flesh that is on the earth."

The Sons of Noah

18 The sons of Noah who went out of the ark were Shem, Ham, and Japheth. Ham was the father of Canaan. 19 These three were the sons of Noah; and from these the whole earth was peopled.

20 Noah, a man of the soil, was the first to plant a vineyard. 21 He drank some of the wine and became drunk, and he lay uncovered in his tent. 22 And Ham, the father of Canaan, saw the nakedness of his father, and told his two brothers outside. 23 Then Shem and Japheth took a garment, laid it on both their shoulders, and walked backward and covered the nakedness of their father; their faces were turned away, and they did not see their father's nakedness. 24 When Noah awoke from his wine and knew what his youngest son had done to him, 25 he said,

"Cursed be Canaan;
    lowest of slaves shall he be to
        his brothers."
26 He also said,
"Blessed by the LORD my God be
        Shem;
    and let Canaan be his slave.
27   May God make space forʸ
            Japheth,
    and let him live in the tents of
        Shem;
    and let Canaan be his slave."

28 After the flood Noah lived three hundred fifty years. 29 All the days of Noah were nine hundred fifty years; and he died.

Nations Descended from Noah

10 These are the descendants of Noah's sons, Shem, Ham, and Japheth; children were born to them after the flood.

x Gk: Heb adds *every animal of the earth*
y Heb *yapht*, a play on *Japheth*

---

nant. Cf. 6.18. **9.11** *That never again . . . destroy the earth.* Cf. 8.21–22. **9.12–17** *Sign of the covenant . . . my bow.* A deity wielding a bow as a weapon is depicted in ancient art. Cf. Lam 2.4; Hab 3.9–11. Hanging up the bow signifies retirement from battle.

9.18–27 An originally independent legend of Noah's life after the flood. The "blameless" Noah (6.9) is less so here, quickly succumbing to the bad habits of settled society. **9.22** *Ham . . . father of Canaan.* The Canaanites, viewed by biblical tradition as later Israel's immediate predecessors in the land, are the chief preoccupation here; cf. vv. 25–27; 10.6, 15–20. *Saw the nakedness of his father* possibly denotes a sexual act; Lev 18.7. On *saw* cf. Gen 3.6; 6.2, 5. **9.23** Shem and Japheth behave with respect toward their father, covering him without looking. **9.24** *Knew*, again a key word; cf. 3.5, 7, 22; 4.1, 17, 25; 8.11. **9.25–27** The hostility toward Canaan is rooted in Israel's memory of Canaan's onetime hegemony in the land under protection of Egyptian might; see note on 10.6.

10.1–11.32 A record of the rise of nations and peoples consisting of two genealogies surrounding the Tower of Babel story. Cf. 9.18–19. **10.1–32** The Table of Nations, with its magnificent geographical sweep, lists many historical peoples, but its lineages should not be taken too literally—the biblical genealogist began with existing political and cultural relations and constructed from them a system of kinship, mingling cities, lands, and peoples as "ancestors." Ham is here progenitor of several large, imperial nations (Egyptians, Babylonians, Hittites, etc.) who were in fact ethnically unrelated peoples. Many names reappear in biblical poetry and prophecy; see especially Isa 7–23; Jer 46–51; Ezek 27–30; 38–39. The branching families of humankind suggest a temporal "tree of life."

2 The descendants of Japheth: Gomer, Magog, Madai, Javan, Tubal, Meshech, and Tiras. ³ The descendants of Gomer: Ashkenaz, Riphath, and Togarmah. ⁴ The descendants of Javan: Elishah, Tarshish, Kittim, and Rodanim.ᶻ ⁵ From these the coastland peoples spread. These are the descendants of Japhethᵃ in their lands, with their own language, by their families, in their nations.

6 The descendants of Ham: Cush, Egypt, Put, and Canaan. ⁷ The descendants of Cush: Seba, Havilah, Sabtah, Raamah, and Sabteca. The descendants of Raamah: Sheba and Dedan. ⁸ Cush became the father of Nimrod; he was the first on earth to become a mighty warrior. ⁹ He was a mighty hunter before the LORD; therefore it is said, "Like Nimrod a mighty hunter before the LORD." ¹⁰ The beginning of his kingdom was Babel, Erech, and Accad, all of them in the land of Shinar. ¹¹ From that land he went into Assyria, and built Nineveh, Rehoboth-ir, Calah, and ¹² Resen between Nineveh and Calah; that is the great city. ¹³ Egypt became the father of Ludim, Anamim, Lehabim, Naphtuhim, ¹⁴ Pathrusim, Casluhim, and Caphtorim, from which the Philistines come.ᵇ

15 Canaan became the father of Sidon his firstborn, and Heth, ¹⁶ and the Jebusites, the Amorites, the Girgashites, ¹⁷ the Hivites, the Arkites, the Sinites, ¹⁸ the Ar-

z Heb Mss Sam Gk See 1 Chr 1.7: MT *Dodanim*
a Compare verses 20, 31. Heb lacks *These are the descendants of Japheth*   b Cn: Heb *Casluhim, from which the Philistines come, and Caphtorim*

10.2 *The descendants of Japheth,* peoples of the Aegean peninsula, Asia Minor and farther east. The best known are *Gomer* (Cimmerians), *Madai* (Medes), and *Javan* (Ionians). *Tubal, Meshech.* Cf. Ezek 27.13; 32.26; 38.2; 39.1. *Tiras,* often identified with the Etruscans or (by Josephus) with the Thracians. **10.3** *Ashkenaz,* probably the Scythians, an Indo-European people; in medieval Hebrew sources it is a term for eastern Europe and its Jews. *Riphath … Togarmah,* in Asia Minor. **10.4** *Elishah,* possibly Alashiah, in Cyprus. Cf. Ezek 27.7. *Tarshish,* possibly Tartessos, in Spain. Cf. Jon 1.3; 4.2. *Kittim and Rodanim,* in Cyprus (or Crete) and Rhodes. The Hebrew text reads "... and Dodanim." **10.6** *Descendants of Ham* here designates peoples of North Africa, Canaan, Arabia, and Mesopotamia. *Cush,* the land south of Egypt, Nubia, or Ethiopia in Greek, Assyrian *Kusu. Put,* a North African people; cf. Jer 46.9; Ezek 30.5; Nah 3.9. *Canaan.* Egypt's close relations with Canaan before the Amarna period and exodus era (fourteenth–thirteenth century B.C.E.) accounts for their kinship here. **10.7** *Seba,* in or near Ethiopia; cf. Ps 72.10; Isa 43.3; 45.14. *Havilah, Sabtah, Raamah,* Arabian locations. *Sabteca.* Location uncertain. *Sheba,* in Arabia. Cf. 1 Kings 10.1–10 (queen of Sheba); see also Job 1.15; Ps 72.15; Isa 60.6; Jer 6.20. *Dedan,* in Edom or northern Arabia; cf. Isa 21.13; Jer 25.23; 49.8; Ezek 25.13. **10.8** *Nimrod,* variously identified with Babylonian deities Marduk and Ninurta, the Greek hunter Orion and other mythic figures, and historical kings such as Sumer's Gilgamesh and Egypt's Amenhotep III. Cf. Mic 5.6 (v. 5 in Hebrew). *The first … mighty warrior.* His rule is singled out for its power and fearsomeness. Cf. *Epic of Gilgamesh* 1.2.9–28. **10.9** *A mighty hunter before the LORD* can imply either divine favor or disapproval. *Therefore, it is said,* quoting a popular adage or royal epithet. **10.10** *Beginning,* or "mainstay." *Babel,* Babylon; see note on 11.9. *Erech,* Babylonian *Uruk,* city of Gilgamesh. *Accad,* Sumerian *Agade,* an important Mesopotamian city and state. *Shinar,* the land of Babylon. **10.11–12** *Nineveh,* capital of Assyria, near modern Mosul. Cf. 2 Kings 19.36 (Isa 37.37); Jon 1.2; 3.2–7; 4.11. *Rehoboth-ir; Calah, Resen,* towns in environs of Nineveh. *That is the great city,* Greater Nineveh; cf. Jon 1.2; 3.2–3; 4.11. **10.13–14** Identifications uncertain, probably regions of Egypt or its closely allied peoples. *Caphtorim,* probably people of Crete (Kaphtor). *Philistines,* one of the "Sea Peoples" who migrated from the Aegean basin to settle on the southern Canaanite shore. Israelite-Philistine relations are recounted extensively in Judges and 1 and 2 Samuel. **10.15–20** *Canaan* is described as the ancestor of various peoples in and around Palestine; cf. lists of Canaanite peoples in 15.19–21; Ex 23.23; 34.11. **10.15** *Sidon,* Phoenician port on the Lebanese coast. *Firstborn* of Canaan, Sidon is treated as the founding father of Phoenicia. *Heth,* eponymous ancestor of the Hittites, an Anatolian people of Indo-European origin allegedly living in Canaan (Canaanite "Hittites" were more likely Semites); cf. 23.3–20; 2 Sam 11.3; 23.39. **10.16** *Jebusites,* pre-Israelite inhabitants of Jerusalem; cf. 24.16–25; Josh 15.8; 18.28; Judg 1.21; 19.10. *Amorites,* Akkadian *Amurru,* actually Semites of western Palestine and Syria; the term sometimes overlaps with "Canaanite." Cf. 15.16; Num 13.29; Deut 1.7, 19, 20, 44; Ezek 16.3. *Girgashites,* name found also in 15.21; Deut 7.1; Josh 3.10; 24.11; Neh 9.8. The region of their origin is uncertain. **10.17–18** *Hivites,* a people probably of central Palestine. *Arkites … Hamathites,* a list of

[handwritten: Priestly writer]

[handwritten top right: connecting to God (Sin)]

[handwritten: Jupiter] *[handwritten: Building Zigarat]*

vadites, the Zemarites, and the Hamath-ites. Afterward the families of the Canaanites spread abroad. 19 And the territory of the Canaanites extended from Sidon, in the direction of Gerar, as far as Gaza, and in the direction of Sodom, Gomorrah, Admah, and Zeboiim, as far as Lasha. 20 These are the descendants of Ham, by their families, their languages, their lands, and their nations.

21 To Shem also, the father of all the children of Eber, the elder brother of Japheth, children were born. 22 The descendants of Shem: Elam, Asshur, Arpachshad, Lud, and Aram. 23 The descendants of Aram: Uz, Hul, Gether, and Mash. 24 Arpachshad became the father of Shelah; and Shelah became the father of Eber. 25 To Eber were born two sons: the name of the one was Peleg,c for in his days the earth was divided, and his brother's name was Joktan. 26 Joktan became the father of Almodad, Sheleph, Hazarmaveth, Jerah, 27 Hadoram, Uzal, Diklah, 28 Obal, Abimael, Sheba, 29 Ophir, Havilah, and Jobab; all these were the descendants of Joktan. 30 The territory in which they lived extended from Mesha in the direction of Sephar, the hill country of the east. 31 These are the descendants of Shem, by their families, their languages, their lands, and their nations.

32 These are the families of Noah's sons, according to their genealogies, in their nations; and from these the nations spread abroad on the earth after the flood.

The Tower of Babel

11 Now the whole earth had one language and the same words. 2 And as they migrated from the east,d they came upon a plain in the land of Shinar and settled there. 3 And they said to one another, "Come, let us make bricks, and burn them thoroughly." And they had brick for stone, and bitumen for mortar. 4 Then they said, "Come, let us build ourselves a city, and a tower with its top in the heavens, and let us make a name for ourselves; otherwise we shall be scattered abroad upon the face of the whole earth." 5 The LORD came down to see the city and the tower, which mortals had built. 6 And the LORD said, "Look, they are one people, and they have all one language; and this is only the beginning of what they will do; nothing that they propose to do will now be impossible for them. 7 Come, let us go down, and confuse their language there, so that they will not understand one another's speech." 8 So the LORD scattered them abroad from there over the face of all the earth, and they left off building the city. 9 Therefore it was called Babel, because there the LORD confusede the language of all the earth; and from there the LORD scattered them abroad over the face of all the earth.

[handwritten: No Act of Gracious Mercy !!]

Descendants of Shem

10 These are the descendants of Shem. When Shem was one hundred

c That is *Division*   d Or *migrated eastward*
e Heb *balal*, meaning *to confuse*

---

peoples of Phoenician cities. **10.19** *Gerar.* Cf. 20.1; 26.1. *Sodom . . . Zeboiim.* Cf. 13.10–13; 14.1–16; 18.16–19.29. **10.21–31** The children of Shem; cf. 11.10–26. **10.21** *Eber,* eponymous ancestor of the Hebrews. The identification of this term with Akkadian *'apiru/habiru* ("migrant, transient") is uncertain, but see note on 14.13. **10.22** *Elam,* a non-Semitic people east of Babylonia. *Asshur,* Assyria. *Arpachshad.* Name's origin uncertain. *Lud,* possibly another version of "Ludim" (10.13), perhaps Lydians, an Anatolian people. *Aram,* the Arameans (i.e., Syrians); see note on 22.20–24. **10.25** *Peleg,* lit. "Division," associated etiologically with the division of nations described in this chapter. **10.26–29** *Joktan . . . Jobab,* Arabic tribal names, including two given earlier (Sheba, Havilah; see 10.7).

11.1–9 A brief allegorical tale about the sepa-

ration of languages and peoples already described in ch. 10 (see esp. 10.5, 20, 31). Like the garden of Eden story, it is a folktale of human pride and folly, here with a decidedly antiurban bias. **11.2** *Shinar.* See note on 10.10. **11.3** *Come, let us . . .* is repeated throughout (11.2, 4, 7). **11.4** *A tower with its top in the heavens*, probably a ziggurat, a pyramidic temple tower such as Entemenanki in Babylon. *Otherwise we shall be scattered.* The root of overweening ambition is often fear. **11.6** Cf. 3.22–23; 11.3. **11.7** *And confuse*, in Hebrew a wordplay on "Babel." **11.8** *So the LORD scattered them abroad.* Their worst fear is realized (see v. 4). **11.9** *Babel,* Akkadian *Bab-ilani,* "Gate of the gods." *Confused,* in Hebrew a continuation of the wordplay on "Babel" (see v. 7).

11.10–26 Another version of 10.21–30, continuing the concern for chronology introduced in

years old, he became the father of Arpachshad two years after the flood; 11 and Shem lived after the birth of Arpachshad five hundred years, and had other sons and daughters.

12 When Arpachshad had lived thirty-five years, he became the father of Shelah; 13 and Arpachshad lived after the birth of Shelah four hundred three years, and had other sons and daughters.

14 When Shelah had lived thirty years, he became the father of Eber; 15 and Shelah lived after the birth of Eber four hundred three years, and had other sons and daughters.

16 When Eber had lived thirty-four years, he became the father of Peleg; 17 and Eber lived after the birth of Peleg four hundred thirty years, and had other sons and daughters.

18 When Peleg had lived thirty years, he became the father of Reu; 19 and Peleg lived after the birth of Reu two hundred nine years, and had other sons and daughters.

20 When Reu had lived thirty-two years, he became the father of Serug; 21 and Reu lived after the birth of Serug two hundred seven years, and had other sons and daughters.

22 When Serug had lived thirty years, he became the father of Nahor; 23 and Serug lived after the birth of Nahor two hundred years, and had other sons and daughters.

24 When Nahor had lived twenty-nine years, he became the father of Terah; 25 and Nahor lived after the birth of Terah one hundred nineteen years, and had other sons and daughters.

26 When Terah had lived seventy years, he became the father of Abram, Nahor, and Haran.

Descendants of Terah

27 Now these are the descendants of Terah. Terah was the father of Abram, Nahor, and Haran; and Haran was the father of Lot. 28 Haran died before his fa-

---

ch. 5. Unlike 10.21–30, this genealogy places less emphasis on sibling relationships and more on a favored successor — a tension between these viewpoints animates all of Genesis. This and the following section provide a bridge from world history to the Israelite ancestral history beginning in ch. 12.

11.27–32 The branch of Shem, via Terah, that leads to Abraham. **11.27** *Abram* is Abraham's name until 17.5. *Lot.* See 12.4; 13.2–13;

THE ABRAHAM CYCLE (GENESIS 11–25)

The episodes in the Abraham story cycle have a complex symmetry. Their arrangement in this table shows parallel relationships between traditions and motifs. Materials violating the symmetry are given in square brackets.

A   Genealogical framework (11.10–32)
  B   Migration from Haran; separation from Nahor ([12.1–3] 12.4–5a)
   C   Building of altars; land promised (12.5b–9 [13.14–18])
    D   "Wife-sister" episode (12.10–20)
     E   Border agreement with Lot (13.1–13)
      F   Sodom episode and rescue of Lot (14.1–24)
       G   Covenant of sacrifice (15.1–21)
        X   Expulsion and rescue of Hagar (16.1–16)
       G'   Covenant of circumcision (17.1–27)
      F'   Sodom episode and rescue of Lot (18.1–19.38)
     [E'   Border agreement with Abimelech (21.22–34)]
    D'   "Wife-sister" episode (20.1–18)
   C'   Building of altar (22.6); land secured (22.17b; 23.1–20)
  B'   Migration to Haran; reunification with Nahor's line (24.1–67)
A'   Genealogical framework ([22.20–24] 25.1–18)

ther Terah in the land of his birth, in Ur of the Chaldeans. 29 Abram and Nahor took wives; the name of Abram's wife was Sarai, and the name of Nahor's wife was Milcah. She was the daughter of Haran the father of Milcah and Iscah. 30 Now Sarai was barren; she had no child.

31 Terah took his son Abram and his grandson Lot son of Haran, and his daughter-in-law Sarai his son Abram's wife, and they went out together from Ur of the Chaldeans to go into the land of Canaan; but when they came to Haran, they settled there. 32 The days of Terah were two hundred five years; and Terah died in Haran.

The Call of Abram

12 Now the LORD said to Abram, "Go from your country and your kindred and your father's house to the land that I will show you. 2 I will make of you a great nation, and I will bless you, and make your name great, so that you will be a blessing. 3 I will bless those who bless you, and the one who curses you I will curse; and in you all the families of the earth shall be blessed."f

4 So Abram went, as the LORD had

told him; and Lot went with him. Abram was seventy-five years old when he departed from Haran. 5 Abram took his wife Sarai and his brother's son Lot, and all the possessions that they had gathered, and the persons whom they had acquired in Haran; and they set forth to go to the land of Canaan. When they had come to the land of Canaan, 6 Abram passed through the land to the place at Shechem, to the oakg of Moreh. At that time the Canaanites were in the land. 7 Then the LORD appeared to Abram, and said, "To your offspringh I will give this land." So he built there an altar to the LORD, who had appeared to him. 8 From there he moved on to the hill country on the east of Bethel, and pitched his tent, with Bethel on the west and Ai on the east; and there he built an altar to the LORD and invoked the name of the LORD. 9 And Abram journeyed on by stages toward the Negeb.

Abram and Sarai in Egypt

10 Now there was a famine in the land. So Abram went down to Egypt to reside there as an alien, for the famine

f Or by you all the families of the earth shall bless themselves   g Or terebinth   h Heb seed

---

14.12–16; 19.1–29. **11.28** *Died before his father*, the gravest of family tragedies. Abraham, Isaac, and Jacob will each be informed of a son's death or mortal endangerment. **11.28, 31** *Ur*, ancient Mesopotamian city. *Chaldeans*, Semitic-, possibly Aramaic-speaking peoples of Mesopotamia. 12.1, 5 identifies Haran (see note on 11.31) as Abraham's birthplace. **11.29** *Sarai*, Sarah's name until 17.15. *Nahor's wife ... Milcah*. The fuller significance of Nahor's household will become clear in 22.20–24; 24.1–67. **11.30** *Sarai was barren*. It is unusual for a genealogy to record the *lack* of children—this dearth forms the thematic linchpin of the entire Abraham cycle. **11.31** *To go into ... Canaan*. An effort to settle Canaan antedates Abraham's journey there. *Haran* (place-name unrelated to the person Haran), an important city of the Hurrians located in northern Mesopotamia.

11.27–25.18 The Abraham cycle recounts the life history of the first ancestor of Israel to settle in Canaan. It describes his migrations and sites of worship, promises from and covenants with God, dealings with the land's inhabitants, and domestic life. Gradually, it focuses on the all-important question of an heir to Abraham and on the status of his two sons, Ishmael and Isaac. Most of the cycle's elements form a symmetry whose

center is ch. 16. **12.1** *The LORD said*. None of Abram's earlier life is considered relevant. *Go from your country ... and your father's house*. Separation of parent and child echoes throughout Genesis; see 2.24; 22.2; 27.41–45; 37.12–36. *To the land that I will show you*. The exact goal unspecified, as if a test of faith; cf. 22.2. **12.2–3** Divine promise of land and posterity echoes throughout Genesis; cf. 13.15–17; 15.5, 7, 18–21; 17.2–8; 22.17–18; 24.60; 26.2–4; 28.3–4, 13–15 and the formula of fulfillment in Solomon's time (1 Kings 4.20). **12.4** *So Abram went as the LORD had told him*. Abram's obedience is immediate and unquestioning; cf. 22.3. *Abram was seventy-five years old*. Cf. other chronological references in the cycle: 16.3, 16; 17.1, 17, 24, 25; 21.5; 23.1; 25.7, 17. **12.5** *The persons whom they had acquired*, as servants, companions, and co-religionists. **12.6** *Shechem*, site of the twelve-tribe covenant of confederacy formed under Joshua's leadership (Josh 24.1–28). *At that time*, then but no longer, or simply "by then." **12.7–9** *He built ... an altar ... and invoked*. Abram's devotions are further depicted in 13.3–4, 18; 15.10–11; 22.13. *From there he moved on*. Cf. Josh 24.3; Abram's journeys suggest the eventual range of Israelite settlement. *Negeb*, the present-day Negev desert.

12.10–20 Abram, forced by famine to take

[handwritten margin notes: "blessed despite actions", "moral wealth"]

was severe in the land. 11When he was about to enter Egypt, he said to his wife Sarai, "I know well that you are a woman beautiful in appearance; 12and when the Egyptians see you, they will say, 'This is his wife'; then they will kill me, but they will let you live. 13Say you are my sister, so that it may go well with me because of you, and that my life may be spared on your account." 14When Abram entered Egypt the Egyptians saw that the woman was very beautiful. 15When the officials of Pharaoh saw her, they praised her to Pharaoh. And the woman was taken into Pharaoh's house. 16And for her sake he dealt well with Abram; and he had sheep, oxen, male donkeys, male and female slaves, female donkeys, and camels.

17 But the LORD afflicted Pharaoh and his house with great plagues because of Sarai, Abram's wife. 18So Pharaoh called Abram, and said, "What is this you have done to me? Why did you not tell me that she was your wife? 19Why did you say, 'She is my sister,' so that I took her for my wife? Now then, here is your wife, take her, and be gone." 20And Pharaoh gave his men orders concerning him; and they set him on the way, with his wife and all that he had.

Abram and Lot Separate

13 So Abram went up from Egypt, he and his wife, and all that he had, and Lot with him, into the Negeb. 2 Now Abram was very rich in livestock, in silver, and in gold. 3He journeyed on by stages from the Negeb as far as Bethel, to the place where his tent had been at the beginning, between Bethel and Ai, 4to the place where he had made

an altar at the first; and there Abram called on the name of the LORD. 5Now Lot, who went with Abram, also had flocks and herds and tents, 6so that the land could not support both of them living together; for their possessions were so great that they could not live together, 7and there was strife between the herders of Abram's livestock and the herders of Lot's livestock. At that time the Canaanites and the Perizzites lived in the land.

8 Then Abram said to Lot, "Let there be no strife between you and me, and between your herders and my herders; for we are kindred. 9Is not the whole land before you? Separate yourself from me. If you take the left hand, then I will go to the right; or if you take the right hand, then I will go to the left." 10Lot looked about him, and saw that the plain of the Jordan was well watered everywhere like the garden of the LORD, like the land of Egypt, in the direction of Zoar; this was before the LORD had destroyed Sodom and Gomorrah. 11So Lot chose for himself all the plain of the Jordan, and Lot journeyed eastward; thus they separated from each other. 12Abram settled in the land of Canaan, while Lot settled among the cities of the Plain and moved his tent as far as Sodom. 13Now the people of Sodom were wicked, great sinners against the LORD.

14 The LORD said to Abram, after Lot had separated from him, "Raise your eyes now, and look from the place where you are, northward and southward and eastward and westward; 15for all the land that you see I will give to you and to your offspring[i] forever. 16I will make your off-

i Heb *seed*

---

up alien status in a foreign land (cf. 20.1; 26.1; 46.1–4), represents his wife as his sister (cf. 20.2; 26.7). The episode, like its parallels, emphasizes a moment when the destined line of Isaac was nearly lost before it began because of erroneous appropriation of the ancestral mother by a foreign king. **12.17** *Great plagues* foretoken the plagues visited on Egypt in Ex 7.14–12.32. **12.20** *They set him on his way,* foretokening the exodus. *With his wife and all that he had.* The Israelites, too, would leave Egypt with their families and a wealth of possessions; see 12.16; 15.14; 20.14–16; Ex 12.36. **13.1–18** The separation between Abram and his nephew Lot. Despite Lot's departure, Abra-

ham remains concerned for his welfare in 14.14–16; 18.23–33. **13.3** *Where his tent had been.* See 12.8. **13.7** *And there was strife.* A similar amicably settled dispute over servants' actions arises between Abraham and Abimelech in 21.25–34. *At that time.* See note on 12.6. **13.10–13** Lot's choice will prove to be shortsighted. *Like the garden . . . like . . . Egypt* connects the story thematically with both the garden of Eden story and the future episodes of Israelites in Egypt. *The people of Sodom were wicked,* as 18.16–19.29 will make clearer. **13.14** *Raise your eyes now.* Lot's shortsightedness and Abram's foresight here contrast. *Northward . . . westward* anticipates Israel's maximum expansion in the era of

spring like the dust of the earth; so that if one can count the dust of the earth, your offspring also can be counted. 17 Rise up, walk through the length and the breadth of the land, for I will give it to you." 18 So Abram moved his tent, and came and settled by the oaks *j* of Mamre, which are at Hebron; and there he built an altar to the LORD.

Lot's Captivity and Rescue

14 In the days of King Amraphel of Shinar, King Arioch of Ellasar, King Chedorlaomer of Elam, and King Tidal of Goiim, 2 these kings made war with King Bera of Sodom, King Birsha of Gomorrah, King Shinab of Admah, King Shemeber of Zeboiim, and the king of Bela (that is, Zoar). 3 All these joined forces in the Valley of Siddim (that is, the Dead Sea).*k* 4 Twelve years they had served Chedorlaomer, but in the thirteenth year they rebelled. 5 In the fourteenth year Chedorlaomer and the kings

who were with him came and subdued the Rephaim in Ashteroth-karnaim, the Zuzim in Ham, the Emim in Shaveh-kiriathaim, 6 and the Horites in the hill country of Seir as far as El-paran on the edge of the wilderness; 7 then they turned back and came to En-mishpat (that is, Kadesh), and subdued all the country of the Amalekites, and also the Amorites who lived in Hazazon-tamar. 8 Then the king of Sodom, the king of Gomorrah, the king of Admah, the king of Zeboiim, and the king of Bela (that is, Zoar) went out, and they joined battle in the Valley of Siddim 9 with King Chedorlaomer of Elam, King Tidal of Goiim, King Amraphel of Shinar, and King Arioch of Ellasar, four kings against five. 10 Now the Valley of Siddim was full of bitumen pits; and as the kings of Sodom and Gomorrah fled, some fell into them, and the rest fled to the hill country. 11 So the enemy took all the goods of Sodom and Gomorrah, and

j Or *terebinths*   *k* Heb *Salt Sea*

Solomon; see 1 Kings 4.20–25. **13.18** *The oaks of Mamre . . . at Hebron.* Cf. "oak of Moreh" at Shechem (12.6). The hill country from Shechem to Hebron will comprise the core of later Israelite settlement.

14.1–24 A military exploit by Abram to rescue Lot from capture by an alliance of eastern kings at war with cities in the Jordan plain. The account, whose origins are difficult to identify, contains authentic Bronze Age names, but corresponds to no known events, portraying Abram as a figure of world-historical importance—an *apiru*-type military chieftain (see note on 14.13), a man of dignity and scrupulousness who, in rescuing his kinsman, decisively aided a faltering local rebellion against Mesopotamian rule. **14.1** *Amraphel.* Once identified with Hammurabi of Babylon, the name is of uncertain origin. *Shinar,* probably Babylon. *Arioch.* Scholars have suggested identifications with Sumerian *Eri-aku* or Mari *Arriwuk* but the actual identity is uncertain. *Ellasar.* Identification with Larsa uncertain. *Chedorlaomer. Kudur-lagamar* is an authentic Elamite name. *Elam.* See 10.22. *Tidal* resembles Hittite *Tudhalia. Goiim,* lit. "nations," possibly a city-state league. **14.2** Some ancient and modern commentators have seen these names of kings as allegorical (e.g., *Bera,* "In Evil," *Birsha,* "In Wickedness"), but they, like the city names, are problematical. *Sodom, Gomorrah.* See ch. 19. *Admah, Zeboiim.* Cf. 10.19; Deut 29.23 (v. 22 in Hebrew); Hos 11.8. *Zoar.* Cf. 19.20–23. **14.3** *All these joined forces in,* the four eastern kings lit. "came in league against." The

Valley of Siddim. The name is unattested elsewhere, although it probably means "Valley of Demons," i.e., spirits of the dead. **14.4** *They had served,* as vassal states, paying tribute in taxes. **14.5** *Chedorlaomer,* here the league's leader. *Rephaim,* lit. "Shades, Spirits." The term is used to refer to pre-Israelite inhabitants of Palestine (15.20), while geographic areas such as Ashtaroth, the capital city of Og, are said to be of the "land of the Rephaim." (See also Deut 2.11; 1 Chr 20.4.) *Asteroth-karnaim,* lit. "Two-Horned Astarte" a place-name (cf. Am 6.13). *Zuzim.* Place unknown. One Greek manuscript tradition reads Zamzum-mim (Deut 2.20). *Ham.* Place unknown. *Emim,* in Deut 2.10–11 another race of Canaanite giants. *Shaveh-kiriathaim,* a Transjordanian city (probably near modern el-Qereiyat; cf. Num 32.37; Josh 13.19). **14.6** *Horites,* a Semitic people (therefore, not Hurrians) said to have dwelt in *Seir* before the Edomites; cf. Deut 2.12, 22; in Gen 36.2 they are called "Hivites." *El-paran,* lit. "Tree of Paran," possibly to be identified with Elath (Deut 2.8). **14.7** *En-mishpat . . . Kadesh,* probably modern 'Ayn-Gedeirat. Cf. Ex 17.7; Num 20.1; Deut 1.2. *Amalekites,* a Negev people, historical enemies of Israel; cf. Ex 17.8–16; Num 14.43–45; 1 Sam 15.5–33. *Amorites.* See note on 10.16. *Hazazon-tamar,* possibly En-gedi (cf. 2 Chr 20.2) or Tamar (1 Kings 9.18; cf. Ezek 47.19; 48.28). **14.10** *Kings of Sodom and Gomorrah.* All five Canaanite kings are meant here. *Some,* not the king of Sodom; cf. 14.21. *Fled to the hill country.* Cf.

all their provisions, and went their way;
12 they also took Lot, the son of Abram's
brother, who lived in Sodom, and his
goods, and departed.

13   Then one who had escaped came
and told Abram the Hebrew, who was living by the oaks*l* of Mamre the Amorite,
brother of Eshcol and of Aner; these were
allies of Abram. 14 When Abram heard
that his nephew had been taken captive,
he led forth his trained men, born in his
house, three hundred eighteen of them,
and went in pursuit as far as Dan. 15 He
divided his forces against them by night,
he and his servants, and routed them and
pursued them to Hobah, north of Damascus. 16 Then he brought back all the
goods, and also brought back his nephew
Lot with his goods, and the women and
the people.

Abram Blessed by Melchizedek

17   After his return from the defeat of
Chedorlaomer and the kings who were
with him, the king of Sodom went out to
meet him at the Valley of Shaveh (that is,
the King's Valley). 18 And King Melchizedek of Salem brought out bread and

wine; he was priest of God Most High.*m*
19 He blessed him and said,
    "Blessed be Abram by God Most
        High,*m*
    maker of heaven and earth;
20   and blessed be God Most High,*m*
    who has delivered your enemies
        into your hand!"
And Abram gave him one-tenth of everything. 21 Then the king of Sodom said to
Abram, "Give me the persons, but take
the goods for yourself." 22 But Abram said
to the king of Sodom, "I have sworn to the
LORD, God Most High,*m* maker of heaven
and earth, 23 that I would not take a
thread or a sandal-thong or anything that
is yours, so that you might not say, 'I have
made Abram rich.' 24 I will take nothing
but what the young men have eaten, and
the share of the men who went with me —
Aner, Eshcol, and Mamre. Let them take
their share."

God's Covenant with Abram

15 After these things the word of the
LORD came to Abram in a vision,
"Do not be afraid, Abram, I am your

l Or *terebinths*   *m* Heb *El Elyon*

19.20–29. **14.12** *Son of Abram's brother* estab-
lishes the tale's first connection to Abram.
14.13 *Hebrew*, later a term for an Israelite used
chiefly by (or when addressing) foreigners; cf.
38.14; 41.12; Jon 1.9. Cf. Canaanite-Akkadian
'apiru or *habiru* ("migrant, transient"), a Bronze
Age sojourner, but see note on 10.21. *Mamre*.
See 13.18. *Eshcol*, lit. "Grape-cluster," a Hebronite
place-name in Num 13.23–24; Deut 1.24.
Aner. Reference uncertain. **14.14** *Nephew*, lit.
"brother, kinsman." *Led forth*, lit. "unsheathed."
Trained men, born in his house, proven warriors and
trusted associates. *Three hundred eighteen*, a miraculously small number against such formidable foes;
cf. note on 14.15. **14.15** *Pursued them . . . north of
Damascus*, an exaggeration in keeping with the
tale's miraculous character. *Hobah*, possibly Ube,
in Bronze Age sources, a land whose capital was
Damascus.
14.17–24   Abram's victorious return from
battle. Vv. 18–20 comprise an independent tradition about Abram's meeting with King Melchizedek of Salem. **14.17** *Valley of Shaveh . . . the
King's Valley*, sometimes identified with the valley
of Absalom's monument, near Jerusalem (see
2 Sam 18.18). **14.18** *King Melchizedek*, a Canaanite priest-king. *Salem*, identified with Jerusalem in

Ps 76.3, in extrabiblical sources with *Uru-Salim*.
God Most High, or *El Elyon*, was a Canaanite deity
whose identity here is merged with Abram's
God. **14.20** *Abram gave . . . one-tenth*, possibly an
explanation of the Israelite law of tithing; cf.
28.22; Deut 14.22–29. **14.21–24** Abram's refusal makes him more than a mere mercenary
and places the kings of the region enduringly in
his debt, a further sign of his foothold in the
promised land.
15.1–21   The first of two episodes (cf. ch. 17)
describing a divine covenant with Abraham. The
chapter continues the dual-promise theme (land
and posterity) begun in chs. 12–13. **15.1** *After
these things*. Cf. 22.1, 20; 39.7; 40.1; 48.1. *The word
of the LORD came . . . in a vision* draws attention
more explicitly than in previous episodes to prophetic revelation. *Do not be afraid*, a formula common in oracles of promise (cf., e.g., 26.24; 46.3;
Deut 1.21; Judg 6.23; Isa 41.10). Divine reassurance perhaps makes best sense after Lot's departure in ch. 13 — Abram is now left with no
potential heir. But ch. 14 deepens the effect:
Abram's concern about an heir assails him precisely at a moment of worldly triumph. *Shield*. Cf.
Deut 33.29; Pss 18.2, 30 (vv. 3, 31 in Hebrew);

shield; your reward shall be very great."
2 But Abram said, "O Lord GOD, what will
you give me, for I continue childless, and
the heir of my house is Eliezer of Damascus?"*n* 3 And Abram said, "You have
given me no offspring, and so a slave born
in my house is to be my heir." 4 But the
word of the LORD came to him, "This man
shall not be your heir; no one but your
very own issue shall be your heir." 5 He
brought him outside and said, "Look toward heaven and count the stars, if you
are able to count them." Then he said to
him, "So shall your descendants be."
6 And he believed the LORD; and the
LORD*o* reckoned it to him as righteousness.

7 Then he said to him, "I am the LORD
who brought you from Ur of the Chaldeans, to give you this land to possess." 8 But
he said, "O Lord GOD, how am I to know
that I shall possess it?" 9 He said to him,
"Bring me a heifer three years old, a female goat three years old, a ram three
years old, a turtledove, and a young pigeon." 10 He brought him all these and cut
them in two, laying each half over against
the other; but he did not cut the birds in
two. 11 And when birds of prey came
down on the carcasses, Abram drove them
away.

12 As the sun was going down, a deep
sleep fell upon Abram, and a deep and
terrifying darkness descended upon him.
13 Then the LORD*o* said to Abram, "Know
this for certain, that your offspring shall
be aliens in a land that is not theirs, and
shall be slaves there, and they shall be oppressed for four hundred years; 14 but I
will bring judgment on the nation that
they serve, and afterward they shall come
out with great possessions. 15 As for yourself, you shall go to your ancestors in
peace; you shall be buried in a good old
age. 16 And they shall come back here in
the fourth generation; for the iniquity of
the Amorites is not yet complete."

17 When the sun had gone down and
it was dark, a smoking fire pot and a flaming torch passed between these pieces.
18 On that day the LORD made a covenant
with Abram, saying, "To your descendants I give this land, from the river of
Egypt to the great river, the river Euphrates, 19 the land of the Kenites, the Keniz-
zites, the Kadmonites, 20 the Hittites, the
Perizzites, the Rephaim, 21 the Amorites,
the Canaanites, the Girgashites, and the
Jebusites."

n Meaning of Heb uncertain   *o* Heb *he*

84.11; 144.2. **15.2** *O Lord GOD,* Hebrew *'adonai
YHWH* ("Lord YHWH"), a form of address often
used in scenes of prophetic call (cf. Judg 6.22; Jer
1.6). *What will you give me?* Abram desires a sign or
reassurance—or perhaps he means: What is "reward" worth without an heir? Abram's doubts and
God's reassurances again foreshadow scenes of
prophetic call (cf. Ex 3; Judg 6.11–27; Isa
6.1–13; Jer 1.1–19). Here the prophetic "mission" is not to preach but to procreate. *Eliezer of
Damascus,* lit. "The Damascan, Eliezer" perhaps
Abram's chief steward (cf. 24.2). Abram possibly
exaggerates for emphasis; Eliezer is not necessarily his legal heir. **15.4** After promises of "innumerable" offspring and a "nation" from Abram's
loins, the first reference to a *specific* heir; cf. note
on 16.11. **15.5** Cf. 13.16. **15.6** Abraham's legendary reputation for faith (cf. Gal 3.6–9; Heb
11.8–12) is rooted in this verse. **15.7** Cf. Ex
20.2. **15.8** *How am I to know?* Abram's doubt
about posterity is matched by doubt about
the promised land. **15.9–11** God's answer is
indirect—Abram must now reformulate his question as a ritual of oracle seeking. Cf. v. 13.
15.12 *Deep sleep.* The same word is used in 2.21.
15.13–21 The sole reference in Genesis to events

of the exodus. While never mentioned by
name, Egypt is clearly intended in vv. 13–14.
15.13 *Know . . . for certain* recalls Abram's question in 15.8. See note on 9.24. *Aliens.* See note on
23.4. *They shall be oppressed.* See note on 16.6. *Four
hundred years,* a schematic figure; the total Egyptian sojourn is later reckoned at 430 years (Ex
12.40). **15.14** *Judgment,* the ten plagues. *With
great possessions.* Cf. Ex 12.35–36. **15.15** *Old age,*
lit. "gray hairs"; cf. 25.8; 42.38. **15.16** *The fourth
generation.* A four-generation cycle of divine justice is implied; cf. Ex 20.5; 34.7; Num 14.18; Deut
5.9. The Egyptian sojourn begins in the fourth
generation after Abraham, the exodus in the
fourth generation after Jacob. *The iniquity of the
Amorites is not yet complete.* A society's evil can take
as long as four generations to mature before war-
ranting divine retribution against the whole people. Possession of Canaan is hinged on the
justness of its inhabitants. Cf. Ex 23.23–33; Lev
26.3–13; Deut 28.1–68. **15.17** *A smoking fire pot
. . . between these pieces* indicates divine acceptance
of the offering. **15.18** *From the river of Egypt to
. . . the river Euphrates.* Cf. 13.14–17; Deut 11.24;
1 Kings 4.21. **15.19–21** Ten nations are mentioned, in contrast to six in Ex 23.23; 34.11, and

The Birth of Ishmael

16 Now Sarai, Abram's wife, bore him no children. She had an Egyptian slave-girl whose name was Hagar, 2 and Sarai said to Abram, "You see that the LORD has prevented me from bearing children; go in to my slave-girl; it may be that I shall obtain children by her." And Abram listened to the voice of Sarai. 3 So, after Abram had lived ten years in the land of Canaan, Sarai, Abram's wife, took Hagar the Egyptian, her slave-girl, and gave her to her husband Abram as a wife. 4 He went in to Hagar, and she conceived; and when she saw that she had conceived, she looked with contempt on her mistress. 5 Then Sarai said to Abram, "May the wrong done to me be on you! I gave my slave-girl to your embrace, and when she saw that she had conceived, she looked on me with contempt. May the LORD judge between you and me!" 6 But Abram said to Sarai, "Your slave-girl is in your power; do to her as you please." Then Sarai dealt harshly with her, and she ran away from her.

7 The angel of the LORD found her by a spring of water in the wilderness, the spring on the way to Shur. 8 And he said, "Hagar, slave-girl of Sarai, where have you come from and where are you going?" She said, "I am running away from my mistress Sarai." 9 The angel of the LORD said to her, "Return to your mistress, and submit to her." 10 The angel of the LORD also said to her, "I will so greatly multiply your offspring that they cannot be counted for multitude." 11 And the angel of the LORD said to her,

"Now you have conceived and
     shall bear a son;
you shall call him Ishmael,P
     for the LORD has given heed to
     your affliction.
12 He shall be a wild ass of a man,
     with his hand against everyone,
     and everyone's hand
         against him;
and he shall live at odds with all
     his kin."

13 So she named the LORD who spoke to her, "You are El-roi";q for she said, "Have I really seen God and remained alive after seeing him?"r 14 Therefore the well was called Beer-lahai-roi;s it lies between Kadesh and Bered.

15 Hagar bore Abram a son; and Abram named his son, whom Hagar bore, Ishmael. 16 Abram was eighty-six years old when Hagar bore himt Ishmael.

p That is *God hears*   q Perhaps *God of seeing* or *God who sees*   r Meaning of Heb uncertain s That is *the Well of the Living One who sees me* t Heb *Abram*

---

seven in Deut 7.1. See note on 10.15–20.
16.1–16 The birth of Abram's first child, Ishmael, through his servant Hagar—our first close glimpse of life in Abram's household and the basis for much that will happen later. **16.1** *An Egyptian slave-girl.* Hagar's Egyptian identity is important to the story; see note on 16.6. **16.2** *Obtain children by her.* Sarai's plan, probably common practice in slave-owning households (cf. 30.3, 9), represents a moral compromise, for Hagar's rights as mother will be subordinate to Sarai's. Cf. Ex 2.1–10. *Abram listened*, in Hebrew a play on "Ishmael"—the same verb occurs in v. 11; 17.20; 21.17. Cf. its use in 3.10, 17. **16.3** *Ten years*, a natural time for pondering the future. *Took . . . and gave.* Cf. use of these verbs in 3.6. **16.4** *She looked with contempt.* Cf. 1 Sam 1.6. **16.5** Cf. Sarah's demand for Abraham's intervention in 21.10 and the situations in 31.53; Ex 5.21; 1 Sam 24.12. **16.6** Sarai *dealt harshly with her*, lit. "oppressed her." Harkening back to 15.13 and foreshadowing Ex 1.11, this connects Sarai's oppression of an Egyptian with the Egyptians' oppression of Sarai's descendants. Indeed, in 37.28

it is Ishmaelites, Hagar's descendants, who transport the enslaved Joseph to Egypt. **16.7** *Angel of the LORD.* Cf. 18.1–16; 19.1–22; 21.17; 22.11–18. *Shur*, near the ancient border of Egypt. **16.9** *Return . . . and submit*, thus explaining Hagar's continued presence in the household of Abraham and Sarah. Hagar is otherwise vindicated in the words that follow. **16.10** Essentially the same promise given to Abram in 13.16; 15.5, but conspicuously understated. Cf. 21.18. **16.11** The promise of a child to Abram now gains additional definition: the mother is identified and the child's name mentioned—but Abram's problem of succession is still by no means solved. **16.12** Possibly a description cherished by early Ishmaelites themselves—cf. the defiant tribal mottoes in Jacob's blessing, especially 49.17, 27. **16.13–14** Both Ishmael and Isaac are the subject of narratives that turn conspicuously on the verb "see"; cf. 21.9, 16, 19; 22.4, 8, 13, 14. **16.15** *Abram named his son . . . Ishmael.* Abram either listened to Hagar (cf. v. 2), or divine will influenced his choice of name. **16.16** This verse continues the preoccupation with chronology expressed in v. 3.

The Sign of the Covenant

17 When Abram was ninety-nine years old, the LORD appeared to Abram, and said to him, "I am God Almighty;[u] walk before me, and be blameless. 2 And I will make my covenant between me and you, and will make you exceedingly numerous." 3 Then Abram fell on his face; and God said to him, 4 "As for me, this is my covenant with you: You shall be the ancestor of a multitude of nations. 5 No longer shall your name be Abram,[v] but your name shall be Abraham;[w] for I have made you the ancestor of a multitude of nations. 6 I will make you exceedingly fruitful; and I will make nations of you, and kings shall come from you. 7 I will establish my covenant between me and you, and your offspring after you throughout their generations, for an everlasting covenant, to be God to you and to your offspring[x] after you. 8 And I will give to you, and to your offspring after you, the land where you are now an alien, all the land of Canaan, for a perpetual holding; and I will be their God."

9 God said to Abraham, "As for you, you shall keep my covenant, you and your offspring after you throughout their generations. 10 This is my covenant, which you shall keep, between me and you and your offspring after you: Every male among you shall be circumcised. 11 You shall circumcise the flesh of your foreskins, and it shall be a sign of the covenant between me and you. 12 Throughout your generations every male among you shall be circumcised when he is eight days old, including the slave born in your house and the one bought with your money from any foreigner who is not of your offspring. 13 Both the slave born in your house and the one bought with your money must be circumcised. So shall my covenant be in your flesh an everlasting covenant. 14 Any uncircumcised male who is not circumcised in the flesh of his foreskin shall be cut off from his people; he has broken my covenant."

15 God said to Abraham, "As for Sarai your wife, you shall not call her Sarai, but Sarah shall be her name. 16 I will bless her, and moreover I will give you a son by her. I will bless her, and she shall give rise to nations; kings of peoples shall come from her." 17 Then Abraham fell on his face and laughed, and said to himself, "Can a child be born to a man who is a hundred years old? Can Sarah, who is ninety years old, bear a child?" 18 And Abraham said to God, "O that Ishmael might live in your sight!" 19 God said, "No, but your wife Sarah shall bear you a son, and you shall name him Isaac.[y] I will establish my covenant with him as an everlasting covenant for his offspring after him. 20 As for Ishmael, I have heard you; I will bless him

u Traditional rendering of Heb *El Shaddai*
v That is *exalted ancestor*   w Here taken to mean *ancestor of a multitude*   x Heb *seed*   y That is *he laughs*

17.1–27 An alternate version of the covenant concluded in ch. 15—here thirteen years after Ishmael's birth. The rite of circumcision is instituted, and Abram's and Sarai's names are changed to their more familiar forms. **17.1** *God Almighty*, in Hebrew *El Shaddai*, a name prominent in Priestly tradition; see Introduction; 28.3; 35.11; 48.3. In Ex 6.3, the name is restricted to the ancestral era. *Shaddai* is also common in other expressions of blessing (cf., e.g., Gen 43.14; 49.25; Num 24.4, 16) and occurs extensively throughout Job. **17.4** *Covenant* is a recurring motif throughout the chapter; see vv. 7, 9, 10, 11, 13, 14, 19, 21. **17.5** *Abram, Abraham*. The first name means "Ab [a divine name] is lofty"; the second is construed to mean "Father of a multitude." *A multitude of nations*. Cf. v. 6. Among non-Israelites, the Arabs, notably, claim descent from Abraham through Ishmael. On Abraham in Islamic tradition, cf. Qur'an 14.35–42. **17.8** *Ca-*naan, *for a perpetual holding*. The idea did not always match the reality—it implicitly contradicts the perspective of 15.13–16, where justice alone determines the land's ownership. **17.10** *Every male . . . circumcised*. The rite is practiced today among Jews and Moslems. On its importance, see Ex 4.24–26. **17.12** *When he is eight days old*, the present practice among Jews; among Moslems, the rite is administered at age thirteen; cf. v. 25. **17.14** *Shall be cut off*. On excommunication, a severe penalty in biblical law, see Ex 30.33, 38; 31.14; Lev 7.20–27; 17.9. **17.15–16** The first time that a child is promised explicitly to Sarah. **17.17** Cf. Sarah's incredulity in 18.12–15. In Hebrew *laughed* is a play on "Isaac"; see also v. 19; 21.6–7. **17.18** Cf. Abraham's concern in 21.11. **17.19** *My covenant with him*, with Isaac. This anticipates the Sinaitic revelation in Ex 20–24; see note on 17.21. **17.20** *I have heard you*, in Hebrew, another play on "Ishmael"; see note

see Gen 25:12-18

and make him fruitful and exceedingly numerous; he shall be the father of twelve princes, and I will make him a great nation. 21 But my covenant I will establish with Isaac, whom Sarah shall bear to you at this season next year." 22 And when he had finished talking with him, God went up from Abraham.

23   Then Abraham took his son Ishmael and all the slaves born in his house or bought with his money, every male among the men of Abraham's house, and he circumcised the flesh of their foreskins that very day, as God had said to him. 24 Abraham was ninety-nine years old when he was circumcised in the flesh of his foreskin. 25 And his son Ishmael was thirteen years old when he was circumcised in the flesh of his foreskin. 26 That very day Abraham and his son Ishmael were circumcised; 27 and all the men of his house, slaves born in the house and those bought with money from a foreigner, were circumcised with him.

A Son Promised to Abraham and Sarah

18 The LORD appeared to Abraham*z* by the oaks*a* of Mamre, as he sat at the entrance of his tent in the heat of the day. 2 He looked up and saw three men standing near him. When he saw them, he ran from the tent entrance to meet them, and bowed down to the ground. 3 He said, "My lord, if I find favor with you, do not pass by your servant. 4 Let a little water be brought, and wash your feet, and rest yourselves under the tree. 5 Let me bring a little bread, that you may refresh yourselves, and after that you may pass on—since you have come to your servant." So they said, "Do as you have said." 6 And Abraham hastened into the tent to Sarah, and said, "Make ready quickly three measures*b* of choice flour, knead it, and make cakes." 7 Abraham ran to the herd, and took a calf, tender and good, and gave it to the servant, who hastened to prepare it. 8 Then he took curds and milk and the calf that he had prepared, and set it before them; and he stood by them under the tree while they ate.

9   They said to him, "Where is your wife Sarah?" And he said, "There, in the tent." 10 Then one said, "I will surely return to you in due season, and your wife Sarah shall have a son." And Sarah was listening at the tent entrance behind him. 11 Now Abraham and Sarah were old, advanced in age; it had ceased to be with Sarah after the manner of women. 12 So Sarah laughed to herself, saying, "After I have grown old, and my husband is old, shall I have pleasure?" 13 The LORD said to Abraham, "Why did Sarah laugh, and say, 'Shall I indeed bear a child, now that I am old?' 14 Is anything too wonderful for the LORD? At the set time I will return to you, in due season, and Sarah shall have a son." 15 But Sarah denied, saying, "I did not laugh"; for she was afraid. He said, "Oh yes, you did laugh."

z Heb *him*   a Or *terebinths*   b Heb *seahs*

---

on 16.2. *Make him fruitful.* Cf. 16.10. *Father of twelve princes.* See 25.12–16. **17.21** Thus, two senses of "covenant" apply in this story: circumcision (applicable to both sons) and Sinaitic revelation (to Isaac alone).

18.1–19.38 God's destruction of Sodom and Gomorrah and its aftermath. **18.1–15** Another version of the annunciation of Isaac told in 17.15–21, the news here brought by the same emissaries who carry out the destruction in ch. 19. **18.1** *The LORD appeared* makes clear that the three strangers described next are not earthly beings. *Oaks of Mamre*, in Hebron; cf. 13.18; 14.13. *In the heat of the day*, a natural time for travelers to seek shelter. **18.2** The unearthly identity of the *three men* is not apparent to Abraham; he bestows on them the same generous hospitality he might show any human visitor. *He ran . . . and bowed.* The text emphasizes his exertions in their honor; cf. the verbs of hastening in vv. 6–7. **18.3** *My lord* can mean "my lords," "my lord" (spoken to one visitor on behalf of all three), or "my Lord" (meaning God). The Hebrew text is vocalized to indicate the third possibility, but the first or second is more appropriate to the immediate situation. **18.8** *Stood by them*, out of concern for their comfort. **18.10** *One said*, lit. "He [God] said." God seems to speak directly in the exchange that follows, not through emissaries. **18.11** *It had ceased . . . the manner of women.* Sarah no longer had menstrual periods. **18.12** *Laughed*, in Hebrew another play on "Isaac"; see note on 17.17. *Pleasure*, i.e., sexual enjoyment. **18.14** *Too wonderful for the LORD*, i.e., beyond God's powers; cf. Num 11.23. **18.15** *Sarah denied.* She seeks to cancel or retract her laughter. *Oh yes, you did laugh*, not an accusation, but provoking the reflection that will result in her child's name.

The Fate of Sodom

16 Then the men set out from there, and they looked toward Sodom; and Abraham went with them to set them on their way. 17 The Lord said, "Shall I hide from Abraham what I am about to do, 18 seeing that Abraham shall become a great and mighty nation, and all the nations of the earth shall be blessed in him?[c] 19 No, for I have chosen[d] him, that he may charge his children and his household after him to keep the way of the Lord by doing righteousness and justice; so that the Lord may bring about for Abraham what he has promised him." 20 Then the Lord said, "How great is the outcry against Sodom and Gomorrah and how very grave their sin! 21 I must go down and see whether they have done altogether according to the outcry that has come to me; and if not, I will know."

22 So the men turned from there, and went toward Sodom, while Abraham remained standing before the Lord.[e] 23 Then Abraham came near and said, "Will you indeed sweep away the righteous with the wicked? 24 Suppose there are fifty righteous within the city; will you then sweep away the place and not forgive it for the fifty righteous who are in it? 25 Far be it from you to do such a thing, to slay the righteous with the wicked, so that the righteous fare as the wicked! Far be that from you! Shall not the Judge of all the earth do what is just?" 26 And the Lord said, "If I find at Sodom fifty righteous in the city, I will forgive the whole place for their sake." 27 Abraham answered, "Let me take it upon myself to speak to the Lord, I who am but dust and ashes. 28 Suppose five of the fifty righteous are lacking? Will you destroy the whole city for lack of five?" And he said, "I will not destroy it if I find forty-five there." 29 Again he spoke to him, "Suppose forty are found there." He answered, "For the sake of forty I will not do it." 30 Then he said, "Oh do not let the Lord be angry if I speak. Suppose thirty are found there." He answered, "I will not do it, if I find thirty there." 31 He said, "Let me take it upon myself to speak to the Lord. Suppose twenty are found there." He answered, "For the sake of twenty I will not destroy it." 32 Then he said, "Oh do not let the Lord be angry if I speak just once more. Suppose ten are found there." He answered, "For the sake of ten I will not destroy it." 33 And the Lord went his way, when he had finished speaking to Abraham; and Abraham returned to his place.

The Depravity of Sodom

19 The two angels came to Sodom in the evening, and Lot was sitting in the gateway of Sodom. When Lot saw them, he rose to meet them, and bowed down with his face to the ground. 2 He

c Or and all the nations of the earth shall bless themselves by him   d Heb known   e Another ancient tradition reads while the Lord remained standing before Abraham

---

18.16–33 A discussion between Abraham and God over the fate of Sodom, where Lot dwells, deepening the theme of moral justice introduced in 13.13; 15.16. Sodom's inhabitants represent the first people displaced from the land for moral depravity (cf. 13.13; 15.16)—yet even a righteous few could save the whole. 18.16 And Abraham went with them, as hospitality demanded. 18.17 A unique moment of divine reflection suggesting God's esteem for Abraham, implicitly a confirmation of Abraham's standing as a prophet or seer; cf. 20.7, 17; 21.22. 18.18 All the nations of the earth shall be blessed in him. Cf. 12.3. 18.19 I have chosen, lit. "known"; cf. notes on 9.24; 15.13. The way of the Lord anticipates the Sinai covenant in Ex 20–24. 18.20 Outcry against, lit. "cry of," perhaps the raucous noise of their violence and merriment; cf. Ex 32.17–18. 18.21 I must go down and see, through the emissaries in 19.1–11. 18.23 Abraham came near, a measure of his courage and daring. 18.23–33 In "bargaining" for God's promise to spare Sodom and Gomorrah for the sake of ten righteous inhabitants, Abraham presents an important quandary: What is the power (and limitation) of righteousness to sway God's intentions? 18.25 Shall not the Judge of all the earth do what is just? This question is the core of the issue and crucial to the events of ch. 22. 18.32 Just once more. The discussion considers no fewer than ten—God's forbearance for a smaller number's sake cannot be predicted.

19.1–11 A close glimpse of a community whose evil places them beyond redemption. This episode strongly resembles Judg 19.10–30. 19.1–3 These events recall Abraham's hospitality in 18.1–8. Lot's kindnesses are less impressive, but enough to show him as righteous, however minimally. 19.1 Two angels, as if the third of the three (18.2) had been God himself, who remained

said, "Please, my lords, turn aside to your servant's house and spend the night, and wash your feet; then you can rise early and go on your way." They said, "No; we will spend the night in the square." 3 But he urged them strongly; so they turned aside to him and entered his house; and he made them a feast, and baked unleavened bread, and they ate. 4 But before they lay down, the men of the city, the men of Sodom, both young and old, all the people to the last man, surrounded the house; 5 and they called to Lot, "Where are the men who came to you tonight? Bring them out to us, so that we may know them." 6 Lot went out of the door to the men, shut the door after him, 7 and said, "I beg you, my brothers, do not act so wickedly. 8 Look, I have two daughters who have not known a man; let me bring them out to you, and do to them as you please; only do nothing to these men, for they have come under the shelter of my roof." 9 But they replied, "Stand back!" And they said, "This fellow came here as an alien, and he would play the judge! Now we will deal worse with you than with them." Then they pressed hard against the man Lot, and came near the door to break it down. 10 But the men inside reached out their hands and brought Lot into the house with them, and shut the door. 11 And they struck with blindness the men who were at the door of the house, both small and great, so that they were unable to find the door.

Sodom and Gomorrah Destroyed

12 Then the men said to Lot, "Have you anyone else here? Sons-in-law, sons, daughters, or anyone you have in the city —bring them out of the place. 13 For we are about to destroy this place, because the outcry against its people has become great before the LORD, and the LORD has sent us to destroy it." 14 So Lot went out and said to his sons-in-law, who were to marry his daughters, "Up, get out of this place; for the LORD is about to destroy the city." But he seemed to his sons-in-law to be jesting.

15 When morning dawned, the angels urged Lot, saying, "Get up, take your wife and your two daughters who are here, or else you will be consumed in the punishment of the city." 16 But he lingered; so the men seized him and his wife and his two daughters by the hand, the LORD being merciful to him, and they brought him out and left him outside the city. 17 When they had brought them outside, they f said, "Flee for your life; do not look back or stop anywhere in the Plain; flee to the hills, or else you will be consumed." 18 And Lot said to them, "Oh, no, my lords; 19 your servant has found favor with you, and you have shown me great kindness in saving my life; but I cannot flee to the hills, for fear the disaster will overtake me and I die. 20 Look, that city is near enough to flee to, and it is a little one. Let me escape there—is it not a little one?—and my life will be saved!" 21 He said to him, "Very well, I grant you this favor too, and will not overthrow the city of which you have spoken. 22 Hurry, escape there, for I can do nothing until you arrive there." Therefore the city was called Zoar.g 23 The sun had risen on the earth when Lot came to Zoar.

24 Then the LORD rained on Sodom and Gomorrah sulfur and fire from the LORD out of heaven; 25 and he overthrew those cities, and all the Plain, and all the inhabitants of the cities, and what grew on the ground. 26 But Lot's wife, behind him, looked back, and she became a pillar of salt.

27 Abraham went early in the morn-

f Gk Syr Vg: Heb *he*   g That is *Little*

---

to converse with Abraham. **19.4** *Young and old . . . to the last man* stresses the completeness of their iniquity, conspicuously recalling 15.16. **19.5** *That we may know them,* i.e., sexually; cf. Judg 19.22. **19.8** *Look, I have two daughters . . . do to them as you please.* Lot's solution is less than exemplary; cf. Judg 19.24–25 and see note on 19.30–38. **19.9** *He would play the judge,* a ready rationalization by those accused of wrongdoing; cf. Ex 2.14; Num 16.13. **19.11** *Blindness,* or "blinding light"; cf. 2 Kings 6.18.

19.12–29 The final step in the angels' mission, the destruction of Sodom and Gomorrah. **19.14** *Seemed . . . to be jesting.* Their refusal to take Lot seriously seals their doom; cf. v. 31. **19.15** *Your wife and . . . daughters.* The number saved narrows conspicuously. **19.18** *My lords.* See note on 18.3. **19.25** *Overthrew.* Cf. Jon 3.4. **19.26** *Pillar of salt,* possibly a local landmark. The number saved now shrinks to three. **19.27–29** The story returns to the context established in 18.23–33.

ing to the place where he had stood be-fore the Lord; 28 and he looked down toward Sodom and Gomorrah and toward all the land of the Plain and saw the smoke of the land going up like the smoke of a furnace.

29 So it was that, when God destroyed the cities of the Plain, God remembered Abraham, and sent Lot out of the midst of the overthrow, when he overthrew the cities in which Lot had settled.

The Origin of Moab and Ammon

30 Now Lot went up out of Zoar and settled in the hills with his two daughters, for he was afraid to stay in Zoar; so he lived in a cave with his two daughters. 31 And the firstborn said to the younger, "Our father is old, and there is not a man on earth to come in to us after the manner of all the world. 32 Come, let us make our father drink wine, and we will lie with him, so that we may preserve offspring through our father." 33 So they made their father drink wine that night; and the firstborn went in, and lay with her father; he did not know when she lay down or when she rose. 34 On the next day, the firstborn said to the younger, "Look, I lay last night with my father; let us make him drink wine tonight also; then you go in and lie with him, so that we may preserve offspring through our father." 35 So they made their father drink wine that night also; and the younger rose, and lay with him; and he did not know when she lay down or when she rose. 36 Thus both the daughters of Lot became pregnant by their father. 37 The firstborn bore a son, and named him Moab; he is the ancestor of the Moabites to this day. 38 The younger also bore a son and named him Ben-ammi; he is the ancestor of the Ammonites to this day.

Abraham and Sarah at Gerar

20 From there Abraham journeyed toward the region of the Negeb, and settled between Kadesh and Shur. While residing in Gerar as an alien, 2 Abraham said of his wife Sarah, "She is my sister." And King Abimelech of Gerar sent and took Sarah. 3 But God came to Abimelech in a dream by night, and said to him, "You are about to die because of the woman whom you have taken; for she is a married woman." 4 Now Abimelech had not approached her; so he said, "Lord, will you destroy an innocent people? 5 Did he not himself say to me, 'She is my sister'? And she herself said, 'He is my brother.' I did this in the integrity of my heart and the innocence of my hands." 6 Then God said to him in the dream, "Yes, I know that you did this in the integrity of your heart; furthermore it was I who kept you from sinning against me. Therefore I did not let you touch her. 7 Now then, return the man's wife; for he is a prophet, and he will pray for you and you shall live. But if you do not restore her, know that you shall surely die, you and all that are yours."

8 So Abimelech rose early in the morning, and called all his servants and told them all these things; and the men were very much afraid. 9 Then Abimelech called Abraham, and said to him, "What have you done to us? How have I sinned against you, that you have brought such great guilt on me and my kingdom? You have done things to me that ought not to be done." 10 And Abimelech said to Abraham, "What were you thinking of, that

---

19.30–38 The aftermath of Lot's escape from Sodom, explaining the origin of the Ammonites and Moabites, two Transjordanian peoples adjoining the Canaanites. This unflattering episode constitutes a fitting recompense for Lot's carelessness about his daughters' welfare in 19.8. But from Moab will eventually come Ruth, ancestor of King David (see Ruth 4.13–18). **19.31** *To come in . . . after the manner of all the world*, to cohabit sexually. **19.32–35** This passage recalls the drunkenness of Noah and resultant sexual indiscretion by one of his offspring in 9.18–27. **19.37–38** *Moab*, in the Hebrew a play on "[Of] the Same Father," as the Septuagint makes explicit. *Ben-ammi* can be translated "Son of My Paternal Kin" as glossed in the Septuagint. Both sons' names play on the incest theme.

20.1–18 An echo of the "wife-sister" episode of 12.10–20. Here the locale, as in 26.1–17, is Gerar. **20.1** *From there*, presumably from the oaks of Mamre in Hebron; cf. 13.18; 14.13; 18.1. On *Kadesh*, cf. 14.7. On *Shur*, cf. 16.7. *Gerar*, possibly a town in the Negev. Exact location uncertain. **20.6** *I . . . kept you from sinning.* Cf. 12.17; 20.18. **20.7** *For he is a prophet*, the sole reference to Abraham as a prophet, but consistent with "prophetic call" motifs of ch. 15; see note on

you did this thing?" 11Abraham said, "I did it because I thought, There is no fear of God at all in this place, and they will kill me because of my wife. 12Besides, she is indeed my sister, the daughter of my father but not the daughter of my mother; and she became my wife. 13And when God caused me to wander from my father's house, I said to her, 'This is the kindness you must do me: at every place to which we come, say of me, He is my brother.'" 14Then Abimelech took sheep and oxen, and male and female slaves, and gave them to Abraham, and restored his wife Sarah to him. 15Abimelech said, "My land is before you; settle where it pleases you." 16To Sarah he said, "Look, I have given your brother a thousand pieces of silver; it is your exoneration before all who are with you; you are completely vindicated." 17Then Abraham prayed to God; and God healed Abimelech, and also healed his wife and female slaves so that they bore children. 18For the LORD had closed fast all the wombs of the house of Abimelech because of Sarah, Abraham's wife.

The Birth of Isaac

21 The LORD dealt with Sarah as he had said, and the LORD did for Sarah as he had promised. 2Sarah conceived and bore Abraham a son in his old age, at the time of which God had spoken to him. 3Abraham gave the name Isaac to his son whom Sarah bore him. 4And Abraham circumcised his son Isaac when he was eight days old, as God had commanded him. 5Abraham was a hundred years old when his son Isaac was born to him. 6Now Sarah said, "God has brought laughter for me; everyone who hears will laugh with me." 7And she said, "Who would ever have said to Abraham that Sarah would nurse children? Yet I have borne him a son in his old age."

Hagar and Ishmael Sent Away

8 The child grew, and was weaned; and Abraham made a great feast on the day that Isaac was weaned. 9But Sarah saw the son of Hagar the Egyptian, whom she had borne to Abraham, playing with her son Isaac.h 10So she said to Abraham, "Cast out this slave woman with her son; for the son of this slave woman shall not inherit along with my son Isaac." 11The matter was very distressing to Abraham on account of his son. 12But God said to Abraham, "Do not be distressed because of the boy and because of your slave woman; whatever Sarah says to you, do as she tells you, for it is through Isaac that offspring shall be named for you. 13As for the son of the slave woman, I will make a nation of him also, because he is your offspring." 14So Abraham rose early in the morning, and took bread and a skin of water, and gave it to Hagar, putting it on her shoulder, along with the child, and sent her away. And she departed, and wandered about in the wilderness of Beer-sheba.

15 When the water in the skin was gone, she cast the child under one of the

h Gk Vg: Heb lacks with her son Isaac

15.2. **20.11** There is no fear of God at all in this place, a notion explicitly contradicted by 20.8. Cf. 21.22. This people's "iniquity . . . is not yet complete" (see 15.16). **20.12** An unanticipated rationale for the disguise undertaken in 20.2. Sarah's parentage is otherwise unmentioned; cf. 11.29. **20.14–16** Abimelech's generosity to Abraham recalls Pharaoh's in 12.16; cf. note on 12.20. **20.17** Abraham prayed, confirming his role as prophetic intercessor. **20.18** For the LORD . . . house of Abimelech recalls the plague visited on Egypt in 12.17. **21.1–7** The fulfillment of the promise made to Abraham and Sarah in 17.15–27; 18.1–15. **21.1** As he had said . . . as he had promised, probably referring to 18.15. **21.4** This verse continues the preoccupation with circumcision introduced in ch. 17. **21.6** Laughter, in Hebrew another play on "Isaac"; cf. 17.17; 18.12–15. **21.8–21** A repetition of the chief events of the domestic struggle portrayed in ch. 16: vying of Sarah and Hagar (cf. 16.4–6); Hagar's journey into the wilderness (cf. 16.7); encounter with an angel (cf. 16.7–8); consolations of Hagar (cf. 16.9–12); and miracle at a well (cf. 16.13–14). **21.9** Sarah saw. As in ch. 16, the verb "see" reverberates throughout. Playing, Hebrew metzacheq, a further play on "Isaac" (Yitzchaq). The word could signify "mocking," as Sarah's reaction suggests. **21.11** Distressing, lit. "evil," recalling Sarah's harsh treatment of Hagar in 16.6 (see note on 16.6; cf. 17.18), but Sarah is vindicated in the next verse. **21.12–13** Cf. 17.20–21. **21.14** Abraham's provisions for Hagar and Ishmael are conspicuously

bushes. 16Then she went and sat down opposite him a good way off, about the distance of a bowshot; for she said, "Do not let me look on the death of the child." And as she sat opposite him, she lifted up her voice and wept. 17And God heard the voice of the boy; and the angel of God called to Hagar from heaven, and said to her, "What troubles you, Hagar? Do not be afraid; for God has heard the voice of the boy where he is. 18Come, lift up the boy and hold him fast with your hand, for I will make a great nation of him." 19Then God opened her eyes and she saw a well of water. She went, and filled the skin with water, and gave the boy a drink.

20 God was with the boy, and he grew up; he lived in the wilderness, and became an expert with the bow. 21He lived in the wilderness of Paran; and his mother got a wife for him from the land of Egypt.

Abraham and Abimelech Make a Covenant

22 At that time Abimelech, with Phicol the commander of his army, said to Abraham, "God is with you in all that you do; 23now therefore swear to me here by God that you will not deal falsely with me or with my offspring or with my posterity, but as I have dealt loyally with you, you will deal with me and with the land where you have resided as an alien." 24And Abraham said, "I swear it."

25 When Abraham complained to Abimelech about a well of water that

Abimelech's servants had seized, 26Abimelech said, "I do not know who has done this; you did not tell me, and I have not heard of it until today." 27So Abraham took sheep and oxen and gave them to Abimelech, and the two men made a covenant. 28Abraham set apart seven ewe lambs of the flock. 29And Abimelech said to Abraham, "What is the meaning of these seven ewe lambs that you have set apart?" 30He said, "These seven ewe lambs you shall accept from my hand, in order that you may be a witness for me that I dug this well." 31Therefore that place was called Beer-sheba;*i* because there both of them swore an oath. 32When they had made a covenant at Beer-sheba, Abimelech, with Phicol the commander of his army, left and returned to the land of the Philistines. 33Abraham*j* planted a tamarisk tree in Beer-sheba, and called there on the name of the LORD, the Everlasting God.*k* 34And Abraham resided as an alien many days in the land of the Philistines.

The Command to Sacrifice Isaac

22 After these things God tested Abraham. He said to him, "Abraham!" And he said, "Here I am." 2He said, "Take your son, your only son Isaac, whom you love, and go to the land of Moriah, and offer him there as a burnt offering on one of the mountains that I shall

i That is *Well of seven* or *Well of the oath*
j Heb *He*   *k* Or *the* LORD, *El Olam*

---

minimal. Also cf. 25.5–6. **21.16** *Do not let me look.* See note on 21.9. **21.17** *Heard, has heard* in Hebrew plays on the name "Ishmael"; see note on 16.2. **21.21** *A wife for him from . . . Egypt,* in keeping with Hagar's own origins and in contrast to Abraham's plans for Isaac; cf. 24.2–8.

21.22–34 A return to Abraham's dealings with King Abimelech, begun in ch. 20. **21.22** *God is with you.* See note on 20.11. **21.25** *When Abraham complained.* See note on 13.7. **21.31** An etiological conclusion explaining a place-name; cf. 16.14; 19.22. **21.32** *Land of the Philistines,* an anachronism. Philistines did not arrive in Canaan until the era of Judges; cf. 10.14; 26.1; Judg 3.31; 13.1. **21.33** *Everlasting God,* possibly the name of a local Canaanite deity; cf. "El Elyon" (God Most High) in 14.19–20.

22.1–19 These verses narrate an extraordinary test of faith placed upon Abraham in the aftermath of Hagar's expulsion, an ironic culmi-

nation of the hopes and promises centered on Isaac throughout the cycle. The chief events of the narrative echo the two Hagar episodes: a journey into the wilderness, encounter with an angel, divine consolation, miracle at the site, and naming of the site. Cf. note on 21.8–21. **22.1** *After these things.* Cf. 15.1. *God tested.* The command is not in earnest, but Abraham does not know this. Cf. Job 1.12; 2.6. *Here I am,* archetypal response of the faithful servant of God; cf. 22.11; 31.11; 46.2; Ex 3.4; 1 Sam 3.4. **22.2** *Take your only son . . . whom you love,* in the Hebrew, "Take your son, your only son whom you love, Isaac." Not until Isaac's name is reached is the command's object clearly known; the phrase conceptually echoes 12.1. Although Ishmael is not mentioned, the verse presupposes his expulsion (21.8–14) and the strife over inheritance. *Land of Moriah.* Location unknown, later identified with the temple mount in Jerusalem (2 Chr 3.1); cf. note on 22.14. *On one of the moun-*

show you." 3 So Abraham rose early in the morning, saddled his donkey, and took two of his young men with him, and his son Isaac; he cut the wood for the burnt offering, and set out and went to the place in the distance that God had shown him. 4 On the third day Abraham looked up and saw the place far away. 5 Then Abraham said to his young men, "Stay here with the donkey; the boy and I will go over there; we will worship, and then we will come back to you." 6 Abraham took the wood of the burnt offering and laid it on his son Isaac, and he himself carried the fire and the knife. So the two of them walked on together. 7 Isaac said to his father Abraham, "Father!" And he said, "Here I am, my son." He said, "The fire and the wood are here, but where is the lamb for a burnt offering?" 8 Abraham said, "God himself will provide the lamb for a burnt offering, my son." So the two of them walked on together.

9 When they came to the place that God had shown him, Abraham built an altar there and laid the wood in order. He bound his son Isaac, and laid him on the altar, on top of the wood. 10 Then Abraham reached out his hand and took the knife to kill[1] his son. 11 But the angel of the LORD called to him from heaven, and said, "Abraham, Abraham!" And he said, "Here I am." 12 He said, "Do not lay your hand on the boy or do anything to him; for now I know that you fear God, since

you have not withheld your son, your only son, from me." 13 And Abraham looked up and saw a ram, caught in a thicket by its horns. Abraham went and took the ram and offered it up as a burnt offering instead of his son. 14 So Abraham called that place "The LORD will provide";[m] as it is said to this day, "On the mount of the LORD it shall be provided."[n]

15   The angel of the LORD called to Abraham a second time from heaven, 16 and said, "By myself I have sworn, says the LORD: Because you have done this, and have not withheld your son, your only son, 17 I will indeed bless you, and I will make your offspring as numerous as the stars of heaven and as the sand that is on the seashore. And your offspring shall possess the gate of their enemies, 18 and by your offspring shall all the nations of the earth gain blessing for themselves, because you have obeyed my voice." 19 So Abraham returned to his young men, and they arose and went together to Beer-sheba; and Abraham lived at Beer-sheba.

The Children of Nahor

20   Now after these things it was told Abraham, "Milcah also has borne children, to your brother Nahor: 21 Uz the firstborn, Buz his brother, Kemuel the father of Aram, 22 Chesed, Hazo, Pildash,

1 Or to slaughter   m Or will see; Heb traditionally transliterated *Jehovah Jireh   n Or he shall be seen*

---

tains *that I shall show you.* See note on 12.1. **22.3** Abraham's obedience is unquestioning (cf. 12.4); cf. his exertions on behalf of Sodom to avert the impending action in 18.16–33. **22.4** *And saw,* continuing plays on the verb "see"; cf. notes on 16.13–14; 21.9; 22.14. **22.5** *We will worship, and . . . come back.* Abraham either anticipates a favorable outcome or conceals the nature of his mission. **22.6** *Fire,* a torch, probably not yet ignited, for kindling the offering. **22.7** Isaac's question deepens the pathos of the events. *Here I am,* an ironic echo of 22.1; cf. note there. **22.8** *Will provide,* lit. "will see [to]," further echoing this key verb; see note on 22.4. **22.12** *Now I know* continues the plays on "know" throughout Genesis. *Fear* in Hebrew plays further on "see" (22.4). **22.13** The miraculous substitution of a ram for Isaac vindicates Abraham's act of faith. *And saw.* See note on 22.4. **22.14** *The LORD will provide,* Hebrew *YHWH yir'eh,* lit. "The LORD sees." *On the mount . . . provided.* The verb *yera'eh,* better left untranslated, carries a threefold pun:

(1) He (God) appears. (2) It (a ram) is provided. (3) One should appear, for pilgrim festivals (see Ex 23.17; 34.23). If the locale is Jerusalem, there is a further pun on its name, *Yeru-Shalem/Yerushalayim,* and on "Moriah." Cf. note on 14.18. **22.15–18** The promise of "innumerable" offspring (cf. 12.2; 13.16; 15.5) is restated—now as reward for Abraham's act of faith. **22.17** *Your offspring shall possess the gate of their enemies,* the first explicit declaration that Israel's later inheritance of Canaan will entail war; cf. 15.18–21; 24.60. **22.18** *Obeyed,* lit. "heard"; cf. plays on that verb in the Hagar episodes (see notes on 16.2; 17.20; 21.17).

22.20–24   An implicit confirmation of the repeated promise of offspring through Isaac. *Aram,* eponymous ancestor of the Arameans (Syrians), whose language, Aramaic, was the *lingua franca* of the Near East between 700 B.C.E. and 600 C.E. and still survives today. *Bethuel became father of Rebekah* alludes to 24.1–67, where a bride for Isaac is secured. Cf. 11.29.

Jidlaph, and Bethuel." 23 Bethuel became the father of Rebekah. These eight Milcah bore to Nahor, Abraham's brother. 24 Moreover, his concubine, whose name was Reumah, bore Tebah, Gaham, Tahash, and Maacah.

Sarah's Death and Burial

23 Sarah lived one hundred twenty-seven years; this was the length of Sarah's life. 2 And Sarah died at Kiriath-arba (that is, Hebron) in the land of Canaan; and Abraham went in to mourn for Sarah and to weep for her. 3 Abraham rose up from beside his dead, and said to the Hittites, 4 "I am a stranger and an alien residing among you; give me property among you for a burying place, so that I may bury my dead out of my sight." 5 The Hittites answered Abraham, 6 "Hear us, my lord; you are a mighty prince among us. Bury your dead in the choicest of our burial places; none of us will withhold from you any burial ground for burying your dead." 7 Abraham rose and bowed to the Hittites, the people of the land. 8 He said to them, "If you are willing that I should bury my dead out of my sight, hear me, and entreat for me Ephron son of Zohar, 9 so that he may give me the cave of Machpelah, which he owns; it is at the end of his field. For the full price let him give it to me in your presence as a possession for a burying place." 10 Now Ephron was sitting among the Hittites; and Ephron the Hittite answered Abraham in the hearing of the Hittites, of all who went in at the gate of his city, 11 "No, my lord, hear me; I give you the field, and I give you the cave that is in it; in the presence of my people I give it to you; bury your dead." 12 Then Abraham bowed down before the people of the land. 13 He said to Ephron in the hearing of the people of the land, "If you only will listen to me! I will give the price of the field; accept it from me, so that I may bury my dead there." 14 Ephron answered Abraham, 15 "My lord, listen to me; a piece of land worth four hundred shekels of silver—what is that between you and me? Bury your dead." 16 Abraham agreed with Ephron; and Abraham weighed out for Ephron the silver that he had named in the hearing of the Hittites, four hundred shekels of silver, according to the weights current among the merchants.

17 So the field of Ephron in Machpelah, which was to the east of Mamre, the field with the cave that was in it and all the trees that were in the field, throughout its whole area, passed 18 to Abraham as a possession in the presence of the Hittites, in the presence of all who went in at the gate of his city. 19 After this, Abraham buried Sarah his wife in the cave of the field of Machpelah facing Mamre (that is, Hebron) in the land of Canaan. 20 The field and the cave that is in it passed from the Hittites into Abraham's possession as a burying place.

The Marriage of Isaac and Rebekah

24 Now Abraham was old, well advanced in years; and the LORD had blessed Abraham in all things. 2 Abraham said to his servant, the oldest of his house, who had charge of all that he had,

---

23.1–20 Abraham's purchase of the cave of Machpelah and surrounding field near Kiriath-arba (Hebron) as burial ground for Sarah and family plot. Ownership of burial land is a crucial step in establishing legal residence. 23.1 The juxtaposition of the information in this verse to the preceding episode prompts—perhaps intentionally—many unanswerable questions about Sarah's reaction to its events and about her final days. 23.3 Hittites, lit. "children of Heth" (see 10.15), not the historical Hittites but a term for pre-Israelite inhabitants of Palestine. On the region's "Hittite" heritage, cf. Ezek 16.3, 45. 23.4 Stranger . . . residing, lit. "stranger and resident," in contrast to 'am ha'aretz, "people of the land, natives" (vv. 7, 12). Cf. 12.10; 15.13; 19.9. Bury my dead. The phrase "bury [one's] dead" oc- curs often here, suggesting a legal formula. 23.6 Mighty prince, lit. "one lifted up by God" or "favored of God." 23.7 Entreat for me, a necessary ritual or legal formality. Ephron son of Zohar. The names are Semitic, not Hittite; cf. 26.34; 2 Sam 11.3. 23.10 Who went in at the gate, who deliberated official matters. 23.11 Ephron offers the plot as a gift, but Abraham will insist on clearer title. 23.13 If only you will listen to me! Abraham's plea for close attention suggests the legal nature of his request. I will give counters Ephron's "I give" in the previous verse. 23.15 Four hundred shekels of silver. Ephron makes the sum seem trifling, but the price is quite high. 23.16 Agreed, lit. "heard." The verb occurs conspicuously throughout (vv. 6, 11, 13). 24.1–67 The securing of a bride for Isaac

"Put your hand under my thigh [3] and I will make you swear by the LORD, the God of heaven and earth, that you will not get a wife for my son from the daughters of the Canaanites, among whom I live, [4] but will go to my country and to my kindred and get a wife for my son Isaac." [5] The servant said to him, "Perhaps the woman may not be willing to follow me to this land; must I then take your son back to the land from which you came?" [6] Abraham said to him, "See to it that you do not take my son back there. [7] The LORD, the God of heaven, who took me from my father's house and from the land of my birth, and who spoke to me and swore to me, 'To your offspring I will give this land,' he will send his angel before you, and you shall take a wife for my son from there. [8] But if the woman is not willing to follow you, then you will be free from this oath of mine; only you must not take my son back there." [9] So the servant put his hand under the thigh of Abraham his master and swore to him concerning this matter.

10 Then the servant took ten of his master's camels and departed, taking all kinds of choice gifts from his master; and he set out and went to Aram-naharaim, to the city of Nahor. [11] He made the camels kneel down outside the city by the well of water; it was toward evening, the time when women go out to draw water. [12] And he said, "O LORD, God of my master Abraham, please grant me success today

and show steadfast love to my master Abraham. [13] I am standing here by the spring of water, and the daughters of the townspeople are coming out to draw water. [14] Let the girl to whom I shall say, 'Please offer your jar that I may drink,' and who shall say, 'Drink, and I will water your camels'— let her be the one whom you have appointed for your servant Isaac. By this I shall know that you have shown steadfast love to my master."

15 Before he had finished speaking, there was Rebekah, who was born to Bethuel son of Milcah, the wife of Nahor, Abraham's brother, coming out with her water jar on her shoulder. [16] The girl was very fair to look upon, a virgin, whom no man had known. She went down to the spring, filled her jar, and came up. [17] Then the servant ran to meet her and said, "Please let me sip a little water from your jar." [18] "Drink, my lord," she said, and quickly lowered her jar upon her hand and gave him a drink. [19] When she had finished giving him a drink, she said, "I will draw for your camels also, until they have finished drinking." [20] So she quickly emptied her jar into the trough and ran again to the well to draw, and she drew for all his camels. [21] The man gazed at her in silence to learn whether or not the LORD had made his journey successful.

22 When the camels had finished drinking, the man took a gold nose-ring weighing a half shekel, and two bracelets

---

from among Abraham's kin in Aram-naharaim through the efforts of Abraham's servant, who journeys there. This elaborate tale marks the last, decisive step toward fulfillment of the promise of progeny through Isaac, providing a luxuriantly rounded conclusion to the narratives of the Abraham cycle. **24.1** *Abraham was old*, therefore succession is urgent. *Blessed . . . in all things*, pending, that is, the conclusion of the following narrative. **24.2** *Under my thigh*, near the organs of procreation, signifying the solemnity of the oath that follows. **24.3–4** Cf. 26.34–35; 27.46–29.9. **24.5** The servant's hesitation follows naturally from the mission's importance. *Perhaps the woman may not be willing.* See note on 24.58. **24.6** *Do not take my son back there.* Abraham clings firmly to two conflicting imperatives: attachment to his distant kin and attachment to his present land. **24.7** *From my father's house . . . the land of my birth.* Cf. 12.1. *And who spoke . . . I will give this land.* See 12.7; 13.15. *Will send his angel*, i.e., will protect

you on this mission and ensure its success; cf. Ex 23.20, 23; 33.2; Mal 3.1. **24.10** *Ten . . . camels.* See note on 24.61. *Aram-naharaim . . . city of Nahor*, Haran; see 11.31.
24.11–49 An encounter at a well forms the core of two other stories of betrothal, 29.1–14 (Jacob and Rachel) and Ex 2.15–22 (Moses and Zipporah). **24.12** Divine guidance is a preoccupation in this tale (cf. vv. 7, 21, 27, 40, 42, 48, 56). **24.14** *Steadfast love*, Hebrew *chesed*, a kindness beyond measure. Cf. vv. 27, 49. **24.15** The text belabors Rebekah's lineage—the goal is at hand. Cf. vv. 24, 47. **24.16** *Very fair . . . a virgin*, further sign of the mission's success. **24.17–19** The wording differs from the servant's envisioning in vv. 13–14, but events transpire as anticipated. **24.18** *Drink, my lord.* She does not know he is a servant. His own retelling (vv. 44, 46) omits "my lord." **24.21** *To learn*, lit. "to know." **24.22** *The man took . . . bracelets*, to place upon her; cf. vv. 30, 47.

for her arms weighing ten gold shekels,
23 and said, "Tell me whose daughter you
are. Is there room in your father's house
for us to spend the night?" 24 She said to
him, "I am the daughter of Bethuel son of
Milcah, whom she bore to Nahor." 25 She
added, "We have plenty of straw and fodder and a place to spend the night."
26 The man bowed his head and worshiped the LORD 27 and said, "Blessed be
the LORD, the God of my master Abraham, who has not forsaken his steadfast
love and his faithfulness toward my master. As for me, the LORD has led me on
the way to the house of my master's kin."

28 Then the girl ran and told her
mother's household about these things.
29 Rebekah had a brother whose name was
Laban; and Laban ran out to the man, to
the spring. 30 As soon as he had seen the
nose-ring, and the bracelets on his sister's
arms, and when he heard the words of his
sister Rebekah, "Thus the man spoke to
me," he went to the man, and there he
was, standing by the camels at the spring.
31 He said, "Come in, O blessed of the
LORD. Why do you stand outside when I
have prepared the house and a place for
the camels?" 32 So the man came into the
house; and Laban unloaded the camels,
and gave him straw and fodder for the
camels, and water to wash his feet and the
feet of the men who were with him.
33 Then food was set before him to eat;
but he said, "I will not eat until I have told
my errand." He said, "Speak on."

34 So he said, "I am Abraham's servant. 35 The LORD has greatly blessed my
master, and he has become wealthy; he
has given him flocks and herds, silver and
gold, male and female slaves, camels and
donkeys. 36 And Sarah my master's wife
bore a son to my master when she was old;
and he has given him all that he has. 37 My
master made me swear, saying, 'You shall
not take a wife for my son from the
daughters of the Canaanites, in whose
land I live; 38 but you shall go to my father's house, to my kindred, and get a

wife for my son.' 39 I said to my master,
'Perhaps the woman will not follow me.'
40 But he said to me, 'The LORD, before
whom I walk, will send his angel with you
and make your way successful. You shall
get a wife for my son from my kindred,
from my father's house. 41 Then you will
be free from my oath, when you come to
my kindred; even if they will not give her
to you, you will be free from my oath.'

42 "I came today to the spring, and
said, 'O LORD, the God of my master
Abraham, if now you will only make successful the way I am going! 43 I am standing here by the spring of water; let the
young woman who comes out to draw, to
whom I shall say, "Please give me a little
water from your jar to drink," 44 and who
will say to me, "Drink, and I will draw for
your camels also" — let her be the woman
whom the LORD has appointed for my
master's son.'

45 "Before I had finished speaking in
my heart, there was Rebekah coming out
with her water jar on her shoulder; and
she went down to the spring, and drew. I
said to her, 'Please let me drink.' 46 She
quickly let down her jar from her shoulder, and said, 'Drink, and I will also water
your camels.' So I drank, and she also watered the camels. 47 Then I asked her,
'Whose daughter are you?' She said, 'The
daughter of Bethuel, Nahor's son, whom
Milcah bore to him.' So I put the ring on
her nose, and the bracelets on her arms.
48 Then I bowed my head and worshiped
the LORD, and blessed the LORD, the God
of my master Abraham, who had led me
by the right way to obtain the daughter of
my master's kinsman for his son. 49 Now
then, if you will deal loyally and truly with
my master, tell me; and if not, tell me, so
that I may turn either to the right hand or
to the left."

50 Then Laban and Bethuel answered, "The thing comes from the LORD;
we cannot speak to you anything bad or
good. 51 Look, Rebekah is before you,
take her and go, and let her be the wife of

24.24 *I am the daughter . . . bore to Nahor* confirms
that she is the one anticipated.   **24.25** Her hospitality is further sign of the mission's success.
24.30 *Thus the man spoke to me.* Further words of
hers are assumed.   **24.41** *Then you will be free from
my oath.* Abraham (v. 8) had freed him from responsibility if the mission *failed.* The servant feels

obligated until its completion—only as an after-
thought (next clause) does he envisage earlier release. *Even if they will not give her to you.* Actually
the stipulation was if *she* refused.   **24.49** *Deal
loyally,* lit. "do *chesed*"; see note on 24.14.
24.50 *Cannot speak . . . bad or good.* Cf. 2 Sam

your master's son, as the LORD has spoken."

52 When Abraham's servant heard their words, he bowed himself to the ground before the LORD. 53 And the servant brought out jewelry of silver and of gold, and garments, and gave them to Rebekah; he also gave to her brother and to her mother costly ornaments. 54 Then he and the men who were with him ate and drank, and they spent the night there. When they rose in the morning, he said, "Send me back to my master." 55 Her brother and her mother said, "Let the girl remain with us a while, at least ten days; after that she may go." 56 But he said to them, "Do not delay me, since the LORD has made my journey successful; let me go that I may go to my master." 57 They said, "We will call the girl, and ask her." 58 And they called Rebekah, and said to her, "Will you go with this man?" She said, "I will." 59 So they sent away their sister Rebekah and her nurse along with Abraham's servant and his men. 60 And they blessed Rebekah and said to her,

"May you, our sister, become
    thousands of myriads;
may your offspring gain
    possession
of the gates of their foes."

61 Then Rebekah and her maids rose up, mounted the camels, and followed the man; thus the servant took Rebekah, and went his way.

62 Now Isaac had come from*o* Beer-lahai-roi, and was settled in the Negeb. 63 Isaac went out in the evening to walk*p*

in the field; and looking up, he saw camels coming. 64 And Rebekah looked up, and when she saw Isaac, she slipped quickly from the camel, 65 and said to the servant, "Who is the man over there, walking in the field to meet us?" The servant said, "It is my master." So she took her veil and covered herself. 66 And the servant told Isaac all the things that he had done. 67 Then Isaac brought her into his mother Sarah's tent. He took Rebekah, and she became his wife; and he loved her. So Isaac was comforted after his mother's death.

Abraham Marries Keturah

25 Abraham took another wife, whose name was Keturah. 2 She bore him Zimran, Jokshan, Medan, Midian, Ishbak, and Shuah. 3 Jokshan was the father of Sheba and Dedan. The sons of Dedan were Asshurim, Letushim, and Leummim. 4 The sons of Midian were Ephah, Epher, Hanoch, Abida, and Eldaah. All these were the children of Keturah. 5 Abraham gave all he had to Isaac. 6 But to the sons of his concubines Abraham gave gifts, while he was still living, and he sent them away from his son Isaac, eastward to the east country.

The Death of Abraham

7 This is the length of Abraham's life, one hundred seventy-five years. 8 Abraham breathed his last and died in a good

o Syr Tg: Heb *from coming to*   *p* Meaning of Heb word is uncertain

---

13.22. **24.53** *Jewelry . . . and garments*, gifts, not a bride-price; see v. 10. **24.54** *The men who were with him*, the first mention of an entourage with the servant. **24.58** Rebekah's consent is crucial to the mission, as already envisaged in v. 5. **24.60** See note on 22.17. **24.61** *Rebekah and her maids . . . mounted the camels* explains why the servant had brought ten camels. **24.62** *Beer-lahai-roi*, site of the annunciation of Ishmael's birth to Hagar; see 16.14. Isaac's emergence *from* there has symbolic resonance—henceforth he will have his own posterity. **24.65** *It is my master.* Throughout the story his master has been Abraham; henceforth it is Isaac.

25.1–18 Information, in the style of an archive, about Abraham's children by Keturah (vv. 1–6), Abraham's death and burial (vv. 7–11), and Ishmael's offspring (vv. 12–18) paralleling the archival traditions of 11.10–32, which preface

the Abraham cycle. The emphasis here is on the secondary lines of Abraham's—those displaced by Isaac. **25.1–6** In a situation similar to Hagar's (cf. 16.3), *Keturah* is called both wife and concubine. She, too, is sent away with her children, and Isaac named as heir. Her best-known child is *Midian*, here ancestor of a powerful nomadic people that biblical passages place in Sinai, Canaan, the Jordan Valley, Moab, and Transjordan; cf. Judg 8.22–24. According to Ex 2.15–22; 18.1, Moses' father-in-law was Midianite. Like Hagar's offspring, the Midianites are said to assist in bringing Joseph to Egypt as a slave (37.28, 36; see note on 16.6). **25.7–11** The death of Abraham, ripe in years, in a time of tranquility and plenty. He is buried beside Sarah at Machpelah (cf. 23.1–20). Notably, Isaac and Ishmael appear in peaceful relations, and Isaac settles at Beer-lahai-roi (cf. 16.13–14; see note on 24.62).

old age, an old man and full of years, and was gathered to his people. 9His sons Isaac and Ishmael buried him in the cave of Machpelah, in the field of Ephron son of Zohar the Hittite, east of Mamre, 10the field that Abraham purchased from the Hittites. There Abraham was buried, with his wife Sarah. 11After the death of Abraham God blessed his son Isaac. And Isaac settled at Beer-lahai-roi.

Ishmael's Descendants

Blessed → Abraham

12   These are the descendants of Ishmael, Abraham's son, whom Hagar the Egyptian, Sarah's slave-girl, bore to Abraham. 13These are the names of the sons of Ishmael, named in the order of their birth: Nebaioth, the firstborn of Ishmael; and Kedar, Adbeel, Mibsam, 14Mishma, Dumah, Massa, 15Hadad, Tema, Jetur, Naphish, and Kedemah. 16These are the sons of Ishmael and these are their names, by their villages and by their encampments, twelve princes according to their tribes. 17(This is the length of the life of Ishmael, one hundred thirty-seven years; he breathed his last and died, and was gathered to his people.) 18They settled from Havilah to Shur, which is opposite Egypt in the direction of Assyria;

he settled down*q* alongside of*r* all his people.

The Birth and Youth of Esau and Jacob

19   These are the descendants of Isaac, Abraham's son: Abraham was the father of Isaac, 20and Isaac was forty years old when he married Rebekah, daughter of Bethuel the Aramean of Paddan-aram, sister of Laban the Aramean. 21Isaac prayed to the LORD for his wife, because she was barren; and the LORD granted his prayer, and his wife Rebekah conceived. 22The children struggled together within her; and she said, "If it is to be this way, why do I live?"*s* So she went to inquire of the LORD. 23And the LORD said to her,

"Two nations are in your womb,
   and two peoples born of you
      shall be divided;
the one shall be stronger than the
      other,
   the elder shall serve the
      younger."

24When her time to give birth was at hand, there were twins in her womb. 25The first came out red, all his body like a hairy mantle; so they named him Esau. 26Afterward his brother came out, with

q Heb *he fell*   r Or *down in opposition to*
s Syr: Meaning of Heb uncertain

25.12–18 A record of the line of Ishmael and his death at 137. Like later Israel, the Ishmaelites constitute twelve tribes, settled chiefly in Arabia.   **25.16** *By their villages and ... encampments.* Cf. formula in 10.31. Here the phrase is meant to reflect a partly settled, partly nomadic culture. **25.18** *From Havilah to Shur,* frontier limits; cf. 2.11; 10.29; 16.7. *Settled ... alongside of,* or "fell upon, made raids against"; cf. 16.12.

25.19–36.43 A well-defined cycle of stories about Jacob, recounting the origins of the people Israel in the life history of their eponymous ancestor, Jacob/Israel (cf. 32.28). Like the Abraham cycle, it is roughly symmetrical, its centerpiece being the birth of Jacob's children in 29.31–30.24. Legends about twins or siblings (cf., e.g., Romulus and Remus, Castor and Pollux) often characterize the early history of civilizations. The rivalry of Jacob and Esau, expressing the historical opposition of Israel and Edom, finds a counterpart in that between Rachel and Leah, expressing the historical opposition between Israel and Judah—the northern and southern Israelite kingdoms, whose parallel histories are told in 1 Kings 12–2 Kings 25.
25.19–28 A condensed rendition of the ri-

valry between Jacob and Esau, which forms the cycle's principal conflict. Each of its discrete traditions presents a facet of the brothers' opposition. **25.19** *These are the descendants.* See note on 2.4.   **25.20** *Isaac was forty years old.* Cf. other chronological references in the cycle: 25.26; 26.34; 35.28. *Bethuel the Aramean, Laban the Aramean.* Bethuel and Laban are termed "Arameans," descendants of Aram, here to show their connection to Aram (see 22.20–23). They are, strictly speaking, portrayed as uncle and cousin to Aram, not descendants. *Paddan-aram,* lit. "Road of Aram." The name overlaps with Aram-naharaim, "Mesopotamian Aram," the locale of Haran (see notes on 11.31; 24.10).   **25.21** Like Sarah (and later Rachel) Rebekah was *barren.* **25.22–23** A tradition from the early monarchy, here anticipating Israel's dominance over Edom in the era of David and Solomon. **25.22** *Why do I live?* How can I endure the pain? **25.24–26** An etiological tradition stressing the twins' striking difference in appearance. *Red,* in Hebrew a play on "Edom," Esau's other name (cf. 36.1). *Hairy mantle,* in Hebrew a play on "Seir," where Esau settled; see 36.8, 20.   **25.26** An etiological tradition rooting the name *Jacob* in the Hebrew word for

his hand gripping Esau's heel; so he was named Jacob.[t] Isaac was sixty years old when she bore them.

27 When the boys grew up, Esau was a skillful hunter, a man of the field, while Jacob was a quiet man, living in tents. 28 Isaac loved Esau, because he was fond of game; but Rebekah loved Jacob.

Esau Sells His Birthright

29 Once when Jacob was cooking a stew, Esau came in from the field, and he was famished. 30 Esau said to Jacob, "Let me eat some of that red stuff, for I am famished!" (Therefore he was called Edom.[u]) 31 Jacob said, "First sell me your birthright." 32 Esau said, "I am about to die; of what use is a birthright to me?" 33 Jacob said, "Swear to me first."[v] So he swore to him, and sold his birthright to Jacob. 34 Then Jacob gave Esau bread and lentil stew, and he ate and drank, and rose and went his way. Thus Esau despised his birthright.

Isaac and Abimelech

26 Now there was a famine in the land, besides the former famine that had occurred in the days of Abraham. And Isaac went to Gerar, to King Abimelech of the Philistines. 2 The LORD appeared to Isaac[w] and said, "Do not go down to Egypt; settle in the land that I shall show you. 3 Reside in this land as an alien, and I will be with you, and will bless you; for to you and to your descendants I will give all these lands, and I will fulfill the oath that I swore to your father Abra-

ham. 4 I will make your offspring as numerous as the stars of heaven, and will give to your offspring all these lands; and all the nations of the earth shall gain blessing for themselves through your offspring, 5 because Abraham obeyed my voice and kept my charge, my commandments, my statutes, and my laws."

6 So Isaac settled in Gerar. 7 When the men of the place asked him about his wife, he said, "She is my sister"; for he was afraid to say, "My wife," thinking, "or else the men of the place might kill me for the sake of Rebekah, because she is attractive in appearance." 8 When Isaac had been there a long time, King Abimelech of the Philistines looked out of a window and saw him fondling his wife Rebekah. 9 So Abimelech called for Isaac, and said, "So she is your wife! Why then did you say, 'She is my sister'?" Isaac said to him, "Because I thought I might die because of her." 10 Abimelech said, "What is this you have done to us? One of the people might easily have lain with your wife, and you would have brought guilt upon us." 11 So Abimelech warned all the people, saying, "Whoever touches this man or his wife shall be put to death."

12 Isaac sowed seed in that land, and in the same year reaped a hundredfold. The LORD blessed him, 13 and the man became rich; he prospered more and more until he became very wealthy. 14 He had possessions of flocks and herds, and a great household, so that the Philistines envied him. 15 (Now the Philistines had

t That is *He takes by the heel* or *He supplants*
u That is *Red*   v Heb *today*   w Heb *him*

"heel." **25.27** An etiological tradition stressing the brothers' (or their offspring's) contrasting ways of life. **25.28** A folkloric tradition expressing the brothers' opposition as opposed preferences of the parents. As in Abraham's case, the wife's preference eventually prevails. *Because he was fond of game*, lit. "Game [was] in his mouth" or "Game [was brought] at his behest."
25.29–34 An etiological tradition offering an additional reason for Jacob's (Israel's) dominance over Esau (Edom). **25.30** *Red stuff*, in Hebrew a play on "Edom." **25.31** *Birthright*, in Hebrew a play on "blessing," a key theme later in the cycle (see esp. 27.1–45; 28.10–17; 32.22–32). On the birthright, cf. Deut 21.15–17.
26.1–33 The only traditions about Isaac in the prime of life. Both concern Isaac's dealings with Abimelech of Gerar and are essentially vari-

ants of traditions about Abraham in Gerar; see 20.1–18; 21.22–34. **26.1** *Former famine*. See 12.10. *Philistines*. See note on 21.32. **26.2** *Do not go down to Egypt*. Isaac is the only patriarch who spends no time outside Canaan. **26.3** *Alien*. See note on 23.4. *Oath . . . I swore*, the often repeated double promise—progeny and land. **26.5** Again, moral justice is pivotal to divine promise; see notes on 15.16; 18.16–33. **26.8** *Fondling*, in Hebrew another play on "Isaac"; cf. 17.17; 18.12–15; 21.6, 9. **26.12–14** All three patriarchs are said to be rich (cf. 12.16; 13.2; 24.1; 30.43), in conformance with divine blessing, but the memory reflects some ambivalence—wealth is also a source of strife and envy; see vv. 15–22. **26.14, 16** Local distrust of a powerful alien also underlies 21.22–23; Ex 1.9–10. But similar tensions can arise among kin; cf. 13.2–13. **26.15** If

stopped up and filled with earth all the wells that his father's servants had dug in the days of his father Abraham.) 16 And Abimelech said to Isaac, "Go away from us; you have become too powerful for us."

17 So Isaac departed from there and camped in the valley of Gerar and settled there. 18 Isaac dug again the wells of water that had been dug in the days of his father Abraham; for the Philistines had stopped them up after the death of Abraham; and he gave them the names that his father had given them. 19 But when Isaac's servants dug in the valley and found there a well of spring water, 20 the herders of Gerar quarreled with Isaac's herders, saying, "The water is ours." So he called the well Esek,x because they contended with him. 21 Then they dug another well, and they quarreled over that one also; so he called it Sitnah.y 22 He moved from there and dug another well, and they did not quarrel over it; so he called it Rehoboth,z saying, "Now the LORD has made room for us, and we shall be fruitful in the land."

23 From there he went up to Beersheba. 24 And that very night the LORD appeared to him and said, "I am the God of your father Abraham; do not be afraid, for I am with you and will bless you and make your offspring numerous for my servant Abraham's sake." 25 So he built an altar there, called on the name of the LORD, and pitched his tent there. And there Isaac's servants dug a well.

26 Then Abimelech went to him from Gerar, with Ahuzzath his adviser and Phicol the commander of his army. 27 Isaac said to them, "Why have you come to me, seeing that you hate me and have sent me away from you?" 28 They said, "We see

plainly that the LORD has been with you; so we say, let there be an oath between you and us, and let us make a covenant with you 29 so that you will do us no harm, just as we have not touched you and have done to you nothing but good and have sent you away in peace. You are now the blessed of the LORD." 30 So he made them a feast, and they ate and drank. 31 In the morning they rose early and exchanged oaths; and Isaac set them on their way, and they departed from him in peace. 32 That same day Isaac's servants came and told him about the well that they had dug, and said to him, "We have found water!" 33 He called it Shibah;a therefore the name of the city is Beer-shebab to this day.

Esau's Hittite Wives

34 When Esau was forty years old, he married Judith daughter of Beeri the Hittite, and Basemath daughter of Elon the Hittite; 35 and they made life bitter for Isaac and Rebekah.

Isaac Blesses Jacob

27 When Isaac was old and his eyes were dim so that he could not see, he called his elder son Esau and said to him, "My son"; and he answered, "Here I am." 2 He said, "See, I am old; I do not know the day of my death. 3 Now then, take your weapons, your quiver and your bow, and go out to the field, and hunt game for me. 4 Then prepare for me savory food, such as I like, and bring it to

x That is *Contention*   y That is *Enmity*   z That is *Broad places* or *Room*   a A word resembling the word for *oath*   b That is *Well of the oath* or *Well of seven*

---

parenthetic, this anticipates v. 18. Otherwise it is expression of the envy just mentioned. **26.18–22** The background to vv. 26–31. The place-names play on the strife and resolution depicted throughout ch. 26. **26.23–25** An altar tradition analogous to 12.7–8; 13.4. *And there Isaac's servants dug a well* returns the narrative to the well dispute theme. **26.26–31** Isaac's pact with Abimelech resolves all disputes hitherto described. As in 21.22–34, it culminates in the naming of Beer-sheba. **26.26** *Phicol.* Cf. 21.22, 32. **26.27** *Sent me away.* See v. 16. **26.28** *The LORD has been with you.* Cf. 21.22. **26.30** *They ate and drank,* covenant formalities. **26.32** An early tradition; with vv. 18–25 it brackets the Abimelech

pact. **26.33** *Shibah,* a play on Hebrew *shebu'ah,* "oath," and *sheba',* "seven."

26.34–35 A tradition about Esau's Hittite wives. Cf. 24.3–4; 27.46–28.9. As in 23.8, these "Hittites" bear Semitic names.

27.1–40 The story of Jacob's deception of his blind father and theft of his brother's blessing, an elaborated variant of the "birthright" tradition in 25.29–34 and the background for the reconciliation in ch. 33. Jacob here acts on Rebekah's initiative (cf. 25.28); she disguises him as Esau and later arranges his escape. **27.1** *His eyes were dim.* The many plays on "see" in ch. 22 are relevant here. Cf. note on 27.27. **27.3** *Hunt game.* Cf. 25.28. **27.4** *That I may bless,* lit. "that my soul may bless"

me to eat, so that I may bless you before I die."

5 Now Rebekah was listening when Isaac spoke to his son Esau. So when Esau went to the field to hunt for game and bring it, 6 Rebekah said to her son Jacob, "I heard your father say to your brother Esau, 7 'Bring me game, and prepare for me savory food to eat, that I may bless you before the LORD before I die.' 8 Now therefore, my son, obey my word as I command you. 9 Go to the flock, and get me two choice kids, so that I may prepare from them savory food for your father, such as he likes; 10 and you shall take it to your father to eat, so that he may bless you before he dies." 11 But Jacob said to his mother Rebekah, "Look, my brother Esau is a hairy man, and I am a man of smooth skin. 12 Perhaps my father will feel me, and I shall seem to be mocking him, and bring a curse on myself and not a blessing." 13 His mother said to him, "Let your curse be on me, my son; only obey my word, and go, get them for me." 14 So he went and got them and brought them to his mother; and his mother prepared savory food, such as his father loved. 15 Then Rebekah took the best garments of her elder son Esau, which were with her in the house, and put them on her younger son Jacob; 16 and she put the skins of the kids on his hands and on the smooth part of his neck. 17 Then she handed the savory food, and the bread that she had prepared, to her son Jacob.

18 So he went in to his father, and said, "My father"; and he said, "Here I am; who are you, my son?" 19 Jacob said to his father, "I am Esau your firstborn. I have done as you told me; now sit up and eat of my game, so that you may bless me." 20 But Isaac said to his son, "How is it that you have found it so quickly, my son?" He answered, "Because the LORD your God granted me success." 21 Then

Isaac said to Jacob, "Come near, that I may feel you, my son, to know whether you are really my son Esau or not." 22 So Jacob went up to his father Isaac, who felt him and said, "The voice is Jacob's voice, but the hands are the hands of Esau." 23 He did not recognize him, because his hands were hairy like his brother Esau's hands; so he blessed him. 24 He said, "Are you really my son Esau?" He answered, "I am." 25 Then he said, "Bring it to me, that I may eat of my son's game and bless you." So he brought it to him, and he ate; and he brought him wine, and he drank. 26 Then his father Isaac said to him, "Come near and kiss me, my son." 27 So he came near and kissed him; and he smelled the smell of his garments, and blessed him, and said,

"Ah, the smell of my son
     is like the smell of a field that
          the LORD has blessed.
28 May God give you of the dew of
          heaven,
     and of the fatness of the earth,
          and plenty of grain and wine.
29 Let peoples serve you,
          and nations bow down to you.
     Be lord over your brothers,
          and may your mother's sons
               bow down to you.
     Cursed be everyone who *foreshadows*
          curses you,
     and blessed be everyone who
          blesses you!"

Esau's Lost Blessing

30 As soon as Isaac had finished blessing Jacob, when Jacob had scarcely gone out from the presence of his father Isaac, his brother Esau came in from his hunting. 31 He also prepared savory food, and brought it to his father. And he said to his father, "Let my father sit up and eat of his son's game, so that you may bless me." 32 His father Isaac said to him, "Who are

---

(cf. vv. 19, 25, 31), suggesting the act's ritual and legal importance. **27.11–12** Cf. 25.25. **27.13** *Let your curse be on me.* Rebekah indeed suffers the consequences—after Jacob's flight she will probably never see him again. **27.19** *I am ... your firstborn* underscores that inheritance is at stake. **27.20–27** Isaac's suspicions heighten the tension and confirm the reason for Rebekah's disguise. Hearing, feeling, and smelling are prominent here, underscoring Isaac's blindness.

27.23 *Recognize*, a key verb in 31.32; 37.32–33; 38.25–26; 42.7–8. **27.27** *Ah,* lit. "See!" **27.29** *Be lord over your brothers.* No traditions exist of other brothers beside Esau; the plural, in context, suggests "your brother's children." See note on 27.37. In the next generation, the notion expressed here will return to haunt Jacob (cf. 37.5–11, 32–35).

27.30–40 The return and reaction of Esau.

you?" He answered, "I am your firstborn son, Esau." 33 Then Isaac trembled violently, and said, "Who was it then that hunted game and brought it to me, and I ate it all[c] before you came, and I have blessed him?—yes, and blessed he shall be!" 34 When Esau heard his father's words, he cried out with an exceedingly great and bitter cry, and said to his father, "Bless me, me also, father!" 35 But he said, "Your brother came deceitfully, and he has taken away your blessing." 36 Esau said, "Is he not rightly named Jacob?[d] For he has supplanted me these two times. He took away my birthright; and look, now he has taken away my blessing." Then he said, "Have you not reserved a blessing for me?" 37 Isaac answered Esau, "I have already made him your lord, and I have given him all his brothers as servants, and with grain and wine I have sustained him. What then can I do for you, my son?" 38 Esau said to his father, "Have you only one blessing, father? Bless me, me also, father!" And Esau lifted up his voice and wept.

39 Then his father Isaac answered him:

"See, away from[e] the fatness of
    the earth shall your
    home be,
and away from[f] the dew of
    heaven on high.
40 By your sword you shall live,
    and you shall serve your
    brother;
but when you break loose,[g]
    you shall break his yoke from
    your neck."

Jacob Escapes Esau's Fury

41 Now Esau hated Jacob because of the blessing with which his father had blessed him, and Esau said to himself, "The days of mourning for my father are approaching; then I will kill my brother Jacob." 42 But the words of her elder son Esau were told to Rebekah; so she sent and called her younger son Jacob and said to him, "Your brother Esau is consoling himself by planning to kill you. 43 Now therefore, my son, obey my voice; flee at once to my brother Laban in Haran, 44 and stay with him a while, until your brother's fury turns away— 45 until your brother's anger against you turns away, and he forgets what you have done to him; then I will send, and bring you back from there. Why should I lose both of you in one day?"

46 Then Rebekah said to Isaac, "I am weary of my life because of the Hittite women. If Jacob marries one of the Hittite women such as these, one of the women of the land, what good will my life be to me?"

28 Then Isaac called Jacob and blessed him, and charged him, "You shall not marry one of the Canaanite women. 2 Go at once to Paddan-aram to the house of Bethuel, your mother's father; and take as wife from there one of the daughters of Laban, your mother's brother. 3 May God Almighty[h] bless you and make you fruitful and numerous,

c Cn: Heb of all   *d* That is He supplants or He takes by the heel   *e* Or See, of   *f* Or and of   *g* Meaning of Heb uncertain   *h* Traditional rendering of Heb El Shaddai

---

27.34 The narrative's sympathy here for Esau is genuine, contrasting with the scorn of 25.34. But cf. note on 27.37. Esau is as much a victim of Isaac's rigidity as of Jacob's trickery. 27.35 Like an oath, a blessing, once conferred, cannot be retracted. 27.36 *Jacob . . . has supplanted.* See text note *d* and the note on 25.26. *Birthright . . . blessing.* See note on 25.31. 27.37 This and v. 29 make clear the drastic nature of Isaac's preferential policy, supplying more justification for Rebekah's ruse. 27.39 *Away from . . . away from.* The double meaning in Hebrew *mi-* ("of" and "away from") carries the ambivalence of this blessing. 27.40 *By your sword . . . serve your brother.* Cf. the oracle about Ishmael in 16.12—contentiousness will partly compensate for historical eclipse. *But when you break loose . . .*

from your neck. Cf. 2 Kings 8.20, 22.
27.41–28.5 Jacob's escape. 27.41 *Then I will kill,* after mourning for Isaac is completed. 27.42 *The words . . . were told.* Esau's secret intentions became publicly known. *Is consoling himself.* Rebekah sees Esau's anger as temporary. 27.44–45 *Until . . . he forgets.* Rebekah's suggestion will hold true (see ch. 33), but she greatly miscalculates the time involved; see note on 27.13. *Lose both,* lit. "be bereaved of both." Rebekah anticipates Esau's death by execution or blood vengeance if he kills Jacob. 27.46 *Because of the Hittite women.* Cf. 24.3; 26.35. 28.1 *Then Isaac called Jacob and blessed him.* Any distress over the deception (cf. 27.33) remains unmentioned. The blessing is for his journey, not a duplicate of the earlier blessing. 28.2 *Paddan-aram.* See note on

that you may become a company of peoples. 4 May he give to you the blessing of Abraham, to you and to your offspring with you, so that you may take possession of the land where you now live as an alien —land that God gave to Abraham." 5 Thus Isaac sent Jacob away; and he went to Paddan-aram, to Laban son of Bethuel the Aramean, the brother of Rebekah, Jacob's and Esau's mother.

Esau Marries Ishmael's Daughter

6 Now Esau saw that Isaac had blessed Jacob and sent him away to Paddan-aram to take a wife from there, and that as he blessed him he charged him, "You shall not marry one of the Canaanite women," 7 and that Jacob had obeyed his father and his mother and gone to Paddan-aram. 8 So when Esau saw that the Canaanite women did not please his father Isaac, 9 Esau went to Ishmael and took Mahalath daughter of Abraham's son Ishmael, and sister of Nebaioth, to be his wife in addition to the wives he had.

Jacob's Dream at Bethel

10 Jacob left Beer-sheba and went toward Haran. 11 He came to a certain place and stayed there for the night, because the sun had set. Taking one of the stones of the place, he put it under his head and lay down in that place. 12 And he dreamed that there was a ladder[i] set up on the earth, the top of it reaching to heaven; and the angels of God were ascending and descending on it. 13 And the LORD stood beside him[j] and said, "I am the LORD, the God of Abraham your father and the God of Isaac; the land on which you lie I will give to you and to your off-

spring; 14 and your offspring shall be like the dust of the earth, and you shall spread abroad to the west and to the east and to the north and to the south; and all the families of the earth shall be blessed[k] in you and in your offspring. 15 Know that I am with you and will keep you wherever you go, and will bring you back to this land; for I will not leave you until I have done what I have promised you." 16 Then Jacob woke from his sleep and said, "Surely the LORD is in this place—and I did not know it!" 17 And he was afraid, and said, "How awesome is this place! This is none other than the house of God, and this is the gate of heaven."

18 So Jacob rose early in the morning, and he took the stone that he had put under his head and set it up for a pillar and poured oil on the top of it. 19 He called that place Bethel;[l] but the name of the city was Luz at the first. 20 Then Jacob made a vow, saying, "If God will be with me, and will keep me in this way that I go, and will give me bread to eat and clothing to wear, 21 so that I come again to my father's house in peace, then the LORD shall be my God, 22 and this stone, which I have set up for a pillar, shall be God's house; and of all that you give me I will surely give one-tenth to you."

Jacob Meets Rachel

29 Then Jacob went on his journey, and came to the land of the people of the east. 2 As he looked, he saw a well in the field and three flocks of sheep lying there beside it; for out of that well the flocks were watered. The stone on the

---

i Or stairway or ramp   j Or stood above it
k Or shall bless themselves   l That is House of God

25.20. **28.3–4** The familiar double promise (land/progeny) is reiterated here. *God Almighty.* See note on 17.1. **28.5** *Bethuel the Aramean.* See note on 25.20. **28.6–9** An addendum mentioning Esau's efforts to please his parents by finding a wife from among kin, although he does not renounce his Hittite wives (v. 9). **28.10–22** Jacob's first vision of God, here at Bethel (cf. 35.1–15). **28.13–15** The double promise again (land/progeny). **28.15** *I am with you,* even though you depart from the land; cf. 46.4. **28.16** *And I did not know it.* Otherwise Jacob would not have slept there; see v. 11.

28.17 *House of God,* in Hebrew a play on "Bethel"; cf. v. 19. **28.18** Probably an allusion to a local landmark. **28.19** *Luz,* lit. "Almond tree"; cf. 35.6; 48.3; Josh 16.2; 18.13; Judg 1.23. **28.20–22** Jacob's faith is more markedly contractual than Abraham's; cf. 15.6; 22.3. **28.22** *One-tenth.* See note on 14.20.
   29.1–14 Jacob's meeting with Rachel, daughter of his uncle, Laban. This is a less-elaborated version of the genre represented by ch. 24 and culminates, similarly, in betrothal. **29.1** *People of the east,* of the Syrian-Arabian desert northeast of Canaan. Cf. 25.6; Judg 6.3, 33; Isa 11.14; Jer

well's mouth was large, 3 and when all the flocks were gathered there, the shepherds would roll the stone from the mouth of the well, and water the sheep, and put the stone back in its place on the mouth of the well.

4 Jacob said to them, "My brothers, where do you come from?" They said, "We are from Haran." 5 He said to them, "Do you know Laban son of Nahor?" They said, "We do." 6 He said to them, "Is it well with him?" "Yes," they replied, "and here is his daughter Rachel, coming with the sheep." 7 He said, "Look, it is still broad daylight; it is not time for the animals to be gathered together. Water the sheep, and go, pasture them." 8 But they said, "We cannot until all the flocks are gathered together, and the stone is rolled from the mouth of the well; then we water the sheep."

9 While he was still speaking with them, Rachel came with her father's sheep; for she kept them. 10 Now when Jacob saw Rachel, the daughter of his mother's brother Laban, and the sheep of his mother's brother Laban, Jacob went up and rolled the stone from the well's mouth, and watered the flock of his mother's brother Laban. 11 Then Jacob kissed Rachel, and wept aloud. 12 And Jacob told Rachel that he was her father's kinsman, and that he was Rebekah's son; and she ran and told her father.

13 When Laban heard the news about his sister's son Jacob, he ran to meet him; he embraced him and kissed him, and brought him to his house. Jacob[m] told Laban all these things, 14 and Laban said to him, "Surely you are my bone and my flesh!" And he stayed with him a month.

Jacob Marries Laban's Daughters

15 Then Laban said to Jacob, "Because you are my kinsman, should you therefore serve me for nothing? Tell me, what shall your wages be?" 16 Now Laban had two daughters; the name of the elder was Leah, and the name of the younger was Rachel. 17 Leah's eyes were lovely,[n] and Rachel was graceful and beautiful. 18 Jacob loved Rachel; so he said, "I will serve you seven years for your younger daughter Rachel." 19 Laban said, "It is better that I give her to you than that I should give her to any other man; stay with me." 20 So Jacob served seven years for Rachel, and they seemed to him but a few days because of the love he had for her.

21 Then Jacob said to Laban, "Give me my wife that I may go in to her, for my time is completed." 22 So Laban gathered together all the people of the place, and made a feast. 23 But in the evening he took his daughter Leah and brought her to Jacob; and he went in to her. 24 (Laban gave his maid Zilpah to his daughter Leah to be her maid.) 25 When morning came, it was Leah! And Jacob said to Laban, "What is this you have done to me? Did I not serve with you for Rachel? Why then have you deceived me?" 26 Laban said, "This is not done in our country—giving the younger before the firstborn. 27 Complete the week of this one, and we will give you the other also in return for serving me another seven years." 28 Jacob did so, and completed her week; then Laban gave him his daughter Rachel as a wife. 29 (Laban gave his maid Bilhah to his

m Heb He   n Meaning of Heb uncertain

49.38. **29.10** *His mother's brother Laban* occurs thrice, underscoring their kinship. *Rolled the stone*, a prodigious feat for one person—a measure of Jacob's elation at seeing his kinswoman. **29.11** *Kissed ... and wept*, gestures common for kin long separated; cf. 33.4; 45.14–15. **29.14** *My bone and my flesh*, a frequent expression for acknowledging kinship; cf. 2.23; Judg 9.2; 2 Sam 5.1; 19.13–14.

29.15–30 Jacob's marriage to Laban's daughters, his agreement to serve Laban for fourteen years, and the birth of his children. **29.15** An overture typical of Laban's calculating character—why should service be mentioned at all? Laban perhaps already perceives Jacob's love

for Rachel (v. 18) and undertakes to exploit it. **29.17** *Lovely*, or "soft, weak," suggesting, conversely, a defect in her beauty; cf. v. 18. *Rachel was graceful and beautiful*, as Sarah (12.11) and Rebekah (24.16) had been; here the language is even more emphatic. **29.18** *I will serve*. See note on 31.15–16. **29.23** Laban's personality further reveals itself. But the exchange of brides under cloak of darkness enacts divine justice as well, for Jacob had similarly defrauded his blind father. Cf. note on 29.26. **29.24** A detail commonly mentioned in Hurrian marriage contracts; cf. v. 29. **29.26** This recalls Jacob's violation of firstborn protocol in ch. 27. **29.27** *Complete the week*, of nuptial festivities; cf. Judg 14.10, 12.

daughter Rachel to be her maid.) [30] So Jacob went in to Rachel also, and he loved Rachel more than Leah. He served Laban[o] for another seven years.

The Birth of Jacob's Children

[31] When the LORD saw that Leah was unloved, he opened her womb; but Rachel was barren. [32] Leah conceived and bore a son, and she named him Reuben;[p] for she said, "Because the LORD has looked on my affliction; surely now my husband will love me." [33] She conceived again and bore a son, and said, "Because the LORD has heard[q] that I am hated, he has given me this son also"; and she named him Simeon. [34] Again she conceived and bore a son, and said, "Now this time my husband will be joined[r] to me, because I have borne him three sons"; therefore he was named Levi. [35] She conceived again and bore a son, and said, "This time I will praise[s] the LORD"; therefore she named him Judah; then she ceased bearing.

30 When Rachel saw that she bore Jacob no children, she envied her sister; and she said to Jacob, "Give me children, or I shall die!" [2] Jacob became very angry with Rachel and said, "Am I in the place of God, who has withheld from you the fruit of the womb?" [3] Then she said, "Here is my maid Bilhah; go in to her, that she may bear upon my knees and that I too may have children through her." [4] So she gave him her maid Bilhah as a wife; and Jacob went in to her. [5] And Bilhah conceived and bore Jacob a son. [6] Then Rachel said, "God has judged me, and has also heard my voice and given me a son"; therefore she named him Dan.[t] [7] Rachel's maid Bilhah conceived again and bore Jacob a second son. [8] Then Rachel said, "With mighty wrestlings I have

wrestled[u] with my sister, and have prevailed"; so she named him Naphtali.

[9] When Leah saw that she had ceased bearing children, she took her maid Zilpah and gave her to Jacob as a wife. [10] Then Leah's maid Zilpah bore Jacob a son. [11] And Leah said, "Good fortune!" so she named him Gad.[v] [12] Leah's maid Zilpah bore Jacob a second son. [13] And Leah said, "Happy am I! For the women will call me happy"; so she named him Asher.[w]

[14] In the days of wheat harvest Reuben went and found mandrakes in the field, and brought them to his mother Leah. Then Rachel said to Leah, "Please give me some of your son's mandrakes." [15] But she said to her, "Is it a small matter that you have taken away my husband? Would you take away my son's mandrakes also?" Rachel said, "Then he may lie with you tonight for your son's mandrakes." [16] When Jacob came from the field in the evening, Leah went out to meet him, and said, "You must come in to me; for I have hired you with my son's mandrakes." So he lay with her that night. [17] And God heeded Leah, and she conceived and bore Jacob a fifth son. [18] Leah said, "God has given me my hire[x] because I gave my maid to my husband"; so she named him Issachar. [19] And Leah conceived again, and she bore Jacob a sixth son. [20] Then Leah said, "God has endowed me with a good dowry; now my husband will honor[y] me, because I have borne him six sons"; so she named him Zebulun. [21] Afterwards she bore a daughter, and named her Dinah.

[22] Then God remembered Rachel, and God heeded her and opened her

o Heb *him* p That is *See, a son* q Heb *shama*
r Heb *lawah* s Heb *hodah* t That is *He judged* u Heb *niphtal* v That is *Fortune*
w That is *Happy* x Heb *sakar* y Heb *zabal*

29.30 *He loved Rachel more than Leah.* The "loved" wife and the "disliked" wife were legally recognized (but not sanctioned) categories; cf. Deut 21.15–17; note on Gen 29.31.
29.31–30.24 The core of the Jacob cycle, recounting the birth of Jacob's children and, so, of the tribes of Israel. Each child's name plays on the events accompanying its conception or birth. **29.31** *When the LORD saw.* Disapproval of Jacob's preferential treatment is implied. Cf. 1 Sam 1.5. **29.32–33** *Reuben, Simeon.* The plays on "see" and "hear" recall the narratives about Abraham's chil-

dren; see notes on 16.2; 16.13–14. The tribes of Reuben and Simeon were absorbed into Judah early in Israel's history. **29.34–35** From the tribes of *Levi* and *Judah* will come Moses and David, respectively, Israel's two historically most pivotal leaders. **30.3** Cf. 16.2. **30.14** *Mandrakes,* or mandragora, an herb thought to confer fertility. **30.15** As favored wife, Rachel effectively has primary right of cohabitation and can barter it temporarily for concessions. **30.21** *Dinah.* No reason for the name is given. Dinah will be the subject of ch. 34 but is not herself a tribal

womb. 23She conceived and bore a son, and said, "God has taken away my reproach"; 24and she named him Joseph,z saying, "May the LORD add to me another son!"

Jacob Prospers at Laban's Expense

25 When Rachel had borne Joseph, Jacob said to Laban, "Send me away, that I may go to my own home and country. 26Give me my wives and my children for whom I have served you, and let me go; for you know very well the service I have given you." 27But Laban said to him, "If you will allow me to say so, I have learned by divination that the LORD has blessed me because of you; 28name your wages, and I will give it." 29Jacob said to him, "You yourself know how I have served you, and how your cattle have fared with me. 30For you had little before I came, and it has increased abundantly; and the LORD has blessed you wherever I turned. But now when shall I provide for my own household also?" 31He said, "What shall I give you?" Jacob said, "You shall not give me anything; if you will do this for me, I will again feed your flock and keep it: 32let me pass through all your flock today, removing from it every speckled and spotted sheep and every black lamb, and the spotted and speckled among the goats; and such shall be my wages. 33So my honesty will answer for me later, when you come to look into my wages with you. Every one that is not speckled and spotted among the goats and black among the lambs, if found with me, shall be counted stolen." 34Laban said, "Good! Let it be as you have said." 35But that day Laban removed the male goats that were striped and spotted, and all the female goats that were speckled and spotted, every one that had white on it, and every lamb that was black, and put them in charge of his sons; 36and he set a distance of three days' journey between himself and Jacob, while Jacob was pasturing the rest of Laban's flock.

37 Then Jacob took fresh rods of poplar and almond and plane, and peeled white streaks in them, exposing the white of the rods. 38He set the rods that he had peeled in front of the flocks in the troughs, that is, the watering places, where the flocks came to drink. And since they bred when they came to drink, 39the flocks bred in front of the rods, and so the flocks produced young that were striped, speckled, and spotted. 40Jacob separated the lambs, and set the faces of the flocks toward the striped and the completely black animals in the flock of Laban; and he put his own droves apart, and did not put them with Laban's flock. 41Whenever the stronger of the flock were breeding, Jacob laid the rods in the troughs before the eyes of the flock, that they might breed among the rods, 42but for the feebler of the flock he did not lay them there; so the feebler were Laban's, and the stronger Jacob's. 43Thus the man grew exceedingly rich, and had large flocks, and male and female slaves, and camels and donkeys.

Jacob Flees with Family and Flocks

31 Now Jacob heard that the sons of Laban were saying, "Jacob has taken all that was our father's; he has gained all this wealth from what belonged to our father." 2And Jacob saw that Laban did not regard him as favorably as he

z That is *He adds*

---

ancestor. **30.22** *Then God remembered.* Cf. 21.1; 25.21; 1 Sam 1.27. **30.23** *Has taken away,* Hebrew *'asaf,* an additional play on "Joseph"; cf. v. 24.

30.25–43 How Jacob obtains partial redress for the disadvantageous deal struck in 29.15–30. **30.27** *Divination,* a practice condemned in other threads in the Hebrew Bible (see 2 Kings 21.6; cf. Gen 44.5, 15). **30.28** *Name your wages,* another deceitful overture; cf. 29.15; 30.33. **30.32** *Speckled and spotted.* All references to markings indicate white markings; see note on 30.35. **30.33** *When you come to look into my wages,* when you later take inventory by breed to determine what is mine and

yours. **30.35** *Every one that had white on it,* white markings, indicating Jacob's sheep. In Hebrew "white" is a play on "Laban." **30.36** *Set a distance . . . between himself and Jacob,* thereby avoiding answerability for the injustice. Jacob, at this point, has been swindled again. **30.37–42** Jacob's strategy presupposes that the offspring's coloration is determined by what its parents see during mating.

31.1–21 Jacob's preparations for departure from Laban as their relations worsen. Jacob heads toward Canaan, ending twenty years of exile. **31.1–2** Jacob's newfound wealth has clearly ex-

did before. 3 Then the LORD said to Jacob, "Return to the land of your ancestors and to your kindred, and I will be with you." 4 So Jacob sent and called Rachel and Leah into the field where his flock was, 5 and said to them, "I see that your father does not regard me as favorably as he did before. But the God of my father has been with me. 6 You know that I have served your father with all my strength; 7 yet your father has cheated me and changed my wages ten times, but God did not permit him to harm me. 8 If he said, 'The speckled shall be your wages,' then all the flock bore speckled; and if he said, 'The striped shall be your wages,' then all the flock bore striped. 9 Thus God has taken away the livestock of your father, and given them to me.

10   During the mating of the flock I once had a dream in which I looked up and saw that the male goats that leaped upon the flock were striped, speckled, and mottled. 11 Then the angel of God said to me in the dream, 'Jacob,' and I said, 'Here I am!' 12 And he said, 'Look up and see that all the goats that leap on the flock are striped, speckled, and mottled; for I have seen all that Laban is doing to you. 13 I am the God of Bethel,[a] where you anointed a pillar and made a vow to me. Now leave this land at once and return to the land of your birth.' " 14 Then Rachel and Leah answered him, "Is there any portion or inheritance left to us in our father's house? 15 Are we not regarded by him as foreigners? For he has sold us, and he has been using up the money given for

us. 16 All the property that God has taken away from our father belongs to us and to our children; now then, do whatever God has said to you."

17   So Jacob arose, and set his children and his wives on camels; 18 and he drove away all his livestock, all the property that he had gained, the livestock in his possession that he had acquired in Paddan-aram, to go to his father Isaac in the land of Canaan.

19   Now Laban had gone to shear his sheep, and Rachel stole her father's household gods. 20 And Jacob deceived Laban the Aramean, in that he did not tell him that he intended to flee. 21 So he fled with all that he had; starting out he crossed the Euphrates,[b] and set his face toward the hill country of Gilead.

Laban Overtakes Jacob

22   On the third day Laban was told that Jacob had fled. 23 So he took his kinsfolk with him and pursued him for seven days until he caught up with him in the hill country of Gilead. 24 But God came to Laban the Aramean in a dream by night, and said to him, "Take heed that you say not a word to Jacob, either good or bad."

25   Laban overtook Jacob. Now Jacob had pitched his tent in the hill country, and Laban with his kinsfolk camped in the hill country of Gilead. 26 Laban said to Jacob, "What have you done? You have deceived me, and carried away my daugh-

a Cn: Meaning of Heb uncertain   b Heb *the river*

---

acerbated tensions. **31.8** In 30.25–43, it was Jacob who set the wages, and it was his cunning, more than divine providence, that brought success. But he speaks subjectively here and is essentially correct; see note on 31.10. **31.10** This now makes 30.37–42 a divinely mandated strategy. Biblical narrative typically withholds information until the moment is ripe for it. Cf. notes on 20.12; 31.13, 14–16, 15–16. **31.12** This drastically simplifies the strategy of 30.37–42 for storytelling purposes. **31.13** See 28.10–22. This suggests strongly that Jacob has always viewed his exilic experience in the light of those events. **31.14–16** Rachel and Leah now air, for the first time, their bitterness toward their father. **31.15–16** The wealth earned by Jacob's indentured labor was meant for Rachel and Leah's support and welfare, not Laban's personal enrichment. **31.19** *Household gods*, Hebrew *teraphim*,

figurines common in Syria and Palestine, even among Israelites, throughout the preexilic period. Talismanic, cultic, and legal significance accrued to their possession; cf. Judg 17.5; 18.17, 20; Ezek 21.21. **31.20** *Deceived.* Open declaration of intent to leave would provoke unwanted conflict and forestall departure. *Aramean.* See note on 25.20. **31.21** *Gilead*, in northeast Transjordan, adjacent to Canaan. Cf. Num 26.29–30; Josh 17.1, 3; Judg 5.17.

31.22–42 Laban's pursuit of Jacob and their exchange of grievances. **31.22** *On the third day.* The figure is approximate, a storytelling formula; cf. 22.4; 34.25. **31.23** *Seven days*, again, a formulaic approximation. **31.24** Laban's restraint in what follows can be attributed to this warning; cf. v. 29. **31.26–30** Laban's grievances, sounding quite reasonable, ignore his longtime misuse

ters like captives of the sword. 27 Why did you flee secretly and deceive me and not tell me? I would have sent you away with mirth and songs, with tambourine and lyre. 28 And why did you not permit me to kiss my sons and my daughters farewell? What you have done is foolish. 29 It is in my power to do you harm; but the God of your father spoke to me last night, saying, 'Take heed that you speak to Jacob neither good nor bad.' 30 Even though you had to go because you longed greatly for your father's house, why did you steal my gods?" 31 Jacob answered Laban, "Because I was afraid, for I thought that you would take your daughters from me by force. 32 But anyone with whom you find your gods shall not live. In the presence of our kinsfolk, point out what I have that is yours, and take it." Now Jacob did not know that Rachel had stolen the gods.*c*

33 So Laban went into Jacob's tent, and into Leah's tent, and into the tent of the two maids, but he did not find them. And he went out of Leah's tent, and entered Rachel's. 34 Now Rachel had taken the household gods and put them in the camel's saddle, and sat on them. Laban felt all about in the tent, but did not find them. 35 And she said to her father, "Let not my lord be angry that I cannot rise before you, for the way of women is upon me." So he searched, but did not find the household gods.

36 Then Jacob became angry, and upbraided Laban. Jacob said to Laban, "What is my offense? What is my sin, that you have hotly pursued me? 37 Although you have felt about through all my goods, what have you found of all your household goods? Set it here before my kinsfolk and your kinsfolk, so that they may decide between us two. 38 These twenty years I have been with you; your ewes and your female goats have not miscarried, and I have not eaten the rams of your flocks. 39 That which was torn by wild beasts I did not bring to you; I bore the loss of it myself; of my hand you required it, whether stolen by day or stolen by night. 40 It was like this with me: by day the heat consumed me, and the cold by night, and my sleep fled from my eyes. 41 These twenty years I have been in your house; I served you fourteen years for your two daughters, and six years for your flock, and you have changed my wages ten times. 42 If the God of my father, the God of Abraham and the Fear*d* of Isaac, had not been on my side, surely now you would have sent me away empty-handed. God saw my affliction and the labor of my hands, and rebuked you last night."

Laban and Jacob Make a Covenant

43 Then Laban answered and said to Jacob, "The daughters are my daughters, the children are my children, the flocks are my flocks, and all that you see is mine. But what can I do today about these daughters of mine, or about their children whom they have borne? 44 Come now, let us make a covenant, you and I; and let it be a witness between you and me." 45 So Jacob took a stone, and set it up as a pillar. 46 And Jacob said to his kinsfolk, "Gather stones," and they took stones, and made a heap; and they ate there by the heap. 47 Laban called it Jegarsahadutha:*e* but Jacob called it Galeed.*f*

c Heb *them*   *d* Meaning of Heb uncertain
e In Aramaic *The heap of witness*   *f* In Hebrew *The heap of witness*

---

of Jacob's household. **31.27** *I would have sent you away . . . with tambourine and lyre.* This action is unlikely, given his past resistance to their departure. **31.31** Jacob's words are not a reply to the question of v. 30, but to what preceded it. Cf. v. 32. **31.32** *But anyone with whom you find your gods shall not live.* The words prove unintentionally prophetic—Rachel will indeed soon die (35.16–20). *In the presence of our kinsfolk,* in effect, a public litigation. **31.35** *The way of women,* her menstrual period; contact with anything she sits upon is probably taboo (cf. Lev 15.20). **31.36–42** Jacob's impassioned defense is masterfully convincing. Its rhetorical form is the *riv* (Hebrew, "upbraiding"; see v. 36), common in biblical legal discourse. Cf. Job 31. **31.39** Contrary to common practice, which did not require restitution (cf. *Code of Hammurabi* 266; Ex 22.13). **31.40** *By day . . . by night.* Cf. Pss 91.5–6; 121.6. **31.42** *Fear of Isaac,* an unusual name. Some scholars suggest "Kinsman of Isaac." Isaac's ordeal in ch. 22 naturally comes to mind.

31.43–55 The conclusion of the dispute, resulting in a treaty between the opponents. The passage is etiological, concerned with later Israelite-Aramean relations and with the place-names "Gilead" and "Mizpah" (vv. 47–48). **31.43** Without admitting error, Laban effectively concedes defeat. **31.47** *Jegar-sahadutha,* an Aramaic name. The oldest surviving Aramaic texts

48 Laban said, "This heap is a witness between you and me today." Therefore he called it Galeed, 49 and the pillar*g* Mizpah,*h* for he said, "The LORD watch between you and me, when we are absent one from the other. 50 If you ill-treat my daughters, or if you take wives in addition to my daughters, though no one else is with us, remember that God is witness between you and me."

51 Then Laban said to Jacob, "See this heap and see the pillar, which I have set between you and me. 52 This heap is a witness, and the pillar is a witness, that I will not pass beyond this heap to you, and you will not pass beyond this heap and this pillar to me, for harm. 53 May the God of Abraham and the God of Nahor"—the God of their father—"judge between us." So Jacob swore by the Fear*i* of his father Isaac, 54 and Jacob offered a sacrifice on the height and called his kinsfolk to eat bread; and they ate bread and tarried all night in the hill country.

55*j* Early in the morning Laban rose up, and kissed his grandchildren and his daughters and blessed them; then he departed and returned home.

32 Jacob went on his way and the angels of God met him; 2 and when Jacob saw them he said, "This is God's camp!" So he called that place Mahanaim.*k*

Jacob Sends Presents to Appease Esau

3 Jacob sent messengers before him to his brother Esau in the land of Seir, the country of Edom, 4 instructing them, "Thus you shall say to my lord Esau: Thus says your servant Jacob, 'I have lived with Laban as an alien, and stayed until now; 5 and I have oxen, donkeys, flocks, male and female slaves; and I have sent to tell my lord, in order that I may find favor in your sight.'"

6 The messengers returned to Jacob, saying, "We came to your brother Esau, and he is coming to meet you, and four hundred men are with him." 7 Then Jacob was greatly afraid and distressed; and he divided the people that were with him, and the flocks and herds and camels, into two companies, 8 thinking, "If Esau comes to the one company and destroys it, then the company that is left will escape."

9 And Jacob said, "O God of my father Abraham and God of my father Isaac, O LORD who said to me, 'Return to your country and to your kindred, and I will do you good,' 10 I am not worthy of the least of all the steadfast love and all the faithfulness that you have shown to your servant, for with only my staff I crossed this Jordan; and now I have become two companies. 11 Deliver me, please, from the hand of my brother, from the hand of Esau, for I am afraid of him; he may come and kill us all, the mothers with the children. 12 Yet you have said, 'I will surely do you good, and make your offspring as the sand of the sea, which cannot be counted because of their number.'"

13 So he spent that night there, and from what he had with him he took a present for his brother Esau, 14 two hundred female goats and twenty male goats, two hundred ewes and twenty rams, 15 thirty milch camels and their colts, forty

g Compare Sam: MT lacks *the pillar*   *h* That is *Watchpost*   *i* Meaning of Heb uncertain   *j* Ch 32.1 in Heb   *k* Here taken to mean *Two camps*

---

date from the tenth century B.C.E. Biblical Aramaic is also present in Ezra 4.8–6.18; 7.12–26; Dan 2.4–7.28; Jer 10.11. *Galeed*, probably a folk etymology for "Gilead," site of the present episode (cf. vv. 21, 23). **31.48** *Mizpah*, or Mizpah-Gilead; cf. Judg 10.17; 11.11, 29, 34; Hos 5.1. **31.53** *The God of their father*, probably a gloss, as the third person indicates. *Fear of . . . Isaac.* See note on 31.42. **32.1–2** These verses properly belong to the episode that follows. **32.1** *Angels.* The same Hebrew word signifies "messengers" in 32.3. **32.2** *Mahanaim*, lit. "Two Camps"; cf. the "ascending" and "descending" angels in 28.12. The "doubleness" of the angelic hosts is a foreshadowing of the twin-brother theme that dominates chs. 32–33; cf. note on 32.7. **32.3–32** Jacob's preparations for reunion with his brother, culminating in the remarkable divine encounter of vv. 22–32, which to modern readers suggests the nightmare of a distraught traveler, anxious about what lies ahead. **32.3** *Land of Seir.* Cf. 14.6; 36.20–21. *Edom.* Cf. 36.1, 6. **32.5** Jacob abruptly dwells on his possessions, a measure of his anxiety. Cf. vv. 13–16. **32.6** *Four hundred men*, seemingly portending a military confrontation. **32.7** *He divided . . . into two companies* continues the "doubleness" motif begun in v. 2. **32.10** *Steadfast love.* See note on 24.14. *Two companies.* See notes on 32.2; 32.7.

cows and ten bulls, twenty female donkeys and ten male donkeys. [16] These he delivered into the hand of his servants, every drove by itself, and said to his servants, "Pass on ahead of me, and put a space between drove and drove." [17] He instructed the foremost, "When Esau my brother meets you, and asks you, 'To whom do you belong? Where are you going? And whose are these ahead of you?' [18] then you shall say, 'They belong to your servant Jacob; they are a present sent to my lord Esau; and moreover he is behind us.'" [19] He likewise instructed the second and the third and all who followed the droves, "You shall say the same thing to Esau when you meet him, [20] and you shall say, 'Moreover your servant Jacob is behind us.'" For he thought, "I may appease him with the present that goes ahead of me, and afterwards I shall see his face; perhaps he will accept me." [21] So the present passed on ahead of him; and he himself spent that night in the camp.

Jacob Wrestles at Peniel

22   The same night he got up and took his two wives, his two maids, and his eleven children, and crossed the ford of the Jabbok. [23] He took them and sent them across the stream, and likewise everything that he had. [24] Jacob was left alone; and a man wrestled with him until daybreak [25] When the man saw that he did not prevail against Jacob, he struck him on the hip socket; and Jacob's hip was put out of joint as he wrestled with him. [26] Then he said, "Let me go, for the day is breaking." But Jacob said, "I will not let you go, unless you bless me." [27] So he said to him, "What is your name?" And he said, "Jacob." [28] Then the man[l] said, "You shall no longer be called Jacob, but Israel,[m] for you have striven with God and with humans,[n] and have prevailed." [29] Then Jacob asked him, "Please tell me your name." But he said, "Why is it that you ask my name?" And there he blessed him. [30] So Jacob called the place Peniel,[o] saying, "For I have seen God face to face, and yet my life is preserved." [31] The sun rose upon him as he passed Penuel, limping because of his hip. [32] Therefore to this day the Israelites do not eat the thigh muscle that is on the hip socket, because he struck Jacob on the hip socket at the thigh muscle.

Jacob and Esau Meet

33   Now Jacob looked up and saw Esau coming, and four hundred men with him. So he divided the children among Leah and Rachel and the two

l Heb *he*   *m* That is *The one who strives with God* or *God strives*   *n* Or *with divine and human beings*   *o* That is *The face of God*

32.15 *Milch*, nursing, milk-producing.   **32.16** *Put a space between drove and drove*. Jacob's gifts are made to seem like decoys; cf. vv. 8, 17–20. **32.20** *His face*. "Face, presence" (Hebrew *panim*) is a key word throughout chs. 32–33, on which the folk etymology of Peniel/Penuel (vv. 30–31) depends.   **32.22** *Jabbok*, possibly a play on "Jacob." The river is an eastern tributary of the Jordan originating near present-day Amman.   **32.24** *Jacob was left alone*, a pregnant moment suggesting Jacob's anguished apprehensions before meeting Esau. *And a man*. No preparation or context is supplied, suggesting the event's internal or supernatural nature. *Wrestled*, in Hebrew a play on "Jabbok" and "Jacob."   **32.25** *Hip socket*, or fleshy part of the thigh. Injury to the reproductive organs is hinted, and indeed with Benjamin already conceived Jacob will beget no further children. Cf. note on 32.31.   **32.26–28** *He said*. Confusion of the two speakers is intentional, suggesting the confusion of their melee, their "twinlike" equivalence as combatants, and their complete standoff.   **32.26** *Unless you bless*. The theme of blessing, surfacing here in a dreamlike way, again reminds us that Jacob is preoccupied with the brother whose blessing he stole.   **32.28** *Israel*. At the very moment Jacob reaches full maturity, his descendants acquire their national name. Later Israel's encounters with God will similarly entail intense struggle, with divine and human alike. **32.29** *Why is it that you ask my name?* See note on 33.15. *And there he blessed him*. Curiously, the blessing's words are not mentioned—the moment remains private and mysterious.   **32.30** *Peniel*. Its variant, Penuel, appears in v. 31. *Face to face*. On this problematic notion, cf. Ex 33.11–23; Deut 5.4; 34.10; Judg 6.22.   **32.31** *Limping*, a frequent motif in myth and legend (Oedipus, too, limps), suggesting maturation, both personal and cultural—parallel, in certain ways, to the ordeal of Abraham and Isaac at Moriah. This "diminished" Jacob is paradoxically more complete. **32.32** A version of this prohibition survives in Jewish dietary laws. This is the Hebrew Bible's sole reference to the practice.   **33.1–17** The meeting of Jacob and Esau after twenty years apart. Their encounter proves unexpectedly cordial, and their long-deferred conflict

maids. 2 He put the maids with their children in front, then Leah with her children, and Rachel and Joseph last of all. 3 He himself went on ahead of them, bowing himself to the ground seven times, until he came near his brother.

4   But Esau ran to meet him, and embraced him, and fell on his neck and kissed him, and they wept. 5 When Esau looked up and saw the women and children, he said, "Who are these with you?" Jacob said, "The children whom God has graciously given your servant." 6 Then the maids drew near, they and their children, and bowed down; 7 Leah likewise and her children drew near and bowed down; and finally Joseph and Rachel drew near, and they bowed down. 8 Esau said, "What do you mean by all this company that I met?" Jacob answered, "To find favor with my lord." 9 But Esau said, "I have enough, my brother; keep what you have for yourself." 10 Jacob said, "No, please; if I find favor with you, then accept my present from my hand; for truly to see your face is like seeing the face of God—since you have received me with such favor. 11 Please accept my gift that is brought to you, because God has dealt graciously with me, and because I have everything I want." So he urged him, and he took it.

12   Then Esau said, "Let us journey on our way, and I will go alongside you." 13 But Jacob said to him, "My lord knows that the children are frail and that the flocks and herds, which are nursing, are a care to me; and if they are overdriven for one day, all the flocks will die. 14 Let my lord pass on ahead of his servant, and I will lead on slowly, according to the pace of the cattle that are before me and according to the pace of the children, until I come to my lord in Seir."

15   So Esau said, "Let me leave with you some of the people who are with me." But he said, "Why should my lord be so kind to me?" 16 So Esau returned that day on his way to Seir. 17 But Jacob journeyed to Succoth,p and built himself a house, and made booths for his cattle; therefore the place is called Succoth.

Jacob Reaches Shechem

18   Jacob came safely to the city of Shechem, which is in the land of Canaan, on his way from Paddan-aram; and he camped before the city. 19 And from the sons of Hamor, Shechem's father, he bought for one hundred pieces of moneyq the plot of land on which he had pitched his tent. 20 There he erected an altar and called it El-Elohe-Israel. r

The Rape of Dinah

34   Now Dinah the daughter of Leah, whom she had borne to Jacob, went out to visit the women of the region. 2 When Shechem son of Hamor the Hivite, prince of the region, saw her, he seized her and lay with her by force. 3 And his soul was drawn to Dinah daugh-

p That is Booths   q Heb one hundred qesitah
r That is God, the God of Israel

---

seems resolved. **33.1** *So he divided.* See note on 32.7. **33.2** Jacob's most cherished household members are placed farthest from Esau's grasp. **33.4** *Kissed ... wept.* See note on 29.11. **33.10** *Like seeing the face of God,* a courtly exaggeration, but containing a measure of truth. It alludes to 32.22–32, which was, by its timing and verbal associations, closely tied to the present encounter. Cf. Hos 12.3. **33.14** *Until I come to ... Seir,* a puzzling detail—no trip to Seir is reported. **33.15** *But he said.* The speaker here is presumably Jacob, but the ambiguity may be intentional. Like the divine encounter in 32.22–32, this one ends with an unanswered question. **33.17** *Succoth,* a Transjordanian town near the Jordan Valley. Cf. Josh 13.27; Judg 8.5–9, 14–16; 1 Kings 7.46. **33.18–20** Jacob's arrival at Shechem, as for Abraham (12.6) the first encampment in Canaan. *Shechem's father* carries a double meaning—Hamor's son is named She-

chem, and Hamor is a "city father." *El-Elohe-Israel,* a Canaanite type ("El") divine name. Cf. El Elyon (14.19), El Shaddai (17.1), El Olam (21.33), and El-bethel (35.7).

34.1–31 The Jacob cycle's last elaborated narrative recounts the rape of Jacob's daughter, Dinah, by Hamor's son Shechem and its violent avenging by Jacob's sons Simeon and Levi—the first acts of violence between Canaanites and Israelites, disrupting otherwise peaceful relations. **34.1** Much time has elapsed since the previous episode; Jacob's children are young adults. *To visit the women of the region.* Relations with Canaanites were cordial, and the women of both peoples moved about freely. **34.2** *Hivite.* Cf. 10.17; Josh 9.7; 11.3, 19. The Septuagint reads "Horites" (cf. notes on 14.6; 36.20). **34.2–3** Without condoning the rape, the narrator presupposes it as compatible with love; here, indeed, love complicates the situation meaningfully. Dinah's reactions go

ter of Jacob; he loved the girl, and spoke tenderly to her. 4 So Shechem spoke to his father Hamor, saying, "Get me this girl to be my wife."

5 Now Jacob heard that Shechem[s] had defiled his daughter Dinah; but his sons were with his cattle in the field, so Jacob held his peace until they came. 6 And Hamor the father of Shechem went out to Jacob to speak with him, 7 just as the sons of Jacob came in from the field. When they heard of it, the men were indignant and very angry, because he had committed an outrage in Israel by lying with Jacob's daughter, for such a thing ought not to be done.

8 But Hamor spoke with them, saying, "The heart of my son Shechem longs for your daughter; please give her to him in marriage. 9 Make marriages with us; give your daughters to us, and take our daughters for yourselves. 10 You shall live with us; and the land shall be open to you; live and trade in it, and get property in it." 11 Shechem also said to her father and to her brothers, "Let me find favor with you, and whatever you say to me I will give. 12 Put the marriage present and gift as high as you like, and I will give whatever you ask me; only give me the girl to be my wife."

13 The sons of Jacob answered Shechem and his father Hamor deceitfully, because he had defiled their sister Dinah. 14 They said to them, "We cannot do this thing, to give our sister to one who is uncircumcised, for that would be a disgrace to us. 15 Only on this condition will we consent to you: that you will become as we are and every male among you be circumcised. 16 Then we will give our daughters to you, and we will take your daughters for ourselves, and we will live among you and become one people. 17 But if you will not listen to us and be circumcised, then

we will take our daughter and be gone."

18 Their words pleased Hamor and Hamor's son Shechem. 19 And the young man did not delay to do the thing, because he was delighted with Jacob's daughter. Now he was the most honored of all his family. 20 So Hamor and his son Shechem came to the gate of their city and spoke to the men of their city, saying, 21 "These people are friendly with us; let them live in the land and trade in it, for the land is large enough for them; let us take their daughters in marriage, and let us give them our daughters. 22 Only on this condition will they agree to live among us, to become one people: that every male among us be circumcised as they are circumcised. 23 Will not their livestock, their property, and all their animals be ours? Only let us agree with them, and they will live among us." 24 And all who went out of the city gate heeded Hamor and his son Shechem; and every male was circumcised, all who went out of the gate of his city.

Dinah's Brothers Avenge Their Sister

25 On the third day, when they were still in pain, two of the sons of Jacob, Simeon and Levi, Dinah's brothers, took their swords and came against the city unawares, and killed all the males. 26 They killed Hamor and his son Shechem with the sword, and took Dinah out of Shechem's house, and went away. 27 And the other sons of Jacob came upon the slain, and plundered the city, because their sister had been defiled. 28 They took their flocks and their herds, their donkeys, and whatever was in the city and in the field. 29 All their wealth, all their little ones and their wives, all that was in the houses, they captured and made their prey. 30 Then

s Heb he

---

unrecorded.   **34.7** *An outrage in Israel*, i.e., among our people. Jacob's children manifest the sense of nationhood that the tale's audience took for granted. On the expression, cf. Judg 20.6 (and 19.1–20.5); 2 Sam 13.12.   **34.9–10** These overtures are problematic in the light of the admonitions of Ex 23.23–33; Deut 7.1–11. **34.13** *Deceitfully*. Cf. 31.20. The justice of their deceit is neither affirmed nor denied by the narrator; cf. notes on 34.2–3; 34.30–31.   **34.19** *The most honored*, i.e., in the eyes of their townspeople, perhaps explaining why the townsmen consent to

circumcision (v. 24).   **34.23** They either reveal here their own baser motives or use material incentives to sway their compatriots.   **34.24** *All who went out of the city gate*, those held fit for military service, able-bodied adult males.   **34.25** *On the third day*. See note on 31.22. *Still in pain*. The operation entails temporary incapacitation, forestalling their self-defense.   **34.27** The inclusion of *the other sons* makes the avenging more than a rash adventure by Simeon and Levi, but cf. v. 30 and 49.5–7, which focus blame on the two. Jacob's later retreat from Shechem (35.1) suggests mili-

Jacob said to Simeon and Levi, "You have brought trouble on me by making me odious to the inhabitants of the land, the Canaanites and the Perizzites; my numbers are few, and if they gather themselves against me and attack me, I shall be destroyed, both I and my household." 31 But they said, "Should our sister be treated like a whore?"

Jacob Returns to Bethel

35 God said to Jacob, "Arise, go up to Bethel, and settle there. Make an altar there to the God who appeared to you when you fled from your brother Esau." 2 So Jacob said to his household and to all who were with him, "Put away the foreign gods that are among you, and purify yourselves, and change your clothes; 3 then come, let us go up to Bethel, that I may make an altar there to the God who answered me in the day of my distress and has been with me wherever I have gone." 4 So they gave to Jacob all the foreign gods that they had, and the rings that were in their ears; and Jacob hid them under the oak that was near Shechem.

5 As they journeyed, a terror from God fell upon the cities all around them, so that no one pursued them. 6 Jacob came to Luz (that is, Bethel), which is in the land of Canaan, he and all the people who were with him, 7 and there he built an altar and called the place El-bethel,ᵗ because it was there that God had revealed himself to him when he fled from his brother. 8 And Deborah, Rebekah's nurse, died, and she was buried under an oak

below Bethel. So it was called Allonbacuth.ᵘ

9 God appeared to Jacob again when he came from Paddan-aram, and he blessed him. 10 God said to him, "Your name is Jacob; no longer shall you be called Jacob, but Israel shall be your name." So he was called Israel. 11 God said to him, "I am God Almighty:ᵛ be fruitful and multiply; a nation and a company of nations shall come from you, and kings shall spring from you. 12 The land that I gave to Abraham and Isaac I will give to you, and I will give the land to your offspring after you." 13 Then God went up from him at the place where he had spoken with him. 14 Jacob set up a pillar in the place where he had spoken with him, a pillar of stone; and he poured out a drink offering on it, and poured oil on it. 15 So Jacob called the place where God had spoken with him Bethel.

The Birth of Benjamin and the Death of Rachel

16 Then they journeyed from Bethel; and when they were still some distance from Ephrath, Rachel was in childbirth, and she had hard labor. 17 When she was in her hard labor, the midwife said to her, "Do not be afraid; for now you will have another son." 18 As her soul was departing (for she died), she named him Ben-oni;ʷ but his father called him Benjamin.ˣ 19 So Rachel died, and she was buried on the

t That is *God of Bethel*　　u That is *Oak of weeping*
v Traditional rendering of Heb *El Shaddai*
w That is *Son of my sorrow*　　x That is *Son of the right hand* or *Son of the South*

---

tary defeat. **34.30–31** Jacob's objections seem motivated more by pragmatism than by honor or justice; the sons, in turn, ignore the dishonorable implications of their deceit. The story offers no easy answer to the dilemma. Sadly, other than in 46.15 Dinah is not mentioned again.

35.1–15 Jacob's return to Bethel, site of his first divine vision during his escape from Esau (see 28.10–22). Chs. 35–36 represent a typical conclusion, in archival style, to the Jacob cycle; cf. 10.1–32; 11.10–32; 25.1–18. **35.2** *Put away the foreign gods*. Cf. Josh 24.14. *Purify yourselves and change your clothes*. Cf. Ex 19.10–14. **35.4** *Under the oak . . . near Shechem*. Cf. Josh 24.26. **35.5** After the hostilities exchanged at Shechem (ch. 34), Canaanites were no longer assumed to be friendly. **35.6** *Luz*. See note on 28.19. **35.7** *El-*

bethel. See note on 33.18–20. **35.8** *Deborah, Rebekah's nurse*. Cf. 24.59, where her last name is unmentioned. **35.10** Cf. 32.27–28. Unlike Abraham's, Jacob's new name is used interchangeably with the old. **35.11** *God Almighty*. See note on 17.1. **35.14** Cf. 28.18.

35.16–29 The birth of Jacob's youngest child, Benjamin; the death of Rachel; Reuben's transgression; the list of Jacob's sons; and Isaac's death. **35.16** *Ephrath*. Cf. Ruth 1.2; 1 Sam 17.12. **35.18** *Ben-oni . . . Benjamin*. Jacob reverses the tragic implications of the child's name to mean "son of the right hand"/"son of fortune" or "son of the south." The latter would express the vantage point of northern-based Israelites. **35.19** *Bethlehem*, a small town about five miles south of Jerusalem. Cf. Judg 17.7–9; 19.1–2, 18;

way to Ephrath (that is, Bethlehem),
20 and Jacob set up a pillar at her grave; it
is the pillar of Rachel's tomb, which is
there to this day. 21 Israel journeyed on,
and pitched his tent beyond the tower of
Eder.

22 While Israel lived in that land,
Reuben went and lay with Bilhah his father's concubine; and Israel heard of it.

Now the sons of Jacob were twelve.
23 The sons of Leah: Reuben (Jacob's firstborn), Simeon, Levi, Judah, Issachar, and
Zebulun. 24 The sons of Rachel: Joseph
and Benjamin. 25 The sons of Bilhah, Rachel's maid: Dan and Naphtali. 26 The
sons of Zilpah, Leah's maid: Gad and
Asher. These were the sons of Jacob who
were born to him in Paddan-aram.

The Death of Isaac

27 Jacob came to his father Isaac at
Mamre, or Kiriath-arba (that is, Hebron),
where Abraham and Isaac had resided as
aliens. 28 Now the days of Isaac were one
hundred eighty years. 29 And Isaac
breathed his last; he died and was gathered to his people, old and full of days;
and his sons Esau and Jacob buried him.

Esau's Descendants

36 These are the descendants of
Esau (that is, Edom). 2 Esau took
his wives from the Canaanites: Adah
daughter of Elon the Hittite, Oholibamah
daughter of Anah son*y* of Zibeon the Hivite, 3 and Basemath, Ishmael's daughter,
sister of Nebaioth. 4 Adah bore Eliphaz to
Esau; Basemath bore Reuel; 5 and Oholibamah bore Jeush, Jalam, and Korah.

These are the sons of Esau who were born
to him in the land of Canaan.

6 Then Esau took his wives, his sons,
his daughters, and all the members of his
household, his cattle, all his livestock, and
all the property he had acquired in the
land of Canaan; and he moved to a land
some distance from his brother Jacob.
7 For their possessions were too great for
them to live together; the land where they
were staying could not support them because of their livestock. 8 So Esau settled
in the hill country of Seir; Esau is Edom.

9 These are the descendants of Esau,
ancestor of the Edomites, in the hill country of Seir. 10 These are the names of
Esau's sons: Eliphaz son of Adah the wife
of Esau; Reuel, the son of Esau's wife Basemath. 11 The sons of Eliphaz were Teman, Omar, Zepho, Gatam, and Kenaz.
12 (Timna was a concubine of Eliphaz,
Esau's son; she bore Amalek to Eliphaz.)
These were the sons of Adah, Esau's wife.
13 These were the sons of Reuel: Nahath,
Zerah, Shammah, and Mizzah. These
were the sons of Esau's wife, Basemath.
14 These were the sons of Esau's wife
Oholibamah, daughter of Anah son*z* of
Zibeon: she bore to Esau Jeush, Jalam,
and Korah.

Clans and Kings of Edom

15 These are the clans*a* of the sons of
Esau. The sons of Eliphaz the firstborn of
Esau: the clans*a* Teman, Omar, Zepho,
Kenaz, 16 Korah, Gatam, and Amalek;
these are the clans*a* of Eliphaz in the land
of Edom; they are the sons of Adah.

y Sam Gk Syr: Heb *daughter*   *z* Gk Syr: Heb
daughter   *a* Or *chiefs*

---

1 Sam 16.1. **35.20** *Rachel's tomb.* Present-day
Bethlehem still honors the reputed site.
35.21 *Tower of Eder*, between Bethlehem and Hebron. **35.22a** Cf. 49.3–4; Deut 33.6; 1 Chr
5.1. **35.22b–26** A Priestly genealogy (see Introduction), the first complete listing of Jacob's
twelve sons and so of Israel's tribal groups (Joseph's descendants comprised two tribes, Manasseh and Ephraim; see note on 48.1–22).
35.26 *Born to him in Paddan-aram*, except Benjamin, born between Bethel and Ephrath.
35.27–29 Another Priestly tradition (see Introduction), notable for showing Esau and Jacob in
peaceful relations (v. 29). Since Isaac was virtually
on his deathbed twenty years earlier, this tradition
may appear here for reasons other than strictly

chronological ones.
36.1–43 A lengthy appendix in archival style
about Esau's descendants, the nation Edom, south
of the Dead Sea. The historical Edomites (like the
Canaanites) spoke a language similar to Hebrew.
The chapter contains several lists, each with a different emphasis: Esau's wives (vv. 1–5); Esau's
sons and grandsons (vv. 9–14); Esauite clans
(vv. 15–19); the proto-Edomite Horites (vv. 20–
30); the earliest kings of Edom (vv. 31–39); and
another Esauite clan list (vv. 40–43). The brief
notation about Esau's migration (vv. 6–8) resembles that concerning Lot's departure from Abraham (13.3–13). **36.12** *Amalek.* See note on
14.7. **36.15** *Eliphaz ... Teman.* Cf. Eliphaz the

17 These are the sons of Esau's son Reuel: the clans*b* Nahath, Zerah, Shammah, and Mizzah; these are the clans*b* of Reuel in the land of Edom; they are the sons of Esau's wife Basemath. 18 These are the sons of Esau's wife Oholibamah: the clans*b* Jeush, Jalam, and Korah; these are the clans*b* born of Esau's wife Oholibamah, the daughter of Anah. 19 These are the sons of Esau (that is, Edom), and these are their clans.*b*

20   These are the sons of Seir the Horite, the inhabitants of the land: Lotan, Shobal, Zibeon, Anah, 21 Dishon, Ezer, and Dishan; these are the clans*b* of the Horites, the sons of Seir in the land of Edom. 22 The sons of Lotan were Hori and Heman; and Lotan's sister was Timna. 23 These are the sons of Shobal: Alvan, Manahath, Ebal, Shepho, and Onam. 24 These are the sons of Zibeon: Aiah and Anah; he is the Anah who found the springs*c* in the wilderness, as he pastured the donkeys of his father Zibeon. 25 These are the children of Anah: Dishon and Oholibamah daughter of Anah. 26 These are the sons of Dishon: Hemdan, Eshban, Ithran, and Cheran. 27 These are the sons of Ezer: Bilhan, Zaavan, and Akan. 28 These are the sons of Dishan: Uz and Aran. 29 These are the clans*b* of the Horites: the clans*b* Lotan, Shobal, Zibeon, Anah, 30 Dishon, Ezer, and Dishan; these are the clans*b* of the Horites, clan by clan*d* in the land of Seir.

31   These are the kings who reigned in the land of Edom, before any king reigned over the Israelites. 32 Bela son of Beor reigned in Edom, the name of his city being Dinhabah. 33 Bela died, and Jobab son of Zerah of Bozrah succeeded him as king. 34 Jobab died, and Husham of the land of the Temanites succeeded him as king. 35 Husham died, and Hadad son of Bedad, who defeated Midian in the country of Moab, succeeded him as king, the name of his city being Avith. 36 Hadad died, and Samlah of Masrekah succeeded him as king. 37 Samlah died, and Shaul of Rehoboth on the Euphrates succeeded him as king. 38 Shaul died, and Baalhanan son of Achbor succeeded him as king. 39 Baal-hanan son of Achbor died, and Hadar succeeded him as king, the name of his city being Pau; his wife's name was Mehetabel, the daughter of Matred, daughter of Me-zahab.

40   These are the names of the clans*b* of Esau, according to their families and their localities by their names: the clans*b* Timna, Alvah, Jetheth, 41 Oholibamah, Elah, Pinon, 42 Kenaz, Teman, Mibzar, 43 Magdiel, and Iram; these are the clans*b* of Edom (that is, Esau, the father of Edom), according to their settlements in the land that they held.

Joseph Dreams of Greatness

37 Jacob settled in the land where his father had lived as an alien, the land of Canaan. 2 This is the story of the family of Jacob.

Joseph, being seventeen years old, was

b Or *chiefs*   *c* Meaning of Heb uncertain
d Or *chief by chief*

Temanite in Job 2.11. **36.20** *Horite.* These Horites are Semites, not Hurrians; cf. note on 14.6. The name may mean "cave dweller." **36.31–39** The kingship of Edom was apparently elective, not hereditary.
37.1–50.26 The final narrative sequence in Genesis, the magisterial saga of Joseph and his brothers. Joseph is not a patriarch in the same sense as Abraham, Isaac, and Jacob, but the ancestor of two Israelite tribes, Manasseh and Ephraim, which produced some of Israel's most important leaders (Joshua, Gideon, Samuel) between the eras of Moses and David. Properly speaking, this is not a story about Joseph alone, but about all twelve sons of Jacob. Yet, for reasons of storytelling (and because of the course of later Israelite history), two brothers occupy the forefront of the narrative, Joseph and Judah. And it is Joseph's unique vantage point that gives the tale its dramatic force. He is the first offspring of Jacob to experience slavery in Egypt; and his dazzling rise to power in his adopted country and his poignant reunion with his brothers and aged father enact a drama of divine providence that ties together all the themes and concerns of Genesis. Like the rest of Genesis, the saga is built out of earlier traditions, here reworked extensively by a literary artist of refined imagination. Its function is twofold: to supply a fitting conclusion to the ancestral narratives that precede it and to provide a bridge to the exodus story that follows.
37.1–11 The stage is set for the saga by recounting Joseph's boyhood interaction with his father and brothers and the resentments he aroused. **37.2** *This is the story of the family*, lit. "These are the generations"; see note on 2.4. *Wives*, i.e., concubines, introduced here in order to include in the narrative most of the brothers

shepherding the flock with his brothers; he was a helper to the sons of Bilhah and Zilpah, his father's wives; and Joseph brought a bad report of them to their father. 3 Now Israel loved Joseph more than any other of his children, because he was the son of his old age; and he had made him a long robe with sleeves.*e* 4 But when his brothers saw that their father loved him more than all his brothers, they hated him, and could not speak peaceably to him.

5 Once Joseph had a dream, and when he told it to his brothers, they hated him even more. 6 He said to them, "Listen to this dream that I dreamed. 7 There we were, binding sheaves in the field. Suddenly my sheaf rose and stood upright; then your sheaves gathered around it, and bowed down to my sheaf." 8 His brothers said to him, "Are you indeed to reign over us? Are you indeed to have dominion over us?" So they hated him even more because of his dreams and his words.

9 He had another dream, and told it to his brothers, saying, "Look, I have had another dream: the sun, the moon, and eleven stars were bowing down to me." 10 But when he told it to his father and to his brothers, his father rebuked him, and said to him, "What kind of dream is this that you have had? Shall we indeed come, I and your mother and your brothers, and bow to the ground before you?" 11 So his brothers were jealous of him, but his father kept the matter in mind.

Joseph Is Sold by His Brothers

12 Now his brothers went to pasture their father's flock near Shechem. 13 And Israel said to Joseph, "Are not your brothers pasturing the flock at Shechem? Come, I will send you to them." He answered, "Here I am." 14 So he said to him, "Go now, see if it is well with your brothers and with the flock; and bring word back to me." So he sent him from the valley of Hebron.

He came to Shechem, 15 and a man found him wandering in the fields; the man asked him, "What are you seeking?" 16 "I am seeking my brothers," he said; "tell me, please, where they are pasturing the flock." 17 The man said, "They have gone away, for I heard them say, 'Let us go to Dothan.'" So Joseph went after his brothers, and found them at Dothan. 18 They saw him from a distance, and before he came near to them, they conspired to kill him. 19 They said to one another, "Here comes this dreamer. 20 Come now, let us kill him and throw him into one of the pits; then we shall say that a wild animal has devoured him, and we shall see what will become of his dreams." 21 But when Reuben heard it, he delivered him out of their hands, saying, "Let us not take his life." 22 Reuben said to them, "Shed no blood; throw him into this pit here in the wilderness, but lay no hand on him"—that he might rescue him out of their hand and restore him to his father. 23 So when Joseph came to his brothers, they stripped him of his robe, the long robe with sleeves*f* that he wore; 24 and they took him and threw him into a pit. The pit was empty; there was no water in it.

e Traditional rendering (compare Gk): *a coat of many colors;* Meaning of Heb uncertain   f See note on 37.3

whose names are not mentioned. *Brought a bad report.* Cf. note on 42.9. **37.3** *Israel loved Joseph.* Again, favoritism will be the root of conflict. *The son of his old age,* a designation more appropriate to Benjamin, who, similarly, was a child of Rachel, Jacob's favorite wife. Benjamin, however, being associated with Rachel's death (35.16–20), was perhaps less favored. *Long robe with sleeves,* or a "striped coat." **37.4** *Peaceably.* The word *shalom* (Hebrew, "peace") is a key word throughout the saga. **37.5–11** In each of the story's three dreaming episodes (cf. 40.5–23; 41.1–36), two dreams are told. Here Joseph's dreams prophesy the events of chs. 42–50. **37.10** *And your mother.* Jacob speaks as if Rachel were still alive—her memory is still a living reality for him and appropriate to his rebuke. **37.11** *Kept the matter in mind.* Jacob already knew the importance of dreams (cf. 28.10–17) and so took the matter seriously. **37.14** *If it is well,* lit. "if [there is] peace." Cf. note on 37.4. **37.15** *A man,* a mysterious stranger who may play the role of divine messenger, but who is not identified directly as such. **37.17** *Dothan,* a site near Shechem. **37.21–24, 28a** Here, Reuben restrains his brothers and Midianites carry Joseph to Egypt; cf. vv. 25–27, 28b. **37.23** *They stripped him.* Cf. 39.12. In 41.14 Joseph's donning of new clothes marks a turning point in his fortunes; see also 41.42. **37.25–27, 28b** Here, in contrast to

25 Then they sat down to eat; and looking up they saw a caravan of Ishmaelites coming from Gilead, with their camels carrying gum, balm, and resin, on their way to carry it down to Egypt. 26 Then Judah said to his brothers, "What profit is it if we kill our brother and conceal his blood? 27 Come, let us sell him to the Ishmaelites, and not lay our hands on him, for he is our brother, our own flesh." And his brothers agreed. 28 When some Midianite traders passed by, they drew Joseph up, lifting him out of the pit, and sold him to the Ishmaelites for twenty pieces of silver. And they took Joseph to Egypt.

29 When Reuben returned to the pit and saw that Joseph was not in the pit, he tore his clothes. 30 He returned to his brothers, and said, "The boy is gone; and I, where can I turn?" 31 Then they took Joseph's robe, slaughtered a goat, and dipped the robe in the blood. 32 They had the long robe with sleeves*g* taken to their father, and they said, "This we have found; see now whether it is your son's robe or not." 33 He recognized it, and said, "It is my son's robe! A wild animal has devoured him; Joseph is without doubt torn to pieces." 34 Then Jacob tore his garments, and put sackcloth on his loins, and mourned for his son many days. 35 All his sons and all his daughters sought to comfort him; but he refused to be comforted, and said, "No, I shall go down to Sheol to my son, mourning." Thus his father bewailed him. 36 Meanwhile the Midianites had sold him in Egypt to Potiphar, one of Pharaoh's officials, the captain of the guard.

Judah and Tamar

38 It happened at that time that Judah went down from his brothers and settled near a certain Adullamite whose name was Hirah. 2 There Judah saw the daughter of a certain Canaanite whose name was Shua; he married her and went in to her. 3 She conceived and bore a son; and he named him Er. 4 Again she conceived and bore a son whom she named Onan. 5 Yet again she bore a son, and she named him Shelah. She*h* was in Chezib when she bore him. 6 Judah took a wife for Er his firstborn; her name was Tamar. 7 But Er, Judah's firstborn, was wicked in the sight of the LORD, and the LORD put him to death. 8 Then Judah said to Onan, "Go in to your brother's wife and perform the duty of a brother-in-law to her; raise up offspring for your brother." 9 But since Onan knew that the offspring would not be his, he spilled his semen on the ground whenever he went in to his brother's wife, so that he would not give offspring to his brother. 10 What he did was displeasing in the sight of the LORD, and he put him to death also. 11 Then Judah said to his daughter-in-law Tamar, "Remain a widow in your father's house until my son Shelah grows up" — for he feared that he too would die, like his brothers. So Tamar went to live in her father's house.

12 In course of time the wife of Judah, Shua's daughter, died; when Judah's time of mourning was over,*i* he went up to Timnah to his sheepshearers, he and his friend Hirah the Adullamite. 13 When

g See note on 37.3   h Gk: Heb He
i Heb when Judah was comforted

vv. 21–24, 28a, it is Judah who restrains his brothers and Ishmaelites (see 39.1) who carry Joseph to Egypt. On the significance of both Ishmaelites and Midianites to the providential scheme enacted in Genesis, see notes on 16.6; 25.1–6. **37.32** *See now*, lit. "Recognize, please." See note on 38.25. **37.34** *Tore his garments*, the traditional gesture of mourning; cf. v. 29; 2 Sam 3.31.

38.1–30 An important subplot to the saga concerned with Judah's begetting of Perez and Zerah. Judah's neglect of the levirate obligation (see note on 38.8) to his daughter-in-law, Tamar, leads to an elaborate artifice on her part to conceive offspring by him. The event's significance was well known in ancient Israel, for from the line of Perez will come King David; cf. Ruth 3.11–13;

4.1–22; which likewise turn on the levirate theme. **38.1** *Adullamite*, a Canaanite from the Judean hills. Cf. 1 Sam 22.1–2. **38.7** *But Er . . . was wicked.* No details are given, nor are they necessary to the story. **38.8** *Perform the duty of a brother-in-law.* The rest of the verse explains the obligation, known as levirate law; see Deut 25.5–10. **38.9** *Onan . . . spilled his semen.* The offense at issue is neither masturbation as such ("onanism") nor the efforts at birth control, but failure to fulfill the levirate obligation. **38.11** *Remain a widow . . . until . . . Shelah grows up.* Judah effectively consigns Tamar to oblivion — he apparently has no true intention of giving Shelah to her in marriage; cf. v. 14. **38.12** *Timnah*, a town in the southern hill country (see Josh 15.57);

Tamar was told, "Your father-in-law is going up to Timnah to shear his sheep,"
14she put off her widow's garments, put
on a veil, wrapped herself up, and sat
down at the entrance to Enaim, which is
on the road to Timnah. She saw that Shelah was grown up, yet she had not been
given to him in marriage. 15When Judah
saw her, he thought her to be a prostitute,
for she had covered her face. 16He went
over to her at the roadside, and said,
"Come, let me come in to you," for he did
not know that she was his daughter-in-
law. She said, "What will you give me, that
you may come in to me?" 17He answered,
"I will send you a kid from the flock."
And she said, "Only if you give me a
pledge, until you send it." 18He said,
"What pledge shall I give you?" She replied, "Your signet and your cord, and
the staff that is in your hand." So he gave
them to her, and went in to her, and she
conceived by him. 19Then she got up and
went away, and taking off her veil she put
on the garments of her widowhood.

20 When Judah sent the kid by his
friend the Adullamite, to recover the
pledge from the woman, he could not
find her. 21He asked the townspeople,
"Where is the temple prostitute who was
at Enaim by the wayside?" But they said,
"No prostitute has been here." 22So he returned to Judah, and said, "I have not
found her; moreover the townspeople
said, 'No prostitute has been here.' " 23Ju-
dah replied, "Let her keep the things as
her own, otherwise we will be laughed at;

you see, I sent this kid, and you could not
find her."

24 About three months later Judah
was told, "Your daughter-in-law Tamar
has played the whore; moreover she is
pregnant as a result of whoredom." And
Judah said, "Bring her out, and let her be
burned." 25As she was being brought out,
she sent word to her father-in-law, "It was
the owner of these who made me pregnant." And she said, "Take note, please,
whose these are, the signet and the cord
and the staff." 26Then Judah acknowledged them and said, "She is more in the
right than I, since I did not give her to my
son Shelah." And he did not lie with her
again.

27 When the time of her delivery
came, there were twins in her womb.
28While she was in labor, one put out a
hand; and the midwife took and bound
on his hand a crimson thread, saying,
"This one came out first." 29But just then
he drew back his hand, and out came his
brother; and she said, "What a breach you
have made for yourself!" Therefore he
was named Perez.j 30Afterward his
brother came out with the crimson thread
on his hand; and he was named Zerah.k

Joseph and Potiphar's Wife

39 Now Joseph was taken down to
Egypt, and Potiphar, an officer of
Pharaoh, the captain of the guard, an
Egyptian, bought him from the Ishmael-

j That is *A breach*   k That is *Brightness*; perhaps
alluding to the crimson thread

---

cf. note on 38.14. **38.14** *Entrance to Enaim*, lit.
"opening of the eyes," a wordplay, just as Timnah
plays on the Hebrew word for "conceal."
38.18 Tamar's foresight in requesting the items
from Judah will become clear as the tale unfolds. **38.21** *Temple prostitute*, Hebrew *kedēshah*,
lit. "sacred woman." Cultic prostitution was common in Mesopotamia and Canaan. In v. 15 the
term is simply the less-esteemed "prostitute"
(*zonah*, perhaps lit. "one who whores for sustenance"). Hirah attempts to dignify Judah's actions
according to the era's customs. *No prostitute*, i.e.
kedēshah. **38.23** *Otherwise we will be laughed at.* An
atmosphere of gossip and scandal clearly prevails
and is important to the tale's conclusion; see notes
on 38.25; 38.26. **38.24** *Played the whore.* The
verb is related to *zonah*, the less respectable term
(see note on 38.21). *Let her be burned.* Judah still
does not realize his own role in the events.

38.25 *Take note, please*, lit. "Recognize, please" —
the same words used in 37.32, thus here a preliminary justice for Judah's role in the sale of Joseph
and deception of Jacob. **38.26** *Acknowledged*, lit.
"recognized." Judah's embarrassment is complete,
and he takes the only dignified way out —
admission of his error and protection of Tamar.
He did not lie with her again, thus reconfirming his
in-law (and exclusively levirate) relation to her.
38.27 *Twins in her womb.* Cf. 25.22–23. Here, similarly, the second-born usurps first place.
38.28–30 An etiological conclusion, explaining
the children's names. Perez will be an ancestor of
King David.

39.1–23 The resumption of Joseph's tale recounting his experiences while serving in the
household of Potiphar, Pharaoh's chief steward,
who treats Joseph kindly until a false accusation
arises. **39.1** *Pharaoh*, from Egyptian for "great

ites who had brought him down there. ²The Lord was with Joseph, and he became a successful man; he was in the house of his Egyptian master. ³His master saw that the Lord was with him, and that the Lord caused all that he did to prosper in his hands. ⁴So Joseph found favor in his sight and attended him; he made him overseer of his house and put him in charge of all that he had. ⁵From the time that he made him overseer in his house and over all that he had, the Lord blessed the Egyptian's house for Joseph's sake; the blessing of the Lord was on all that he had, in house and field. ⁶So he left all that he had in Joseph's charge; and, with him there, he had no concern for anything but the food that he ate.

Now Joseph was handsome and good-looking. ⁷And after a time his master's wife cast her eyes on Joseph and said, "Lie with me." ⁸But he refused and said to his master's wife, "Look, with me here, my master has no concern about anything in the house, and he has put everything that he has in my hand. ⁹He is not greater in this house than I am, nor has he kept back anything from me except yourself, because you are his wife. How then could I do this great wickedness, and sin against God?" ¹⁰And although she spoke to Joseph day after day, he would not consent to lie beside her or to be with her. ¹¹One day, however, when he went into the house to do his work, and while no one else was in the house, ¹²she caught hold of his garment, saying, "Lie with me!" But he left his garment in her hand, and fled and ran outside. ¹³When she saw that he had left his garment in her hand and had fled outside, ¹⁴she called out to the members of her household and said to them, "See, my husband[1] has brought among us a Hebrew to insult us! He came in to me to lie with me, and I cried out with a loud voice; ¹⁵and when he heard me raise my voice and cry out, he left his garment beside me, and fled outside." ¹⁶Then she kept his garment by her until his master came home, ¹⁷and she told him the same story, saying, "The Hebrew servant, whom you have brought among us, came in to me to insult me; ¹⁸but as soon as I raised my voice and cried out, he left his garment beside me, and fled outside."

19 When his master heard the words that his wife spoke to him, saying, "This is the way your servant treated me," he became enraged. ²⁰And Joseph's master took him and put him into the prison, the place where the king's prisoners were confined; he remained there in prison. ²¹But the Lord was with Joseph and showed him steadfast love; he gave him favor in the sight of the chief jailer. ²²The chief jailer committed to Joseph's care all the prisoners who were in the prison, and whatever was done there, he was the one who did it. ²³The chief jailer paid no heed to anything that was in Joseph's care, because the Lord was with him; and whatever he did, the Lord made it prosper.

The Dreams of Two Prisoners

40 Some time after this, the cup-bearer of the king of Egypt and his baker offended their lord the king of Egypt. ²Pharaoh was angry with his two officers, the chief cupbearer and the chief

1 Heb *he*

---

house," here and elsewhere a generic term (though wielded like a name) for the king of Egypt, whose given name is never mentioned. *Ishmaelites.* See note on 37.25–27, 28b. **39.2** *He was in the house.* Normally a slave would serve in the fields or at construction. **39.4** *Overseer . . . in charge of all,* a rehearsal for Joseph's more exalted role in the future. **39.5** *The blessing of the Lord was on all that he had, in house and field,* as later it would be upon Egypt through Joseph's leadership.
39.7–18   These events are frequently compared to an Egyptian tale, "Story of Two Brothers." Joseph's self-restraint contrasts markedly with Judah's patronage of prostitution (38.16). **39.9** *God.* The name YHWH, translated "Lord" in nrsv, is never used in conversation with non-Israelites. **39.14** *A Hebrew.* See note on 14.13. **39.20** The significance of *the place where the king's prisoners were confined* will become clear in ch. 40. Joseph's punishment is surprisingly mild, given the allegation's seriousness and Potiphar's high station. **39.21** *Steadfast love.* See note on 24.14; cf. 24.27, 49; 32.10. *Gave him favor.* As in v. 4, a strange turnabout for one who so persistently alienated his brothers. **39.22** *Committed to Joseph's care.* In every circumstance, Joseph demonstrates his capacity for leadership. **39.23** *The chief jailer paid no heed to anything,* just as Potiphar "had no concern for anything" (v. 6). **40.1–23**   Joseph's interpretation of the dreams of two fellow prisoners, servants of Phar-

baker, 3 and he put them in custody in the house of the captain of the guard, in the prison where Joseph was confined. 4 The captain of the guard charged Joseph with them, and he waited on them; and they continued for some time in custody. 5 One night they both dreamed—the cupbearer and the baker of the king of Egypt, who were confined in the prison—each his own dream, and each dream with its own meaning. 6 When Joseph came to them in the morning, he saw that they were troubled. 7 So he asked Pharaoh's officers, who were with him in custody in his master's house, "Why are your faces downcast today?" 8 They said to him, "We have had dreams, and there is no one to interpret them." And Joseph said to them, "Do not interpretations belong to God? Please tell them to me."

9 So the chief cupbearer told his dream to Joseph, and said to him, "In my dream there was a vine before me, 10 and on the vine there were three branches. As soon as it budded, its blossoms came out and the clusters ripened into grapes. 11 Pharaoh's cup was in my hand; and I took the grapes and pressed them into Pharaoh's cup, and placed the cup in Pharaoh's hand." 12 Then Joseph said to him, "This is its interpretation: the three branches are three days; 13 within three days Pharaoh will lift up your head and restore you to your office; and you shall place Pharaoh's cup in his hand, just as you used to do when you were his cupbearer. 14 But remember me when it is well with you; please do me the kindness

to make mention of me to Pharaoh, and so get me out of this place. 15 For in fact I was stolen out of the land of the Hebrews; and here also I have done nothing that they should have put me into the dungeon."

16 When the chief baker saw that the interpretation was favorable, he said to Joseph, "I also had a dream: there were three cake baskets on my head, 17 and in the uppermost basket there were all sorts of baked food for Pharaoh, but the birds were eating it out of the basket on my head." 18 And Joseph answered, "This is its interpretation: the three baskets are three days; 19 within three days Pharaoh will lift up your head—from you!—and hang you on a pole; and the birds will eat the flesh from you."

20 On the third day, which was Pharaoh's birthday, he made a feast for all his servants, and lifted up the head of the chief cupbearer and the head of the chief baker among his servants. 21 He restored the chief cupbearer to his cupbearing, and he placed the cup in Pharaoh's hand; 22 but the chief baker he hanged, just as Joseph had interpreted to them. 23 Yet the chief cupbearer did not remember Joseph, but forgot him.

Joseph Interprets Pharaoh's Dream

41 After two whole years, Pharaoh dreamed that he was standing by the Nile, 2 and there came up out of the Nile seven sleek and fat cows, and they grazed in the reed grass. 3 Then seven

---

aoh who had fallen from favor. **40.1** *Some time after this.* As in 15.1; 22.1; 22.20; 39.7, this formula and the words immediately following are a heading for the whole episode; the next verse, therefore, is not redundant. **40.5** *Each his own dream.* Like Joseph's two boyhood dreams (37.5–11), these are parallel but, unlike them, differ drastically in the outcomes they portend. **40.8** *Do not interpretations belong to God?* After his boyhood dreams, it was others who did the interpreting; here Joseph takes on the task, acknowledging the interpreter's debt to God. Cf. note on 41.32. On the name "God," see note on 39.9. **40.9–11** See note on 40.16–17. **40.13** *Will lift up your head* conceals a double meaning; see note on 40.19. **40.14** See note on 40.23. **40.15** *Stolen out of the land of the Hebrews.* See note on 45.4. **40.16–17** In the cupbearer's dream, Pharaoh was being nourished; here Pharaoh is deprived of

nourishment. This contrast portends Joseph's eventual role as provider of food for all Egypt. **40.17** *The birds were eating it.* Preservation of precious food supplies against the ravages of nature will eventually be the key to Egypt's salvation; cf. 41.25–36. **40.19** *Will lift up your head—from you!* "Lift up . . . [the] head" means both "favor, forgive" and "behead." Cf. v. 20b. **40.20** *On the third day.* See note on 31.22. **40.23** Had the cupbearer obtained Joseph's release *before* Pharaoh's dreams (ch. 41), the historically critical moment for Joseph's services would have been wasted. Joseph's powers are recalled when the need is greatest.

41.1–36 The saga's central episode, recounting the turning point in Joseph's career: his interpreting of Pharaoh's two dreams, which portend for Egypt seven years of plenty and seven years of famine. **41.1** *Pharaoh dreamed.* The previous

other cows, ugly and thin, came up out of the Nile after them, and stood by the other cows on the bank of the Nile. 4 The ugly and thin cows ate up the seven sleek and fat cows. And Pharaoh awoke. 5 Then he fell asleep and dreamed a second time; seven ears of grain, plump and good, were growing on one stalk. 6 Then seven ears, thin and blighted by the east wind, sprouted after them. 7 The thin ears swallowed up the seven plump and full ears. Pharaoh awoke, and it was a dream. 8 In the morning his spirit was troubled; so he sent and called for all the magicians of Egypt and all its wise men. Pharaoh told them his dreams, but there was no one who could interpret them to Pharaoh.

9 Then the chief cupbearer said to Pharaoh, "I remember my faults today. 10 Once Pharaoh was angry with his servants, and put me and the chief baker in custody in the house of the captain of the guard. 11 We dreamed on the same night, he and I, each having a dream with its own meaning. 12 A young Hebrew was there with us, a servant of the captain of the guard. When we told him, he interpreted our dreams to us, giving an interpretation to each according to his dream. 13 As he interpreted to us, so it turned out; I was restored to my office, and the baker was hanged."

14 Then Pharaoh sent for Joseph, and he was hurriedly brought out of the dungeon. When he had shaved himself and changed his clothes, he came in before Pharaoh. 15 And Pharaoh said to Joseph, "I have had a dream, and there is no one who can interpret it. I have heard it said of you that when you hear a dream you can interpret it." 16 Joseph answered Pharaoh, "It is not I; God will give Pharaoh a favorable answer." 17 Then Pharaoh said to Joseph, "In my dream I was stand-

ing on the banks of the Nile; 18 and seven cows, fat and sleek, came up out of the Nile and fed in the reed grass. 19 Then seven other cows came up after them, poor, very ugly, and thin. Never had I seen such ugly ones in all the land of Egypt. 20 The thin and ugly cows ate up the first seven fat cows, 21 but when they had eaten them no one would have known that they had done so, for they were still as ugly as before. Then I awoke. 22 I fell asleep a second time *m* and I saw in my dream seven ears of grain, full and good, growing on one stalk, 23 and seven ears, withered, thin, and blighted by the east wind, sprouting after them; 24 and the thin ears swallowed up the seven good ears. But when I told it to the magicians, there was no one who could explain it to me."

25 Then Joseph said to Pharaoh, "Pharaoh's dreams are one and the same; God has revealed to Pharaoh what he is about to do. 26 The seven good cows are seven years, and the seven good ears are seven years; the dreams are one. 27 The seven lean and ugly cows that came up after them are seven years, as are the seven empty ears blighted by the east wind. They are seven years of famine. 28 It is as I told Pharaoh; God has shown to Pharaoh what he is about to do. 29 There will come seven years of great plenty throughout all the land of Egypt. 30 After them there will arise seven years of famine, and all the plenty will be forgotten in the land of Egypt; the famine will consume the land. 31 The plenty will no longer be known in the land because of the famine that will follow, for it will be very grievous. 32 And the doubling of Pharaoh's dream means that the thing is

m Gk Syr Vg: Heb lacks *I fell asleep a second time*

---

dreamers, Joseph's fellow prisoners (ch. 40), were at the bottom of the social ladder; this one is at the top. Joseph's interpretive vision encompasses the whole. **41.2, 5** *Cows, ears of grain.* The two dreams concern the heart of Egypt's economy: livestock and agriculture. Throughout Genesis, food is a core preoccupation. **41.2** The Hebrew words for *Nile* and *reed grass* are of Egyptian origin; similar Egyptian touches occur throughout the saga. Cf. 41.42–45. For Egypt, the Nile (lit. "the River") is the source of all sustenance and life. **41.7** *Pharaoh awoke, and it was a dream.* The disorientation of one awakening is shown here.

41.8 *No one who could interpret.* Cf. the consternation in the royal court in Esth 6.1–13; Dan 2.1–16. The king's courtiers fail where a wise outsider succeeds. **41.9** *I remember my faults today.* See note on 40.23; cf. 42.21. **41.12** *A young Hebrew.* See note on 14.13. **41.14** *Changed his clothes.* See note on 37.23. **41.16** *Not I; God will give.* Again, Joseph credits God for the interpretation he will advance; cf. 40.8; 41.32. **41.17–24** As in ch. 24, in the retelling of an event the wording is subtly varied. Pharaoh's description is more detailed and emotional than the narrator's. **41.25** *One and the same.* See note on

fixed by God, and God will shortly bring it about. 33 Now therefore let Pharaoh select a man who is discerning and wise, and set him over the land of Egypt. 34 Let Pharaoh proceed to appoint overseers over the land, and take one-fifth of the produce of the land of Egypt during the seven plenteous years. 35 Let them gather all the food of these good years that are coming, and lay up grain under the authority of Pharaoh for food in the cities, and let them keep it. 36 That food shall be a reserve for the land against the seven years of famine that are to befall the land of Egypt, so that the land may not perish through the famine."

Joseph's Rise to Power

37 The proposal pleased Pharaoh and all his servants. 38 Pharaoh said to his servants, "Can we find anyone else like this — one in whom is the spirit of God?" 39 So Pharaoh said to Joseph, "Since God has shown you all this, there is no one so discerning and wise as you. 40 You shall be over my house, and all my people shall order themselves as you command; only with regard to the throne will I be greater than you." 41 And Pharaoh said to Joseph, "See, I have set you over all the land of Egypt." 42 Removing his signet ring from his hand, Pharaoh put it on Joseph's hand; he arrayed him in garments of fine linen, and put a gold chain around his neck. 43 He had him ride in the chariot of his second-in-command; and they cried out in front of him, "Bow the knee!"n Thus he set him over all the land of Egypt. 44 Moreover Pharaoh said to Joseph, "I am Pharaoh, and without your consent no one shall lift up hand or foot in all the land of Egypt." 45 Pharaoh gave Joseph the name Zaphenath-paneah; and he gave him Asenath daughter of Potiphera, priest of On, as his wife. Thus Joseph gained authority over the land of Egypt.

46 Joseph was thirty years old when he entered the service of Pharaoh king of Egypt. And Joseph went out from the presence of Pharaoh, and went through all the land of Egypt. 47 During the seven plenteous years the earth produced abundantly. 48 He gathered up all the food of the seven years when there was plentyo in the land of Egypt, and stored up food in the cities; he stored up in every city the food from the fields around it. 49 So Joseph stored up grain in such abundance — like the sand of the sea — that he stopped measuring it; it was beyond measure.

50 Before the years of famine came, Joseph had two sons, whom Asenath daughter of Potiphera, priest of On, bore to him. 51 Joseph named the firstborn Manasseh,p "For," he said, "God has made me forget all my hardship and all my father's house." 52 The second he named Ephraim,q "For God has made me fruitful in the land of my misfortunes."

53 The seven years of plenty that prevailed in the land of Egypt came to an end; 54 and the seven years of famine began to come, just as Joseph had said. There was famine in every country, but throughout the land of Egypt there was bread. 55 When all the land of Egypt was

n Abrek, apparently an Egyptian word similar in sound to the Hebrew word meaning to kneel
o Sam Gk: MT the seven years that were   p That is Making to forget   q From a Hebrew word meaning to be fruitful

---

41.32.   41.32 The doubling, a delayed explanation for the double occurrence of dreams in 37.5–9; 40.5, 9–11, 16–17; 41.1–7 — it is God who causes the doubling in order to convey a message. 41.33 Discerning and wise. Cf. v. 39. Cf. also the pairing of these and comparable traits in 1 Kings 3.12; Job 12.2–3; Prov 8.14. 41.37–57 Joseph's sudden rise to power as chief overseer of Egypt, to carry out his recommended plan. 41.38 Spirit of God. Since the pharaohs were themselves regarded as gods, this one's sincere obeisance to God seems unusual. Cf. 20.8; 21.22. On God, see note on 39.9. 41.40 Joseph's third and most consequential appointment to responsibility over others; cf. 39.4–6, 22–23. 41.42 Again, Joseph's garments mirror his fortunes; cf. 37.3, 23, 31–32; 39.12; 41.14. 41.43 He had him ride. Cf. Esth 6.7–11. Bow the knee! No agreement exists about the meaning of the Egyptian word exclaimed here, but as a Hebrew expression it anticipates 42.6. 41.45 Zaphenath-paneah. Jewish commentary reads this Egyptian name as the Hebrew words "He Deciphers the Concealed." Potiphera, a variant of "Potiphar," probably indicating another person. 41.51–52 The names Manasseh and Ephraim are made to signify the psychological remoteness of Joseph's native land — in context a profound (if thus far rare) glimpse of Joseph's inner life. Paradoxically, the tribes of Manasseh and Ephraim are later said to settle the heart of Canaan and adjacent Transjordan; see Josh

famished, the people cried to Pharaoh for bread. Pharaoh said to all the Egyptians, "Go to Joseph; what he says to you, do." 56 And since the famine had spread over all the land, Joseph opened all the storehouses,r and sold to the Egyptians, for the famine was severe in the land of Egypt. 57 Moreover, all the world came to Joseph in Egypt to buy grain, because the famine became severe throughout the world.

Joseph's Brothers Go to Egypt

42 When Jacob learned that there was grain in Egypt, he said to his sons, "Why do you keep looking at one another? 2 I have heard," he said, "that there is grain in Egypt; go down and buy grain for us there, that we may live and not die." 3 So ten of Joseph's brothers went down to buy grain in Egypt. 4 But Jacob did not send Joseph's brother Benjamin with his brothers, for he feared that harm might come to him. 5 Thus the sons of Israel were among the other people who came to buy grain, for the famine had reached the land of Canaan.

6 Now Joseph was governor over the land; it was he who sold to all the people of the land. And Joseph's brothers came and bowed themselves before him with their faces to the ground. 7 When Joseph saw his brothers, he recognized them, but he treated them like strangers and spoke harshly to them. "Where do you come from?" he said. They said, "From the land of Canaan, to buy food." 8 Although Jo-

seph had recognized his brothers, they did not recognize him. 9 Joseph also remembered the dreams that he had dreamed about them. He said to them, "You are spies; you have come to see the nakedness of the land!" 10 They said to him, "No, my lord; your servants have come to buy food. 11 We are all sons of one man; we are honest men; your servants have never been spies." 12 But he said to them, "No, you have come to see the nakedness of the land!" 13 They said, "We, your servants, are twelve brothers, the sons of a certain man in the land of Canaan; the youngest, however, is now with our father, and one is no more." 14 But Joseph said to them, "It is just as I have said to you; you are spies! 15 Here is how you shall be tested: as Pharaoh lives, you shall not leave this place unless your youngest brother comes here! 16 Let one of you go and bring your brother, while the rest of you remain in prison, in order that your words may be tested, whether there is truth in you; or else, as Pharaoh lives, surely you are spies." 17 And he put them all together in prison for three days.

18 On the third day Joseph said to them, "Do this and you will live, for I fear God: 19 if you are honest men, let one of your brothers stay here where you are imprisoned. The rest of you shall go and carry grain for the famine of your households, 20 and bring your youngest brother to me. Thus your words will be verified, and you shall not die." And they agreed to

r Gk Vg Compare Syr: Heb *opened all that was in* (or, *among*) *them*

13.29–33; 16.1–17.18; Judg 1.22–29. **41.57** As before (cf. 12.10), the surrounding lands look to Egypt for food in time of famine. Joseph's role in saving his kin in Canaan is central to the saga; cf. 45.5–8. This verse serves as a bridge to the next chapter, which returns to Jacob's household. **42.1–25** The first journey to Egypt by Joseph's brothers to buy grain for their father's household. Joseph immediately recognizes them but pretends not to know them while observing their behavior. They do not recognize him but remember well their betrayal of Joseph years before. **42.1** *Learned*, lit. "saw," continuing the echo of this important verb. See, e.g., notes on 16.13–14; 21.9; 22.14. *Looking at one another*, lit. "seeing one another," or possibly "showing yourselves [before me]." **42.4** *Did not send . . . Benjamin*. With Joseph gone, Jacob's protectiveness naturally shifts to Benjamin. *Joseph's brother*, i.e.,

full brother; cf. note on 43.29. **42.6** *Joseph's brothers came and bowed*. Joseph's early dreams (37.5–9) have come true (cf. v. 9). **42.7** *He recognized*. Cf. 37.32–33; 38.25–26. *Treated them like strangers*, lit. "played the stranger." The Hebrew word plays on "recognized"; see v. 8. **42.9** *Remembered the dreams*. See note on 42.6. *You are spies* recalls Joseph's own spying on his brothers (37.2)—indeed, he spies on them now. *To see the nakedness of the land*. The language of sexual transgression (cf. 9.22; Lev 18.6) emphasizes their illegitimacy of purpose. **42.13** They omit mentioning their role in Joseph's enslavement. **42.17** Joseph makes them relive his own uncertainty and helplessness when sold as a slave. *Put*, in Hebrew a play on "Joseph"; cf. 30.23. **42.18** *On the third day*. See note on 31.22. *For I fear God*. Joseph neither wishes their death nor will behave unjustly. **42.19** *Honest men*, and not

do so. 21 They said to one another, "Alas, we are paying the penalty for what we did to our brother; we saw his anguish when he pleaded with us, but we would not listen. That is why this anguish has come upon us." 22 Then Reuben answered them, "Did I not tell you not to wrong the boy? But you would not listen. So now there comes a reckoning for his blood." 23 They did not know that Joseph understood them, since he spoke with them through an interpreter. 24 He turned away from them and wept; then he returned and spoke to them. And he picked out Simeon and had him bound before their eyes. 25 Joseph then gave orders to fill their bags with grain, to return every man's money to his sack, and to give them provisions for their journey. This was done for them.

Joseph's Brothers Return to Canaan

26 They loaded their donkeys with their grain, and departed. 27 When one of them opened his sack to give his donkey fodder at the lodging place, he saw his money at the top of the sack. 28 He said to his brothers, "My money has been put back; here it is in my sack!" At this they lost heart and turned trembling to one another, saying, "What is this that God has done to us?"

29 When they came to their father Jacob in the land of Canaan, they told him all that had happened to them, saying, 30 "The man, the lord of the land, spoke harshly to us, and charged us with spying on the land. 31 But we said to him, 'We are honest men, we are not spies. 32 We are twelve brothers, sons of our father; one is

no more, and the youngest is now with our father in the land of Canaan.' 33 Then the man, the lord of the land, said to us, 'By this I shall know that you are honest men: leave one of your brothers with me, take grain for the famine of your households, and go your way. 34 Bring your youngest brother to me, and I shall know that you are not spies but honest men. Then I will release your brother to you, and you may trade in the land.' "

35 As they were emptying their sacks, there in each one's sack was his bag of money. When they and their father saw their bundles of money, they were dismayed. 36 And their father Jacob said to them, "I am the one you have bereaved of children: Joseph is no more, and Simeon is no more, and now you would take Benjamin. All this has happened to me!" 37 Then Reuben said to his father, "You may kill my two sons if I do not bring him back to you. Put him in my hands, and I will bring him back to you." 38 But he said, "My son shall not go down with you, for his brother is dead, and he alone is left. If harm should come to him on the journey that you are to make, you would bring down my gray hairs with sorrow to Sheol."

The Brothers Return to Egypt with Benjamin

43 Now the famine was severe in the land. 2 And when they had eaten up the grain that they had brought from Egypt, their father said to them, "Go again, buy us a little more food." 3 But Judah said to him, "The man solemnly warned us, saying, 'You shall not see my face unless your brother is with you.' 4 If

---

spies; cf. v. 34. **42.20** *They agreed to do so*, lit. "They did so (Hebrew *ken*)," a play on *kenim* ("honest") in v. 19. **42.21** *Saw . . . but would not listen*. These two key verbs now sum up their crime in ch. 37. *This anguish*. For the first time, they view the sale of Joseph from his perspective. **42.22** *Did I not tell you . . . you would not listen*. See 37.21–22. *A reckoning for his blood*. Cf. 4.10; 9.5. **42.23** This emphasizes that Joseph's self-disguise continues. Cf. note on 43.32. **42.24** *Simeon* (cf. 29.33) plays on "we would not listen" (v. 21); Joseph virtually imprisons their ears for the crime of heedlessness. **42.25** *Return every man's money*. The reason becomes clearer in vv. 27–28, 35; 43.12, 20–23.

42.26–38 The brothers' return to Canaan and Jacob's reactions to their journey. **42.32** Again (see v. 13) they restate the situation of ch. 37, but now Joseph is mentioned before Benjamin, for he is fresher in their minds. **42.35a** One had already found his money (v. 27); the rest now discover what they were afraid to check for then (v. 28). **42.36** *Bereaved*. Cf. Rebekah's use of this word translated "lose" in 27.45; see also 43.14. **42.38** *Bring down . . . to Sheol*. Cf. 37.35. On *gray hairs*, see note on 15.15.
43.1–34 The brothers' second trip to Egypt, this time with Benjamin. Joseph, still unrecognized by them, receives them amicably and invites them to dine—but sits apart. **43.3** *Shall not see*

you will send our brother with us, we will go down and buy you food; 5 but if you will not send him, we will not go down, for the man said to us, 'You shall not see my face, unless your brother is with you.'" 6 Israel said, "Why did you treat me so badly as to tell the man that you had another brother?" 7 They replied, "The man questioned us carefully about ourselves and our kindred, saying, 'Is your father still alive? Have you another brother?' What we told him was in answer to these questions. Could we in any way know that he would say, 'Bring your brother down'?" 8 Then Judah said to his father Israel, "Send the boy with me, and let us be on our way, so that we may live and not die — you and we and also our little ones. 9 I myself will be surety for him; you can hold me accountable for him. If I do not bring him back to you and set him before you, then let me bear the blame forever. 10 If we had not delayed, we would now have returned twice."

11 Then their father Israel said to them, "If it must be so, then do this: take some of the choice fruits of the land in your bags, and carry them down as a present to the man — a little balm and a little honey, gum, resin, pistachio nuts, and almonds. 12 Take double the money with you. Carry back with you the money that was returned in the top of your sacks; perhaps it was an oversight. 13 Take your brother also, and be on your way again to the man; 14 may God Almighty[s] grant you mercy before the man, so that he may send back your other brother and Benjamin. As for me, if I am bereaved of my children, I am bereaved." 15 So the men took the present, and they took double the money with them, as well as Benjamin. Then they went on their way down to Egypt, and stood before Joseph.

16 When Joseph saw Benjamin with them, he said to the steward of his house, "Bring the men into the house, and

slaughter an animal and make ready, for the men are to dine with me at noon." 17 The man did as Joseph said, and brought the men to Joseph's house. 18 Now the men were afraid because they were brought to Joseph's house, and they said, "It is because of the money, replaced in our sacks the first time, that we have been brought in, so that he may have an opportunity to fall upon us, to make slaves of us and take our donkeys." 19 So they went up to the steward of Joseph's house and spoke with him at the entrance to the house. 20 They said, "Oh, my lord, we came down the first time to buy food; 21 and when we came to the lodging place we opened our sacks, and there was each one's money in the top of his sack, our money in full weight. So we have brought it back with us. 22 Moreover we have brought down with us additional money to buy food. We do not know who put our money in our sacks." 23 He replied, "Rest assured, do not be afraid; your God and the God of your father must have put treasure in your sacks for you; I received your money." Then he brought Simeon out to them. 24 When the steward[t] had brought the men into Joseph's house, and given them water, and they had washed their feet, and when he had given their donkeys fodder, 25 they made the present ready for Joseph's coming at noon, for they had heard that they would dine there.

26 When Joseph came home, they brought him the present that they had carried into the house, and bowed to the ground before him. 27 He inquired about their welfare, and said, "Is your father well, the old man of whom you spoke? Is he still alive?" 28 They said, "Your servant our father is well; he is still alive." And they bowed their heads and did obeisance. 29 Then he looked up and saw his brother

s Traditional rendering of Heb *El Shaddai*
t Heb *the man*

---

my face, their own words (cf. 42.19–20). The language recalls 32.30; 33.10. **43.7** *Questioned us carefully,* again, their embellishment. See also 44.19. **43.8** *Judah said* anticipates Judah's key role in 44.18–34. *Live and not die.* Cf. 42.2, 20. **43.10** *Twice.* The motif of "doubling" (cf. 41.32) returns here and in vv. 12, 15. **43.14** *God Almighty.* See note on 17.1. **43.23** *Rest assured,* lit. "Be at peace"; cf. note on 37.4. *Brought Simeon out*

to them, ending the detention begun in 42.24. **43.26** *And bowed* now gives new meaning to the doubling of Joseph's early dream (35.5–9) — it prophesied *two* obeisances. **43.27** *Welfare,* lit. "peace." *Is your father well,* lit. "Is your father [at] peace"; cf. note on 37.4. **43.27–28** *Still alive.* See note on 45.5. **43.29** *Looked up and saw.* Cf. 22.4. *His mother's son.* Their common descent through Rachel is stressed, associating both of

Benjamin, his mother's son, and said, "Is this your youngest brother, of whom you spoke to me? God be gracious to you, my son!" 30 With that, Joseph hurried out, because he was overcome with affection for his brother, and he was about to weep. So he went into a private room and wept there. 31 Then he washed his face and came out; and controlling himself he said, "Serve the meal." 32 They served him by himself, and them by themselves, and the Egyptians who ate with him by themselves, because the Egyptians could not eat with the Hebrews, for that is an abomination to the Egyptians. 33 When they were seated before him, the firstborn according to his birthright and the youngest according to his youth, the men looked at one another in amazement. 34 Portions were taken to them from Joseph's table, but Benjamin's portion was five times as much as any of theirs. So they drank and were merry with him.

Joseph Detains Benjamin

44 Then he commanded the steward of his house, "Fill the men's sacks with food, as much as they can carry, and put each man's money in the top of his sack. 2 Put my cup, the silver cup, in the top of the sack of the youngest, with his money for the grain." And he did as Joseph told him. 3 As soon as the morning was light, the men were sent away with their donkeys. 4 When they had gone only a short distance from the city, Joseph said to his steward, "Go, follow after the men; and when you overtake them, say to them, 'Why have you returned evil for good?

Why have you stolen my silver cup?^{u} 5 Is it not from this that my lord drinks? Does he not indeed use it for divination? You have done wrong in doing this.' "

6 When he overtook them, he repeated these words to them. 7 They said to him, "Why does my lord speak such words as these? Far be it from your servants that they should do such a thing! 8 Look, the money that we found at the top of our sacks, we brought back to you from the land of Canaan; why then would we steal silver or gold from your lord's house? 9 Should it be found with any one of your servants, let him die; moreover the rest of us will become my lord's slaves." 10 He said, "Even so; in accordance with your words, let it be: he with whom it is found shall become my slave, but the rest of you shall go free." 11 Then each one quickly lowered his sack to the ground, and each opened his sack. 12 He searched, beginning with the eldest and ending with the youngest; and the cup was found in Benjamin's sack. 13 At this they tore their clothes. Then each one loaded his donkey, and they returned to the city.

14 Judah and his brothers came to Joseph's house while he was still there; and they fell to the ground before him. 15 Joseph said to them, "What deed is this that you have done? Do you not know that one such as I can practice divination?" 16 And Judah said, "What can we say to my lord? What can we speak? How can we clear ourselves? God has found out the guilt of your servants; here we are then, my lord's

---

u Gk Compare Vg: Heb lacks *Why have you stolen my silver cup?*

---

them with their father's favor. **43.30–31** Cf. 42.24. **43.32** The eating arrangements are a measure of how distant Joseph has become from his native ways, at least outwardly; cf. 41.51–52; 42.23. **43.33** *The firstborn ... to his youth,* a formality imposed by the Egyptian court, not their natural protocol, given Reuben's and Simeon's ostracism at home (see 34.30; 35.22; 49.3–7). Their *amazement* is understandable. Cf. v. 34. **43.34** *Benjamin's portion ... five times as much.* Paradoxically, the youngest, being full brother to Joseph, receives preferential treatment. **44.1–17** The brothers again find themselves in trouble, and Joseph demands Benjamin's detention. **44.2** Joseph continues his scheme to embarrass his brothers. **44.4** *Evil for good.* This classic dyad (cf. 2.9) recalls the garden of

Eden story, which echoes throughout Genesis. **44.5** *Does he not indeed use it for divination,* an affectation — Joseph's divinatory powers are surely more direct. Cf. v. 9. The word "divination," associated with Laban in 30.27, increases the similarity between this scene and 31.22–35. **44.9** *Let him die.* These words, recalling Jacob's in 31.32, unintentionally place Benjamin in mortal danger, at least in theory (Joseph's ultimate intention is in fact not yet clear). **44.10** *Shall become my slave.* See note on 44.16. **44.12** *Beginning with the eldest,* "Egyptian" protocol (see note on 43.33), increasing suspense to explosive proportions by the time Benjamin is reached. **44.15** *Divination.* See note on 44.5. **44.16** *Here we are then, my lord's slaves.* Their former sale of Joseph has come full

slaves, both we and also the one in whose possession the cup has been found." 17 But he said, "Far be it from me that I should do so! Only the one in whose possession the cup was found shall be my slave; but as for you, go up in peace to your father."

Judah Pleads for Benjamin's Release

18 Then Judah stepped up to him and said, "O my lord, let your servant please speak a word in my lord's ears, and do not be angry with your servant; for you are like Pharaoh himself. 19 My lord asked his servants, saying, 'Have you a father or a brother?' 20 And we said to my lord, 'We have a father, an old man, and a young brother, the child of his old age. His brother is dead; he alone is left of his mother's children, and his father loves him.' 21 Then you said to your servants, 'Bring him down to me, so that I may set my eyes on him.' 22 We said to my lord, 'The boy cannot leave his father, for if he should leave his father, his father would die.' 23 Then you said to your servants, 'Unless your youngest brother comes down with you, you shall see my face no more.' 24 When we went back to your servant my father we told him the words of my lord. 25 And when our father said, 'Go again, buy us a little food,' 26 we said, 'We cannot go down. Only if our youngest brother goes with us, will we go down; for we cannot see the man's face unless our youngest brother is with us.' 27 Then your servant my father said to us, 'You know that my wife bore me two sons; 28 one left me, and I said, Surely he has been torn to pieces; and I have never seen him since. 29 If you take this one also from me, and harm comes to him, you will bring down

my gray hairs in sorrow to Sheol.' 30 Now therefore, when I come to your servant my father and the boy is not with us, then, as his life is bound up in the boy's life, 31 when he sees that the boy is not with us, he will die; and your servants will bring down the gray hairs of your servant our father with sorrow to Sheol. 32 For your servant became surety for the boy to my father, saying, 'If I do not bring him back to you, then I will bear the blame in the sight of my father all my life.' 33 Now therefore, please let your servant remain as a slave to my lord in place of the boy; and let the boy go back with his brothers. 34 For how can I go back to my father if the boy is not with me? I fear to see the suffering that would come upon my father."

Joseph Reveals Himself to His Brothers

45 Then Joseph could no longer control himself before all those who stood by him, and he cried out, "Send everyone away from me." So no one stayed with him when Joseph made himself known to his brothers. 2 And he wept so loudly that the Egyptians heard it, and the household of Pharaoh heard it. 3 Joseph said to his brothers, "I am Joseph. Is my father still alive?" But his brothers could not answer him, so dismayed were they at his presence.

4 Then Joseph said to his brothers, "Come closer to me." And they came closer. He said, "I am your brother, Joseph, whom you sold into Egypt. 5 And now do not be distressed, or angry with yourselves, because you sold me here; for God sent me before you to preserve life. 6 For the famine has been in the land these two years; and there are five more

---

circle. **44.17** *Go up*, the standard term for migration toward Canaan/Israel. *In peace*. See note on 37.4.

44.18–34 One of the longest in biblical narrative, this speech marks the turning point in the brothers' present dealings with Joseph. Judah is the hero of this scene, remarkably retelling the entire story up to now. **44.34** *I fear ... upon my father*. This final remark, more than any other, touches Joseph deeply; cf. note on 42.21.

45.1–28 The saga's dramatic culmination presents two of biblical narrative's most fundamental moments: acknowledgement of kinship and reunion after long absence. Cf. the more sub-

dued reunion of Jacob and Esau in ch. 33. **45.1** *Send everyone away*, i.e., members of the Egyptian court. *When Joseph made himself known*. Again, "knowledge" is a key theme. See, e.g., Gen 31.32; 38.16; 42.23. **45.2** *And he wept*. For the third and most decisive time, Joseph is overcome with emotion; cf. 42.24; 43.30–31. **45.4** *Whom you sold*. Joseph's first explicit declaration of blame, though it is tempered in the next verse. **45.5** *To preserve life*. The often repeated "that we may live ..." finds culmination here and is echoed in 46.30. Joseph's statement has both a familial and world-historical dimension. **45.6** *Neither plowing nor harvest*, no plowing that will lead to

years in which there will be neither plowing nor harvest. 7God sent me before you
to preserve for you a remnant on earth,
and to keep alive for you many survivors.
8So it was not you who sent me here, but
God; he has made me a father to Pharaoh, and lord of all his house and ruler
over all the land of Egypt. 9Hurry and go
up to my father and say to him, 'Thus says
your son Joseph, God has made me lord
of all Egypt; come down to me, do not
delay. 10You shall settle in the land of Goshen, and you shall be near me, you and
your children and your children's children, as well as your flocks, your herds,
and all that you have. 11I will provide for
you there—since there are five more
years of famine to come—so that you and
your household, and all that you have,
will not come to poverty.' 12And now your
eyes and the eyes of my brother Benjamin
see that it is my own mouth that speaks to
you. 13You must tell my father how
greatly I am honored in Egypt, and all
that you have seen. Hurry and bring my
father down here." 14Then he fell upon
his brother Benjamin's neck and wept,
while Benjamin wept upon his neck.
15And he kissed all his brothers and wept
upon them, and after that his brothers
talked with him.

16   When the report was heard in
Pharaoh's house, "Joseph's brothers have
come," Pharaoh and his servants were
pleased. 17Pharaoh said to Joseph, "Say to
your brothers, 'Do this: load your animals
and go back to the land of Canaan.
18Take your father and your households
and come to me, so that I may give you
the best of the land of Egypt, and you may
enjoy the fat of the land.' 19You are further charged to say, 'Do this: take wagons
from the land of Egypt for your little ones
and for your wives, and bring your father,
and come. 20Give no thought to your pos-

sessions, for the best of all the land of
Egypt is yours.'"

21   The sons of Israel did so. Joseph
gave them wagons according to the instruction of Pharaoh, and he gave them
provisions for the journey. 22To each one
of them he gave a set of garments; but to
Benjamin he gave three hundred pieces
of silver and five sets of garments. 23To
his father he sent the following: ten donkeys loaded with the good things of
Egypt, and ten female donkeys loaded
with grain, bread, and provision for his
father on the journey. 24Then he sent his
brothers on their way, and as they were
leaving he said to them, "Do not quarrel v
along the way."

25   So they went up out of Egypt and
came to their father Jacob in the land of
Canaan. 26And they told him, "Joseph is
still alive! He is even ruler over all the
land of Egypt." He was stunned; he could
not believe them. 27But when they told
him all the words of Joseph that he had
said to them, and when he saw the wagons
that Joseph had sent to carry him, the
spirit of their father Jacob revived. 28Is-
rael said, "Enough! My son Joseph is still
alive. I must go and see him before I die."

Jacob Brings His Whole Family to Egypt

46   When Israel set out on his jour-
      ney with all that he had and came
to Beer-sheba, he offered sacrifices to the
God of his father Isaac. 2God spoke to
Israel in visions of the night, and said, "Jacob, Jacob." And he said, "Here I am."
3Then he said, "I am God,w the God of
your father; do not be afraid to go down
to Egypt, for I will make of you a great
nation there. 4I myself will go down with
you to Egypt, and I will also bring you up

v Or *be agitated*   w Heb *the God*

---

harvest. **45.7** *A remnant on earth.* See note on
6.8. **45.8** *A father to Pharaoh,* a protector and
benefactor. **45.10** *Land of Goshen.* See note on
46.28. *And your children and your children's children.*
This last intention will be imperiled by the Israelite servitude after Joseph's lifetime. **45.11** *So
that you . . . will not come to poverty.* See note on
45.10. **45.20** *For the best of all the land of Egypt is
yours,* a decision with problematic consequences;
see note on 47.13–26. **45.22** *But to Benjamin . . .
garments,* as if to underscore the previous verse's
theme of favoritism. **45.24** *Do not quarrel.* If

translated thus, the remark supplies a humorous
rounding off of Joseph's ancient quarrel with
them. **45.27–28** *Revived, alive.* Cf. 46.30 and
note on 45.5. **45.28** *Enough!* In his excitement
over Joseph, Jacob does not dwell on the brothers'
former treachery, perhaps in silent acknowledgement of his own implicit role in what happened.
46.1–27 Jacob's migration to Egypt with his
children and grandchildren, a divine revelation
sanctioning the move, and a list of Jacob's children and grandchildren. **46.2** *Here I am.* See
note on 22.1. **46.3** *Do not be afraid.* Cf. 28.13;

again; and Joseph's own hand shall close your eyes."

5 Then Jacob set out from Beersheba; and the sons of Israel carried their father Jacob, their little ones, and their wives, in the wagons that Pharaoh had sent to carry him. 6 They also took their livestock and the goods that they had acquired in the land of Canaan, and they came into Egypt, Jacob and all his offspring with him, 7 his sons, and his sons' sons with him, his daughters, and his sons' daughters; all his offspring he brought with him into Egypt.

8 Now these are the names of the Israelites, Jacob and his offspring, who came to Egypt. Reuben, Jacob's firstborn, 9 and the children of Reuben: Hanoch, Pallu, Hezron, and Carmi. 10 The children of Simeon: Jemuel, Jamin, Ohad, Jachin, Zohar, and Shaul,ˣ the son of a Canaanite woman. 11 The children of Levi: Gershon, Kohath, and Merari. 12 The children of Judah: Er, Onan, Shelah, Perez, and Zerah (but Er and Onan died in the land of Canaan); and the children of Perez were Hezron and Hamul. 13 The children of Issachar: Tola, Puvah, Jashub,ʸ and Shimron. 14 The children of Zebulun: Sered, Elon, and Jahleel 15 (these are the sons of Leah, whom she bore to Jacob in Paddanaram, together with his daughter Dinah; in all his sons and his daughters numbered thirty-three). 16 The children of Gad: Ziphion, Haggi, Shuni, Ezbon, Eri, Arodi, and Areli. 17 The children of Asher: Imnah, Ishvah, Ishvi, Beriah, and their sister Serah. The children of Beriah: Heber and Malchiel 18 (these are the children of Zilpah, whom Laban gave to his daughter Leah; and these she bore to

Jacob—sixteen persons). 19 The children of Jacob's wife Rachel: Joseph and Benjamin. 20 To Joseph in the land of Egypt were born Manasseh and Ephraim, whom Asenath daughter of Potiphera, priest of On, bore to him. 21 The children of Benjamin: Bela, Becher, Ashbel, Gera, Naaman, Ehi, Rosh, Muppim, Huppim, and Ard 22 (these are the children of Rachel, who were born to Jacob—fourteen persons in all). 23 The children of Dan: Hashum.ᶻ 24 The children of Naphtali: Jahzeel, Guni, Jezer, and Shillem 25 (these are the children of Bilhah, whom Laban gave to his daughter Rachel, and these she bore to Jacob—seven persons in all). 26 All the persons belonging to Jacob who came into Egypt, who were his own offspring, not including the wives of his sons, were sixty-six persons in all. 27 The children of Joseph, who were born to him in Egypt, were two; all the persons of the house of Jacob who came into Egypt were seventy.

Jacob Settles in Goshen

28 Israelᵃ sent Judah ahead to Joseph to lead the way before him into Goshen. When they came to the land of Goshen, 29 Joseph made ready his chariot and went up to meet his father Israel in Goshen. He presented himself to him, fell on his neck, and wept on his neck a good while. 30 Israel said to Joseph, "I can die now, having seen for myself that you are still alive." 31 Joseph said to his brothers and to his father's household, "I will go up and tell

x Or *Saul*   y Compare Sam Gk Num 26.24;
1 Chr 7.1: MT *Iob*   z Gk: Heb *Hushim*
a Heb *He*

26.2. **46.4** *You,* i.e., your descendants and your remains; cf. 47.30; 49.29–50.13. *Joseph's own hand shall close your eyes.* Cf. 50.1. **46.7** *Daughters . . . sons' daughters.* The women of Jacob's extended family, not daughters as such (Dinah is mentioned separately in v. 15). **46.8** *Now these are the names.* Cf. Ex 1.1. Cf. lists in Ex 1.1–7; 6.14–25; Num 1.1–47; 26.1–65; 1 Chr 2–8. **46.12** *Er and Onan died.* See 38.7–10. **46.15** *Together with . . . Dinah.* Dinah, in fact, seems excluded from the thirty-three, but cf. note on 46.26. **46.18** *Children of Zilpah.* Each concubine has half as many children and grandchildren as her mistress; cf. v. 25. **46.21** *Children of Benjamin.* The reference is anachronistic—Benjamin is still a young man. **46.26** *Sixty-six.* This includes Dinah, but excludes

Er, Onan, Joseph, Manasseh, and Ephraim. **46.27** *Who came into Egypt,* i.e., who lived there after the migration, whether immigrant or native. *Seventy.* This adds to the preceding number: Jacob, Joseph, Manasseh, and Ephraim. On "seventy," cf. Ex 1.5; 24.1–9; Num 11.16; Deut 10.22. This list constitutes the entire people Israel in miniature, marking a transition to the collective history narrated from Exodus onward. **46.28–47.12** The tearful reunion of Jacob (Israel) with Joseph, the newcomers' introduction to Pharaoh, and Pharaoh's invitation to settle in Goshen. **46.28** *Goshen,* in the northeast part of the Nile Delta, chiefly suitable for sheep grazing. **46.29** *Fell on his neck, and wept.* Cf. 33.4; 45.14–15. **46.30** See notes on 45.5; 45.27–28.

Pharaoh, and will say to him, 'My brothers and my father's household, who were in the land of Canaan, have come to me. 32 The men are shepherds, for they have been keepers of livestock; and they have brought their flocks, and their herds, and all that they have.' 33 When Pharaoh calls you, and says, 'What is your occupation?' 34 you shall say, 'Your servants have been keepers of livestock from our youth even until now, both we and our ancestors'—in order that you may settle in the land of Goshen, because all shepherds are abhorrent to the Egyptians."

47 So Joseph went and told Pharaoh, "My father and my brothers, with their flocks and herds and all that they possess, have come from the land of Canaan; they are now in the land of Goshen." 2 From among his brothers he took five men and presented them to Pharaoh. 3 Pharaoh said to his brothers, "What is your occupation?" And they said to Pharaoh, "Your servants are shepherds, as our ancestors were." 4 They said to Pharaoh, "We have come to reside as aliens in the land; for there is no pasture for your servants' flocks because the famine is severe in the land of Canaan. Now, we ask you, let your servants settle in the land of Goshen." 5 Then Pharaoh said to Joseph, "Your father and your brothers have come to you. 6 The land of Egypt is before you; settle your father and your brothers in the best part of the land; let them live in the land of Goshen; and if you know that there are capable men among them, put them in charge of my livestock."

7 Then Joseph brought in his father Jacob, and presented him before Pharaoh, and Jacob blessed Pharaoh. 8 Pharaoh said to Jacob, "How many are the years of your life?" 9 Jacob said to Pharaoh, "The years of my earthly sojourn are one hundred thirty; few and hard have been the years of my life. They do not compare with the years of the life of my ancestors during their long sojourn." 10 Then Jacob blessed Pharaoh, and went out from the presence of Pharaoh. 11 Joseph settled his father and his brothers, and granted them a holding in the land of Egypt, in the best part of the land, in the land of Rameses, as Pharaoh had instructed. 12 And Joseph provided his father, his brothers, and all his father's household with food, according to the number of their dependents.

The Famine in Egypt

13 Now there was no food in all the land, for the famine was very severe. The land of Egypt and the land of Canaan languished because of the famine. 14 Joseph collected all the money to be found in the land of Egypt and in the land of Canaan, in exchange for the grain that they bought; and Joseph brought the money into Pharaoh's house. 15 When the money from the land of Egypt and from the land of Canaan was spent, all the Egyptians came to Joseph, and said, "Give us food! Why should we die before your eyes? For our money is gone." 16 And Joseph answered, "Give me your livestock, and I will give you food in exchange for your livestock, if your money is gone." 17 So they brought their livestock to Joseph; and Joseph gave them food in exchange

---

46.31 *I will . . . tell Pharaoh.* Pharaoh has already approved their migration; see 45.16–20. 46.34 *All shepherds are abhorrent,* probably all *foreign* shepherds, not shepherds as such—but, being a threat to agriculture, shepherding was perhaps confined to the outskirts of settled areas. 47.7, 10 *Jacob blessed Pharaoh,* perhaps alluding to 12.3. 47.8–9 Preoccupation with Jacob's life span underscores the transience of a generation, implicitly reminding readers of a Pharaoh to come "who did not know Joseph" (Ex 1.8). *Few and hard* recalls Jacob's harsh sojourn with Laban (cf. 31.38–42), the years of famine, and his grief over Joseph's absence—remote, indeed, seems the blessedness of Abraham! 47.11 *Land of Rameses,* a synonym for Goshen. The city's founder, Ramses II (1279–1212 B.C.E.),

postdates the purported era of Jacob.
47.13–26 A variant of 41.46–57 emphasizing the Egyptian populace's gradual impoverishment and enslavement under Joseph's authority, resulting in concentration of Egypt's wealth into the hands of Pharaoh and his priests. This dismaying description, combined with traditions about preferential treatment of Joseph's kin (45.20; 47.6), provides a cogent explanation of the backlash soon to erupt against Israelites under the next Pharaoh (see Ex 1.8–14)—recalling the scheme of reciprocal justice first suggested in 15.16; 16.6 (see notes there). 47.14–25 A four-step process of impoverishment: money (vv. 14–15), livestock (vv. 16–17), land (vv. 18–20), and freedom (vv. 21–25). 47.15 *Why should we die?* Cf. "life/death" theme presented in 42.2, 18; 43.27–28;

for the horses, the flocks, the herds, and the donkeys. That year he supplied them with food in exchange for all their livestock. 18 When that year was ended, they came to him the following year, and said to him, "We can not hide from my lord that our money is all spent; and the herds of cattle are my lord's. There is nothing left in the sight of my lord but our bodies and our lands. 19 Shall we die before your eyes, both we and our land? Buy us and our land in exchange for food. We with our land will become slaves to Pharaoh; just give us seed, so that we may live and not die, and that the land may not become desolate." 20 So Joseph bought all the land of Egypt for Pharaoh. All the Egyptians sold their fields, because the famine was severe upon them; and the land became Pharaoh's. 21 As for the people, he made slaves of them*b* from one end of Egypt to the other. 22 Only the land of the priests he did not buy; for the priests had a fixed allowance from Pharaoh, and lived on the allowance that Pharaoh gave them; therefore they did not sell their land. 23 Then Joseph said to the people, "Now that I have this day bought you and your land for Pharaoh, here is seed for you; sow the land. 24 And at the harvests you shall give one-fifth to Pharaoh, and four-fifths shall be your own, as seed for the field and as food for yourselves and your households, and as food for your little ones." 25 They said, "You have saved our lives; may it please my lord, we will be slaves to Pharaoh." 26 So Joseph made it a statute concerning the land of Egypt, and it stands to this day, that Pharaoh should have the fifth. The land of the priests alone did not become Pharaoh's.

The Last Days of Jacob

27 Thus Israel settled in the land of Egypt, in the region of Goshen; and they gained possessions in it, and were fruitful and multiplied exceedingly. 28 Jacob lived in the land of Egypt seventeen years; so the days of Jacob, the years of his life, were one hundred forty-seven years. 29 When the time of Israel's death drew near, he called his son Joseph and said to him, "If I have found favor with you, put your hand under my thigh and promise to deal loyally and truly with me. Do not bury me in Egypt. 30 When I lie down with my ancestors, carry me out of Egypt and bury me in their burial place." He answered, "I will do as you have said." 31 And he said, "Swear to me"; and he swore to him. Then Israel bowed himself on the head of his bed.

Jacob Blesses Joseph's Sons

48 After this Joseph was told, "Your father is ill." So he took with him his two sons, Manasseh and Ephraim. 2 When Jacob was told, "Your son Joseph has come to you," he*c* summoned his strength and sat up in bed. 3 And Jacob said to Joseph, "God Almighty*d* appeared to me at Luz in the land of Canaan, and he blessed me, 4 and said to me, 'I am go-

b Sam Gk Compare Vg: MT *He removed them to the cities*   *c* Heb *Israel*   *d* Traditional rendering of Heb *El Shaddai*

45.3, 5.   **47.19, 21** *Slaves*. See note on 47.25. **47.20** *So Joseph bought ... for Pharaoh*. Joseph's policies stem foremost from his identification of Pharaoh's welfare with Egypt's, ignoring the long-term social consequences.   **47.22** *Fixed allowances*. On the priestly allowance, cf. Ex 29.28; Lev 10.12–15 (Hebrew term identical).   **47.25** The thrice-mentioned word *slaves* (cf. vv. 19, 21) stresses that slavery is the main preoccupation of this section, in anticipation of the events of Ex 1.8–14.

47.27–31   Introduction to Jacob's deathbed addresses, recording the prosperity of his final days, and his orders to Joseph to bury him beside his departed kin in Canaan.   **47.27** Following immediately upon the preceding section, this verse reemphasizes the growing strength of the Israelites in Egypt.   **47.29** *Hand under my thigh*.

See note on 24.2.   **47.30** *Their burial place*, at Machpelah cave; see 23.1–20; 25.9; 49.29–52. **47.31** *Bowed himself*, i.e., nodded in reclinement, approving the oath.

48.1–22   Jacob's next deathbed pronouncement is the blessing of Manasseh and Ephraim — these sons of Joseph are adopted as full sons of Jacob, standing for the children Rachel might have provided if she had lived (see v. 7). This tradition may stem from two needs: to confer full Israelite status on children born of an Egyptian mother; and to explain the eventual use of Manasseh and Ephraim as tribal names (in lieu of Joseph) and the prominence of the two tribes in Israel's later history. Cf. notes on 41.51–52; 48.19.   **48.1** *Your father is ill*. His condition has worsened; he was already bedridden.   **48.3** *God*

ing to make you fruitful and increase your numbers; I will make of you a company of peoples, and will give this land to your offspring after you for a perpetual holding.' 5 Therefore your two sons, who were born to you in the land of Egypt before I came to you in Egypt, are now mine; Ephraim and Manasseh shall be mine, just as Reuben and Simeon are. 6 As for the offspring born to you after them, they shall be yours. They shall be recorded under the names of their brothers with regard to their inheritance. 7 For when I came from Paddan, Rachel, alas, died in the land of Canaan on the way, while there was still some distance to go to Ephrath; and I buried her there on the way to Ephrath" (that is, Bethlehem).

8 When Israel saw Joseph's sons, he said, "Who are these?" 9 Joseph said to his father, "They are my sons, whom God has given me here." And he said, "Bring them to me, please, that I may bless them." 10 Now the eyes of Israel were dim with age, and he could not see well. So Joseph brought them near him; and he kissed them and embraced them. 11 Israel said to Joseph, "I did not expect to see your face; and here God has let me see your children also." 12 Then Joseph removed them from his father's knees,e and he bowed himself with his face to the earth. 13 Joseph took them both, Ephraim in his right hand toward Israel's left, and Manasseh in his left hand toward Israel's right, and brought them near him. 14 But Israel stretched out his right hand and laid it on the head of Ephraim, who was the younger, and his left hand on the head of Manasseh, crossing his hands, for Manasseh was the firstborn. 15 He blessed Joseph, and said,

"The God before whom my
    ancestors Abraham and
    Isaac walked,
the God who has been my
    shepherd all my life to
    this day,
16 the angel who has redeemed me
    from all harm, bless the
    boys;
and in them let my name be
    perpetuated, and the name
    of my ancestors Abraham
    and Isaac;
and let them grow into a
    multitude on the earth."

17 When Joseph saw that his father laid his right hand on the head of Ephraim, it displeased him; so he took his father's hand, to remove it from Ephraim's head to Manasseh's head. 18 Joseph said to his father, "Not so, my father! Since this one is the firstborn, put your right hand on his head." 19 But his father refused, and said, "I know, my son, I know; he also shall become a people, and he also shall be great. Nevertheless his younger brother shall be greater than he, and his offspring shall become a multitude of nations." 20 So he blessed them that day, saying,

"By youf Israel will invoke
    blessings, saying,
'God make youf like Ephraim
    and like Manasseh.' "

So he put Ephraim ahead of Manasseh. 21 Then Israel said to Joseph, "I am about to die, but God will be with you and will bring you again to the land of your ances-

e Heb from his knees   f you here is singular in Heb

Almighty. See note on 17.1.   **48.5** *Just as Reuben and Simeon are*, i.e., of my flesh and of their generation. Jacob's choice of his two least-favored sons as examples makes clear that he has these factors in mind, rather than favoredness per se. But he perhaps also wishes Joseph's sons to be "firstborn," in lieu of Reuben and Simeon (see note on 48.22).   **48.6** That is, children born to Joseph from now on shall take the place of Ephraim and Manasseh in the line of inheritance, though no other children are said to be born to Joseph. **48.7** *Paddan*, Paddan-aram. *Rachel, alas, died* stresses that Manasseh and Ephraim are symbolically *her* children. *Ephrath*. See note on 35.16. **48.8** *Who are these?* Jacob's intelligence does not falter—his eyesight is dim (v. 10) and he must as-

certain if they are the children he has been discussing.   **48.13** Joseph, with his left hand, sends Manasseh toward Jacob's right, the favored position.   **48.14** *Crossing his hands*, placing his hand of favor on the younger son. *For Manasseh was*, "although Manasseh was."   **48.15** *He blessed Joseph*, with Joseph's children betokening Joseph. **48.17** *It displeased him*. Cf. Joseph's "firstborn" protocol in 43.33.   **48.19** Cf. God's reassurance of Abraham about Ishmael (17.20; 21.13). *Younger . . . shall be greater*. Israel's two most prominent leaders in the confederate era after Moses were Ephraimite (Joshua and Samuel); a third was Manassite (Gideon).   **48.20** *By you Israel will invoke . . . like Manasseh*, a widespread household custom that has continued into Jewish practice down to

tors. 22 I now give to you one portion*g*
more than to your brothers, the portion*g*
that I took from the hand of the Amorites
with my sword and with my bow."

Jacob's Last Words to His Sons

49 Then Jacob called his sons, and
said: "Gather around, that I may
tell you what will happen to you in days to
come.
2   Assemble and hear, O sons of
        Jacob;
    listen to Israel your father.

3   Reuben, you are my firstborn,
        my might and the first fruits of
        my vigor,
    excelling in rank and excelling
        in power.
4   Unstable as water, you shall no
        longer excel
    because you went up onto your
        father's bed;
    then you defiled it—you*h* went
        up onto my couch!

5   Simeon and Levi are brothers;
        weapons of violence are their
        swords.
6   May I never come into their
        council;
    may I not be joined to their
        company—
    for in their anger they
        killed men,

and at their whim they
    hamstrung oxen.
7   Cursed be their anger, for it is
        fierce,
    and their wrath, for it is cruel!
    I will divide them in Jacob,
        and scatter them in Israel.

8   Judah, your brothers shall
        praise you;
    your hand shall be on the neck
        of your enemies;
    your father's sons shall bow
        down before you.
9   Judah is a lion's whelp;
        from the prey, my son, you
        have gone up.
    He crouches down, he stretches
        out like a lion,
    like a lioness—who dares rouse
        him up?
10 The scepter shall not depart from
        Judah,
    nor the ruler's staff from
        between his feet,
    until tribute comes to him;*i*
        and the obedience of the
        peoples is his.
11 Binding his foal to the vine
        and his donkey's colt to the
        choice vine,
    he washes his garments in wine

g Or mountain slope (Heb *shekem*, a play on the
name of the town and district of Shechem)
h Gk Syr Tg: Heb *he*   *i Or until Shiloh comes* or
until he comes to Shiloh or (with Syr) *until he comes to
whom it belongs*

the present. **48.22** *One portion*, lit. "a shoulder-
height," a play on the town name Shechem. *That I
took from . . . the Amorites.* Cf. 33.18–20; 34.25–31.
Shechem sits near the later tribal borders between
Manasseh and Ephraim. Its mention here links
the adoption of Joseph's sons with the censure of
Simeon and Levi in 34.30; 49.5–7. Joseph was
eventually buried there (Josh 24.32).
49.1–28   Vv. 3–27 are a lengthy and ancient
poetic composition whose contents concern the
era of the judges and the monarchy. Woven from
once-independent songs or mottoes, it glimpses
the tribes of Israel in their early days in Canaan
with occasional references to later history. The
language is obscure; translation is necessarily approximate. Cf. Judg 5; Deut 33, which similarly
deal with Israel's early history, the latter, like Gen
49, placed near the book's end to signify the close
of a historical era (cf. 2 Sam 1.19–27; 22.2–51).
49.1 Jacob's ability to envisage *days to come* stems

from his implicit status (like Abraham's) as a
prophet. **49.3–4** *Because you went up . . . onto my
bed*, based on 35.22; cf. Deut 33.6; 1 Chr 5.1.
49.5–7 Based on 34.25–31. Simeon is missing
from Deut 33, and Levi's "violence" is there
changed to reflect Ex 32.25–29. **49.7** *I will divide . . . and scatter.* Simeon was eventually absorbed into Judah (see Josh 19.9), and Levi,
perhaps decimated by wars, became the landless
levitical priesthood; see Num 18.6–7, 20;
35.1–8. **49.8** *Shall praise you*, in Hebrew a play
on "Judah." Vv. 8–10 anticipate the monarchy
under Judah's descendant David. **49.10** *Until
tribute comes to him*, see text note *i*. Shiloh was an
early Israelite military and religious center (see
Josh 18.1; 22.9, 12; Judg 18.31; 1 Sam 1.1–2), but
it suffered disaster (1 Sam 4) and later symbolized
northern Israel's desolation (Jer 7.12–14; 26.6,
9). This obscure phrase could thus express Judah's later hopes for renewal of dominion over

and his robe in the blood of
    grapes;
12 his eyes are darker than wine,
    and his teeth whiter than milk.

13 Zebulun shall settle at the shore
    of the sea;
he shall be a haven for ships,
    and his border shall be at
    Sidon.

14 Issachar is a strong donkey,
    lying down between the
    sheepfolds;
15 he saw that a resting place was
    good,
    and that the land was pleasant;
so he bowed his shoulder to the
    burden,
    and became a slave at forced
    labor.

16 Dan shall judge his people
    as one of the tribes of Israel.
17 Dan shall be a snake by the
    roadside,
    a viper along the path,
that bites the horse's heels
    so that its rider falls backward.

18 I wait for your salvation, O Lord.

19 Gad shall be raided by raiders,
    but he shall raid at their heels.

20 Asher's*j* food shall be rich,
    and he shall provide royal
    delicacies.

21 Naphtali is a doe let loose
    that bears lovely fawns.*k*

22 Joseph is a fruitful bough,
    a fruitful bough by a spring;
his branches run over the
    wall.*l*

23 The archers fiercely
    attacked him;
    they shot at him and pressed
    him hard.
24 Yet his bow remained taut,
    and his arms*m* were made agile
by the hands of the Mighty One
    of Jacob,
    by the name of the Shepherd,
    the Rock of Israel,
25 by the God of your father, who
    will help you,
    by the Almighty*n* who will
    bless you
with blessings of heaven above,
blessings of the deep that lies
    beneath,
blessings of the breasts and of
    the womb.
26 The blessings of your father
    are stronger than the blessings
    of the eternal mountains,
    the bounties*o* of the everlasting
    hills;
may they be on the head of
    Joseph,
    on the brow of him who was set
    apart from his brothers.

27 Benjamin is a ravenous wolf,
    in the morning devouring the
    prey,
    and at evening dividing the
    spoil."

28 All these are the twelve tribes of Israel, and this is what their father said to
them when he blessed them, blessing each
one of them with a suitable blessing.

j Gk Vg Syr: Heb *From Asher*   *k* Or *that gives
beautiful words*   *l* Meaning of Heb uncertain
m Heb *the arms of his hands*   *n* Traditional
rendering of Heb *Shaddai*   *o* Cn Compare Gk:
Heb *of my progenitors to the boundaries*

---

northern Israel. **49.13** *Zebulun shall settle*, a possible play on Hebrew *zabal*, "dwell." Zebulun's territory was in southern Galilee. The *sea* is perhaps
Lake Chinnereth (Sea of Galilee), although most
scholars suggest the Mediterranean Sea. Cf. Josh
19.10–16. *Border ... at Sidon*, a poetic overstate-
ment or a suggestion that Zebulun adopted Phoenician culture. **49.14–15** A play on Issachar's
name to suggest "hired" man. Cf. 30.18.
49.16–17 *Shall judge*, Hebrew *yadin*, playing on

"Dan." The passage depicts the brigand existence
of Israel's early confederate days; cf. v. 27.
49.19 *Raided, raiders, shall raid*, in Hebrew, all
plays on "Gad."   **49.22** *Fruitful bough*, Hebrew
ben porat, plays implicitly on "Ephraim." Many
translations are possible for this obscure term.
49.25 *Blessings of the breasts and of the womb*, blessings of plenitude and fertility. **49.28** This verse
makes clear the identification of the sons with
tribes and concludes the section.

Jacob's Death and Burial

29 Then he charged them, saying to them, "I am about to be gathered to my people. Bury me with my ancestors—in the cave in the field of Ephron the Hittite, 30 in the cave in the field at Machpelah, near Mamre, in the land of Canaan, in the field that Abraham bought from Ephron the Hittite as a burial site. 31 There Abraham and his wife Sarah were buried; there Isaac and his wife Rebekah were buried; and there I buried Leah— 32 the field and the cave that is in it were purchased from the Hittites." 33 When Jacob ended his charge to his sons, he drew up his feet into the bed, breathed his last, and was gathered to his people.

50 Then Joseph threw himself on his father's face and wept over him and kissed him. 2 Joseph commanded the physicians in his service to embalm his father. So the physicians embalmed Israel; 3 they spent forty days in doing this, for that is the time required for embalming. And the Egyptians wept for him seventy days.

4 When the days of weeping for him were past, Joseph addressed the household of Pharaoh, "If now I have found favor with you, please speak to Pharaoh as follows: 5 My father made me swear an oath; he said, 'I am about to die. In the tomb that I hewed out for myself in the land of Canaan, there you shall bury me.' Now therefore let me go up, so that I may bury my father; then I will return." 6 Pharaoh answered, "Go up, and bury your father, as he made you swear to do."

7 So Joseph went up to bury his father. With him went up all the servants of Pharaoh, the elders of his household, and all the elders of the land of Egypt, 8 as well as all the household of Joseph, his brothers, and his father's household. Only their children, their flocks, and their herds were left in the land of Goshen. 9 Both chariots and charioteers went up with him. It was a very great company. 10 When they came to the threshing floor of Atad, which is beyond the Jordan, they held there a very great and sorrowful lamentation; and he observed a time of mourning for his father seven days. 11 When the Canaanite inhabitants of the land saw the mourning on the threshing floor of Atad, they said, "This is a grievous mourning on the part of the Egyptians." Therefore the place was named Abel-mizraim;p it is beyond the Jordan. 12 Thus his sons did for him as he had instructed them. 13 They carried him to the land of Canaan and buried him in the cave of the field at Machpelah, the field near Mamre, which Abraham bought as a burial site from Ephron the Hittite. 14 After he had buried his father, Joseph returned to Egypt with his brothers and all who had gone up with him to bury his father.

Joseph Forgives His Brothers

15 Realizing that their father was dead, Joseph's brothers said, "What if Joseph still bears a grudge against us and pays us back in full for all the wrong that we did to him?" 16 So they approachedq Joseph, saying, "Your father gave this instruction before he died, 17 'Say to Joseph: I beg you, forgive the crime of your brothers and the wrong they did in harming you.' Now therefore please forgive the crime of the servants of the God of your father." Joseph wept when they spoke to him. 18 Then his brothers also wept,r fell down before him, and said, "We are here

p That is *mourning* (or *meadow*) *of Egypt*
q Gk Syr: Heb *they commanded*   r Cn: Heb *also came*

49.29–50.14 The conclusion of the traditions about Jacob, recounting his death and his burial in Canaan at Machpelah cave. **49.29–33** A variant of the tradition recorded in 49.29–31; together with 50.12–13, it encloses the main narrative. On Machpelah, see ch. 23. **50.2** *To embalm*, an Egyptian, not an Israelite, practice. Its presence here underscores Joseph's Egyptian ways and the esteem of the Egyptians (see vv. 3, 7) and perhaps intends to explain the corpse's preservation until burial in Canaan. **50.5–6** This benign encounter with Pharaoh to request permission for departure foreshadows Moses' repeated entreaties beginning in Ex 5.1. **50.8** *Only their children . . . in the land of Goshen* stresses the temporary nature of their departure.

50.15–21 The brothers' anxiety that, with their father dead (cf. 27.41), Joseph might revenge the wrongs once done to him. Joseph, however, reassures them of his continued loyalty and care. **50.17–18** *Servants, slaves*. These words (identical in Hebrew) continue the preoccupation with servitude and foreshadow Ex 1.8–14.

as your slaves." 19But Joseph said to them, "Do not be afraid! Am I in the place of God? 20Even though you intended to do harm to me, God intended it for good in order to preserve a numerous people, as he is doing today. 21So have no fear; I myself will provide for you and your little ones." In this way he reassured them, speaking kindly to them.

Joseph's Last Days and Death

22 So Joseph remained in Egypt, he and his father's household; and Joseph lived one hundred ten years. 23Joseph saw Ephraim's children of the third generation; the children of Machir son of Manasseh were also born on Joseph's knees.

24 Then Joseph said to his brothers, "I am about to die; but God will surely come to you, and bring you up out of this land to the land that he swore to Abraham, to Isaac, and to Jacob." 25So Joseph made the Israelites swear, saying, "When God comes to you, you shall carry up my bones from here." 26And Joseph died, being one hundred ten years old; he was embalmed and placed in a coffin in Egypt.

50.19 *Am I in the place of God*, an intriguing echo of Jacob's words to Joseph's mother-to-be in 30.2. **50.20** *Even though you intended to do harm* [lit. "evil"] *to me, God intended it for good*, a restatement of the book's theme of "good and evil." *To preserve*, lit. "to give life."

50.22–26 An account of Joseph's last days and his death. He assures his brothers of God's intention to bring the Israelites out of Egypt and extracts from them a promise to bring his bones from there—which is fulfilled in Ex 13.19.

EXODUS

Name and Content

THE NAME EXODUS, DERIVED FROM GREEK, refers to the first of the two central narrative events in the book—the liberation of the Israelites from Egyptian bondage (chs. 1–15). The other event, the Lord's covenant-forging revelation to Israel at Mount Sinai (chs. 19–24), and the laws and instructions that ensue from it complete the book.

The book's Hebrew name, "These are the names," derives from the first words of the text's prologue (1.1–7), which harks back to and abridges the genealogy in Gen 46.8–27. In one sense Exodus directly continues the story of Jacob's clan in Egypt (Gen 37–50). The Lord is said to rescue Israel on account of his covenant with their ancestors (2.24; cf. 3.6, 15–16; 4.5; 6.2–4). In another sense, Exodus is a distinct book, relating the story of Israel's formation as a people and its covenant with God. The second part of the story is dependent on the first: by redeeming the Israelite slaves from Egypt, the Lord earns the right to "enslave" them to himself (Lev 25.42, 55) by binding them to the covenant obligations.

Biblical Context

Covenant law issuing immediately or indirectly from the Sinai event makes up most of what follows Exodus in the Pentateuch. Moses has the people recommit themselves to the covenant before he dies (Deut 29–30). In the next generation the Israelites twice reaffirm the covenant (Josh 4–5, 24), an act that will be expressly repeated only centuries later (2 Kings 22–23) and again after the Babylonian exile (Neh 8–10). Precedent for renewing, or restoring, the covenant is set within Exodus itself, following the golden calf incident (ch. 34).

Although biblical tradition links the exodus with a (geographically unspecified) covenant (e.g., Deut 4.45; 6.21–25; 29.25; 1 Kings 8.9, 21; Jer 11.2–4, 6–7; 31.32; 34.13), it is the exodus itself that chiefly exercises the biblical memory. Within the Pentateuch, or Torah, the recent exodus provides a motive for worshiping the Lord (e.g., Ex 20.2; 29.46; Lev 26.13; Deut 6.12; 13.6–10; cf. Josh 24.17) and observing the law (e.g., Lev 11.45; 22.32–33; Num 15.41;

Deut 5.15; 8.11–14; 29.2), especially those precepts protecting the disadvantaged (e.g., Lev 19.35; 25.38, 42, 55), because the experience of slavery is meant to instill empathy for them (e.g., Ex 23.9; Lev 19.34; Deut 10.19; 15.15; 16.12; 24.22; and see Jer 34.13–14). Moreover, the rescue of Israel from Egypt serves as a paradigm of divine saving power, within the Torah (e.g., Lev 26.24–25; Num 23.22; 24.8; Deut 6.21–22; 20.1; 26.8) as well as among the prophets (e.g., Isa 11.16; 51.10; Jer 16.14–15; 23.7–8; 32.20–21; Am 2.10; 9.7; Mic 6.4; 7.15; cf. also Dan 9.15) and psalmists (e.g., Pss 77; 78; 81; 105; 106; 136). Unlike the Sinai revelation, the exodus event functions as a point of chronological reference (e.g., Num 1.1; 9.1; Deut 9.7; Judg 19.30; 1 Sam 8.8; 2 Sam 7.6; 1 Kings 6.1; 8.16; 2 Kings 21.15; Jer 7.25).

Historical Context

The present text seems to incorporate a variety of once independent sources (e.g., 4.24–26; 15.1–18; 20.2–17; chs. 21–23). The narratives of complaint during the wilderness trek (15.22–17.7) overlap with stories in Numbers; the plagues narrative (chs. 7–11) and Passover passage (ch. 12) manifest the kinds of duplication and dissonance that suggest the presence of different traditions. Comparison of Exodus with folklore and myth suggests the story is already the stuff of legend. Historical reconstruction is accordingly obstructed by a centuries-long process of literary formation that can hardly be retraced.

Nevertheless, the sojourn of Israelites in Egypt, plagues, and crossing the sea and wilderness are traditions on which diverse biblical sources inside and outside the Torah agree. The details of the narrative, however, frequently conflict or make little sense; for example, though the Israelites are said to live apart in Goshen (e.g., Gen 47.1–6; Ex 8.22; 9.26), they borrow valuable objects from their Egyptian neighbors (3.21–22) and the Lord must pass over Israelite homes to strike Egyptian households in the tenth plague (12.12–13). External factors lead many to place the historical exodus in the late thirteenth century B.C.E.; but historical references in Exodus are slim, vague, or problematic, and there is no archaeological record of the exodus in Egypt.   *Edward L. Greenstein*

[handwritten: from his line = Moses]

1 These are the names of the sons of Israel who came to Egypt with Jacob, each with his household: 2 Reuben, Simeon, Levi, and Judah, 3 Issachar, Zebulun, and Benjamin, 4 Dan and Naphtali, Gad and Asher. 5 The total number of people born to Jacob was seventy. Joseph was already in Egypt. 6 Then Joseph died, and all his brothers, and that whole generation. 7 But the Israelites were fruitful and prolific; they multiplied and grew exceedingly strong, so that the land was filled with them.

The Israelites Are Oppressed

8 Now a new king arose over Egypt, who did not know Joseph. 9 He said to his people, "Look, the Israelite people are more numerous and more powerful than we. 10 Come, let us deal shrewdly with them, or they will increase and, in the event of war, join our enemies and fight against us and escape from the land." 11 Therefore they set taskmasters over them to oppress them with forced labor. They built supply cities, Pithom and Rameses, for Pharaoh. 12 But the more they were oppressed, the more they multiplied and spread, so that the Egyptians came to dread the Israelites. 13 The Egyptians became ruthless in imposing tasks on the Israelites, 14 and made their lives bitter with hard service in mortar and brick and in every kind of field labor. They were ruth-

[handwritten margin: beginning of "slavery"]

1.1–7 The prologue returns to a point prior to the conclusion of Genesis (see Introduction). The story of the Israelite population explosion in Egypt fulfills the Lord's promise of numerous progeny to the patriarchs (Gen 13.16; 15.5; 22.17; 26.4; 32.13). **1.1** *Israel*, the patriarch Jacob (Gen 32.29; 35.10). **1.2–4** The list of Jacob's sons separates the sons of his wives, Leah and Rachel, from those of his concubines, Bilhah and Zilpah. Daughter Dinah (Gen 30.21; 34) is, like other women, omitted in this enumeration. **1.5** *Born to Jacob*, lit. "coming out of Jacob's thigh," which was impaired (Gen 32.26, 32). *Seventy*, counting only Jacob's sons and grandsons, a very close approximation. **1.6** *Joseph's* death and mummification conclude Genesis. *Generation*, the unit of patriarchal periodization; cf. note on 12.40. **1.7** *Israelites*, lit. "the sons of Israel" (cf. v. 1), but here referring to the "children of Israel" as a people. *Fruitful . . . and multiplied.* See Gen 47.27; cf. Gen 1.28; 9.1, 7; 17.6, 20. *Prolific*. The unusual Hebrew term (cf. Gen 9.7) connotes the proliferation of animals (e.g., Gen 1.21; 8.17; Ex 8.3). Israel's populousness motivates the pharaoh's attempts at genocide. **1.8–22** The episode of the midwives recalls such fairy tales as "Snow White": a monarch orders a servant of the opposite sex to murder a child of the monarch's sex who is feared as a threat to the throne. **1.8** The *new king* seems to initiate a new policy toward the Asian foreigners, but *did not know* might mean "did not care about" (the same Hebrew verb is translated *took notice* in 2.25). The king remains anonymous, although many identify him with Ramses II (ca. 1290–1224 B.C.E.) on the basis of v. 11 and the mention of "Israel" within Canaan on a monument of the succeeding pharaoh, Merneptah (ca. 1224–1211). **1.9** *The Israelite people*, in contrast to *his* (the king's) *people. Numerous . . . powerful*, in

Hebrew cognate to the verbs rendered *multiplied* and *grew strong* in v. 7; both terms may refer to strength in numbers (cf. e.g., Num 32.1; Deut 26.5; Joel 1.6). The assertion that Israel outnumbers Egypt is surely hyperbolic. **1.10** *Shrewdly*, lit. "wisely"—an earlier pharaoh had called Joseph incomparably "wise" (Gen 41.39); the king may resent Egypt's debt to Joseph. *Join*, the same Hebrew verb (*nosaf*) as the name Joseph (*yosef*). *Escape*, lit. "go up," more aptly referring to taking control ("rising over") rather than leaving. Letters from Egypt's agents in Canaan to pharaohs of the fourteenth century B.C.E. at el-Amarna complain of landless "Apiru" joining forces with rebellious towns. Scholars have suggested a link between these landless folk and the "Hebrews," a term that may be related to "Apiru." **1.11** *They set.* The king's people cooperate. *Taskmasters*, lit. "officers of the corvée" (cf. 1 Kings 5.13–14). *To oppress*, used prophetically of the Egyptian bondage (Gen 15.13) and of Sarai's affliction of Hagar (Gen 16.6, 9, 11). *Pithom*, Egyptian *Per-Atum*, "House of (the sun god) Atum," and *Rameses*, "(House of) Rameses," sites in the region presumably inhabited by the Israelites in the eastern Nile Delta, the latter possibly Tanis, the capital of Rameses II, but also possibly a first-millennium B.C.E. city. *Pharaoh*, Egyptian *Per-ʿo*, "Great House," used to refer to the king of Egypt as though it were a proper name. **1.12** *They were oppressed*, lit. "they (namely, the Egyptians) oppressed him (namely, the Israelite people)," emphasizing the Egyptians' role. *The more they multiplied.* The Hebrew *ken yirbeh* mocks the pharaoh's words in v. 10, *pen yirbeh*, or ("lest") *they will increase. Spread*, the same Hebrew verb rendered "grew . . . rich" in Gen 30.43; Israel's proliferation in the face of Pharaoh's measures echoes Jacob's increase despite Laban's scheme. The Hebrew verb, which means lit. "to explode," sounds like a contraction of *were fruitful*

less in all the tasks that they imposed on them.

15 The king of Egypt said to the Hebrew midwives, one of whom was named Shiphrah and the other Puah, 16"When you act as midwives to the Hebrew women, and see them on the birthstool, if it is a boy, kill him; but if it is a girl, she shall live." 17But the midwives feared God; they did not do as the king of Egypt commanded them, but they let the boys live. 18So the king of Egypt summoned the midwives and said to them, "Why have you done this, and allowed the boys to live?" 19The midwives said to Pharaoh, "Because the Hebrew women are not like the Egyptian women; for they are vigorous and give birth before the midwife comes to them." 20So God dealt well with the midwives; and the people multiplied and became very strong. 21And because the midwives feared God, he gave them families. 22Then Pharaoh commanded all his people, "Every boy that is born to the Hebrews[a] you shall throw into the Nile, but you shall let every girl live."

Birth and Youth of Moses

2 Now a man from the house of Levi went and married a Levite woman. 2The woman conceived and bore a son; and when she saw that he was a fine baby, she hid him three months. 3When she could hide him no longer she got a papyrus basket for him, and plastered it with bitumen and pitch; she put the child in it and placed it among the reeds on the bank of the river. 4His sister stood at a distance, to see what would happen to him.

5 The daughter of Pharaoh came down to bathe at the river, while her attendants walked beside the river. She saw the basket among the reeds and sent her maid to bring it. 6When she opened it, she saw the child. He was crying, and she

a Sam Gk Tg: Heb lacks to the Hebrews

---

and prolific (v. 7), an ironic reversal of the pharaoh's plan to contain Hebrew reproduction. Came to dread. Cf. Num 22.3. **1.13** More precisely, "The Egyptians made the Israelites work to the point of collapse," a practice explicitly forbidden in Lev 25.43, 46; this is repeated in v. 14. **1.14** Made . . . bitter. See 12.8. Mortar, more likely "bitumen" as in another text tradition; the Hebrew words are spelled the same but vocalized differently (cf. Gen 11.3). Field labor, including digging irrigation canals (see Deut 11.10). **1.15** Hebrew midwives. Despite the Semitic names of the midwives, the Hebrew may be interpreted as "midwives of the Hebrews," i.e., Egyptian women serving the Israelites. Unlike the pharaoh, these heroic women are named. **1.16** In ancient Israel ethnicity was patrilineal, so that eliminating the males suffices to wipe out the people. **1.17** For the motif of a Gentile acknowledging Israel's God, see 18.1–12; Gen 14.18–20; Num 24.1; Josh 2.10–11; 2 Kings 5.15; Jon 1.16. The midwives precede both Israel and Egypt in recognizing Israel's national God as the true one. **1.19** Vigorous, lit. "lively," probably "quick." **1.20** Multiplied and became . . . strong, the same verbs as in vv. 7, 9; see note on 1.9. **1.21** Families; lit. "house(hold)s." **1.22** All his people, and not only the midwives (see note on 1.15). Since all Egyptians are involved in the genocide, all Egyptian households will suffer the plagues (chs. 7–12). Every boy. See v. 16. Nile, Hebrew ye'or, "river" in Egyptian.

2.1–10 The story of Moses' exposure and miraculous survival resembles diverse folktales of a hero's birth, especially that of Sargon of Akkad (probably from the late eighth century B.C.E.). **2.1** The parents are unnamed as in folktales; they are identified as Amram and Jochebed in 6.20. A Levite woman, or, since in 6.20 Amram marries his father's sister, "a daughter of (the tribal namesake) Levi." Moses' Levitical pedigree is emphasized; cf. 6.14–27. **2.2** That he was . . . fine, the same phrase rendered "that it was good" in the creation story (e.g., Gen 1.10, 12, 18). Baby, not in the Hebrew. **2.3** Papyrus, a seaworthy material (cf. Isa 18.2). Basket, an Egyptian loanword, used only here and of Noah's ark (e.g., Gen 6.14), another rudderless box under the deity's protection. Plastered, from the same Hebrew root as "bitumen" (see note on 1.14); different from the term rendered "pitch" (Gen 6.14). The river, lit. "the Nile"; cf. 1.22. **2.4** His sister is unnamed, but later identified with Miriam, who is introduced as Aaron's sister in 15.20 and cited as Moses' sister in Num 26.59. Stood, more precisely "stationed herself." Would happen, lit. "would be done." **2.5** The daughter of Pharaoh too is unnamed. The river, both times lit. "the Nile"; see note on 2.3. **2.6** He was crying, rather "and here: a lad crying," indicating that that is what she saw. Children, lit. "boys." Although "boy" in Hebrew is a generic term for "child," she seems to recognize him as a boy. The daughter's compassion contrasts with

took pity on him. "This must be one of the Hebrews' children," she said. 7 Then his sister said to Pharaoh's daughter, "Shall I go and get you a nurse from the Hebrew women to nurse the child for you?" 8 Pharaoh's daughter said to her, "Yes." So the girl went and called the child's mother. 9 Pharaoh's daughter said to her, "Take this child and nurse it for me, and I will give you your wages." So the woman took the child and nursed it. 10 When the child grew up, she brought him to Pharaoh's daughter, and she took him as her son. She named him Moses,b "because," she said, "I drew him outc of the water."

Moses Flees to Midian

11 One day, after Moses had grown up, he went out to his people and saw their forced labor. He saw an Egyptian beating a Hebrew, one of his kinsfolk. 12 He looked this way and that, and seeing no one he killed the Egyptian and hid him in the sand. 13 When he went out the next day, he saw two Hebrews fighting; and he said to the one who was in the wrong, "Why do you strike your fellow Hebrew?"

14 He answered, "Who made you a ruler and judge over us? Do you mean to kill me as you killed the Egyptian?" Then Moses was afraid and thought, "Surely the thing is known." 15 When Pharaoh heard of it, he sought to kill Moses.

But Moses fled from Pharaoh. He settled in the land of Midian, and sat down by a well. 16 The priest of Midian had seven daughters. They came to draw water, and filled the troughs to water their father's flock. 17 But some shepherds came and drove them away. Moses got up and came to their defense and watered their flock. 18 When they returned to their father Reuel, he said, "How is it that you have come back so soon today?" 19 They said, "An Egyptian helped us against the shepherds; he even drew water for us and watered the flock." 20 He said to his daughters, "Where is he? Why did you leave the man? Invite him to break bread." 21 Moses agreed to stay with the man, and he gave Moses his daughter Zipporah in marriage. 22 She bore a son, and he named him Gershom; for he said, "I

b Heb Mosheh   c Heb mashah

---

her father's brutality. **2.8** *Girl*, one who is past puberty (cf. Gen 24.43; Isa 7.14). **2.9** *Take*, better "take away," echoing "Go!" (rendered *Yes*) in v. 8. **2.10** *She took him as her son*, lit. "he became a son to her," an idiom indicating adoption. *Moses* in Hebrew means "the one who draws out," not, as the punning princess implies, the one she has drawn out. The name may derive from Egyptian "child of" (e.g., Thutmose) and/or be related to the Levitical clan of Mushites (e.g., 6.19; Num 3.20, 33; 26.58).

2.11–22 Moses' flight prior to a comeback as national deliverer parallels the stories of Jacob (Gen 27–33), Jephthah (Judg 11), and David (e.g., 1 Sam 20), as well as the extrabiblical stories of the Egyptian Sinuhe and the Syrian Idrimi (fifteenth century B.C.E.). The flight eastward and dispute with the Hebrews anticipates the exodus and later confrontations (15.22–17.7; Num 11; 14; 16). The episode at the well in Midian (vv. 15–21) evokes a traditional motif (Gen 24; 29); the present version highlights Moses' role as savior (v. 17). **2.11** *One day*, rather "in those days" of oppression. *His people*, lit. "his brothers," the same word translated *his kinsfolk* in the next sentence; Moses seems to identify with the Israelites. *Their forced labor*. See 1.11. *Beating*. The retributive plagues use the same Hebrew verb (translated *strike*; e.g., 3.20; 7.17, 20, 25; 8.16–17; 9.15; 12.12–13, 29). **2.12** *Killed*, lit. "struck,"

the same Hebrew word translated *beating* in v. 11. *Hid*, used mostly of burying in the ground, a different Hebrew word from that translated *hid/hide* in vv. 2–3. **2.13** *Strike*, the same Hebrew word translated *beat* in v. 11 and *kill* in v. 12. **2.14** *Kill*, not the Hebrew term translated *strike* in vv. 11–13. *Surely*, contrary to what I thought (e.g., Gen 28.16). **2.15** *Kill*, the verb used in v. 14. *Midian*. The Midianites, described in Gen 25.2 as nomadic offspring of Abraham and Keturah, range from the Sinai Peninsula to northern Arabia. **2.16** *Priest*, probably a position of leadership, like Moses' later role. *Seven*, a round number, characteristic of folktales. **2.17** *Came to their defense*, rendered *saved* in 14.30, foreshadows the rescue of Israel. **2.18** *Reuel*, meaning "Friend of God" in Hebrew, is of the same root as *fellow* (v. 13) and echoes the Hebrew *ro'eh*, "shepherd" (v. 17). Different traditions name him Jethro (e.g., 3.1; 18.1) and Hobab (Num 10.29, where he is Reuel's son); in Judg 4.11 he is a Kenite, traced to the nomadic Cain (Gen 4.12, 14); concerning the hypothesis of diverse sources, see note on 4.2–5. **2.19** *Egyptian*. Raised in Pharaoh's household, Moses still looks Egyptian. *Drew water*. Moses' generosity recalls Rebekah's (Gen 24.19). **2.21** *In marriage*, lit. "as a wife," added to the Hebrew text on the basis of some versions. There is a parallel in the Egyptian tale of Sinuhe. **2.22** *Gershom*, interpreted by wordplay

have been an alien*d* residing in a foreign land."

23 After a long time the king of Egypt died. The Israelites groaned under their slavery, and cried out. Out of the slavery their cry for help rose up to God. 24 God heard their groaning, and God remembered his covenant with Abraham, Isaac, and Jacob. 25 God looked upon the Israelites, and God took notice of them.

Moses at the Burning Bush

3 Moses was keeping the flock of his father-in-law Jethro, the priest of Midian; he led his flock beyond the wilderness, and came to Horeb, the mountain of God. 2 There the angel of the LORD appeared to him in a flame of fire out of a bush; he looked, and the bush was blazing, yet it was not consumed. 3 Then Moses said, "I must turn aside and look at this great sight, and see why the bush is not burned up." 4 When the LORD saw that he had turned aside to see, God called to him out of the bush, "Moses, Moses!" And he said, "Here I am." 5 Then he said, "Come no closer! Remove the sandals from your feet, for the place on which you are standing is holy ground." 6 He said further, "I am the God of your father, the God of Abraham, the God of Isaac, and the God of Jacob." And Moses hid his face, for he was afraid to look at God.

7 Then the LORD said, "I have ob-

d Heb *ger*

---

here and in 18.3 as *ger-sham*, Hebrew, "an alien there," referring to Midian or possibly Egypt; the letters of the name also echo *drove them away* (v. 17). **2.23–25** God's renewed attention to the Israelites' plight is conditioned by the covenant with Israel's ancestors. **2.23** *A long time*, lit. "in those many days" of Moses' exile and/or Israel's oppression; see v. 11. *The king of Egypt died*. The stage is set for Moses' return; see 4.19. *Slavery*, the term rendered *tasks* and *service* in 1.13–14, a reference more to hard labor than to slavery per se. *Cried out*, supplication, not merely an outcry (e.g., Judg 3.9; 1 Sam 7.9; Ps 107.13; Jer 11.11–12, Jon 1.5); the plea is not directed to the Lord (cf. 14.10). **2.24** *Groaning*, the sound of the oppressed (see Judg 2.18). *Remembered*. Hebrew does not distinguish "to remember" from "to pay mind to," which seems more apt in context. *Abraham*. Cf. Gen 17.7–8. *Isaac*. Cf. Gen 17.19, 21. *Jacob*. Cf. Gen 35.11–12; 46.3–4. **2.25** *Looked upon*, in the sense of "took note." *Took notice*. See note on 1.8.
3.1–12 The commissioning of Moses begins with a numinous experience, appropriate to the wonder-working task that awaits him. **3.1** *Moses was*, lit. "Now Moses, he was . . . ," indicating that the ensuing episode takes place simultaneously with the preceding (2.23–25). *Keeping*, from the same Hebrew root as *shepherd* (2.17), a distinctively Hebrew occupation (Gen 46.32–34; 47.3–4). Moses' future role is betokened: "shepherd" is a metaphor for leader (see Num 27.17; 2 Sam 5.2; Jer 22.22; Ezek 34.2); David, too, was a shepherd (2 Sam 7.8). *Jethro*. See note on 2.18. *He led*, apparently intentionally; see note on 4.18–20. *Beyond*. The odd Hebrew has "behind." *Horeb*, the name of Mount Sinai in a tradition ascribed by scholars to the putative Elohist and Deuteronomic sources, that is, to traditions in

Genesis–Exodus and Deuteronomy (e.g., 17.6; 33.6; Deut 1.2, 6). *Mountain of God*, the narrator's anticipation or Moses knowledge prior to the revelation to follow that it was a holy mountain; see note on 4.18–20. **3.2** *Fire*, a conventional medium of the divine presence (e.g., Gen 15.17; Judg 13.20). *A bush*, in Hebrew "the bush," another hint that the site was known to be sacred. The Hebrew term for "bush," *seneh*, suggests the mountain's name, Sinai, Yahweh's original location according to Deut 33.2; Judg 5.5 and site of the Lord's appearance before all Israel (chs. 19–20). *It*. The Hebrew repeats "the bush." **3.3** *Look* and *sight* are from the same root in Hebrew. *And see*, is not in the Hebrew, where *why* begins Moses' question to himself. *Is not burned up*, rather "does not burn." **3.4** *The LORD*. Although it was an *angel* that appeared in v. 2, there is no substantive difference between the deity and his agents. *Moses, Moses!* Doubling the name may serve to reassure that it is not mirage (cf. Gen 22.11; 1 Sam 3.10). *Here I am*, an obliging gesture on Moses' part (e.g., Gen 22.1; 1 Sam 3.4). **3.5** *No closer*. Cf. 19.12, 21–24. *Remove . . . holy ground*. Cf. Josh 5.15. **3.6** *God of . . . Jacob*. Cf. 2.24. *Hid his face*, a phrase elsewhere used mostly of God's shutting out human affairs, e.g., Deut 31.17–18; Ps 44.24; Isa 8.17; Ezek 39.23–24. *Afraid to look*. Gazing directly into the deity's face is said to be fatal (see 33.20; cf. Isa 6.5), but seeing an angel or a mitigated divine vision does no harm; see Gen 32.30; Ex 24.11; 33.23; Judg 6.22–23; 13.22–23; cf. Ex. 33.11. **3.7–9** An elaboration of 2.23–25. **3.7** *Observed*, the same Hebrew term rendered *looked upon* (2.25), *looked/look* (3.2–3), and *saw* (3.4). *Misery*, or "affliction," cognate to *oppress* (1.11). *Their cry*, "outcry," connoting moral outrage (e.g., Gen 18.21; Isa 5.7). *Sufferings*, physical pain (e.g., Isa

Hebrew destination

served the misery of my people who are in Egypt; I have heard their cry on account of their taskmasters. Indeed, I know their sufferings, 8 and I have come down to deliver them from the Egyptians, and to bring them up out of that land to a good and broad land, a land flowing with milk and honey, to the country of the Canaanites, the Hittites, the Amorites, the Perizzites, the Hivites, and the Jebusites. 9 The cry of the Israelites has now come to me; I have also seen how the Egyptians oppress them. 10 So come, I will send you to Pharaoh to bring my people, the Israelites, out of Egypt." 11 But Moses said to God, "Who am I that I should go to Pharaoh, and bring the Israelites out of Egypt?" 12 He said, "I will be with you; and this shall be the sign for you that it is I who sent you: when you have brought the people out of Egypt, you shall worship God on this mountain."

The Divine Name Revealed

13 But Moses said to God, "If I come to the Israelites and say to them, 'The God of your ancestors has sent me to you,' and they ask me, 'What is his name?' what shall I say to them?" 14 God said to Moses, "I AM WHO I AM."e He said further,

"Thus you shall say to the Israelites, 'I AM has sent me to you.'" 15 God also said to Moses, "Thus you shall say to the Israelites, 'The LORD,f the God of your ancestors, the God of Abraham, the God of Isaac, and the God of Jacob, has sent me to you':

This is my name forever,
    and this my title for all
        generations.

16 Go and assemble the elders of Israel, and say to them, 'The LORD, the God of your ancestors, the God of Abraham, of Isaac, and of Jacob, has appeared to me, saying: I have given heed to you and to what has been done to you in Egypt. 17 I declare that I will bring you up out of the misery of Egypt, to the land of the Canaanites, the Hittites, the Amorites, the Perizzites, the Hivites, and the Jebusites, a land flowing with milk and honey.' 18 They will listen to your voice; and you and the elders of Israel shall go to the king of Egypt and say to him, 'The LORD, the God of the Hebrews, has met with us; let us now go a three days' journey into

e Or *I AM WHAT I AM* or *I WILL BE WHAT I WILL BE*
f The word "LORD" when spelled with capital letters stands for the divine name, *YHWH*, which is here connected with the verb *hayah*, "to be"

53.4; Jer 20.15; 51.8). **3.8** *Have come down*, from God's abode in the sky (e.g., 19.11, 20; Gen 11.5; 18.21; 28.13; Ps 18.7–20). *Milk and honey*, the first instance of this cliché for the land of Israel (e.g., 13.5; 33.3; Lev 20.24; Num 13.27; Deut 6.3). *Canaanites . . . Jebusites*, six of the indigenous Canaanite peoples, recapitulated in v. 17. Gen 15.19–21 lists ten, but not the Hivites. *Hittites*, a people originally from Asia Minor who populated Canaan beginning about 1400 B.C.E. *Amorites*, a generic term for western Semites. *Jebusites*, inhabitants of Jerusalem, conquered by David (2 Sam 5.6–7). **3.9** *Seen*, the same Hebrew term rendered *observed* in v. 7. *Oppress*, different from the term in 1.11–12; used twice in the Hebrew phrasing, it has the root sense of "press"; cf. 22.20; 23.9. **3.10** *So*. The Hebrew is stronger: "Now then." *Send*. This verb defines the prophet's role as a messenger from God. *Pharaoh*. Moses may not know the pharaoh; the one he knew has died (2.23; see note on 4.18–20). *Bring . . . out*, the causative verb "to have them go out," the etymology of "exodus," a themeword of the narrative and a term by which the delivering Lord will be identified (e.g., 6.6–7; 20.2). **3.11** A pragmatic concern or a display of Moses' famed modesty (Num 12.3). Moses plays the reluctant

prophet (cf. Judg 6.15; Isa 6.8; Jer 1). **3.12** The deity echoes Moses' language. Although not reflected in the English, the Hebrew particle "that, indeed" is used twice by Moses in v. 11 and twice by God in this verse. *Sign*, a key term throughout this and the ensuing narrative. Signs authenticate those who perform them and demonstrate the Lord's power. **3.13–22** The Lord is revealed as the God of Israel's ancestors, and the exodus is previewed. **3.13** *Ask*, the same Hebrew verb rendered *say* here twice. **3.14** *I AM WHO I AM*, on the basis of 33.19 (*I will be gracious to whom I will be gracious . . .*), "I will be whatever I will be." The name puns on the divine name Yahweh and in the present context would seem to connote "being there" for Moses and the Israelites. **3.15** The speech is punctuated by a parallel, adding drama and/or solemnity. *My title*, the name by which I shall be invoked or memorialized; cf. 20.24 where *cause my name to be remembered* uses the same Hebrew root; cf. 23.13. **3.16** Moses will convince his people only after the Lord has performed wonders. **3.18** The ruse will not fool Pharaoh (5.1–4; 8.21–24; 10.8–11). *Sacrifice*. The term in Hebrew connotes slaughtering an animal, part of which is offered to the deity; it lacks the English word's

the wilderness, so that we may sacrifice to the LORD our God.' 19I know, however, that the king of Egypt will not let you go unless compelled by a mighty hand.*g* 20So I will stretch out my hand and strike Egypt with all my wonders that I will perform in it; after that he will let you go. 21I will bring this people into such favor with the Egyptians that, when you go, you will not go empty-handed; 22each woman shall ask her neighbor and any woman living in the neighbor's house for jewelry of silver and of gold, and clothing, and you shall put them on your sons and on your daughters; and so you shall plunder the Egyptians."

Moses' Miraculous Power

4 Then Moses answered, "But suppose they do not believe me or listen to me, but say, 'The LORD did not appear to you.'" 2The LORD said to him, "What is that in your hand?" He said, "A staff." 3And he said, "Throw it on the ground." So he threw the staff on the ground, and it became a snake; and Moses drew back

from it. 4Then the LORD said to Moses, "Reach out your hand, and seize it by the tail"—so he reached out his hand and grasped it, and it became a staff in his hand— 5"so that they may believe that the LORD, the God of their ancestors, the God of Abraham, the God of Isaac, and the God of Jacob, has appeared to you."

6 Again, the LORD said to him, "Put your hand inside your cloak." He put his hand into his cloak; and when he took it out, his hand was leprous,*h* as white as snow. 7Then God said, "Put your hand back into your cloak"—so he put his hand back into his cloak, and when he took it out, it was restored like the rest of his body— 8"If they will not believe you or heed the first sign, they may believe the second sign. 9If they will not believe even these two signs or heed you, you shall take some water from the Nile and pour it on the dry ground; and the water that you shall take from the Nile will become blood on the dry ground."

g Gk Vg: Heb *no, not by a mighty hand*   *h* A term for several skin diseases; precise meaning uncertain

---

connotation of surrender.   **3.19** *Let . . . go*, not the same Hebrew verb as in v. 20 and in the recurrent liberation formula usually rendered *let go* (e.g., 4.23; 5.1; 7.16). The latter are from the root "to send." *Compelled*, added for clarity. *Mighty hand*. The difficult, textually uncertain Hebrew leaves open whether God will force Pharaoh's hand (cf. 13.9) or whether Pharaoh will force Israel out (cf. 6.1).   **3.20** *Stretch out . . . hand*, lit. "send (the) hand," an idiom for inflicting harm (e.g., 1 Sam 22.17; Esth 2.21). *Strike*, translated *beat* in (see note on) 2.11. *Wonders*, a term used within the exodus story only here and in 34.10 but commonly in later texts referring to the exodus (e.g., Judg 6.13; Pss 78.4, 11; 106.22; Mic 7.15). *Let you go*. See note on 3.19.   **3.21** The Israelites will not leave *empty-handed*, the way Jacob (Israel) left Laban (Gen 31.42); when the Israelites become autonomous, they must not "release" their slaves (Deut 15.13) or worship God (23.15; 34.20; Deut 16.16) empty-handed. Cf. Gen 15.14.   **3.22** *Plunder*, lit. "stripping," divine compensation for Egypt's exploitation of the Hebrews; cf. Gen 12.16; 20.14–16. The "borrowing" is effected in 12.35–36, echoing the terms of vv. 21–22 here but in reverse (chiastic) order, indicating completion of the thematic unit (see notes on 4.30–31; 6.26–27; 17.7). Later Jewish traditions suggest that the women do the borrowing because they will dress their children in the

Egyptians' clothes and jewels.

4.1–17   Moses suggests two further impediments: credibility (vv. 1–9) and problematic speech (vv. 10–16).   **4.1** *They*, the elders (3.16). *Believe*, in the sense of trust (19.9); cf. 14.31; in v. 5 below *believe* in the sense of "accept as true" is more apt.   **4.2–5** Some explain the wondrous signs naturalistically, pointing here to the fact that some snakes stiffen when one grasps their tails. V. 2 makes clear that the snake began as Moses' staff. The deity's power is demonstrated by producing the fantastic from the ordinary. Moses will use none of the three signs to convince the Israelites; Aaron will turn the staff into a "serpent" (a different word in the Hebrew) in an attempt to persuade Pharaoh (7.8–13). On account of discrepancies like this (different word, actor, storyline) some scholars suppose that the text is woven from different sources; others do not expect the text to be consistent or smooth.   **4.3** *Drew back*, lit. "fled" (14.27). Gen 3.15 posits a normal human phobia of snakes.   **4.4** *Reach out*, lit. "send" (see note on 3.20).   **4.5** Cf. 3.16.   **4.6–9** The third sign anticipates the first plague (7.14–25). In view of this, the second sign, which is never used, may anticipate the plague of boils (9.8–12); and the first may suggest the plague of frogs, which is initiated by stretching the staff over Egypt's waterways (8.5–6).   **4.7** *Rest of his body*, lit. "his flesh."   **4.9** *Dry ground* anticipates the Is-

10 But Moses said to the Lord, "O my Lord, I have never been eloquent, neither in the past nor even now that you have spoken to your servant; but I am slow of speech and slow of tongue." 11 Then the Lord said to him, "Who gives speech to mortals? Who makes them mute or deaf, seeing or blind? Is it not I, the Lord? 12 Now go, and I will be with your mouth and teach you what you are to speak." 13 But he said, "O my Lord, please send someone else." 14 Then the anger of the Lord was kindled against Moses and he said, "What of your brother Aaron the Levite? I know that he can speak fluently; even now he is coming out to meet you, and when he sees you his heart will be glad. 15 You shall speak to him and put the words in his mouth; and I will be with your mouth and with his mouth, and will teach you what you shall do. 16 He indeed shall speak for you to the people; he shall serve as a mouth for you, and you shall serve as God for him. 17 Take in your hand this staff, with which you shall perform the signs."

Moses Returns to Egypt

18 Moses went back to his father-in-law Jethro and said to him, "Please let me go back to my kindred in Egypt and see whether they are still living." And Jethro said to Moses, "Go in peace." 19 The Lord said to Moses in Midian, "Go back to Egypt; for all those who were seeking your life are dead." 20 So Moses took his wife and his sons, put them on a donkey, and went back to the land of Egypt; and Moses carried the staff of God in his hand.

21 And the Lord said to Moses, "When you go back to Egypt, see that you perform before Pharaoh all the wonders

---

raelites' crossing the sea on dry ground (14.22). **4.10** *Eloquent*, lit. "a man of words," of the same Hebrew root as *spoken*. *Slow of speech*, lit. "heavy of mouth." *Slow of tongue*, lit. "heavy of tongue"; see 6.12, 30. "Heavy" in various forms will figure throughout the plagues and exodus narrative (see, e.g., 5.9; notes on 4.21; 9.3; 10.14; 14.4; 14.25). Moses' "heavy" speech may entail a physical impediment (so comparative evidence) or an inability to wax eloquent in Egyptian (see Ezek 3.6, where foreign speech is indicated); in this story, however, Egyptians speak Hebrew (see 2.10). **4.11** *Speech*, lit. "a mouth"; Moses, whose mouth will be accompanied by the Lord (vv. 12, 15), will put the necessary words into Aaron's mouth (v. 15). Prophecy consists of the deity's very words (e.g., Deut 18.18; Jer 1.9; Ezek 2.7–3.3; 3.4, 10). **4.13** *Someone else*, rather "whomever you will send," a construction resembling *I am who I am* in 3.14. **4.14** *Speak fluently.* Cf. the historical role of the Levites as transmitters of divine instructions (Deut 33.10); cf. 18.15, where Moses the Levite functions as an oracle. **4.15–16** Aaron will play the role of oracle (*mouth*) to Moses' role as God, the source of revelation; see 7.1, where the analogy is: Moses is to Aaron as God is to a prophet. For God as an oracular source, see 18.15; 21.6; 22.7.

4.18–31 The anticipation of the tenth plague—the slaying of Egypt's firstborn (v. 23)— provides background to the assault on Moses or his firstborn (vv. 24–26). The perilous meeting with the Lord en route to Egypt contrasts with Aaron's meeting Moses (v. 27): the return to Egypt is hazardous; the journey away is smooth; cf. Deut 17.16. **4.18–20** In v. 19 the Lord or-

ders Moses back to Egypt as though the preceding dialogue has not taken place; it implies that Moses' reluctance to return stems from the same fear that led to his flight (2.15). The language of 3.1 suggests that Moses has gone to the mountain for a purpose. Vv. 18–20 may reflect a different tradition from 3.1–4.17, one in which Moses, in the manner of other fugitive heroes, goes to Sinai/Horeb seeking an oracle, to learn if it is safe to go home to Egypt and see his kin (4.18). **4.18** *Jethro*. The Hebrew has the variant "Jether"; see note on 2.18. *Kindred*, lit. "brothers"; see note on 2.11. **4.19** See 2.23. **4.20** *Sons*. The birth of only one of Moses' sons has been reported (2.22); see 18.2–6. Apart from the episode in vv. 24–26, Moses' Midianite family plays no role in the exodus story. *Staff of God*, perhaps one given to him by God (cf. v. 17), not the one he used as a shepherd. **4.21** *Wonders*, better "signs" (so too 7.3, 9; 11.9–10), synonymous with the Hebrew word translated *sign* in 4.8–9, 30, not the same as *wonders* in 3.20, a word from a different Hebrew root. *Your power*, lit. "your hand"; the three signs given in vv. 2–9 are all indeed performed by one hand. *Harden his heart*. In 3.19 the Lord says that Pharaoh will be stubborn, but here the Lord claims responsibility for "stiffening" the Egyptian's will; as the story unfolds Pharaoh's heart will "stiffen" or "grow heavy" (see note on 4.10) by Pharaoh's own will (7.13–14, 22–23; 8.15, 19, 32; 9.7, 34–35) or it will be stiffened, made heavy, or hardened by the Lord (9.12; 10.1, 20, 27; 11.10; 14.8). The hardening prolongs the plagues and ensures that Egypt will suffer the punishment it deserves and witness the Lord's power; see note on 1.22; cf. 7.3–5; 14.4.

that I have put in your power; but I will harden his heart, so that he will not let the people go. 22 Then you shall say to Pharaoh, 'Thus says the LORD: Israel is my firstborn son. 23 I said to you, "Let my son go that he may worship me." But you refused to let him go; now I will kill your firstborn son.'"

24 On the way, at a place where they spent the night, the LORD met him and tried to kill him. 25 But Zipporah took a flint and cut off her son's foreskin, and touched Moses'[i] feet with it, and said, "Truly you are a bridegroom of blood to me!" 26 So he let him alone. It was then she said, "A bridegroom of blood by circumcision."

27 The LORD said to Aaron, "Go into the wilderness to meet Moses." So he went; and he met him at the mountain of God and kissed him. 28 Moses told Aaron all the words of the LORD with which he had sent him, and all the signs with which he had charged him. 29 Then Moses and

Aaron went and assembled all the elders of the Israelites. 30 Aaron spoke all the words that the LORD had spoken to Moses, and performed the signs in the sight of the people. 31 The people believed; and when they heard that the LORD had given heed to the Israelites and that he had seen their misery, they bowed down and worshiped.

Bricks Without Straw

5 Afterward Moses and Aaron went to Pharaoh and said, "Thus says the LORD, the God of Israel, 'Let my people go, so that they may celebrate a festival to me in the wilderness.'" 2 But Pharaoh said, "Who is the LORD, that I should heed him and let Israel go? I do not know the LORD, and I will not let Israel go." 3 Then they said, "The God of the Hebrews has revealed himself to us; let us go a three days' journey into the wilderness to sacri-

i Heb *his*

4.22–23 The metaphor of Israel's election as the Lord's *firstborn son* (see Jer 31.9; Hos 11.1) lends the tenth plague a quality of poetic justice. *Worship*, the same Hebrew verb as "to serve, work, act-as-a-slave" (see note on 2.23); the Hebrews are to be the Lord's servants, not Pharaoh's (cf. Lev 25.42, 55). **4.24–26** The unmotivated divine assault is made even stranger by its ambiguous use of pronouns: it remains unclear whether Moses or his son is the victim. The juxtaposition with Pharaoh's *firstborn son* (v. 23) suggests that Moses' son may be the one at risk. The episode runs against the larger narrative sequence in which Moses has two sons (4.20; 18.2–6). **4.24** *At a place . . . night.* The laconic Hebrew has only "at-the-lodging-place" (*bammalon*). *Tried*, the same Hebrew verb rendered "seeking" in v. 19. **4.25** In the context of Exodus the ritual blood produced by the circumcision serves to protect against destructive divine power, like the blood of the paschal lamb (12.7, 12–13, 21–27). *Zipporah*, a priest's daughter, may be acquainted with ritual procedures. *Flint*, sharpened stone used in circumcision; e.g., Josh 5.2–3. *Cut off*, not the Hebrew term "to circumcise." *Moses' feet*, lit. "his feet" (see text note *i*), possibly a euphemism for the genitals (cf. 2 Kings 18.27; Isa 6.2; 7.20), Moses' or his son's. *Bridegroom*, either Moses (since among certain Semites a bridegroom was circumcised by his father-in-law; the Hebrew term for "father-in-law" means "one who circumcises") or his son (since among some Semites a boy undergoing circumcision is called a bridegroom). **4.26** *He*, the Lord. *Let him alone*, more precisely "let him loose."

A bridegroom . . . circumcision, an apparent byword, the meaning of which, like the historical sense of the episode, has been lost. **4.27** *He met him.* See note on 4.18–31. *Mountain of God*, Sinai/Horeb (see note on 3.1). *Kissed him* evokes Gen 33.4; 45.14–15. **4.29** According to the instructions in 3.16. **4.30–31** Aaron's role (v. 30) answers to Moses' fourth objection (vv. 10–17) and the people's acceptance (v. 31) obviates the need for the signs provided in response to Moses' objection in vv. 1–9. The reverse (chiastic) sequence closes the passage; cf. note on 3.22. **4.31** *People*, not only the elders (v. 29). *Worshiped*, lit. "prostrated themselves," which signifies obedience to God (see 12.27).

5.1–6.1 Pharaoh reacts to Moses and Aaron by making matters worse, vindicating the Lord's prediction (3.19) and further justifying the plagues. **5.1** *Moses and Aaron.* The elders are not included as the Lord ordained (3.18). *The LORD*, the first time in this story that the Lord's name is announced in Egypt; cf. v. 23. *Celebrate a festival*, one verb in Hebrew; the Hebrew cognate noun *hag* (cf. Arabic *haj*) denotes a pilgrimage. They do not yet ask for three days' leave (as in 3.18; 5.3). **5.2** *Who is the LORD*, an echo of what Moses said in 3.11. *Heed him*, lit. "listen to his voice," an echo of what Moses said in 4.1. *I do not know.* Cf. 1.8. To know the Lord is a main theme of the succeeding narrative (e.g., 7.5, 17; 8.10; 9.14; 14.18). **5.3** A recapitulation of 3.18 with the addition *or* ("lest") *he will fall . . . sword*, an ironic hint of the plagues that will beset Egypt; *pestilence* is used of the fifth plague (9.3), *the sword* foreshadows the quasi-

fice to the LORD our God, or he will fall upon us with pestilence or sword." 4 But the king of Egypt said to them, "Moses and Aaron, why are you taking the people away from their work? Get to your labors!" 5 Pharaoh continued, "Now they are more numerous than the people of the land *j* and yet you want them to stop working!" 6 That same day Pharaoh commanded the taskmasters of the people, as well as their supervisors, 7 "You shall no longer give the people straw to make bricks, as before; let them go and gather straw for themselves. 8 But you shall require of them the same quantity of bricks as they have made previously; do not diminish it, for they are lazy; that is why

they cry, 'Let us go and offer sacrifice to our God.' 9 Let heavier work be laid on them; then they will labor at it and pay no attention to deceptive words."

10 So the taskmasters and the supervisors of the people went out and said to the people, "Thus says Pharaoh, 'I will not give you straw. 11 Go and get straw yourselves, wherever you can find it; but your work will not be lessened in the least.'" 12 So the people scattered throughout the land of Egypt, to gather stubble for straw. 13 The taskmasters were urgent, saying, "Complete your work, the same daily assignment as when you were given straw."

j Sam: Heb *The people of the land are now many*

---

battle at the sea (see 15.9). **5.4** *King of Egypt.* By avoiding "Pharaoh" here a pun in Hebrew is averted on the verb *taking away from. Labors,* imposed in 1.11. **5.5** *More numerous.* See 1.9. *You want them to stop,* lit. "you are stopping them." The Hebrew verb translated *stop* is the root of "sabbath" (see note on 16.23); the Lord, in contrast to Pharaoh, ordains a break from labor (see Deut 5.12–15). **5.6** *Taskmasters,* lit. "oppressors," used

in 3.7 and below in vv. 10, 13, 14, not the term rendered *taskmasters* in 1.11. Egyptian art depicts laborers being overseen, and sometimes beaten, by rod-wielding taskmasters. *Supervisors,* apparently Israelites (see v. 14). **5.7** *As before.* Only brick making was assigned in 1.14. **5.9** *Deceptive words,* rather "lies," that the Hebrews' God has appeared to Moses. **5.11** *Lessened,* translated *diminish* in v. 8. *Your work . . . in the least,* lit. "not a thing

Asiatic captives making bricks under Thutmose III, ruler of Egypt in the fifteenth century B.C.E., for the temple of Amon at Thebes. Line drawing of an illustration from the tomb of Rekhmara. (From S. R. Driver, The Book of Exodus.)

14 And the supervisors of the Israelites, whom Pharaoh's taskmasters had set over them, were beaten, and were asked, "Why did you not finish the required quantity of bricks yesterday and today, as you did before?"

15 Then the Israelite supervisors came to Pharaoh and cried, "Why do you treat your servants like this? 16 No straw is given to your servants, yet they say to us, 'Make bricks!' Look how your servants are beaten! You are unjust to your own people."*k* 17 He said, "You are lazy, lazy; that is why you say, 'Let us go and sacrifice to the LORD.' 18 Go now, and work; for no straw shall be given you, but you shall still deliver the same number of bricks." 19 The Israelite supervisors saw that they were in trouble when they were told, "You shall not lessen your daily number of bricks." 20 As they left Pharaoh, they came upon Moses and Aaron who were waiting to meet them. 21 They said to them, "The LORD look upon you and judge! You have brought us into bad odor with Pharaoh and his officials, and have put a sword in their hand to kill us."

22 Then Moses turned again to the LORD and said, "O LORD, why have you mistreated this people? Why did you ever send me? 23 Since I first came to Pharaoh to speak in your name, he has mistreated this people, and you have done nothing at all to deliver your people."

Israel's Deliverance Assured

6 Then the LORD said to Moses, "Now you shall see what I will do to Pharaoh: Indeed, by a mighty hand he will let them go; by a mighty hand he will drive them out of his land."

2 God also spoke to Moses and said to him: "I am the LORD. 3 I appeared to Abraham, Isaac, and Jacob as God Almighty,*l* but by my name 'The LORD'*m* I did not make myself known to them. 4 I also established my covenant with them, to give them the land of Canaan, the land in which they resided as aliens. 5 I have also heard the groaning of the Israelites whom the Egyptians are holding as slaves, and I have remembered my covenant. 6 Say therefore to the Israelites, 'I am the LORD, and I will free you from the burdens of the Egyptians and deliver you from slavery to them. I will redeem you with an outstretched arm and with mighty acts of judgment. 7 I will take you as my people, and I will be your God. You shall know that I am the LORD your God, who has freed you from the burdens of the Egyptians. 8 I will bring you into the land that I swore to give to Abraham, Isaac, and Jacob; I will give it to you for a possession. I am the LORD.' " 9 Moses told this

k Gk Compare Syr Vg: Heb *beaten, and the sin of your people* *l* Traditional rendering of Heb *El Shaddai* *m* Heb *YHWH*; see note at 3.15

---

will be removed from your work." **5.14** *Were beaten.* Cf. 2.11. **5.15** *Cried* connotes complaining, as in 14.15 and perhaps in 5.8. *Servants*, the same term as that for the slaves they oversee. **5.16** *You are unjust*, rather "you sin against," as in 9.27. **5.17** Cf. v. 8. **5.19** *Trouble*, lit. "bad, evil." **5.21** *You have brought us into a bad odor with Pharaoh*, lit. "You have made our smell stink in the eyes of Pharaoh." Bad odor will attend the first two plagues (see 7.21; 8.10). **5.22** *Turned again*, returned to Mount Sinai. *Mistreated*, of the same Hebrew root as the word translated *trouble* in v. 19. **5.23** *First*, not in the Hebrew. *You have done nothing at all to deliver*, rather "you have not (yet) rescued, not rescued." *Your name* and *your people* stress the Lord's responsibility and evoke Moses' diffidence at the burning bush (chs. 3–4); cf. 32.7, 11. **6.1** *Mighty hand*. Cf. 3.19–20.

6.2–13 Cf. the parallel passage, chs. 3–4, which scholars trace to a different tradition. In context, the present passage presupposes the Isra-

elites' discouragement after the initial confrontation with Pharaoh (v. 9), and the divine charge to go to Pharaoh (v. 11) is a reassurance. **6.2** *Also*, not in the Hebrew. **6.3** *Almighty*. Etymologically the name suggests "One of the Mountain," appropriate for a deity who reveals himself on Horeb/Sinai; cf. Gen 17.1; 28.3; 35.11. *The Lord*, Abraham, Isaac, and Jacob each use this name (Gen 12.8; 26.22; 32.10); the present passage seems to know a different tradition. **6.4** *Resided as aliens*. In this context merely "resided" might be more accurate (cf. Gen 26.3). The verse echoes Gen 17.7–8. **6.5** This verse echoes 2.24. **6.6** *Free*. See 3.10, where the same Hebrew verb is rendered *bring . . . out*. The Hebrew word translated *burdens* is rendered *forced labor* in 1.11; 2.11 and *labors* in 5.4. *Redeem* connotes the ransom of indentured kin; cf. Lev 25.47–49. **6.7** *Know*. See note on 5.2. The relationship between God and Israel is expressed as a legal adoption; cf., e.g., Lev 26.12; 2 Sam 7.14. **6.8** *I swore*, expressed idiomatically in Hebrew by a gesture of

to the Israelites; but they would not listen to Moses, because of their broken spirit and their cruel slavery.

10 Then the LORD spoke to Moses, 11 "Go and tell Pharaoh king of Egypt to let the Israelites go out of his land." 12 But Moses spoke to the LORD, "The Israelites have not listened to me; how then shall Pharaoh listen to me, poor speaker that I am?"n 13 Thus the LORD spoke to Moses and Aaron, and gave them orders regarding the Israelites and Pharaoh king of Egypt, charging them to free the Israelites from the land of Egypt.

The Genealogy of Moses and Aaron

14 The following are the heads of their ancestral houses: the sons of Reuben, the firstborn of Israel: Hanoch, Pallu, Hezron, and Carmi; these are the families of Reuben. 15 The sons of Simeon: Jemuel, Jamin, Ohad, Jachin, Zohar, and Shaul,o the son of a Canaanite woman; these are the families of Simeon. 16 The following are the names of the sons of Levi according to their genealogies: Gershon,p Kohath, and Merari, and the length of Levi's life was one hundred thirty-seven years. 17 The sons of Gershon:p Libni and Shimei, by their families. 18 The sons of Kohath: Amram, Izhar, Hebron, and Uzziel, and the length of Kohath's life was one hundred thirty-three years. 19 The sons of Merari: Mahli and Mushi. These are the families of the Levites according to their genealogies. 20 Amram married Jochebed his father's sister and she bore him Aaron and Moses, and the length of Amram's life was one hundred thirty-seven years. 21 The sons of Izhar: Korah, Nepheg, and Zichri. 22 The sons of Uzziel: Mishael, Elzaphan, and Sithri. 23 Aaron married Elisheba, daughter of Amminadab and sister of Nahshon, and she bore him Nadab, Abihu, Eleazar, and Ithamar. 24 The sons of Korah: Assir, Elkanah, and Abiasaph; these are the families of the Korahites. 25 Aaron's son Eleazar married one of the daughters of Putiel, and she bore him Phinehas. These are the heads of the ancestral houses of the Levites by their families.

26 It was this same Aaron and Moses to whom the LORD said, "Bring the Israelites out of the land of Egypt, company by company." 27 It was they who spoke to Pharaoh king of Egypt to bring the Israelites out of Egypt, the same Moses and Aaron.

n Heb *me? I am uncircumcised of lips*   o Or *Saul*
p Also spelled *Gershom*; see 2.22

---

oath-taking, "I have raised my hand" (e.g., Deut 32.40). **6.9** *Broken spirit*, lit. "shortness of breath," frustration perhaps. *Cruel slavery*, the same phrase translated *hard service* in 1.14. **6.11** *Tell*, the substance of the preceding revelation. *To let*, rather "so that he (Pharaoh) will let." **6.12** *Poor speaker*. See note on 4.10. **6.13** *Aaron*. Cf. 4.14.

6.14–27 The narrative is interrupted by a genealogy that places Moses and Aaron within the lineage of the Israelite tribe and among the various Levitical clans. Vv. 26–27 repeat the contents of vv. 10–13 and resume the narrative. The genealogy breaks off after Levi, giving the impression that the text is excerpted from a fuller list, such as Gen 46.8–27. See the more ramified genealogy in Num 26. **6.14** *Ancestral houses*, lit. "father's houses," denotes tribal divisions. **6.16** *Merari*, an Egyptian name. *One hundred thirty-seven*. The limit of 120 years (Gen 6.3) only applies from Moses' generation on. **6.20** *Father's sister*. See note on 2.1. This is incest according to Lev 18.12. Heroes' births are often marked by the illicit; cf. the birth of Isaac from a brother and half-sister (Gen 20.12), David from a Moabite (Ruth), and Solomon from the once-adulterous couple, David and Bathsheba. *Aaron and Moses*. Some versions add here "and Miriam their sister" (see Num 26.59). **6.23** *Elisheba*, "Elizabeth" in the Greek version. *Amminadab*, clan head of Judah (Num 1.7). *Sister of Nahshon*. An unmarried woman is sometimes identified by her eldest brother, who may play a role in arranging her marriage (see Gen 24); cf. Ex 15.20; Gen 25.20; 28.9. *Nahshon* is the military chieftain of Judah (Num 2.3). *Nadab . . . Ithamar*. The Hebrew couples "Nadab and Abihu, Eleazar and Ithamar"; the older pair will die (Lev 10.1–5) and the younger will succeed to priestly leadership; cf. note on 7.7. **6.24** *Korah*, rebel (Num 16) and namesake of the Second Temple gatekeepers (1 Chr 9.19). **6.25** *Putiel*, an Egyptian name; cf. Potiphar (Gen 39.1), Potiphera (Gen 41.45). *Phinehas*, an Egyptian name. A large number of Egyptian names are concentrated in the Levite tribe (e.g., Moses, Aaron, Miriam, Merari, Hophni), leading some to trace only the Levites to Egypt. **6.26–27** The resumptive unit begins with the sequence *Aaron and Moses* and ends chiastically with *Moses and Aaron*. **6.26** *Company*, in a military sense (see Num 2); see 12.41; cf. 7.4; 12.51; 13.18.

Moses and Aaron Obey God's Commands

28 On the day when the LORD spoke to Moses in the land of Egypt, 29 he said to him, "I am the LORD; tell Pharaoh king of Egypt all that I am speaking to you." 30 But Moses said in the LORD's presence, "Since I am a poor speaker,*q* why would Pharaoh listen to me?"

7 The LORD said to Moses, "See, I have made you like God to Pharaoh, and your brother Aaron shall be your prophet. 2 You shall speak all that I command you, and your brother Aaron shall tell Pharaoh to let the Israelites go out of his land. 3 But I will harden Pharaoh's heart, and I will multiply my signs and wonders in the land of Egypt. 4 When Pharaoh does not listen to you, I will lay my hand upon Egypt and bring my people the Israelites, company by company, out of the land of Egypt by great acts of judgment. 5 The Egyptians shall know that I am the LORD, when I stretch out my hand against Egypt and bring the Israelites out from among them." 6 Moses and Aaron did so; they did just as the LORD commanded them. 7 Moses was eighty years old and Aaron eighty-three when they spoke to Pharaoh.

Aaron's Miraculous Rod

8 The LORD said to Moses and Aaron, 9 "When Pharaoh says to you, 'Perform a wonder,' then you shall say to Aaron, 'Take your staff and throw it down before Pharaoh, and it will become a snake.'" 10 So Moses and Aaron went to Pharaoh and did as the LORD had commanded; Aaron threw down his staff before Pharaoh and his officials, and it became a snake. 11 Then Pharaoh summoned the wise men and the sorcerers; and they also, the magicians of Egypt, did the same by their secret arts. 12 Each one threw down his staff, and they became snakes; but Aaron's staff swallowed up theirs. 13 Still Pharaoh's heart was hardened, and he would not listen to them, as the LORD had said.

The First Plague: Water Turned to Blood

14 Then the LORD said to Moses, "Pharaoh's heart is hardened; he refuses to let the people go. 15 Go to Pharaoh in the morning, as he is going out to the water; stand by at the river bank to meet him, and take in your hand the staff that was turned into a snake. 16 Say to him, 'The LORD, the God of the Hebrews, sent me to you to say, "Let my people go, so that they may worship me in the wilderness." But until now you have not lis-

q Heb *am uncircumcised of lips*; see 6.12

6.28–7.7 A recapitulation of earlier passages, underscoring the fact that when Moses and Aaron address Pharaoh, they represent the Lord. **6.30** An echo of 6.12. **7.1–2** An echo of 4.16. **7.2** An echo of 6.11. **7.3–5** An echo of 3.19–20; 4.21. **7.3** *Wonders* anticipates vv. 8–13. **7.4** *Great acts of judgment* echoes 6.6; cf. 12.12. **7.5** *Shall know* echoes 6.7 and anticipates v. 17. *Stretch out my hand* (see note on 3.20) echoes 6.6 and anticipates the first three plagues (see 7.19; 8.5–6, 16–17). **7.7** In traditional literature and regularly in the narrative traditions of the Hebrew Bible, the older brother is subordinated to the younger. **7.8–13** See note on 4.2. Here, as in the first three plagues, Aaron performs the signs with his own staff and not Israel but Pharaoh is the object. **7.9** *Snake.* See note on 4.2–5; in Ezek 29.3; 32.2 the term is used to describe a pharaoh as a "dragon." **7.11** *Magicians.* The Hebrew is a loanword from Egyptian, used in the Pentateuch only of Egyptians. **7.12** *Swallowed.* Cf. 15.12. The one staff swallowing the many recalls the dream Egypt's magicians could not interpret (Gen 41.1–7). The magicians' competition with Aaron here and in the first three plagues prefigures the contest between the Lord and Pharaoh. **7.13** *Hardened*, "stiffened"; see note on 4.21. **7.14–12.32** The ten plagues appear to comprise different traditions; Pss 78; 105 count no more than eight of them. Here they are arranged in three sets of three plus a climatic tenth. Although some see the plagues as a plausible series of natural disasters, the narrative distinguishes their incredible, unprecedented (9.18, 24; 10.6, 14; 11.6) character; the tenth admits of no "natural" explanation. **7.14–25** Afflicting Egypt's deified life source recalls the genocide at the Nile (1.22). **7.14** *Hardened*, lit. "heavy"; see note on 4.21. **7.15** Each set of three plagues begins with Moses alone confronting Pharaoh in the morning (cf. 8.20; 9.13). Moses' concern in 3.11 was for naught. *Turned* anticipates the coming plague (see vv. 17, 20). *Snake*, the term used in 4.3. **7.16** An

can't drink

tened. 17 Thus says the LORD, "By this you shall know that I am the LORD." See, with the staff that is in my hand I will strike the water that is in the Nile, and it shall be turned to blood. 18 The fish in the river shall die, the river itself shall stink, and the Egyptians shall be unable to drink water from the Nile.' " 19 The LORD said to Moses, "Say to Aaron, 'Take your staff and stretch out your hand over the waters of Egypt—over its rivers, its canals, and its ponds, and all its pools of water—so that they may become blood; and there shall be blood throughout the whole land of Egypt, even in vessels of wood and in vessels of stone.' "

20 Moses and Aaron did just as the LORD commanded. In the sight of Pharaoh and of his officials he lifted up the staff and struck the water in the river, and all the water in the river was turned into blood, 21 and the fish in the river died. The river stank so that the Egyptians could not drink its water, and there was blood throughout the whole land of Egypt. 22 But the magicians of Egypt did the same by their secret arts; so Pharaoh's heart remained hardened, and he would not listen to them, as the LORD had said. 23 Pharaoh turned and went into his house, and he did not take even this to heart. 24 And all the Egyptians had to dig along the Nile for water to drink, for they could not drink the water of the river.

25 Seven days passed after the LORD had struck the Nile.

The Second Plague: Frogs

8 r Then the LORD said to Moses, "Go to Pharaoh and say to him, 'Thus says the LORD: Let my people go, so that they may worship me. 2 If you refuse to let them go, I will plague your whole country with frogs. 3 The river shall swarm with frogs; they shall come up into your palace, into your bedchamber and your bed, and into the houses of your officials and of your people,s and into your ovens and your kneading bowls. 4 The frogs shall come up on you and on your people and on all your officials.' " 5 t And the LORD said to Moses, "Say to Aaron, 'Stretch out your hand with your staff over the rivers, the canals, and the pools, and make frogs come up on the land of Egypt.' " 6 So Aaron stretched out his hand over the waters of Egypt; and the frogs came up and covered the land of Egypt. 7 But the magicians did the same by their secret arts, and brought frogs up on the land of Egypt.

8 Then Pharaoh called Moses and Aaron, and said, "Pray to the LORD to take away the frogs from me and my people, and I will let the people go to sacrifice to the LORD." 9 Moses said to Pharaoh, "Kindly tell me when I am to pray for you and for your officials and for your people, that the frogs may be removed from you and your houses and be left only in the Nile." 10 And he said, "Tomorrow." Moses said, "As you say! So that you may know that there is no one like the LORD

can't cook

r Ch 7.26 in Heb   s Gk: Heb upon your people
t Ch 8.1 in Heb

---

allusion to 5.1–4. **7.17** *Know.* See note on 5.2. *It,* the water. **7.18** *Shall stink.* Cf. 5.21. **7.19** *Canals,* plural of the same word translated "Nile." *Pools of water,* a term used in Gen 1.10, suggesting perhaps that the plagues, like the flood, reverse the order of creation. *Vessels,* added for clarity; this fact differentiates the plague from a "natural" disaster of the Nile. **7.20** *Struck.* See note on 2.11. **7.20–21** *The river,* in Hebrew refers to "the Nile." **7.22** Where the *magicians* found water to turn to blood is not explained. *Hardened,* "stiffened." See note on 4.21. The sentence repeats v. 13 verbatim, lending coherence to the narrative. **7.23** *Turned,* did an about-face. **7.25** *Seven days,* a round number. The unusual waiting period allows the Nile to return to normal and serve as the source of the next plague (see 8.3). *Struck.* See v. 20.

8.1–15 The first of four plagues connected with animals is remarkable for its extent. The magicians can produce frogs, ironically compounding the plague, but they cannot remove them. **8.1** Cf. 7.16. **8.3** *The river,* "the Nile." *Swarm.* Cf. Gen 1.20; see note on Ex 1.7, in whose light the plague is poetic justice. *Kneading bowls.* The first plague made it impossible to drink, the second to cook. **8.5** *Stretch out.* See note on 7.5; an echo of 7.19. **8.6** *Covered,* a motif recurring in the plagues of hail, locusts, and darkness. **8.8** Recalling 7.22, one is surprised that now *Pharaoh calls Moses and Aaron. Pray,* entreat. *From me.* The plague was directed at Pharaoh first (vv. 3–4). **8.9** *That the frogs may be removed.* In Hebrew the verb is active, "to cut off the frogs." **8.10** *Know.* See 7.17; Moses is "calling the shot" to demonstrate the plague is directed by Yahweh.

our God, 11 the frogs shall leave you and your houses and your officials and your people; they shall be left only in the Nile." 12 Then Moses and Aaron went out from Pharaoh; and Moses cried out to the LORD concerning the frogs that he had brought upon Pharaoh.u 13 And the LORD did as Moses requested: the frogs died in the houses, the courtyards, and the fields. 14 And they gathered them together in heaps, and the land stank. 15 But when Pharaoh saw that there was a respite, he hardened his heart, and would not listen to them, just as the LORD had said.

The Third Plague: Gnats

16   Then the LORD said to Moses, "Say to Aaron, 'Stretch out your staff and strike the dust of the earth, so that it may become gnats throughout the whole land of Egypt.'" 17 And they did so; Aaron stretched out his hand with his staff and struck the dust of the earth, and gnats came on humans and animals alike; all the dust of the earth turned into gnats throughout the whole land of Egypt. 18 The magicians tried to produce gnats by their secret arts, but they could not. There were gnats on both humans and animals. 19 And the magicians said to Pharaoh, "This is the finger of God!" But Pharaoh's heart was hardened, and he would not listen to them, just as the LORD had said.

The Fourth Plague: Flies

20   Then the LORD said to Moses, "Rise early in the morning and present yourself before Pharaoh, as he goes out to the water, and say to him, 'Thus says the LORD: Let my people go, so that they may worship me. 21 For if you will not let my people go, I will send swarms of flies on you, your officials, and your people, and into your houses; and the houses of the Egyptians shall be filled with swarms of flies; so also the land where they live. 22 But on that day I will set apart the land of Goshen, where my people live, so that no swarms of flies shall be there, that you may know that I the LORD am in this land. 23 Thus I will make a distinctionv between my people and your people. This sign shall appear tomorrow.'" 24 The LORD did so, and great swarms of flies came into the house of Pharaoh and into his officials' houses; in all of Egypt the land was ruined because of the flies.

u Or frogs, as he had agreed with Pharaoh
v Gk Vg: Heb will set redemption

8.12 *Cried out*, used in 14.15; 15.25 as well as in 3.7; 12.30. 8.13 *Died in*, in Hebrew "died from," meaning that the frogs in these areas died; for a similar usage, see 9.6–7. 8.14 *They*, the Egyptians. 8.15 *Hardened*, "made heavy"; see note on 4.21.

8.16–19   The term *gnats*, or mosquitoes, which are indigenous to Egypt, has also been interpreted as "lice," which are not. The last plague in each set of three is narrated briefly; there is no encounter with Pharaoh and no mention of removing the pest. 8.17 *Animals*. As in the flood story of Gen 6–9, animals are innocent victims, here afflicted to punish the Egyptians. *All the dust of the earth turned into gnats*, an impossible, therefore amazing, feat; cf. 7.19. 8.18 See v. 7. 8.19 *This is . . . God*. To acknowledge God's power was an explicit purpose of the preceding two plagues (7.17; 8.10). *Hardened*, "stiffened." See note on 4.21.

8.20–32   The Hebrew word translated *flies* occurs only in connection with this plague and is not precisely defined. It may derive from the sense of "swarm"; Jewish tradition interprets "wild animals." The word resembles the word for "locusts" (eighth plague) and the sense of "fly" suits Ps 78.45. 8.20 *Morning*. See note on 7.15. *Present yourself*, "position yourself," as in 2.4; 7.15 in which the term is translated with the verb "to stand." 8.21 This verse is an echo of vv. 3–4, forging coherence with the second plague. *Flies*. See note on 8.20–32. *Send*. The Hebrew term is of the same root as *let . . . go*. *Filled*, a verbal link with the first plague, rendered *passed* in 7.25. 8.22 *Set apart*. As in the fifth (9.4), seventh (9.26), ninth (10.23), and tenth (11.7; 12.23) plagues the Israelites are miraculously spared; see also note on 14.1–31. Segregating the Hebrews, by which Egypt had asserted its superiority (Gen 43.32; 46.34), is turned to Israel's advantage. *Goshen*. See Gen 45.10; the name may derive from Arabs who spread into Egypt in the seventh century B.C.E. *Know*. See note on 8.19. *In this land*, lit. "in the midst of the land." 8.23 *Sign*, as in 4.8–9. *Tomorrow* recalls 8.10. 8.24 *The LORD* effects this plague without the intermediation of Moses or Aaron. *Great swarms of flies*, lit. "a heavy swarm-of-flies"; see note on 4.10. *Ruined* evokes "corrupt"

25 Then Pharaoh summoned Moses and Aaron, and said, "Go, sacrifice to your God within the land." 26 But Moses said, "It would not be right to do so; for the sacrifices that we offer to the LORD our God are offensive to the Egyptians. If we offer in the sight of the Egyptians sacrifices that are offensive to them, will they not stone us? 27 We must go a three days' journey into the wilderness and sacrifice to the LORD our God as he commands us." 28 So Pharaoh said, "I will let you go to sacrifice to the LORD your God in the wilderness, provided you do not go very far away. Pray for me." 29 Then Moses said, "As soon as I leave you, I will pray to the LORD that the swarms of flies may depart tomorrow from Pharaoh, from his officials, and from his people; only do not let Pharaoh again deal falsely by not letting the people go to sacrifice to the LORD." 30 So Moses went out from Pharaoh and prayed to the LORD. 31 And the LORD did as Moses asked: he removed the swarms of flies from Pharaoh, from his officials, and from his people; not one remained. 32 But Pharaoh hardened his heart this time also, and would not let the people go.

The Fifth Plague: Livestock Diseased

9 Then the LORD said to Moses, "Go to Pharaoh, and say to him, 'Thus says the LORD, the God of the Hebrews: Let my people go, so that they may worship me. 2 For if you refuse to let them go and still hold them, 3 the hand of the LORD will strike with a deadly pestilence your livestock in the field: the horses, the donkeys, the camels, the herds, and the flocks. 4 But the LORD will make a distinction between the livestock of Israel and the livestock of Egypt, so that nothing shall die of all that belongs to the Israelites.'" 5 The LORD set a time, saying, "Tomorrow the LORD will do this thing in the land." 6 And on the next day the LORD did so; all the livestock of the Egyptians died, but of the livestock of the Israelites not one died. 7 Pharaoh inquired and found that not one of the livestock of the Israelites was dead. But the heart of Pharaoh was hardened, and he would not let the people go.

The Sixth Plague: Boils

8 Then the LORD said to Moses and Aaron, "Take handfuls of soot from the kiln, and let Moses throw it in the air in the sight of Pharaoh. 9 It shall become

---

and "destroy" from the same Hebrew root in Gen 6.11–13. **8.25–27** Cf. 5.3. **8.26** The Hebrew terms for *right* and *so* play on the same root. *Offensive*, an "abomination." See note on 8.22. Egypt abominates Israelite sheepherding (Gen 46.34), and Israel would offer sheep to its God; cf. 12.3–5. **8.29** *Tomorrow*, emphasized in the Hebrew. *Only*, rendered *provided* in v. 28; Moses' reply plays on Pharaoh's rhetoric. *Deal falsely*, play a dirty trick (e.g., Gen 31.7). **8.31** *Removed*, lit. "caused to depart," the Hebrew root used in v. 29 and of the removal of the frogs in vv. 9–11. *Remained*, another verbal link with the second plague (translated *be left* in v. 9). **8.32** *Hardened*, "made heavy" (see 8.15).

9.1–7 The affliction of Egypt's animals, anticipated in the third plague (see note on 8.17), is resumed in the sixth (vv. 9–10), seventh (9.19–22, 25), and tenth (11.5; 12.29) plagues. The Israelites' livestock is spared and will accompany them out of Egypt (10.26; 12.32, 38). Pestilence becomes a curse for the Israelites to shun (Lev 26.25; Deut 28.21). **9.1** The freedom refrain (7.16; 8.1, 20). **9.2** *Hold*, the Hebrew root of *hardened* in 7.13, 22; 8.19 (see note on 4.21). **9.3** *The LORD*, as in the preceding plague (see note on 8.24). *Strike with a deadly pestilence*, lit. "will be there . . . , a very heavy pestilence." "Will-be-there" is of the same root as the divine name (see note on 3.14); on "heavy," see note on 4.10. *Camels*, an anachronism; camels weren't used in Israel in substantial numbers until ca. 600 B.C.E. and in Egypt even later. **9.4** *Distinction*, as in the preceding plague (8.22–23). **9.5** See 8.10, 23. *Thing*, Hebrew *davar*, also used in *nothing* (v. 4) and in the phrase translated *did so* (v. 6), a play on *pestilence* (Hebrew *dever*) in v. 3. **9.6** *All the livestock*, a detail that, like *all the water* in 7.20, is inconsistent with what follows; some of Egypt's livestock will be explicitly affected by the sixth (9.10), seventh (9.19–21), and tenth (11.5; 12.29) plagues. **9.7** *Inquired*, lit. "sent," an ironic play in Hebrew on the cognate *let go* (v. 1). *Was hardened*, lit. "became heavy" (see 8.15, 32).

9.8–12 See note on 8.16–19; Pharaoh is not addressed, but he is to witness the transformation of soot into boils. Boils is the first plague to affect humans directly; the "boils of Egypt" is a curse (Deut 28.27). **9.8** The Hebrew terms for *handful* and *soot* form a wordplay. *Moses*. Moses and Aaron collect the soot, but only Moses effects the plague by throwing the soot. **9.8, 10** *In the air,*

fine dust all over the land of Egypt, and shall cause festering boils on humans and animals throughout the whole land of Egypt." 10 So they took soot from the kiln, and stood before Pharaoh, and Moses threw it in the air, and it caused festering boils on humans and animals. 11 The magicians could not stand before Moses because of the boils, for the boils afflicted the magicians as well as all the Egyptians. 12 But the LORD hardened the heart of Pharaoh, and he would not listen to them, just as the LORD had spoken to Moses.

The Seventh Plague: Thunder and Hail

13 Then the LORD said to Moses, "Rise up early in the morning and present yourself before Pharaoh, and say to him, 'Thus says the LORD, the God of the Hebrews: Let my people go, so that they may worship me. 14 For this time I will send all my plagues upon you yourself, and upon your officials, and upon your people, so that you may know that there is no one like me in all the earth. 15 For by now I could have stretched out my hand and struck you and your people with pestilence, and you would have been cut off from the earth. 16 But this is why I have let you live: to show you my power, and to make my name resound through all the earth. 17 You are still exalting yourself against my people, and will not let them go. 18 Tomorrow at this time I will cause the heaviest hail to fall that has ever fallen in Egypt from the day it was founded until now. 19 Send, therefore, and have your livestock and everything that you have in the open field brought to a secure place; every human or animal that is in the open field and is not brought under shelter will die when the hail comes down upon them.' " 20 Those officials of Pharaoh who feared the word of the LORD hurried their slaves and livestock off to a secure place. 21 Those who did not regard the word of the LORD left their slaves and livestock in the open field.

22 The LORD said to Moses, "Stretch out your hand toward heaven so that hail may fall on the whole land of Egypt, on humans and animals and all the plants of the field in the land of Egypt." 23 Then Moses stretched out his staff toward heaven, and the LORD sent thunder and hail, and fire came down on the earth. And the LORD rained hail on the land of Egypt; 24 there was hail with fire flashing continually in the midst of it, such heavy hail as had never fallen in all the land of Egypt since it became a nation. 25 The hail struck down everything that was in the

---

lit. "heavenward." **9.11** The *magicians*, who increasingly fail, are not only beaten but ridiculed. *Could not*, a motif; cf. 7.18 (*be unable*); 7.21, 24; 8.18. **9.12** *Hardened*, lit. "stiffened"; this is the first time the Lord brings on Pharaoh's stubbornness; see note on 4.21.

9.13–35 The first in the third set of plagues (see note on 7.15) is drawn out. Moses explains the reason for prolonging the plagues (vv. 14–16). The hail is extraordinary for its combination with fire, its unprecedented extent (vv. 18, 23–24), and the exemption of the Israelites (v. 26). Pharaoh's temporary surrender (v. 27) is an anticlimax. **9.13** *Present yourself*. See note on 8.20. The rest of the verse echoes 9.1. **9.14** *All my plagues*. This is curious; perhaps it refers to the severity of the plague, or *this time* refers to the set of three plagues. *There is no one like me*. The claim carries greater conviction following the utter defeat of the magicians. **9.15** *Stretched*, rendered *send* in v. 14; cf. note on 3.20. *Struck*. See note on 2.11. Until now only the cattle have been afflicted with *pestilence* (v. 3). **9.16** *To make ... resound*, lit. "to tell"; cf. 10.2; 12.27–28; 13.8; cf. Ps 78.1–6. **9.17** *Exalting*, elevating (see Prov 4.8). **9.18** *Tomorrow*. See 8.10. *Heaviest hail*, a close echo in Hebrew of "a very heavy pestilence" (see note on 9.3). *Has ever fallen*. See note on 7.14–12.32. **9.19** *Send*, proclaim through messengers. *Livestock*. According to v. 6, all the livestock of the Egyptians died in the fifth plague; see note on 9.6. The plague is directed against life supports, not life itself. **9.20** *Officials*. See 7.10. *A secure place*; rather *shelters* (v. 19). **9.21** *Did not regard*, a faint echo of *did not take ... to heart* (7.23). Egypt's willfulness is ultimately responsible for its catastrophic fate; see note on 1.22. **9.22** *Stretch*. See note on 7.5. *Toward heaven*, a link with vv. 8, 10. *Whole land ... on humans and animals* seems dissonant with vv. 20–21; for consistency one assumes that the persons and livestock of the God-fearing are excepted. *Plants of the field*, also in v. 25, evokes Gen 2.5; see note on 7.19. **9.23** Extending the arm (v. 22) and extending the *staff* are viewed as the same act, as in 10.12–13; 14.16, 21. *Thunder* (lit. "sounds") and *fire* anticipate the Sinai revelation (19.16, 18). The combination of *heaven*, *fire*, and *rained* recalls the destruction of Sodom and Gomorrah (Gen 19.24). **9.24** *Flashing*, elsewhere only in Ezek 1.4. *Such ... hail*, an echo of *no one like me* (v. 14); the incomparable deity effects unprecedented phenomena; cf. also v. 18.

open field throughout all the land of Egypt, both human and animal; the hail also struck down all the plants of the field, and shattered every tree in the field. 26 Only in the land of Goshen, where the Israelites were, there was no hail.

27 Then Pharaoh summoned Moses and Aaron, and said to them, "This time I have sinned; the LORD is in the right, and I and my people are in the wrong. 28 Pray to the LORD! Enough of God's thunder and hail! I will let you go; you need stay no longer." 29 Moses said to him, "As soon as I have gone out of the city, I will stretch out my hands to the LORD; the thunder will cease, and there will be no more hail, so that you may know that the earth is the LORD's. 30 But as for you and your officials, I know that you do not yet fear the LORD God." 31 (Now the flax and the barley were ruined, for the barley was in the ear and the flax was in bud. 32 But the wheat and the spelt were not ruined, for they are late in coming up.) 33 So Moses left Pharaoh, went out of the city, and stretched out his hands to the LORD; then the thunder and the hail ceased, and the rain no longer poured down on the earth. 34 But when Pharaoh saw that the rain and the hail and the thunder had ceased, he sinned once more and hardened his heart, he and his officials. 35 So the heart of Pharaoh was hardened, and he would not let the Israelites go, just as the LORD had spoken through Moses.

The Eighth Plague: Locusts

10 Then the LORD said to Moses, "Go to Pharaoh; for I have hardened his heart and the heart of his officials, in order that I may show these signs of mine among them, 2 and that you may tell your children and grandchildren how I have made fools of the Egyptians and what signs I have done among them—so that you may know that I am the LORD."

3 So Moses and Aaron went to Pharaoh, and said to him, "Thus says the LORD, the God of the Hebrews, 'How long will you refuse to humble yourself before me? Let my people go, so that they may worship me. 4 For if you refuse to let my people go, tomorrow I will bring locusts into your country. 5 They shall cover the surface of the land, so that no one will be able to see the land. They shall devour the last remnant left you after the hail, and they shall devour every tree of yours that grows in the field. 6 They shall fill your houses, and the houses of all your officials and of all the Egyptians—something that neither your parents nor your grandparents have seen, from the day they came on earth to this day.'" Then he turned and went out from Pharaoh.

9.25 *Struck . . . shattered*, parallelism (see note on 3.15); cf. Ps 29.5. **9.26** See note on 8.22. **9.27** *Summoned*, lit. "sent and called for," using the Hebrew rendered *send* in v. 19. *In the right*, legal terminology (e.g., Deut 25.1) suggesting the Lord's superiority is proved by the evidence of the plagues. *In the right* and *in the wrong* also connote the "righteous" and "wicked," again evoking Sodom and Gomorrah (see note on v. 23; cf. Gen 18.23). **9.28** *Pray*. Cf. 8.28. *Enough*, lit. "it is (too) great"; cf. 1.9, where *more numerous* is lit. "too great." *God's thunder*, idiomatic for "very great thunder." **9.29** *Out of the city*, an indication of leaving the royal precincts or possibly a suggestion that the Lord may be contacted only outside the pagan site. *Stretch*, or "spread," a gesture of prayer (e.g., 1 Kings 8.22; Isa 1.15). *You may know* echoes v. 14. **9.30** Moses explains why he needed to provide additional proof that God is the supreme power by predicting the end of the plague. **9.31–32** Some crops had to survive to serve as fodder for the locusts in the next plague (10.5, 12, 15). **9.33** *Stretched*. See note on 9.29. *Rain*, not mentioned except in *cause . . . to fall* (v. 18). **9.34** *Sinned*. See v. 27. *Hardened*, "made heavy" (see note on 4.21). **9.35** *Hardened*, "stiffened" by itself (see note on 4.21).

10.1–20 The locusts devour the remaining vegetation and cover the land (vv. 5, 15), providing a transition from the devastation of crops by hail to the darkness that follows. For the first time Pharaoh is pressured to release the Hebrews (v. 7), anticipating the tenth plague (12.33). Locusts are a curse (Deut 28.38); cf. note on 9.8–12. **10.1** *Hardened*, "made heavy," as in 9.34. **10.2** *Tell*. See note on 9.16. **10.3** *How long*, a rhetorical addition to the formula in 9.13. *Humble yourself*, the same Hebrew root translated *oppress* in 1.11–12; Pharaoh must receive poetic justice. **10.4** An echo of 8.2. *Tomorrow*. See 8.10. **10.5** The imagery is elaborated in Joel 1; cf. Judg 6.5; 7.12. Here human and animal life are only indirectly affected, as the severest plague is saved for last. *Cover the surface*. Cf. Num 22.5, 11. *Remnant*. See note on 9.31–32. **10.6** Another echo of the frog plague (8.3–6), whose relative harmlessness contrasts with the severity of the locust plague. *Turned*, "faced" away, foreshadow-

7 Pharaoh's officials said to him, "How long shall this fellow be a snare to us? Let the people go, so that they may worship the LORD their God; do you not yet understand that Egypt is ruined?" 8 So Moses and Aaron were brought back to Pharaoh, and he said to them, "Go, worship the LORD your God! But which ones are to go?" 9 Moses said, "We will go with our young and our old; we will go with our sons and daughters and with our flocks and herds, because we have the LORD's festival to celebrate." 10 He said to them, "The LORD indeed will be with you, if ever I let your little ones go with you! Plainly, you have some evil purpose in mind. 11 No, never! Your men may go and worship the LORD, for that is what you are asking." And they were driven out from Pharaoh's presence.

12 Then the LORD said to Moses, "Stretch out your hand over the land of Egypt, so that the locusts may come upon it and eat every plant in the land, all that the hail has left." 13 So Moses stretched out his staff over the land of Egypt, and the LORD brought an east wind upon the land all that day and all that night; when morning came, the east wind had brought the locusts. 14 The locusts came upon all the land of Egypt and settled on the whole country of Egypt, such a dense swarm of locusts as had never been before, nor ever shall be again. 15 They covered the surface of the whole land, so that the land was black; and they ate all the plants in the land and all the fruit of the trees that the hail had left; nothing green was left, no tree, no plant in the field, in all the land of Egypt. 16 Pharaoh hurriedly summoned Moses and Aaron and said, "I have sinned against the LORD your God, and against you. 17 Do forgive my sin just this once, and pray to the LORD your God that at the least he remove this deadly thing from me." 18 So he went out from Pharaoh and prayed to the LORD. 19 The LORD changed the wind into a very strong west wind, which lifted the locusts and drove them into the Red Sea; w not a single locust was left in all the country of Egypt. 20 But the LORD hardened Pharaoh's heart, and he would not let the Israelites go.

The Ninth Plague: Darkness

21 Then the LORD said to Moses, "Stretch out your hand toward heaven so

w Or *Sea of Reeds*

---

ing vv. 28–29. **10.7** *How long* echoes v. 3. *This fellow*, lit. "this" (see note on 32.1). *Snare.* Cf., e.g., 23.33; 34.12; Deut 7.16. *People.* The Hebrew has "persons," not the collective term "people." *Ruined*, not the Hebrew term so translated in 8.24. **10.8** In contrast to 8.8 and v. 16 below, Pharaoh does not directly summon *Moses and Aaron. Which ones.* Pharaoh is prepared to make a concession as in 8.25–28, but again with restrictions. **10.9** *Festival to celebrate.* See note on 5.1. **10.10** *Evil* may pun in Hebrew on the name of the Egyptian god Ra (Re). **10.11** *No, never*, or "No indeed," echoing *indeed* in v. 10. *Men*, as in 23.17; 34.23; Deut 16.16. *They were driven*, lit. "he drove them"; some versions read "they drove them." *Presence*, "face," again (see note on 10.6) foreshadowing vv. 28–29. **10.12** *Stretch*, as in 9.22; see note on 7.5. **10.13** *Staff.* See note on 9.23. *East wind*, an anticipation of 14.21. *All that night*, "all night," exactly as in 14.20. **10.14** *Dense swarm*, lit. "very heavy"; see note on 4.10. **10.15** *Covered.* See note on 10.5. *The land was black*, or "and the land became dark," anticipating the plague of darkness (vv. 21–22). *All the plants*, inconsistent with the Israelites' use of herbs and hyssop (12.8, 22) unless Goshen is spared. **10.16** *Hurriedly* foreshadows 12.33. *Summoned.* See note on 10.8. *Sinned.* Phar-

aoh has said this before (9.27). **10.17** *Pray* as in 8.8, 28; 9.28. *Deadly thing*, lit. "death," hyperbole here but foreshadowing the tenth plague. **10.19** *West wind*, lit. "sea wind," an Israelite perspective since the Mediterranean lies west of Israel; cf. note on 26.18. References to "sea," *wind*, and *Red Sea* anticipate 14.21–28. *Drove into*, not toward but lit. "into," different from *driven out* in v. 11; cf. Joel 2.20. *Red Sea*, the "Sea of Reeds," possibly one of the lagoons along the Mediterranean coast of the Sinai Peninsula; see note on 14.2. Few of the geographical sites in the Exodus narrative can be identified, and it is possible the Red Sea is meant; although it is unrealistic here, it may have been adopted to present a later Israelite audience with a well-known body of water. *Not a single . . . was left*, the same Hebrew phrase rendered *not one remained* in 8.31, an anticipation of 14.28. **10.20** *Hardened*, "stiffened," as in 9.35.

10.21–29 Because light symbolizes freedom (e.g., Isa 9.1; Lam 3.1–2, where darkness and "oppression" are juxtaposed), the plague of darkness gives Egypt a taste of enslavement (see v. 23) and Israel a foretaste of liberation. The darkness also foreshadows the tenth plague (see 12.29). Cf. Deut 28.29. **10.21** *Stretch*, as in v. 12; see note on 7.5. That the darkness *can be felt* distinguishes

that there may be darkness over the land of Egypt, a darkness that can be felt." 22 So Moses stretched out his hand toward heaven, and there was dense darkness in all the land of Egypt for three days. 23 People could not see one another, and for three days they could not move from where they were; but all the Israelites had light where they lived. 24 Then Pharaoh summoned Moses, and said, "Go, worship the LORD. Only your flocks and your herds shall remain behind. Even your children may go with you." 25 But Moses said, "You must also let us have sacrifices and burnt offerings to sacrifice to the LORD our God. 26 Our livestock also must go with us; not a hoof shall be left behind, for we must choose some of them for the worship of the LORD our God, and we will not know what to use to worship the LORD until we arrive there." 27 But the LORD hardened Pharaoh's heart, and he was unwilling to let them go. 28 Then Pharaoh said to him, "Get away from me! Take care that you do not see my face again, for on the day you see my face you shall die." 29 Moses said, "Just as you say! I will never see your face again."

Warning of the Final Plague

11 The LORD said to Moses, "I will bring one more plague upon Pharaoh and upon Egypt; afterwards he will let you go from here; indeed, when he lets you go, he will drive you away. 2 Tell the people that every man is to ask his neighbor and every woman is to ask her neighbor for objects of silver and gold." 3 The LORD gave the people favor in the sight of the Egyptians. Moreover, Moses himself was a man of great importance in the land of Egypt, in the sight of Pharaoh's officials and in the sight of the people.

4 Moses said, "Thus says the LORD: About midnight I will go out through Egypt. 5 Every firstborn in the land of Egypt shall die, from the firstborn of Pharaoh who sits on his throne to the firstborn of the female slave who is behind the handmill, and all the firstborn of the livestock. 6 Then there will be a loud cry throughout the whole land of Egypt, such as has never been or will ever be again. 7 But not a dog shall growl at any of the Israelites — not at people, not at animals — so that you may know that the

---

it from ordinary darkness. **10.22** *Three days*, the only notice of a plague's duration since 7.25, forming a frame around the first nine plagues. **10.23** *The Israelites had light*. See note on 8.22. **10.24** Pharaoh reverses himself (see v. 10). **10.25** *Let us have*, lit. "give into our hands"; Pharaoh must contribute toward, and not merely tolerate, Israelite cult *sacrifices*, slaughtered animals that are partly burned on the altar and partly eaten by the worshiper. **10.26** *What to use*, or "how." **10.27** *Hardened*, "stiffened," as in v. 20. **10.28** *Take care*, be on your guard. **10.29** It was Pharaoh who summoned Moses in the eighth and ninth plagues; and he will summon Moses and Aaron after the tenth (12.31). Moses defies Pharaoh's warning (11.8).

11.1–10 The tenth plague has been adumbrated since 4.22–23. In light of 13.1–2, another purpose to slaying both human and animal (v. 5) firstborns is suggested: the Lord exercises his right to collect, as it were, all firstborn males. **11.1** The Hebrew term translated *plague* is of the root "touch" and connotes disease; it is different from the word also translated *plague* in 9.14; and *strike* in 12.23. "Touch" figured in 4.25, just after the firstborn plague was first revealed. *Upon*, against. *Afterwards*, as predicted in 3.20. *Drive you away*. The Hebrew adds "completely"; others in-

terpret "as he would divorce a bride." **11.2** Predicted in 3.22 (see note there). *Tell*, lit. "say now in the ears of." *And gold*, lit. "and objects of gold." 3.22; 12.35 mention *clothing*, which term is also found here in some versions. **11.3** *Sight*, lit. "eyes"; that the people found favor is predicted in 3.21. *Man ... importance*, ironic (see 10.28–29). Again (see 10.7) Pharaoh's underlings arrive at the truth before he does. **11.4** It is surprising, in view of 10.28–29 and the omission of any reference to Pharaoh here, that this speech is addressed to Pharaoh in person (see v. 8). *Midnight*, an hour associated with death (Job 34.20; cf. Gen 32.23–25; Ex 4.24). *Go out*, the verb denoting "exodus" (see note on 3.10). **11.5** *Firstborn*, that is "firstborn male"; see note on 13.1–2. *Female slave*. Egypt had other than Hebrew slaves. *Handmill*, a stationary horizontal round stone with a mobile upper grinding stone; using it was the most menial chore (Isa 47.1–2). The *livestock* were all said to have perished (see note on 9.6). **11.6** *Cry*, poetic justice: see note on 3.7. *Never been*. See note on 7.14–12.32. *Will ... again* echoes *never ... again* in 10.28–29. **11.7** *Growl*, lit. "chop with the tongue," hence "bark"; cf. Josh 10.21. While Egypt is beset by unprecedented screams, Israel will not be disturbed by so much as a barking dog. *Distinction*. Cf. *distinction* in 9.4, *set apart* in 8.22;

LORD makes a distinction between Egypt and Israel. 8 Then all these officials of yours shall come down to me, and bow low to me, saying, 'Leave us, you and all the people who follow you.' After that I will leave." And in hot anger he left Pharaoh.

9 The LORD said to Moses, "Pharaoh will not listen to you, in order that my wonders may be multiplied in the land of Egypt." 10 Moses and Aaron performed all these wonders before Pharaoh; but the LORD hardened Pharaoh's heart, and he did not let the people of Israel go out of his land.

The First Passover Instituted

12 The LORD said to Moses and Aaron in the land of Egypt: 2 This month shall mark for you the beginning of months; it shall be the first month of the year for you. 3 Tell the whole congregation of Israel that on the tenth of this month they are to take a lamb for each family, a lamb for each household. 4 If a household is too small for a whole lamb, it shall join its closest neighbor in obtaining one; the lamb shall be divided in proportion to the number of people who eat of it. 5 Your lamb shall be without blemish, a year-old male; you may take it from the sheep or from the goats. 6 You shall keep it until the fourteenth day of this month; then the whole assembled congregation of Israel shall slaughter it at twilight. 7 They shall take some of the blood and put it on the two doorposts and the lintel of the houses in which they eat it. 8 They shall eat the lamb that same night; they shall eat it roasted over the fire with unleavened bread and bitter herbs. 9 Do not eat any of it raw or boiled in water, but roasted over the fire, with its

---

see note on 8.22. **11.8** *Officials*, lit. "servants," who will now "serve" the Lord. In Hebrew *these* and *to me* sound alike, reinforcing the sense that Pharaoh's courtiers will render homage to God. *Left Pharaoh*. See note on 11.4. **11.9** The plagues narrative pauses, echoing the story's beginning (7.3–4). **11.10** *Hardened*. See note on 4.21.
12.1–28 Although the Passover ceremony may have its origins in a spring fertility rite, it serves two functions here: the immediate one of warding off the plague (vv. 7, 13, 22–23) and the perennial one of commemorating the exodus redemption (vv. 14, 24–27). The week-long Festival of Unleavened Bread (vv. 14–20), which immediately follows (Lev 23.5–6; Num 28.16–17) and coalesces with Passover (Deut 16.1–8; but see Ex 23.15; 34.18), is not celebrated before leaving Egypt but is ordained here as it, too, comes to commemorate the exodus (vv. 15–20; 13.3–10). **12.1** *Egypt*. The Egyptian Passover is distinguished from the perennial one (vv. 17, 20). Deut 16.1–8 centralizes the rite at a single shrine (cf. 2 Kings 23.21–23). **12.2** The Bible's cultic calendar begins with the exodus season. The "priestly" term *first month* (Lev 23.5; Num 28.16) is Abib (Hebrew "new ear of grain") elsewhere in the Pentateuch (Ex 13.4; 23.15; 34.18; Deut 16.1) and Nisan (from Babylonian) in postexilic books (Neh 2.1; Esth 3.7). The agricultural calendar begins with the seventh month; see 23.17 and the tenth-century B.C.E. Gezer inscription, which lists agricultural tasks by month. *Mark*, lit. "be." *Beginning*, lit. "head," cognate to *first*. **12.3** *Israel* has not expressly heard from Moses and Aaron since 6.12; its cooperation now reflects the impact of the Lord's wonders. The *tenth* day of the seventh month is the Day of Atonement (Lev 23.27). *Family*, lit. "house of fathers." **12.4** *It shall join . . . in obtaining*, lit. "he and his neighbor closest to his house will take." *The lamb . . . eat of it*, "according to the number of persons, each by how much he eats, you shall divide the lamb." **12.5** *Without blemish*, a stipulation for all sacrificial offerings (e.g., Lev 1.3, 10). *A year-old male*, a typical sacrificial offering (e.g., Num 28.3; 29.2). **12.6** The *fourteenth*, the full moon, a propitious time when the night is brightest; see also Lev 23.34. *The whole assembled congregation*, or "the entire assembly," which does not imply that everyone performed the rite together. *Twilight*, lit. "between the two settings," apparently between sunset and the last of the residual light in the sky. **12.7** See note on 4.25. By performing this apotropaic ritual Israel is again "set apart" from Egypt (11.7). *They eat*, lit. "they shall eat." **12.8** *Same night*. See Num 9.12; Deut 16.4. The sacred meal may also serve to protect the household. *Roasted*. See note on 12.9. *Unleavened bread*, minimally cooked, biscuitlike "matsah" bread used generally in ritual offerings (e.g., Lev 2.4–5; 6.9); leavening removes the flour further from its natural, created state. See the symbolic interpretation in vv. 33–34. *Bitter herbs*, the species is uncertain, but see 1.14. The three components of the offering signify a complete meal. **12.9** The prohibition against eating the offering *raw or boiled* means that it must be *roasted*, which ensures that the blood, the protective element, is removed. Blood, the symbol of life (Gen 9.4; Lev 17.11, 14), is divine property and must be returned to the deity whenever meat is eaten (Lev 17.3–6; Deut 12.16); cf. Deut 16.7, which is har-

head, legs, and inner organs. 10 You shall let none of it remain until the morning; anything that remains until the morning you shall burn. 11 This is how you shall eat it: your loins girded, your sandals on your feet, and your staff in your hand; and you shall eat it hurriedly. It is the passover of the LORD. 12 For I will pass through the land of Egypt that night, and I will strike down every firstborn in the land of Egypt, both human beings and animals; on all the gods of Egypt I will execute judgments: I am the LORD. 13 The blood shall be a sign for you on the houses where you live: when I see the blood, I will pass over you, and no plague shall destroy you when I strike the land of Egypt.

14   This day shall be a day of remembrance for you. You shall celebrate it as a festival to the LORD; throughout your generations you shall observe it as a perpetual ordinance. 15 Seven days you shall eat unleavened bread; on the first day you shall remove leaven from your houses, for whoever eats leavened bread from the first day until the seventh day shall be cut

off from Israel. 16 On the first day you shall hold a solemn assembly, and on the seventh day a solemn assembly; no work shall be done on those days; only what everyone must eat, that alone may be prepared by you. 17 You shall observe the festival of unleavened bread, for on this very day I brought your companies out of the land of Egypt: you shall observe this day throughout your generations as a perpetual ordinance. 18 In the first month, from the evening of the fourteenth day until the evening of the twenty-first day, you shall eat unleavened bread. 19 For seven days no leaven shall be found in your houses; for whoever eats what is leavened shall be cut off from the congregation of Israel, whether an alien or a native of the land. 20 You shall eat nothing leavened; in all your settlements you shall eat unleavened bread.

21   Then Moses called all the elders of Israel and said to them, "Go, select lambs for your families, and slaughter the passover lamb. 22 Take a bunch of hyssop, dip it in the blood that is in the basin, and

---

monized in 2 Chr 35.13. *With its . . . organs*, in contradistinction to the wholly burnt offering (Lev 1.8–9). **12.10** *Let none of it remain*, lest it be profaned; cf. 23.18; Lev 7.15; see notes on 12.8; 10.19. **12.11** *Passover*. The name of the offering and its festival are related to the cognate verb *pass over* in vv. 13, 23, 27. **12.12** *Pass through*, not pass over (see note on 12.11). *Strike*. See note on 2.11. *Firstborn*. See note on 13.1–2. *Gods*. See Num 33.4. By causing so severe a catastrophe in Egypt, the Lord, who has sought acknowledgment among the Egyptians (see 9.14; cf. note on 5.2), defeats Egypt's gods, who, like Pharaoh's magicians (see notes on 7.12; 9.11), prove powerless. Deities other than the Lord are assumed to exist, even if they are ineffectual; cf. 15.11. **12.13** *No plague shall destroy*, rather "no plague will be a destroyer," the demonic agent that brings death ("ravager" in Isa 54.16), distinguished from the deity in v. 23. **12.14** *Celebrate . . . festival*. See note on 5.1. *Perpetual*. See note on 12.1; cf. v. 17. **12.15** See note on 12.1–28. *Remove*, lit. "cause to stop" (see note on 5.5). *Cut off*, a punishment imposed in the priestly Torah literature primarily for serious ritual infractions (e.g., Lev 17.4); because it contrasts with capital punishment (31.14), it may entail divine retribution for transgressions that escape human detection. **12.16** See Lev 23.7–8; Num 28.18,25. *Assembly*, or "convocation." The preparation of food for immediate consumption is permitted during the festival but

prohibited on the sabbath (16.23; 35.3). **12.17** *I brought*. The Passover in Egypt is seen as past. *Companies*. See note on 6.26. **12.18** *Until*, up to the eve of the twenty-first if the festivals of Passover and Unleavened Bread have coalesced (see note on 12.1–28), up through the eve of the twenty-first if the festivals are discrete. **12.19** Cf. v. 15. *Alien*. Aliens who reside among the Israelites by dint of marriage or another circumstance and are circumcised (v. 48) are enjoined to observe most laws (so v. 49) and are protected from abuse (e.g., 22.20–22). **12.20** *Settlements* refers to Israel's future circumstances, as in v. 17. **12.21–28** An elaboration of the laws in vv. 1–13. The Festival of Unleavened Bread, which does not take place the night of the plague, is omitted. **12.21** *Moses*. Cf. v. 28, which includes Aaron. *Lambs*, rather "small cattle," sheep or goats; see v. 5. *Families*, not the term used in v. 3. *Select . . . and slaughter the passover lamb*. The instruction presupposes that the ritual is already familiar; the term *passover* is introduced in v. 11 only after the offering has been described. **12.22** *Hyssop*, a brushlike plant of uncertain identity, used also in purification rites (e.g., Lev 14.4, 6; Num 19.6). *Basin*, to collect the blood of the Passover animal. *Touch*. Cf. 4.25. *None . . . go outside*. The phrasing, absent from the foregoing instructions, suggests the protective function of the ritual; see notes on 12.8; 12.42; see also v. 46.

touch the lintel and the two doorposts with the blood in the basin. None of you shall go outside the door of your house until morning. 23 For the LORD will pass through to strike down the Egyptians; when he sees the blood on the lintel and on the two doorposts, the LORD will pass over that door and will not allow the destroyer to enter your houses to strike you down. 24 You shall observe this rite as a perpetual ordinance for you and your children. 25 When you come to the land that the LORD will give you, as he has promised, you shall keep this observance. 26 And when your children ask you, 'What do you mean by this observance?' 27 you shall say, 'It is the passover sacrifice to the LORD, for he passed over the houses of the Israelites in Egypt, when he struck down the Egyptians but spared our houses'" And the people bowed down and worshiped.

28 The Israelites went and did just as the LORD had commanded Moses and Aaron.

The Tenth Plague: Death of the Firstborn

29 At midnight the LORD struck down all the firstborn in the land of Egypt, from the firstborn of Pharaoh who sat on his throne to the firstborn of the prisoner who was in the dungeon, and all the firstborn of the livestock. 30 Pharaoh arose in the night, he and all his officials and all the Egyptians; and there was a loud cry in Egypt, for there was not a house without someone dead. 31 Then he summoned Moses and Aaron in the night, and said, "Rise up, go away from my people, both you and the Israelites! Go, worship the LORD, as you said. 32 Take your flocks and your herds, as you said, and be gone. And bring a blessing on me too!"

The Exodus: From Rameses to Succoth

33 The Egyptians urged the people to hasten their departure from the land, for they said, "We shall all be dead." 34 So the people took their dough before it was leavened, with their kneading bowls wrapped up in their cloaks on their shoulders. 35 The Israelites had done as Moses told them; they had asked the Egyptians for jewelry of silver and gold, and for clothing, 36 and the LORD had given the people favor in the sight of the Egyptians, so that they let them have what they asked. And so they plundered the Egyptians.

37 The Israelites journeyed from Rameses to Succoth, about six hundred thousand men on foot, besides children. 38 A mixed crowd also went up with them, and livestock in great numbers, both flocks and herds. 39 They baked unleavened cakes of the dough that they had brought out of Egypt; it was not leavened, because they were driven out of Egypt and could not wait, nor had they prepared any provisions for themselves.

12.23 *Pass through.* See note on 12.12. *Strike down,* or "afflict with plague" (twice), cognate to *plague* (v. 13). *The destroyer.* See note on 12.13. **12.24** *Rite,* lit. "word," command. **12.25** Cf., e.g., 3.8, 17; 6.8–9. The topic of rites to be observed once Israel is settled in Canaan is resumed in 13.5. **12.26** See note on 9.16. **12.27** *Struck down.* See note on 12.23. *Worshiped.* See note on 4.31. **12.28** *Aaron.* See note on 12.21.

12.29–30 The fulfillment of 11.4–6, with some variations; cf. note on 11.1–10. **12.29** *Prisoner,* more severe than the image in 11.5. *Dungeon,* lit. "pit," alluding perhaps to Gen 41.14. **12.30** *Arose,* aroused by the outcry. **12.31** *Summoned.* See note on 10.29. Pharaoh's implicit surrender to the Lord is a reversal (see 5.2). **12.32** Pharaoh reverses his refusal in 10.24. *Bring a blessing on me too,* "bless me too" when you worship the Lord. **12.33** *Egyptians.* Cf. 10.7. *Urged,* ironically another rendering of the Hebrew verb used of "stiffening" Pharaoh's heart in 14.4, 8

(hardened; see note on 4.21). *Hasten.* See note on 10.16. *All.* They fear the tenth plague is not the last. **12.34** *Leavened,* a symbolic interpretation of v. 8 (cf. v. 11) and of the Festival of Unleavened Bread; see v. 39. *Kneading bowls,* an echo of 8.3 (7.28 in Hebrew). **12.35** *Told them.* It has not been reported that Moses gave the instruction to ask for jewelry and clothing, although he was so ordered (3.21–22; 11.2–3). *Clothing,* the *cloaks* of v. 34. *Plundered.* See note on 3.22. **12.37** *Rameses.* See 1.11. *Succoth,* hebraization ("Booths") of an Egyptian name, in the area of Pithom (see 1.11). Num 33.4 adds a macabre detail. *Six hundred thousand.* 603,550 in Num 1.46, excluding 8,580 Levite men (Num 4.48). Counting women, children, and the elderly, the total would well exceed 2 million; a large army comprised perhaps 20,000 soldiers. **12.38** *Mixed,* intermarried (Neh 13.3); see Num 11.4; cf. Lev 24.10. The Hebrew term recalls the fourth plague's flies. *Great numbers,* "very heavy" (see note on 4.10). **12.39** See

40 The time that the Israelites had lived in Egypt was four hundred thirty years. 41 At the end of four hundred thirty years, on that very day, all the companies of the LORD went out from the land of Egypt. 42 That was for the LORD a night of vigil, to bring them out of the land of Egypt. That same night is a vigil to be kept for the LORD by all the Israelites throughout their generations.

Directions for the Passover

43 The LORD said to Moses and Aaron: This is the ordinance for the passover: no foreigner shall eat of it, 44 but any slave who has been purchased may eat of it after he has been circumcised; 45 no bound or hired servant may eat of it. 46 It shall be eaten in one house; you shall not take any of the animal outside the house, and you shall not break any of its bones. 47 The whole congregation of Israel shall celebrate it. 48 If an alien who resides with you wants to celebrate the passover to the LORD, all his males shall be circumcised; then he may draw near to celebrate it; he shall be regarded as a native of the land. But no uncircumcised person shall eat of it; 49 there shall be one law for the native and for the alien who resides among you.

50 All the Israelites did just as the LORD had commanded Moses and Aaron.

51 That very day the LORD brought the Israelites out of the land of Egypt, company by company.

13 The LORD said to Moses: 2 Conse-crate to me all the firstborn; whatever is the first to open the womb among the Israelites, of human beings and animals, is mine.

dedicate to sacred purpose

The Festival of Unleavened Bread

3 Moses said to the people, "Remember this day on which you came out of Egypt, out of the house of slavery, because the LORD brought you out from there by strength of hand; no leavened bread shall be eaten. 4 Today, in the month of Abib, you are going out. 5 When the LORD brings you into the land of the Canaanites, the Hittites, the Amorites, the Hivites, and the Jebusites, which he swore to your ancestors to give you, a land flowing with milk and honey, you shall keep this observance in this month. 6 Seven days you shall eat unleavened bread, and on the seventh day there shall be a festival to the LORD. 7 Unleavened bread shall be eaten for seven days; no leavened bread shall be seen in your possession, and no leaven shall be seen among you in all your territory. 8 You shall tell your child on that day, 'It is because of what the LORD did for me when I came out of Egypt.' 9 It

---

note on 12.34. **12.40** *The time . . . lived,* lit. "The dwelling . . . dwelled." *Four hundred thirty.* It is 400 years in Gen 15.13. Gen 15.16 predicts four generations (160 years), a count that conforms to 6.16–20, in which Moses is the fourth generation in Egypt. **12.41** *Companies.* See note on 6.26. **12.42** If the *vigil* is Israel's and not the Lord's (the Hebrew is ambiguous), a protective function for the Passover rite is again suggested (see notes on 12.8; 12.22; see also v. 46). **12.43–49** A resumption of the instructions for the Passover night ritual (vv. 1–13, 21–27); cf. v. 19. Since vv. 14, 28 seems to close the preceding units, the present passage appears to be a codicil. See also Num 9.1–14. **12.43** *Foreigner,* not *alien* (vv. 19, 48–49). **12.44** *Purchased.* The Hebrew adds "for silver" (cf. Gen 37.28). **12.45** *Bound . . . servant,* more likely a transient "resident"; cf. a similar distinction in Lev 22.10–11. **12.46** *Outside.* See note on 12.22. *Bones.* See Num 9.12; cf. Jn 19.36. **12.48** *Alien.* See note on 12.19. *All his males shall be circumcised,* like Abraham and the males of his household (Gen 17.10–14, 23–27). **12.49** *Law,* lit. "instruction" (Hebrew *torah*).

Cf. Lev 24.22. **12.51** A repetition of v. 41, enclosing the codicil. *Company.* See note on 6.26. **13.1–2** The law to consecrate Israel's human and animal firstborn is juxtaposed with the slaying of Egypt's firstborn, as in 34.18–20; Deut 15.19–16.8; see note on 11.1–10. It is assumed on the basis of vv. 12, 15 and all parallel passages that only males are meant (cf. 11.5; 12.29). The elaboration in vv. 11–26 is paralleled by 34.19–20; Num 18.15–18. The parallel law in 22.29–30 does not elaborate a method of consecration. Cf. the practices in Num 18; Deut 15.19–23 (which does not relate to firstborn humans) and the motive in Num 3.11–13, 41, 45; 8.17. **13.3–10** Cf. 12.14–20; differences suggest diverse traditions. **13.3** Cf. 12.14. *House of slavery.* Cf. 20.2. *Strength of hands.* See vv. 9, 14, 16; cf. *mighty hand* (6.1, from the same root) and 3.19. *No leavened bread.* Cf. 12.15. **13.4** *Abib.* See note on 12.2. **13.5** Cf. 3.17; see note on 12.25. **13.6** *Seventh day.* See 12.16. **13.7** In Hebrew *your possession* and *among you* are expressed identically, creating a parallelism (see note on 3.15). **13.8** Cf. 12.26. **13.9** *On your hand, on your fore-*

shall serve for you as a sign on your hand and as a reminder on your forehead, so that the teaching of the LORD may be on your lips; for with a strong hand the LORD brought you out of Egypt. 10 You shall keep this ordinance at its proper time from year to year.

The Consecration of the Firstborn

11 "When the LORD has brought you into the land of the Canaanites, as he swore to you and your ancestors, and has given it to you, 12 you shall set apart to the LORD all that first opens the womb. All the firstborn of your livestock that are males shall be the LORD's. 13 But every firstborn donkey you shall redeem with a sheep; if you do not redeem it, you must break its neck. Every firstborn male among your children you shall redeem. 14 When in the future your child asks you, 'What does this mean?' you shall answer, 'By strength of hand the LORD brought us out of Egypt, from the house of slavery. 15 When Pharaoh stubbornly refused to let us go, the LORD killed all the firstborn in the land of Egypt, from human firstborn to the firstborn of animals. Therefore I sacrifice to the LORD every male that first opens the womb, but every firstborn of my sons I redeem.' 16 It shall serve as a sign on your hand and as an emblem^x on

your forehead that by strength of hand the LORD brought us out of Egypt."

The Pillars of Cloud and Fire

17 When Pharaoh let the people go, God did not lead them by way of the land of the Philistines, although that was nearer; for God thought, "If the people face war, they may change their minds and return to Egypt." 18 So God led the people by the roundabout way of the wilderness toward the Red Sea.^y The Israelites went up out of the land of Egypt prepared for battle. 19 And Moses took with him the bones of Joseph who had required a solemn oath of the Israelites, saying, "God will surely take notice of you, and then you must carry my bones with you from here." 20 They set out from Succoth, and camped at Etham, on the edge of the wilderness. 21 The LORD went in front of them in a pillar of cloud by day, to lead them along the way, and in a pillar of fire by night, to give them light, so that they might travel by day and by night. 22 Neither the pillar of cloud by day nor the pillar of fire by night left its place in front of the people.

x Or *as a frontlet*; Meaning of Heb uncertain
y Or *Sea of Reeds*

---

head, places where people would string identifying seals or ornaments; as in v. 16 a metaphor for a reminder (cf. Deut 6.8; Song 8.6). **13.11–16** An elaboration of vv. 1–2. Firstborn redemption, like the Feast of Unleavened Bread (v. 6), is to be interpreted to the next generations in connection with the exodus (v. 14). **13.11** Cf. v. 5. **13.12** *Males*. See note on 13.1–2. **13.13** The *donkey* is ritually tainted (Lev 11.3); the *sheep* is pure. *Break its neck*, to kill the animal without ritually slaughtering it since it is tainted; the animal is rightfully God's and may not be used. Lev 27.27 stipulates that the tainted animal must be redeemed at 120 percent its value, which favors the priests, who suffer a loss here because a sheep is worth less than a donkey. *Children*, lit. "sons" (see note on 13.1–2). *Redeem*. The sum is not fixed; Num 18.16 specifies 5 shekels. **13.14** Cf. v. 8. *Strength of hand*. Cf. vv. 3, 9, 16. **13.15** *Stubbornly refused*, lit. "made hard" (see note on 4.21). *Therefore*, a formula introducing an explanation of origins (etiology). *Sacrifice*. See note on 3.18. *Every male*, of the pure animals (see v. 13). **13.16** *Em-*

blem, a pendant or headband, interpreted in Judaism as phylacteries; see note on 13.9. **13.17** *Philistines*, apparently anachronistic; the Philistines would only have begun to settle the coast of Canaan at the time of the exodus; yet a Philistine presence there is taken for granted (see 15.14; cf. Gen 21.34; 26.1). *Thought*, lit. "said"; the apprehension anticipates 14.10–11. *Change their minds*, or "repent," a pun in Hebrew on *lead them*. **13.18** *Led . . . roundabout*, lit. "had go around" (Hebrew *wayyasev*) plays on "Sea of Reeds" (*yam suf*); see note on 10.19. *Prepared for battle*, or "armed" (Judg 7.11). **13.19** See Gen 50.25. **13.20** *Succoth*. See note on 12.37, whose narrative is resumed here. *Etham*. The site is uncertain; Num 33.8 places the Etham wilderness on the far side of the water Israel will cross; see 14.2. **13.21** The Lord, depicted as a storm god (see chs. 15, 19), radiates light from within a cover of cloud (cf. Ps 18.9–13). The two pillars are one (see 14.25): by day only the cloud is visible, by night only the light; cf. 24.15–17; 40.34–38.

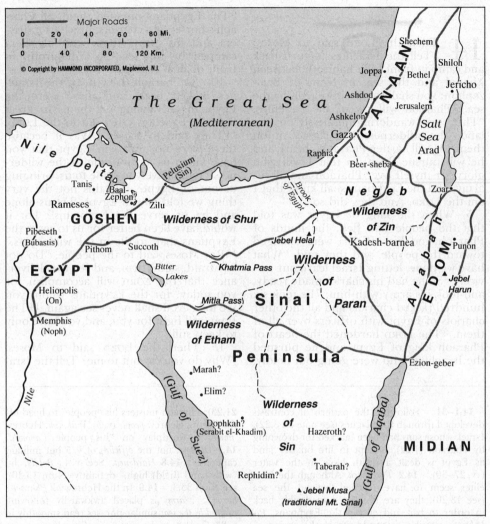

The geographical setting of the narratives in Exodus and Numbers.

Crossing the Red Sea

14 Then the LORD said to Moses: 2 Tell the Israelites to turn back and camp in front of Pi-hahiroth, between Migdol and the sea, in front of Baal-zephon; you shall camp opposite it, by the sea. 3 Pharaoh will say of the Israelites, "They are wandering aimlessly in the land; the wilderness has closed in on them." 4 I will harden Pharaoh's heart, and he will pursue them, so that I will gain glory for myself over Pharaoh and all his army; and the Egyptians shall know that I am the LORD. And they did so.

5 When the king of Egypt was told that the people had fled, the minds of Pharaoh and his officials were changed toward the people, and they said, "What have we done, letting Israel leave our service?" 6 So he had his chariot made ready, and took his army with him; 7 he took six hundred picked chariots and all the other chariots of Egypt with officers over all of them 8 The LORD hardened the heart of Pharaoh king of Egypt and he pursued the Israelites, who were going out boldly.

9 The Egyptians pursued them, all Pharaoh's horses and chariots, his chariot drivers and his army; they overtook them camped by the sea, by Pi-hahiroth, in front of Baal-zephon.

10 As Pharaoh drew near, the Israelites looked back, and there were the Egyptians advancing on them. In great fear the Israelites cried out to the LORD. 11 They said to Moses, "Was it because there were no graves in Egypt that you have taken us away to die in the wilderness? What have you done to us, bringing us out of Egypt? 12 Is this not the very thing we told you in Egypt, 'Let us alone and let us serve the Egyptians'? For it would have been better for us to serve the Egyptians than to die in the wilderness." 13 But Moses said to the people, "Do not be afraid, stand firm, and see the deliverance that the LORD will accomplish for you today; for the Egyptians whom you see today you shall never see again. 14 The LORD will fight for you, and you have only to keep still."

15 Then the LORD said to Moses, "Why do you cry out to me? Tell the Isra-

---

14.1–31 Following the pattern of contrasts developed through the plagues (see note on 8.22), Israel, whose sons had been marked for drowning by Pharaoh (1.22), is kept in life on dry land as Egypt is dealt a death blow in the water (vv. 27–30). **14.2** *Turn back.* Although the Israelites seem to have reached beyond the sea (see 13.20), they are instructed to double back in order to bait and entrap the Egyptians. *Pi-hahiroth*, possibly a temple site in the region of Succoth (13.20). *Migdol*, "Tower" in Hebrew, probably a fortification against Assyria north of the Bitter Lakes built in the seventh century B.C.E. (cf. Jer 44.1). If *Baal-zephon* is the Zeus Casius temple that juts into Lake Sarbonis, the other sites too are located along the northern Sinai coast, and Lake Sarbonis is the *sea*. *Baal* is the Canaanite storm god; "Zaphon" is known as his home on the north Syrian coast, probably Mount Casius. **14.3** *Closed in on*, or "enclosed" (cf. Josh 6.1). **14.4** *Harden*, "stiffen" (see note on 4.21) a strong link with the plagues narratives. *Gain glory for myself*, lit. "prove heavy"; see v. 18; note on 4.10. *Know.* See note on 5.2; cf. also Josh 4.24. **14.5** *The people ... fled*, as if Egypt had not pressed them to leave (12.31–33); or it has dawned on the Egyptians that the Israelites had left for more than three days (5.3). **14.6** *He had ... made ready*, lit. "he (himself) harnessed"; see also note on 14.25. *Army*, lit. "people" (cf. Num

21.23); Pharaoh musters his "people" to head off the fleeing Hebrew *people* (v. 5). *With him*, Hebrew *'immo*, a wordplay on "his people (*'ammo*)." **14.7** *Officers*, not the *officials* of v. 5 but military captains. **14.8** *Hardened.* See v. 4. *Boldly*, lit. "with hand (held) high," defiantly (Num 15.30); see Num 33.3. **14.9** In the Hebrew *all Pharaoh's horses ... army* is placed awkwardly following *camped by the sea*; similar phrases read smoothly in v. 23. On the anachronistic use of cavalry, see note on 15.1. **14.10** *Pharaoh.* The king is in focus even though the entire army is in pursuit; cf. v. 6. *There were*, "here: ..."; see note on 2.6. *Advancing.* In the Hebrew the verb is singular, suggesting that the Egyptian army is perceived as a single horde. *In great fear.* Cf. Moses' reply in v. 13. *Cried out to the LORD.* Cf. 2.23, where the prayer is undirected, and 5.15, where appeal is made to Pharaoh. **14.11–12** *Egypt* is used five times in two verses. **14.11** Cf. Num 11.18–20; 14.2–4. **14.12** *The very thing*, not exactly; see 5.20–21. **14.13** *Deliverance*, in Hebrew cognate to *came to their defense* in 2.17 and *saved* in 14.30; it anticipates 15.2, where it is rendered *salvation*. *Never see again* echoes 10.28–29. **14.14** *Will fight* anticipates the cognate *warrior* in 15.3. God's fighting on Israel's behalf (see Deut 1.30; 3.22; 20.4) is developed in Joshua (10.14, 42; 23.3, 10). **14.15** It is presupposed that, beside responding to the people's complaint (vv. 13–14), Moses ap-

elites to go forward. 16But you lift up your staff, and stretch out your hand over the sea and divide it, that the Israelites may go into the sea on dry ground. 17Then I will harden the hearts of the Egyptians so that they will go in after them; and so I will gain glory for myself over Pharaoh and all his army, his chariots, and his chariot drivers. 18And the Egyptians shall know that I am the Lord, when I have gained glory for myself over Pharaoh, his chariots, and his chariot drivers."

19 The angel of God who was going before the Israelite army moved and went behind them; and the pillar of cloud moved from in front of them and took its place behind them. 20It came between the army of Egypt and the army of Israel. And so the cloud was there with the darkness, and it lit up the night; one did not come near the other all night.

21 Then Moses stretched out his hand over the sea. The Lord drove the sea back by a strong east wind all night, and turned the sea into dry land; and the waters were divided. 22The Israelites went into the sea on dry ground, the waters forming a wall for them on their right and on their left. 23The Egyptians pursued, and went into the sea after them, all of Pharaoh's horses, chariots, and chariot drivers. 24At the morning watch the Lord in the pillar of fire and cloud looked down upon the Egyptian army, and threw the Egyptian army into panic. 25He clogged[z] their chariot wheels so that they turned with difficulty. The Egyptians said, "Let us flee from the Israelites, for the Lord is fighting for them against Egypt."

The Pursuers Drowned

26 Then the Lord said to Moses, "Stretch out your hand over the sea, so that the water may come back upon the Egyptians, upon their chariots and chariot drivers." 27So Moses stretched out his hand over the sea, and at dawn the sea returned to its normal depth. As the Egyptians fled before it, the Lord tossed the Egyptians into the sea. 28The waters returned and covered the chariots and the chariot drivers, the entire army of Pharaoh that had followed them into the sea; not one of them remained. 29But the Israelites walked on dry ground through the sea, the waters forming a wall for them on their right and on their left.

30 Thus the Lord saved Israel that day from the Egyptians; and Israel saw

z Sam Gk Syr: MT removed

---

pealed to the Lord, as in 5.22–23. **14.16** *Staff* (see note on 7.8–13) and *stretch out your hand* (see note on 7.5) recall the plagues (e.g., 10.12–13). *Divide.* Splitting the sea evokes an Israelite creation myth in which the Lord cuts through the primeval sea monster (Isa 51.9; Job 26.13); Isa 51.10 in fact compares the exodus to creation. The nature myth, shared with other Near Eastern cultures, in which the Lord cleaves the hostile sea monster is transformed here into a historical drama in which the Lord divides an inanimate sea and slays his enemies in it. *Dry ground,* an allusion to a version of the creation myth in which the Lord dries up the primeval sea (Ps 74.13–15; Isa 50.2; 51.10; Nah 1.4). **14.17** *Gain glory.* See note on 14.4. **14.19** *Angel,* a divine manifestation in the cloud and fire, *the Lord* in v. 24; see note on 3.4. *Army,* lit. "camp" here and in vv. 20, 24. **14.20** *It . . . it,* apparently the *angel.* The divine presence, glowing within the cloud, blocks the oncoming Egyptians; see note on 13.21; cf. Josh 24.7. *One . . . the other,* the Israelite and Egyptian camps. **14.21** See note on 14.16. *Strong* anticipates *my strength* in 15.2. *East wind.* See 10.13. *Dry land,* different from Hebrew term rendered *dry ground* in vv. 16, 22; used in Gen 7.22; Josh 3.17;

4.18. **14.23** The Hebrew defers *into the sea* to the verse's end. **14.24** *The Lord.* See note on 14.19. *Looked down.* The radiant face of the Lord, no longer veiled by cloud, "panics" the Egyptians, who recognize him (v. 25). Mesopotamian kings boasted that the mere sight of their divine auras would terrify the enemy. **14.25** *Clogged,* lit. "removed" or "turned aside." Greek and other manuscript traditions read lit. "he bound," thus having the Lord mirror Pharaoh, who "binds" or "harnesses," preparing his chariot in v. 6 (see note on 14.6). *Difficulty,* lit. "heaviness"; in vv. 4, 17 the Lord says he will "prove heavy" for Pharaoh's army (see note on 14.4). *Fighting.* See note on 14.14. **14.27** *Normal depth,* lit. "full strength." *Egyptians,* lit. "Egypt," which occurs twice mid-verse, is enclosed by *sea,* twice before and once after, as the Egyptians are enveloped by the water. **14.28** *Not one . . . remained,* an echo of the plagues (see note on 10.19). **14.29** *Walked.* The Hebrew syntax may be better understood as "had walked"; see v. 22, whose echo here frames the episode of drowning; the frame highlights Israel's salvation. **14.30** *Saved.* See note on 14.13. *From the Egyptians,* lit. "from Egypt's hand," contrasting with the Lord's marvelous "hand," rendered *work*

the Egyptians dead on the seashore. [31] Israel saw the great work that the LORD did against the Egyptians. So the people feared the LORD and believed in the LORD and in his servant Moses.

The Song of Moses

15 Then Moses and the Israelites sang this song to the LORD:

"I will sing to the LORD, for he
    has triumphed gloriously;
horse and rider he has thrown
    into the sea.
2 The LORD is my strength and my
    might,[a]
and he has become my
    salvation;
this is my God, and I will
    praise him,
my father's God, and I will
    exalt him.
3 The LORD is a warrior;
    the LORD is his name.

4 "Pharaoh's chariots and his army
    he cast into the sea;
his picked officers were sunk in
    the Red Sea.[b]
5 The floods covered them;

they went down into the depths
    like a stone.
6 Your right hand, O LORD,
    glorious in power—
your right hand, O LORD,
    shattered the enemy.
7 In the greatness of your majesty
    you overthrew your
    adversaries;
you sent out your fury, it
    consumed them like
    stubble.
8 At the blast of your nostrils the
    waters piled up,
the floods stood up in a heap;
    the deeps congealed in the
    heart of the sea.
9 The enemy said, 'I will pursue, I
    will overtake,
I will divide the spoil, my desire
    shall have its fill of them.
I will draw my sword, my hand
    shall destroy them.'
10 You blew with your wind, the sea
    covered them;
they sank like lead in the
    mighty waters.

a Or *song*   *b* Or *Sea of Reeds*

---

in v. 31. **14.31** *The Egyptians*, lit. "Egypt," referring perhaps to the wonders the Lord performed there. *Believed*. See note on 4.1.
15.1–19 The song of Moses proper, vv. 1b–18, written in "high," archaic Hebrew verse, extensively using parallelism, expresses Israel's trust (14.31; cf. Ps 106.12). Although the song refers to the events related in ch. 14, it does not narrate them in sequence and the descriptions do not entirely match. **15.1** *Moses*. See note on 15.21. *Israelites*. Since the song is formulated in the first-person singular, perhaps Moses sings a line and the Israelites respond antiphonally. *I will sing*, or "let me sing." The Hebrew rendered *triumphed gloriously* is used elsewhere of the sea's excrescence (e.g., Ps 89.9) and of human arrogance (e.g., Isa 2.12); the basic sense is "to be high," a polar contrast to the Egyptians (see vv. 5, 10). *Horse*. Egyptian reliefs and paintings of the late second millennium B.C.E. show horses pulling chariots but not being ridden. Biblical texts of the eighth century B.C.E. (e.g., Isa 31.1) know of Egyptians traveling on horseback. *Rider*, lit. "its rider." *Thrown*. Ironically, homonymous with "high" in "high hand" (see note on 14.8). **15.2** *The LORD*, the short name "Yah," placed at the end of the clause in Hebrew, meaning that the Israelites declare that "Yah"—and no other—is

their God; see v. 11. *Salvation*. See note on 14.13. *Praise*, lit. "enshrine." *My father's God*. Cf. 3.15–16. *Exalt*, cognate to "high" in (see note on) 14.8. **15.3** *Warrior*, lit. "man of war," typical of a storm god (see notes on 9.23; 13.21); cf. Ps 24.8. *Name*. See 3.13–15; 6.3. **15.4** The language recalls 14.7. *Red Sea*. See note on 10.19. **15.5** This verse chronologically follows vv. 8–10. *Floods*, plural of "the deep" (Gen 1.2). **15.7** *Majesty*; in Hebrew cognate to *triumphed* (v. 1). The first clause of this verse forms the third line of the distinctively Canaanite "staircase" parallelism begun in v. 6; other "staircases" are vv. 11, 16b–17a. Staircases have a retarding effect. *Fury* connotes burning. **15.8** The mobile is turned stationary. *Nostrils*. Cf. Ps 18.8; cf. also Ex 14.21; Deut 11.4. *Floods* denotes "flow," a different Hebrew term from that translated *floods* in v. 5. In Hebrew this clause alliterates. *Heap*, used nearly always of water; cf. *wall* in 14.22, 29. *Deeps*, rendered *floods* in v. 5. *The sea*, or "Sea," a name of the Canaanite sea god; see note on 14.16. **15.9** The first five Hebrew words (through *spoil*) alliterate. *Destroy*, lit. "dispossess," an intention at cross-purposes with the Lord's (see v. 17). **15.10** *Blew*, a rare verb in Hebrew. *Sank*, a different Hebrew verb from that translated *sunk* in v. 4, echoing *depths* in v. 5. *Lead*. Cf. *stone* in v. 5. *Mighty*, in Hebrew cognate to *glo-*

Spiffed up?
Added verse or two

11 "Who is like you, O Lord, among
   the gods?
   Who is like you, majestic in
   holiness,
   awesome in splendor, doing
   wonders?
12 You stretched out your right
   hand,
   the earth swallowed them.

13 "In your steadfast love you led
   the people whom you
   redeemed;
   you guided them by your
   strength to your holy
   abode.
14 The peoples heard, they
   trembled;
   pangs seized the inhabitants of
   Philistia.
15 Then the chiefs of Edom were
   dismayed;
   trembling seized the leaders of
   Moab;
   all the inhabitants of Canaan
   melted away.
16 Terror and dread fell upon
   them;

by the might of your arm, they
   became still as a stone
until your people, O Lord,
   passed by,
until the people whom you
   acquired passed by.
17 You brought them in and planted
   them on the mountain of
   your own possession,
   the place, O Lord, that you
   made your abode,
   the sanctuary, O Lord, that
   your hands have
   established.   *Temple of Solomon*
18 The Lord will reign forever and
   ever."

19 When the horses of Pharaoh with
his chariots and his chariot drivers went
into the sea, the Lord brought back the
waters of the sea upon them; but the Israelites walked through the sea on dry
ground.

The Song of Miriam

20 Then the prophet Miriam, Aaron's
sister, took a tambourine in her hand; and
all the women went out after her with

---

rious in v. 6.   **15.11** The second praise in direct
address, also a "staircase" parallelism (see note on
15.7). *Gods.* See note on 12.12; cf. 2 Sam 7.22–23;
Ps 86.8–10. *Majestic,* rendered *glorious* in v. 6, a
repetition enhancing coherence. *In holiness,* or
"among the holy ones" (so too in Ps 68.17 and
perhaps 16.24).   **15.12** *Stretched.* See note on
14.16. *Right hand.* See v. 6. *Earth,* probably connoting the netherworld (e.g., Eccl 3.21; Isa 14.12),
whose *swallow* (Num 16.32) is figurative of burial;
cf. Isa 5.14 and the voracious appetite of the Canaanite death god Mot.   **15.13** The song turns to
the Lord's guidance of Israel to its land, using
pastoral language: *led, abode* (lit. "pasture") as in
Ps 23.2–3. *Steadfast love,* used of covenantal as
well as personal devotion. *Redeemed.* See note on
6.6. *Strength* recalls v. 2, lending coherence. *Abode,*
in Hebrew cognate to *exalt* (v. 2), the land of Israel
(see v. 17).   **15.14–16** Anachronistic anticipation
of the reaction in the east to the news of Egypt's
destruction; cf. 18.1; Josh 2.9–11; but see note on
15.15.   **15.14** *Philistia.* See note on 13.17.
15.15 The widespread dread suggested here (cf.
Josh 9.9–10) is contradicted by the succeeding
narrative; neither the Edomites (Num 20.14–21),
the southern Canaanites (Num 21.1), nor the Amorites (Num 21.21–23) are intimidated by Israel;
Moab conspires with Midian to defeat Israel by
magic (Num 22.2–7). The terminology *chiefs,* lit.

"bulls," and *leaders,* lit. "rams," reflects ancient Canaanite usage.   **15.16** Ps 105.38 attributes the
same *dread* to the post-plague Egyptians. *As a
stone.* The simile's repetition (see v. 5) links the
second part of the song with the first. The Israelites *passed by* the peoples situated en route to Canaan (cf. Deut 29.16). *Acquired.* "Created" is more
in keeping with archaic usage (e.g., Gen 14.19, 22;
Deut 32.6; Pss 74.2; 78.54; 139.13; Prov 8.22).
15.17 *Mountain of . . . possession,* an archaic expression referring either anachronistically to
Mount Zion or to hilly Canaan (e.g., Deut 3.25).
Abode, not the same Hebrew word as that rendered *abode* in v. 13 but cognate to *established* here.
Sanctuary, the Jerusalem temple or a holy abode in
general (cf. Ps 78.54). When Israel takes possession of the land, it becomes the Lord's holy (designated) place (Ps 114.2).   **15.18** Proclaiming the
deity king is customary in Near Eastern creation
myths; cf., e.g., Deut 33.5; Ps 29.10.   **15.19** This
verse recapitulates and resumes the narrative in
14.27–29.   **15.20** *Prophet,* Miriam, so called only
here; cf. Num 12.1–9; see Mic 6.4. *Miriam.* See
note on 2.4. *Aaron's sister.* See note on 6.23; she
conspires with Aaron in Num 12. *Tambourine.* Archaeological finds depict a hand drum without
jingles. *Dancing,* a form of (not only female) rel
gious praise; e.g., 32.19; Judg 21.21; 2 Sam

tambourines and with dancing. 21 And
Miriam sang to them:

"Sing to the LORD, for he has
        triumphed gloriously;
horse and rider he has thrown
        into the sea."

Bitter Water Made Sweet

22   Then Moses ordered Israel to set
out from the Red Sea,c and they went
into the wilderness of Shur. They went
three days in the wilderness and found no
water. 23 When they came to Marah, they
could not drink the water of Marah because it was bitter. That is why it was
called Marah.d 24 And the people complained against Moses, saying, "What shall
we drink?" 25 He cried out to the LORD;
and the LORD showed him a piece of
wood;e he threw it into the water, and
the water became sweet.

There the LORD f made for them a statute and an ordinance and there he put
them to the test. 26 He said, "If you will
listen carefully to the voice of the LORD
your God, and do what is right in his
sight, and give heed to his commandments and keep all his statutes, I will not
bring upon you any of the diseases that I
brought upon the Egyptians; for I am the
LORD who heals you."

27   Then they came to Elim, where
there were twelve springs of water and
seventy palm trees; and they camped
there by the water.

Bread from Heaven

16   The whole congregation of the
        Israelites set out from Elim; and
Israel came to the wilderness of Sin,
which is between Elim and Sinai, on the
fifteenth day of the second month after
they had departed from the land of
Egypt. 2 The whole congregation of the
Israelites complained against Moses and
Aaron in the wilderness. 3 The Israelites
said to them, "If only we had died by the
hand of the LORD in the land of Egypt,
when we sat by the fleshpots and ate our
fill of bread; for you have brought us out
into this wilderness to kill this whole assembly with hunger."

4   Then the LORD said to Moses, "I am
going to rain bread from heaven for you,
and each day the people shall go out and
gather enough for that day. In that way I
will test them, whether they will follow my
instruction or not. 5 On the sixth day,
when they prepare what they bring in, it
will be twice as much as they gather on

c Or Sea of Reeds   d That is Bitterness   e Or a
tree   f Heb he

Pss 149.3; 150.4.   **15.21** The victory song typically belongs to women (see Judg 11.34; 1 Sam
18.6–7); Miriam and her cohort may in an earlier
tradition have initiated the song; note the exhortation *sing* in contrast to "let me sing" in v. 1; but
in the present context the women answer the
men.   **15.22–27** In parallel episodes in Numbers, Israel is punished for its complaints.
15.22 *Shur*, the site of an oasis (see Gen 16.7),
located between the Negev and Egypt (Gen
20.1).   **15.23** *Marah*, often identified with Hawwarah, the site of a bitter spring down the eastern
coast of the Gulf of Suez.   **15.24** *Complained*, the
key verb in virtually all the complaint episodes.
15.25 *Showed*, unusual usage of "to instruct"
("teach" in Deut 33.10), punning on the soundalike *Marah* and on *statute and . . . ordinance*, synonyms of the Hebrew cognate *torah*, "instruction."
The reference of *statute and . . . ordinance* is unclear; see 16.4. *He put them*. The Hebrew "he put
him" is ambiguous; Israel may be testing God's
reliability too.   **15.26** *Diseases*, not necessarily the
plagues; Egypt is also otherwise portrayed as a
diseased land (e.g., Deut 7.15). *Heals*, used of purifying water in a similar miracle tale ("made . . .
wholesome" in 2 Kings 2.21–22), making the

analogy plain: I can cure you as I cured the
water—if you obey me.   **15.27** *Elim*, often identified with Wadi Gharandel, south of Hawwarah
(see note on 15.23). The round numbers set a legendary tone.   **16.1–36** In the parallel episode in Num 11,
God produces the quails only after the manna
fails to suffice.   **16.1** *The whole . . . came*, lit.
"They set out from Elim, and the whole congregation came," an irregular variant on the typical
travel formula (see Num 33). *Sin*, of uncertain
identification, similar to *Sinai*. *Second month*. They
have traveled exactly one month (see 12.6,
17–18), and this is the seventh stop (see 12.37;
13.20; 14.9; 15.22, 23, 27) and the third complaint (see 14.11; 15.24). *Departed*, the theme
word "exodus" (see note on 3.10).   **16.2** *Aaron*.
In 15.24 the people *complain* against Moses alone.
In the wilderness, superfluous information, suggesting perhaps that the wilderness is a factor (see
v. 3).   **16.3** Cf. 14.11; Num 20.3–5.   **16.4** *Rain*.
Cf. the hail the Lord "rained down" on Egypt
(rendered *cause to fall* in 9.18). *Test*. Cf. 15.25–26;
Deut 8.16. *Instruction*, Hebrew *torah*; see note on
15.25.   **16.5** *Prepare*, in the sense of "set aside"
(e.g., 23.20; Josh 4.3) or "measure" ("calculate" in

other days." 6 So Moses and Aaron said to all the Israelites, "In the evening you shall know that it was the LORD who brought you out of the land of Egypt, 7 and in the morning you shall see the glory of the LORD, because he has heard your complaining against the LORD. For what are we, that you complain against us?" 8 And Moses said, "When the LORD gives you meat to eat in the evening and your fill of bread in the morning, because the LORD has heard the complaining that you utter against him — what are we? Your complaining is not against us but against the LORD."

9 Then Moses said to Aaron, "Say to the whole congregation of the Israelites, 'Draw near to the LORD, for he has heard your complaining.'" 10 And as Aaron spoke to the whole congregation of the Israelites, they looked toward the wilderness, and the glory of the LORD appeared in the cloud. 11 The LORD spoke to Moses and said, 12 "I have heard the complaining of the Israelites; say to them, 'At twilight you shall eat meat, and in the morning you shall have your fill of bread; then you shall know that I am the LORD your God.'"

13 In the evening quails came up and covered the camp; and in the morning there was a layer of dew around the camp. 14 When the layer of dew lifted, there on the surface of the wilderness was a fine flaky substance, as fine as frost on the ground. 15 When the Israelites saw it, they said to one another, "What is it?"g For they did not know what it was. Moses said to them, "It is the bread that the LORD has given you to eat. 16 This is what the LORD has commanded: 'Gather as much of it as each of you needs, an omer to a person according to the number of persons, all providing for those in their own tents.'" 17 The Israelites did so, some gathering more, some less. 18 But when they measured it with an omer, those who gathered much had nothing over, and those who gathered little had no shortage; they gathered as much as each of them needed. 19 And Moses said to them, "Let no one leave any of it over until morning." 20 But they did not listen to Moses; some left part of it until morning, and it bred worms and became foul. And Moses was angry with them. 21 Morning by morning they gathered it, as much as each needed; but when the sun grew hot, it melted.

22 On the sixth day they gathered twice as much food, two omers apiece. When all the leaders of the congregation came and told Moses, 23 he said to them, "This is what the LORD has commanded: 'Tomorrow is a day of solemn rest, a holy sabbath to the LORD; bake what you want

g Or "It is manna" (Heb man hu, see verse 31)

Deut 19.3) as in v. 18. *Twice as much*, so that one portion can be saved for the sabbath, on which gathering is forbidden (Num 15.32–36); see vv. 22–30. **16.6–7** There is no mention of quail, as in v. 13. *Know.* See note on 5.2; cf. v. 12. *Glory*, the divine aura (e.g., v. 10; 24.16; 33.18–23; 40.34–35; see notes on 13.21; 14.24), lit. "heaviness" (see note on 4.10). *We*, an unusual Aramaic-like form, repeated in v. 8; see note on 16.15. **16.8** *Meat*, quail (v. 13). *Bread*, manna (vv. 13–15). **16.9** *To the LORD*, lit. "before the LORD," perhaps an anachronistic reference to the tabernacle; cf. vv. 33–34. **16.10** Cf. Num 16.42. **16.12** *Twilight* evokes Passover (12.6). *Know.* See v. 6; note on 5.2. **16.13** Cf. Num 11.31–32. Quails migrate across the Red Sea to Europe in the spring, landing for rest at night. **16.14** *Lifted*, rendered *came up* in v. 13. *Flaky substance*, an unusual word in Hebrew, possibly related to "sherd" in Aramaic; see note on 16.15. **16.15** *What is it*, possibly Aramaic, a popular etymology of *manna* (v. 31); note the Aramaic coloring of the preceding passage (vv. 7–8, 14?).

What it was, the Hebrew equivalent of *what is it*. **16.16** *Each of you*, lit. "(each) man"; apparently the head of each household collected for his family. *Needs*, in Hebrew "eats," another (see note on 16.11) evocation of the Passover (see note on 12.4). *Omer.* See v. 36. *A person*, lit. *a head* (as in 38.26). *All*, lit. "(each) man." **16.18** *No shortage*, quoted in 2 Cor 8.15. *Needed*, lit. "eats"; each took the quantity appropriate to his family size. **16.19** *Leave ... over*, another evocation of the Passover (rendered *let ... remain* in 12.10). **16.20** *Bred*, a unique Hebrew verb meaning "to crawl with," cognate to *worms* in v. 24. *Foul*, rendered *stank*, in 7.21. *Was angry*. The root meaning is "to foam (at the mouth)." **16.21** *Each needed*. See note on 16.16. **16.22** *Twice as much*. See note on 16.5. *Leaders*, lit. the "elevated," tribal chiefs (Num 8). **16.23** *Commanded*, lit. "spoken," rendered "meant" in Lev 10.3, where it likewise introduces an explanation of the mysterious. *Day of solemn rest*, lit., "a (time of) cessation (from work)," cognate to *sabbath* (*rested* in v. 30; Gen 2.2–3). Cooking is forbidden on the sabbath (cf. 35.3). *To*

to bake and boil what you want to boil, and all that is left over put aside to be kept until morning.'" 24 So they put it aside until morning, as Moses commanded them; and it did not become foul, and there were no worms in it. 25 Moses said, "Eat it today, for today is a sabbath to the LORD; today you will not find it in the field. 26 Six days you shall gather it; but on the seventh day, which is a sabbath, there will be none."

27 On the seventh day some of the people went out to gather, and they found none. 28 The LORD said to Moses, "How long will you refuse to keep my commandments and instructions? 29 See! The LORD has given you the sabbath, therefore on the sixth day he gives you food for two days; each of you stay where you are; do not leave your place on the seventh day." 30 So the people rested on the seventh day.

31 The house of Israel called it manna; it was like coriander seed, white, and the taste of it was like wafers made with honey. 32 Moses said, "This is what the LORD has commanded: 'Let an omer of it be kept throughout your generations, in order that they may see the food with which I fed you in the wilderness, when I brought you out of the land of Egypt.'" 33 And Moses said to Aaron, "Take a jar,

and put an omer of manna in it, and place it before the LORD, to be kept throughout your generations." 34 As the LORD commanded Moses, so Aaron placed it before the covenant,*h* for safekeeping. 35 The Israelites ate manna forty years, until they came to a habitable land; they ate manna, until they came to the border of the land of Canaan. 36 An omer is a tenth of an ephah.

Water from the Rock

17 From the wilderness of Sin the whole congregation of the Israelites journeyed by stages, as the LORD commanded. They camped at Rephidim, but there was no water for the people to drink. 2 The people quarreled with Moses, and said, "Give us water to drink." Moses said to them, "Why do you quarrel with me? Why do you test the LORD?" 3 But the people thirsted there for water; and the people complained against Moses and said, "Why did you bring us out of Egypt, to kill us and our children and livestock with thirst?" 4 So Moses cried out to the LORD, "What shall I do with this people? They are almost ready to stone me." 5 The LORD said to Moses, "Go on ahead of the people, and take some of the elders of Is-

h Or *treaty* or *testimony*; Heb *eduth*

---

be kept, another evocation of the Passover (12.6). **16.24** See note on 16.20. **16.26** God, like Israel, ceases to labor on the sabbath (Gen 2.2–3); the formula anticipates 20.9–10. **16.27** *Some*, lit. "they." **16.28** *You*, plural. *Instructions*. See v. 4. **16.29** *Stay . . . do not leave*. The positive-negative combination typifies laws contrary to natural inclination, e.g., Deut 9.7; 15.7–8, 12–13. Jewish law interprets this to prohibit travel on the sabbath. **16.31** *House of Israel*, a rare usage, elsewhere in Exodus only in 40.38, possibly evoking the Passover again (12.3–4, 27). *Manna*. See note on 16.15. *Coriander*. Cf. Num 11.7. *Made with*, or dipped in (the Hebrew is elliptical). *Honey*. See Num 11.7. **16.32** *An omer*, lit. "an omerful." See v. 16. *Be kept*. See note on 16.23; cf. the commemorative aspect of Passover (12.24–27). **16.33** *To Aaron* anticipates his priestly function; see note on 19.22. *Before the LORD*. See note on 16.9. **16.34** *Covenant*, the two stone tablets (25.16) or (metonymically) the ark (30.36), which would be anachronistic; but see note on 17.4–6. *For safekeeping*, rendered *to be kept* in vv. 23, 32. **16.35** A retrospective comment. *Canaan*. Cf. Josh 5.12. **16.36** An explanation called for by the fact that

elsewhere in the Torah an *omer* is a sheaf of grain, not a measure, and that elsewhere a tenth of an ephah is an *issaron* (one-tenth in 29.40). An *ephah* is 22 liters. **17.1–7** Another version of the incident appears in Num 20.2–13. **17.1** *Stages*, journey stops; cf. Num 33.1. *There was no water . . . to drink*. Hebrew syntax favors "there was not (enough) water for the people to drink." **17.2** *Quarreled*, not *complained* (as in v. 3; see note on 15.24); the term is one root of the site's new compound name (v. 7; Num 20.3, 13). *Moses*. In 16.2; Num 20.2 Aaron too is addressed. *Test*, an echo of the two preceding episodes (15.25–26; 16.4) and root of the site's new name (v. 7), but unreflected in Num 20. The two verbs are arranged in parallel clauses (see note on 3.15). **17.3** See note on 16.3. Although some versions read *us . . . our*, the traditional Hebrew text has the more personal "me . . . my." **17.4** *Cried*, as in 14.15; 15.25. Unlike in Num 20.6, there is no shrine here at which to seek divine counsel. *Stone*. See 1 Sam 30.6. **17.5** *Struck the Nile*, and removed drinkable water from Egypt (7.21, 24). Num 20.8 lacks such a reference, perhaps on account of its magical aspect.

rael with you; take in your hand the staff with which you struck the Nile, and go. 6 I will be standing there in front of you on the rock at Horeb. Strike the rock, and water will come out of it, so that the people may drink." Moses did so, in the sight of the elders of Israel. 7 He called the place Massah*i* and Meribah,*j* because the Israelites quarreled and tested the LORD, saying, "Is the LORD among us or not?"

Amalek Attacks Israel and Is Defeated

8 Then Amalek came and fought with Israel at Rephidim. 9 Moses said to Joshua, "Choose some men for us and go out, fight with Amalek. Tomorrow I will stand on the top of the hill with the staff of God in my hand." 10 So Joshua did as Moses told him, and fought with Amalek, while Moses, Aaron, and Hur went up to the top of the hill. 11 Whenever Moses held up his hand, Israel prevailed; and whenever he lowered his hand, Amalek prevailed. 12 But Moses' hands grew

weary; so they took a stone and put it under him, and he sat on it. Aaron and Hur held up his hands, one on one side, and the other on the other side; so his hands were steady until the sun set. 13 And Joshua defeated Amalek and his people with the sword.

14 Then the LORD said to Moses, "Write this as a reminder in a book and recite it in the hearing of Joshua: I will utterly blot out the remembrance of Amalek from under heaven." 15 And Moses built an altar and called it, The LORD is my banner. 16 He said, "A hand upon the banner of the LORD *k* The LORD will have war with Amalek from generation to generation."

Jethro's Advice

18 Jethro, the priest of Midian, Moses' father-in-law, heard of all that God had done for Moses and for his people Israel, how the LORD had brought

i That is *Test*   *j* That is *Quarrel*
k Cn: Meaning of Heb uncertain

17.6 *I*, the Lord, visibly (see note on 13.21; see also Gen 18.22). *Horeb.* See note on 3.1. According to 19.1–2; Num 33.15, Sinai is the next journey stop. *Strike.* In Num 20.8 Moses and Aaron are to "command" the rock, making the same point that the Lord is responsible for the water but without manifesting the Lord's presence there physically. **17.7** *Massah and Meribah.* Only the latter name is used in Num 20.13. Deut 33.8–9 pairs the two names in reference to an opaque episode in which the Levites proved loyal to God in time of rebellion (cf. 32.25–28); *Massah* alone occurs in Deut 6.16; 9.22. A chiastic parallelism (*Test, Quarrel, quarrel, test*) closes the unit (see note on 3.22). *Among us.* See v. 6. **17.8–15** Typically, as in Assyrian annals and Xenophon's *Anabasis*, a raggedy group on march is attacked by marauders. In the light of the preceding episode, the unmotivated attack may be a fight over water rights; but cf. Deut 25.7–9; 1 Sam 30.1–20. **17.8** *Amalek,* an Edomite tribe (Gen 36.12), said to dwell in the Negev (Num 13.29). *Rephidim.* See v. 1; note on 17.6. **17.9** *Joshua,* Moses' field commander, mentioned without his patronym, "son of Nun," as if he were already introduced; he is described elsewhere as Moses' young assistant (e.g., 33.11) and made his successor in Num 27. The name in Hebrew means "The LORD saves" (cf. Ex 2.17, which uses the same verb; see note on 2.17). *Staff.* See v. 5. **17.10** *Hur,* apparently a notable of the tribe of Judah, grandfather of the artisan Bezalel

(31.2), paired here and in 24.14 with *Aaron,* who married Judean nobility (6.23); cf. note on 31.2. **17.11** The raised arms symbolize power and inspire morale. It is unclear whether Moses is holding up the staff (v. 9); cf. Josh 8.18–19. *Prevailed,* or "proved strong," unrelated to the term rendered "prevailed" in Gen 32.28. **17.12** *Weary,* lit. "heavy" (see note on 14.24). *Steady,* in Hebrew cognate to *believed* in 14.31. **17.13** *Defeated,* lit. "weakened," here antonymous to *steady* (v. 12); the Samaritan version adds "and smote." *Sword.* See 13.18. **17.14** *Reminder.* Cf. 16.32–33. *Book,* any document (see note on 17.16); this is the first text Moses is told to write. *Remembrance,* judging by curses typical of ancient royal inscriptions a reference to posterity as well to the name *Amalek;* cf. Deut 25.17–19. King Saul is ordered to obliterate the Amalekites (1 Sam 15.2–3) but fails (see 2 Sam 1.1–10; Esth 3.1). **17.15** *Altar,* for commemoration, not necessarily thanksgiving (e.g., Judg 6.24). *Banner,* a Hebrew term from a root similar to *test* (v. 2). **17.16** *Hand upon,* or "monument to" (e.g., 1 Sam 15.12), perhaps a stele on which he wrote the inscription. *Banner.* The translation assumes a scribal error; the Hebrew and ancient versions have "seat," referring perhaps to the stone on which Moses sat, hands raised (v. 12). The utterance is often understood as an oath gesture. *The LORD,* "Yah" (see note on 15.2). *Generation,* see Num 14.43–45; Judg 3.13; 6.3; 1 Sam 30.1–2.

18.1–27 Although Moses' establishment of a

Israel out of Egypt. 2After Moses had sent away his wife Zipporah, his father-in-law Jethro took her back, 3along with her two sons. The name of the one was Gershom (for he said, "I have been an alien*l* in a foreign land"), 4and the name of the other, Eliezer*m* (for he said, "The God of my father was my help, and delivered me from the sword of Pharaoh"). 5Jethro, Moses' father-in-law, came into the wilderness where Moses was encamped at the mountain of God, bringing Moses' sons and wife to him. 6He sent word to Moses, "I, your father-in-law Jethro, am coming to you, with your wife and her two sons." 7Moses went out to meet his father-in-law; he bowed down and kissed him; each asked after the other's welfare, and they went into the tent. 8Then Moses told his father-in-law all that the LORD had done to Pharaoh and to the Egyptians for Israel's sake, all the hardship that had beset them on the way, and how the LORD had delivered them. 9Jethro rejoiced for all the good that the LORD had done to

Israel, in delivering them from the Egyptians.

10 Jethro said, "Blessed be the LORD, who has delivered you from the Egyptians and from Pharaoh. 11Now I know that the LORD is greater than all gods, because he delivered the people from the Egyptians,*n* when they dealt arrogantly with them." 12And Jethro, Moses' father-in-law, brought a burnt offering and sacrifices to God; and Aaron came with all the elders of Israel to eat bread with Moses' father-in-law in the presence of God.

13 The next day Moses sat as judge for the people, while the people stood around him from morning until evening. 14When Moses' father-in-law saw all that he was doing for the people, he said, "What is this that you are doing for the people? Why do you sit alone, while all the people stand around you from morning until evening?" 15Moses said to his

l Heb *ger*   *m* Heb *Eli*, my God; *ezer*, help
n The clause *because . . . Egyptians* has been transposed from verse 10

---

judicial system appears to precede the legislation that follows, v. 5 places it at what seems to be Sinai, where the Israelites are reported to arrive in 19.1–2. To the juxtaposition of the Midianite priest Jethro and the Amalekites here, cf. the conjunction of Midian and Amalek in Judg 6.3, 33; 7.12. The chapter is marked by uncommon usages of biblical language: *sent away* (v. 2), *rejoiced* (v. 9), *wear . . . out* (v. 18), *teach* (v. 20), *look for* (v. 21), and the forms of *them* (v. 20) and *decided* (v. 26); some linguistic features are shared by 20.22–23.33. **18.1** *Jethro.* See note on 2.18. *Heard.* Cf. 15.14; see note on 1.17. **18.2–4** A comment resolving the contradiction between vv. 5–6 and (see note on) 4.20. **18.2** *Sent away*, in Deut 24.1 a term for divorce. **18.3** *Gershom.* See note on 2.22. **18.4** *Father.* See 3.6. *Help.* Cf. Gen 49.25. *Pharaoh.* See 2.15; 4.19. **18.5** *Bringing*, added in English to smooth the syntax; the verse reads lit. "Jethro, Moses' father-in-law, and his sons and his wife, came . . ." *Mountain of God.* See 3.1; and note on 18.1–27. **18.6** *Sent word*, in Hebrew "said," but see v. 7. *With . . . sons.* In Hebrew the phrase sounds tacked on. **18.7** No reference is made here or below to Moses' wife and sons; cf. note on 4.20. Unlike Genesis, Exodus through Deuteronomy concerns the entire people and not families per se. *Bowed down and kissed.* Cf., e.g., Gen 33.4–7; 2 Sam 14.33. *Tent*, presumably Jethro's. **18.8** *Told*, as in 10.2 (*tell*). *Egyptians.* See note on 14.31. *For Israel's sake*, rather "about" (Gen 21.25) or "on account of" (Gen 21.11) "Israel." *Hardship*, in Hebrew cognate to *unable*

(7.18), rendered "adversity" in Num 20.14. *On the way.* See 15.22–17.16. **18.9** *Good*, acts of good. *To*, for. *From the Egyptians*, lit. "from the hand of Egypt," somewhat echoing v. 4; see note on 18.10. **18.10** *Blessed be the LORD.* Cf. Gen 14.20; see note on 1.17. *Delivered*, the verb used in vv. 4, 8–9, not the one translated "delivered" in Gen 14.20. *From the Egyptians and from Pharaoh*, lit. "from the hand of Egypt and from the hand of Pharaoh," echoing (see note on) 14.30. **18.11** *I know.* Cf. 5.2. *Gods.* See note on 15.11. *From the Egyptians*, lit. "from under the hand of Egypt," an idiom for overturning foreign rule (e.g., 2 Kings 8.20; 13.5). The transposed clause (see text note *n*) may well belong in v. 10: Jethro celebrates the divine deliverance expansively. *Dealt arrogantly with*, or "acted with malice against" (see e.g., 1.10), in Hebrew cognate to *willfully attacks* in 21.14 and alluded to in Neh 9.10. **18.12** *Burnt offering*, one wholly incinerated on an altar (20.24). *Sacrifices.* See note on 10.25. *Bread*, in the sense of "food" (Lev 3.11). The homage ritual often entails a meal shared by the deity and worshiper (e.g., 24.11; 32.6) just as ancient pacts were often so sealed (e.g., Gen 26.30). *In the presence of God*, in front of the mountain (v. 5). **18.13–16** Moses legislates ad hoc, case by case, in advance of the code that will issue from the Sinai revelation (chs. 20–23). **18.13** *Sat*, according to ancient custom (e.g., Judg 4.5), illustrated already in Ugaritic epic (mid-second millennium B.C.E.). **18.14** *This*, Hebrew "this thing (lit. word)," a pun on *dispute* (v. 16). **18.15** *To inquire of God*, to seek an oracle (cf., e.g.,

father-in-law, "Because the people come to me to inquire of God. 16When they have a dispute, they come to me and I decide between one person and another, and I make known to them the statutes and instructions of God." 17Moses' father-in-law said to him, "What you are doing is not good. 18You will surely wear yourself out, both you and these people with you. For the task is too heavy for you; you cannot do it alone. 19Now listen to me. I will give you counsel, and God be with you! You should represent the people before God, and you should bring their cases before God; 20teach them the statutes and instructions and make known to them the way they are to go and the things they are to do. 21You should also look for able men among all the people, men who fear God, are trustworthy, and hate dishonest gain; set such men over them as officers over thousands, hundreds, fifties and tens. 22Let them sit as judges for the people at all times; let them bring every important case to you, but decide every

minor case themselves. So it will be easier for you, and they will bear the burden with you. 23If you do this, and God so commands you, then you will be able to endure, and all these people will go to their home in peace."

24 So Moses listened to his father-in-law and did all that he had said. 25Moses chose able men from all Israel and appointed them as heads over the people, as officers over thousands, hundreds, fifties, and tens. 26And they judged the people at all times; hard cases they brought to Moses, but any minor case they decided themselves. 27Then Moses let his father-in-law depart, and he went off to his own country.

The Israelites Reach Mount Sinai

19 On the third new moon after the Israelites had gone out of the land of Egypt, on that very day, they came into the wilderness of Sinai. 2They had journeyed from Rephidim, entered the

---

Gen 25.22; see notes on 4.14; 4.15–16; 4.18–20); used of seeking prophetic oracles (e.g., 1 Sam 9.9; 2 Kings 8.8; Ezek 20.1) and later of scriptural exegesis (Ezra 7.10).   **18.16** *Dispute*, a legal case (v. 19), lit. "a word." *They come*, in Hebrew "he (the people, v. 15) comes" or "it (the case) comes"; 22.9 favors the latter. *Person*, lit. "man"; it is unclear whether a woman could personally initiate or appear in a litigation. *Another*, lit. "his fellow." *Instructions*. See note on 16.4. The Hebrew cognate verb is used of priestly "instruction" or "teaching" (e.g., Deut 17.10; 33.10).   **18.17–23** In Deut 1.9–18 Moses credits himself with setting up the judicial system.   **18.17** *What*, Hebrew "the thing" (see note on 18.14).   **18.18** *Wear ... out*, the less common form of the Hebrew verbal root, punning on the verbs "to be foolhardy" (e.g., Deut 32.6; 1 Sam 25.25) and "to confound" (e.g., Gen 11.7, 9). *Task*, lit. "thing" (see note on 18.14). *Alone*, the same word rendered "all by myself" in Deut 1.12.   **18.19** *Counsel*. See Num 10.29–32. *God*, the oracle (see note on 18.15), punning in Hebrew on *God be with you*. *Cases*, another pun (see note on 18.16) since an oracle "speaks" (see notes on 4.14; 4.15–16). Typically (cf. Abigail, 1 Sam 25.2, 25) Jethro's wisdom is demonstrated by his wit.   **18.20** *Teach* connotes illumining and admonishing. *The way*. Israel's actual way in the wilderness is attributed to Jethro's eyes (Num 10.31). *Things*, lit. "acts."   **18.21** *You should also*, or "You yourself." *Look for*, and find (cf. the use of "see," rendered "provided" in Gen 22.8; 1 Sam 16.1), elsewhere "to prophesy" and

therefore perhaps another pun (see note on 18.19). *Able*. Other nuances are "worthy" (1 Kings 1.42) and "valiant" (1 Sam 14.52). *Dishonest gain*. Cf. 23.6–8. *Officers*, elsewhere where used militarily; the judicial levels and divisions seem artificial.   **18.22** *Sit as judges*, lit. "judge," but see vv. 13–14. *You*. Under the monarchy the king acts as chief judge (e.g., 2 Sam 15.2; 1 Kings 3.16–28). *Decide*, "judge." *Easier*, lit. "lighter," the antithesis of *heavy* (v. 18).   **18.23** *This*. See note on 18.14. *And God so commands you*, or "when the oracle directs you." *Endure*, lit. "stand," punning perhaps on *sat/sit* (vv. 13–14). *Home*, lit. "place."   **18.24** *Listened*. See v. 19.   **18.26** *Brought ... decided*, "would bring ... would judge" (see note on 18.22).   **18.27** *Let ... depart*, the same Hebrew verb rendered *let ... go* in the liberation formula (see note on 3.19).

19.1–24.18   The Sinai revelation, in which context the Ten Commandments (34.28) and the Book of the Covenant (24.7) are presented, is comprised of several units beginning with 19.1–9. The arrangement of diverse sections seems to conclude at 24.18. The laws are surrounded by a covenant framework (19.3–6; 24.1–14) to which the people commit themselves (19.7–25; 24.3–8). Israel remains encamped at Sinai until Num 10.11–12 (second year, second month, twentieth day). Moses' repeated trips up and down the mountain together with his exclusive admission to the divine presence (cf. 3.5) strengthen his image as divine mediator.   **19.1** The *Sinai* Peninsula contains a large mountainous center; several

wilderness of Sinai, and camped in the wilderness; Israel camped there in front of the mountain. 3 Then Moses went up to God; the LORD called to him from the mountain, saying, "Thus you shall say to the house of Jacob, and tell the Israelites: 4 You have seen what I did to the Egyptians, and how I bore you on eagles' wings and brought you to myself. 5 Now therefore, if you obey my voice and keep my covenant, you shall be my treasured possession out of all the peoples. Indeed, the whole earth is mine, 6 but you shall be for me a priestly kingdom and a holy nation. These are the words that you shall speak to the Israelites."

7 So Moses came, summoned the elders of the people, and set before them all these words that the LORD had commanded him. 8 The people all answered as one: "Everything that the LORD has spoken we will do." Moses reported the words of the people to the LORD. 9 Then the LORD said to Moses, "I am going to come to you in a dense cloud, in order that the people may hear when I speak with you and so trust you ever after."

The People Consecrated

When Moses had told the words of the people to the LORD, 10 the LORD said to Moses: "Go to the people and consecrate them today and tomorrow. Have them wash their clothes 11 and prepare for the third day, because on the third day the LORD will come down upon Mount Sinai in the sight of all the people. 12 You shall set limits for the people all around, saying, 'Be careful not to go up the mountain or to touch the edge of it. Any who touch the mountain shall be put to death. 13 No hand shall touch them, but they shall be stoned or shot with arrows;*o* whether animal or human being, they shall not live.' When the trumpet sounds a long blast, they may go up on the mountain." 14 So Moses went down from the mountain to the people. He consecrated the people, and they washed their clothes. 15 And he said to the people, "Prepare for the third day; do not go near a woman."

16 On the morning of the third day there was thunder and lightning, as well

o Heb lacks *with arrows*

---

peaks have been proposed for Mount Sinai, and one in the south-central peninsula (e.g., Jebel Musa, Jebel Serbal) is most consistent with earlier locations on the route (see 15.23, 27). On the chronology, see introduction; note on 18.1–27. **19.2** *Had journeyed.* The Hebrew means only "journeyed"; v. 2 chronologically precedes v. 1, making v. 1 look like an overview. **19.3** *Then Moses went.* Hebrew syntax favors "Moses had gone . . ." It is unclear in what manifestation the Lord addresses Moses; he is said to descend onto the mountain only on the *third day* (vv. 16–20). *Thus . . . Israelites,* expressed in parallelism (see note on 3.15). **19.4** *You have seen,* a motif phrase unifying the larger passage (see 20.22; 20.18, where *witnessed* is lit. "seen"); in Deut 4.12, 15 the aural experience is favored. *Eagle's wings.* Cf. Deut 32.11. **19.5** *Treasured.* For the literal root of the metaphor see 1 Chr 29.3; cf. Deut 7.6; 14.2; 26.18–19; Ps 135.4. *Indeed,* or "because"; the Lord has the right to covenant with any people he wants; see Deut 10.14–15. **19.6** *But,* not expressed in Hebrew. *Priestly.* Israel is meant to maintain a degree of holiness higher than that of other nations just as priests observe more stringent purity rules than other Israelites; see v. 10. Isa 61.6 uses a similar metaphor of restored Judah, and 1 Pet 2.5, 9; Rev 1.6 apply it to the Christian community. **19.7** *Elders.* Cf. e.g., 3.16; 4.29; 12.21. Typically the Torah does not report that

the elders fulfill the mediating function. **19.9** *Hear,* that the Lord speaks directly to Moses; the people do not seem to discern the words themselves; see 20.18–21; cf. Deut 4.10, 12; 5.22; see note on 19.25. *Trust.* Cf. 14.31. *When,* not expressed in Hebrew. Syntactically the phrase, which seems to duplicate v. 8b, may belong to what precedes rather than to what follows. **19.10** *Consecrate,* by rituals of purification and avoidance of defilement (see v. 15); the people must be in a priestly state for the divine encounter (cf. 28.41); cf., e.g., 1 Sam 16.5. *Clothes.* See Num 8.21. **19.11** *Third day.* Priests undergo a seven-day rite (29.35). *Sight.* See note on 19.4. **19.12** *Limits,* physical boundaries (Deut 20.14). *Edge,* even the edge. **19.13** *No hand shall touch* lest the executioner become contaminated or transgress the limit. *Stoned or shot,* from outside the limit. Vv. 22, 24 describe direct extermination by God, whose holy presence will tolerate no contact with the impure, even impure animals. *Trumpet,* ram's horn, used for signaling (Josh 6.5), by metonymy the jubilee (Lev 25.9–10). **19.15** *The third day,* lit. "three days." *Do not go near a woman* and through the sexual act become ritually defiled for a day (Deut 23.10–11); cf. 1 Sam 21.4; only adult males are addressed. **19.16–24** The Lord (Yahweh) is described in the conventional imagery of a Canaanite storm god, as in ch. 15

Don't really see God [handwritten note]

as a thick cloud on the mountain, and a blast of a trumpet so loud that all the people who were in the camp trembled. 17 Moses brought the people out of the camp to meet God. They took their stand at the foot of the mountain. 18 Now Mount Sinai was wrapped in smoke, because the LORD had descended upon it in fire; the smoke went up like the smoke of a kiln, while the whole mountain shook violently. 19 As the blast of the trumpet grew louder and louder, Moses would speak and God would answer him in thunder. 20 When the LORD descended upon Mount Sinai, to the top of the mountain, the LORD summoned Moses to the top of the mountain, and Moses went up. 21 Then the LORD said to Moses, "Go down and warn the people not to break through to the LORD to look; otherwise many of them will perish. 22 Even the priests who approach the LORD must consecrate themselves or the LORD will break out against them." 23 Moses said to the LORD, "The people are not permitted to come up to Mount Sinai; for you yourself warned us, saying, 'Set limits around the mountain and keep it holy.' " 24 The LORD said to him, "Go down, and come up bringing Aaron with you; but do not let either the priests or the people break through to come up to the LORD; otherwise he will break out against them." 25 So Moses went down to the people and told them.

The Ten Commandments

20 Then God spoke all these words: 2 I am the LORD your God, who brought you out of the land of Egypt, out of the house of slavery; 3 you shall have no other gods beforeP me.

4 You shall not make for yourself an idol, whether in the form of anything that is in heaven above, or that is on the earth beneath, or that is in the water under the earth. 5 You shall not bow down to them or worship them; for I the LORD your

p Or *besides*

---

and Pss 18; 29; 68. **19.16** *Morning*, more precisely "daybreak." *Thick*, lit. "heavy." *Trumpet*, the more common term, not the one so translated in v. 13. The storm god is a warrior (see 15.3), and the trumpet signals battle (Num 10.9); cf. Zech 9.14. *So ... that*, not in the Hebrew. **19.18** *Wrapped in smoke*, lit. "all smoking." *Shook*, the same Hebrew term rendered *trembled* in v. 16. In Ugaritic epic and Pss 18.7; 68.8 the earth quakes at the storm god's appearance. **19.19** *Thunder*, different in form from *thunder* in v. 16, more probably "(human) voice" (see 33.11; 1 Sam 3.4–8). **19.20** *When*, not in the Hebrew, added because v. 18 already reports the Lord's descent; but *The LORD summoned ... Moses went up* seems prior to v. 19. **19.21** *To look*, at odds with 20.18–21; Deut 5.5, 25–27. *Otherwise*, lit. "and (as a result)." *Perish*, lit. "fall" (32.28) through a divine outburst (see vv. 22, 24; 2 Sam 6.6–8). **19.22** *Priests*, anachronistic since the priests are not yet commissioned (Lev 8–9). *Break out*, not the Hebrew word for *break through* in vv. 21, 24 but the root rendered *break out* in v. 24 and "burst forth" in 2 Sam 6.8; see note on 19.13. The divine presence neutralizes any encroachment; cf. also Lev 10.1–5. **19.23** *Limits*. See note on 19.12. **19.24** A repetition of vv. 21–22, adding an order to *bring Aaron*, vaguely anticipating 24.1. *Break out*. See note on 19.22. **19.25** *Told them*, rather "said to them," apparently governing 20.1–17. Moses seems to relate the laws to the people (see note on 19.9).
20.1–17 The Decalogue comprises a core of ten rules (lit. *words*, 34.28), essentially prohibitions, addressed to the individual, with no penalties and few details spelled out. Nine of the rules appear variously elsewhere in the Torah, and the core Decalogue is elaborated differently in Deut 5.6–21. Prophets hold Israel accountable for the rules (e.g., Jer 7.9; 29.23; Ezek 18.5–18; 22.6–12; Hos 4.2), and psalms allude to them (e.g., Pss 50.16–19; 81.9–10); see also Mk 10.19; Lk 18.20; Rom 13.9. The severity of the commandments is such that violation of most of them is elsewhere said to be punishable by death. The Decalogue may have served as a creed, as it did later in Judaism and Christianity. The text of the Decalogue will be inscribed by God (31.18; 32.16) and placed in the ark of the covenant (Deut 10.1–5; cf. Ex 25.16, 22). **20.2** A prologue. **20.3** The first rule; cf. 23.24; 34.14; Deut 6.13. *Gods*. See note on 12.12. **20.4–6** Cf. v. 23; 34.17; Lev 19.4; 26.1; Deut 4.15–20. **20.4** *Water under the earth*, the subterranean ocean (e.g., Gen 49.25; Ps 24.2). For the division heaven-earth-water, cf. Gen 1. The tabernacle's iconography depicts creatures not of this world; see note on 25.18. **20.5** *Worship*. See note on 4.22–23. *Jealous*. The Hebrew term also connotes zeal (e.g., Num 25.11); cf. Deut 4.24; 6.15. *Punishing children for the iniquity of parents*, lit. "accounting the sins of the fathers to the sons" (cf. 34.7); that God punishes vicariously is denied by Jer 31.29–30; Ezek 18. In contrast to other ancient Near Eastern legislation, vicarious punishment is prohibited in criminal matters (Deut 24.16); but see Josh 7.24; 2 Kings 9.26.

God am a jealous God, punishing children for the iniquity of parents, to the third and the fourth generation of those who reject me, 6but showing steadfast love to the thousandth generation*q* of those who love me and keep my commandments.

7 You shall not make wrongful use of the name of the LORD your God, for the LORD will not acquit anyone who misuses his name.

8 Remember the sabbath day, and keep it holy. 9Six days you shall labor and do all your work. 10But the seventh day is a sabbath to the LORD your God; you shall not do any work—you, your son or your daughter, your male or female slave, your livestock, or the alien resident in your towns. 11For in six days the LORD made heaven and earth, the sea, and all that is in them, but rested the seventh day; therefore the LORD blessed the sabbath day and consecrated it.

12 Honor your father and your mother, so that your days may be long in the land that the LORD your God is giving you.

13 You shall not murder.*r*

14 You shall not commit adultery.

15 You shall not steal.

16 You shall not bear false witness against your neighbor.

17 You shall not covet your neighbor's house; you shall not covet your neighbor's wife, or male or female slave, or ox, or donkey, or anything that belongs to your neighbor.

18 When all the people witnessed the thunder and lightning, the sound of the trumpet, and the mountain smoking, they were afraid*s* and trembled and stood at a distance, 19and said to Moses, "You speak to us, and we will listen; but do not let God speak to us, or we will die." 20Moses said to the people, "Do not be afraid; for God has come only to test you and to put

q Or *to thousands*   *r* Or *kill*   *s* Sam Gk Syr Vg: MT *they saw*

Reject, lit. "hate." **20.6** *Steadfast love.* See note on 15.13; see also Deut 7.9. *Thousandth generation.* See Deut 7.9. **20.7** *Make wrongful use,* particularly in an oath (Lev 6.3; 19.12; Ps 24.4), in which the deity's name is typically invoked (Deut 6.13; 10.20; cf., e.g., Gen 14.22; 24.3). *Acquit,* rendered *clear . . . the guilty* in 34.7. *Misuses,* the same Hebrew term rendered *makes wrongful use of.* For a thematic link between this commandment and the preceding two, see 23.13. **20.8–11** Cf. 23.12; 31.12–17; 34.21; 35.1–3; Lev 23.3; Jer 17.19–27. **20.8** *Remember.* See note on 2.24; in Deut 5.12, "observe" (or "keep"). *Sabbath.* See note on 16.23. Mesopotamians sought to avoid evil spirits on the seventh, fourteenth, twenty-first and twenty-eighth days of the (lunar) month; the Torah's proscriptions of fire and work/movement outdoors on the sabbath are consonant with an original motive to avoid danger. *Keep . . . holy,* "hallow" in Gen 2.3 and *consecrate* in v. 11; by observing the sabbath one does what God does. **20.10** Major textual versions add "on it" after *do.* *Livestock.* Deut 5.14 adds here "or your ox or your donkey" and at the end "so that your . . . slave may rest as well as you" in accordance with the motive there. *Alien resident.* See Introduction. *Towns,* lit. "city gates," a locution characteristic of Deut (e.g., 12.12, 18). **20.11** *Therefore.* Cf. Gen 2.3; cf. 23.12; Deut 5.15. **20.12** Cf. Lev 19.3; Prov 19.26; 28.24; elsewhere this commandment is formulated as a prohibition (Ex 21.15, 17; Lev 20.9; Deut 27.16; and see Deut 21.18–21); for linking the positive and negative formulations, see Mt 15.4. Honoring parents serves as a metaphor for the covenant between God and Israel (e.g., Deut 32.16–21; Isa 1.2; Mal 1.6). *Long,* an expression characteristic of Deuteronomy (e.g., 4.40; 22.6–7). **20.13** *Murder.* Cf. 21.12; Lev 24.17; Num 35.30–34; Deut 19.11–13; see Gen 9.5–6. **20.14** Since men may be polygamous, adultery is intercourse between a married woman and any man but her husband; cf. Lev 18.20; 20.10; Deut 22.22; also cf. Num 5.11–31. For adultery as a metaphor for apostasy, cf., e.g., Hos 1–3; Mal 2.13–16. In some versions this commandment precedes v. 13. **20.15** Cf. 22.1–12; Lev 19.11. *Steal,* possibly referring to kidnapping (21.16; Deut 24.7; cf. Gen 40.15). **20.16** Witnesses not only testify but bring charges (e.g., Deut 19.15–19; 1 Kings 21.13). Cf. Ex 23.1; Num 35.30; Deut 19.16–21; Prov 6.19; 14.5, 25; 19.5, 9. **20.17** *Covet,* to the point of theft (see 34.24; Deut 7.25; Josh 7.21; Mic 2.2; cf. 2 Sam 11; 1 Kings 21, although the term *covet* is not employed there). *House,* household, including the wife, whom Deut 5.21 separates as an individual. **20.18–21** A different perspective from that of 19.16–23; cf. Deut 5.5, 22–27. The passage serves to incorporate the succeeding laws into the Sinai revelation. **20.18** *Witnessed.* See note on 19.4. The paradoxical "seeing" *the thunder* lends mystique to the revelation. *Lightning,* lit. "torches," not the Hebrew term so translated in 19.16. *Trembled,* different from the term used in 19.16, but the same as the term translated "shook" in Isa 7.2. **20.19** *And we will listen,* rather "so that we may listen/hear." *Or we will die,* "lest we die"; cf. Deut 4.33; 5.23–26. **20.20** *Test.* Cf. 16.4;

the fear of him upon you so that you do not sin." 21 Then the people stood at a distance, while Moses drew near to the thick darkness where God was.

Book of the Covenant (handwritten)

Laws Concerning Worship

22   The LORD said to Moses: Thus you shall say to the Israelites: "You have seen for yourselves that I spoke with you from heaven. 23 You shall not make gods of silver alongside me, nor shall you make for yourselves gods of gold. 24 You need make for me only an altar of earth and sacrifice on it your burnt offerings and your offerings of well-being, your sheep and your oxen; in every place where I cause my name to be remembered I will come to you and bless you. 25 But if you make for me an altar of stone, do not build it of hewn stones; for if you use a chisel upon it you profane it. 26 You shall

not go up by steps to my altar, so that your nakedness may not be exposed on it."

The Law Concerning Slaves

21   These are the ordinances that you shall set before them:
2   When you buy a male Hebrew slave, he shall serve six years, but in the seventh he shall go out a free person, without debt. 3 If he comes in single, he shall go out single; if he comes in married, then his wife shall go out with him. 4 If his master gives him a wife and she bears him sons or daughters, the wife and her children shall be her master's and he shall go out alone. 5 But if the slave declares, "I love my master, my wife, and my children; I will not go out a free person," 6 then his master shall bring him before

---

Judg 2.22–23.   **20.21** *Thick darkness*, or "fog" (e.g., Ps 18.10), synonymous with *cloud* (19.9, 16). References to Moses' approach to God here and in 24.2, where *come near* is the same as *drew near* here, frame the corpus of law that follows.
20.22–23.33   The so-called Book of the Covenant (see 24.7) is generally regarded as the oldest legislation in the Bible, dating perhaps to premonarchical times. Parallels to Mesopotamian law abound, and subsequent biblical texts may be taken to repeat and revise the law found here. Sections of ritual and civil/criminal law alternate. The archaic language has some features in common with ch. 18 (see note on 18.1–27).
20.22–26   The laws of worship elaborate the second commandment (vv. 4–6), adding positive injunctions to the commandment's prohibitions.
20.22 *Seen*, a link to the preceding section (see note on 19.4). *With you*, in tension with 20.18–21 (see note there).   **20.23** *Silver . . . gold* is an ancient and common word pair in parallelism (see note on 3.15).   **20.24** *Altar of earth*. Such a primitive altar was found at Mari, a northwest Mesopotamian city of the eighteenth century B.C.E. with a West Semitic population; see 2 Kings 5.17; cf. 27.1–8; 1 Kings 8.64. *Sacrifice*. See note on 3.18. *Burnt offerings*. See note on 18.12. *Well-being*, or "goodwill," for propitiation; cf. Lev 3.1–16; 7.11–18. *Every place*. Many local altars are implied; cf., e.g., Judg 6.24; 1 Sam 14.35; cf. Deut 12.5–14, which is taken to originate centuries later. On the *altar* as a place where God is *remembered*, see note on 17.15 or *invoked* (as in 23.13; see note on 3.15).   **20.25** *Stone*. See Deut 27.5–6; Josh 8.30–31; 1 Kings 18.31–32; 1 Macc 4.47; cf. Judg 13.19; 1 Sam 6.14; 1 Kings 1.9. Early Israel-

ite religion favors the natural; cf. note on 12.8; cf. 27.1–8. *Use*, in a sweeping motion. *Chisel*, a cutting tool (or weapon) specified as iron in Deut 27.5; Josh 8.31. Metal tools taint the sanctuary (1 Kings 6.7).   **20.26** *Steps*. Cf. Ezek 43.17; the eighth-century B.C.E. altar at Dan, too, was reached by steps. *Nakedness*. Cf. 28.42. It is implied that sacrificers — who are not necessarily priests — wear full-length garments, like God (Isa 6.1); cf. 28.42. Cultic practices had no sexual aspect in Israelite religion; accordingly, women did not serve in the cult, to avoid the aspect of a sexual relationship to the Lord, who is conceived as male.
21.1–22.17   Civil and criminal laws mostly formulated casuistically ("When/if . . . then . . .") in the fashion of other ancient Near Eastern collections.   **21.2–11** Laws involving slavery, a prominent theme of the exodus (see Introduction) and in the prologue to the Decalogue (20.2).   **21.1** *These*, "And these"; the succeeding laws are attached to the foregoing.   **21.2** *Buy*. The law is seller-oriented; cf. Lev 25.39; Deut 15.12. *Male*. Deut 15.12–17 treats the female as an individual. *Seventh*. Cf. Lev 25.40. *Without debt*, "gratis" ("for nothing" in Gen 29.15); see v. 11; note on 3.21.   **21.3** *Married*, lit. "master of a woman." The provisions in vv. 3–5 are irrelevant to Deut 15.12–17 (see note on 21.2).   **21.5** *Master*. Cf. Deut 15.16.   **21.6** *God*, the household gods, an oracle (see note on 4.15–16), or the local shrine; omitted in Deut 15.17. *Door*, of the master's house. *Ear*. The wound disappears, but the blood on the doorpost signifies the permanent attachment of the person to the household. *For life*. Slavery of Israelites is a vocation, taken on to re-

God.*t* He shall be brought to the door or the doorpost; and his master shall pierce his ear with an awl; and he shall serve him for life.

7 When a man sells his daughter as a slave, she shall not go out as the male slaves do. 8 If she does not please her master, who designated her for himself, then he shall let her be redeemed; he shall have no right to sell her to a foreign people, since he has dealt unfairly with her. 9 If he designates her for his son, he shall deal with her as with a daughter. 10 If he takes another wife to himself, he shall not diminish the food, clothing, or marital rights of the first wife.*u* 11 And if he does not do these three things for her, she shall go out without debt, without payment of money.

The Law Concerning Violence

12 Whoever strikes a person mortally shall be put to death. 13 If it was not premeditated, but came about by an act of God, then I will appoint for you a place to which the killer may flee. 14 But if someone willfully attacks and kills another by treachery, you shall take the killer from my altar for execution.

15 Whoever strikes father or mother shall be put to death.

16 Whoever kidnaps a person, whether that person has been sold or is still held in possession, shall be put to death.

17 Whoever curses father or mother shall be put to death.

18 When individuals quarrel and one strikes the other with a stone or fist so that the injured party, though not dead, is confined to bed, 19 but recovers and walks around outside with the help of a staff, then the assailant shall be free of liability, except to pay for the loss of time, and to arrange for full recovery.

t Or *to the judges*   *u* Heb *of her*

---

pay debts (see v. 7; 22.3; Lev 25.39; 2 Kings 4.1; Neh 5.4–5); foreign slaves are permanent (Lev 25.44–46). **21.7** *Daughter.* The Code of Hammurabi sets a three-year term on family members sold to repay a debt. Israelite sons, who could also be sold (see note on 21.6), seemed to go free after six years (v. 2) since the present law deals only with the contingencies of selling a daughter. No such situation is treated in Deut 15.12–17. Lev 25.41 treats indentured children the same as parents. *Slave*, a term designating a woman often purchased for concubinage ("slave woman" in Gen 21.10–13; Judg 9.18; 19.19, where the translation omits "slave" before "woman"). **21.8** *Designated her*, as a concubine (see note on 21.7); cf. Lev 19.20. *Foreign people*, or "another clan" than hers (taking *people* in its archaic sense); redemption is the clan's duty (see Ruth 3.13, where "act as next-of-kin" translates the verb elsewhere rendered "redeem" and Ezek 11.15, where Hebrew "people of your redemption" denotes kin; cf. Lev 25.25). *Dealt unfairly*, rather "broken faith" (e.g., Jer 3.20), reneged. **21.9** *As with a daughter*, more precisely "according to the rule of (free) daughters." **21.10–11** These verses resume the situation on v. 8. **21.10** *Wife.* The Hebrew has "another (female)," probably a concubine. *Food*, lit. "meat." *Marital rights*, the traditional conjugal understanding. Etymology and Islamic parallels favor "lodging"; Mesopotamian parallels favor "(cosmetic) oil" (cf. Hos 2.8). **21.11** *Without debt.* See note on 21.2.
21.12–17 Capital crimes corresponding to rules on murder, honoring parents, and theft in the Decalogue (20.12–15; see notes there). **21.12** *Put to death*, by the "avenger of blood" (Num 35.19, 21; Deut 19.12; 2 Sam 14.11). Hittite laws (see note on 3.8) provide for compensation. **21.13** *Not premeditated*, lit. "If he did not hunt"; cf. Num 35.20. Num 35.11, 15; Deut 19.4 are less graphic. *Act of God.* For illustrations, see Num 35.22–23; Deut 19.5. *A place*, elaborated as the six cities of refuge (Num 35.9–28; Deut 19.1–13; Josh 20). **21.14** *Willfully attacks.* See note on 18.11. *Altar.* See 1 Kings 1.50–53; 2.28–34. The altar, like the cities of refuge (see note on 21.13), apparently protects accidental slayers. **21.15** *Strikes*, less than fatally (cf. v. 12). The Code of Hammurabi prescribes cutting off the hand. **21.16** *Kidnaps*, the same Hebrew term rendered *steal* in 20.15. *Person.* Deut 24.7 and ancient translations of the present verse indicate that an Israelite is meant. *Sold*, as a slave (e.g., Gen 37.27–28, 36; Joel 3.6). *Death*, the punishment also in the Code of Hammurabi; Hittite laws (see note on 3.8) penalize economically. **21.17** *Curses*, rejects the authority of or denounces (cf. 2 Sam 16.5–8), in Hebrew cognate to "dishonors" (Deut 27.16); cf. Lev 20.9; Deut 21.18–21; Prov 20.20. Various ancient Near Eastern laws punish rejection of parents with disinheritance or enslavement.

21.18–27 A resumption of the topic of vv. 12–14, treating less than fatal "striking" of persons by persons. **21.18** *Injured party*, supplied for clarity. *Not dead.* If death is caused, the culprit presumably seeks asylum (v. 13); other Near Eastern codes fix a fine. *Is confined*, lit. "falls." **21.19** *But*, lit. "if he." *Recovers*, lit. "gets up." *To*

(margin annotations: "okays slavery", "forgiveness?")

20 When a slaveowner strikes a male or female slave with a rod and the slave dies immediately, the owner shall be punished. 21 But if the slave survives a day or two, there is no punishment; for the slave is the owner's property.

22 When people who are fighting injure a pregnant woman so that there is a miscarriage, and yet no further harm follows, the one responsible shall be fined what the woman's husband demands, paying as much as the judges determine. 23 If any harm follows, then you shall give life for life, 24 eye for eye, tooth for tooth, hand for hand, foot for foot, 25 burn for burn, wound for wound, stripe for stripe.

26 When a slaveowner strikes the eye of a male or female slave, destroying it, the owner shall let the slave go, a free person, to compensate for the eye. 27 If the owner knocks out a tooth of a male or female slave, the slave shall be let go, a free person, to compensate for the tooth.

Laws Concerning Property

28 When an ox gores a man or a woman to death, the ox shall be stoned, and its flesh shall not be eaten; but the owner of the ox shall not be liable. 29 If the ox has been accustomed to gore in the past, and its owner has been warned but has not restrained it, and it kills a man or a woman, the ox shall be stoned, and its owner also shall be put to death. 30 If a ransom is imposed on the owner, then the owner shall pay whatever is imposed for the redemption of the victim's life. 31 If it gores a boy or a girl, the owner shall be dealt with according to this same rule. 32 If the ox gores a male or female slave, the owner shall pay to the slaveowner thirty shekels of silver, and the ox shall be stoned.

33 If someone leaves a pit open, or digs a pit and does not cover it, and an ox or a donkey falls into it, 34 the owner of the pit shall make restitution, giving money to its owner, but keeping the dead animal.

35 If someone's ox hurts the ox of another, so that it dies, then they shall sell the live ox and divide the price of it; and the dead animal they shall also divide. 36 But if it was known that the ox was accustomed to gore in the past, and its owner has not restrained it, the owner shall restore ox for ox, but keep the dead animal.

Laws of Restitution

22 v When someone steals an ox or a sheep, and slaughters it or sells it, the thief shall pay five oxen for an ox, and four sheep for a sheep. w The thief shall make restitution, but if unable to do so,

v Ch 21.37 in Heb   w Verses 2, 3, and 4 rearranged thus: 3b, 4, 2, 3a

---

pay, lit. "he must pay." *Loss of time*, unemployment compensation. *Recovery*, lit. "healing." **21.20** *Slaveowner*, lit. "a man," but a woman too might abuse her slave (e.g., Gen 16.6). *A . . . slave*, "his (own) . . . slave." *Punished*, lit. "avenged," by the victim's kin or another party (see Num 35.16–19). **21.21** *Survives*, lit. "stands." *Property*. The economic loss is sufficient punishment. **21.22** *Harm*, to the woman. *Demands*, *imposes* as in v. 30. Vv. 12–14 do not apply because the fetus is legally not a person. **21.23** *Life for life*, life of the perpetrator for the life of the woman. The Code of Hammurabi requires the life of the perpetrator's daughter; biblical law opposes vicarious punishment (see note on 20.5). **21.24** *Eye*. Cf. Lev 24.19–21; Deut 19.21. Unlike other Near Eastern codes, biblical law puts no price on limbs as it puts none on life (Num 35.31). **21.26** *Slaveowner*. See note on 21.20. *A . . . slave*, "his (own) . . . slave." *Free person*. Cf. v. 2. Near Eastern codes generally penalize economically.

21.28–36 Personal injuries caused by animals or negligence. **21.28** *Stoned*. See Gen 9.5. *Not be* eaten, because the animal is not properly slaughtered (22.31; Lev 17; Deut 12.15–16) and/or because it is polluted by bloodguilt (cf. Deut 21.1–9). **21.29** *Death*, in theory (see v. 30); the Code of Hammurabi imposes a fine and in no case has the animal killed. **21.30** *Ransom*. Compensation is allowed, contra Num 35.31, because this is not premeditated murder. *Imposed*, by the victim's kin. **21.31** *A boy or a girl*, lit. "a son . . . or a daughter." Vicarious punishment (see note on 21.23) is ruled out; in the Code of Hammurabi if a builder's faulty work kills a citizen's child, his own child is executed. **21.32** *Thirty*. Cf. Gen 37.28. **21.34** *Keeping*, for its hide and for food if Lev 17.15; Deut 14.21 do not yet hold. **21.35** *Divide*, lit. "halve." **21.36** *If it was known*, "If he (the owner) was informed." *Restore*, "pay." *Keep*. See note on 21.34.

22.1 *Oxen*, any "large cattle." *Five . . . and four*, ten and six in Hittite laws (see note on 3.8); cf. 2 Sam 12.6. *Sheep*, any "small cattle." *Make restitution*, "pay" restitution plus the fine. *Unable to do so*, lit. "he doesn't have it." *Sold*. See note on

shall be sold for the theft. 4 When the animal, whether ox or donkey or sheep, is found alive in the thief's possession, the thief shall pay double.

2x If a thief is found breaking in, and is beaten to death, no bloodguilt is incurred; 3 but if it happens after sunrise, bloodguilt is incurred.

5 When someone causes a field or vineyard to be grazed over, or lets livestock loose to graze in someone else's field, restitution shall be made from the best in the owner's field or vineyard.

6 When fire breaks out and catches in thorns so that the stacked grain or the standing grain or the field is consumed, the one who started the fire shall make full restitution.

7 When someone delivers to a neighbor money or goods for safekeeping, and they are stolen from the neighbor's house, then the thief, if caught, shall pay double. 8 If the thief is not caught, the owner of the house shall be brought before God,y to determine whether or not the owner had laid hands on the neighbor's goods.

9 In any case of disputed ownership involving ox, donkey, sheep, clothing, or any other loss, of which one party says, "This is mine," the case of both parties shall come before God;y the one whom

God condemnsz shall pay double to the other.

10 When someone delivers to another a donkey, ox, sheep, or any other animal for safekeeping, and it dies or is injured or is carried off, without anyone seeing it, 11 an oath before the LORD shall decide between the two of them that the one has not laid hands on the property of the other; the owner shall accept the oath, and no restitution shall be made. 12 But if it was stolen, restitution shall be made to its owner. 13 If it was mangled by beasts, let it be brought as evidence; restitution shall not be made for the mangled remains.

14 When someone borrows an animal from another and it is injured or dies, the owner not being present, full restitution shall be made. 15 If the owner was present, there shall be no restitution; if it was hired, only the hiring fee is due.

Social and Religious Laws

16 When a man seduces a virgin who is not engaged to be married, and lies with her, he shall give the bride-price for her and make her his wife. 17 But if her father refuses to give her to him, he shall pay an

x Ch 22.1 in Heb   y Or before the judges
z Or the judges condemn

21.6. Hammurabi's laws would have the insolent thief executed. **22.4** *Double*, restitution plus fine; cf. vv. 7, 9. **22.2** *Breaking in*, the Hebrew root means "to dig"; "digging" is figurative for "in the act"; cf. Job 24.16. *Is beaten to death*, rather "is struck and dies." *Bloodguilt*, "blood" (plural) criminally spilled; cf. Gen 4.10. *Incurred*. Greek and Roman law similarly allow for defense against thieves. **22.3** *After sunrise*, lit. "the sun shone on him," the thief is caught sometime after the crime, which is typically perpetrated at night (see Job 24.14–17). *Bloodguilt is incurred*, because the slaying is premeditated. **22.5** *Restitution . . . vineyard* or "(the perpetrator) shall pay the best (highest potential yield) of (the owner's) field or vineyard." **22.6** *Thorns*, used to hedge a field (Sir 28.24), removed to this day by burning. *Started the fire*, in Hebrew plays on *causes . . . to be grazed* (v. 5); it is a case of negligence. *Restitution*, according the principle in v. 5. **22.7–15** On the safekeeping and use of another's property. **22.7** *Goods*, "utensils." *Double*, as in v. 4. **22.8** *Be brought*, rather "approach." *God*, an oracle (see note on 21.6). *To determine*, not in the Hebrew; rather, the householder swears (the words rendered *whether or not* are an oath formula) "he did

not lay a hand . . ." *Goods*, *property* as in v. 11, not *goods* as in v. 7. **22.9** *God*. See note on 22.8; cf. 1 Kings 8.31–32. *Condemns*, or "declares to be in the wrong" (as in Deut 25.1). *Double*, as in v. 4. The Code of Hammurabi condemns the culprit to death. **22.10** *Carried off*. Cf. Job 1.14–17. **22.11** *Before the LORD*, or "(taking) the LORD's (name)" (see note on 21.6); cf. 1 Kings 2.43. *That*, the oath formula (see note on 22.8), taken by the safekeeper. *No restitution shall be made*, "(one) does not pay" restitution plus fine (see v. 9). **22.12** *Restitution shall be made*, because the safekeeper's negligence, spelled out in Hammurabi's laws, is assumed. **22.13** *Evidence*. Cf. 1 Sam 17.34–35; Am 3.12. *Restitution . . . remains*. In Gen 31.39 Jacob goes beyond the law. **22.14** *An animal*, not in the Hebrew; any borrowed property may be meant. *Injured*, "broken," referring to an animal or object. **22.15** *If the owner was present*. The owner could have prevented a mishap as well as the borrower. *It*, the object or animal. *The hiring fee is due* because the renter paid for a sound implement or animal. **22.16** *A virgin*, a young woman. *Is not*, more precisely "has never been." *Bride-price*. Cf. Gen 24.12; 1 Sam 18.25. Deut 22.29 specifies 50 shekels. Cf. Deut 22.23–27

amount equal to the bride-price for virgins.

18 You shall not permit a female sorcerer to live.

19 Whoever lies with an animal shall be put to death.

20 Whoever sacrifices to any god, other than the LORD alone, shall be devoted to destruction.

21 You shall not wrong or oppress a resident alien, for you were aliens in the land of Egypt. 22 You shall not abuse any widow or orphan. 23 If you do abuse them, when they cry out to me, I will surely heed their cry; 24 my wrath will burn, and I will kill you with the sword, and your wives shall become widows and your children orphans. *favors oppressed*

25 If you lend money to my people, to the poor among you, you shall not deal with them as a creditor; you shall not exact interest from them. 26 If you take your neighbor's cloak in pawn, you shall restore it before the sun goes down; 27 for it may be your neighbor's only clothing to use as cover; in what else shall that person sleep? And if your neighbor cries out to

me, I will listen, for I am compassionate.

28 You shall not revile God, or curse a leader of your people.

29 You shall not delay to make offerings from the fullness of your harvest and from the outflow of your presses.[a] The firstborn of your sons you shall give to me. 30 You shall do the same with your oxen and with your sheep: seven days it shall remain with its mother; on the eighth day you shall give it to me.

31 You shall be people consecrated to me; therefore you shall not eat any meat that is mangled by beasts in the field; you shall throw it to the dogs.

Justice for All

23 You shall not spread a false report. You shall not join hands with the wicked to act as a malicious witness. 2 You shall not follow a majority in wrongdoing; when you bear witness in a lawsuit, you shall not side with the majority so as to pervert justice; 3 nor shall you be partial to the poor in a lawsuit.

4 When you come upon your enemy's

a Meaning of Heb uncertain

(rape). **22.17** *If her father refuses.* Deut 22.29 excludes the circumstance so that the girl's marriage is guaranteed. *For virgins.* Cf. the legal principle implied in (see note on) 22.5. **22.18–22** These laws are formulated apodictically (*you shall/shall not*) like the Ten Commandments. **22.18** *Female sorcerer,* from the Hebrew for "to cast a spell," singled out perhaps for her popularity (cf. 1 Sam 28; Ezek 13.17–23); for the popularity of sorcery generally, see, e.g., 2 Kings 23.24; Isa 3.2–3. The Torah abominates any form of divine manipulation other than a direct approach to the Lord; cf. Lev 19.26, 31; 20.6, 27; Deut 18.9–14. **22.19** Cf. Lev 18.23; 20.15–16; Deut 27.21. **22.20** *Devoted* to destruction, placed under ban; see Deut 13.12–17; cf. Lev 27.28–29; Josh 6.21, 7; Judg 21.5–11; 1 Sam 15.1–9. **22.21** *Oppress.* See 3.9; cf. 23.9. *Aliens.* See Introduction. **22.22** *Abuse.* See 1.11–12. *Orphan.* Protecting the "fatherless," along with the indigent *widow,* is an expressed duty of Near Eastern monarchs as well as the Lord (e.g., Deut 10.18; Ps 68.5); cf., e.g., Deut 24.17; Isa 1.17; Jer 7.6; 22.3; Zech 7.10. **22.23** *Cry.* See 3.7. **22.24** *Sword,* in war (cf. Isa 9.11–17). *Wives.* Men are addressed (see note on 19.15). The grim poetic justice underscores the idea that Israel was liberated for the purpose of establishing a just society. **22.25** *People,* Israel. Cf. Lev 25.36–37; Deut 23.19–20; Ps 15.5; Prov 28.8; Ezek 18.8, 13, 17. **22.26–27** Cf. Deut

24.6, 10–13; Ezek 18.12, 16; 33.15. **22.26** *Cloak.* Cf. Am 2.8. An Israelite letter from the seventh century B.C.E. complains that a laborer's garment was distrained for unsatisfactory work. **22.27** *For . . . cover,* lit. "for it is his only covering, it is his cloak for his skin." Cf. Job 22.6; 24.7. *Compassionate* anticipates 34.6 (rendered *gracious* there). **22.28** *Revile,* rather "curses," as in Lev 24.11–16, 23; cf. 1 Kings 21.13; Job 2.9–10; Isa 8.21. *Leader.* See note on 16.22; cf. 2 Sam 16.5–13. Quoted in Acts 23.5. **22.29** *Offerings,* added in translation, inferred from such passages as Num 18.11–12, 26–30; Deut 26.1–15; the juxtaposition with the firstborn law suggests first fruits (23.19) are meant, but tithes (Num 18.21–32; Deut 14.22–29) too may be intended. *Firstborn.* See note on 13.1–2. **22.30** *On the eighth day,* following a seven-day period for overcoming the ritual pollution that accompanies birth (Lev 12.2–3); see Lev 22.27; cf. Ex 29.35–37. **22.31** *Consecrated,* or "who are holy," as in Lev 19.2, a similar context. *Mangled.* See note on 21.28.

23.1–3 Laws addressed to potential witnesses. **23.1** *False.* Cf. (and see note on) 20.16; Lev 19.16; Deut 5.20. *Malicious.* See Pss 27.12; 35.11. The penalty would seem to be as in Deut 19.18–19 (and in the Code of Hammurabi). **23.3** *Partial.* See Deut 16.19. *To the poor,* in light of Lev 19.15; Deut 1.17; and especially v. 6 below,

ox or donkey going astray, you shall bring it back.

5 When you see the donkey of one who hates you lying under its burden and you would hold back from setting it free, you must help to set it free.[b]

6 You shall not pervert the justice due to your poor in their lawsuits. 7 Keep far from a false charge, and do not kill the innocent and those in the right, for I will not acquit the guilty. 8 You shall take no bribe, for a bribe blinds the officials, and subverts the cause of those who are in the right.

9 You shall not oppress a resident alien; you know the heart of an alien, for you were aliens in the land of Egypt.

Sabbatical Year and Sabbath

10 For six years you shall sow your land and gather in its yield; 11 but the seventh year you shall let it rest and lie fallow, so that the poor of your people may eat; and what they leave the wild animals may eat. You shall do the same with your vineyard, and with your olive orchard.

12 Six days you shall do your work, but on the seventh day you shall rest, so that your ox and your donkey may have relief, and your homeborn slave and the resident alien may be refreshed. 13 Be attentive to all that I have said to you. Do not invoke the names of other gods; do not let them be heard on your lips.

The Annual Festivals

14 Three times in the year you shall hold a festival for me. 15 You shall observe the festival of unleavened bread; as I commanded you, you shall eat unleavened bread for seven days at the appointed time in the month of Abib, for in it you came out of Egypt.

No one shall appear before me empty-handed.

16 You shall observe the festival of harvest, of the first fruits of your labor, of what you sow in the field. You shall observe the festival of ingathering at the end of the year, when you gather in from the field the fruit of your labor. 17 Three times in the year all your males shall appear before the Lord GOD.

18 You shall not offer the blood of my

b Meaning of Heb uncertain

"(even) to the poor," for whom sympathy is natural (for the style see v. 4). **23.4** *Your enemy's,* "(even) your enemy's" (see note on 23.3), anyone's; cf. Deut 22.1–3. On overcoming hatred, cf. Lev 19.17–18. **23.5** *One who hates,* a poetic synonym of *enemy* (e.g., Ps 21.8). *Setting it free,* or "unloading it"; cf. Deut 22.4, where loading or "lifting up," a more demanding activity is called for. **23.6–9** These verses resume vv. 1–3 and address judges. **23.6** See note on 23.3; cf. Ps 82.3–4; Isa 10.2; Jer 5.28; Am 2.6–7; 5.12. **23.7** *False charge.* Cf. v. 1. *Kill,* by erroneous condemnation; cf. Ps 94.6–7. *Acquit,* "declare in the right" (as in Deut 25.1); cf. Ex 34.7. **23.8** See Deut 1.17; 16.19; 27.25; cf. Ps 26.9–10; Prov 17.23; Isa 1.23; 5.23; Ezek 22.12; Mic 3.11. **23.9** See 22.21; Introduction. **23.10–11** Cf. the cultic emphasis of Lev 25.1–7, 20–22 and the socioeconomic emphasis of Deut 15. **23.12** *Refreshed,* like the Lord after creation (31.17). See note on 20.8–11; cf. the motive in 23.11; Deut 5.14–15. **23.13** *Invoke* may be taken to elaborate 20.3; cf. Josh 23.7; Hos 2.17; Zech 13.2. The repetitive, impressionistic style called "parallelism" brings the section to closure. **23.14–17** On the calendar, see note on 12.2. **23.14** *Hold a festival.* See note on 5.1. **23.15** *Commanded.* See 12.14–20; 13.3–10. The Passover offering, a home ritual (see 12.1–11), is not mentioned here

(see note on 12.1–28). *Abib.* See note on 12.2. *Appear before me,* lit. "see my face," an idiom meaning "to worship," devolving from the practice of seeing a god's image in a shrine (e.g., Ps 42.2; Isa 1.12). *Empty-handed.* See note on 3.21. **23.16** *Festival of harvest,* the Festival of Weeks (34.22; Num 28.26; Deut 16.10; cf. Lev 23.15), so named for its timing seven weeks after Passover (Lev 23.15; Deut 16.9). *First fruits.* The first produce of each crop, like human and animal firstborn (see note on 13.1–2), is rendered to God; cf. v. 19. Deut 26.1–11 does not connect first fruits with a particular festival. The crop is elsewhere described as *wheat* (34.22), "new grain" (Lev 23.16; Num 28.26), and "standing grain" (Deut 16.9). *Festival of ingathering,* the Festival of Booths (Lev 23.34; Deut 16.13). The priestly traditions reflected in Lev 23.34; Num 29.12 date it to the fifteenth day of the seventh month. *Fruit of your labor.* See Deut 16.13. **23.17** *Males.* See note on 10.11. *Appear before,* "see the face of" (see note on 23.15). *Lord, master* in 21.4–6, implying the Israelites are the Lord's servants (Lev 25.55). *GOD,* the name Yahweh, elsewhere rendered LORD. **23.18** *Leavened,* in light of 34.25; Deut 16.3–4, an addendum to v. 15. *Fat,* the hard, inedible coating of the entrails, burned into smoke (e.g., 29.12; Lev 3.5) and savored by God, signifying acceptance (e.g., Gen 8.21; Lev 26.31). *Until the morn-*

sacrifice with anything leavened, or let the fat of my festival remain until the morning.

19 The choicest of the first fruits of your ground you shall bring into the house of the LORD your God.

You shall not boil a kid in its mother's milk.

The Conquest of Canaan Promised

20 I am going to send an angel in front of you, to guard you on the way and to bring you to the place that I have prepared. 21 Be attentive to him and listen to his voice; do not rebel against him, for he will not pardon your transgression; for my name is in him.

22 But if you listen attentively to his voice and do all that I say, then I will be an enemy to your enemies and a foe to your foes.

23 When my angel goes in front of you, and brings you to the Amorites, the Hittites, the Perizzites, the Canaanites, the Hivites, and the Jebusites, and I blot them out, 24 you shall not bow down to their gods, or worship them, or follow their practices, but you shall utterly demolish them and break their pillars in pieces. 25 You shall worship the LORD your God, and I c will bless your bread and your water; and I will take sickness away from among you. 26 No one shall miscarry or be barren in your land; I will fulfill the number of your days. 27 I will send my terror in front of you, and will throw into confusion all the people against whom you shall come, and I will make all your enemies turn their backs to you. 28 And I will send the pestilence d in front of you, which shall drive out the Hivites, the Canaanites, and the Hittites from before you. 29 I will not drive them out from before you in one year, or the land would become desolate and the wild animals would multiply against you. 30 Little by little I will drive them out from before you, until you have increased and possess the land. 31 I will set your borders from the Red Sea e to the sea of the Philistines, and from the wilderness to the Euphrates; for I will hand over to you the inhabitants of the land, and

c Gk Vg: Heb *he*   d Or *hornets*: Meaning of Heb uncertain   e Or *Sea of Reeds*

---

ing. See note on 12.10.   **23.19** *Choicest, best* in 34.26; an addendum to v. 16. The amount depends on individual ability (Deut 16.17). *House*, a temple such as that at Shiloh (Judg 18.31; 1 Sam 1.17) or Jerusalem (1 Kings 8.10). *You shall not . . . milk*. Mixing death with a life fluid is ritually polluting (cf. blood or semen loss from a reproductive organ, Lev 12; 15). The context here and in 34.26 is opaque, but in Deut 14.21 the law occurs among eating regulations.

23.20–33 Biblical law is presented through the analogy of Near Eastern treaty conditions that an overlord (the Lord) imposes on a vassal (Israel). Such treaties conclude with curses to befall the vassal should it disobey. Blessings and curses conclude legislation in Lev 26; Deut 28. Here they are intermixed with commands because the legislation does not end but resumes with cultic law. The passage is elaborated in Deut 7.12–26. **23.20** *Angel*. Cf. 14.19; see Josh 5.13–15; Judg 2.1–5.   **23.21** *Name*, a concretization of the deity; e.g., Deut 12.5, 11; Pss 20.1; 54.1. **23.22** *Foe*, Hebrew *tsar*, perhaps a play on Egypt (*mitzrayim*). Cf. Lev 26.7–8; Deut 28.7. The last two clauses are parallel (see note on 3.15). **23.23** *Jebusites*. Cf. 3.17; Josh 3.10; 24.11. *Blot . . . out*, as Pharaoh has been (the same Hebrew verb rendered *cut off* in 9.15).   **23.24** *Bow down . . . worship*. Cf. 20.5; Deut 28.14. *Pillars*, steles, representing deities, on which libations are poured,

well attested archaeologically in Canaan; cf. 34.13; Deut 12.3. Israelite pillars are eventually forbidden (Lev 26.1; Deut 16.22; 2 Kings 18.4; 23.14).   **23.25** *Bread*. Cf. Lev 26.5, 26. *Sickness*, such as God brought upon Egypt (the same Hebrew word translated *diseases* in 15.26); cf. Lev 26.16; Deut 28.21–22, 58–61.   **23.26** Cf. Lev 26.9; Deut 28.4, 11; also cf. Lev 26.22 ("bereave" is the same Hebrew verb as *miscarry* here); Deut 28.18, 63.   **23.27** *Terror*. Cf. 15.14–16; see note on 14.24. *Throw into confusion*, as the Lord has done to Egypt (14.24, where *threw into panic* is the same verb); cf. Josh 10.10; also cf. Lev 26.36–37; Deut 28.20, 28–29. *Turn their backs*, as Israel must do when it is punished (Josh 7.8, 12); cf. Lev 26.7–8; Deut 28.7; 28.25.   **23.28** *Pestilence*, Hebrew *tsir'ah*, personified angel of destruction as in v. 20 and like "the destroyer" the Hebrew of 12.13 (see note there); in Hebrew it echoes *foe* in v. 22; cf. Deut 7.20; Josh 24.12. *Hivites . . . Hittites*, a list abridged from v. 23.   **23.29** *In one year*, as in Josh 10–11, but gradually as in Josh 13; Judg 1. *Wild animals*. Cf. Lev 26.22; Lam 5.18.   **23.30** *Increased*, as you began to do in Egypt (1.7, 12). *Possess*, inherit (e.g., Josh 14.1); cf. Josh 13.6–7. **23.31** *Sea of the Philistines*: the Mediterranean ("Western Sea" in Deut 11.24; "Great Sea" in Josh 1.4). *Wilderness*, the Negev (cf. Deut 11.24; Josh 1.4). *Euphrates*, lit. "the river" (see Deut 11.24). Cf. the extent of Solomon's kingdom (1 Kings 4.21).

you shall drive them out before you. **32**You shall make no covenant with them and their gods. 33 They shall not live in your land, or they will make you sin against me; for if you worship their gods, it will surely be a snare to you.

The Blood of the Covenant

24 Then he said to Moses, "Come up to the LORD, you and Aaron, Nadab, and Abihu, and seventy of the elders of Israel, and worship at a distance. 2 Moses alone shall come near the LORD; but the others shall not come near, and the people shall not come up with him."

3 Moses came and told the people all the words of the LORD and all the ordinances; and all the people answered with one voice, and said, "All the words that the LORD has spoken we will do." 4 And Moses wrote down all the words of the LORD. He rose early in the morning, and built an altar at the foot of the mountain, and set up twelve pillars, corresponding to the twelve tribes of Israel. 5 He sent young men of the people of Israel, who offered burnt offerings and sacrificed oxen as offerings of well-being to the LORD. 6 Moses took half of the blood and put it in basins, and half of the blood he dashed against the altar. 7 Then he took the book of the covenant, and read it in the hearing of the people; and they said, "All that the LORD has spoken we will do, and we will be obedient." 8 Moses took the blood and dashed it on the people, and said, "See the blood of the covenant that the LORD has made with you in accordance with all these words."

On the Mountain with God

9 Then Moses and Aaron, Nadab, and Abihu, and seventy of the elders of Israel went up, 10 and they saw the God of Israel. Under his feet there was something like a pavement of sapphire stone, like the very heaven for clearness. 11 God f did not lay his hand on the chief men of the people of Israel; also they beheld God, and they ate and drank.

12 The LORD said to Moses, "Come up to me on the mountain, and wait there; and I will give you the tablets of stone,

f Heb He

23.32–33 These verses are elaborated in 34.11–16; cf. Josh 23.12–13; Judg 2.2–3; and note the trick in Josh 9. **23.33** *A snare*, eventually leading to disaster; cf. Judg 8.27; 1 Sam 18.21. **24.1–8** Ritual ratification of the covenant (cf. note on 19.1–9), an apparent but imprecise sequel to 19.24 (see 20.21). **24.1** *To Moses*. Cf. the address to all Israel (20.22). *To the LORD*. The Lord refers to himself in the third person as in 19.24. *Nadab and Abihu*. Cf. 6.23. *Seventy*, a full complement (cf. 1.5). Cf. Num 11.16–17, 24–25. *Elders*. Cf. 19.7. *Worship*, lit. "bow down." *At a distance*. Cf. 20.18, 21. **24.3** *Came*, presumably prior to fulfilling the command in vv. 1–2; see note on 24.9–11. *Ordinances*, in 20.23–23.19. *Do*. Cf. v. 7; 19.8; see note on 19.1–9. The repetition of *all* suggests completion. **24.4** *Wrote down*. Cf. 17.14. The *book* (v. 7), presumably parchment since stone is not specified (as in v. 12; 31.18), may be understood to be deposited in the ark (25.16, 21) as was customary with treaty documents. *Pillars*, as witnesses (Gen 31.44–48; Josh 24.26–27); cf. note on 23.24. **24.5** *Young men*, acting as cultic assistants prior to the establishment of the hereditary priesthood (cf. 1 Sam 2.11–18). *Oxen*, rather "bulls"; the term occurs at the end of the sentence in the Hebrew, meaning that both types of offering consist of bulls. *Well-*

being. See note on 20.24. The people eat the flesh of this offering (see Lev 3) so that both parties partake. **24.6** The Hebrew term translated *basins* here is never used of implements in priestly practices. *Altar*, the Lord's surrogate in the ceremony. **24.7** *Read it*. Cf. Deut 31.9–13; 2 Kings 23.1–3; Neh 8.1–8. *Be obedient*, the same term rendered *listen* in 20.19. **24.8** *People*, or the pillars (v. 4) as their surrogates. Dashing blood, elsewhere an instrument of purification and atonement, on the two parties signifies somehow that the onus is on both; cf. Heb 9.18–22. **24.9–11** A resumption of vv. 1–2. **24.10** *Saw*. See note on 19.4. *Something like*, more precisely "like the construction of" (e.g., Ezek 1.16). *Sapphire*, as in Ezek 1.26–28; God's upper body is not directly perceived (cf. Ex 33.20). **24.11** *Lay his hand*. The command in vv. 1–2 supersedes 19.24. *Chief men*, presumably the *elders* (v. 9). *Beheld*, elsewhere used of prophetic visions (e.g., 1 Kings 22.19; Isa 6.1 where *beheld* is translated "to see"). *Ate and drank*. See note on 18.12. **24.12–18** Since Moses is already on the mountain, this resumes v. 8 or takes place after the others mentioned in v. 9 descend (see v. 14). **24.12** *Wait*, lit. "be," the root of God's name (see note on 3.14). *And I will*, rather "so that I may." *Tablets of stone*. Cf. 31.18; 34.1; Deut 4.13; called "tablets of the covenant" in Deut 9.9. *Law* (He-

with the law and the commandment, which I have written for their instruction." 13 So Moses set out with his assistant Joshua, and Moses went up into the mountain of God. 14 To the elders he had said, "Wait here for us, until we come to you again; for Aaron and Hur are with you; whoever has a dispute may go to them."

15   Then Moses went up on the mountain, and the cloud covered the mountain. 16 The glory of the LORD settled on Mount Sinai, and the cloud covered it for six days; on the seventh day he called to Moses out of the cloud. 17 Now the appearance of the glory of the LORD was like a devouring fire on the top of the mountain in the sight of the people of Israel. 18 Moses entered the cloud, and went up on the mountain. Moses was on the mountain for forty days and forty nights.

Offerings for the Tabernacle

25 The LORD said to Moses: 2 Tell the Israelites to take for me an offering; from all whose hearts prompt them to give you shall receive the offering for me. 3 This is the offering that you shall receive from them: gold, silver, and bronze, 4 blue, purple, and crimson yarns and fine linen, goats' hair, 5 tanned rams' skins, fine leather,g acacia wood, 6 oil for the lamps, spices for the anointing oil and for the fragrant incense, 7 onyx stones and gems to be set in the ephod and for the breastpiece. 8 And have them make me a sanctuary, so that I may dwell among them. 9 In accordance with all that I show you concerning the pattern of the tabernacle and of all its furniture, so you shall make it.

The Ark of the Covenant

10   They shall make an ark of acacia wood; it shall be two and a half cubits long, a cubit and a half wide, and a cubit and a half high. 11 You shall overlay it with pure gold, inside and outside you shall overlay it, and you shall make a molding of gold upon it all around. 12 You shall cast four rings of gold for it and put them on its four feet, two rings on the one side of it, and two rings on the other side.

g Meaning of Heb uncertain

---

brew *torah*) is cognate to the verb translated *instruction*; see note on 18.16.   **24.13** *Joshua*. See note on 17.9. Joshua appears to station himself partway up the mountain (cf. 32.17). *Mountain of God*. See 3.1.   **24.14** *Wait here*. See Gen 22.5. The vagueness sets the stage for 32.1. *Hur*. See note on 17.10; Hur fulfills Moses' judicial duties (18.26) along with Aaron. *Dispute*. See note on 18.16. **24.15–16** These verses anticipate 40.34–35. **24.15** *Cloud*. Cf. 19.9, 16; 20.21.   **24.16** *Glory*. See note on 16.6–7. *Settled*, the same term rendered *dwell* in 25.8, used of making the divine presence, in whatever form, immanent. *Six days*, double the period the people underwent sanctification merely to witness the divine presence (see 19.11).   **24.17** *Devouring fire*. Cf. Isa 30.30; Ezek 1.4; note on 13.21.   **24.18** *Forty*, a stereotypical number indicating a full period; cf. 34.28; Deut 9.9–11, 18, 25.
25.1–31.18   Moses learns how to set up a mobile dwelling (tabernacle) for the deity in the midst of the Israelite camp and to establish its priesthood. The dwelling serves as a shrine for worship and as an oracular source (29.43–44), the tent of meeting (27.21); cf. note on 33.7. The construction of the dwelling follows the golden calf incident (ch. 32) and consequent renewal of the covenant (chs. 33–34). It is uncertain whether the tabernacle described here corresponds to any historical edifice.   **25.2** *Offering*, from the Hebrew for "to raise," unrelated to term for sacrificial offerings, a "donation" (Num 15.19–21; Deut 12.6, 11, 17) to the priests and cult. *You*, plural, Israel at large.   **25.3** *Gold, ... bronze*. Like descriptions of the tabernacle and its paraphernalia generally, the three metals are presented in descending order of value. The holier the object (the more immediately it impinges upon the divine presence), the more valuable the materials of which it is made.   **25.4** *Blue, purple*, dyes fit for royalty (Esth 1.6; 8.15), taken from the sea (Ezek 27.7), a staple of Canaanite industry. *Fine linen*, an Egyptian export (Ezek 27.7), worn by nobility (Gen 41.42).   **25.5** *Tanned*, lit. "reddened." *Fine leather*, cognate to Akkadian (Mesopotamian Semitic) "dyed sheep/goat leather." *Acacia*, found locally.   **25.6** *Oil*, of olives (27.20). *Spices*. See 30.23–38. *Incense*. See 30.34–38.   **25.7** *Onyx*. Cf. Gen 2.12; Ezek 28.13. *Ephod*. See 28.6–14. *Breastpiece*. See 28.15–30.   **25.8** Cf. 29.43–46.   **25.9** *Pattern*, structural design, from the Hebrew "to build." Ascribing a temple's blueprint to its god is attested, too, in Mesopotamia and Egypt.   **25.10–22** That the Lord sits between and above two cherubim in the manner of ancient Near Eastern kings indicates that the ark is the divine throne or its footstool; cf. Ps 99.1. **25.10** *Ark*, lit. "box, chest," not the Hebrew term translated "ark" in Gen 6.14 (see note on 2.3).   **25.11** *Molding*, an ornamented ridge. **25.12** *Feet*, bottom corners. *Side*, the shorter side, so that the divine presence always faces forward;

13 You shall make poles of acacia wood, and overlay them with gold. 14 And you shall put the poles into the rings on the sides of the ark, by which to carry the ark. 15 The poles shall remain in the rings of the ark; they shall not be taken from it. 16 You shall put into the ark the covenant[h] that I shall give you.

17 Then you shall make a mercy seat[i] of pure gold; two cubits and a half shall be its length, and a cubit and a half its width. 18 You shall make two cherubim of gold; you shall make them of hammered work, at the two ends of the mercy seat.[j] 19 Make one cherub at the one end, and one cherub at the other; of one piece with the mercy seat[j] you shall make the cherubim at its two ends. 20 The cherubim shall spread out their wings above, overshadowing the mercy seat[j] with their wings. They shall face one to another; the faces of the cherubim shall be turned toward the mercy seat.[j] 21 You shall put the mercy seat[j] on the top of the ark; and in the ark you shall put the covenant[h] that I shall give you. 22 There I will meet with you, and from above the mercy seat,[j] from between the two cherubim that are on the ark of the covenant,[h] I will deliver to you all my commands for the Israelites.

The Table for the Bread of the Presence

23 You shall make a table of acacia wood, two cubits long, one cubit wide, and a cubit and a half high. 24 You shall overlay it with pure gold, and make a molding of gold around it. 25 You shall make around it a rim a handbreadth wide, and a molding of gold around the rim. 26 You shall make for it four rings of gold, and fasten the rings to the four corners at its four legs. 27 The rings that hold the poles used for carrying the table shall be close to the rim. 28 You shall make the poles of acacia wood, and overlay them with gold, and the table shall be carried with these. 29 You shall make its plates and dishes for incense, and its flagons and bowls with which to pour drink offerings; you shall make them of pure gold. 30 And you shall set the bread of the Presence on the table before me always.

The Lampstand

31 You shall make a lampstand of pure gold. The base and the shaft of the lampstand shall be made of hammered work; its cups, its calyxes, and its petals shall be of one piece with it; 32 and there shall be six branches going out of its sides, three branches of the lampstand out of one side of it and three branches of the lampstand out of the other side of it; 33 three cups shaped like almond blossoms, each with calyx and petals, on one

h Or treaty, or testimony; Heb eduth   i Or a cover
j Or the cover

the poles, which are never removed (v. 15), are perpendicular to the ark's length (cf. 1 Kings 8.8). **25.15** Once the tablets of the covenant (vv. 16, 21) are deposited in it (40.20), the ark itself becomes too holy to handle (see 2 Sam 6.6–7). **25.16** Covenant, the Ten Commandments (31.18). **25.17** Pure gold, solid gold, not plated like the rest of the ark, because God sits directly above it (cf. note on 25.3). **25.18** Cherubim, winged sphinxes with the body of a bull or lion and a human head; representations of these creatures are abundant in the archaeological evidence. Cf. Ezek 1; 10; 41.18–20; cf. the size and position of the cherubim in 1 Kings 6.23–28. These hybrid creatures represent the various animal powers over which God has control; cf. Gen 3.24; Ps 18.10. **25.20** Spread, to support the divine presence; cf. Ezek 1.11. Overshadowing, "screening over," so that the entire divine presence is seated above the lid (mercy seat). **25.22** Meet. See note on 25.1–31.18. I will deliver to you all my commands, lit. "I will speak with you

all I will command you"; cf. Num 7.89. **25.23** For the table's placement, see 26.35. **25.25** Rim, more precisely "frame"; the area between it and the molding above it gives a sunken look, described by the historian Josephus and depicted on the Arch of Titus (70 C.E.). **25.27** That hold the poles, lit. "for houses for the poles," a rhyming phrase in Hebrew. **25.29** For incense, added in translation, assuming that this is the purpose of the dishes (cf. Lev 24.7). With which, or "into which." To pour, or "can be poured"; in fact no liquid is poured into or out of these (cf. 30.9). Drink offerings, added in translation. **25.30** Bread, laid out for presentation but consumed by the priests (Lev 24.5–9; 1 Sam 21.1–6). Since the deity does not eat or drink, setting the table is a show of hospitality. Presence, lit. "face" (cf. note on 23.15). Always, rather "regularly" (as in 27.20), every sabbath (Lev 24.8; 1 Chr 9.32). **25.31** For the placement of the lampstand, see 26.35. Pure, solid. Calyxes, "capitals" in Am 9.1. Petals, "flowers." **25.32** Branches, the same

branch, and three cups shaped like almond blossoms, each with calyx and petals, on the other branch—so for the six branches going out of the lampstand. 34On the lampstand itself there shall be four cups shaped like almond blossoms, each with its calyxes and petals. 35There shall be a calyx of one piece with it under the first pair of branches, a calyx of one piece with it under the next pair of branches, and a calyx of one piece with it under the last pair of branches—so for the six branches that go out of the lampstand. 36Their calyxes and their branches shall be of one piece with it, the whole of it one hammered piece of pure gold. 37You shall make the seven lamps for it; and the lamps shall be set up so as to give light on the space in front of it. 38Its snuffers and trays shall be of pure gold. 39It, and all these utensils, shall be made from a talent of pure gold. 40And see that you make them according to the pattern for them, which is being shown you on the mountain.

The Tabernacle

26 Moreover you shall make the tabernacle with ten curtains of fine twisted linen, and blue, purple, and crimson yarns; you shall make them with cherubim skillfully worked into them. 2The length of each curtain shall be twenty-eight cubits, and the width of each curtain four cubits; all the curtains shall be of the same size. 3Five curtains shall be joined to one another; and the other five curtains shall be joined to one another. 4You shall make loops of blue on the edge of the outermost curtain in the first set; and likewise you shall make loops on the edge of the outermost curtain in the second set. 5You shall make fifty loops on the one curtain, and you shall make fifty loops on the edge of the curtain that is in the second set; the loops shall be opposite one another. 6You shall make fifty clasps of gold, and join the curtains to one another with the clasps, so that the tabernacle may be one whole.

7 You shall also make curtains of goats' hair for a tent over the tabernacle; you shall make eleven curtains. 8The length of each curtain shall be thirty cubits, and the width of each curtain four cubits; the eleven curtains shall be of the same size. 9You shall join five curtains by themselves, and six curtains by themselves, and the sixth curtain you shall double over at the front of the tent. 10You shall make fifty loops on the edge of the curtain that is outermost in one set, and fifty loops on the edge of the curtain that is outermost in the second set.

11 You shall make fifty clasps of bronze, and put the clasps into the loops, and join the tent together, so that it may be one whole. 12The part that remains of the curtains of the tent, the half curtain that remains, shall hang over the back of the tabernacle. 13The cubit on the one side, and the cubit on the other side, of what remains in the length of the curtains of the tent, shall hang over the sides of the tabernacle, on this side and that side, to cover it. 14You shall make for the tent a covering of tanned rams' skins and an outer covering of fine leather.*k*

---

k Meaning of Heb uncertain

---

word translated *shaft* in v. 31. **25.34** *Itself*, the center shaft. **25.37** *Shall be set*, lit. "he (Aaron) shall set," every evening (30.8), treating the deity like a royal guest. **25.38** *Snuffers*, "tongs" for adjusting the wicks and removing their charred remains. **25.39** *Talent*, an "ingot" weighing 3,000 shekels.

26.1–14 Four layers cover the frame of the tabernacle, the "dwelling" proper (not including the courtyard and its altar). **26.1** *Ten*. Segmenting the curtain facilitates transport. *Curtains*, to be laid over the top of the structure along the shorter side. *Cherubim*. See note on 25.18. The design of the bottommost curtain is visible only on the inside. *Skillfully worked into them*, lit. "the work of a designer" (cf. 35.32), woven in. **26.2** *Twenty-eight*. This decorative curtain is a cubit off the ground on both ends. *Four*, making the total length of all ten 40, covering the 30-cubit length of the tabernacle and overlapping the front and back (vv. 12–13). **26.4** *Set*, in Hebrew cognate to *join* in v. 3. **26.6** *Whole*, added in translation. The *goats' hair* was woven into a heavy cloth, a practice still current among Bedouin. *Tent*, a cover for the curtain beneath. *Eleven*, the extra length (cf. v. 1) makes a portal (v. 9). **26.11** *Bronze*. See note on 25.3. **26.12** *Part*, more precisely "extension," cognate to *hang over*. **26.14** *Fine leather*. See note on 25.6. The two

The Framework

15 You shall make upright frames of acacia wood for the tabernacle. 16 Ten cubits shall be the length of a frame, and a cubit and a half the width of each frame. 17 There shall be two pegs in each frame to fit the frames together; you shall make these for all the frames of the tabernacle. 18 You shall make the frames for the tabernacle: twenty frames for the south side; 19 and you shall make forty bases of silver under the twenty frames, two bases under the first frame for its two pegs, and two bases under the next frame for its two pegs; 20 and for the second side of the tabernacle, on the north side twenty frames, 21 and their forty bases of silver, two bases under the first frame, and two bases under the next frame; 22 and for the rear of the tabernacle westward you shall make six frames. 23 You shall make two frames for corners of the tabernacle in the rear; 24 they shall be separate beneath, but joined at the top, at the first ring; it shall be the same with both of them; they shall form the two corners. 25 And so there shall be eight frames, with their bases of silver, sixteen bases; two bases under the first frame, and two bases under the next frame.

26 You shall make bars of acacia wood, five for the frames of the one side of the tabernacle, 27 and five bars for the frames of the other side of the tabernacle, and five bars for the frames of the side of the tabernacle at the rear westward. 28 The middle bar, halfway up the frames, shall pass through from end to end. 29 You shall overlay the frames with gold, and shall make their rings of gold to hold the bars; and you shall overlay the bars with gold. 30 Then you shall erect the tabernacle according to the plan for it that you were shown on the mountain.

The Curtain

31 You shall make a curtain of blue, purple, and crimson yarns, and of fine twisted linen; it shall be made with cherubim skillfully worked into it. 32 You shall hang it on four pillars of acacia overlaid with gold, which have hooks of gold and rest on four bases of silver. 33 You shall hang the curtain under the clasps, and bring the ark of the covenant *l* in there, within the curtain; and the curtain shall separate for you the holy place from the most holy. 34 You shall put the mercy seat*m* on the ark of the covenant *l* in the most holy place. 35 You shall set the table outside the curtain, and the lampstand on the south side of the tabernacle opposite the table; and you shall put the table on the north side.

36 You shall make a screen for the entrance of the tent, of blue, purple, and crimson yarns, and of fine twisted linen, embroidered with needlework. 37 You

l Or *treaty*, or *testimony*; Heb *eduth*   *m* Or *the cover*

---

outer layers are weatherproofing. **26.15** *Upright frames*, "planks," which, placed side by side, form the 10-by-30-cubit structure. **26.17** *Pegs*, tenons on the bottom edge to be inserted into the bases (v. 19). *To fit the frames together*, rather "each (peg) parallel to the other," perpendicular to the bottom edge of the plank. **26.18** *South*, lit. "toward the Negev, southward," an orientation assuming a setting in the land of Israel. **26.19** *Bases*, sockets. *Silver*. See note on 25.3. **26.22** *Westward*, lit. "toward the (Mediterranean) sea"; see notes on v. 18; 10.19. **26.23** *Corners*, to enclose the open space left by the six planks in the rear, which cover only 9 cubits of the length. **26.24** *Separate*, rather "congruent" ("twinned"); the spaces on each side of the rear planks are to be symmetrical. *But joined*, rather "and identically (in the same pattern) will they end" (a Hebrew play on "congruent"). *First ring*, or "one ring," a crux, possibly a single band holding the planks together around the top of the perimeter. **26.25** *Eight*, the six planks plus the two corners. **26.26** *Bars*, to stabilize the planks in the middle. *Side*, "flank," different from *side* in vv. 18, 20. **26.28** *Halfway up*, "in the middle" (cognate to *middle*). *Pass through*, cognate to *bar*. The other bars, surely to be arranged in parallel, above and below the middle, do not extend all the way across. **26.30** *Plan*, *ordinance* in 21.1 and "rule" in 21.9 (see note there). Cf. 25.40. **26.31** *Curtain*, close in sound to *mercy seat* (25.17), referred to in v. 34. *Cherubim*. Cf. 26.1. *Skillfully worked*. See note on 26.1. The curtain matches the draped walls and ceiling of the *most holy place* (v. 34). **26.32** The construction is the same as the tabernacle framework. **26.33** *Under the clasps*, i.e., under the ceiling drape; see 26.6. **26.34** *Most holy place*, "holy of holies," the 10-cubit cube on the western end of the tabernacle proper, where the divine presence rests. Symmetry of space signifies holiness; cf. 27.1. **26.36** *Embroidered*, not woven in like the curtain (v. 31) since it is farther from the divine presence.

shall make for the screen five pillars of acacia, and overlay them with gold; their hooks shall be of gold, and you shall cast five bases of bronze for them.

The Altar of Burnt Offering

27 You shall make the altar of acacia wood, five cubits long and five cubits wide; the altar shall be square, and it shall be three cubits high. 2 You shall make horns for it on its four corners; its horns shall be of one piece with it, and you shall overlay it with bronze. 3 You shall make pots for it to receive its ashes, and shovels and basins and forks and firepans; you shall make all its utensils of bronze. 4 You shall also make for it a grating, a network of bronze; and on the net you shall make four bronze rings at its four corners. 5 You shall set it under the ledge of the altar so that the net shall extend halfway down the altar. 6 You shall make poles for the altar, poles of acacia wood, and overlay them with bronze; 7 the poles shall be put through the rings, so that the poles shall be on the two sides of the altar when it is carried. 8 You shall make it hollow, with boards. They shall be made just as you were shown on the mountain.

The Court and Its Hangings

9 You shall make the court of the tabernacle. On the south side the court shall have hangings of fine twisted linen one hundred cubits long for that side; 10 its twenty pillars and their twenty bases shall be of bronze, but the hooks of the pillars and their bands shall be of silver. 11 Likewise for its length on the north side there shall be hangings one hundred cubits long, their pillars twenty and their bases twenty, of bronze, but the hooks of the pillars and their bands shall be of silver. 12 For the width of the court on the west side there shall be fifty cubits of hangings, with ten pillars and ten bases. 13 The width of the court on the front to the east shall be fifty cubits. 14 There shall be fifteen cubits of hangings on the one side, with three pillars and three bases. 15 There shall be fifteen cubits of hangings on the other side, with three pillars and three bases. 16 For the gate of the court there shall be a screen twenty cubits long, of blue, purple, and crimson yarns, and of fine twisted linen, embroidered with needlework; it shall have four pillars and with them four bases. 17 All the pillars around the court shall be banded with silver; their hooks shall be of silver, and their bases of bronze. 18 The length of the court shall be one hundred cubits, the width fifty, and the height five cubits, with hangings of fine twisted linen and bases of bronze. 19 All the utensils of the tabernacle for every use, and all its pegs and all the pegs of the court, shall be of bronze.

The Oil for the Lamp

20 You shall further command the Israelites to bring you pure oil of beaten olives for the light, so that a lamp may be set up to burn regularly. 21 In the tent of meeting, outside the curtain that is before

---

27.1–8 The courtyard altar, the altar of burnt offering (38.1), is bronze (cf. 30.3; note on 25.3); also cf. 20.24–25. **27.1** *Square.* See note on 26.34; the *altar* is called *most holy* (29.37). **27.2** *Horns,* a symbol of God (cf. Num 23.22 and note that the Canaanite god Baal is depicted with horns on his helmet) or the animals offered; cf. 1 Kings 1.50–53; 2.28–34. Stone altars with "horns" at the four corners have been excavated at several Israelite sites. **27.4** *Grating,* to support the ledge (v. 5), on which the officiating priests presumably stood. **27.5** *Down,* lit. "up" from the ground. **27.8** *Boards,* panels, the same word translated *tablets* (e.g., 24.12). *Shown.* Cf. 25.40; 26.30. **27.9–19** The 50-by-100-cubit rectangular court, a topless tent, surrounds the tabernacle in its western half and the bronze altar in its eastern half; it is assumed that the ark and altar were situated at the centers of their respective squares, in which case the eastern edge of the tabernacle proper lies on the line that bisects the court's length. **27.10** *Bases,* sockets. *Hooks,* for holding the hangings. *Bands,* decoration encircling the pillars; see v. 17; 38.17, which also mentions capitals. **27.13** Oriented eastward, the tabernacle fills with sunlight in the morning. **27.16** The *gate* stands in front of an open entryway in the middle of the eastern edge. *Screen,* like the one in 26.36 but narrower. **27.19** *Use,* a term for cultic "service" (cognate to *worship* in 4.23). *Pegs,* tent-pins whose cords (35.18) stabilize the pillars. **27.20** *To burn,* not in the Hebrew. *Regularly,* every evening (v. 21). The instructions return to service within the tabernacle itself. **27.21** *Tent of meeting,* the tabernacle proper (see note on 25.1–31.18). *Covenant,* elliptical for *ark of the cove-*

the covenant,[n] Aaron and his sons shall tend it from evening to morning before the LORD. It shall be a perpetual ordinance to be observed throughout their generations by the Israelites.

Vestments for the Priesthood

28 Then bring near to you your brother Aaron, and his sons with him, from among the Israelites, to serve me as priests—Aaron and Aaron's sons, Nadab and Abihu, Eleazar and Ithamar. [2]You shall make sacred vestments for the glorious adornment of your brother Aaron. [3]And you shall speak to all who have ability, whom I have endowed with skill, that they make Aaron's vestments to consecrate him for my priesthood. [4]These are the vestments that they shall

make: a breastpiece, an ephod, a robe, a checkered tunic, a turban, and a sash. When they make these sacred vestments for your brother Aaron and his sons to serve me as priests, [5]they shall use gold, blue, purple, and crimson yarns, and fine linen.

The Ephod

6 They shall make the ephod of gold, of blue, purple, and crimson yarns, and of fine twisted linen, skillfully worked. [7]It shall have two shoulder-pieces attached to its two edges, so that it may be joined together. [8]The decorated band on it shall be of the same workmanship and materials, of gold, of blue, purple, and crimson

n Or *treaty*, or *testimony*; Heb *eduth*

---

nant (25.22). *Aaron and his sons*, whoever of Aaron's lineage is the chief priest at the time (see Lev 24.3). *Tend*, lit. "arrange," fill the lamp every evening with enough fuel to burn till daybreak (cf. 1 Sam 3.3). *Perpetual*, and not the one time implied by 25.1–7. *To be observed*, added for clarity.

28.1–43 The description up to v. 40 concerns the vestments only the chief priest (Aaron) wears, only when officiating inside the tabernacle. **28.1** Cf. 6.23. **28.3** *To all who have ability*, lit. "to all wise of heart," cognate to *skill*. *To consecrate*. See 29.5–6; Lev 8.6–13. *For my priesthood, to*

serve me as priest (vv. 1, 4). **28.4** *Checkered*, or "fringed," cognate to *filigree* (e.g., v. 11). **28.6** *Ephod*, a long vest (1 Sam 2.18; 2 Sam 6.14) made of the same materials as the curtain (26.31), open at the bottom and fastened at the top; it is possibly derived from the questionable cult object of the same name (e.g., Judg 8.27; 17.5; 1 Sam 21.9; Hos 3.4) used as an oracle (1 Sam 23.9–12; 30.7–8). **28.7** *Attached*, permanently (sewn on). The Hebrew is unclear; *to its two edges* may modify *it may be joined*, i.e., it is to be fastened at the top corner edges, on the shoulders. **28.8** *Decorated band*, a girdle around the middle, perhaps more

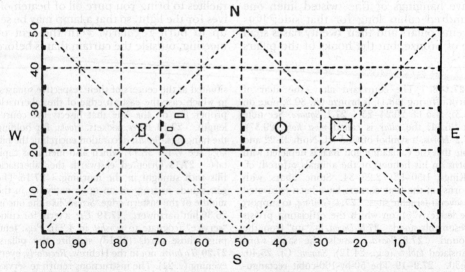

This plan approximates the court of the tabernacle as it is described in Exodus 27. The 50-by-100-cubit rectangular court, a topless tent, surrounds the tabernacle in its western half and the bronze courtyard altar, the altar of burnt offering, in its eastern half. (From S. R. Driver, The Book of Exodus.*)*

yarns, and of fine twisted linen. 9You shall take two onyx stones, and engrave on them the names of the sons of Israel, 10six of their names on the one stone, and the names of the remaining six on the other stone, in the order of their birth. 11As a gem-cutter engraves signets, so you shall engrave the two stones with the names of the sons of Israel; you shall mount them in settings of gold filigree. 12You shall set the two stones on the shoulder-pieces of the ephod, as stones of remembrance for the sons of Israel; and Aaron shall bear their names before the LORD on his two shoulders for remembrance. 13You shall make settings of gold filigree, 14and two chains of pure gold, twisted like cords; and you shall attach the corded chains to the settings.

The Breastplate

15 You shall make a breastpiece of judgment, in skilled work; you shall make it in the style of the ephod; of gold, of blue and purple and crimson yarns, and of fine twisted linen you shall make it. 16It shall be square and doubled, a span in length and a span in width. 17You shall set in it four rows of stones. A row of carnelian,o chrysolite, and emerald shall be the first row; 18and the second row a turquoise, a sapphirep and a moonstone; 19and the third row a jacinth, an agate, and an amethyst; 20and the fourth row a beryl, an onyx, and a jasper; they shall be set in gold filigree. 21There shall be twelve stones with names corresponding

to the names of the sons of Israel; they shall be like signets, each engraved with its name, for the twelve tribes. 22You shall make for the breastpiece chains of pure gold, twisted like cords; 23and you shall make for the breastpiece two rings of gold, and put the two rings on the two edges of the breastpiece. 24You shall put the two cords of gold in the two rings at the edges of the breastpiece; 25the two ends of the two cords you shall attach to the two settings, and so attach it in front to the shoulder-pieces of the ephod. 26You shall make two rings of gold, and put them at the two ends of the breastpiece, on its inside edge next to the ephod. 27You shall make two rings of gold, and attach them in front to the lower part of the two shoulder-pieces of the ephod, at its joining above the decorated band of the ephod. 28The breastpiece shall be bound by its rings to the rings of the ephod with a blue cord, so that it may lie on the decorated band of the ephod, and so that the breastpiece shall not come loose from the ephod. 29So Aaron shall bear the names of the sons of Israel in the breastpiece of judgment on his heart when he goes into the holy place, for a continual remembrance before the LORD. 30In the breastpiece of judgment you shall put the Urim and the Thummim, and they shall be on Aaron's heart when he goes in before the LORD; thus Aaron shall bear the judgment of the Is-

o The identity of several of these stones is uncertain   p Or lapis lazuli

---

precisely "the band of the vest." Decorated is a play on skillfully worked (v. 6); band is cognate to ephod. 28.10 In the order of their birth (see Gen 29–30; 35), or "according to their lineages," in order by mother (cf. Gen 46; Num 1). 28.12 Remembrance, to call Israel, the covenant partner the priest represents, to the Lord's attention; cf. v. 29; 2.24; 30.16; Num 10.10; 31.54. 28.13 Settings, in the shoulder-pieces of the ephod (v. 7). 28.14 Chains, to attach the breastpiece (vv. 22–28) to the ephod. 28.15 Breastpiece, or "pouch." Judgment, in the sense of divine messages (cf. 22.9) mediated by the Urim and Thummim (v. 30; see note on 28.30). 28.16 Square. Cf. 27.1. Doubled, to form the pouch (see note on 28.15). 28.17 In it. The Hebrew adds "settings of stone." Stones. The gems in all but row three (v. 19) are said by Ezekiel (28.13) to adorn "Eden, the garden of God" (cf. Gen 2.12) and the king of

Tyre; cf. Rev 21.19–20. 28.23 On the ... edges, at the shoulders (cf. note on 28.7). 28.25 Settings. See v. 13. In front, more precisely "opposite the face (front)"; the ephod will double under (v. 26). 28.26 On its inside edge next to the ephod, more precisely "on its lip (hemmed edge) (running) along the ephod on the inside." 28.27 See notes on 28.7; 28.8. 28.28 Bound, linked. Blue. See note on 25.4; cf. Num 15.38. Lie on, more precisely "be (right) over." 28.29 In, or "on." Holy place, the outer part of the tabernacle proper, location of the lampstand and table. Continual, rendered regularly in 27.20. Remembrance. Cf. v. 12. 28.30 Urim and Thummim. Comparative evidence suggests they are light and dark stones, extracted from the pouch for the purposes of divination (see 1 Sam 14.41; cf. Num 27.21; Deut 33.8; 1 Sam 28.6; Ezra 2.63). Bear the judgment, carry the divining medium (cf. note on 28.15).

raelites on his heart before the LORD continually.

Other Priestly Vestments

31 You shall make the robe of the ephod all of blue. 32 It shall have an opening for the head in the middle of it, with a woven binding around the opening, like the opening in a coat of mail,*q* so that it may not be torn. 33 On its lower hem you shall make pomegranates of blue, purple, and crimson yarns, all around the lower hem, with bells of gold between them all around—34 a golden bell and a pomegranate alternating all around the lower hem of the robe. 35 Aaron shall wear it when he ministers, and its sound shall be heard when he goes into the holy place before the LORD, and when he comes out, so that he may not die.

36 You shall make a rosette of pure gold, and engrave on it, like the engraving of a signet, "Holy to the LORD." 37 You shall fasten it on the turban with a blue cord; it shall be on the front of the turban. 38 It shall be on Aaron's forehead, and Aaron shall take on himself any guilt incurred in the holy offering that the Israelites consecrate as their sacred donations; it shall always be on his forehead, in order that they may find favor before the LORD.

39 You shall make the checkered tunic of fine linen, and you shall make a turban of fine linen, and you shall make a sash embroidered with needlework.

40 For Aaron's sons you shall make tunics and sashes and headdresses; you shall make them for their glorious adornment. 41 You shall put them on your brother Aaron, and on his sons with him, and shall anoint them and ordain them and consecrate them, so that they may serve me as priests. 42 You shall make for them linen undergarments to cover their naked flesh; they shall reach from the hips to the thighs; 43 Aaron and his sons shall wear them when they go into the tent of meeting, or when they come near the altar to minister in the holy place; or they will bring guilt on themselves and die. This shall be a perpetual ordinance for him and for his descendants after him.

The Ordination of the Priests

29 Now this is what you shall do to them to consecrate them, so that they may serve me as priests. Take one young bull and two rams without blemish, 2 and unleavened bread, unleavened

q Meaning of Heb uncertain

28.31 The *robe* is worn underneath the ephod; it is woven 39.22). *All*, or "of one piece of," in Hebrew plays on the sound of *blue*. *Blue*. See note on 25.4. **28.33** *Hem*, of fine twisted linen (39.24). *Pomegranates*, a common decorative pattern; cf. the almond blossoms in 25.33–34. **28.34** *Alternating*, lit. "a golden bell and a pomegranate," which rhyme in Hebrew, creating euphony; the rhythmic and sound patterns that adorn the descriptions are lost in translation. **28.35** The *sound* of the bells shows courtesy to the deity, who, like a monarch, may not be approached without announcement; cf. note on 25.10–22. *So that he may not die*, an admonition accompanying various cultic instructions (e.g., 30.20, 21; Lev 8.35; 10.9). **28.36** *Rosette*, lit. "flower," but more probably "shiny plate" (some Hebrew verbs for sprouting denote shining too) on which an inscription could be engraved; cf. 39.30. *Holy to*, or "sacred property of" (singular in Hebrew of *sacred donations* in v. 38). **28.37** *Blue cord*. Cf. v. 28. **28.38** *On*, or "above, over." *Incurred*. Cf. Lev 22.3, 9, 15–16. The head-plate may act like a lightning rod, mitigating divine reaction against unwitting desecrations (cf. notes on 19.13; 19.21). *Always*, regularly (27.20), when he enters the *holy place*

(v. 35). *They*, the sacred donations (cf., e.g., Lev 22.20). **28.39** *Checkered*. See note on 28.4. *Tunic*, woven of one cloth (39.27). *Turban*, worn by at least one Judean king (Ezek 21.26). *Sash*, worn by nobility (Isa 22.21). *With needlework*, added for clarity. The *sash* exhibits the royal hues that adorn the chief priest's vestments; see 39.29. **28.40** The *headdresses* are apparently wound on like a turban into a conical shape. See 29.9, where the headdresses are *tied* or lit. "wound" on. *Glorious adornment*. Cf. v. 2. **28.41** *Ordain*, lit. "fill the hands" ("mandate"). The verse previews ch. 29. **28.42** *Undergarments*, drawers; see note on 20.26. **28.43** *Tent of meeting*. See note on 27.21. *Holy place*, here the tabernacle and its court, where the altar stands (e.g., 36.1). *Die*. See note on 28.35.

29.1–35 The ordination procedure includes washing, investiture, and anointing (vv. 4–9), purification (vv. 10–14), propitiation (vv. 15–18), ordination (vv. 19–21), and homage (vv. 22–27). The ordination is performed in Lev 8–9. **29.1** *You*, Moses (25.1). *Them*, Aaron and his sons (28.43). *Without blemish*, lit. "whole." **29.2** *Unleavened*. See note on 12.8. *Cakes . . . wafers*. Cf. Lev 2.4. *Spread*, elsewhere translated "anointed" (e.g.,

cakes mixed with oil, and unleavened wafers spread with oil. You shall make them of choice wheat flour. 3 You shall put them in one basket and bring them in the basket, and bring the bull and the two rams. 4 You shall bring Aaron and his sons to the entrance of the tent of meeting, and wash them with water. 5 Then you shall take the vestments, and put on Aaron the tunic and the robe of the ephod, and the ephod, and the breastpiece, and gird him with the decorated band of the ephod; 6 and you shall set the turban on his head, and put the holy diadem on the turban. 7 You shall take the anointing oil, and pour it on his head and anoint him. 8 Then you shall bring his sons, and put tunics on them, 9 and you shall gird them with sashes r and tie headdresses on them; and the priesthood shall be theirs by a perpetual ordinance. You shall then ordain Aaron and his sons.

10 You shall bring the bull in front of the tent of meeting. Aaron and his sons shall lay their hands on the head of the bull, 11 and you shall slaughter the bull before the Lord, at the entrance of the tent of meeting, 12 and shall take some of the blood of the bull and put it on the horns of the altar with your finger, and all the rest of the blood you shall pour out at the base of the altar. 13 You shall take all the fat that covers the entrails, and the appendage of the liver, and the two kidneys with the fat that is on them, and turn them into smoke on the altar. 14 But the flesh of the bull, and its skin, and its dung, you shall burn with fire outside the camp; it is a sin offering.

15 Then you shall take one of the

rams, and Aaron and his sons shall lay their hands on the head of the ram, 16 and you shall slaughter the ram, and shall take its blood and dash it against all sides of the altar. 17 Then you shall cut the ram into its parts, and wash its entrails and its legs, and put them with its parts and its head, 18 and turn the whole ram into smoke on the altar; it is a burnt offering to the Lord; it is a pleasing odor, an offering by fire to the Lord.

19 You shall take the other ram; and Aaron and his sons shall lay their hands on the head of the ram, 20 and you shall slaughter the ram, and take some of its blood and put it on the lobe of Aaron's right ear and on the lobes of the right ears of his sons, and on the thumbs of their right hands, and on the big toes of their right feet, and dash the rest of the blood against all sides of the altar. 21 Then you shall take some of the blood that is on the altar, and some of the anointing oil, and sprinkle it on Aaron and his vestments and on his sons and his sons' vestments with him; then he and his vestments shall be holy, as well as his sons and his sons' vestments.

22 You shall also take the fat of the ram, the fat tail, the fat that covers the entrails, the appendage of the liver, the two kidneys with the fat that is on them, and the right thigh (for it is a ram of ordination), 23 and one loaf of bread, one cake of bread made with oil, and one wafer, out of the basket of unleavened bread that is before the Lord; 24 and you shall place all these on the palms of Aaron and

r Gk: Heb sashes, Aaron and his sons

Ex 29.36). **29.3** *In*, "on," suggesting an open basket or tray. *Bring*, "bring near," used of cultic offerings and approaching the deity, often repeated in this section. **29.5** *Vestments.* See ch. 28. The *undergarments* (28.42) are not mentioned because the priests put them on alone. *Gird*, in Hebrew cognate to *ephod*. **29.6** *Diadem*, the rosette (28.36), also used of a royal crown (e.g., 2 Sam 1.10). **29.7** *Anointing oil.* See 30.22–33. Anointing, performed also on kings, signifies luxury and privilege (cf., e.g., Ps 23.5; Eccl 9.8). **29.9** *Ordain.* See note on 28.41. **29.10** *Lay their hands,* to signify it is theirs (e.g., Lev 1.4); cf. Lev 4.4. **29.12** *The rest of,* added for clarity. **29.13** *Fat.* See note on 23.18. **29.14** *Outside the camp,* because the offering pollutes; cf. Num 19. *Sin offering,* or "purification offering" (from the verb

"cleanse," Lev 14.52). Its purpose is to remove ritual pollution and transform to a state of purity, a prerequisite to approaching God (cf. note on 19.10); it is used of purifying the altar in vv. 36–37. **29.16** *Dashing* the blood signifies its return to God (cf. Lev 17.6, 11). **29.17** *Parts,* in Hebrew cognate to "cut"; cf. Lev 1.6. *With,* rather "on top of." **29.18** *Odor.* See note on 23.18. **29.19–28** The ordination rite adapts the well-being offering (Lev 3). **29.20** *Blood,* a divine substance (cf. Lev 17.11) and therefore an agent of purification and safeguard against ritual pollution (see v. 21). Cf. Lev 14.14. *The rest of,* added for clarity. **29.22** *Fat tail,* part of the fat (Lev 3.9). *Right thigh,* ordinarily eaten by the priests (Lev 7.32–33), here served to God; the offering symbolizes a meal (see v. 25). **29.23** *Loaf,* more

on the palms of his sons, and raise them as an elevation offering before the LORD. 25 Then you shall take them from their hands, and turn them into smoke on the altar on top of the burnt offering of pleasing odor before the LORD; it is an offering by fire to the LORD.

26 You shall take the breast of the ram of Aaron's ordination and raise it as an elevation offering before the LORD; and it shall be your portion. 27 You shall consecrate the breast that was raised as an elevation offering and the thigh that was raised as an elevation offering from the ram of ordination, from that which belonged to Aaron and his sons. 28 These things shall be a perpetual ordinance for Aaron and his sons from the Israelites, for this is an offering; and it shall be an offering by the Israelites from their sacrifice of offerings of well-being, their offering to the LORD.

29 The sacred vestments of Aaron shall be passed on to his sons after him; they shall be anointed in them and ordained in them. 30 The son who is priest in his place shall wear them seven days, when he comes into the tent of meeting to minister in the holy place.

31 You shall take the ram of ordination, and boil its flesh in a holy place; 32 and Aaron and his sons shall eat the flesh of the ram and the bread that is in the basket, at the entrance of the tent of meeting. 33 They themselves shall eat the food by which atonement is made, to ordain and consecrate them, but no one else shall eat of them, because they are holy. 34 If any of the flesh for the ordination, or of the bread, remains until the morning, then you shall burn the remainder with fire; it shall not be eaten, because it is holy.

35 Thus you shall do to Aaron and to his sons, just as I have commanded you; through seven days you shall ordain them. 36 Also every day you shall offer a bull as a sin offering for atonement. Also you shall offer a sin offering for the altar, when you make atonement for it, and shall anoint it, to consecrate it. 37 Seven days you shall make atonement for the altar, and consecrate it, and the altar shall be most holy; whatever touches the altar shall become holy.

The Daily Offerings

38 Now this is what you shall offer on the altar: two lambs a year old regularly each day. 39 One lamb you shall offer in the morning, and the other lamb you shall offer in the evening; 40 and with the first lamb one-tenth of a measure of choice flour mixed with one-fourth of a hin of beaten oil, and one-fourth of a hin of wine for a drink offering. 41 And the other lamb you shall offer in the evening, and shall offer with it a grain offering and its drink offering, as in the morning, for a pleasing odor, an offering by fire to the LORD. 42 It shall be a regular burnt offering throughout your generations at the entrance of the tent of meeting before the LORD, where I will meet with you, to speak to you there. 43 I will meet with the Israelites there, and it shall be sanctified by my glory; 44 I will consecrate the tent of meeting and the altar; Aaron also and his sons I will consecrate, to serve me as priests. 45 I will dwell among the Israelites, and I will be their God. 46 And they shall

---

precisely "a (flat) round." **29.24** *Raise*, in Hebrew cognate to *elevation*; on the significance of the presentation, cf. note on 25.30. *Before the LORD*, in front of the tent of meeting (v. 4). **29.26** *You*, Moses, who partakes of the offering since he functions here as priest; cf. Lev 7.30–31. **29.27** *Consecrate*, render as cultic property. The second occurrence of *elevation offering* in this verse translates a generic Hebrew term for cultic donations (see note on 25.2), rendered *offering* in v. 28. The first occurrence translates a different Hebrew word, also in v. 26. **29.28** *Perpetual*. See Lev 7.28–36; Num 18.8, 18–19. **29.29** See Num 20.26. **29.30** *Seven days*. See vv. 35–37. *When he comes*, rather "who will come," in apposition to *priest*. **29.31** A resumption of v. 27.

29.33 *No one else*, an outsider (Num 1.51; 3.10, 38; 16.40; 18.4, 7) or nonpriest, here applied to any but the chief priests (as in Num 16.40). **29.34** *Holy*, rendered *sacred donations* in 28.38. **29.36** *Sin offering*. See note on 29.14. *Atonement*, in the sense of expurgating ritual pollution, such as that of the altar; cf. Lev 16. **29.37** *Seven days*. Cf. Ezek 43.26. *Most holy*, "holy of holies"; cf. 40.10. *Holy*, cultic property (a noun); see note on 29.34; cf. Num 16.37–39. **29.38–42** A digression on the use of the *altar*; cf. Num 28.3–6. **29.39** *In the evening*, rather *at twilight*, as translated in 12.6. **29.40** *A measure*, an ephah (see note on 16.36). *Hin*, one-sixth of a bath, the liquid equivalent of an ephah. **29.42** *Meet*. See note on 25.1–31.18. **29.43** *Glory*. See note on 16.6–7.

know that I am the LORD their God, who brought them out of the land of Egypt that I might dwell among them; I am the LORD their God.

The Altar of Incense

30 You shall make an altar on which to offer incense; you shall make it of acacia wood. 2 It shall be one cubit long, and one cubit wide; it shall be square, and shall be two cubits high; its horns shall be of one piece with it. 3 You shall overlay it with pure gold, its top, and its sides all around and its horns; and you shall make for it a molding of gold all around. 4 And you shall make two golden rings for it; under its molding on two opposite sides of it you shall make them, and they shall hold the poles with which to carry it. 5 You shall make the poles of acacia wood, and overlay them with gold. 6 You shall place it in front of the curtain that is above the ark of the covenant,ˢ in front of the mercy seatᵗ that is over the covenant,ˢ where I will meet with you. 7 Aaron shall offer fragrant incense on it; every morning when he dresses the lamps he shall offer it, 8 and when Aaron sets up the lamps in the evening, he shall offer it, a regular incense offering before the LORD throughout your generations. 9 You shall not offer unholy incense on it, or a burnt offering, or a grain offering; and you shall not pour a drink offering on it. 10 Once a year Aaron shall perform the rite of atonement on its horns. Through-

out your generations he shall perform the atonement for it once a year with the blood of the atoning sin offering. It is most holy to the LORD.

The Half Shekel for the Sanctuary

11 The LORD spoke to Moses: 12 When you take a census of the Israelites to register them, at registration all of them shall give a ransom for their lives to the LORD, so that no plague may come upon them for being registered. 13 This is what each one who is registered shall give: half a shekel according to the shekel of the sanctuary (the shekel is twenty gerahs), half a shekel as an offering to the LORD. 14 Each one who is registered, from twenty years old and upward, shall give the LORD's offering. 15 The rich shall not give more, and the poor shall not give less, than the half shekel, when you bring this offering to the LORD to make atonement for your lives. 16 You shall take the atonement money from the Israelites and shall designate it for the service of the tent of meeting; before the LORD it will be a reminder to the Israelites of the ransom given for your lives.

The Bronze Basin

17 The LORD spoke to Moses: 18 You shall make a bronze basin with a bronze stand for washing. You shall put it between the tent of meeting and the altar, and you shall put water in it; 19 with the

s Or *treaty*, or *testimony*; Heb *eduth*   t Or *the cover*

29.45 *Dwell.* See note on 25.1–31.18. **29.46** *Know.* Cf. note on 5.2; cf. 20.2.
30.1–5 The incense altar is constructed like that of the courtyard, but it is of more precious material since it will stand in the "holy place"; cf. note on 27.1–8. **30.1** *Offer*, in Hebrew cognate to *incense*, lit. "(aromatic) smoke." **30.4** *On two opposite sides*, lit. "on its two flanks, on its two sides." **30.6** *It*, the altar (v. 1). *Above*, rather "over" (see 26.31–33; 35.12). *Meet.* See 25.21–22. **30.7** *Offer*, burn (see note on v. 1). *Every morning*, lit. "in the morning, in the morning." *Dresses*, or cleans. **30.8** *Sets up.* Cf. 27.21. *In the evening.* See note on 29.39. **30.9** *Unholy*, lit. "alien"; cf. Lev 10.1; see note on 29.33. **30.10** *Once a year*, presumably on the Day of Atonement, although this rite is not specified in Lev 16. *Atonement.* See note on 29.36. *Most holy.* See note on 29.37. **30.11–16** The levy gives the Israelites a share in the tabernacle and protects

them against the demonic attack that a head count attracts; cf. 2 Sam 24; also cf. the harmless military census in Num 1. For the use of the levy, see 38.25–28; cf. 2 Chr 24.4–10; Mt 17.24. **30.12** *Take a census*, lit. "raise the head" (see Num 1.2). *Register*, rendered "take a census" in 2 Sam 24.2. *Plague*, the Hebrew term also rendered *plague* in 12.13 but not the one rendered "pestilence" in 2 Sam 24.15. **30.13** *Each one*, only males (cf. Num 1.2). *Twenty gerahs.* Cf. Lev 27.25; Num 3.47; 18.16. *Offering.* See note on 25.2. **30.14** *Twenty.* Cf. Num 1.3. **30.15** *To make atonement*, "ransom," in Hebrew cognate to *ransom* in v. 12; the same phrase is translated as *ransom* in v. 16 (see note there). **30.16** *To the Israelites*, rather "of the Israelites" *before the LORD*; see note on 28.12. *Of the ransom given for your lives*, rather "to ransom your lives." **30.18** *Basin*, or "laver," a different Hebrew term from the one so rendered in 24.6; the term is used in 1 Kings 7.38, where,

water[u] Aaron and his sons shall wash their hands and their feet. 20 When they go into the tent of meeting, or when they come near the altar to minister, to make an offering by fire to the LORD, they shall wash with water, so that they may not die. 21 They shall wash their hands and their feet, so that they may not die: it shall be a perpetual ordinance for them, for him and for his descendants throughout their generations.

The Anointing Oil and Incense

22 The LORD spoke to Moses: 23 Take the finest spices: of liquid myrrh five hundred shekels, and of sweet-smelling cinnamon half as much, that is, two hundred fifty, and two hundred fifty of aromatic cane, 24 and five hundred of cassia—measured by the sanctuary shekel—and a hin of olive oil; 25 and you shall make of these a sacred anointing oil blended as by the perfumer; it shall be a holy anointing oil. 26 With it you shall anoint the tent of meeting and the ark of the covenant,[v] 27 and the table and all its utensils, and the lampstand and its utensils, and the altar of incense, 28 and the altar of burnt offering with all its utensils, and the basin with its stand; 29 you shall consecrate them, so that they may be most holy; whatever touches them will become holy. 30 You shall anoint Aaron and his sons, and consecrate them, in order that they may serve me as priests. 31 You shall say to the Isra-

elites, "This shall be my holy anointing oil throughout your generations. 32 It shall not be used in any ordinary anointing of the body, and you shall make no other like it in composition; it is holy, and it shall be holy to you. 33 Whoever compounds any like it or whoever puts any of it on an unqualified person shall be cut off from the people."

34 The LORD said to Moses: Take sweet spices, stacte, and onycha, and galbanum, sweet spices with pure frankincense (an equal part of each), 35 and make an incense blended as by the perfumer, seasoned with salt, pure and holy; 36 and you shall beat some of it into powder, and put part of it before the covenant[v] in the tent of meeting where I shall meet with you; it shall be for you most holy. 37 When you make incense according to this composition, you shall not make it for yourselves; it shall be regarded by you as holy to the LORD. 38 Whoever makes any like it to use as perfume shall be cut off from the people.

Bezalel and Oholiab

31 The LORD spoke to Moses: 2 See, I have called by name Bezalel son of Uri son of Hur, of the tribe of Judah: 3 and I have filled him with divine spirit,[w] with ability, intelligence, and knowledge

u Heb it   v Or treaty, or testimony; Heb eduth
w Or with the spirit of God

---

unlike here, dimensions are given. **30.19** *With the water*, rather "from it," from the basin. **30.20** *Die*. See note on 28.35. **30.21** A parallelism effects closure (cf. note on 23.13). **30.22–38** For the actual anointing, see Lev 8.10–12. **30.23** *Finest spices*. Cf. Song 4.14. *Liquid*, or "solidified" (resinous), contrasting with the flowing state described in Song 5.5, 13. *Aromatic*, cognate to *spice* and *sweet-smelling*. **30.24** *Hin*. See note on 29.40. **30.25** *Blended as by the perfumer*. The Hebrew plies the same root three ways. *Holy*, the same Hebrew term rendered *sacred*; see also v. 32. **30.29** *Holy*. See note on 29.37. **30.30** *And his sons*. 29.7, 29 direct only that Aaron and his vestments be anointed; to resolve the discrepancy, cf. note on 27.21. **30.31** Cf. 1 Chr 9.30. **30.32** *It shall not be used in any ordinary anointing of the body*, lit. "On (ordinary) human flesh it shall not be poured." **30.33** *Compounds*, in Hebrew cognate to *blend*, rendered *perfumer* in v. 25. *Unqualified person*. See note on 30.9 (where the term is translated *unholy*). *Cut off*. See

note on 12.15. **30.34** *Sweet spices*, a different Hebrew term from (aromatic) *spices* in v. 23 and *fragrant* (spices) in 25.6. *An equal part of each*, lit. "part like part shall it be." **30.35** *Make*, lit. "make of them." *Blended*. Cf. v. 25. *Seasoned with salt*, rather "salted." *Pure*, ritually pure (not as in v. 34, which uses a different term). *Holy*. See note on 29.37. **30.36** *Part*, the same Hebrew term rendered *some*. *Covenant*. See note on 27.21. **30.38** *To use as perfume*, lit. "to smell by it." *Cut off*. Cf. v. 33.

31.1–11 The primary role of a Judahite versus the secondary role of a Danite in constructing the tabernacle presages the superiority of the Jerusalem temple of Solomon (of Judah; 1 Kings 6) over Jeroboam's shrine at Dan (1 Kings 12.25–30); cf. note on 32.1–35. The passage is reprised in 35.30–36.1. **31.2** *Called by name*, idiomatic for "designated" (e.g., Isa 43.1). *Bezalel* in Hebrew means "In-the-Shade (Protection)-of-God." *Hur*. See note on 17.10. Hur, Uri, and Bezalel are descendants of the Judahite Caleb (Num 13.6) in 1 Chr 2.18–20. **31.3** *Divine spirit*. Cf.

in every kind of craft, 4to devise artistic designs, to work in gold, silver, and bronze, 5in cutting stones for setting, and in carving wood, in every kind of craft. 6Moreover, I have appointed with him Oholiab son of Ahisamach, of the tribe of Dan; and I have given skill to all the skillful, so that they may make all that I have commanded you: 7the tent of meeting, and the ark of the covenant,x and the mercy seaty that is on it, and all the furnishings of the tent, 8the table and its utensils, and the pure lampstand with all its utensils, and the altar of incense, 9and the altar of burnt offering with all its utensils, and the basin with its stand, 10and the finely worked vestments, the holy vestments for the priest Aaron and the vestments of his sons, for their service as priests, 11and the anointing oil and the fragrant incense for the holy place. They shall do just as I have commanded you.

The Sabbath Law

12 The LORD said to Moses: 13You yourself are to speak to the Israelites: "You shall keep my sabbaths, for this is a sign between me and you throughout your generations, given in order that you may know that I, the LORD, sanctify you. 14You shall keep the sabbath, because it is holy for you; everyone who profanes it shall be put to death; whoever does any

work on it shall be cut off from among the people. 15Six days shall work be done, but the seventh day is a sabbath of solemn rest, holy to the LORD; whoever does any work on the sabbath day shall be put to death. 16Therefore the Israelites shall keep the sabbath, observing the sabbath throughout their generations, as a perpetual covenant. 17It is a sign forever between me and the people of Israel that in six days the LORD made heaven and earth, and on the seventh day he rested, and was refreshed."

The Two Tablets of the Covenant

18 When Godz finished speaking with Moses on Mount Sinai, he gave him the two tablets of the covenant,x tablets of stone, written with the finger of God.

The Golden Calf

32 When the people saw that Moses delayed to come down from the mountain, the people gathered around Aaron, and said to him, "Come, make gods for us, who shall go before us; as for this Moses, the man who brought us up out of the land of Egypt, we do not know what has become of him." 2Aaron said to them, "Take off the gold rings that are on

x Or treaty, or testimony; Heb eduth   y Or the cover
z Heb he

Gen 41.38. *Craft*, rendered *work* in 20.9. **31.4** *Devise*, in Hebrew cognate to *designs*. **31.5** *Setting*. Cf., e.g., 25.7. *Carving*, the same word rendered *cutting*. *In*. The Hebrew adds "doing," which is assonant with *setting*. **31.6** *Oholiab* in Hebrew means "My-Tent-is-the-Father (God)." *Skill to all the skillful*, lit. "wisdom in the heart of every wise of heart"; cf. note on 28.3. **31.7** *Furnishings*, the same term rendered *utensils* in vv. 8–9. **31.10** *Finely worked*, some ancient manuscript traditions read "service," of a root similar to *to minister* (e.g., 30.20). **31.12–17** The sacred time of the sabbath is analogous to the sacred space of the tabernacle; see Lev 19.30; cf. Ex 39.32; 40.34; Gen 2.1–2; also cf. Ex 39.43; Gen 2.3. See also Ex 16.22–26; 20.8–11; 23.12; 34.21; 35.2–3. **31.13** *You yourself*, a rhetorical indication of a new topic (27.20; 28.1; 30.23), not an emphasis on Moses' personal performance. *Keep*. See note on 20.8 (where the term is translated *remember*); cf. Lev 19.3, 30. *Sign*. Cf. Gen 9.12–13; 17.11. *Know*. Cf. 29.46; see Ezek 20.12. **31.14** *Holy*. See note on 29.37. *Profanes*, used of the sanctuary (e.g., Lev 21.12, 23; Ezek 23.39) as

well as the sabbath (e.g., Ezek 20.13). *Put to death*, by the community; cf. Num 15.32–36. *Work*. Cf. 20.9. *Cut off*. See note on 12.15. **31.15** *Solemn rest*. See note on 16.23. **31.17** *Rested*. Cf. Gen 2.2. *Refreshed*. Cf. 23.12. **31.18** *He gave him*. In Hebrew the phrase prominently begins the verse. *Tablets*. See 24.12.
    32.1–35 Making the golden calf violates 20.4, 23; cf. King Jeroboam's calves (1 Kings 12.25–33; see note on 32.4), which functioned historically not as idols but as pedestals for the deity (like the cherubim; see note on 25.18), but which are viewed as idolatrous in 2 Kings 17.16; Hos 8.4–6; 10.5–6; 13.2. Cf. the variations in Deut 9.8–21, 25–29; also Neh 9.16–18. **32.1** *Delayed*. Readers know Moses will be on the mountain forty days (24.18), but the Israelites do not. *Around*, rather "against" (e.g., Num 16.3). *Aaron*. See 24.14. *Gods*, or "a god." *This*, an expression of contempt (e.g., 1 Sam 10.27; 21.15). *The man*, or "this man Moses." **32.2** *Rings*, associated in Gen 35.4 with foreign gods that must be suppressed at Bethel, one of Jeroboam's cult sites (see note on 32.1–35).

the ears of your wives, your sons, and your daughters, and bring them to me." ³So all the people took off the gold rings from their ears, and brought them to Aaron. ⁴He took the gold from them, formed it in a mold,ᵃ and cast an image of a calf; and they said, "These are your gods, O Israel, who brought you up out of the land of Egypt!" ⁵When Aaron saw this, he built an altar before it; and Aaron made proclamation and said, "Tomorrow shall be a festival to the LORD." ⁶They rose early the next day, and offered burnt offerings and brought sacrifices of well-being; and the people sat down to eat and drink, and rose up to revel.

7   The LORD said to Moses, "Go down at once! Your people, whom you brought up out of the land of Egypt, have acted perversely; ⁸they have been quick to turn aside from the way that I commanded them; they have cast for themselves an image of a calf, and have worshiped it and sacrificed to it, and said, 'These are your gods, O Israel, who brought you up out of the land of Egypt!'" ⁹The LORD said to Moses, "I have seen this people, how stiff-necked they are. ¹⁰Now let me alone, so that my wrath may burn hot against them and I may consume them; and of you I will make a great nation."

11   But Moses implored the LORD his God, and said, "O LORD, why does your wrath burn hot against your people, whom you brought out of the land of Egypt with great power and with a mighty hand? ¹²Why should the Egyptians say, 'It was with evil intent that he brought them out to kill them in the mountains, and to consume them from the face of the earth'? Turn from your fierce wrath; change your mind and do not bring disaster on your people. ¹³Remember Abraham, Isaac, and Israel, your servants, how you swore to them by your own self, saying to them, 'I will multiply your descendants like the stars of heaven, and all this land that I have promised I will give to your descendants, and they shall inherit it forever.'" ¹⁴And the LORD changed his mind about the disaster that he planned to bring on his people.

15   Then Moses turned and went down from the mountain, carrying the two tablets of the covenantᵇ in his hands, tablets that were written on both sides, written on the front and on the back. ¹⁶The tablets were the work of God, and the writing was the writing of God, engraved upon the tablets. ¹⁷When Joshua heard the noise of the people as they shouted, he said to Moses, "There is a noise of war in the camp." ¹⁸But he said,

"It is not the sound made by
    victors,
or the sound made by losers;
it is the sound of revelers that I
    hear."

¹⁹As soon as he came near the camp and saw the calf and the dancing, Moses' an-

---

ᵃ Or *fashioned it with a graving tool*; Meaning of Heb uncertain   ᵇ Or *treaty*, or *testimony*; Heb *eduth*

32.4 *Image.* "Molten" is connoted. *Calf*, or young bull (cf. Ps 106.19–20, where the word translated "ox" means "bull"), an image applied to leading Canaanite gods; but see note on 32.1–35. *These.* The plural pronoun, which is more appropriate in 1 Kings 12.28 (a verse in which the words are virtually identical to this one), evokes Jeroboam's calves; cf. Neh 9.18. **32.5** *Saw.* Cf. v. 1. *Altar.* Cf. the legitimate altar (27.1–8). *It*, the calf (v. 4). *Festival.* Cf. 23.14–17. **32.6** *Revel.* Cf. v. 19; the verb has sexual overtones ("fondling" in Gen 26.8). The ritual seems to parody 24.5, 11; see also note on 32.8. **32.7** *Go down*, counterposed to v. 1. *Your . . . you.* The Lord follows suit in disavowing the people; cf., e.g., 20.2; 29.46. *Perversely*, translated "corrupt" in Gen 6.11–12; "dealt falsely" in Deut 32.5a. **32.8** *Worshiped.* Cf. 24.1; see note on 4.31. *These.* See note on 32.4. **32.9** *Seen.* Cf. v. 5. *Stiff-necked*, like an unresponsive draft animal (cf. Num 22.23). **32.10** *Consume*, in the sense of "put to an end," perhaps a pun in Hebrew on "devour" (Deut 4.24). *Great nation.* See Gen 12.2; cf. Num 14.12. Moses responds in v. 32. **32.11** *Your people.* Cf. v. 7; 33.13. **32.12** *Egyptians.* Cf. Num 14.13–16. *Mountains.* See note on 19.1. *Consume.* See note on 32.10. *Fierce*, burning (vv. 10–11). *Change your mind*, in Hebrew a pun on *let me alone* (v. 10); cf. Jon 3.9–10. *Disaster*, the same term rendered *evil intent.* **32.13** *Israel*, not *Jacob* as in 2.24, reiterating the bond between the people and its namesake. *Swore.* See Gen 22.16–17. *Forever.* See Gen 17.7–8. **32.14** *His people.* See v. 11. **32.15** *Turned*, "about-faced" (see note on 32.11). *Carrying*, not in the Hebrew. *Hands*, "hand" in Hebrew. **32.17** *Joshua.* See note on 24.13. *Noise*, the same term rendered *sound* in v. 18. *As they shouted*, in Hebrew a pun on *with evil intent* (v. 12). **32.18** *Made by victors*, more precisely "of singing triumph," as in 15.1–18. *Made by losers*, more precisely "of singing defeat." *Revelers*, "singing" (the same Hebrew verb as in 15.21; Isa 27.2).

ger burned hot, and he threw the tablets from his hands and broke them at the foot of the mountain. 20 He took the calf that they had made, burned it with fire, ground it to powder, scattered it on the water, and made the Israelites drink it.

21 Moses said to Aaron, "What did this people do to you that you have brought so great a sin upon them?" 22 And Aaron said, "Do not let the anger of my lord burn hot; you know the people, that they are bent on evil. 23 They said to me, 'Make us gods, who shall go before us; as for this Moses, the man who brought us up out of the land of Egypt, we do not know what has become of him.' 24 So I said to them, 'Whoever has gold, take it off'; so they gave it to me, and I threw it into the fire, and out came this calf!"

25 When Moses saw that the people were running wild (for Aaron had let them run wild, to the derision of their enemies), 26 then Moses stood in the gate of the camp, and said, "Who is on the Lord's side? Come to me!" And all the sons of Levi gathered around him. 27 He said to them, "Thus says the Lord, the God of Israel, 'Put your sword on your side, each of you! Go back and forth from gate to gate throughout the camp, and each of you kill your brother, your friend, and your neighbor.' " 28 The sons of Levi did as Moses commanded, and about three thousand of the people fell on that day. 29 Moses said, "Today you have ordained yourselvesc for the service of the Lord, each one at the cost of a son or a brother,

and so have brought a blessing on yourselves this day."

30 On the next day Moses said to the people, "You have sinned a great sin. But now I will go up to the Lord; perhaps I can make atonement for your sin." 31 So Moses returned to the Lord and said, "Alas, this people has sinned a great sin; they have made for themselves gods of gold. 32 But now, if you will only forgive their sin—but if not, blot me out of the book that you have written." 33 But the Lord said to Moses, "Whoever has sinned against me I will blot out of my book. 34 But now go, lead the people to the place about which I have spoken to you; see, my angel shall go in front of you. Nevertheless, when the day comes for punishment, I will punish them for their sin."

35 Then the Lord sent a plague on the people, because they made the calf—the one that Aaron made.

The Command to Leave Sinai

33 The Lord said to Moses, "Go, leave this place, you and the people whom you have brought up out of the land of Egypt, and go to the land of which I swore to Abraham, Isaac, and Jacob, saying, 'To your descendants I will give it.' 2 I will send an angel before you, and I will drive out the Canaanites, the Amorites, the Hittites, the Perizzites, the Hivites, and the Jebusites. 3 Go up to a land flowing with milk and honey; but I will not go up among you, or I would con-

c Gk Vg Compare Tg: Heb *Today ordain yourselves*

32.19 *Dancing,* as in 15.20. *Anger.* Cf. Num 20.10–11. *Burned hot.* Cf. vv. 10–11. **32.20** *Drink it,* a detail that goes beyond Deut 9.21; cf. Num 5.24. The calf is annihilated like a god in Ugaritic myth. **32.22** *Aaron* echoes Moses in v. 11. *Bent on evil.* The soundalike *running wild* (v. 25) is read here by another version. **32.23** Cf. v. 1. **32.24** *Threw* echoes Moses' action in v. 19; cf. v. 4. In Deut 9.20 Moses prays for Aaron's life. **32.25** *Let them run wild.* The Hebrew (*pera'o*) puns on "Pharaoh" and perhaps "Peor" (Num 25); see note on 32.28. **32.26** *Gate,* the place of assembly (e.g., Gen 23.10; Ruth 4.1). *Camp.* Cf. 19.2; see also Num 2. *On the Lord's side,* lit. "for the Lord." *Levi.* The Levites are subordinated to Aaron narratively in Num 16–18; cf. Deut 10.8–9; they are first consecrated for cultic service in Num 8. **32.27** *Neighbor,* or "relative"; cf. Deut 33.9. **32.28** Cf. Num 25.6–12.

32.29 *Ordained.* See note on 28.41. *For the service of,* Hebrew "for," as in v. 26 (see note on 32.26). *So have brought,* rather "so that he (the Lord) will bring." **32.30** *Great sin.* Cf. v. 21. **32.31** *Returned,* ironic for Moses, who had begged the Lord to *turn* (same Hebrew verb, v. 12). *Gods.* See note on 32.1. **32.32** *Book.* See note on 17.14. That the names of those who are to live is recorded on high is an ancient Near Eastern tradition; cf. Ps 69.28; Isa 4.3; Mal 3.16; also cf. Num 11.15. **32.34** *Lead,* a play in Hebrew on *let me alone* (v. 10). *Angel.* See 33.2. *For punishment*; lit. "of my accounting" (cf. 20.5). **32.35** *Plague.* See note on 30.12; the plague may result from the account in v. 20.

33.1 *Leave,* lit. "go up" (cf. 32.7). *You.* Cf. 32.7. *Jacob.* See note on 32.13. **33.2** *Angel.* Cf. 23.20. *Drive out.* Cf. 23.28; 34.11. **33.3** *Milk and honey.* Cf. 3.8. *I will not.* See vv. 16–17. Or, "lest," an

sume you on the way, for you are a stiff-
necked people."

4 When the people heard these harsh
words, they mourned, and no one put on
ornaments. 5 For the LORD had said to
Moses, "Say to the Israelites, 'You are a
stiff-necked people; if for a single moment I should go up among you, I would
consume you. So now take off your ornaments, and I will decide what to do to
you.'" 6 Therefore the Israelites stripped
themselves of their ornaments, from
Mount Horeb onward.

The Tent Outside the Camp

7 Now Moses used to take the tent and
pitch it outside the camp, far off from the
camp; he called it the tent of meeting.
And everyone who sought the LORD
would go out to the tent of meeting,
which was outside the camp. 8 Whenever
Moses went out to the tent, all the people
would rise and stand, each of them, at the
entrance of their tents and watch Moses
until he had gone into the tent. 9 When
Moses entered the tent, the pillar of cloud
would descend and stand at the entrance
of the tent, and the LORD would speak
with Moses. 10 When all the people saw
the pillar of cloud standing at the entrance of the tent, all the people would
rise and bow down, all of them, at the entrance of their tent. 11 Thus the LORD
used to speak to Moses face to face, as one
speaks to a friend. Then he would return

to the camp; but his young assistant,
Joshua son of Nun, would not leave the
tent.

Moses' Intercession

12 Moses said to the LORD, "See, you
have said to me, 'Bring up this people';
but you have not let me know whom you
will send with me. Yet you have said, 'I
know you by name, and you have also
found favor in my sight.' 13 Now if I have
found favor in your sight, show me your
ways, so that I may know you and find
favor in your sight. Consider too that this
nation is your people." 14 He said, "My
presence will go with you, and I will give
you rest." 15 And he said to him, "If your
presence will not go, do not carry us up
from here. 16 For how shall it be known
that I have found favor in your sight, I
and your people, unless you go with us?
In this way, we shall be distinct, I and
your people, from every people on the
face of the earth."

17 The LORD said to Moses, "I will do
the very thing that you have asked, for
you have found favor in my sight, and I
know you by name." 18 Moses said, "Show
me your glory, I pray." 19 And he said, "I
will make all my goodness pass before
you, and will proclaim before you the
name, 'The LORD';d and I will be gracious
to whom I will be gracious, and will show

d Heb YHWH; see note at 3.15

---

anticipation of rebellions to come (e.g., Num 11,
14). *Consume.* See note on 32.10. **33.4** *Harsh*
or "disastrous" (see 32.12). *Ornaments.* Cf. Jdt
10.1–4. In contrast to vv. 5–6, here the people
take the initiative. **33.5** *For the LORD had said,* lit.
"The LORD said," which would seem to precede
v. 4. *And I will decide,* lit. "so that I will know,"
in Hebrew a pun on *ornaments.* **33.6** *Horeb.* See
note on 3.1. **33.7** *Pitch it.* The Hebrew adds "for
himself." Moses pitches the tent to administer the
oracle (see v. 9; cf. note on 25.1–31.18). This *tent
of meeting* is the precursor of the tabernacle, also
called the tent of meeting (e.g., 27.21), which
will be located at the center of the camp (Num
2.2). The *tent* cannot be situated in the camp until
the camp can be cleansed of ritual pollution
through appropriate cultic activity (cf. Num
5.1–4). **33.9** *Cloud.* See notes on 13.21; 24.15;
cf. 40.34–38; Num 11.25; 12.5; Deut 31.15. *Entrance.* Cf. 25.22. **33.11** *Face to face,* figurative
for immediate contact (see vv. 20–23); cf. Num
12.8 (lit. "mouth to mouth"); Deut 34.10. *Joshua.*

See note on 17.9. **33.12–23** Note the key words
see, face (cf. v. 11), and *know.* **33.12** *See,* responding to vv. 1–3. *Whom.* In light of v. 2, Moses would
be asking for the angel's name (see Gen 32.29;
Judg 13.17–18; cf. 3.13). *Know,* lit. "have known,"
an idiom for "to elect" (Jer 1.5; Hos 13.5). Moses
anticipates the Lord (v. 17). **33.13** *Show me,* lit.
"let me know." *Ways.* See v. 19; 34.6–7; cf. Ps
103.7–18. *Consider,* rendered *see* in v. 12. *Your,* responding to v. 1; cf. 32.11. **33.14** *Presence,* lit.
"face" (also v. 15), replying to vv. 2–3 and anticipating 34.9. *Go.* Cf. 32.1. *Give you rest,* a play in
Hebrew on *lead* (32.34) and referring to the settlement of Israel in Canaan (see Deut 3.20; 12.10;
Josh 22.4). **33.15** *Carry . . . up,* the same Hebrew
verb rendered *bring up* in v. 12. **33.16** *Be distinct.*
See note on 11.7; cf. Deut 7.6. **33.17** *Know.* See
note on 33.12. **33.18** *Show me,* lit. "let me see."
Glory. See note on 16.6–7. **33.19** *Goodness,* or
"splendor" ("fair" in Hos 10.11). *LORD.* See note
on 3.14. *Gracious,* in Hebrew cognate to *favor*

mercy on whom I will show mercy. 20But," he said, "you cannot see my face; for no one shall see me and live." 21And the LORD continued, "See, there is a place by me where you shall stand on the rock; 22and while my glory passes by I will put you in a cleft of the rock, and I will cover you with my hand until I have passed by; 23then I will take away my hand, and you shall see my back; but my face shall not be seen."

Moses Makes New Tablets

34 The LORD said to Moses, "Cut two tablets of stone like the former ones, and I will write on the tablets the words that were on the former tablets, which you broke. 2Be ready in the morning, and come up in the morning to Mount Sinai and present yourself there to me, on the top of the mountain. 3No one shall come up with you, and do not let anyone be seen throughout all the mountain; and do not let flocks or herds graze in front of that mountain." 4So Moses cut two tablets of stone like the former ones; and he rose early in the morning and went up on Mount Sinai, as the LORD had commanded him, and took in his hand the two tablets of stone. 5The LORD descended in the cloud and stood with him there, and proclaimed the name, "The LORD."e 6The LORD passed before him, and proclaimed,
"The LORD, the LORD,
   a God merciful and gracious,
   slow to anger,
   and abounding in steadfast love
      and faithfulness,

7 keeping steadfast love for the
      thousandth generation,f
   forgiving iniquity and
      transgression and sin,
   yet by no means clearing the
      guilty,
   but visiting the iniquity of the
      parents
   upon the children
   and the children's children,
   to the third and the fourth
      generation."
8And Moses quickly bowed his head toward the earth, and worshiped. 9He said, "If now I have found favor in your sight, O Lord, I pray, let the Lord go with us. Although this is a stiff-necked people, pardon our iniquity and our sin, and take us for your inheritance."

The Covenant Renewed

10 He said: I hereby make a covenant. Before all your people I will perform marvels, such as have not been performed in all the earth or in any nation; and all the people among whom you live shall see the work of the LORD; for it is an awesome thing that I will do with you.

11 Observe what I command you today. See, I will drive out before you the Amorites, the Canaanites, the Hittites, the Perizzites, the Hivites, and the Jebusites. 12Take care not to make a covenant with the inhabitants of the land to which you are going, or it will become a snare among you. 13You shall tear down their altars, break their pillars, and cut down their

e Heb YHWH; see note at 3.15   f Or for thousands

(vv. 12, 13, 16, 17). Cf. 34.6. **33.20** See note on 3.6. **33.21** See, lit. "here." Place. Cf. 3.5. Stand. See note on 2.4. The Hebrew term is rendered present yourself in 34.2. Rock. Cf. 17.6. **33.22** Passed. See 1 Kings 19.11–12. **33.23** For the effect, see 34.29.

34.1–8 Following the pardon of the people's apostasy, the Lord dispenses another covenant-forging revelation. **34.1** Cut. Cf. v. 28. I will write. Cf. v. 28; see Deut 10.1–2, 4. **34.2** Be ready and morning evoke the Sinai revelation (see 19.11, 15, 16; the Hebrew term rendered prepare there is the same one rendered ready here). Top. Cf. 19.20. **34.3** No one. Cf. 24.2, 12; 19.24. Be seen. Cf. 19.12–13, 21–24. **34.5** The cloud, lit. "a cloud"; cf. 19.9, 16; 24.15; see note on 13.21. Stood. See note on 33.21. Proclaimed. Cf. 33.19; or

"invoked" (e.g., Gen 12.8), the subject being Moses. **34.6–7** See notes on 20.5; 20.6; 20.7. Variants are quoted in Num 14.18; Neh 9.17; Pss 86.15; 103.8; 145.8; Jer 32.18; Joel 2.13; Jon 4.2; Nah 1.3. **34.8** Toward the earth. Bowing the head "to the ground" was a conventional gesture of homage and is depicted in ancient art. **34.9** See note on 33.14. **34.10–26** In view of Israel's deviance in the golden calf incident (ch. 32), a reiteration of some fundamental covenantal laws. **34.10** Marvels, translated wonders in 3.20 and similar to the term rendered set apart in 8.22. Performed, rather "created"; cf. Num 16.30; Deut 4.32–34. **34.11** Cf. 23.28; 33.2. **34.12** Cf. 23.32–33. **34.13** Pillars. Cf. 23.24. Sacred poles, stylized trees (Deut 16.21); the Hebrew term for them asherim, is cognate to Asherah, the Canaan-

sacred poles*g* 14(for you shall worship no other god, because the LORD, whose name is Jealous, is a jealous God). 15You shall not make a covenant with the inhabitants of the land, for when they prostitute themselves to their gods and sacrifice to their gods, someone among them will invite you, and you will eat of the sacrifice. 16And you will take wives from among their daughters for your sons, and their daughters who prostitute themselves to their gods will make your sons also prostitute themselves to their gods.

17 You shall not make cast idols.

18 You shall keep the festival of unleavened bread. Seven days you shall eat unleavened bread, as I commanded you, at the time appointed in the month of Abib; for in the month of Abib you came out from Egypt.

19 All that first opens the womb is mine, all your male*h* livestock, the firstborn of cow and sheep. 20The firstborn of a donkey you shall redeem with a lamb, or if you will not redeem it you shall break its neck. All the firstborn of your sons you shall redeem.

No one shall appear before me empty-handed.

21 Six days you shall work, but on the seventh day you shall rest; even in plowing time and in harvest time you shall rest. 22You shall observe the festival of weeks, the first fruits of wheat harvest, and the festival of ingathering at the turn of the year. 23Three times in the year all your males shall appear before the LORD God, the God of Israel. 24For I will cast out na-

tions before you, and enlarge your borders; no one shall covet your land when you go up to appear before the LORD your God three times in the year.

25 You shall not offer the blood of my sacrifice with leaven, and the sacrifice of the festival of the passover shall not be left until the morning.

26 The best of the first fruits of your ground you shall bring to the house of the LORD your God.

You shall not boil a kid in its mother's milk.

27 The LORD said to Moses: Write these words; in accordance with these words I have made a covenant with you and with Israel. 28He was there with the LORD forty days and forty nights; he neither ate bread nor drank water. And he wrote on the tablets the words of the covenant, the ten commandments.*i*

The Shining Face of Moses

29 Moses came down from Mount Sinai. As he came down from the mountain with the two tablets of the covenant*j* in his hand, Moses did not know that the skin of his face shone because he had been talking with God. 30When Aaron and all the Israelites saw Moses, the skin of his face was shining, and they were afraid to come near him. 31But Moses called to them; and Aaron and all the leaders of the congregation returned to

g Heb *Asherim*   *h* Gk Theodotion Vg Tg: Meaning of Heb uncertain   *i* Heb *words*
j Or *treaty*, or *testimony*; Heb *eduth*

---

ite fertility goddess (cf. Judg 6.25); cf. Deut 7.5; 12.3. **34.14** *Jealous*, perhaps a play on the Lord's name, Yahweh, whose root can mean "crave" (Prov 10.3). Cf. 20.3, 5. **34.15** *Prostitute themselves.* See Num 25.1–2; cf. Lev 17.7; 20.5–6; Deut 31.16; Judg 2.17; 8.33. **34.16** Cf. Judg 3.6. **34.17** Cf. 20.4, 23; Lev 19.4. **34.18** In contrast to 23.12–15, the *festival of unleavened bread* is mentioned here before the sabbath and is separated from the other two pilgrimages, perhaps by virtue of its immediate connection to the exodus. **34.19–20** Cf. 13.12–13. *No one . . . empty-handed* pertains to the preceding law (v. 18; see 23.15); in ch. 13, too, the law about the firstborn is juxtaposed with the *Festival of Unleavened Bread.* **34.21** Cf. 23.12. **34.22–23** Cf. 23.16–17. For the name *festival of weeks*, see Deut 16.9–10. **34.22** *Turn*, lit. "(completed) circuit." **34.24** *Cast out*, lit. "dispossess" (Deut 9.5); cf.

23.23, 27–31; Deut 4.38 (where "driving out" translates the same verb). *Enlarge.* Cf. Deut 12.20 (where "territory" translates the same word as *borders* here). *Covet.* See note on 20.17; cf. the allaying fear in 23.29–30. *Go up*, an anticipation of the Jerusalem temple (e.g., 1 Kings 12.27). **34.25–26** Cf. 23.18–19. **34.27** *These words*, vv. 11–26. **34.28** *Forty.* Cf. 24.18. Here a second forty-day period is indicated; cf. Deut 10.10. *Neither ate bread nor drank water.* Cf. Deut 9.9, 18; a semidivine state is suggested. *Wrote.* See note on 34.1. *Commandments.* See v. 1. **34.29** *Moses came*, rather, "As Moses came." *Shone*, in Hebrew cognate to "rays" (Hab 3.4); see note on 13.21; 14.24. *God*, lit. "him," some of whose radiance was imparted to Moses (see 33.17–23). **34.30** *They were afraid*, because Moses looked like a god; see v. 20; cf. 14.24. **34.31** *Returned*, rather "turned."

him, and Moses spoke with them. 32 Afterward all the Israelites came near, and he gave them in commandment all that the LORD had spoken with him on Mount Sinai. 33 When Moses had finished speaking with them, he put a veil on his face; 34 but whenever Moses went in before the LORD to speak with him, he would take the veil off, until he came out; and when he came out, and told the Israelites what he had been commanded, 35 the Israelites would see the face of Moses, that the skin of his face was shining; and Moses would put the veil on his face again, until he went in to speak with him.

Sabbath Regulations

35 Moses assembled all the congregation of the Israelites and said to them: These are the things that the LORD has commanded you to do: 2 Six days shall work be done, but on the seventh day you shall have a holy sabbath of solemn rest to the LORD; whoever does any work on it shall be put to death. 3 You shall kindle no fire in all your dwellings on the sabbath day.

Preparations for Making the Tabernacle

4 Moses said to all the congregation of the Israelites: This is the thing that the LORD has commanded: 5 Take from among you an offering to the LORD; let whoever is of a generous heart bring the LORD's offering: gold, silver, and bronze; 6 blue, purple, and crimson yarns, and fine linen; goats' hair, 7 tanned rams' skins, and fine leather;*k* acacia wood, 8 oil for the light, spices for the anointing oil and for the fragrant incense, 9 and onyx stones and gems to be set in the ephod and the breastpiece.

10 All who are skillful among you shall come and make all that the LORD has commanded: the tabernacle, 11 its tent and its covering, its clasps and its frames, its bars, its pillars, and its bases; 12 the ark with its poles, the mercy seat,*l* and the curtain for the screen; 13 the table with its poles and all its utensils, and the bread of the Presence; 14 the lampstand also for the light, with its utensils and its lamps, and the oil for the light; 15 and the altar of incense, with its poles, and the anointing oil and the fragrant incense, and the screen for the entrance, the entrance of the tabernacle; 16 the altar of burnt offering, with its grating of bronze, its poles, and all its utensils, the basin with its stand; 17 the hangings of the court, its pillars and its bases, and the screen for the gate of the court; 18 the pegs of the tabernacle and the pegs of the court, and their cords; 19 the finely worked vestments for ministering in the holy place, the holy vestments for the priest Aaron, and the vestments of his sons, for their service as priests.

Offerings for the Tabernacle

20 Then all the congregation of the Israelites withdrew from the presence of Moses. 21 And they came, everyone whose heart was stirred, and everyone whose spirit was willing, and brought the LORD's offering to be used for the tent of meeting, and for all its service, and for the sacred vestments. 22 So they came, both men and women; all who were of a willing

k Meaning of Heb uncertain   *l* Or *the cover*

34.33 *Veil.* Cf. the cloud covering the deity's glory (e.g., 24.16). **34.34** *Before the LORD*, into the tent of meeting, see 33.7; Num 7.89. **35.1–3** Moses begins his instructions to the Israelites with the last matter in which he was instructed before descending the mountain (31.12–17); in this way the preceding topic of building the tabernacle (chs. 25–31) is resumed in what follows (chs. 35–40). The preparations for and construction of the tabernacle repeat the language of the instructions nearly verbatim, though with several ellipses. **35.2** Cf. 31.15. **35.3** Cf. 16.23; see note on 20.8. **35.4–9** Cf. 25.2–7. The tabernacle's purpose (see 25.8; 29.45–46) is omitted. **35.10–19** An expansive parallel to 31.6–11; the list is pervaded by rhythmic repetition, assonance, and rhyme (cf. note on 28.34). The description moves from the holy of holies to the tabernacle proper to the court, each closed on the east by a screen (vv. 12, 10, 17). **35.10** *Skillful.* See note on 28.3 **35.12** *Curtain for the screen*, called a *screen* only here; cf. 26.31–33, where no screen is mentioned, but see 40.3 for an association between the terms screen and curtain. **35.14** *Also*, not in the Hebrew. **35.20–29** The overwhelming response (see also 36.3–7) redeems the people's contributions to the illicit cult (32.2–3). Cf. 2 Chr 24.4–14. **35.20** *The presence of*, or "attendance upon." **35.22** *Earrings.* Cf. 32.2–3. *Offering*, rendered *elevation offering* in 29.27, here in a general sense (as in 38.24).

heart brought brooches and earrings and signet rings and pendants, all sorts of gold objects, everyone bringing an offering of gold to the LORD. 23 And everyone who possessed blue or purple or crimson yarn or fine linen or goats' hair or tanned rams' skins or fine leather,*m* brought them. 24 Everyone who could make an offering of silver or bronze brought it as the LORD's offering; and everyone who possessed acacia wood of any use in the work, brought it. 25 All the skillful women spun with their hands, and brought what they had spun in blue and purple and crimson yarns and fine linen; 26 all the women whose hearts moved them to use their skill spun the goats' hair. 27 And the leaders brought onyx stones and gems to be set in the ephod and the breastpiece, 28 and spices and oil for the light, and for the anointing oil, and for the fragrant incense. 29 All the Israelite men and women whose hearts made them willing to bring anything for the work that the LORD had commanded by Moses to be done, brought it as a freewill offering to the LORD.

Bezalel and Oholiab

30 Then Moses said to the Israelites: See, the LORD has called by name Bezalel son of Uri son of Hur, of the tribe of Judah; 31 he has filled him with divine spirit,*n* with skill, intelligence, and knowledge in every kind of craft, 32 to devise artistic designs, to work in gold, silver, and bronze, 33 in cutting stones for setting, and in carving wood, in every kind of craft. 34 And he has inspired him to teach, both him and Oholiab son of Ahisamach, of the tribe of Dan. 35 He has filled them with skill to do every kind of work done by an artisan or by a designer or by an embroiderer in blue, purple, and crimson yarns, and in fine linen, or by a weaver—by any sort of artisan or skilled designer.

36 Bezalel and Oholiab and every skillful one to whom the LORD has given skill and understanding to know how to do any work in the construction of the sanctuary shall work in accordance with all that the LORD has commanded.

2 Moses then called Bezalel and Oholiab and every skillful one to whom the LORD had given skill, everyone whose heart was stirred to come to do the work; 3 and they received from Moses all the freewill offerings that the Israelites had brought for doing the work on the sanctuary. They still kept bringing him freewill offerings every morning, 4 so that all the artisans who were doing every sort of task on the sanctuary came, each from the task being performed, 5 and said to Moses, "The people are bringing much more than enough for doing the work that the LORD has commanded us to do." 6 So Moses gave command, and word was proclaimed throughout the camp: "No man or woman is to make anything else as an offering for the sanctuary." So the people were restrained from bringing; 7 for what they had already brought was more than enough to do all the work.

Construction of the Tabernacle

8 All those with skill among the workers made the tabernacle with ten curtains; they were made of fine twisted linen, and blue, purple, and crimson yarns, with cherubim skillfully worked into them. 9 The length of each curtain was twenty-eight cubits, and the width of each curtain four cubits; all the curtains were of the same size.

10 He joined five curtains to one another, and the other five curtains he joined to one another. 11 He made loops

m Meaning of Heb uncertain   *n* Or *the spirit of God*

35.23 *Fine leather.* See note on 25.5. **35.30–33** Cf. 31.1–5. **35.34–35** A more elaborate version of 31.6, adding notably *to teach* the artisans. **36.1** *In the construction of,* rather "in connection with the service (i.e., sacrificial cult)" (see 39.40); cf. note on 27.19. **36.2** *Come,* "come near" (see note on 29.3). **36.3** *Received,* "took." *Freewill offering,* rather *an offering* (as in v. 6). *Doing the work,* or "the work of the service" (see note on 36.1). **36.4** *Task,* rendered *work* in vv. 1–2.

36.5–7 Cf. Pharaoh's complaint (5.4–9).

36.8–39.31 Unlike the instructions, which tend to treat the holiest objects first, the construction follows a practical sequence in which the holiest objects are not made until their protective surroundings are. Portions of instructions that deal with the use of the ritual paraphernalia are typically omitted. **36.8–19** Cf. 26.1–14. **36.10** *He,* Bezalel (35.30–35; cf. 37.1).

of blue on the edge of the outermost curtain of the first set; likewise he made them
on the edge of the outermost curtain of
the second set; 12 he made fifty loops on
the one curtain, and he made fifty loops
on the edge of the curtain that was in the
second set; the loops were opposite one
another. 13 And he made fifty clasps of
gold, and joined the curtains one to the
other with clasps; so the tabernacle was
one whole.

14 He also made curtains of goats'
hair for a tent over the tabernacle; he
made eleven curtains. 15 The length of
each curtain was thirty cubits, and the
width of each curtain four cubits; the
eleven curtains were of the same size.
16 He joined five curtains by themselves,
and six curtains by themselves. 17 He
made fifty loops on the edge of the outermost curtain of the one set, and fifty loops
on the edge of the other connecting curtain. 18 He made fifty clasps of bronze to
join the tent together so that it might be
one whole. 19 And he made for the tent a
covering of tanned rams' skins and an
outer covering of fine leather.o

20   Then he made the upright frames
for the tabernacle of acacia wood. 21 Ten
cubits was the length of a frame, and a
cubit and a half the width of each frame.
22 Each frame had two pegs for fitting together; he did this for all the frames of
the tabernacle. 23 The frames for the tabernacle he made in this way: twenty
frames for the south side; 24 and he made
forty bases of silver under the twenty
frames, two bases under the first frame
for its two pegs, and two bases under the
next frame for its two pegs. 25 For the second side of the tabernacle, on the north
side, he made twenty frames 26 and their
forty bases of silver, two bases under the
first frame and two bases under the next
frame. 27 For the rear of the tabernacle
westward he made six frames. 28 He made
two frames for corners of the tabernacle
in the rear. 29 They were separate beneath, but joined at the top, at the first
ring; he made two of them in this way, for
the two corners. 30 There were eight
frames with their bases of silver: sixteen
bases, under every frame two bases.

31   He made bars of acacia wood, five
for the frames of the one side of the tabernacle, 32 and five bars for the frames of
the other side of the tabernacle, and five
bars for the frames of the tabernacle at
the rear westward. 33 He made the middle
bar to pass through from end to end halfway up the frames. 34 And he overlaid the
frames with gold, and made rings of gold
for them to hold the bars, and overlaid
the bars with gold.

35   He made the curtain of blue, purple, and crimson yarns, and fine twisted
linen, with cherubim skillfully worked
into it. 36 For it he made four pillars of
acacia, and overlaid them with gold; their
hooks were of gold, and he cast for them
four bases of silver. 37 He also made a
screen for the entrance to the tent, of
blue, purple, and crimson yarns, and fine
twisted linen, embroidered with needlework; 38 and its five pillars with their
hooks. He overlaid their capitals and their
bases with gold, but their five bases were
of bronze.

Making the Ark of the Covenant

37 Bezalel made the ark of acacia
wood; it was two and a half cubits
long, a cubit and a half wide, and a cubit
and a half high. 2 He overlaid it with pure
gold inside and outside, and made a
molding of gold around it. 3 He cast for it
four rings of gold for its four feet, two
rings on its one side and two rings on its
other side. 4 He made poles of acacia
wood, and overlaid them with gold, 5 and
put the poles into the rings on the sides of
the ark, to carry the ark. 6 He made a
mercy seatp of pure gold; two cubits and
a half was its length, and a cubit and a half
its width. 7 He made two cherubim of
hammered gold; at the two ends of the
mercy seatq he made them, 8 one cherub
at the one end, and one cherub at the
other end; of one piece with the mercy
seatq he made the cherubim at its two
ends. 9 The cherubim spread out their
wings above, overshadowing the mercy
seatq with their wings. They faced one

o Meaning of Heb uncertain   p Or a cover
q Or the cover

36.20–34 Cf. 26.15–29. The command to
erect the tabernacle (26.30) is fulfilled not here
but in 40.17–19. Most other details of setting up

parts of the tabernacle are altogether omitted.
36.35–38 Cf. 26.31–32, 36–37.
37.1–9 Cf. 25.10–14, 17–20. **37.1** Bezalel,

another; the faces of the cherubim were turned toward the mercy seat.[r]

Making the Table for the Bread of the Presence

10 He also made the table of acacia wood, two cubits long, one cubit wide, and a cubit and a half high. 11 He overlaid it with pure gold, and made a molding of gold around it. 12 He made around it a rim a handbreadth wide, and made a molding of gold around the rim. 13 He cast for it four rings of gold, and fastened the rings to the four corners at its four legs. 14 The rings that held the poles used for carrying the table were close to the rim. 15 He made the poles of acacia wood to carry the table, and overlaid them with gold. 16 And he made the vessels of pure gold that were to be on the table, its plates and dishes for incense, and its bowls and flagons with which to pour drink offerings.

Making the Lampstand

17 He also made the lampstand of pure gold. The base and the shaft of the lampstand were made of hammered work; its cups, its calyxes, and its petals were of one piece with it. 18 There were six branches going out of its sides, three branches of the lampstand out of one side of it and three branches of the lampstand out of the other side of it; 19 three cups shaped like almond blossoms, each with calyx and petals, on one branch, and three cups shaped like almond blossoms, each with calyx and petals, on the other branch — so for the six branches going out of the lampstand. 20 On the lampstand itself there were four cups shaped like almond blossoms, each with its calyxes and petals. 21 There was a calyx of one piece with it under the first pair of branches, a calyx of one piece with it under the next pair of branches, and a calyx of one piece with it under the last pair of branches. 22 Their calyxes and their branches were

of one piece with it, the whole of it one hammered piece of pure gold. 23 He made its seven lamps and its snuffers and its trays of pure gold. 24 He made it and all its utensils of a talent of pure gold.

Making the Altar of Incense

25 He made the altar of incense of acacia wood, one cubit long, and one cubit wide; it was square, and was two cubits high; its horns were of one piece with it. 26 He overlaid it with pure gold, its top, and its sides all around, and its horns; and he made for it a molding of gold all around, 27 and made two golden rings for it under its molding, on two opposite sides of it, to hold the poles with which to carry it. 28 And he made the poles of acacia wood, and overlaid them with gold.

Making the Anointing Oil and the Incense

29 He made the holy anointing oil also, and the pure fragrant incense, blended as by the perfumer.

Making the Altar of Burnt Offering

38 He made the altar of burnt offering also of acacia wood; it was five cubits long, and five cubits wide; it was square, and three cubits high. 2 He made horns for it on its four corners; its horns were of one piece with it, and he overlaid it with bronze. 3 He made all the utensils of the altar, the pots, the shovels, the basins, the forks, and the firepans: all its utensils he made of bronze. 4 He made for the altar a grating, a network of bronze, under its ledge, extending halfway down. 5 He cast four rings on the four corners of the bronze grating to hold the poles; 6 he made the poles of acacia wood, and overlaid them with bronze. 7 And he put the poles through the rings on the sides of the altar, to carry it with them; he made it hollow, with boards.

r Or the cover

Moses according to Deut 10.3, 5. **37.10–16** Cf. 25.23–29. **37.17–24** Cf. 25.31–39. **37.25–28** Cf. 30.1–5. **37.29** A summary of 30.22–25, 34–35. **38.1–7** Cf. 27.1–8. **38.1** *Altar of burnt offering*, in contradistinction to the altar of incense (37.25–28). **38.2** *He*, Bezalel, but Eleazar according to Num 16.38–39. **38.8** *Basin of bronze.*

Cf. 30.18. *From the mirrors ... tent of meeting* provides new information, possibly alluding to a lost episode similar to the one in 1 Sam 2.22 in which the women who served were made to surrender their mirrors on account of sexual misconduct; for ritual paraphernalia as a reminder of misdeeds, see Num 16.36–40. The reference is out of

8   He made the basin of bronze with its stand of bronze, from the mirrors of the women who served at the entrance to the tent of meeting.

Making the Court of the Tabernacle

9   He made the court; for the south side the hangings of the court were of fine twisted linen, one hundred cubits long; 10 its twenty pillars and their twenty bases were of bronze, but the hooks of the pillars and their bands were of silver. 11 For the north side there were hangings one hundred cubits long; its twenty pillars and their twenty bases were of bronze, but the hooks of the pillars and their bands were of silver. 12 For the west side there were hangings fifty cubits long, with ten pillars and ten bases; the hooks of the pillars and their bands were of silver. 13 And for the front to the east, fifty cubits. 14 The hangings for one side of the gate were fifteen cubits, with three pillars and three bases. 15 And so for the other side; on each side of the gate of the court were hangings of fifteen cubits, with three pillars and three bases. 16 All the hangings around the court were of fine twisted linen. 17 The bases for the pillars were of bronze, but the hooks of the pillars and their bands were of silver; the overlaying of their capitals was also of silver, and all the pillars of the court were banded with silver. 18 The screen for the entrance to the court was embroidered with needlework in blue, purple, and crimson yarns and fine twisted linen. It was twenty cubits long and, along the width of it, five cubits high, corresponding to the hangings of the court. 19 There were four pillars; their four bases were of bronze, their hooks of silver, and the overlaying of their capitals and their bands of silver. 20 All the pegs for the tabernacle and for the court all around were of bronze.

Materials of the Tabernacle

21   These are the records of the tabernacle, the tabernacle of the covenant,[s] which were drawn up at the commandment of Moses, the work of the Levites being under the direction of Ithamar son of the priest Aaron. 22 Bezalel son of Uri son of Hur, of the tribe of Judah, made all that the LORD commanded Moses; 23 and with him was Oholiab son of Ahisamach, of the tribe of Dan, engraver, designer, and embroiderer in blue, purple, and crimson yarns, and in fine linen.

24   All the gold that was used for the work, in all the construction of the sanctuary, the gold from the offering, was twenty-nine talents and seven hundred thirty shekels, measured by the sanctuary shekel. 25 The silver from those of the congregation who were counted was one hundred talents and one thousand seven hundred seventy-five shekels, measured by the sanctuary shekel; 26 a beka a head (that is, half a shekel, measured by the sanctuary shekel), for everyone who was counted in the census, from twenty years old and upward, for six hundred three thousand, five hundred fifty men. 27 The hundred talents of silver were for casting the bases of the sanctuary, and the bases of the curtain; one hundred bases for the hundred talents, a talent for a base. 28 Of the thousand seven hundred seventy-five shekels he made hooks for the pillars, and overlaid their capitals and made bands for them. 29 The bronze that was contributed was seventy talents, and two thousand four hundred shekels; 30 with it he made the bases for the entrance of the tent of meeting, the bronze altar and the bronze grating for it and all the utensils of the altar, 31 the bases all around the court, and the bases of the gate of the court, all the pegs of the tabernacle, and all the pegs around the court.

s Or *treaty*, or *testimony*; Heb *eduth*

---

place here since the tent has not yet been erected. **38.9–20** Cf. 27.9–19. **38.21–31** The inventory of metals presupposes the census that is prescribed in 30.12–16 but performed only in Num 1, dated a month later than the erection of the tabernacle (cf. 40.17; Num 1.1). **38.21** *Records*, rather "tally" (rendered *counted*, *census* in vv. 25–26). *Drawn up*, rather "counted." *Levites*, anachronistic (see Num 3.5–13). *Ithamar*.

Cf. Num 4.33; the death of Aaron's older sons (Lev 10.1–2) seems to be assumed. **38.22–23** Cf. 31.2–6; 35.30–35. **38.24** *Talents*. See note on 25.39. **38.25** There is also freely donated silver (25.2–3; 35.5, 24). **38.26** *Beka*, the term found as a label on excavated weights of that size. *Census*. Cf. Num 1.45–46. **38.30** The *basin* is omitted; see v. 8.

Making the Vestments for the Priesthood

39 Of the blue, purple, and crimson yarns they made finely worked vestments, for ministering in the holy place; they made the sacred vestments for Aaron; as the LORD had commanded Moses. 2 He made the ephod of gold, of blue, purple, and crimson yarns, and of fine twisted linen. 3 Gold leaf was hammered out and cut into threads to work into the blue, purple, and crimson yarns and into the fine twisted linen, in skilled design. 4 They made for the ephod shoulder-pieces, joined to it at its two edges. 5 The decorated band on it was of the same materials and workmanship, of gold, of blue, purple, and crimson yarns, and of fine twisted linen; as the LORD had commanded Moses.

6 The onyx stones were prepared, enclosed in settings of gold filigree and engraved like the engravings of a signet, according to the names of the sons of Israel. 7 He set them on the shoulder-pieces of the ephod, to be stones of remembrance for the sons of Israel; as the LORD had commanded Moses.

8 He made the breastpiece, in skilled work, like the work of the ephod, of gold, of blue, purple, and crimson yarns, and of fine twisted linen. 9 It was square; the breastpiece was made double, a span in length and a span in width when doubled. 10 They set in it four rows of stones. A row of carnelian,[t] chrysolite, and emerald was the first row; 11 and the second row, a turquoise, a sapphire,[u] and a moonstone; 12 and the third row, a jacinth, an agate, and an amethyst; 13 and the fourth row, a beryl, an onyx, and a jasper; they were enclosed in settings of gold filigree. 14 There were twelve stones with names corresponding to the names of the sons of Israel; they were like signets, each engraved with its name, for the twelve tribes. 15 They made on the breastpiece chains of pure gold, twisted like cords; 16 and they made two settings of gold filigree and two gold rings, and put the two rings on the two edges of the breastpiece; 17 and they put the two cords of gold in the two rings at the edges of the breastpiece. 18 Two ends of the two cords they had attached to the two settings of filigree; in this way they attached it in front to the shoulder-pieces of the ephod. 19 Then they made two rings of gold, and put them at the two ends of the breastpiece, on its inside edge next to the ephod. 20 They made two rings of gold, and attached them in front to the lower part of the two shoulder-pieces of the ephod, at its joining above the decorated band of the ephod. 21 They bound the breastpiece by its rings to the rings of the ephod with a blue cord, so that it should lie on the decorated band of the ephod, and that the breastpiece should not come loose from the ephod; as the LORD had commanded Moses.

22 He also made the robe of the ephod woven all of blue yarn; 23 and the opening of the robe in the middle of it was like the opening in a coat of mail,[v] with a binding around the opening, so that it might not be torn. 24 On the lower hem of the robe they made pomegranates of blue, purple, and crimson yarns, and of fine twisted linen. 25 They also made bells of pure gold, and put the bells between the pomegranates on the lower hem of the robe all around, between the pomegranates; 26 a bell and a pomegranate, a bell and a pomegranate all around on the lower hem of the robe for ministering; as the LORD had commanded Moses.

27 They also made the tunics, woven of fine linen, for Aaron and his sons, 28 and the turban of fine linen, and the headdresses of fine linen, and the linen undergarments of fine twisted linen, 29 and the sash of fine twisted linen, and of blue, purple, and crimson yarns, embroidered with needlework; as the LORD had commanded Moses.

t The identification of several of these stones is uncertain   *u* Or *lapis lazuli*   *v* Meaning of Heb uncertain

---

39.1–31 Cf. ch. 28. **39.1** *Of the blue . . . yarns* harks back to 38.23 (accordingly the use here of *they*, Bezalel and Oholiab) but *fine linen* is omitted. *As the LORD*, a sevenfold refrain in the passage, recalling the structure of Gen 1.1–2.4. **39.2** *He*, Bezalel (37.1). **39.3** *Gold leaf*, an additional detail. *Was hammered out*, rather "they hammered out," the volunteers (36.2, 4), who apparently also made the curtains, screen, and hangings (26.1–14, 31, 36; 27.9–15) that are omitted from

30 They made the rosette of the holy diadem of pure gold, and wrote on it an inscription, like the engraving of a signet, "Holy to the Lord." 31 They tied to it a blue cord, to fasten it on the turban above; as the Lord had commanded Moses.

The Work Completed

32 In this way all the work of the tabernacle of the tent of meeting was finished; the Israelites had done everything just as the Lord had commanded Moses. 33 Then they brought the tabernacle to Moses, the tent and all its utensils, its hooks, its frames, its bars, its pillars, and its bases; 34 the covering of tanned rams' skins and the covering of fine leather,w and the curtain for the screen; 35 the ark of the covenantx with its poles and the mercy seat;y 36 the table with all its utensils, and the bread of the Presence; 37 the pure lampstand with its lamps set on it and all its utensils, and the oil for the light; 38 the golden altar, the anointing oil and the fragrant incense, and the screen for the entrance of the tent; 39 the bronze altar, and its grating of bronze, its poles, and all its utensils; the basin with its stand; 40 the hangings of the court, its pillars, and its bases, and the screen for the gate of the court, its cords, and its pegs; and all the utensils for the service of the tabernacle, for the tent of meeting; 41 the finely worked vestments for ministering in the holy place, the sacred vestments for the priest Aaron, and the vestments of his sons to serve as priests. 42 The Israelites had done all of the work just as the Lord had commanded Moses. 43 When Moses saw that they had done all the work just as the Lord had commanded, he blessed them.

The Tabernacle Erected and Its Equipment Installed

40 The Lord spoke to Moses: 2 On the first day of the first month you shall set up the tabernacle of the tent of meeting. 3 You shall put in it the ark of the covenant,x and you shall screen the ark with the curtain. 4 You shall bring in the table, and arrange its setting; and you shall bring in the lampstand, and set up its lamps. 5 You shall put the golden altar for incense before the ark of the covenant,x and set up the screen for the entrance of the tabernacle. 6 You shall set the altar of burnt offering before the entrance of the tabernacle of the tent of meeting, 7 and place the basin between the tent of meeting and the altar, and put water in it. 8 You shall set up the court all around, and hang up the screen for the gate of the court. 9 Then you shall take the anointing oil, and anoint the tabernacle and all that is in it, and consecrate it and all its furniture, so that it shall become holy. 10 You shall also anoint the altar of burnt offering and all its utensils, and consecrate the altar, so that the altar shall be most holy. 11 You shall also anoint the basin with its stand, and consecrate it. 12 Then you shall bring Aaron and his sons to the entrance of the tent of meeting, and shall wash them with water, 13 and put on Aaron the sacred vestments, and you shall anoint him and consecrate him, so that he may serve me as priest. 14 You shall bring his sons also and put tunics on them, 15 and anoint them, as you anointed their father, that they may serve me as priests: and their anointing shall admit them to a perpetual priesthood throughout all generations to come.

16 Moses did everything just as the

w Meaning of Heb uncertain   x Or treaty, or testimony; Heb eduth   y Or the cover

---

the account; cf. v. 42. **39.30** Diadem. Cf. 29.6. **39.32** In this way, not in the Hebrew. Finished. Cf. Gen 2.1; also cf. Ex 40.33; Gen 2.2; see note on 39.43. Near Eastern myth, e.g., the Babylonian Enuma Elish, associates temple building with creation; see note on 40.2. **39.33–41** Cf. 35.11–19. **39.42** Israelites. See note on 39.3. Work connotes service in maintaining the cultic or religious life of the community (see note on 36.1), different from the term translated work in v. 43. **39.43** Work, as in Gen 2.2–3. Blessed. Cf. Gen 2.3.

40.2 First month, the new year according to the rhythms of the ritual life of the community; see 12.2; note on 39.32. New year, temple (or tabernacle) building, and creation are associated in Israelite worldview. Cf. v. 17. You. See 25.9. **40.3** Screen. Cf. 35.12. **40.4** Setting. See 25.29–30. **40.5** Before, but outside the curtain (see 30.6). **40.9** Furniture, translated utensils in v. 10. Holy. See note on 29.37. **40.10** Most holy. See note on 29.37. **40.12** Bring. See note on 29.3; see also v. 14. **40.15** Perpetual. Cf. 29.9;

LORD had commanded him. 17 In the first month in the second year, on the first day of the month, the tabernacle was set up. 18 Moses set up the tabernacle; he laid its bases, and set up its frames, and put in its poles, and raised up its pillars; 19 and he spread the tent over the tabernacle, and put the covering of the tent over it; as the LORD had commanded Moses. 20 He took the covenant*z* and put it into the ark, and put the poles on the ark, and set the mercy seat*a* above the ark; 21 and he brought the ark into the tabernacle, and set up the curtain for screening, and screened the ark of the covenant;*z* as the LORD had commanded Moses. 22 He put the table in the tent of meeting, on the north side of the tabernacle, outside the curtain, 23 and set the bread in order on it before the LORD; as the LORD had commanded Moses. 24 He put the lampstand in the tent of meeting, opposite the table on the south side of the tabernacle, 25 and set up the lamps before the LORD; as the LORD had commanded Moses. 26 He put the golden altar in the tent of meeting before the curtain, 27 and offered fragrant incense on it; as the LORD had commanded Moses. 28 He also put in place the screen for the entrance of the tabernacle. 29 He set the altar of burnt offering at the entrance of the tabernacle of the tent of meeting, and offered on it the burnt offering and the grain offering as the LORD had commanded Moses. 30 He set the basin between the tent of meeting and the altar, and put water in it for washing, 31 with which Moses and Aaron and his sons washed their hands and their feet. 32 When they went into the tent of meeting, and when they approached the altar, they washed; as the LORD had commanded Moses. 33 He set up the court around the tabernacle and the altar, and put up the screen at the gate of the court. So Moses finished the work.

The Cloud and the Glory

34 Then the cloud covered the tent of meeting, and the glory of the LORD filled the tabernacle. 35 Moses was not able to enter the tent of meeting because the cloud settled upon it, and the glory of the LORD filled the tabernacle. 36 Whenever the cloud was taken up from the tabernacle, the Israelites would set out on each stage of their journey; 37 but if the cloud was not taken up, then they did not set out until the day that it was taken up. 38 For the cloud of the LORD was on the tabernacle by day, and fire was in the cloud*b* by night, before the eyes of all the house of Israel at each stage of their journey.

z Or *treaty*, or *testimony*; Heb *eduth*   *a* Or *the cover*
b Heb *it*

Num 25.11–13.   **40.17** See note on 40.2. **40.18** *Moses.* Cf. v. 2.   **40.19** *Tent.* See 26.7, 11. *Covering.* See 26.14.   **40.20** *Poles.* See note on 25.12. *Above,* rather "on top of" (25.21). **40.22** *Tent of meeting.* See note on 27.21. **40.27** *Offered.* See note on 30.1.   **40.28** *For the entrance,* aligned with but at some remove (see note on 27.9–19).   **40.29** *Burnt offering.* See 28.38–39. *Grain offering.* See 28.40. Mention of the offerings provides a transition to Leviticus, which begins with the burnt offering (ch. 1) and grain offering (ch. 2).   **40.31** *Washed,* or "would wash."   **40.32** *Went ... approached ... washed.* Rather, in the Hebrew the tense is present, de-scribing ongoing activity and interrupting the in-vestiture and anointing ceremony (vv. 13–15), which is resumed in Lev 8.   **40.33** *Finished.* See note on 39.32.   **40.34–38** The descent of the divine presence into the "dwelling" (*tabernacle*) parallels the *settling* (same Hebrew verb) of the Lord atop Mount Sinai (24.15–16).   **40.34** *Cloud.* See note on 13.21. *Glory.* See note on 16.6–7; cf. 24.16–17.   **40.35** Cf. 1 Kings 8.10–11. **40.36–38** An institutionalization of the *pillars* in 13.21–22; cf. Num 9.15–23.   **40.38** *At each stage ... journey,* lit. "in each of their journeys"; cf. Num 10.11–36.

LEVITICUS

THE BOOK OF LEVITICUS is more aptly described by its tannaitic, or early rabbinic, name, *Torat Kohanim*, the Priests' Manual. It is thematically an independent entity. Priestly material in the book of Exodus describes the construction of the Israelite cultic implements (the sacred religious objects used in ritual—the tabernacle, its contents, and the priestly vestments); in Leviticus this static picture is converted into scenes from the living cult. The book of Numbers which follows concentrates on the cultic laws of the camp in motion. Since the transport of the sacred paraphernalia and their protection against encroachment by impurity is the function of the Levites, it is no accident that all the cultic laws pertaining to the Levites are in Numbers, and none are in Leviticus.

The Priesthood

Although the Priests' Manual focuses on the priesthood, few laws are reserved for priests alone (Lev 8–10; 16.1–28; 21.1–22.16). Their role is defined in pedagogic terms: to teach the distinctions "between the holy and the common, and between the unclean and the clean" (10.10 [cf. 14.57]; 15.31). They must do this because Israel's moral sins and physical impurities are leading to the pollution of the sanctuary and the expulsion of Israel from its land. The priests, then, are charged with a double task: to instruct Israel not to cause defilement and to purge the sanctuary whenever it is defiled. However, Leviticus is not just a collection of rituals. On the contrary, the ethical element fuses with and even informs the ritual, so that one may seek a moral basis behind each ritual act.

Israel's priests were not an insular elite. They were military chaplains, accompanying Israel's armies in distant and dangerous battlefields (Num 31.6). They were called outside the sanctuary and, indeed, outside the settlements to quarantine and certify carriers of scale disease (Lev 14.2). The responsibility of the priesthood for the welfare of all Israel is nowhere better exemplified than in the relationship of priests and laity in the sacrificial service. The preliminary rites with the sacrificial animal are performed by the offerer: hand-leaning, slaughtering, flaying, quartering, and washing (1.1–9). The priest takes over at the altar and continues the sacrificial ritual in silence. By virtue of his sacred status, the priest acts as the offerer's (silent) intermediary before God. But he is more than a mere technician. In effect, he is the cultic counterpart of the prophet. Both represent the Israelites before God. Both intercede on their behalf, one through ritual, the other through prayer. The welfare of Israel depends on both a Moses and an Aaron.

Ideas of Holiness and Pollution According to P and H

The book of Leviticus comprises two priestly sources, known as P (Priestly code) and H (Holiness code). They are not homogeneous; each betrays the work of schools. For example, two P strata are discernible in ch. 11 (a later P stratum in vv. 24–38, 47), as are two H strata in ch. 23 (a later H stratum in vv. 2–3, 39–43). Whether material belongs to P or H can be determined by two criteria: ideology and terminology.

The most important ideological distinction between the two codes rests in their contrasting concepts of holiness. For P, spatial holiness is limited to the sanctuary; for H, it is coextensive with the promised land. As for the holiness of persons, P restricts it to priests and Nazirites (cf. Num 6.5–8); H extends it to all of Israel. This expansion follows logically from H's doctrine of spatial holiness: since the land is holy, all who reside on it are to keep it that way. All adult Israelites are enjoined to attain holiness by observing God's commandments, and even resident aliens must heed the prohibitive commandments, the violation of which threatens to pollute the land for all (e.g., 18.26).

P's doctrine of holiness is static; H's is dynamic. P constricts holiness to the sanctuary and its priests, assiduously avoiding the root of the word "holy" even in describing the Levites. Although H concedes that only priests are innately holy, it repeatedly calls upon Israel to strive for holiness. The dynamic quality of H's concept is highlighted by the term "sanctify," used to describe the holiness of the laity and the priesthood. Sanctification is an ongoing process for priests (21.8, 15, 23; 22.9, 16) as well as for all Israelites (21.8; 22.32). The holiness of the priests and Israelites expands or contracts in proportion to their adherence to God's commandments.

The converse, the doctrine of pollution, also varies sharply. P holds that the sanctuary is polluted by Israel's moral and ritual violations (4.2) committed anywhere in the camp (but not outside) and that this pollution can and must be effaced by the violator's purification offering and, if committed deliberately, by priestly sacrifice and confession (16.3–22) H, however, concentrates instead on the polluting effects of Israel's violations of the covenant (26.15), for example, incest (18; 20.11–24), idolatry (20.1–6), and depriving the land of its sabbaths (26.34–35). Pollution for H is nonritualistic, as shown by its metaphoric usage (e.g., 18.20, 24; 19.31) and by the fact that the polluted land cannot be expiated by ritual. Violations irrevocably lead to the expulsion of its inhabitants (18.24–29; 20.22).

The distinctive vocabularies of P and H emerge in their use of homonyms and synonyms. For example, in P *shiqqetz* means "defile (by ingestion)" (translated "unclean" in 11.8) and *timmē'* means "defile (by contact)" (translated "detestable" in 11.11), whereas in H they are used interchangeably (20.25). P's term for "law" or "statute" is always given in the feminine form *chuqqah, chuqqot* (e.g., 10.9), whereas H also resorts to masculine *choq, chuqqim* (e.g., 26.46). The term "commit sacrilege" in P is *ma'al*, translated "commit a trespass" (6.2), and in H is *chillel*, translated "profaned" (19.8). The pervasive intrusion of H characteristics into the P text points to the strong possibility that H is not only subsequent to P but is also P's redactor.

His original document, P afterwards

Structure

Generally, the book of Leviticus divides into the main P text (chs. 1–16), comprising descriptions of the sacrificial system, the inaugural service at the sanctuary, and the laws of impurities; the H text (chs. 17–26); and a section on commutation of gifts to the sanctuary (ch. 27).   *Jacob Milgrom*

The Burnt Offering

1 The LORD summoned Moses and spoke to him from the tent of meeting, saying: 2 Speak to the people of Israel and say to them: When any of you bring an offering of livestock to the LORD, you shall bring your offering from the herd or from the flock.

3 If the offering is a burnt offering from the herd, you shall offer a male without blemish; you shall bring it to the

---

1.1–7.38 The sacrificial system. Sacrifice is a flexible symbol that conveys a variety of possible meanings. The quintessential sacrificial act is the transference of property from the profane to the sacred realm, in other words, a gift to the deity. That this notion is also basic to Israelite sacrifice is demonstrated by fundamental sacrificial terms that connote a gift, such as *mattanah* (23.38), *minchah*, rendered *grain offering* (2.1), and *'isheh, an offering by fire* (see 1.9). It explains why game and fish were unacceptable as sacrifices: "I will not offer burnt offerings to the LORD my God that cost me nothing" (2 Sam 24.24). To date, however, no single theory can encompass the sacrificial system of any society, even the most primitive. In chs. 1–5 the sacrifices are characterized by donor: chs. 1–3 speak of sacrifices brought spontaneously (burnt, cereal, well-being); chs. 4–5, of sacrifices required for expiation (purification and reparation). Chs. 6–7 regroup these sacrifices in order of their sanctity. The common denominator of the sacrifices discussed in these chapters is that they arise in answer to an unpredictable religious or emotional need and are thereby set apart from the sacrifices of the public feasts and fasts that are fixed by the calendar (chs. 9, 16, 23; cf. Num 28–29).

1.1–17 The burnt offering is the only sacrifice that is entirely consumed on the altar (cf. Deut 33.10; 1 Sam 7.9). Vv. 3–5 summarize the major concepts of the sacrificial system: imposition of hands, acceptance, expiation, slaughter, blood manipulation, and entrance to the tent of meeting. The donor is an active participant in the ritual. The burnt offering must be an unblemished male animal from an eligible species of livestock or birds. It is probably the oldest and most popular sacrifice (*Tosefta Zebachim* 13.1). Its function here is expiatory (v. 4; cf. 9.7; 14.20; Job 1.5; 42.8) and finds parallels in Ugaritic texts found at Ras Shamra on the coast of Syria dating to the middle of the second millennium B.C.E, but in H (see Introduction), the burnt offering by an individual marks a joyous occasion (cf. Lev 22.17–21; Num 15.1–11). **1.2** *Any of you.* The text can be read "any person among you," thereby explaining the third person in the Hebrew of vv. 2, 3, 4, 10, translated by the second person in the NRSV. **1.3** *Without blemish.* The significance of this requirement is vividly underscored by the prophet: "When you offer blind animals in sacrifice, is that not wrong? And when you offer those that are lame or sick, is that not wrong? Try presenting that to your governor, will he be pleased with you

entrance of the tent of meeting, for acceptance in your behalf before the LORD. 4You shall lay your hand on the head of the burnt offering, and it shall be acceptable in your behalf as atonement for you. 5The bull shall be slaughtered before the LORD; and Aaron's sons the priests shall offer the blood, dashing the blood against all sides of the altar that is at the entrance of the tent of meeting. 6The burnt offering shall be flayed and cut up into its parts. 7The sons of the priest Aaron shall put fire on the altar and arrange wood on the fire. 8Aaron's sons the priests shall arrange the parts, with the head and the suet, on the wood that is on the fire on the altar; 9but its entrails and its legs shall be washed with water. Then the priest shall turn the whole into smoke on the altar as a burnt offering, an offering by fire of pleasing odor to the LORD.

10 If your gift for a burnt offering is from the flock, from the sheep or goats, your offering shall be a male without blemish. 11It shall be slaughtered on the north side of the altar before the LORD, and Aaron's sons the priests shall dash its blood against all sides of the altar. 12It shall be cut up into its parts, with its head and its suet, and the priest shall arrange them on the wood that is on the fire on the altar; 13but the entrails and the legs shall be washed with water. Then the priest shall offer the whole and turn it into smoke on the altar; it is a burnt offering, an offering by fire of pleasing odor to the LORD.

14 If your offering to the LORD is a burnt offering of birds, you shall choose your offering from turtledoves or pigeons. 15The priest shall bring it to the altar and wring off its head, and turn it into smoke on the altar; and its blood shall be drained out against the side of the altar. 16He shall remove its crop with its contentsa and throw it at the east side of the altar, in the place for ashes. 17He shall tear it open by its wings without severing it. Then the priest shall turn it into smoke on the altar, on the wood that is on the fire; it is a burnt offering, an offering by fire of pleasing odor to the LORD.

Grain Offerings

2 When anyone presents a grain offering to the LORD, the offering shall be of choice flour; the worshiper shall pour oil on it, and put frankincense on it, 2and

a Meaning of Heb uncertain

---

or show you favor? says the LORD of hosts" (Mal 1.8). *Tent of meeting*, a term referring to the wilderness sanctuary, also called the tabernacle, which was contained within a collapsible and portable tent and itself contained an incense altar, a table for the bread of Presence, a lampstand, and, separated from these sacred objects by a curtain, the ark of the covenant (Ex 25.10–40). Its name is derived from its function; see Ex 29.42–43. The tent of meeting was surrounded by a fenced courtyard. The whole courtyard from its entrance to the entrance of the tent was accessible to the lay offerer and was where he performed the preliminary sacrificial rites (see Introduction). **1.4** *Lay your hand* (cf. 3.2, 8, 12; 4.4, 15, 24), lit. "lean your hand." This rite required pressure. Its purpose is to signify ownership, so that the benefits of the sacrifice will be accrued to the donor. Hand-leaning was not required whenever the offering could be carried by hand — cases where ownership was obvious — such as the burnt offering of birds, the grain offering, and the reparation-offering money (e.g., 5.14–6.7). *Atonement*. Originally the burnt offering may have been the only expiatory sacrifice. However, once the exclusively expiatory purification and reparation offerings came into being (see chs. 4–5), the sole expiatory function

remaining for the burnt offering was to atone for neglected performative commandments or for sinful thoughts (see Job 1.5). **1.9** *Turn ... into smoke*. This term is carefully distinguished from "burn," the normal term for nonsacrificial incineration, to indicate that the offering is not destroyed but transformed into smoke so that it can ascend to heaven above, the dwelling place of God. *An offering by fire* (cf 1.13, 17; 2.3, 10), more accurately "a food gift." **1.16** *Crop with its contents*, or "crissum by its feathers." The waste material inside the bird is removed by cutting around and pulling its tail.

2.1–16 In non-priestly texts the term "grain offering" connotes a present made to secure goodwill (e.g., Gen 32.13–21) or a tribute brought by subjects to their overlords, both human (Judg 3.15–18) and divine. This sacrifice may be brought in either animal or vegetable form (Gen. 4.3; 1 Sam 2.17). In P, however, (see Introduction) it is exclusively grain, semolina (Lev 2.1–3), semolina cakes (2.4–10), or roasted grain (2.14–16). Because leaven and honey (fruit syrup) ferment and salt preserves, the first two are forbidden, and salt is required on the altar (2.11–13). Leaven, however, is permitted as a first-fruit offering to the priest (23.17; 2 Chr

bring it to Aaron's sons the priests. After taking from it a handful of the choice flour and oil, with all its frankincense, the priest shall turn this token portion into smoke on the altar, an offering by fire of pleasing odor to the LORD. 3 And what is left of the grain offering shall be for Aaron and his sons, a most holy part of the offerings by fire to the LORD.

4 When you present a grain offering baked in the oven, it shall be of choice flour: unleavened cakes mixed with oil, or unleavened wafers spread with oil. 5 If your offering is grain prepared on a griddle, it shall be of choice flour mixed with oil, unleavened; 6 break it in pieces, and pour oil on it; it is a grain offering. 7 If your offering is grain prepared in a pan, it shall be made of choice flour in oil. 8 You shall bring to the LORD the grain offering that is prepared in any of these ways; and when it is presented to the priest, he shall take it to the altar. 9 The priest shall remove from the grain offering its token portion and turn this into smoke on the altar, an offering by fire of

pleasing odor to the LORD. 10 And what is left of the grain offering shall be for Aaron and his sons; it is a most holy part of the offerings by fire to the LORD.

11 No grain offering that you bring to the LORD shall be made with leaven, for you must not turn any leaven or honey into smoke as an offering by fire to the LORD. 12 You may bring them to the LORD as an offering of choice products, but they shall not be offered on the altar for a pleasing odor. 13 You shall not omit from your grain offerings the salt of the covenant with your God; with all your offerings you shall offer salt.

14 If you bring a grain offering of first fruits to the LORD, you shall bring as the grain offering of your first fruits coarse new grain from fresh ears, parched with fire. 15 You shall add oil to it and lay frankincense on it; it is a grain offering. 16 And the priest shall turn a token portion of it into smoke — some of the coarse grain and oil with all its frankincense; it is an offering by fire to the LORD.

31.5). The restriction to grain emphasizes that people's tribute to God should be from the fruits of their labors on the soil. As in other ancient Near Eastern cultures, the burnt offering could appease the deity's anger. Because grain was abundant and cheap, it became the poor person's burnt offering (Philo *On the Special Laws* 1.271; *Leviticus Rabbah* 8.4). **2.1** *Choice flour*, more specifically "semolina," or coarsely ground flour that remains after the fine flour has been extracted from the wheat (cf. *Mishnah 'Abot* 5.15). *Frankincense*, a fragrant and costly gum-resin tapped from three species of the Boswellia tree native only to southern Arabia (see Jer 6.20) and Somaliland. It was also the main ingredient in the incense burned on the incense altar (Ex 30.7–8, 34–36). **2.2** *Token portion*. The entire grain offering should go up in smoke, but only a portion does, *pars pro toto*. **2.3** *Most holy* defines the burnt, grain, purification, and reparation offerings (6.17, 25; 7.6), as distinct from the rest of the offerings designated by the term "holy," namely, the well-being offering, the devoted thing, and the first of animals, fruits, and processed foods (Num 18.12–19). **2.4–10** Four different preparations of the grain offering are here included: oven-baked (two varieties), griddle-toasted, and pan-fried. Their common denominator is that they are all cooked, unleavened semolina. Frankincense is not required for these cooked grain offerings, possibly as a deliberate concession to

the poor. **2.10** This verse stands in flat contradiction to 7.9, which assigns the cooked grain offering to the officiating priest. This may reflect different sanctuary traditions: the officiating priest was recompensed at the small, local sanctuary, whereas the priestly corps distributed the perquisites equitably at the Jerusalem temple (see also 7.31–33). **2.12** *An offering of choice products*, or "a first-processed offering." The gift of the first fruits is due not only from the first-ripe crops but also from certain foods processed from these crops, namely, grain, new wine (must), new (olive) oil, fruit syrup, leavened food, and meal dough. **2.13** *Salt of the covenant*. Since salt was the preservative par excellence in antiquity, it made the ideal symbol for the perdurability of a covenant, and it is likely that salt played a prominent role at the solemn meal that sealed a covenant in the ancient Near East. **2.14** *First fruits* refers to barley, which Arab peasants roast to this day, but not to wheat because of its flat taste (note the absence of the term "semolina"). It may refer to the offering originally required of each Israelite barley grower (see 23.10–11). *Coarse new grain from fresh ears*, more specifically "milky grain, groats of the first ear." Hebrew *'abib*, "milky grain," represents the intermediate (milky) stage between mere stalks and fully ripe grain; Hebrew *geres* (rabbinic *gerisim*) means "groats"; and *karmel* refers to the grain, namely the "fresh ear" (cf. 2 Kings 4.42).

Offerings of Well-Being

3 If the offering is a sacrifice of well-being, if you offer an animal of the herd, whether male or female, you shall offer one without blemish before the LORD. 2 You shall lay your hand on the head of the offering and slaughter it at the entrance of the tent of meeting; and Aaron's sons the priests shall dash the blood against all sides of the altar. 3 You shall offer from the sacrifice of well-being, as an offering by fire to the LORD, the fat that covers the entrails and all the fat that is around the entrails; 4 the two kidneys with the fat that is on them at the loins, and the appendage of the liver, which he shall remove with the kidneys. 5 Then Aaron's sons shall turn these into smoke on the altar, with the burnt offering that is on the wood on the fire, as an offering by fire of pleasing odor to the LORD.

6 If your offering for a sacrifice of well-being to the LORD is from the flock, male or female, you shall offer one without blemish. 7 If you present a sheep as your offering, you shall bring it before the LORD 8 and lay your hand on the head of the offering. It shall be slaughtered before the tent of meeting, and Aaron's sons shall dash its blood against all sides of the altar. 9 You shall present its fat from the sacrifice of well-being, as an offering by fire to the LORD: the whole broad tail, which shall be removed close to the backbone, the fat that covers the entrails, and

all the fat that is around the entrails; 10 the two kidneys with the fat that is on them at the loins, and the appendage of the liver, which you shall remove with the kidneys. 11 Then the priest shall turn these into smoke on the altar as a food offering by fire to the LORD.

12 If your offering is a goat, you shall bring it before the LORD 13 and lay your hand on its head; it shall be slaughtered before the tent of meeting; and the sons of Aaron shall dash its blood against all sides of the altar. 14 You shall present as your offering from it, as an offering by fire to the LORD, the fat that covers the entrails, and all the fat that is around the entrails; 15 the two kidneys with the fat that is on them at the loins, and the appendage of the liver, which you shall remove with the kidneys. 16 Then the priest shall turn these into smoke on the altar as a food offering by fire for a pleasing odor.

All fat is the LORD's. 17 It shall be a perpetual statute throughout your generations, in all your settlements: you must not eat any fat or any blood.

Purification Offerings

4 The LORD spoke to Moses, saying, 2 Speak to the people of Israel, saying: When anyone sins unintentionally in any of the LORD's commandments about things not to be done, and does any one of them:

3 If it is the anointed priest who sins,

3.1–17 The well-being offering never serves as expiation (but cf. ch. 17). Its basic function is simply to permit the consumption of meat. The motivation was usually spontaneous and occasioned by a sense of elation. The rules are similar to those of the burnt offering except that the victims may be female but not birds. Also, being of lesser sanctity, its portions are assigned to the donor as well as to God. The choicest internal fats (suet) are turned to smoke. **3.1** *You* (and throughout the chapter), lit. "he"/"him." *Without blemish.* See 1.3. **3.3** *Fat* (and throughout the chapter), more specifically "suet," referring to the layer of fat beneath the surface of the animal's skin and around its organs, which can be peeled off, in contrast to the fat that is inextricably entwined in the musculature. **3.4** *Appendage,* i.e., the caudate lobe of the liver. **3.9** *Backbone,* rather the "sacrum," the lowest part of the spine closest to the broad tail. **3.16** *All fat is the LORD's.*

Hence all sacrificial meat must initially be brought to the altar. Together with v. 17, this phrase is probably an H supplement (see Introduction). **4.1–35** The purpose of the purification offering (not properly *sin offering*) is to remove the impurity inflicted upon the sanctuary by the inadvertent violation of prohibitions. The brazen violation of these laws is punishable by death through divine agency (Num 15.27–31). Such serious violations include defilement of holy days (e.g., the Day of Atonement, Lev 23.29–30), contamination of sacred objects (7.20–21), prohibited ritual acts (17.3–4, 8–9), and illicit sex (18.29). The greater the sin, the deeper the penetration into the sanctuary compound and the more extensive the purification required (cf. vv. 3–21, 22–35; see note on 16.1–34). **4.3** *Anointed priest,* the title of the high priest in preexilic times. *Guilt on,* more accurately "harm to," the consequential meaning of the Hebrew noun *'asham,* "guilt" (cf.

thus bringing guilt on the people, he shall offer for the sin that he has committed a bull of the herd without blemish as a sin offering to the LORD. 4 He shall bring the bull to the entrance of the tent of meeting before the LORD and lay his hand on the head of the bull; the bull shall be slaughtered before the LORD. 5 The anointed priest shall take some of the blood of the bull and bring it into the tent of meeting. 6 The priest shall dip his finger in the blood and sprinkle some of the blood seven times before the LORD in front of the curtain of the sanctuary. 7 The priest shall put some of the blood on the horns of the altar of fragrant incense that is in the tent of meeting before the LORD; and the rest of the blood of the bull he shall pour out at the base of the altar of burnt offering, which is at the entrance of the tent of meeting. 8 He shall remove all the fat from the bull of sin offering: the fat that covers the entrails and all the fat that is around the entrails; 9 the two kidneys with the fat that is on them at the loins; and the appendage of the liver, which he shall remove with the kidneys, 10 just as these are removed from the ox of the sacrifice of well-being. The priest shall turn them into smoke upon the altar of burnt offering. 11 But the skin of the bull and all its flesh, as well as its head, its legs, its entrails, and its dung— 12 all the rest of the bull—he shall carry out to a clean place outside the camp, to the ash heap, and shall burn it on a wood fire; at the ash heap it shall be burned.

13 If the whole congregation of Israel errs unintentionally and the matter escapes the notice of the assembly, and they do any one of the things that by the LORD's commandments ought not to be done and incur guilt; 14 when the sin that they have committed becomes known, the assembly shall offer a bull of the herd for a sin offering and bring it before the tent of meeting. 15 The elders of the congregation shall lay their hands on the head of the bull before the LORD, and the bull shall be slaughtered before the LORD. 16 The anointed priest shall bring some of the blood of the bull into the tent of meeting, 17 and the priest shall dip his finger in the blood and sprinkle it seven times before the LORD, in front of the curtain. 18 He shall put some of the blood on the horns of the altar that is before the LORD in the tent of meeting; and the rest of the blood he shall pour out at the base of the altar of burnt offering that is at the entrance of the tent of meeting. 19 He shall remove all its fat and turn it into smoke

---

Gen 26.10; Jer 51.5b). **4.6** *Sprinkle ... blood seven times.* Sevenfold sprinkling is attested for the blood of the purification offering (4.6, 17; 16.14, 15, 19; Num 19.4), for the oil and mixture of blood and water used in the purification of the healed leper (Lev 14.7, 16, 27, 51), and for anointing oil on the altar (8.11). In this chapter the blood of the purification offering acts as a ritual detergent purging the sanctuary of Israel's impurities. Seven is the number of completion and occurs frequently in the cultic calendar: seventh day (sabbath), seventh week (Pentecost), seventh month (Tishri), seventh year (sabbatical), and forty-ninth (seven times seven) year (jubilee). Even the magical use of seven is attested in the Bible: Balaam requires seven altars, seven bulls, and seven rams for his divination (Num 23.1); Job's friends require the same sacrifices (Job 42.8); Naaman bathes seven times in the Jordan (2 Kings 5.10, 14); Elijah's servant scans the skies seven times for signs of rain (1 Kings 18.43); Joshua's armies circuit Jericho seven times on the seventh day (Josh 6.15). **4.7** *Horns.* The altar's horns are right-angle tetrahedra projecting from the four corners and are of one piece with the altar (Ex 27.2; 30.2), as illustrated by archaeological finds from Megiddo and Beer-sheba. Their daubing with the purification blood meant the purgation of the entire altar by the principle of *pars pro toto.* **4.12** *Clean place.* Though the sacrificial carcass has symbolically absorbed the sanctuary's impurities, it is still sacred and must be treated as such. *Ash heap.* That there actually existed a special dump for the sacrificial ashes outside Solomon's temple is shown by Jer 31.40 and by the discovery of a huge ash dump just north of ancient Jerusalem at the Mandelbaum Gate (the former passageway between East and West Jerusalem) consisting exclusively of remains of animal flesh, bones, and teeth. **4.13–21** This passage forms a single case with vv. 1–12. The high priest has erred in judgment, causing the people who follow his ruling also to err (v. 3). Because both errors comprise inadvertent violations of prohibitive commandments (vv. 2, 13) that pollute the shrine, each party is responsible for purging the shrine with the blood of a similar sacrifice, a purification-offering bull. **4.13** *Incur guilt.* The nuance is to feel guilt (see vv. 22, 27), the psychological component of the verb *'asham* (cf. 5.2–5, 17; 6.4a). **4.15** *Elders* act on behalf of the congregation (9.1; see Ex 3.16; 4.29; 12.21; 17.6;

on the altar. 20He shall do with the bull just as is done with the bull of sin offering; he shall do the same with this. The priest shall make atonement for them, and they shall be forgiven. 21He shall carry the bull outside the camp, and burn it as he burned the first bull; it is the sin offering for the assembly.

22 When a ruler sins, doing unintentionally any one of all the things that by commandments of the LORD his God ought not to be done and incurs guilt, 23once the sin that he has committed is made known to him, he shall bring as his offering a male goat without blemish. 24He shall lay his hand on the head of the goat; it shall be slaughtered at the spot where the burnt offering is slaughtered before the LORD; it is a sin offering. 25The priest shall take some of the blood of the sin offering with his finger and put it on the horns of the altar of burnt offering, and pour out the rest of its blood at the base of the altar of burnt offering. 26All its fat he shall turn into smoke on the altar, like the fat of the sacrifice of well-being. Thus the priest shall make atonement on his behalf for his sin, and he shall be forgiven.

27 If anyone of the ordinary people among you sins unintentionally in doing any one of the things that by the LORD's commandments ought not to be done and incurs guilt, 28when the sin that you have committed is made known to you, you shall bring a female goat without blemish as your offering, for the sin that you have committed. 29You shall lay your hand on the head of the sin offering; and the sin offering shall be slaughtered at the place of the burnt offering. 30The priest shall take some of its blood with his finger and put it on the horns of the altar of burnt offering, and he shall pour out the rest of

its blood at the base of the altar. 31He shall remove all its fat, as the fat is removed from the offering of well-being, and the priest shall turn it into smoke on the altar for a pleasing odor to the LORD. Thus the priest shall make atonement on your behalf, and you shall be forgiven.

32 If the offering you bring as a sin offering is a sheep, you shall bring a female without blemish. 33You shall lay your hand on the head of the sin offering; and it shall be slaughtered as a sin offering at the spot where the burnt offering is slaughtered. 34The priest shall take some of the blood of the sin offering with his finger and put it on the horns of the altar of burnt offering, and pour out the rest of its blood at the base of the altar. 35You shall remove all its fat, as the fat of the sheep is removed from the sacrifice of well-being, and the priest shall turn it into smoke on the altar, with the offerings by fire to the LORD. Thus the priest shall make atonement on your behalf for the sin that you have committed, and you shall be forgiven.

5 When any of you sin in that you have heard a public adjuration to testify and—though able to testify as one who has seen or learned of the matter—do not speak up, you are subject to punishment. 2Or when any of you touch any unclean thing—whether the carcass of an unclean beast or the carcass of unclean livestock or the carcass of an unclean swarming thing—and are unaware of it, you have become unclean, and are guilty. 3Or when you touch human uncleanness —any uncleanness by which one can become unclean—and are unaware of it, when you come to know it, you shall be guilty. 4Or when any of you utter aloud a rash oath for a bad or a good purpose, whatever people utter in an oath, and are

18.12; 24.9). **4.20** *Sin offering*, that is, the "purification offering." *And*, better "so that." Only God determines the efficacy of sacrifice. **4.22** *A ruler*, more specifically "a (tribal) chieftain."

5.1–13 Rabbinic tradition distinguishes between the purification offering of ch. 4 and that of 5.1–13, calling the latter "the scaled offering" because it is geared not to status but to the financial means of the offender. This separate offering probably arises from the failure or inability to cleanse impurity immediately upon its incurrence. **5.1** *Any of you*; see 1.2. *Public adjuration*, lit. "imprecation." Thus Micah is induced by his

mother's imprecation to confess that he had stolen her silver (Judg 17.1–5). A striking parallel to this case is cited in Prov 29.24, which might be translated "He who shares with a thief is his own enemy; he hears the imprecation and does not testify." **5.2–4** *Are unaware of it*. The fact escapes him, i.e., he has perhaps repressed the matter. *You have become unclean . . . you come to know it* might be translated "though he has become unclean . . . though he has known it," i.e., he knows he did wrong before amnesia set in and prolonged his impure state. *Are guilty . . . shall be*

unaware of it, when you come to know it, you shall in any of these be guilty. 5 When you realize your guilt in any of these, you shall confess the sin that you have committed. 6 And you shall bring to the LORD, as your penalty for the sin that you have committed, a female from the flock, a sheep or a goat, as a sin offering; and the priest shall make atonement on your behalf for your sin.

7 But if you cannot afford a sheep, you shall bring to the LORD, as your penalty for the sin that you have committed, two turtledoves or two pigeons, one for a sin offering and the other for a burnt offering. 8 You shall bring them to the priest, who shall offer first the one for the sin offering, wringing its head at the nape without severing it. 9 He shall sprinkle some of the blood of the sin offering on the side of the altar, while the rest of the blood shall be drained out at the base of the altar; it is a sin offering. 10 And the second he shall offer for a burnt offering according to the regulation. Thus the priest shall make atonement on your behalf for the sin that you have committed, and you shall be forgiven.

11 But if you cannot afford two turtledoves or two pigeons, you shall bring as your offering for the sin that you have committed one-tenth of an ephah of choice flour for a sin offering; you shall not put oil on it or lay frankincense on it, for it is a sin offering. 12 You shall bring it to the priest, and the priest shall scoop up a handful of it as its memorial portion,

and turn this into smoke on the altar, with the offerings by fire to the LORD; it is a sin offering. 13 Thus the priest shall make atonement on your behalf for whichever of these sins you have committed, and you shall be forgiven. Like the grain offering, the rest shall be for the priest.

Reparation Offerings

14 The LORD spoke to Moses, saying: 15 When any of you commit a trespass and sin unintentionally in any of the holy things of the LORD, you shall bring, as your guilt offering to the LORD, a ram without blemish from the flock, convertible into silver by the sanctuary shekel; it is a guilt offering. 16 And you shall make restitution for the holy thing in which you were remiss, and shall add one-fifth to it and give it to the priest. The priest shall make atonement on your behalf with the ram of the guilt offering, and you shall be forgiven.

17 If any of you sin without knowing it, doing any of the things that by the LORD's commandments ought not to be done, you have incurred guilt, and are subject to punishment. 18 You shall bring to the priest a ram without blemish from the flock, or the equivalent, as a guilt offering; and the priest shall make atonement on your behalf for the error that you committed unintentionally, and you shall be forgiven. 19 It is a guilt offering; you have incurred guilt before the LORD.

---

guilty, feels guilt (see 4.13). **5.5** Confess. The Septuagint translates "declare," i.e., articulate the confession, as distinct from the silent "confession" mandated for the inadvertent wrongdoer. Confession must be verbalized because it is the act that counts, not just the intention. By the same token, neither can mere thought bear consequences. For a curse to incur penalty, it must be pronounced and the name of God articulated (see 24.16). Confession is never required for inadvertences but only for deliberate sins (5.1–4; 16.21; 26.40; Num 5.6–7). Confession converts deliberate sins into inadvertences, thereby qualifying them for sacrificial expiation (see 6.1–7).
5.14–6.7 The reparation offering is prescribed for trespass upon divine or human property, the latter through the use of a false oath. The sin to which it relates is desecration: the sacred objects (holy things) or the name of God have become desanctified (as opposed to cases of the

purification offering in ch. 4, where the sin is contamination of sacred objects). Sins brazenly committed against God (i.e., a lying oath) can be commuted retroactively to inadvertent sins by subsequent repentance. **5.14–16** Reparation offerings for malevolent sacrilege against sacred objects. **5.15** Trespass, more accurately "sacrilege," the legal term for the wrong that is redressed by the reparation offering. Convertible into silver. The priest charges the supplicant the amount of the desecrated sacred object plus the amount needed to purchase the requisite reparation animal. Guilt offering, better "reparation offering." God must be compensated for the desecrated sacred object. **5.16** And give it to the priest, or "when he gives it to the priest." **5.17–19** Reparation for suspected trespass against sacred objects. **5.17** You have incurred guilt. He feels guilt (cf. 4.13), though he only suspects he has sinned. **5.18** The equivalent, its

6 *b* The LORD spoke to Moses, saying:
² When any of you sin and commit a trespass against the LORD by deceiving a neighbor in a matter of a deposit or a pledge, or by robbery, or if you have defrauded a neighbor, ³ or have found something lost and lied about it — if you swear falsely regarding any of the various things that one may do and sin thereby — ⁴ when you have sinned and realize your guilt, and would restore what you took by robbery or by fraud or the deposit that was committed to you, or the lost thing that you found, ⁵ or anything else about which you have sworn falsely, you shall repay the principal amount and shall add one-fifth to it. You shall pay it to its owner when you realize your guilt. ⁶ And you shall bring to the priest, as your guilt offering to the LORD, a ram without blemish from the flock, or its equivalent, for a guilt offering. ⁷ The priest shall make atonement on your behalf before the LORD, and you shall be forgiven for any of the things that one may do and incur guilt thereby.

Instructions Concerning Sacrifices

8 *c* The LORD spoke to Moses, saying: ⁹ Command Aaron and his sons, saying: This is the ritual of the burnt offering. The burnt offering itself shall remain on the hearth upon the altar all night until the morning, while the fire on the altar shall be kept burning. ¹⁰ The priest shall put on his linen vestments after putting on his linen undergarments next to his body; and he shall take up the ashes to which the fire has reduced the burnt offering on the altar, and place them beside the altar. ¹¹ Then he shall take off his vestments and put on other garments, and carry the ashes out to a clean place outside the camp. ¹² The fire on the altar shall be kept burning; it shall not go out. Every morning the priest shall add wood to it, lay out the burnt offering on it, and turn into smoke the fat pieces of the offerings of well-being. ¹³ A perpetual fire shall be kept burning on the altar; it shall not go out.

14   This is the ritual of the grain offering: The sons of Aaron shall offer it before the LORD, in front of the altar. ¹⁵ They shall take from it a handful of the choice flour and oil of the grain offering, with all the frankincense that is on the offering, and they shall turn its memorial portion into smoke on the altar as a pleasing odor to the LORD. ¹⁶ Aaron and his sons shall eat what is left of it; it shall be eaten as unleavened cakes in a holy place; in the court of the tent of meeting they shall eat it. ¹⁷ It shall not be baked with leaven. I have given it as their portion of my offerings by fire; it is most holy, like the sin offering and the guilt offering. ¹⁸ Every male among the descendants of Aaron shall eat of it, as their perpetual due throughout your generations, from

b Ch 5.20 in Heb   *c* Ch 6.1 in Heb

---

assessment in sanctuary-weighed silver.   **6.2** *Deposit.* The neighbor was entrusted with the safekeeping of an object. *A pledge,* probably an investment.   **6.2, 4** *Defrauded,* better "withheld from." The specific case is withholding wages from an employee (19.13).   **6.6** *Equivalent.* See 5.18.

6.8–7.38   Supplementary instructions for sacrifices. Since the well-being offering is eaten chiefly by the donor, the rules pertain mainly to him (7.11–34, esp. 23, 29). Otherwise they are the concerns of the officiating priest. The subjects are the altar fire (6.8–13); the manner and place for eating the grain offering (6.14–18); the daily grain offering of the high priest and the voluntary one of the ordinary priest (6.19–23); safeguards in sacrificing the purification offering (6.24–30); the ritual for the reparation offering (7.1–7, missing in ch. 5); the priestly share in the burnt and cereal offerings (7.8–10); the types of well-being offering and their taboos (7.11–21); the prohibition against eating suet and blood (7.22–27); the priestly share of the well-being offering, set aside by the donor (7.28–36); and the summation (7.37–38).   **6.10** *Body,* a euphemism for genitals.   **6.11** *Other garments.* These must be nonsacral, profane clothes, as the priest was forbidden to wear his priestly vestments outside the sanctuary (see Ezek 44.19).   **6.13** *A perpetual fire.* The sacrifices offered up at the inauguration of the public cult were consumed miraculously by a divine fire (9.24), and it is this fire that is not allowed to die out, so that all subsequent sacrifices might claim divine acceptance (see Philo *On the Special Laws* 1.286).   **6.14** *The grain offering,* the raw type described in 2.1–3.   **6.18** *Anything,* but not anyone. The priestly legists

the Lord's offerings by fire; anything that touches them shall become holy.

19 The Lord spoke to Moses, saying: 20 This is the offering that Aaron and his sons shall offer to the Lord on the day when he is anointed: one-tenth of an ephah of choice flour as a regular offering, half of it in the morning and half in the evening. 21 It shall be made with oil on a griddle; you shall bring it well soaked, as a grain offering of baked*d* pieces, and you shall present it as a pleasing odor to the Lord. 22 And so the priest, anointed from among Aaron's descendants as a successor, shall prepare it; it is the Lord's —a perpetual due—to be turned entirely into smoke. 23 Every grain offering of a priest shall be wholly burned; it shall not be eaten.

24 The Lord spoke to Moses, saying: 25 Speak to Aaron and his sons, saying: This is the ritual of the sin offering. The sin offering shall be slaughtered before the Lord at the spot where the burnt offering is slaughtered; it is most holy. 26 The priest who offers it as a sin offering shall eat of it; it shall be eaten in a holy place, in the court of the tent of meeting. 27 Whatever touches its flesh shall become holy; and when any of its blood is spattered on a garment, you shall wash the bespattered part in a holy place. 28 An earthen vessel in which it was boiled shall be broken; but if it is boiled in a bronze vessel, that shall be scoured and rinsed in water. 29 Every male among the priests shall eat of it; it is most holy. 30 But no sin offering shall be eaten from which any blood is brought into the tent of meeting for atonement in the holy place; it shall be burned with fire.

7 This is the ritual of the guilt offering. It is most holy; 2 at the spot where the burnt offering is slaughtered, they shall slaughter the guilt offering, and its blood shall be dashed against all sides of the altar. 3 All its fat shall be offered: the broad tail, the fat that covers the entrails, 4 the two kidneys with the fat that is on them at the loins, and the appendage of the liver, which shall be removed with the kidneys. 5 The priest shall turn them into smoke on the altar as an offering by fire to the Lord; it is a guilt offering. 6 Every male among the priests shall eat of it; it shall be eaten in a holy place; it is most holy.

7 The guilt offering is like the sin offering, there is the same ritual for them; the priest who makes atonement with it shall have it. 8 So, too, the priest who offers anyone's burnt offering shall keep the skin of the burnt offering that he has offered. 9 And every grain offering baked in the oven, and all that is prepared in a pan or on a griddle, shall belong to the priest who offers it. 10 But every other grain offering, mixed with oil or dry, shall belong to all the sons of Aaron equally.

Further Instructions

11 This is the ritual of the sacrifice of the offering of well-being that one may offer to the Lord. 12 If you offer it for thanksgiving, you shall offer with the thank offering unleavened cakes mixed with oil, unleavened wafers spread with oil, and cakes of choice flour well soaked in oil. 13 With your thanksgiving sacrifice of well-being you shall bring your offer-

d Meaning of Heb uncertain

have limited that which is subject to contagion to things. **6.20** *On the day*, or "from the time." The high priest's grain offering is sacrificed every day. **6.27–30** Paradoxically, the purification offering, though it is most holy, pollutes objects that it contacts because it absorbs the impurities it purges. However, if it purges severe impurity, i.e., one that polluted the shrine, it must be eliminated by burning. **7.1–6** Since one liable for a reparation offering was expected to bring its monetary equivalent to the sanctuary (5.15), the procedure for the sacrifice is given here in the administrative unit addressed to the priests (6.8–7.38) rather than in the didactic order addressed to the laity (1.1–6.7). Once the lay offerer purchases the requisite reparation animal from

the priest, the latter makes certain that the proper sacrificial procedure is followed. **7.7–10** The priestly prebends belong to the officiating priest. The sole exception is the raw grain offering, which is divided equally among all the priests, a development that probably reflects the Jerusalem temple and its large priestly corps (see also vv. 31–33). **7.11** *That one may offer to the Lord*, an admission that it is permitted to eat the meat of pure, nonsacrificial animals. **7.12–21, 28–32** *You*. All second-person pronouns are actually third person in the Hebrew. **7.13, 15** *Thanksgiving sacrifice of well-being*. P's conflation of two sacrifices, the thanksgiving offering and the well-being offering, which H treats as distinct sacrifices (22.21, 29). On P

ing with cakes of leavened bread. 14 From this you shall offer one cake from each offering, as a gift to the LORD; it shall belong to the priest who dashes the blood of the offering of well-being. 15 And the flesh of your thanksgiving sacrifice of well-being shall be eaten on the day it is offered; you shall not leave any of it until morning. 16 But if the sacrifice you offer is a votive offering or a freewill offering, it shall be eaten on the day that you offer your sacrifice, and what is left of it shall be eaten the next day; 17 but what is left of the flesh of the sacrifice shall be burned up on the third day. 18 If any of the flesh of your sacrifice of well-being is eaten on the third day, it shall not be acceptable, nor shall it be credited to the one who offers it; it shall be an abomination, and the one who eats of it shall incur guilt.

19 Flesh that touches any unclean thing shall not be eaten; it shall be burned up. As for other flesh, all who are clean may eat such flesh. 20 But those who eat flesh from the LORD's sacrifice of well-being while in a state of uncleanness shall be cut off from their kin. 21 When any one of you touches any unclean thing—human uncleanness or an unclean animal or any unclean creature—and then eats flesh from the LORD's sacrifice of well-being, you shall be cut off from your kin.

22 The LORD spoke to Moses, saying: 23 Speak to the people of Israel, saying: You shall eat no fat of ox or sheep or goat. 24 The fat of an animal that died or was torn by wild animals may be put to any other use, but you must not eat it. 25 If any one of you eats the fat from an animal of which an offering by fire may be made

to the LORD, you who eat it shall be cut off from your kin. 26 You must not eat any blood whatever, either of bird or of animal, in any of your settlements. 27 Any one of you who eats any blood shall be cut off from your kin.

28 The LORD spoke to Moses, saying: 29 Speak to the people of Israel, saying: Any one of you who would offer to the LORD your sacrifice of well-being must yourself bring to the LORD your offering from your sacrifice of well-being. 30 Your own hands shall bring the LORD's offering by fire; you shall bring the fat with the breast, so that the breast may be raised as an elevation offering before the LORD. 31 The priest shall turn the fat into smoke on the altar, but the breast shall belong to Aaron and his sons. 32 And the right thigh from your sacrifices of well-being you shall give to the priest as an offering; 33 the one among the sons of Aaron who offers the blood and fat of the offering of well-being shall have the right thigh for a portion. 34 For I have taken the breast of the elevation offering, and the thigh that is offered, from the people of Israel, from their sacrifices of well-being, and have given them to Aaron the priest and to his sons, as a perpetual due from the people of Israel. 35 This is the portion allotted to Aaron and to his sons from the offerings made by fire to the LORD, once they have been brought forward to serve the LORD as priests; 36 these the LORD commanded to be given them, when he anointed them, as a perpetual due from the people of Israel throughout their generations.

37 This is the ritual of the burnt offering, the grain offering, the sin offering,

---

and H, see Introduction. **7.16** *Votive offering*, brought following the successful fulfillment of a vow (e.g., 2 Sam 15.7–8; Prov 7.14). *Freewill offering*, brought as the spontaneous by-product of one's happiness, whatever its cause (e.g., Num 15.3, 8; Ezek 46.12). **7.18** *It shall not be acceptable*. The sacrifice retains its holiness until the time of its elimination. **7.20, 21, 25** *Cut off from their/your kin*, extermination of the line by God. In consonance with the sacrificial system, which clearly recognizes the principle of intention (chs. 4–5), it must be assumed that if any impure person inadvertently, not deliberately, eats sacred food, his wrong will be expiated by a purification offering. **7.21** *Unclean creature*, any of the eight quadrupeds singled out in 11.29–31 whose contact is defiling. **7.22–27** This passage differs

from the rest of the chapter by employing the second person in the Hebrew rather than the third. Furthermore, the banning of the suet of all sacrificial animals differs from P, which allows for profane slaughter, and is a telltale sign of H (cf. 3.16–17; 17.3–5). On P and H, see Introduction. **7.28–32** *You*. See 7.12–21. **7.30** The *elevation offering* transfers the object from the offerer to the deity (represented by the priest). Thus the hands of both the offerer and the priest are placed under the offering in the performance of this rite. **7.31–33** The breast belongs to the entire priestly corps, whereas the right thigh is awarded the officiating priest, the latter prebend probably reflecting the older custom prevailing in any of the small sanctuaries attended by a single priestly family (e.g., Shiloh). **7.37** *The offering of*

the guilt offering, the offering of ordination, and the sacrifice of well-being, [38] which the LORD commanded Moses on Mount Sinai, when he commanded the people of Israel to bring their offerings to the LORD, in the wilderness of Sinai.

The Rites of Ordination

8 The LORD spoke to Moses, saying: [2] Take Aaron and his sons with him, the vestments, the anointing oil, the bull of sin offering, the two rams, and the basket of unleavened bread; [3] and assemble the whole congregation at the entrance of the tent of meeting. [4] And Moses did as the LORD commanded him. When the congregation was assembled at the entrance of the tent of meeting, [5] Moses said to the congregation, "This is what the LORD has commanded to be done."

6 Then Moses brought Aaron and his sons forward, and washed them with water. [7] He put the tunic on him, fastened the sash around him, clothed him with the robe, and put the ephod on him. He then put the decorated band of the ephod around him, tying the ephod to him with it. [8] He placed the breastpiece on him, and in the breastpiece he put the Urim and the Thummim. [9] And he set the turban on his head, and on the turban, in front, he set the golden ornament, the holy crown, as the LORD commanded Moses.

10 Then Moses took the anointing oil and anointed the tabernacle and all that was in it, and consecrated them. [11] He sprinkled some of it on the altar seven times, and anointed the altar and all its utensils, and the basin and its base, to consecrate them. [12] He poured some of the anointing oil on Aaron's head and anointed him, to consecrate him. [13] And Moses brought forward Aaron's sons, and clothed them with tunics, and fastened sashes around them, and tied headdresses on them, as the LORD commanded Moses.

14 He led forward the bull of sin offering; and Aaron and his sons laid their hands upon the head of the bull of sin offering, [15] and it was slaughtered. Moses took the blood and with his finger put some on each of the horns of the altar, purifying the altar; then he poured out the blood at the base of the altar. Thus he consecrated it, to make atonement for it. [16] Moses took all the fat that was around the entrails, and the appendage of the liver, and the two kidneys with their fat, and turned them into smoke on the altar. [17] But the bull itself, its skin and flesh and its dung, he burned with fire outside the camp, as the LORD commanded Moses.

18 Then he brought forward the ram of burnt offering. Aaron and his sons laid their hands on the head of the ram, [19] and it was slaughtered. Moses dashed the

---

ordination. The mention of this offering before the well-being offering suggests that a section based on Ex 29 originally preceded 7.11.
8.1–10.20 In chs. 8–10, which follow logically and chronologically upon Ex 35–40, the priests are inducted into service after the priestly vestments and the tabernacle are completed. It is not Aaron, however, but Moses who dominates the scene. He conducts the inaugural service, consecrates the priests, and apportions all tasks, while Aaron is clearly answerable to him (see 10.16–20). Strikingly, the superiority of prophet over priest is insisted upon by the priestly document.
8.1–36 *To ordain you* (v. 33), lit. "to fill your hands." In scripture this phrase is used exclusively for the consecration of priests (Ex 32.29; Judg 17.5, 12; 1 Kings 13.33), but in other ancient Near Eastern texts it refers to the distribution of booty. Thus, the Hebrew idiom indicates that installation rites officially entitle the priests to their

share of the revenues and sacrifices brought to the sanctuary. *As the LORD commanded Moses* concludes each phase of the consecration ceremony, a reminder that this chapter is a repetition of the instructions in Ex 29. **8.7** *Ephod,* a garment, shaped like an apron, covering the loins and suspended from two shoulder pieces (Ex 28.6–14). It must be distinguished from the linen ephod attributed in non-priestly sources to the ordinary priest (1 Sam. 2.18; 22.18; 2 Sam. 6.14) and from the oracular ephod (1 Sam 23.6, 9; Hos 3.4). **8.8** *The Urim and the Thummim,* a form of oracle placed inside the pocket-shaped breastpiece worn by the high priest on his chest. Their shape and function are still undetermined. **8.9** *Ornament.* The Hebrew word means "flower." Possibly it took the shape of a plate (so the Septuagint) containing a floral decoration. **8.10** *Anointing oil.* For consecration see vv. 10–13, 30 and Ex 30.23–24. *Tabernacle.* See 1.3. **8.11** *Sprinkled ... seven.* See 4.6. **8.16** *Turned ... into smoke.*

blood against all sides of the altar. 20 The ram was cut into its parts, and Moses turned into smoke the head and the parts and the suet. 21 And after the entrails and the legs were washed with water, Moses turned into smoke the whole ram on the altar; it was a burnt offering for a pleasing odor, an offering by fire to the LORD, as the LORD commanded Moses.

22   Then he brought forward the second ram, the ram of ordination. Aaron and his sons laid their hands on the head of the ram, 23 and it was slaughtered. Moses took some of its blood and put it on the lobe of Aaron's right ear and on the thumb of his right hand and on the big toe of his right foot. 24 After Aaron's sons were brought forward, Moses put some of the blood on the lobes of their right ears and on the thumbs of their right hands and on the big toes of their right feet; and Moses dashed the rest of the blood against all sides of the altar. 25 He took the fat — the broad tail, all the fat that was around the entrails, the appendage of the liver, and the two kidneys with their fat — and the right thigh. 26 From the basket of unleavened bread that was before the LORD, he took one cake of unleavened bread, one cake of bread with oil, and one wafer, and placed them on the fat and on the right thigh. 27 He placed all these on the palms of Aaron and on the palms of his sons, and raised them as an elevation offering before the LORD. 28 Then Moses took them from their hands and turned

them into smoke on the altar with the burnt offering. This was an ordination offering for a pleasing odor, an offering by fire to the LORD. 29 Moses took the breast and raised it as an elevation offering before the LORD; it was Moses' portion of the ram of ordination, as the LORD commanded Moses.

30   Then Moses took some of the anointing oil and some of the blood that was on the altar and sprinkled them on Aaron and his vestments, and also on his sons and their vestments. Thus he consecrated Aaron and his vestments, and also his sons and their vestments.

31   And Moses said to Aaron and his sons, "Boil the flesh at the entrance of the tent of meeting, and eat it there with the bread that is in the basket of ordination offerings, as I was commanded, 'Aaron and his sons shall eat it'; 32 and what remains of the flesh and the bread you shall burn with fire. 33 You shall not go outside the entrance of the tent of meeting for seven days, until the day when your period of ordination is completed. For it will take seven days to ordain you; 34 as has been done today, the LORD has commanded to be done to make atonement for you. 35 You shall remain at the entrance of the tent of meeting day and night for seven days, keeping the LORD's charge so that you do not die; for so I am commanded." 36 Aaron and his sons did all the things that the LORD commanded through Moses.

See 1.9.   8.23–24 In the ancient Near East, incantations recited during the ritual smearing of persons, statues of gods, and buildings testify that its purpose is purificatory and apotropaic: to wipe off and ward off the incursions of menacing forces. Always it is the vulnerable parts of bodies (extremities) and structures (corners, entrances) that are smeared with magical substances. 8.27 Elevation offering. See 7.30. Because the right thigh is given directly by its offerer to the officiating priest without the benefit of a ritual (7.32–33), it is imperative that it undergo the rite of elevation to indicate that it no longer belongs to the offerer but now belongs to God and must be offered up on the altar. 8.28 Ordination offering. In 7.30, this sacrifice stands between the most holy offerings (burnt, grain, purification, reparation) and holy offerings (well-being). Like the most holy offerings it is eaten only by male priests in the sanctuary court (v. 31; cf. 6.16, 26; 7.6); the

priestly prebends of the well-being offering may be eaten by the priest's family at any pure place. Of the three kinds of well-being offering (7.11–16), it resembles most the thanksgiving offering in that it is also accompanied by bread offerings (v. 2; cf. Ex 29.2; Lev 7.12) and is consumed on the same day. It is a transitional offering and it corresponds with the transitional nature of its offerers, the priestly consecrands, who are passing from the realm of the profane to the realm of the sacred. 8.29 Moses receives the breast as his prebend (from God but not from the offerers, the priests) but not the thigh, lest that make him in the people's eyes a priest (see 7.34). 8.30 Whereas the blood daubing is for purification (vv. 23–24), the blood sprinkling is for consecration (16.19). 8.33, 35 The seven-day priestly consecration is a rite of passage from the profane to the sacred sphere, a liminal state fraught with peril for initiates.

Aaron's Priesthood Inaugurated

9 On the eighth day Moses summoned Aaron and his sons and the elders of Israel. 2 He said to Aaron, "Take a bull calf for a sin offering and a ram for a burnt offering, without blemish, and offer them before the LORD. 3 And say to the people of Israel, 'Take a male goat for a sin offering; a calf and a lamb, yearlings without blemish, for a burnt offering; 4 and an ox and a ram for an offering of well-being to sacrifice before the LORD; and a grain offering mixed with oil. For today the LORD will appear to you.'" 5 They brought what Moses commanded to the front of the tent of meeting; and the whole congregation drew near and stood before the LORD. 6 And Moses said, "This is the thing that the LORD commanded you to do, so that the glory of the LORD may appear to you." 7 Then Moses said to Aaron, "Draw near to the altar and sacrifice your sin offering and your burnt offering, and make atonement for yourself and for the people; and sacrifice the offering of the people, and make atonement for them; as the LORD has commanded."

8 Aaron drew near to the altar, and slaughtered the calf of the sin offering, which was for himself. 9 The sons of Aaron presented the blood to him, and he dipped his finger in the blood and put it on the horns of the altar; and the rest of the blood he poured out at the base of the altar. 10 But the fat, the kidneys, and the appendage of the liver from the sin offering he turned into smoke on the altar, as the LORD commanded Moses; 11 and the flesh and the skin he burned with fire outside the camp.

12 Then he slaughtered the burnt offering. Aaron's sons brought him the blood, and he dashed it against all sides of the altar. 13 And they brought him the burnt offering piece by piece, and the head, which he turned into smoke on the altar. 14 He washed the entrails and the legs and, with the burnt offering, turned them into smoke on the altar.

15 Next he presented the people's offering. He took the goat of the sin offering that was for the people, and slaughtered it, and presented it as a sin offering like the first one. 16 He presented the burnt offering, and sacrificed it according to regulation. 17 He presented the grain offering, and, taking a handful of it, he turned it into smoke on the altar, in addition to the burnt offering of the morning.

18 He slaughtered the ox and the ram as a sacrifice of well-being for the people. Aaron's sons brought him the blood, which he dashed against all sides of the altar, 19 and the fat of the ox and of the ram—the broad tail, the fat that covers the entrails, the two kidneys and the fat on them,e and the appendage of the liver. 20 They first laid the fat on the breasts, and the fat was turned into smoke on the altar; 21 and the breasts and the right thigh Aaron raised as an elevation offering before the LORD, as Moses had commanded.

22 Aaron lifted his hands toward the people and blessed them; and he came down after sacrificing the sin offering, the burnt offering, and the offering of well-being. 23 Moses and Aaron entered the tent of meeting, and then came out and blessed the people; and the glory of the LORD appeared to all the people. 24 Fire came out from the LORD and consumed

e Gk: Heb *the broad tail, and that which covers, and the kidneys*

9.1–24 On the eighth day following the week of consecration, the priests begin their official duties. They offer up special sacrifices for the people *that the glory of the LORD may appear* (9.6; also 9.4, 9.23). Indeed, the whole purpose of the sacrificial system is revelation, the assurance that God is with his people. However, God's presence is never assumed to be a coefficient of the ritual performed; it is always viewed as an act of his grace. **9.2** *Sin offering*, more accurately "purification offering"; see note on 4.1–35. **9.9** *Horns.* See 7.7. **9.10** *Turned into smoke.* See 1.9. **9.12** *Burnt offering.* See note on 1.1–17. **9.17** *Grain offering.* See note on 2.1–16. *Burnt offering of the morning.* See Ex 29.38–42. **9.18** *Sacrifice of well-being.* See note on 3.1–17. **9.21** *Elevation offering.* See 7.30. **9.22** *Blessed them,* probably with the priestly blessing of Num 6.24–26. *He came down.* Presumably, the blessing was recited from the top of the altar. **9.23** *The glory of the LORD appeared,* in the form of fire. Israel will be guided in the wilderness not by God's voiced commands but by his visible presence, a cloud-encased fire (Ex 40.38) identified with God's "glory" (Ex 24.17; Ezek 1.27–28; 2 Chr 7.3). **9.24** *Fire came out from the LORD,* presumably

the burnt offering and the fat on the altar; and when all the people saw it, they shouted and fell on their faces.

Nadab and Abihu

10 Now Aaron's sons, Nadab and Abihu, each took his censer, put fire in it, and laid incense on it; and they offered unholy fire before the LORD, such as he had not commanded them. 2 And fire came out from the presence of the LORD and consumed them, and they died before the LORD. 3 Then Moses said to Aaron, "This is what the LORD meant when he said,

'Through those who are near me
I will show myself holy,
and before all the people
I will be glorified.'"

And Aaron was silent.

4 Moses summoned Mishael and Elzaphan, sons of Uzziel the uncle of Aaron, and said to them, "Come forward, and carry your kinsmen away from the front of the sanctuary to a place outside the camp." 5 They came forward and carried them by their tunics out of the camp, as Moses had ordered. 6 And Moses said to Aaron and to his sons Eleazar and Ithamar, "Do not dishevel your hair, and do not tear your vestments, or you will die and wrath will strike all the congregation; but your kindred, the whole house of Israel, may mourn the burning that the LORD has sent. 7 You shall not go outside the entrance of the tent of meeting, or you will die; for the anointing oil of the LORD is on you." And they did as Moses had ordered.

8 And the LORD spoke to Aaron: 9 Drink no wine or strong drink, neither you nor your sons, when you enter the tent of meeting, that you may not die; it is a statute forever throughout your generations. 10 You are to distinguish between the holy and the common, and between the unclean and the clean; 11 and you are to teach the people of Israel all the statutes that the LORD has spoken to them through Moses.

12 Moses spoke to Aaron and to his remaining sons, Eleazar and Ithamar:

---

from the adytum (the innermost part of the tabernacle), where God's "glory" rested between the outspread wings of the cherubim flanking the ark (Ex 25.22). The theophany functioned to legitimize the Aaronite priesthood. **10.1–20** Ch. 10 continues the material from ch. 9. Grain and well-being offerings are eaten by the priests in accordance with the injunctions of 6.16; 7.28–34. But the procedure for the purification offering is switched from the individual to the communal form: the disposal of blood (9.9; 10.18) has been carried out in accordance with 4.30 but not the disposal of the flesh (10.18), which follows 4.12 rather than 6.26. The death of Nadab and Abihu has intervened. Aaron follows the more stringent procedure of destroying rather than eating the sacrificial meat because it has been doubly polluted by the sin and death of his sons. **10.1** *Unholy fire*, "unauthorized coals" (cf. Num 16.37, 40). **10.2** *And fire came out from the presence of the LORD*, a measure-for-measure principle: those who sinned by fire are punished by fire. **10.3** *What the LORD meant when he said*, more accurately "what the LORD has decreed, saying" (see Gen 24.51). *Those who are near me*, i.e., the priests (Ezek 42.13, translated "who approach"). The greater responsibility of the priests is evidenced in the rules dealing with the crime of encroaching upon the sacred spaces and objects (Num 18.1, 3, 7). The penalty is that of Nadab and Abihu—death by divine agency. The Lord becomes sanctified and glorified through punishment (see Ezek 28.22). *And Aaron was silent*, contrasting starkly with the people's shouting moments earlier (9.24). **10.4** *Mishael and Elzaphan* are Levites, not priests, hence, permitted to come in contact with the dead. **10.6** *Dishevel your hair . . . tear your vestments*, signs of mourning (e.g., Gen 37.29, 34; Lev 13.45). Although Eleazar and Ithamar, the surviving sons of Aaron, were permitted to mourn their brothers (21.1–3), they were on duty, assisting their father in the performance of the sacrifices (9.9, 12, 18) and had yet to eat the sacred meat (10.17). Moreover, they were anointed, in contrast to their priestly successors (Ex 40.15). Hence they were forbidden to mourn as their father was (21.10–11) because *the anointing oil of the LORD is on you* (v. 7). **10.9** *Strong drink*, probably "ale." The existence of a beer industry in Israel is attested by the prevalence of the beer jug in archaeological excavations. *When you enter the tent of meeting*, also forbidden to a priest if he was improperly washed (Ex 30.20), physically blemished (Lev 21.23), or improperly dressed (Ex 28.43). **10.10** Teaching these distinctions is essential to the priestly function (see Ezek 44.21–23). **10.11** *To them*, to Israel, not to the priests. The priests carry no new instruction; they transmit the old, the teaching imparted to Israel through the mediation of Moses. This may be a telltale sign of H (see Introduction). **10.12** *Grain offering*. See note on 2.1–16. *Most holy*. See 2.3.

Take the grain offering that is left from the LORD's offerings by fire, and eat it unleavened beside the altar, for it is most holy; 13 you shall eat it in a holy place, because it is your due and your sons' due, from the offerings by fire to the LORD; for so I am commanded. 14 But the breast that is elevated and the thigh that is raised, you and your sons and daughters as well may eat in any clean place; for they have been assigned to you and your children from the sacrifices of the offerings of well-being of the people of Israel. 15 The thigh that is raised and the breast that is elevated they shall bring, together with the offerings by fire of the fat, to raise for an elevation offering before the LORD; they are to be your due and that of your children forever, as the LORD has commanded.

16 Then Moses made inquiry about the goat of the sin offering, and—it had already been burned! He was angry with Eleazar and Ithamar, Aaron's remaining sons, and said, 17 "Why did you not eat the sin offering in the sacred area? For it is most holy, and God f has given it to you that you may remove the guilt of the congregation, to make atonement on their behalf before the LORD. 18 Its blood was not brought into the inner part of the sanctuary. You should certainly have eaten it in the sanctuary, as I commanded." 19 And Aaron spoke to Moses, "See, today they offered their sin offering and their burnt offering before the LORD; and yet such things as these have befallen me! If I had eaten the sin offering today, would it have been agreeable to the LORD?" 20 And when Moses heard that, he agreed.

Clean and Unclean Foods

11 The LORD spoke to Moses and Aaron, saying to them: 2 Speak to the people of Israel, saying:

From among all the land animals, these are the creatures that you may eat. 3 Any animal that has divided hoofs and is cleft-

f Heb he

10.13 Holy place. See 6.16.   10.14 Offerings of well-being. See note on 3.1–12.   10.15 Elevation offering. See 7.30.   10.16 Sin offering, better "purification offering." See note on 4.1–35. He was angry; Moses was angry. The purification offering, whose blood is daubed on the horns of the outer altar (4.25, 30, 34) but not brought inside the tent of meeting (6.30), must be eaten by the officiating priest (6.26), namely, Aaron, and what he cannot finish must be eaten by the rest of the priestly cadre (6.29), namely, his remaining sons, Eleazar and Ithamar. Moses may have become angry because the reluctance of the priests to eat this sacrifice would engender the suspicion that they were afraid of the harm that might befall them if they ate the impurity-laden meat, a belief that was current in Israel's contemporary world but that the Priestly source (P) assiduously attempted to eradicate.   10.17 Remove the guilt, remove the iniquity by ingesting the purificatory offering. This sacrifice is the analogic counterpart to the high priest's golden plate (8.9). Just as the latter symbolically draws to itself all the impurities of Israel's sacred offerings (Ex 28.38) so the former, by the blood manipulation, draws out the pollution of the sanctuary caused by Israel's impurities and iniquities (see notes on 4.1–35; 16.1–34).   10.18 In accordance with 6.26, 30.   10.19 Aaron's excuse; see note on 10.1–20.   10.20 That the ministrations of Aaron and his sons require the approval not only of God but also of Moses strikingly proves that the Priestly source acknowledges the superiority of the prophet (Moses) over the priest (Aaron).

11.1–16.34   Laws dealing with four sources of impurity: carcasses (ch. 11), childbirth (ch. 12), scale disease (chs. 13–14), and genital discharges (ch. 15). (A fifth source, the corpse, is dealt with in Num 19.) The common denominator of these impurity sources is that they stand for death. Blood and semen represent the forces of life and their loss, death. The wasting of the body, the characteristic of scale disease, symbolizes the death process (cf. Num 12.12) as much as the loss of blood and semen. Carcasses and corpses obviously are the epitome of death and therefore of impurity. Since impurity and holiness are semantic opposites, it is incumbent upon Israel to prevent impurity or, at least, to control its occurrence, lest it impinge upon the sanctuary, the realm of the holy God.   11.1–23   Clean and unclean foods.   11.1–8 Cf. vv. 3–4 with Deut 14.4–6, where the permitted land animals are named. The classification is the result not of empirical medical knowledge but of the universal need to classify phenomena by establishing beneficent and destructive categories.   11.2 Land animals, i.e., quadrupeds.   11.3 Divided hoofs, rather "hoofs." Israel's access is thus limited to the main domestic species—cattle, sheep, and goats (plus several wild but virtually unobtainable animals, Deut 14.4–5). Chews the cud excludes the pig (v. 7), regarded as an abomination particularly because it was revered in chthonic cults that penetrated into Israel as late as the sixth century B.C.E., arousing the wrath of

footed and chews the cud—such you may eat. 4 But among those that chew the cud or have divided hoofs, you shall not eat the following: the camel, for even though it chews the cud, it does not have divided hoofs; it is unclean for you. 5 The rock badger, for even though it chews the cud, it does not have divided hoofs; it is unclean for you. 6 The hare, for even though it chews the cud, it does not have divided hoofs; it is unclean for you. 7 The pig, for even though it has divided hoofs and is cleft-footed, it does not chew the cud; it is unclean for you. 8 Of their flesh you shall not eat, and their carcasses you shall not touch; they are unclean for you.

9 These you may eat, of all that are in the waters. Everything in the waters that has fins and scales, whether in the seas or in the streams—such you may eat. 10 But anything in the seas or the streams that does not have fins and scales, of the swarming creatures in the waters and among all the other living creatures that are in the waters—they are detestable to you 11 and detestable they shall remain. Of their flesh you shall not eat, and their carcasses you shall regard as detestable. 12 Everything in the waters that does not have fins and scales is detestable to you.

13 These you shall regard as detestable among the birds. They shall not be eaten; they are an abomination: the eagle, the vulture, the osprey, 14 the buzzard, the kite of any kind; 15 every raven of any kind; 16 the ostrich, the nighthawk, the sea gull, the hawk of any kind; 17 the little owl, the cormorant, the great owl, 18 the water hen, the desert owl, g the carrion vulture, 19 the stork, the heron of any kind, the hoopoe, and the bat. h

20 All winged insects that walk upon all fours are detestable to you. 21 But among the winged insects that walk on all fours you may eat those that have jointed legs above their feet, with which to leap on the ground. 22 Of them you may eat: the locust according to its kind, the bald locust according to its kind, the cricket according to its kind, and the grasshopper according to its kind. 23 But all other winged insects that have four feet are detestable to you.

Unclean Animals

24 By these you shall become unclean; whoever touches the carcass of any of them shall be unclean until the evening, 25 and whoever carries any part of the carcass of any of them shall wash his clothes and be unclean until the evening. 26 Every animal that has divided hoofs but is not cleft-footed or does not chew the cud is unclean for you; everyone who touches one of them shall be unclean. 27 All that walk on their paws, among the animals that walk on all fours, are unclean for you; whoever touches the carcass of any of them shall be unclean until the evening, 28 and the one who carries the carcass shall wash his clothes and be unclean until the evening; they are unclean for you.

g Or *pelican*   h Identification of several of the birds in verses 13-19 is uncertain

prophet and priest alike (Isa 66.3, 17; cf. 65.4–5). **11.5–6** The *rock badger* and *hare* are not true ruminants, but the sideward movement of their jaws gives them the appearance of one. Their habit of chewing their food twice also creates the impression that they are incessantly chewing food. **11.9–12** That neither prohibited nor permitted fish are enumerated (either here or in Deut 14.9) may be explained by the relatively limited variety of species of sea life in the Mediterranean prior to the construction of the Suez Canal. Fish—alone among the creatures—were not named by Adam (Gen 2.19–20). **11.13–19** No criteria are stated for *birds*. The fact that only impure birds are enumerated implies that the species of pure birds are innumerable (*Sipre Deuteronomy* 103). **11.20–23** *Winged insects*. The reason for exempting locusts is not clear. It may be related to Israel's pastoral life in its presettlement period, when the community subsisted on its herds as well as on the sporadic visits of locusts, just as bedouin do to this day (cf. Mt 3.4; Mk 1.6). **11.24–40** Impurity by contact with carcasses. This section is an insertion from another source, since it interrupts the fourfold classification (11.46) of creatures that may not be eaten. Nonporous articles polluted by cadavers of the species listed in vv. 29–30 must be washed, but contaminated earthenware (porous and absorbent, 6.28) may never be reused. Food and seed grain are immune to impurity except when moist, since water is an impurity carrier. Only the carcasses of quadrupeds and eight reptiles contaminate by touch; all others contaminate by ingestion. **11.24** *Unclean until evening.* Bathing is presumed, but impurity also needs time to completely dissipate, in the case of minor impurities, until evening. **11.25** *Wash his clothes.* Bathing is pre-

29 These are unclean for you among the creatures that swarm upon the earth: the weasel, the mouse, the great lizard according to its kind, 30 the gecko, the land crocodile, the lizard, the sand lizard, and the chameleon. 31 These are unclean for you among all that swarm; whoever touches one of them when they are dead shall be unclean until the evening. 32 And anything upon which any of them falls when they are dead shall be unclean, whether an article of wood or cloth or skin or sacking, any article that is used for any purpose; it shall be dipped into water, and it shall be unclean until the evening, and then it shall be clean. 33 And if any of them falls into any earthen vessel, all that is in it shall be unclean, and you shall break the vessel. 34 Any food that could be eaten shall be unclean if water from any such vessel comes upon it; and any liquid that could be drunk shall be unclean if it was in any such vessel. 35 Everything on which any part of the carcass falls shall be unclean; whether an oven or stove, it shall be broken in pieces; they are unclean, and shall remain unclean for you. 36 But a spring or a cistern holding water shall be clean, while whatever touches the carcass in it shall be unclean. 37 If any part of their carcass falls upon any seed set aside for sowing, it is clean; 38 but if water is put on the seed and any part of their carcass falls on it, it is unclean for you.

39 If an animal of which you may eat dies, anyone who touches its carcass shall be unclean until the evening. 40 Those who eat of its carcass shall wash their clothes and be unclean until the evening; and those who carry the carcass shall wash

their clothes and be unclean until the evening.

41 All creatures that swarm upon the earth are detestable; they shall not be eaten. 42 Whatever moves on its belly, and whatever moves on all fours, or whatever has many feet, all the creatures that swarm upon the earth, you shall not eat; for they are detestable. 43 You shall not make yourselves detestable with any creature that swarms; you shall not defile yourselves with them, and so become unclean. 44 For I am the LORD your God; sanctify yourselves therefore, and be holy, for I am holy. You shall not defile yourselves with any swarming creature that moves on the earth. 45 For I am the LORD who brought you up from the land of Egypt, to be your God; you shall be holy, for I am holy.

46 This is the law pertaining to land animal and bird and every living creature that moves through the waters and every creature that swarms upon the earth, 47 to make a distinction between the unclean and the clean, and between the living creature that may be eaten and the living creature that may not be eaten.

Purification of Women After Childbirth

12 The LORD spoke to Moses, saying: 2 Speak to the people of Israel, saying:

If a woman conceives and bears a male child, she shall be ceremonially unclean seven days; as at the time of her menstruation, she shall be unclean. 3 On the eighth day the flesh of his foreskin shall be circumcised. 4 Her time of blood purifi-

---

sumed. **11.29–30** These eight named land swarmers differ from the rest of their kind (vv. 41–43) in that they contaminate not only by ingestion but also by touch (v. 31), a characteristic they share with the impure quadrupeds (vv. 8, 24–28). These eight would commonly be found in the kitchen, and, being small, might be found inside vessels (vv. 32–38). **11.33** Contaminated earthenware must be broken because it absorbs impurities that cannot be removed. **11.34** Once wetted by liquid, food becomes susceptible to impurity (v. 38). **11.35** Ovens and stoves are made of earthenware. **11.36** Water sources are, however, not susceptible to impurity because they are embedded in the ground. **11.39–40** The carcasses of clean (i.e., edible) animals also defile. **11.41–42** These verses on swarming things

continue 11.23. **11.43–45** Israel enjoined to be holy. An interpolation from H (see Introduction). **11.46–47** A summary of the entire chapter.

12.1–8 For seven days following the birth of a male child and fourteen days following that of a female child, no conjugal relations are allowed. For an additional period of thirty-three and sixty-six days respectively, contact with sacred spaces and objects is proscribed. That sacrifices are brought only after the impurity has totally disappeared is proof that their function is neither apotropaic nor medicinal; only ritual impurity adheres, which time and ablutions remove. The rite is scaled to economic circumstances (5.7–13; 14.21–32). **12.2** *Conceives*, lit. "produces seed." **12.3** *Flesh of his foreskin*, or "foreskin of his mem-

cation shall be thirty-three days; she shall not touch any holy thing, or come into the sanctuary, until the days of her purification are completed. 5 If she bears a female child, she shall be unclean two weeks, as in her menstruation; her time of blood purification shall be sixty-six days.

6 When the days of her purification are completed, whether for a son or for a daughter, she shall bring to the priest at the entrance of the tent of meeting a lamb in its first year for a burnt offering, and a pigeon or a turtledove for a sin offering. 7 He shall offer it before the LORD, and make atonement on her behalf; then she shall be clean from her flow of blood. This is the law for her who bears a child, male or female. 8 If she cannot afford a sheep, she shall take two turtledoves or two pigeons, one for a burnt offering and the other for a sin offering; and the priest shall make atonement on her behalf, and she shall be clean.

Scale Disease, Varieties and Symptoms

13 The LORD spoke to Moses and Aaron, saying:
2 When a person has on the skin of his body a swelling or an eruption or a spot, and it turns into a leprous*i* disease on the skin of his body, he shall be brought to Aaron the priest or to one of his sons the priests. 3 The priest shall examine the disease on the skin of his body, and if the hair in the diseased area has turned white and the disease appears to be deeper than the skin of his body, it is a leprous*i* disease; after the priest has examined him he shall pronounce him ceremonially unclean. 4 But if the spot is white in the skin of his body, and appears no deeper than the skin, and the hair in it has not turned white, the priest shall confine the diseased person for seven days. 5 The priest shall examine him on the seventh day, and if he sees that the disease is checked and the disease has not spread in the skin, then the priest shall confine him seven days more. 6 The priest shall examine him again on the seventh day, and if the disease has abated and the disease has not spread in the skin, the priest shall pronounce him clean; it is only an eruption; and he shall wash his clothes, and be clean. 7 But if the eruption spreads in the skin after he has shown himself to the priest for his cleansing, he shall appear again before the priest. 8 The priest shall make an examination, and if the eruption has spread in the skin, the priest shall pronounce him unclean; it is a leprous*i* disease.

9 When a person contracts a leprous*i* disease, he shall be brought to the priest. 10 The priest shall make an examination, and if there is a white swelling in the skin

i A term for several skin diseases; precise meaning uncertain

---

ber." **12.5** The reason for the disparity between the sexes is unknown. **12.6** The rendering *sin offering* seems especially misleading in this case. What sin has the new mother committed? A better rendering would be "purification offering" merely indicating that her postpartum blood flow has engendered a ritual impurity that has contaminated the sanctuary, for which a purification offering is mandated once she is completely healed (see expressly 14.19). **12.7** *Flow*, lit. "source."

13.1–14.57 The priest is instructed to identify and isolate those afflicted with scale disease, traditionally but not properly translated "leprosy" (Hansen's disease). It is mainly a noncontagious condition, probably vitiligo or, less likely, psoriasis. (Regarding these examples of scale disease as ritually contaminating, see note on 11.1–16.34.) Scaling is the common denominator of all the skin ailments described in ch. 13, as follows: boils (vv. 18–23), burns (vv. 24–28), scalls, i.e., infection of the hairy parts of the head (vv. 29–37), tetters and normal baldness (pure manifestations;

vv. 38–41); and impure baldness (vv. 42–44). The comportment of a certified scale-disease carrier is described in 13.45–46 and his or her purificatory rites in 14.1–20. Lev 13.47–59 describes the deterioration of garments probably because of mildew or fungus, and 14.33–53 describes the infection of houses because of the spread of saltpeter or moss, in which case quarantine procedures are also enforced. Unusual considerations for property are reflected in 14.36: the priest clears the house prior to his inspection so that the contents will not be condemned with the house. The priest is not a physician. His rituals commence only after the disease has passed. Both disease and healing stem from the one God. Chs. 13–14 are summarized in 14.54–57. **13.2** *A swelling or an eruption or a spot.* A preferable translation might be "a discoloration or a scab or a shining mark." Vv. 2–8 deal with shining marks and vv. 9–17 with discolorations. Nonspreading scabs are not impure (vv. 7–8). **13.3** *Leprous disease*, rather "scale disease" (so throughout; see

that has turned the hair white, and there is quick raw flesh in the swelling, 11 it is a chronic leprous*j* disease in the skin of his body. The priest shall pronounce him unclean; he shall not confine him, for he is unclean. 12 But if the disease breaks out in the skin, so that it covers all the skin of the diseased person from head to foot, so far as the priest can see, 13 then the priest shall make an examination, and if the disease has covered all his body, he shall pronounce him clean of the disease; since it has all turned white, he is clean. 14 But if raw flesh ever appears on him, he shall be unclean; 15 the priest shall examine the raw flesh and pronounce him unclean. Raw flesh is unclean, for it is a leprous*j* disease. 16 But if the raw flesh again turns white, he shall come to the priest; 17 the priest shall examine him, and if the disease has turned white, the priest shall pronounce the diseased person clean. He is clean.

18   When there is on the skin of one's body a boil that has healed, 19 and in the place of the boil there appears a white swelling or a reddish-white spot, it shall be shown to the priest. 20 The priest shall make an examination, and if it appears deeper than the skin and its hair has turned white, the priest shall pronounce him unclean; this is a leprous*j* disease, broken out in the boil. 21 But if the priest examines it and the hair on it is not white, nor is it deeper than the skin but has abated, the priest shall confine him seven days. 22 If it spreads in the skin, the priest shall pronounce him unclean; it is diseased. 23 But if the spot remains in one place and does not spread, it is the scar of the boil; the priest shall pronounce him clean.

24   Or, when the body has a burn on the skin and the raw flesh of the burn becomes a spot, reddish-white or white, 25 the priest shall examine it. If the hair in the spot has turned white and it appears deeper than the skin, it is a leprous*j* disease; it has broken out in the burn, and the priest shall pronounce him unclean. This is a leprous*j* disease. 26 But if the priest examines it and the hair in the spot is not white, and it is no deeper than the skin but has abated, the priest shall confine him seven days. 27 The priest shall examine him the seventh day; if it is spreading in the skin, the priest shall pronounce him unclean. This is a leprous*j*

disease. 28 But if the spot remains in one place and does not spread in the skin but has abated, it is a swelling from the burn, and the priest shall pronounce him clean; for it is the scar of the burn.

29   When a man or woman has a disease on the head or in the beard, 30 the priest shall examine the disease. If it appears deeper than the skin and the hair in it is yellow and thin, the priest shall pronounce him unclean; it is an itch, a leprous*j* disease of the head or the beard. 31 If the priest examines the itching disease, and it appears no deeper than the skin and there is no black hair in it, the priest shall confine the person with the itching disease for seven days. 32 On the seventh day the priest shall examine the itch; if the itch has not spread, and there is no yellow hair in it, and the itch appears to be no deeper than the skin, 33 he shall shave, but the itch he shall not shave. The priest shall confine the person with the itch for seven days more. 34 On the seventh day the priest shall examine the itch; if the itch has not spread in the skin and it appears to be no deeper than the skin, the priest shall pronounce him clean. He shall wash his clothes and be clean. 35 But if the itch spreads in the skin after he was pronounced clean, 36 the priest shall examine him. If the itch has spread in the skin, the priest need not seek for the yellow hair; he is unclean. 37 But if in his eyes the itch is checked, and black hair has grown in it, the itch is healed, he is clean; and the priest shall pronounce him clean.

38   When a man or a woman has spots on the skin of the body, white spots, 39 the priest shall make an examination, and if the spots on the skin of the body are of a dull white, it is a rash that has broken out on the skin; he is clean.

40   If anyone loses the hair from his head, he is bald but he is clean. 41 If he loses the hair from his forehead and temples, he has baldness of the forehead but he is clean. 42 But if there is on the bald head or the bald forehead a reddish-white diseased spot, it is a leprous*j* disease breaking out on his bald head or his bald forehead. 43 The priest shall examine him; if the diseased swelling is reddish-white on his bald head or on his bald forehead, which resembles a leprous*j* disease in the skin of the body, 44 he is leprous,*j*

j A term for several skin diseases; precise meaning uncertain

he is unclean. The priest shall pronounce him unclean; the disease is on his head.

45 The person who has the leprous[k] disease shall wear torn clothes and let the hair of his head be disheveled; and he shall cover his upper lip and cry out, "Unclean, unclean." 46He shall remain unclean as long as he has the disease; he is unclean. He shall live alone; his dwelling shall be outside the camp.

47 Concerning clothing: when a leprous[k] disease appears in it, in woolen or linen cloth, 48in warp or woof of linen or wool, or in a skin or in anything made of skin, 49if the disease shows greenish or reddish in the garment, whether in warp or woof or in skin or in anything made of skin, it is a leprous[k] disease and shall be shown to the priest. 50The priest shall examine the disease, and put the diseased article aside for seven days. 51He shall examine the disease on the seventh day. If the disease has spread in the cloth, in warp or woof, or in the skin, whatever be the use of the skin, this is a spreading leprous[k] disease; it is unclean. 52He shall burn the clothing, whether diseased in warp or woof, woolen or linen, or anything of skin, for it is a spreading leprous[k] disease; it shall be burned in fire.

53 If the priest makes an examination, and the disease has not spread in the clothing, in warp or woof or in anything of skin, 54the priest shall command them to wash the article in which the disease appears, and he shall put it aside seven days more. 55The priest shall examine the diseased article after it has been washed. If the diseased spot has not changed color, though the disease has not spread, it is unclean; you shall burn it in fire, whether the leprous[k] spot is on the inside or on the outside.

56 If the priest makes an examination, and the disease has abated after it is washed, he shall tear the spot out of the cloth, in warp or woof, or out of skin. 57If it appears again in the garment, in warp or woof, or in anything of skin, it is spreading; you shall burn with fire that in which the disease appears. 58But the cloth, warp or woof, or anything of skin from which the disease disappears when you have washed it, shall then be washed a second time, and it shall be clean.

59 This is the ritual for a leprous[k] disease in a cloth of wool or linen, either in warp or woof, or in anything of skin, to decide whether it is clean or unclean.

Purification of Scale-Diseased Persons and Houses

14 The LORD spoke to Moses, saying: 2This shall be the ritual for the leprous[k] person at the time of his cleansing:

He shall be brought to the priest; 3the priest shall go out of the camp, and the priest shall make an examination. If the disease is healed in the leprous[k] person, 4the priest shall command that two living clean birds and cedarwood and crimson yarn and hyssop be brought for the one who is to be cleansed. 5The priest shall command that one of the birds be slaughtered over fresh water in an earthen vessel. 6He shall take the living bird with the cedarwood and the crimson yarn and the hyssop, and dip them and the living bird in the blood of the bird that was slaughtered over the fresh water. 7He shall sprinkle it seven times upon the one who is to be cleansed of the leprous[k] disease; then he shall pronounce him clean, and he shall let the living bird go into the open field. 8The one who is to be cleansed shall wash his clothes, and shave off all his hair, and bathe himself in water, and he shall be clean. After that he shall come into the camp, but shall live outside his tent seven

k A term for several skin diseases; precise meaning uncertain

---

note on 13.1–14.57). **13.43** Diseased swelling, or "discolored affliction." **13.45** The certified scale-diseased person adopts the manner of a mourner. **13.51** Spreading, a malignant disease (also 14.44).

14.1–32 Three separate purificatory ceremonies are required for a healed scale-diseased person: for the first day (vv. 2–8; also invoked for houses, vv. 48–53), for the seventh day (v. 9), and for the eighth day (vv. 10–32). They constitute a

rite of passage whereby the person is successively reintegrated into the community. **14.2** He shall be brought to the priest, preferably "When it is reported to the priest," in view of the subsequent statement the priest shall go out of the camp. **14.4–8** The living bird, dipped in the blood of the slain bird, carries off enough ritual impurity to allow the erstwhile "leper" to reenter the camp after he shaves and bathes but not to reenter his (or any) tent lest he contaminate it (see 14.46).

days. 9 On the seventh day he shall shave all his hair: of head, beard, eyebrows; he shall shave all his hair. Then he shall wash his clothes, and bathe his body in water, and he shall be clean.

10 On the eighth day he shall take two male lambs without blemish, and one ewe lamb in its first year without blemish, and a grain offering of three-tenths of an ephah of choice flour mixed with oil, and one log*l* of oil. 11 The priest who cleanses shall set the person to be cleansed, along with these things, before the LORD, at the entrance of the tent of meeting. 12 The priest shall take one of the lambs, and offer it as a guilt offering, along with the log*l* of oil, and raise them as an elevation offering before the LORD. 13 He shall slaughter the lamb in the place where the sin offering and the burnt offering are slaughtered in the holy place; for the guilt offering, like the sin offering, belongs to the priest: it is most holy. 14 The priest shall take some of the blood of the guilt offering and put it on the lobe of the right ear of the one to be cleansed, and on the thumb of the right hand, and on the big toe of the right foot. 15 The priest shall take some of the log*l* of oil and pour it into the palm of his own left hand, 16 and dip his right finger in the oil that is in his left hand and sprinkle some oil with his finger seven times before the LORD. 17 Some of the oil that remains in his hand the priest shall put on the lobe of the right ear of the one to be cleansed, and on the thumb of the right hand, and on the big toe of the right foot, on top of the blood of the guilt offering. 18 The rest of the oil that is in the priest's hand he shall put on the head of the one to be cleansed. Then the priest shall make atonement on his behalf before the LORD: 19 the priest shall offer the sin offering, to make atonement for the one to be cleansed from his uncleanness. Afterward he shall slaughter the burnt offering; 20 and the priest shall offer the burnt offering and the grain offering on the altar. Thus the priest shall

make atonement on his behalf and he shall be clean.

21 But if he is poor and cannot afford so much, he shall take one male lamb for a guilt offering to be elevated, to make atonement on his behalf, and one-tenth of an ephah of choice flour mixed with oil for a grain offering and a log*l* of oil; 22 also two turtledoves or two pigeons, such as he can afford, one for a sin offering and the other for a burnt offering. 23 On the eighth day he shall bring them for his cleansing to the priest, to the entrance of the tent of meeting, before the LORD; 24 and the priest shall take the lamb of the guilt offering and the log*l* of oil, and the priest shall raise them as an elevation offering before the LORD. 25 The priest shall slaughter the lamb of the guilt offering and shall take some of the blood of the guilt offering, and put it on the lobe of the right ear of the one to be cleansed, and on the thumb of the right hand, and on the big toe of the right foot. 26 The priest shall pour some of the oil into the palm of his own left hand, 27 and shall sprinkle with his right finger some of the oil that is in his left hand seven times before the LORD. 28 The priest shall put some of the oil that is in his hand on the lobe of the right ear of the one to be cleansed, and on the thumb of the right hand, and the big toe of the right foot, where the blood of the guilt offering was placed. 29 The rest of the oil that is in the priest's hand he shall put on the head of the one to be cleansed, to make atonement on his behalf before the LORD. 30 And he shall offer, of the turtledoves or pigeons such as he can afford, 31 one*m* for a sin offering and the other for a burnt offering, along with a grain offering; and the priest shall make atonement before the LORD on behalf of the one being cleansed. 32 This is the ritual for the one

l A liquid measure   *m* Gk Syr: Heb *afford,* 31 *such as he can afford, one*

14.9 After his second shaving and ablution on the seventh day, he resumes normal intercourse with family. 14.10–20 The final stage of his purification takes place the following day when he brings a reparation offering for having possibly desecrated a sacred object or space (see 5.17–19), the blood of which together with sanctified oil is

smeared on his extremities to purify him (see 8.30); a purification offering (not properly *sin offering*) for having contaminated the sanctuary by his impurity (see esp. v. 19); and a burnt offering and a grain offering to expiate for neglected performative commandments or sinful thoughts (see 1.4). 14.16 *Seven times before the*

[handwritten margin notes: "deeper meaning: —ancient Israel no sep secular/religion —deep concern for poor"; "Not be so dismissive"; "When people lived in cities"; "mold mildew"; "not healthy"]

who has a leprous[n] disease, who cannot afford the offerings for his cleansing.

33 The LORD spoke to Moses and Aaron, saying:

34 When you come into the land of Canaan, which I give you for a possession, and I put a leprous[n] disease in a house in the land of your possession, 35 the owner of the house shall come and tell the priest, saying, "There seems to me to be some sort of disease in my house." 36 The priest shall command that they empty the house before the priest goes to examine the disease, or all that is in the house will become unclean; and afterward the priest shall go in to inspect the house. 37 He shall examine the disease; if the disease is in the walls of the house with greenish or reddish spots, and if it appears to be deeper than the surface, 38 the priest shall go outside to the door of the house and shut up the house seven days. 39 The priest shall come again on the seventh day and make an inspection; if the disease has spread in the walls of the house, 40 the priest shall command that the stones in which the disease appears be taken out and thrown into an unclean place outside the city. 41 He shall have the inside of the house scraped thoroughly, and the plaster that is scraped off shall be dumped in an unclean place outside the city. 42 They shall take other stones and put them in the place of those stones, and take other plaster and plaster the house.

43 If the disease breaks out again in the house, after he has taken out the stones and scraped the house and plastered it, 44 the priest shall go and make inspection; if the disease has spread in the house, it is a spreading leprous[n] disease in the house; it is unclean. 45 He shall have the house torn down, its stones and timber and all the plaster of the house, and taken outside the city to an unclean place.

46 All who enter the house while it is shut up shall be unclean until the evening; 47 and all who sleep in the house shall wash their clothes; and all who eat in the house shall wash their clothes.

48 If the priest comes and makes an inspection, and the disease has not spread in the house after the house was plastered, the priest shall pronounce the house clean; the disease is healed. 49 For the cleansing of the house he shall take two birds, with cedarwood and crimson yarn and hyssop, 50 and shall slaughter one of the birds over fresh water in an earthen vessel, 51 and shall take the cedarwood and the hyssop and the crimson yarn, along with the living bird, and dip them in the blood of the slaughtered bird and the fresh water, and sprinkle the house seven times. 52 Thus he shall cleanse the house with the blood of the bird, and with the fresh water, and with the living bird, and with the cedarwood and hyssop and crimson yarn; 53 and he shall let the living bird go out of the city into the open field; so he shall make atonement for the house, and it shall be clean. *[handwritten: Urban renewal — Chicago — S. Bronx]*

54 This is the ritual for any leprous[n] disease: for an itch, 55 for leprous[n] diseases in clothing and houses, 56 and for a swelling or an eruption or a spot, 57 to determine when it is unclean and when it is clean. This is the ritual for leprous[n] diseases.

Concerning Bodily Discharges

15 The LORD spoke to Moses and Aaron, saying: 2 Speak to the people of Israel and say to them:

When any man has a discharge from his member,[o] his discharge makes him cere-

---

n A term for several skin diseases; precise meaning uncertain   o Heb *flesh*

LORD, to consecrate the oil (see 4.6). **14.36** Persons and objects that were in the house prior to its quarantine by the priest are declared pure. **14.46** *All who enter* points to the extraordinary power of the fungous house to contaminate by overhang, that is, to contaminate anyone under its roof, proof that scale disease (and all severe impurities) emits a miasma that contaminates the sanctuary at a distance and, in the case of scale disease and corpse contamination (see Num 19.14), defiles persons and objects inside a house. **14.49–52** For the cleansing of the house only the

first-day rite for scale disease (vv. 4–8) is required since the impurity generated by the house is not strong enough to contaminate the sanctuary from afar.

15.1–33 Ch. 15 is composed of two sections: natural discharges of men and women (15.16–18; 15.19–24, respectively), an impurity removed simply by bathing, and pathological discharges (15.2–15; 15.25–30, respectively), which require sacrificial expiation. The eight-day ritual for the latter, as for the scale-diseased person, is a rite of passage from death to life. **15.2** *Discharge*, an

monially unclean. 3 The uncleanness of his discharge is this: whether his member*P* flows with his discharge, or his member*P* is stopped from discharging, it is uncleanness for him. 4 Every bed on which the one with the discharge lies shall be unclean; and everything on which he sits shall be unclean. 5 Anyone who touches his bed shall wash his clothes, and bathe in water, and be unclean until the evening. 6 All who sit on anything on which the one with the discharge has sat shall wash their clothes, and bathe in water, and be unclean until the evening. 7 All who touch the body of the one with the discharge shall wash their clothes, and bathe in water, and be unclean until the evening. 8 If the one with the discharge spits on persons who are clean, then they shall wash their clothes, and bathe in water, and be unclean until the evening. 9 Any saddle on which the one with the discharge rides shall be unclean. 10 All who touch anything that was under him shall be unclean until the evening, and all who carry such a thing shall wash their clothes, and bathe in water, and be unclean until the evening. 11 All those whom the one with the discharge touches without his having rinsed his hands in water shall wash their clothes, and bathe in water, and be unclean until the evening.

12 Any earthen vessel that the one with the discharge touches shall be broken; and every vessel of wood shall be rinsed in water.

13 When the one with a discharge is cleansed of his discharge, he shall count seven days for his cleansing; he shall wash his clothes and bathe his body in fresh water, and he shall be clean. 14 On the eighth day he shall take two turtledoves or two pigeons and come before the LORD to the entrance of the tent of meeting and give them to the priest. 15 The priest shall offer them, one for a sin offering and the other for a burnt offering; and the priest shall make atonement on his behalf before the LORD for his discharge.

16 If a man has an emission of semen, he shall bathe his whole body in water, and be unclean until the evening. 17 Everything made of cloth or of skin on which the semen falls shall be washed with water, and be unclean until the evening. 18 If a man lies with a woman and has an emission of semen, both of them shall bathe in water, and be unclean until the evening.

19 When a woman has a discharge of blood that is her regular discharge from her body, she shall be in her impurity for seven days, and whoever touches her shall be unclean until the evening. 20 Every-

p Heb *flesh*

---

abnormal one, usually but not exclusively identified with gonorrhea. **15.3** The loss of semen and genital blood (vv. 19–30) generates impurity since it represents the loss of life and, hence, is opposed to the Lord, the source of holiness and life (see note on 11.1–16.34). **15.5** This extrastrength impurity, affecting persons and objects at a second (even a third, v. 23) remove, is limited to objects directly underneath those having genital discharges. **15.11** *Rinsed his hands.* Whoever takes this precaution may touch persons and objects. Thus he may live at home, a far-reaching leniency. **15.12** See 11.33. **15.13** *Fresh water.* Fresh, lit. "living," water is also required in two other cases: corpse contamination (Num 19.17) and scale disease (Lev 14.5–6, 50–52). Together with genital discharges they comprise all the sources of severe impurity (lasting seven days or more). Since impurity is symbolic of death, its antidote is that which fosters life. **15.15** *Sin offering,* more accurately "purification offering" (see note on 4.1–35), for having polluted the sanctuary with his impurity. The function of the *burnt offering* here is to provide adequate substance for the altar, since the meat is assigned to the offici-

ating priest (6.26). So too must every other purification-offering bird be accompanied by a burnt-offering bird (5.7; 12.8; 14.30–31). **15.16** Natural emissions of semen, as opposed to pathological ones, constitute only a minor impurity of one day's duration. **15.18** In many ancient cultures sexual intercourse disqualified a person from participating in religious ritual. The rite frequently prescribed for purification from sexual impurity is bathing, but the Bible uniquely adds one stipulation: for the impurity to be completely eliminated one must wait until evening (see 11.24). One can understand that seminal emissions, being a total loss of life-giving fluids, were regarded as impure. But in conjugal union, the act of procreation? Obviously, the priestly legists were aware of the fact that it is the rare seed that results in procreation; mostly it is wasted. **15.19** Laundering and bathing at the end of seven days must be presumed. **15.19–23** The menstruant is not banished but remains at home. She may prepare meals and perform her household chores. The family, in turn, has to avoid lying in her bed, sitting in her chair, or touching

thing upon which she lies during her impurity shall be unclean; everything also upon which she sits shall be unclean. 21 Whoever touches her bed shall wash his clothes, and bathe in water, and be unclean until the evening. 22 Whoever touches anything upon which she sits shall wash his clothes, and bathe in water, and be unclean until the evening; 23 whether it is the bed or anything upon which she sits, when he touches it he shall be unclean until the evening. 24 If any man lies with her, and her impurity falls on him, he shall be unclean seven days; and every bed on which he lies shall be unclean.

25 If a woman has a discharge of blood for many days, not at the time of her impurity, or if she has a discharge beyond the time of her impurity, all the days of the discharge she shall continue in uncleanness; as in the days of her impurity, she shall be unclean. 26 Every bed on which she lies during all the days of her discharge shall be treated as the bed of her impurity; and everything on which she sits shall be unclean, as in the uncleanness of her impurity. 27 Whoever touches these things shall be unclean, and shall wash his clothes, and bathe in water, and be unclean until the evening. 28 If she is

cleansed of her discharge, she shall count seven days, and after that she shall be clean. 29 On the eighth day she shall take two turtledoves or two pigeons and bring them to the priest at the entrance of the tent of meeting. 30 The priest shall offer one for a sin offering and the other for a burnt offering; and the priest shall make atonement on her behalf before the LORD for her unclean discharge.

31 Thus you shall keep the people of Israel separate from their uncleanness, so that they do not die in their uncleanness by defiling my tabernacle that is in their midst.

32 This is the ritual for those who have a discharge: for him who has an emission of semen, becoming unclean thereby, 33 for her who is in the infirmity of her period, for anyone, male or female, who has a discharge, and for the man who lies with a woman who is unclean.

The Day of Atonement

16 The LORD spoke to Moses after the death of the two sons of Aaron, when they drew near before the LORD and died. 2 The LORD said to Moses: Tell your brother Aaron not to come just at any time into the sanctuary inside

---

her. **15.23** *The bed or anything*, more precisely "on the bed or on anything." An object can be contaminated at a third remove provided it is in unbroken contact with the menstruant. **15.24** *If any man ... on him* may be translated "if any man lies with her, her impurity will fall upon him," implying that copulation may have been a deliberate act, punishable by excision (20.18). The severe, seven-day impurity may be due to the loss of both life-giving semen and genital blood. **15.25** *The days of her impurity*, lit. "the days of her menstrual impurity," a reference to vv. 20, 22. **15.27** *These things*. Possibly with Septuagint read "her," in conformance with the law concerning men's *discharge* (v. 7). **15.30** See v. 15. **15.31** *Defiling my tabernacle*. Severe impurity incurred anywhere in the community will pollute the sanctuary. For this spatial notion of impurity, see chs. 4 and 16. **16.1–34** The annual Day of Atonement for the sanctuary and people. According to v. 1, ch. 16 follows upon ch. 10. Thus, chs. 11–15 are an insert listing the specific impurities that will contaminate the sanctuary (15.31) for which the purification ritual of ch. 16 is mandated. The impurities of the sanctuary are eliminated by purification offerings (16.16–19). The iniquities of the

people are eliminated by the confession of the high priest over the dispatched goat while the people fast (vv. 21–22, 29–31). The text strongly suggests that the original form of the purgation rite described in vv. 2–28 was an emergency measure invoked by the high priest whenever he felt that the entire sanctuary had to be purged. It is the appendix, vv. 29–34, that fixes this rite as an annual observance. That it comprises an appendix is ascertained by the change of person (direct address to Israel); the fact that not Aaron but his descendants are officiating (v. 32); a change in terminology (e.g., the adytum is now called "the holiest part of the sanctuary"; see v. 33); only here is the date specified at the end (vv. 29, 34), whereas all other festival prescriptions begin with the date; and the unexpected inclusion of resident aliens, its first occurrence in the book of Leviticus. All seventeen subsequent attestations in chs. 17–24 are, by common scholarly consent, attributed to H (see Introduction). **16.1** *Drew near before*, better "encroached upon." **16.2** *In the cloud*, by means of the screen of incense raised by the high priest (v. 13). **16.2–3** *Sanctuary/holy place*, the adytum, innermost part of the tabernacle. *Sin offering*, better "purification offering" (see

the curtain before the mercy seat*q* that is upon the ark, or he will die; for I appear in the cloud upon the mercy seat.*q* 3 Thus shall Aaron come into the holy place: with a young bull for a sin offering and a ram for a burnt offering. 4 He shall put on the holy linen tunic, and shall have the linen undergarments next to his body, fasten the linen sash, and wear the linen turban; these are the holy vestments. He shall bathe his body in water, and then put them on. 5 He shall take from the congregation of the people of Israel two male goats for a sin offering, and one ram for a burnt offering.

6 Aaron shall offer the bull as a sin offering for himself, and shall make atonement for himself and for his house. 7 He shall take the two goats and set them before the LORD at the entrance of the tent of meeting; 8 and Aaron shall cast lots on the two goats, one lot for the LORD and the other lot for Azazel.*r* 9 Aaron shall present the goat on which the lot fell for the LORD, and offer it as a sin offering; 10 but the goat on which the lot fell for Azazel*r* shall be presented alive before the LORD to make atonement over it, that it may be sent away into the wilderness to Azazel.*r*

11 Aaron shall present the bull as a sin offering for himself, and shall make atonement for himself and for his house; he shall slaughter the bull as a sin offering

for himself. 12 He shall take a censer full of coals of fire from the altar before the LORD, and two handfuls of crushed sweet incense, and he shall bring it inside the curtain 13 and put the incense on the fire before the LORD, that the cloud of the incense may cover the mercy seat*q* that is upon the covenant,*s* or he will die. 14 He shall take some of the blood of the bull, and sprinkle it with his finger on the front of the mercy seat,*q* and before the mercy seat*q* he shall sprinkle the blood with his finger seven times.

15 He shall slaughter the goat of the sin offering that is for the people and bring its blood inside the curtain, and do with its blood as he did with the blood of the bull, sprinkling it upon the mercy seat*q* and before the mercy seat.*q* 16 Thus he shall make atonement for the sanctuary, because of the uncleannesses of the people of Israel, and because of their transgressions, all their sins; and so he shall do for the tent of meeting, which remains with them in the midst of their uncleannesses. 17 No one shall be in the tent of meeting from the time he enters to make atonement in the sanctuary until he comes out and has made atonement for himself and for his house and for all the assembly of Israel. 18 Then he shall go out to the altar that is before the LORD and

q Or *the cover*   *r* Traditionally rendered *a scapegoat*   *s* Or *treaty*, or *testament*; Heb *eduth*

note on 4.1–35). **16.4** The high priest donned linen garments perhaps because entering the adytum was equivalent to being admitted to the heavenly council, whose members, the angels, were also dressed in linen (Ezek 9.2–3, 11; 10.2; Dan 10.5) **16.6** *Offer*, lit. "bring forward," as in v. 11, "present." **16.8** *Azazel*, probably the name of a demon who has been stripped of his alleged powers by the priestly legists. No longer a personality but just a name, he designates the place to which Israel's impurities and sins are banished. **16.10** *To make atonement over it*, by the confession of Israel's sins (v. 21). **16.11** The high priest must purge the sanctuary of the impurities he and his fellow priests have caused before he is eligible to do the same for the people. **16.12–13** If the purpose of the incense is to raise a cloud of smoke that screens the high priest's view of the ark, how could it be that he lights the incense only *after* he enters the adytum? The clue to the solution is supplied by the fact that the lit incense by itself does not produce a cloud of smoke. Thus another smoke-raising ingredient has to be added to the

incense and it, not the incense, was ignited by the high priest before he entered the adytum and ignited the incense. The incense, then, would have functioned to placate God for the high priest's presumption in entering before his presence. *The covenant*, short for "the ark of the covenant." **16.14** *On the front of*, lit. "on the surface of . . . the east side." Since the high priest could not see the ark cover, he merely threw the drop of blood toward it but made sure it landed on its east side, namely, before it. Thus symbolically the ark was purged, as was the entire adytum, by the sevenfold blood sprinkling on the adytum floor. **16.16** *Make atonement for the sanctuary*, purge the adytum. *Transgressions*. In the priestly theology it is the transgressions, the willful, brazen impurities committed by the people, that have penetrated into the adytum, requiring its purgation by the high priest on the annual Day of Atonement. *So he shall do for the tent of meeting*. The purgation rite of 4.6–7, 17–18 is presumed. The tent of meeting here refers to the outer room, the shrine. **16.18** *On its behalf*, better "upon it." Purification-

make atonement on its behalf, and shall take some of the blood of the bull and of the blood of the goat, and put it on each of the horns of the altar. 19 He shall sprinkle some of the blood on it with his finger seven times, and cleanse it and hallow it from the uncleannesses of the people of Israel.

20 When he has finished atoning for the holy place and the tent of meeting and the altar, he shall present the live goat. 21 Then Aaron shall lay both his hands on the head of the live goat, and confess over it all the iniquities of the people of Israel, and all their transgressions, all their sins, putting them on the head of the goat, and sending it away into the wilderness by means of someone designated for the task.t 22 The goat shall bear on itself all their iniquities to a barren region; and the goat shall be set free in the wilderness.

23 Then Aaron shall enter the tent of meeting, and shall take off the linen vestments that he put on when he went into the holy place, and shall leave them there. 24 He shall bathe his body in water in a holy place, and put on his vestments; then he shall come out and offer his burnt offering and the burnt offering of the people, making atonement for himself and for the people. 25 The fat of the sin offering he shall turn into smoke on the altar. 26 The one who sets the goat free for Azazelu shall wash his clothes and bathe his body in water, and afterward may come into the camp. 27 The bull of the sin offering and the goat of the sin offering, whose blood was brought in to make atonement in the holy place, shall be taken outside the camp; their skin and their flesh and their dung shall be consumed in fire. 28 The one who burns them shall wash his clothes and bathe his body in water, and afterward may come into the camp.

29 This shall be a statute to you forever: In the seventh month, on the tenth day of the month, you shall deny yourselves,v and shall do no work, neither the citizen nor the alien who resides among you. 30 For on this day atonement shall be made for you, to cleanse you; from all your sins you shall be clean before the LORD. 31 It is a sabbath of complete rest to you, and you shall deny yourselves;v it is a statute forever. 32 The priest who is anointed and consecrated as priest in his father's place shall make atonement, wearing the linen vestments, the holy vestments. 33 He shall make atonement for the sanctuary, and he shall make atonement for the tent of meeting and for the altar, and he shall make atonement for the priests and for all the people of the assembly. 34 This shall be an everlasting statute for you, to make atonement for the people of Israel once in the year for all their sins. And Moses did as the LORD had commanded him.

The Slaughtering of Animals

17 The LORD spoke to Moses:
2 Speak to Aaron and his sons and to all the people of Israel and say to them: This is what the LORD has com-

t Meaning of Heb uncertain   u Traditionally rendered a scapegoat   v Or shall fast

---

offering blood is put directly on the sacrificial altar (see Ex 29.36). **16.18–19** The daubing of the blood on the altar purifies it (see 4.7, 25; 8.15); the sprinkling rite sanctifies it (see 8.11). **16.21** *Lay*, lit. "lean" (see 1.4). *Both his hands*, an act of transference (as in 24.14), in contrast with sacrificial, one-handed hand-leaning, an act of ownership (1.4). *Iniquities*. Whereas the blood rites in the sanctuary purge it of Israel's impurities (*uncleanness*, v. 16), the hand-leaning on the confession over the live goat purge the people of their sins by transferring them to the head of the goat and dispatching it into the wilderness. *Confess*. Confession is required only for brazen, presumptuous sins (5.5; 26.40; Num 5.7). **16.22** *And*. Translate "when" and connect with v. 23 to avoid a redundancy with v. 21b. **16.23** *Leave them there*, because they contracted the extreme sanctity of the adytum. **16.24** *His vestments*, i.e., the ornate ones he always wore while officiating at the altar (8.6–9). **16.26–28** The handlers of the slain and live purification offerings are contaminated, but not the high priest who is immune to impurity while officiating. **16.29** *Deny yourselves*. "Afflict yourselves, from food, drink, and from enjoying bathing, and from anointing, and from sexual intercourse" (*Targum Pseudo-Jonathan*). **16.29–31** See also 23.26–32. **16.32** *Priest in his father's place*. In contrast to vv. 2–28, which speak solely of Aaron, this verse focuses on his successors. **16.33** *The sanctuary*, rather "the holiest part of the sanctuary," i.e., the adytum.

17.1–26.46 The Holiness source (H). The remainder of the book of Leviticus (excluding ch. 27), it is often held, consists largely of an independent code in which moral and ritual laws alter-

manded. 3 If anyone of the house of Israel slaughters an ox or a lamb or a goat in the camp, or slaughters it outside the camp, 4 and does not bring it to the entrance of the tent of meeting, to present it as an offering to the LORD before the tabernacle of the LORD, he shall be held guilty of bloodshed; he has shed blood, and he shall be cut off from the people. 5 This is in order that the people of Israel may bring their sacrifices that they offer in the open field, that they may bring them to the LORD, to the priest at the entrance of the tent of meeting, and offer them as sacrifices of well-being to the LORD. 6 The priest shall dash the blood against the altar of the LORD at the entrance of the tent of meeting, and turn the fat into smoke as a pleasing odor to the LORD, 7 so that they may no longer offer their sacrifices for goat-demons, to whom they prostitute themselves. This shall be a statute forever to them throughout their generations.

8 And say to them further: Anyone of the house of Israel or of the aliens who reside among them who offers a burnt offering or sacrifice, 9 and does not bring it to the entrance of the tent of meeting, to sacrifice it to the LORD, shall be cut off from the people.

Eating Blood Prohibited

10 If anyone of the house of Israel or of the aliens who reside among them eats any blood, I will set my face against that person who eats blood, and will cut that person off from the people. 11 For the life of the flesh is in the blood; and I have given it to you for making atonement for your lives on the altar; for, as life, it is the blood that makes atonement. 12 Therefore I have said to the people of Israel: No person among you shall eat blood, nor shall any alien who resides among you eat blood. 13 And anyone of the people of Israel, or of the aliens who reside among them, who hunts down an animal or bird that may be eaten shall pour out its blood and cover it with earth.

---

nate, motivated by holiness. This, however, is questionable. Ch. 17, the alleged beginning of the code, is connected thematically and verbally with the preceding chapters. Chs. 25–26, which are often alleged to be the conclusion, form an independent scroll, to judge from the unique vocabulary (e.g., 25.18–19; 26.5), theme (25.8–13; 26.34–35, 43), and redaction (25.1; 26.46). Nonetheless, much of the language and some ideas in chs. 17–26 differ from the first part of Leviticus. For a fuller discussion of H and of the relationship between P and H, see the Introduction.
17.1–16 Whoever kills a sacrificial animal outside the sanctuary is guilty of murder (17.3–4). Sacrifice to goat-demons or "satyrs" is thus abolished (17.5–9), and expiation for killing the animal is assured through a ritual by which its lifeblood is returned to its creator, either upon the altar (17.10–12) or by being drained and covered by earth in the case of game animals (17.13–14; cf. Deut 12.16). V. 11 has nothing to do with the expiation of sin in general.
17.3–7 No common slaughter. **17.3** *Outside the camp*, but within easy access of the sanctuary. **17.4** *Guilty of bloodshed*, a capital crime. *Cut off from the people*, i.e., extinction of his line by divine agency, a capital punishment (see 7.20). **17.5** *In the open field*, for chthonic worship (see v. 7). *Sacrifices of well-being to the LORD*. Henceforth, common slaughter is strictly forbidden. Meat for the table must initially be a sacrifice. **17.7** *Goat-demons*. It is possible that the demon Azazel (the first ele-

ment of which means "goat"; see 16.8) was also a satyr. *Prostitute themselves*, a metaphor for idolatry (Ex 34.15–16; Lev 20.5, 6; Deut 31.16).
17.8–9 No sacrifices to other gods. **17.8** If *aliens* wish to have meat, they need not bring their animals to the sanctuary (a performative commandment), but they are forbidden to worship other gods (a prohibitive commandment). *Burnt offering or sacrifice*. The latter refers to the well-being (including the thanksgiving) offering. Thus, the purification and reparation offerings are excluded, possibly a reflex of the popular religion, which knew only the burnt offering as the exclusive expiatory sacrifice (see also 22.17–21).
17.10–12 Blood of sacrificial animals may not be ingested. Vv. 11–12 are an aside to Moses; only the law is given to Israel, not its rationale.
17.10 *Aliens* are forbidden to ingest blood, a prohibitive commandment. *Eats*, proof that the blood is ingested in the course of eating meat. **17.11** *To you*, to Israel, but not to aliens who may slaughter animals at home. *For making atonement*, or "to ransom" (see Ex 30.12, 15, 16). Animal slaughter is murder except at the authorized altar, where the offered blood ransoms the donor's life. *As life, it is the blood that makes atonement*, or "it is the blood that ransoms by means of life."
17.13–14 The blood of game may not be ingested. Assumed is the knowledge of 11.13–19, 24–28. **17.13** *Cover it with earth*: so that the blood will not be used in chthonic worship (e.g., for divination) but returned to God, who en-

14 For the life of every creature—its blood is its life; therefore I have said to the people of Israel: You shall not eat the blood of any creature, for the life of every creature is its blood; whoever eats it shall be cut off. 15 All persons, citizens or aliens, who eat what dies of itself or what has been torn by wild animals, shall wash their clothes, and bathe themselves in water, and be unclean until the evening; then they shall be clean. 16 But if they do not wash themselves or bathe their body, they shall bear their guilt.

Sexual Relations

18 The LORD spoke to Moses, saying: 2 Speak to the people of Israel and say to them: I am the LORD your God. 3 You shall not do as they do in the land of Egypt, where you lived, and you shall not do as they do in the land of Canaan, to which I am bringing you. You shall not follow their statutes. 4 My ordinances you shall observe and my statutes you shall keep, following them: I am the LORD your God. 5 You shall keep my statutes and my ordinances; by doing so one shall live: I am the LORD.

6 None of you shall approach anyone near of kin to uncover nakedness: I am the LORD. 7 You shall not uncover the nakedness of your father, which is the nakedness of your mother; she is your mother, you shall not uncover her nakedness. 8 You shall not uncover the nakedness of your father's wife; it is the nakedness of your father. 9 You shall not uncover the nakedness of your sister,

dowed animals as well as humans with *nefesh* (Hebrew), "life, soul." **17.14** The third aside to Moses providing rationales for required actions (in addition to vv. 5–7, 11–12), virtually repeating vv. 10–11a. **17.15–16** Eating of a carcass requires purification. **17.15** Lest they pollute the land, *aliens* must also purify themselves after eating of a carcass. **17.16** *Guilt,* or "punishment." If their impurity is prolonged, leading to the pollution of the sanctuary, they will be punished by the excision of their line (see 5.1–13).

18.1–20.27 On being holy. Though chs. 18–20 were originally independent, they are thematically united: ch. 20 prescribes the penalties for the illicit relations and homicidal cult practices proscribed in ch. 18 (20.1–5) and for violating the ban on magic put into effect in 19.31 (20.6). Moreover, the entire unit is framed by a single goal: separation of the Israelites from the Canaanites, who are portrayed as engaging in idolatrous and immoral practices, which pollute the divinely chosen land (18.3; 18.24–30; 20.22–24). The arrangement of Ezek 22 contains a mixture of ethical and ritual sins based solely on these chapters, indicating that their written formulation is preexilic.

The key word in this section is *holy.* This word clusters in the food prohibitions (Lev 11.44–47; 20.23–26) and significantly in only one other context, the rules concerning the priesthood, 21.6–8. The priesthood, Israel, and humankind form three rings of decreasing holiness about the center, God. Ideally, all Israel shall be "a priestly kingdom and a holy nation" (Ex 19.6). If Israel is to attain its higher level of holiness, it must abide by a more rigid code of behavior than that practiced by other nations, just as the priests live by

more stringent standards than common Israelites. Holiness, then, implies separation and is so defined in 20.26. The positive aspect of holiness is discussed in ch. 19.

18.1–30 The list of prohibitions is framed by passages (18.1–5; 18.24–30) castigating the sexual mores of the Egyptians and the Canaanites. Israel is charged with an exacting code of family purity whose violation means death (20.10–16). Only the Holiness source proclaims the sanctity of the land of Canaan; hence both Israelites and resident strangers are responsible for maintaining its sanctity (18.26–27; 20.2; 24.22). The moral justification for its conquest (18.27–28; 20.22) is also a warning: if guilty of the same infractions, Israel too will be "vomited out." **18.2** *I am the LORD your God,* or "I the LORD am your God." Hence, you must follow my laws. **18.3** *Egypt* and *Canaan* are accused by biblical authors of consanguineous, incestuous, promiscuous, and homosexual unions (Gen 9.24; 19.5; 34.2; 39.7; Ezek 16.26; 23.3, 20). **18.5** *I am the LORD,* or "I the LORD," i.e., "I the LORD have spoken," equivalent to the prophetic "says the LORD" (e.g., Amos 2.16; 3.15). **18.6** *Approach,* a euphemism for "have sex with." *Near of kin,* lit. "flesh of his flesh," i.e., the nearest kin, one's mother, sister, and daughter, the last two otherwise missing in this list. *Uncover nakedness,* another euphemism for having sex with, given here in this initial law for emphasis. **18.7** *The nakedness of your father,* i.e., your father's exclusive possession (18.8; 20.11; Deut 22.30; cf. Lev 20.20, 21). **18.9** *Born at home or born abroad,* i.e., whether she belongs to your kin group or another kin group; that is, even if your half sister is totally unrelated to you by blood, she is forbid-

your father's daughter or your mother's daughter, whether born at home or born abroad. 10 You shall not uncover the nakedness of your son's daughter or of your daughter's daughter, for their nakedness is your own nakedness. 11 You shall not uncover the nakedness of your father's wife's daughter, begotten by your father, since she is your sister. 12 You shall not uncover the nakedness of your father's sister; she is your father's flesh. 13 You shall not uncover the nakedness of your mother's sister, for she is your mother's flesh. 14 You shall not uncover the nakedness of your father's brother, that is, you shall not approach his wife; she is your aunt. 15 You shall not uncover the nakedness of your daughter-in-law: she is your son's wife; you shall not uncover her nakedness. 16 You shall not uncover the nakedness of your brother's wife; it is your brother's nakedness. 17 You shall not uncover the nakedness of a woman and her daughter, and you shall not take*w* her son's daughter or her daughter's daughter to uncover her nakedness; they are your*x* flesh; it is depravity. 18 And you shall not take*w* a woman as a rival to her sister, uncovering her nakedness while her sister is still alive.

19 You shall not approach a woman to uncover her nakedness while she is in her menstrual uncleanness. 20 You shall not have sexual relations with your kinsman's wife, and defile yourself with her. 21 You shall not give any of your offspring to sacrifice them*y* to Molech, and so profane the name of your God: I am the LORD. 22 You shall not lie with a male as with a woman; it is an abomination. 23 You shall not have sexual relations with any animal and defile yourself with it, nor shall any woman give herself to an animal to have sexual relations with it: it is perversion.

24 Do not defile yourselves in any of these ways, for by all these practices the nations I am casting out before you have defiled themselves. 25 Thus the land became defiled; and I punished it for its iniquity, and the land vomited out its inhabitants. 26 But you shall keep my statutes and my ordinances and commit none of these abominations, either the citizen or the alien who resides among you 27 (for the inhabitants of the land, who were before you, committed all of these abominations, and the land became defiled); 28 otherwise the land will vomit you out for defiling it, as it vomited out the nation that was before you. 29 For whoever commits any of these abominations shall be cut off from their people. 30 So keep my charge not to commit any of these abominations that were done before you, and not to defile yourselves by them: I am the LORD your God.

w Or marry   *x Gk: Heb lacks* your   *y Heb to pass them over*

---

den. But see Gen 20.12 in which Abraham married his half sister. **18.11** *Begotten by your father*, rather "of your father's kin." But if she belongs to a different kin group, marriage is permissible. **18.12** Amram married Jochebed, his paternal aunt (they were the parents of Aaron and Moses), despite this prohibition. Reflecting sensitivity to this discrepancy, the Septuagint in Ex 6.20 reads "the daughter of his father's brother," i.e., his cousin. Perhaps for this reason the birth of Moses is attributed to anonymous Levite parents (Ex 2.1). **18.15** Judah married his daughter-in-law, Tamar, despite this prohibition—an early form of levirate marriage (cf. Gen 38; Deut 25.5–10). **18.16** Ostensibly, the verse is opposed to the institution of levirate marriage (Deut 25.5–10; see Lev 20.21). **18.18** Despite this prohibition, Jacob married two sisters, Rachel and Leah, while both were alive (Gen 29.15–30). The obvious answer to all four above-mentioned marital discrepancies with vv. 9, 12, 18 is that they occurred before the Sinaitic law code became operative. **18.20** *Kins-* man's, rather "neighbor's" (cf. Ezek 18.6, 15). **18.21** *Give ... offspring to sacrifice.* See 2 Kings 23.10; cf. Deut 12.31; 2 Kings 16.3; Jer 7.31; 19.5; 32.35. *Molech* may stand for *melek*, "king (of the underworld)," who was probably identified by his worshipers with Israel's God (cf. Jer 7.31; 19.5). If it were another god, the sacrifice would have been condemned as murder. See further in 20.2. *Profane the name of your God*, since the rite is dedicated to him. **18.23** Different species should be kept apart, following God's example at creation (Gen 1); see further in Lev 19.19. **18.25** Moral sins pollute the earth, e.g., those of Adam and Eve (Gen 3.17), Cain (Gen 4.10–12), and Noah's generation (see Gen 8.21). Here, however, the pollution is confined to the land of Canaan (Ezek 36.17; see Num 35.33; Deut 21.23; Jer 2.7). Therein lies the theological basis of the concept of the holy land, namely, that all who reside on this land, including all aliens, must observe God's prohibitive commandments (see Lev 17.8, 10; esp. 24.16).

Ritual and Moral Holiness

19 The LORD spoke to Moses, saying:
2 Speak to all the congregation of the people of Israel and say to them: You shall be holy, for I the LORD your God am holy. 3 You shall each revere your mother and father, and you shall keep my sabbaths: I am the LORD your God. 4 Do not turn to idols or make cast images for yourselves: I am the LORD your God.

5 When you offer a sacrifice of well-being to the LORD, offer it in such a way that it is acceptable in your behalf. 6 It shall be eaten on the same day you offer it, or on the next day; and anything left over until the third day shall be consumed in fire. 7 If it is eaten at all on the third day, it is an abomination; it will not be acceptable. 8 All who eat it shall be subject to punishment, because they have profaned what is holy to the LORD; and any such person shall be cut off from the people.

9 When you reap the harvest of your land, you shall not reap to the very edges of your field, or gather the gleanings of your harvest. 10 You shall not strip your vineyard bare, or gather the fallen grapes of your vineyard; you shall leave them for the poor and the alien: I am the LORD your God.

11 You shall not steal; you shall not deal falsely; and you shall not lie to one another. 12 And you shall not swear falsely by my name, profaning the name of your God: I am the LORD.

13 You shall not defraud your neighbor; you shall not steal; and you shall not keep for yourself the wages of a laborer until morning. 14 You shall not revile the deaf or put a stumbling block before the blind; you shall fear your God: I am the LORD.

15 You shall not render an unjust judgment; you shall not be partial to the poor or defer to the great: with justice you shall judge your neighbor. 16 You shall not go around as a slanderer z among your people, and you shall not profit by the blood a of your neighbor: I am the LORD.

17 You shall not hate in your heart anyone of your kin; you shall reprove your neighbor, or you will incur guilt yourself. 18 You shall not take vengeance or bear a grudge against any of your people, but you shall love your neighbor as yourself: I am the LORD.

19 You shall keep my statutes. You shall not let your animals breed with a different kind; you shall not sow your field with two kinds of seed; nor shall you put on a garment made of two different materials.

20 If a man has sexual relations with a woman who is a slave, designated for an-

z Meaning of Heb uncertain   a Heb *stand against the blood*

19.1–37 For Israel, "holy" means more than that which is unapproachable. It becomes a positive concept, an inspiration and a goal associated with God's nature and his desire for humans to be holy: *You shall be holy; for I . . . am holy* (19.2). That which humans are not, nor can ever fully be, but which they are commanded to emulate and approximate is what the Bible calls "holy." Holiness means *imitatio Dei*—the life of godliness. How can human beings imitate God? The answer of Lev 19 is given in a series of ethical and ritual commands, above which soars the commandment to love all persons (19.18), including aliens (19.34). Such love must be concretely expressed in deeds: equality in civil justice (24.22; Num 35.15), free loans (Lev 25.35–38; Deut 10.18; 23.20), and free gleanings (Lev 19.9–10). **19.5–8** Here the well-being sacrifice is limited to the freewill and votive offerings, in contrast to 7.11–16, which includes the thanksgiving offering. **19.10** The widow and orphan fall under the category of the *poor*. The poor, however, do not appear as a separate category in the humanitarian legislation of Deuteronomy, which instead ordains for them loans (Deut 15.7–11); i.e., they can work off their debt, something that widows and orphans cannot. *I am the LORD your God*, "for the LORD pleads their cause and despoils of life those who despoil them" (Prov 22.23). **19.11** *Deal falsely*, e.g., deny you possessed your neighbor's property (6.2). **19.13** *Steal*, rather "rob" (cf. v. 11). **19.16** *Profit*, lit. "stand," i.e., don't stand by idle when your neighbor is in danger. **19.17** *Guilt*, i.e., "punishment." *Yourself*, more accurately "because of him," i.e., you are likely to take action against him that may be sinful. **19.18** *Love*, reach out, befriend. Love here is not an emotion. *Neighbor*, i.e., an Israelite (cf. v. 34). *As yourself*, i.e., as you love yourself, or "who is like you," since he or she is also created by God. **19.19** *Two kinds of seed, two different materials*. (See Deut 22.9.) God separated everything according to its species (Gen 1). The human world should mirror the natural world. Israel, therefore, may not mix with other nations, but be holy,

other man but not ransomed or given her freedom, an inquiry shall be held. They shall not be put to death, since she has not been freed; 21 but he shall bring a guilt offering for himself to the LORD, at the entrance of the tent of meeting, a ram as guilt offering. 22 And the priest shall make atonement for him with the ram of guilt offering before the LORD for his sin that he committed; and the sin he committed shall be forgiven him.

23 When you come into the land and plant all kinds of trees for food, then you shall regard their fruit as forbidden;*b* three years it shall be forbidden*c* to you, it must not be eaten. 24 In the fourth year all their fruit shall be set apart for rejoicing in the LORD. 25 But in the fifth year you may eat of their fruit, that their yield may be increased for you: I am the LORD your God.

26 You shall not eat anything with its blood. You shall not practice augury or witchcraft. 27 You shall not round off the hair on your temples or mar the edges of your beard. 28 You shall not make any gashes in your flesh for the dead or tattoo any marks upon you: I am the LORD.

29 Do not profane your daughter by making her a prostitute, that the land not become prostituted and full of depravity. 30 You shall keep my sabbaths and reverence my sanctuary: I am the LORD.

31 Do not turn to mediums or wizards; do not seek them out, to be defiled by them: I am the LORD your God.

32 You shall rise before the aged, and defer to the old; and you shall fear your God: I am the LORD.

33 When an alien resides with you in your land, you shall not oppress the alien. 34 The alien who resides with you shall be to you as the citizen among you; you shall love the alien as yourself, for you were aliens in the land of Egypt: I am the LORD your God.

35 You shall not cheat in measuring length, weight, or quantity. 36 You shall have honest balances, honest weights, an honest ephah, and an honest hin: I am the LORD your God, who brought you out of the land of Egypt. 37 You shall keep all my statutes and all my ordinances, and observe them: I am the LORD.

Penalties for Violations of Holiness

20 The LORD spoke to Moses, saying: 2 Say further to the people of Israel:

Any of the people of Israel, or of the aliens who reside in Israel, who give any of their offspring to Molech shall be put to death; the people of the land shall stone them to death. 3 I myself will set my face against them, and will cut them off

b Heb *as their uncircumcision*
c Heb *uncircumcision*

---

set apart for God. **19.20–22** A marginal case. Though not guilty before humans (not adulterous), he is guilty before God; hence he brings a reparation offering. **19.24** *Set apart . . . in the* LORD, lit. "holy . . . before the LORD," i.e., at the sanctuary. **19.26** *With*, lit. "over," a chthonic rite for the purpose of consulting the dead spirits (see v. 31; 17.5–7, 13–14; 20.6; 1 Sam 14.32–35). Instead, the blood should be offered on the altar (Lev 17.3–4, 11). **19.27–28** Pagan mourning rites. **19.31** Mediums, or "ancestral spirits" (see v. 26; 20.27). **19.33** *Oppress*, or "cheat." **19.34** The summit of biblical ethics.
20.1–27 The penalties for illicit sexual relations are graded according to their severity: vv. 10–16, death by humans; vv. 17–19, death by God; vv. 20–21, childlessness. Of illicit worship of God, only Molech worship and oracles through mediums are singled out, the former because of its monstrousness and the latter because of its prevalence (Deut 18.9–12; 1 Sam 28.9; Isa 8.19). The absence of the lofty pronouncements of ch. 19 from this list is mute evidence that ethics

are really unenforceable. **20.2** Since *aliens* reside in the Lord's land, they are required to observe all the prohibitive commandments (see 17.8, 10). The *Molech* cult is expressly mentioned in 18.21; 20.2–5; 2 Kings 23.10; Jer 32.35 and alluded to in Isa 57.9; Jer 7.31; 19.5. Though the Leviticus texts use the ambiguous verbs "give" and "pass over" (alternative translation of "give" in 18.21), other references explicitly use the verb "burn" (Jer 7.31; 19.5; cf. 32.35; Isa 30.33). The reason this prohibition is set among the sexual offenses (note the sexual imagery in v. 5) is that it (and, indeed, all idolatry) was regarded as spiritual adultery (Ex 34.15–16; cf. Jer 3). Molech is probably identical with the Canaanite god *mlk*, who in Akkadian sources is called Malik and is equated with the underworld god Nergal. The sacrifices to Molech were offered in the Valley of Hinnom, just outside Jerusalem (2 Kings 23.10; cf. Jer 7.31, 32.35). **20.3** *Defiling my sanctuary.* Since Molech worship was practiced just beneath the temple mount in the Valley of Hinnom (Jer 32.35), it was feasible to worship at both sites the

[handwritten margin notes: "more appropriet then law?", "grossly inappropriet"]

from the people, because they have given of their offspring to Molech, defiling my sanctuary and profaning my holy name. 4 And if the people of the land should ever close their eyes to them, when they give of their offspring to Molech, and do not put them to death, 5 I myself will set my face against them and against their family, and will cut them off from among their people, them and all who follow them in prostituting themselves to Molech.

6 If any turn to mediums and wizards, prostituting themselves to them, I will set my face against them, and will cut them off from the people. 7 Consecrate yourselves therefore, and be holy; for I am the LORD your God. 8 Keep my statutes, and observe them; I am the LORD; I sanctify you. 9 All who curse father or mother shall be put to death; having cursed father or mother, their blood is upon them.

10 If a man commits adultery with the wife of[d] his neighbor, both the adulterer and the adulteress shall be put to death. 11 The man who lies with his father's wife has uncovered his father's nakedness; both of them shall be put to death; their blood is upon them. 12 If a man lies with his daughter-in-law, both of them shall be put to death; they have committed perversion, their blood is upon them. 13 If a man lies with a male as with a woman, both of them have committed an abomination; they shall be put to death; their blood is upon them. 14 If a man takes a wife and her mother also, it is depravity; they shall be burned to death, both he and they, that there may be no depravity among you. 15 If a man has sexual relations with an animal, he shall be put to death; and you shall kill the animal. 16 If a woman approaches any animal and has sexual relations with it, you shall kill the woman and the animal; they shall be put to death, their blood is upon them.

17 If a man takes his sister, a daughter of his father or a daughter of his mother, and sees her nakedness, and she sees his nakedness, it is a disgrace, and they shall be cut off in the sight of their people; he has uncovered his sister's nakedness, he shall be subject to punishment. 18 If a man lies with a woman having her sickness and uncovers her nakedness, he has laid bare her flow and she has laid bare her flow of blood; both of them shall be cut off from their people. 19 You shall not uncover the nakedness of your mother's sister or of your father's sister, for that is to lay bare one's own flesh; they shall be subject to punishment. 20 If a man lies with his un-

[vertical margin text: Reservation]

d Heb repeats *if a man commits adultery with the wife of*

---

same day (Ezek 23.32–39), an indication that its devotees felt that its worship was compatible with the worship of and, indeed, demanded by the Lord. **20.5** *Them*, i.e., the Molech worshipers. *Their family*. The family may have protected them. **20.5–6** *People*, better "(deceased) kin." The Lord imposes a measure-for-measure punishment: he cuts off from ancestral spirits the one who tries to placate them. **20.6** It is no accident that this prohibition against turning to mediums and wizards (for the purpose of consulting the ancestral spirits; see 19.26) is cojoined with the Molech prohibition. Both are directed against chthonic worship, which especially prevailed in Judah at the end of the eighth and beginning of the seventh century B.C.E. The Judean kings of this period, Ahaz and Manasseh, are accused of practicing Molech worship (2 Kings 16.3; 21.6), and Isaiah (eighth century) reports the resort to mediums and wizards (19.3 explicitly mentions its goal: "[to] consult . . . the spirits of the dead") — further indication that the Holiness source (H) originates from this period. **20.8** *I am the* LORD; *I sanctify you*, or "I, the LORD, sanctify you." Israel acquires holiness by observing the commandments (22.32; cf. Ex 31.13; Ezek 20.12; 37.28). **20.9** *Curse*, perhaps "insult, dishonor" (see Ex 21.17; Prov 20.20; Mt 15.4; Mk 7.10). *Their blood is upon them*, that is, their executioner need not fear that their blood will be "on his head" (see Josh 2.14; 2 Sam 1.16; 1 Kings 2.37), namely, that God will hold him responsible for spilling their blood. **20.10** The text begins *If a man commits adultery with the wife of his neighbor*. The specification "his neighbor" limits the penalty to Israelites. Though adultery is listed last among the illicit heterosexual relations (18.20), it is first when it comes to these penalties since it concerns not only private morality but the stability and welfare of the community. **20.11** *His father's wife*. His mother is assumed (18.7–8). **20.12** See 18.15. **20.13** See 18.22. **20.14** *Takes*, in marriage or by common consent. See 18.17. **20.15–16** See 18.23. **20.15** *Kill the animal*, which has also sinned (cf. Ex 21.28–29). **20.17** See 18.9. *Sees her nakedness . . . sees his nakedness*, a willful act. *Subject to punishment*, probably excision. **20.18** *Sickness*, not just menstruation but any genital flow (15.25, 33), an expansion of 18.19. **20.19** See 18.12–13. *One's own flesh*, actually "the

cle's wife, he has uncovered his uncle's nakedness; they shall be subject to punishment; they shall die childless. 21 If a man takes his brother's wife, it is impurity; he has uncovered his brother's nakedness; they shall be childless.

22 You shall keep all my statutes and all my ordinances, and observe them, so that the land to which I bring you to settle in may not vomit you out. 23 You shall not follow the practices of the nation that I am driving out before you. Because they did all these things, I abhorred them. 24 But I have said to you: You shall inherit their land, and I will give it to you to possess, a land flowing with milk and honey. I am the LORD your God; I have separated you from the peoples. 25 You shall therefore make a distinction between the clean animal and the unclean, and between the unclean bird and the clean; you shall not bring abomination on yourselves by animal or by bird or by anything with which the ground teems, which I have set apart for you to hold unclean. 26 You shall be holy to me; for I the LORD am holy, and I have separated you from the other peoples to be mine.

27 A man or a woman who is a medium or a wizard shall be put to death; they shall be stoned to death, their blood is upon them.

The Holiness of Priests

21 The LORD said to Moses: Speak to the priests, the sons of Aaron, and say to them:

No one shall defile himself for a dead person among his relatives, 2 except for his nearest kin: his mother, his father, his son, his daughter, his brother; 3 likewise, for a virgin sister, close to him because she has had no husband, he may defile himself for her. 4 But he shall not defile himself as a husband among his people and so profane himself. 5 They shall not make bald spots upon their heads, or shave off the edges of their beards, or make any gashes in their flesh. 6 They shall be holy to their God, and not profane the name of their God; for they offer the LORD's offerings by fire, the food of their God; therefore they shall be holy. 7 They shall not marry a prostitute or a woman who has been defiled; neither shall they marry a woman divorced from her husband. For they are holy to their God, 8 and you shall treat them as holy, since they offer the

---

flesh of one's flesh." **20.20** See 18.14. **20.21** A rejection of the levirate (Deut 25.5), whereby the name of the deceased husband is preserved through the progeny born of his wife and his brother. *Childless.* Once again, the divine measure-for-measure punishment is manifest: his wish to have a child from his brother's widow will be denied. **20.24** *Honey,* date syrup (Deut 8.8). **20.25** Making distinctions between the animals that form one's diet teaches one to make distinctions in human contact. **20.27** *Is a medium,* lit. "has inside him an ancestral spirit." An appendix. Whereas those who consult mediums are punished by God (v. 6), the mediums themselves are put to death by people.

21.1–22.33 Restrictions are placed upon the priests to guard against moral and ritual defilement, which might entail dire consequences for them and the people (22.9, 15–16; cf. 4.3; 15.31). Disqualifications of sacrifices are also enumerated (22.21–24). Ritual impurity stems from three sources: certain scale diseases (see chs. 13–14), genital fluxes, both male and female (see ch. 15), and carcasses (see ch. 11) or corpses (Num 19, a knowledge of which is presumed here). Contamination by corpses is the most severe of the ritual impurities because a person becomes contaminated merely by being under the same roof as a

corpse (Num 19.14) and because the impurity lasts for seven days (Num 19.14, 16) and can only be eliminated by the unique rite of being aspersed with the ashes of a red cow (Num 19.17–19). There is no prohibition against coming in contact with a corpse (it is assumed that one may, and indeed should, bury the dead). The only restriction is that the purificatory rite may not be overlooked or even delayed (Num 19.13, 19). This allowance, however, does not hold for a priest. He is holy, and the contact between holiness and impurity not only is forbidden; it is lethal (see 7.20–21; 22.9). Thus, the permission given to priests to bury their closest blood relatives (their nuclear family; 21.1–4) constitutes a concession. **21.4** *People,* rather "kin" (see 20.5–6), implying that the priest may not defile himself for the burial of his wife or any of her relatives. If, however, the words "as a husband" are deleted (a possible dittography of the following word), then the prohibition repeats and forms an inclusion with v. 1, a structure repeated in vv. 17b, 21. **21.5** These mourning rites are also forbidden to Israelites (19.27–28). **21.7** *Woman who has been defiled,* probably raped, which carries no stigma for her if she is the daughter of a layman (Deut 22.28–29; cf. Lev 21.9). *Divorced,* but not a widow; the criterion is reputation. **21.8** *Treat them as*

food of your God; they shall be holy to you, for I the LORD, I who sanctify you, am holy. 9 When the daughter of a priest profanes herself through prostitution, she profanes her father; she shall be burned to death.

10 The priest who is exalted above his fellows, on whose head the anointing oil has been poured and who has been consecrated to wear the vestments, shall not dishevel his hair, nor tear his vestments. 11 He shall not go where there is a dead body; he shall not defile himself even for his father or mother. 12 He shall not go outside the sanctuary and thus profane the sanctuary of his God; for the consecration of the anointing oil of his God is upon him: I am the LORD. 13 He shall marry only a woman who is a virgin. 14 A widow, or a divorced woman, or a woman who has been defiled, a prostitute, these he shall not marry. He shall marry a virgin of his own kin, 15 that he may not profane his offspring among his kin, for I am the LORD; I sanctify him.

16 The LORD spoke to Moses, saying: 17 Speak to Aaron and say: No one of your offspring throughout their generations who has a blemish may approach to offer the food of his God. 18 For no one who has a blemish shall draw near, one who is blind or lame, or one who has a mutilated face or a limb too long, 19 or one who has a broken foot or a broken hand, 20 or a hunchback, or a dwarf, or a man with a blemish in his eyes or an itching disease or scabs or crushed testicles. 21 No descendant of Aaron the priest who has a blemish shall come near to offer the

LORD's offerings by fire; since he has a blemish, he shall not come near to offer the food of his God. 22 He may eat the food of his God, of the most holy as well as of the holy. 23 But he shall not come near the curtain or approach the altar, because he has a blemish, that he may not profane my sanctuaries; for I am the LORD; I sanctify them. 24 Thus Moses spoke to Aaron and to his sons and to all the people of Israel.

The Use of Holy Offerings

22 The LORD spoke to Moses, saying: 2 Direct Aaron and his sons to deal carefully with the sacred donations of the people of Israel, which they dedicate to me, so that they may not profane my holy name; I am the LORD. 3 Say to them: If anyone among all your offspring throughout your generations comes near the sacred donations, which the people of Israel dedicate to the LORD, while he is in a state of uncleanness, that person shall be cut off from my presence: I am the LORD. 4 No one of Aaron's offspring who has a leprous[e] disease or suffers a discharge may eat of the sacred donations until he is clean. Whoever touches anything made unclean by a corpse or a man who has had an emission of semen, 5 and whoever touches any swarming thing by which he may be made unclean or any human being by whom he may be made unclean— whatever his uncleanness may be— 6 the person who touches any such shall be un-

e A term for several skin diseases; precise meaning uncertain

---

holy, by seeing to it that your daughters qualify as their wives (vv. 7, 9). *Sanctify you*. One may read "sanctify them" with Septuagint, the Samaritan Pentateuch, and a Dead Sea Scroll fragment of Leviticus written in the old Hebrew alphabet (11QpaleoLev). **21.9** *She profanes her father*, just as a wife's character reflects on her husband (v. 7). **21.10** *The priest ... exalted above his fellows*, i.e., the high priest, may not engage even in permitted mourning rites. **21.11** Sight of a corpse also contaminates a high priest. **21.12** He may not leave the sanctuary to follow the bier (see 10.7). **21.13** Since he is appointed during the lifetime of his father (6.22; 16.32), he could be young and unmarried. **21.17, 21** *Approach ... come near*, more precisely "qualify." **21.23** *Near the curtain*, i.e., officiate, the prerogative only of the high priest. *My sanctuaries*, literally, "my holy

things." *I sanctify them*. Though the priests are invariably holy, their sanctity is enhanced by their observance of these prohibitions. **22.2** *Deal carefully with*, lit. "separate themselves from" (see Num 6.3; Ezek 14.7). *Sacred donations* include all the sacrifices and offerings to the sanctuary, both the less holy (e.g., the well-being offering, v. 21) and the most holy (e.g., the purification offering, 6.25) from which the priest receives stipulated prebends (see 6.25; 7.31–32) and which he would defile if he ate them in a state of impurity (vv. 4–8). **22.3** *Comes near*, or "encroaches upon." **22.4** *Has a leprous disease or suffers a discharge*. See chs. 13–15. The third source of contamination, the corpse, is assumed. *Anything*, more accurately "anyone" (similarly "it" in Num 19.22 should read "him"). **22.6–7** *Washed ... When*, rather "first washed ... Then when."

clean until evening and shall not eat of the sacred donations unless he has washed his body in water. 7 When the sun sets he shall be clean; and afterward he may eat of the sacred donations, for they are his food. 8 That which died or was torn by wild animals he shall not eat, becoming unclean by it: I am the Lord. 9 They shall keep my charge, so that they may not incur guilt and die in the sanctuary[f] for having profaned it: I am the Lord; I sanctify them. 10 No lay person shall eat of the sacred donations. No bound or hired servant of the priest shall eat of the sacred donations; 11 but if a priest acquires anyone by purchase, the person may eat of them; and those that are born in his house may eat of his food. 12 If a priest's daughter marries a layman, she shall not eat of the offering of the sacred donations; 13 but if a priest's daughter is widowed or divorced, without offspring, and returns to her father's house, as in her youth, she may eat of her father's food. No lay person shall eat of it. 14 If a man eats of the sacred donation unintentionally, he shall add one-fifth of its value to it, and give the sacred donation to the priest. 15 No one shall profane the sacred donations of the people of Israel, which they offer to the Lord, 16 causing them to bear guilt requiring a guilt offering, by eating their sacred donations: for I am the Lord; I sanctify them.

Acceptable Offerings

17 The Lord spoke to Moses, saying: 18 Speak to Aaron and his sons and all the people of Israel and say to them: When anyone of the house of Israel or of the aliens residing in Israel presents an offering, whether in payment of a vow or as a freewill offering that is offered to the Lord as a burnt offering, 19 to be accept-

able in your behalf it shall be a male without blemish, of the cattle or the sheep or the goats. 20 You shall not offer anything that has a blemish, for it will not be acceptable in your behalf.

21 When anyone offers a sacrifice of well-being to the Lord, in fulfillment of a vow or as a freewill offering, from the herd or from the flock, to be acceptable it must be perfect; there shall be no blemish in it. 22 Anything blind, or injured, or maimed, or having a discharge or an itch or scabs—these you shall not offer to the Lord or put any of them on the altar as offerings by fire to the Lord. 23 An ox or a lamb that has a limb too long or too short you may present for a freewill offering; but it will not be accepted for a vow. 24 Any animal that has its testicles bruised or crushed or torn or cut, you shall not offer to the Lord; such you shall not do within your land, 25 nor shall you accept any such animals from a foreigner to offer as food to your God; since they are mutilated, with a blemish in them, they shall not be accepted in your behalf.

26 The Lord spoke to Moses, saying: 27 When an ox or a sheep or a goat is born, it shall remain seven days with its mother, and from the eighth day on it shall be acceptable as the Lord's offering by fire. 28 But you shall not slaughter, from the herd or the flock, an animal with its young on the same day. 29 When you sacrifice a thanksgiving offering to the Lord, you shall sacrifice it so that it may be acceptable in your behalf. 30 It shall be eaten on the same day; you shall not leave any of it until morning: I am the Lord.

31 Thus you shall keep my commandments and observe them: I am the Lord. 32 You shall not profane my holy name, that I may be sanctified among the people

f Vg: Heb *incur guilt for it and die in it*

For they are his food, a concession. Note that Ezek 44.26 requires more rigorous purification. **22.8** Not forbidden to laypersons (17.15). **22.9** *Keep my charge,* i.e., "observe my prohibitions." *Incur guilt and die in the sanctuary for having profaned it,* more precisely, "incur punishment and die for it, having profaned it (the prohibition)." **22.10** *Bound or hired servant,* a resident laborer. **22.15** *No one,* i.e., no priest. **22.16** *Guilt requiring a guilt offering,* a penalty of reparation. **22.18** *Payment of a vow or as a freewill offering.* See 7.16. **22.21–24** The defects that disqualify

animals from the altar closely resemble those that disqualify priests from officiating at it (21.16–23). **22.21** *In fulfillment of a,* or "for an explicit." **22.28** *An animal,* i.e., a mother. **22.29** *Thanksgiving offering.* In H this offering is not a well-being offering (v. 21; 19.5; cf. 7.11–15 [P]; on H and P, see Introduction). **22.32** *I sanctify you,* namely, Israel (see v. 33). However, Israel is not innately holy as are the priests (21.7); Israel is enjoined to strive for a holy life by obeying the Lord's commandments (v. 31; see note on 19.1–37).

of Israel: I am the LORD; I sanctify you, 33 I who brought you out of the land of Egypt to be your God: I am the LORD.

Appointed Festivals

23 The LORD spoke to Moses, saying: 2 Speak to the people of Israel and say to them: These are the appointed festivals of the LORD that you shall proclaim as holy convocations, my appointed festivals.

The Sabbath, Passover, and Unleavened Bread

3 Six days shall work be done; but the seventh day is a sabbath of complete rest, a holy convocation; you shall do no work: it is a sabbath to the LORD throughout your settlements.

4 These are the appointed festivals of the LORD, the holy convocations, which you shall celebrate at the time appointed for them. 5 In the first month, on the fourteenth day of the month, at twilight,g there shall be a passover offering to the LORD, 6 and on the fifteenth day of the same month is the festival of unleavened bread to the LORD; seven days you shall eat unleavened bread. 7 On the first day you shall have a holy convocation; you shall not work at your occupations. 8 For seven days you shall present the LORD's offerings by fire; on the seventh day there shall be a holy convocation: you shall not work at your occupations.

The Offering of First Fruits

9 The LORD spoke to Moses: 10 Speak to the people of Israel and say to them: When you enter the land that I am giving you and you reap its harvest, you shall bring the sheaf of the first fruits of your harvest to the priest. 11 He shall raise the sheaf before the LORD, that you may find acceptance; on the day after the sabbath the priest shall raise it. 12 On the day when you raise the sheaf, you shall offer a lamb a year old, without blemish, as a burnt offering to the LORD. 13 And the grain offering with it shall be two-tenths of an ephah of choice flour mixed with oil, an offering by fire of pleasing odor to the LORD; and the drink offering with it shall be of wine, one-fourth of a hin. 14 You shall eat no bread or parched grain or fresh ears until that very day, until you have brought the offering of your God: it is a statute forever throughout your generations in all your settlements.

The Festival of Weeks

15 And from the day after the sabbath, from the day on which you bring the sheaf of the elevation offering, you shall count off seven weeks; they shall be complete. 16 You shall count until the day after the seventh sabbath, fifty days; then you shall present an offering of new grain to the LORD. 17 You shall bring from your

g Heb *between the two evenings*

23.1–44 H's listing of the festivals is distinguished from the Old Epic (JE) tradition (Ex 23.14–17; 34.21–23; see Introduction to Genesis) and the Deuteronomical influence (Deut 16; see Introduction to Deuteronomy) by emphasis on natural and agricultural data. Because Lev 23 addresses laypeople like farmers, rather than priests, the New Moon festival is omitted (on this day the Israelites have no special duties or prohibitions). Indeed, with the exception of vv. 13, 18–20, all requirements of the priestly, public cult are ignored, and only the offerings of individual farmers are enumerated. **23.3** This verse dealing with the sabbath is a later interpolation, possibly from exilic times, since it mentions no sacrifices. Its incongruity in this chapter is emphasized by the fact that the sabbath is not an appointed festival (v. 2) and that the original beginning of this chapter is clearly v. 4. **23.5–8** Passover and the Festival of Unleavened Bread were originally discrete festivals. The Pass-over was observed at home (Ex 12) and the pilgrimage to the local sanctuary took place on the seventh day (Ex 13.6). When worship was centralized, the Passover sacrifice was observed at the Jerusalem temple and the pilgrimage was transferred to the first day, thus amalgamating the two festivals (Deut 16.1–8). **23.8** *The LORD's offerings,* enumerated in Num 28.16–25. **23.10** *Sheaf,* or "armful." *First fruits of your harvest,* i.e., barley. See 2.14. **23.11** *That you may find acceptance,* so that the Lord will bless your crop. *The day after the sabbath.* Three opinions about the day were recorded in Second Temple times — the day after the Passover, Nisan 16 (Pharisees); the Sunday falling during the festival (Sadducees); and the Sunday after the festival (Qumran) — creating confusion when to celebrate the Festival of Weeks. This phrase (also in v. 15) is probably a gloss, and originally each farmer brought the first grain offering whenever it ripened. **23.15** *Seven weeks,* lit. "seven sabbaths," i.e., seven weeks, each

settlements two loaves of bread as an elevation offering, each made of two-tenths
of an ephah; they shall be of choice flour,
baked with leaven, as first fruits to the
LORD. 18 You shall present with the bread
seven lambs a year old without blemish,
one young bull, and two rams; they shall
be a burnt offering to the LORD, along
with their grain offering and their drink
offerings, an offering by fire of pleasing
odor to the LORD. 19 You shall also offer
one male goat for a sin offering, and two
male lambs a year old as a sacrifice of well-
being. 20 The priest shall raise them with
the bread of the first fruits as an elevation
offering before the LORD, together with
the two lambs; they shall be holy to the
LORD for the priest. 21 On that same day
you shall make proclamation; you shall
hold a holy convocation; you shall not
work at your occupations. This is a statute
forever in all your settlements throughout
your generations.
22   When you reap the harvest of your
land, you shall not reap to the very edges
of your field, or gather the gleanings of
your harvest; you shall leave them for the
poor and for the alien: I am the LORD
your God.

The Festival of Trumpets

23   The LORD spoke to Moses, saying:
24 Speak to the people of Israel, saying: In
the seventh month, on the first day of the
month, you shall observe a day of complete rest, a holy convocation commemo-
rated with trumpet blasts. 25 You shall not
work at your occupations; and you shall
present the LORD's offering by fire.

The Day of Atonement

26   The LORD spoke to Moses, saying:
27 Now, the tenth day of this seventh
month is the day of atonement; it shall be

a holy convocation for you: you shall deny
yourselves[h] and present the LORD's offering by fire; 28 and you shall do no work
during that entire day; for it is a day of
atonement, to make atonement on your
behalf before the LORD your God. 29 For
anyone who does not practice self-denial[i]
during that entire day shall be cut off
from the people. 30 And anyone who does
any work during that entire day, such a
one I will destroy from the midst of the
people. 31 You shall do no work: it is a
statute forever throughout your generations in all your settlements. 32 It shall be
to you a sabbath of complete rest, and you
shall deny yourselves;[h] on the ninth day
of the month at evening, from evening to
evening you shall keep your sabbath.

The Festival of Booths

33   The LORD spoke to Moses, saying:
34 Speak to the people of Israel, saying:
On the fifteenth day of this seventh
month, and lasting seven days, there shall
be the festival of booths[j] to the LORD.
35 The first day shall be a holy convocation; you shall not work at your occupations. 36 Seven days you shall present the
LORD's offerings by fire; on the eighth
day you shall observe a holy convocation
and present the LORD's offerings by fire;
it is a solemn assembly; you shall not work
at your occupations.
37   These are the appointed festivals
of the LORD, which you shall celebrate as
times of holy convocation, for presenting
to the LORD offerings by fire—burnt
offerings and grain offerings, sacrifices
and drink offerings, each on its proper
day— 38 apart from the sabbaths of the
LORD, and apart from your gifts, and
apart from all your votive offerings, and

h Or shall fast   i Or does not fast
j Or tabernacles: Heb succoth

---

ending with the sabbath. **23.16** *New grain*, i.e.,
wheat. **23.18–19** The sacrifices are enumerated
since they differ slightly from those specified in
Num 28.26–31. **23.22** Closing statement for
both the barley and wheat harvests (cf.
19.9–10). **23.24, 39** *Complete rest*, not complete,
since only occupational work is forbidden (v. 25).
Trumpet, rather "horn" (Hebrew *shofar*; cf. Ps.
81.3). Its use marks the beginning of the old,
agricultural calendar when the fates of humans
and nature (i.e., adequate rain) were decided.
23.25 *LORD's offering*, prescribed in Num

29.1–6. **23.27** *LORD's offering*, prescribed in
Num 29.7–11. **23.28** Prescriptions for the *day of
atonement* are given in 16.1–28. **23.29** *Self-
denial*. See 16.29. **23.30** *I will destroy*. Work, a
public act, is a worse violation than eating, a private act, evoking God's immediate retribution.
23.36 *LORD's offerings*, prescribed in Num
29.12–34, 35–38. The *solemn assembly*, the purpose of which is to pray for rain, is an important
function of all the festivals of the seventh month
(cf. Joel 2.15). **23.38** *Apart from the sabbaths*—
proof that the prescription for the sabbath

apart from all your freewill offerings, which you give to the LORD.

39 Now, the fifteenth day of the seventh month, when you have gathered in the produce of the land, you shall keep the festival of the LORD, lasting seven days; a complete rest on the first day, and a complete rest on the eighth day. 40 On the first day you shall take the fruit of majestic^k trees, branches of palm trees, boughs of leafy trees, and willows of the brook; and you shall rejoice before the LORD your God for seven days. 41 You shall keep it as a festival to the LORD seven days in the year; you shall keep it in the seventh month as a statute forever throughout your generations. 42 You shall live in booths for seven days; all that are citizens in Israel shall live in booths, 43 so that your generations may know that I made the people of Israel live in booths when I brought them out of the land of Egypt: I am the LORD your God

44 Thus Moses declared to the people of Israel the appointed festivals of the LORD.

The Lamp

24 The LORD spoke to Moses, saying: 2 Command the people of Israel to bring you pure oil of beaten olives for the lamp, that a light may be kept burning regularly. 3 Aaron shall set it up in the tent of meeting, outside the curtain of the covenant,^{l} to burn from evening to morning before the LORD regularly; it shall be a statute forever throughout your generations. 4 He shall set up the lamps on the lampstand of pure gold^m before the LORD regularly.

The Bread for the Tabernacle

5 You shall take choice flour, and bake twelve loaves of it; two-tenths of an ephah shall be in each loaf. 6 You shall place them in two rows, six in a row, on the table of pure gold.^{n} 7 You shall put pure frankincense with each row, to be a token offering for the bread, as an offering by fire to the LORD. 8 Every sabbath day Aaron shall set them in order before the LORD regularly as a commitment of the people of Israel, as a covenant forever. 9 They shall be for Aaron and his descendants, who shall eat them in a holy place, for they are most holy portions for him from the offerings by fire to the LORD, a perpetual due.

Blasphemy and Its Punishment

10 A man whose mother was an Israelite and whose father was an Egyptian came out among the people of Israel; and the Israelite woman's son and a certain Israelite began fighting in the camp. 11 The Israelite woman's son blasphemed the Name in a curse. And they brought him

k Meaning of Heb uncertain   l Or treaty, or testament; Heb eduth   m Heb pure lampstand   n Heb pure table

---

(vv. 2b–3) was not originally part of this chapter. **23.40** *Fruit of majestic trees*, traditionally, the citron. *Leafy trees*, identified with the myrtle. *Seven days*, to be spent at the sanctuary. **23.42** Possibly the *booths* were to accommodate the vast number of pilgrims at the sanctuary (cf. Hos 12.9). *Citizens*, but not aliens, who are not bound by performative commandments. **23.43** *Booths* (Hebrew *sukkot*), possibly a topographical name referring to the first station in the wilderness after the exodus (Ex 12.37; Num 33.5).

24.1–23 Instructions on the lamp, the bread, and blasphemy. **24.1–4** The lamp oil. Since the lampstand stood inside the sanctuary, its greater sanctity required the use of pure oil and also required it to be lighted by the high priest (Ex 30.7; Num 8.1–4; "sons" in Ex 27.21 is a probable error). **24.2** *For the lamp, that a light*, or "for lighting, so that a lamp." **24.3** *Curtain of the covenant*, short for "curtain that is over the ark of the covenant" (Ex 30.6). **24.5–9** The bread of the Pres-

ence. **24.5** Moses provides the loaves the first time; thereafter, they are provided by the Israelites (v. 8). **24.6** *Rows*, i.e., piles. **24.7** The *token offering* is always offered up with part of the grain offering (2.9), but here, since none of the bread goes on the altar, the text must state that the token offering comprises solely the frankincense. **24.8** *Every sabbath day* Aaron should remove the old loaves and set up the new. **24.10–14, 23** The law of blasphemy. Blasphemy means more than speaking contemptuously of God, for which there is no stated penalty (Ex 22.28). It must involve the additional offense of uttering the sacred name of God, the Tetragrammaton (YHWH), and it is the combination of the two (24.15–16) that warrants the death penalty. The Tetragrammaton's power affects not only the speaker but the hearers; their contamination is literally transferred back to the blasphemer by the ritual of the imposition of hands. **24.11** *The Name*, a circumlocution for the divine name.

to Moses—now his mother's name was Shelomith, daughter of Dibri, of the tribe of Dan— 12and they put him in custody, until the decision of the LORD should be made clear to them.

13 The LORD said to Moses, saying: 14Take the blasphemer outside the camp; and let all who were within hearing lay their hands on his head, and let the whole congregation stone him. 15And speak to the people of Israel, saying: Anyone who curses God shall bear the sin. 16One who blasphemes the name of the LORD shall be put to death; the whole congregation shall stone the blasphemer. Aliens as well as citizens, when they blaspheme the Name, shall be put to death. 17Anyone who kills a human being shall be put to death. 18Anyone who kills an animal shall make restitution for it, life for life. 19Anyone who maims another shall suffer the same injury in return: 20fracture for fracture, eye for eye, tooth for tooth; the injury inflicted is the injury to be suffered. 21One who kills an animal shall make restitution for it; but one who kills a human being shall be put to death. 22You shall have one law for the alien and for the citizen: for I am the LORD your God. 23Moses spoke thus to the people of Israel; and they took the blasphemer outside the camp, and stoned him to death. The people of Israel did as the LORD had commanded Moses.

The Sabbatical Year

25 The LORD spoke to Moses on Mount Sinai, saying: 2Speak to the people of Israel and say to them: When you enter the land that I am giving you, the land shall observe a sabbath for the LORD. 3Six years you shall sow your field, and six years you shall prune your vineyard, and gather in their yield; 4but in the seventh year there shall be a sabbath of complete rest for the land, a sabbath for the LORD: you shall not sow your field or prune your vineyard. 5You shall not reap the aftergrowth of your harvest or gather the grapes of your unpruned vine: it shall be a year of complete rest for the land. 6You may eat what the land yields during its sabbath—you, your male and female slaves, your hired and your bound laborers who live with you; 7for your livestock also, and for the wild animals in your land all its yield shall be for food.

The Year of Jubilee

8 You shall count off seven weeks*o* of years, seven times seven years, so that the period of seven weeks of years gives forty-nine years. 9Then you shall have the trumpet sounded loud; on the tenth day of the seventh month—on the day of atonement—you shall have the trumpet

o Or *sabbaths*

24.14 The purpose of the hand-leaning was to transfer the pollution generated by the blasphemy back to its source. **24.15–22** An appendix of civil-damage laws. The extension of *lex talionis* (Ex 21.23–25; Deut 19.21) to the stranger is one of the great moral achievements of the legislation preserved in Leviticus. Every distinction is eradicated not only between the powerful and the helpless but even between the Israelite and the non-Israelite. The interpolation of these civil statutes, with their emphasis upon the resident alien, is due to the legal status of the half-Israelite offender. **24.15–16** One who *curses God*, in secret, will be punished by God; one who *blasphemes*, in public, will be punished by human agency. **24.16** *Aliens*, thereby including the blasphemer of vv. 10–11, the son of a non-Israelite father. **24.18** *Life for life* perhaps originally began the talion formula of v. 20. **24.21** A repetition of vv. 17–18 for the sake of an envelope structure.
25.1–55 Each seventh year is a sabbath of liberating respite for Hebrew slaves (Ex 21.2–6;

Deut 15.12–18), and the land (Ex 23.10–11). In H (see Introduction), this "full" sabbatical is reserved for the jubilee, whereas the seventh-year sabbatical applies only to the land. These two laws are not in conflict. Exodus refers to members of a *landless* class who voluntarily sell themselves into slavery. Lev 25 deals with impoverished *landed* Israelites who are free to sell themselves as slaves but who may not be treated as slaves and who return to their land at the jubilee or when they are redeemed (vv. 39–42). Deuteronomy extends the sabbatical release to debtors (Deut 15.1–11). **25.1** *Mount Sinai* forms an inclusion with 26.46, indicating that, originally, chs. 25–26 formed a separate scroll. **25.2** *The land shall observe a sabbath.* All who reside on it, including aliens, must observe it. **25.3–5, 11** *Sow ... reap*, proof that the sabbatical and jubilee years begin in the fall. **25.6** This verse alters Ex 23.11 by denying the sabbatical aftergrowth to the poor and endowing it to the owner and his household. H (see Introduction) makes other, ongoing provisions for the

sounded throughout all your land. 10 And you shall hallow the fiftieth year and you shall proclaim liberty throughout the land to all its inhabitants. It shall be a jubilee for you: you shall return, every one of you, to your property and every one of you to your family. 11 That fiftieth year shall be a jubilee for you: you shall not sow, or reap the aftergrowth, or harvest the unpruned vines. 12 For it is a jubilee; it shall be holy to you: you shall eat only what the field itself produces.

13 In this year of jubilee you shall return, every one of you, to your property. 14 When you make a sale to your neighbor or buy from your neighbor, you shall not cheat one another. 15 When you buy from your neighbor, you shall pay only for the number of years since the jubilee; the seller shall charge you only for the remaining crop years. 16 If the years are more, you shall increase the price, and if the years are fewer, you shall diminish the price; for it is a certain number of harvests that are being sold to you. 17 You shall not cheat one another, but you shall fear your God; for I am the LORD your God.

18 You shall observe my statutes and faithfully keep my ordinances, so that you may live on the land securely. 19 The land will yield its fruit, and you will eat your fill and live on it securely. 20 Should you ask, "What shall we eat in the seventh year, if we may not sow or gather in our crop?" 21 I will order my blessing for you in the sixth year, so that it will yield a crop for three years. 22 When you sow in the eighth year, you will be eating from the old crop; until the ninth year, when its produce comes in, you shall eat the old. 23 The land shall not be sold in perpetuity, for the land is mine; with me you are but aliens and tenants. 24 Throughout the land that you hold, you shall provide for the redemption of the land.

25 If anyone of your kin falls into difficulty and sells a piece of property, then the next of kin shall come and redeem what the relative has sold. 26 If the person has no one to redeem it, but then prospers and finds sufficient means to do so, 27 the years since its sale shall be computed and the difference shall be refunded to the person to whom it was sold, and the property shall be returned. 28 But if there are not sufficient means to recover it, what was sold shall remain with the purchaser until the year of jubilee; in the jubilee it shall be released, and the property shall be returned.

29 If anyone sells a dwelling house in a walled city, it may be redeemed until a year has elapsed since its sale; the right of redemption shall be one year. 30 If it is not redeemed before a full year has elapsed, a house that is in a walled city shall pass in perpetuity to the purchaser, throughout the generations; it shall not be released in the jubilee. 31 But houses in villages that have no walls around them shall be classed as open country; they may be redeemed, and they shall be released in the jubilee. 32 As for the cities of the Levites,

---

poor (19.9–10; 23.20).   **25.10** *Liberty.* Hebrew *deror* is related to Akkadian *duraru*, which could also entail the emancipation of indentured slaves, the return of confiscated land, and the cancellation of debts. However, it was episodic, occasionally proclaimed on the ascension of the Mesopotamian king to the throne. Also its purpose was strictly economic, to relieve the plight of the poor, whereas in Israel its goal was social as well, to preserve the clan structure by restoring its landholdings. *For you,* not for the land or for the release of alien slaves (vv. 45–46). Note that the term "sabbath" is absent in the jubilee provisions. **25.15** *Pay,* i.e., deduct.   **25.20–22** The sixth to ninth years, mentioned here, are reckoned by the spring calendar. Hence the sabbatical and succeeding jubilee years, which follow the fall calendar, must begin in the fall of the sixth and seventh years and terminate in the spring of the seventh and eighth years, respectively. Thus, what is sown in the eighth year will be reaped in the ninth, and the harvest of the sixth year must therefore last three years. **25.23** *In perpetuity,* Hebrew *tzemitut,* related to the Akkadian verb *tzamatu,* "financially hand over (real estate)"; i.e., neither the seller nor his heirs may ever revoke the sale. **25.25–55** Four cases of worsening impoverishment: selling part of the land, depending upon an Israelite (probably a kinsman) for support, selling oneself as a resident laborer to an Israelite (probably a kinsman), selling oneself as a slave to a resident alien.   **25.25** Since the purpose of the jubilee is to preserve the clan holdings, the redeemer (a close kinsman) probably keeps the land until the jubilee (as shown by v. 33 below) as compensation for his purchase. **25.29–34** Unwalled (Canaanite) cities, not having been allocated to the tribal clans, are not subject to the jubilee. Redemption and jubilee, however, apply to the al-

the Levites shall forever have the right of redemption of the houses in the cities belonging to them. 33 Such property as may be redeemed from the Levites—houses sold in a city belonging to them—shall be released in the jubilee; because the houses in the cities of the Levites are their possession among the people of Israel. 34 But the open land around their cities may not be sold; for that is their possession for all time.

35 If any of your kin fall into difficulty and become dependent on you,p you shall support them; they shall live with you as though resident aliens. 36 Do not take interest in advance or otherwise make a profit from them, but fear your God; let them live with you. 37 You shall not lend them your money at interest taken in advance, or provide them food at a profit. 38 I am the LORD your God, who brought you out of the land of Egypt, to give you the land of Canaan, to be your God.

39 If any who are dependent on you become so impoverished that they sell themselves to you, you shall not make them serve as slaves. 40 They shall remain with you as hired or bound laborers. They shall serve with you until the year of the jubilee. 41 Then they and their children with them shall be free from your authority; they shall go back to their own family and return to their ancestral property. 42 For they are my servants, whom I brought out of the land of Egypt; they shall not be sold as slaves are sold. 43 You shall not rule over them with harshness, but shall fear your God. 44 As for the male and female slaves whom you may have, it is from the nations around you that you may acquire male and female slaves. 45 You may also acquire them from among the aliens residing with you, and from their families that are with you, who have been born in your land; and they may be your property. 46 You may keep

them as a possession for your children after you, for them to inherit as property. These you may treat as slaves, but as for your fellow Israelites, no one shall rule over the other with harshness.

47 If resident aliens among you prosper, and if any of your kin fall into difficulty with one of them and sell themselves to an alien, or to a branch of the alien's family, 48 after they have sold themselves they shall have the right of redemption; one of their brothers may redeem them, 49 or their uncle or their uncle's son may redeem them, or anyone of their family who is of their own flesh may redeem them; or if they prosper they may redeem themselves. 50 They shall compute with the purchaser the total from the year when they sold themselves to the alien until the jubilee year; the price of the sale shall be applied to the number of years: the time they were with the owner shall be rated as the time of a hired laborer. 51 If many years remain, they shall pay for their redemption in proportion to the purchase price; 52 and if few years remain until the jubilee year, they shall compute thus: according to the years involved they shall make payment for their redemption. 53 As a laborer hired by the year they shall be under the alien's authority, who shall not, however, rule with harshness over them in your sight. 54 And if they have not been redeemed in any of these ways, they and their children with them shall go free in the jubilee year. 55 For to me the people of Israel are servants; they are my servants whom I brought out from the land of Egypt: I am the LORD your God.

Rewards for Obedience

26 You shall make for yourselves no idols and erect no carved images or pillars, and you shall not place figured stones in your land, to worship at them;

p Meaning of Heb uncertain

---

located cities of the Levites. **25.33** The first half of this verse reads better as "Whoever of the Levites redeems the house, which was sold in the city of his possession [so Septuagint], must be released in the jubilee." **25.36** Otherwise make a profit, rather "accrued interest." **25.37** A profit, or "accrued interest." **25.39–43** The fact that female slaves are not mentioned here (cf. v. 44) implies that the Holiness (H) source did not permit, or

perhaps even contemplate, female slavery. Cf. Ex 21.7–11; Deut 15.12–18 where, however, the context speaks of Hebrews (i.e., impoverished, landless Israelites; see note on 25.1–55) who sell their daughters for the purpose of marriage. **25.40** Or bound, rather "resident." **25.42** My servants, not yours. The heart of this chapter; cf. also v. 55.

26.1–46 The threat of total destruction and

for I am the LORD your God. 2 You shall
keep my sabbaths and reverence my sanctuary: I am the LORD.

3 If you follow my statutes and keep
my commandments and observe them
faithfully, 4 I will give you your rains in
their season, and the land shall yield its
produce, and the trees of the field shall
yield their fruit. 5 Your threshing shall
overtake the vintage, and the vintage shall
overtake the sowing; you shall eat your
bread to the full, and live securely in your
land. 6 And I will grant peace in the land,
and you shall lie down, and no one shall
make you afraid; I will remove dangerous
animals from the land, and no sword shall
go through your land. 7 You shall give
chase to your enemies, and they shall fall
before you by the sword. 8 Five of you
shall give chase to a hundred, and a hundred of you shall give chase to ten thousand; your enemies shall fall before you
by the sword. 9 I will look with favor upon
you and make you fruitful and multiply
you; and I will maintain my covenant with
you. 10 You shall eat old grain long stored,
and you shall have to clear out the old to
make way for the new. 11 I will place my
dwelling in your midst, and I shall not abhor you. 12 And I will walk among you,
and will be your God, and you shall be my
people. 13 I am the LORD your God who
brought you out of the land of Egypt, to
be their slaves no more; I have broken the
bars of your yoke and made you walk
erect.

Penalties for Disobedience

14 But if you will not obey me, and do
not observe all these commandments, 15 if
you spurn my statutes, and abhor my ordinances, so that you will not observe all

my commandments, and you break my
covenant, 16 I in turn will do this to you: I
will bring terror on you; consumption and
fever that waste the eyes and cause life to
pine away. You shall sow your seed in
vain, for your enemies shall eat it. 17 I will
set my face against you, and you shall be
struck down by your enemies; your foes
shall rule over you, and you shall flee
though no one pursues you. 18 And if in
spite of this you will not obey me, I will
continue to punish you sevenfold for your
sins. 19 I will break your proud glory, and
I will make your sky like iron and your
earth like copper. 20 Your strength shall
be spent to no purpose: your land shall
not yield its produce, and the trees of the
land shall not yield their fruit.

21 If you continue hostile to me, and
will not obey me, I will continue to plague
you sevenfold for your sins. 22 I will let
loose wild animals against you, and they
shall bereave you of your children and destroy your livestock; they shall make you
few in number, and your roads shall be
deserted.

23 If in spite of these punishments
you have not turned back to me, but continue hostile to me, 24 then I too will continue hostile to you: I myself will strike
you sevenfold for your sins. 25 I will bring
the sword against you, executing vengeance for the covenant; and if you with-
draw within your cities, I will send
pestilence among you, and you shall be
delivered into enemy hands. 26 When I
break your staff of bread, ten women
shall bake your bread in a single oven,
and they shall dole out your bread by
weight; and though you eat, you shall not
be satisfied.

27 But if, despite this, you disobey me,
and continue hostile to me, 28 I will con-

---

exile appears in three other books of the Bible:
Deuteronomy, Jeremiah, and Ezekiel (whose es-
chatology is largely based on Lev 26). These books
also share with this chapter a view that cultic
transgressions alone, as here defined, cause the
nation's collapse; idolatry (26.1) and the neglect
of the sabbatical system (26.2, 34–35) are specified here. Since the events in chs. 25–26 are attributed to Israel's sojourn at Mount Sinai (25.1;
26.46), these may well constitute the text of
the Sinaitic covenant according to the Holiness
source. **26.1** *Carved images* even of Israel's God
(Ex 20.4, 23). *Pillars.* This prohibition was origi-

nally restricted to worship of foreign gods (Ex
23.24), but beginning with Hezekiah and Josiah,
kings of the eighth and seventh centuries B.C.E.
respectively, it was extended to include Israel's
God (Deut 16.22). *At,* rather "on." For similar language see Gen 47.31. **26.2** *Sabbaths,* i.e., the
weekly sabbaths (19.3, 30), which may account for
the inclusion of vv. 1–2 in this chapter to remind
readers that not only neglecting the sabbatical
year (vv. 34–35) but also the sabbath day accounts
for Israel's exile. **26.3–13** The conditionality
of the blessing is also found in ancient Near Eastern treaties. **26.14–39** Comparable curses are

tinue hostile to you in fury; I in turn will punish you myself sevenfold for your sins. 29 You shall eat the flesh of your sons, and you shall eat the flesh of your daughters. 30 I will destroy your high places and cut down your incense altars; I will heap your carcasses on the carcasses of your idols. I will abhor you. 31 I will lay your cities waste, will make your sanctuaries desolate, and I will not smell your pleasing odors. 32 I will devastate the land, so that your enemies who come to settle in it shall be appalled at it. 33 And you I will scatter among the nations, and I will unsheathe the sword against you; your land shall be a desolation, and your cities a waste.

34   Then the land shall enjoyq its sabbath years as long as it lies desolate, while you are in the land of your enemies; then the land shall rest, and enjoyq its sabbath years. 35 As long as it lies desolate, it shall have the rest it did not have on your sabbaths when you were living on it. 36 And as for those of you who survive, I will send faintness into their hearts in the lands of their enemies; the sound of a driven leaf shall put them to flight, and they shall flee as one flees from the sword, and they shall fall though no one pursues. 37 They shall stumble over one another, as if to escape a sword, though no one pursues; and you shall have no power to stand against your enemies. 38 You shall perish among the nations, and the land of your enemies shall devour you. 39 And those of you who survive shall languish in the land of your enemies because of their iniquities; also they shall languish because of the iniquities of their ancestors.

40   But if they confess their iniquity and the iniquity of their ancestors, in that they committed treachery against me and, moreover, that they continued hostile to me— 41 so that I, in turn, continued hostile to them and brought them into the land of their enemies; if then their uncircumcised heart is humbled and they make amends for their iniquity, 42 then will I remember my covenant with Jacob; I will remember also my covenant with Isaac and also my covenant with Abraham, and I will remember the land. 43 For the land shall be deserted by them, and enjoyq its sabbath years by lying desolate without them, while they shall make amends for their iniquity, because they dared to spurn my ordinances, and they abhorred my statutes. 44 Yet for all that, when they are in the land of their enemies, I will not spurn them, or abhor them so as to destroy them utterly and break my covenant with them; for I am the Lord their God; 45 but I will remember in their favor the covenant with their ancestors whom I brought out of the land of Egypt in the sight of the nations, to be their God: I am the Lord.

46   These are the statutes and ordinances and laws that the Lord established between himself and the people of Israel on Mount Sinai through Moses.

Votive Offerings and Dedications

27 The Lord spoke to Moses, saying: 2 Speak to the people of Israel and say to them: When a person makes an explicit vow to the Lord concerning the equivalent for a human being,

q Or *make up for*

---

appended to ancient Near Eastern treaties. **26.31** *Sanctuaries*, the multiple sanctuaries throughout the land before Hezekiah's reform. **26.34** *Sabbath years* refers to the sabbaticals, but not the jubilees since the term "sabbath" is inappropriate for the jubilee.   **26.40** *Confess*. For the priestly tradition confession must be a coefficient of sacrifice (e.g. 5.5–6), but obviously not in exile. **27.1–34**   An appendix closely associated with ch. 25 by its theme, the redemption of dedications (not votive offerings). It is organized as follows: (1) Redemption does not apply to humans since only their value, not their person, may be dedicated (vv. 1–28; but cf. v. 29). (2) Only impure animals may be redeemed; offerable ones must be sacrificed (vv. 9–13). (3) All land is redeemable because land is unofferable (vv. 14–19, 22–25);

only *cherem* (Hebrew, "devoted") dedications (man, animal, or land, vv. 20–21, 28–29) may not be redeemed. (4) Firstlings (vv. 26–27) must be sacrificed unless they are defective or impure, in which case they are redeemed or sold. (5) Offerable crop tithe is redeemable; offerable animal tithe is unredeemable (vv. 30–33). One postulate explains these gradations: offerable animals are irredeemable because they must be sacrificed, whereas nonofferable animals and other "holy things" (see 5.14–6.7) are redeemable unless they are *cherem* (see note on 27.28–29).   **27.1–8** The values in this section probably prevailed in the slave markets. Note that the price of a male infant (v. 6) above the age of one month corresponds with the redemption price of a male firstborn (Num 3.47; 18.16) and that the priest is enjoined

3 the equivalent for a male shall be: from twenty to sixty years of age the equivalent shall be fifty shekels of silver by the sanctuary shekel. 4 If the person is a female, the equivalent is thirty shekels. 5 If the age is from five to twenty years of age, the equivalent is twenty shekels for a male and ten shekels for a female. 6 If the age is from one month to five years, the equivalent for a male is five shekels of silver, and for a female the equivalent is three shekels of silver. 7 And if the person is sixty years old or over, then the equivalent for a male is fifteen shekels, and for a female ten shekels. 8 If any cannot afford the equivalent, they shall be brought before the priest and the priest shall assess them; the priest shall assess them according to what each one making a vow can afford.

9 If it concerns an animal that may be brought as an offering to the Lord, any such that may be given to the Lord shall be holy. 10 Another shall not be exchanged or substituted for it, either good for bad or bad for good, and if one animal is substituted for another, both that one and its substitute shall be holy. 11 If it concerns any unclean animal that may not be brought as an offering to the Lord, the animal shall be presented before the priest. 12 The priest shall assess it: whether good or bad, according to the assessment of the priest, so it shall be. 13 But if it is to be redeemed, one-fifth must be added to the assessment.

14 If a person consecrates a house to the Lord, the priest shall assess it: whether good or bad, as the priest assesses it, so it shall stand. 15 And if the one who consecrates the house wishes to redeem it, one-fifth shall be added to its assessed value, and it shall revert to the original owner.

16 If a person consecrates to the Lord any inherited landholding, its assessment shall be in accordance with its seed requirements: fifty shekels of silver to a homer of barley seed. 17 If the person consecrates the field as of the year of jubilee, that assessment shall stand; 18 but if the field is consecrated after the jubilee, the priest shall compute the price for it according to the years that remain until the year of jubilee, and the assessment shall be reduced. 19 And if the one who consecrates the field wishes to redeem it, then one-fifth shall be added to its assessed value, and it shall revert to the original owner; 20 but if the field is not redeemed, or if it has been sold to someone else, it shall no longer be redeemable. 21 But when the field is released in the jubilee, it shall be holy to the Lord as a devoted field; it becomes the priest's holding. 22 If someone consecrates to the Lord a field that has been purchased, which is not a part of the inherited landholding, 23 the priest shall compute for it the proportionate assessment up to the year of jubilee, and the assessment shall be paid as of that day, a sacred donation to the Lord. 24 In the year of jubilee the field shall return to the one from whom it was bought, whose holding the land is. 25 All assessments shall be by the sanctuary shekel: twenty gerahs shall make a shekel.

26 A firstling of animals, however, which as a firstling belongs to the Lord, cannot be consecrated by anyone; whether ox or sheep, it is the Lord's. 27 If it is an unclean animal, it shall be ransomed at its assessment, with one-fifth added; if it is not redeemed, it shall be sold at its assessment.

28 Nothing that a person owns that has been devoted to destruction for the Lord, be it human or animal, or inherited landholding, may be sold or redeemed; every devoted thing is most holy to the Lord. 29 No human beings who have been devoted to destruction can be ransomed; they shall be put to death.

30 All tithes from the land, whether

---

to adjust the price according to the economic conditions of the vower (v. 8). **27.13** *If it is . . . redeemed.* This rule applies only to the owner, but the sanctuary may sell it to anyone else for the assessment price (v. 27). **27.20** *Has,* rather "had." The owner dedicated his field after he sold it. **27.21** *Devoted field,* i.e., *cherem* dedications are irredeemable. **27.28–29** *Devoted to destruction,* more precisely "totally dedicated," the distinction

being that *cherem* (Hebrew, "devoted") animals and lands become the permanent property of the sanctuary, whereas *cherem* persons—probably prisoners of war resulting from *cherem* vows taken against an enemy (e.g., Num 21.1–3; 1 Sam 15.3, 33)—must be destroyed. **27.30** These tithes differ from those of Num 18.21 (P) and Deut 14.22–29 (D) in that they are assigned to the sanc-

the seed from the ground or the fruit from the tree, are the LORD's; they are holy to the LORD. 31 If persons wish to redeem any of their tithes, they must add one-fifth to them. 32 All tithes of herd and flock, every tenth one that passes under the shepherd's staff, shall be holy to the LORD. 33 Let no one inquire whether it is good or bad, or make substitution for it; if one makes substitution for it, then both it and the substitute shall be holy and cannot be redeemed.

34   These are the commandments that the LORD gave to Moses for the people of Israel on Mount Sinai.

---

tuary; those in Numbers belong to the Levites and those in Deuteronomy to the owner. **27.32** The only recorded instance of the animal tithe is during the reign of Hezekiah (2 Chr 31.6), an indication that H formed the basis of Hezekiah's reform. (On P and H, see Introduction.)

NUMBERS

NUMBERS IS THE FOURTH BOOK of the Bible and therefore the fourth in the Pentateuch ("five scrolls"), or Torah, as the first five books are known collectively. Numbers takes its English name from *Arithmoi*, the title of the book in the ancient Greek translation called the Septuagint, begun in the third century B.C.E. In Hebrew the book is called *Bemidbar*, "in the wilderness," a word in the first verse of the book and perhaps a more appropriate title given its contents. The book of Numbers begins with the Israelites in the wilderness of Sinai and spans the forty years of the wilderness wanderings, ending with the people on the east side of the Jordan River, in the "plains of Moab," poised for the conquest of Canaan. Lack of faith (chs. 13–14) leads to the almost complete destruction of the exodus generation, which is to be replaced by a new generation born in the wilderness and looking forward to Canaan rather than backward to Egypt.

Structure and Sources

The structure of the book follows the geographical sequence of the account as well as the change in generations over the forty years of wandering. Geographically, Numbers can be divided into three fairly neat sections: in the wilderness of Sinai, 1.1–10.10; the march through the wilderness to Transjordan, 10.11–22.1; and in the plains of Moab, 22.2–36.13. The book is also, however, divided into two sections by the two military censuses in chs. 1 and 26, which represent the doubting exodus generation and the new generation that takes its place. These two censuses, as well as several other counting episodes, have led to the impression that "numbers" are the principal topic of the book, hence its title in the Septuagint.

Modern scholars believe that the material in the Pentateuch, and therefore in the book of Numbers, was brought together from several sources. It is useful to

---

Map opposite: *The major places and routes that figure in the narratives of Israel's migration into Canaan (Numbers, Joshua, and Judges).*

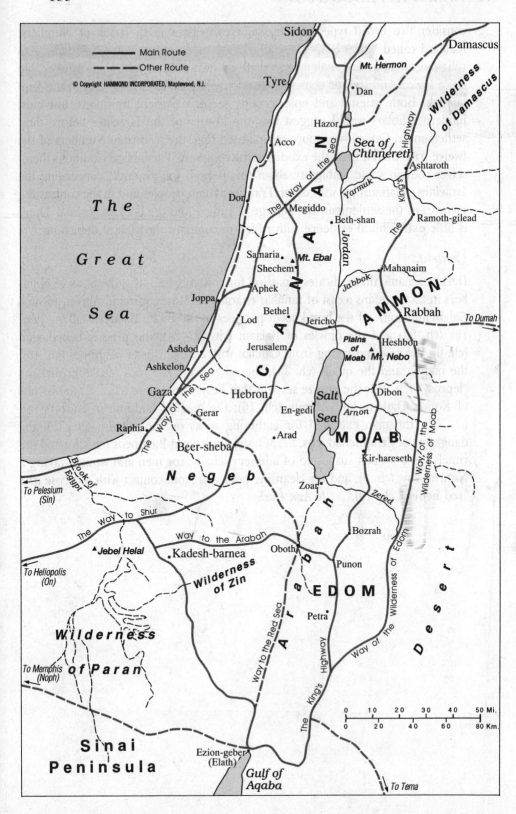

consider two broad types of these sources evident in the book of Numbers: material called "priestly" because of its interest in cultic matters pertaining to religious ritual and genealogy and material drawn from "old epic" sources that has a lexical and stylistic consistency with similar material elsewhere in the Pentateuch. Both priestly and epic sections preserve ancient traditions, but most modern scholars would suggest that the history of the Israelites before their settlement in Canaan was more complicated than the picture in Numbers of the twelve-tribe march from the exodus to the conquest. The biblical traditions themselves contain some ambiguity about this period, for example, concerning the Israelites' relationships with other Transjordanian peoples and in the contrasting pictures of the settlement that emerge in Judg 1 and the book of Joshua. There is little extrabiblical evidence with which to compare the biblical depictions.

Content

Despite a name that indicates a passion for counting and lists, the book of Numbers in fact contains a cast of familiar characters (Moses, Miriam, Aaron, Joshua, Caleb) and some of the best-known passages in the Bible: Balaam's talking donkey (ch. 22) and the oracles of Balaam (chs. 23–24); the priestly benediction (ch. 6); the spies returning from Canaan with a huge cluster of grapes (ch. 13); the manna and the quails (ch. 11); the water from the rock (ch. 20); Miriam's "leprosy" (ch. 12); the bronze serpent that healed snakebite (ch. 21); the revolts of Korah, Dathan, and Abiram (ch. 16); the magical budding of Aaron's rod (ch. 17); the man executed for gathering sticks on the sabbath (ch. 15); the daughters of Zelophehad (chs. 27, 36); the apostasy at Baal-peor (ch. 25); and the rituals for a woman suspected of adultery (ch. 5), for men and women taking a Nazirite vow (ch. 6), and for cleansing pollution from contact with a corpse (the "red heifer," ch. 19).   *Jo Ann Hackett*

The First Census of Israel

1 The LORD spoke to Moses in the wilderness of Sinai, in the tent of meeting, on the first day of the second month, in the second year after they had come out of the land of Egypt, saying: 2 Take a census of the whole congregation of Israelites, in their clans, by ancestral houses, according to the number of names, every male individually; 3 from twenty years old and upward, everyone in Israel able to go to war. You and Aaron shall enroll them, company by company. 4 A man from each tribe shall be with you, each man the head of his ancestral house. 5 These are the names of the men who shall assist you:

From Reuben, Elizur son of
    Shedeur.
6 From Simeon, Shelumiel son of
    Zurishaddai.
7 From Judah, Nahshon son of
    Amminadab.
8 From Issachar, Nethanel son of
    Zuar.
9 From Zebulun, Eliab son of
    Helon.
10 From the sons of Joseph:
    from Ephraim, Elishama son of
    Ammihud;
    from Manasseh, Gamaliel son of
    Pedahzur.
11 From Benjamin, Abidan son of
    Gideoni.
12 From Dan, Ahiezer son of
    Ammishaddai.
13 From Asher, Pagiel son of
    Ochran.
14 From Gad, Eliasaph son of Deuel.
15 From Naphtali, Ahira son of
    Enan.

16 These were the ones chosen from the congregation, the leaders of their ancestral tribes, the heads of the divisions of Israel.

17 Moses and Aaron took these men who had been designated by name, 18 and on the first day of the second month they assembled the whole congregation together. They registered themselves in their clans, by their ancestral houses, according to the number of names from twenty years old and upward, individually, 19 as the LORD commanded Moses. So

---

1.1–54 Moses, Aaron, and one man from each tribe are commanded to take a census of all males age twenty and older who are able to serve in the military. The expeditions envisioned are the battles to conquer the promised land, but in fact, with the exception of Joshua and Caleb, these are the men of the generation who will die in the wilderness because of their lack of faith (see chs. 13–14). The similar census reported in ch. 26 then counts a new generation of men to fight those battles (26.64–65). **1.1** The setting of the beginning of the book of Numbers is the *wilderness of Sinai*, where the Israelites have been encamped since the third month after the exodus (Ex 19.1, 2). The *tent of meeting* is the goat-hair tent that covers the tabernacle, which houses the ark of the covenant, first described in Ex 26.7. The date is one month after the setting up of the tabernacle (Ex 40.17). **1.2** A tribe in Israel is made up of several *clans*, and each clan of several *ancestral houses*. Each individual male counted is to be identified by ancestral house and clan within each tribe. **1.3** Ex 30.11–12 reports the belief that a military census could result in a plague (see 2 Sam 24; 1 Chr 21), and so a tax was to be paid to the sanctuary as a "ransom" for the lives of those counted. (See also Ex 38.25–28.) The word here translated *company* can also be translated "army" or "host" and refers to a group organized for war. **1.5–15** These same names also occur in lists in 2.3–31; 7.12–83; 10.14–28. The order in which the tribes are listed in these verses is based for the most part on subgroupings characterized as Jacob's sons born of the same mother, according to Gen 29.31–30.24; 35.16–18. Reuben, Simeon, Judah, Issachar, and Zebulun were sons of Leah. Levi was Leah's third son, but the tribe of Levi is not here listed as part of the military census (see Num 1.47–54). To compensate for the loss of Levi and preserve the number twelve for the total number of tribes, the tribe of Joseph is divided into Ephraim and Manasseh (see Gen 48.8–20) and listed along with Benjamin. Joseph and Benjamin were Rachel's sons in Genesis. Of the final four tribes, Dan and Naphtali were the sons of Rachel's maid Bilhah, and Gad and Asher were the sons of Leah's maid Zilpah. (Naphtali and Asher have switched positions in the list here.) **1.17–46** The tribes are listed in the same order as in vv. 5–15, except that Gad has shifted position. Gad occupies the third slot in this list, right after Reuben and Simeon. This shift seems to be based on Gad's position in the arrangement of tribes in the camp described in ch. 2. There Gad is joined with Simeon and Reuben on the south side (see 2.10–16). The total of 603,550 military men (v. 46) has seemed unrealistically high to commentators, as has the similar number,

he enrolled them in the wilderness of Sinai.

20 The descendants of Reuben, Israel's firstborn, their lineage, in their clans, by their ancestral houses, according to the number of names, individually, every male from twenty years old and upward, everyone able to go to war: 21 those enrolled of the tribe of Reuben were forty-six thousand five hundred.

22 The descendants of Simeon, their lineage, in their clans, by their ancestral houses, those of them that were numbered, according to the number of names, individually, every male from twenty years old and upward, everyone able to go to war: 23 those enrolled of the tribe of Simeon were fifty-nine thousand three hundred.

24 The descendants of Gad, their lineage, in their clans, by their ancestral houses, according to the number of the names, from twenty years old and upward, everyone able to go to war: 25 those enrolled of the tribe of Gad were forty-five thousand six hundred fifty.

26 The descendants of Judah, their lineage, in their clans, by their ancestral houses, according to the number of names, from twenty years old and upward, everyone able to go to war: 27 those enrolled of the tribe of Judah were seventy-four thousand six hundred.

28 The descendants of Issachar, their lineage, in their clans, by their ancestral houses, according to the number of names, from twenty years old and upward, everyone able to go to war: 29 those enrolled of the tribe of Issachar were fifty-four thousand four hundred.

30 The descendants of Zebulun, their lineage, in their clans, by their ancestral houses, according to the number of names, from twenty years old and upward, everyone able to go to war: 31 those enrolled of the tribe of Zebulun were fifty-seven thousand four hundred.

32 The descendants of Joseph, namely, the descendants of Ephraim, their lineage, in their clans, by their ancestral houses, according to the number of names, from twenty years old and upward, everyone able to go to war: 33 those enrolled of the tribe of Ephraim were forty thousand five hundred.

34 The descendants of Manasseh, their lineage, in their clans, by their ancestral houses, according to the number of names, from twenty years old and upward, everyone able to go to war: 35 those enrolled of the tribe of Manasseh were thirty-two thousand two hundred.

36 The descendants of Benjamin, their lineage, in their clans, by their ancestral houses, according to the number of names, from twenty years old and upward, everyone able to go to war: 37 those enrolled of the tribe of Benjamin were thirty-five thousand four hundred.

38 The descendants of Dan, their lineage, in their clans, by their ancestral houses, according to the number of names, from twenty years old and upward, everyone able to go to war: 39 those enrolled of the tribe of Dan were sixty-two thousand seven hundred.

40 The descendants of Asher, their lineage, in their clans, by their ancestral houses, according to the number of names, from twenty years old and upward, everyone able to go to war: 41 those enrolled of the tribe of Asher were forty-one thousand five hundred.

42 The descendants of Naphtali, their lineage, in their clans, by their ancestral houses, according to the number of names, from twenty years old and upward, everyone able to go to war: 43 those enrolled of the tribe of Naphtali were fifty-three thousand four hundred.

44 These are those who were enrolled, whom Moses and Aaron enrolled with the help of the leaders of Israel, twelve men, each representing his ancestral house. 45 So the whole number of the Israelites, by their ancestral houses, from twenty years old and upward, everyone able to go to war in Israel— 46 their whole number was six hundred three thousand five hundred fifty. 47 The Levites, however, were not numbered by their ancestral tribe along with them.

48 The LORD had said to Moses: 49 Only the tribe of Levi you shall not enroll, and you shall not take a census of them with the other Israelites. 50 Rather

---

601,730, in the second census in ch. 26 (v. 51). **1.47–54** The tribe of Levi is to be considered separately from the "landed" tribes and dedicated

entirely to service at the tabernacle (see also, e.g., Deut 10.8–9; 12.12; Josh 13.14, 33). Levi is left out of the tribal list in the poem in Judg 5.

you shall appoint the Levites over the tabernacle of the covenant,ª and over all its equipment, and over all that belongs to it; they are to carry the tabernacle and all its equipment, and they shall tend it, and shall camp around the tabernacle. 51 When the tabernacle is to set out, the Levites shall take it down; and when the tabernacle is to be pitched, the Levites shall set it up. And any outsider who comes near shall be put to death. 52 The other Israelites shall camp in their respective regimental camps, by companies; 53 but the Levites shall camp around the tabernacle of the covenant,ª that there may be no wrath on the congregation of the Israelites; and the Levites shall perform the guard duty of the tabernacle of the covenant.ª 54 The Israelites did so; they did just as the LORD commanded Moses.

The Order of Encampment and Marching

2 The LORD spoke to Moses and Aaron, saying: 2 The Israelites shall camp each in their respective regiments, under ensigns by their ancestral houses; they shall camp facing the tent of meeting on every side. 3 Those to camp on the east side toward the sunrise shall be of the regimental encampment of Judah by companies. The leader of the people of Judah

shall be Nahshon son of Amminadab, 4 with a company as enrolled of seventy-four thousand six hundred. 5 Those to camp next to him shall be the tribe of Issachar. The leader of the Issacharites shall be Nethanel son of Zuar, 6 with a company as enrolled of fifty-four thousand four hundred. 7 Then the tribe of Zebulun: The leader of the Zebulunites shall be Eliab son of Helon, 8 with a company as enrolled of fifty-seven thousand four hundred. 9 The total enrollment of the camp of Judah, by companies, is one hundred eighty-six thousand four hundred. They shall set out first on the march.

10 On the south side shall be the regimental encampment of Reuben by companies. The leader of the Reubenites shall be Elizur son of Shedeur, 11 with a company as enrolled of forty-six thousand five hundred. 12 And those to camp next to him shall be the tribe of Simeon. The leader of the Simeonites shall be Shelumiel son of Zurishaddai, 13 with a company as enrolled of fifty-nine thousand three hundred. 14 Then the tribe of Gad: The leader of the Gadites shall be Eliasaph son of Reuel, 15 with a company as enrolled of forty-five thousand six hundred fifty. 16 The total enrollment of the camp of Reuben, by companies, is one

a Or *treaty*, or *testimony*; Heb *eduth*

1.50, 53 The tabernacle is called *tabernacle of the covenant* elsewhere only in Ex 38.21; Num 10.11. **1.51** The term *outsider* here refers to anyone who is not a Levite (see also 3.10, 38; 18.7; cf. 16.40). **1.52** The word translated *regiment* probably originally referred to a standard or banner that was used to mark a military unit and then was extended to denote the unit itself, as here (cf. the translation, *standard*, of the same word in 10.14, 18, 22, 25). In fifth-century B.C.E. texts from the Jewish colony at Elephantine in Egypt, this word can even represent a larger legal entity that includes the families of military men. **1.53** The *wrath* of the Lord would be brought on by any non-Levitical trespasser who came into contact with the tabernacle. The Levites are literally its guards.
2.1–34 The tabernacle within the tent of meeting stands at the center of the camp in this description (cf. Ex 33.7–11, where the tent is set up outside the camp). At each of the cardinal points around the tent are three tribes, separated from the tent by Levites (v. 17; 1.52–53). Each group of three is arranged in a camp named for the dominant tribe of the three. The order in

which they camp is also the order in which they march, the tribes on the east leading the march. The sequence in which the tribes are named in this chapter is based on the genealogically organized list in 1.5–15 with minor changes; see vv. 3–9, 10–16. The leaders are those in the lists in 1.5–15; 7.12–83; 10.14–28. **2.2** *Ensign* or "sign" here suggests that each ancestral house had its own symbol that could be displayed. **2.3–9** Judah is the preeminent tribe in this scheme: it is the first tribe listed on the east side of the tabernacle and so leads the march. Judah takes with it Issachar and Zebulun from the list in ch. 1 to make up the *camp of Judah* (v. 9). **2.10–16** The tribes on the south side are next, headed by Reuben, the traditional firstborn. Since Judah is now at the head of the entire list, the *camp of Reuben* (v. 16) includes Gad, in the position Judah held in the list in ch. 1. Gad is the tribe to be moved up either because Reuben and Gad are associated as Transjordanian tribes or because the earlier tribes have all been "Leah" tribes (see 1.5–15) and Gad is the firstborn of Leah's maid Zilpah (Gen 30.9–11). **2.14** For *Reuel*, read "Deuel," following 1.14 and several ancient

hundred fifty-one thousand four hundred fifty. They shall set out second.

17 The tent of meeting, with the camp of the Levites, shall set out in the center of the camps; they shall set out just as they camp, each in position, by their regiments.

18 On the west side shall be the regimental encampment of Ephraim by companies. The leader of the people of Ephraim shall be Elishama son of Ammihud, 19with a company as enrolled of forty thousand five hundred. 20Next to him shall be the tribe of Manasseh. The leader of the people of Manasseh shall be Gamaliel son of Pedahzur, 21with a company as enrolled of thirty-two thousand two hundred. 22Then the tribe of Benjamin: The leader of the Benjaminites shall be Abidan son of Gideoni, 23with a company as enrolled of thirty-five thousand four hundred. 24The total enrollment of the camp of Ephraim, by companies, is one hundred eight thousand one hundred. They shall set out third on the march.

25 On the north side shall be the regimental encampment of Dan by companies. The leader of the Danites shall be Ahiezer son of Ammishaddai, 26with a company as enrolled of sixty-two thousand seven hundred. 27Those to camp next to him shall be the tribe of Asher. The leader of the Asherites shall be Pagiel son of Ochran, 28with a company as enrolled of forty-one thousand five hundred. 29Then the tribe of Naphtali: The leader of the Naphtalites shall be Ahira son of Enan, 30with a company as enrolled of fifty-three thousand four hundred. 31The total enrollment of the camp of Dan is one hundred fifty-seven thousand six hundred. They shall set out last, by companies.*b*

32 This was the enrollment of the Israelites by their ancestral houses; the total enrollment in the camps by their companies was six hundred three thousand five hundred fifty. 33Just as the LORD had commanded Moses, the Levites were not enrolled among the other Israelites.

34 The Israelites did just as the LORD had commanded Moses: They camped by regiments, and they set out the same way, everyone by clans, according to ancestral houses.

The Sons of Aaron

3 This is the lineage of Aaron and Moses at the time when the LORD spoke with Moses on Mount Sinai. 2These are the names of the sons of Aaron: Nadab the firstborn, and Abihu, Eleazar, and Ithamar; 3these are the names of the sons of Aaron, the anointed priests, whom he ordained to minister as priests. 4Nadab and Abihu died before the LORD when they offered unholy fire before the LORD in the wilderness of Sinai, and they had no children. Eleazar and Ithamar served as priests in the lifetime of their father Aaron.

The Duties of the Levites

5 Then the LORD spoke to Moses, saying: 6Bring the tribe of Levi near, and set them before Aaron the priest, so that they may assist him. 7They shall perform duties for him and for the whole congregation in front of the tent of meeting, doing service at the tabernacle; 8they shall be in charge of all the furnishings of the tent of meeting, and attend to the duties for the Israelites as they do service at the tabernacle. 9You shall give the Levites to Aaron

b Compare verses 9, 16, 24: Heb *by their regiments*

---

manuscripts. **2.18–24** Ephraim heads the western camp because in Genesis he became the dominant son of Jacob's favorite son, Joseph (Gen 48.13–20). **2.25–31** Dan is first in the northern camp because he was the eldest son born to a concubine of Jacob (Bilhah, Gen 30.1–6). **2.33** See 1.48–49.
3.1–51 The duties, arrangement, and numbers of the tribe of Levi. **3.1** *Aaron* is listed before *Moses* here because Aaron is the firstborn. This verse is set at *Mount Sinai* (cf. 1.1; 3.14), when Nadab and Abihu were alive (see v. 4). In reverting to Mount Sinai for a few verses, the nar-

rative implies that the information in vv. 5–13 was already understood at the time the rest of the activity in this chapter takes place. **3.2** See also Ex 6.23. **3.3** *He.* It was Moses who ordained the sons of Aaron (Lev 8.30; see also Ex 29.21; 30.30; 40.12–15; cf. Lev 8.12). **3.4** See Lev 10.1–2.
3.5–10 A distinction is made between Aaron and his descendants (the anointed priests) and the rest of the tribe of Levi, to which both Aaron and Moses belong. The rest of the Levites will *assist* (v. 6) Aaron and his descendants. **3.7–8** One of the *duties* of the Levites is to guard the tabernacle from intrusion. **3.9** Instead of *to him,* several

and his descendants; they are unreservedly given to him from among the Israelites. 10 But you shall make a register of Aaron and his descendants; it is they who shall attend to the priesthood, and any outsider who comes near shall be put to death.

11 Then the LORD spoke to Moses, saying: 12 I hereby accept the Levites from among the Israelites as substitutes for all the firstborn that open the womb among the Israelites. The Levites shall be mine, 13 for all the firstborn are mine; when I killed all the firstborn in the land of Egypt, I consecrated for my own all the firstborn in Israel, both human and animal; they shall be mine. I am the LORD.

A Census of the Levites

14 Then the LORD spoke to Moses in the wilderness of Sinai, saying: 15 Enroll the Levites by ancestral houses and by clans. You shall enroll every male from a month old and upward. 16 So Moses enrolled them according to the word of the LORD, as he was commanded. 17 The following were the sons of Levi, by their names: Gershon, Kohath, and Merari. 18 These are the names of the sons of Gershon by their clans: Libni and Shimei. 19 The sons of Kohath by their clans: Am-

ram, Izhar, Hebron, and Uzziel. 20 The sons of Merari by their clans: Mahli and Mushi. These are the clans of the Levites, by their ancestral houses.

21 To Gershon belonged the clan of the Libnites and the clan of the Shimeites; these were the clans of the Gershonites. 22 Their enrollment, counting all the males from a month old and upward, was seven thousand five hundred. 23 The clans of the Gershonites were to camp behind the tabernacle on the west, 24 with Eliasaph son of Lael as head of the ancestral house of the Gershonites. 25 The responsibility of the sons of Gershon in the tent of meeting was to be the tabernacle, the tent with its covering, the screen for the entrance of the tent of meeting, 26 the hangings of the court, the screen for the entrance of the court that is around the tabernacle and the altar, and its cords — all the service pertaining to these.

27 To Kohath belonged the clan of the Amramites, the clan of the Izharites, the clan of the Hebronites, and the clan of the Uzzielites; these are the clans of the Kohathites. 28 Counting all the males, from a month old and upward, there were eight thousand six hundred, attending to the duties of the sanctuary. 29 The clans of the Kohathites were to camp on

---

manuscripts have "to me," as in 8.16; see also 3.12; 18.6. **3.10** *Outsider.* See 1.51. **3.11–13** See 8.16–18. **3.12** Earlier laws had required that human *firstborn* (males are usually specified) be consecrated to the Lord (to a life of religious service), redeemed, or perhaps even sacrificed, presumably to ensure continued fertility (see Ex 13.2, 11–15; 22.29b–30; 34.19–20; see also Num 18.15).

3.14–39 Census of the Levites and recording of their duties. **3.14** This verse returns to the narrative's present time and place, in the *wilderness of Sinai.* **3.15–16** Cf. 1.47–49. The prohibition apparently does not extend to a separate census of the Levites. **3.15** *By ancestral houses and by clans.* Note the reverse order in 1.2 and throughout ch. 1. Unlike the earlier military census, which counted males twenty and older, this census of the Levites counts *every male from a month old and upward,* because they will be substitutes for Israelite firstborn males a month old and upward (vv. 40–41). One month seems to be the age at which personhood was believed to begin; see Lev 27.6. **3.17–20** See Gen 46.11; Ex 6.16–19. **3.21–39** The Levitical clans are to encamp between the tabernacle and the Israelites on three

sides of the tabernacle and are given the responsibility to protect and to transport the tabernacle and its accessories, including the tent of meeting. **3.21–26** The first Levitical clan discussed is the Gershonites; see v. 17. **3.23, 25** The Gershonites encamp on the west side of the tabernacle and have custody over the accessories made of fabric (see also 4.25–26): the *tabernacle,* the innermost tent housing the ark, made of blue (or violet), purple, and crimson linen curtains with a cherubim design (Ex 26.1); the *tent* of meeting, made of goat-hair curtains (Ex 26.7), and its ramskin and leather *covering* (Ex 26.14); the linen *screen* for the entrance to the tent (Ex 26.36); the linen *hangings* for the court surrounding the tabernacle (Ex 27.9); and the linen *screen* for the entrance to the court (Ex 27.16) and its *cords* (Ex 39.40). **3.27–32** *Kohathites.* See v. 17. **3.28** *Eight thousand six hundred.* The Septuagint has "eight thousand three hundred," which accords with the total of twenty-two thousand reported in v. 39. The difference between the Hebrew words for "six" and "three" is only one consonant. **3.29, 31** The Kohathites camp on the *south side* of the tabernacle and have custody over the most sacred items: the *ark* itself (Ex 25.10–22) and its

the south side of the tabernacle, 30with Elizaphan son of Uzziel as head of the ancestral house of the clans of the Kohathites. 31Their responsibility was to be the ark, the table, the lampstand, the altars, the vessels of the sanctuary with which the priests minister, and the screen—all the service pertaining to these. 32Eleazar son of Aaron the priest was to be chief over the leaders of the Levites, and to have oversight of those who had charge of the sanctuary.

33 To Merari belonged the clan of the Mahlites and the clan of the Mushites: these are the clans of Merari. 34Their enrollment, counting all the males from a month old and upward, was six thousand two hundred. 35The head of the ancestral house of the clans of Merari was Zuriel son of Abihail; they were to camp on the north side of the tabernacle. 36The responsibility assigned to the sons of Merari was to be the frames of the tabernacle, the bars, the pillars, the bases, and all their accessories—all the service pertaining to these; 37also the pillars of the court all around, with their bases and pegs and cords.

38 Those who were to camp in front of the tabernacle on the east—in front of the tent of meeting toward the east—were Moses and Aaron and Aaron's sons, having charge of the rites within the sanctuary, whatever had to be done for the Israelites; and any outsider who came near was to be put to death. 39The total enrollment of the Levites whom Moses and Aaron enrolled at the commandment of the LORD, by their clans, all the males from a month old and upward, was twenty-two thousand.

The Redemption of the Firstborn

40 Then the LORD said to Moses: Enroll all the firstborn males of the Israelites, from a month old and upward, and count their names. 41But you shall accept the Levites for me—I am the LORD—as substitutes for all the firstborn among the Israelites, and the livestock of the Levites as substitutes for all the firstborn among the livestock of the Israelites. 42So Moses enrolled all the firstborn among the Israelites, as the LORD commanded him. 43The total enrollment, all the firstborn males from a month old and upward, counting the number of names, was twenty-two thousand two hundred seventy-three.

44 Then the LORD spoke to Moses, saying: 45Accept the Levites as substitutes for all the firstborn among the Israelites, and the livestock of the Levites as substitutes for their livestock; and the Levites shall be mine. I am the LORD. 46As the price of redemption of the two hundred

---

immediate surroundings—the *table* that holds the bread of the Presence (Ex 25.23–30; 35.13; 39.36); the *lampstand* (Ex 25.31–40); the two horned *altars*, one covered with bronze in the court (Ex 27.1–8) and one covered with gold for burning incense (Ex 30.1–10); the *vessels of the sanctuary*, also translated "utensils" (e.g., Ex 27.19; 30.17–21, 26–29; 37.16; 38.3), enumerated in Num 4.5–15; and the *screen* (not one of the screens in vv. 25–26, but rather the curtain that sets off the holiest portion of the tabernacle, otherwise always called the "curtain," the "screening curtain," the "curtain for the screen," or the "curtain for screening," e.g., Ex 26.31–35; 35.12; 39.34; 40.21). **3.32** *Eleazar* (see also 4.16), like Aaron and Moses, is a Kohathite (Ex 6.16, 18, 20, 23). **3.33–37** Merarites; see v. 17. **3.35–36** The Merarites camp on the *north side* of the tabernacle and have custody over the supporting structure of the tabernacle, i.e., the wooden *frames, bars, pillars*, silver *bases*, and *accessories* (Ex 26.15–30; 35.10–11; 39.33; 40.18; see also Num 4.31), and of the surrounding court, its wooden *pillars*, its bronze *bases* and *pegs*, and its *cords* (Ex

27.10–19; 35.17–18; 39.40). **3.38** The preeminent position to the *east* of the tabernacle is taken by Moses, Aaron, and the descendants of Aaron, set apart from the other Levites (see 3.5–10). *Outsider*. See 1.51. **3.39** *Twenty-two thousand*. The numbers in the text actually total twenty-two thousand, three hundred; see 3.28.

3.40–51 The Levites are substitutes for firstborn males (3.14–15). **3.41** Even the Levites' *livestock* are substituted for the livestock of the firstborn (see also v. 45, but cf. 18.17). **3.43** The number of firstborn males (22,273) is very low compared to the census numbers reported in 1.17–46. **3.46–48** Since each Levite could redeem only one firstborn male, a ransom of *five shekels* each had to be paid for the 273 above and beyond the number of Levites (unless that number should actually be 300 higher; see vv. 28, 39). Archaeological evidence suggests that the shekel in ancient Israel weighed about 11.4 grams, though it is possible that there were two systems at work simultaneously, as in ancient Mesopotamia, and that *the shekel of the sanctuary* (v. 47) was

seventy-three of the firstborn of the Israelites, over and above the number of the Levites, 47you shall accept five shekels apiece, reckoning by the shekel of the sanctuary, a shekel of twenty gerahs. 48Give to Aaron and his sons the money by which the excess number of them is redeemed. 49So Moses took the redemption money from those who were over and above those redeemed by the Levites; 50from the firstborn of the Israelites he took the money, one thousand three hundred sixty-five shekels, reckoned by the shekel of the sanctuary; 51and Moses gave the redemption money to Aaron and his sons, according to the word of the LORD, as the LORD had commanded Moses.

The Kohathites

4 The LORD spoke to Moses and Aaron, saying: 2Take a census of the Kohathites separate from the other Levites, by their clans and their ancestral houses, 3from thirty years old up to fifty years old, all who qualify to do work relating to the tent of meeting. 4The service of the Kohathites relating to the tent of meeting concerns the most holy things.

5 When the camp is to set out, Aaron and his sons shall go in and take down the screening curtain, and cover the ark of the covenant*c* with it; 6then they shall put on it a covering of fine leather,*d* and spread over that a cloth all of blue, and shall put its poles in place. 7Over the table of the bread of the Presence they shall spread a blue cloth, and put on it the plates, the dishes for incense, the bowls,

and the flagons for the drink offering; the regular bread also shall be on it; 8then they shall spread over them a crimson cloth, and cover it with a covering of fine leather,*d* and shall put its poles in place. 9They shall take a blue cloth, and cover the lampstand for the light, with its lamps, its snuffers, its trays, and all the vessels for oil with which it is supplied; 10and they shall put it with all its utensils in a covering of fine leather,*d* and put it on the carrying frame. 11Over the golden altar they shall spread a blue cloth, and cover it with a covering of fine leather,*d* and shall put its poles in place; 12and they shall take all the utensils of the service that are used in the sanctuary, and put them in a blue cloth, and cover them with a covering of fine leather,*d* and put them on the carrying frame. 13They shall take away the ashes from the altar, and spread a purple cloth over it; 14and they shall put on it all the utensils of the altar, which are used for the service there, the firepans, the forks, the shovels, and the basins, all the utensils of the altar; and they shall spread on it a covering of fine leather,*d* and shall put its poles in place. 15When Aaron and his sons have finished covering the sanctuary and all the furnishings of the sanctuary, as the camp sets out, after that the Kohathites shall come to carry these, but they must not touch the holy things, or they will die. These are the things of the tent of meeting that the Kohathites are to carry.

16 Eleazar son of Aaron the priest

c Or *treaty*, or *testimony*; Heb *eduth*   *d* Meaning of Heb uncertain

---

heavier than the common shekel (see also the "shekels by the king's weight" in 2 Sam 14.26). **3.49–50** The ransom money will be paid by the firstborn (v. 50) or by a portion of them (v. 49). **4.1–49** The second Levitical census, to determine the number of Levites between the ages of thirty and fifty, the years in which they are qualified to perform their priestly duties (but cf. 8.24–26). **4.2–4** In 3.14–37 Gershon was counted first because Gershon is the "firstborn" (3.17, 21–26). Here, the Kohathites are counted first and are singled out *from the other Levites* because they have custody over *the most holy things* (v. 4; see also 3.31). **4.5–14** The most holy things are prepared for the march by Aaron and his sons. **4.5** *Screening curtain.* See 3.31. **4.6** The *poles* are for carrying the ark (Ex 25.13–15). **4.7** *Table of the bread of the Presence.*

See 3.31. The *plates, dishes for incense, bowls*, and *flagons for the drink offering* (Ex 25.29; 37.16). The *regular bread* is the bread that is continually on the table (Ex 25.30; Lev 24.5–9). **4.8** *Poles* for carrying the table (Ex 25.28). **4.9** *Lampstand.* See 3.31. **4.11** The *golden altar* for burning incense. See 3.31 (its *poles*, Ex 30.4–5). **4.12** The *utensils of the service that are used in the sanctuary* are those that are used inside the tent itself and are most sacred (see 3.31). The *blue* (or violet) *cloth* and *fine leather* indicate the very sacred status of these items, which are placed within the tent while the camp is at rest. **4.13–14** The *altar* here is the bronze altar for sacrifice in the court that surrounds the tabernacle (see 3.31) with its *utensils* (Ex 27.3) and its *poles* (Ex 27.6–7). **4.15** *Or they will die.* See Ex 19.20–24 (cf. Ex 19.12–13); 1 Sam 6.19 (Hebrew text in note *v*); 2 Sam 6.6–15.

shall have charge of the oil for the light, the fragrant incense, the regular grain offering, and the anointing oil, the oversight of all the tabernacle and all that is in it, in the sanctuary and in its utensils.

17 Then the LORD spoke to Moses and Aaron, saying: 18 You must not let the tribe of the clans of the Kohathites be destroyed from among the Levites. 19 This is how you must deal with them in order that they may live and not die when they come near to the most holy things: Aaron and his sons shall go in and assign each to a particular task or burden. 20 But the Kohathites[e] must not go in to look on the holy things even for a moment; otherwise they will die.

The Gershonites and Merarites

21 Then the LORD spoke to Moses, saying: 22 Take a census of the Gershonites also, by their ancestral houses and by their clans; 23 from thirty years old up to fifty years old you shall enroll them, all who qualify to do work in the tent of meeting. 24 This is the service of the clans of the Gershonites, in serving and bearing burdens: 25 They shall carry the curtains of the tabernacle, and the tent of meeting with its covering, and the outer covering of fine leather[f] that is on top of it, and the screen for the entrance of the tent of meeting, 26 and the hangings of the court, and the screen for the entrance of the gate of the court that is around the tabernacle and the altar, and their cords, and all the equipment for their service; and they shall do all that needs to be done with regard to them. 27 All the service of the Gershonites shall be at the command of Aaron and his sons, in all that they are to carry, and in all that they have to do; and you shall assign to their charge all that they are to carry. 28 This is the service of the clans of the Gershonites relating to the tent of meeting, and their responsibilities are to be under the oversight of Ithamar son of Aaron the priest.

29 As for the Merarites, you shall enroll them by their clans and their ancestral houses; 30 from thirty years old up to fifty years old you shall enroll them, everyone who qualifies to do the work of the tent of meeting. 31 This is what they are charged to carry, as the whole of their service in the tent of meeting: the frames of the tabernacle, with its bars, pillars, and bases, 32 and the pillars of the court all around with their bases, pegs, and cords, with all their equipment and all their related service; and you shall assign by name the objects that they are required to carry. 33 This is the service of the clans of the Merarites, the whole of their service relating to the tent of meeting, under the hand of Ithamar son of Aaron the priest.

Census of the Levites

34 So Moses and Aaron and the leaders of the congregation enrolled the Kohathites, by their clans and their ancestral houses, 35 from thirty years old up to fifty years old, everyone who qualified for work relating to the tent of meeting; 36 and their enrollment by clans was two thousand seven hundred fifty. 37 This was the enrollment of the clans of the Kohathites, all who served at the tent of meeting, whom Moses and Aaron enrolled according to the commandment of the LORD by Moses.

38 The enrollment of the Gershonites, by their clans and their ancestral houses, 39 from thirty years old up to fifty years old, everyone who qualified for work relating to the tent of meeting— 40 their enrollment by their clans and their ancestral houses was two thousand six hundred thirty. 41 This was the enrollment of the clans of the Gershonites, all who served at the tent of meeting, whom Moses and Aaron enrolled according to the commandment of the LORD.

42 The enrollment of the clans of the Merarites, by their clans and their ancestral houses, 43 from thirty years old up to

e Heb they   f Meaning of Heb uncertain

4.16 See 3.32.   4.19 Burden, i.e., that which he is to transport.   4.21–28 The census of the Gershonites aged thirty to fifty and the items they are to transport; see 3.21–26.   4.28 As Eleazar is supervisor for the Kohathites and any work having to do with the tabernacle itself, Aaron's other living son, Ithamar (see 3.1–4), is responsible for the Gershonites and the Merarites (v. 33) and the rest of the Levitical service.   4.29–33 The census of the Merarites aged thirty to fifty and the items they are to transport; see 3.33–37.   4.33 See v. 28.   4.36, 40, 44, 48 The numbers here refer only to male Levites aged thirty to fifty; cf. 3.22, 28, 34, 39.

fifty years old, everyone who qualified for work relating to the tent of meeting — 44their enrollment by their clans was three thousand two hundred. 45This is the enrollment of the clans of the Merarites, whom Moses and Aaron enrolled according to the commandment of the LORD by Moses.

46 All those who were enrolled of the Levites, whom Moses and Aaron and the leaders of Israel enrolled, by their clans and their ancestral houses, 47from thirty years old up to fifty years old, everyone who qualified to do the work of service and the work of bearing burdens relating to the tent of meeting, 48their enrollment was eight thousand five hundred eighty. 49According to the commandment of the LORD through Moses they were appointed to their several tasks of serving or carrying; thus they were enrolled by him, as the LORD commanded Moses.

Unclean Persons

5 The LORD spoke to Moses, saying: 2Command the Israelites to put out of the camp everyone who is leprous,g or has a discharge, and everyone who is unclean through contact with a corpse; 3you shall put out both male and female, putting them outside the camp; they must not defile their camp, where I dwell among them. 4The Israelites did so, putting them outside the camp; as the LORD had spoken to Moses, so the Israelites did.

Confession and Restitution

5 The LORD spoke to Moses, saying: 6Speak to the Israelites: When a man or a woman wrongs another, breaking faith with the LORD, that person incurs guilt 7and shall confess the sin that has been committed. The person shall make full restitution for the wrong, adding one-fifth to it, and giving it to the one who was wronged. 8If the injured party has no next of kin to whom restitution may be made for the wrong, the restitution for wrong shall go to the LORD for the priest, in addition to the ram of atonement with which atonement is made for the guilty party. 9Among all the sacred donations of the Israelites, every gift that they bring to the priest shall be his. 10The sacred donations of all are their own; whatever anyone gives to the priest shall be his.

Concerning an Unfaithful Wife

11 The LORD spoke to Moses, saying: 12Speak to the Israelites and say to them: If any man's wife goes astray and is unfaithful to him, 13if a man has had intercourse with her but it is hidden from her husband, so that she is undetected though she has defiled herself, and there is no witness against her since she was not caught in the act; 14if a spirit of jealousy comes on him, and he is jealous of his wife who has defiled herself; or if a spirit of jealousy comes on him, and he is jealous of his wife, though she has not defiled herself; 15then the man shall bring his wife to the priest. And he shall bring the offering required for her, one-tenth of an ephah of barley flour. He shall pour no oil on it and put no frankincense on it, for

g A term for several skin diseases; precise meaning uncertain

---

5.1–4 The entire encampment is treated as sacred because of the presence of the tabernacle, the place, the Lord says, *where I dwell among them* (v. 3). Any impurity, therefore, that is "contagious" must be kept outside the camp. Here the possibility of contagion comes from people ritually "unclean" because of a skin condition (Lev 13, esp. vv. 45–46), because of a bodily discharge (presumably, as in Lev 15, from the genitalia), or because of contact with a corpse (see Num 19.11–20). **5.5–8** A supplement to Lev 6.1–7, for the case in which the injured party has died and there is no next of kin. **5.8** *Next of kin*, lit. "redeemer." See Lev 25.25–26, 48–49; Num 35.12. *Ram of atonement.* Lev 6.6–7. **5.9–10** An instruction providing that Israelites can earmark their donations for individual priests (see Lev 7.7–9, 14, 32–33; cf. 7.10, 31). **5.11–31** The instruction for a woman who is suspected of adultery. **5.12–14** Vv. 12–13 describe a wife who has in fact committed adultery, although there is no proof available. *Is unfaithful to him* uses the same Hebrew phrase as *breaking faith with the LORD* in v. 6. V. 14 describes a husband who is jealous without knowing whether his wife has in fact committed adultery. This instruction, then, concerns two types of cases in which a woman's guilt or innocence cannot be proven by the usual means. **5.15** An *ephah* is estimated to be between three-eighths and two-thirds of a bushel. *Oil* and *frankincense* (or oil alone, Lev 2.4–7; 14.10, 21; Num 6.15) were usually poured on a grain offering, and the grain is usually choice wheat flour, not barley flour (Lev 2.1; 6.14–15;

it is a grain offering of jealousy, a grain offering of remembrance, bringing iniquity to remembrance.

16 Then the priest shall bring her near, and set her before the LORD; 17 the priest shall take holy water in an earthen vessel, and take some of the dust that is on the floor of the tabernacle and put it into the water. 18 The priest shall set the woman before the LORD, dishevel the woman's hair, and place in her hands the grain offering of remembrance, which is the grain offering of jealousy. In his own hand the priest shall have the water of bitterness that brings the curse. 19 Then the priest shall make her take an oath, saying, "If no man has lain with you, if you have not turned aside to uncleanness while under your husband's authority, be immune to this water of bitterness that brings the curse. 20 But if you have gone astray while under your husband's authority, if you have defiled yourself and some man other than your husband has had intercourse with you," 21 — let the priest make the woman take the oath of the curse and say to the woman — "the LORD make you an execration and an oath among your people, when the LORD makes your uterus drop, your womb discharge; 22 now may this water that brings the curse enter your bowels and make your womb discharge, your uterus drop!" And the woman shall say, "Amen. Amen."

23 Then the priest shall put these curses in writing, and wash them off into the water of bitterness. 24 He shall make the woman drink the water of bitterness that brings the curse, and the water that brings the curse shall enter her and cause bitter pain. 25 The priest shall take the grain offering of jealousy out of the woman's hand, and shall elevate the grain offering before the LORD and bring it to the altar; 26 and the priest shall take a handful of the grain offering, as its memorial portion, and turn it into smoke on the altar, and afterward shall make the woman drink the water. 27 When he has made her drink the water, then, if she has defiled herself and has been unfaithful to her husband, the water that brings the curse shall enter into her and cause bitter pain, and her womb shall discharge, her uterus drop, and the woman shall become an execration among her people. 28 But if the woman has not defiled herself and is clean, then she shall be immune and be able to conceive children.

29 This is the law in cases of jealousy, when a wife, while under her husband's authority, goes astray and defiles herself, 30 or when a spirit of jealousy comes on a man and he is jealous of his wife; then he shall set the woman before the LORD, and the priest shall apply this entire law to her. 31 The man shall be free from iniquity, but the woman shall bear her iniquity.

---

cf. Lev 5.11). **5.16** *Before the LORD,* probably before the altar of burnt offering in the court surrounding the tabernacle (see 3.31; 1 Kings 8.31–32). **5.17** *Holy water.* See Ex 30.17–21, 28–29. An *earthen vessel* can be broken after use so that its contents do not pollute or endanger (see Lev 6.24–28; 11.33; 14.5, 50; 15.12). *Dust that is on the floor of the tabernacle* is presumably thought to be powerful because of its association with the tabernacle. **5.18** *Dishevel the woman's hair,* a sign of mourning in Lev 10.6; 21.10, and of uncleanness because of skin disease in Lev 13.45. **5.19–22** The woman suspected of adultery must take an oath that she has not been unfaithful (see Ex 22.10–11). It is on the basis of this oath that the ordeal in vv. 23–28 operates. If she has sworn falsely, the *water of bitterness* (v. 19) will have an immediate negative effect on her body; if what she has sworn is the truth, there will be no effect. **5.21** *The LORD make you an execration and an oath among your people.* See Job 30.9; Jer 29.21–23. *Uterus drop . . . womb discharge.* The symptoms the woman is warned of seem to describe a prolapsed uterus. **5.22** *"Amen, amen"* signals the woman's acceptance of the consequences of a false oath, the equivalent of taking an oath that she has not committed adultery. A guilty woman would hesitate to take the oath. See also Deut 27.15–26; Neh 5.13. **5.23–28** The ordeal. The *water of bitterness* (vv. 23, 24) will test the truth of the woman's oath. **5.23** The priest writes on something that would allow the writing to dissolve in water. The water then carries the force of the curse. See Jer 51.59–64; Ezek 3.1–4. **5.24** The *bitterness* is etymologized as causing *bitter (pain),* presumably to a guilty woman only. (See Ex 32.20, 35.) V. 24 (perhaps vv. 23–24) is anticipatory, as the entire procedure is spelled out in vv. 25–27. **5.25** On elevating the guilt offering, see Lev 14.12, 21, 24. **5.26** For a *handful of the grain offering* as a *memorial portion,* see Lev 2.2, 9, 16 (there translated "token portion"). **5.28** The punishment for the one who swears falsely is a condition that precludes

The Nazirites

6 The LORD spoke to Moses, saying: 2 Speak to the Israelites and say to them: When either men or women make a special vow, the vow of a nazirite,ʰ to separate themselves to the LORD, 3 they shall separate themselves from wine and strong drink; they shall drink no wine vinegar or other vinegar, and shall not drink any grape juice or eat grapes, fresh or dried. 4 All their days as nazirites* they shall eat nothing that is produced by the grapevine, not even the seeds or the skins.

5 All the days of their nazirite vow no razor shall come upon the head; until the time is completed for which they separate themselves to the LORD, they shall be holy; they shall let the locks of the head grow long. 6 All the days that they separate themselves to the LORD they shall not go near a corpse. 7 Even if their father or mother, brother or sister, should die, they may not defile themselves; because their consecration to God is upon the head. 8 All their days as nazirites* they are holy to the LORD.

9 If someone dies very suddenly nearby, defiling the consecrated head, then they shall shave the head on the day of their cleansing; on the seventh day they shall shave it. 10 On the eighth day they shall bring two turtledoves or two young pigeons to the priest at the entrance of the tent of meeting, 11 and the priest shall offer one as a sin offering and the other as a burnt offering, and make atonement for them, because they incurred guilt by reason of the corpse. They shall sanctify the head that same day, 12 and separate themselves to the LORD for their days as nazirites,* and bring a male lamb a year old as a guilt offering. The former time shall be void, because the consecrated head was defiled.

13 This is the law for the nazirites* when the time of their consecration has been completed: they shall be brought to the entrance of the tent of meeting, 14 and they shall offer their gift to the LORD, one male lamb a year old without blemish as a burnt offering, one ewe lamb a year old without blemish as a sin offering, one ram without blemish as an offering of well-being, 15 and a basket of unleavened bread, cakes of choice flour mixed with oil and unleavened wafers spread with oil, with their grain offering and their drink offerings. 16 The priest shall present them before the LORD and offer their sin offering and burnt offering, 17 and shall offer the ram as a sacrifice of well-being to the LORD, with the basket of unleavened

h That is *one separated* or *one consecrated*   i That is *those separated* or *those consecrated*

bearing children. **5.31** The husband will not be punished for putting even an innocent wife through the oath and ordeal; it is his right to ask for the procedure. The wife's punishment or lack of it will depend on the outcome of the ordeal.
6.1–21 The temporary Nazirite vow. **6.2** For women's vows, see also 30.3–16. On the Nazirite, see also Judg 13.2–14; 16.4–31; 1 Sam 1.11; Am 2.11–12. **6.3–4** Nazirites must abstain from all products of the vine; cf. the Rechabites (Jer 35; 2 Kings 10.15–28). *Other vinegar,* lit. "vinegar from (any) intoxicant." Even Samson's pregnant mother was to abstain from intoxicants and other grape products (Judg 13.4, 7, 14). See also 1 Sam 1.11; Am 2.11–12. *All their days as nazirites* (vv. 4, 5, 6, 8, 12), instructions for a temporary naziriteship, unlike Samson's and Samuel's, which were lifelong. **6.5** *Locks . . . grow long.* The Nazirites' uncut hair was their most important feature. See vv. 7, 9, 18 and the story of Samson's naziriteship (Judg 13.5; 16.4–31). (See also Lev 25.5, 11, where the unpruned vine is called in Hebrew *nazir.*) **6.6–7** Like the high priest, Nazirites were to avoid contact with a corpse, even of a close member of the family (see Lev 21.10–11; cf. vv. 1–3). **6.9–12** Accidental contact with a corpse requires purification and rededication. **6.9** *Suddenly* implies there was no time for the Nazirite to avoid contact. *Seventh day.* See 19.11–12, 19. **6.10–12** Even priests who were contaminated by contact with a corpse were not required to undergo such a purification (see 19.11–12; cf. Ezek 44.25–27; see Lev 12.6–8; 14.10–32; 15.13–15, 28–30 for similar purification rituals). *Sanctify the head,* in preparation for a new vow of naziriteship, beginning the period of separation over again (v. 12). **6.13–20** The instruction for the ritual upon the completion of the Nazirite vow. **6.14–17** Regulations for the *burnt offering* are in Lev 1, for the *sin offering* in Lev 4.1–5.13, for the *offering of well-being* in Lev 3, and for the *grain offering* in Lev 2. For *drink offerings,* see Ex 29.40; 30.9; Lev 23.13. The extent of the ritual indicates the seriousness

bread; the priest also shall make the accompanying grain offering and drink offering. 18Then the naziritesⱼ shall shave the consecrated head at the entrance of the tent of meeting, and shall take the hair from the consecrated head and put it on the fire under the sacrifice of well-being. 19The priest shall take the shoulder of the ram, when it is boiled, and one unleavened cake out of the basket, and one unleavened wafer, and shall put them in the palms of the nazirites,ⱼ after they have shaved the consecrated head. 20Then the priest shall elevate them as an elevation offering before the Lord; they are a holy portion for the priest, together with the breast that is elevated and the thigh that is offered. After that the naziritesⱼ may drink wine.

21 This is the law for the naziritesⱼ who take a vow. Their offering to the Lord must be in accordance with the naziritek vow, apart from what else they can afford. In accordance with whatever vow they take, so they shall do, following the law for their consecration.

The Priestly Benediction

22 The Lord spoke to Moses, saying: 23Speak to Aaron and his sons, saying, Thus you shall bless the Israelites: You shall say to them,
24 The Lord bless you and
          keep you;

25 the Lord make his face to shine
          upon you, and be gracious
          to you;
26 the Lord lift up his countenance
          upon you, and give you
          peace.
27 So they shall put my name on the Israelites, and I will bless them.

Offerings of the Leaders

7 On the day when Moses had finished setting up the tabernacle, and had anointed and consecrated it with all its furnishings, and had anointed and consecrated the altar with all its utensils, 2the leaders of Israel, heads of their ancestral houses, the leaders of the tribes, who were over those who were enrolled, made offerings. 3They brought their offerings before the Lord, six covered wagons and twelve oxen, a wagon for every two of the leaders, and for each one an ox; they presented them before the tabernacle. 4Then the Lord said to Moses: 5Accept these from them, that they may be used in doing the service of the tent of meeting, and give them to the Levites, to each according to his service. 6So Moses took the wagons and the oxen, and gave them to the Levites. 7Two wagons and four oxen he gave to the Gershonites, according to their service; 8and four wagons and eight oxen he gave to the Merarites, according

ⱼ That is *those separated* or *those consecrated*
k That is *one separated* or *one consecrated*

---

of the transformation from a state of consecration back to a mundane life. **6.18** The sacrifice of hair is not uncommon among the world's religions. Here the hair must be burned, *put on the fire,* because it is holy (see Lev 7.16–17; 19.5–8). **6.20** See Ex 29.26–28; Lev 7.32–34; 10.14–15. **6.22–27** The ancient and lovely priestly benediction which appears here need not be connected with its immediate context; it is in general a function of the priesthood to bless the worshiping community; see Lev 9.22–23; Deut 10.8; 21.5; 2 Chr 30.27; Ps 118.26. **6.24–26** Portions of this blessing appear on two tiny silver scroll-amulets found in a tomb in Jerusalem from the seventh or sixth century B.C.E. **6.25** The *shining* face of the Lord is a sign of protection (Pss 4.6; 31.16; 44.3; 80.3; 89.15; cf. Deut 31.17–18). **6.26** The lifting up of the Lord's *countenance* is a sign of favor; the Hebrew is similar in Gen 19.21;

32.20; Job 42.8–9; Mal 1.8–9. *Peace,* i.e., well-being, wholeness. **6.27** Putting the Lord's name on the Israelites implies ownership; see Deut 12.5; 28.10; Jer 7.10–11; 14.9. This command may have been taken literally, i.e., by wearing the name of God as part of an amulet (see note on 6.24–26).

7.1–9 *On the day.* Even though set one month earlier than the beginning of the book of Numbers (v. 1; see Ex 40.17; cf. Num 1.1), this description of the gifts offered presumes the information presented just prior to this section: the *wagons* and *oxen* are given to transport the sanctuary items assigned to the Levites in chs. 3–4, except for the items the Kohathites were to carry on their shoulders. The Merarites are given twice as many oxen and wagons as the Gershonites, since transporting the supporting structure of the tabernacle would be more burdensome than transporting its vari-

to their service, under the direction of Ithamar son of Aaron the priest. 9 But to the Kohathites he gave none, because they were charged with the care of the holy things that had to be carried on the shoulders.

10   The leaders also presented offerings for the dedication of the altar at the time when it was anointed; the leaders presented their offering before the altar. 11 The LORD said to Moses: They shall present their offerings, one leader each day, for the dedication of the altar.

12   The one who presented his offering the first day was Nahshon son of Amminadab, of the tribe of Judah; 13 his offering was one silver plate weighing one hundred thirty shekels, one silver basin weighing seventy shekels, according to the shekel of the sanctuary, both of them full of choice flour mixed with oil for a grain offering; 14 one golden dish weighing ten shekels, full of incense; 15 one young bull, one ram, one male lamb a year old, for a burnt offering; 16 one male goat for a sin offering; 17 and for the sacrifice of well-being, two oxen, five rams, five male goats, and five male lambs a year old. This was the offering of Nahshon son of Amminadab.

18   On the second day Nethanel son of Zuar, the leader of Issachar, presented an offering; 19 he presented for his offering one silver plate weighing one hundred thirty shekels, one silver basin weighing seventy shekels, according to the shekel of the sanctuary, both of them full of choice flour mixed with oil for a grain offering; 20 one golden dish weighing ten shekels, full of incense; 21 one young bull, one ram, one male lamb a year old, as a burnt offering; 22 one male goat as a sin offering; 23 and for the sacrifice of well-being, two oxen, five rams, five male goats, and five male lambs a year old. This was the offering of Nethanel son of Zuar.

24   On the third day Eliab son of Helon, the leader of the Zebulunites: 25 his offering was one silver plate weighing one hundred thirty shekels, one silver basin weighing seventy shekels, according to the shekel of the sanctuary, both of them full of choice flour mixed with oil for a grain offering; 26 one golden dish weighing ten shekels, full of incense; 27 one young bull, one ram, one male lamb a year old, for a burnt offering; 28 one male goat for a sin offering; 29 and for the sacrifice of well-being, two oxen, five rams, five male goats, and five male lambs a year old. This was the offering of Eliab son of Helon.

30   On the fourth day Elizur son of Shedeur, the leader of the Reubenites: 31 his offering was one silver plate weighing one hundred thirty shekels, one silver basin weighing seventy shekels, according to the shekel of the sanctuary, both of them full of choice flour mixed with oil for a grain offering; 32 one golden dish weighing ten shekels, full of incense; 33 one young bull, one ram, one male lamb a year old, for a burnt offering; 34 one male goat for a sin offering; 35 and for the sacrifice of well-being, two oxen, five rams, five male goats, and five male lambs a year old. This was the offering of Elizur son of Shedeur.

36   On the fifth day Shelumiel son of Zurishaddai, the leader of the Simeonites: 37 his offering was one silver plate weighing one hundred thirty shekels, one silver basin weighing seventy shekels, according to the shekel of the sanctuary, both of them full of choice flour mixed with oil for a grain offering; 38 one golden dish weighing ten shekels, full of incense; 39 one young bull, one ram, one male lamb a year old, for a burnt offering; 40 one male goat for a sin offering; 41 and for the sacrifice of well-being, two oxen, five rams, five male goats, and five male lambs a year old. This was the offering of Shelumiel son of Zurishaddai.

42   On the sixth day Eliasaph son of Deuel, the leader of the Gadites: 43 his offering was one silver plate weighing one hundred thirty shekels, one silver basin weighing seventy shekels, according to the shekel of the sanctuary, both of them full of choice flour mixed with oil for a grain offering; 44 one golden dish weighing ten shekels, full of incense; 45 one young bull, one ram, one male lamb a year old, for a burnt offering; 46 one male goat for a sin

___

ous cloth items; see 3.23, 25, 35–37. **7.10** See vv. 1, 4–9. **7.12–83** The leaders are those in 1.5–15; 2.3–31; and 10.14–28, presented in the order of the list in 2.3–31. The dedication offerings are the same from each tribe. **7.13** *Shekel of the sanctuary*. See 3.46–48. **7.17** *Oxen* here does not indicate castrated bulls, but simply male bovines. Castrated animals would not have been

offering; 47and for the sacrifice of well-being, two oxen, five rams, five male goats, and five male lambs a year old. This was the offering of Eliasaph son of Deuel.

48 On the seventh day Elishama son of Ammihud, the leader of the Ephraimites: 49his offering was one silver plate weighing one hundred thirty shekels, one silver basin weighing seventy shekels, according to the shekel of the sanctuary, both of them full of choice flour mixed with oil for a grain offering; 50one golden dish weighing ten shekels, full of incense; 51one young bull, one ram, one male lamb a year old, for a burnt offering; 52one male goat for a sin offering; 53and for the sacrifice of well-being, two oxen, five rams, five male goats, and five male lambs a year old. This was the offering of Elishama son of Ammihud.

54 On the eighth day Gamaliel son of Pedahzur, the leader of the Manassites: 55his offering was one silver plate weighing one hundred thirty shekels, one silver basin weighing seventy shekels, according to the shekel of the sanctuary, both of them full of choice flour mixed with oil for a grain offering; 56one golden dish weighing ten shekels, full of incense; 57one young bull, one ram, one male lamb a year old, for a burnt offering; 58one male goat for a sin offering; 59and for the sacrifice of well-being, two oxen, five rams, five male goats, and five male lambs a year old. This was the offering of Gamaliel son of Pedahzur.

60 On the ninth day Abidan son of Gideoni, the leader of the Benjaminites: 61his offering was one silver plate weighing one hundred thirty shekels, one silver basin weighing seventy shekels, according to the shekel of the sanctuary, both of them full of choice flour mixed with oil for a grain offering; 62one golden dish weighing ten shekels, full of incense; 63one young bull, one ram, one male lamb a year old, for a burnt offering; 64one male goat for a sin offering; 65and for the sacrifice of well-being, two oxen, five rams, five male goats, and five male lambs a year old. This was the offering of Abidan son of Gideoni.

66 On the tenth day Ahiezer son of Ammishaddai, the leader of the Danites: 67his offering was one silver plate weighing one hundred thirty shekels, one silver basin weighing seventy shekels, according to the shekel of the sanctuary, both of

them full of choice flour mixed with oil for a grain offering; 68one golden dish weighing ten shekels, full of incense; 69one young bull, one ram, one male lamb a year old, for a burnt offering; 70one male goat for a sin offering; 71and for the sacrifice of well-being, two oxen, five rams, five male goats, and five male lambs a year old. This was the offering of Ahiezer son of Ammishaddai.

72 On the eleventh day Pagiel son of Ochran, the leader of the Asherites: 73his offering was one silver plate weighing one hundred thirty shekels, one silver basin weighing seventy shekels, according to the shekel of the sanctuary, both of them full of choice flour mixed with oil for a grain offering; 74one golden dish weighing ten shekels, full of incense; 75one young bull, one ram, one male lamb a year old, for a burnt offering; 76one male goat for a sin offering; 77and for the sacrifice of well-being, two oxen, five rams, five male goats, and five male lambs a year old. This was the offering of Pagiel son of Ochran.

78 On the twelfth day Ahira son of Enan, the leader of the Naphtalites: 79his offering was one silver plate weighing one hundred thirty shekels, one silver basin weighing seventy shekels, according to the shekel of the sanctuary, both of them full of choice flour mixed with oil for a grain offering; 80one golden dish weighing ten shekels, full of incense; 81one young bull, one ram, one male lamb a year old, for a burnt offering; 82one male goat for a sin offering; 83and for the sacrifice of well-being, two oxen, five rams, five male goats, and five male lambs a year old. This was the offering of Ahira son of Enan.

84 This was the dedication offering for the altar, at the time when it was anointed, from the leaders of Israel: twelve silver plates, twelve silver basins, twelve golden dishes, 85each silver plate weighing one hundred thirty shekels and each basin seventy, all the silver of the vessels two thousand four hundred shekels according to the shekel of the sanctuary, 86the twelve golden dishes, full of incense, weighing ten shekels apiece according to the shekel of the sanctuary, all the gold of the dishes being one hundred twenty shekels; 87all the livestock for the burnt offering twelve bulls, twelve rams, twelve male lambs a year old, with their grain offering; and twelve male goats for

a sin offering; 88 and all the livestock for the sacrifice of well-being twenty-four bulls, the rams sixty, the male goats sixty, the male lambs a year old sixty. This was the dedication offering for the altar, after it was anointed.

89 When Moses went into the tent of meeting to speak with the LORD,*l* he would hear the voice speaking to him from above the mercy seat*m* that was on the ark of the covenant*n* from between the two cherubim; thus it spoke to him.

The Seven Lamps

8 The LORD spoke to Moses, saying: 2 Speak to Aaron and say to him: When you set up the lamps, the seven lamps shall give light in front of the lampstand. 3 Aaron did so; he set up its lamps to give light in front of the lampstand, as the LORD had commanded Moses. 4 Now this was how the lampstand was made, out of hammered work of gold. From its base to its flowers, it was hammered work; according to the pattern that the LORD had shown Moses, so he made the lampstand.

Consecration and Service of the Levites

5 The LORD spoke to Moses, saying: 6 Take the Levites from among the Israelites and cleanse them. 7 Thus you shall do to them, to cleanse them: sprinkle the water of purification on them, have them shave their whole body with a razor and wash their clothes, and so cleanse themselves. 8 Then let them take a young bull and its grain offering of choice flour mixed with oil, and you shall take another young bull for a sin offering. 9 You shall bring the Levites before the tent of meeting, and assemble the whole congregation of the Israelites. 10 When you bring the Levites before the LORD, the Israelites shall lay their hands on the Levites, 11 and Aaron shall present the Levites before the LORD as an elevation offering from the Israelites, that they may do the service of the LORD. 12 The Levites shall lay their hands on the heads of the bulls, and he shall offer the one for a sin offering and the other for a burnt offering to the LORD, to make atonement for the Levites. 13 Then you shall have the Levites stand

l Heb *him*   *m* Or *the cover*   *n* Or *treaty*, or *testimony*; Heb *eduth*

---

considered suitable for sacrifice. **7.84, 88** See vv. 1, 4–9. **7.89** This short notice has no obvious connection with what precedes or follows, except that it concerns the sanctuary. The *mercy seat* with the two cherubim is the cover of the ark, and it is from above the mercy seat, between the *cherubim*, that the Lord promises to meet with Moses (Ex 25.17–22; 30.6, 36). In 1 Chr 28.2 the ark is called God's "footstool" (see also Pss 99.5; 132.7), and the Lord is said to be enthroned upon the cherubim (1 Sam 4.4; 2 Sam 6.2; 2 Kings 19.15; 1 Chr 13.6; Pss 80.1; 99.1). Such a throne for a deity is also known from Canaanite iconography. **8.1** The setting is presumably still that of Ex 40.17 (see Num 7.1–9). **8.2–4** *In front of*. That the lamps should throw light forward (northward) toward the ark, the incense altar, and the table of the bread of the Presence was specified in the command to build the lampstand in Ex 25.31–40 (see v. 37), but not in the report of its construction in Ex 37.17–24. See also Ex 27.20–21; 30.7–8; Lev 24.4; 1 Sam 3.3. *Pattern.* See Ex 25.9, 40.

8.5–26 The Levites (presumably those twenty-five and older; see vv. 24–26) are purified by cleansing and sacrifice so that they will be in an appropriate state to handle the sanctuary items (v. 15). Cf. the anointing and ordination of the

priests in Ex 29; Lev 8. **8.6–7** *From among the Israelites.* See 1.48–54; 3.11–13. *Cleanse*, i.e., make ritually "clean." *Water of purification.* See also 19.9, 17–19, 21; 31.23; the "water of cleansing" would seem to be the same as the "water of purification" (see also Ezek 36.25), but it is not the "holy water" for the priests mentioned in Num 5.17. In 8.7, "purification" or "purification offering" is the same Hebrew word generally translated "sin" or "sin offering." *Have them shave their whole body with a razor*, lit. "make a razor pass over their entire body" (cf. 6.9). Then they are to *wash their clothes* and presumably themselves (see Lev 13.29–34; 14.8–9; Num 19.19). See also Lev 8; 11; 16; 17 for various rituals involving washing of clothes or persons. **8.8** The first *young bull* is to be a burnt offering; see v. 12. **8.9–11** *Before the LORD*, i.e., at the entrance to the tent (cf., e.g., Ex 29.11, 42; Num 16.16–18). The laying on of *hands* identifies the sacrificer with the sacrificial victim (Lev 1.4; and see Num 8.12). The Levites have become the sacrifice, i.e., they have been dedicated to the Lord and serve as Israel's representatives in the sanctuary. **8.12** The Levites offer a sin offering and a burnt offering to atone for any possible sin (Lev 1.4; 4.20); see v. 15. **8.13** As an *elevation offering* the Levites also belong to Aaron and his descendants (see Ex 29.26–28; Lev 7.34–36;

before Aaron and his sons, and you shall present them as an elevation offering to the LORD. 14 Thus you shall separate the Levites from among the other Israelites, and the Levites shall be mine. 15 Thereafter the Levites may go in to do service at the tent of meeting, once you have cleansed them and presented them as an elevation offering. 16 For they are unreservedly given to me from among the Israelites; I have taken them for myself, in place of all that open the womb, the firstborn of all the Israelites. 17 For all the firstborn among the Israelites are mine, both human and animal. On the day that I struck down all the firstborn in the land of Egypt I consecrated them for myself, 18 but I have taken the Levites in place of all the firstborn among the Israelites. 19 Moreover, I have given the Levites as a gift to Aaron and his sons from among the Israelites, to do the service for the Israelites at the tent of meeting, and to make atonement for the Israelites, in order that there may be no plague among the Israelites for coming too close to the sanctuary.

20 Moses and Aaron and the whole congregation of the Israelites did with the Levites accordingly; the Israelites did with the Levites just as the LORD had commanded Moses concerning them. 21 The Levites purified themselves from sin and washed their clothes; then Aaron presented them as an elevation offering before the LORD, and Aaron made atonement for them to cleanse them. 22 Thereafter the Levites went in to do their service in the tent of meeting in attendance on Aaron and his sons. As the LORD had commanded Moses concerning the Levites, so they did with them.

23 The LORD spoke to Moses, saying: 24 This applies to the Levites: from twenty-five years old and upward they shall begin to do duty in the service of the tent of meeting; 25 and from the age of fifty years they shall retire from the duty of the service and serve no more. 26 They may assist their brothers in the tent of meeting in carrying out their duties, but they shall perform no service. Thus you shall do with the Levites in assigning their duties.

The Passover at Sinai

9 The LORD spoke to Moses in the wilderness of Sinai, in the first month of the second year after they had come out of the land of Egypt, saying: 2 Let the Israelites keep the passover at its appointed time. 3 On the fourteenth day of this month, at twilight,o you shall keep it at its appointed time; according to all its statutes and all its regulations you shall keep it. 4 So Moses told the Israelites that they should keep the passover. 5 They kept the passover in the first month, on the fourteenth day of the month, at twilight,o in the wilderness of Sinai. Just as the LORD had commanded Moses, so the Israelites did. 6 Now there were certain people who were unclean through touching a corpse, so that they could not keep the passover on that day. They came before Moses and Aaron on that day, 7 and said to him, "Although we are unclean through touching a corpse, why must we be kept from presenting the LORD's offering at its appointed time among the Israelites?" 8 Moses spoke to them, "Wait, so

o Heb between the two evenings

10.12–15). **8.14** See vv. 6–7. **8.16–18** See 3.11–13. **8.19** As a gift to Aaron and his sons. See 3.5–9. Because the Levites stood between the Israelites and the sanctuary, the Israelites were less likely to trespass in dangerous proximity to the sanctuary; see 1.51–53; 2.17. **8.23–26** On the age limits for Levitical duty, cf. 4.3, 23, 30. Num 8 liberalizes the age limits, and other writings expand them even more (see 1 Chr 23.3, 24, 27; 2 Chr 31.17; Ezra 3.8). The differences are presumably due to variations over time in the numbers and duties of the Levites; an upper age limit is more appropriate for those doing heavy work such as transporting (Num 3–4); in v. 26 Levites over fifty could still assist in the tent of

meeting. When the tabernacle was stationary within the temple (see 1 Kings 8.1–13), no such duties would fall to the Levites. Differences in lower age limits may be due to changing numbers of available Levite males (see Ezra 2.1–2, 40; Neh 7.6–7, 43). **9.1–5** The Passover is kept in the wilderness of Sinai. This second Passover is celebrated immediately before the people set out on a march, as was the first (Ex 12–13). **9.1** One month before the date in 1.1; see 7.1–9. **9.2–4** See Ex 12.1–27, 43–49. **9.6** Unclean through touching a corpse. See 19.11–20; also 5.2. Aaron seems to be an addition here; the rest of the narrative involves

that I may hear what the LORD will command concerning you."

9 The LORD spoke to Moses, saying: 10Speak to the Israelites, saying: Anyone of you or your descendants who is unclean through touching a corpse, or is away on a journey, shall still keep the passover to the LORD. 11In the second month on the fourteenth day, at twilight,p they shall keep it; they shall eat it with unleavened bread and bitter herbs. 12They shall leave none of it until morning, nor break a bone of it; according to all the statute for the passover they shall keep it. 13But anyone who is clean and is not on a journey, and yet refrains from keeping the passover, shall be cut off from the people for not presenting the LORD's offering at its appointed time; such a one shall bear the consequences for the sin. 14Any alien residing among you who wishes to keep the passover to the LORD shall do so according to the statute of the passover and according to its regulation; you shall have one statute for both the resident alien and the native.

The Cloud and the Fire

15 On the day the tabernacle was set up, the cloud covered the tabernacle, the tent of the covenant;q and from evening until morning it was over the tabernacle, having the appearance of fire. 16It was always so: the cloud covered it by dayr and the appearance of fire by night. 17Whenever the cloud lifted from over the tent, then the Israelites would set out; and in the place where the cloud settled down, there the Israelites would camp. 18At the command of the LORD the Israelites would set out, and at the command of the LORD they would camp. As long as the cloud rested over the tabernacle, they would remain in camp. 19Even when the cloud continued over the tabernacle many days, the Israelites would keep the charge of the LORD, and would not set out. 20Sometimes the cloud would remain a few days over the tabernacle, and according to the command of the LORD they would remain in camp; then according to the command of the LORD they would set out. 21Sometimes the cloud would remain from evening until morning; and when the cloud lifted in the morning, they would set out, or if it continued for a day and a night, when the cloud lifted they would set out. 22Whether it was two days, or a month, or a longer time, that the cloud continued over the tabernacle, resting upon it, the Israelites would remain in camp and would not set out; but when it lifted they would set out. 23At the com-

p Heb *between the two evenings*   q Or *treaty*, or *testimony*; Heb *eduth*   r Gk Syr Vg: Heb lacks *by day*

9.10 *Unclean . . . corpse.* See 9.6. Being *away on a journey* was not part of the original question and seems to assume a settled life in Canaan (note the phrase *or your descendants*). **9.11** Supplemental instructions adapt the older regulations to unaddressed circumstances (see also 2 Chr 30.1–3, 15). **9.12** See Ex 12.10, 46; see also Ex 29.34; Lev 7.15; 22.29–30. **9.13** Commentators are divided on the precise meaning of the phrase *cut off from the people* as to whether the guilty person is killed or his family line is cut off, but most agree the phrase implies punishment by divine rather than human agency. For a clearer case, see 15.30–31. **9.14** The resident *alien* is not a native Israelite, but rather someone who has taken up permanent residence among the Israelites and finds protection in that community. Resident aliens, in contrast to foreigners passing through or living only temporarily in the Israelite community (Ex 12.43), were allowed to participate in the Passover as long as their males were circumcised (Ex 12.48–49), but they were not punished for not participating as native Israelites would be (Num 9.13).

9.15–23 The setting of these verses is the march from the wilderness of Sinai, although the beginning of the march is not reported until 10.11. **9.15–16** *Day . . . was set up.* On the date, see v. 1. *The cloud covered the tabernacle, the tent of the covenant:* among earlier mentions of the cloud, see Ex 13.21–22, where the cloud and the fire are described separately, the cloud by day and the fire by night; see other variations in Ex 16.10; 24.15–18; 33.9–10; 40.34–38; Lev 16.2. See also Ex 14.19, 24; Num 14.14; Deut 31.15; Neh 9.12, 19. The fire that is in the cloud in some descriptions has been associated with the "glory" of the Lord, and such descriptions have led commentators to describe this "glory"-cloud as a kind of glowing aura, like the "radiance" of Mesopotamian gods (see, e.g., Ex 16.10; 24.16–18; also 40.34–35; Num 16.42; Ezek 1.28; 10.4). **9.16** Cf. Pss 78.14; 105.39. **9.17–23** See, e.g., Ex 40.36–37; Num 10.11–13. **9.17** *Settled down,* lit. "tabernacled." Presumably the cloud stopped at the point where the tabernacle was to be set up, determining, then, the position of the rest of the camp (ch. 2).

mand of the LORD they would camp, and
at the command of the LORD they would
set out. They kept the charge of the LORD,
at the command of the LORD by Moses.

The Silver Trumpets

10 The LORD spoke to Moses, saying: 2 Make two silver trumpets;
you shall make them of hammered work;
and you shall use them for summoning
the congregation, and for breaking camp.
3 When both are blown, the whole congregation shall assemble before you at the entrance of the tent of meeting. 4 But if only
one is blown, then the leaders, the heads
of the tribes of Israel, shall assemble before you. 5 When you blow an alarm, the
camps on the east side shall set out;
6 when you blow a second alarm, the
camps on the south side shall set out. An
alarm is to be blown whenever they are to
set out. 7 But when the assembly is to be
gathered, you shall blow, but you shall not
sound an alarm. 8 The sons of Aaron, the
priests, shall blow the trumpets; this shall
be a perpetual institution for you
throughout your generations. 9 When you
go to war in your land against the adversary who oppresses you, you shall sound
an alarm with the trumpets, so that you
may be remembered before the LORD

your God and be saved from your enemies. 10 Also on your days of rejoicing, at
your appointed festivals, and at the beginnings of your months, you shall blow the
trumpets over your burnt offerings and
over your sacrifices of well-being; they
shall serve as a reminder on your behalf
before the LORD your God: I am the LORD
your God.

Departure from Sinai

11 In the second year, in the second
month, on the twentieth day of the
month, the cloud lifted from over the tabernacle of the covenant.*s* 12 Then the Israelites set out by stages from the
wilderness of Sinai, and the cloud settled
down in the wilderness of Paran. 13 They
set out for the first time at the command
of the LORD by Moses. 14 The standard of
the camp of Judah set out first, company
by company, and over the whole company
was Nahshon son of Amminadab. 15 Over
the company of the tribe of Issachar was
Nethanel son of Zuar; 16 and over the
company of the tribe of Zebulun was Eliab
son of Helon.

17 Then the tabernacle was taken
down, and the Gershonites and the Mera-

s Or *treaty*, or *testimony*; Heb *eduth*

10.1–10 Moses is to make two silver trumpets
to be used during the march from the wilderness
of Sinai. **10.2** There are several Hebrew words
translated *trumpets*. The trumpets in this narrative
are made of metal, not animal horns, and are
used almost entirely for sacred and not secular
purposes. They are blown by priests (see v. 8).
According to Josephus and as depicted on later
coins, they were slender with a wide mouth and
about one foot long. **10.4** *The leaders, the heads of
the tribes of Israel.* See 1.16. **10.5–6** Many commentators suggest that an *alarm* is a series of
short blasts, as distinguished from a *blow*, a long
blast (v. 7). The Hebrew word translated "alarm"
here is commonly a battle cry (e.g., v. 9; 31.6; Josh
6.5, 20; 2 Chr 13.12–16) but can also be a shout
for joy (e.g., 2 Sam 6.15; Ps 33.3). Presumably an
alarm is blown for the tribes on the west and
north as well (so the Septuagint). **10.7** *Blow.*
See 10.5–6. **10.8** On these particular trumpets
as *priestly* instruments, see v. 2. **10.10** *Days of rejoicing,* e.g., the coronation of King Joash (2 Kings
11.14) or the laying of the foundation of the second temple (Ezra 3.10). *Appointed festivals.* See
Num 28–29; Lev 23. *Beginnings of your months.* See
Num 28.11–15.

10.11–22.1 The march from the wilderness
of Sinai to Transjordan. **10.11–36** Cf. Deut
1.6–8. **10.11–12** *Second year . . . month.* The
date is nineteen days after the census in 1.1 and
eleven months and nineteen days after the Israelites arrived at the wilderness of Sinai (Ex 19.1).
Cloud. See 9.15–23. For the *stages* of their journey, see also 33.1–49. In the first stage, the people move from the wilderness of Sinai to the
wilderness of Paran (see also 11.3, 35; 12.16). Paran seems to refer to the entire area of the northern Sinai between Egypt and Midian (1 Kings
11.18). **10.14–28** For the order of the march,
see ch. 2. Positions of the Levitical families during
the march are not quite symmetrically assigned.
Those who are *over the company* parallel the lists of
leaders in 1.5–15; 2.3–31; 7.12–83. For the *standard* of a tribe (vv. 14, 18, 22, and 25), see 1.52.
There are three tribes for each standard as there
are three tribes for each "regimental encampment" in ch. 2. A regimental encampment consists
of the tribes who camp under the same standard.
Company by company. See 1.3. **10.17** The Gershonites and Merarites presumably also took
down the parts of the tabernacle that they transported on wagons (7.1–9) and put the structure

rites, who carried the tabernacle, set out. 18 Next the standard of the camp of Reuben set out, company by company; and over the whole company was Elizur son of Shedeur. 19 Over the company of the tribe of Simeon was Shelumiel son of Zurishaddai, 20 and over the company of the tribe of Gad was Eliasaph son of Deuel.

21 Then the Kohathites, who carried the holy things, set out; and the tabernacle was set up before their arrival. 22 Next the standard of the Ephraimite camp set out, company by company, and over the whole company was Elishama son of Ammihud. 23 Over the company of the tribe of Manasseh was Gamaliel son of Pedahzur, 24 and over the company of the tribe of Benjamin was Abidan son of Gideoni.

25 Then the standard of the camp of Dan, acting as the rear guard of all the camps, set out, company by company, and over the whole company was Ahiezer son of Ammishaddai. 26 Over the company of the tribe of Asher was Pagiel son of Ochran, 27 and over the company of the tribe of Naphtali was Ahira son of Enan. 28 This was the order of march of the Israelites, company by company, when they set out.

29 Moses said to Hobab son of Reuel the Midianite, Moses' father-in-law, "We are setting out for the place of which the LORD said, 'I will give it to you'; come with us, and we will treat you well; for the LORD has promised good to Israel." 30 But he said to him, "I will not go, but I will go back to my own land and to my kindred." 31 He said, "Do not leave us, for you know where we should camp in the wilderness, and you will serve as eyes for us. 32 Moreover, if you go with us, whatever good the LORD does for us, the same we will do for you."

33 So they set out from the mount of the LORD three days' journey with the ark of the covenant of the LORD going before them three days' journey, to seek out a resting place for them, 34 the cloud of the LORD being over them by day when they set out from the camp.

[35] Whenever the ark set out, Moses would say,

"Arise, O LORD, let your enemies
        be scattered,
    and your foes flee before you."
36 And whenever it came to rest, he would say,

"Return, O LORD of the ten
        thousand thousands of
        Israel." *t*

Complaining in the Desert

11 Now when the people complained in the hearing of the LORD about their misfortunes, the LORD heard it and his anger was kindled. Then

t Meaning of Heb uncertain

---

up again when the people camped (see 10.21). The descendants of Aaron pack up the most sacred items of the tabernacle structure for the Kohathites to carry (v. 21 here; 3.31–32; 4.5–20), and the dismantling of the rest is perhaps implied in 4.27–28, 32b–33. For the items that the Gershonites and Merarites transport, see 3.25–26, 36–37; 4.24–26, 31–32a. **10.21** See 10.17. **10.25** *Rear guard*, lit. "gatherer"; see also Josh 6.9, 13; Isa 52.12. **10.29–36** At this point old epic materials return, interrupting the so-called priestly materials (see Introduction) that have been the source of the narrative since Ex 35. **10.29–32** *Hobab son of Reuel the Midianite, Moses' father-in-law* is persuaded to accompany the people on their march. Elsewhere called Jethro (Ex 3.1; 4.18; 18.1–12) or even Reuel (Ex 2.18), Hobab is mentioned again in Judg 4.11 and in the Septuagint in Judg 1.16. Moses is frequently associated with Midianites or with the related Kenites, and his father-in-law is a priest of the Lord (Ex 2.16) even before Moses' encounter with the deity at the burning bush (Ex 3). Moses' and Israel's relations with Midianites or Kenites are sometimes described positively (Ex 2.11–22; 3.1–6; 4.18–20; 18; Judg 1.16; 4.11; 1 Sam 15.6; 27.8–12; 30.26–31), but sometimes a tradition of animosity against Midian is evident (Num 22.4, 7; 25; 31; Josh 13.21–23; Judg 6–8; Ps 83.9; Isa 9.4; 10.26). **10.33–34** *Mount of the LORD.* See Deut 1.6. For the *cloud* that was over the people by day, see 9.15–23. That the ark went before them *three days' journey* makes little sense; the temporal phrase is perhaps repeated mistakenly from earlier in the verse. Cf. Josh 3.1–4. **10.35–36** Two very short pieces that appear to be ancient battle cries. *"Arise, O LORD"* and *"Return, O LORD"* imply that the ark represents the presence of the Lord among the people (see 7.89; 14.44; Ex 25.10–22; 1 Sam 4.1–7.2; 2 Sam 6.1–19; 2 Chr 6.41; Pss 68.1; 132.8). In Hebrew manuscripts, this two-verse portion is set off by an inverted Hebrew letter *nun* at the beginning and end, indicating that ancient Jewish tradition considered these verses special in some way and took pains to mark them as such.

the fire of the LORD burned against them, and consumed some outlying parts of the camp. 2 But the people cried out to Moses; and Moses prayed to the LORD, and the fire abated. 3 So that place was called Taberah,u because the fire of the LORD burned against them.

4 The rabble among them had a strong craving; and the Israelites also wept again, and said, "If only we had meat to eat! 5 We remember the fish we used to eat in Egypt for nothing, the cucumbers, the melons, the leeks, the onions, and the garlic; 6 but now our strength is dried up, and there is nothing at all but this manna to look at."

7 Now the manna was like coriander seed, and its color was like the color of gum resin. 8 The people went around and gathered it, ground it in mills or beat it in mortars, then boiled it in pots and made cakes of it; and the taste of it was like the taste of cakes baked with oil. 9 When the dew fell on the camp in the night, the manna would fall with it.

10 Moses heard the people weeping throughout their families, all at the entrances of their tents. Then the LORD became very angry, and Moses was displeased. 11 So Moses said to the LORD, "Why have you treated your servant so badly? Why have I not found favor in your sight, that you lay the burden of all this people on me? 12 Did I conceive all this people? Did I give birth to them, that you should say to me, 'Carry them in your bosom, as a nurse carries a sucking child,' to the land that you promised on oath to their ancestors? 13 Where am I to get meat to give to all this people? For they come weeping to me and say, 'Give us meat to eat!' 14 I am not able to carry all this peo-

u That is Burning

11.1–35 The stories in ch. 11 appear to be a doublet of the set of incidents in Ex 15.22–16.36. In each case there is a three-day march (Ex 15.22; Num 10.33), a set of complaints (Ex 15.24; 16.2–3; Num 11.1, 4, 10), and the provision of manna and quails for the people to eat (Ex 16.4, 13–15, 31–36; Num 11.7–9, 31–32). **11.1–3** A schematic story of complaint. This is the first appearance in Numbers of the common motif of the people's complaining because of the hardship of their life in the desert. They long for the settled life of Egypt and regret that they left what was familiar to make the dangerous trek through the unknown. Typically they complain and are punished by the Lord. In some of the stories, Moses intercedes with the Lord on behalf of the people, and in some the name of the place where the complaining happens is etymologized with reference to some incident or element within the story. Such stories begin in Ex 14.10; 15.24; 16.2; 17.2; (32.1); Num 11.1; 11.4; 14.1; 16.41; 20.3; and 21.4. (See also Pss 78.15–31; 106.13–15.) **11.1** The *misfortunes* mentioned here are unspecified. *Fire of the LORD* is probably lightning (see Ex 9.23–24; 19.18; 2 Kings 1.9–14). **11.2** Moses *prayed* for the people, suggesting the prophet's role as intercessor. Complaint stories often include some intercession by Moses; see further in vv. 10–15. **11.3** *Fire of the LORD.* See v. 1. *Taberah*, presumably a place in the wilderness of Paran (see 10.11–12; Deut 9.22; cf. Num 33.16–17). **11.4–9** Another complaint, this time first voiced by the *rabble* (v. 4). **11.4** The word for *rabble*, lit. "a collection," occurs only here and means a mixed group of people, i.e., non-Israelites who were attached to the people (see Ex 12.38; Lev 24.10). This verse is evidence of a tradition that the Israelites did not have animals with them on the march; cf. Ex 10.24–26; 12.32, 38; 17.3; 34.3; Num 14.33; 32.1. **11.5** The foods listed here are typical in Egypt. Note that none is precisely "meat"; in fact, most are vegetables. **11.6–9** *Manna.* See Ex 16.14–21, 31. **11.8** *Cakes baked with oil,* a loose translation (see Ex 16.31); a literal translation would be "cream of oil," perhaps rich or choice cream. **11.10–15** In a very unusual passage, Moses, like the people, complains of his lot and says he would prefer death to a continuation of the current situation. Moses' complaint is that the Lord has not been responsible in caring for the Israelites, even though their situation is a result of the Lord's previous activity and promises; he feels caught in the middle between a complaining throng and an unconcerned deity (see v. 14). Moses' role as intercessor is not unusual (see v. 3; 14.13–19; 16.22; 21.7; see also Abraham in Gen 18.22–32), but in several instances his pleas are rather extended and in some of these, as here, he is surprisingly indignant about his own role (see Ex 17.2–4; 32.11–14, 30–32; 33.12–16; cf. Ex 14.15–18, which seems to be a response to such an outcry, now lost). **11.12** The use of an extra Hebrew pronoun *I* twice lends emphasis to Moses' implication here that it was indeed the Lord who conceived and gave birth to Israel. (It is used again in v. 14.) The female imagery used here of the Lord and of Moses (he has been designated Israel's wet nurse) is unusual, but not unique (see Deut 32.18; also Isa 42.14; 66.13). *Carry them in your bosom,* a wet nurse's activity (see Isa 40.11 for the same image as a description of a shepherd with lambs). **11.14** Cf. Ex 18.17–18.

ple alone, for they are too heavy for me. 15 If this is the way you are going to treat me, put me to death at once—if I have found favor in your sight—and do not let me see my misery."

The Seventy Elders

16 So the LORD said to Moses, "Gather for me seventy of the elders of Israel, whom you know to be the elders of the people and officers over them; bring them to the tent of meeting, and have them take their place there with you. 17 I will come down and talk with you there; and I will take some of the spirit that is on you and put it on them; and they shall bear the burden of the people along with you so that you will not bear it all by yourself. 18 And say to the people: Consecrate yourselves for tomorrow, and you shall eat meat; for you have wailed in the hearing of the LORD, saying, 'If only we had meat to eat! Surely it was better for us in Egypt.' Therefore the LORD will give you meat, and you shall eat. 19 You shall eat not only one day, or two days, or five days, or ten days, or twenty days, 20 but for a whole month—until it comes out of your nostrils and becomes loathsome to you—because you have rejected the LORD who is among you, and have wailed before him, saying, 'Why did we ever leave Egypt?' " 21 But Moses said, "The people I am with number six hundred thousand on foot; and you say, 'I will give them meat, that they may eat for a whole month'! 22 Are there enough flocks and herds to slaughter for them? Are there enough fish in the sea to catch for them?"

23 The LORD said to Moses, "Is the LORD's power limited? v Now you shall see whether my word will come true for you or not."

24 So Moses went out and told the people the words of the LORD; and he gathered seventy elders of the people, and placed them all around the tent. 25 Then the LORD came down in the cloud and spoke to him, and took some of the spirit that was on him and put it on the seventy elders; and when the spirit rested upon them, they prophesied. But they did not do so again.

26 Two men remained in the camp, one named Eldad, and the other named Medad, and the spirit rested on them; they were among those registered, but they had not gone out to the tent, and so they prophesied in the camp. 27 And a young man ran and told Moses, "Eldad and Medad are prophesying in the camp." 28 And Joshua son of Nun, the assistant of Moses, one of his chosen men, w said, "My lord Moses, stop them!" 29 But Moses said to him, "Are you jealous for my sake? Would that all the LORD's people were prophets, and that the LORD would put his spirit on them!" 30 And Moses and the elders of Israel returned to the camp.

The Quails

31 Then a wind went out from the LORD, and it brought quails from the sea and let them fall beside the camp, about a day's journey on this side and a day's journey on the other side, all around the

v Heb LORD's hand too short?   w Or of Moses from his youth

11.15 See Ex 32.32.
    11.16–17 See a similar solution in Ex 18.13–26. 11.16 Seventy of the elders. See also Ex 24.1, 9. In the old epic traditions represented here (see Introduction) the tent of meeting is outside the camp (see vv. 26, 30), as in Ex 33.7–11 (note Joshua's role there also); Num 12.4; 19.1–4; it is pitched quite simply by Moses (Ex 33.7). The tradition that reports the tent outside the camp presents it as the site where anyone can obtain an oracle from the Lord (Ex 33.7) as Miriam and Aaron do in 12.4–9. 11.17 I will come down and talk with you there. See 7.89. Leaders and prophets are commonly perceived to possess a special spirit (see, e.g., 24.2–3; Judg 3.10; Ezek 2.2), and that spirit can be passed to others (Num 11.24–29;

1 Sam 10.5–10; 19.18–24; 2 Kings 2.9–15). 11.18 Consecrate yourselves, implying an upcoming encounter with the divine or the sacred. 11.20 See 14.27; 1 Sam 8.7; 10.19. 11.21 The six hundred thousand on foot are the soldiers (see Ex 12.37; cf. Num 1.46). 11.23 Is the LORD's power limited? See text note v. See Isa 50.2; 59.1 for the same image. 11.24–30 See 11.17. 11.25 The prophesying was a temporary condition and not a permanent occupation. 11.26, 30 The tent of meeting is outside the camp.
    11.31–34 This section returns to the topic of vv. 18–24a; see Ps 105.40. 11.31 Wind provides a verbal connection with the preceding section because "wind" and "spirit" are the same word in Hebrew. Quails. See Ex 16.13. Two cubits, about

camp, about two cubits deep on the ground. 32 So the people worked all that day and night and all the next day, gathering the quails; the least anyone gathered was ten homers; and they spread them out for themselves all around the camp. 33 But while the meat was still between their teeth, before it was consumed, the anger of the LORD was kindled against the people, and the LORD struck the people with a very great plague. 34 So that place was called Kibroth-hattaavah,ˣ because there they buried the people who had the craving. 35 From Kibroth-hattaavah the people journeyed to Hazeroth.

Aaron and Miriam Jealous of Moses

12 While they were at Hazeroth, Miriam and Aaron spoke against Moses because of the Cushite woman whom he had married (for he had indeed married a Cushite woman); 2 and they said, "Has the LORD spoken only through Moses? Has he not spoken through us also?" And the LORD heard it. 3 Now the man Moses was very humble,ʸ more so than anyone else on the face of the earth. 4 Suddenly the LORD said to Moses, Aaron, and Miriam, "Come out, you three, to the tent of meeting." So the three of them came out. 5 Then the LORD came down in a pillar of cloud, and stood at the entrance of the tent, and called Aaron and Miriam; and they both came forward. 6 And he said, "Hear my words:

When there are prophets
    among you,
I the LORD make myself known
    to them in visions;
I speak to them in dreams.
7 Not so with my servant Moses;
    he is entrusted with all my
    house.
8 With him I speak face to face—
    clearly, not in riddles;

---

x That is *Graves of craving*   y Or *devout*

---

one yard. **11.32** Some sources indicate a *homer* is about 6 bushels, others that it is as high as 14 bushels. They *spread out* the quails to dry and preserve them. **11.33** On the Lord's anger resulting in a plague, see Ex 9.15; Lev 26.21; Num 12.9–10; 14.11–12, 36–37; 16.45–46; 21.5–6 (serpents); 25.1–9, 18; Deut 28.15, 27; 1 Sam 4.5–8; 2 Sam 24.10–17; 1 Chr 21.1–17; Jer 14.10–12. **11.34** The mention of *craving* here forms an inclusio with v. 4, in which the rabble had a strong craving. Taken literally, the use of this phrase suggests that only the rabble were affected by the plague. **11.35** The next stage on the journey. *Kibroth-hattaavah.* See 33.16–17; Deut 9.22. *Hazeroth.* See Num 12.1, 16; 33.17–18; Deut 1.1; cf. Num 10.11–12.

12.1 *Hazeroth.* See 11.35. *Miriam and Aaron* are Moses' sister and brother (Ex 4.14; 15.20). *A Cushite woman.* Cush often refers to Ethiopia in the Bible, and the Septuagint translates "Ethiopian" here. There is also a place called Cush in northern Arabia, however, and, given Hab 3.7 where "Cushan" is used in parallel with Midian, it must be the north Arabian Cush that is referred to here. Thus the Cushite woman would be Zipporah, a Midianite (Ex 2.15–21; 3.1; Num 10.29), more specifically a member of the Midianite subgroup the Kenites (Judg 1.16; 4.11). **12.2** In this verse Miriam and Aaron offer a different reason for their speaking against their brother Moses: he should not be considered the only intermediary for Israel since they also have received communications from the Lord (see Ex 4.14–16; 15.20–21;

Mic 6.4). At question here is Moses' unique position as the leader of the people; this passage probably reflects issues of a later day when groups who traced their authority to Moses were involved in a power struggle with groups who traced their authority to Miriam or Aaron. **12.3** This verse, because of its laudatory third-person reference to Moses, was a stumbling block to earlier readers who understood the entire Pentateuch to have been written by Moses himself. **12.4** *Come out ... to the tent.* See 11.16, 26, 30. **12.5** See 9.15–16. **12.6** *Visions* and *dreams* are a valid form of communication from the Lord in Israel (see Joel 2.28; also Gen 15.1; 40–41), but dreams are often distinguished from communications through prophets (Deut 13.1, 3, 5; 1 Sam 28.6, 15; Jer 27.9; 29.8), and sometimes dreams are ranked below a prophet's communications (Jer 23.28). The verbs in this verse are habitual or customary: this is how it is usually done. **12.7** Moses is distinguished from all other prophets, from what is customary (v. 6). The Lord's *house* is Israel (Jer 12.7; Hos 8.1); see also Gen 24.2; 39.4–6; 41.40; and the frequent reference to Israel as "the house of Israel" (as in Ex 16.31; 40.38). **12.8** *Face to face* is not meant to be taken literally here; the literal translation in this verse would be "mouth to mouth." That the Lord spoke to Moses "face to face" perhaps always means simply that they spoke directly, without an intermediary or a medium such as a dream (Ex 33.11; Deut 34.10 [both lit. "face to face"]; Num 14.14; Isa 52.8 [both lit. "eye to eye"]). Moses *beholds the form of the*

and he beholds the form of the LORD. Why then were you not afraid to speak against my servant Moses?" 9 And the anger of the LORD was kindled against them, and he departed.

10 When the cloud went away from over the tent, Miriam had become leprous,z as white as snow. And Aaron turned towards Miriam and saw that she was leprous. 11 Then Aaron said to Moses, "Oh, my lord, do not punish usª for a sin that we have so foolishly committed. 12 Do not let her be like one stillborn, whose flesh is half consumed when it comes out of its mother's womb." 13 And Moses cried to the LORD, "O God, please heal her." 14 But the LORD said to Moses, "If her father had but spit in her face, would she not bear her shame for seven days? Let her be shut out of the camp for seven days, and after that she may be brought in again." 15 So Miriam was shut out of the camp for seven days; and the people did not set out on the march until Miriam had been brought in again. 16 After that the people set out from Hazeroth, and camped in the wilderness of Paran.

Spies Sent into Canaan

13 The LORD said to Moses, 2 "Send men to spy out the land of Canaan, which I am giving to the Israelites; from each of their ancestral tribes you shall send a man, every one a leader among them." 3 So Moses sent them from the wilderness of Paran, according to the command of the LORD, all of them leading men among the Israelites. 4 These were their names: From the tribe of Reuben, Shammua son of Zaccur; 5 from the tribe of Simeon, Shaphat son of Hori; 6 from the tribe of Judah, Caleb son of Jephunneh; 7 from the tribe of Issachar, Igal son of Joseph; 8 from the tribe of Ephraim, Hoshea son of Nun; 9 from the tribe of Benjamin, Palti son of Raphu; 10 from the tribe of Zebulun, Gaddiel son of Sodi; 11 from the tribe of Joseph (that is, from the tribe of Manasseh), Gaddi son of Susi; 12 from the tribe of Dan, Ammiel son of Gemalli; 13 from the tribe of Asher, Sethur son of Michael; 14 from the tribe of Naphtali, Nahbi son of Vophsi; 15 from the tribe of Gad, Geuel son of Machi. 16 These were the names of the men whom Moses sent to spy out the land. And Moses changed the name of Hoshea son of Nun to Joshua.

17 Moses sent them to spy out the land of Canaan, and said to them, "Go up there into the Negeb, and go up into the hill country, 18 and see what the land is like, and whether the people who live in it are strong or weak, whether they are few or many, 19 and whether the land they live in is good or bad, and whether the towns that they live in are unwalled or fortified, 20 and whether the land is rich or poor, and whether there are trees in it or not. Be bold, and bring some of the fruit of

z A term for several skin diseases; precise meaning uncertain　　a Heb do not lay sin upon us

---

LORD, however (see Ex 33.17–23; cf. Deut 4.12, 15, where the people behold no form; Ps 17.15). **12.10** Leprous. See text note z and vv. 13–15. We do not know why Miriam is punished, but not Aaron. Aaron, in v. 11, asks that Moses not punish the two of them, as if he too is suffering or about to suffer. **12.11** Aaron addresses Moses as my lord, ironically acknowledging Moses' superiority in his plea for help. Do not punish us. See 12.10. **12.13** Moses' intercession on behalf of Miriam is typical. See 11.10–15. **12.14** Spit in her face. On spitting as a sign of humiliation, see Deut 25.9; Job 30.10; Isa 50.6. **12.15** See Lev 13.1–17, especially v. 4; 14.1–32, especially v. 8. **12.16** Either this verse means that the people are still in the wilderness of Paran, or else the old epic traditions represented here (see Introduction) do not consider that they enter the wilderness of Paran until they leave Hazeroth.

13.1–3 Like those who helped with the census, 1.4, the men sent to spy out the land for the people at the Lord's command (cf. Deut 1.22–25) are chosen because each is a leader in one of the twelve tribes. The setting is the wilderness of Paran; see 12.16. **13.4–16** The order in which the tribes are listed is similar to that in 1.5–15, but the leaders are not the same. This list of names is not duplicated. **13.6** Elsewhere (32.12; Josh 14.6, 14) Caleb is called a Kenizzite; see Num 14.24. **13.17** Negeb (pronounced "negev"), the generally dry waste country just north of the Sinai Peninsula, south of what is later Judah, and to the west and south of the Dead Sea. The hill country referred to here is either the highlands of the Negeb itself (see 14.40; Deut 1.20) or the highlands of Judah (Judg 1.19), part of the central spine of hills that runs north and south through Canaan. **13.20** The season of the first ripe grapes

the land." Now it was the season of the first ripe grapes.

21 So they went up and spied out the land from the wilderness of Zin to Rehob, near Lebo-hamath. 22 They went up into the Negeb, and came to Hebron; and Ahiman, Sheshai, and Talmai, the Anakites, were there. (Hebron was built seven years before Zoan in Egypt.) 23 And they came to the Wadi Eshcol, and cut down from there a branch with a single cluster of grapes, and they carried it on a pole between two of them. They also brought some pomegranates and figs. 24 That place was called the Wadi Eshcol,*b* because of the cluster that the Israelites cut down from there.

The Report of the Spies

25 At the end of forty days they returned from spying out the land. 26 And they came to Moses and Aaron and to all the congregation of the Israelites in the wilderness of Paran, at Kadesh; they brought back word to them and to all the congregation, and showed them the fruit of the land. 27 And they told him, "We came to the land to which you sent us; it flows with milk and honey, and this is its fruit. 28 Yet the people who live in the land are strong, and the towns are fortified and very large; and besides, we saw the descendants of Anak there. 29 The Amalekites live in the land of the Negeb; the Hittites, the Jebusites, and the Amorites live in the hill country; and the Canaanites live by the sea, and along the Jordan."

30 But Caleb quieted the people be-

b That is *Cluster*

---

in July/August. **13.21–24** Cf. Deut 1.24–25a. **13.21** Another note from the priestly traditions (see Introduction). While the following old epic story (vv. 22–24) locates the reconnoitering entirely in the area of the Negeb and Judah, the priestly traditions state that the spies went from the far southern end of the promised land in the *wilderness of Zin* (see 34.1–4; Josh 15.1–3) to the far northern end at *Rehob* or Beth-rehob, described as near *Lebo-hamath* (lit. "the entrance to Hamath" in southern Syria), often mentioned as part of Israel's northern border (see 34.7–8; Judg 18.27–28; 2 Sam 10.6, 8). **13.22** *Negeb*. See 13.17. *Hebron*, an important city in Judah, especially in the family narratives in Genesis, is about twenty miles south of Jerusalem. The *Anakites* are one of several groups described as the indigenous peoples of Canaan, many of whom are remembered as giants; see vv. 32–33 (see also Gen 6.1–4); Deut 2.9–11, 19–21; 9.1–2; Josh 11.21–22; 14.12–15; 15.13–14; Judg 1.10, 20; see also Gen 14.5; 15.20; Deut 3.11, 13; Josh 12.4–5; 13.12; 17.15; 1 Chr 20.4. *Ahiman, Sheshai, and Talmai*. See Josh 15.14; Judg 1.10. *Zoan in Egypt*, in the eastern Delta (Ex 1.11). **13.23–24** *Wadi Eshcol*, site unknown, is etymologized by being tied to the spies' acquisition of oversized fruit there. In Hebrew an *eshcol* is a cluster of grapes; see text note *b*. *Grapes, pomegranates*, and *figs* do grow in the Hebron area, as well as many other areas of Palestine. **13.25–33** See Deut 1.25b. **13.25** *Forty days* is a stereotyped expression of time in biblical literature; see, e.g., Gen 7.4; Ex 24.18; 1 Sam 17.16; 1 Kings 19.8; Ezek 4.6. **13.26** This is the first mention of the oasis *Kadesh* (Kadesh-barnea; see, e.g., 32.8), where much of the forty years in the wilderness will be spent (including the events in chs. 13–20). According to the priestly traditions (see Introduction), Kadesh is in the wilderness of Zin (20.1); it is placed in the wilderness of Paran in the old epic traditions. Kadesh-barnea was probably one of a group of oases located about fifty miles south of Beer-sheba, one of which is still called "the spring Kadesh." (See Ex 17.7.) **13.27** The spies say the land *flows with milk and honey* in the first use in the book of Numbers of the well-known phrase. See also 14.8; 16.13 (used of Egypt!), 14; Ex 3.8. **13.28** The *descendants of Anak* are the Anakites of v. 22. A common Semitic way of designating the members of a group is to call them "the descendants/children" of an eponymous ancestor or of a typical member of the group: "the children of Israel" are the Israelites; "the sons of the prophets" in 1 Kings 20.35 (see text note *r*), are themselves prophets. **13.29** The *Amalekites* are a perennial enemy of the Israelites (e.g., Gen 14.7; Ex 17.8–16; Judg 3.12–13; 1 Sam 15.1–9) who apparently inhabited the Negeb area where the people are to spend the next forty years. On the *Hittites, Jebusites, Amorites*, and *Canaanites*, see Ex 3.8. The spies' listing of these indigenous peoples divides the land into its constituent parts: the Negeb, the central hill country, the seacoast, and the Jordan Valley. Cf. 14.25, 45, for a slightly different arrangement of peoples. **13.30–31** In this old epic passage (see Introduction) Caleb is the only

---

Map opposite: *The "Land of Canaan" at the end of the second millennium B.C.E., showing possible routes into Canaan from Sinai.*

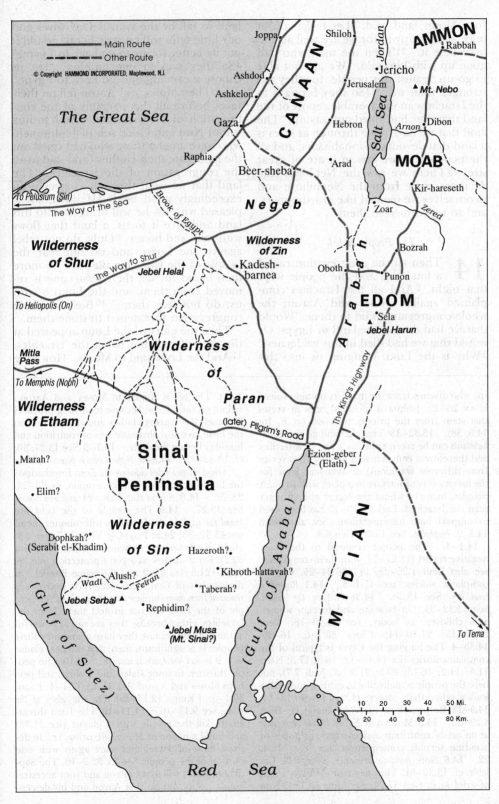

fore Moses, and said, "Let us go up at once and occupy it, for we are well able to overcome it." 31 Then the men who had gone up with him said, "We are not able to go up against this people, for they are stronger than we." 32 So they brought to the Israelites an unfavorable report of the land that they had spied out, saying, "The land that we have gone through as spies is a land that devours its inhabitants; and all the people that we saw in it are of great size. 33 There we saw the Nephilim (the Anakites come from the Nephilim); and to ourselves we seemed like grasshoppers, and so we seemed to them."

The People Rebel

14 Then all the congregation raised a loud cry, and the people wept that night. 2 And all the Israelites complained against Moses and Aaron; the whole congregation said to them, "Would that we had died in the land of Egypt! Or would that we had died in this wilderness! 3 Why is the LORD bringing us into this land to fall by the sword? Our wives and our little ones will become booty; would it not be better for us to go back to Egypt?" 4 So they said to one another, "Let us choose a captain, and go back to Egypt."

5 Then Moses and Aaron fell on their faces before all the assembly of the congregation of the Israelites. 6 And Joshua son of Nun and Caleb son of Jephunneh, who were among those who had spied out the land, tore their clothes 7 and said to all the congregation of the Israelites, "The land that we went through as spies is an exceedingly good land. 8 If the LORD is pleased with us, he will bring us into this land and give it to us, a land that flows with milk and honey. 9 Only, do not rebel against the LORD; and do not fear the people of the land, for they are no more than bread for us; their protection is removed from them, and the LORD is with us; do not fear them." 10 But the whole congregation threatened to stone them.

Then the glory of the LORD appeared at the tent of meeting to all the Israelites. 11 And the LORD said to Moses, "How long

spy who dissents from the majority opinion voiced in vv. 28–29. Joshua is included only in verses that stem from the priestly tradition (vv. 8, 16; 14.6, 38). **13.32–33** That the land *devours its inhabitants* can be taken either as a sign of infertility and therefore a contradiction of v. 27 (two verses from different traditions) or as a metaphor for the inevitability of warfare in a place with so many peoples, many of whom are bigger and stronger than the Israelites. Ezek 36.13–15 has been used to support both interpretations. See also Num 14.3, 9. *Nephilim.* See 13.22; Gen 6.4. **14.1–4** The people respond to the spies' negative report (13.27–33) with their complaints; see also Deut 1.26–28; Ps 106.24–25. On the complaint stories, see 11.1–3. **14.1** *Raised a loud cry.* See 13.30. **14.3a** *Fall by the sword.* See 13.32–33. On Israelite and foreign women and children as booty, see 31.13–18; Deut 20.10–15; 21.10–14; 1 Sam 30.1–6, 16–20. **14.3b–4** The longing for Egypt is typical of the complaint stories (Ex 14.10–12; 16.3; 17.3; Num 11.5; 14.2; 16.13; 20.5; 21.5; cf. Josh 7.7), but here the people actually plot to return, and with a leader other than Moses; cf. ch. 12; 16.12–14. **14.5–12** Responses to the complaints; cf. Deut 1.29–33. **14.5** Moses and Aaron *fell on their faces* as an act of contrition and entreaty, in hopes of avoiding terrible consequences; see, e.g., 16.4, 22. **14.6** Note *Joshua*'s presence along with Caleb's; cf. 13.30–31. They *tore their clothes* as a sign of grief (e.g., Gen 37.29, 34; Judg 11.35; 2 Sam

1.11). The act is similar to Moses' and Aaron's falling on their faces, because mourning practices in Israel, like tearing clothes and putting dirt on the head, are also obviously acts of contrition and humility before the deity. **14.7–9** See 13.27, 30; cf. 13.32–33. **14.8–9** *If the LORD is pleased with us . . . Only, do not rebel against the LORD* foreshadows the Lord's rejection of this generation, vv. 20–24, 28–35. **14.8** *A land that flows with milk and honey.* See 13.27. **14.9** The people of the land are *bread for us,* i.e., the Israelites will conquer them; see 13.32–33; 24.8; Pss 14.4; 53.4; 79.7; Jer 2.3; 10.25. *Protection,* lit. "shadow" (Judg 9.15; Isa 32.2). For a shadow as a god's protection, see Pss 91.1; 121.5; Isa 25.4; and the name Bezalel, "in the shadow of God," Ex 31.2. *Their protection is removed from them* implies that the gods of the people of the land will not protect them from the Israelites, either because they are not as powerful as the Lord or because they have abandoned their people. It is significant, then, that the next clause in v. 9 is *and the LORD is with us.* **14.10** The people threaten to stone Caleb and Joshua, and perhaps Moses and Aaron also (cf. Ex 17.1–4; 1 Sam 30.1–6; 1 Kings 12.17–18). On the *glory of the LORD,* see 9.15–16. **14.11–12** The Lord threatens to kill the people with a plague (see 11.33) and build a nation of Moses' offspring, i.e., to destroy most of Israel and start again with one portion of the people. See Ex 32.9–10. The Septuagint has "I will make of you and your ancestral house . . ." (v. 12), so that Aaron and his descen-

will this people despise me? And how long will they refuse to believe in me, in spite of all the signs that I have done among them? 12 I will strike them with pestilence and disinherit them, and I will make of you a nation greater and mightier than they."

Moses Intercedes for the People

13 But Moses said to the LORD, "Then the Egyptians will hear of it, for in your might you brought up this people from among them, 14 and they will tell the inhabitants of this land. They have heard that you, O LORD, are in the midst of this people; for you, O LORD, are seen face to face, and your cloud stands over them and you go in front of them, in a pillar of cloud by day and in a pillar of fire by night. 15 Now if you kill this people all at one time, then the nations who have heard about you will say, 16 'It is because the LORD was not able to bring this people into the land he swore to give them that he has slaughtered them in the wilderness.' 17 And now, therefore, let the power of the LORD be great in the way that you promised when you spoke, saying,

18   'The LORD is slow to anger,
    and abounding in steadfast love,
    forgiving iniquity and
        transgression,
    but by no means clearing the
        guilty,

visiting the iniquity of the parents
    upon the children
to the third and the fourth
    generation.'
19 Forgive the iniquity of this people according to the greatness of your steadfast love, just as you have pardoned this people, from Egypt even until now."

20   Then the LORD said, "I do forgive, just as you have asked; 21 nevertheless — as I live, and as all the earth shall be filled with the glory of the LORD — 22 none of the people who have seen my glory and the signs that I did in Egypt and in the wilderness, and yet have tested me these ten times and have not obeyed my voice, 23 shall see the land that I swore to give to their ancestors; none of those who despised me shall see it. 24 But my servant Caleb, because he has a different spirit and has followed me wholeheartedly, I will bring into the land into which he went, and his descendants shall possess it. 25 Now, since the Amalekites and the Canaanites live in the valleys, turn tomorrow and set out for the wilderness by the way to the Red Sea."[c]

An Attempted Invasion Is Repulsed

26   And the LORD spoke to Moses and to Aaron, saying: 27 How long shall this wicked congregation complain against

c Or Sea of Reeds

---

dants are also included in the promise. After Moses' intercession, the Lord's threat will be tempered so that, although this generation of Israel will not see the promised land (vv. 20–24, 28–35), Israel will not be entirely destroyed. **14.13–19** Moses argues that the Lord should not destroy Israel, for the Egyptians and the people of Canaan will assume it was the Lord's failure to settle the people in the land that forced the annihilation (see Deut 32.26–27; Josh 7.6–9; Ezek 20.8–9; 36.18–32; 39.21–29); furthermore, the Lord has promised (Ex 34.6–7) to "forgive iniquity" and Moses urges the Lord to do so in this instance. This is not the first time Moses has interceded for the people; see Num 11.10–15. **14.14** Face to face, lit. "eye to eye"; see 12.8. Your cloud. See 9.15–16. Pillar of cloud, pillar of fire. See 12.5. **14.18** Abbreviated from Ex 34.6–7. **14.20–25** The Lord's response to Moses' intercession; cf. Deut 1.34–36. The Lord replies that he will acquiesce to Moses' wishes and not exterminate Israel, but none of the Israelites who rebelled will be allowed to see the promised land;

see also vv. 28–35; 26.64–65; 32.10–12. Only Caleb is exempt (Deut 1.35 also, but see Num 14.30; 32.12). **14.21** As I live, a typical oath formula. Although people usually swear on the life of the Lord or a ruler (e.g., Gen 42.15–16; Ruth 3.13; 1 Sam 14.39, 45; 25.26, 34; 28.10; 2 Sam 15.21), the Lord must swear "on my life" (e.g., Gen 22.16; Num 14.28; Isa 49.18). **14.22** Ten times, i.e., frequently (see, e.g., Gen 31.7, 41). **14.23** The Septuagint has here that their innocent children will be given the land, as in v. 31; Deut 1.39. **14.24** On Caleb alone, see 13.30–31. Caleb's inheriting of a portion of the land, foretold here, is reported in Josh 14.6–14. Commentators have long suggested that Caleb represents a family group rather than an individual (perhaps the "dog clan" since the name Caleb means "dog"), one that eventually joined with the tribe of Judah. **14.25** In the valleys. Cf. 13.29; 14.45. Turn, i.e., turn back, because this generation is not to move forward but to remain in the wilderness. By the way to the Red Sea, see text note c. The Hebrew is "Sea of Reeds"; see Ex 10.19.

me? I have heard the complaints of the Israelites, which they complain against me. 28 Say to them, "As I live," says the LORD, "I will do to you the very things I heard you say: 29 your dead bodies shall fall in this very wilderness; and of all your number, included in the census, from twenty years old and upward, who have complained against me, 30 not one of you shall come into the land in which I swore to settle you, except Caleb son of Jephunneh and Joshua son of Nun. 31 But your little ones, who you said would become booty, I will bring in, and they shall know the land that you have despised. 32 But as for you, your dead bodies shall fall in this wilderness. 33 And your children shall be shepherds in the wilderness for forty years, and shall suffer for your faithlessness, until the last of your dead bodies lies in the wilderness. 34 According to the number of the days in which you spied out the land, forty days, for every day a year, you shall bear your iniquity, forty years, and you shall know my displeasure." 35 I the LORD have spoken; surely I will do thus to all this wicked congregation gathered together against me: in this wilderness they shall come to a full end, and there they shall die.

36 And the men whom Moses sent to spy out the land, who returned and made all the congregation complain against him by bringing a bad report about the land — 37 the men who brought an unfavorable report about the land died by a plague before the LORD. 38 But Joshua son of Nun and Caleb son of Jephunneh alone remained alive, of those men who went to spy out the land.

39 When Moses told these words to all the Israelites, the people mourned greatly. 40 They rose early in the morning and went up to the heights of the hill country, saying, "Here we are. We will go up to the place that the LORD has promised, for we have sinned." 41 But Moses said, "Why do you continue to transgress the command of the LORD? That will not succeed. 42 Do not go up, for the LORD is not with you; do not let yourselves be struck down before your enemies. 43 For the Amalekites and the Canaanites will confront you there, and you shall fall by the sword; because you have turned back from following the LORD, the LORD will not be with you." 44 But they presumed to go up to the heights of the hill country, even though the ark of the covenant of the LORD, and Moses, had not left the camp. 45 Then the Amalekites and the Canaanites who lived in that hill country

---

14.26–35 Continuation of the Lord's response. Cf. Deut 1.37–40 (although nothing in Num 14.26–35 corresponds to Deut 1.37); Ps 106.26–27. **14.27** They *complain against me.* See 11.20. **14.28–35** Their punishment corresponds to the Israelites' fears. **14.28** *As I live.* See 14.21. **14.29** *Your dead bodies shall fall in this very wilderness.* The immediate referent is v. 2. *Included in the census,* lit. "your enrolled ones," in the census in ch. 1. Note that this leaves ambiguous the fate of the Levites, who were not counted in the census in ch. 1; see 1.49; 3.15. There were also no Levites represented among the spies. Moreover, Aaron's son Eleazar, surely twenty years old by now (see 3.32; 4.16), does enter the land (e.g., Josh 14.1; 17.4; 24.33). **14.30** *I swore,* lit. "I raised my hand"; see also Gen 14.22; Ex 6.8; Ps 106.26. On the inclusion of Joshua, see 13.30–31. **14.31a** On children as booty, see 14.3. **14.33** *Forty years* is a typical biblical expression for one generation (see Gen 25.20; 26.34). **14.34** *Forty days, for every day a year.* See 13.25. See the similar phrase in Ezek 4.6. The tradition that Israel spent forty years in the wilderness is reported also in the early prophets (Am 2.10; 5.25; see also Hos 2.14–15), although there is no sense in these passages that the wilderness sojourn is a punishment; cf. Ps 95.10. **14.36–38** The spies, except for Joshua and Caleb, are killed by the Lord. **14.36** See 13.32; 14.1–4. **14.37** *Plague.* See 11.33. The Hebrew word used here simply means some form of death, lit. "a smiting." **14.38** On *Joshua* and *Caleb,* see 13.30–31. **14.39–45** An abortive attempt to enter the land from the south; cf. Deut 1.41–45. **14.39–40** The people change their minds when they hear their punishment. **14.40** *They rose early in the morning.* Cf. "tomorrow" in v. 25. **14.41** Moses explains that it is no better to go when the Lord has commanded them to turn back (v. 25) than it was to refuse to go when the Lord commanded them to go. **14.42–43** Moses says that the Lord will not be with them in this venture. Cf. v. 9 and see also v. 44; in Deut 1.42 it is the Lord who says this. **14.43, 45** *Amalekites, Canaanites.* See 14.25. On the enmity between Israelites and Amalekites, see 13.29 (cf. Deut 1.44: "Amorites"). *Fall by the sword.* See 14.3, 28–35. **14.44** This verse makes clear what it means that the Lord will not be with the people: the ark will not go up with them; see 7.89; 10.35–36. **14.45** *Hormah,* in the extreme south of Israel's possessions; see 21.1–3

came down and defeated them, pursuing them as far as Hormah.

Various Offerings

15 The LORD spoke to Moses, saying: 2Speak to the Israelites and say to them: When you come into the land you are to inhabit, which I am giving you, 3and you make an offering by fire to the LORD from the herd or from the flock—whether a burnt offering or a sacrifice, to fulfill a vow or as a freewill offering or at your appointed festivals—to make a pleasing odor for the LORD, 4then whoever presents such an offering to the LORD shall present also a grain offering, one-tenth of an ephah of choice flour, mixed with one-fourth of a hin of oil. 5Moreover, you shall offer one-fourth of a hin of wine as a drink offering with the burnt offering or the sacrifice, for each lamb. 6For a ram, you shall offer a grain offering, two-tenths of an ephah of choice flour mixed with one-third of a hin of oil; 7and as a drink offering you shall offer one-third of a hin of wine, a pleasing odor to the LORD. 8When you offer a bull as a burnt offering or a sacrifice, to fulfill a vow or as an offering of well-being to the LORD, 9then you shall present with the bull a grain offering, three-tenths of an ephah of choice flour, mixed with half a hin of oil, 10and you shall present as a drink offering half a hin of wine, as an offering by fire, a pleasing odor to the LORD.

11 Thus it shall be done for each ox or ram, or for each of the male lambs or the kids. 12According to the number that you offer, so you shall do with each and every one. 13Every native Israelite shall do these things in this way, in presenting an offering by fire, a pleasing odor to the LORD. 14An alien who lives with you, or who takes up permanent residence among you, and wishes to offer an offering by fire, a pleasing odor to the LORD, shall do as you do. 15As for the assembly, there shall be for both you and the resident alien a single statute, a perpetual statute throughout your generations; you and the alien shall be alike before the LORD. 16You and the alien who resides with you shall have the same law and the same ordinance.

17 The LORD spoke to Moses, saying: 18Speak to the Israelites and say to them: After you come into the land to which I am bringing you, 19whenever you eat of the bread of the land, you shall present a donation to the LORD. 20From your first batch of dough you shall present a loaf as a donation; you shall present it just as you present a donation from the threshing floor. 21Throughout your generations you shall give to the LORD a donation from the first of your batch of dough.

22 But if you unintentionally fail to observe all these commandments that the LORD has spoken to Moses— 23every-

---

(where the name is etymologized as "destruction"); Judg 1.16–17 (with the same etymology); 1 Sam 30.26–31. In Deut 1.44 it is associated with Seir, i.e., Edom. **15.1–16** These verses prescribe grain and drink offerings to go along with burnt offerings and offerings of well-being. Cf. Ezek 46.4–15; see also Num 28–29; Ex 29.38–42. **15.2** *When you come into the land.* The prescribed offerings reflect a settled agricultural life. There is irony in this verse: this generation will not, in fact, "come into the land"; see 14.20–24, 28–35. **15.3** *An offering by fire* perhaps is not specifically a fire offering, but simply any offering, cognate to a word for "gift" in the language of the ancient city of Ugarit. *From the herd or from the flock,* i.e., domestic animals, not wild, are used for sacrifice. On various offerings, see 6.14–17. *Sacrifice,* here the equivalent of an offering of well-being, i.e., an offering in which the worshiper participates. Lev 7.11–18 describes the three kinds of offerings of

well-being: thanksgiving, votive, and freewill, two of which are named in Num 15.3 as well. *A pleasing odor for the LORD* describes an acceptable offering; see Gen 8.20–22. **15.4** *Ephah.* See 5.15 (note the grain offering mixed with oil). A *hin* was approximately 12 pints. **15.5** *For each lamb.* See v. 11 where both lambs and goats are included. **15.6–10** The amounts of the accompanying grain and drink offerings increase with the size of the animal offered. **15.11–16** The same rules apply to resident *aliens* as to Israelites; see 9.14; also 15.26, 29. **15.16** See also Ex 12.43–49; cf. Deut 14.21. **15.19** A *donation* is simply an offering dedicated to the Lord, in this case for the priests. **15.20** An offering from the *first batch of dough* is like a first-fruits offering; see Neh 10.36–37; Ezek 44.30; see also Ex 22.29a; 23.19a; 34.26a; Lev 23.9–14; Num 18.13–18; Deut 26.1–11. *A donation from the threshing floor.* See 18.27. **15.22–29** Atonement for unintentional sins; see also Lev 4–5. **15.22** *You* here is plural

thing that the LORD has commanded you by Moses, from the day the LORD gave commandment and thereafter, throughout your generations— 24 then if it was done unintentionally without the knowledge of the congregation, the whole congregation shall offer one young bull for a burnt offering, a pleasing odor to the LORD, together with its grain offering and its drink offering, according to the ordinance, and one male goat for a sin offering. 25 The priest shall make atonement for all the congregation of the Israelites, and they shall be forgiven; it was unintentional, and they have brought their offering, an offering by fire to the LORD, and their sin offering before the LORD, for their error. 26 All the congregation of the Israelites shall be forgiven, as well as the aliens residing among them, because the whole people was involved in the error.

27 An individual who sins unintentionally shall present a female goat a year old for a sin offering. 28 And the priest shall make atonement before the LORD for the one who commits an error, when it is unintentional, to make atonement for the person, who then shall be forgiven. 29 For both the native among the Israelites and the alien residing among them—you shall have the same law for anyone who acts in error. 30 But whoever acts highhandedly, whether a native or an alien, affronts the LORD, and shall be cut off from among the people. 31 Because of having despised the word of the LORD and broken his commandment, such a person shall be utterly cut off and bear the guilt.

Penalty for Violating the Sabbath

32 When the Israelites were in the wilderness, they found a man gathering sticks on the sabbath day. 33 Those who found him gathering sticks brought him to Moses, Aaron, and to the whole congregation. 34 They put him in custody, because it was not clear what should be done to him. 35 Then the LORD said to Moses, "The man shall be put to death; all the congregation shall stone him outside the camp." 36 The whole congregation brought him outside the camp and stoned him to death, just as the LORD had commanded Moses.

Fringes on Garments

37 The LORD said to Moses: 38 Speak to the Israelites, and tell them to make fringes on the corners of their garments throughout their generations and to put a blue cord on the fringe at each corner. 39 You have the fringe so that, when you see it, you will remember all the commandments of the LORD and do them, and not follow the lust of your own heart and your own eyes. 40 So you shall remember and do all my commandments, and you shall be holy to your God. 41 I am the LORD your God, who brought you out of the land of Egypt, to be your God: I am the LORD your God.

The Revolt of Korah, Dathan, and Abiram

16 Now Korah son of Izhar son of Kohath son of Levi, along with Dathan and Abiram sons of Eliab, and On son of Peleth—descendants of Reuben—

---

in Hebrew. **15.24** *According to the ordinance,* i.e., vv. 1–16. **15.25** It is the priest who makes *atonement* for the ones who are in error; see Ex 29.10–37; Lev 1.4; Num 8.10–11. *An offering by fire.* See 15.3. **15.28** See 15.25. **15.30–31** Intentional sins. One who *acts high-handedly* sins boldly; see the translation "boldly" for "highhandedly" in 33.3; Ex 14.8. *Cut off.* See 9.13. Here execution is plainly meant; see 15.35–36, especially "just as" in v. 36. **15.32–36** See the similar story in Lev 24.10–23. Intentional violation of the sabbath carries the death penalty (Ex 31.14–15; 35.2). **15.34** *They put him in custody* until a decision was made; see also Lev 24.12. **15.35–36** The man was stoned outside the camp so as not to disturb the sanctity of the camp; see also Lev 24.14, 23; 1 Kings 21.10, 23–24.

15.37–41 *Fringes on ... garments.* Cf. Deut 22.12. **15.38** The fringes apparently resembled locks of hair; see the translation "lock (of hair)" for the same word in Ezek 8.3. Fringe on garments is known elsewhere in the ancient Near East from pictorial representations. Fringes are still worn on the prayer shawl or *tallit* of Orthodox Jewish men. *Blue* or violet, the same color as some of the hangings of the tabernacle enclosure; see 4.5–12. **15.41** For variations on the formulaic sayings in this verse, see, e.g., Ex 6.6–7; 20.2; Lev 26.13; Deut 5.6; cf. Gen 15.7.

16.1–40 In this section on the revolt of Korah, Dathan, and Abiram, there is some mixing of traditions: the complaints are against Moses or Aaron or both; the complaints are about secular or sacred leadership; either Levites or Reubenites,

took ²two hundred fifty Israelite men, leaders of the congregation, chosen from the assembly, well-known men,*d* and they confronted Moses. ³They assembled against Moses and against Aaron, and said to them, "You have gone too far! All the congregation are holy, every one of them, and the LORD is among them. So why then do you exalt yourselves above the assembly of the LORD?" ⁴When Moses heard it, he fell on his face. ⁵Then he said to Korah and all his company, "In the morning the LORD will make known who is his, and who is holy, and who will be allowed to approach him; the one whom he will choose he will allow to approach him. ⁶Do this: take censers, Korah and all your*e* company, ⁷and tomorrow put fire in them, and lay incense on them before the LORD; and the man whom the LORD chooses shall be the holy one. You Levites have gone too far!" ⁸Then Moses said to Korah, "Hear now, you Levites! ⁹Is it too little for you that the God of Israel has separated you from the congregation of Israel, to allow you to approach him in order to perform the duties of the LORD's tabernacle, and to stand before the congregation and serve them? ¹⁰He has allowed you to approach him, and all your brother Levites with you; yet you seek the priesthood as well! ¹¹Therefore you and all your company have gathered together against the LORD. What is Aaron that you rail against him?"

12   Moses sent for Dathan and Abiram sons of Eliab; but they said, "We will not come! ¹³Is it too little that you have brought us up out of a land flowing with milk and honey to kill us in the wilderness, that you must also lord it over us? ¹⁴It is clear you have not brought us into a land flowing with milk and honey, or given us an inheritance of fields and vineyards. Would you put out the eyes of these men? We will not come!"

15   Moses was very angry and said to the LORD, "Pay no attention to their offering. I have not taken one donkey from

d Cn: Heb *and they confronted Moses, and two hundred fifty men . . . well-known men*   *e* Heb *his*

---

or even the whole community are the rebels; the rebels are swallowed whole or are burned by fire from the Lord. Commentators have divided these stories into two major strands (with subplots within them): a priestly strand with the story of Korah's rebellion and an old epic strand with a secular rebellion led by Reubenites (see Introduction). The two strands are combined by vv. 1, 24, 27a, 32b. Cf. Deut 11.6; Ps 106.16–18.   **16.1** For *Korah*'s genealogy, see Ex 6.16–21. See also the titles to Pss 42; 44–49; 84–85; 87–88. Korah is apparently the eponymous ancestor of a group of temple singers (1 Chr 6.16–38).   **16.2** *Well-known men*, lit. "men of name." A similar phrase is used in Gen 6.4, there translated "warriors of renown"; 1 Chr 5.24; 12.30. In Job 30.8, the "disreputable brood" are "those without name" in Hebrew.   **16.3** There are actually two levels of priestly conflict in this Korah narrative: in one level, Korah argues that *all the congregation are holy, every one of them, and the LORD is among them*, thus denying any prerogatives the descendants of Levi might have, whether Aaronite priests or Levites. (See 5.3; 15.40; Ex 19.5–6; Deut 7.6; 14.2, 21a; 28.9; Isa 61.6). In this level, we assume Korah and his followers are not Levites (see 27.1–3, where a Manassite's family feel they must defend their father against any suspicion that he was part of Korah's group) and that the censer test is a matter of non-Levitical people using censers, something that had been a prerogative of the Levites. On a second level, however, Korah's group is addressed as Levites attempting to usurp the prerogatives of the Aaronite priesthood (vv. 1, 7b, 8–11), and the test is one of lesser-ranked Levites using the censers of the Aaronite priesthood (see v. 40; 1 Chr 6.49; 2 Chr 26.16–21). With Korah's complaint here, cf. 12.1–2. *Exalt yourselves.* See 16.13; cf. Ex 2.14.   **16.4** *Fell on his face.* See 14.5; 16.22, 45; 20.6.   **16.5** *Who will be allowed to approach him*, i.e., who will be allowed to approach the altar.   **16.6–7** The *censers* were apparently trays that would hold coals onto which incense could be placed (see Ex 25.38; 27.3; 37.23; 38.3; Lev 10.1–2; 16.12). *Before the LORD*, at the entrance to the tent of meeting; see vv. 18–19. **16.9** On the Levites' prescribed *duties*, see 1.47–54; 3; 4; 8.   **16.10** *You seek the priesthood as well!* See 3.5–10; 8.5–22, especially vv. 19, 22. **16.11** *What is Aaron that you rail against him?* Cf. Ex 16.8.   **16.12–14** The Reubenites' complaint. It is logical that Reubenites should lead a civil revolt since they had once been the preeminent tribe; see Gen 35.22–26; 49.3–4.   **16.13–14** This is a typical complaint narrative; see 11.1–3. Here it is Moses' leadership on the march that is in question.   **16.13** *A land flowing with milk and honey,* here used anomalously of Egypt instead of Canaan; see 13.27. *Lord it over us.* See 16.3; Ex 2.14.   **16.14** *Put out the eyes,* i.e., deceive them. Cf. the modern phrase "pull the wool over the eyes."   **16.15** *Pay no attention to their offering,* a metaphor for withholding favor; see the rejection

them, and I have not harmed any one of them." 16 And Moses said to Korah, "As for you and all your company, be present tomorrow before the LORD, you and they and Aaron; 17 and let each one of you take his censer, and put incense on it, and each one of you present his censer before the LORD, two hundred fifty censers; you also, and Aaron, each his censer." 18 So each man took his censer, and they put fire in the censers and laid incense on them, and they stood at the entrance of the tent of meeting with Moses and Aaron. 19 Then Korah assembled the whole congregation against them at the entrance of the tent of meeting. And the glory of the LORD appeared to the whole congregation.

20   Then the LORD spoke to Moses and to Aaron, saying: 21 Separate yourselves from this congregation, so that I may consume them in a moment. 22 They fell on their faces, and said, "O God, the God of the spirits of all flesh, shall one person sin and you become angry with the whole congregation?"

23   And the LORD spoke to Moses, saying: 24 Say to the congregation: Get away from the dwellings of Korah, Dathan, and Abiram. 25 So Moses got up and went to Dathan and Abiram; the elders of Israel followed him. 26 He said to the congregation, "Turn away from the tents of these wicked men, and touch nothing of theirs, or you will be swept away for all their sins." 27 So they got away from the dwellings of Korah, Dathan, and Abiram; and Dathan and Abiram came out and stood at the entrance of their tents, together with their wives, their children, and their little ones. 28 And Moses said, "This is how you shall know that the LORD has sent me to do all these works; it has not been of my own accord: 29 If these people die a natural death, or if a natural fate comes on them, then the LORD has not sent me. 30 But if the LORD creates something new, and the ground opens its mouth and swallows them up, with all that belongs to them, and they go down alive into Sheol, then you shall know that these men have despised the LORD."

31   As soon as he finished speaking all these words, the ground under them was split apart. 32 The earth opened its mouth and swallowed them up, along with their households—everyone who belonged to Korah and all their goods. 33 So they with all that belonged to them went down alive

---

of Cain in Gen 4. *I have not taken one donkey from them.* Cf. 1 Sam 12.1–5. **16.16–17** These verses repeat the information in vv. 6–7, but the addition of Aaron moves the story from the level of congregation vs. Levites to Levites vs. Aaronite priests; see 16.3. **16.16** *Before the LORD,* i.e., at the entrance to the tent of meeting; see vv. 18–19. **16.19** *The glory of the LORD appeared.* See 9.15–16. **16.21** The Lord threatens to *consume* the congregation; see also 16.45; 14.11–12. *In a moment.* This generation will die in the desert, 14.28–30, but here the Lord threatens to kill them immediately. **16.22** *Fell on their faces,* see 16.4; 14.5. *The God of the spirits of all flesh* is used elsewhere only in 27.16. But the Hebrew word for "spirit" also means "breath," and the Lord is frequently described as the giver and taker of human breath. See Gen 2.7 (with a different Hebrew word for "breath"); Isa 42.5. *Shall one person sin.* Dathan and Abiram are not at issue here in this strand of the narrative. Cf. Abraham's intercession in Gen 18.23–33. On prophetic intercession, see 11.10–15. **16.24** The number of the punished is reduced to the rebels and their families, in response to Moses and Aaron's intercession (v. 22). The word for *dwellings* (singular in Hebrew) here and in v. 27 is the same as the word commonly used for the Lord's tabernacle and is elsewhere never used in the singular to mean a secular dwelling. Commentators have suggested that this part of the text has been disturbed by the attempt to connect Korah and his followers to the story of the punishment of Dathan and Abiram. **16.25** On the *elders* who accompany Moses, see 11.16–30. **16.26** The people are told to *touch nothing* that belongs to the rebels because their sins are polluting. Elsewhere, similar commands convey the belief that holiness itself is dangerous, improper contact with it is polluting and life-threatening; see Ex 19.12–13; Num 4.15; 2 Sam 6.6–7; 1 Chr 13.9–10. Even seeing holy things can be dangerous: Num 4.20; cf. the Hebrew of 1 Sam 6.19. **16.27–33** These verses express the belief in corporate guilt and in the family as the extension of the (usually male) head of the family; see Josh 7.24–26. **16.30, 33** *Sheol* is the underworld home of the dead (see Gen 37.35; 1 Sam 28.11–14; Isa 14.9–11). In Isa 5.14 Sheol opens its mouth to eat the doomed. **16.32** Dathan and Abiram are not mentioned here and instead we have only *everyone who belonged to Korah.* Commentators have assumed this phrase displaced the mention of Dathan and Abiram in an editor's attempt to combine the two strands; cf. Deut 11.6; Ps 106.17. This verse does not say that Korah himself was killed, but cf.

into Sheol; the earth closed over them, and they perished from the midst of the assembly. 34 All Israel around them fled at their outcry, for they said, "The earth will swallow us too!" 35 And fire came out from the LORD and consumed the two hundred fifty men offering the incense.

36 f Then the LORD spoke to Moses, saying: 37 Tell Eleazar son of Aaron the priest to take the censers out of the blaze; then scatter the fire far and wide. 38 For the censers of these sinners have become holy at the cost of their lives. Make them into hammered plates as a covering for the altar, for they presented them before the LORD and they became holy. Thus they shall be a sign to the Israelites. 39 So Eleazar the priest took the bronze censers that had been presented by those who were burned; and they were hammered out as a covering for the altar — 40 a reminder to the Israelites that no outsider, who is not of the descendants of Aaron, shall approach to offer incense before the LORD, so as not to become like Korah and his company — just as the LORD had said to him through Moses.

41 On the next day, however, the whole congregation of the Israelites rebelled against Moses and against Aaron, saying, "You have killed the people of the LORD." 42 And when the congregation had assembled against them, Moses and Aaron turned toward the tent of meeting;

the cloud had covered it and the glory of the LORD appeared. 43 Then Moses and Aaron came to the front of the tent of meeting, 44 and the LORD spoke to Moses, saying, 45 "Get away from this congregation, so that I may consume them in a moment." And they fell on their faces. 46 Moses said to Aaron, "Take your censer, put fire on it from the altar and lay incense on it, and carry it quickly to the congregation and make atonement for them. For wrath has gone out from the LORD; the plague has begun." 47 So Aaron took it as Moses had ordered, and ran into the middle of the assembly, where the plague had already begun among the people. He put on the incense, and made atonement for the people. 48 He stood between the dead and the living; and the plague was stopped. 49 Those who died by the plague were fourteen thousand seven hundred, besides those who died in the affair of Korah. 50 When the plague was stopped, Aaron returned to Moses at the entrance of the tent of meeting.

The Budding of Aaron's Rod

17 g The LORD spoke to Moses, saying: 2 Speak to the Israelites, and get twelve staffs from them, one for each ancestral house, from all the leaders of their ancestral houses. Write each man's

f Ch 17.1 in Heb   g Ch 17.16 in Heb

16.40; 26.10–11. **16.35** The *two hundred fifty* who are elsewhere "the company of Korah" are killed separately by fire from the Lord; see 11.1. Cf. Lev 10.1–2. In Num 16.17, it is assumed that the two hundred and fifty are Levites; each has his own censer. V. 2, however, implies they came from all the tribes; see 27.1–3. **16.37–39** It is *Eleazar* instead of Aaron who has contact with the censers, perhaps because of a rule like the one in Lev 21.10–11. See also Num 19.3. The censers *have become holy at the cost of* [the rebels'] *lives*, i.e., they are holy because they were presented before the Lord, but since they were offered by those who were not qualified to offer incense, the offering was at the cost of those men's lives. These verses present an etiology of the bronze covering of the altar that is different from Ex 27.1–2; 38.1–2. **16.40** This event has served to reinforce the prerogatives of Aaron and his descendants; thus, commentators have assumed that the Korah narrative reflects conflicts in later rival priestly groups, with Aaronite priests claiming supremacy based on this story and others

like it (see 16.3; 12.2).

16.41–50 Revolt of the whole congregation; see 11.1–3. Since it is "the whole congregation" that is at fault, the intercession in 16.22 is no longer valid. The complaint this time concerns the deaths of Korah, Dathan, Abiram, and their families and followers. **16.41** There is in the Hebrew an extra pronoun "you" for emphasis in *You have killed the people of the LORD*, so that one might translate "It is you who killed the people of the LORD," i.e., Moses and Aaron and not really God. **16.42** On the *tent*, the *cloud*, and the *glory*, see 7.89; 9.15–16; 12.5. **16.45** On the Lord's *consuming* the congregation, see 16.21. *Fell on their faces.* See 16.4; 14.5. **16.46** The priest makes *atonement*; see 15.25. Incense is not the usual medium of atonement, but it is fitting in this story; cf. 5.21; 21.6–9. On the Lord's *wrath* and *plague*, see 11.33. **16.48** See Lev 21.10–11; such an instruction underlines the seriousness of Aaron's act here. **16.49** *Those who died in the affair of Korah*, i.e., the two hundred and fifty (v. 35).

17.1–13 Another proof that the tribe of Levi

name on his staff, ³and write Aaron's name on the staff of Levi. For there shall be one staff for the head of each ancestral house. ⁴Place them in the tent of meeting before the covenant,ʰ where I meet with you. ⁵And the staff of the man whom I choose shall sprout; thus I will put a stop to the complaints of the Israelites that they continually make against you. ⁶Moses spoke to the Israelites; and all their leaders gave him staffs, one for each leader, according to their ancestral houses, twelve staffs; and the staff of Aaron was among theirs. ⁷So Moses placed the staffs before the LORD in the tent of the covenant.ʰ

8 When Moses went into the tent of the covenantʰ on the next day, the staff of Aaron for the house of Levi had sprouted. It put forth buds, produced blossoms, and bore ripe almonds. ⁹Then Moses brought out all the staffs from before the LORD to all the Israelites, and they looked, and each man took his staff. ¹⁰And the LORD said to Moses, "Put back the staff of Aaron before the covenant,ʰ

to be kept as a warning to rebels, so that you may make an end of their complaints against me, or else they will die." ¹¹Moses did so; just as the LORD commanded him, so he did.

12 The Israelites said to Moses, "We are perishing; we are lost, all of us are lost! ¹³Everyone who approaches the tabernacle of the LORD will die. Are we all to perish?"

Responsibility of Priests and Levites

18 The LORD said to Aaron: You and your sons and your ancestral house with you shall bear responsibility for offenses connected with the sanctuary, while you and your sons alone shall bear responsibility for offenses connected with the priesthood. ²So bring with you also your brothers of the tribe of Levi, your ancestral tribe, in order that they may be joined to you, and serve you while you and your sons with you are in front of the tent of the covenant.ʰ ³They shall perform duties for you and for the whole

ʰ Or treaty, or testimony; Heb eduth

---

and Aaron as their leader are chosen above the rest of the community in ritual affairs, necessary because of the renewed rebellion in 16.41–50. **17.2** The *staff* referred to here is a symbol of a leader's authority (see Jer 48.17) and as the symbol of a tribal leader had come itself to mean "tribe," as in Num 1.16 and elsewhere. The double meaning of the word is appropriate here since the staff/tribe that buds is the one chosen by the Lord. *Leaders.* See 16.2, where they were part of the rebellion. **17.2–3** The command to Moses to *write each man's name on his staff* assumes Moses was literate (see also Ex 17.14; 24.4; 34.27; Num 33.2; Deut 31.9). **17.3** For Aaron's descent from *Levi,* see Ex 6.16–20. There is no hint here of the rivalry between Aaronite priests and other Levites; see 16.3, 40. **17.4** *In the tent of meeting before the covenant,* i.e., in front of the ark. See Ex 31.18; 34.29; also Ex 25.16, 21; 40.20; on the name "ark of the covenant," see, e.g., Ex 30.26; 40.3; Num 4.5; 7.89. *Where I meet with you.* See 7.89. **17.5** *The man whom I choose,* i.e., to approach the Lord in ritual; see 16.5, 7. The immediate referent for the *complaints* is 16.41–50, but see 11.1–3 for the complaint stories in general. **17.6–7** Moses carries out the Lord's commands, although the narrative does not report the writing of the names. **17.7** *Before the LORD* must mean "before the ark" here; see 17.4. **17.7–8** For *tent of the covenant,* see also 9.15; 18.2. For the tent in general, see 1.1; 2.1–34. **17.8** For other stories

of Aaron's miraculous staff, see Ex 7.8–8.19. Other narratives of blossoming staffs, clubs, or spears from many cultures have been noted by folklorists. **17.10** The Hebrew word for *warning* is the same as the word translated "sign" in 16.38. *Against me.* Cf. v. 5 ("you" plural in Hebrew); Ex 16.8. **17.12–13** The Israelites are convinced that only the tribe of Levi should approach the most holy parts of the tabernacle, but they take the warning in v. 10 so seriously that they become afraid that they will always be in danger of trespassing and dying. These verses serve as an introduction to ch. 18, where the Levites are said to guard the tent from trespass by unqualified persons (18.21–22). **18.1–7** See also 1.50–53; 3.5–10, 14–38; 16. **18.1** A distinction is made in this chapter between Aaron and his descendants on the one hand and the rest of the tribe of Levi on the other. See 3.5–10; 16.3, 40; cf. Ezek 44.10–16. *Bear responsibility for offenses,* i.e., suffer the consequences for any offense. This charge is meant to allay the fears expressed in 17.12–13. For offenses connected with the priesthood, see v. 3; Ex 28.38; e.g., Ex 30.20–21; 28.42–43; Lev 10.8–9; 16.2; 21.16–23. **18.2** The Levites are *joined to* Aaron and his descendants, a pun in Hebrew on the name Levi (see Gen 29.34), and they *serve* them; see 3.5–10; 8.14–22. *Tent of the covenant.* See 17.7–8. **18.3** The *altar* is the bronze altar;

tent. But they must not approach either the utensils of the sanctuary or the altar, otherwise both they and you will die. 4 They are attached to you in order to perform the duties of the tent of meeting, for all the service of the tent; no outsider shall approach you. 5 You yourselves shall perform the duties of the sanctuary and the duties of the altar, so that wrath may never again come upon the Israelites. 6 It is I who now take your brother Levites from among the Israelites; they are now yours as a gift, dedicated to the LORD, to perform the service of the tent of meeting. 7 But you and your sons with you shall diligently perform your priestly duties in all that concerns the altar and the area behind the curtain. I give your priesthood as a gift; *i* any outsider who approaches shall be put to death.

The Priests' Portion

8 The LORD spoke to Aaron: I have given you charge of the offerings made to me, all the holy gifts of the Israelites; I have given them to you and your sons as a priestly portion due you in perpetuity. 9 This shall be yours from the most holy things, reserved from the fire: every offering of theirs that they render to me as a most holy thing, whether grain offering, sin offering, or guilt offering, shall belong to you and your sons. 10 As a most holy thing you shall eat it; every male may eat it; it shall be holy to you. 11 This also is yours: I have given to you, together with your sons and daughters, as a perpetual due, whatever is set aside from the gifts of all the elevation offerings of the Israelites; everyone who is clean in your house may eat them. 12 All the best of the oil and all the best of the wine and of the grain, the choice produce that they give to the LORD, I have given to you. 13 The first fruits of all that is in their land, which they bring to the LORD, shall be yours; everyone who is clean in your house may eat of it. 14 Every devoted thing in Israel shall be yours. 15 The first issue of the womb of all creatures, human and animal, which is offered to the LORD, shall be yours; but the firstborn of human beings you shall redeem, and the firstborn of unclean animals you shall redeem. 16 Their redemption price, reckoned from one

i Heb *as a service of gift*

---

see 3.29, 31; 4.13–14; 16.38–39. *Both they and you will die*, i.e., the priests will die along with the trespassers, because the priests did not guard the sanctuary properly. See also 4.5–15. **18.4** It is the duty of the Levites to keep non-Levitical people from the most sacred areas; see 1.51. **18.5** For ritual as a means of avoiding the Lord's *wrath*, see 16.46. **18.6** For the Levites as a *gift* to the Aaronites, see 3.9; 8.19. **18.7** The *area behind the curtain* is where the Holy of Holies is, with the ark and the gold altar; see 3.29, 31.
18.8–20 The Aaronite priests' portion. This section stipulates that the priests are to receive, except for those portions that are burned on the altar, all of the grain offerings, sin offerings, and guilt offerings, which may be eaten by any Aaronite males (vv. 9–10). Further, the contributed part of the offerings of well-being, the best of the oil, wine, and grain, the first-fruit offerings, "devoted" things, and the firstborn of clean animals can be eaten by any ritually clean member of an Aaronite household, male or female. Finally, the redemption price for firstborn human beings and unclean animals also is to go to the priests (vv. 15–16). See 1 Sam 2.12–17 for a narrative involving the misuse of this provision. **18.8** The Lord has ordained that part of the Israelites' offerings is to be a means of support for the priesthood and the sanctuary. The word translated *charge* here might also be translated "that which is kept back" from the fire, held back for the priests. **18.9–10** The *most holy things* include the offerings listed in v. 9; see Lev 6.14–17. Note the absence of the burnt offering, of which only the skin goes to the priest (Lev 7.8). For that which is not *reserved from the fire*, see, e.g., Lev 2.2, 9, 16; 3.3–5; 5.12; 6.15–16; 7.3–5. **18.11** *Whatever is set aside*, i.e., contributed to the priests. *Elevation offerings*. See 8.13. For the parts set aside from elevation offerings, see, e.g., 18.18; Lev 7.28–36; Num 6.19–20; and the offerings of well-being listed in 6.17–18. *Everyone who is clean*. See Lev 22.3–7; 1 Sam 21.1–6. *In your house*. See Lev 22.10–16. **18.12–13** See also Deut 18.4; Ex 23.19a; Num 15.17–21. **18.14** *Devoted thing*. See Lev 27.21, 28. Here it is devoted to the service of the Lord, but something "devoted" is often "devoted to destruction" or "put to the ban," including in other circumstances human beings (see, e.g., Lev 27.29; Deut 13.12–18; Josh 6.15–21). **18.15–16** On the *firstborn* and redemption of firstborn males, see 3.12, 15, 40–51. Here in Num 18 there is no specification of the sex of the firstborn human being who is to be redeemed. *Their redemption price* refers to the redemption of human beings. The redemption price of unclean animals depended on the valuation by the priest (see Lev 27.11–13, 27). *Shekel of the sanctuary.*

month of age, you shall fix at five shekels of silver, according to the shekel of the sanctuary (that is, twenty gerahs). 17 But the firstborn of a cow, or the firstborn of a sheep, or the firstborn of a goat, you shall not redeem; they are holy. You shall dash their blood on the altar, and shall turn their fat into smoke as an offering by fire for a pleasing odor to the LORD; 18 but their flesh shall be yours, just as the breast that is elevated and as the right thigh are yours. 19 All the holy offerings that the Israelites present to the LORD I have given to you, together with your sons and daughters, as a perpetual due; it is a covenant of salt forever before the LORD for you and your descendants as well. 20 Then the LORD said to Aaron: You shall have no allotment in their land, nor shall you have any share among them; I am your share and your possession among the Israelites. 21 To the Levites I have given every tithe in Israel for a possession in return for the service that they perform, the service in the tent of meeting. 22 From now on the Israelites shall no longer approach the tent of meeting, or else they will incur guilt and die. 23 But the Levites shall perform the service of the tent of meeting, and they shall bear responsibility for their own offenses; it shall be a perpetual statute throughout your generations. But among the Israelites they shall have no allotment, 24 because I have given to the Levites as their portion the tithe of the Israelites, which they set apart as an offering to the LORD. Therefore I have said of them that they shall have no allotment among the Israelites.

25 Then the LORD spoke to Moses, saying: 26 You shall speak to the Levites, saying: When you receive from the Israelites the tithe that I have given you from them for your portion, you shall set apart an offering from it to the LORD, a tithe of the tithe. 27 It shall be reckoned to you as your gift, the same as the grain of the threshing floor and the fullness of the wine press. 28 Thus you also shall set apart an offering to the LORD from all the tithes that you receive from the Israelites; and from them you shall give the LORD's offering to the priest Aaron. 29 Out of all the gifts to you, you shall set apart every offering due to the LORD; the best of all of them is the part to be consecrated. 30 Say also to them: When you have set apart the best of it, then the rest shall be reckoned to the Levites as produce of the threshing floor, and as produce of the wine press. 31 You may eat it in any place, you and your households; for it is your payment for your service in the tent of meeting. 32 You shall incur no guilt by reason of it, when you have offered the best of it. But you shall not profane the holy gifts of the Israelites, on pain of death.

Ceremony of the Red Heifer

19 The LORD spoke to Moses and Aaron, saying: 2 This is a statute of the law that the LORD has commanded: Tell the Israelites to bring you a red

---

See 3.46–48. **18.17–18.** Cf. the description of offerings of well-being in Ex 29.26–28; Lev 7.28–36; 10.14–15. The firstborn of all clean animals belong to the Lord (Lev 27.26) and they are here assigned to the priests as part of their portion. *A pleasing odor to the LORD.* See 15.3. **18.19** The phrase *covenant of salt* apparently refers to an ancient custom of sharing food as part of a covenant ceremony (see Gen 31.54; Ex 24.9–11; cf. Ezra 4.14). A covenant of salt was perhaps one that could not be broken (see 2 Chr 13.5). Salt was to be added to all sacrifices according to Lev 2.13; see also Ezek 43.18–24. **18.20** The Aaronite priests are supposed to have no tribal inheritance; see 26.62; Josh 14.3. Their only support is cultic donations. Cities are provided for all those of the tribe of Levi, however, so that they will have homes and pasture land (but no agricultural land); see 35.1–8; Josh 21.1–42; 1 Chr 6.54–81. Cf. 1 Kings 2.26.

18.21–32 Those Levites other than the Aaronite priests have as their portion the Israelites' tithes, here of agricultural products only; see also Neh 10.37; 13.5, 12. Cf. Lev 27.30–33; 2 Chr 31.6; Deut 14.22–29; 26.12–15. **18.22** *Approach.* See 17.12–13; also 1.51. **18.23–24** See 18.20. **18.25–29** The Levites themselves must tithe and pay their offering to the Aaronite priests. **18.30–32** Once the Levites have tithed, their "income" is like any other Israelite's. Even though the tithes are technically offered to the Lord and are therefore sacred, the Levites may eat their portion without incurring guilt as long as they have first offered their tithe to the priests. If, however, they have not been faithful in their treatment of their "income," its essentially sacred nature will ensure their deaths.

19.1–22 31.19–24 assumes this chapter; see also Lev 5.3–6; 21.1–4, 10–11; 22.3–7; Num 5.1–3; 6.6–12; 9.6–7, 10–11. The need for ritual

heifer without defect, in which there is no blemish and on which no yoke has been laid. 3 You shall give it to the priest Eleazar, and it shall be taken outside the camp and slaughtered in his presence. 4 The priest Eleazar shall take some of its blood with his finger and sprinkle it seven times towards the front of the tent of meeting. 5 Then the heifer shall be burned in his sight; its skin, its flesh, and its blood, with its dung, shall be burned. 6 The priest shall take cedarwood, hyssop, and crimson material, and throw them into the fire in which the heifer is burning. 7 Then the priest shall wash his clothes and bathe his body in water, and afterwards he may come into the camp; but the priest shall remain unclean until evening. 8 The one who burns the heifer*j* shall wash his clothes in water and bathe his body in water; he shall remain unclean until evening. 9 Then someone who is clean shall gather up the ashes of the heifer, and deposit them outside the camp in a clean place; and they shall be kept for the congregation of the Israelites for the water for cleansing. It is a purification offering. 10 The one who gathers the ashes of the heifer shall wash his clothes and be unclean until evening.

This shall be a perpetual statute for the Israelites and for the alien residing among them. 11 Those who touch the dead body of any human being shall be unclean seven days. 12 They shall purify

j Heb *it*

---

after contact with a corpse is felt in many cultures, including other ancient Near Eastern ones. **19.2** The English meaning of *heifer* as a young cow that has not yet calved is not implied by the Hebrew word here. "Cow" is a better translation. Cf. the use of the same Hebrew word in 1 Sam 6.7, 10; Job 21.10. It is not clear why the animal should be red (or brownish-red, cf. Gen 25.29–34) unless it is the color of blood and so, like the *crimson material* in v. 6, symbolically increases the purifying blood in the ritual. Red is a common color choice for sacrificial animals in the ancient world. *Without defect . . . no blemish* (see also, e.g., Lev 4.28; 14.10; 22.20; 21.17–23 for the priests themselves). The cow to be used is one *on which no yoke has been laid*; certain special animals in biblical rituals were to be those that had never been used for profane work; see Deut 15.19; 21.3–4 (a different word for "heifer," meaning a young cow); 1 Sam 6.7. **19.3** *Eleazar*, Aaron's son. See, e.g., Ex 6.23; Num 3.1–4; 16.37–40. That the entire ceremony of this cow is to take place *outside the camp* makes it something other than ordinary sacrifice, which was performed at the altar. The uniqueness of this ritual must lie in its connection with the pollution associated with corpses. *In his presence,* i.e., the priest must officiate. **19.4** *Seven times.* Seven is often a sacred number in the Bible (e.g., Gen 2.3; 7.2; Lev 4.6; 8.11; Num 23.1–2). *Towards the front of the tent of meeting,* (the eastern side), i.e., towards the Lord. **19.5** The dung and skin of a sacrificial animal are sometimes burned (Ex 29.14; Lev 4.11–12; 8.17; 16.27), but never its blood. See 19.2. **19.6** On *cedarwood, hyssop, and crimson material,* see Lev 14.4–6, 49–53; cf. Num 19.18. Cedarwood is perhaps a symbol for endurance since it preserves. "Hyssop" may not be a correct translation for the next term since hyssop is not native to Palestine, but some aromatic, climbing plant is meant (1 Kings 4.33; see also Ex 12.22; Ps 51.7). The crimson material may simply be another symbol of purifying blood; see 19.2. Similar materials (aromatic woods, crimson yarn) are used in rituals elsewhere in the ancient world. **19.7–10a** The priest, who burns the cow, and the one who gathers its ashes must cleanse themselves and remain ritually unclean until evening; see, e.g., Lev 11.24–25, 28, 40; 15; 16.26, 28; 22.3–7. **19.9** The cow's ashes have been made sacred because the cow was an offering (a *purification offering;* see 8.6–7); no one unclean may deal with the ashes and the ashes should be kept ritually clean. *Water for cleansing,* sometimes translated "water of impurity," but here correctly identified as water to *cleanse* from impurity (see 8.6–7; also 31.23; Zech 13.1). On special mixtures of water used for ritual purposes, cf. also Ex 32.20; Num 5.16–28. **19.10** Contact with the sacred can make one "unclean." See 16.26. Both pollution and holiness are outside everyday life and so both require ritual attention before the people in question are once more "clean," i.e., before they can reenter their usual, mundane life for which they must be untouched by the unusual. Holiness can be dangerous (see Ex 19.10–15, 21–24; Num 16.26) and, like pollution, can even be considered contagious, though this is rare (Lev 6.25–29; Ezek 44.19; 46.20; cf. Hag 2.12–13). See 16.37–39, where only Eleazar the priest is to touch the censers made holy by the fire. A *perpetual statute.* See also 19.21; 10.8; 15.15; 18.23. **19.11–22** Uses of the water for cleansing, for people defiled by contact with a corpse or other vestige of human death. See also 31.19–24. **19.11** For people unclean through contact with a corpse, see note on 19.1–22. For a seven-day period of "uncleanness," see also the birth of a male child, Lev 12.2; skin disease, Lev 14.9; menstruation and bodily discharges, Lev 15. **19.12** *With*

themselves with the water on the third day and on the seventh day, and so be clean; but if they do not purify themselves on the third day and on the seventh day, they will not become clean. 13 All who touch a corpse, the body of a human being who has died, and do not purify themselves, defile the tabernacle of the LORD; such persons shall be cut off from Israel. Since water for cleansing was not dashed on them, they remain unclean; their uncleanness is still on them.

14 This is the law when someone dies in a tent: everyone who comes into the tent, and everyone who is in the tent, shall be unclean seven days. 15 And every open vessel with no cover fastened on it is unclean. 16 Whoever in the open field touches one who has been killed by a sword, or who has died naturally,k or a human bone, or a grave, shall be unclean seven days. 17 For the unclean they shall take some ashes of the burnt purification offering, and running water shall be added in a vessel; 18 then a clean person shall take hyssop, dip it in the water, and sprinkle it on the tent, on all the furnishings, on the persons who were there, and on whoever touched the bone, the slain, the corpse, or the grave. 19 The clean person shall sprinkle the unclean ones on the third day and on the seventh day, thus

purifying them on the seventh day. Then they shall wash their clothes and bathe themselves in water, and at evening they shall be clean. 20 Any who are unclean but do not purify themselves, those persons shall be cut off from the assembly, for they have defiled the sanctuary of the LORD. Since the water for cleansing has not been dashed on them, they are unclean.

21 It shall be a perpetual statute for them. The one who sprinkles the water for cleansing shall wash his clothes, and whoever touches the water for cleansing shall be unclean until evening. 22 Whatever the unclean person touches shall be unclean, and anyone who touches it shall be unclean until evening.

The Waters of Meribah

20 The Israelites, the whole congregation, came into the wilderness of Zin in the first month, and the people stayed in Kadesh. Miriam died there, and was buried there.

2 Now there was no water for the congregation; so they gathered together against Moses and against Aaron. 3 The people quarreled with Moses and said, "Would that we had died when our kin-

k Heb lacks naturally

---

the water, Hebrew "with it," either the water or the collection of ashes (vv. 9–10). **19.13** Such people would defile the tabernacle (see Lev 15.31) because, since the camp is holy (see 5.1–4), any possible contact with uncleanness could endanger the holiness of the tabernacle at the center. Cut off. See 9.13. **19.14–22** A repetition of information in vv. 11–13, but with more detail. **19.14–15** The uncleanness of a tent (or, probably, any dwelling; the Septuagint translates "house, dwelling") where someone has died is like that from contact with a corpse (see v. 11). The uncleanness is envisioned as contagion that can spread even to open containers. **19.16** This verse treats contact with human death in an environment opposite from the dwelling of vv. 14–15, an open field. **19.17–20** Instructions for making and using the water for cleansing (v. 9). **19.17** The burnt purification offering is that of the red cow, vv. 2–10, and the ashes are mentioned in vv. 9–10. Running water, Hebrew "living water," is water that flows continuously, as from a spring, and cannot become stagnant. See also the various translations in Gen 26.19; Lev 14.5, 50; 15.13; Song 4.15; Jer 2.13; 17.13; Zech 14.8.

19.18–19 For hyssop, see 19.6. Here the purification process is a matter of being sprinkled with the water for cleansing, of washing clothes, and of bathing. The instruction in v. 12 is less explicit. **19.20** See 19.13. **19.21–22** See 19.10.

20.1–13 This narrative takes place after the forty years of wandering. **20.1** V. 1 presents many chronological and geographical problems. Wilderness of Zin. See 13.21. In the first month, but the year is not specified. Most commentators propose the fortieth year because of the date of Aaron's death given in 33.38. The people stayed in Kadesh, but the length of time is not given. V. 12 indicates that forty years have passed: the Israelites in this narrative are to be allowed into the promised land, hence the conclusion that the old generation had died (see 14.21–24, 28–35); note the resumption of the march in v. 22. On Miriam, see ch. 12. **20.2–13** The complaint and the waters of Meribah. On complaint stories in general, see 11.1–3. Compare this story to its doublet in Ex 17.1–7. This narrative is also referred to in Deut 33.8; Pss 78.15–16, 20; 81.7; 95.8–11; 106.32–33. **20.3** Quarreled, from the same root as Meribah, hence the etymology in v. 13. When

dred died before the LORD! 4 Why have you brought the assembly of the LORD into this wilderness for us and our livestock to die here? 5 Why have you brought us up out of Egypt, to bring us to this wretched place? It is no place for grain, or figs, or vines, or pomegranates; and there is no water to drink." 6 Then Moses and Aaron went away from the assembly to the entrance of the tent of meeting; they fell on their faces, and the glory of the LORD appeared to them. 7 The LORD spoke to Moses, saying: 8 Take the staff, and assemble the congregation, you and your brother Aaron, and command the rock before their eyes to yield its water. Thus you shall bring water out of the rock for them; thus you shall provide drink for the congregation and their livestock.

9 So Moses took the staff from before the LORD, as he had commanded him. 10 Moses and Aaron gathered the assembly together before the rock, and he said to them, "Listen, you rebels, shall we bring water for you out of this rock?" 11 Then Moses lifted up his hand and struck the rock twice with his staff; water came out abundantly, and the congregation and their livestock drank. 12 But the LORD said to Moses and Aaron, "Because you did not trust in me, to show my holiness before the eyes of the Israelites, therefore you shall not bring this assembly into the land that I have given them." 13 These are the waters of Meribah,¹ where the people of Israel quarreled with the LORD, and by which he showed his holiness.

Passage Through Edom Refused

14 Moses sent messengers from Kadesh to the king of Edom, "Thus says your brother Israel: You know all the adversity that has befallen us: 15 how our ancestors went down to Egypt, and we lived in Egypt a long time; and the Egyptians oppressed us and our ancestors; 16 and when we cried to the LORD, he heard our voice, and sent an angel and brought us out of Egypt; and here we are in Kadesh,

1 That is *Quarrel*

---

our kindred died before the LORD, i.e., in the Korah, Dathan, and Abiram affair, ch. 16 (esp. vv. 32–33, 35, 49). **20.4** *Livestock*. See 11.4. **20.5** *No . . . figs, or vines, or pomegranates*. Cf. 13.23. **20.6** *Fell on their faces*. See 14.5; 16.4. *Glory*. See 9.15–16. **20.8–9** The mention of *the staff* is phrased in such a way that a particular staff seems to be meant. Since it is taken *from before the LORD* it must be Aaron's staff of 17.10–11; but see v. 11. See also Ex 7.8–8.19. The reference to *the rock* also implies a known entity, perhaps a well-known feature at Kadesh. The Hebrew word for rock here, *sela*, is also the name of a city in Edom (see Judg 1.36; 2 Kings 14.7) and may be a literary link to the Edom narrative in vv. 14–21. **20.10** For Israel as *rebels*, see 17.10, also concerned with the staff. **20.12** No satisfying explanation has ever been given for the punishment of Moses and Aaron for this incident. Their "sin" is described here as unbelief; in v. 24 and 27.14 it is rebellion; in Deut 32.50–52 they are said to have "broken faith" with the Lord. Ps 106.32–33 blames Moses' "rash words" (perhaps v. 10), and yet other explanations, not always referring to this narrative at all, are given in Deut 1.37; 3.25–26; 4.21. Commentators have made many suggestions about the nature of the "sin," but none of these explanations is widely accepted. Aaron's death is reported in v. 28, Moses' in Deut 34.5. That *this assembly* will be taken into the promised land implies that this must be the new

generation, grown up after the old has died during forty years in the wilderness. *To show my holiness* might also be translated "to treat me as holy." **20.13** *Quarreled*. See 20.3. For the etymologies of place-names, see, e.g., 11.1–3; 13.24; 21.3. *With the LORD*. See Ex 16.8; 17.7.

20.14–21 The relationship between Edom and Israel in the Bible is complicated: sometimes friendly, sometimes hostile (e.g., the stories of Jacob/Israel and Esau/Edom, Gen 25.27–34; 27.1–28.9; 32.3–33.17; and elsewhere, Num 24.18; 1 Sam 14.47; 2 Sam 8.13–14; 1 Kings 11.14–17; 2 Kings 3.4–27; Isa 34.5–7; Ob). **20.14** *King*. There is no archaeological evidence that Edom was an organized kingdom in the early Iron Age; probably the passages that report "chieftains" of Edom are more accurate (see text notes to Gen 36.15–19, 40–43; Ex 15.15). The message in vv. 14–17 is worded in the same way as a typical ancient Near Eastern letter: addressee, sender, message. Moses calls Israel Edom's *brother* in typical diplomatic language. Use of the term "brother" indicates that the message sender believes the two parties to be equals and allies. In this case, of course, there is a double meaning since Israel (Jacob) and Edom (Esau) are recorded as biological brothers in the stories in Genesis (e.g., 25.21–26). **20.16** *Angel*. See Ex 14.19; 23.20–33; 32.34. As in many biblical stories, the "angel" is probably meant to be in fact some aspect of the Lord (see, e.g., Gen 16.7–13; Num

a town on the edge of your territory. 17 Now let us pass through your land. We will not pass through field or vineyard, or drink water from any well; we will go along the King's Highway, not turning aside to the right hand or to the left until we have passed through your territory." 18 But Edom said to him, "You shall not pass through, or we will come out with the sword against you." 19 The Israelites said to him, "We will stay on the highway; and if we drink of your water, we and our livestock, then we will pay for it. It is only a small matter; just let us pass through on foot." 20 But he said, "You shall not pass through." And Edom came out against them with a large force, heavily armed. 21 Thus Edom refused to give Israel passage through their territory; so Israel turned away from them.

The Death of Aaron

22 They set out from Kadesh, and the Israelites, the whole congregation, came to Mount Hor. 23 Then the LORD said to Moses and Aaron at Mount Hor, on the border of the land of Edom, 24 "Let Aaron be gathered to his people. For he shall not enter the land that I have given to the Israelites, because you rebelled against my command at the waters of Meribah. 25 Take Aaron and his son Eleazar, and bring them up Mount Hor; 26 strip Aaron of his vestments, and put them on his son Eleazar. But Aaron shall be gathered to his people,*m* and shall die there." 27 Moses did as the LORD had commanded; they went up Mount Hor in the sight of the whole congregation. 28 Moses stripped Aaron of his vestments, and put them on his son Eleazar; and Aaron died there on the top of the mountain. Moses and Eleazar came down from the mountain. 29 When all the congregation saw that Aaron had died, all the house of Israel mourned for Aaron thirty days.

The Defeat of Arad

21 When the Canaanite, the king of Arad, who lived in the Negeb, heard that Israel was coming by the way of Atharim, he fought against Israel and took some of them captive. 2 Then Israel made a vow to the LORD and said, "If you will indeed give this people into our hands, then we will utterly destroy their towns." 3 The LORD listened to the voice of Israel, and handed over the Canaan-

m Heb lacks *to his people*

22.22–35). **20.17** Because their attack from the south had failed many years earlier (14.39–45), the Israelites are now planning to invade Canaan from the east. To do so they must either pass directly through Edom or make a long detour around. The *King's Highway* was the north-south Transjordanian route connecting the Gulf of Aqaba with Syria. Such a route is still in use today. **20.18** The Edomites refuse, although without explanation. See Judg 11.17–18, but cf. Deut 2.2–8, 26–29. See the similar plot in the narrative of Jacob and Esau in Gen 32–33. **20.21** See 21.4: the Israelites go south of Edom when they continue their march.

20.22–29 Aaron's successor installed; Aaron dies. **20.22** *They set out.* See 10.11–12. *Mount Hor.* Site unknown, but see v. 23; 33.37; cf. Deut 10.6; Num 33.30–31, 37. **20.24** That an Israelite is *gathered to his people* probably usually refers to burial in a family tomb; see Gen 25.8–10. *Because you rebelled.* "You" is plural; see v. 12; Deut 32.50–52. **20.26** Aaron's son *Eleazar* (see 19.3) will take Aaron's place as chief priest; see also Deut 10.6. On his *vestments*, see Ex 28; Lev 8.7–9. **20.28** Moses will also die on top of a *mountain;* see Deut 32.50; 34.1–6. Num 33.38 places Aaron's death at the first day of the fifth month, year forty. **20.29** The Israelites mourn for Aaron *thirty days,* as they do for Moses (Deut 34.8). The usual period of mourning was seven days (Gen 50.10; 1 Sam 31.13).

21.1–3 The defeat of the king of Arad. This appears to be another story of an attack on the promised land from the south (see v. 4). For other battles of Hormah, see 14.39–45; Judg 1.16–17. **21.1** For *Canaanites* in this region, see also 14.25, 45. *Arad* is approximately fifty miles north of the oases of which Kadesh was a part. For the *king of Arad,* see Josh 12.14. *Negeb.* See 13.17; Judg 1.16. The *way of Atharim.* Site unknown. **21.2–3** See Judg 11.30–31. *We will utterly destroy their towns* is a vow to wage "holy war." See Ex 17.14; Num 18.14; Deut 20.16–18. Such a practice is known also from ancient Moab. *Hormah* is from the same Hebrew root as "utterly destroy," hence this narrative provides an etymology of the place name Hormah, as does Judg 1.17. It is odd that, having achieved a victory in the Negeb, the Israelites still turn to the southeast to go through Transjordan and attack Canaan from the east (v. 4), rather than continuing northward into Canaan. Commentators have suggested, therefore, that vv. 1–3 are out of place in their current position.

ites; and they utterly destroyed them and their towns; so the place was called Hormah.*n*

The Bronze Serpent

4 From Mount Hor they set out by the way to the Red Sea,*o* to go around the land of Edom; but the people became impatient on the way. 5 The people spoke against God and against Moses, "Why have you brought us up out of Egypt to die in the wilderness? For there is no food and no water, and we detest this miserable food." 6 Then the LORD sent poisonous*p* serpents among the people, and they bit the people, so that many Israelites died. 7 The people came to Moses and said, "We have sinned by speaking against the LORD and against you; pray to the LORD to take away the serpents from us." So Moses prayed for the people. 8 And the LORD said to Moses, "Make a poisonous*q* serpent, and set it on a pole; and everyone

who is bitten shall look at it and live." 9 So Moses made a serpent of bronze, and put it upon a pole; and whenever a serpent bit someone, that person would look at the serpent of bronze and live.

The Journey to Moab

10 The Israelites set out, and camped in Oboth. 11 They set out from Oboth, and camped at Iye-abarim, in the wilderness bordering Moab toward the sunrise. 12 From there they set out, and camped in the Wadi Zered. 13 From there they set out, and camped on the other side of the Arnon, in*r* the wilderness that extends from the boundary of the Amorites; for the Arnon is the boundary of Moab, between Moab and the Amorites. 14 Wherefore it is said in the Book of the Wars of the LORD,

n Heb *Destruction*   *o* Or *Sea of Reeds*
p Or *fiery*; Heb *seraphim*   *q* Or *fiery*; Heb *seraph*
r Gk: Heb *which is in*

21.4–9 The bronze serpent. This is the last of the complaint stories (see 11.1–3) and the most serious since the people complain directly against God as well as Moses (v. 5, although cf. Ex 16.8; Num 14.3). **21.4** *They set out.* This is part of the itinerary reported in 33.41. *By the way to the Red Sea.* The Hebrew actually says "Reed Sea," as in 14.25. In this passage, however, Red Sea makes sense, regardless of where the miracle at the sea was thought to have taken place. The Israelites have turned to the Gulf of Aqaba in order *to go around the land of Edom*, because they have been denied passage; see 20.14–21. **21.5** *Against God and against Moses.* See notes 21.4–9. This phrasing is unique. **21.6–7** *Poisonous serpents*, lit. "fiery snakes," so called perhaps because of the burning of their bites. Poisonous snakes do exist in the Sinai and the Negeb. **21.8–9** *Make a poisonous serpent*, lit. "make a fiery one," presumably a "fiery snake." In Isa 30.6 the same word (a flying "fiery one," translated as a flying "serpent") describes an animal of the Negeb. *Set it on a pole*, so that it could be held up for victims to see. Looking at the serpent cures the victims, a process here described as a sort of sympathetic magic (although see Wis 16.5–7). The phrase *serpent of bronze* is a pun in Hebrew, both words derived from the same root. Also from that root is Nehushtan, the bronze serpent King Hezekiah destroys because it has become an object of worship; see 2 Kings 18.4. This story in Numbers serves as an etiology for the serpent of Hezekiah's time. Serpent worship is attested elsewhere in the ancient world, as is the belief in a relationship between snakes and healing.

21.10–11 Cf. 33.41–44, with stops at Zalmonah and Punon not listed in ch. 21 (see v. 4). The location of *Oboth* is unknown. *Iye-abarim*, possibly "the ruins of the Abarim." Abarim, from the root that means "across," i.e., across the Jordan (from the point of view of an Israelite writer), is a word that describes an area or mountain range in Moab (see 27.12; 33.47). Here the text seems to place the Israelites to the east of Moab, below the Arnon (v. 13); cf. v. 12 where they appear to be south of Moab. **21.12** The style of the itinerary changes in this verse, and the stopping places no longer correspond to the list of "stages" in Num 33 (see 33.45), so commentators generally see a shift to the old epic sources rather than the priestly tradition (see Introduction; 10.29–36). In Deut 2.8–25, the *Wadi Zered* appears to be the southern boundary of Moab, between Moab and Edom, probably modern Wadi el-Hesa. **21.13** The *Arnon*, modern Wadi el-Mujib, was at some periods the northern boundary of Moab. A ninth-century B.C.E. Moabite inscription attributed to King Mesha (2 Kings 3.4–27) describes his regaining the territory north of the Arnon from Israel, in whose control it had been since the time of the Israelite king Omri (1 Kings 16.21–30). The inscription was indeed found north of the Arnon. The *other side* of the Arnon must refer to the north side, since the Israelites were marching from the south. **21.14–15** *The Book of the Wars of the LORD* is otherwise unknown. Cf. the Book of Jashar (Josh 10.13; 2 Sam 1.18). These fragments suggest the existence of collec-

"Waheb in Suphah and the wadis.
The Arnon [15] and the slopes of
the wadis
that extend to the seat of Ar,
and lie along the border of
Moab." [s]

16 From there they continued to
Beer; [t] that is the well of which the LORD
said to Moses, "Gather the people together, and I will give them water."
[17] Then Israel sang this song:
"Spring up, O well! — Sing to it! —
18   the well that the leaders sank,
that the nobles of the people dug,
with the scepter, with the staff."
From the wilderness to Mattanah, [19] from
Mattanah to Nahaliel, from Nahaliel to
Bamoth, [20] and from Bamoth to the valley
lying in the region of Moab by the top of
Pisgah that overlooks the wasteland. [u]

King Sihon Defeated

21 Then Israel sent messengers to
King Sihon of the Amorites, saying,
[22] "Let me pass through your land; we will
not turn aside into field or vineyard; we
will not drink the water of any well; we
will go by the King's Highway until
we have passed through your territory."

23 But Sihon would not allow Israel to pass
through his territory. Sihon gathered all
his people together, and went out against
Israel to the wilderness; he came to Jahaz,
and fought against Israel. [24] Israel put
him to the sword, and took possession of
his land from the Arnon to the Jabbok, as
far as to the Ammonites; for the boundary of the Ammonites was strong. [25] Israel
took all these towns, and Israel settled in
all the towns of the Amorites, in Heshbon,
and in all its villages. [26] For Heshbon was
the city of King Sihon of the Amorites,
who had fought against the former king
of Moab and captured all his land as far as
the Arnon. [27] Therefore the ballad singers say,
"Come to Heshbon, let it be built;
let the city of Sihon be
established.
28   For fire came out from Heshbon,
flame from the city of Sihon.
It devoured Ar of Moab,
and swallowed up [v] the heights
of the Arnon.
29   Woe to you, O Moab!

s Meaning of Heb uncertain   t That is *Well*
u Or *Jeshimon*   v Gk: Heb *and the lords of*

---

tions of poems about Israel's early wars of conquest. Such wars were called "the wars of the
LORD" because of the Israelites' belief that the
Lord led them in battle (i.e., "holy wars," see, e.g.,
Josh 6; Judg 4.14–16; 11.30–33; 1 Sam 14.6–10,
23; 18.17; 25.28). The translation of the poem
is problematical. For *Ar* as a town in Moab,
see 21.28; Deut 2.18. The name probably means
"town," in fact. The *seat* of Ar could refer to
its location or to some dwelling in the town.
21.16–18 An otherwise unknown miraculous
provision of water; cf. Ex 17.1–7; Num 20.2–11,
although the "Song of the Well" could obviously
be sung about any well. **21.19** *Mattanah* and *Nahaliel* are unknown. *Bamoth*, "high places," could
refer to a number of sites, e.g., Bamoth-baal,
22.41; Josh 13.17; Beth-bamoth in the Mesha inscription (see 21.13). **21.20** *Valley* here could refer to a valley within a series of hills and need not
clash with *the top of Pisgah*. For Pisgah as hills, see,
e.g., 23.14; Deut 3.17, 27; 34.1. Pisgah is on the
Moabite plateau above the Jordan Valley (Deut
34.1), and so the march has come northwest to
this point. The *wasteland* referred to in this verse
must be the area north of the Dead Sea and east
of the Jordan River. The same word is used of
that area on the west side of the river as well.
21.21–35 The defeat of kings Sihon and Og.

See the similar narratives in Deut 2.24–3.7; Judg
11.19–22; and many other mentions such as Josh
12.1–5; 13.10–12; Jer 48.45. **21.21** *Amorites*.
See 13.29; Gen 10.16. **21.22** Cf. 20.17, 19. The
Israelites still need to move farther north in order
to press their attack on Canaan from the east, and
this brings them to the border of Amorite territory. *The King's Highway*. See 20.17. **21.23** Cf.
20.18, 20–21. *Jahaz* (also mentioned in the Mesha
Inscription, see 21.13) seems to be the limit of
Moab's land (Isa 15.4; Jer 48.34) and was probably near Dibon (see 21.30). **21.24** In ch. 20 Israel bypassed Edom, but here the Israelites fight
with the Amorites. The *Jabbok* is modern Wadi
Zerqa. On the *Ammonites*, see Gen 19.38. The area
of Ammon in the highlands east of the Jordan
Valley was already widely settled in the middle of
the second millennium B.C.E. **21.25–26** *All these
towns* has no obvious referent. The site of *Heshbon*
in this early period has not been certainly identified, but was probably in the highlands east of
the Jordan Valley, opposite Jericho. *Villages*, lit.
"daughters," i.e., dependent towns. According to
these verses, the territory in question (north of
the Arnon) had once been Moabite, just as in King
Mesha's inscription (see 21.13). **21.27–30** The
Song of Heshbon is a song in praise of an Amorite
victory over Moab. **21.29** *Chemosh* is the national

You are undone, O people of
Chemosh!
He has made his sons fugitives,
and his daughters captives,
to an Amorite king, Sihon.
30 So their posterity perished
from Heshbon w to Dibon,
and we laid waste until fire
spread to Medeba." x
31 Thus Israel settled in the land of
the Amorites. 32 Moses sent to spy out Jazer; and they captured its villages, and
dispossessed the Amorites who were
there.

King Og Defeated

33 Then they turned and went up the
road to Bashan; and King Og of Bashan
came out against them, he and all his people, to battle at Edrei. 34 But the LORD said
to Moses, "Do not be afraid of him; for I
have given him into your hand, with all
his people, and all his land. You shall do

to him as you did to King Sihon of the
Amorites, who ruled in Heshbon." 35 So
they killed him, his sons, and all his people, until there was no survivor left; and
they took possession of his land.

Balak Summons Balaam to Curse Israel

22 The Israelites set out, and
camped in the plains of Moab
across the Jordan from Jericho. 2 Now Balak son of Zippor saw all that Israel had
done to the Amorites. 3 Moab was in great
dread of the people, because they were so
numerous; Moab was overcome with fear
of the people of Israel. 4 And Moab said to
the elders of Midian, "This horde will
now lick up all that is around us, as an ox
licks up the grass of the field." Now Balak
son of Zippor was king of Moab at that
time. 5 He sent messengers to Balaam son
of Beor at Pethor, which is on the Eu-

w Gk: Heb we have shot at them; Heshbon has perished
x Compare Sam Gk: Meaning of MT uncertain

god of Moab, known also from the Mesha Inscription (see 21.13); see also 1 Kings 11.7, 33; 2 Kings
23.13; Jer 48.7, 13, 46; cf. Judg 11.12–24. Cf.
"the people of Chemosh" here and in Jer 48.46
with Israel as "the people of the LORD" in Num
11.29; 2 Kings 9.6; Ezek 36.20; Zeph 2.10.
21.30 *Dibon*, about thirty miles southwest of
Amman, and *Medeba*, about twenty miles southwest of Amman. See 33.45; Josh 13.8–9. The Hebrew of v. 30 is not at all clear.   **21.32** *Jazer*.
Site unknown; see 32.1–4; Josh 13.24–25.
21.33–35 The defeat of King Og, another Amorite king. *Bashan* is northern Transjordan, a plateau of volcanic origin and famous in biblical
passages as a fertile land; see Ps 22.12; Isa 2.13;
33.9; Jer 50.19; Ezek 27.6; 39.18; Mic 7.14; Nah
1.4; Zech 11.2. *Edrei*, about sixty miles south of
Damascus; see Deut 3.8–10.   **21.34** *Do not be
afraid of him; for I have given him into your hand.* Cf.
Josh 10.8.
22.1 The last stage in the journey from the
wilderness of Sinai, before the crossing of the
Jordan River; see Num 33.48–49; 36.13; Deut
1.1–5; Josh 3.1.
22.2–24.25 The story of Balaam, son of
Beor. The biblical stories of Balaam have been
supplemented by the discovery at Tell Deir Alla
in Jordan of a plaster inscription dating to the
eighth century B.C.E. The text, which is probably
non-Israelite, relates that Balaam, son of Beor, a
"seer of the gods," receives an upsetting night visit
from the gods and then reports to his people that
he has seen a divine council meeting (see Gen
1.26) where impending disaster is apparently

planned for the earth. The Balaam story in Num
22–24 combines epic and poetic sources, resulting
in a few apparent contradictions: on the one
hand, Balaam's journey to Balak seems rather
short, with a donkey and two servants (22.21–35),
while, on the other, he is said to come from upper
Syria (22.5); he is outspokenly loyal to the God of
Israel, but his failure to curse Israel continues to
surprise Balak; he is portrayed as both prophet
and diviner. The connection, if any, between Balaam and Bela son of Beor (an Edomite king, Gen
36.32–33; 1 Chr 1.43–44) is obscure. Some of the
mentions of Balaam in the Bible refer to the narrative in chs. 22–24; some refer to the negative
Balaam tradition in 31.8, 16; and others have
slightly different traditions from either of these
(see Deut 23.3–6; Josh 13.22; 24.9–10; Judg
11.25; Neh 13.1–2; Mic 6.5).   **22.2** *Balak* is mentioned only in these chapters and in references to
them (Josh 24.9; Judg 11.25; Mic 6.5). *All that
Israel had done to the Amorites.* See 21.21–35.
22.3 *Moab was overcome with fear of the people of
Israel.* Cf. Josh 2.8–11.   **22.4** On the connection
between Balaam and *Midian*, see 31.8, 16.   **22.5**
Pethor, possibly Pitru on the upper Euphrates,
where Syrian and Mesopotamian cultures came
together; see also 23.7; Deut 23.4. This identification for Pethor, however, accords badly with
vv. 21–35 where a short journey seems envisioned
(see notes on 22.2–24.25). *Amaw*, or "his people";
see the text note y and cf. 24.14. There is a place-
name in northern Syria that might correspond to
Hebrew Amaw. Amaw might also be a scribal error for Ammon. *They have spread over the face of the*

phrates, in the land of Amaw,*y* to summon him, saying, "A people has come out of Egypt; they have spread over the face of the earth, and they have settled next to me. 6Come now, curse this people for me, since they are stronger than I; perhaps I shall be able to defeat them and drive them from the land; for I know that whomever you bless is blessed, and whomever you curse is cursed."

7 So the elders of Moab and the elders of Midian departed with the fees for divination in their hand; and they came to Balaam, and gave him Balak's message. 8He said to them, "Stay here tonight, and I will bring back word to you, just as the LORD speaks to me"; so the officials of Moab stayed with Balaam. 9God came to Balaam and said, "Who are these men with you?" 10Balaam said to God, "King Balak son of Zippor of Moab, has sent me this message: 11'A people has come out of Egypt and has spread over the face of the earth; now come, curse them for me; perhaps I shall be able to fight against them and drive them out.'" 12God said to Balaam, "You shall not go with them; you shall not curse the people, for they are blessed." 13So Balaam rose in the morning, and said to the officials of Balak, "Go to your own land, for the LORD has refused to let me go with you." 14So the officials of Moab rose and went to Balak, and said, "Balaam refuses to come with us."

15 Once again Balak sent officials, more numerous and more distinguished than these. 16They came to Balaam and said to him, "Thus says Balak son of Zip-

por: 'Do not let anything hinder you from coming to me; 17for I will surely do you great honor, and whatever you say to me I will do; come, curse this people for me.'" 18But Balaam replied to the servants of Balak, "Although Balak were to give me his house full of silver and gold, I could not go beyond the command of the LORD my God, to do less or more. 19You remain here, as the others did, so that I may learn what more the LORD may say to me." 20That night God came to Balaam and said to him, "If the men have come to summon you, get up and go with them; but do only what I tell you to do." 21So Balaam got up in the morning, saddled his donkey, and went with the officials of Moab.

Balaam, the Donkey, and the Angel

22 God's anger was kindled because he was going, and the angel of the LORD took his stand in the road as his adversary. Now he was riding on the donkey, and his two servants were with him. 23The donkey saw the angel of the LORD standing in the road, with a drawn sword in his hand; so the donkey turned off the road, and went into the field; and Balaam struck the donkey, to turn it back onto the road. 24Then the angel of the LORD stood in a narrow path between the vineyards, with a wall on either side. 25When the donkey saw the angel of the LORD, it scraped against the wall, and scraped Balaam's foot against the wall; so he struck it again. 26Then the angel of the LORD went

y Or *land of his kinsfolk*

earth; cf. the same expression used of locusts in Ex 10.5, 15. **22.6** Balaam's role here is one who blesses and curses; cf. vv. 7, 40; 23.1–3. **22.7** *Fees for divination.* See the negative interpretation of Balaam's role as diviner in Josh 13.22; see also Deut 18.10–14. Divination was a common ancient cultic practice designed to discover information by interpretation of some object or event, such as the configuration of the entrails of a sacrificed animal or the pattern oil drops on water. Diviners learned traditional interpretations preserved in long lists of many possible configurations of the various media. **22.8** Balaam, a non-Israelite, maintains unexpectedly that he must confer with the Lord, i.e., with Yahweh, the God of Israel; see also vv. 12–13, 18; Gen 26.28. Not unexpectedly, the God of Israel does not give Balaam permission to curse Israel for Balak king of

Moab (v. 6). Equally unusual, the Moabites and Midianites in the story seem to accept that Balaam is dependent on the Lord for his blessings and curses, as if the Lord were the only god Balaam could possibly call on. Cf. 21.29. Balaam here reflects a tradition in which a prophet is the mouthpiece for a deity. See Deut 18.18; also Num 22.18–20, 35, 38; 23.3, 15, 17, 26; 24.13. **22.18** *My God.* Balaam here refers to the Lord as his own god. Cf. v. 8. **22.20** Balaam is given permission to go with the men, but not to curse Israel.

22.22–35 The story of Balaam's talking donkey is a fable that perhaps pokes fun at Balaam — the seer whose donkey can see more than he can. Cf. the story of trees talking in Judg 9.7–15. **22.22** God's *anger* is unexplained in the text as we have it; cf. v. 20. **22.23a** Cf. Josh 5.13–15.

ahead, and stood in a narrow place, where there was no way to turn either to the right or to the left. 27 When the donkey saw the angel of the LORD, it lay down under Balaam; and Balaam's anger was kindled, and he struck the donkey with his staff. 28 Then the LORD opened the mouth of the donkey, and it said to Balaam, "What have I done to you, that you have struck me these three times?" 29 Balaam said to the donkey, "Because you have made a fool of me! I wish I had a sword in my hand! I would kill you right now!" 30 But the donkey said to Balaam, "Am I not your donkey, which you have ridden all your life to this day? Have I been in the habit of treating you this way?" And he said, "No."

31 Then the LORD opened the eyes of Balaam, and he saw the angel of the LORD standing in the road, with his drawn sword in his hand; and he bowed down, falling on his face. 32 The angel of the LORD said to him, "Why have you struck your donkey these three times? I have come out as an adversary, because your way is perverse[z] before me. 33 The donkey saw me, and turned away from me these three times. If it had not turned away from me, surely just now I would have killed you and let it live." 34 Then Balaam said to the angel of the LORD, "I have sinned, for I did not know that you were standing in the road to oppose me. Now therefore, if it is displeasing to you, I will return home." 35 The angel of the LORD said to Balaam, "Go with the men; but speak only what I tell you to speak." So Balaam went on with the officials of Balak.

36 When Balak heard that Balaam had come, he went out to meet him at Ir-moab, on the boundary formed by the Ar-non, at the farthest point of the boundary. 37 Balak said to Balaam, "Did I not send to summon you? Why did you not come to me? Am I not able to honor you?" 38 Balaam said to Balak, "I have come to you now, but do I have power to say just anything? The word God puts in my mouth, that is what I must say." 39 Then Balaam went with Balak, and they came to Kiriath-huzoth. 40 Balak sacrificed oxen and sheep, and sent them to Balaam and to the officials who were with him.

Balaam's First Oracle

41 On the next day Balak took Balaam and brought him up to Bamoth-baal; and from there he could see part of the people of Israel.[a]

23 1 Then Balaam said to Balak, "Build me seven altars here, and prepare seven bulls and seven rams for me." 2 Balak did as Balaam had said; and Balak and Balaam offered a bull and a ram on each altar. 3 Then Balaam said to Balak, "Stay here beside your burnt offerings while I go aside. Perhaps the LORD will come to meet me. Whatever he shows me I will tell you." And he went to a bare height.

4 Then God met Balaam; and Balaam said to him, "I have arranged the seven altars, and have offered a bull and a ram on each altar." 5 The LORD put a word in Balaam's mouth, and said, "Return to Balak, and this is what you must say." 6 So he returned to Balak,[b] who was standing beside his burnt offerings with all the officials of Moab. 7 Then Balaam[c] uttered his oracle, saying:

z Meaning of Heb uncertain   a Heb lacks of Israel   b Heb him   c Heb he

---

22.28 *Opened the mouth of the donkey.* Cf. v. 31 (although a different Hebrew word is used for "open"). **22.31** *The LORD opened the eyes of Balaam,* so that he could see something supernatural; cf. 2 Kings 6.15–17. **22.32** The *angel* seems to be, in some sense, the Lord; see also 20.16. **22.35** *Angel.* Cf. 22.20, 32. **22.36–39** Balak comes to meet Balaam when he gets to Moab's border. **22.36** *Ir-moab,* or "the city of Moab," perhaps the same as Ar in Moab; see 21.15, 28; Deut 2.9, 18, 29; Isa 15.1. On the *Arnon* as the northern boundary of Moab, see 21.13. **22.39** *Kiriath-huzoth,* "the town of streets." Site unknown. **22.40** The sacrifices could be part of Balaam's divining; see v. 7; 23.2, 14; cf. 24.1.

22.41 *Bamoth-baal, Pisgah* (23.14), and *Peor* (23.28) are in the hills above the eastern Jordan Valley; see 21.19–20; Deut 3.27; 34.1; Josh 13.17–20. **23.1–2** See 22.40. **23.3** See 22.8. **23.5** See 22.8; the *word* is the following oracle, vv. 7–10. **23.7–10** The first of Balaam's oracles. Commentators generally consider oracles one and two separately from oracles three and four. The first and second oracles would make little sense without the prose that surrounds them, while the third and fourth have little necessary connection with the prose narrative. Many would date oracles three and four earlier than one and two, and see

"Balak has brought me from
Aram,
the king of Moab from the
eastern mountains:
'Come, curse Jacob for me;
Come, denounce Israel!'
8 How can I curse whom God has
not cursed?
How can I denounce those
whom the LORD has not
denounced?
9 For from the top of the crags I
see him,
from the hills I behold him;
Here is a people living alone,
and not reckoning itself among
the nations!
10 Who can count the dust of Jacob,
or number the dust-cloud[d] of
Israel?
Let me die the death of the
upright,
and let my end be like his!"

11 Then Balak said to Balaam, "What
have you done to me? I brought you to
curse my enemies, but now you have done
nothing but bless them." 12 He answered,
"Must I not take care to say what the LORD
puts into my mouth?"

Balaam's Second Oracle

13 So Balak said to him, "Come with
me to another place from which you may
see them; you shall see only part of them,
and shall not see them all; then curse
them for me from there." 14 So he took
him to the field of Zophim, to the top of
Pisgah. He built seven altars, and offered
a bull and a ram on each altar. 15 Balaam
said to Balak, "Stand here beside your
burnt offerings, while I meet the LORD

over there." 16 The LORD met Balaam, put
a word into his mouth, and said, "Return
to Balak, and this is what you shall say."
17 When he came to him, he was standing
beside his burnt offerings with the officials of Moab. Balak said to him, "What
has the LORD said?" 18 Then Balaam uttered his oracle, saying:

"Rise, Balak, and hear;
listen to me, O son of Zippor:
19 God is not a human being, that
he should lie,
or a mortal, that he should
change his mind.
Has he promised, and will he not
do it?
Has he spoken, and will he not
fulfill it?
20 See, I received a command to
bless;
he has blessed, and I cannot
revoke it.
21 He has not beheld misfortune in
Jacob;
nor has he seen trouble in
Israel
The LORD their God is with them,
acclaimed as a king among
them.
22 God, who brings them out of
Egypt,
is like the horns of a wild ox
for them.
23 Surely there is no enchantment
against Jacob,
no divination against Israel;
now it shall be said of Jacob and
Israel,
'See what God has done!'

d Or fourth part

---

some deliberate literary dependence of two on
three; see vv. 22, 24. See notes on 24.3–4, 8–9,
15–16, 17–18. **23.7** *Aram* (Syria). See 22.5. Jacob and Israel are equivalent terms used in parallel in this typical poetic construction; see Gen
32.27–28; 35.9–10. **23.8** See 22.8. **23.9** *Him*
is Jacob/Israel. *A people living alone* is a phrase that
connotes security; see Jer 49.31; Deut 33.28.
23.10 *Who can count the dust of Jacob*. See Gen
13.16; 28.14. **23.11–12** See 22.8.

23.13 *You shall see only part of them*. This phrase
(see also 22.41) implies a vast number of people
camped beyond them (see 22.3–6). **23.14** *The
field of Zophim*, "Sentinels' Field." Site unknown.
Pisgah (see 22.41) was not a particular mountain-

top, but a highland range, so "the field of Zophim" could be a part of the Pisgah highlands. On
the sacrifices, see 22.40; 23.1–2. **23.16** See
v. 5. **23.18–24** The second oracle; see 23.7–10.
23.18 See 23.7. **23.19** Balaam and Balak's petitions (and, by implication, all such petitions) are
not effective with God who, not being a human
being, is not swayed from a course already chosen. See also vv. 20, 23; but cf., e.g., Gen
18.22–33, and Moses' many acts of intercession
(see 11.10–15). **23.21** Here the Lord is referred
to specifically as the *God* of Israel; see 22.8, 18.
23.22 *Horns of a wild ox*. See 24.8. **23.23** Israel's
success as a nation reflects well on the Lord. Cf.
Moses' suggestion that the opposite is also true

24 Look, a people rising up like a
    lioness,
  and rousing itself like a lion!
It does not lie down until it has
    eaten the prey
  and drunk the blood of the
    slain."
25 Then Balak said to Balaam, "Do not curse them at all, and do not bless them at all." 26 But Balaam answered Balak, "Did I not tell you, 'Whatever the LORD says, that is what I must do'?"
27 So Balak said to Balaam, "Come now, I will take you to another place; perhaps it will please God that you may curse them for me from there." 28 So Balak took Balaam to the top of Peor, which overlooks the wasteland. e 29 Balaam said to Balak, "Build me seven altars here, and prepare seven bulls and seven rams for me." 30 So Balak did as Balaam had said, and offered a bull and a ram on each altar.

Balaam's Third Oracle

24 Now Balaam saw that it pleased the LORD to bless Israel, so he did not go, as at other times, to look for omens, but set his face toward the wilderness. 2 Balaam looked up and saw Israel camping tribe by tribe. Then the spirit of God came upon him, 3 and he uttered his oracle, saying:

"The oracle of Balaam son of
    Beor,
  the oracle of the man whose
    eye is clear, f
4 the oracle of one who hears the
    words of God,
  who sees the vision of the
    Almighty, g
  who falls down, but with eyes
    uncovered:
5 how fair are your tents, O Jacob,
  your encampments, O Israel!
6 Like palm groves that stretch far
    away,
  like gardens beside a river,
  like aloes that the LORD has
    planted,
  like cedar trees beside the
    waters.
7 Water shall flow from his buckets,
  and his seed shall have
    abundant water,
  his king shall be higher than
    Agag,
  and his kingdom shall be
    exalted.
8 God who brings him out of
    Egypt,
  is like the horns of a wild ox
    for him;

e Or overlooks Jeshimon   f Or closed or open
g Traditional rendering of Heb Shaddai

(14.13–19). **23.24** For a fierce people portrayed as a *lion*, see 24.9; Gen 49.9; Deut 33.20, 22; Isa 5.29; Ezek 19.1–9; Joel 1.6; Nah 2.11–12. **23.25–26** See 22.8. **23.28** *Peor.* See 22.41. *Which overlooks the wasteland.* Cf. 21.20. **23.29–30** See 23.1–2.

24.1–14 Balaam's third oracle. The third and fourth oracles are generally considered older than the first two (see 23.7–10), with very little connection to the narrative context, although see v. 9. **24.1–2** The preparation for the third oracle is different from that for the first two. *As at other times, to look for omens.* See 22.40. *The spirit of God came upon him.* See 11.17. **24.3–9** The third oracle itself is a general blessing of Israel and, along with the fourth oracle, has literary connections to other poetry thought by many to be quite early—not from the time of Balaam and Moses, but perhaps from the early monarchy (see 24.7, 17–18). **24.3–4** That Balaam seems to be introduced here and in vv. 15–16 is one reason commentators have suggested this Balak narrative is not the original context for oracles three and

four. *The oracle of the man whose eye is clear.* See text note *f.* The translation is uncertain. See also 2 Sam 23.1; Prov 30.1 (similar in Hebrew). *The Almighty.* See text note *g.* One group of gods in the Deir Alla inscription (see 22.2–24.25), to whose council meeting Balaam was privy, is called the "Shaddai gods." *Who falls down,* perhaps a reference to ecstatic behavior; see also 11.24–29; 1 Sam 10.5–13; 19.20–24. **24.7** *Agag.* Those who would date oracles three and four during the early monarchy compare this verse to the story of Saul's victory over the Amalekites and their king Agag in 1 Sam 15. Amalek is also mentioned in Num 24.20. **24.8–9** Some verses in oracles three and four are often compared to other early poetry, particularly the tribal lists in Gen 49 and Deut 33. *Horns of a wild ox.* See 23.22; Deut 33.17. The Hebrew word translated "horns" here and in 23.22 is not entirely clear. For lion imagery, see 23.24; note especially Gen 49.9; Deut 33.20, 22. The theme of blessing and cursing (see the blessing of Jacob in Gen 27.29) is the suggested literary link that ties oracles three and four

he shall devour the nations that
are his foes
and break their bones.
He shall strike with his
arrows.*h*
9 He crouched, he lay down like a
lion,
and like a lioness; who will
rouse him up?
Blessed is everyone who
blesses you,
and cursed is everyone who
curses you."

10 Then Balak's anger was kindled against Balaam, and he struck his hands together. Balak said to Balaam, "I summoned you to curse my enemies, but instead you have blessed them these three times. 11 Now be off with you! Go home! I said, 'I will reward you richly,' but the LORD has denied you any reward." 12 And Balaam said to Balak, "Did I not tell your messengers whom you sent to me, 13 'If Balak should give me his house full of silver and gold, I would not be able to go beyond the word of the LORD, to do either good or bad of my own will; what the LORD says, that is what I will say'? 14 So now, I am going to my people; let me advise you what this people will do to your people in days to come."

Balaam's Fourth Oracle

15 So he uttered his oracle, saying:
"The oracle of Balaam son of
Beor,
the oracle of the man whose
eye is clear,*i*
16 the oracle of one who hears the
words of God,

and knows the knowledge of
the Most High,*j*
who sees the vision of the
Almighty,*k*
who falls down, but with his
eyes uncovered:
17 I see him, but not now;
I behold him, but not near—
a star shall come out of Jacob,
and a scepter shall rise out of
Israel;
it shall crush the borderlands*l* of
Moab,
and the territory*m* of all the
Shethites.
18 Edom will become a possession,
Seir a possession of its
enemies,*n*
while Israel does valiantly.
19 One out of Jacob shall rule,
and destroy the survivors
of Ir."

20 Then he looked on Amalek, and uttered his oracle, saying:
"First among the nations was
Amalek,
but its end is to perish forever."
21 Then he looked on the Kenite, and uttered his oracle, saying:
"Enduring is your dwelling place,
and your nest is set in the rock;
22 yet Kain is destined for burning.
How long shall Asshur take you
away captive?"
23 Again he uttered his oracle, saying:
"Alas, who shall live when God
does this?

h Meaning of Heb uncertain   *i* Or *closed* or *open*
j Or *of Elyon*   *k* Traditional rendering of Heb
Shaddai   *l* Or *forehead*   *m* Some Mss read *skull*
n Heb *Seir, its enemies, a possession*

to an otherwise unrelated narrative context; see 24.1–14. **24.10** Balak *struck his hands together* in contempt. See Job 27.23; Lam 2.15. **24.11** *I said, 'I will reward you richly.'* See 22.17–18, 37. **24.12–13** See 22.8, 18; 23.3, 5, 8, 11–12, 21, 25–26. **24.14** *My people.* See 22.5.
24.15–24 The fourth oracle is a prediction that Israel will rule over the Transjordanian kingdoms (see 2 Sam 8–12). Many commentators believe that vv. 21–24 are later additions, some that v. 20 is not original to this oracle. **24.15–16** Slightly expanded over vv. 3–4. *The Most High.* See Gen 14.18–24; Deut 32.8. **24.17–18** These verses have been read as referring to King David's victories over Moab and

Edom (2 Sam 8.2, 11–14), again pointing to the early monarchy as a setting for these two oracles. *I see him, but not now; I behold him, but not near.* See 23.9. *Scepter.* See Gen 49.10. *Shethites*, perhaps a reference to the nomadic Sutu, a people known from second-millennium B.C.E. documents. On *Seir* for Edom, see Gen 32.3; Judg 5.4. **24.19** *Ir.* See 22.36. **24.20** On *Amalek*, see 13.29; see also 24.7, 15–24. **24.21–22** *Kenite.* See 10.29–32. *Kain*, the eponymous ancestor of the Kenites, is the same in Hebrew as Cain in Gen 4.1–17 and Tubal-cain in Gen 4.22. *Your nest is set in the rock* contains a pun in Hebrew: the Hebrew word for "nest" is very similar to "Kain." *Asshur* is Assyria, and the Neo-Assyrian Empire was especially fa-

24   But ships shall come from
            Kittim
   and shall afflict Asshur and Eber;
   and he also shall perish
            forever."
25 Then Balaam got up and went
back to his place, and Balak also went
his way.

Worship of Baal of Peor and the Incident of the Midianite Woman

25 While Israel was staying at Shittim, the people began to have sexual relations with the women of Moab. ²These invited the people to the sacrifices of their gods, and the people ate and bowed down to their gods. ³Thus Israel yoked itself to the Baal of Peor, and the LORD's anger was kindled against Israel. ⁴The LORD said to Moses, "Take all the chiefs of the people, and impale them in the sun before the LORD, in order that the fierce anger of the LORD may turn away from Israel." ⁵And Moses said to the judges of Israel, "Each of you shall kill any of your people who have yoked themselves to the Baal of Peor."

6   Just then one of the Israelites came and brought a Midianite woman into his family, in the sight of Moses and in the sight of the whole congregation of the Israelites, while they were weeping at the entrance of the tent of meeting. ⁷When Phinehas son of Eleazar, son of Aaron the priest, saw it, he got up and left the con-

mous for deporting conquered populations (see 2 Kings 17.5–41). **24.24** The term *Kittim* refers to Cyprus in Jer 2.10; Ezek 27.6 and is used elsewhere to represent the Greeks (Gen 10.4; 1 Macc 1.1; 8.5) and even the Romans (Dan 11.30 and in the Dead Sea Scrolls). *Asshur.* See v. 22. *Eber*, perhaps the eponymous ancestor of the Hebrews (Gen 10.21–25; 11.10–16), more likely a land "beyond" the river (as in Josh 24.3; Isa 7.20), i.e., Mesopotamia or specifically Babylonia, used here along with Assyria. *He also shall perish forever.* See v. 20.
25.1–18 This chapter is a combination of two different stories about Israelite men and foreign women: one in vv. 1–5 involving Moabite women, sacrifices, and Baal of Peor and another in vv. 6–15 involving an apparent marriage between a Midianite woman and a Simeonite man. The two are combined by vv. 16–18, and the combined narrative is known to 31.8, 15–16; Josh 22.17; Ps 106.28–31. **25.1–5** See also Deut 4.3–4; Hos 9.10. **25.1–2** *Shittim*, "the acacias." Site unknown. See the full name Abel-shittim in 33.49, there located in the plains of Moab where the Israelites have camped since 22.1. See also Josh 2.1; 3.1; Mic 6.5 (for Gilgal, see Josh 4.19–24): Shittim is the place where the conquest of the land west of the Jordan begins. *Began.* By a change in the vowels this word could read "defiled themselves." *To have sexual relations with*, lit. "to prostitute themselves with," which phrase can be used of sexual relations or of religious apostasy. *The women of Moab.* Cf. vv. 17–18; 31.15–16. *Sacrifices of their gods*, or "god" (the same Hebrew word can be used for both singular and plural) since only one god is mentioned in v. 3; see Ps 106.28–31, where these sacrifices are said to be part of a cult of the dead. *The people ate*, i.e., they participated in the sacrifices; see, e.g., Ex 32.6; Lev 7.11–18; 1 Sam 1.4, 9. Cf. vv. 1–2; Ex

34.15–16. **25.3** *Baal*, lit. "lord," originally an epithet that came to be used as the equivalent of a personal name for the Syrian storm god Hadad (cf. the Aramean king's name Hadadezer, "Hadad is help," 2 Sam 8.3–12). *Peor* is a place-name; see 23.28. **25.4** *Impale*, sometimes translated "crucify" or "expose." The narrative nowhere states that the execution of the *chiefs of the people* takes place, unless v. 8 is the equivalent. **25.5** Moses' command to the *judges of Israel* (some ancient translations have "tribes of Israel") is not the same as the Lord's command in v. 4. Here Moses asks only that the guilty parties be executed. Again, there is no indication in the narrative that this was done. **25.6–15** See also Josh 22.17–18; Ps 106.28–31. **25.6** *Into his family*, lit. "to his brothers." For "brother" as kin in general, see, e.g., 16.10; Gen 13.8; 29.12. What was the offense involved in this story? Perhaps simply bringing home, i.e., marrying, a Midianite woman. That it was done *in the sight of Moses* takes on a special significance then. Even though Moses was aware of the offense, he did nothing about it. Vv. 6–18 are an anti-Midianite story used also to elevate Aaron's family over Moses'; see 12.2; 16.3, 40. Moses could hardly punish an Israelite man for marrying a Midianite woman when he had done so himself (see 10.29–32); there is more than one attitude toward intermarriage in the Hebrew Bible; cf. Ex 34.15–16; Deut 7.2–4; Josh 23.12–13. Although the reason is not given until v. 8, the people were apparently *weeping at the entrance of the tent of meeting* because of a plague. Once the two stories in this chapter are combined, the plague becomes a punishment for the worship of Baal of Peor (see v. 18 [a third punishment, the ones in vv. 4–5 apparently not having been carried out]), and the people are weeping before the tent in supplication to the Lord (see 7.89; 16.16–18). **25.7** *Phinehas son of Eleazar.* See Ex

gregation. Taking a spear in his hand, [8]he went after the Israelite man into the tent, and pierced the two of them, the Israelite and the woman, through the belly. So the plague was stopped among the people of Israel. [9]Nevertheless those that died by the plague were twenty-four thousand.

10 The LORD spoke to Moses, saying: [11]"Phinehas son of Eleazar, son of Aaron the priest, has turned back my wrath from the Israelites by manifesting such zeal among them on my behalf that in my jealousy I did not consume the Israelites. [12]Therefore say, 'I hereby grant him my covenant of peace. [13]It shall be for him and for his descendants after him a covenant of perpetual priesthood, because he was zealous for his God, and made atonement for the Israelites.'"

14 The name of the slain Israelite man, who was killed with the Midianite woman, was Zimri son of Salu, head of an ancestral house belonging to the Simeonites. [15]The name of the Midianite woman who was killed was Cozbi daughter of Zur, who was the head of a clan, an ancestral house in Midian.

16 The LORD said to Moses, [17]"Harass the Midianites, and defeat them; [18]for they have harassed you by the trickery with which they deceived you in the affair of Peor, and in the affair of Cozbi, the daughter of a leader of Midian, their sister; she was killed on the day of the plague that resulted from Peor."

A Census of the New Generation

26 After the plague the LORD said to Moses and to Eleazar son of Aaron the priest, [2]"Take a census of the whole congregation of the Israelites, from twenty years old and upward, by their ancestral houses, everyone in Israel able to go to war." [3]Moses and Eleazar the priest spoke with them in the plains of Moab by the Jordan opposite Jericho, saying, [4]"Take a census of the people,[o] from twenty years old and upward," as the LORD commanded Moses.

The Israelites, who came out of the land of Egypt, were:

5 Reuben, the firstborn of Israel. The descendants of Reuben: of Hanoch, the

o Heb lacks *take a census of the people*: Compare verse 2

6.23–25; Num 20.22–29.   **25.8** The Hebrew word for *tent* here is not the usual one. In fact, this word is used in the Hebrew Bible only here. The meaning is uncertain, but it was probably a domed tent; it has been suggested that this term is an alternate word for the tabernacle. *Pierced the two of them*, i.e., at once, implying sexual intercourse or some positioning in which the two bodies could be pierced with one thrust of the spear. *Through the belly*. The Hebrew is difficult but seems to mean "through *her* belly." The Hebrew word for "belly" here, though, is very similar to the word for a special tent earlier in this verse, and one ancient translation has "in the tent" at this point.   **25.8–9** *Plague*. See v. 6.   **25.10–13** The event becomes the grounds for praise of the Aaronite priestly family (see 1 Chr 6.3–15, 49–53), and an indirect criticism of Moses, who apparently failed to carry out either form of punishment in vv. 4–5 and did nothing about the trespass in v. 6.   **25.12** *My covenant of peace*. See Isa 54.10; Ezek 34.25; 37.26; Mal 2.4–5.   **25.13** *Perpetual priesthood*. See also Ex 29.9; 40.15.   **25.14–15** Both the Israelite man and the Midianite woman were important people in their own groups; see also v. 18 and *Zur* in 31.8.   **25.16–18** See ch. 31.   **25.18** This verse ties together the two stories in this chapter by pairing the Midianites with the Moabites in the *affair of*

Peor and by asserting that the plague mentioned in vv. 8–9 was the result of the same Peor incident. *Trickery*, presumably the women's use of sexual contact to draw the Israelite men to sacrifices to a god other than the Lord; see 31.16.

26.1–65 The last obstacle to the conquest is overcome when the plague of ch. 25 apparently kills the remaining Israelites of the wilderness generation (see 26.64), those who were condemned to die because of the incident of the spies in chs. 13–14 (see 14.20–25, 28–35). At this point a new military census is taken, parallel to the census in ch. 1, and from this point the people of Israel are not the condemned generation of the forty years' wandering but rather a new generation that will live to conquer the promised land.   **26.1** *After the plague* is v. 19 of ch. 25 in Hebrew. The plague is the one in 25.8–9, 18. *To Moses and to Eleazar son of Aaron*. Cf. 1.3; 20.22–29.   **26.2** Cf. 1.2–3.   **26.4** *Who came out of the land of Egypt* is an odd introduction to the following list since these are precisely not those people (vv. 64–65). The phrase may simply mean those who were on the way from Egypt to Canaan.   **26.5–50** Cf. 1.20–43. The ordering of the tribes here is different from that in ch. 1, but similar to that in ch. 2; the eastern and southern threesomes have traded places so that Reuben, the traditional firstborn, is first, and Manasseh and Ephraim are

clan of the Hanochites; of Pallu, the clan of the Palluites; 6of Hezron, the clan of the Hezronites; of Carmi, the clan of the Carmites. 7These are the clans of the Reubenites; the number of those enrolled was forty-three thousand seven hundred thirty. 8And the descendants of Pallu: Eliab. 9The descendants of Eliab: Nemuel, Dathan, and Abiram. These are the same Dathan and Abiram, chosen from the congregation, who rebelled against Moses and Aaron in the company of Korah, when they rebelled against the Lord, 10and the earth opened its mouth and swallowed them up along with Korah, when that company died, when the fire devoured two hundred fifty men; and they became a warning. 11Notwithstanding, the sons of Korah did not die.

12 The descendants of Simeon by their clans: of Nemuel, the clan of the Nemuelites; of Jamin, the clan of the Jaminites; of Jachin, the clan of the Jachinites; 13of Zerah, the clan of the Zerahites; of Shaul, the clan of the Shaulites.p 14These are the clans of the Simeonites, twenty-two thousand two hundred.

15 The children of Gad by their clans: of Zephon, the clan of the Zephonites; of Haggi, the clan of the Haggites; of Shuni, the clan of the Shunites; 16of Ozni, the clan of the Oznites; of Eri, the clan of the Erites; 17of Arod, the clan of the Arodites; of Areli, the clan of the Arelites. 18These are the clans of the Gadites: the number of those enrolled was forty thousand five hundred.

19 The sons of Judah: Er and Onan; Er and Onan died in the land of Canaan. 20The descendants of Judah by their clans were: of Shelah, the clan of the Shelanites; of Perez, the clan of the Perezites; of Zerah, the clan of the Zerahites. 21The descendants of Perez were: of Hezron, the clan of the Hezronites; of Hamul, the clan of the Hamulites. 22These are the clans of Judah: the number of those enrolled was seventy-six thousand five hundred.

23 The descendants of Issachar by their clans: of Tola, the clan of the Tolaites; of Puvah, the clan of the Punites; 24of Jashub, the clan of the Jashubites; of Shimron, the clan of the Shimronites. 25These are the clans of Issachar: sixty-four thousand three hundred enrolled.

26 The descendants of Zebulun by their clans: of Sered, the clan of the Seredites; of Elon, the clan of the Elonites; of Jahleel, the clan of the Jahleelites. 27These are the clans of the Zebulunites; the number of those enrolled was sixty thousand five hundred.

28 The sons of Joseph by their clans: Manasseh and Ephraim. 29The descendants of Manasseh: of Machir, the clan of the Machirites; and Machir was the father of Gilead; of Gilead, the clan of the Gileadites. 30These are the descendants of Gilead: of Iezer, the clan of the Iezerites; of Helek, the clan of the Helekites; 31and of Asriel, the clan of the Asrielites; and of Shechem, the clan of the Shechemites; 32and of Shemida, the clan of the Shemidaites; and of Hepher, the clan of the Hepherites. 33Now Zelophehad son of Hepher had no sons, but daughters: and the names of the daughters of Zelophehad were Mahlah, Noah, Hoglah, Milcah, and Tirzah. 34These are the clans of Manasseh; the number of those enrolled was fifty-two thousand seven hundred.

35 These are the descendants of Ephraim according to their clans: of Shuthelah, the clan of the Shuthelahites; of Becher, the clan of the Becherites; of Tahan, the clan of the Tahanites. 36And these are the descendants of Shuthelah: of Eran, the clan of the Eranites. 37These are the clans of the Ephraimites: the number of those enrolled was thirty-two thousand five hundred. These are the descendants of Joseph by their clans.

38 The descendants of Benjamin by their clans: of Bela, the clan of the Belaites; of Ashbel, the clan of the Ashbelites; of Ahiram, the clan of the Ahiramites; 39of Shephupham, the clan of the Shuphamites; of Hupham, the clan of the Huphamites. 40And the sons of Bela were Ard and Naaman: of Ard, the clan of the Ardites; of Naaman, the clan of the Naamites. 41These are the descendants of

p Or Saul ... Saulites

switched within the western threesome (cf. Gen 41.50–52; 48.8–20). In this second military census in Numbers, furthermore, the clans of each tribe are listed along with the tribe's totals (cf. Gen 46.8–27). The totals in this list differ from the totals in ch. 1, clan by clan and for Israel as a whole. **26.9–10** *Dathan and Abiram.* See ch. 16. **26.11** On the Korahites, see 16.1. **26.19** See

Benjamin by their clans; the number of those enrolled was forty-five thousand six hundred.

42 These are the descendants of Dan by their clans: of Shuham, the clan of the Shuhamites. These are the clans of Dan by their clans. 43 All the clans of the Shuhamites: sixty-four thousand four hundred enrolled.

44 The descendants of Asher by their families: of Imnah, the clan of the Imnites; of Ishvi, the clan of the Ishvites; of Beriah, the clan of the Beriites. 45 Of the descendants of Beriah: of Heber, the clan of the Heberites; of Malchiel, the clan of the Malchielites. 46 And the name of the daughter of Asher was Serah. 47 These are the clans of the Asherites: the number of those enrolled was fifty-three thousand four hundred.

48 The descendants of Naphtali by their clans: of Jahzeel, the clan of the Jahzeelites; of Guni, the clan of the Gunites; 49 of Jezer, the clan of the Jezerites; of Shillem, the clan of the Shillemites. 50 These are the Naphtalites*q* by their clans: the number of those enrolled was forty-five thousand four hundred.

51 This was the number of the Israelites enrolled: six hundred and one thousand seven hundred thirty.

52 The LORD spoke to Moses, saying: 53 To these the land shall be apportioned for inheritance according to the number of names. 54 To a large tribe you shall give a large inheritance, and to a small tribe you shall give a small inheritance; every tribe shall be given its inheritance according to its enrollment. 55 But the land shall be apportioned by lot; according to the names of their ancestral tribes they shall inherit. 56 Their inheritance shall be apportioned according to lot between the larger and the smaller.

57 This is the enrollment of the Le-

vites by their clans: of Gershon, the clan of the Gershonites; of Kohath, the clan of the Kohathites; of Merari, the clan of the Merarites. 58 These are the clans of Levi: the clan of the Libnites, the clan of the Hebronites, the clan of the Mahlites, the clan of the Mushites, the clan of the Korahites. Now Kohath was the father of Amram. 59 The name of Amram's wife was Jochebed daughter of Levi, who was born to Levi in Egypt; and she bore to Amram: Aaron, Moses, and their sister Miriam. 60 To Aaron were born Nadab, Abihu, Eleazar, and Ithamar. 61 But Nadab and Abihu died when they offered unholy fire before the LORD. 62 The number of those enrolled was twenty-three thousand, every male one month old and upward; for they were not enrolled among the Israelites because there was no allotment given to them among the Israelites.

63 These were those enrolled by Moses and Eleazar the priest, who enrolled the Israelites in the plains of Moab by the Jordan opposite Jericho. 64 Among these there was not one of those enrolled by Moses and Aaron the priest, who had enrolled the Israelites in the wilderness of Sinai. 65 For the LORD had said of them, "They shall die in the wilderness." Not one of them was left, except Caleb son of Jephunneh and Joshua son of Nun.

The Daughters of Zelophehad

27 Then the daughters of Zelophehad came forward. Zelophehad was son of Hepher son of Gilead son of Machir son of Manasseh son of Joseph, a member of the Manassite clans. The names of his daughters were: Mahlah, Noah, Hoglah, Milcah, and Tirzah. 2 They stood before Moses, Eleazar the priest, the leaders, and all the congrega-

q Heb *clans of Naphtali*

Gen 38. **26.33** See 27.1–11; 36.1–12. **26.51** See 1.46. **26.52–56** A new reason for taking a census is given here, in addition to the need for knowing military power (v. 2), i.e., that after the conquest of Canaan, land will be apportioned based on the size of the tribes. **26.57–62** Cf. 3.14–39. **26.61** See Lev 10.1–2. **26.62** *Every male one month old and up.* See 3.15, 40–41. *Not enrolled among the Israelites.* See 1.48–49. *No allotment given to them.* See, e.g., 18.23–24. **26.64–65** See 14.20–25, 28–35.

27.1–11 In Israel, property was passed from father to son, but any patrilineal system must have alternative inheritance arrangements for a man who has no sons (ancestral land is not to be sold; see 1 Kings 21.1–19; Mic 2.1–5). One such arrangement, known also from other ancient Near Eastern documents, is that daughters may inherit, and that solution is here given Mosaic sanction. A restriction is added in 36.1–12, and the decision is carried out in Josh 17.3–6. For alternative solutions, see Deut 25.5–10 (cf. Gen 38.6–11; Ruth); Jer 32.6–15; Lev 25.8–31. **27.1** See 26.33.

tion, at the entrance of the tent of meeting, and they said, 3 "Our father died in the wilderness; he was not among the company of those who gathered themselves together against the LORD in the company of Korah, but died for his own sin; and he had no sons. 4 Why should the name of our father be taken away from his clan because he had no son? Give to us a possession among our father's brothers."

5 Moses brought their case before the LORD. 6 And the LORD spoke to Moses, saying: 7 The daughters of Zelophehad are right in what they are saying; you shall indeed let them possess an inheritance among their father's brothers and pass the inheritance of their father on to them. 8 You shall also say to the Israelites, "If a man dies, and has no son, then you shall pass his inheritance on to his daughter. 9 If he has no daughter, then you shall give his inheritance to his brothers. 10 If he has no brothers, then you shall give his inheritance to his father's brothers. 11 And if his father has no brothers, then you shall give his inheritance to the nearest kinsman of his clan, and he shall possess it. It shall be for the Israelites a statute and ordinance, as the LORD commanded Moses."

Joshua Appointed Moses' Successor

12 The LORD said to Moses, "Go up this mountain of the Abarim range, and see the land that I have given to the Isra-elites. 13 When you have seen it, you also shall be gathered to your people, as your brother Aaron was, 14 because you rebelled against my word in the wilderness of Zin when the congregation quarreled with me.ʳ You did not show my holiness before their eyes at the waters." (These are the waters of Meribath-kadesh in the wilderness of Zin.) 15 Moses spoke to the LORD, saying, 16 "Let the LORD, the God of the spirits of all flesh, appoint someone over the congregation 17 who shall go out before them and come in before them, who shall lead them out and bring them in, so that the congregation of the LORD may not be like sheep without a shepherd." 18 So the LORD said to Moses, "Take Joshua son of Nun, a man in whom is the spirit, and lay your hand upon him; 19 have him stand before Eleazar the priest and all the congregation, and commission him in their sight. 20 You shall give him some of your authority, so that all the congregation of the Israelites may obey. 21 But he shall stand before Eleazar the priest, who shall inquire for him by the decision of the Urim before the LORD; at his word they shall go out, and at his word they shall come in, both he and all the Israelites with him, the whole congregation." 22 So Moses did as the LORD commanded him. He took Joshua and had him stand before Eleazar the priest and the whole congregation; 23 he laid his hands on him and commissioned him—as the LORD had directed through Moses.

r Heb lacks *with me*

27.3 See ch. 16. That Zelophehad, a Manassite, might have been part of Korah's rebellion marks this mention as dependent on the strand of tradition in which Korah and his group are not Levites (see 16.3). *For his own sin*, perhaps simply a reference to chs. 13–14. 27.4 On the *name*, cf. Deut 25.5–7. The son perpetuates the father's name in his genealogy. Presumably in the case of Zelophehad's daughters, the daughters' sons would carry on as Zelophehad's descendants and would inherit his property, an arrangement also known from other ancient Near Eastern documents; see also 1 Chr 2.34–36; Ezra 2.61; Neh 7.63. The complication that the sons will be part of their fathers' lineages as well is resolved in ch. 36, again in typical fashion. *Father's brothers*, i.e., male members of his clan. 27.5 *Before the LORD*, i.e., at the tent of meeting; see v. 2. 27.8–11 The line of inheritance approved here favors direct descendants, male or female, over other relatives, then moves from near to more distant male relatives. 27.12 See 21.11. 27.13 See 20.22–29. 27.14 See 20.12. 27.16 *The God of the spirits of all flesh*. See 16.22. 27.17 *Go out before them and come in before them* is a phrase often used as a technical military term for the battle march; see v. 21; Josh 14.11; 1 Sam 18.13, 16; 29.6. *Sheep without a shepherd*. See 1 Kings 22.17; Ezek 34.1–10; Zech 11. 27.18 On *Joshua*, besides the book of Joshua, see especially Ex 17.8–14; 24.13; 33.11; Num 11.28; 13.8, 16; 14.6, 30, 38. *A man in whom is the spirit*. See 11.16–30. *Lay your hand upon him*, a form of transfer, in this case, of Moses' authority (v. 20). See also 8.10–11; Deut 34.9. 27.21 *Eleazar*, not Joshua, is to perform the role of intermediary, using the Urim to determine the Lord's will; see Ex 28.29–30; 1 Sam 14.41; 28.6; Ezra 2.63. *Go out, and ... come in*. See v. 17. 27.23 See v. 18.

Daily Offerings

28 The LORD spoke to Moses, saying: ²Command the Israelites, and say to them: My offering, the food for my offerings by fire, my pleasing odor, you shall take care to offer to me at its appointed time. ³And you shall say to them, This is the offering by fire that you shall offer to the LORD: two male lambs a year old without blemish, daily, as a regular offering. ⁴One lamb you shall offer in the morning, and the other lamb you shall offer at twilight;ˢ ⁵also one-tenth of an ephah of choice flour for a grain offering, mixed with one-fourth of a hin of beaten oil. ⁶It is a regular burnt offering, ordained at Mount Sinai for a pleasing odor, an offering by fire to the LORD. ⁷Its drink offering shall be one-fourth of a hin for each lamb; in the sanctuary you shall pour out a drink offering of strong drink to the LORD. ⁸The other lamb you shall offer at twilightˢ with a grain offering and a drink offering like the one in the morning; you shall offer it as an offering by fire, a pleasing odor to the LORD.

Sabbath Offerings

9 On the sabbath day: two male lambs a year old without blemish, and two-tenths of an ephah of choice flour for a grain offering, mixed with oil, and its drink offering— ¹⁰this is the burnt offering for every sabbath, in addition to the regular burnt offering and its drink offering.

Monthly Offerings

11 At the beginnings of your months you shall offer a burnt offering to the LORD: two young bulls, one ram, seven male lambs a year old without blemish; ¹²also three-tenths of an ephah of choice flour for a grain offering, mixed with oil, for each bull; and two-tenths of choice flour for a grain offering, mixed with oil, for the one ram; ¹³and one-tenth of choice flour mixed with oil as a grain offering for every lamb—a burnt offering of pleasing odor, an offering by fire to the LORD. ¹⁴Their drink offerings shall be half a hin of wine for a bull, one-third of a hin for a ram, and one-fourth of a hin for a lamb. This is the burnt offering of every month throughout the months of the year. ¹⁵And there shall be one male goat for a sin offering to the LORD; it shall be offered in addition to the regular burnt offering and its drink offering.

Offerings at Passover

16 On the fourteenth day of the first month there shall be a passover offering to the LORD. ¹⁷And on the fifteenth day of this month is a festival; seven days shall unleavened bread be eaten. ¹⁸On the first day there shall be a holy convocation. You shall not work at your occupations. ¹⁹You shall offer an offering by fire, a burnt offering to the LORD: two young bulls, one ram, and seven male lambs a year old; see that they are without blemish. ²⁰Their grain offering shall be of choice flour mixed with oil: three-tenths of an ephah shall you offer for a bull, and two-tenths for a ram; ²¹one-tenth shall you offer for each of the seven lambs; ²²also one male goat for a sin offering, to make atonement for you. ²³You shall offer these in addition to the burnt offering of the morning, which belongs to the regular burnt offering. ²⁴In the same way you shall offer daily, for seven days, the food of an offering by fire, a pleasing odor to the LORD; it shall be offered in addition to the regular burnt offering and its drink offering. ²⁵And on the seventh day you shall have a holy convocation; you shall not work at your occupations.

Offerings at the Festival of Weeks

26 On the day of the first fruits, when you offer a grain offering of new grain to the LORD at your festival of weeks, you

s Heb *between the two evenings*

28.1–29.40 Offerings are described for a number of occasions. Lev 23 has a similar cultic calendar; cf. also Ex 23.14–17; 34.18–24; Deut 16.1–17; Ezek 45.17–46.15. **28.2** *Offerings by fire* and *my pleasing odor*. See 15.3. **28.3–8** Cf. Ex 29.38–42. **28.11** *Beginnings of your months*. See 10.10; 1 Sam 20.5, 24; 2 Kings 4.23; Isa 1.14; Hos 2.11; Am 8.5. **28.16** On the *passover*, see 9.1–14; Ex 12.1–27. No offerings are described here; the celebration is described elsewhere and assumed here. **28.17–25** The festival of *unleavened bread* (Ex 13.3–10), originally a separate festival, is combined with the Passover. **28.26** Fifty days after the Festival of

shall have a holy convocation; you shall not work at your occupations. 27 You shall offer a burnt offering, a pleasing odor to the LORD: two young bulls, one ram, seven male lambs a year old. 28 Their grain offering shall be of choice flour mixed with oil, three-tenths of an ephah for each bull, two-tenths for one ram, 29 one-tenth for each of the seven lambs; 30 with one male goat, to make atonement for you. 31 In addition to the regular burnt offering with its grain offering, you shall offer them and their drink offering. They shall be without blemish.

Offerings at the Festival of Trumpets

29 On the first day of the seventh month you shall have a holy convocation; you shall not work at your occupations. It is a day for you to blow the trumpets, 2 and you shall offer a burnt offering, a pleasing odor to the LORD: one young bull, one ram, seven male lambs a year old without blemish. 3 Their grain offering shall be of choice flour mixed with oil, three-tenths of one ephah for the bull, two-tenths for the ram, 4 and one-tenth for each of the seven lambs; 5 with one male goat for a sin offering, to make atonement for you. 6 These are in addition to the burnt offering of the new moon and its grain offering, and the regular burnt offering and its grain offering, and their drink offerings, according to the ordinance for them, a pleasing odor, an offering by fire to the LORD.

Offerings on the Day of Atonement

7 On the tenth day of this seventh month you shall have a holy convocation, and deny yourselves;*t* you shall do no work. 8 You shall offer a burnt offering to the LORD, a pleasing odor: one young bull, one ram, seven male lambs a year old. They shall be without blemish. 9 Their grain offering shall be of choice flour mixed with oil, three-tenths of an ephah for the bull, two-tenths for the one ram, 10 one-tenth for each of the seven lambs; 11 with one male goat for a sin offering, in addition to the sin offering of atonement, and the regular burnt offering and its grain offering, and their drink offerings.

Offerings at the Festival of Booths

12 On the fifteenth day of the seventh month you shall have a holy convocation; you shall not work at your occupations. You shall celebrate a festival to the LORD seven days. 13 You shall offer a burnt offering, an offering by fire, a pleasing odor to the LORD: thirteen young bulls, two rams, fourteen male lambs a year old. They shall be without blemish. 14 Their grain offering shall be of choice flour mixed with oil, three-tenths of an ephah for each of the thirteen bulls, two-tenths for each of the two rams, 15 and one-tenth for each of the fourteen lambs; 16 also one male goat for a sin offering, in addition to the regular burnt offering, its grain offering and its drink offering.

17 On the second day: twelve young bulls, two rams, fourteen male lambs a year old without blemish, 18 with the grain offering and the drink offerings for the bulls, for the rams, and for the lambs, as prescribed in accordance with their number; 19 also one male goat for a sin offering, in addition to the regular burnt offering and its grain offering, and their drink offerings.

20 On the third day: eleven bulls, two rams, fourteen male lambs a year old without blemish, 21 with the grain offering and the drink offerings for the bulls, for the rams, and for the lambs, as prescribed in accordance with their number; 22 also one male goat for a sin offering, in addition to the regular burnt offering and its grain offering and its drink offering.

23 On the fourth day: ten bulls, two

t Or *and fast*

Unleavened Bread, at the beginning of the wheat harvest (June), is the *festival of weeks*, Shavuoth (Lev 23.15–21), or the festival of harvest (Ex 23.16). **29.1** *The first day of the seventh month* is traditionally New Year's Day (Rosh Hashanah; see Ex 23.16; 34.22 for the end of the year); many commentators have argued that Israel once had an "agricultural year" calendar in which the first month came in the autumn, following the harvest thanksgiving festival (see v. 12). *To blow the trumpets.* See 10.1–10. **29.6** See 28.2. **29.7–11** The Day of Atonement, Yom Kippur; see Lev 16.29–34; 23.26–32. **29.12–34** The Festival of Booths, Sukkoth (Lev 23.33–36; Deut 16.13–15), or Festival of Ingathering (Ex 23.16; 34.22), is the harvest thanksgiving festival.

rams, fourteen male lambs a year old without blemish, 24 with the grain offering and the drink offerings for the bulls, for the rams, and for the lambs, as prescribed in accordance with their number; 25 also one male goat for a sin offering, in addition to the regular burnt offering, its grain offering and its drink offering.

26 On the fifth day: nine bulls, two rams, fourteen male lambs a year old without blemish, 27 with the grain offering and the drink offerings for the bulls, for the rams, and for the lambs, as prescribed in accordance with their number; 28 also one male goat for a sin offering, in addition to the regular burnt offering and its grain offering and its drink offering.

29 On the sixth day: eight bulls, two rams, fourteen male lambs a year old without blemish, 30 with the grain offering and the drink offerings for the bulls, for the rams, and for the lambs, as prescribed in accordance with their number; 31 also one male goat for a sin offering, in addition to the regular burnt offering, its grain offering, and its drink offerings.

32 On the seventh day: seven bulls, two rams, fourteen male lambs a year old without blemish, 33 with the grain offering and the drink offerings for the bulls, for the rams, and for the lambs, as prescribed in accordance with their number; 34 also one male goat for a sin offering, besides the regular burnt offering, its grain offering, and its drink offering.

35 On the eighth day you shall have a solemn assembly; you shall not work at your occupations. 36 You shall offer a burnt offering, an offering by fire, a pleasing odor to the LORD: one bull, one ram, seven male lambs a year old without blemish, 37 and the grain offering and the drink offerings for the bull, for the ram, and for the lambs, as prescribed in accordance with their number; 38 also one male goat for a sin offering, in addition to the

regular burnt offering and its grain offering and its drink offering.

39 These you shall offer to the LORD at your appointed festivals, in addition to your votive offerings and your freewill offerings, as your burnt offerings, your grain offerings, your drink offerings, and your offerings of well-being.

40 u So Moses told the Israelites everything just as the LORD had commanded Moses.

Vows Made by Women

30 Then Moses said to the heads of the tribes of the Israelites: This is what the LORD has commanded. 2 When a man makes a vow to the LORD, or swears an oath to bind himself by a pledge, he shall not break his word; he shall do according to all that proceeds out of his mouth.

3 When a woman makes a vow to the LORD, or binds herself by a pledge, while within her father's house, in her youth, 4 and her father hears of her vow or her pledge by which she has bound herself, and says nothing to her; then all her vows shall stand, and any pledge by which she has bound herself shall stand. 5 But if her father expresses disapproval to her at the time that he hears of it, no vow of hers, and no pledge by which she has bound herself, shall stand; and the LORD will forgive her, because her father had expressed to her his disapproval.

6 If she marries, while obligated by her vows or any thoughtless utterance of her lips by which she has bound herself, 7 and her husband hears of it and says nothing to her at the time that he hears, then her vows shall stand, and her pledges by which she has bound herself shall stand. 8 But if, at the time that her husband hears of it, he expresses disapproval to her, then he shall nullify the vow

u Ch 30.1 in Heb

29.35–38 Although the Feast of Booths is a grand seven-day festival (see v. 12), these regulations add still an eighth day, with far fewer offerings. 30.1–16 Ch. 30 focuses on vows made by women and the limits that husbands and fathers may place on those vows (note the mention of vows in 29.39). 30.3–5 Vows made while a woman is under her father's authority. 30.4–5

The father must speak up as soon as he hears of his daughter's vow, if he disapproves. *The LORD will forgive her*, i.e., will not punish her or require atonement from her for breaking her vow. 30.6–8 A woman under a vow at the time of her marriage, one that, presumably, her father did not annul. *Thoughtless*, perhaps "impulsive" or "rash" would be a better translation; cf. the same root in Lev 5.4; Ps 106.33.

by which she was obligated, or the thoughtless utterance of her lips, by which she bound herself; and the LORD will forgive her. 9(But every vow of a widow or of a divorced woman, by which she has bound herself, shall be binding upon her.) 10And if she made a vow in her husband's house, or bound herself by a pledge with an oath, 11and her husband heard it and said nothing to her, and did not express disapproval to her, then all her vows shall stand, and any pledge by which she bound herself shall stand. 12But if her husband nullifies them at the time that he hears them, then whatever proceeds out of her lips concerning her vows, or concerning her pledge of herself, shall not stand. Her husband has nullified them, and the LORD will forgive her. 13Any vow or any binding oath to deny herself,^{v} her husband may allow to stand, or her husband may nullify. 14But if her husband says nothing to her from day to day,^{w} then he validates all her vows, or all her pledges, by which she is obligated; he has validated them, because he said nothing to her at the time that he heard of them. 15But if he nullifies them some time after he has heard of them, then he shall bear her guilt.

16 These are the statutes that the LORD commanded Moses concerning a husband and his wife, and a father and his daughter while she is still young and in her father's house.

War Against Midian

31 The LORD spoke to Moses, saying, 2"Avenge the Israelites on the Midianites; afterward you shall be gathered to your people." 3So Moses said to the people, "Arm some of your number

for the war, so that they may go against Midian, to execute the LORD's vengeance on Midian. 4You shall send a thousand from each of the tribes of Israel to the war." 5So out of the thousands of Israel, a thousand from each tribe were conscripted, twelve thousand armed for battle. 6Moses sent them to the war, a thousand from each tribe, along with Phinehas son of Eleazar the priest,^{x} with the vessels of the sanctuary and the trumpets for sounding the alarm in his hand. 7They did battle against Midian, as the LORD had commanded Moses, and killed every male. 8They killed the kings of Midian: Evi, Rekem, Zur, Hur, and Reba, the five kings of Midian, in addition to others who were slain by them; and they also killed Balaam son of Beor with the sword. 9The Israelites took the women of Midian and their little ones captive; and they took all their cattle, their flocks, and all their goods as booty. 10All their towns where they had settled, and all their encampments, they burned, 11but they took all the spoil and all the booty, both people and animals. 12Then they brought the captives and the booty and the spoil to Moses, to Eleazar the priest, and to the congregation of the Israelites, at the camp on the plains of Moab by the Jordan at Jericho.

Return from the War

13 Moses, Eleazar the priest, and all the leaders of the congregation went to meet them outside the camp. 14Moses became angry with the officers of the army, the commanders of thousands and the commanders of hundreds, who had come

v Or to fast w Or from that day to the next
x Gk: Heb adds to the war

30.7–8 See 30.4–5.   30.9 A *widow* or *divorced woman* is presumably not under any man's authority.   30.10–15 Vows made while under a husband's authority.   30.11–12 See 30.4–5.   30.13 A specific instance, in which a woman vows to *deny herself* or to fast (see text note v; cf. the same phrase in 29.7).   30.14–15 *He shall bear her guilt.* See 30.4–5. The husband may change his mind at a later date and keep her from carrying out her vow, but the Lord will hold him responsible, not her (see Deut 23.21–23).
31.2 *Avenge the Israelites* because of the incident at Peor (25.6–18). Moses' death is predicted (see also 27.13).   31.3–12 The war against Mid-

ian is described in holy-war terms (see, e.g., Deut 20; 21.10–14; 23.9–14; 24.5; Josh 6.1–21). 31.5 Compared to 26.2, 51, *twelve thousand* is a very small number. Cf. Deut 20.5–8; Judg 7.2–8; 1 Sam 14.6–15; 2 Sam 17.1; 1 Kings 10.26. 31.6 *Phinehas* instead of Eleazar. See 16.37–39; 25.7. *Trumpets.* See 10.9. The presence of the priest and items from the sanctuary indicates holy war; see Deut 20.2–4. 31.7 *Killed every male.* See Deut 20.12–13. 31.8 The five kings. See also Josh 13.21. *Zur.* See 25.15. *Balaam.* See 31.16; chs. 22–25. 31.9–12 See Deut 20.14–15; 21.10–14; but cf. Num 31.14–18. 31.14 See

from service in the war. 15 Moses said to them, "Have you allowed all the women to live? 16 These women here, on Balaam's advice, made the Israelites act treacherously against the LORD in the affair of Peor, so that the plague came among the congregation of the LORD. 17 Now therefore, kill every male among the little ones, and kill every woman who has known a man by sleeping with him. 18 But all the young girls who have not known a man by sleeping with him, keep alive for yourselves. 19 Camp outside the camp seven days; whoever of you has killed any person or touched a corpse, purify yourselves and your captives on the third and on the seventh day. 20 You shall purify every garment, every article of skin, everything made of goats' hair, and every article of wood."

21 Eleazar the priest said to the troops who had gone to battle: "This is the statute of the law that the LORD has commanded Moses: 22 gold, silver, bronze, iron, tin, and lead— 23 everything that can withstand fire, shall be passed through fire, and it shall be clean. Nevertheless it shall also be purified with the water for purification; and whatever cannot withstand fire, shall be passed through the water. 24 You must wash your clothes on the seventh day, and you shall be clean; afterward you may come into the camp."

Disposition of Captives and Booty

25 The LORD spoke to Moses, saying, 26 "You and Eleazar the priest and the heads of the ancestral houses of the congregation make an inventory of the booty captured, both human and animal. 27 Divide the booty into two parts, between the warriors who went out to battle and all the congregation. 28 From the share of the warriors who went out to battle, set aside as tribute for the LORD, one item out of every five hundred, whether persons, oxen, donkeys, sheep, or goats. 29 Take it from their half and give it to Eleazar the priest as an offering to the LORD. 30 But from the Israelites' half you shall take one out of every fifty, whether persons, oxen, donkeys, sheep, or goats—all the animals —and give them to the Levites who have charge of the tabernacle of the LORD."

31 Then Moses and Eleazar the priest did as the LORD had commanded Moses:

32 The booty remaining from the spoil that the troops had taken totaled six hundred seventy-five thousand sheep, 33 seventy-two thousand oxen, 34 sixty-one thousand donkeys, 35 and thirty-two thousand persons in all, women who had not known a man by sleeping with him.

36 The half-share, the portion of those who had gone out to war, was in number three hundred thirty-seven thousand five hundred sheep and goats, 37 and the LORD's tribute of sheep and goats was six hundred seventy-five. 38 The oxen were thirty-six thousand, of which the LORD's tribute was seventy-two. 39 The donkeys were thirty thousand five hundred, of which the LORD's tribute was sixty-one. 40 The persons were sixteen thousand, of which the LORD's tribute was thirty-two persons. 41 Moses gave the tribute, the offering for the LORD, to Eleazar the priest, as the LORD had commanded Moses.

42 As for the Israelites' half, which Moses separated from that of the troops, 43 the congregation's half was three hundred thirty-seven thousand five hundred sheep and goats, 44 thirty-six thousand oxen, 45 thirty thousand five hundred donkeys, 46 and sixteen thousand persons. 47 From the Israelites' half Moses took one of every fifty, both of persons and of animals, and gave them to the Levites who had charge of the tabernacle of the LORD; as the LORD had commanded Moses.

---

also 1 Sam 15.10–19. **31.15** See 31.9. **31.16** Cf. ch. 25. Although Balaam is not mentioned there, ch. 25 is juxtaposed to the Balaam narrative, and Balaam is said to be at Peor in 23.28. See also Josh 13.21–22. Midianite women, plural, seem here to be merged with Moabite women (Num 25.1–5, 16–18). **31.17–18** Even male children are killed, presumably to ensure the extermination of Midian, but cf. Judg 6–8. The women who are to be killed are all those who might have been involved in sexual relations with Israelite men; see 31.16; 25.1. **31.19–24** See 19.1–22. **31.19** On the third and on the seventh day. See 19.12, 19. **31.20** See Lev 11.29–32. **31.23** Water for purification. See 19.9, 11–22. **31.27–30** Provision for the sanctuary from the living booty (see also 18.8–32), a smaller amount taken from the warriors' share for the priests and a larger amount taken from the rest for the Levites; see also 1 Sam 30.21–25. **31.35** See 31.14–18.

48 Then the officers who were over the thousands of the army, the commanders of thousands and the commanders of hundreds, approached Moses, 49 and said to Moses, "Your servants have counted the warriors who are under our command, and not one of us is missing. 50 And we have brought the LORD's offering, what each of us found, articles of gold, armlets and bracelets, signet rings, earrings, and pendants, to make atonement for ourselves before the LORD." 51 Moses and Eleazar the priest received the gold from them, all in the form of crafted articles. 52 And all the gold of the offering that they offered to the LORD, from the commanders of thousands and the commanders of hundreds, was sixteen thousand seven hundred fifty shekels. 53 (The troops had all taken plunder for themselves.) 54 So Moses and Eleazar the priest received the gold from the commanders of thousands and of hundreds, and brought it into the tent of meeting as a memorial for the Israelites before the LORD.

Conquest and Division of Transjordan

32 Now the Reubenites and the Gadites owned a very great number of cattle. When they saw that the land of Jazer and the land of Gilead was a good place for cattle, 2 the Gadites and the Reubenites came and spoke to Moses, to Eleazar the priest, and to the leaders of the congregation, saying, 3 "Ataroth, Dibon, Jazer, Nimrah, Heshbon, Elealeh, Sebam, Nebo, and Beon— 4 the land that the LORD subdued before the congregation of Israel—is a land for cattle; and your servants have cattle." 5 They continued, "If we have found favor in your sight, let this land be given to your servants for a possession; do not make us cross the Jordan."

6 But Moses said to the Gadites and to the Reubenites, "Shall your brothers go to war while you sit here? 7 Why will you discourage the hearts of the Israelites from going over into the land that the LORD has given them? 8 Your fathers did this, when I sent them from Kadesh-barnea to see the land. 9 When they went up to the Wadi Eshcol and saw the land, they discouraged the hearts of the Israelites from going into the land that the LORD had given them. 10 The LORD's anger was kindled on that day and he swore, saying, 11 'Surely none of the people who came up out of Egypt, from twenty years old and upward, shall see the land that I swore to give to Abraham, to Isaac, and to Jacob, because they have not unreservedly followed me— 12 none except Caleb son of Jephunneh the Kenizzite and Joshua son of Nun, for they have unreservedly followed the LORD.' 13 And the LORD's anger was kindled against Israel, and he made them wander in the wilderness for forty years, until all the generation that had done evil in the sight of the LORD had disappeared. 14 And now you, a brood of sinners, have risen in place of your fathers, to increase the LORD's fierce anger against Israel! 15 If you turn away from following him, he will again abandon them in the wilderness; and you will destroy all this people."

16 Then they came up to him and said, "We will build sheepfolds here for our flocks, and towns for our little ones, 17 but we will take up arms as a vanguard^y before the Israelites, until we have brought them to their place. Mean-

y Cn: Heb hurrying

31.49 The Israelite officers inform Moses that they lost no one in the battle. **31.50** For a possible explanation for the officers' need for *atonement*, see Ex 30.11–16. On the Midianites' *gold*, see Judg 8.24–26. **31.53** The *troops*, i.e., as opposed to the officers. **31.54** *As a memorial* in the tent of meeting; see also 16.39–40; Ex 30.11–16.

32.1–42 See also Deut 3.12–20; Josh 13.8–32; 22. **32.1–5** The Reubenites and the Gadites have cattle and they point out that Israel has already won good cattle land. **32.1** *Jazer*. See 21.32. *Gilead*, the fertile highland east of the Jordan River; see Gen 31.21, 47–48. **32.2**

Eleazar. See 19.3; 20.22–29. **32.6** See Judg 5.16–17, 23. **32.8–15** Moses interprets the request of the Reubenites and Gadites as a fear of failure in war, as in the disastrous earlier incident of the spies, chs. 13–14. This passage is one of several that are negative toward the tribes east of the Jordan. See also 16.1; Gen 35.22a; 49.3–4; Josh 22.10–34; Judg 11.29–40; 1 Chr 5.1, 23–26. **32.16–27** The parties reach a compromise: the Reubenites and Gadites will both inherit the land they want and fight in the remaining battles of conquest on the west side of the Jordan. **32.17** *Before the Israelites*, as if these people are not

while our little ones will stay in the forti-fied towns because of the inhabitants of the land. 18 We will not return to our homes until all the Israelites have obtained their inheritance. 19 We will not inherit with them on the other side of the Jordan and beyond, because our inheritance has come to us on this side of the Jordan to the east."

20 So Moses said to them, "If you do this—if you take up arms to go before the LORD for the war, 21 and all those of you who bear arms cross the Jordan before the LORD, until he has driven out his enemies from before him 22 and the land is subdued before the LORD—then after that you may return and be free of obligation to the LORD and to Israel, and this land shall be your possession before the LORD. 23 But if you do not do this, you have sinned against the LORD; and be sure your sin will find you out. 24 Build towns for your little ones, and folds for your flocks; but do what you have promised."

25 Then the Gadites and the Reubenites said to Moses, "Your servants will do as my lord commands. 26 Our little ones, our wives, our flocks, and all our livestock shall remain there in the towns of Gilead; 27 but your servants will cross over, everyone armed for war, to do battle for the LORD, just as my lord orders."

28 So Moses gave command concerning them to Eleazar the priest, to Joshua son of Nun, and to the heads of the ancestral houses of the Israelite tribes. 29 And Moses said to them, "If the Gadites and the Reubenites, everyone armed for battle before the LORD, will cross over the Jordan with you and the land shall be subdued before you, then you shall give them the land of Gilead for a possession; 30 but if they will not cross over with you armed, they shall have possessions among you in

the land of Canaan." 31 The Gadites and the Reubenites answered, "As the LORD has spoken to your servants, so we will do. 32 We will cross over armed before the LORD into the land of Canaan, but the possession of our inheritance shall remain with us on this side of z the Jordan."

33 Moses gave to them—to the Gadites and to the Reubenites and to the half-tribe of Manasseh son of Joseph—the kingdom of King Sihon of the Amorites and the kingdom of King Og of Bashan, the land and its towns, with the territories of the surrounding towns. 34 And the Gadites rebuilt Dibon, Ataroth, Aroer, 35 Atroth-shophan, Jazer, Jogbehah, 36 Beth-nimrah, and Beth-haran, fortified cities, and folds for sheep. 37 And the Reubenites rebuilt Heshbon, Elealeh, Kiriathaim, 38 Nebo, and Baal-meon (some names being changed), and Sibmah; and they gave names to the towns that they rebuilt. 39 The descendants of Machir son of Manasseh went to Gilead, captured it, and dispossessed the Amorites who were there; 40 so Moses gave Gilead to Machir son of Manasseh, and he settled there. 41 Jair son of Manasseh went and captured their villages, and renamed them Havvoth-jair.a 42 And Nobah went and captured Kenath and its villages, and renamed it Nobah after himself.

The Stages of Israel's Journey from Egypt

33 These are the stages by which the Israelites went out of the land of Egypt in military formation under the leadership of Moses and Aaron. 2 Moses wrote down their starting points, stage by stage, by command of the LORD; and these are their stages according to their starting places. 3 They set out from Rame-

z Heb *beyond*   a That is *the villages of Jair*

---

part of Israel (see v. 22). **32.22** *Free of obligation to the* LORD *and to Israel* reads almost as if they will no longer be part of the tribal federation. See also 34.1–2, 10–12; Josh 22.9, 21–29. It is also possible that "free of obligation" simply means that they will have participated fully in the holy war of conquest. **32.28** See 32.2. Moses must *give a command* because he will not be with the Israelites (see 20.12; 27.13–14). *Joshua.* See 27.12–23. **32.30** *They shall have possessions among you in the land of Canaan,* i.e., they will not be given the choice land they desire. **32.33** Note the addition of half of *Manasseh. Sihon.* See 21.21–32. *Og.*

See 21.33–35. **32.34–38** Cf. Josh 13.15–28. As described here in Numbers, the boundary between Reuben and Gad is not clear-cut. **32.39–42** Not only Reuben and Gad but also half the tribe of *Manasseh* lived east of the Jordan (see v. 33; Josh 13.29–32, and cf. Josh 17.1–13. On Manasseh's descendants, see Num 26.29–34; 1 Chr 7.14–19; Gen 50.23. These verses are similar to the descriptions of tribal conquests in Judg 1. **32.39** *Gilead.* Cf. 32.1–4. **32.41** *Havvoth-jair.* See Deut 3.14; Judg 10.3–4; 1 Chr 2.21–23. **32.42** On *Nobah* and *Kenath,* see Judg 8.11; 1 Chr 2.23.

ses in the first month, on the fifteenth day of the first month; on the day after the passover the Israelites went out boldly in the sight of all the Egyptians, 4while the Egyptians were burying all their firstborn, whom the LORD had struck down among them. The LORD executed judgments even against their gods.

5 So the Israelites set out from Rameses, and camped at Succoth. 6They set out from Succoth, and camped at Etham, which is on the edge of the wilderness. 7They set out from Etham, and turned back to Pi-hahiroth, which faces Baal-zephon; and they camped before Migdol. 8They set out from Pi-hahiroth, passed through the sea into the wilderness, went a three days' journey in the wilderness of Etham, and camped at Marah. 9They set out from Marah and came to Elim; at Elim there were twelve springs of water and seventy palm trees, and they camped there. 10They set out from Elim and camped by the Red Sea.b 11They set out from the Red Seab and camped in the wilderness of Sin. 12They set out from the wilderness of Sin and camped at Doph-kah. 13They set out from Dophkah and camped at Alush. 14They set out from Alush and camped at Rephidim, where there was no water for the people to drink. 15They set out from Rephidim and camped in the wilderness of Sinai. 16They set out from the wilderness of Sinai and camped at Kibroth-hattaavah. 17They set out from Kibroth-hattaavah and camped at Hazeroth. 18They set out from Haze-roth and camped at Rithmah. 19They set out from Rithmah and camped at Rimmon-perez. 20They set out from Rimmon-perez and camped at Libnah. 21They set out from Libnah and camped at Rissah. 22They set out from Rissah and camped at Kehelathah. 23They set out from Kehelathah and camped at Mount Shepher. 24They set out from Mount Shepher and camped at Haradah. 25They set out from Haradah and camped at Makheloth. 26They set out from Makhe-loth and camped at Tahath. 27They set out from Tahath and camped at Terah. 28They set out from Terah and camped at Mithkah. 29They set out from Mithkah and camped at Hashmonah. 30They set out from Hashmonah and camped at Mo-seroth. 31They set out from Moseroth and camped at Bene-jaakan. 32They set out from Bene-jaakan and camped at Hor-haggidgad. 33They set out from Hor-haggidgad and camped at Jotbathah. 34They set out from Jotbathah and camped at Abronah. 35They set out from Abronah and camped at Ezion-geber. 36They set out from Ezion-geber and camped in the wilderness of Zin (that is, Kadesh). 37They set out from Kadesh and camped at Mount Hor, on the edge of the land of Edom.

38 Aaron the priest went up Mount Hor at the command of the LORD and died there in the fortieth year after the Israelites had come out of the land of Egypt, on the first day of the fifth month. 39Aaron was one hundred twenty-three years old when he died on Mount Hor.

40 The Canaanite, the king of Arad, who lived in the Negeb in the land of Ca-naan, heard of the coming of the Is-raelites.

41 They set out from Mount Hor and camped at Zalmonah. 42They set out from Zalmonah and camped at Punon. 43They set out from Punon and camped at Oboth. 44They set out from Oboth and camped at Iye-abarim, in the territory of Moab. 45They set out from Iyim and camped at Dibon-gad. 46They set out from Dibon-gad and camped at Almon-diblathaim. 47They set out from Almon-diblathaim and camped in the mountains of Abarim, before Nebo. 48They set out from the mountains of Abarim and camped in the plains of Moab by the Jor-dan at Jericho; 49they camped by the Jor-dan from Beth-jeshimoth as far as Abel-shittim in the plains of Moab.

Directions for the Conquest of Canaan

50 In the plains of Moab by the Jor-dan at Jericho, the LORD spoke to Moses, saying: 51Speak to the Israelites, and say to them: When you cross over the Jordan

b Or *Sea of Reeds*

33.3–5   See Ex 12.37. **33.6–15** From Succoth to the wilderness of Sinai. See Ex 13.17–19.1. **33.16–49** From the wilderness of Sinai to the plains of Moab. See 10.11–22.1.

33.38–39 See 20.22–29.
33.50–56 See also, e.g., Ex 23.23–33; 34.11–16; Deut 7.1–6; 12.2–4; cf. Josh 23.4–8; Judg 1.1–2.5; 2.11–3.6.

into the land of Canaan, 52 you shall drive out all the inhabitants of the land from before you, destroy all their figured stones, destroy all their cast images, and demolish all their high places. 53 You shall take possession of the land and settle in it, for I have given you the land to possess. 54 You shall apportion the land by lot according to your clans; to a large one you shall give a large inheritance, and to a small one you shall give a small inheritance; the inheritance shall belong to the person on whom the lot falls; according to your ancestral tribes you shall inherit. 55 But if you do not drive out the inhabitants of the land from before you, then those whom you let remain shall be as barbs in your eyes and thorns in your sides; they shall trouble you in the land where you are settling. 56 And I will do to you as I thought to do to them.

The Boundaries of the Land

34 The LORD spoke to Moses, saying: 2 Command the Israelites, and say to them: When you enter the land of Canaan (this is the land that shall fall to you for an inheritance, the land of Canaan, defined by its boundaries), 3 your south sector shall extend from the wilderness of Zin along the side of Edom. Your southern boundary shall begin from the end of the Dead Sea[c] on the east; 4 your boundary shall turn south of the ascent of Akrabbim, and cross to Zin, and its outer limit shall be south of Kadesh-barnea; then it shall go on to Hazar-addar, and cross to Azmon; 5 the boundary shall turn from Azmon to the Wadi of Egypt, and its termination shall be at the Sea.

6 For the western boundary, you shall have the Great Sea and its[d] coast; this shall be your western boundary.
7 This shall be your northern boundary: from the Great Sea you shall mark out your line to Mount Hor; 8 from Mount Hor you shall mark it out to Lebo-hamath, and the outer limit of the boundary shall be at Zedad; 9 then the boundary shall extend to Ziphron, and its end shall be at Hazar-enan; this shall be your northern boundary.
10 You shall mark out your eastern boundary from Hazar-enan to Shepham; 11 and the boundary shall continue down from Shepham to Riblah on the east side of Ain; and the boundary shall go down, and reach the eastern slope of the sea of Chinnereth; 12 and the boundary shall go down to the Jordan, and its end shall be at the Dead Sea.[c] This shall be your land with its boundaries all around.
13 Moses commanded the Israelites, saying: This is the land that you shall inherit by lot, which the LORD has commanded to give to the nine tribes and to the half-tribe; 14 for the tribe of the Reubenites by their ancestral houses and the tribe of the Gadites by their ancestral houses have taken their inheritance, and also the half-tribe of Manasseh; 15 the two tribes and the half-tribe have taken their inheritance beyond the Jordan at Jericho eastward, toward the sunrise.

Tribal Leaders

16 The LORD spoke to Moses, saying: 17 These are the names of the men who shall apportion the land to you for inheri-

c Heb *Salt Sea*   d Syr: Heb lacks *its*

34.1–15 The boundaries of the promised land given here are ideal and do not correspond to Israel's actual boundaries at any time, especially in the case of the western border. They do, however, correspond to the territory "Canaan" as ruled by Egypt in the second half of the second millennium B.C.E. Cf. Josh 13–19; Ezek 47.13–20; 48.1–7, 23–29. **34.1–2** The "promised land" here is the land west of the Jordan only; see vv. 10–12; 32.22. **34.3** *Wilderness of Zin.* See 13.21, 26; 20.1. **34.4** *Ascent of Akrabbim,* "ascent of scorpions." Site unknown. *Kadesh-barnea.* See 13.26. *Hazar-addar.* Cf. Hezron and Addar in Josh 15.3. **34.4–5** *Azmon.* Site unknown. The *Wadi of Egypt* is modern Wadi el-Arish, south of Gaza, between the Negeb and the

Sinai. **34.6–7** The *Great Sea* is the Mediterranean. **34.7–8** *Mount Hor* here cannot be the southern mountain where Aaron died (20.22–29). *Lebo-hamath.* See 13.21. *Zedad,* probably a site northeast of Damascus and east of Byblos. **34.9** *Ziphron* and *Hazar-enan.* Sites unknown. **34.10–11** *Shepham, Riblah,* and *Ain.* Sites unknown. The *sea of Chinnereth* is the Sea of Galilee. **34.11–12** These verses exclude the Transjordanian holdings (see also vv. 13–15; 32.17, 22; 35.14). **34.13–15** See 32.33–42. **34.16–29** Other than Caleb and Joshua, these leaders have not been mentioned before. The tribes are listed south to north, except for Manasseh, which is listed before the more southern Ephraim because Manasseh was the firstborn

tance: the priest Eleazar and Joshua son of Nun. 18 You shall take one leader of every tribe to apportion the land for inheritance. 19 These are the names of the men: Of the tribe of Judah, Caleb son of Jephunneh. 20 Of the tribe of the Simeonites, Shemuel son of Ammihud. 21 Of the tribe of Benjamin, Elidad son of Chislon. 22 Of the tribe of the Danites a leader, Bukki son of Jogli. 23 Of the Josephites: of the tribe of the Manassites a leader, Hanniel son of Ephod, 24 and of the tribe of the Ephraimites a leader, Kemuel son of Shiphtan. 25 Of the tribe of the Zebulunites a leader, Eli-zaphan son of Parnach. 26 Of the tribe of the Issacharites a leader, Paltiel son of Azzan. 27 And of the tribe of the Asherites a leader, Ahihud son of Shelomi. 28 Of the tribe of the Naphtalites a leader, Pedahel son of Ammihud. 29 These were the ones whom the LORD commanded to apportion the inheritance for the Israelites in the land of Canaan.

Cities for the Levites

35 In the plains of Moab by the Jordan at Jericho, the LORD spoke to Moses, saying: 2 Command the Israelites to give, from the inheritance that they possess, towns for the Levites to live in; you shall also give to the Levites pasture lands surrounding the towns. 3 The towns shall be theirs to live in, and their pasture lands shall be for their cattle, for their livestock, and for all their animals. 4 The pasture lands of the towns, which you shall give to the Levites, shall reach from the wall of the town outward a thousand cubits all around. 5 You shall measure, outside the town, for the east side two thousand cubits, for the south side two thousand cubits, for the west side two thousand cubits, and for the north side two thousand cubits, with the town in the middle; this shall belong to them as pasture land for their towns.

6 The towns that you give to the Levites shall include the six cities of refuge, where you shall permit a slayer to flee, and in addition to them you shall give forty-two towns. 7 The towns that you give to the Levites shall total forty-eight, with their pasture lands. 8 And as for the towns that you shall give from the possession of the Israelites, from the larger tribes you shall take many, and from the smaller tribes you shall take few; each, in proportion to the inheritance that it obtains, shall give of its towns to the Levites.

Cities of Refuge

9 The LORD spoke to Moses, saying: 10 Speak to the Israelites, and say to them: When you cross the Jordan into the land of Canaan, 11 then you shall select cities to be cities of refuge for you, so that a slayer who kills a person without intent may flee there. 12 The cities shall be for you a refuge from the avenger, so that the slayer may not die until there is a trial before the congregation. 13 The cities that you designate shall be six cities of refuge for you: 14 you shall designate three cities beyond the Jordan, and three cities in the land of Canaan, to be cities of refuge. 15 These six cities shall serve as refuge for the Israelites, for the resident or transient alien among them, so that anyone who kills a person without intent may flee there.

Concerning Murder and Blood Revenge

16 But anyone who strikes another with an iron object, and death ensues, is a murderer; the murderer shall be put to death. 17 Or anyone who strikes another with a stone in hand that could cause death, and death ensues, is a murderer;

(Gen 41.50–52). **34.17** *Eleazar* has replaced Aaron (20.22–29), and *Joshua* will replace Moses when the people cross over into Canaan (27.12–23).
35.1–8 See also Josh 21; 1 Chr 6.54–81. The Levites were not allotted land as the other tribes were (see 18.20–24). **35.4–5** *A thousand cubits* and *two thousand cubits*, about 500 yards and 1000 yards. **35.6** *Cities of refuge.* See 35.9–15. **35.8** See 26.52–56. **35.9–15** Cities of refuge were necessary to protect a killer from blood vengeance before a trial could be held; see Ex 21.12–14; Deut 4.41–43; 19.1–13; Josh 20. **35.12** On the *avenger*, see the order of those who "redeem" (the same Hebrew verb) in Lev 25.25, 47–49 ("uncle" here is father's brother); see also Num 5.8. **35.14** The area *beyond the Jordan* is Transjordan, the term "beyond" betraying the point of view of a narrator from the west. **35.16–34** The distinction is made between murder (including negligence resulting in death) and unintentional killing; see also Ex 21.13–14, but cf.

the murderer shall be put to death. 18 Or anyone who strikes another with a weapon of wood in hand that could cause death, and death ensues, is a murderer; the murderer shall be put to death. 19 The avenger of blood is the one who shall put the murderer to death; when they meet, the avenger of blood shall execute the sentence. 20 Likewise, if someone pushes another from hatred, or hurls something at another, lying in wait, and death ensues, 21 or in enmity strikes another with the hand, and death ensues, then the one who struck the blow shall be put to death; that person is a murderer; the avenger of blood shall put the murderer to death, when they meet.

22 But if someone pushes another suddenly without enmity, or hurls any object without lying in wait, 23 or, while handling any stone that could cause death, unintentionally*e* drops it on another and death ensues, though they were not enemies, and no harm was intended, 24 then the congregation shall judge between the slayer and the avenger of blood, in accordance with these ordinances; 25 and the congregation shall rescue the slayer from the avenger of blood. Then the congregation shall send the slayer back to the original city of refuge. The slayer shall live in it until the death of the high priest who was anointed with the holy oil. 26 But if the slayer shall at any time go outside the bounds of the original city of refuge, 27 and is found by the avenger of blood outside the bounds of the city of refuge, and is killed by the avenger, no bloodguilt shall be incurred. 28 For the slayer must remain in the city of refuge until the death of the high priest; but after the death of the high priest the slayer may return home.

29 These things shall be a statute and ordinance for you throughout your generations wherever you live.

30 If anyone kills another, the murderer shall be put to death on the evidence of witnesses; but no one shall be put to death on the testimony of a single witness. 31 Moreover you shall accept no ransom for the life of a murderer who is subject to the death penalty; a murderer must be put to death. 32 Nor shall you accept ransom for one who has fled to a city of refuge, enabling the fugitive to return to live in the land before the death of the high priest. 33 You shall not pollute the land in which you live; for blood pollutes the land, and no expiation can be made for the land, for the blood that is shed in it, except by the blood of the one who shed it. 34 You shall not defile the land in which you live, in which I also dwell; for I the LORD dwell among the Israelites.

Marriage of Female Heirs

36 The heads of the ancestral houses of the clans of the descendants of Gilead son of Machir son of Manasseh, of the Josephite clans, came forward and spoke in the presence of Moses and the leaders, the heads of the ancestral houses of the Israelites; 2 they said, "The LORD commanded my lord to give the land for inheritance by lot to the Israelites; and my lord was commanded by the LORD to give the inheritance of our brother Zelophehad to his daughters. 3 But if they are married into another Israelite tribe, then their inheritance will be taken from the inheritance of our ancestors and added to the inheritance of the tribe into which they marry; so it will be taken away from the allotted portion of our inheritance.

e Heb *without seeing*

Ex 21.20–21; Deut 4.42; 19.4–6. **35.19, 21** The execution of the murderer is by the *avenger*; see v. 12. **35.20–23** The concern with whether there was *hatred* or *enmity* between the killer and victim helps to establish intention; see also Deut 4.42; 19.4; Josh 20.3–5. **35.25–28** The blood of the victim *pollutes the land* (v. 33) and that pollution, in the case of unintentional killing, is only masked by the exile of the killer to a city of refuge until the high priest's death atones for the victim's blood; see also Josh 20.6. If the killer steps outside the city of refuge, the pollution is released again and the avenger is justified in destroying the cause of pollution; cf. 2 Sam 19.18–23; 1 Kings 2.36–46. **35.33** *Pollutes the land.* See 35.25–28; Gen 4.10–11. **35.34** The land is holy because the Lord dwells there. See 5.1–4.

36.1–12 See 27.1–11. **36.1** See 27.1. **36.2** *Brother.* See 25.6; 27.4. **36.3** The complaint in this verse assumes that a wife's property became her husband's upon marriage. In such a case, the solution in 27.7–8 that daughters could inherit might mean that ancestral land would be moved from one tribe to another, a possibility not considered in framing that earlier solution

4 And when the jubilee of the Israelites comes, then their inheritance will be added to the inheritance of the tribe into which they have married; and their inheritance will be taken from the inheritance of our ancestral tribe."

5 Then Moses commanded the Israelites according to the word of the LORD, saying, "The descendants of the tribe of Joseph are right in what they are saying. 6 This is what the LORD commands concerning the daughters of Zelophehad, 'Let them marry whom they think best; only it must be into a clan of their father's tribe that they are married, 7 so that no inheritance of the Israelites shall be transferred from one tribe to another; for all Israelites shall retain the inheritance of their ancestral tribes. 8 Every daughter who possesses an inheritance in any tribe

of the Israelites shall marry one from the clan of her father's tribe, so that all Israelites may continue to possess their ancestral inheritance. 9 No inheritance shall be transferred from one tribe to another; for each of the tribes of the Israelites shall retain its own inheritance.' "

10 The daughters of Zelophehad did as the LORD had commanded Moses. 11 Mahlah, Tirzah, Hoglah, Milcah, and Noah, the daughters of Zelophehad, married sons of their father's brothers. 12 They were married into the clans of the descendants of Manasseh son of Joseph, and their inheritance remained in the tribe of their father's clan.

13 These are the commandments and the ordinances that the LORD commanded through Moses to the Israelites in the plains of Moab by the Jordan at Jericho.

---

and one that was to be avoided (see 27.1–11). **36.4** On *the jubilee of the Israelites,* see Lev 25.8–55; 27.16–25. Since the land was not sold, even the jubilee regulations would not bring it back to its original owners; cf. Lev 25.13–17, 28, 31, 33. **36.6–9** A regulation that women who

inherit must marry within a specific family group (or else forfeit their property) is common among societies with patrilineal inheritance laws, including other ancient Near Eastern societies. **36.13** See 22.1; 26.3, 63; 33.48–50; 35.1; Deut 34.1, 8.

DEUTERONOMY

Name and Canonical Significance

DEUTERONOMY IS THE NAME FOR THE FIFTH BOOK of the Hebrew Bible and the last of those traditionally ascribed to Moses comprising the Torah or Pentateuch. The name reflects the Greek word *deuteronomion* (meaning "second law" or "repeated law"), which is a somewhat erroneous and misleading translation of a Hebrew phrase in Deut 17.18, *mishneh hattorah hazzot*, meaning "copy of this law." In Jewish tradition, the book is generally known by its opening words, *'elleh haddevarim* ("these are the words"), frequently shortened to *devarim* ("words").

Deuteronomy is the only book of the Pentateuch to identify itself explicitly and repeatedly as a record of Mosaic torah (see 1.5; 4.8, 44; 17.18–19; 27.3, 8, 26; 28.58, 61; 29.21; 30.10; 31.9, 11, 12, 24, 26; 32.46). *Torah* here has the sense of comprehensive and divinely sanctioned instruction. In the context of the book, it may be characterized as the authoritative, inspired "polity" (or, "political constitution") that Moses, unable himself to lead Israel across the Jordan, enacts for the people as a normative guide to their corporate existence in the land they are about to occupy. In short, this authoritative instruction is a virtual surrogate for Moses himself in his capacity as the preeminent mediator of the divine word to Israel (see 5.4–5, 23–31). From the perspective of the Jewish canon, Deuteronomy is not merely a parenetic appendix to the pentateuchal narrative of Israel's prehistory and religious formation under the leadership of Moses. Rather, as Mosaic instruction par excellence Deuteronomy is the interpretative key to the Pentateuch understood as a whole to mediate the abiding revelation of God's will for the ongoing life of the covenant people.

In similar fashion Deuteronomy also provides the crucial point of reference for an understanding of the canonical unity of the following collection of "the Prophets" in Jewish scripture. Significantly, affirmations of the Mosaic torah in its characteristically Deuteronomic form bracket the collection as a whole (see Josh 1.7–8; Mal 3.22). Deuteronomic influence and perspectives are especially evident in the "Former Prophets," consisting of the books of Joshua, Judges, 1 and 2 Samuel, 1 and 2 Kings (see, e.g., Josh 1.1–9; 23; Judg 2.11–23;

1 Sam 7.3–14; 12.1–25; 2 Sam 7.1–29; 1 Kings 9.1–9; 11.1–13, 29–39; 14.1–16; 2 Kings 17.7–23; 21.1–23.27). For this reason these books are also known as the "Deuteronomistic History" in contemporary biblical scholarship. Many believe that the book of Deuteronomy at one stage during its literary history was part of the Deuteronomistic History, before it was detached and incorporated into the Pentateuch. In its dual character of both remembering Israel's past and anticipating its future, the book occupies a pivotal position, both literarily and theologically, in the canon of the Hebrew Bible.

Literary Character, Structure, and Content

Deuteronomy is cast in the form of a series of testamentary speeches and acts of Moses. Four editorial superscriptions (1.1–5; 4.44–49; 29.1; 33.1) introduce the coordinated segments of the work, and describe the particular character and content of each major part. The first part (1.1–4.43) consists chiefly of Mosaic memoirs on Israel's journey from Horeb/Sinai to Transjordan (1.6–3.29), followed by a hortatory discourse on Israel's destiny as God's people (4.1–40) and a brief narrative appendix concerning designated cities of refuge (4.41–43). The second and central part of the book (4.44–28.68) is the most significant section around which the entire book is constructed. It contains the authoritative law (*torah*) mediated through Moses to Israel. *Torah* here may be defined as covenantal law or the divinely authorized social order that Israel must implement in order to secure its collective political existence as the people of God. Three further subdivisions making up this central section are sermonic reflections and admonitions elaborating the basic terms of the Horeb covenant (5.1–11.30); promulgation of the statutory rulings (11.31–26.15); and covenantal ratification, rites, and sanctions (26.16–28.68). The third part of the book (29.1–32.52) alludes to another covenant Moses was to make with Israel in Moab. It also relates the commissioning of Joshua, the written consignment of the law, and the recitation of a song. The fourth and final part of the book (33.1–34.12) contains a testamentary blessing of the tribes of Israel and a prose narrative about Moses' death and burial, along with a concluding epitaph.

Composition

While Deuteronomy exhibits a remarkable coherence in comparison with the preceding books of the Pentateuch, it cannot be considered a unitary literary product. The internal evidence of the book points to a lengthy and complex growth process over several centuries. Among the sources utilized are the Decalogue (which appears in a form different from that of Ex 20), legislation in the Book of the Covenant (Ex 20–23) together with the supplement in Ex 33–34, narrative traditions of earlier pentateuchal books, and the poems in chs. 32–33. While some of the antecedent traditions of Deuteronomy may well be older, the major stages in the compositional history of the book can with some confidence be dated to the two centuries between the fall of Samaria (721 B.C.E.) and the beginning of the Judean restoration (ca. 535 B.C.E.) after the exile to Babylonia. Since the beginning of the nineteenth century, critical scholarship has built a convincing case for relating at least a central portion of the book to the document recovered from the Jerusalem temple archives during the reign of King Josiah (621 B.C.E.). Many of the characteristic provisions of the book find a close correspondence in the reforms instituted by that king. Yet in its received form the editing of the traditions points to an exilic setting—when the older Mosaic constitution may have been set within an expanded frame of Moses' valedictory addresses to Israel. Authors must be sought among those who bore particular responsibility for the transmission, interpretation, and implementation of the Mosaic legacy of covenantal law. While arguments have been set forth on behalf of royal scribes, prophets, or elders, most likely are those identified in the book itself as "levitical priests," whose functions included judicial decision making as well as officiating in worship. Maintenance of the covenant relationship between Israel and its divine sovereign through the rule of faith and law within the community is the principal concern of Deuteronomy. *S. Dean McBride, Jr.*

Editorial Preface

1 These are the words that Moses spoke to all Israel beyond the Jordan—in the wilderness, on the plain opposite Suph, between Paran and Tophel, Laban, Hazeroth, and Di-zahab. 2 (By the way of Mount Seir it takes eleven days to reach Kadesh-barnea from Horeb.) 3 In the fortieth year, on the first day of the eleventh month, Moses spoke to the Israelites just as the LORD had commanded him to speak to them. 4 This was after he had defeated King Sihon of the Amorites, who reigned in Heshbon, and King Og of Bashan, who reigned in Ashtaroth and[a] in Edrei. 5 Beyond the Jordan in the land of Moab, Moses undertook to expound this law as follows:

Israel's Marching Orders

6 The LORD our God spoke to us at Horeb, saying, "You have stayed long enough at this mountain. 7 Resume your journey, and go into the hill country of the Amorites as well as into the neighbor-

a Gk Syr Vg Compare Josh 12.4: Heb lacks *and*

1.1–5 The preface understands Moses' address in 1.6–4.40 to be an expository introduction to the Deuteronomic *law* (v. 5); see 4.44. **1.1** *These are the words* constitutes the book's title in Jewish tradition (see Introduction). *The plain opposite Suph* and following toponymns may define a natural amphitheater in the valley near Bethpeor; see 3.29. **1.2** Perhaps a comment on 1.19. *Mount Seir*, the Edomite highlands flanking the rift valley from the Dead Sea southward. Once thought to be the mountain refuge of Petra, *Kadesh-barnea* is now usually identified with the oases of 'Ain al-Qudeirat in northern Sinai. In Deuteronomy and some other sources (cf. Ex 3.1) *Horeb* is preferred over "Sinai" as the name for the wilderness mount of revelation. **1.3** The date, counting from the first Passover (Ex 12.2),

when Moses completed his word as God's spokesman. **1.4** As prelude to the campaign west of the Jordan, these victories vindicate Israel's trust in divine providence; see 2.26–3.22; 4.46–48; cf. Ps 135.10–12. **1.6–3.29** A review of what happened to Israel and why during the post-Horeb epoch of Moses' career. The chief lesson is that Israel's national well-being requires strict observance of all that God commands. **1.6–8** The order to depart from Horeb was an oracular summons to invade and occupy the promised homeland west of the Jordan. **1.7** *The hill country of the Amorites* (also 1.19–20) and *the land of the Canaanites* (cf. Ex 13.11; Ezek 16.3) are comprehensive terms for western Palestine, using general designations for the land's pre-Israelite occupants. Component re-

ing regions—the Arabah, the hill country, the Shephelah, the Negeb, and the seacoast—the land of the Canaanites and the Lebanon, as far as the great river, the river Euphrates. 8 See, I have set the land before you; go in and take possession of the land that I b swore to your ancestors, to Abraham, to Isaac, and to Jacob, to give to them and to their descendants after them."

9 At that time I said to you, "I am unable by myself to bear you. 10 The LORD your God has multiplied you, so that today you are as numerous as the stars of heaven. 11 May the LORD, the God of your ancestors, increase you a thousand times more and bless you, as he has promised you! 12 But how can I bear the heavy burden of your disputes all by myself? 13 Choose for each of your tribes individuals who are wise, discerning, and reputable to be your leaders." 14 You answered me, "The plan you have proposed is a good one." 15 So I took the leaders of your tribes, wise and reputable individuals, and installed them as leaders over you, commanders of thousands, commanders of hundreds, commanders of fifties, commanders of tens, and officials, throughout your tribes. 16 I charged your judges at that time: "Give the members of your community a fair hearing, and judge rightly between one person and another, whether citizen or resident alien. 17 You must not be partial in judging: hear out the small and the great alike; you shall not

be intimidated by anyone, for the judgment is God's. Any case that is too hard for you, bring to me, and I will hear it." 18 So I charged you at that time with all the things that you should do.

Rebellion and Defeat

19 Then, just as the LORD our God had ordered us, we set out from Horeb and went through all that great and terrible wilderness that you saw, on the way to the hill country of the Amorites, until we reached Kadesh-barnea. 20 I said to you, "You have reached the hill country of the Amorites, which the LORD our God is giving us. 21 See, the LORD your God has given the land to you; go up, take possession, as the LORD, the God of your ancestors, has promised you; do not fear or be dismayed."

22 All of you came to me and said, "Let us send men ahead of us to explore the land for us and bring back a report to us regarding the route by which we should go up and the cities we will come to." 23 The plan seemed good to me, and I selected twelve of you, one from each tribe. 24 They set out and went up into the hill country, and when they reached the Valley of Eshcol they spied it out 25 and gathered some of the land's produce, which they brought down to us. They brought back a report to us, and said, "It

b Sam Gk: MT the LORD

gions are the *Arabah* (the Jordan rift valley), the central highland ridge, the western hills of the *Shephelah*, the *Negeb* slope of southern Judah, and the Mediterranean coastal plain. Territory to the northeast, called the *Lebanon* range, which extends into Syria toward the upper reach of the *Euphrates*, was controlled by Aramaean states during most of the earlier Iron Age; Israel claimed hegemony over the region in the era of Davidic-Solomonic empire (2 Sam 8.3–12; 1 Kings 4.21, 24) and briefly again in the heyday of Jeroboam II's reign (2 Kings 14.25). **1.8** See Gen 15.12–21; 17.8; 26.4–5; 28.13–14. **1.9–18** Before setting out, a plan of military command and tribal judiciary was implemented to lighten Moses' burden of governance (cf. Ex 18.13–26; Num 11.10–30). **1.10–11** See Gen 15.5; 22.17; 26.4; Ex 32.13. **1.16–17** Because the judges act on God's behalf, all who participate in the life of the community, including alien sojourners, must be given equal access to justice (cf. 10.17–19;

16.18–20). On Moses' role as arbiter in cases *too hard* for tribal courts to resolve, see 17.8–11. **1.18** Perhaps an allusion to Ex 24.3–8.
1.19–45 This review (see Num 13–14) highlights how Israel's countermanding of divine orders (vv. 26, 43) reversed the expected outcome of the initial march of conquest. **1.21** A war oracle reiterating the earlier command (vv. 7–8) and urging bold compliance as the requisite response (cf. 20.2–4; Ex 14.13–14). **1.22–33** The communal decision to reconnoiter the route of attack is not faulted here, nor is the spies' report (cf. Num 13.32). The fertile *Valley of Eshcol* (v. 24) lies in the Judean hill country near Hebron, a region whose aborigines were the formidable *Anakim* (v. 28; cf. 2.10–11, 21; 9.2; Num 13.22–33; Josh 14.15). Dread of this foe fueled a grass-roots revolt that imputed malice to the Lord, whose salvific presence had been amply shown to the generation that experienced the exodus from Egypt and swift passage through the wilderness

is a good land that the LORD our God is giving us."

26 But you were unwilling to go up. You rebelled against the command of the LORD your God; 27 you grumbled in your tents and said, "It is because the LORD hates us that he has brought us out of the land of Egypt, to hand us over to the Amorites to destroy us. 28 Where are we headed? Our kindred have made our hearts melt by reporting, 'The people are stronger and taller than we; the cities are large and fortified up to heaven! We actually saw there the offspring of the Anakim!' " 29 I said to you, "Have no dread or fear of them. 30 The LORD your God, who goes before you, is the one who will fight for you, just as he did for you in Egypt before your very eyes, 31 and in the wilderness, where you saw how the LORD your God carried you, just as one carries a child, all the way that you traveled until you reached this place. 32 But in spite of this, you have no trust in the LORD your God, 33 who goes before you on the way to seek out a place for you to camp, in fire by night, and in the cloud by day, to show you the route you should take."

34 When the LORD heard your words, he was wrathful and swore: 35 "Not one of these—not one of this evil generation—shall see the good land that I swore to give to your ancestors, 36 except Caleb son of Jephunneh. He shall see it, and to him and to his descendants I will give the land on which he set foot, because of his complete fidelity to the LORD." 37 Even with me the LORD was angry on your account, saying, "You also shall not enter there. 38 Joshua son of Nun, your assistant, shall enter there; encourage him, for he is the one who will secure Israel's possession of it. 39 And as for your little ones, who you thought would become booty, your chil-

dren, who today do not yet know right from wrong, they shall enter there; to them I will give it, and they shall take possession of it. 40 But as for you, journey back into the wilderness, in the direction of the Red Sea." c

41 You answered me, "We have sinned against the LORD! We are ready to go up and fight, just as the LORD our God commanded us." So all of you strapped on your battle gear, and thought it easy to go up into the hill country. 42 The LORD said to me, "Say to them, 'Do not go up and do not fight, for I am not in the midst of you; otherwise you will be defeated by your enemies.' " 43 Although I told you, you would not listen. You rebelled against the command of the LORD and presumptuously went up into the hill country. 44 The Amorites who lived in that hill country then came out against you and chased you as bees do. They beat you down in Seir as far as Hormah. 45 When you returned and wept before the LORD, the LORD would neither heed your voice nor pay you any attention.

Starting Over

46 After you had stayed at Kadesh as many days as you did, 1 we journeyed back into the wilderness, in the direction of the Red Sea, c as the LORD had told me and skirted Mount Seir for many days. 2 Then the LORD said to me: 3 "You have been skirting this hill country long enough. Head north, 4 and charge the people as follows: You are about to pass through the territory of your kindred, the descendants of Esau, who live in Seir. They will be afraid of you, so, be very careful 5 not to engage in battle with them, for I will not give you

c Or *Sea of Reeds*

(vv. 19, 30–33; cf. Ex 13.21–22). **1.36** Among seniors, *Caleb* alone modeled the zeal demanded of the Lord's warriors; for his reward, see Josh 14.6–14; 15.13–14. **1.39** *Know right from wrong.* The age of accountable discretion (cf. Isa 7.15) was twenty years according to Num 14.29–30. **1.40** *Red Sea,* here the Gulf of Aqaba; cf. 2.8. **1.41–44** Attack on Canaan from the south was not only a foolhardy initiative, resulting in the militia's rout, but another act of brazen rebellion against divine orders. **1.44** *Hormah,* a site in the southeastern Negeb near Arad (cf. Num 21.1–3; Judg 1.16–17).

1.46–2.25 Full renewal of the mandate for conquest accompanied the demise of the rebellious generation. **2.1** Reversing direction away from Canaan and toward Egypt was at least a return to obedience (1.40). **2.3** *Head north,* apparently along the desert route east of the Arabah (see 2.8). **2.4–8** Esau, elder brother of Jacob (Israel) and forefather of the Edomites (Gen 25.21–26; 36.1–19), had title to the Seir hill country by grant from the Lord; hence Israel had neither right (vv. 5–6) nor reason (v. 7) to challenge Edom's sovereignty. (Num 20.14–21 gives a different account of the passage.) **2.8** *Elath and*

even so much as a foot's length of their land, since I have given Mount Seir to Esau as a possession. 6 You shall purchase food from them for money, so that you may eat; and you shall also buy water from them for money, so that you may drink. 7 Surely the LORD your God has blessed you in all your undertakings; he knows your going through this great wilderness. These forty years the LORD your God has been with you; you have lacked nothing." 8 So we passed by our kin, the descendants of Esau who live in Seir, leaving behind the route of the Arabah, and leaving behind Elath and Ezion-geber.

When we had headed out along the route of the wilderness of Moab, 9 the LORD said to me: "Do not harass Moab or engage them in battle, for I will not give you any of its land as a possession, since I have given Ar as a possession to the descendants of Lot." 10 (The Emim — a large and numerous people, as tall as the Anakim — had formerly inhabited it. 11 Like the Anakim, they are usually reckoned as Rephaim, though the Moabites call them Emim. 12 Moreover, the Horim had formerly inhabited Seir, but the descendants of Esau dispossessed them, destroying them and settling in their place, as Israel has done in the land that the LORD gave them as a possession.) 13 "Now then, proceed to cross over the Wadi Zered."

So we crossed over the Wadi Zered. 14 And the length of time we had traveled from Kadesh-barnea until we crossed the Wadi Zered was thirty-eight years, until

the entire generation of warriors had perished from the camp, as the LORD had sworn concerning them. 15 Indeed, the LORD's own hand was against them, to root them out from the camp, until all had perished.

16 Just as soon as all the warriors had died off from among the people, 17 the LORD spoke to me, saying, 18 "Today you are going to cross the boundary of Moab at Ar. 19 When you approach the frontier of the Ammonites, do not harass them or engage them in battle, for I will not give the land of the Ammonites to you as a possession, because I have given it to the descendants of Lot." 20 (It also is usually reckoned as a land of Rephaim. Rephaim formerly inhabited it, though the Ammonites call them Zamzummim, 21 a strong and numerous people, as tall as the Anakim. But the LORD destroyed them from before the Ammonites so that they could dispossess them and settle in their place. 22 He did the same for the descendants of Esau, who live in Seir, by destroying the Horim before them so that they could dispossess them and settle in their place even to this day. 23 As for the Avvim, who had lived in settlements in the vicinity of Gaza, the Caphtorim, who came from Caphtor, destroyed them and settled in their place.) 24 "Proceed on your journey and cross the Wadi Arnon. See, I have handed over to you King Sihon the Amorite of Heshbon, and his land. Begin to take possession by engaging him in battle. 25 This day I will begin to put the dread and fear of you upon the peoples

---

Ezion-geber, ports on the Gulf of Aqaba; cf. 1 Kings 9.26. **2.9** *Ar*, the portion of greater Moab between the Zered (2.13) and the Arnon (2.24) which the Lord granted to Lot's Moabite lineage (also 2.18, 29; cf. Gen 19.36–38; Num 21.13–15, 28). **2.10–12** An editorial comment on aboriginal folk dispossessed by Moab and Edom (cf. 2.20–23; 3.11). Both *Emim* (Hebrew, "Frighteners") and Anakim (cf. 1.28) are identified as *Rephaim*, giant warriors of yore who are variously implicated in Israelite and Ugaritic folklore with the antediluvian Nephilim and other defunct heroes (cf. Gen 6.4; 14.5; Num 13.33). On the *Horim* of Seir (perhaps "Troglodytes" rather than ethnic "Hurrians"), see Gen 14.6; 36.20–30. **2.13–15** *Zered*, the Wadi el-Hesa, which flows westward into the southern end of the Dead Sea. Crossing of this physical boundary between Edom and Moab marked Israel's com-munal passage, hastened by divine agency, to a new generation of warriors. **2.19** Lot's Ammonite descendants also (cf. 2.9) received by divine grant their homeland on the plateau northeast of Moabite Ar (cf. 2.37). **2.20–23** Folklore with theological commentary continuing vv. 10–12. *Zamzummim* (Hebrew, "Mumblers"?), another subset of Rephaim; cf. "Zuzim" in Gen 14.5. *Avvim* (Hebrew, "Ruiners"?). Cf. Josh 13.3. *Caphtorim . . . from Caphtor*, Philistines or a related people from Crete; cf. Gen 10.14; Jer 47.4; Am 9.7. **2.24** Consignment of *Sihon*'s realm to Israel renewed the Lord's war against the Amorites (cf. Gen 15.16; Am 2.9–10). Other ancient claimants to the rich tableland north of the *Arnon* gorge (Wadi el-Mujib) included Ammon (Judg 11.4–33; cf. 1 Sam 11.1–11) and Moab (Num 21.13–15; Jer 48; cf. the Mesha Inscription). **2.25** Cf. Ex 15.14–16.

everywhere under heaven; when they hear report of you, they will tremble and be in anguish because of you."

Conquests in Transjordan

26 So I sent messengers from the wilderness of Kedemoth to King Sihon of Heshbon with the following terms of peace: 27 "If you let me pass through your land, I will travel only along the road; I will turn aside neither to the right nor to the left. 28 You shall sell me food for money, so that I may eat, and supply me water for money, so that I may drink. Only allow me to pass through on foot— 29 just as the descendants of Esau who live in Seir have done for me and likewise the Moabites who live in Ar—until I cross the Jordan into the land that the LORD our God is giving us." 30 But King Sihon of Heshbon was not willing to let us pass through, for the LORD your God had hardened his spirit and made his heart defiant in order to hand him over to you, as he has now done.

31 The LORD said to me, "See, I have begun to give Sihon and his land over to you. Begin now to take possession of his land." 32 So when Sihon came out against us, he and all his people for battle at Jahaz, 33 the LORD our God gave him over to us; and we struck him down, along with his offspring and all his people. 34 At that time we captured all his towns, and in each town we utterly destroyed men, women, and children. We left not a single survivor. 35 Only the livestock we kept as spoil for ourselves, as well as the plunder of the towns that we had captured. 36 From Aroer on the edge of the Wadi Arnon (including the town that is in the wadi itself) as far as Gilead, there was no citadel too high for us. The LORD our God gave everything to us. 37 You did not encroach, however, on the land of the Ammonites, avoiding the whole upper region of the Wadi Jabbok as well as the towns of the hill country, just as[d] the LORD our God had charged.

3 When we headed up the road to Bashan, King Og of Bashan came out against us, he and all his people, for battle at Edrei. 2 The LORD said to me, "Do not fear him, for I have handed him over to you, along with his people and his land. Do to him as you did to King Sihon of the Amorites, who reigned in Heshbon." 3 So the LORD our God also handed over to us King Og of Bashan and all his people. We struck him down until not a single survivor was left. 4 At that time we captured all his towns; there was no citadel that we did not take from them—sixty towns, the whole region of Argob, the kingdom of Og in Bashan. 5 All these were fortress towns with high walls, double gates, and bars, besides a great many villages. 6 And

d Gk Tg: Heb *and all*

2.26–3.7 The era of Israel's conquests began under Moses' command (as promised, Ex 34.10), with model holy-war campaigns against the forces of Sihon and Og in Transjordan (cf. Num 21.13–35). 2.26 *Kedemoth*, at the desert's edge east of Ar, near the Arnon's upper reach; cf. Josh 13.18. *Heshbon*, Sihon's capital, near mid-point on the plateau stretching north from the Arnon to Gilead; cf. Josh 12.2; Jer 48.45; Song 7.4. 2.27–29 Though a bit puzzling, the request for peaceful passage may be understood in context (vv. 24–25, 30–31) as the means to draw Sihon into battle (cf. 2.6; 23.3–4). 2.30 Divine action to promote Sihon's bellicose obstinacy and downfall recalls the "hardening of Pharaoh's heart" theme of the exodus drama (e.g. Ex 4.21; 7.3; 14.4; cf. 1 Sam 16.14; 1 Kings 22.20–23; Isa 6.10). 2.32 *Jahaz*, a fortified town on the plateau south of Heshbon; cf. Josh 13.17–18; Isa 15.4. 2.33–35 The "ban" (Hebrew *cherem*) enforced here and against Bashan (3.6–7) straddles the rules of war given in 20.10–17: the human populations are totally annihilated (20.16–17) but livestock as well as goods are exempted (20.13–15); cf. Josh 8.2, 26–27; 11.10–15; Josh 6.17–19; 7.1; 1 Sam 15.3–9. 2.36–37 *Aroer* (the place now called in Arabic 'Ara'ir), a fortress commanding the Arnon's north rim; cf. Josh 13.9. *Gilead*, the fertile hill country of central Transjordan; it is bisected by the *Jabbok* (now Arabic Nahr ez-Zerqa), a major eastern tributary of the Jordan, which descends from the heights of Ammon; cf. Gen 32.22; Josh 12.2. 3.1 *Bashan*, a region of rich highland forests, pastures, and fields in northern Transjordan, reaching beyond Gilead across the Yarmuk River into Syria; cf. 32.13–14; Ezek 27.6; 39.18. *Edrei* (modern Dar'a). The battle site, near the upper reach of the Yarmuk's southern tributary, was apparently one of Og's two royal cities (the other was Ashtaroth); cf. 1.4; Josh 9.10; 12.4. 3.4 *Argob* seems here to designate the broad expanse of south-central Bashan, from the Golan Heights eastward to the Hauran massif (modern Jebel Druze); cf. 3.13–14.

we utterly destroyed them, as we had done to King Sihon of Heshbon, in each city utterly destroying men, women, and children. 7 But all the livestock and the plunder of the towns we kept as spoil for ourselves.

Allotment of the Territories

8 So at that time we took from the two kings of the Amorites the land beyond the Jordan, from the Wadi Arnon to Mount Hermon 9 (the Sidonians call Hermon Sirion, while the Amorites call it Senir), 10 all the towns of the tableland, the whole of Gilead, and all of Bashan, as far as Salecah and Edrei, towns of Og's kingdom in Bashan. 11 (Now only King Og of Bashan was left of the remnant of the Rephaim. In fact his bed, an iron bed, can still be seen in Rabbah of the Ammonites. By the common cubit it is nine cubits long and four cubits wide.) 12 As for the land that we took possession of at that time, I gave to the Reubenites and Gadites the territory north of Aroer,*e* that is on the edge of the Wadi Arnon, as well as half the hill country of Gilead with its towns, 13 and I gave to the half-tribe of Manasseh the rest of Gilead and all of Bashan, Og's kingdom. (The whole region of Argob: all that portion of Bashan used to be called a land of Rephaim; 14 Jair the Manassite acquired the whole region of Argob as far as the border of the Geshurites and the Maacathites, and he named them—that is, Bashan—after himself, Havvoth-jair,*f* as it is to this day.) 15 To Machir I gave Gil-

ead. 16 And to the Reubenites and the Gadites I gave the territory from Gilead as far as the Wadi Arnon, with the middle of the wadi as a boundary, and up to the Jabbok, the wadi being boundary of the Ammonites; 17 the Arabah also, with the Jordan and its banks, from Chinnereth down to the sea of the Arabah, the Dead Sea,*g* with the lower slopes of Pisgah on the east.

18 At that time, I charged you as follows: "Although the LORD your God has given you this land to occupy, all your troops shall cross over armed as the vanguard of your Israelite kin. 19 Only your wives, your children, and your livestock— I know that you have much livestock— shall stay behind in the towns that I have given to you. 20 When the LORD gives rest to your kindred, as to you, and they too have occupied the land that the LORD your God is giving them beyond the Jordan, then each of you may return to the property that I have given to you." 21 And I charged Joshua as well at that time, saying: "Your own eyes have seen everything that the LORD your God has done to these two kings; so the LORD will do to all the kingdoms into which you are about to cross. 22 Do not fear them, for it is the LORD your God who fights for you."

A Personal Entreaty

23 At that time, too, I entreated the LORD, saying: 24 "O Lord GOD, you have

e Heb *territory from Aroer*   *f* That is *Settlement of Jair*   *g* Heb *Salt Sea*

3.8–22 A brief report on the apportionment of conquered regions among the tribes of Reuben, Gad, and Manasseh (cf. Num 32; Josh 13.8–32) plus instructions concerning participation of their militias in the invasion of the land west of the Jordan. **3.8–9** *Mount Hermon* (now in Arabic Jebel esh-Sheikh), the towering southern spur of the Anti-Lebanon range, known also as *Sirion* and *Senir,* marks the northern limit of Israel's primary territorial claims; cf. 4.48; Josh 11.16–17; Ps 29.6; Song 4.8. **3.10** *Salecah,* a town on the eastern boundary of Bashan; cf. Josh 12.5; 13.11. **3.11** The note offers an intriguing glimpse into lore about Og, here not an "Amorite" (cf. v. 8) but last of the giant Rephaim (cf. Josh 12.4; 13.12). His massive *iron bed* (about 13 by 6 feet) may have been a megalith or sarcophagus of black basalt. *Rabbah* (modern Amman), the Ammonite royal citadel. **3.13–15** Major

clans of eastern *Manasseh* (*half* [of the] *tribe*) include *Jair,* here allotted most of Bashan (cf. Num 32.41; Judg 10.3–5; 1 Kings 4.13), and *Machir,* receiving Gilead (cf. Num 26.29; 32.39–40; Josh 17.1). *Geshurites and the Maacathites,* Aramaean clans occupying the Golan Heights; cf. Gen 22.24; Josh 13.13; 2 Sam 3.3; 15.8. **3.17** *Chinnereth,* the Sea of Galilee or Gennesaret. *Pisgah,* the northwestern flank of Mount Nebo; cf. 3.27; 32.49; 34.1. **3.18–20** For the outcome, see Josh 1.12–18; 4.12; 22.1–6. The promised *rest* means not only relief from the urgency of war but the Lord's gift to Israel of a stable life in a secure homeland, thus bringing to completion the plan that began to unfold with the exodus (cf. 12.8–9; Ex 3.7–8; 15.17; 33.14; Josh 21.43–45; 1 Kings 8.56). **3.21–22** See note on 1.4; cf. 2.25; 31.3–8.

3.23–29 Moses, who so often had interceded

only begun to show your servant your greatness and your might; what god in heaven or on earth can perform deeds and mighty acts like yours! 25 Let me cross over to see the good land beyond the Jordan, that good hill country and the Lebanon." 26 But the LORD was angry with me on your account and would not heed me. The LORD said to me, "Enough from you! Never speak to me of this matter again! 27 Go up to the top of Pisgah and look around you to the west, to the north, to the south, and to the east. Look well, for you shall not cross over this Jordan. 28 But charge Joshua, and encourage and strengthen him, because it is he who shall cross over at the head of this people and who shall secure their possession of the land that you will see." 29 So we remained in the valley opposite Beth-peor.

The Discipline of Faith

4 So now, Israel, give heed to the statutes and ordinances that I am teaching you to observe, so that you may live to enter and occupy the land that the LORD, the God of your ancestors, is giving you. 2 You must neither add anything to what I command you nor take away anything from it, but keep the commandments of the LORD your God with which I am charging you. 3 You have seen for yourselves what the LORD did with regard to the Baal of Peor—how the LORD your God destroyed from among you everyone who followed the Baal of Peor, 4 while those of you who held fast to the LORD your God are all alive today.

5 See, just as the LORD my God has charged me, I now teach you statutes and ordinances for you to observe in the land that you are about to enter and occupy. 6 You must observe them diligently, for this will show your wisdom and discernment to the peoples, who, when they hear all these statutes, will say, "Surely this great nation is a wise and discerning people!" 7 For what other great nation has a god so near to it as the LORD our God is whenever we call to him? 8 And what other great nation has statutes and ordinances as just as this entire law that I am setting before you today?

9 But take care and watch yourselves closely, so as neither to forget the things that your eyes have seen nor to let them slip from your mind all the days of your life; make them known to your children and your children's children— 10 how you once stood before the LORD your God at Horeb, when the LORD said to me, "Assemble the people for me, and I will let them hear my words, so that they may learn to fear me as long as they live on the earth, and may teach their children so"; 11 you approached and stood at the foot of

---

successfully on behalf of others (e.g., 9.20, 25–29; Ex 32.11–14; Num 11.2; 21.7), could not secure divine permission to cross with the new generation of Israel into the land beyond the Jordan. **3.24** Moses' plea begins with hymnic praise extolling the Lord's incomparability (cf. Ex 15.11, 16; 2 Sam 7.22–24; Pss 89.5–8; 113.5–6). **3.26–27** The Lord's rebuke is softened by allowing Moses to survey visually the full expanse of Israel's national homeland (see 32.48–52; 34.1–4). **3.28** See 31.7–8. **3.29** The *valley* (now in Arabic Wadi ʿAyun Musa) lies beneath the northwest slope of Pisgah, where Moses is addressing the people (see 1.1, 5; cf. Num 21.20). *Beth-peor*, the "house" or sanctuary of the Baal of Peor; see 4.3–4.

4.1–40 This grand peroration advances the claim that diligent observance of God's law, as taught by Moses, is the wellspring of Israel's life and hence also the discipline that shapes its unique theological witness. **4.1–8** The thesis stated. **4.1** *So now* is a rhetorical device (cf. 10.12; 26.10), here marking a shift in Moses' address from the foregoing memoirs to climactic exhortation and admonition. **4.2–4** *Neither add . . . nor take away*. Because Moses' instruction in what God demands is both authoritative and complete, it is the only guide to life that Israel ever need or should follow (see 12.32; cf. 30.11–14; Prov 30.5–6; Eccl 3.14). The consequences of conflicting claims on Israel's loyalty were demonstrated by the Lord's discriminating judgment in *the Baal of Peor* affair (cf. Num 25.1–13; Ps 106.28; Hos 9.10). **4.5–8** Israel will be counted as a *great nation* (cf. 26.5; Gen 12.2; 18.18; 46.3; Ex 32.10) by virtue of its ethical character and the responsive nearness of its divine sovereign (cf. Ex 3.7; Judg 3.9, 15; 4.3; Ps 145.18; Isa 55.6–7). *This entire law*, whose just provisions and prudent observance by Israel will gain acclaim from other nations (cf. Ezra 7.25; Pss 19.7–10; 147.19–20), is the Mosaic law preserved in Deuteronomy; see 4.44–45. **4.9–31** The case against idolatry. **4.9** Transmission through the generations of Israel's normative experience and polity is a major Deuteronomic concern (e.g., 6.7, 20–25; 11.19–21; 29.29; 31.12–13). **4.10–11** Cf.

the mountain while the mountain was blazing up to the very heavens, shrouded in dark clouds. 12 Then the LORD spoke to you out of the fire. You heard the sound of words but saw no form; there was only a voice. 13 He declared to you his covenant, which he charged you to observe, that is, the ten commandments;*h* and he wrote them on two stone tablets. 14 And the LORD charged me at that time to teach you statutes and ordinances for you to observe in the land that you are about to cross into and occupy.

15 Since you saw no form when the LORD spoke to you at Horeb out of the fire, take care and watch yourselves closely, 16 so that you do not act corruptly by making an idol for yourselves, in the form of any figure—the likeness of male or female, 17 the likeness of any animal that is on the earth, the likeness of any winged bird that flies in the air, 18 the likeness of anything that creeps on the ground, the likeness of any fish that is in the water under the earth. 19 And when you look up to the heavens and see the sun, the moon, and the stars, all the host of heaven, do not be led astray and bow down to them and serve them, things that the LORD your God has allotted to all the peoples everywhere under heaven. 20 But the LORD has taken you and brought you out of the iron-smelter, out of Egypt, to become a people of his very own possession, as you are now.

21 The LORD was angry with me because of you, and he vowed that I should

not cross the Jordan and that I should not enter the good land that the LORD your God is giving for your possession. 22 For I am going to die in this land without crossing over the Jordan, but you are going to cross over to take possession of that good land. 23 So be careful not to forget the covenant that the LORD your God made with you, and not to make for yourselves an idol in the form of anything that the LORD your God has forbidden you. 24 For the LORD your God is a devouring fire, a jealous God.

25 When you have had children and children's children, and become complacent in the land, if you act corruptly by making an idol in the form of anything, thus doing what is evil in the sight of the LORD your God, and provoking him to anger, 26 I call heaven and earth to witness against you today that you will soon utterly perish from the land that you are crossing the Jordan to occupy; you will not live long on it, but will be utterly destroyed. 27 The LORD will scatter you among the peoples; only a few of you will be left among the nations where the LORD will lead you. 28 There you will serve other gods made by human hands, objects of wood and stone that neither see, nor hear, nor eat, nor smell. 29 From there you will seek the LORD your God, and you will find him if you search after him with all your heart and soul. 30 In your distress, when all these things have happened to you in time to come, you will return to the LORD

h Heb *the ten words*

5.4–5; Ex 19.7–25; 20.18–21.   **4.12** Key motifs in the expository argument are *fire . . . no form . . . voice* (see vv. 15–16, 23–25, 33, 36).   **4.13–14** The Horeb *covenant* was essentially defined by the stipulations of the Decalogue; teaching Israel how to implement them in its national life was Moses' charge. Cf. 5.2–31; 10.4; Ex 34.27–28. **4.15–19** An exposition of 5.8 (Ex 20.4) argues that Israel's imageless worship (cf. Ex 20.23; 34.17; Lev 19.4; 26.1) is a consequence of the visual formlessness of the Lord's presence at Horeb. **4.20** By *iron-smelter* is meant the harshness of servitude in Egypt (cf. 1 Kings 8.51; Isa 48.10; Jer 11.4). In the exodus, Israel became the Lord's *very own possession* or "heritage" (cf. 32.8–9; 9.26, 29; 1 Sam 10.1; 1 Kings 8.53; Ps 33.12). **4.21–23** The fact of Moses' absence ought never again give rise to idolatry, as happened in the golden calf episode (cf. 9.12–14; Ex 32.1–10). **4.24** Especially in combination, the epithets *de-*

vouring fire (9.3; Ex 24.17) and *jealous God* (5.9; 6.15; Ex 34.14) express the vehement passion of the Lord's self-defense against idolatry and other acts of profanation (cf. 32.19–22; Lev 10.1–3; Num 16.35; 25.11).   **4.25–27** In view here is the exilic Dispersion as an actualization of curses due to Israel's breach of covenant (cf. 28.64–67; Lev 26.30–39). *Heaven and earth* are invoked as enduring witnesses that Moses had foreseen this fate (cf. 30.19; 31.28; 32.1; Isa 1.2).   **4.28** Cf. 29.17; Pss 115.4–8; 135.15–18; Isa 44.9–20.   **4.29–31** In view too is a renewal of covenant, predicated on Israel's genuinely remorseful seeking of the Lord (on *all your heart and soul*; see 6.5) and the Lord's perennial graciousness (cf. 5.10; 30.1–5; Lev 26.40–45; 1 Kings 8.46–51; Jer 29.10–14; Hos 14.1–7). The latter attribute is invoked by the liturgical epithet *merciful God* (Ex 34.6–7; cf. Neh 9.17, 31; Pss 103.8–14; 145.8–9; Jon 4.2).

your God and heed him. 31 Because the LORD your God is a merciful God, he will neither abandon you nor destroy you; he will not forget the covenant with your ancestors that he swore to them.

32 For ask now about former ages, long before your own, ever since the day that God created human beings on the earth; ask from one end of heaven to the other: has anything so great as this ever happened or has its like ever been heard of? 33 Has any people ever heard the voice of a god speaking out of a fire, as you have heard, and lived? 34 Or has any god ever attempted to go and take a nation for himself from the midst of another nation, by trials, by signs and wonders, by war, by a mighty hand and an outstretched arm, and by terrifying displays of power, as the LORD your God did for you in Egypt before your very eyes? 35 To you it was shown so that you would acknowledge that the LORD is God; there is no other besides him. 36 From heaven he made you hear his voice to discipline you. On earth he showed you his great fire, while you heard his words coming out of the fire. 37 And because he loved your ancestors, he chose their descendants after them. He brought you out of Egypt with his own presence, by his great power, 38 driving out before you nations greater and mightier than yourselves, to bring you in, giving you their land for a possession, as it is still today. 39 So acknowledge today and take to heart that the LORD is God in heaven above and on the earth beneath; there is no other. 40 Keep his statutes and his commandments, which I am commanding you today for your own well-being and that of your descendants after you, so that you may long remain in the land that the LORD your God is giving you for all time.

Cities of Refuge in the Transjordan

41 Then Moses set apart on the east side of the Jordan three cities 42 to which a homicide could flee, someone who unintentionally kills another person, the two not having been at enmity before; the homicide could flee to one of these cities and live: 43 Bezer in the wilderness on the tableland belonging to the Reubenites, Ramoth in Gilead belonging to the Gadites, and Golan in Bashan belonging to the Manassites.

Preface to the Articles of the Horeb Covenant

44 This is the law that Moses set before the Israelites. 45 These are the decrees and the statutes and ordinances that Moses spoke to the Israelites when they had come out of Egypt, 46 beyond the Jordan in the valley opposite Beth-peor, in the land of King Sihon of the Amorites, who reigned at Heshbon, whom Moses and the Israelites defeated when they came out of Egypt. 47 They occupied his land and the land of King Og of Bashan, the two kings of the Amorites on the eastern side of the Jordan: 48 from Aroer, which is on the edge of the Wadi Arnon, as far as Mount Sirion[i] (that is, Hermon), 49 together with all the Arabah on the east side of the Jordan as far as the Sea of the Arabah, under the slopes of Pisgah.

Initiation of the Covenant

5 Moses convened all Israel, and said to them:

Hear, O Israel, the statutes and ordinances that I am addressing to you today; you shall learn them and observe them

i Syr: Heb Sion

4.32–40 The Lord's incomparability (see note on 3.24) has its counterpart in Israel's unique experiences of divine providence. The unprecedented events of the exodus (vv. 34, 37–38) and the revelation at Horeb (vv. 33, 36) give empirical support to Israel's monotheistic creed: the Lord (Yahweh) is God and there is no other (vv. 35, 39). Cf. 32.39; 1 Kings 8.60; Isa 43.10–13; 44.6; Joel 2.27. 4.41–43 An appended note reports that Moses himself designated three cities in the Transjordan to serve as places of refuge for persons who commit unintentional homicide (19.1–13; cf. Num 35.10–28; Josh 20). 4.44–48 A second preface (cf. 1.1–5) intro-

duces the covenantal traditions promulgated through Moses. 4.44–45 The comprehensive Hebrew term for this corpus is Torah (always translated law in the NRSV of Deuteronomy, e.g., 4.8; 17.18–19; 30.10; 31.11–12). Primary components of the law are the decrees (also 6.17, 20; cf. Ps 25.10), the basic "terms" of the covenant, i.e., the Ten Commandments, and the statutes and ordinances (e.g., 5.1; 11.32–12.1; 26.16), a compound designation for the constitutional rules, procedures, and precedents set forth in 12.2–26.15. 4.46–48 See 2.26–3.29.

5.1–12.1 This first major section of Mosaic torah consists of a series of hortatory keynotes

diligently. 2 The LORD our God made a covenant with us at Horeb. 3 Not with our ancestors did the LORD make this covenant, but with us, who are all of us here alive today. 4 The LORD spoke with you face to face at the mountain, out of the fire. 5 (At that time I was standing between the LORD and you to declare to you the words*j* of the LORD; for you were afraid because of the fire and did not go up the mountain.) And he said:

6 I am the LORD your God, who brought you out of the land of Egypt, out of the house of slavery; 7 you shall have no other gods before*k* me.

8 You shall not make for yourself an idol, whether in the form of anything that is in heaven above, or that is on the earth beneath, or that is in the water under the earth. 9 You shall not bow down to them or worship them; for I the LORD your God am a jealous God, punishing children for the iniquity of parents, to the third and fourth generation of those who reject me, 10 but showing steadfast love to the thousandth generation*l* of those who love me and keep my commandments.

11 You shall not make wrongful use of the name of the LORD your God, for the LORD will not acquit anyone who misuses his name.

12 Observe the sabbath day and keep it holy, as the LORD your God commanded you. 13 Six days you shall labor and do all your work. 14 But the seventh day is a sabbath to the LORD your God; you shall not do any work—you, or your son or your daughter, or your male or female slave, or your ox or your donkey, or any of your livestock, or the resident alien in your towns, so that your male and female slave may rest as well as you. 15 Remember that you were a slave in the land of Egypt, and the LORD your God brought you out from there with a mighty hand and an outstretched arm; therefore the LORD your God commanded you to keep the sabbath day.

16 Honor your father and your mother, as the LORD your God commanded you, so that your days may be long and that it may go well with you in the land that the LORD your God is giving you.

17 You shall not murder.*m*

18 Neither shall you commit adultery.

19 Neither shall you steal.

---

j Q Mss Sam Gk Syr Vg Tg: MT *word*
k Or *besides*   *l* Or *to thousands*   *m* Or *kill*

(5.1–6.3; 6.4–8.20; 9.1–10.11; 10.12–12.1) treating fundamental aspects of the covenant relationship, especially the demand that Israel give undivided allegiance to the Lord. **5.1–6.3** The Israelites at Horeb heard only the Decalogue communicated directly by the Lord; they authorized Moses to receive and transmit to them the rest of the Lord's covenantal instructions. See, in brief, 4.13–14. **5.1–5** The assembly at Horeb. **5.1–3** Moses' audience *today* and their *ancestors* who had originally assembled at Horeb are generational manifestations of the corporate "Israel" with whom the Lord enacts this covenant (cf. 26.16–19; 29.10–15). **5.4** *Face to face.* The Lord's presence was articulate and direct (cf. 34.10; Num 12.8). **5.5** *At that time . . . mountain* anticipating Moses' appointment as intermediary probably alludes to Ex 19.3–25. **5.6–21** There are some substantive as well as minor differences between this version of the Decalogue ("the ten words") and the one in Ex 20.2–17. **5.6–10** These verses, cast in the divine first person, form a coherent "word" and comprise a single paragraph in the Hebrew Masoretic Text. The Lord's assertion of sovereignty over Israel (v. 6) introduces a series of three injunctions that prohibit association of *other gods* or any form of idolatry with worship of the Lord (vv. 7–9a); the final clauses proclaim the chief dimensions of the Lord's steadfastness, which should motivate Israel's fidelity to the bond of covenant (vv. 9b–10; cf. 4.24, 31; 7.9–10). **5.9** *Punishing children . . . parents.* See note on 7.10. **5.11** *Wrongful use,* invocation of the divine name in false oaths or for any magical, malicious, or blasphemous purpose (cf. Lev 19.12; 24.10–23; Ps 24.4; Jer 29.23; Hos 4.2). **5.12–15** The command to hallow the *sabbath day* through observance of broadly inclusive communal rest is connected here with remembrance of the Lord's intervention to free Israel from slavery in Egypt (cf. Ex 20.8–11; 23.12; 31.12–17; 34.21; Isa 58.13–14; Jer 17.21–27). **5.16** *Honor,* respect for parental authority and dignity (cf. 21.18–21; 27.16; Ex 21.15, 17) and faithful performance of filial duties, such as care for aging parents (cf. Sir 3.1–16). **5.17** *Murder,* negligent or premeditated homicide (cf. Ex 21.12–14, 29; Num 35.16–34). **5.18–21** *Neither,* lit. "and not"; i.e., the final terse prohibitions are linked in series. **5.18** *Adultery.* Cf. Lev 18.20; 20.10; Prov 6.23–29; Jer 7.9. **5.19** *Steal,* whether persons or property (cf. 24.7; Ex 21.16;

20 Neither shall you bear false witness against your neighbor.

21 Neither shall you covet your neighbor's wife.

Neither shall you desire your neighbor's house, or field, or male or female slave, or ox, or donkey, or anything that belongs to your neighbor.

Moses' Mandate

22 These words the LORD spoke with a loud voice to your whole assembly at the mountain, out of the fire, the cloud, and the thick darkness, and he added no more. He wrote them on two stone tablets, and gave them to me. 23 When you heard the voice out of the darkness, while the mountain was burning with fire, you approached me, all the heads of your tribes and your elders; 24 and you said, "Look, the LORD our God has shown us his glory and greatness, and we have heard his voice out of the fire. Today we have seen that God may speak to someone and the person may still live. 25 So now why should we die? For this great fire will consume us; if we hear the voice of the LORD our God any longer, we shall die. 26 For who is there of all flesh that has heard the voice of the living God speaking out of fire, as we have, and remained alive? 27 Go near, you yourself, and hear all that the LORD our God will say. Then tell us everything that the LORD our God tells you, and we will listen and do it."

28 The LORD heard your words when you spoke to me, and the LORD said to me: "I have heard the words of this people, which they have spoken to you; they are right in all that they have spoken. 29 If only they had such a mind as this, to fear me and to keep all my commandments always, so that it might go well with them and with their children forever! 30 Go say to them, 'Return to your tents.' 31 But you, stand here by me, and I will tell you all the commandments, the statutes and the ordinances, that you shall teach them, so that they may do them in the land that I am giving them to possess." 32 You must therefore be careful to do as the LORD your God has commanded you; you shall not turn to the right or to the left. 33 You must follow exactly the path that the LORD your God has commanded you, so that you may live, and that it may go well with you, and that you may live long in the land that you are to possess.

6 Now this is the commandment—the statutes and the ordinances—that the LORD your God charged me to teach you to observe in the land that you are about to cross into and occupy, 2 so that you and your children and your children's children may fear the LORD your God all the days of your life, and keep all his decrees and his commandments that I am commanding you, so that your days may be long. 3 Hear therefore, O Israel, and observe them diligently, so that it may go well with you, and so that you may multiply greatly in a land flowing with milk and honey, as the LORD, the God of your ancestors, has promised you.

22.1). **5.20** *False witness.* Cf. 19.15–19; Ex 23.1–3; 1 Kings 21.5–14; Prov 25.18. **5.21** The ninth and tenth "words" both prohibit covetousness but distinguish lust to possess a neighbor's *wife* (cf. Prov 6.25) from compulsive desire to alienate a neighbor's *house* or other properties (cf. Isa 5.8; Mic 2.2).

5.22–6.3 Moses' authority to legislate and instruct in matters of the covenant was established through formal agreement at Horeb. **5.22** Like *all Israel* in developed Deuteronomic usage (cf. 5.1; 12.7, 12, 18; 29.2, 10–13), *whole assembly* seems to mean the full constituency of the covenant people, inclusive of women and children (cf. 31.12–13, 30; 16.16; 23.1–8; Ex 19.15; cf. Josh 8.35; 2 Kings 23.1–3). The *tablets* document Israel's receipt of the Decalogue as the basic terms of the covenant (see 4.13; 9.9–11, 17; 10.1–5; cf. 31.9, 26). **5.24** *Glory and greatness,* the awesome visual display of the Lord's presence, which served as accompaniment to the divine speaking (cf. 4.10–12; Ex 19.9, 16–18; 24.9, 15–18; Num 16.19; cf. also Ex 33.18–23; 1 Kings 19.11–13). **5.26** *Living God,* the God whose rule is manifest through word and deed (e.g., Josh 3.10; 1 Sam 17.26; 2 Kings 19.4, 16; Jer 10.10; 23.36). **5.27** *Listen and do it.* Israel agreed to heed Moses' voice as God's own. **5.28–31** The Lord ratified Israel's choice of Moses as intermediary, empowering him not only to transmit divine commandments but to teach their application. **5.32–6.1** *Now,* a generation later, Moses is about to fulfill his commission, by providing Israel with the divinely sanctioned charter for its life in the land. **6.2** *Fear the LORD* means to revere and obey the Lord as trustworthy sovereign (e.g., 4.10; 5.29; 6.13, 24; 10.12). **6.3** See Ex 3.8.

The Lord Alone Is Israel's God

4 Hear, O Israel: The Lord is our God, the Lord alone.[n] 5 You shall love the Lord your God with all your heart, and with all your soul, and with all your might. 6 Keep these words that I am commanding you today in your heart. 7 Recite them to your children and talk about them when you are at home and when you are away, when you lie down and when you rise. 8 Bind them as a sign on your hand, fix them as an emblem[o] on your forehead, 9 and write them on the doorposts of your house and on your gates.

10 When the Lord your God has brought you into the land that he swore to your ancestors, to Abraham, to Isaac, and to Jacob, to give you—a land with fine, large cities that you did not build, 11 houses filled with all sorts of goods that you did not fill, hewn cisterns that you did not hew, vineyards and olive groves that you did not plant—and when you have eaten your fill, 12 take care that you do not forget the Lord, who brought you out of the land of Egypt, out of the house of slavery. 13 The Lord your God you shall fear; him you shall serve, and by his name alone you shall swear. 14 Do not follow other gods, any of the gods of the peoples who are all around you, 15 because the Lord your God, who is present with you, is a jealous God. The anger of the Lord your God would be kindled against you and he would destroy you from the face of the earth.

16 Do not put the Lord your God to the test, as you tested him at Massah. 17 You must diligently keep the commandments of the Lord your God, and his decrees, and his statutes that he has commanded you. 18 Do what is right and good in the sight of the Lord, so that it may go well with you, and so that you may go in and occupy the good land that the Lord swore to your ancestors to give you, 19 thrusting out all your enemies from before you, as the Lord has promised.

20 When your children ask you in time to come, "What is the meaning of the decrees and the statutes and the ordinances that the Lord our God has commanded you?" 21 then you shall say to your children, "We were Pharaoh's slaves in Egypt, but the Lord brought us out of Egypt with a mighty hand. 22 The Lord displayed before our eyes great and awesome signs and wonders against Egypt, against Pharaoh and all his household.

n Or The Lord our God is one Lord, or The Lord our God, the Lord is one, or The Lord is our God, the Lord is one   o Or as a frontlet

---

6.4–8.20 This section offers Moses' instruction in how Israel, when it comes into possession of a national homeland, must conduct its life by disciplined devotion to the Lord. **6.4–9** In Jewish liturgy, this is the lead paragraph of the Shema (which means *Hear*, the unit's initial word, in Hebrew), which the faithful are instructed to recite twice daily (cf. *Mishnah Berakot* 1.1–3.6). In the synoptic Gospels, the creedal injunction of vv. 4–5 is affirmed as the "Great Commandment," which, together with the requirement to love one's neighbor (Lev 19.18), epitomizes the Mosaic law (Mt 22.36–40; Mk 12.28–34; cf. Lk 10.25–28). **6.4–5** *Love* is commanded as the fullest measure of the loyalty that Israel owes the Lord (Yahweh), its only divine sovereign (cf. 5.6–10). *Heart*, connoting the human intellect and will, and *soul*, meaning the vitality of selfhood, are often so conjoined in Deuteronomic rhetoric (e.g., 4.29; 10.12; 26.16; Josh 23.14; 2 Kings 23.3); the final item, *might*, or "capacity," appears only here and in a tribute to King Josiah (2 Kings 23.25). **6.6–9** Moses' instruction is to be internalized by the faithful (cf. Ps 37.31; Prov 3.3; Isa 51.7; Jer 31.33) and outwardly displayed in witness to personal and communal identity among the Lord's people. **6.10–19** A concise exposition of 5.6–9, framed as a warning that Israel must never compromise its reliance on the Lord's providence. **6.10–11** Cf. 8.7–14; 32.11–15; Neh 9.25. **6.13** A summary of positive duties; see also 10.20. *Swear.* Cf. Josh 23.6–8; Isa 48.1; Jer 4.2; 5.7; 12.16. **6.14–15** The perennial injunction and threat; see, e.g., 4.23–26; 8.19–20; 11.16–17; 13.12–18; 29.24–28; 30.17–18; Josh 24.14; Judg 2.11–15; 2 Kings 17.7–18. **6.16** *Test*, by questioning God's presence with or benevolent intentions toward Israel, as exemplified by the incident at *Massah*; see Ex 17.1–7; cf. 1.26–33; Num 14.22; Ps 95.8–9. **6.19** For the divine promise, see Ex 23.27; 34.11–12 (cf. Josh 2.22–24). **6.20–25** This catechesis illustrates observance of the instruction in 6.6–9, i.e., how a new generation should be led to acknowledgment of Mosaic statutes and ordinances as central to God's gracious design for Israel's well-being (cf. Ex 12.26; 13.14–15; Josh 4.6–7, 21–22). **6.21–23** *We.* The response is succinct, confessional, and experiential; see also 26.5–10 (cf. 5.3;

23 He brought us out from there in order to bring us in, to give us the land that he promised on oath to our ancestors. 24 Then the LORD commanded us to observe all these statutes, to fear the LORD our God, for our lasting good, so as to keep us alive, as is now the case. 25 If we diligently observe this entire commandment before the LORD our God, as he has commanded us, we will be in the right."

Israel and the Peoples of Canaan

7 When the LORD your God brings you into the land that you are about to enter and occupy, and he clears away many nations before you—the Hittites, the Girgashites, the Amorites, the Canaanites, the Perizzites, the Hivites, and the Jebusites, seven nations mightier and more numerous than you— 2 and when the LORD your God gives them over to you and you defeat them, then you must utterly destroy them. Make no covenant with them and show them no mercy. 3 Do not intermarry with them, giving your daughters to their sons or taking their daughters for your sons, 4 for that would turn away your children from following

me, to serve other gods. Then the anger of the LORD would be kindled against you, and he would destroy you quickly. 5 But this is how you must deal with them: break down their altars, smash their pillars, hew down their sacred poles,p and burn their idols with fire. 6 For you are a people holy to the LORD your God; the LORD your God has chosen you out of all the peoples on earth to be his people, his treasured possession.

7 It was not because you were more numerous than any other people that the LORD set his heart on you and chose you —for you were the fewest of all peoples. 8 It was because the LORD loved you and kept the oath that he swore to your ancestors, that the LORD has brought you out with a mighty hand, and redeemed you from the house of slavery, from the hand of Pharaoh king of Egypt. 9 Know therefore that the LORD your God is God, the faithful God who maintains covenant loyalty with those who love him and keep his commandments, to a thousand generations, 10 and who repays in their own person those who reject him. He does not

p Heb *Asherim*

6.4). **6.24–25** The chief aim of the law is to secure life (cf. 4.1–4; 30.15–20). *Be in the right,* a verdict of acquittal, anticipated here because of meritorious discharge of covenantal obligations (cf. 24.13; Gen 15.6; Ezek 18.5–9). **7.1–26** In order to safeguard its allegiance to the Lord, Israel must extirpate the nations of Canaan along with their idolatrous cults (cf. Ex 23.23–33; 34.11–16; Num 33.51–56). **7.1–6** Prescription. **7.1** Like *Canaanites* and *Amorites* (see 1.7), *Hittites* may be a generic label for Israel's predecessors (cf. Gen 10.15; 23.3–20; 49.29–30; Num 13.29; Josh 1.4; Ezek 16.3, 45). Anatolian antecedents are possible for the *Girgashites* (cf. Gen 10.16), the *Perizzites* (cf. Gen 13.7; 34.30; Josh 17.15; Judg 1.4–5), and Jerusalem's *Jebusites* (cf. Josh 15.63; 2 Sam 5.6–8). *Hivites,* perhaps from north Syria, are associated with Shechem and the Gibeonite cities (cf. Gen 34.2; Josh 9.1–7; Judg 3.3; 2 Sam 21.2). *Seven nations* appear also in Josh 3.10; 24.11; such lists most often have six of the names (e.g., Ex 3.8; Josh 9.1; Judg 3.5; cf. Gen 15.19–21; 1 Kings 9.20). **7.2** *Utterly destroy.* The ban is a radical solution (cf. 20.16–18; Josh 10.40; 11.11–12) that, if enforced, would make the commands of vv. 2b–5 superfluous. *No covenant.* Cf. Ex 23.32–33; 34.12, 15; Josh 9.3–27; 11.19; Judg 2.2–3. **7.3–4** See Ex 34.16; Josh 23.12–13; Judg 3.5–6 (cf. Gen 34.9–10;

1 Kings 11.1–6). *Me,* apparently Moses, speaking as the Lord's surrogate; see 5.27 (cf. 11.13–15; 17.3; 28.20; 29.5). **7.5** Eradication of Canaanizing cult places and practices is a Deuteronomic priority (12.2–4, 29–31; 16.21–22; 18.9–14; cf. the measures attributed to kings Hezekiah and Josiah in 2 Kings 18.4; 23.4–24). *Pillars,* commemorative steles (cf. Gen 28.18; 35.14; Ex 24.4; Lev 26.1; 2 Kings 10.26–27). *Asherim* (see text note p) were probably *poles* or trees symbolizing fertility and associated with the goddess Asherah, who was sometimes venerated as the Lord's consort (cf. Judg 6.25–30; 1 Kings 14.22–24; 2 Kings 17.16; Isa 27.9; Jer 17.2; Mic 5.14). **7.6** See 14.2, 21; 26.18–19; 32.8–12. Cf. Ex 19.5–6; Ps 135.4; Mal 3.17. **7.7–16** God's election of Israel is motivated solely by God's love and faithfulness and not by the nation's intrinsic value (variations on 5.6–10). **7.7** *Set his heart,* was smitten with love (10.14–15; cf. 21.11; Gen 34.8; Hos 11.1). **7.8** See 5.6. *Redeemed,* emancipated or ransomed (also 9.26; 13.5; 15.15; 21.8; 24.18; cf. Num 18.15–17; Ps 78.42; Hos 13.14). **7.9** See 5.10 (cf. Neh 1.5; 9.32; Dan 9.4; Jon 4.2). *Faithful,* trustworthy, consistent, diligent (cf. 32.4; Pss 89.1–2; 98.3; Isa 49.7). *Covenant loyalty,* lit. "the covenant and the steadfast love" (also v. 12; cf. 1 Kings 8.23–24; Ps 89.24, 28, 33–34; Isa 54.10; 55.3; Mic 7.20). **7.10** An emphatic revi-

delay but repays in their own person those who reject him. 11 Therefore, observe diligently the commandment—the statutes and the ordinances—that I am commanding you today.

12 If you heed these ordinances, by diligently observing them, the LORD your God will maintain with you the covenant loyalty that he swore to your ancestors; 13 he will love you, bless you, and multiply you; he will bless the fruit of your womb and the fruit of your ground, your grain and your wine and your oil, the increase of your cattle and the issue of your flock, in the land that he swore to your ancestors to give you. 14 You shall be the most blessed of peoples, with neither sterility nor barrenness among you or your livestock. 15 The LORD will turn away from you every illness; all the dread diseases of Egypt that you experienced, he will not inflict on you, but he will lay them on all who hate you. 16 You shall devour all the peoples that the LORD your God is giving over to you, showing them no pity; you shall not serve their gods, for that would be a snare to you.

17 If you say to yourself, "These nations are more numerous than I; how can I dispossess them?" 18 do not be afraid of them. Just remember what the LORD your God did to Pharaoh and to all Egypt, 19 the great trials that your eyes saw, the signs and wonders, the mighty hand and the outstretched arm by which the LORD your God brought you out. The LORD your God will do the same to all the peo-

ples of whom you are afraid. 20 Moreover, the LORD your God will send the pestilence q against them, until even the survivors and the fugitives are destroyed. 21 Have no dread of them, for the LORD your God, who is present with you, is a great and awesome God. 22 The LORD your God will clear away these nations before you little by little; you will not be able to make a quick end of them, otherwise the wild animals would become too numerous for you. 23 But the LORD your God will give them over to you, and throw them into great panic, until they are destroyed. 24 He will hand their kings over to you and you shall blot out their name from under heaven; no one will be able to stand against you, until you have destroyed them. 25 The images of their gods you shall burn with fire. Do not covet the silver or the gold that is on them and take it for yourself, because you could be ensnared by it; for it is abhorrent to the LORD your God. 26 Do not bring an abhorrent thing into your house, or you will be set apart for destruction like it. You must utterly detest and abhor it, for it is set apart for destruction.

The LORD Provides

8 This entire commandment that I command you today you must diligently observe, so that you may live and increase, and go in and occupy the land that the LORD promised on oath to your

q Or *hornets*: Meaning of Heb uncertain

---

sion of 5.9b (cf. Ex 34.6–7; Num 14.18). Instead of corporate punishment, which might affect several generations, retribution for breach of covenant is now targeted against individual offenders (cf. 24.16; Jer 31.29–30; 32.18–19; Ezek 18.1–24). **7.13–14** Cf. 15.6; 28.4–14; Ex 23.25–26. *Grain . . . wine . . . oil*, the chief agricultural products of Canaan (11.14; 12.17; 14.23; 18.4; 28.51; cf. Hos 2.8, 22). **7.15** *Diseases of Egypt*, presumably exemplified by the plagues of Ex 9.3, 9 (cf. Deut 28.27, 60; Ex 15.26; Am 4.10). **7.16** Cf. 5.7–9a; Ex 23.32–33; 34.14. **7.17–26** Implementation (the conquest theme). **7.17–19** Cf. 1.28–30; 3.22; 4.34, 37–38; 9.1–3; 20.1; 29.2–3; Josh 23.3, 9–10. **7.20** *Pestilence*, perhaps a metaphor for terror as a weapon of divine warfare (cf. 2.25; 32.23–24; Ex 15.14–16; 23.27–28; Josh 24.12; Hab 3.5). **7.22** *Little by little*. Cf. Ex 23.29–30; Judg 2.3, 20–23; 3.1–6. **7.23** *Panic*. Cf. 28.20; 1 Sam 5.9–11; 14.18–20.

7.24 Cf. 11.25; Josh 13. **7.25–26** *Images . . . you shall burn*. See 9.21; 1 Kings 15.13; 2 Kings 10.26–27; 23.4, 11, 15. *Do not covet*. This and the following provisions foreshadow Josh 6.18–19 and the aftermath in Josh 7; cf. Judg 8.24–27; 17.2–4. *Abhorrent to the LORD* is a label used to proscribe things, practices, and persons deemed fraudulent, idolatrous, or otherwise morally repugnant (e.g., 12.31; 17.1; 18.12; 22.5; 23.18; 24.4; 25.16; Prov 3.32; 6.16; 15.8–9, 26; cf. Gen 43.32; Ex 8.26). **8.1–20** The theme of affluent life in Canaan encouraging haughtiness and apostasy is a familiar one in prophetic as well as Deuteronomic sources (cf. 4.25; 31.20; 32.13–18; Isa 5.1–7; Jer 2.1–13; Hos 13.4–6; Am 6.1–8). Here the issue is addressed in light of Israel's experience of divine providence during the wilderness era. **8.1–10** Exhortation (*remember*, v. 2; *know*, v. 5;

ancestors. 2 Remember the long way that the LORD your God has led you these forty years in the wilderness, in order to humble you, testing you to know what was in your heart, whether or not you would keep his commandments. 3 He humbled you by letting you hunger, then by feeding you with manna, with which neither you nor your ancestors were acquainted, in order to make you understand that one does not live by bread alone, but by every word that comes from the mouth of the LORD.r 4 The clothes on your back did not wear out and your feet did not swell these forty years. 5 Know then in your heart that as a parent disciplines a child so the LORD your God disciplines you. 6 Therefore keep the commandments of the LORD your God, by walking in his ways and by fearing him. 7 For the LORD your God is bringing you into a good land, a land with flowing streams, with springs and underground waters welling up in valleys and hills, 8 a land of wheat and barley, of vines and fig trees and pomegranates, a land of olive trees and honey, 9 a land where you may eat bread without scarcity, where you will lack nothing, a land whose stones are iron and from whose hills you may mine copper. 10 You shall eat your fill and bless the LORD your God for the good land that he has given you.

11 Take care that you do not forget the LORD your God, by failing to keep his commandments, his ordinances, and his statutes, which I am commanding you today. 12 When you have eaten your fill and have built fine houses and live in them, 13 and when your herds and flocks have multiplied, and your silver and gold is multiplied, and all that you have is multiplied, 14 then do not exalt yourself, forgetting the LORD your God, who brought you out of the land of Egypt, out of the house of slavery, 15 who led you through the great and terrible wilderness, an arid wasteland with poisonouss snakes and scorpions. He made water flow for you from flint rock, 16 and fed you in the wilderness with manna that your ancestors did not know, to humble you and to test you, and in the end to do you good. 17 Do not say to yourself, "My power and the might of my own hand have gotten me this wealth." 18 But remember the LORD your God, for it is he who gives you power to get wealth, so that he may confirm his covenant that he swore to your ancestors, as he is doing today. 19 If you do forget the LORD your God and follow other gods to serve and worship them, I solemnly warn you today that you shall surely perish. 20 Like the nations that the LORD is destroying before you, so shall you perish, because you would not obey the voice of the LORD your God.

The Covenant Broken and Restored

9 Hear, O Israel! You are about to cross the Jordan today, to go in and dispossess nations larger and mightier than you, great cities, fortified to the

r Or by anything that the LORD decrees   s Or fiery; Heb seraph

---

keep, v. 6). **8.2** Forty years. Cf. 1.3; 29.5; Ps 95.10; Am 2.10. The Israelites were humbled in the wilderness, treated in an abusive and humiliating manner (e.g., 21.14; 22.24; 26.6; Ex 22.22–23; Ps 90.15), to test their willingness to obey. **8.3** Israel survived on manna (cf. Ex 16; Num 11.5–9; Josh 5.12), which was "miserable food" (Num 21.5), because that is what the Lord provided. The lesson: life is ordered and sustained not by human preferences but by anything and everything that the Lord alone decrees (cf. Ps 104; Prov 30.8). **8.4** Cf. 29.5; Neh 9.21. **8.5** On divine and parental discipline, see, e.g., 4.36; 11.2; 21.18; Jer 31.18; Ps 94.12; Prov 3.11–12; 19.18; 29.17; Hos 11.1–4. **8.7–9** An encomium on Canaan's bounties (cf. 1.25; 11.9–12; 32.13–14; 33.28; Num 20.5; also the Egyptian "Tale of Sinuhe" 81–84). **8.10** Eat . . . bless, return praise to the Lord for the blessings received (cf. Gen 24.48; Neh 9.5; Pss 34.1; 145.1–2; also Mishnah Berakot 6). **8.11–20** Admonition (Do not forget, v. 11; Do not say, v. 17). **8.11–14** See 6.10–12. **8.15** Snakes. Cf. Num 21.6–9. Flint rock. See 32.13; cf. Ex 17.6; Num 20.8–11; Ps 114.8. **8.17–18** Because the Lord provides the means to acquire wealth (cf. Gen 34.29; Job 5.5; Prov 13.22; Ezek 28.4–5), prosperity must always be acknowledged as a divine gift and never claimed as a personal right (see also 9.4–5; 12.5–7; 14.28–29; 15.4–18; 26.1–15). **8.19** Solemnly warn, testify against or threaten (cf. 4.26; 30.19; 32.46; 1 Sam 8.9; 2 Kings 17.13).

9.1–10.11 This section offers a preemptive challenge to national self-righteousness and triumphalism by reviewing Israel's history of rebelliousness during the wilderness era. **9.1–7** Introduction (continuing the conquest theme). **9.1–2** A new generation of Israel must

heavens, 2 a strong and tall people, the offspring of the Anakim, whom you know. You have heard it said of them, "Who can stand up to the Anakim?" 3 Know then today that the LORD your God is the one who crosses over before you as a devouring fire; he will defeat them and subdue them before you, so that you may dispossess and destroy them quickly, as the LORD has promised you.

4 When the LORD your God thrusts them out before you, do not say to yourself, "It is because of my righteousness that the LORD has brought me in to occupy this land"; it is rather because of the wickedness of these nations that the LORD is dispossessing them before you. 5 It is not because of your righteousness or the uprightness of your heart that you are going in to occupy their land; but because of the wickedness of these nations the LORD your God is dispossessing them before you, in order to fulfill the promise that the LORD made on oath to your ancestors, to Abraham, to Isaac, and to Jacob.

6 Know, then, that the LORD your God is not giving you this good land to occupy because of your righteousness; for you are a stubborn people. 7 Remember and do not forget how you provoked the LORD your God to wrath in the wilderness; you have been rebellious against the LORD from the day you came out of the land of Egypt until you came to this place. 8 Even at Horeb you provoked the LORD to wrath, and the LORD was so angry with you that he was ready to destroy you.

9 When I went up the mountain to receive the stone tablets, the tablets of the covenant that the LORD made with you, I remained on the mountain forty days and forty nights; I neither ate bread nor drank water. 10 And the LORD gave me the two stone tablets written with the finger of God; on them were all the words that the LORD had spoken to you at the mountain out of the fire on the day of the assembly. 11 At the end of forty days and forty nights the LORD gave me the two stone tablets, the tablets of the covenant. 12 Then the LORD said to me, "Get up, go down quickly from here, for your people whom you have brought from Egypt have acted corruptly. They have been quick to turn from the way that I commanded them; they have cast an image for themselves." 13 Furthermore the LORD said to me, "I have seen that this people is indeed a stubborn people. 14 Let me alone that I may destroy them and blot out their name from under heaven; and I will make of you a nation mightier and more numerous than they."

15 So I turned and went down from the mountain, while the mountain was ablaze; the two tablets of the covenant were in my two hands. 16 Then I saw that you had indeed sinned against the LORD your God, by casting for yourselves an image of a calf; you had been quick to turn from the way that the LORD had commanded you. 17 So I took hold of the two tablets and flung them from my two hands, smashing them before your eyes.

---

face the threats that undid its predecessor; see 1.28, 41–45; 2.10–11; Num 13.28. **9.3** A reply to the preceding adage: the Lord, leading as a *devouring fire* (see 4.24), will defeat the formidable enemy on Israel's behalf (cf. 31.3–6). *Quickly.* See notes on 6.19; 7.22. **9.4–5** Were the issue to be litigated (cf. 25.1), Israel could not gain title to its homeland on grounds of its own "innocence," *righteousness*, or "integrity," *uprightness of heart* (cf. Pss 32.11; 97.11). The Lord is evicting the nations because of their "guilt," *wickedness* (see 20.18; Gen 15.16; Lev 18.24; 2 Kings 17.8; 21.2); the land only passes to Israel in fulfillment of the divine promise to the patriarchs (see 1.8). **9.6** *Stubborn* or "stiff-necked," indicates an obstinate refusal to heed orders (cf. also 9.13; 10.16; 31.27; Ex 32.9; 33.3; 34.9; Isa 48.4; Jer 17.23; 19.15). **9.7** *From . . . Egypt.* Cf. Ex 14.10–14; 15.22–26; Jer 7.25–26; 2 Kings 21.15. **9.8–24** Rebellions of the wilderness era. **9.8–9** The apostasy at Ho-

reb, passed over in Moses' earlier reviews (chs. 1, 4–5), is now introduced as the paradigm case of Israel's unfaithfulness. **9.9** *Tablets of the covenant.* See notes on 4.13–14; 5.22; cf. Ex 24.12. *Forty days . . . nights* is a leitmotif; see also 9.11, 18, 25; 10.10; 1 Kings 19.8; Jon 3.4. **9.10** Cf. Ex 31.18. *The day of the assembly*; when the full convocation heard the Lord speak directly (also 10.4; 18.16; see note on 5.22). **9.12–14** *Your people whom you have brought.* Israel, already in violation of the chief commandment (5.6–10), was disclaimed by the Lord, who proposed to start over with Moses; see Ex 32.7–10 (cf. Num 14.12). **9.15–17** The metallic *calf*, whether meant to represent the Lord or some other deity, made the case prima facie against Israel for breach of covenant (cf. Ex 32.1–8; 1 Kings 12.28–30; Ps 106.19–22; Hos 8.4–6; 10.5–6; 13.1–2). Moses signaled annulment of the treaty by *smashing* the

18 Then I lay prostrate before the LORD as before, forty days and forty nights; I neither ate bread nor drank water, because of all the sin you had committed, provoking the LORD by doing what was evil in his sight. 19 For I was afraid that the anger that the LORD bore against you was so fierce that he would destroy you. But the LORD listened to me that time also. 20 The LORD was so angry with Aaron that he was ready to destroy him, but I interceded also on behalf of Aaron at that same time. 21 Then I took the sinful thing you had made, the calf, and burned it with fire and crushed it, grinding it thoroughly, until it was reduced to dust; and I threw the dust of it into the stream that runs down the mountain.

22 At Taberah also, and at Massah, and at Kibroth-hattaavah, you provoked the LORD to wrath. 23 And when the LORD sent you from Kadesh-barnea, saying, "Go up and occupy the land that I have given you," you rebelled against the command of the LORD your God, neither trusting him nor obeying him. 24 You have been rebellious against the LORD as long as he has[t] known you.

25 Throughout the forty days and forty nights that I lay prostrate before the LORD when the LORD intended to destroy you, 26 I prayed to the LORD and said, "Lord GOD, do not destroy the people who are your very own possession, whom you redeemed in your greatness, whom you brought out of Egypt with a mighty

hand. 27 Remember your servants, Abraham, Isaac, and Jacob; pay no attention to the stubbornness of this people, their wickedness and their sin, 28 otherwise the land from which you have brought us might say, 'Because the LORD was not able to bring them into the land that he promised them, and because he hated them, he has brought them out to let them die in the wilderness.' 29 For they are the people of your very own possession, whom you brought out by your great power and by your outstretched arm."

10 At that time the LORD said to me, "Carve out two tablets of stone like the former ones, and come up to me on the mountain, and make an ark of wood. 2 I will write on the tablets the words that were on the former tablets, which you smashed, and you shall put them in the ark." 3 So I made an ark of acacia wood, cut two tablets of stone like the former ones, and went up the mountain with the two tablets in my hand. 4 Then he wrote on the tablets the same words as before, the ten commandments[u] that the LORD had spoken to you on the mountain out of the fire on the day of the assembly; and the LORD gave them to me. 5 So I turned and came down from the mountain, and put the tablets in the ark that I had made; and there they are, as the LORD commanded me.

6 (The Israelites journeyed from

t Sam Gk: MT *I have*   u Heb *the ten words*

tablets. **9.18–19** *Prostrate*, the posture of supplication (cf. Num 16.22). *As before* and *that time also* suppose this to be Moses' second successful intercession in the affair (cf. vv. 25–29; Ex 32.11–14, 30–34). **9.20** The exodus account recognizes *Aaron's* guilt (32.1–6, 21–25, 35) but says nothing about special pleading on his behalf. **9.21** Cf. Ex 32.20; see note on 7.25–26. **9.22–24** Other incidents are tersely noted by toponyms to establish a pattern of rebelliousness (cf. 31.27): *Taberah* (Num 11.1–3); *Massah* (see Deut 6.16); *Kibroth-hattaavah* (Num 11.31–34; 33.16); and *Kadesh-barnea* (see 1.19–33). **9.25–10.11** Restoration of the covenant. **9.25–29** Moses' intercessory prayer boldly responded to the Lord's disowning of and threats against Israel in vv. 12–14 (cf. Ex 32.11–14). **9.26** *Your very own possession*; lit. "your people and your possession" (also v. 29; cf. 4.20); i.e., the people belong not to Moses (9.12) but to the Lord who *redeemed* them from slavery in Egypt (see 7.8). **9.27–28** Despite Israel's obstinacy (9.13–14) there are reasons for divine restraint: the merit of the ancestors (cf. 7.8) and the Lord's own reputation (cf. 32.26–27; Num 14.13–16; Josh 7.7–9; Ps 115.1–2). **10.1–5** The covenant was reconstituted, on its original terms (the Decalogue, vv. 2, 4), when a duplicate set of *tablets* was inscribed by the Lord and transmitted to Israel through Moses (cf. 4.13; 5.22; Ex 34.1–4, 27–29). **10.1** In the tradition represented here, the *ark* was a wooden "chest" (cf. Gen 50.26, "coffin"; 2 Kings 12.9–10) built by Moses for the specific purpose of transporting the stone tablets of the covenant (cf. 10.8; 31.9, 24–26; 1 Kings 8.9 with various views in, e.g., Ex 25.10–22; 37.1–9; Num 10.35–36; 1 Sam 4.3–11; Ps 132.8). **10.6–9** Two appended notes supply data on priestly personnel. **10.6–7** Segments of a wilderness itinerary (with another version in Num 33.31–33) frame a notice on Aaron's death and the succession of his son *Eleazar* to priestly leadership (cf. Num 3.1–4, 32; 20.22–29;

Beeroth-bene-jaakan[v] to Moserah. There Aaron died, and there he was buried; his son Eleazar succeeded him as priest. 7From there they journeyed to Gudgodah, and from Gudgodah to Jotbathah, a land with flowing streams. 8At that time the LORD set apart the tribe of Levi to carry the ark of the covenant of the LORD, to stand before the LORD to minister to him, and to bless in his name, to this day. 9Therefore Levi has no allotment or inheritance with his kindred; the LORD is his inheritance, as the LORD your God promised him.)

10 I stayed on the mountain forty days and forty nights, as I had done the first time. And once again the LORD listened to me. The LORD was unwilling to destroy you. 11The LORD said to me, "Get up, go on your journey at the head of the people, that they may go in and occupy the land that I swore to their ancestors to give them."

The Essence of the Covenant

12 So now, O Israel, what does the LORD your God require of you? Only to fear the LORD your God, to walk in all his ways, to love him, to serve the LORD your God with all your heart and with all your soul, 13and to keep the commandments of the LORD your God[w] and his decrees that I am commanding you today, for your own well-being. 14Although heaven and

the heaven of heavens belong to the LORD your God, the earth with all that is in it, 15yet the LORD set his heart in love on your ancestors alone and chose you, their descendants after them, out of all the peoples, as it is today. 16Circumcise, then, the foreskin of your heart, and do not be stubborn any longer. 17For the LORD your God is God of gods and Lord of lords, the great God, mighty and awesome, who is not partial and takes no bribe, 18who executes justice for the orphan and the widow, and who loves the strangers, providing them food and clothing. 19You shall also love the stranger, for you were strangers in the land of Egypt. 20You shall fear the LORD your God; him alone you shall worship; to him you shall hold fast, and by his name you shall swear. 21He is your praise; he is your God, who has done for you these great and awesome things that your own eyes have seen. 22Your ancestors went down to Egypt seventy persons; and now the LORD your God has made you as numerous as the stars in heaven.

11 You shall love the LORD your God, therefore, and keep his charge, his decrees, his ordinances, and his commandments always. 2Remember today that it was not your children (who have not known or seen the discipline of

v Or the wells of the Bene-jaakan   w Q Ms Gk Syr: MT lacks your God

---

26.63–64; 24.33). **10.8–9** Another supplement reports the commissioning of the *tribe of Levi* to perform ritual service. For their duties and prebends, see notes on 18.1–8; 21.5; 33.8–11 (cf. Ex 32.25–29; Num 6.23–27; 8.5–26). **10.10–11** The review ends at the point where Moses' memoirs begin in 1.6 (cf. Ex 33.1). **10.12–12.1** In this finale to Moses' preliminary instruction, primary themes of the preceding sections (5.1–6.3; 6.4–8.20; 9.1–10.11) are rhetorically highlighted, with particular emphasis on love of the Lord as the crux of covenantal obedience (cf. 5.10; 6.5; 7.9; 10.12; 11.1, 13, 22). **10.12–22** The Lord's requirements epitomized. **10.12–13** *So now.* See note on 4.1. The question and answer scheme suggests liturgical usage (cf. Pss 15; 24.3–5, 8, 10; Mic 6.8). The terms of response are thoroughly Deuteronomic (e.g., 5.29–33; 6.2, 13, 24; 8.6; 11.13, 22). **10.14–15** Cf. 7.7–8; Ex 19.5–6. *Heaven of heavens* or "the highest heaven" (cf. 1 Kings 8.27; Neh 9.6; Ps 148.4). **10.16** *Circumcise . . . the foreskin of your heart*, a call to conversion that identifies recal-

citrant human minds or individual wills as the barrier to knowing and doing what the Lord requires (cf. 30.6; Lev 26.41; Jer 4.4; 6.10; 9.26; Ezek 44.7, 9). **10.17–18** Both the hymnic titles (cf. Ex 15.3, 11; Ps 47.2; Dan 2.47) and the social agenda of resolute justice (cf. 1.16–17; 16.19; Pss 68.5–6; 99.1–5; 146.5–9) are prerogatives of the Lord's universal suzerainty. **10.19** *You shall also love.* Israel is to imitate the Lord's zeal for egalitarian justice (cf. 24.17–22; Ex 22.21–24; 23.6–9; Lev 19.33–34; also Isa 61.1–9). **10.21** *Your praise*, the one to whom you give praise (cf. Ps 109.1; Jer 17.14). **10.22** *Seventy persons.* See Gen 46.8–27; Ex 1.5; cf. Deut 1.10. **11.1–17** The Lord's providential care. **11.1** *Keep his charge*, perform loyal service as prescribed (cf. Gen 26.5; Lev 8.35; Josh 22.3; 1 Kings 2.3). **11.2** By *discipline* is meant here lessons learned through normative experience of the Lord's sovereign presence (cf. 4.9, 33–39; 5.29; 8.5), i.e., the creedal lore that each generation must assimilate and faithfully transmit to the next (cf.

the LORD your God), but it is you who must acknowledge his greatness, his mighty hand and his outstretched arm, [3] his signs and his deeds that he did in Egypt to Pharaoh, the king of Egypt, and to all his land; [4] what he did to the Egyptian army, to their horses and chariots, how he made the water of the Red Sea[x] flow over them as they pursued you, so that the LORD has destroyed them to this day; [5] what he did to you in the wilderness, until you came to this place; [6] and what he did to Dathan and Abiram, sons of Eliab son of Reuben, how in the midst of all Israel the earth opened its mouth and swallowed them up, along with their households, their tents, and every living being in their company; [7] for it is your own eyes that have seen every great deed that the LORD did.

8 Keep, then, this entire commandment that I am commanding you today, so that you may have strength to go in and occupy the land that you are crossing over to occupy, [9] and so that you may live long in the land that the LORD swore to your ancestors to give them and to their descendants, a land flowing with milk and honey. [10] For the land that you are about to enter to occupy is not like the land of Egypt, from which you have come, where you sow your seed and irrigate by foot like a vegetable garden. [11] But the land that you are crossing over to occupy is a land of hills and valleys, watered by rain from the sky, [12] a land that the LORD your God looks after. The eyes of the LORD your God are always on it, from the beginning of the year to the end of the year.

13 If you will only heed his every commandment[y] that I am commanding you today—loving the LORD your God, and serving him with all your heart and with all your soul— [14] then he[z] will give the rain for your land in its season, the early rain and the later rain, and you will gather in your grain, your wine, and your oil; [15] and he[z] will give grass in your fields for your livestock, and you will eat your fill. [16] Take care, or you will be seduced into turning away, serving other gods and worshiping them, [17] for then the anger of the LORD will be kindled against you and he will shut up the heavens, so that there will be no rain and the land will yield no fruit; then you will perish quickly off the good land that the LORD is giving you.

18 You shall put these words of mine in your heart and soul, and you shall bind them as a sign on your hand, and fix them as an emblem[a] on your forehead. [19] Teach them to your children, talking about them when you are at home and when you are away, when you lie down and when you rise. [20] Write them on the doorposts of your house and on your gates, [21] so that your days and the days of your children may be multiplied in the land that the LORD swore to your ancestors to give them, as long as the heavens are above the earth.

22 If you will diligently observe this entire commandment that I am commanding you, loving the LORD your God, walking in all his ways, and holding fast to him, [23] then the LORD will drive out all these nations before you, and you will dispossess nations larger and mightier than yourselves. [24] Every place on which you set foot shall be yours; your territory shall

x Or *Sea of Reeds*   y Compare Gk: Heb *my commandments*   z Sam Gk Vg: MT *I*   a Or *as a frontlet*

6.20–25). **11.3–4** The emphasis here on the Lord's victory at the *Red Sea* is singular among the book's witnesses to the exodus (cf. 6.21–22; 7.18–19; 26.8; 29.2–3; 34.11; Josh 24.5–7; Ps 106.7–12). **11.6** In the expansive version of Num 16 (usually ascribed to the "priestly" tradition, or "P"), the insurrectionist party of the Reubenites *Dathan and Abiram* is subordinated to the ecclesial revolt led by the Levite Korah, unmentioned here (cf. Ps 106.16–18). **11.8–9** Cf. 5.32–6.3. **11.10–12** While Egypt's agricultural productivity (cf. Gen 13.10; 41.53–57; Num 11.5) is based on irrigation, exploiting the regularity of the Nile, Canaan's prosperity requires seasonal rains that attest the Lord's special care.

11.13–15 Rainfall in autumn and spring (*the early rain and the later rain*; see Jer 3.3; 5.24; Job 29.23) and the fertility it creates are divine blessings, granted to reward performance of covenantal duties (cf. 7.12–14; 28.12; Lev 26.4–5; Isa 30.23–24; Jer 14.21–22). **11.16** On the danger of entrapment in idolatry (*seduced*), see 7.1–6; 13.1–15. **11.17** *Shut up the heavens*, to withhold rain (cf. 28.23–24; Gen 7.11; Lev 26.19; 1 Kings 8.35–36; Job 38.25–27). **11.18–12.1** Transition to the Mosaic legislation. **11.18–21** Rhetorical echoes of 6.6–9; 6.1–3 recall attention to the chief aim of the address. **11.21** *As long as the heavens are above the earth*, i.e., forever (cf. Ps 89.29; Jer 31.36–37; 33.25–26). **11.22–23** Cf.

extend from the wilderness to the Lebanon and from the River, the river Euphrates, to the Western Sea. 25 No one will be able to stand against you; the LORD your God will put the fear and dread of you on all the land on which you set foot, as he promised you.

26 See, I am setting before you today a blessing and a curse: 27 the blessing, if you obey the commandments of the LORD your God that I am commanding you today; 28 and the curse, if you do not obey the commandments of the LORD your God, but turn from the way that I am commanding you today, to follow other gods that you have not known.

29 When the LORD your God has brought you into the land that you are entering to occupy, you shall set the blessing on Mount Gerizim and the curse on Mount Ebal. 30 As you know, they are beyond the Jordan, some distance to the west, in the land of the Canaanites who live in the Arabah, opposite Gilgal, beside the oak *b* of Moreh.

31 When you cross the Jordan to go in to occupy the land that the LORD your God is giving you, and when you occupy it and live in it, 32 you must diligently observe all the statutes and ordinances that I am setting before you today.

12 These are the statutes and ordinances that you must diligently observe in the land that the LORD, the God of your ancestors, has given you to occupy all the days that you live on the earth.

The Place the LORD Will Choose

2 You must demolish completely all the places where the nations whom you are about to dispossess served their gods, on the mountain heights, on the hills, and under every leafy tree. 3 Break down their altars, smash their pillars, burn their sacred poles *c* with fire, and hew down the idols of their gods, and thus blot out their name from their places. 4 You shall not worship the LORD your God in such ways.

b Gk Syr: Compare Gen 12.6; Heb *oaks* or *terebinths*
c Heb *Asherim*

10.12–13, 20; 9.1. **11.24** *Every place ... yours.* Josh 1.3 cites this promise. *Your territory.* The boundaries encompass the broad expanse of Syro-Palestine and correspond approximately to the scope of Davidic hegemony in the early tenth century B.C.E. (see note on 1.7; cf. Ex 23.31). *The Western Sea,* the Mediterranean. **11.25** For the promise, see 2.25. **11.26–28** *A blessing and a curse* are the alternatives of weal and woe posed by the constant choice that Israel must make between fidelity to the Lord and apostasy (cf. 30.15–20; Josh 24.14–28). These fundamental options are sanctioned by the specific lists of conditional "blessings" and "curses" in ch. 28 (see also Lev 26). **11.28** *Gods that you have not known,* gods whose effective presence you have not experienced (cf. 4.32–39; 32.16–17; Judg 2.11–13; 5.8). **11.29** This anticipates the rites prescribed in ch. 27 (cf. Josh 8.30–35). Ancient Shechem was situated in the valley between *Mount Gerizim* on the south and *Mount Ebal* on the north. **11.30** Geographical sense is not evident in the association of Canaanite inhabitants of the *Arabah* (cf. Num 13.29) with the site of *Gilgal* near Jericho (see Josh 4–5) and the distant *oak of Moreh* at Shechem (Gen 12.6; 35.4; cf. Josh 24.26). **11.31–12.1** These verses form a rhetorical seam between the general instructions, now completed, and the following promulgation of *the statutes and ordinances*; see note on 4.44–45. **12.2–26.15** Articles of the covenantal polity are arranged in five broad topical divisions: the single sanctuary (12.2–28); communal service of the Lord (12.29–17.13); constitutional offices (17.14–18.22); major juridical principles and precedents (19.1–25.19); and liturgical reaffirmations of fidelity (26.1–15). **12.2–28** In this initial division, four complementary articles (vv. 2–7, 8–12, 13–19, 20–28) develop a bold reinterpretation of the sanctuary law in Ex 20.24–26. The revision's chief concern correlates closely with reforms attributed to the Judean kings Hezekiah at the end of the eighth century B.C.E. (2 Kings 18.3–6, 22) and Josiah in the later seventh (2 Kings 23.4–19): suppression of apostasy and cultic pluralism by restricting Israel's performance of sacrificial rites and related ceremonies to the temple in Jerusalem. **12.2–7** A categorical distinction is drawn between the manifold cultic installations that Israel must destroy while conquering its homeland and the single, divinely designated place where Israel's own national worship center will be established. **12.2–3** Antecedent injunctions are Ex 23.23–24; 34.11–14 (cf. also Deut 7.5; Num 33.51–52). *Heights ... leafy tree.* See, e.g., 2 Kings 16.4; Jer 2.20. *Their name,* the sovereignty claimed by the defunct nations but also the immanence of putative gods associated with the installations (cf. 7.24–25; 25.19; Gen 35.14–15; Ex 20.24; Josh 23.7). **12.4** According to many witnesses, this is just what happened. See, e.g., Judg 17.3–5; 1 Kings 12.28–30; 14.22–24; 2 Kings 17.8–12; Jer 3.6–10; 17.1–3; Ezek 6.2–7; 18.6; Hos

5 But you shall seek the place that the LORD your God will choose out of all your tribes as his habitation to put his name there. You shall go there, 6 bringing there your burnt offerings and your sacrifices, your tithes and your donations, your votive gifts, your freewill offerings, and the firstlings of your herds and flocks. 7 And you shall eat there in the presence of the LORD your God, you and your households together, rejoicing in all the undertakings in which the LORD your God has blessed you.

8 You shall not act as we are acting here today, all of us according to our own desires, 9 for you have not yet come into the rest and the possession that the LORD your God is giving you. 10 When you cross over the Jordan and live in the land that the LORD your God is allotting to you, and when he gives you rest from your enemies all around so that you live in safety, 11 then you shall bring everything that I command you to the place that the LORD your God will choose as a dwelling for his name: your burnt offerings and your sacrifices, your tithes and your donations, and all your choice votive gifts that you vow to the LORD. 12 And you shall rejoice before the LORD your God, you together with your sons and your daughters, your male and female slaves, and the Levites who reside in your towns (since they have no allotment or inheritance with you).

13 Take care that you do not offer your burnt offerings at any place you happen to see. 14 But only at the place that the LORD will choose in one of your tribes —there you shall offer your burnt offerings and there you shall do everything I command you.

15 Yet whenever you desire you may slaughter and eat meat within any of your towns, according to the blessing that the LORD your God has given you; the unclean and the clean may eat of it, as they would of gazelle or deer. 16 The blood, however, you must not eat; you shall pour it out on the ground like water. 17 Nor may you eat within your towns the tithe of

---

4.12–13; 10.8. **12.5** Israel should seek the Lord in worship not at "every place" commemorating the divine name (Ex 20.24) but only at the one *place* chosen *out of all your tribes*, i.e., Jerusalem's acropolis, where David's tent shrine for the ark was soon replaced by the Solomonic temple (cf. 2 Sam 6.17; 7.6–7, 13; 24.18–25; 1 Kings 8.16–21; 11.32; 14.21; 2 Kings 21.7; Ps 132). While in Deuteronomic theology the transcendent God does not "reside" in any earthly abode, the Lord's *name* is localized at the one sanctuary as a manifestation of divine presence and cosmic attentiveness (26.15; 1 Kings 8.27–30, 43, 48–49; cf. Ex 23.20; Ps 74.7; Isa 18.7; Jer 3.17; 7.12–14; Tob 13.11). Hence *as his habitation* is a dubious rendering; the Hebrew may be translated instead "to establish it (the divine name)," similarly in 12.11; 14.23; 16.2, 6, 11; 26.2. **12.6** *Burnt offerings*, "holocausts" in which flayed animal carcasses were wholly consumed by fire on the altar, sustained the system of expiatory sacrifices (cf. Lev 1.3–17; 6.9–13; Num 28.2–8, 23–24; Am 5.22). Other *sacrifices* were usually consumed in part by the worshipers who presented them and also by priestly officiants (cf. 18.1–3; Lev 3; 7.29–36). *Tithes . . . firstlings*, i.e., all types of sacred dues (14.22–27; 15.19–23; 23.21–23; 26.12–15; cf. Lev 27.1–8; Num 15.18–21; 30.2–15; Am 4.4–5). **12.7** Emphasis on inclusive religious celebrations is characteristic of the Deuteronomic legislation (cf. 12.12, 18–19; 14.26–27; 15.20; 16.11, 14; 26.11).

12.8–12 A temporal distinction is made between divergent practices *today* and the centralization of worship that will become normative for Israel. **12.8** *We are acting . . . all of us according to our own desires*, lit. "each person (doing) what is right in his own sight": individual willfulness reigns (cf. Judg 17.6; 21.25) rather than divine authority (*what is right in the sight of the LORD*; cf. 6.18; 12.25, 28). **12.9–10** *Rest and possession*, secure territorial dominion (see notes on 3.18–20; 11.24; cf. 33.28–29). According to developed Deuteronomic tradition, the conditions were only met with the creation of David's empire (cf. Josh 23.1–5; 2 Sam 7.1–16; 1 Kings 5.3–5; 8.56). **12.11** *As a dwelling for his name*, better "to establish his name"; see note on 12.5. **12.12** *Levites*. See notes on 10.8–9; 18.1–8. **12.13–19** Two key functional distinctions are made here, one between extant cultic "places" (cf. Ex 20.24; 1 Sam 7.16; Josh 22.10–34), which are not or no longer to be used for sacrificial worship, and the chosen *place* and the other between altar sacrifices and animals slaughtered for food. **12.15** *Whenever you desire*, as your appetite dictates (cf. 18.6; Prov 23.2) and the Lord's *blessing* permits (cf. 7.13). *The unclean and the clean may eat of it*. Since domestic slaughter of livestock is no different than the killing of game (*gazelle or deer*) for edible meat, rules of purity that pertain to the consumption of sacrificial offerings and other sacral dues are not applicable (cf. also 12.20–22; 15.22; Lev 7.19–21; 17.3–9). **12.16** *Blood* is the essence of animal "life" and must not be consumed (cf. 12.23; 15.23; Gen 9.4–5; Lev 17.10–14; 19.26; 1 Sam

your grain, your wine, and your oil, the firstlings of your herds and your flocks, any of your votive gifts that you vow, your freewill offerings, or your donations; 18these you shall eat in the presence of the LORD your God at the place that the LORD your God will choose, you together with your son and your daughter, your male and female slaves, and the Levites resident in your towns, rejoicing in the presence of the LORD your God in all your undertakings. 19Take care that you do not neglect the Levite as long as you live in your land.

20 When the LORD your God enlarges your territory, as he has promised you, and you say, "I am going to eat some meat," because you wish to eat meat, you may eat meat whenever you have the desire. 21If the place where the LORD your God will choose to put his name is too far from you, and you slaughter as I have commanded you any of your herd or flock that the LORD has given you, then you may eat within your towns whenever you desire. 22Indeed, just as gazelle or deer is eaten, so you may eat it; the unclean and the clean alike may eat it. 23Only be sure that you do not eat the blood; for the blood is the life, and you shall not eat the life with the meat. 24Do not eat it; you shall pour it out on the ground like water. 25Do not eat it, so that all may go well with you and your children after you, because you do what is right in the sight of the LORD. 26But the sacred donations that are due from you, and your votive gifts, you shall bring to the place that the LORD will choose. 27You shall present your burnt offerings, both the meat and the blood, on the altar of the LORD your God; the blood of your other sacrifices shall be poured out beside d the altar of the LORD your God, but the meat you may eat.

28 Be careful to obey all these words that I command you today,e so that it may go well with you and with your children after you forever, because you will be doing what is good and right in the sight of the LORD your God.

Warning Against Apostasy

29 When the LORD your God has cut off before you the nations whom you are about to enter to dispossess them, when you have dispossessed them and live in their land, 30take care that you are not snared into imitating them, after they have been destroyed before you: do not inquire concerning their gods, saying, "How did these nations worship their gods? I also want to do the same." 31You must not do the same for the LORD your God, because every abhorrent thing that the LORD hates they have done for their gods. They would even burn their sons and their daughters in the fire to their gods. 32f You must diligently observe everything that I command you; do not add to it or take anything from it.

d Or on   e Gk Sam Syr: MT lacks today
f Ch 13.1 in Heb

14.31–35).   **12.20–28** A summary paragraph emphasizes orthopraxy and its motives: though nonsacrificial slaughter is permitted as a geographical necessity (*When the LORD . . . enlarges your territory*; cf. 14.24; 19.8–9; Ex 34.24), sacrificial slaughter remains preferable whenever the altar of the single sanctuary is near enough for use (vv. 20–22, 27; cf. Lev 17.3–9).   **12.23** The restriction on eating *blood* must never be relaxed (vv. 23–25; cf. 12.16; Lev 17.10–14); requisite offerings and sacral dues must be presented regularly at the sanctuary (vv. 26–27; cf. 14.22–27; 15.19–20; 16.16–17; 26.1–15).   **12.28** The paragraph and pericope conclude with an exhortation composed of familiar phrases (e.g., 4.40; 5.29; 6.3, 17–18; 12.25).

12.29–17.13 This division treats corporate obligations and institutional structures designed to maintain Israel's national identity as the covenant people of God. **12.29–32** Specific provisions are introduced by another warning against any compromise of Israel's distinctiveness as defined by the Mosaic legislation (cf. 4.1–2; 5.32–6.3; 11.31–12.1).   **12.30** *Snared*, here through attraction to aboriginal religious culture rather than by political or nuptial alliance with the condemned nations (cf. 7.1–5, 25; Ex 23.33; 34.12; Judg 2.3).   **12.31** *Abhorrent*. See note on 7.25–26. Immolation of children by *fire* is particularly associated with the cult of Molech, practiced during the monarchical era in the Hinnom Valley southwest of Jerusalem (Lev 18.21; 20.2–5; 2 Kings 23.10; Jer 7.31; 19.5; cf. also 18.10; 2 Kings 3.27; 16.3; 21.6).   **12.32** *Everything*, neither less nor more, because worship of the Lord augmented with pagan practices becomes paganism (cf. 2 Kings 17.7–41).

Counteracting Sedition

13 *g* If prophets or those who divine by dreams appear among you and promise you omens or portents, 2 and the omens or the portents declared by them take place, and they say, "Let us follow other gods" (whom you have not known) "and let us serve them," 3 you must not heed the words of those prophets or those who divine by dreams; for the LORD your God is testing you, to know whether you indeed love the LORD your God with all your heart and soul. 4 The LORD your God you shall follow, him alone you shall fear, his commandments you shall keep, his voice you shall obey, him you shall serve, and to him you shall hold fast. 5 But those prophets or those who divine by dreams shall be put to death for having spoken treason against the LORD your God—who brought you out of the land of Egypt and redeemed you from the house of slavery—to turn you from the way in which the LORD your God commanded you to walk. So you shall purge the evil from your midst.

6 If anyone secretly entices you—even if it is your brother, your father's son or *h* your mother's son, or your own son or daughter, or the wife you embrace, or your most intimate friend—saying, "Let us go worship other gods," whom neither you nor your ancestors have known, 7 any of the gods of the peoples that are around you, whether near you or far away from you, from one end of the earth to the other, 8 you must not yield to or heed any such persons. Show them no pity or compassion and do not shield them. 9 But you shall surely kill them; your own hand shall be first against them to execute them, and afterwards the hand of all the people. 10 Stone them to death for trying to turn you away from the LORD your God, who brought you out of the land of Egypt, out of the house of slavery. 11 Then all Israel shall hear and be afraid, and never again do any such wickedness.

12 If you hear it said about one of the towns that the LORD your God is giving you to live in, 13 that scoundrels from among you have gone out and led the inhabitants of the town astray, saying, "Let us go and worship other gods," whom you have not known, 14 then you shall inquire and make a thorough investigation. If the charge is established that such an abhorrent thing has been done among you, 15 you shall put the inhabitants of that

g Ch 13.2 in Heb   *h* Sam Gk Compare Tg: MT lacks *your father's son or*

13.1–18 Three cases are summarized to prescribe severe, unyielding retribution against instigators of sedition. **13.1–5** Mantic incitement to apostasy is a criminal offense, never credible even when supported by accurate prognostication. **13.1–3** *Divine by dreams.* See, e.g., Gen 37.5–10; Num 12.6; Judg 7.13–14; Jer 23.25; 27.9; Joel 2.28. *Omens or portents*, any forecasts or signs offered to authenticate claims of divine empowerment (see 34.11; Ex 4.1–9, 21; 7.9; Judg 6.17–21, 36–40). *Testing.* See 8.2, 16. **13.4** An emphatic restatement of allegiance to the Lord alone (cf. 10.20; 11.22). **13.5** *Spoken treason* also describes prophetic duplicity in Jer 28.16; 29.32. *So you shall purge the evil from your midst.* The formula emphasizes communal responsibility to eradicate perpetrators of virulent evil from Israel's midst (also 17.7, 12; 19.19; 21.21; 22.21, 22, 24; 24.7). **13.6–11** Clandestine enticement to apostasy must be confronted with equal resolve and severe punishment. **13.6–8** Loyalty to Israel's divine sovereign takes precedence over even the closest human bonds of kinship, marriage, and collegiality. **13.6** *Intimate friend*, one as beloved as one's own self; cf. 1 Sam 18.3. **13.8** *No pity.* Cf. 7.16; 19.13, 21; 25.12. **13.9–10** To *kill*

offenders by stoning on presumption of guilt legitimates communal lynching (cf. 1 Sam 30.6; 1 Kings 12.18). But the Septuagint may preserve the preferable reading, that an accuser must first "decry" or "publicly charge" a culprit, thereby initiating judicial proceedings that may result in capital punishment carried out by accuser and communal court (cf. 17.4–7; 21.18–21; 22.20–24; Josh 7.10–26; 1 Kings 21.8–14). **13.11** Publicized execution in such circumstances is meant as a deterrent (cf. 17.12–13; 21.21). **13.12–18** This case outlines judicial procedure and martial retribution in the event that an entire town in Israel becomes contaminated by apostasy. **13.13** *Scoundrels,* lit. "sons without worth," "outlaws" who defy legitimate authority (cf. Judg 19.22; 20.13; 1 Sam 2.12). **13.14** *Inquire* could connote oracular consultation (cf. Judg 20.18, 23; Josh 7.13–21) but the clear purport of this Deuteronomic usage is judicial initiative to gather empirical evidence (see 17.4, 9; 19.18; cf. Josh 22.10–34). **13.15–17** The apostate town becomes anathema, like the former nations whose practices it assimilated (12.29–30); thus a comprehensive ban must be implemented against it,

town to the sword, utterly destroying it and everything in it—even putting its livestock to the sword. 16 All of its spoil you shall gather into its public square; then burn the town and all its spoil with fire, as a whole burnt offering to the LORD your God. It shall remain a perpetual ruin, never to be rebuilt. 17 Do not let anything devoted to destruction stick to your hand, so that the LORD may turn from his fierce anger and show you compassion, and in his compassion multiply you, as he swore to your ancestors, 18 if you obey the voice of the LORD your God by keeping all his commandments that I am commanding you today, doing what is right in the sight of the LORD your God.

Avoiding Defilement

14 You are children of the LORD your God. You must not lacerate yourselves or shave your forelocks for the dead. 2 For you are a people holy to the LORD your God; it is you the LORD has chosen out of all the peoples on earth to be his people, his treasured possession.

3 You shall not eat any abhorrent thing. 4 These are the animals you may eat: the ox, the sheep, the goat, 5 the deer, the gazelle, the roebuck, the wild goat, the ibex, the antelope, and the mountain-sheep. 6 Any animal that divides the hoof and has the hoof cleft in two, and chews the cud, among the animals, you may eat. 7 Yet of those that chew the cud or have the hoof cleft you shall not eat these: the camel, the hare, and the rock badger, because they chew the cud but do not divide the hoof; they are unclean for you. 8 And the pig, because it divides the hoof but does not chew the cud, is unclean for you. You shall not eat their meat, and you shall not touch their carcasses.

9 Of all that live in water you may eat these: whatever has fins and scales you may eat. 10 And whatever does not have fins and scales you shall not eat; it is unclean for you.

11 You may eat any clean birds. 12 But these are the ones that you shall not eat: the eagle, the vulture, the osprey, 13 the buzzard, the kite of any kind; 14 every raven of any kind; 15 the ostrich, the nighthawk, the sea gull, the hawk of any kind; 16 the little owl and the great owl, the water hen 17 and the desert owl,*i* the carrion vulture and the cormorant, 18 the stork, the heron of any kind; the hoopoe and the bat.*j* 19 And all winged insects are unclean for you; they shall not be eaten. 20 You may eat any clean winged creature.

21 You shall not eat anything that dies of itself; you may give it to aliens residing in your towns for them to eat, or you may

i Or *pelican*   *j* Identification of several of the birds in verses 12-18 is uncertain

---

lest Israel as a whole incur the wrath of God (20.16–18; cf. 7.25–26). **13.16** *Whole burnt offering;* a sacrificial conflagration (33.10; Lev 6.22–23; 1 Sam 7.9; cf. Isa 34.6–7). *Perpetual ruin,* like Ai (Josh 8.28; cf. Jer 49.2).

14.1–21 Select rules pertaining to Israel's comportment as the Lord's holy people. **14.1** *Children of the LORD,* referring to the covenant community, is language elsewhere attested especially in prophetic contexts treating Israel's filial waywardness (32.5–6, 19–20; Ps 103.13; Isa 1.2, 4; 30.1; Jer 3.14, 19, 22; cf. Jer 31.9, 20; Hos 1.10; 11.1–4). *Lacerate, shave . . . forelocks.* Self-laceration and tonsure are perhaps prohibited because they were associated with pagan rites (cf. Lev 19.27–28; 21.5; 1 Kings 18.28; Jer 16.6–7; 41.4–5; 47.5; Am 8.10). **14.2** A restatement of covenantal integrity based on Ex 19.5–6 (cf. 7.6) introduces a series of dietary rules. **14.3** *Abhorrent* in the general prohibition makes foods excluded from Israel's diet a matter of the Lord's discretion (see note on 7.25–26; cf. Ex 8.26). **14.4–20** The basic categories of land animals (vv. 4–8), fish (vv. 9–10), and flying creatures (vv. 11–20) reflect the familiar taxonomy of the created order (Gen 1.20–25; 9.2–3). A common antecedent tradition as well as some mutual influence at a late stage of textual formation best account for the detailed similarities and differences between this classification of clean and unclean creatures and its counterpart in Lev 11.2–23. Some of the species identifications, especially of the birds, remain uncertain. **14.21** *Anything that dies of itself,* i.e., carrion or the carcass of an otherwise edible animal from which the blood was not drained (cf. 12.16, 22–27; with Ex 22.31; Lev 17.15; 22.8; Ezek 44.31). The issue is ritual purity, not health per se; hence the affected meat could be eaten by those who did not belong to the sacral community (resident *aliens* or a *foreigner*). The old prohibition against cooking *a kid in its mother's milk* (Ex 23.19; 34.26) concludes the series of rules. The original significance of this prohibition is a matter of some dispute. Some see it as proscribing Canaanite religious practices, others as being directed against the unnatural and callous treatment of animals. The later Jewish dietary practice of not mixing meat and dairy

sell it to a foreigner. For you are a people holy to the LORD your God.

You shall not boil a kid in its mother's milk.

Tithes

22 Set apart a tithe of all the yield of your seed that is brought in yearly from the field. 23 In the presence of the LORD your God, in the place that he will choose as a dwelling for his name, you shall eat the tithe of your grain, your wine, and your oil, as well as the firstlings of your herd and flock, so that you may learn to fear the LORD your God always. 24 But if, when the LORD your God has blessed you, the distance is so great that you are unable to transport it, because the place where the LORD your God will choose to set his name is too far away from you, 25 then you may turn it into money. With the money secure in hand, go to the place that the LORD your God will choose; 26 spend the money for whatever you wish—oxen, sheep, wine, strong drink, or whatever you desire. And you shall eat there in the presence of the LORD your God, you and your household rejoicing together. 27 As for the Levites resident in your towns, do not neglect them, because they have no allotment or inheritance with you.

28 Every third year you shall bring out the full tithe of your produce for that year, and store it within your towns; 29 the Levites, because they have no allotment or inheritance with you, as well as the resident aliens, the orphans, and the widows in your towns, may come and eat their fill so that the LORD your God may bless you in all the work that you undertake.

The Sabbatical Year of Remission

15 Every seventh year you shall grant a remission of debts. 2 And this is the manner of the remission: every creditor shall remit the claim that is held against a neighbor, not exacting it of a neighbor who is a member of the community, because the LORD's remission has been proclaimed. 3 Of a foreigner you may exact it, but you must remit your claim on whatever any member of your community owes you. 4 There will, however, be no one in need among you, because the LORD is sure to bless you in the land that the LORD your God is giving you as a possession to occupy, 5 if only you will obey the LORD your God by diligently observing this entire commandment that I command you today. 6 When the LORD your God has blessed you, as he promised you, you will lend to many nations, but you will not borrow; you will rule over many nations, but they will not rule over you.

7 If there is among you anyone in

---

products is based on this law. **14.22–29** The *tithe* probably originated as a 10 percent tax on agricultural produce (*all the yield of your seed*), usually paid in kind to the land's sovereign or designated government officials (cf. Gen 14.20; 28.22; Lev 27.30–33; Num 18.21–32; 1 Sam 8.15, 17; Am 4.4). Here the ancient practice is roughly adapted to the circumstances of centralization of worship. **14.23** *As a dwelling for his name.* See notes on 12.5; 12.11. The three annual pilgrimage festivals (see 16.16–17) are presumably meant as primary occasions for presentation of both agricultural tithes and *firstlings* of livestock (see also 12.17; 15.19–23). **14.24–27** Emphasis again falls on promoting inclusive celebrations (cf. note on 12.7); important social, economic, and administrative implications are ignored (cf. 2 Chr 31.2–19; Neh 12.44; Mk 11.15; Jn 2.13–14). **14.28–29** However, provision is added for local storage and distribution of tithes from produce harvested *every third year*, to sustain dispersed Levitical clans as well as to provide for others in need of charity (cf. 26.12–15; Ex 22.21–24). **15.1–18** This remarkable revision of older

laws (Ex 21.2–11; 22.25; 23.10–11) seeks to strengthen procedures for redressing economic imbalances within Israelite society resulting from usury and debt slavery. (For the abusive practices at issue, see Neh 5.1–13; Job 24.9; Ezek 18.16–18; Am 2.6–8.) **15.1–3** Sabbatical *remission of debts* (Hebrew *shemitta*, only in 15.1, 2, 9; 31.10) regularizes proclamation on the Lord's behalf of "liberty" for Israel's oppressed from burdens of indebtedness (cf. 10.17–18; Lev 25; Isa 61.1–2; Jer 34.8–22). **15.2** *Claim*, the debt itself, but also the surety pledged for a loan or taken as distraint after default (cf. 2 Kings 4.1; Prov 6.1–5; 17.18; 22.26–27). **15.3** Debts of a *foreigner* are unaffected (cf. Prov 20.16; 27.13). **15.4–6** Homiletical motivation: fidelity to the covenant will assure ample blessings for all citizens to share, making Israel preeminent among nations (cf. 7.12–14; 26.15; 28.1–14). **15.7–11** These exhortations anticipate that periodic cancellation of debts could seriously curtail lending, thus aggravating the plight of those in need (cf. *Mishnah Shebi'it* 10). Enforcement must be left to the Lord's devices of reward and punish-

need, a member of your community in any of your towns within the land that the LORD your God is giving you, do not be hard-hearted or tight-fisted toward your needy neighbor. 8 You should rather open your hand, willingly lending enough to meet the need, whatever it may be. 9 Be careful that you do not entertain a mean thought, thinking, "The seventh year, the year of remission, is near," and therefore view your needy neighbor with hostility and give nothing; your neighbor might cry to the LORD against you, and you would incur guilt. 10 Give liberally and be ungrudging when you do so, for on this account the LORD your God will bless you in all your work and in all that you undertake. 11 Since there will never cease to be some in need on the earth, I therefore command you, "Open your hand to the poor and needy neighbor in your land."

12 If a member of your community, whether a Hebrew man or a Hebrew woman, is sold*k* to you and works for you six years, in the seventh year you shall set that person free. 13 And when you send a male slave*l* out from you a free person, you shall not send him out empty-handed. 14 Provide liberally out of your flock, your threshing floor, and your wine press, thus giving to him some of the bounty with which the LORD your God has blessed you. 15 Remember that you were a slave in the land of Egypt, and the LORD your God redeemed you; for this reason I lay this command upon you today. 16 But if he says to you, "I will not go out from you," because he loves you and your household, since he is well off with you, 17 then you

shall take an awl and thrust it through his earlobe into the door, and he shall be your slave*m* forever.
You shall do the same with regard to your female slave.*n*

18 Do not consider it a hardship when you send them out from you free persons, because for six years they have given you services worth the wages of hired laborers; and the LORD your God will bless you in all that you do.

The Firstborn of Livestock

19 Every firstling male born of your herd and flock you shall consecrate to the LORD your God; you shall not do work with your firstling ox nor shear the firstling of your flock. 20 You shall eat it, you together with your household, in the presence of the LORD your God year by year at the place that the LORD will choose. 21 But if it has any defect—any serious defect, such as lameness or blindness—you shall not sacrifice it to the LORD your God; 22 within your towns you may eat it, the unclean and the clean alike, as you would a gazelle or deer. 23 Its blood, however, you must not eat; you shall pour it out on the ground like water.

Pilgrimage Festivals

16 Observe the month*o* of Abib by keeping the passover to the LORD your God, for in the month of Abib the LORD your God brought you out of

k Or *sells himself or herself*   *l* Heb *him*
m Or *bondman*   *n* Or *bondwoman*   *o* Or *new moon*

---

ment (cf. 24.19; Ps 37.21–22; Prov 19.17). **15.9** *Cry.* An appeal to the divine judge for redress (24.15; cf. Ex 2.23–24; 22.23–24, 27). **15.12–18** In context, this reworking of older laws of manumission (Ex 21.2–11) apparently favors a collective release of both male and female bondslaves in the fixed sabbatical year of remission (cf. 31.10–13; Jer 34.8–14). **15.12** *Hebrew,* which seems to mean client status in Ex 21.2, here simply denotes a fellow Israelite; *member of your community,* lit. "your brother," rendered inclusively as sense requires. *Sold,* e.g., as a debtor or distrainee, or indentured by judicial authority to make restitution for a theft (cf. Ex 22.3). **15.13–15** Generous provision for those released is urged as appropriate imitation of the Lord's liberality in redeeming Israel from Egyptian slavery (cf. 5.14–15; 10.17–22; 16.12; 24.18, 22; 26.6–10).

Empty-handed. Cf. 16.16; also Ex 3.21–22. **15.16–18** A noteworthy revision of Ex 21.2–11 includes the general presumption against permanent enslavement of Israelites as well as the equal treatment now accorded a bondwoman. **15.19–23** Provision is made here for disposal of firstlings in accord with the requirements of the single sanctuary. (For antecedent and alternate rulings, see Ex 13.2, 11–16; 22.29–30; 34.19–20; Lev 22.26–27; 27.26–27; Num 18.15–18.) **15.19–20** Though male *firstlings* of livestock must not be used productively, a flexible schedule (*year by year*) is allowed for sacrificial presentation (cf. 12.6–7, 17–18; 14.23; 16.16; Ex 22.30). **15.21–22** Rules of local slaughter (12.15–16, 22–24) apply to any firstling unacceptable for sacrifice because of *serious defect* (cf. 17.1; Lev 22.17–25; Mal 1.8).

Egypt by night. 2 You shall offer the passover sacrifice to the LORD your God, from the flock and the herd, at the place that the LORD will choose as a dwelling for his name. 3 You must not eat with it anything leavened. For seven days you shall eat unleavened bread with it — the bread of affliction — because you came out of the land of Egypt in great haste, so that all the days of your life you may remember the day of your departure from the land of Egypt. 4 No leaven shall be seen with you in all your territory for seven days; and none of the meat of what you slaughter on the evening of the first day shall remain until morning. 5 You are not permitted to offer the passover sacrifice within any of your towns that the LORD your God is giving you. 6 But at the place that the LORD your God will choose as a dwelling for his name, only there shall you offer the passover sacrifice, in the evening at sunset, the time of day when you departed from Egypt. 7 You shall cook it and eat it at the place that the LORD your God will choose; the next morning you may go back to your tents. 8 For six days you shall continue to eat unleavened bread, and on the seventh day there shall be a solemn assembly for the LORD your God, when you shall do no work.

9 You shall count seven weeks; begin to count the seven weeks from the time the sickle is first put to the standing grain. 10 Then you shall keep the festival of weeks to the LORD your God, contributing a freewill offering in proportion to the blessing that you have received from the LORD your God. 11 Rejoice before the LORD your God — you and your sons and your daughters, your male and female slaves, the Levites resident in your towns, as well as the strangers, the orphans, and the widows who are among you — at the place that the LORD your God will choose as a dwelling for his name. 12 Remember that you were a slave in Egypt, and diligently observe these statutes.

13 You shall keep the festival of booths[p] for seven days, when you have gathered in the produce from your threshing floor and your wine press. 14 Rejoice during your festival, you and your sons and your daughters, your male and female slaves, as well as the Levites, the strangers, the orphans, and the widows resident in your towns. 15 Seven days you shall keep the festival to the LORD your God at the place that the LORD will choose; for the LORD your God will bless you in all your produce and in all your undertakings, and you shall surely celebrate.

16 Three times a year all your males shall appear before the LORD your God at the place that he will choose: at the festi-

p Or *tabernacles*; Heb *succoth*

16.1–17 Deuteronomic restriction of Israel's ritual sacrifices and related ceremonies to a single sanctuary (12.5) culminates in this sketch of a revised liturgical calendar (see Ex 23.14–18; 34.18–24; cf. Lev 23.4–44; Num 28.11–29.39; Ezek 45.18–25). **16.1–8** Communal celebration of the Passover sacrifice (vv. 1–2, 4b–7) is closely correlated with the week-long consumption of unleavened bread (vv. 3–4a, 8) to commemorate the exodus from Egypt (see Ex 12–13; 23.15; 34.18; cf. Josh 5.10–12; 2 Kings 23.21–23; 2 Chr 30; 35.1–19). **16.1** According to the oldest traditions, the nocturnal escape from Egypt occurred on the "new moon" (preferable to *month*) of *Abib*, the season in early spring when ears of barley began to ripen (cf. Ex 12.29–32, 41–42; 13.3–4; Num 29.6; 1 Sam 20.5, 18; Isa 1.13; Am 8.5). **16.2** Presumably firstlings of livestock (*flock* and *herd*) were to provide the sacrificial meals during the full term of festivities (cf. Ex 12.5; 2 Chr 30.17–24; 35.7–13). **16.2, 6** *As a dwelling for his name.* See notes on 12.5; 12.11. **16.7** *Cook,* or "boil" (1 Sam 2.13, 15); cf. Ex 12.9; 2 Chr 35.13.

16.8 *Solemn assembly.* A sacral convocation concludes the festivities (cf. Ex 13.6; Lev 23.36; Num 29.35; Isa 1.13; Am 5.21). **16.9–12** *Weeks,* later known as Pentecost (e.g., Acts 2.1), is the "harvest" festival of early summer, when first fruits of grain were to be presented at the sanctuary (cf. Ex 23.16; 34.22; Num 28.26). **16.10** *Freewill offering,* apparently in addition to the mandatory tithe of agricultural produce (cf. 12.6, 17). **16.11** *As a dwelling for his name.* See notes on 12.5; 12.11. **16.13–15** *Booths* (cf. Lev 23.34, 42–43; Ezra 3.4; Neh 8.14) is the old autumn festival of "ingathering" at the end of the agricultural year (Ex 23.16; 34.22). It seems to have been the occasion for King Josiah's renewal of the covenant (cf. 31.10–13; 2 Kings 23.1–3) as well as Solomon's dedication of the temple two centuries earlier (1 Kings 8.2, 62–66). **16.16–17** In this summary, the spring pilgrimage is designated only as *unleavened bread*; specification of *males* as participants reflects older practice (Ex 23.17; 34.23) rather than the Deuteronomic emphasis on inclusivity (vv. 11, 14; see note on 12.7).

val of unleavened bread, at the festival of weeks, and at the festival of booths.q They shall not appear before the LORD empty-handed; 17all shall give as they are able, according to the blessing of the LORD your God that he has given you.

Administration of Justice

18 You shall appoint judges and officials throughout your tribes, in all your towns that the LORD your God is giving you, and they shall render just decisions for the people. 19You must not distort justice; you must not show partiality; and you must not accept bribes, for a bribe blinds the eyes of the wise and subverts the cause of those who are in the right. 20Justice, and only justice, you shall pursue, so that you may live and occupy the land that the LORD your God is giving you.

21 You shall not plant any tree as a sacred poler beside the altar that you make for the LORD your God; 22nor shall you set up a stone pillar—things that the LORD your God hates.

17 You must not sacrifice to the LORD your God an ox or a sheep that has a defect, anything seriously wrong; for that is abhorrent to the LORD your God.

2 If there is found among you, in one of your towns that the LORD your God is giving you, a man or woman who does what is evil in the sight of the LORD your

God, and transgresses his covenant 3by going to serve other gods and worshiping them—whether the sun or the moon or any of the host of heaven, which I have forbidden— 4and if it is reported to you or you hear of it, and you make a thorough inquiry, and the charge is proved true that such an abhorrent thing has occurred in Israel, 5then you shall bring out to your gates that man or that woman who has committed this crime and you shall stone the man or woman to death. 6On the evidence of two or three witnesses the death sentence shall be executed; a person must not be put to death on the evidence of only one witness. 7The hands of the witnesses shall be the first raised against the person to execute the death penalty, and afterward the hands of all the people. So you shall purge the evil from your midst.

8 If a judicial decision is too difficult for you to make between one kind of bloodshed and another, one kind of legal right and another, or one kind of assault and another—any such matters of dispute in your towns—then you shall immediately go up to the place that the LORD your God will choose, 9where you shall consult with the levitical priests and the judge who is in office in those days; they shall announce to you the decision in the case. 10Carry out exactly the decision that they announce to you from the place that the LORD will choose, diligently observing

q Or *tabernacles*; Heb *succoth*   r Heb *Asherah*

16.18–17.13 The burden of theocratic governance within Israel is to be born by a two-tiered judiciary comprised of city courts in tribal jurisdictions and a consultative council associated with the single sanctuary. **16.18–20** The whole community (*you*) authorizes judicial administration by a corps of professional *judges and officials*, probably consisting in large part of dispersed Levitical personnel (cf. 1.13–17; 19.17; 21.5; Ex 32.26–29; Josh 21.1–42; 1 Chr 23.2–6; 26.29; 2 Chr 17.7–9; 19.5–11). **16.19** On the injunctions against *partiality* and taking *bribes*, see 1.16–17; 10.17–18 (cf. Ex 23.2–3, 6–8; Lev 19.15; Prov 17.23; 18.5; Isa 1.23; Mic 7.3). **16.21–17.1** In context, these prohibitions suggest that maintenance of ritual purity is to be a primary judicial concern. For the themes, see 7.5; 15.21 (cf. 2 Kings 23.6, 15). **17.2–7** Due process in adjudicating capital offenses is illustrated by reviewing prosecution of a case of apostasy (cf.

13.1–11). **17.2–3** *Transgresses his covenant.* Cf. Josh 7.11, 15; 23.16; Judg 2.20; 2 Kings 18.12; Jer 34.18; Hos 6.7; 8.1. *Sun ... moon ... host of heaven.* Cf. 4.19; 2 Kings 17.16; 21.3; 23.5; Jer 8.2; Ezek 8.16. **17.4–5** See 13.10. **17.6** See 19.15–21; cf. Num 35.30. **17.7** See 13.5, 9; note on 13.5. **17.8–13** Moses' authority to arbitrate in cases *too difficult* for resolution by local courts (cf. 1.17; Ex 18.22, 26) is institutionalized in a judicial council consisting mainly of Levitical priests. (This tribunal resembles the one attributed to King Jehoshaphat in 2 Chr 19.8–11.) **17.8** *One kind of bloodshed and another*, e.g., between murder and accidental homicide (cf. 19.4–13). **17.9–12** Levitical competence in judicial affairs seems here to be associated with transmission and authoritative application of Mosaic law (*the law that they interpret*); cf. 17.18; 31.9; 33.10; 2 Kings 17.27–28; Ezra 7.25–26. *Judge*, perhaps the king or civil governor (cf. 2 Sam

everything they instruct you. 11 You must carry out fully the law that they interpret for you or the ruling that they announce to you; do not turn aside from the decision that they announce to you, either to the right or to the left. 12 As for anyone who presumes to disobey the priest appointed to minister there to the LORD your God, or the judge, that person shall die. So you shall purge the evil from Israel. 13 All the people will hear and be afraid, and will not act presumptuously again.

Kingship

14 When you have come into the land that the LORD your God is giving you, and have taken possession of it and settled in it, and you say, "I will set a king over me, like all the nations that are around me," 15 you may indeed set over you a king whom the LORD your God will choose. One of your own community you may set as king over you; you are not permitted to put a foreigner over you, who is not of your own community. 16 Even so, he must not acquire many horses for himself, or return the people to Egypt in order to acquire more horses, since the LORD has said to you, "You must never return that way again." 17 And he must not acquire many wives for himself, or else his heart will turn away; also silver and gold he must not acquire in great quantity for himself. 18 When he has taken the throne

of his kingdom, he shall have a copy of this law written for him in the presence of the levitical priests. 19 It shall remain with him and he shall read in it all the days of his life, so that he may learn to fear the LORD his God, diligently observing all the words of this law and these statutes, 20 neither exalting himself above other members of the community nor turning aside from the commandment, either to the right or to the left, so that he and his descendants may reign long over his kingdom in Israel.

The Levitical Priesthood

18 The levitical priests, the whole tribe of Levi, shall have no allotment or inheritance within Israel. They may eat the sacrifices that are the LORD's portion[s] 2 but they shall have no inheritance among the other members of the community; the LORD is their inheritance, as he promised them.

3 This shall be the priests' due from the people, from those offering a sacrifice, whether an ox or a sheep: they shall give to the priest the shoulder, the two jowls, and the stomach. 4 The first fruits of your grain, your wine, and your oil, as well as the first of the fleece of your sheep, you shall give him. 5 For the LORD your God has chosen Levi[t] out of all your

[s] Meaning of Heb uncertain   [t] Heb him

14.3–20; 1 Kings 3.9; Prov 16.10). **17.13** See 13.11.

17.14–18.22 Offices held by virtue of divine election rather than communal empowerment are treated in this central section of the polity. **17.14–20** While monarchy is a permissible instrument of theocratic governance, major restrictions are placed on the exercise of royal authority (cf. 1 Sam 10.25). **17.14** When . . . and settled in it, a formulaic introduction; cf. 26.1. Like all the nations. Cf. 1 Sam 8.5, 20. **17.15** On divine designation of kings, usually through prophetic agency, see, e.g., 1 Sam 10.24; 16.1–13; 1 Kings 19.15–16; 2 Kings 9.1–13 (cf. Hos 8.4). One of your own community, lit. "from among your brothers," i.e., a fellow Israelite (cf. 18.15, 18). **17.16–17** These injunctions against abuse of royal power seem to have Solomon's excesses in specific view (1 Kings 10.6–11.8; cf. 1 Sam 8.10–18; Isa 2.7). **17.18** A copy of this law (see 4.44–45). The interpretive rendering in the Septuagint, Greek to deuteronomion touto ("this reiter-

ated law"; cf. Josh 8.32), underlies the familiar name "Deuteronomy." **17.19–20** The king's only stated task is to model obedience to the covenantal law incumbent on Israel as a whole; so too, dynastic succession and national tenure in the land are parallel rewards for fidelity (cf. 5.32–6.2; 2 Sam 7.10–16; 1 Kings 2.4; Ps 132.11–18). **18.1–8** Other texts sketch the broader scope of work performed by the Levitical bureaucracy (cf. 10.8–9; 17.8–12, 18; 20.2–9; 21.5; 31.9; 33.8–11). Here the concern is to establish the perquisites of Levites who serve at the single sanctuary. **18.1–2** The sacerdotal profession, supported chiefly by sacral prebends, is a prerogative distinguishing the clans or guilds that comprise the whole tribe of Levi from Israelite tribes granted territorial dominion (cf. Josh 13.14, 33; 18.7; 21.1–42; 2 Chr 31.2–19). **18.3** The priests' due. Cf. Lev 7.28–36; Num 18.8–20. **18.4** First fruits, "choice" portions representing the tithes of agricultural produce (cf. 14.22–29; 26.1–15; Num 18.21–32; Neh 13.10–13). **18.5** See 10.8;

tribes, to stand and minister in the name of the LORD, him and his sons for all time.

6 If a Levite leaves any of your towns, from wherever he has been residing in Israel, and comes to the place that the LORD will choose (and he may come whenever he wishes), 7 then he may minister in the name of the LORD his God, like all his fellow-Levites who stand to minister there before the LORD. 8 They shall have equal portions to eat, even though they have income from the sale of family possessions. [u]

Israel's Prophets

9 When you come into the land that the LORD your God is giving you, you must not learn to imitate the abhorrent practices of those nations. 10 No one shall be found among you who makes a son or daughter pass through fire, or who practices divination, or is a soothsayer, or an augur, or a sorcerer, 11 or one who casts spells, or who consults ghosts or spirits, or who seeks oracles from the dead. 12 For whoever does these things is abhorrent to the LORD; it is because of such abhorrent practices that the LORD your God is driving them out before you. 13 You must remain completely loyal to the LORD your God. 14 Although these nations that you are about to dispossess do give heed to soothsayers and diviners, as for you, the LORD your God does not permit you to do so.

15 The LORD your God will raise up for you a prophet [v] like me from among your own people; you shall heed such a prophet. [w] 16 This is what you requested of the LORD your God at Horeb on the day of the assembly when you said: "If I hear the voice of the LORD my God any more, or ever again see this great fire, I will die." 17 Then the LORD replied to me: "They are right in what they have said. 18 I will raise up for them a prophet [v] like you from among their own people; I will put my words in the mouth of the prophet, [x] who shall speak to them everything that I command. 19 Anyone who does not heed the words that the prophet [y] shall speak in my name, I myself will hold accountable. 20 But any prophet who speaks in the name of other gods, or who presumes to speak in my name a word that I have not commanded the prophet to speak — that prophet shall die." 21 You may say to yourself, "How can we recognize a word that the LORD has not spoken?" 22 If a prophet speaks in the name of the LORD but the thing does not take place or prove true, it is a word that the LORD has not spoken. The prophet has spoken it presumptuously; do not be frightened by it.

u Meaning of Heb uncertain   v Or *prophets*
w Or *such prophets*   x Or *mouths of the prophets*
y Heb *he*

---

cf. Ex 32.25–29; 1 Sam 2.27–28; Jer 33.17–22; Mal 2.2–7. **18.6–7** *Residing.* Lacking their own tribal territory, Levites "sojourn" among the land-holding tribes (cf. Judg 17.7; 19.1). Eligible Levites retain the right to officiate at the single sanctuary (cf. 2 Kings 23.8–9; 2 Chr 11.13–15). **18.8** *Income,* apparently, e.g., from the sale or lease of family fields and homes (cf. Lev 25.32–34; Num 35.1–8; Jer 32.6–15). **18.9–22** Although prophecy, in contrast to pagan divinatory practices, is a legitimate medium of revelation, individual prophetic claims to speak on the Lord's behalf must be rigorously assessed. **18.9–12** Polemic against *abhorrent practices* of the erstwhile nations (see 12.29–31; 20.17–18; note on 7.25–26) frames proscription of various types of occultism (cf. Ex 22.18; Lev 19.31; 20.6, 27; 1 Sam 28.3–19; Isa 8.19–20; Ezek 21.21). **18.10** Child sacrifice (*pass through fire;* see note on 12.31) is also associated with mantic practices in Deuteronomic indictments of both the Northern Kingdom, Israel, and King Manasseh of Judah (2 Kings 17.17; 21.6), while Josiah is credited with implementing the prohibitions (2 Kings 23.10, 24). **18.13** *Completely loyal* connotes personal "integrity" or "blamelessness" (e.g., Gen 6.9; 17.1; Job 12.4; Ps 18.23; Prov 11.5). **18.15–18** Prophecy, manifest as an authoritative role rather than in a fixed office, is legitimated on the model of Moses' mediation between God and Israel at Horeb (5.23–33; Ex 20.18–21; cf. 2 Kings 17.13; Jer 7.25–26). **18.15** *Like me,* i.e., a fellow Israelite (cf. 17.15; 34.10 is different). **18.18** *I will put my words in the mouth of the prophet.* Cf. Ex 4.12–16; Jer 1.9; 15.19; Ezek 3.1–4. **18.19** Cf. Jer 11.21–23; Am 7.10–17. **18.20** Unauthorized prophesying, whether in *the name of other gods* or the Lord, is a capital offense; see 13.1–5 (cf. Jer 14.13–16; 23.9–40; 28.12–17; Ezek 13). **18.21–22** On the criterion's utility, cf. 1 Kings 22.5–28; Jer 18.5–12; 28; Ezek 12.21–28; 33.30–33; Jon 3.10–4.5; Hab 2.1–3.

Cities of Refuge

19 When the LORD your God has cut off the nations whose land the LORD your God is giving you, and you have dispossessed them and settled in their towns and in their houses, 2 you shall set apart three cities in the land that the LORD your God is giving you to possess. 3 You shall calculate the distances^z and divide into three regions the land that the LORD your God gives you as a possession, so that any homicide can flee to one of them.

4 Now this is the case of a homicide who might flee there and live, that is, someone who has killed another person unintentionally when the two had not been at enmity before: 5 Suppose someone goes into the forest with another to cut wood, and when one of them swings the ax to cut down a tree, the head slips from the handle and strikes the other person who then dies; the killer may flee to one of these cities and live. 6 But if the distance is too great, the avenger of blood in hot anger might pursue and overtake and put the killer to death, although a death sentence was not deserved, since the two had not been at enmity before. 7 Therefore I command you: You shall set apart three cities.

8 If the LORD your God enlarges your territory, as he swore to your ancestors — and he will give you all the land that he promised your ancestors to give you, 9 provided you diligently observe this entire commandment that I command you today, by loving the LORD your God and walking always in his ways — then you shall add three more cities to these three, 10 so that the blood of an innocent person may not be shed in the land that the LORD your God is giving you as an inheritance, thereby bringing bloodguilt upon you.

11 But if someone at enmity with another lies in wait and attacks and takes the life of that person, and flees into one of these cities, 12 then the elders of the killer's city shall send to have the culprit taken from there and handed over to the avenger of blood to be put to death. 13 Show no pity; you shall purge the guilt of innocent blood from Israel, so that it may go well with you.

Proscription of Encroachment

14 You must not move your neighbor's boundary marker, set up by former generations, on the property that will be allotted to you in the land that the LORD your God is giving you to possess.

Witnesses

15 A single witness shall not suffice to convict a person of any crime or wrongdoing in connection with any offense that may be committed. Only on the evidence of two or three witnesses shall a charge be sustained. 16 If a malicious witness comes

z Or *prepare roads to them*

19.1–25.19 The diverse articles of this division exemplify principles of social justice and practices meant to protect individual life and livelihood within the covenant community. **19.1–13** This adaptation of Ex 21.12–14 emphasizes communal responsibility to facilitate legitimate asylum in cases of accidental homicide without compromising either prosecution of those guilty of premeditated murder or, implicitly, the ban on local altars (cf. 4.41–43; Num 35.9–28; Josh 20). **19.1–3** A formulaic introduction to the division echoing 12.29 is followed by prescriptions for establishment of *three cities* that provide regionally accessible places of refuge. **19.4–7** Rationale for the institution is given in the form of an illustrative case. **19.4** *Unintentionally*, not premeditated (lit. "without knowledge"; cf. Job 35.16; 36.12; 38.2). **19.6** *Avenger of blood*, the agent designated (by the family of the deceased or a city court?) to inflict retaliatory punishment on the murderer (cf. 2 Sam 14.11). *In*

hot anger, impetuously (lit. "because his heart is hot"; cf. Ps 39.3). **19.8–9** Provision for an additional three cities when *the* LORD ... *enlarges your territory*; cf. 12.20; also 11.22–25. **19.10** *Bloodguilt*, the onus or pollution of illegitimate "bloodshed"; cf. 21.8–9; Ex 22.2; 1 Sam 25.26, 33; 2 Sam 21.1; Ps 51.14; Hos 4.2. **19.11–12** Cf. Josh 20.4–6. **19.12** On the jurisdiction of city *elders*, cf. 21.1–9, 19–20; 22.15–19; 25.7–9. **19.13** *No pity*. See 13.5, 8. **19.14** Concern for the integrity of cairns and the like delimiting familial plots of arable land is widely attested in biblical and other ancient sources (see 27.17; Job 24.2; Prov 22.28; Hos 5.10; cf. *Instruction of Amenemope* 7.11–19).
19.15–21 In view here is protection of individuals from pernicious accusation and perjured witness (cf. 5.20; Ex 20.16; 23.1). **19.15** The requirement of corroborative testimony to sustain a guilty verdict in capital cases (17.6; Num 35.30) is restated as a general rule of judicial evidence.

forward to accuse someone of wrongdoing, 17 then both parties to the dispute
shall appear before the Lord, before the
priests and the judges who are in office in
those days, 18 and the judges shall make a
thorough inquiry. If the witness is a false
witness, having testified falsely against another, 19 then you shall do to the false witness just as the false witness had meant to
do to the other. So you shall purge the evil
from your midst. 20 The rest shall hear
and be afraid, and a crime such as this
shall never again be committed among
you. 21 Show no pity: life for life, eye for
eye, tooth for tooth, hand for hand, foot
for foot.

Conduct of Warfare

20 When you go out to war against
your enemies, and see horses and
chariots, an army larger than your own,
you shall not be afraid of them; for the
Lord your God is with you, who brought
you up from the land of Egypt. 2 Before
you engage in battle, the priest shall come
forward and speak to the troops, 3 and
shall say to them: "Hear, O Israel! Today
you are drawing near to do battle against
your enemies. Do not lose heart, or be
afraid, or panic, or be in dread of them;
4 for it is the Lord your God who goes
with you, to fight for you against your enemies, to give you victory." 5 Then the of-

ficials shall address the troops, saying,
"Has anyone built a new house but not
dedicated it? He should go back to his
house, or he might die in the battle and
another dedicate it. 6 Has anyone planted
a vineyard but not yet enjoyed its fruit?
He should go back to his house, or he
might die in the battle and another be
first to enjoy its fruit. 7 Has anyone become engaged to a woman but not yet
married her? He should go back to his
house, or he might die in the battle and
another marry her." 8 The officials shall
continue to address the troops, saying, "Is
anyone afraid or disheartened? He
should go back to his house, or he might
cause the heart of his comrades to melt
like his own." 9 When the officials have
finished addressing the troops, then the
commanders shall take charge of them.
10 When you draw near to a town to
fight against it, offer it terms of peace.
11 If it accepts your terms of peace and
surrenders to you, then all the people in it
shall serve you at forced labor. 12 If it does
not submit to you peacefully, but makes
war against you, then you shall besiege it;
13 and when the Lord your God gives it
into your hand, you shall put all its males
to the sword. 14 You may, however, take as
your booty the women, the children, livestock, and everything else in the town, all
its spoil. You may enjoy the spoil of your

19.16 *Malicious witness*, one intent on doing injury
or "violence" to another (cf. Gen 6.13; Job 19.7;
Ps 35.11). *Wrongdoing* is the capital offense of incitement to "treason" in 13.5 (cf. Isa 59.13).
19.17 *Both parties*, accuser and accused. *Before the
Lord* refers to divine presence at the (single) sanctuary (e.g., 12.18; 14.23), here represented by the
judicial council (17.8–12; cf. 1.17). **19.18** Cf.
13.14; 17.4. **19.19–21** Just retribution as well as
effective deterrence (cf. 13.11) commend punishment corresponding to the harm that the culprit
intended to do to the victim. The talion formula
life for life . . . foot for foot (cf. Ex 21.23–25) is invoked to underscore the principle of reciprocity.
20.1–20 Protocols of holy war, sketched in
this and subsequent units (21.10–14; 23.9–14;
24.5), are one of the features distinguishing the
Deuteronomic polity from other bodies of biblical
law. The martial program of the later Judean
monarchy (cf. 2 Kings 18.7–19.35; 23.29) as well
as the ideology of the conquest era (e.g., 7.1–2,
17–26; 9.1–3; 31.3–8) seem to be reflected in
these texts. **20.1** Because the Lord is present as

warrior with Israel to give victory (cf. 1.30; 3.22;
Ex 14.14; 15.1–4; Judg 4.14), the militia should
not be intimidated by a foe's superior numbers
and weaponry. *Horses and chariots*. Cf. Josh 11.4;
1 Kings 20.25; Isa 31.1. **20.2–9** The levy.
20.2–4 The only stated task of the *priest* is to deliver a vestigial war oracle (cf. 1.20–21, 29–31;
9.1–3); cf., e.g., Num 31.6; Judg 20.25–28; 1 Sam
7.7–11; 14.36–42. **20.5–8** On the administrative role of the *officials*, see 16.18 (cf. 1.15; Josh
1.10). Implementation of these provisions for exemption is specifically noted in 1 Macc 3.56 (cf.
Deut 24.5; Judg 7.3). *Dedicated*, or "inaugurated";
cf. 1 Kings 8.63 (of the temple); also cf. Deut
28.30 (*live in*). **20.6** *Enjoyed its fruit*, made "profane" or ordinary use of the harvest (Jer 31.5;
cf. Lev 19.23–25). **20.7** *Engaged*, formally
betrothed; cf. 2 Sam 3.14. **20.9** *Commanders*,
lit. "officers of hosts" (cf. 1.15; 1 Kings 2.5).
20.10–20 Rules of engagement. **20.10–11** *Terms
of peace*, surrender followed by vassalage (cf.
2.26; Josh 9.3–27; 11.19; Judg 21.13; 2 Sam
10.19). **20.12–15** A mitigated ban is applicable

enemies, which the LORD your God has given you. 15 Thus you shall treat all the towns that are very far from you, which are not towns of the nations here. 16 But as for the towns of these peoples that the LORD your God is giving you as an inheritance, you must not let anything that breathes remain alive. 17 You shall annihilate them — the Hittites and the Amorites, the Canaanites and the Perizzites, the Hivites and the Jebusites — just as the LORD your God has commanded, 18 so that they may not teach you to do all the abhorrent things that they do for their gods, and you thus sin against the LORD your God.

19 If you besiege a town for a long time, making war against it in order to take it, you must not destroy its trees by wielding an ax against them. Although you may take food from them, you must not cut them down. Are trees in the field human beings that they should come under siege from you? 20 You may destroy only the trees that you know do not produce food; you may cut them down for use in building siegeworks against the town that makes war with you, until it falls.

Purgation of Bloodguilt

21 If, in the land that the LORD your God is giving you to possess, a body is found lying in open country, and it is not known who struck the person down, 2 then your elders and your judges shall come out to measure the distances to the towns that are near the body. 3 The elders of the town nearest the body shall take a heifer that has never been worked, one that has not pulled in the yoke; 4 the elders of that town shall bring the heifer down to a wadi with running water, which is neither plowed nor sown, and shall break the heifer's neck there in the wadi. 5 Then the priests, the sons of Levi, shall come forward, for the LORD your God has chosen them to minister to him and to pronounce blessings in the name of the LORD, and by their decision all cases of dispute and assault shall be settled. 6 All the elders of that town nearest the body shall wash their hands over the heifer whose neck was broken in the wadi, 7 and they shall declare: "Our hands did not shed this blood, nor were we witnesses to it. 8 Absolve, O LORD, your people Israel, whom you redeemed; do not let the guilt of innocent blood remain in the midst of your people Israel." Then they will be absolved of bloodguilt. 9 So you shall purge the guilt of innocent blood from your midst, because you must do what is right in the sight of the LORD.

Treatment of Female Captives

10 When you go out to war against your enemies, and the LORD your God hands them over to you and you take them captive, 11 suppose you see among the captives a beautiful woman whom you desire and want to marry, 12 and so you bring her home to your house: she shall

---

against distant or external foes (cf. 2.33–35; 3.6–7; Num 31.7–54). **20.16–18** A total ban must be inflicted upon the proscribed nations of Canaan (see 7.1–2; cf. 12.29–31). *Anything that breathes*, livestock as well as the human populations (cf. Gen 7.22; Josh 10.40; 11.11, 14; 1 Kings 15.29). **20.19–20** For the tactics called into question, cf. 2 Kings 3.19, 25; Josephus *Jewish War* 5.523; 6.5–6.

21.1–9 This case sketches procedures for restricting communal liability and exculpating bloodguilt in event of a rural homicide in which the culprit cannot be found and prosecuted (cf. 19.4–13; Num 35.30–34). **21.2** Appointed *judges* (cf. 16.18) exercise concurrent jurisdiction with local *elders* (cf. 19.12) in determining the town nearest the scene of the crime. **21.3–4** Transfer or expurgation of liability is enacted by nonsacrificial slaughter (*break the . . . neck*; cf. Ex 13.13; 34.20) of an unworked *heifer*

(cf. Num 19.2; 1 Sam 6.7) in a pristine locale. *Running water*. The "constant flow" (cf. Ps 74.15; Am 5.24) presumably effects the removal of bloodguilt. **21.5** For the jurisdiction of *the priests, the sons of Levi* (also 31.9; cf. 18.1), see 17.8–13. **21.6–8** An exculpatory act (hand washing) and declaration of innocence accompany petitionary prayer for removal of bloodguilt. **21.8** *Absolve*, "cleanse," "forgive," or "expiate" (e.g., 32.43; Ex 32.30; 2 Sam 21.3). **21.9** Cf. 13.5, 18; 19.13.

21.10–21 These three articles (vv. 10–14, 15–17, 18–21) impose restraints on the exercise of authority by male heads of household. **21.10–14** Here a foreign woman acquired as a spoil of war (cf. 20.14) who then becomes a man's slave-wife or concubine may not later be sold for profit by the husband (cf. Ex 21.7–11). **21.12–13** The rites mark a transition, separating the woman from her former identity and captive

shave her head, pare her nails, 13 discard her captive's garb, and shall remain in your house a full month, mourning for her father and mother; after that you may go in to her and be her husband, and she shall be your wife. 14 But if you are not satisfied with her, you shall let her go free and not sell her for money. You must not treat her as a slave, since you have dishonored her.

Primogeniture

15 If a man has two wives, one of them loved and the other disliked, and if both the loved and the disliked have borne him sons, the firstborn being the son of the one who is disliked, 16 then on the day when he wills his possessions to his sons, he is not permitted to treat the son of the loved as the firstborn in preference to the son of the disliked, who is the firstborn. 17 He must acknowledge as firstborn the son of the one who is disliked, giving him a double portion*a* of all that he has; since he is the first issue of his virility, the right of the firstborn is his.

Prosecution of an Incorrigible Son

18 If someone has a stubborn and rebellious son who will not obey his father and mother, who does not heed them when they discipline him, 19 then his father and his mother shall take hold of him and bring him out to the elders of his town at the gate of that place. 20 They shall say to the elders of his town, "This son of ours is stubborn and rebellious. He will not obey us. He is a glutton and a drunkard." 21 Then all the men of the town shall stone him to death. So you shall purge the evil from your midst; and all Israel will hear, and be afraid.

Burial of a Criminal's Corpse

22 When someone is convicted of a crime punishable by death and is executed, and you hang him on a tree, 23 his corpse must not remain all night upon the tree; you shall bury him that same day, for anyone hung on a tree is under God's curse. You must not defile the land that the Lord your God is giving you for possession.

Return of Lost Property

22 You shall not watch your neighbor's ox or sheep straying away and ignore them; you shall take them back to their owner. 2 If the owner does not reside near you or you do not know who the owner is, you shall bring it to your own house, and it shall remain with you until the owner claims it; then you shall return it. 3 You shall do the same with a neighbor's donkey; you shall do the same with a neighbor's garment; and you shall do the same with anything else that your neighbor loses and you find. You may not withhold your help.

a Heb *two-thirds*

---

status in preparation for her role as bride. **21.14** *Go free* may denote manumission rather than divorce (cf. 15.12–13; Jer 34.16; cf. 22.19, 29; 24.1–3). *As a slave*; i.e., as chattel. *Dishonored* or "violated" often refers to coerced sexual intercourse (e.g., 22.24, 29; Gen 34.2; Judg 19.24; 2 Sam 13.12). **21.15–17** The legal status of *firstborn* son, with an attendant share of inheritance, is fixed by priority of birth rather than paternal decision. (Cf., e.g., Gen 21.9–13; 27.1–40; 48.13–49.4; 1 Kings 1.15–21; 1 Chr 5.1–2; *Code of Hammurabi* 165–170.) **21.15** *Disliked*. Cf. Gen 29.31–33. **21.17** *Double portion*, "two-thirds" of the total estate (cf. 2 Kings 2.9; Zech 13.8). *Virility*. Cf. Gen 49.3; Ps 105.36. **21.18–21** The local community, represented by its elders, has jurisdiction in the capital case of a son charged with chronically dishonorable conduct in defiance of parental authority (cf. 5.16; 27.16; Ex 21.15, 17; Lev 20.9). **21.19** Both parents must appear as plaintiffs before the court (at the *town gate*; cf. Isa 29.21; Am 5.10, 12, 15). **21.20** *Stubborn and rebellious*, obstinately unruly (cf. Jer 5.23; Ps 78.8). *A glutton and a drunkard*, dissolute (cf. Prov 23.20–21; 28.7; see also Mt 11.19; Lk 7.34). **21.21** Public execution by stoning treats the offense as comparable to treason; cf. 13.5, 10–11; 22.21, 24; Lev 20.2; 24.14–16.

21.22–23 Limitation on public display of the corpse of an executed criminal; cf. Josh 8.29; 10.26–27; 1 Sam 31.10; 2 Sam 4.12. Exposure of the body (*hang on a tree*) was presumably meant to revile the crime by degrading its perpetrator, supposed to be *under God's curse*. Same-day burial prevented the corpse from becoming carrion (cf. 2 Sam 21.10; Ezek 39.17–20).

22.1–3 This redraft of Ex 23.4 prescribes initiatives to aid fellow Israelites in the recovery of straying livestock (cf. 1 Sam 9.3) and, by extension, any other lost property.

Assorted Duties and Restrictions

4 You shall not see your neighbor's donkey or ox fallen on the road and ignore it; you shall help to lift it up.

5 A woman shall not wear a man's apparel, nor shall a man put on a woman's garment; for whoever does such things is abhorrent to the LORD your God.

6 If you come on a bird's nest, in any tree or on the ground, with fledglings or eggs, with the mother sitting on the fledglings or on the eggs, you shall not take the mother with the young. 7 Let the mother go, taking only the young for yourself, in order that it may go well with you and you may live long.

8 When you build a new house, you shall make a parapet for your roof; otherwise you might have bloodguilt on your house, if anyone should fall from it.

9 You shall not sow your vineyard with a second kind of seed, or the whole yield will have to be forfeited, both the crop that you have sown and the yield of the vineyard itself.

10 You shall not plow with an ox and a donkey yoked together.

11 You shall not wear clothes made of wool and linen woven together.

12 You shall make tassels on the four corners of the cloak with which you cover yourself.

The Accused Bride

13 Suppose a man marries a woman, but after going in to her, he dislikes her 14 and makes up charges against her, slandering her by saying, "I married this woman; but when I lay with her, I did not find evidence of her virginity." 15 The father of the young woman and her mother shall then submit the evidence of the young woman's virginity to the elders of the city at the gate. 16 The father of the young woman shall say to the elders: "I gave my daughter in marriage to this man but he dislikes her; 17 now he has made up charges against her, saying, 'I did not find evidence of your daughter's virginity.' But here is the evidence of my daughter's virginity." Then they shall spread out the cloth before the elders of the town. 18 The elders of that town shall take the man and punish him; 19 they shall fine him one hundred shekels of silver (which they shall give to the young woman's father) because he has slandered a virgin of Israel. She shall remain his wife; he shall not be permitted to divorce her as long as he lives.

20 If, however, this charge is true, that evidence of the young woman's virginity was not found, 21 then they shall bring the young woman out to the entrance of her father's house and the men

---

22.4 A reformulation of Ex 23.5. **22.5** Classification of cross-dressing as *abhorrent to the LORD* (cf. note on 7.25–26; 12.31) suggests that the prohibition has in view pagan cultic practices (associated, e.g., with worship of the Mesopotamian goddess Ishtar). **22.6–7** The article urges self-interest (well-being, longevity) as ample motive for ecological sensitivity (cf. 20.19–20; Lev 22.28). **22.8** Flat *roofs* of houses functioned as domestic space (e.g., Josh 2.6). *Bloodguilt* (cf. 19.10). The homeowner was liable for injury or death resulting from negligent construction. **22.9–11** Traditional interpretation understood these and related provisions (Lev 19.19) to exemplify distinctions in the created order that were not to be blurred by human agency; e.g., "nature does not delight in the combination of dissimilar things" (Josephus *Antiquities* 4.228–29; cf. Philo *Special Laws* 4.203–12; *Mishnah Kilayim*). **22.9** *Forfeited* or "hallowed"; i.e., treated like tithed produce (cf. 26.13; Lev 27.10, 21; Josh 6.19). **22.12** Cf. Num 15.38–41 (which develops a theological rationale for the practice). **22.13–21** Emphasis in this case as drafted

falls on constraining a husband who falsely accuses his bride of losing her virginity prior to marital consummation; a codicil sketches punitive response, should the accusation be unrefuted (vv. 20–21). The litigants in contention before the town elders (cf. 21.19–20) are the bride's parents and the husband, whose charges have implicitly defamed them as well as their daughter. **22.13–14** Motive for the slander is not stated; that the husband *dislikes* or "hates" his wife would suffice as grounds for formal divorce (cf. 21.15; 24.1). *Evidence of her virginity*, a sign of blood from a rupture of the hymen (see v. 17). **22.18–19** While *punishment* could include flogging (cf. 21.18; 25.1–3), it most clearly refers to monetary damages awarded the bride's father, which are double the amount specified for rape (22.29; cf. Ex 22.7). Since the husband accused his wife of a capital offense comparable to adultery (cf. vv. 21–24), the preclusion of divorce falls well short of talion in severity (see note on 19.19–21); the woman's wishes are not considered. **22.21** *Disgraceful act*, an "outrage," usually of sexual nature (e.g., Gen 34.7; Judg 19.23–24; 2 Sam

of her town shall stone her to death, because she committed a disgraceful act in Israel by prostituting herself in her father's house. So you shall purge the evil from your midst.

Adultery and Related Offenses

22 If a man is caught lying with the wife of another man, both of them shall die, the man who lay with the woman as well as the woman. So you shall purge the evil from Israel.

23 If there is a young woman, a virgin already engaged to be married, and a man meets her in the town and lies with her, 24 you shall bring both of them to the gate of that town and stone them to death, the young woman because she did not cry for help in the town and the man because he violated his neighbor's wife. So you shall purge the evil from your midst.

25 But if the man meets the engaged woman in the open country, and the man seizes her and lies with her, then only the man who lay with her shall die. 26 You shall do nothing to the young woman; the young woman has not committed an offense punishable by death, because this case is like that of someone who attacks and murders a neighbor. 27 Since he found her in the open country, the engaged woman may have cried for help, but there was no one to rescue her.

28 If a man meets a virgin who is not engaged, and seizes her and lies with her, and they are caught in the act, 29 the man who lay with her shall give fifty shekels of silver to the young woman's father, and she shall become his wife. Because he violated her he shall not be permitted to divorce her as long as he lives.

30 b A man shall not marry his father's wife, thereby violating his father's rights. c

Membership in the Assembly

23 No one whose testicles are crushed or whose penis is cut off shall be admitted to the assembly of the Lord.
2 Those born of an illicit union shall not be admitted to the assembly of the Lord. Even to the tenth generation, none of their descendants shall be admitted to the assembly of the Lord.
3 No Ammonite or Moabite shall be admitted to the assembly of the Lord. Even to the tenth generation, none of their descendants shall be admitted to the assembly of the Lord, 4 because they did not meet you with food and water on your journey out of Egypt, and because they hired against you Balaam son of Beor, from Pethor of Mesopotamia, to curse you. 5 (Yet the Lord your God refused to heed Balaam; the Lord your God turned the curse into a blessing for you, because the Lord your God loved you.) 6 You shall never promote their welfare or their prosperity as long as you live.

b Ch 23.1 in Heb   c Heb uncovering his father's skirt

13.12), threatening to the integrity of the social order. *Purge.* See note on 13.5.
22.22–30 The series of sexual offenses continues, first by prescribing the death penalty in the case of a man caught in adultery with another's wife (cf. 5.18; Ex 20.14; Lev 20.10) and then by reviewing related cases complicated by circumstances or rules of evidence. **22.22** *Both ... shall die,* execution of the pair, presumably by stoning (cf. vv. 21, 24; Lev 20.10; Ezek 16.38–40; Jn 8.5). **22.23–27** Intercourse with an *engaged* or formally betrothed woman is equated with the crime of adultery. The question of the woman's culpability distinguishes the two outcomes: she is punished when there is reason, because of locale, to charge her with complicity. **22.26** *This case is like,* reasoning by analogy to accidental homicide (see 19.4–10). **22.28–29** *Seizes, violated* (cf. 21.14). The wording indicates coercion, but bibli-

cal law does not sharply distinguish between rape and seduction of an unbetrothed woman (cf. Ex 22.16–17). Preclusion of *divorce.* See 22.19. **22.30** *Violating his father's rights.* The categorical prohibition of a son marrying his widowed or divorced step-mother (*father's wife*) is a matter of decency and respect for paternal privilege (cf. 27.20; Gen 49.4; Lev 18.8; 20.11; Ezek 22.10). **23.1–8** These rules understand the Lord's *assembly* to be a cohort of adult male Israelites, i.e., the covenant community functioning as a restricted religious, military, and political association (cf. 16.16; 20.1–9; 33.5 with, e.g., 5.22; 31.30; Isa 56.3–8. Cf. also Judg 20.2; 1 Kings 12.3, 20). **23.1** Exclusion by reason of genital impairment; cf. Lev 21.17–23. **23.2** *Illicit union* was traditionally understood to mean incest (*Mishnah Yebamot* 4.13; cf. Gen 19.30–38; Lev 18.6–18). **23.3–6** Ethnic disqualifications. Cf. Ezra 10.10–44; Neh 13.1–3, 23–27. **23.4** *Ba-*

7 You shall not abhor any of the Edomites, for they are your kin. You shall not abhor any of the Egyptians, because you were an alien residing in their land. 8 The children of the third generation that are born to them may be admitted to the assembly of the LORD.

Purity of the Military Camp

9 When you are encamped against your enemies you shall guard against any impropriety. 10 If one of you becomes unclean because of a nocturnal emission, then he shall go outside the camp; he must not come within the camp. 11 When evening comes, he shall wash himself with water, and when the sun has set, he may come back into the camp. 12 You shall have a designated area outside the camp to which you shall go. 13 With your utensils you shall have a trowel; when you relieve yourself outside, you shall dig a hole with it and then cover up your excrement. 14 Because the LORD your God travels along with your camp, to save you and to hand over your enemies to you, therefore your camp must be holy, so that he may not see anything indecent among you and turn away from you.

Fugitive Slaves

15 Slaves who have escaped to you from their owners shall not be given back to them. 16 They shall reside with you, in your midst, in any place they choose in any one of your towns, wherever they please; you shall not oppress them.

Cultic Exclusions

17 None of the daughters of Israel shall be a temple prostitute; none of the sons of Israel shall be a temple prostitute. 18 You shall not bring the fee of a prostitute or the wages of a male prostitute[d] into the house of the LORD your God in payment for any vow, for both of these are abhorrent to the LORD your God.

Usury

19 You shall not charge interest on loans to another Israelite, interest on money, interest on provisions, interest on anything that is lent. 20 On loans to a foreigner you may charge interest, but on loans to another Israelite you may not charge interest, so that the LORD your God may bless you in all your undertakings in the land that you are about to enter and possess.

Vows

21 If you make a vow to the LORD your God, do not postpone fulfilling it; for the LORD your God will surely require it of you, and you would incur guilt. 22 But if you refrain from vowing, you will not incur guilt. 23 Whatever your lips utter

d Heb *a dog*

---

laam. See Num 22–24. **23.6** *Welfare* ("peace") and *prosperity* may connote political alliance or treaty (cf. Ezra 9.12; Jer 29.7; 38.4); cf. this injunction with 2.9, 19; Isa 16.4. **23.7–8** *Abhor.* Cf. 7.26. *Edomites.* Cf. 2.4–8; Gen 36; Am 1.11. Benevolence toward *Egyptians* is remarkable in view of 24.22; 26.5, 6; 28.60, 68 (but see Gen 12.10–20). *Children,* apparently the descendants of intermarriage.
23.9–14 Specific rules together with theological rationale for maintenance of personal hygiene during holy-war campaigns (cf. 20.1–20; 2 Sam 11.11). **23.10–11** Cf. Lev 15.16–17; also the Dead Sea Scrolls *Temple Scroll* (11QTemple) 45.7–12; 46.18. **23.12** *Designated areas,* privy (lit. "hand"); cf. *Temple Scroll* (11QTemple) 46.13–16. **23.14** *Travels along.* Cf. 1.30; 20.4; 31.6, 8; 2 Sam 7.6–7. *Indecent,* repugnant or "objectionable" (cf. 24.1).
23.15–16 Extradition of *slaves* who seek asylum in Israel is prohibited (cf. 1 Kings 2.39–40;

Code of Hammurabi 15–20).
23.17–18 Proscriptions in defense of Israel's sacral integrity. *Temple prostitute.* The terms refer to "consecrated" persons, associated in biblical usage with Canaanite or otherwise pagan rites (cf. Gen 38.21–22; 1 Kings 14.24; 15.12; 22.46; 2 Kings 23.7; Hos 4.14). On a harlot's "wages" or *fee,* cf. Isa 23.17–18; Ezek 16.31, 34, 41; Hos 9.1; Mic 1.7. *Abhorrent to the LORD.* See note on 7.25–26.
23.19–20 In accord with 15.1–11, distinction is made between interest-free welfare loans to fellow Israelites (cf. 24.10–13; Ex 22.25; Lev 25.35–38) and profit-making commercial loans to foreigners (cf. 15.6; 28.12). *Interest,* increment, lit. "bite," usually taken by the creditor when making the loan (cf. Ezek 18.8, 13, 17; 22.12).
23.21–23 The closely comparable admonitions in Eccl 5.4–6 are derivative. *Vow,* a form of promissory oath, sworn in anticipation of divine favor (e.g., Gen 28.20–22; Num 21.2–3; 1 Sam

you must diligently perform, just as you have freely vowed to the LORD your God with your own mouth.

Limitations on Foraging

24 If you go into your neighbor's vineyard, you may eat your fill of grapes, as many as you wish, but you shall not put any in a container.
25 If you go into your neighbor's standing grain, you may pluck the ears with your hand, but you shall not put a sickle to your neighbor's standing grain.

Restriction of Remarriage

24 Suppose a man enters into marriage with a woman, but she does not please him because he finds something objectionable about her, and so he writes her a certificate of divorce, puts it in her hand, and sends her out of his house; she then leaves his house 2 and goes off to become another man's wife. 3 Then suppose the second man dislikes her, writes her a bill of divorce, puts it in her hand, and sends her out of his house (or the second man who married her dies); 4 her first husband, who sent her away, is not permitted to take her again to be his wife after she has been defiled; for that would be abhorrent to the LORD, and you shall not bring guilt on the land that

the LORD your God is giving you as a possession.

Exemption for the Newlywed

5 When a man is newly married, he shall not go out with the army or be charged with any related duty. He shall be free at home one year, to be happy with the wife whom he has married.

Personal Dignity and Welfare

6 No one shall take a mill or an upper millstone in pledge, for that would be taking a life in pledge.
7 If someone is caught kidnaping another Israelite, enslaving or selling the Israelite, then that kidnaper shall die. So you shall purge the evil from your midst.
8 Guard against an outbreak of a leprous[e] skin disease by being very careful; you shall carefully observe whatever the levitical priests instruct you, just as I have commanded them. 9 Remember what the LORD your God did to Miriam on your journey out of Egypt.
10 When you make your neighbor a loan of any kind, you shall not go into the house to take the pledge. 11 You shall wait outside, while the person to whom you are making the loan brings the pledge out to you. 12 If the person is poor, you shall

e A term for several skin diseases; precise meaning uncertain

---

1.11; Ps 132.1–5).   **23.23** *Whatever,* usually a sacrifice or equivalent monetary payment (cf. Lev 27.2–29; Num 30.2–15; Pss 56.12–13; 66.13–15).
23.24–25 These rulings cogently define the limits of traditional hospitality extended to hungry wayfarers as well as to fieldhands (cf. 25.4; Josephus *Antiquities* 4.234–37).
24.1–4 Unlike the exceptional cases of 22.19, 29, divorce is here left to a husband's discretion (*does not please,* v. 1; *dislikes,* v. 3). But he is prohibited from remarrying a former spouse after she has become another man's wife, thus preventing interpretation of her second marriage as harlotry or wife swapping (so Nachmanides, medieval Jewish Bible commentator).   **24.1** *Something objectionable* (*indecent,* 23.14) apparently means for any cause, though the sense was already disputed in antiquity (cf. Sir 7.26; 25.25–26; Mt 19.3–9; Josephus *Antiquities* 4.253). *Certificate of divorce,* a writ proving the husband had relinquished claim on the woman, freeing her to remarry (cf. Isa 50.1; Jer 3.8; Mt. 5.31; *Mishnah Gitin*).   **24.4** *Been de-*

filed, by the husband, who had enabled or caused her to seek another marriage. *Abhorrent.* See note on 7.25–26. *Guilt on the land,* pollution comparable to that caused by homicide (19.13; 21.9; cf. Jer 3.1–3; Hos 4.2–3).   **24.5** A supplement to 20.7. *Related duty,* e.g., conscripted labor or government service (cf. 1 Sam 8.11–13; 1 Kings 5.13–18; 9.15–21).
24.6–25.4 Most of these otherwise diverse provisions exemplify concern for humane, charitable treatment of persons, especially the economically disadvantaged; together with parallels in other bodies of biblical law, they form the bedrock of biblical social ethics.   **24.6** Legitimate surety for creditors must not compromise the means of debtors to subsist.   **24.7** A redraft of Ex 21.16. *Enslaving or selling,* e.g., abuse of distrainees (cf. 2 Kings 4.1; Job 24.9; Am 2.6). *Purge.* See note on 13.5.   **24.8–9** On priestly dermatology, see Lev 13–14. For the judgment on *Miriam,* see Num 12.10–15.   **24.10–13** Additional restrictions on distraint (see vv. 6, 17, cluding a redraft of Ex 22.26–27 (cf. Job 2.

not sleep in the garment given you as[f] the pledge. 13 You shall give the pledge back by sunset, so that your neighbor may sleep in the cloak and bless you; and it will be to your credit before the LORD your God.

14 You shall not withhold the wages of poor and needy laborers, whether other Israelites or aliens who reside in your land in one of your towns. 15 You shall pay them their wages daily before sunset, because they are poor and their livelihood depends on them; otherwise they might cry to the LORD against you, and you would incur guilt.

16 Parents shall not be put to death for their children, nor shall children be put to death for their parents; only for their own crimes may persons be put to death.

17 You shall not deprive a resident alien or an orphan of justice; you shall not take a widow's garment in pledge. 18 Remember that you were a slave in Egypt and the LORD your God redeemed you from there; therefore I command you to do this.

19 When you reap your harvest in your field and forget a sheaf in the field, you shall not go back to get it; it shall be left for the alien, the orphan, and the widow, so that the LORD your God may bless you in all your undertakings. 20 When you beat your olive trees, do not strip what is left; it shall be for the alien, the orphan, and the widow.

21 When you gather the grapes of your vineyard, do not glean what is left; it shall be for the alien, the orphan, and the widow. 22 Remember that you were a slave in the land of Egypt; therefore I am commanding you to do this.

25 Suppose two persons have a dispute and enter into litigation, and the judges decide between them, declaring one to be in the right and the other to be in the wrong. 2 If the one in the wrong deserves to be flogged, the judge shall make that person lie down and be beaten in his presence with the number of lashes proportionate to the offense. 3 Forty lashes may be given but not more; if more lashes than these are given, your neighbor will be degraded in your sight.

4 You shall not muzzle an ox while it is treading out the grain.

Levirate Marriage

5 When brothers reside together, and one of them dies and has no son, the wife of the deceased shall not be married outside the family to a stranger. Her husband's brother shall go in to her, taking her in marriage, and performing the duty of a husband's brother to her, 6 and the firstborn whom she bears shall succeed to the name of the deceased brother, so that his name may not be blotted out of Israel. 7 But if the man has no desire to marry his brother's widow, then his brother's widow

f Heb lacks *the garment given you as*

Prov 20.16; 27.13; Am 2.8). **24.13** *Be to your credit*, counted as "merit" (cf. 6.25), the converse of 15.9; 24.15. **24.14–15** Daily receipt of wages is a laborer's right (cf. Lev 19.13; Jer 22.13; Mt 20.2–15). On equal treatment for *aliens* ("sojourners"), cf. vv. 17–22; 1.16; 10.17–19; Lev 19.33–34; Ezek 47.22–23. **24.15** *Cry to the* LORD. See note on 15.9. **24.16** This juridical principle limiting liability for capital offenses to the actual perpetrators of crimes is cited in 2 Kings 14.6. (For theological reverberations, cf. Deut 7.10; Jer 31.29, 30; Ezek 18.) **24.17–18** For the theological rationale, see 10.17–19; 15.15; 24.22 (cf. also 27.19; Ex 22.21–24; 23.6, 9). **24.19–22** Provisions on gleaning. Cf. Ex 23.10–11; Lev 19.9–10; 23.22; Ruth 2; *Mishnah Pe'a*. **25.1–3** Flogging, administered as punishment by a court, should be *proportionate to the offense* (cf. the rule of talion, note on 19.19–21), with *forty* stripes fixed as a maximum in order to protect the culprit from cruel humiliation (cf. 2 Cor 11.24; Josephus *Antiq-*

uities 4.238; *Mishnah Makkot* 3). **25.4** Social equity is exemplified by humane treatment of a working ox; cf. 5.14; Prov 12.10; also 1 Cor 9.9; 1 Tim 5.18.

25.5–10 As drafted, this legislation is concerned with resolving the anomalous relationship between a childless but still youthful widow and her deceased husband's family. Custom preferred an endogamous remarriage of the woman to her *husband's brother*, *levir* in Latin, whence the practice is commonly called "levirate marriage." (Cf. the related practices in Gen 38.6–26; Ruth 3–4; also cf. Lev 18.16; 20.21.) **25.5** Though context supports the literal rendering *son*, the sense was later understood to include female offspring (e.g., Septuagint; Josephus *Antiquities* 4.254; Lk 20.28; cf. Num 27.8–11). **25.6** Lineage succession of the male *firstborn* to the *name of the deceased brother* implicitly includes claim to patrimony (cf. 21.15–17; Num 27.4; Ruth 4.5, 10; also 2 Sam 14.7). **25.7–8** Jurisdiction of *elders* in familial

shall go up to the elders at the gate and say, "My husband's brother refuses to perpetuate his brother's name in Israel; he will not perform the duty of a husband's brother to me." 8 Then the elders of his town shall summon him and speak to him. If he persists, saying, "I have no desire to marry her," 9 then his brother's wife shall go up to him in the presence of the elders, pull his sandal off his foot, spit in his face, and declare, "This is what is done to the man who does not build up his brother's house." 10 Throughout Israel his family shall be known as "the house of him whose sandal was pulled off."

Immodest Assault

11   If men get into a fight with one another, and the wife of one intervenes to rescue her husband from the grip of his opponent by reaching out and seizing his genitals, 12 you shall cut off her hand; show no pity.

Honest Weights and Measures

13   You shall not have in your bag two kinds of weights, large and small. 14 You shall not have in your house two kinds of measures, large and small. 15 You shall have only a full and honest weight; you shall have only a full and honest measure, so that your days may be long in the land that the LORD your God is giving you. 16 For all who do such things, all who act dishonestly, are abhorrent to the LORD your God.

Extirpation of Amalek

17   Remember what Amalek did to you on your journey out of Egypt, 18 how he attacked you on the way, when you were faint and weary, and struck down all who lagged behind you; he did not fear God. 19 Therefore when the LORD your God has given you rest from all your enemies on every hand, in the land that the LORD your God is giving you as an inheritance to possess, you shall blot out the remembrance of Amalek from under heaven; do not forget.

Liturgical Declarations

26   When you have come into the land that the LORD your God is giving you as an inheritance to possess, and you possess it, and settle in it, 2 you shall take some of the first of all the fruit of the ground, which you harvest from the land that the LORD your God is giving you, and you shall put it in a basket and go to the place that the LORD your God will choose as a dwelling for his name. 3 You shall go to the priest who is in office at that time, and say to him, "Today I declare to the LORD your God that I have come into the land that the LORD swore to our ancestors to give us." 4 When the priest takes the basket from your hand

---

disputes; cf. 19.12; 21.19–20; 22.17–19. 25.9–10 Public degradation of the unwilling levir (husband's brother); *spitting* is an act of contempt (cf. Num 12.14; Job 17.6; 30.10; Isa 50.6); removal of his *sandal* is a rite of quittance, freeing the widow from further obligation to the husband's family (*house*). 25.11–12   The severe penalty, comparable to talion (see note on 19.19–21), presumes the woman has recklessly endangered the man's procreative capacity (cf. 19.21; Ex 21.22–25; *Mishnah Bava Kamma* 8.1). 25.13–16   Such injunctions and the commercial abuses they address are well attested; e.g., Lev 19.35–36; Prov 16.11; 20.23; Ezek 45.10–12; Hos 12.7; Mic 6.10–11; *Instruction of Amenemope* 17.17–19; 18.14–19.2. 25.16 *Abhorrent*. See note on 7.25–26. 25.17–19   A codicil to 23.3–6 reflecting Ex 17.14–15. On the tradition of enmity between Israel and the Amalekites of northern Sinai, cf.

Num 24.20; Judg 6.3; 10.12; 1 Sam 15.2–33. 25.18   This perfidy goes unreported in Ex 17.8–13.   25.19 *Rest*. Cf. 3.20; 12.9. *Blot out the remembrance*. Cf. 9.14; 25.6; 29.20; 1 Sam 24.21; Pss 9.5–6; 109.13. 26.1–15   This brief concluding section of the polity, which is a counterpart of 12.2–28, prescribes affirmations of covenantal identity that worshipers are to make on particular occasions of pilgrimage to the single sanctuary. 26.1–11 Creedal declarations associated with presentations of first fruits (cf. Lev 23.9–21; Num 28.26–31; *Mishnah Bikkurim*). 26.2 *First* (or "choicest"; cf. Ex 23.19; 34.26) *of all the fruit*, token presentation of each agricultural crop at the sanctuary (*the place*; see 12.5), apparently in conjunction with the annual pilgrimage feasts and as pledge on full payment of tithes (cf. 14.22–23; 16.1–17; 18.4; Ex 22.29; Tob 1.6–7; Philo *Special Law* 2.216–20). *As a dwelling for his name*. See not 12.5; 12.11.   26.3 *Priest*. Cf. 17.9, 12; 18.1

and sets it down before the altar of the LORD your God, 5 you shall make this response before the LORD your God: "A wandering Aramean was my ancestor; he went down into Egypt and lived there as an alien, few in number, and there he became a great nation, mighty and populous. 6 When the Egyptians treated us harshly and afflicted us, by imposing hard labor on us, 7 we cried to the LORD, the God of our ancestors; the LORD heard our voice and saw our affliction, our toil, and our oppression. 8 The LORD brought us out of Egypt with a mighty hand and an outstretched arm, with a terrifying display of power, and with signs and wonders; 9 and he brought us into this place and gave us this land, a land flowing with milk and honey. 10 So now I bring the first of the fruit of the ground that you, O LORD, have given me." You shall set it down before the LORD your God and bow down before the LORD your God. 11 Then you, together with the Levites and the aliens who reside among you, shall celebrate with all the bounty that the LORD your God has given to you and to your house.

12   When you have finished paying all the tithe of your produce in the third year (which is the year of the tithe), giving it to the Levites, the aliens, the orphans, and the widows, so that they may eat their fill within your towns, 13 then you shall say before the LORD your God: "I have removed the sacred portion from the house,

and I have given it to the Levites, the resident aliens, the orphans, and the widows, in accordance with your entire commandment that you commanded me; I have neither transgressed nor forgotten any of your commandments: 14 I have not eaten of it while in mourning; I have not removed any of it while I was unclean; and I have not offered any of it to the dead. I have obeyed the LORD my God, doing just as you commanded me. 15 Look down from your holy habitation, from heaven, and bless your people Israel and the ground that you have given us, as you swore to our ancestors—a land flowing with milk and honey."

Ratification of the Covenant

16   This very day the LORD your God is commanding you to observe these statutes and ordinances; so observe them diligently with all your heart and with all your soul. 17 Today you have obtained the LORD's agreement: to be your God; and for you to walk in his ways, to keep his statutes, his commandments, and his ordinances, and to obey him. 18 Today the LORD has obtained your agreement: to be his treasured people, as he promised you, and to keep his commandments; 19 for him to set you high above all nations that he has made, in praise and in fame and in honor; and for you to be a people holy to the LORD your God, as he promised.

19.17; 20.2. *Swore to our ancestors.* See 1.8, 20–21.   **26.5** *Wandering Aramean* refers to Israel's north Syrian ancestry, traced through Abram (Abraham) (cf. Gen 11.31; 12.1–9; 20.13) as well as Jacob (Israel), who is probably meant here (cf. Gen 29–32). *Few in number.* See 28.62; Ps 105.12 (cf. Gen 34.30; 46.8–27). *Great nation.* See 4.6–8 (cf. Ex 1.7, 9).   **26.6** *Hard labor.* See Ex 1.13–14; 6.9 (cf. 1 Kings 12.4).   **26.7** *Cried to the LORD.* See Ex 14.10, 15; Num 20.16; Josh 24.7. *God of our ancestors.* See, e.g., 1.11; 6.3; 12.1 (cf. Ex 3.15–16).   **26.8** Cf. 4.34; 6.21.   **26.9** *This place.* Cf. Ex 15.17.   **26.11** Cf. 12.7.   **26.12–15** The worshiper's positive and negative declarations of compliance with the rules of triennial tithing (see 14.28–29; cf. *Mishnah Ma'aser Sheni* 5.10–13) are followed by a prayer for continuance of divine blessing on Israel.   **26.13** *Before the LORD,* at the single sanctuary (see, e.g., 14.23; 16.16).   **26.14** Protestations of innocence (cf. Job 31.5–40; Ps 26.4–7) regarding misuse of tithed produce in mortuary rites. *Mourning.* Cf. Jer 16.7;

Ezek 24.17, 22. *Unclean.* Cf. Lev 11.24–25; 22.3; Num 19.11–22; Hos 9.4; Hag 2.13. *To the dead* may refer to a cult of ancestors (cf. 14.1; Tob 4.17; Sir 30.18–20).   **26.15** *Holy habitation . . . heaven.* See, e.g., 1 Kings 8.39, 43, 49; Jer 25.30; Ps 102.19.

26.16–28.68   An archival collection of covenant rites and sanctions concludes the primary corpus of Deuteronomic law (see 4.44–45). **26.16–19** The alliance between God and Israel is formally joined or reaffirmed when each party declares its acceptance of reciprocal roles and obligations. (Cf. the succinct formulation of covenantal identities in, e.g., 29.13; Ex 6.7; Lev 26.12; 2 Sam 7.24; Jer 7.23; 31.33; Ezek 11.20; Hos 2.23.)   **26.16** *This very day,* the liturgical present, or anytime the Israel of subsequent generations is gathered in solemn assembly to hear and recommit itself to this Deuteronomic legislation (cf. 4.4; 5.1–3; 11.32; 27.9).   **26.17** Cf. 8.6; 10.12; 11.22. **26.18–19** Cf. 7.6; 14.2; 28.9; Ex 19.5–6; Jer 13.11; 33.9.

Rites of Reaffirmation

27 Then Moses and the elders of Israel charged all the people as follows: Keep the entire commandment that I am commanding you today. 2 On the day that you cross over the Jordan into the land that the LORD your God is giving you, you shall set up large stones and cover them with plaster. 3 You shall write on them all the words of this law when you have crossed over, to enter the land that the LORD your God is giving you, a land flowing with milk and honey, as the LORD, the God of your ancestors, promised you. 4 So when you have crossed over the Jordan, you shall set up these stones, about which I am commanding you today, on Mount Ebal, and you shall cover them with plaster. 5 And you shall build an altar there to the LORD your God, an altar of stones on which you have not used an iron tool. 6 You must build the altar of the LORD your God of unhewn*g* stones. Then offer up burnt offerings on it to the LORD your God, 7 make sacrifices of well-being, and eat them there, rejoicing before the LORD your God. 8 You shall write on the stones all the words of this law very clearly.

9 Then Moses and the levitical priests spoke to all Israel, saying: Keep silence and hear, O Israel! This very day you have become the people of the LORD your God. 10 Therefore obey the LORD your God, observing his commandments and his statutes that I am commanding you today.

11 The same day Moses charged the people as follows: 12 When you have crossed over the Jordan, these shall stand on Mount Gerizim for the blessing of the people: Simeon, Levi, Judah, Issachar, Joseph, and Benjamin. 13 And these shall stand on Mount Ebal for the curse: Reuben, Gad, Asher, Zebulun, Dan, and Naphtali. 14 Then the Levites shall declare in a loud voice to all the Israelites:

15 "Cursed be anyone who makes an idol or casts an image, anything abhorrent to the LORD, the work of an artisan, and sets it up in secret." All the people shall respond, saying, "Amen!"

16 "Cursed be anyone who dishonors father or mother." All the people shall say, "Amen!"

17 "Cursed be anyone who moves a neighbor's boundary marker." All the people shall say, "Amen!"

18 "Cursed be anyone who misleads a blind person on the road." All the people shall say, "Amen!"

19 "Cursed be anyone who deprives

g Heb *whole*

27.1–26 The narrative transition to the blessings and curses in ch. 28 is augmented with ceremonial lore, apparently gleaned from various sources and loosely conflated to encourage observance of covenant obligations. **27.1** The consortium of *Moses and the elders of Israel* (cf. 31.9) may attest a tradition stratum (the Yahwist or "J" source; see Introduction to *The HarperCollins Study Bible*) also evident in Ex 3.16–18; 17.5–6; 19.7; 24.1, 9–14; Num 11.16–30. **27.2–3, 8** Memorial *stones*, erected after crossing the Jordan, suggest the shrine at Gilgal (cf. 11.30; Josh 4). *Cover them with plaster*, i.e., to produce a stuccoed writing surface. *All the words of this law* (vv. 3, 8): the articles of Deuteronomic legislation (cf. 17.19; 27.26; 28.58; 29.29; 31.12). **27.4** The location at *Mount Ebal* (see 11.29) promotes linkage of vv. 2–3 with vv. 5–7, 12–13 (cf. Josh 8.30–32). **27.5–7** Cf. the covenant-making rites depicted in Ex 24.3–8. **27.5** *Altar of [unhewn] stones.* Cf. Ex 20.24–26; *Mishnah Middot* 3.4. **27.7** The term rendered *sacrifices of well-being* (e.g., Ex 20.24; 24.5; 32.6; Lev 3.1–5) is otherwise unattested in the book of Deuteronomy (cf. 12.6, 11, 26–27). **27.9–10** Rhetorical connection is made between 26.16–19 and 28.1. (Cf. 5.32–6.1; 11.31–12.1.) **27.11–13** Further instruction on promulgation of covenant sanctions in the region of Shechem (see 11.26–30; cf. Josephus *Antiquities* 4.305–308; *Mishnah Sota* 7.5). Implementation, as reported in Josh 8.33–35, relates *the blessing* and *the curse* to the contents of ch. 28. **27.14–26** The liturgy of imprecations and antiphonal responses recorded here comprises a loyalty oath, apparently administered by officiating *Levites* to the membership of Israel's tribal "assembly" (cf. 10.8; 23.1–8; 33.4–5, 8–10). By anathematizing any member who commits one of these clandestine offenses (*in secret*, vv. 15, 24; cf. 13.6; 29.17–21), the list reinforces the basic communal ethos. Specific items are paralleled in the Decalogue and other biblical codes of law; the whole Deuteronomic polity is encompassed by the final curse (cf. vv. 3, 8). **27.15** Cf., e.g., 4.15–20; 5.8–9; Ex 20.23; 34.17; Lev 19.4; 26.1; Hos 13.2. On secretive idolatry, cf. Job 31.26–27; Pss 64.5–6; 115.4–8. *Amen*, or "so be it" (cf. Num 5.22; Jer 11.5; Neh 5.13). **27.16** Cf. 5.16; 21.18–20; Ex 21.17; Lev 20.9. **27.17** See 19.14. **27.18** Cf. Lev 19.14. **27.19** See 24.17 (cf. Ex 22.21–22; 23.9; Lev

the alien, the orphan, and the widow of justice." All the people shall say, "Amen!"

20 "Cursed be anyone who lies with his father's wife, because he has violated his father's rights."[h] All the people shall say, "Amen!"

21 "Cursed be anyone who lies with any animal." All the people shall say, "Amen!"

22 "Cursed be anyone who lies with his sister, whether the daughter of his father or the daughter of his mother." All the people shall say, "Amen!"

23 "Cursed be anyone who lies with his mother-in-law." All the people shall say, "Amen!"

24 "Cursed be anyone who strikes down a neighbor in secret." All the people shall say, "Amen!"

25 "Cursed be anyone who takes a bribe to shed innocent blood." All the people shall say, "Amen!"

26 "Cursed be anyone who does not uphold the words of this law by observing them." All the people shall say, "Amen!"

Covenantal Blessings and Curses

28 If you will only obey the LORD your God, by diligently observing all his commandments that I am commanding you today, the LORD your God will set you high above all the nations of the earth; 2 all these blessings shall come upon you and overtake you, if you obey the LORD your God:

3 Blessed shall you be in the city, and blessed shall you be in the field.

4 Blessed shall be the fruit of your womb, the fruit of your ground, and the fruit of your livestock, both the increase of your cattle and the issue of your flock.

5 Blessed shall be your basket and your kneading bowl.

6 Blessed shall you be when you come in, and blessed shall you be when you go out.

7 The LORD will cause your enemies who rise against you to be defeated before you; they shall come out against you one way, and flee before you seven ways. 8 The LORD will command the blessing upon you in your barns, and in all that you undertake; he will bless you in the land that the LORD your God is giving you. 9 The LORD will establish you as his holy people, as he has sworn to you, if you keep the commandments of the LORD your God and walk in his ways. 10 All the peoples of the earth shall see that you are called by the name of the LORD, and they shall be afraid of you. 11 The LORD will make you abound in prosperity, in the fruit of your womb, in the fruit of your livestock, and in the fruit of your ground in the land that the LORD swore to your ancestors to give you. 12 The LORD will open for you his rich storehouse, the heavens, to give the rain of your land in its season and to bless all your undertakings. You will lend to many nations, but you will not borrow. 13 The LORD will make you the head, and not the tail; you shall be only at the top, and not at the

h Heb uncovered his father's skirt

19.33–34). **27.20–23** Proscribed sexual relations; cf. 22.30; Ex 22.19; Lev 18.7–9, 17, 23; 20.11, 14–17. **27.24** Surreptitious homicide; cf. 21.1; Ex 21.12. **27.25** Abuse of judicial power; cf. 1.16–17; 16.19; Ex 23.6–8. **27.26** Cf. Jer 11.3; also Gal 3.10.

28.1–46 Covenantal blessings and curses. **28.1–14** The blessings affirm that national security, prosperity, and political preeminence are intrinsic consequences of Israel's fidelity to the covenant relationship (see 26.18–19; cf. also 7.12–16; 11.13–15; Lev 26.1–13). **28.1** *Set you high.* The language of royal apotheosis (cf. 2 Sam 7.22–29; Ps 89.27–37; Isa 55.3–5) directly echoes 26.19. **28.3–6** This sixfold benediction, together with its imprecatory counterpart in vv. 16–19, may represent an ancient liturgy (cf. 27.12–13). The paired antonyms in vv. 3, 6 (cf.

6.7) express the fullness of productive labors: *city* and *field*, i.e., wherever you work (e.g., Gen 34.28; 1 Kings 14.11; Jer 14.18); *come in* and *go out*, whatever you do (e.g., 31.2; Ps 121.8). Similarly, the central blessings (vv. 4–5) invoke comprehensive fertility for livestock, fields, and their human caretakers (cf. 7.13–14; 32.13–14; Ex 23.26; Lev 26.4–5, 9). **28.7–14** Emphasized here is divine agency in providing the benefactions that will ensure well-being and exaltation for Israel, contingent upon its continuing observance of the Lord's commands. **28.7** Defeat of *enemies.* Cf. 9.1–3; Ex 23.27–28; Lev 26.6–8. **28.8** Cf. 8.7–10; 11.10–12; Lev 26.10. **28.9** See 26.18–19. **28.10** *Called by the name of the LORD* denotes the Lord's active conservatorship of Israel (cf. 2 Chr 7.14; Isa 61.9; 63.19; Jer 14.9; Am 9.12). **28.11** See v. 4. **28.12** Heavenly *storehouse* of sea-

bottom — if you obey the commandments of the LORD your God, which I am commanding you today, by diligently observing them, 14 and if you do not turn aside from any of the words that I am commanding you today, either to the right or to the left, following other gods to serve them.

15 But if you will not obey the LORD your God by diligently observing all his commandments and decrees, which I am commanding you today, then all these curses shall come upon you and overtake you:

16 Cursed shall you be in the city, and cursed shall you be in the field.

17 Cursed shall be your basket and your kneading bowl.

18 Cursed shall be the fruit of your womb, the fruit of your ground, the increase of your cattle and the issue of your flock.

19 Cursed shall you be when you come in, and cursed shall you be when you go out.

20 The LORD will send upon you disaster, panic, and frustration in everything you attempt to do, until you are destroyed and perish quickly, on account of the evil of your deeds, because you have forsaken me. 21 The LORD will make the pestilence cling to you until it has consumed you off the land that you are entering to possess. 22 The LORD will afflict you with consumption, fever, inflammation, with fiery heat and drought, and with blight and mildew; they shall pursue you until you perish. 23 The sky over your head shall be bronze, and the earth under you iron. 24 The LORD will change the rain of your land into powder, and only dust shall come down upon you from the sky until you are destroyed.

25 The LORD will cause you to be defeated before your enemies; you shall go out against them one way and flee before them seven ways. You shall become an object of horror to all the kingdoms of the earth. 26 Your corpses shall be food for every bird of the air and animal of the earth, and there shall be no one to frighten them away. 27 The LORD will afflict you with the boils of Egypt, with ulcers, scurvy, and itch, of which you cannot be healed. 28 The LORD will afflict you with madness, blindness, and confusion of mind; 29 you shall grope about at noon as blind people grope in darkness, but you shall be unable to find your way; and you shall be continually abused and robbed, without anyone to help. 30 You shall become engaged to a woman, but another man shall lie with her. You shall build a house, but not live in it. You shall plant a vineyard, but not enjoy its fruit. 31 Your ox shall be butchered before your eyes, but you shall not eat of it. Your donkey shall be stolen in front of you, and shall not be restored to you. Your sheep shall be given to your enemies, without anyone to help you. 32 Your sons and daughters shall be given to another people, while you look on; you will strain your eyes looking for them all day but be powerless to do anything. 33 A people whom you do not know shall eat up the fruit of your ground and of all your labors; you shall be continually abused and crushed, 34 and driven mad by the sight that your eyes shall see. 35 The LORD will strike you on the knees and on the legs with grievous boils of which you cannot be healed, from the sole of your foot to the crown of your head. 36 The LORD will bring you, and the king whom you set over you, to a nation that neither you nor your ancestors have known, where you shall serve other gods, of wood and stone. 37 You shall become an object of horror, a proverb, and a byword

---

sonal rains. Cf. Job 38.22; Ps 135.7; Jer 10.13. *Lend, but not borrow.* Cf. 15.6. **28.14** See 5.32. **28.15–19** Introductory threat plus the initial series of curses forms a close antithesis to 28.1–6. **28.20–46** This is an expansive counterpart to 28.7–14. **28.20** The terms *disaster, panic, and frustration* broadly categorize effects of the following curses (vv. 21–44). *Me.* See 7.4. **28.21–22** Debilitation. Cf., e.g., Lev 26.16, 25; 1 Kings 8.37; Jer 14.12; Am 4.9–10; Hag 2.17. **28.23–24** Strikingly parallel curses appear in *Vassal Treaties of Esarhaddon* 526–33. For the imagery,

cf. also Lev 26.19; Job 37.18; 38.38. **28.25** Military rout. Cf. 1.44; 28.7; Lev 26.17–18. *Object of horror* or "revulsion." Cf. 2 Chr 29.8; Jer 15.4; 34.17; Ezek 23.46. **28.26** See Jer 7.33; 34.20; cf. 2 Sam 21.10; Ps 79.2; Ezek 39.17–20. **28.27** *Boils of Egypt.* Cf. 7.15; 28.60; Ex 9.9–11. **28.28–29** Derangement. Cf. Job 5.14; 12.25; Isa 19.14; 59.10; Zech 12.4. **28.30** Cf. 20.5–7; Am 5.11. **28.31–34** Spoliation. Cf., e.g., Jer 5.17; 38.21–23; Lam 5.2–18; Am 7.17. **28.35** Cf. v. 27; Job 2.7. **28.36–37** Captivity. Cf., e.g., 4.27–28; 2 Kings 25.7, 11; Jer 16.13; 24.8–9;

among all the peoples where the LORD will lead you.

38 You shall carry much seed into the field but shall gather little in, for the locust shall consume it. 39 You shall plant vineyards and dress them, but you shall neither drink the wine nor gather the grapes, for the worm shall eat them. 40 You shall have olive trees throughout all your territory, but you shall not anoint yourself with the oil, for your olives shall drop off. 41 You shall have sons and daughters, but they shall not remain yours, for they shall go into captivity. 42 All your trees and the fruit of your ground the cicada shall take over. 43 Aliens residing among you shall ascend above you higher and higher, while you shall descend lower and lower. 44 They shall lend to you but you shall not lend to them; they shall be the head and you shall be the tail.

45 All these curses shall come upon you, pursuing and overtaking you until you are destroyed, because you did not obey the LORD your God, by observing the commandments and the decrees that he commanded you. 46 They shall be among you and your descendants as a sign and a portent forever.

Scenarios of Curse

47 Because you did not serve the LORD your God joyfully and with gladness of heart for the abundance of everything, 48 therefore you shall serve your enemies whom the LORD will send against you, in hunger and thirst, in nakedness and lack of everything. He will put an iron yoke on your neck until he has destroyed you. 49 The LORD will bring a nation from far away, from the end of the earth, to swoop down on you like an eagle, a nation whose language you do not understand, 50 a grim-faced nation showing no respect to the old or favor to the young. 51 It shall consume the fruit of your livestock and the fruit of your ground until you are destroyed, leaving you neither grain, wine, and oil, nor the increase of your cattle and the issue of your flock, until it has made you perish. 52 It shall besiege you in all your towns until your high and fortified walls, in which you trusted, come down throughout your land; it shall besiege you in all your towns throughout the land that the LORD your God has given you. 53 In the desperate straits to which the enemy siege reduces you, you will eat the fruit of your womb, the flesh of your own sons and daughters whom the LORD your God has given you. 54 Even the most refined and gentle of men among you will begrudge food to his own brother, to the wife whom he embraces, and to the last of his remaining children, 55 giving to none of them any of the flesh of his children whom he is eating, because nothing else remains to him, in the desperate straits to which the enemy siege will reduce you in all your towns. 56 She who is the most refined and gentle among you, so gentle and refined that she does not venture to set the sole of her foot on the ground, will begrudge food to the husband whom she embraces, to her own son, and to her own daughter, 57 begrudging even the afterbirth that comes out from between her thighs, and the children that she bears, because she is eating them in secret for lack of anything else, in the desperate straits to which the enemy siege will reduce you in your towns.

58 If you do not diligently observe all the words of this law that are written in

---

25.9–10; Ezek 17.12. **28.38–42** Futility of labors. Cf. v. 18; Lev 26.20; Hos 2.8–13; Mic 6.15. **28.43–44** Reversal of roles. Cf. 15.6; 28.12–13. **28.45** Inclusion (a repetition signaling the beginning and end of a unit), echoing 28.15. **28.46** Perduring effects of curse. Cf. v. 37; also 29.22–28.

28.47–68 Divine retaliation against Israel for breach of covenant is portrayed in scenes (vv. 47–57, 58–68) that threaten reversal of the conquest and even the exodus from Egypt (cf. 6.21–23; 8.11–20; 26.5–9). **28.47–48** Rejection of the Lord's benevolent sovereignty will result in Israel's subjugation to its enemies (cf. Judg 2.11–15). *Joyfully and with gladness of heart* connotes cheerful alacrity (cf. 1 Kings 1.40; 8.66; Esth 5.9). **28.48** *Iron yoke*, heavy, infrangible vassalage (cf. Jer 28.13–14; Mt 11.28–30; *Mishnah Avot* 3.5). **28.49–50** Portrait of the merciless foe wielded by the Lord as a weapon against Israel is conventional (cf. Jer 5.14–17; 6.22–26; Joel 1.6; 2.3–11; Hab 1.6–11). *Grim-faced*, imperious, brazen (cf. Prov 7.13; 21.29; Eccl 8.1; Dan 8.23). **28.51** Cf. 28.4, 18, 33. **28.53–57** Cannibalistic themes epitomize *the desperate straits* of people under prolonged *siege* in Assyrian sources (e.g., *Vassal Treaties of Esarhaddon* 448–50) as well as biblical texts (e.g., Lev 26.29; 2 Kings 6.28–29; Jer 19.9;

this book, fearing this glorious and awesome name, the LORD your God, 59 then the LORD will overwhelm both you and your offspring with severe and lasting afflictions and grievous and lasting maladies. 60 He will bring back upon you all the diseases of Egypt, of which you were in dread, and they shall cling to you. 61 Every other malady and affliction, even though not recorded in the book of this law, the LORD will inflict on you until you are destroyed. 62 Although once you were as numerous as the stars in heaven, you shall be left few in number, because you did not obey the LORD your God. 63 And just as the LORD took delight in making you prosperous and numerous, so the LORD will take delight in bringing you to ruin and destruction; you shall be plucked off the land that you are entering to possess. 64 The LORD will scatter you among all peoples, from one end of the earth to the other; and there you shall serve other gods, of wood and stone, which neither you nor your ancestors have known. 65 Among those nations you shall find no ease, no resting place for the sole of your foot. There the LORD will give you a trembling heart, failing eyes, and a languishing spirit. 66 Your life shall hang in doubt before you; night and day you shall be in dread, with no assurance of your life. 67 In the morning you shall say, "If only it were evening!" and at evening you shall say, "If only it were morning!" — because of the dread that your heart shall feel and the sights that your eyes shall see. 68 The

LORD will bring you back in ships to Egypt, by a route that I promised you would never see again; and there you shall offer yourselves for sale to your enemies as male and female slaves, but there will be no buyer.

The Covenant Enacted in Moab

29 [i] These are the words of the covenant that the LORD commanded Moses to make with the Israelites in the land of Moab, in addition to the covenant that he had made with them at Horeb.

2 [j] Moses summoned all Israel and said to them: You have seen all that the LORD did before your eyes in the land of Egypt, to Pharaoh and to all his servants and to all his land, 3 the great trials that your eyes saw, the signs, and those great wonders. 4 But to this day the LORD has not given you a mind to understand, or eyes to see, or ears to hear. 5 I have led you forty years in the wilderness. The clothes on your back have not worn out, and the sandals on your feet have not worn out; 6 you have not eaten bread, and you have not drunk wine or strong drink — so that you may know that I am the LORD your God. 7 When you came to this place, King Sihon of Heshbon and King Og of Bashan came out against us for battle, but we defeated them. 8 We took their land and gave it as an inheritance to the Reubenites, the Gadites, and the half-tribe of Manasseh. 9 Therefore diligently observe the words

i Ch 28.69 in Heb   j Ch 29.1 in Heb

Lam 2.20; 4.10). **28.58** *All the words of this law . . . written in this book*, the whole Deuteronomic polity, recorded and textually transmitted (cf. 17.18–19; 29.20–21, 27; 30.10; 31.9, 24–26). *Fearing this . . . name* means fidelity to the covenantal oath, sworn in acknowledgment of *the LORD* (Yahweh) as Israel's sole divine sovereign (see 5.6; 6.4, 13; 29.12–13; cf. Ex 6.2–3, 7; Josh 24.14–24). **28.59–61** Cf. 7.15; 28.21–22, 27. **28.62** Reversal of proliferation. Cf. 1.10; 10.22; 26.5. **28.63–67** Dispersion. Cf. 4.26–28; 29.28; Lev 26.33–39. **28.68** Displacement to *Egypt*. Cf. Jer 42–44; also Hos 8.13; 9.3, 6; 11.5. The sense of *in ships . . . by a route that I promised you would never see again* is obscure (cf. 17.16).
29.1–30.20 Principal features of a covenant rite are profiled in this hortatory epilogue to Moses' promulgation of the law. **29.1** The book's third editorial heading (cf. 1.1–5; 4.44–49) introduces the concluding portion of Moses' valedic-

tory address and apparently also introduces the supplemental depositions that follow in chs. 31–32. These varied contents, designated covenantal *words* or "provisions," respond to the crisis of continuity posed by Moses' imminent demise. For the setting near Beth-peor in *Moab*, see 3.29; 4.46. For the *covenant* initiated *at Horeb*, see 4.10–13; 5.1–3 (cf. 1.2). **29.2–9** The retrospect encompasses the era from the exodus through the conquests in the Transjordan (cf. 4.37–38; 6.21–23; 26.5–10). **29.3** *Great trials*, the plagues (cf. 4.34; 7.19). **29.4** *Mind to understand* (lit. "heart to know"), the personal capacity to discern providence (cf. Isa 6.9–10; Jer 5.21; 24.7; Ezek 12.2–3). **29.5–6** Cf. 8.2–5. On the apparent shift from Mosaic to divine speech, cf. note on 7.3–4. **29.7–8** *Sihon* and *Og*. See 1.4; 2.26–3.22. **29.9** *Succeed*, or "prosper," contingent upon obedience; cf. Josh 1.7–8; 1 Kings 2.3.

of this covenant, in order that you may succeed[k] in everything that you do.

10 You stand assembled today, all of you, before the LORD your God—the leaders of your tribes,[l] your elders, and your officials, all the men of Israel, 11 your children, your women, and the aliens who are in your camp, both those who cut your wood and those who draw your water—12 to enter into the covenant of the LORD your God, sworn by an oath, which the LORD your God is making with you today; 13 in order that he may establish you today as his people, and that he may be your God, as he promised you and as he swore to your ancestors, to Abraham, to Isaac, and to Jacob. 14 I am making this covenant, sworn by an oath, not only with you who stand here with us today before the LORD our God, 15 but also with those who are not here with us today. 16 You know how we lived in the land of Egypt, and how we came through the midst of the nations through which you passed. 17 You have seen their detestable things, the filthy idols of wood and stone, of silver and gold, that were among them. 18 It may be that there is among you a man or woman, or a family or tribe, whose heart is already turning away from the LORD our God to serve the gods of those nations. It may be that there is among you a root sprouting poisonous and bitter growth. 19 All who hear the words of this oath and bless themselves, thinking in their hearts, "We are safe even though we go our own stubborn ways" (thus bringing disaster on moist and dry alike)[m]— 20 the LORD will be unwilling to pardon them,

for the LORD's anger and passion will smoke against them. All the curses written in this book will descend on them, and the LORD will blot out their names from under heaven. 21 The LORD will single them out from all the tribes of Israel for calamity, in accordance with all the curses of the covenant written in this book of the law. 22 The next generation, your children who rise up after you, as well as the foreigner who comes from a distant country, will see the devastation of that land and the afflictions with which the LORD has afflicted it— 23 all its soil burned out by sulfur and salt, nothing planted, nothing sprouting, unable to support any vegetation, like the destruction of Sodom and Gomorrah, Admah and Zeboiim, which the LORD destroyed in his fierce anger—24 they and indeed all the nations will wonder, "Why has the LORD done thus to this land? What caused this great display of anger?" 25 They will conclude, "It is because they abandoned the covenant of the LORD, the God of their ancestors, which he made with them when he brought them out of the land of Egypt. 26 They turned and served other gods, worshiping them, gods whom they had not known and whom he had not allotted to them; 27 so the anger of the LORD was kindled against that land, bringing on it every curse written in this book. 28 The LORD uprooted them from their land in anger, fury, and great wrath, and cast them into another land, as is now the case." 29 The secret things belong to the LORD our God,

k Or deal wisely   l Gk Syr: Heb your leaders, your tribes   m Meaning of Heb uncertain

---

29.10–29 Emphasized here is the individual's accountability as well as the social and multigenerational inclusiveness of Israel's covenant community. **29.10–11** See note on 5.22. Cf. 31.12; Josh 8.33, 35; 9.27; 23.2; 2 Kings 23.2–3. **29.12–13** Covenant . . . sworn by an oath. Cf. Gen 26.28; Ezek 17.13–14, 18. See also Deut 26.16–19. **29.14–15** Cf. 5.3. **29.16–17** Detestable things (or "abominations"), filthy idols. Cf., e.g., Lev 26.30; 1 Kings 11.5–7; 21.26; 2 Kings 23.13, 24; Ezek 6.4–6; 20.7–8. **29.18–21** On the threat of secret apostasy, cf. 13.6–11; 27.15. **29.18** Poisonous and bitter growth. Cf., e.g., Jer 9.15; 23.15; Hos 10.4; Am 6.12. **29.19** Our own stubborn ways, individual willfulness (cf. 12.8), lit. "the stubbornness of my own heart" (e.g., Ps 81.11–13; Jer 3.17; 7.24). Obstinate idiosyncrasy may threaten the survival of the whole community (moist and dry alike, apparently an agricultural metaphor; cf. Ps 107.4–9, 33–37; Isa 58.11). **29.20** Divine anger and passion. Cf. v. 27; 4.24; 32.19–22. Blot out their names. Cf. 9.14; 25.19. **29.22–28** Purview shifts to the aftermath of national disaster (cf. 4.25–28). **29.23** Sodom and Gomorrah, Admah and Zeboiim, infamous cities of the Jordan plain (cf., e.g., Gen 10.19; 19.24–25; Isa 1.9–10; Jer 49.18; Hos 11.8). **29.24–28** Cf. the interrogation schema in 1 Kings 9.8–9; Jer 5.19; 9.12–16; 16.10–13; 22.8–9. **29.26** Other gods . . . not allotted to them. Cf. 4.19; 32.8–9. **29.27–28** Cf. vv. 20–21; Jer 21.5; 32.37. **29.29** The maxim apparently affirms that faithful observance of the instruction received through Moses (revealed things) is sufficient to assure Israel's continuance in covenant relationship with God (see 4.2; cf. 6.25; 30.11–14).

but the revealed things belong to us and to our children forever, to observe all the words of this law.

Prescriptions for Renewal of Covenant

30 When all these things have happened to you, the blessings and the curses that I have set before you, if you call them to mind among all the nations where the LORD your God has driven you, 2 and return to the LORD your God, and you and your children obey him with all your heart and with all your soul, just as I am commanding you today, 3 then the LORD your God will restore your fortunes and have compassion on you, gathering you again from all the peoples among whom the LORD your God has scattered you. 4 Even if you are exiled to the ends of the world,[n] from there the LORD your God will gather you, and from there he will bring you back. 5 The LORD your God will bring you into the land that your ancestors possessed, and you will possess it; he will make you more prosperous and numerous than your ancestors.

6 Moreover, the LORD your God will circumcise your heart and the heart of your descendants, so that you will love the LORD your God with all your heart and with all your soul, in order that you may live. 7 The LORD your God will put all these curses on your enemies and on the adversaries who took advantage of you. 8 Then you shall again obey the LORD, observing all his commandments that I am commanding you today, 9 and the LORD your God will make you abundantly prosperous in all your undertakings, in the fruit of your body, in the fruit of your livestock, and in the fruit of your soil. For the LORD will again take delight in prospering you, just as he delighted in prospering your ancestors, 10 when you obey the LORD your God by observing his commandments and decrees that are written in this book of the law, because you turn to the LORD your God with all your heart and with all your soul.

11 Surely, this commandment that I am commanding you today is not too hard for you, nor is it too far away. 12 It is not in heaven, that you should say, "Who will go up to heaven for us, and get it for us so that we may hear it and observe it?" 13 Neither is it beyond the sea, that you should say, "Who will cross to the other side of the sea for us, and get it for us so that we may hear it and observe it?" 14 No, the word is very near to you; it is in your mouth and in your heart for you to observe.

15 See, I have set before you today life and prosperity, death and adversity. 16 If you obey the commandments of the LORD your God[o] that I am commanding you today, by loving the LORD your God, walking in his ways, and observing his commandments, decrees, and ordinances, then you shall live and become numerous, and the LORD your God will bless you in

n Heb of heaven   o Gk: Heb lacks If you obey the commandments of the LORD your God

---

30.1–10 The witness of 4.29–31 to the future of covenant beyond the devastation of curse is now developed as a promise of restoration for those in exile who penitently renew their commitment to the Lord (cf. Lev 26.40–45). **30.1** Call them to mind (lit. "return [them] to your heart"). Continuing reflection on experience yields theological insight; see 4.39 (cf. 1 Kings 8.47; Isa 46.8; Lam 3.21). **30.2** Return . . . with all your heart and . . . soul. Cf. v. 10; also 4.29–30; 1 Kings 8.48; 2 Kings 23.25; Jer 3.10; 24.7. **30.3** Restore your fortunes. See, e.g., Jer 29.14; 33.26; Ezek 39.25; Am 9.14; Zeph 3.20. **30.4** Neh 1.8–9 cites this promise of ingathering, together with the threat of 28.64. For the theme in prophetic sources, see, e.g., Isa 43.5–7; Jer 31.10; 32.37; Ezek 36.24; 37.21. **30.5** Cf. 28.62–63; Jer 23.3; 30.3. **30.6** Divine initiative to overcome human recalcitrance and spiritual fatuity (circumcise your heart; cf. 10.16) accords with the "new covenant" emphases of Jer 31.31–34; 32.37–41; Ezek 11.19–20; 36.26–28 (cf. Ps 51.10). Love the LORD. See 6.5. **30.7** Cf. 7.15. **30.9–10** Cf. 28.4, 11–12, 18; 30.2. This book of the law, the scroll of Deuteronomic legislation (cf. 29.20–21; 31.9, 24–26). **30.11–14** What the Lord requires of Israel is both perspicuous and practicable (cf. 4.5–8; 10.12–13). **30.11** This commandment, the basic protocol of covenantal fidelity, elaborated by Moses (cf. 5.31–6.2; 11.22; 19.9). Not too hard, neither infeasible nor esoteric (cf. Ps 139.6). **30.12–13** Cf. the quest after cosmic "wisdom" portrayed in Bar 3.29–31 (cf. Job 28.12–28). **30.14** Internalization of the word. Cf. 6.6–7; 11.18–19; cf. Jer 1.9. **30.15–20** A climactic appeal for allegiance resounds with familiar expressions. **30.15** The options posed for Israel's decision are "blessing" (life and prosperity) and "curse" (death and adversity); see 11.26–28 (cf. Jer 21.8; Prov 11.19; 14.27). **30.16** Cf. 4.1; 8.1;

the land that you are entering to possess. [17]But if your heart turns away and you do not hear, but are led astray to bow down to other gods and serve them, [18]I declare to you today that you shall perish; you shall not live long in the land that you are crossing the Jordan to enter and possess. [19]I call heaven and earth to witness against you today that I have set before you life and death, blessings and curses. Choose life so that you and your descendants may live, [20]loving the LORD your God, obeying him, and holding fast to him; for that means life to you and length of days, so that you may live in the land that the LORD swore to give to your ancestors, to Abraham, to Isaac, and to Jacob.

Acts of Conveyance and Investiture

31 When Moses had finished speaking all[p] these words to all Israel, [2]he said to them: "I am now one hundred twenty years old. I am no longer able to get about, and the LORD has told me, 'You shall not cross over this Jordan.' [3]The LORD your God himself will cross over before you. He will destroy these nations before you, and you shall dispossess them. Joshua also will cross over before you, as the LORD promised. [4]The LORD will do to them as he did to Sihon and Og, the kings of the Amorites, and to their land, when he destroyed them. [5]The LORD will give them over to you and you shall deal with them in full accord with the command

that I have given to you. [6]Be strong and bold; have no fear or dread of them, because it is the LORD your God who goes with you; he will not fail you or forsake you."

[7] Then Moses summoned Joshua and said to him in the sight of all Israel: "Be strong and bold, for you are the one who will go with this people into the land that the LORD has sworn to their ancestors to give them; and you will put them in possession of it. [8]It is the LORD who goes before you. He will be with you; he will not fail you or forsake you. Do not fear or be dismayed."

[9] Then Moses wrote down this law, and gave it to the priests, the sons of Levi, who carried the ark of the covenant of the LORD, and to all the elders of Israel. [10]Moses commanded them: "Every seventh year, in the scheduled year of remission, during the festival of booths,[q] [11]when all Israel comes to appear before the LORD your God at the place that he will choose, you shall read this law before all Israel in their hearing. [12]Assemble the people — men, women, and children, as well as the aliens residing in your towns — so that they may hear and learn to fear the LORD your God and to observe diligently all the words of this law, [13]and so that their children, who have not known it, may hear and learn to fear the LORD your God, as long as you live in the land

p Q Ms Gk: MT *Moses went and spoke*
q Or *tabernacles*; Heb *succoth*

11.22; cf. Lev 18.4–5. **30.17–18** Cf. 4.19, 25–26; 8.19–20. *30.19 Heaven and earth* as witnesses. See 4.26; 31.28; Ps 50.4. **30.20** See 1.8; 4.1, 40; 10.20; 11.22.

31.1–32.52 With Moses' death again in immediate view (cf. 3.23–28; 4.21–24), the narrative conjoins the provisions for transition in leadership and preservation of the Mosaic legacy of covenantal lore. **31.1–8** Parallel charges reassure the Israelite militia and Joshua of the Lord's own presence as vanguard in the impending conquest west of the Jordan. **31.1** In context, *all these words* should mean the several preceding portions of Moses' valedictory address (see 1.1). **31.2** Moses' age of *one hundred twenty years* spans three normal forty-year generations (cf. 34.7; Ex 7.7; Acts 7.23, 30); according to Gen 6.3 this is the maximum lifetime allowed to any human being (cf. Job 42.16). *To get about*, lit. "to go out and to come in," refers to active leadership, especially exercise of military command (cf. 28.6, 19; Num

27.17, 21; Josh 14.11; 1 Sam 18.16). *You shall not cross.* See 3.27 (cf. 1.37; 4.21–22). **31.3–5** On the vanguard and conquest themes, cf. 1.29–33; 3.21–22, 28; 7.1–5; 9.1–3; 20.16–18. **31.6–8** For the formulaic exhortations to steadfastness and valor, see, e.g., 1.21, 29; Josh 1.6–9; 10.25 (cf. Pss 27.14; 31.24; Isa 7.4). *31.8 He will be with you.* Reassurance invokes the Lord's accompanying presence (cf. v. 23; Ex 3.12; Josh 1.5, 17; 3.7; 2 Sam 7.9; cf. Ex 33.12–16). **31.9–13** Disposition and periodic proclamation of the written Mosaic law; see also vv. 24–27. **31.9** *This law,* the Deuteronomic polity (see 4.44). *Priests, the sons of Levi.* See 21.5 (cf. 10.8–9; 17.18). *Ark of the covenant.* Cf. 10.1–5, 8; Josh 8.33. *All the elders of Israel.* Cf. note on 27.1. **31.10–11** *Year of remission.* See 15.1–11. *Festival of booths.* See 16.13–15. *The place that he will choose.* See 12.5. On public reading of the polity in the liturgical setting of covenant renewal, see 2 Kings 23.2; Neh 8; cf. *Mishnah Sota* 7.8. **31.12–13** Cf. 29.10–15; cf.

that you are crossing over the Jordan to possess."

14 The LORD said to Moses, "Your time to die is near; call Joshua and present yourselves in the tent of meeting, so that I may commission him." So Moses and Joshua went and presented themselves in the tent of meeting, 15 and the LORD appeared at the tent in a pillar of cloud; the pillar of cloud stood at the entrance to the tent.

16 The LORD said to Moses, "Soon you will lie down with your ancestors. Then this people will begin to prostitute themselves to the foreign gods in their midst, the gods of the land into which they are going; they will forsake me, breaking my covenant that I have made with them. 17 My anger will be kindled against them in that day. I will forsake them and hide my face from them; they will become easy prey, and many terrible troubles will come upon them. In that day they will say, 'Have not these troubles come upon us because our God is not in our midst?' 18 On that day I will surely hide my face on account of all the evil they have done by turning to other gods. 19 Now therefore write this song, and teach it to the Israelites; put it in their mouths, in order that this song may be a witness for me against the Israelites. 20 For when I have brought them into the land flowing with milk and honey, which I promised on oath to their ancestors, and they have eaten their fill and grown fat, they will turn to other gods and serve them, despising me and breaking my covenant. 21 And when many terrible troubles come upon them, this song will confront them as a witness, because it will not be lost from the mouths of their descendants. For I know what they are inclined to do even now, before I have brought them into the land that I promised them on oath." 22 That very day Moses wrote this song and taught it to the Israelites.

23 Then the LORD commissioned Joshua son of Nun and said, "Be strong and bold, for you shall bring the Israelites into the land that I promised them; I will be with you."

24 When Moses had finished writing down in a book the words of this law to the very end, 25 Moses commanded the Levites who carried the ark of the covenant of the LORD, saying, 26 "Take this book of the law and put it beside the ark of the covenant of the LORD your God; let it remain there as a witness against you. 27 For I know well how rebellious and stubborn you are. If you already have been so rebellious toward the LORD while I am still alive among you, how much more after my death! 28 Assemble to me all the elders of your tribes and your officials, so that I may recite these words in their hearing and call heaven and earth to witness against them. 29 For I know that after my death you will surely act corruptly, turning aside from the way that I have commanded you. In time to come

---

also 4.9–14; 5.29–6.2. **31.14–23** A brief account of Joshua's installation to succeed Moses as war leader (vv. 14–15; 23) frames a divine charge introducing the Song of Moses as an oracular witness against Israel (vv. 16–22; see also 31.28–32.44). **31.14** *Your time to die is near.* Cf. Gen 47.29; 1 Kings 2.1. *Tent of meeting.* Cf. Ex 25.22; 29.42–45; 33.7–11; Num 11.16–25. **31.15** On *the pillar of cloud* manifesting divine presence at the tent, see Ex 33.9–10; Num 12.5. **31.16** *Lie down with your ancestors.* Cf., e.g., Gen 47.30; 2 Sam 7.12; 1 Kings 2.10; 11.43. Prostitution is frequently used as a metaphor for apostasy, e.g., Ex 34.15–16; Judg 8.27, 33; Hos 4.12; 9.1. Though identified here with *the gods of the land* (Canaan), *foreign gods* most often refers to cultic imports or innovations that compromise Israel's allegiance to the Lord alone (cf. 32.12, 16–17; Gen 35.2–4; Josh 24.2, 20–23; Judg 5.8; 10.16; 1 Kings 11.1–10; 2 Kings 17.29–41). *Breaking my covenant* (also v. 20). Cf. Jer 11.9–10.

31.17–18 Anticipation of 32.19–22. *God is not in our midst.* See 1.42; cf. Ex 17.7; Num 14.14, 42; Jer 14.9. **31.19–22** The written text of the song has a mnemonic function (cf. 6.6–9; Ex 17.14) while also documenting divine prescience of Israel's dire fate (cf. Jer 36). **31.20** *Despising me*, neglect or renunciation of the Lord's sovereignty (see Num 14.11, 23; 2 Sam 12.14; Ps 10.3, 13; Isa 1.4). **31.23** See vv. 7–8; cf. Num 27.15–23 (in the "priestly" tradition). **31.24–29** Preceding themes of the written law (vv. 9–13) and of the Song of Moses as witness (vv. 16–22) are here resumed and conflated; see also 32.44–47. **31.26** The scroll (*this book of the law*, cf. 29.20–21; 30.10) is to be preserved *beside the ark*, i.e., as an authoritative and accessible complement to the tablets of the Decalogue deposited within (cf. 4.13–14; 10.1–5; Ex 40.20; 1 Kings 8.9). **31.27** See 9.6–7, 23–24. **31.28–29** Cf. vv. 12–13, 19–22; cf. also 4.25–26; 11.26–28; 30.17–19.

trouble will befall you, because you will do what is evil in the sight of the LORD, provoking him to anger through the work of your hands."

The Song of Moses

30 Then Moses recited the words of this song, to the very end, in the hearing of the whole assembly of Israel:

32 Give ear, O heavens, and I
will speak;
let the earth hear the words of
my mouth.
2 May my teaching drop like the
rain,
my speech condense like
the dew;
like gentle rain on grass,
like showers on new growth.
3 For I will proclaim the name of
the LORD;
ascribe greatness to our God!

4 The Rock, his work is perfect,
and all his ways are just.
A faithful God, without deceit,
just and upright is he;
5 yet his degenerate children have
dealt falsely with him,[r]
a perverse and crooked
generation.
6 Do you thus repay the LORD,

O foolish and senseless people?
Is not he your father, who
created you,
who made you and
established you?
7 Remember the days of old,
consider the years long past;
ask your father, and he will
inform you;
your elders, and they will
tell you.
8 When the Most High[s]
apportioned the nations,
when he divided humankind,
he fixed the boundaries of the
peoples
according to the number of the
gods;[t]
9 the LORD's own portion was his
people,
Jacob his allotted share.

10 He sustained[u] him in a desert
land,
in a howling wilderness waste;
he shielded him, cared for him,
guarded him as the apple of
his eye.

r Meaning of Heb uncertain   s Traditional rendering of Heb *Elyon*   t Q Ms Compare Gk Tg: MT *the Israelites*   u Sam Gk Compare Tg: MT *found*

31.30 On Israel's plenary *assembly*, see note on 5.22. **32.1–43** The valedictory canticle ascribed to Moses is an eloquent poetic homily on the vicissitudes of the filial relationship between the Lord and Jacob (Israel). While origin and date of composition are disputed, forensic themes and the vivid imagery of divine pathos associate the work closely with traditions of classical Israelite prophecy. Cf. especially Isa 30.1–18; Jer 2–3; Ezek 20.1–44; Hos 13–14; Mic 6.1–5; cf. also Pss 50; 78. **32.1–3** The introductory idiom is both didactic and hymnic. **32.1** On the appeal for *heavens* and *earth* to attend the poet's discourse, cf. 4.26; 30.19; 31.28; Ps 50.4; Isa 1.2. **32.2** *Teaching* or "lore." Cf., e.g., Isa 29.24; Job 11.4; Prov 1.5; 4.2. **32.3** Proclamation of the *name of the LORD* here means public defense of divine providence and honor (cf., e.g., Josh 7.7–9; Ps 96.8; Jer 14.21; 32.20). **32.4–18** Poignant contrast between God's superlative character and the waywardness of God's people (vv. 4–5) is developed through narrative retrospect into an indictment of the poet's audience (*you*, vv. 6–7, 15, 18). **32.4** The Lord's stalwart integrity and trustworthiness are underscored by the epithets *Rock* (also

vv. 15, 18, 30–31; elsewhere, e.g., 2 Sam 22.3; Ps 18.2, 31, 46; Isa 17.10; Hab 1.12) and *faithful God* (cf. 7.9; Pss 33.4; 89.1–2; Isa 25.1; Hos 2.20). **32.5** *Children.* See 14.1. *Dealt falsely* (acted corruptly in 9.12). Cf. Isa 1.2–4; Hos 9.9; Mal 2.8. **32.6** *You.* Accusation stresses the Lord's paternal claim on Israel. *Your father, who created you.* Cf. Ex 4.21–23; Jer 31.8–9; Hos 11.1–3. **32.7** On the appeal for remembrance of primal events (*days of old,* Isa 51.9–10; 63.11; Mic 7.14–15), cf. Deut 4.32–34; Job 8.8–10; Isa 46.8–11; 63.11. **32.8** *Most High* (Hebrew *Elyon*) is an appellation generally expressing the Lord's universal sovereignty (e.g., Gen 14.18–22; Num 24.16; Pss 47.2; 83.18); here and occasionally elsewhere (Isa 14.14; Ps 82) it denotes the executive of the divine assembly, comprising subordinate *gods* (lit., "sons of God," as in Job 1.6; 2.1; Pss 29.1; 89.5–7). **32.9** Cf. 7.6; Jer 10.16; Zech 2.12; Sir 17.17. **32.10–12** For the motives in this portrait of divine providence during the exodus-wilderness era, cf. especially Jer 2.2–3, 6; Hos 2.14–15; 9.10; 13.4–6 (also Deut 1.31; 2.7; Ex 15.13; 19.4; Isa 43.10–21). *Apple of his eye.* Cf. Ps 17.8; Prov 7.2.

11 As an eagle stirs up its nest,
  and hovers over its young;
 as it spreads its wings, takes
    them up,
 and bears them aloft on its
    pinions,
12 the LORD alone guided him;
 no foreign god was with him.
13 He set him atop the heights of
    the land,
 and fed him with^v produce of
    the field;
 he nursed him with honey from
    the crags,
 with oil from flinty rock;
14 curds from the herd, and milk
    from the flock,
 with fat of lambs and rams;
 Bashan bulls and goats,
  together with the choicest
    wheat—
 you drank fine wine from the
    blood of grapes.
15 Jacob ate his fill;^{w}
 Jeshurun grew fat, and kicked.
 You grew fat, bloated, and
    gorged!
 He abandoned God who
    made him,
 and scoffed at the Rock of his
    salvation.
16 They made him jealous with
    strange gods,
 with abhorrent things they
    provoked him.
17 They sacrificed to demons,
    not God,

 to deities they had never
    known,
 to new ones recently arrived,
  whom your ancestors had not
    feared.
18 You were unmindful of the Rock
    that bore you;^{x}
 you forgot the God who gave
    you birth.
19 The LORD saw it, and was
    jealous;^{y}
 he spurned^z his sons and
    daughters.
20 He said: I will hide my face from
    them,
 I will see what their end
    will be;
 for they are a perverse
    generation,
 children in whom there is no
    faithfulness.
21 They made me jealous with what
    is no god,
 provoked me with their idols.
 So I will make them jealous with
    what is no people,
 provoke them with a foolish
    nation.
22 For a fire is kindled by my anger,
 and burns to the depths of
    Sheol;
 it devours the earth and its
    increase,

v Sam Gk Syr Tg: MT *he ate*   w Q Mss Sam Gk:
MT lacks *Jacob ate his fill*   x Or *that begot you*
y Q Mss Gk: MT lacks *was jealous*   z Cn: Heb *he
spurned because of provocation*

32.13–14 Cf. 8.7–9; Ex 15.17; Ps 81.16.
32.13 *Heights of the land*, connoting mountains (cf.
Isa 58.14; Am 4.13; Mic 1.3), refers here to the
highlands of Canaan (see 1.7). **32.14** *Bashan*.
See note on 3.1. **32.15** Cf. 8.12–17; 31.20; Neh
9.25. The appellations *Jacob* and *Jeshurun* are also
paralleled in Isa 44.2; the latter designation (rendered "beloved one, darling" in the Septuagint)
is otherwise attested only in Deut 33.5, 26.
32.16–17 Cf. 31.16; cf. Judg 5.8. **32.16** *Strange
gods*. See Pss 44.20; 81.9; Isa 43.12; cf. note on
Deut 31.16. **32.17** *Demons* are associated with
abhorrent Canaanite rites in Ps 106.34–39.
32.18 For the imagery of divine maternity, com-
plementing vv. 6–7, cf. Isa 49.15.

32.19–42 Divine soliloquy, contemplating appropriate punishment of Israel's apostasy, alter-
nates with the narrator's voice (vv. 19, 28–33,
36). **32.19–21** The judgment announced is

retaliatory, corresponding to the form of the
crime (see note on 19.19–21 on talion). On jealousy as a divine attribute, see 4.24. **32.20** *Hide
my face*, withdrawal of divine favor and protective
presence, i.e., the converse of Num 6.25–26;
see 31.17–18 (cf., e.g., Ps 13.1; Isa 8.17; Jer 33.5;
Ezek 39.23–24). **32.21** *No god* is a categorical
negation of the anonymous deities referred to in
vv. 16–17. So too the anonymous adversary selected as the Lord's instrument of revenge (*no people, foolish nation*) may be intentionally generic;
cf. 28.49–50 (cf. Judg 2.14–15; Ps 79.1–7; Isa
9.11–12). **32.22–25** The onslaught of the
Lord's wrath is graphically plotted. **32.22** On
fire as a weapon of divine warfare, see, e.g., Job
31.12; Ps 50.3; Am 1.4; cf. Deut 4.24. For portrayal of the catastrophic cosmic effects (consuming the *depths of Sheol*, i.e., the netherworld, the
earth's surface, and *foundations of the mountains*),

and sets on fire the foundations
 of the mountains.
23 I will heap disasters upon them,
 spend my arrows against them:
24 wasting hunger,
 burning consumption,
 bitter pestilence.
The teeth of beasts I will send
 against them,
 with venom of things crawling
 in the dust.
25 In the street the sword shall
 bereave,
 and in the chambers terror,
for young man and woman alike,
 nursing child and old gray
 head.
26 I thought to scatter them*a*
 and blot out the memory of
 them from humankind;
27 but I feared provocation by the
 enemy,
 for their adversaries might
 misunderstand
and say, "Our hand is
 triumphant;
 it was not the Lord who did all
 this."

28 They are a nation void of sense;
 there is no understanding in
 them.
29 If they were wise, they would
 understand this;
 they would discern what the
 end would be.
30 How could one have routed a
 thousand,
 and two put a myriad to flight,

unless their Rock had sold them,
 the Lord had given them up?
31 Indeed their rock is not like our
 Rock;
 our enemies are fools.*a*
32 Their vine comes from the
 vinestock of Sodom,
 from the vineyards of
 Gomorrah;
their grapes are grapes of poison,
 their clusters are bitter;
33 their wine is the poison of
 serpents,
 the cruel venom of asps.

34 Is not this laid up in store
 with me,
 sealed up in my treasuries?
35 Vengeance is mine, and
 recompense,
 for the time when their foot
 shall slip;
because the day of their calamity
 is at hand,
 their doom comes swiftly.

36 Indeed the Lord will vindicate
 his people,
 have compassion on his
 servants,
when he sees that their power is
 gone,
 neither bond nor free
 remaining.
37 Then he will say: Where are their
 gods,

a Gk: Meaning of Heb uncertain

---

see especially Ps 18.7–8; Am 7.4. **32.23** Pestilential *arrows* in the Lord's arsenal (cf. also v. 42; Job 6.4; Pss 7.12–13; 18.14; Lam 3.12–13; Ezek 5.16; Hab 3.9) approximate covenantal curses (cf. Deut 28.21–22; Ps 78.49). **32.25** Cf. Jer 6.11; 9.20–22; Lam 1.20; 2.21; Ezek 7.15. **32.26–27** Divine wrath is restrained, short of Israel's extinction, to thwart the foe's triumphalism. **32.26** *Blot out the memory.* Cf. 25.19. *Provocation,* vainglory (cf. Isa 10.5–15). On the implied threat to the Lord's reputation, cf., e.g., 9.26–29; Ex 32.11–14; Ps 74.18; Isa 48.9–11. **32.28–33** Descanting on the Lord's deliberations, the poet or prophetic narrator here reproaches the arrogance and brutish character of the enemy. **32.28** *Void of sense* or "lacking counsel"; cf. Isa 10.13 (boast of Assyria's king) and the ironical interrogation of Edom in Jer 49.7.

32.32 On *Sodom* and *Gomorrah.* See Deut 29.23. **32.34–35** The agent of chastisement will not itself escape judgment; cf. Isa 10.15–16 (Assyria); Jer 49.12–22 (Edom). **32.34** *This,* the foe's transgression, which awaits divine requital (cf. Job 14.17; Hos 13.12). **32.35** *Vengeance,* retribution, vindication (cf., e.g., Judg 16.28; Ps 94.1–3; Isa 61.2). *Recompense,* equitable redress (Isa 59.18; cf. Hos 9.7). *Day of their calamity.* See, e.g., Job 21.30; Ps 18.18; Jer 18.17; Ob 12–13. **32.36–42** Promise of the Lord's intervention as judge and warrior to exact retributive justice. **32.36** Prophetic proclamation of divine intent. *Vindicate* or "judge" refers to judicial review, here divine prosecution on Israel's behalf (cf., e.g., Gen 15.14; Pss 7.8; 9.8; Isa 3.13); note the parallel in Ps 135.14. The sense of *neither bond nor free* seems to be "(almost) no one" (cf. 1 Kings 14.10; 21.21;

the rock in which they took
    refuge,
38 who ate the fat of their sacrifices,
    and drank the wine of their
        libations?
Let them rise up and help you,
    let them be your protection!

39 See now that I, even I, am he;
    there is no god besides me.
I kill and I make alive;
    I wound and I heal;
    and no one can deliver from
        my hand.
40 For I lift up my hand to heaven,
    and swear: As I live forever,
41 when I whet my flashing sword,
    and my hand takes hold on
        judgment;
I will take vengeance on my
    adversaries,
    and will repay those who
        hate me.
42 I will make my arrows drunk with
    blood,
    and my sword shall devour
        flesh —
with the blood of the slain and
    the captives,
    from the long-haired enemy.

43 Praise, O heavens,[b] his people,
    worship him, all you gods![c]
For he will avenge the blood of
    his children,[d]

and take vengeance on his
    adversaries;
he will repay those who
    hate him,[c]
    and cleanse the land for his
        people.[e]

44 Moses came and recited all the
words of this song in the hearing of the
people, he and Joshua[f] son of Nun.
45 When Moses had finished reciting all
these words to all Israel, 46 he said to
them: "Take to heart all the words that I
am giving in witness against you today;
give them as a command to your children,
so that they may diligently observe all the
words of this law. 47 This is no trifling
matter for you, but rather your very life;
through it you may live long in the land
that you are crossing over the Jordan to
possess."

48 On that very day the LORD addressed Moses as follows: 49 "Ascend this
mountain of the Abarim, Mount Nebo,
which is in the land of Moab, across from
Jericho, and view the land of Canaan,
which I am giving to the Israelites for a
possession; 50 you shall die there on the
mountain that you ascend and shall be
gathered to your kin, as your brother
Aaron died on Mount Hor and was gathered to his kin; 51 because both of you

b Q Ms Gk: MT *nations*   c Q Ms Gk: MT lacks
this line   d Q Ms Gk: MT *his servants*   e Q Ms
Sam Gk Vg: MT *his land his people*   f Sam Gk
Syr Vg: MT *Hoshea*

2 Kings 9.8; 14.26). **32.37–38** Interrogation of
Israel (cf. Isa 40.25–31) or its adversaries (cf. Isa
41.1–4) or both (cf. Isa 43.8–13; 44.6–8). On
mockery of impotent *gods* and those who foolishly
profess them, cf. Judg 10.10–14; 1 Kings 18.27;
Isa 46.1–2; Jer 2.26–28. **32.39** The unanswered queries support the Lord's assertion of exclusive sovereignty, as often in the trial scenes of
Second Isaiah (Isa 40.28–31; 41.4; 43.10–13;
44.6); cf. 4.32–40. *Kill and ... make alive*. Cf.
1 Sam 2.6–8; Tob 13.2; Wis 16.13. *I wound and I
heal*. Cf. Job 5.18; Isa 30.26; Hos 6.1–2; cf. Ex
15.26. **32.40–42** Promissory oath of the Divine
Warrior. *As I live forever*. Cf. Isa 49.18; Jer 22.24;
Ezek 5.11; Zeph 2.9. For the themes and carnage
depicted, cf. Isa 1.24; Jer 46.10; Nah 1.2. Por-
traits of the Lord's retribution against Edom
are noteworthy: Isa 34.5–7; 63.1–6; Ezek
25.12–14. **32.43** Concluding summons of the
heavens to celebrate redemption of the Lord's people (cf. Isa 49.13) forms an inclusion (a repetition
signaling the beginning and end of a unit) with

the appeal of v. 1. Subordination of the *gods*
echoes vv. 8, 37. *Cleanse*, or "purify, expiate"; see 21.8. **32.44–47** Principal strands of
chs. 30–31 especially are woven together in this
conclusion to the "Moab Covenant." For the multiple, overlapping connotations of the leitmotif
word(s), cf. 29.1, 9, 19, 29; 30.1 (*things*), 14; 31.1,
12, 24, 28, 30. **32.44** *Joshua* (or *Hoshea*; see text
note *f*; cf. Num 13.8, 16) is now in place as Moses'
successor; see 31.14–15, 23. **32.47** A final admonition recalls the exhortations of 30.11–20 (cf.
4.26, 40; 6.1–2; Lev 18.5). *No trifling matter*, lit.
"no empty word." *Through it*, lit. "by this word."
32.48–52 Transition to the pentateuchal account
of Moses' death in ch. 34. With this resumptive
paraphrase of Num 27.12–14 (priestly tradition),
cf. 3.23–27. **32.49** *Nebo* is a northern promontory of the *Abarim* range that flanks the eastern
shore of the Dead Sea (cf. 3.17, 27; 34.1; Num
33.47–48). **32.50** For Aaron's death *on Mount
Hor*, see the priestly account of Num 20.22–29;
33.38–39; cf. 10.6. **32.51** *Broke faith*. Cf. Ex

broke faith with me among the Israelites
at the waters of Meribath-kadesh in the
wilderness of Zin, by failing to maintain
my holiness among the Israelites. 52 Although you may view the land from a distance, you shall not enter it—the land that
I am giving to the Israelites."

Moses' Testamentary Blessing

33 This is the blessing with which
Moses, the man of God, blessed
the Israelites before his death. 2 He said:
The LORD came from Sinai,
    and dawned from Seir
        upon us; *g*
he shone forth from Mount
        Paran.
With him were myriads of holy
        ones; *h*
    at his right, a host of his own. *i*
3 Indeed, O favorite among *j*
        peoples,
    all his holy ones were in your
        charge;
    they marched at your heels,

accepted direction from you.
4 Moses charged us with the law,
    as a possession for the assembly
        of Jacob.
5 There arose a king in Jeshurun,
    when the leaders of the people
        assembled—
    the united tribes of Israel.

6 May Reuben live, and not die out,
    even though his numbers
        are few.

7 And this he said of Judah:
    O LORD, give heed to Judah,
    and bring him to his people;
    strengthen his hands for him, *k*
    and be a help against his
        adversaries.

8 And of Levi he said:

g Gk Syr Vg Compare Tg: Heb *upon them*
h Cn Compare Gk Sam Syr Vg: MT *He came from
Ribeboth-kodesh,*   *i* Cn Compare Gk: meaning of
Heb uncertain   *j* Or *O lover of the*   *k* Cn: Heb
with his hands he contended

17.1–7; Ps 106.32; Num 20.1–13 (priestly tradition). *Meribath-kadesh in the wilderness of Zin* is apparently identical with the oasis of Kadesh-barnea
in northern Sinai (see note on 1.2; cf. Josh
15.1–3; Ezek 47.19; 48.28). **33.1** The last of the book's four editorial
headings (cf. 1.1–5; 4.44–49; 29.1) anticipates
ch. 34 while specifically introducing Moses' oracular benedictions on the assembled tribes. (For
the genre of testamentary blessings, cf. Gen
27.27–29; 49.1–28.) On the prophetic appellation *the man of God*, also used of Moses in Josh
14.6; Ps 90 (heading), cf., e.g., Judg 13.6, 8;
1 Sam 2.27; 9.6–9; 1 Kings 12.22; 13.1; 17.8.
33.2–29 The composition, which may ultimately
derive from a liturgical celebration of the Israelite
confederacy, perhaps during the era of Saulide
rule (ca. 1000 B.C.E.), is a collocation of tribal
epigrams set within the frame of a victory
hymn (vv. 2–5, 26–29). **33.2–5** Hymnic poem.
33.2–3 The introit rehearses the Lord's
epiphany, advancing into Canaan from *Sinai*
across the southeastern highlands of Edom (*Seir,
Mount Paran*; see 1.2), accompanied by a vast
heavenly cohort and its mundane counterpart, Israel's tribal militia. Variations on this hymnal epic
theme are attested also in Judg 5.4–5; Ps 68.7–8,
17; Hab 3.3–7; cf. Ex 15.13–18. *Dawned, shown
forth* suggest a solar epiphany: cf. Pss 50.1–2;
80.1–2; 94.1; Job 37.15 (lightning). *Myriads of holy
ones, host.* Cf. Num 10.36; 1 Kings 22.19; Pss
68.17; 89.7; Zech 14.5; cf. also Mt 26.53; Rev

5.11. **33.4–5** Though formed in response to divine initiative, the confederation of Jacob (Israel)
(*assembly*; cf. Neh 5.7; *united tribes*) was formally
constituted through Moses' promulgation of law
(Hebrew *torah*; see 4.44). **33.5** *There arose a king*
is perhaps an oblique reference to inauguration
of monarchical governance under Saul (cf. 1 Sam
10.20–25; 11.14–15). The phrase could also be
rendered "let there be a king" or "he became
king"; the latter has traditionally been understood
to mean either the Lord's (so, e.g., RSV; cf. Ex
15.18; Num 23.21; Judg 8.23; Isa 33.17, 22) or
Moses' exaltation to sovereignty over tribal Israel
(cf. Ex 14.31; 34.10). *Jeshurun.* See note on
32.15. **33.6–25** Benedictory pronouncements
about or petitions on behalf of the individual
tribes. Among the traditional twelve tribes, only
Simeon is conspicuously missing; cf., e.g., Gen
35.23; 49.5; Ex 1.2. Cf. Josh 19.1–9. **33.6** Attri-
tion of *Reuben* may be the outcome of warfare
with its Transjordanian neighbors during the
eleventh century B.C.E. (cf. 3.12, 16; Judg
10.7–11.33; 1 Sam 10.27–11.11). **33.7** The petition on behalf of *Judah* perhaps alludes to Philistine hegemony in the central hill country of
Palestine after the defeat of Saul (cf. 1 Sam 31).
33.8–11 This expansive encomium on *Levi* suggests the charter of a clerical guild; see 10.8–9;
18.1–8. *Thummim* and *Urim*, sacred lots; cf. Ex
28.30; Lev 8.8; 1 Sam 14.41–42. The *loyal one* is
presumably Moses himself, *tested at Massah* and

Give to Levi[l] your Thummim,
  and your Urim to your
    loyal one,
whom you tested at Massah,
  with whom you contended at
    the waters of Meribah;
9 who said of his father and
    mother,
  "I regard them not";
he ignored his kin,
  and did not acknowledge his
    children.
For they observed your word,
  and kept your covenant.
10 They teach Jacob your
    ordinances,
  and Israel your law;
they place incense before you,
  and whole burnt offerings on
    your altar.
11 Bless, O Lord, his substance,
  and accept the work of his
    hands;
crush the loins of his adversaries,
  of those that hate him, so that
    they do not rise again.

12 Of Benjamin he said:
The beloved of the Lord rests in
    safety—
  the High God[m] surrounds him all
    day long—
  the beloved[n] rests between his
    shoulders.

13 And of Joseph he said:
Blessed by the Lord be his land,
  with the choice gifts of heaven
    above,
  and of the deep that lies
    beneath;

14 with the choice fruits of the sun,
  and the rich yield of the
    months;
15 with the finest produce of the
    ancient mountains,
  and the abundance of the
    everlasting hills;
16 with the choice gifts of the earth
    and its fullness,
  and the favor of the one who
    dwells on Sinai.[o]
Let these come on the head of
    Joseph,
  on the brow of the prince
    among his brothers.
17 A firstborn[p] bull—majesty is his!
  His horns are the horns of a
    wild ox;
with them he gores the peoples,
  driving them to[q] the ends of
    the earth;
such are the myriads of Ephraim,
  such the thousands of
    Manasseh.

18 And of Zebulun he said:
Rejoice, Zebulun, in your
    going out;
  and Issachar, in your tents.
19 They call peoples to the
    mountain;
there they offer the right
    sacrifices;
for they suck the affluence of the
    seas
  and the hidden treasures of the
    sand.

l Q Ms Gk: MT lacks *Give to Levi*   *m* Heb *above him*   *n* Heb *he*   *o* Cn: Heb *in the bush*   *p* Q Ms Gk Syr Vg: MT *His firstborn*   *q* Cn: Heb *the peoples, together*

Meribah; cf. 6.16; 9.22; 32.51; Ex 17.1–7; Num 20.1–13 (cf. also 1 Sam 2.27–28; Pss 77.20; 99.6; Sir 45.1–5). **33.9** On the declaration *I regard them not*, cf. Ex 32.25–29; cf. also Lk 14.26. **33.10** *Teach*, or "interpret for" (cognate with the Hebrew noun *torah*); cf. 17.10–11; cf. Lev 10.10–11; 2 Kings 17.27–28; Jer 18.18; Ezek 7.26; Hos 4.6; Mic 3.11; Mal 2.4–9. **33.12** This cryptic saying may refer to the location of *Benjamin*'s tribal allotment in the central Palestinian hill country between the major sanctuaries of Bethel and Jerusalem; cf. Josh 18.11–28. *Beloved of the Lord*. Cf. 2 Sam 12.25 (Solomon); Jer 11.15 (Israel). *Rests* (or "tents") *in safety*. Cf. v. 28; 12.10; cf. Prov 1.33; 2.21. *The High God*, Hebrew *'Alu* (also in 1 Sam 2.10), a variant form of the divine appel-

lation *Elyon*; see 32.8. **33.13–17** This expansive encomium indicates the prominence of *Joseph* among the tribes. *Heaven, deep*. See Gen 7.11; 8.2; 49.25; cf. Ps 107.26; Prov 8.27. **33.15** *Mountains, hills*. Cf. Gen 49.26; Hab 3.6. **33.16** *Who dwells* (or "tabernacles") *on Sinai*; cf. Ex 24.16. **33.17** *Horns of a wild ox*. Cf. Num 23.22; 24.8. *Ephraim, Manasseh*. Cf. 3.13–14. **33.18–19** *Zebulun* and *Issachar* are linked as neighboring tribes occupying the hills of southern Galilee and the fertile Esdraelon plain; cf. Josh 19.10–23. **33.19** The *mountain* is probably Tabor, in the central Esdraelon (cf. Judg 4.6, 12–14), though Mount Carmel on the coast is also possible. *Seas* should mean the Mediterranean and the Sea of Galilee (Chinnereth); cf. Gen 49.13.

20 And of Gad he said:
  Blessed be the enlargement
    of Gad!
  Gad lives like a lion;
  he tears at arm and scalp.
21 He chose the best for himself,
    for there a commander's
      allotment was reserved;
  he came at the head of the
    people,
  he executed the justice of the
    LORD,
  and his ordinances for Israel.

22 And of Dan he said:
  Dan is a lion's whelp
    that leaps forth from Bashan.

23 And of Naphtali he said:
  O Naphtali, sated with favor,
  full of the blessing of the
    LORD,
  possess the west and the
    south.

24 And of Asher he said:
  Most blessed of sons be Asher;
  may he be the favorite of his
    brothers,
  and may he dip his foot in oil.
25 Your bars are iron and bronze;
    and as your days, so is your
      strength.

26 There is none like God,
      O Jeshurun,
  who rides through the heavens
    to your help,
  majestic through the skies.
27 He subdues the ancient gods,*r*
    shatters*s* the forces of old;*t*
  he drove out the enemy
    before you,
  and said, "Destroy!"
28 So Israel lives in safety,
    untroubled is Jacob's abode*u*
  in a land of grain and wine,
  where the heavens drop
    down dew.
29 Happy are you, O Israel! Who is
      like you,
  a people saved by the LORD,
  the shield of your help,
  and the sword of your triumph!
  Your enemies shall come fawning
    to you,
  and you shall tread on their
    backs.

Moses' Departure and Epitaph

34 Then Moses went up from the plains of Moab to Mount Nebo, to the top of Pisgah, which is opposite Jeri-

r Or *The eternal God is a dwelling place*
s Cn: Heb *from underneath*   t Or *the everlasting
arms*   u Or *fountain*

33.20–21 Territorial expansion of *Gad* in the Transjordan contrasts sharply with Reuben's diminished condition (v. 6). **33.21** *Chose the best.* See Num 32.1–5. *Commander's allotment* was understood in early rabbinic tradition to refer to Moses' burial place; Mahanaim, which served as royal refuge for Ishbaal after the death of his father, Saul, may be a more likely possibility (cf. 2 Sam 2.8–10). On Gad's military prowess (*like a lion*, v. 18; *head of the people*), cf. 3.18–20; Josh 1.12–14; 1 Chr 12.8–15. *Executed . . . justice* is another royal theme. Cf. 2 Sam 8.15 (David); Ps 72.1–4; Jer 22.15–16; 23.5–6. **33.22** Judah receives the epithet *lion's whelp* in Gen 49.9. *Bashan.* See note on 3.1. On *Dan's* northern provenance, cf. 34.1; Josh 19.47; Judg 18. **33.23** *Naphtali*, situated in the Galilean highlands, is encouraged to expand its holdings. **33.24–25** The territory of *Asher* on the slopes of western Galilee is renowned for its orchards that yielded fine-quality olive *oil.* **33.25** Metallic *bars* perhaps alludes to well-fortified settlements. **33.26–29** The postlude resumes the hymnal epic themes of the Lord's advent and incomparability as warrior, em-powering Israel to achieve victories against its enemies. Cf. 3.24; 4.32–40. **33.26** *Jeshurun.* See note on 32.15. *Who rides*, on the cloud-chariot of the Divine Warrior; cf. Isa 19.1; Pss 18.10; 68.4, 33; 104.3. **33.27** On the theme of the Lord's triumph over otiose gods of Canaan (*ancient gods, forces of old*), cf., e.g., 7.4, 25; Ex 23.23–24; 1 Sam 5.1–7; 2 Sam 7.22–24; Isa 51.9–10. **33.28–29** Cf. 7.12–24; Gen 27.28. **33.29** *Shield of your help.* Cf. Gen 15.1; 2 Sam 22.3; Pss 28.7; 119.114.

34.1–12 This final act of Moses' career, concluding the broad pentateuchal story of Israel's formation, seems perfunctory and impassive in the telling here. That may be the result of editorial design, abridging the extant traditions (some of which may resurface later in Jewish folklore; cf. *Midrash Rabbah*). What took precedence in Israel's memory was not the grave site of the great leader (whether secret or simply forgotten) but his legacy of torah (29.29; 31.9–13; 33.4, 10) and the superlative character of his leadership, handed on through Joshua, even if only in diminished form (vv. 9–12; cf. Josh 1.1–9). **34.1–3** A

cho, and the LORD showed him the whole
land: Gilead as far as Dan, 2 all Naphtali,
the land of Ephraim and Manasseh, all
the land of Judah as far as the Western
Sea, 3 the Negeb, and the Plain—that is,
the valley of Jericho, the city of palm trees
—as far as Zoar. 4 The LORD said to him,
"This is the land of which I swore to Abraham, to Isaac, and to Jacob, saying, 'I will
give it to your descendants'; I have let you
see it with your eyes, but you shall not
cross over there." 5 Then Moses, the servant of the LORD, died there in the land of
Moab, at the LORD's command. 6 He was
buried in a valley in the land of Moab,
opposite Beth-peor, but no one knows his
burial place to this day. 7 Moses was one
hundred twenty years old when he died;
his sight was unimpaired and his vigor

had not abated. 8 The Israelites wept for
Moses in the plains of Moab thirty days;
then the period of mourning for Moses
was ended.

9 Joshua son of Nun was full of the
spirit of wisdom, because Moses had laid
his hands on him; and the Israelites
obeyed him, doing as the LORD had commanded Moses.

10 Never since has there arisen a
prophet in Israel like Moses, whom the
LORD knew face to face. 11 He was un-
equaled for all the signs and wonders that
the LORD sent him to perform in the land
of Egypt, against Pharaoh and all his servants and his entire land, 12 and for all the
mighty deeds and all the terrifying displays of power that Moses performed in
the sight of all Israel.

---

panoramic view of the promised land. *Plains of
Moab to Mount Nebo.* Cf. 32.49; Num 22.1. *Pisgah.*
See 3.17. The view northward extends beyond
Gilead (see 2.36) to Danite territory on the lower
slopes of Mount Hermon (see 3.8; 33.22).
34.2 *Western Sea.* See 11.24.   **34.3** *Negeb.* See
1.7. *Plain,* the basin of the Dead Sea, extending
from *Jericho* in the northwest to *Zoar* in the southeast (cf. Gen 13.10–11; 14.2, 8).   **34.4** Cf. 1.8;
3.27.   **34.5–8** Death, burial, and mourning for
Moses. *Servant of the LORD.* Cf. Ex 14.31; Num
12.7–8; Josh 1.1–2, 7, 13, 15; 1 Kings 8.53, 56;
Mal 4.4. *Valley in the land of Moab, opposite Beth-
peor.* See 3.29.   **34.7** On Moses' ripe old age,
see 31.2; cf. this, together with 1.31, to the notice
on Aaron's death report in Num 33.38–39.

34.8 *Thirty days* of mourning for a deceased
leader was apparently traditional; cf. Num
20.29.   **34.9** Joshua's initial exaltation. *Full of the
spirit of wisdom.* Cf. Ex 28.3; 35.31; 31.3; Num
27.18–23.   **34.10–12** The epitaph affirms, from
an apparent distance, the preeminence of Moses'
work as deliverer; it serves as a colophon to
the completed Pentateuch (cf. 18.15–18; Mal
4.4–5).   **34.10** *Face to face* indicates God's intimate knowledge of Moses: cf. 5.4; Ex 33.11; Num
12.8 (lit. "mouth to mouth"); Sir 45.5.   **34.11**
On *Signs and wonders,* see, e.g., Ex 7.8–12.
34.12 *Mighty deeds, terrifying displays of power.* Moses performed God's own work; cf. 4.34, 37; 26.8;
Ps 77.11–15; see also Ex 4.16, 21; 7.1; 34.10.

JOSHUA

THE BOOK OF JOSHUA is eloquent testimony to the grace and power of Yahweh, whom ancient Israel acknowledged to be sovereign Lord of all. ("Yahweh" is the personal name of the God of Israel, for which Jewish tradition respectfully substitutes the title "LORD.") This book tells the story of the Israelites who, under Joshua's leadership and with benefit of divine intervention, crossed the Jordan River to take control of the land of Canaan. The land was the Lord's gift, as promised to the ancestors in the stories of Gen 12–50, to be held in return for the promise of service to the divine Lord.

Structure

The body of the book shows two main divisions, the "conquest" of the land (chs. 6–12) and its "settlement," the apportionment and redistribution of the land by sacred lot to the tribes of Israel (chs. 13–19). This body of the book is bracketed by specially chosen introductory and concluding material (chs. 1–5 and 20–24, respectively).

Content and Message

At the outset Israel is depicted as a mighty, populous twelve-tribe army. The people are encamped east of the Jordan River in a region known as the "Plains of Moab." There, from a position directly overlooking the northern end of the Dead Sea and the southern Jordan Valley, one commands a sweeping view of the western hill country, the land toward which Moses had led the people in their wanderings for forty years since departure from Mount Sinai/Horeb. In the concluding chapter, Joshua assembles all the tribes of Israel at the city of Shechem in the heart of the northcentral hill country. There Joshua presides at a covenant ceremony in which ancestral gods are repudiated and allegiance to Yahweh alone is affirmed.

Between those first and final chapters, discerning readers will note a tension between sweeping editorial claims for military conquest of "all" the land (11.16, 23) and the few stories of actual warfare (6.1–11.15). To these stories is prefixed a leisurely account of preparations for entrance into the land (ch. 1), the reconnaissance of Jericho (ch. 2), the crossing of the Jordan River and establishment of the camp and religious sanctuary at Gilgal (chs. 3–4), and finally circumcision of all the males (5.2–9) and celebration of the first Passover west of the Jordan (5.10–12). The narrator explains that the entire exodus generation had died out and the rite of circumcision was not practiced during the wilderness wanderings. With the circumcision of the militiamen and celebration of the Passover, all was at last in readiness for the warfare, as signaled by Joshua's encounter, in a vision, with the heavenly commander (5.13–15). In sum, the so-called conquest was interpreted as God's enabling action, for which Israel could claim no credit, graciously reestablishing the ancient people in their homeland.

Throughout these introductory chapters, Israel takes its orders from Joshua, who gets his orders directly from Yahweh. In Canaan Israel is supposed to live as a model theocracy, that is, a people governed directly by the divine Lord.

Concluding chapters share the same perspective. To facilitate justice in cases of homicide while at the same time curbing the practice of blood vengeance within Israel, asylum towns ("cities of refuge") are designated, three on each side of the Jordan (ch. 20). These and other towns are designated in each of the tribes to provide residential and grazing rights for the priestly tribe of Levi (ch. 21).

The Levites are thus dispersed throughout the territorial tribes. It was their responsibility to teach the distinctive ethic, represented by the Decalogue, for example, that shaped the common allegiance of the tribes. That there were deep rifts and rivalries, however, between priestly factions is vividly displayed when the story line resumes. The building of an altar "near the Jordan" (ch. 22) nearly results in intertribal warfare. This is precisely the reverse of intentions for Gilgal near the Jordan at the outset of the era! Joshua's concluding address spirals downward to a stern warning (ch. 23), followed by a great covenanting ceremony at Shechem (ch. 24). The stage is at last set for the story of Israel's life in the land from start (Judges) to finish (2 Kings).

Canonical Context, Sources, and Redaction

A widely accepted hypothesis regards the book of Joshua as part of a historical work that includes also the books of Judges, 1 and 2 Samuel, and 1 and 2 Kings, with the book of Deuteronomy as theological preface or introduction—thus a "Deuteronomistic History." The main edition of the work probably comes from the reign of the reforming King Josiah and the discovery of a long lost Book of the Law during repairs at the Jerusalem temple (ca. 622 B.C.E.; see 2 Kings 22–23). For the era of Joshua, the historian(s) had a collection of stories, lists, and poetic fragments (all of varying antiquity) which they used to present Joshua as military ideal for the Jerusalem king. But Josiah's successes were short-lived. Babylonian armies destroyed Jerusalem in 587 B.C.E., and the History was updated for the last time. The hypothesis may be summarized in the following symbols. *Dtn* stands for Josiah's "Book of the Law," nuclear contents of the canonical book of Deuteronomy (4.44–30.20). Its roots are traceable to older, reform-minded Levites claiming authority by descent from Moses. *Dtr 1* is the bulk of canonical Deut 4.44–2 Kings from the era of King Josiah. It was produced by a historian of the monarchy in Levitical circles close to the Jerusalem throne. *Dtr 2* is the final edition, supplemented by a "loyal opposition," so as to be, ironically, supportive of life in exile.

The details given in stories and archival materials taken up in Joshua may have varying degrees of historicity. The stories were told and the lists preserved to serve the pedagogical interests of earlier Levitical teachers and later editors. Archaeological data frequently provide illustrative light, but rarely decisive evidence. When studied with the aid of social science perspectives, the texts and excavation data combine to yield a clearer picture of the emergence of ancient Israel as Yahweh's alternative kingdom, wherein Joshua was remembered as playing a decisive role, originally as much "diplomatic," it now appears, as military.
Robert G. Boling

God's Commission to Joshua

1 After the death of Moses the servant of the LORD, the LORD spoke to Joshua son of Nun, Moses' assistant, saying, 2 "My servant Moses is dead. Now proceed to cross the Jordan, you and all this people, into the land that I am giving to them, to the Israelites. 3 Every place that the sole of your foot will tread upon I have given to you, as I promised to Moses. 4 From the wilderness and the Lebanon as far as the great river, the river Euphrates, all the land of the Hittites, to the Great Sea in the west shall be your territory. 5 No one shall be able to stand against you all the days of your life. As I was with Moses, so I will be with you; I will not fail you or forsake you. 6 Be strong and courageous; for you shall put this people in possession of the land that I swore to their ancestors to give them. 7 Only be strong and very courageous, being careful to act in accordance with all the law that my servant Moses commanded you; do not turn from it to the right hand or to the left, so that you may be successful wherever you go. 8 This book of the law shall not depart out of your mouth; you shall meditate on it day and night, so that you may be careful to act in accordance with all that is written in it. For then you shall make your way prosperous, and then you shall be successful. 9 I hereby command you: Be strong and courageous; do not be frightened or dismayed, for the LORD your God is with you wherever you go."

10 Then Joshua commanded the officers of the people, 11 "Pass through the

1.1–11 God's commission to Joshua. Vv. 1–9 emphasize qualities required of Joshua and leadership he must provide in taking over the land. The Lord speaks as commander in chief to his field commander Joshua, who in turn is introduced in terms appropriate as a role model in military matters for later kings. **1.1** Action begins *after the death of Moses,* who had been denied entrance into the land (Num 20.12). *Assistant* ("minister" in older translations), better "lieutenant" in this context. **1.4** Canaan lay west of the Jordan, *the great river,* stretching from the *wilderness* (possibly the southern Negeb desert) to a line running east from Lebanon's mountains to the upper Euphrates. The latter describes the southeastern portion of the once-mighty empire of the *Hittites.* **1.6** *Strong and courageous* (repeated in vv. 7, 9, 18). Cf. Deut 31.7, 23. The rhetoric of speeches in Joshua frequently echoes Deuteronomy. **1.8** *This book of the law* (cf. 2 Kings 22.8) refers to an earlier edition of Deuteronomy (hypothetical Dtn; see Introduction) containing legal lore such as is found in Deut 12–28. As in Deuteronomy, so also here is emphasized how important the keeping of this teaching is for continuing life in the promised land. **1.11** *In three days,*

camp, and command the people: 'Prepare your provisions; for in three days you are to cross over the Jordan, to go in to take possession of the land that the LORD your God gives you to possess.' "

Address to the Transjordanian Tribes

12 To the Reubenites, the Gadites, and the half-tribe of Manasseh Joshua said, 13 "Remember the word that Moses the servant of the LORD commanded you, saying, 'The LORD your God is providing you a place of rest, and will give you this land.' 14 Your wives, your little ones, and your livestock shall remain in the land that Moses gave you beyond the Jordan. But all the warriors among you shall cross over armed before your kindred and shall help them, 15 until the LORD gives rest to your kindred as well as to you, and they too take possession of the land that the LORD your God is giving them. Then you shall return to your own land and take possession of it, the land that Moses the servant of the LORD gave you beyond the Jordan to the east."

16 They answered Joshua: "All that you have commanded us we will do, and wherever you send us we will go. 17 Just as we obeyed Moses in all things, so we will obey you. Only may the LORD your God be with you, as he was with Moses! 18 Whoever rebels against your orders and disobeys your words, whatever you com-

mand, shall be put to death. Only be strong and courageous."

Spies Sent to Jericho

2 Then Joshua son of Nun sent two men secretly from Shittim as spies, saying, "Go, view the land, especially Jericho." So they went, and entered the house of a prostitute whose name was Rahab, and spent the night there. 2 The king of Jericho was told, "Some Israelites have come here tonight to search out the land." 3 Then the king of Jericho sent orders to Rahab, "Bring out the men who have come to you, who entered your house, for they have come only to search out the whole land." 4 But the woman took the two men and hid them. Then she said, "True, the men came to me, but I did not know where they came from. 5 And when it was time to close the gate at dark, the men went out. Where the men went I do not know. Pursue them quickly, for you can overtake them." 6 She had, however, brought them up to the roof and hidden them with the stalks of flax that she had laid out on the roof. 7 So the men pursued them on the way to the Jordan as far as the fords. As soon as the pursuers had gone out, the gate was shut.

8 Before they went to sleep, she came up to them on the roof 9 and said to the men: "I know that the LORD has given you the land, and that dread of you has fallen

---

i.e., "the day after tomorrow," reflects liturgical celebration and dramatic reenactment.
1.12–18 It was in territory east of the Jordan, settled by Reuben, Gad, and half of the tribe of Manasseh, that the followers of Moses scored their first successes. The Transjordanian militiamen are now commanded to participate in seizure of land in Canaan, where the other half of Manasseh will settle along with the remainder of the territorial tribes. **1.16–18** The Transjordanian tribes here respond eagerly and exhort Joshua in words echoing his own usage in vv. 7, 9. Their eagerness will turn to reluctance and suspicion in ch. 22 (dispute over an altar near the Jordan), which is a companion framework piece.
2.1–24 This story of spies sent to *view the land* (v. 1), their visit to Rahab's house, her protection of them, and their promise of future protection for her was secondarily connected with Jericho. The story abruptly resumes (6.22–25) after the capture of Jericho. **2.1–3** *Jericho* is named three times in three verses, but not again in this story.

The location of OT Jericho is the heavily excavated mound Tell es-Sultan, some twenty-three miles east of Jerusalem. The only major west-bank oasis in the southern half of the Jordan Valley, Jericho had for millennia controlled several fords and routes of access to the hill country. Archaeology has shown that by the late thirteenth and early twelfth centuries B.C.E. Jericho had fallen on hard times, to become at most a small unfortified village sitting atop the imposing ruins of the formerly walled town. **2.1** *Shittim*, in Hebrew "Acacias." Trees characteristic of desert terrain gave this name to the final desert encampment (Num 25.1) in the eastern Jordan Valley. Other stories of *spies* are found in Num 13; Josh 7.2–5; Judg 18.2–10. *Rahab* is later reckoned among the ancestors of Jesus (Mt 1.5), lauded as an example of living faith (Heb 11.31), and justified by her works (Jas 2.25). Here she uses rhetoric characteristic of Deuteronomy. **2.9** *Inhabitants*, better understood as "rulers" in this passage, represented in negotiations by one of their number.

on us, and that all the inhabitants of the land melt in fear before you. 10 For we have heard how the LORD dried up the water of the Red Sea[a] before you when you came out of Egypt, and what you did to the two kings of the Amorites that were beyond the Jordan, to Sihon and Og, whom you utterly destroyed. 11 As soon as we heard it, our hearts melted, and there was no courage left in any of us because of you. The LORD your God is indeed God in heaven above and on earth below. 12 Now then, since I have dealt kindly with you, swear to me by the LORD that you in turn will deal kindly with my family. Give me a sign of good faith 13 that you will spare my father and mother, my brothers and sisters, and all who belong to them, and deliver our lives from death." 14 The men said to her, "Our life for yours! If you do not tell this business of ours, then we will deal kindly and faithfully with you when the LORD gives us the land."

15 Then she let them down by a rope through the window, for her house was on the outer side of the city wall and she resided within the wall itself. 16 She said to them, "Go toward the hill country, so that the pursuers may not come upon you. Hide yourselves there three days, until the pursuers have returned; then afterward you may go your way." 17 The men said to her, "We will be released from this oath that you have made us swear to you 18 if we invade the land and you do not tie this crimson cord in the window through which you let us down, and you do not gather into your house your father and mother, your brothers, and all your family. 19 If any of you go out of the doors of your house into the street, they shall be responsible for their own death, and we shall be innocent; but if a hand is laid upon any who are with you in the house, we shall bear the responsibility for their death. 20 But if you tell this business of ours, then we shall be released from this oath that you made us swear to you." 21 She said, "According to your words, so be it." She sent them away and they departed. Then she tied the crimson cord in the window.

22 They departed and went into the hill country and stayed there three days, until the pursuers returned. The pursuers had searched all along the way and found nothing. 23 Then the two men came down again from the hill country. They crossed over, came to Joshua son of Nun, and told him all that had happened to them. 24 They said to Joshua, "Truly the LORD has given all the land into our hands; moreover all the inhabitants of the land melt in fear before us."

Israel Crosses the Jordan

3 Early in the morning Joshua rose and set out from Shittim with all the Israelites, and they came to the Jordan. They camped there before crossing over. 2 At the end of three days the officers went through the camp 3 and commanded the people, "When you see the ark of the covenant of the LORD your God being car-

a Or Sea of Reeds

See Num. 10.35f

2.10 The kingdoms of *Sihon and Og*, in central and northern Transjordan, had been conquered under Moses' leadership (Num 21; Deut 1–2); they are the only kings mentioned by name in Josh 1–9. **2.12** *Deal kindly*, i.e., show *chesed*. The Hebrew word stands for the exercise of responsible caring such as grounds a covenant relationship. **2.15** That *she resided within the wall* suggests defensive fortifications of the casemate type, parallel walls divided by cross walls creating chambers that might be used for residence. This may be a standard narrative motif; no such wall system has been found at Tell es-Sultan in Middle or Late Bronze levels (ca. 1900–1200 B.C.E.). **2.16** *Toward the hill country*. Having sent the posse eastward toward the river, Rahab directs the spies westward into the high country to hide out for a few days. Clearly intended as a prime example of negotiating and keeping treaty faith, the story is flatly at odds with the authoritative teaching (Deut 20.10–20). **2.24** *All the land, all the inhabitants*. At Rahab's place the spies found their entire mission crowned with success.

3.1–17 The opening of the waters. The "invasion" of the promised land is told in ways suggestive of a solemn liturgical procession and probably reflects dramatic reenactments in festival celebrations at Gilgal. Israelites in a later time would be exhorted to "remember ... what happened from Shittim to Gilgal" (Mic 6.5). **3.2** *Three days*, the same time interval as in the spy story (2.22). **3.3** *The ark of the covenant* contained the tablets of the Sinai covenant and was conceptualized as the portable throne of the Divine Sovereign, the place of most reliable oracle seeking. The *levitical priests* here comprise a militant cadre

ried by the levitical priests, then you shall set out from your place. Follow it, 4 so that you may know the way you should go, for you have not passed this way before. Yet there shall be a space between you and it, a distance of about two thousand cubits; do not come any nearer to it." 5 Then Joshua said to the people, "Sanctify yourselves; for tomorrow the LORD will do wonders among you." 6 To the priests Joshua said, "Take up the ark of the covenant, and pass on in front of the people." So they took up the ark of the covenant and went in front of the people.

7 The LORD said to Joshua, "This day I will begin to exalt you in the sight of all Israel, so that they may know that I will be with you as I was with Moses. 8 You are the one who shall command the priests who bear the ark of the covenant, 'When you come to the edge of the waters of the Jordan, you shall stand still in the Jordan.' " 9 Joshua then said to the Israelites, "Draw near and hear the words of the LORD your God." 10 Joshua said, "By this you shall know that among you is the living God who without fail will drive out from before you the Canaanites, Hittites, Hivites, Perizzites, Girgashites, Amorites, and Jebusites: 11 the ark of the covenant of the Lord of all the earth is going to pass before you into the Jordan. 12 So now select twelve men from the tribes of Israel, one from each tribe. 13 When the soles of

the feet of the priests who bear the ark of the LORD, the Lord of all the earth, rest in the waters of the Jordan, the waters of the Jordan flowing from above shall be cut off; they shall stand in a single heap."

14 When the people set out from their tents to cross over the Jordan, the priests bearing the ark of the covenant were in front of the people. 15 Now the Jordan overflows all its banks throughout the time of harvest. So when those who bore the ark had come to the Jordan, and the feet of the priests bearing the ark were dipped in the edge of the water, 16 the waters flowing from above stood still, rising up in a single heap far off at Adam, the city that is beside Zarethan, while those flowing toward the sea of the Arabah, the Dead Sea,b were wholly cut off. Then the people crossed over opposite Jericho. 17 While all Israel were crossing over on dry ground, the priests who bore the ark of the covenant of the LORD stood on dry ground in the middle of the Jordan, until the entire nation finished crossing over the Jordan.

Israel at Gilgal

4 When the entire nation had finished crossing over the Jordan, the LORD said to Joshua: 2 "Select twelve men from

b Heb Salt Sea

having responsibility for transport and care of the sacred ark. **3.4** *Two thousand cubits*, roughly one kilometer. **3.5** *Sanctify yourselves*. A variety of prohibitions and ritual purifications were in force as preparation for warfare under Yahweh's command (Deut 20.1–9; 1 Sam 21.4–5). **3.6** The story evokes the image of a commander reviewing troops. **3.7–8** Joshua hears both promise (cf. Ex 3.12) and command. **3.10** *The living God*, better "El the Living" as the descriptive name of the ancestors' God. That there are seven peoples named is an aid to memory; there are twenty-one such lists in the OT, more or less stereotyped. Cf., on the other hand, the list of thirty-one conquered kings in 12.9–24. **3.12** *Twelve ... one from each tribe*, apparently counting two "Joseph" tribes (Ephraim and Manasseh) but not Levi. **3.13–17** The crossing is told as providential. The normally fordable river was at flood stage, but temporarily dammed, as is known to happen there by collapse of soft limestone banks. **3.16** *Adam ... Zarethan*, Tell ed-Damiyeh (twenty-seven kilometers north of Jericho) and Tell es-

Saidiyeh (eighteen kilometers farther north). **3.17** *Middle of the Jordan*. This precise specification seems to have structural significance in relation to the story in 22.10–34.

4.1–5.12 Israel at Gilgal; establishing a foothold. *Gilgal* (v. 19) was a major political and religious center in the premonarchical period; it was where Saul was made king (1 Sam 11.15) and where David's relations with Judah were later repaired (2 Sam 19.15, 40). Gilgal flourished also in the eighth century B.C.E. when it was roundly denounced by prophets (Hos 4.15; 9.15; 12.11; Am 4.4; 5.5). It is perhaps to be identified with the very small site Khirbet el-Mefjir, about one mile north of OT Jericho. **4.1–5.1** These verses appear to describe two sets of twelve stones. The first set, carried from the east bank to midstream, would be underwater and not visible but would provide firm footing for Levites carrying the sacred ark. The second set, taken from midstream, would become a memorial to the crossing, that is, the shrine at Gilgal, which means "Circle." The story highlights responsibilities of the custodians

the people, one from each tribe, 3 and command them, 'Take twelve stones from here out of the middle of the Jordan, from the place where the priests' feet stood, carry them over with you, and lay them down in the place where you camp tonight.'" 4 Then Joshua summoned the twelve men from the Israelites, whom he had appointed, one from each tribe. 5 Joshua said to them, "Pass on before the ark of the LORD your God into the middle of the Jordan, and each of you take up a stone on his shoulder, one for each of the tribes of the Israelites, 6 so that this may be a sign among you. When your children ask in time to come, 'What do those stones mean to you?' 7 then you shall tell them that the waters of the Jordan were cut off in front of the ark of the covenant of the LORD. When it crossed over the Jordan, the waters of the Jordan were cut off. So these stones shall be to the Israelites a memorial forever."

8 The Israelites did as Joshua commanded. They took up twelve stones out of the middle of the Jordan, according to the number of the tribes of the Israelites, as the LORD told Joshua, carried them over with them to the place where they camped, and laid them down there. 9 (Joshua set up twelve stones in the middle of the Jordan, in the place where the feet of the priests bearing the ark of the covenant had stood; and they are there to this day.)

10 The priests who bore the ark remained standing in the middle of the Jordan, until everything was finished that the LORD commanded Joshua to tell the people, according to all that Moses had commanded Joshua. The people crossed over in haste. 11 As soon as all the people had finished crossing over, the ark of the LORD, and the priests, crossed over in front of the people. 12 The Reubenites, the Gadites, and the half-tribe of Manasseh crossed over armed before the Israelites, as Moses had ordered them. 13 About forty thousand armed for war crossed

over before the LORD to the plains of Jericho for battle.

14 On that day the LORD exalted Joshua in the sight of all Israel; and they stood in awe of him, as they had stood in awe of Moses, all the days of his life.

15 The LORD said to Joshua, 16 "Command the priests who bear the ark of the covenant,c to come up out of the Jordan." 17 Joshua therefore commanded the priests, "Come up out of the Jordan." 18 When the priests bearing the ark of the covenant of the LORD came up from the middle of the Jordan, and the soles of the priests' feet touched dry ground, the waters of the Jordan returned to their place and overflowed all its banks, as before.

19 The people came up out of the Jordan on the tenth day of the first month, and they camped in Gilgal on the east border of Jericho. 20 Those twelve stones, which they had taken out of the Jordan, Joshua set up in Gilgal, 21 saying to the Israelites, "When your children ask their parents in time to come, 'What do these stones mean?' 22 then you shall let your children know, 'Israel crossed over the Jordan here on dry ground.' 23 For the LORD your God dried up the waters of the Jordan for you until you crossed over, as the LORD your God did to the Red Sea,d which he dried up for us until we crossed over, 24 so that all the peoples of the earth may know that the hand of the LORD is mighty, and so that you may fear the LORD your God forever."

5 When all the kings of the Amorites beyond the Jordan to the west, and all the kings of the Canaanites by the sea, heard that the LORD had dried up the waters of the Jordan for the Israelites until they had crossed over, their hearts melted, and there was no longer any spirit in them, because of the Israelites.

c Or treaty, or testimony; Heb eduth   d Or Sea of Reeds

---

of the ark of the covenant. **4.12** As in ch. 1, the Transjordanian tribes are the only ones specified. **4.13** *Forty thousand*, better "forty muster units" (approximating perhaps four hundred as a more probable total). **4.19** *The first month*, Abib, i.e., March-April, later called Nisan. **4.24** This etiological story has dual purpose: that *all peoples*

of the earth will acknowledge the power of Yahweh and that Israel's descendants *fear* (hold in reverent awe) *the LORD . . . forever*. **5.1** Validity of the teaching is illustrated by reaction of neighboring *kings*, whose loss of courage made it possible for Israel to engage in the action described in the next section.

Circumcision and Passover

2 At that time the LORD said to Joshua, "Make flint knives and circumcise the Israelites a second time." 3 So Joshua made flint knives, and circumcised the Israelites at Gibeath-haaraloth.*e* 4 This is the reason why Joshua circumcised them: all the males of the people who came out of Egypt, all the warriors, had died during the journey through the wilderness after they had come out of Egypt. 5 Although all the people who came out had been circumcised, yet all the people born on the journey through the wilderness after they had come out of Egypt had not been circumcised. 6 For the Israelites traveled forty years in the wilderness, until all the nation, the warriors who came out of Egypt, perished, not having listened to the voice of the LORD. To them the LORD swore that he would not let them see the land that he had sworn to their ancestors to give us, a land flowing with milk and honey. 7 So it was their children, whom he raised up in their place, that Joshua circumcised; for they were uncircumcised, because they had not been circumcised on the way.

8 When the circumcising of all the nation was done, they remained in their places in the camp until they were healed. 9 The LORD said to Joshua, "Today I have rolled away from you the disgrace of Egypt." And so that place is called Gilgal*f* to this day.

10 While the Israelites were camped in Gilgal they kept the passover in the evening on the fourteenth day of the month in the plains of Jericho. 11 On the day after the passover, on that very day, they ate the produce of the land, unleavened cakes and parched grain. 12 The manna ceased on the day they ate the produce of the land, and the Israelites no longer had manna; they ate the crops of the land of Canaan that year.

Joshua's Vision

13 Once when Joshua was by Jericho, he looked up and saw a man standing before him with a drawn sword in his hand. Joshua went to him and said to him, "Are you one of us, or one of our adversaries?" 14 He replied, "Neither; but as commander of the army of the LORD I have now come." And Joshua fell on his face to the earth and worshiped, and he said to him, "What do you command your servant, my lord?" 15 The commander of the army of the LORD said to Joshua, "Remove the sandals from your feet, for the place where you stand is holy." And Joshua did so.

Jericho Taken and Destroyed

6 Now Jericho was shut up inside and out because of the Israelites; no one came out and no one went in. 2 The LORD said to Joshua, "See, I have handed Jeri-

e That is *the Hill of the Foreskins*   *f* Related to Heb *galal* to roll

---

5.2–12 Circumcision and Passover became especially significant in Judaism as it consolidated during the exile and in the postexilic period. While circumcision was not a uniquely Israelite practice, it became an indispensable sign of Israel's relationship with the Lord; all males participating in the Passover must be circumcised (Ex 12.48). The practice had not been followed during the wilderness period. **5.12** With the militiamen thus prepared and the first Passover celebrated in the land, all was in readiness for life in the land; and so *the manna* was replaced by *the crops of the land of Canaan*. **5.13–15** Somewhere near Jericho, Joshua is granted a theophany—the appearance of a divine being—much in the manner of Gideon (Judg 6.11–12). **5.15** Direct quotation of Ex 3.5 elevates Joshua as direct successor of Moses. With the arrival of Joshua's heavenly counterpart, the chain of command is complete. The warfare sequence may now begin.

6.1–10.43 In this long and major segment of the book everything turns upon the interventions of Yahweh to produce three decisive demonstrations of divine power: at Jericho (ch. 6), at Ai (chs. 7–8), and at Gibeon (chs. 9–10). These three stories embody the idea of the miraculous sign. **6.1–27** Jericho is captured first and placed off-limits for Israelites. The story may reflect a combination of two traditions. In vv. 3–21, the core of the chapter, where the walls collapse at the climax on the seventh day after six days of ceremonial preparation, there is no mention of the city by name, of the king, or of resistance by the inhabitants. This account of ceremonial siege and ritual victory is framed by verses that connect with the Rahab story: vv. 1–2, mentioning the king and soldiers, and vv. 22–25, representing the sequel to ch. 2, the deliverance of Rahab and her household. The frame story thus seems to present the

cho over to you, along with its king and soldiers. ³You shall march around the city, all the warriors circling the city once. Thus you shall do for six days, ⁴with seven priests bearing seven trumpets of rams' horns before the ark. On the seventh day you shall march around the city seven times, the priests blowing the trumpets. ⁵When they make a long blast with the ram's horn, as soon as you hear the sound of the trumpet, then all the people shall shout with a great shout; and the wall of the city will fall down flat, and all the people shall charge straight ahead." ⁶So Joshua son of Nun summoned the priests and said to them, "Take up the ark of the covenant, and have seven priests carry seven trumpets of rams' horns in front of the ark of the LORD." ⁷To the people he said, "Go forward and march around the city; have the armed men pass on before the ark of the LORD."

⁸ As Joshua had commanded the people, the seven priests carrying the seven trumpets of rams' horns before the LORD went forward, blowing the trumpets, with the ark of the covenant of the LORD following them. ⁹And the armed men went before the priests who blew the trumpets; the rear guard came after the ark, while the trumpets blew continually. ¹⁰To the people Joshua gave this command: "You shall not shout or let your voice be heard, nor shall you utter a word, until the day I tell you to shout. Then you shall shout." ¹¹So the ark of the LORD went around the city, circling it once; and they came into the camp, and spent the night in the camp.

¹² Then Joshua rose early in the morning, and the priests took up the ark of the LORD. ¹³The seven priests carrying the seven trumpets of rams' horns before the ark of the LORD passed on, blowing the trumpets continually. The armed men went before them, and the rear guard came after the ark of the LORD, while the trumpets blew continually. ¹⁴On the second day they marched around the city once and then returned to the camp. They did this for six days.

¹⁵ On the seventh day they rose early, at dawn, and marched around the city in the same manner seven times. It was only on that day that they marched around the city seven times. ¹⁶And at the seventh time, when the priests had blown the trumpets, Joshua said to the people, "Shout! For the LORD has given you the city. ¹⁷The city and all that is in it shall be devoted to the LORD for destruction. Only Rahab the prostitute and all who are with her in her house shall live because she hid the messengers we sent. ¹⁸As for you, keep away from the things devoted to destruction, so as not to covet⁰ and take any of the devoted things and make the camp of Israel an object for destruction, bringing trouble upon it. ¹⁹But all silver and gold, and vessels of bronze and iron, are sacred to the LORD; they shall go into the treasury of the LORD." ²⁰So the people

---

g Gk: Heb *devote to destruction* Compare 7.21

---

takeover of the city as an inside job in response to military siege. Cf. the story of Bethel's capture in Judg 1.22–26. Joshua's instruction to spare Rahab and his household (v. 17) splices the two traditions together. **6.1** That *Jericho was shut up inside and out* clearly describes a military siege. Regulations for siege warfare distinguish between cities that lie outside Israel's inheritance (Deut 20.10–15) and those that have belonged to one of the "seven nations" (Deut 20.17 in the Septuagint and Samaritan Pentateuch). This story ostensibly concerns one of the latter. **6.4** *Seven priests bearing seven trumpets.* Repeated use of the sacred number seven and the role of the priests suggest that the story is based in part on liturgical action. **6.15** *Around the city seven times* on one day presupposes a city mostly in ruins, thus putting no obstructions in the path of the marchers. **6.17** *Devoted to the LORD for destruction.* The He-

brew term *cherem* refers to an ad hoc decree (cf. Lev 27.28–29) and was not an exclusively Israelite word or practice. In Israel, it has been suggested, the *cherem* may be understood in connection with efforts at disease control. Epidemic disease, especially bubonic plague, was not uncommon in the aftermath of warfare. **6.19** At Jericho no private spoils were to be taken. Except for valuable metal items, which would go into *the treasury of the LORD* (the common coffers?), the city and everything in it was to be destroyed. Only one other town mentioned in the Joshua stories, Hazor in ch. 11, is consecrated, placed under the *cherem*.

Map opposite: *The conquest of Canaan according to the narratives in Joshua. Other sources and archaeological evidence show different patterns of early Israelite settlement.*

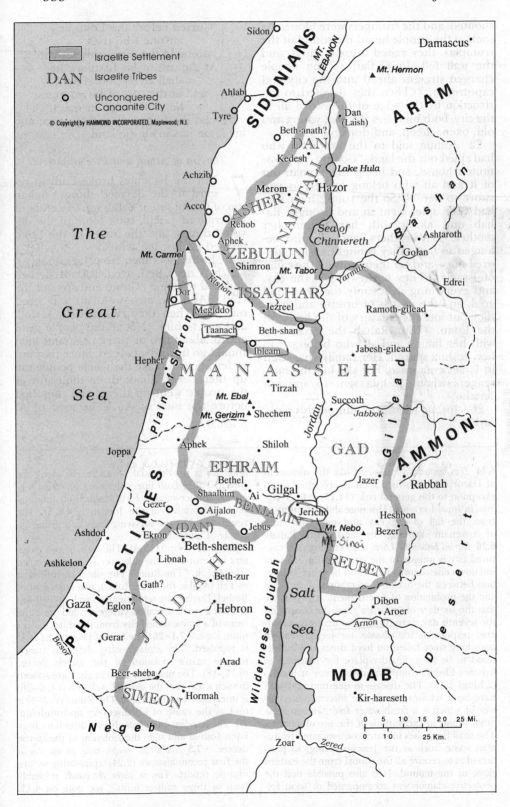

shouted, and the trumpets were blown. As soon as the people heard the sound of the trumpets, they raised a great shout, and the wall fell down flat; so the people charged straight ahead into the city and captured it. 21 Then they devoted to destruction by the edge of the sword all in the city, both men and women, young and old, oxen, sheep, and donkeys.

22 Joshua said to the two men who had spied out the land, "Go into the prostitute's house, and bring the woman out of it and all who belong to her, as you swore to her." 23 So the young men who had been spies went in and brought Rahab out, along with her father, her mother, her brothers, and all who belonged to her—they brought all her kindred out—and set them outside the camp of Israel. 24 They burned down the city, and everything in it; only the silver and gold, and the vessels of bronze and iron, they put into the treasury of the house of the LORD. 25 But Rahab the prostitute, with her family and all who belonged to her, Joshua spared. Her family*h* has lived in Israel ever since. For she hid the messengers whom Joshua sent to spy out Jericho.

26 Joshua then pronounced this oath, saying,

"Cursed before the LORD be
    anyone who tries
    to build this city—this Jericho!
At the cost of his firstborn he
    shall lay its foundation,
    and at the cost of his youngest
    he shall set up its gates!"

27 So the LORD was with Joshua; and his fame was in all the land.

The Sin of Achan and Its Punishment

7 But the Israelites broke faith in regard to the devoted things: Achan son of Carmi son of Zabdi son of Zerah, of the tribe of Judah, took some of the devoted things; and the anger of the LORD burned against the Israelites.

2 Joshua sent men from Jericho to Ai, which is near Beth-aven, east of Bethel, and said to them, "Go up and spy out the land." And the men went up and spied out Ai. 3 Then they returned to Joshua and said to him, "Not all the people need go up; about two or three thousand men should go up and attack Ai. Since they are so few, do not make the whole people toil up there." 4 So about three thousand of the people went up there; and they fled before the men of Ai. 5 The men of Ai

h Heb She

6.24 *They burned down the city*, like the treatment of Hazor (11.11), which itself is presented as an exception to the general rule (11.13). **6.25** *Has lived in Israel ever since*. This note shifts focus away from the fall of the city and onto the story of covenant keeping by and with Rahab. **6.26** *Cursed before the LORD*. This cursing of a captured city is unique in the OT, although it is not unknown elsewhere. There must be some connection between the act of consecration of the ruin and the prohibition of resettlement. It is possible that the six days of "practice" and the clamor on the seventh day were directed at demons considered responsible for disease, for Jericho was an oasis long since fallen on hard times and understood to be an unhealthy place for Israelites to live. See Elisha's complaint about water at Jericho (2 Kings 2.19). The disease in question may well have been schistosomiasis, the intermediate carrier of which is a fresh-water snail, *bulinus truncatus*, found in excavations at the site of Jericho. The snail flourishes in water contaminated by human waste, such as the Jericho spring, so positioned as to receive all the runoff from the eastern slope of the mound. It is also possible that the protective clamor was accompanied or soon followed by a providential seismic event along the Jordan Valley fault line, collapsing surviving segments of once-mighty fortifications (cf. the temporary damming of the Jordan in ch. 3). The result would be the surviving story as a prime example of amazing grace.

7.1–8.29 *Israel at Ai*. The bulk of two chapters is devoted to the takeover of a place called "the Ai," lit. "The Ruin." The site is identified as et-Tell (Arabic for "The Ruin"), two miles east of Bethel. During the settlement period, et-Tell was at most a small unwalled village nestled amid the ruins of a major walled city from the third millennium B.C.E. **7.1–26** The first of two attacks at Ai is repulsed. The embarrassing defeat is traced to one man's violation of the *cherem* decree (6.17–18). The narrative units in ch. 7 are spliced in such a way that the story of Achan (vv. 1, 6–26) is interrupted and defeat at The Ruin (vv. 2–5) is told as the cause of his discovery and undoing. **7.1** *The Israelites broke faith* diverts attention away from Joshua and onto the violation of the *cherem* decree. **7.3** *Not all the people need go up*. As in the first reconnaissance (2.24), spies bring an optimistic report. *Two or three thousand*, probably "two or three muster units"; see note on 4.13.

killed about thirty-six of them, chasing them from outside the gate as far as Shebarim and killing them on the slope. The hearts of the people melted and turned to water.

6 Then Joshua tore his clothes, and fell to the ground on his face before the ark of the LORD until the evening, he and the elders of Israel; and they put dust on their heads. 7 Joshua said, "Ah, Lord GOD! Why have you brought this people across the Jordan at all, to hand us over to the Amorites so as to destroy us? Would that we had been content to settle beyond the Jordan! 8 O Lord, what can I say, now that Israel has turned their backs to their enemies! 9 The Canaanites and all the inhabitants of the land will hear of it, and surround us, and cut off our name from the earth. Then what will you do for your great name?"

10 The LORD said to Joshua, "Stand up! Why have you fallen upon your face? 11 Israel has sinned; they have transgressed my covenant that I imposed on them. They have taken some of the devoted things; they have stolen, they have acted deceitfully, and they have put them among their own belongings. 12 Therefore the Israelites are unable to stand before their enemies; they turn their backs to their enemies, because they have become a thing devoted for destruction themselves. I will be with you no more, unless you destroy the devoted things from among you. 13 Proceed to sanctify the people, and say, 'Sanctify yourselves for tomorrow; for thus says the LORD, the God of Israel, "There are devoted things among you, O Israel; you will be unable to stand before your enemies until you take away the devoted things from among you." 14 In the morning therefore you shall come forward tribe by tribe. The tribe that the LORD takes shall come near by clans, the clan that the LORD takes shall come near by households, and the household that the LORD takes shall come near one by one. 15 And the one who is taken as having the devoted things shall be burned with fire, together with all that he has, for having transgressed the covenant of the LORD, and for having done an outrageous thing in Israel.'"

16 So Joshua rose early in the morning, and brought Israel near tribe by tribe, and the tribe of Judah was taken. 17 He brought near the clans of Judah, and the clan of the Zerahites was taken; and he brought near the clan of the Zerahites, family by family,*i* and Zabdi was taken. 18 And he brought near his household one by one, and Achan son of Carmi son of Zabdi son of Zerah, of the tribe of Judah, was taken. 19 Then Joshua said to Achan, "My son, give glory to the LORD God of Israel and make confession to him. Tell me now what you have done; do not hide it from me." 20 And Achan answered Joshua, "It is true; I am the one who sinned against the LORD God of Israel. This is what I did: 21 when I saw among the spoil a beautiful mantle from Shinar, and two hundred shekels of silver, and a bar of gold weighing fifty shekels, then I coveted them and took them. They now lie hidden in the ground inside my tent, with the silver underneath."

22 So Joshua sent messengers, and they ran to the tent; and there it was, hidden in his tent with the silver underneath. 23 They took them out of the tent and brought them to Joshua and all the Israelites; and they spread them out before the LORD. 24 Then Joshua and all Israel with him took Achan son of Zerah, with the

i Mss Syr: MT *man by man*

7.5 A loss of *about thirty-six* was truly disastrous. 7.6–26 Achan as explanation. 7.6 Exposure of the guilty one begins with rituals of mourning and penitence (cf. 2 Sam 12.15–16; Job 1.20; Jer 16.6–7; Joel 1.8–14) *before the ark of the LORD*. This is the first indication in Joshua of the ark's oracular function. As the portable throne of the Divine King, it was the place of highest legitimate inquiry (see Judg 20.27). 7.13 *Proceed to sanctify ... Sanctify yourselves*. Here the "holiness" root (Hebrew *qdsh*) is used twice. In contrast to 3.5, where all was going smoothly, here Joshua must be prompted. 7.14–18 The elimination proceeds, most likely, by sacred lot, which is explicitly mentioned in the determination of tribal territories (14.2; 18.6). Three concentric circles within which individual identity was established—house, clan, tribe—are the basis of the proceedings. Cf. 1 Sam 10.17–24; 14.37–42. 7.15 The death penalty for breach of covenant is known from other texts (Ex 21.12, 15–17; 22.18–20). Here not only the guilty individual, but also the physically contaminated and disease-laden booty, with all and everything that it has touched, are burned. 7.24 A stone cairn in the *Valley of Achor* (Hebrew, "Trouble"), on the border between Benjamin and

silver, the mantle, and the bar of gold, with his sons and daughters, with his oxen, donkeys, and sheep, and his tent and all that he had; and they brought them up to the Valley of Achor. 25 Joshua said, "Why did you bring trouble on us? The LORD is bringing trouble on you to-day." And all Israel stoned him to death; they burned them with fire, cast stones on them, 26 and raised over him a great heap of stones that remains to this day. Then the LORD turned from his burning anger. Therefore that place to this day is called the Valley of Achor.*j*

Ai Captured by a Stratagem and Destroyed

8 Then the LORD said to Joshua, "Do not fear or be dismayed; take all the fighting men with you, and go up now to Ai. See, I have handed over to you the king of Ai with his people, his city, and his land. 2 You shall do to Ai and its king as you did to Jericho and its king; only its spoil and its livestock you may take as booty for yourselves. Set an ambush against the city, behind it."

3 So Joshua and all the fighting men set out to go up against Ai. Joshua chose thirty thousand warriors and sent them out by night 4 with the command, "You shall lie in ambush against the city, behind it; do not go very far from the city, but all of you stay alert. 5 I and all the people who are with me will approach the city. When they come out against us, as before,

we shall flee from them. 6 They will come out after us until we have drawn them away from the city; for they will say, 'They are fleeing from us, as before.' While we flee from them, 7 you shall rise up from the ambush and seize the city; for the LORD your God will give it into your hand. 8 And when you have taken the city, you shall set the city on fire, doing as the LORD has ordered; see, I have commanded you." 9 So Joshua sent them out; and they went to the place of ambush, and lay between Bethel and Ai, to the west of Ai; but Joshua spent that night in the camp.*k*

10 In the morning Joshua rose early and mustered the people, and went up, with the elders of Israel, before the people to Ai. 11 All the fighting men who were with him went up, and drew near before the city, and camped on the north side of Ai, with a ravine between them and Ai. 12 Taking about five thousand men, he set them in ambush between Bethel and Ai, to the west of the city. 13 So they stationed the forces, the main encampment that was north of the city and its rear guard west of the city. But Joshua spent that night in the valley. 14 When the king of Ai saw this, he and all his people, the inhabitants of the city, hurried out early in the morning to the meeting place facing the Arabah to meet Israel in battle; but he did not know that there was an ambush against him behind the city. 15 And Joshua and all Israel made a pretense of

j That is *Trouble*   *k* Heb *among the people*

Judah, marked the place of execution.

8.1–29 Ambush and victory at Ai. Here Yahweh takes charge, Joshua and Israel strictly obey orders, and victory is secured. The clustering of references to Ai (twenty-two occurrences in the chapter) suggests that two narratives have been combined. Three segments that together mention Ai exactly eleven times (vv. 1–2, 12–19, 26–29) alternate with two other units (vv. 3–11, 20–25). The set of three scans in Hebrew as continuous narrative. Inclusion of vv. 3–11 and 20–25 turned the story of the victory at Ai into a preview of the victory at Gibeah in civil war at the end of the wider era (Judg 20). The terrain around Ai and the terrain around Gibeah are similar enough that it would not be surprising to have the ambush at one place sound so much like the one at the other.   **8.1** *Do not fear or be dismayed,* recurring encouragement in Yahweh's war (Ex 14.13; Deut 1.21; 3.2; 7.18; 20.1; 31.8). Archaeology has

shown that *the king of Ai* ruled at most a small village. It is conceivable that he was the suzerain of kings rallying at The Ruin to oppose Joshua and his followers.   **8.2** *Set an ambush.* The ambush is Yahweh's strategy (cf. Judg 20.29–34).   **8.3** There is no place on the watershed ridge in the vicinity of Ai to hide a force of *thirty thousand;* "thirty muster units" would be more like it (see note on 4.13). To move *by night* from the Jordan Valley near Jericho into position near Ai is not implausible.   **8.10** *The elders,* elsewhere in Joshua only in 7.6; 20.4; 23.2; 24.1, 31. In village and countryside as well as in smaller cities, the elders were responsible for law and order and for maintaining the convenantal ethic. Their relative absence from this book reflects the dominant interest in presenting the leadership of Joshua as model for the later kings (Dtr 1; see Introduction).   **8.12** *Five thousand* (better "five muster units"; see note on 4.13) is a still more plausible

being beaten before them, and fled in the direction of the wilderness. 16 So all the people who were in the city were called together to pursue them, and as they pursued Joshua they were drawn away from the city. 17 There was not a man left in Ai or Bethel who did not go out after Israel; they left the city open, and pursued Israel.

18 Then the LORD said to Joshua, "Stretch out the sword that is in your hand toward Ai; for I will give it into your hand." And Joshua stretched out the sword that was in his hand toward the city. 19 As soon as he stretched out his hand, the troops in ambush rose quickly out of their place and rushed forward. They entered the city, took it, and at once set the city on fire. 20 So when the men of Ai looked back, the smoke of the city was rising to the sky. They had no power to flee this way or that, for the people who fled to the wilderness turned back against the pursuers. 21 When Joshua and all Israel saw that the ambush had taken the city and that the smoke of the city was rising, then they turned back and struck down the men of Ai. 22 And the others came out from the city against them; so they were surrounded by Israelites, some on one side, and some on the other; and Israel struck them down until no one was left who survived or escaped. 23 But the king of Ai was taken alive and brought to Joshua.

24 When Israel had finished slaughtering all the inhabitants of Ai in the open wilderness where they pursued them, and when all of them to the very last had fallen by the edge of the sword, all Israel returned to Ai, and attacked it with the edge of the sword. 25 The total of those who fell that day, both men and women, was twelve thousand—all the people of Ai. 26 For Joshua did not draw back his hand, with which he stretched out the sword, until he had utterly destroyed all the inhabitants of Ai. 27 Only the livestock and the spoil of that city Israel took as their booty, according to the word of the LORD that he had issued to Joshua. 28 So Joshua burned Ai, and made it forever a heap of ruins, as it is to this day. 29 And he hanged the king of Ai on a tree until evening; and at sunset Joshua commanded, and they took his body down from the tree, threw it down at the entrance of the gate of the city, and raised over it a great heap of stones, which stands there to this day.

Joshua Renews the Covenant

30 Then Joshua built on Mount Ebal an altar to the LORD, the God of Israel,

---

number for an ambush than the previously mentioned "thirty" (v. 3). **8.17** *Bethel* is mentioned elsewhere in the story only as a geographical reference point (7.2; 8.9, 12). It may rather refer to the sanctuary (*beth'el*, Hebrew, "house of God") at Ai, left unattended. **8.18** The Hebrew uses a very rare word for the *sword* that Joshua holds high at Yahweh's command. It may refer to the sickle-sword, ubiquitous in Mesopotamian and Egyptian art over two millennia prior to the emergence of Israel as symbol of sovereignty. Cf. the outstretched arms of Moses at the battle with Amalek (Ex 17.11) and reference to the "arm" of Yahweh at Israel's deliverance (Deut 26.8; Ps 44.3; Isa 51.9–11). **8.25** *The total . . . twelve thousand*, more likely "twelve muster units" (see note on 4.13). The losses of Israel in the first battle ("thirty-six" in 7.5) probably set the limits for a total loss of seventy-five to one hundred and fifty in the Israelite victory. Extremely modest proportions of the Iron I occupation at et-Tell (see note on 7.1–8.29) belong to a pattern developing north and south along the watershed ridge in the early twelfth century B.C.E. **8.26–27** The taking of plunder was strictly regulated this time (v. 2).

Here it is explicit that there was a clear distinction between *cherem* and booty.
8.30–35 Covenant renewal at Mount Ebal. Ebal is located about twenty miles north of Ai. This unit fits loosely in its context; in the Greek version it is placed after 9.1–2. In fact the coalescence of Israel and the formation of opposing coalitions may have given reciprocal impetus to each other. Vv. 30–31 show Joshua carrying out Yahweh's command to Moses (Deut 27.4–5). **8.30** *Then*. The same distinctive introduction in the Hebrew in 22.1, beginning the story of the altar near the Jordan, indicates a rhetorical relationship. *Mount Ebal* on the north and Mount Gerizim on the south flank the pass controlled by the great site of Shechem. Whoever commanded the pass below Ebal could control all the hill country from a point not far north of Jerusalem almost to the plain of Esdraelon (or Jezreel). For most of that extensive territory centering in the neighborhood of Shechem, however, there is no conquest tradition. The implication is that it became a part of Yahwist Israel by negotiation, as represented here in liturgical, covenantal dress. The curious fact that Shechem is not mentioned may be due to

31 just as Moses the servant of the LORD
had commanded the Israelites, as it is
written in the book of the law of Moses,
"an altar of unhewn*l* stones, on which no
iron tool has been used"; and they offered
on it burnt offerings to the LORD, and sacrificed offerings of well-being. 32 And
there, in the presence of the Israelites,
Joshua*m* wrote on the stones a copy of the
law of Moses, which he had written. 33 All
Israel, alien as well as citizen, with their
elders and officers and their judges, stood
on opposite sides of the ark in front of the
levitical priests who carried the ark of the
covenant of the LORD, half of them in
front of Mount Gerizim and half of them
in front of Mount Ebal, as Moses the servant of the LORD had commanded at the
first, that they should bless the people of
Israel. 34 And afterward he read all the
words of the law, blessings and curses, according to all that is written in the book of
the law. 35 There was not a word of all that

Moses commanded that Joshua did not
read before all the assembly of Israel, and
the women, and the little ones, and the
aliens who resided among them.

The Gibeonites Save Themselves by Trickery

9 Now when all the kings who were beyond the Jordan in the hill country
and in the lowland all along the coast of
the Great Sea toward Lebanon—the Hittites, the Amorites, the Canaanites, the
Perizzites, the Hivites, and the Jebusites—
heard of this, 2 they gathered together
with one accord to fight Joshua and
Israel.

3 But when the inhabitants of Gibeon
heard what Joshua had done to Jericho
and to Ai, 4 they on their part acted with
cunning: they went and prepared provisions,*n* and took worn-out sacks for their

l Heb *whole*   *m* Heb *he*   *n* Cn: Meaning of
Heb uncertain

---

the fact that the city was destroyed in the mid-
twelfth century B.C.E. (see the story of Abimelech
in Judg 9), while the celebrations of covenant renewal at Ebal presumably lived on. It has been
proposed but is far from certain that a recently
excavated Iron I "sanctuary" at el-Barnat on Ebal
marks the site. **8.31** *Moses*, with the distinctive
title *servant of the LORD*, is mentioned five times in
this brief unit. The *book of the law of Moses* is very
likely the hypothetical Dtn rediscovered during
King Josiah's reign (2 Kings 22) and finally edited
as the book Deuteronomy (see Introduction). The
burnt offerings were consumed entirely by the fire
on the altar, while *offerings of well-being* were par-
tially consumed by the worshipers as sacrifices establishing or maintaining friendship with God.
8.32 He, presumably Joshua, *wrote on the stones*,
i.e., probably on standing stone pillars. Treaty inscriptions might characteristically be written
on plastered stone surfaces (cf. 24.26–27).
8.33 *Alien as well as citizen*. Teaching, which set
forth an egalitarian standard for public policy,
was the special responsibility of *levitical priests who
carried the ark of the covenant*. **8.34** *Blessings and
curses*, standard elements in the suzerainty treaty
form as appropriated in Yahwism. See especially
Deut 27–28. **8.35** The *assembly* (Hebrew *kahal*)
in the era before the monarchy was the totality of
those gathered for one of the pilgrimage feasts.
The assembly was eclipsed by the splendors of the
Jerusalem temple festivities but was revived in the
theology of the postmonarchical period to designate the worshiping congregation.
9.1–27 Royal alliance and special status for
Gibeonites. The sequel to the victory at Ai and the

Ebal covenant is presented in two aspects: formation of a wide-ranging coalition of kings and peoples (vv. 1–2) and a treaty with the people of
Gibeon (vv. 3–27). **9.1** *Hittites . . . Jebusites*. To
this list should probably be added a seventh ("Girgashites") as in 3.10. Initial successes, facilitated
by one or two unusual events in the natural order,
polarized the power elite and existing population
groups. Except for the area dominated by Shechem, the number of independent city-states in
Canaan seems nearly to have doubled between
the fourteenth and twelfth centuries B.C.E. There
is no direct correlation between this list and the
account of six cities (and seven kings) defeated in
10.28–39. **9.2** *With one accord*, under one command. The abrupt conclusion suggests that another battle story once followed at this point,
perhaps something relating to the area west
and north of Shechem (see towns listed in
12.17–18). **9.3–27** The treaty with Gibeon.
Vv. 3–15 deal with the protection of Gibeon,
vv. 16–27 with the exploitation of Gibeon and its
allied towns. The treaty was highly problematical
from Israel's side in view of the prohibitions set
forth in Deut 20.10–18. The tradition's essential
historicity is undergirded by the account of a famine during David's reign that was traced to Saul's
bloodguilt "because he put the Gibeonites to
death" (2 Sam 21.1). **9.3** Deliberations are initiated by the *inhabitants* of a town that has no king.
Gibeon lies on an important east-west road from
Jericho that descends to the coastal plain through
the Valley of Aijalon. It was at most a small village in the twelfth century B.C.E., like Jericho,
Ai, and the other towns in this story (v. 17).

donkeys, and wineskins, worn-out and torn and mended, 5 with worn-out, patched sandals on their feet, and worn-out clothes; and all their provisions were dry and moldy. 6 They went to Joshua in the camp at Gilgal, and said to him and to the Israelites, "We have come from a far country; so now make a treaty with us." 7 But the Israelites said to the Hivites, "Perhaps you live among us; then how can we make a treaty with you?" 8 They said to Joshua, "We are your servants." And Joshua said to them, "Who are you? And where do you come from?" 9 They said to him, "Your servants have come from a very far country, because of the name of the LORD your God; for we have heard a report of him, of all that he did in Egypt, 10 and of all that he did to the two kings of the Amorites who were beyond the Jordan, King Sihon of Heshbon, and King Og of Bashan who lived in Ashta-roth. 11 So our elders and all the inhabi-tants of our country said to us, 'Take provisions in your hand for the journey; go to meet them, and say to them, "We are your servants; come now, make a treaty with us." ' 12 Here is our bread; it was still warm when we took it from our houses as our food for the journey, on the day we set out to come to you, but now, see, it is dry and moldy; 13 these wineskins

were new when we filled them, and see, they are burst; and these garments and sandals of ours are worn out from the very long journey." 14 So the leaders⁰ partook of their provisions, and did not ask direction from the LORD. 15 And Joshua made peace with them, guarantee-ing their lives by a treaty; and the leaders of the congregation swore an oath to them.

16   But when three days had passed af-ter they had made a treaty with them, they heard that they were their neighbors and were living among them. 17 So the Is-raelites set out and reached their cities on the third day. Now their cities were Gib-eon, Chephirah, Beeroth, and Kiriath-jearim. 18 But the Israelites did not attack them, because the leaders of the congre-gation had sworn to them by the LORD, the God of Israel. Then all the congrega-tion murmured against the leaders. 19 But all the leaders said to all the congregation, "We have sworn to them by the LORD, the God of Israel, and now we must not touch them. 20 This is what we will do to them: We will let them live, so that wrath may not come upon us, because of the oath that we swore to them." 21 The leaders said to them, "Let them live." So they be-came hewers of wood and drawers of

o Gk: Heb *men*

9.6–7 Abrupt mention of *Gilgal* is jarring. That the people of Gibeon are *Hivites* suggests ancestral origin in Cilicia, in which case they tell a half-truth; they have come *from a far country*, but not recently.   **9.9–10** Their argument echoes Ra-hab's speech (2.10–11), based on Deut 2.26–3.17 (cf. Josh 12.1–6) and epic tradition (Num 21.21–35).   **9.14** They *did not ask direction from the LORD*. Joshua finds himself having to ratify negotiations undertaken by anonymous Israelites and for which he was not originally responsible. The reading in the Greek, which specifies "the leaders" in this verse, is to be rejected. The "lead-ers" are those who will propose a way out of the predicament in vv. 16–27. Epic tradition explic-itly associates Joshua with the divinatory tech-nique "decision of the Urim" (Num 27.18–21). **9.15b** This half verse is the compiler's splice. **9.16–27** This supplement and sequel is from an independent and very possibly older account. **9.17** Mention of *their cities* is the first hint in the chapter that more than one settlement might be involved. The four named (all very small villages in the twelfth century B.C.E.) controlled the entire northwest quadrant of approaches to Jerusalem.

9.18 *The leaders* appear ten times in Joshua, al-ways in contexts that may be considered contribu-tions of the final redactor (9.15, 18 [twice], 19, 21; 13.21; 17.4; 22.14, 30, 32 ["chiefs"]). There is a strong rhetorical relationship between this story and the altar narrative in ch. 22. *Congregation* (He-brew *'edah*), like the word for "assembly" (Hebrew *kahal* as in 8.35), is nearly nonexistent in texts of Samuel and Kings referring to the monarchical era. Used in this story for the first time in Joshua (vv. 15, 18 [twice], 19, 21, 27), it occurs another six times in the Hebrew text of the altar story (22.12, 16, 17, 18, 20, 30). The words for "assem-bly" and "congregation" reflect the parallel culti-vation of the tradition by different Levitical (priestly) families. With the transition to monar-chy the old deliberative "assembly/congregation" was displaced by royally appointed officials, only to come into prominence again as a term for the worshiping community after destruction of the state and demise of the royal festivals (post 587 B.C.E.).   **9.18–20** The phrase *sworn to them by the LORD/swore to them* is stated three times in quick succession, emphatically locating responsibility. **9.21** Negotiation of status as *hewers of wood and*

water for all the congregation, as the leaders had decided concerning them.

22 Joshua summoned them, and said to them, "Why did you deceive us, saying, 'We are very far from you,' while in fact you are living among us? 23 Now therefore you are cursed, and some of you shall always be slaves, hewers of wood and drawers of water for the house of my God." 24 They answered Joshua, "Because it was told to your servants for a certainty that the LORD your God had commanded his servant Moses to give you all the land, and to destroy all the inhabitants of the land before you; so we were in great fear for our lives because of you, and did this thing. 25 And now we are in your hand: do as it seems good and right in your sight to do to us." 26 This is what he did for them: he saved them from the Israelites; and they did not kill them. 27 But on that day Joshua made them hewers of wood and drawers of water for the congregation and for the altar of the LORD, to continue to this day, in the place that he should choose.

Joshua's Defense of Gibeon

10 When King Adoni-zedek of Jerusalem heard how Joshua had taken Ai, and had utterly destroyed it, doing to Ai and its king as he had done to Jericho and its king, and how the inhabitants of Gibeon had made peace with Israel and were among them, 2 heᵖ became greatly frightened, because Gibeon was a large city, like one of the royal cities, and was larger than Ai, and all its men were

p Heb *they*

---

drawers of water is an ironic inversion of covenantal equality, for in Deut 29.11, which uses exactly these descriptions for the sojourner, the implication of the covenant is precisely to erase distinctions of status that otherwise attach to various subgroups. **9.23** They are *cursed*. For bearing false witness? The *house of my God*. There was almost certainly a Yahwist temple at Shiloh and very possibly one at Gilgal. **9.27** The etiological formula *to continue to this day* signals narrative motivation, providing ironic legitimation for exploitation of Gibeonites. Very likely *the place that he* (Yahweh) *should choose* (Deut 12.5, 11, 14, 18, 21, 26 and repeatedly) was so designated by the presence of the ark of the covenant, as on Mount Ebal in the preceding unit (8.33). The effect is to startle readers by clearing the air for a fresh look at what comes next. Yahweh will honor the problematical treaty.

10.1–39 Defense of Gibeon and a southern campaign. Gibeon is faced with the threat of a coalition headed by the king of Jerusalem (vv. 1–5); Joshua and Israel fulfill their treaty obligation and repel the attackers, thanks to another intervention by the divine commander (vv. 6–11). The latter point is emphasized in a flashback (vv. 12–14). The primary story line then resumes, with the capture of the allied kings (vv. 16–27). To all of this is appended another older unit (vv. 28–39), which focuses on towns destroyed in the south. The units are strung together in a logical sequence without any attempt to harmonize differences. Description of the "southern campaign" seems to make sense militarily. The redactional effect is to present the victories in the south as an unplanned offshoot of Yahweh's third intervention since the crossing of the Jordan (see note on 6.1–10.43). **10.1–15** The treaty with Gibeon and the combined might of five city-states posed the greatest of odds against Israel. **10.1** *Jerusalem*, by this name mentioned here for the first time in the Bible. It is the only member of the coalition that escapes a raid even though its king is eliminated in the defeat of the coalition. Jerusalem remained a Canaanite town until its takeover by King David. **10.2** Gibeon as *a large city* is an exaggeration, but in keeping with the monarchical proportions of Israel that are assumed by the editors (Dtr 1, Dtr 2; see Introduction). Thirty-one *royal cities* in western Palestine alone are listed in 12.7–24. *Warriors*. The Hebrew refers to men trained in combat and prosperous enough to be able to afford such activity, in effect, "knights." Gideon was a notable Israelite example (Judg 6.12). **10.3** In Judg 1.10 capture of *Hebron* is credited to Judah. Hebron, with a monarchical tradition going back to the seventeenth century B.C.E., figures prominently in the stories of Israel's ancestors, especially Abraham and Sarah (see Gen 13.18; 18.1; 23.19). Hebron too had a heavy concentration of non-Semitic people. The local kingdoms dismantled by early Israel were mostly of recent and alien origin. *Jarmuth*, the first of three towns situated in a north-south line in the foothills separating the central mountain range from the coastal road. *Lachish* was a fortified town already half a millennium old when it was destroyed in the mid-twelfth century B.C.E. It is hard to comprehend this date and a thirteenth-century destruction at Hazor (ch. 11) as both falling within one man's lifetime. It appears that the emergence of Israel, out of prolonged struggle for better life in Canaan, has been stylized as occurring all under Joshua's exemplary leadership. Regarding

warriors. [3]So King Adoni-zedek of Jerusalem sent a message to King Hoham of Hebron, to King Piram of Jarmuth, to King Japhia of Lachish, and to King Debir of Eglon, saying, [4]"Come up and help me, and let us attack Gibeon; for it has made peace with Joshua and with the Israelites." [5]Then the five kings of the Amorites—the king of Jerusalem, the king of Hebron, the king of Jarmuth, the king of Lachish, and the king of Eglon—gathered their forces, and went up with all their armies and camped against Gibeon, and made war against it.

[6] And the Gibeonites sent to Joshua at the camp in Gilgal, saying, "Do not abandon your servants; come up to us quickly, and save us, and help us; for all the kings of the Amorites who live in the hill country are gathered against us." [7]So Joshua went up from Gilgal, he and all the fighting force with him, all the mighty warriors. [8]The LORD said to Joshua, "Do not fear them, for I have handed them over to you; not one of them shall stand before you." [9]So Joshua came upon them suddenly, having marched up all night from Gilgal. [10]And the LORD threw them into a

panic before Israel, who inflicted a great slaughter on them at Gibeon, chased them by the way of the ascent of Beth-horon, and struck them down as far as Azekah and Makkedah. [11]As they fled before Israel, while they were going down the slope of Beth-horon, the LORD threw down huge stones from heaven on them as far as Azekah, and they died; there were more who died because of the hailstones than the Israelites killed with the sword.

[12] On the day when the LORD gave the Amorites over to the Israelites, Joshua spoke to the LORD; and he said in the sight of Israel,

"Sun, stand still at Gibeon,
　　and Moon, in the valley of
　　　Aijalon."
[13] And the sun stood still, and the
　　　moon stopped,
　　until the nation took vengeance
　　　on their enemies.

Is this not written in the Book of Jashar? The sun stopped in midheaven, and did not hurry to set for about a whole day. [14]There has been no day like it before or

---

King Debir of Eglon, the tradition may be garbled. *Debir* is a place name in vv. 38–39; 15.7; 21.15. Location of *Eglon* is unknown, possibly Tell Aitun. **10.5** *Amorites*, often a synonym for "Canaanites," may here retain its etymological sense, "westerners." **10.8** *The LORD said* presupposes oracular consultation, presumably by some such means as the sacred dice, Urim and Thummim. Here the Israelites do not repeat the mistake for which they are faulted earlier (9.14). **10.9** A forced march *all night* is plausible (as in the siege of Ai), a straight-line distance of about thirty-two kilometers, but a strenuous, twisting climb mostly uphill, out of the Jordan Valley. **10.10** *And the LORD threw ... chased ... and struck.* It was Yahweh's victory, not Joshua's or Israel's. The *ascent of Beth-horon*, also known as Valley of Aijalon, was a major access route from the northern Shephelah to the hill country. *Azekah* is identified with Tell-Zakariyeh. The location of *Makkedah*, somewhere in the northern Shephelah, is unknown. **10.11** *Stones from heaven* seems to be an unusually severe and unseasonable hailstorm. The coastal plain receives five to eight days of hail per year, mostly in midwinter. **10.12–14** The main thought here is of Yahweh's responsiveness to a human voice. The narrative incorporates an old poetic fragment in which sun and moon are collaborators rather than subordinates serving in the

heavenly army, as in Hab 3.11. Cf. how "the stars fought from heaven" against Sisera (Judg 5.20), probably being regarded as the source of rain that produced a providential flash flood. **10.12** With a restoration from the Greek version, the introduction to the poem becomes chiastic, i.e., successive lines repeat ideas in reverse order: "Then Joshua appealed to the LORD, on the day God gave the Amorites over to the Israelites" parallels "When he (that is, the LORD) attacked them at Gibeon, they were smitten before Israel." Thus the next line, *he* (that is, the LORD) *said in the sight of Israel*, begins the poetic fragment. **10.13** Perhaps sun and moon were ordered to cover opposite escape routes from the pass. *Until the nation took vengeance on their enemies* is better translated: "until he (the LORD) defeated his enemies' force." "To take vengeance," which in the human scene means taking the law into one's own hands, is far from the meaning of the Hebrew here. The same consonants for "the nation," in Hebrew, also spell the military word for a fighting force. *The Book of Jashar* is also quoted in 2 Sam 1.18–27, King David's poetic lament over the deaths of Saul and Jonathan. That the sun did not set *for about a whole day* represents a literal misreading of the poem. **10.14** That *the LORD fought for Israel* may thus be understood in terms of a providential hailstorm seriously impeding the retreat of coali-

since, when the LORD heeded a human voice; for the LORD fought for Israel.

15 Then Joshua returned, and all Israel with him, to the camp at Gilgal.

Five Kings Defeated

16 Meanwhile, these five kings fled and hid themselves in the cave at Makkedah. 17 And it was told Joshua, "The five kings have been found, hidden in the cave at Makkedah." 18 Joshua said, "Roll large stones against the mouth of the cave, and set men by it to guard them; 19 but do not stay there yourselves; pursue your enemies, and attack them from the rear. Do not let them enter their towns, for the LORD your God has given them into your hand." 20 When Joshua and the Israelites had finished inflicting a very great slaughter on them, until they were wiped out, and when the survivors had entered into the fortified towns, 21 all the people returned safe to Joshua in the camp at Makkedah; no one dared to speak*q* against any of the Israelites.

22 Then Joshua said, "Open the mouth of the cave, and bring those five kings out to me from the cave." 23 They did so, and brought the five kings out to him from the cave, the king of Jerusalem, the king of Hebron, the king of Jarmuth, the king of Lachish, and the king of Eglon. 24 When they brought the kings out to Joshua, Joshua summoned all the Israelites, and said to the chiefs of the warriors who had gone with him, "Come near, put your feet on the necks of these kings." Then they came near and put their feet on their necks. 25 And Joshua said to them, "Do not be afraid or dismayed; be strong and courageous; for thus the LORD will do to all the enemies against whom you fight." 26 Afterward Joshua struck them down and put them to death, and he hung them on five trees. And they hung on the trees until evening. 27 At sunset Joshua commanded, and they took them down from the trees and threw them into the cave where they had hidden themselves; they set large stones against the mouth of the cave, which remain to this very day.

Victories in the South

28 Joshua took Makkedah on that day, and struck it and its king with the edge of the sword; he utterly destroyed every person in it; he left no one remaining. And he did to the king of Makkedah as he had done to the king of Jericho.

29 Then Joshua passed on from Makkedah, and all Israel with him, to Libnah, and fought against Libnah. 30 The LORD gave it also and its king into the hand of Israel; and he struck it with the edge of the sword, and every person in it; he left no one remaining in it; and he did to its king as he had done to the king of Jericho.

31 Next Joshua passed on from Libnah, and all Israel with him, to Lachish, and laid siege to it, and assaulted it. 32 The LORD gave Lachish into the hand of Israel, and he took it on the second day, and struck it with the edge of the sword, and every person in it, as he had done to Libnah.

33 Then King Horam of Gezer came up to help Lachish; and Joshua struck

q Heb *moved his tongue*

---

tion forces, giving the advantage to Joshua's force. **10.15** This verse is probably a gloss, supplied by a scribe who did not recognize vv. 12–14 as a digression or flashback.
10.16–27 The sequel to the prose account of the rout of the southern confederacy. The emphasis shifts, ironically, away from Yahweh's salvific action and onto Israel's military achievement. **10.17–21** With *the five kings . . . hidden in the cave at Makkedah*, the opposing forces were in leaderless rout and failed, for the most part, to find refuge inside *the fortified towns.* **10.21** The emphasis is on Israel's increasing military prowess. **10.24** For the manner of execution *feet on their necks,* cf. figurative use in Ps 110.1; 1 Cor 15.25–28. **10.25** *Do not be afraid,* an inclusion with v. 8. Cf. 1.7, 9. **10.26** This is not death by hanging, but public exposure of corpses after execution so as to inspire fear. **10.28–39** It is impossible to fully harmonize this account of the campaign in the south with the description of the coalition in vv. 1–5, because of the way the compiler chose to work by putting together preformed literary units. **10.28** *Destroyed,* i.e., "devoted" (Hebrew root *chrm*); see note on 6.17. **10.29** In the case of *Libnah,* there is no mention of the *cherem* (see note on 6.17). **10.30** Skipping over "the king of Ai" to get to *the king of Jericho* (whose fate is otherwise not described) contributes to closure on the account of warfare in the south. **10.33** *King Horam of Gezer* only now joins the action and is the only one mentioned by name

him and his people, leaving him no survivors.

34 From Lachish Joshua passed on with all Israel to Eglon; and they laid siege to it, and assaulted it; 35 and they took it that day, and struck it with the edge of the sword; and every person in it he utterly destroyed that day, as he had done to Lachish.

36 Then Joshua went up with all Israel from Eglon to Hebron; they assaulted it, 37 and took it, and struck it with the edge of the sword, and its king and its towns, and every person in it; he left no one remaining, just as he had done to Eglon, and utterly destroyed it with every person in it.

38 Then Joshua, with all Israel, turned back to Debir and assaulted it, 39 and he took it with its king and all its towns; they struck them with the edge of the sword, and utterly destroyed every person in it; he left no one remaining; just as he had done to Hebron, and, as he had done to Libnah and its king, so he did to Debir and its king.

40 So Joshua defeated the whole land, the hill country and the Negeb and the lowland and the slopes, and all their kings; he left no one remaining, but utterly destroyed all that breathed, as the LORD God of Israel commanded. 41 And Joshua defeated them from Kadesh-barnea to Gaza, and all the country of Goshen, as far as Gibeon. 42 Joshua took all these kings and their land at one time, because the LORD God of Israel fought for Israel. 43 Then Joshua returned, and all Israel with him, to the camp at Gilgal.

The United Kings of Northern Canaan Defeated

11 When King Jabin of Hazor heard of this, he sent to King Jobab of Madon, to the king of Shimron, to the king of Achshaph, 2 and to the kings who were in the northern hill country, and in the Arabah south of Chinneroth, and in the lowland, and in Naphoth-dor on the west, 3 to the Canaanites in the east and the west, the Amorites, the Hittites, the Perizzites, and the Jebusites in the hill

---

in this recapping of successes in the south. There is a tension, but no necessary contradiction, between this text and other passages in 16.10 and Judg 1.29 (which fault the tribe of Ephraim for failure to oust the Canaanites from Gezer). *Gezer* only became Israelite in Solomon's reign, as a dowry that came with Pharaoh's daughter. **10.34** Location of *Eglon* is uncertain, perhaps Tell Aitun. **10.36–39** In 14.6–15 Caleb is credited with victory at *Hebron* (see also 15.13–14), but "Judah" in general gets the credit in Judg 1.10. It is likely that towns changed hands more than once. The specification *its towns* (satellite villages) is made only for Hebron and Debir. The former remains archaeologically little known due to continuous modern occupation. The name of *Debir* "was formerly Kiriath-sepher" (Judg 1.11), which may be read as "Town of the Treaty Stele," suggesting something of a southern counterpart to the role of Shechem in the north (8.30–35; ch. 24). Debir is probably the small hill country site of Khirbet Rabud, where, again, only restricted areas could be excavated, but no pertinent destruction stratum has been found.

10.40–43 An editorial summary that, like 9.1–2, with which it frames the story about the Gibeonites, covers both more and less than what is reported in the enclosed narrative. **10.40** The *Negeb* is the southern desert stretching from the foot of the Judean hill country into the northern Sinai peninsula. That he *utterly destroyed all that*

breathed is rhetorical exaggeration characteristic of the monarchical edition (Dtr 1; see Introduction); it overlooks previous statements to the contrary in various units. **11.1–15** Victory in the far north. Defeat of the Galilean coalition headed by Hazor is the last of the stories of Joshua's military leadership to be highlighted by the monarchy's historian (Dtr 1; see Introduction). **11.1** *Jabin* was a dynastic name at Hazor. In Judg 4.2, 23, 24 another(?) "Jabin" is "king of Canaan." By the thirteenth century B.C.E., Hazor was greatly reduced in size. What the king of Hazor *heard* was (1) the news of the Ebal covenant, (2) news from the southern hill country, or (3) some combination of the two. Moreover, northern Galilee in the thirteenth century B.C.E. was, for the first time in history, the scene of many new settlements, open and unfortified, occupied by families practicing subsistence farming. This pattern cannot be unrelated to the migrations of groups called Habiru in ancient sources and the Yahwist movement in particular. The hasty formation of a defensive coalition of local elites in Galilee is entirely plausible. *Jobab* and *Madon*, non-Semitic names, traceable to an Anatolian origin. Precise locations of Madon, *Shimron*, and *Achshaph* are uncertain. **11.3** *Hittites, Perizzites, Jebusites, Hivites*, four "nations" with non-Semitic names and backgrounds. *Mizpah*, Hebrew "Watchtower" or "Lookout." *Land of Mizpah* may be a general term for the area overlooked by

country, and the Hivites under Hermon in the land of Mizpah. ⁴ They came out, with all their troops, a great army, in number like the sand on the seashore, with very many horses and chariots. ⁵ All these kings joined their forces, and came and camped together at the waters of Merom, to fight with Israel.

6 And the LORD said to Joshua, "Do not be afraid of them, for tomorrow at this time I will hand over all of them, slain, to Israel; you shall hamstring their horses, and burn their chariots with fire." ⁷ So Joshua came suddenly upon them with all his fighting force, by the waters of Merom, and fell upon them. ⁸ And the LORD handed them over to Israel, who attacked them and chased them as far as Great Sidon and Misrephoth-maim, and eastward as far as the valley of Mizpeh. They struck them down, until they had left no one remaining. ⁹ And Joshua did to them as the LORD commanded him; he hamstrung their horses, and burned their chariots with fire.

10 Joshua turned back at that time, and took Hazor, and struck its king down with the sword. Before that time Hazor was the head of all those kingdoms.

¹¹ And they put to the sword all who were in it, utterly destroying them; there was no one left who breathed, and he burned Hazor with fire. ¹² And all the towns of those kings, and all their kings, Joshua took, and struck them with the edge of the sword, utterly destroying them, as Moses the servant of the LORD had commanded. ¹³ But Israel burned none of the towns that stood on mounds except Hazor, which Joshua did burn. ¹⁴ All the spoil of these towns, and the livestock, the Israelites took for their booty; but all the people they struck down with the edge of the sword, until they had destroyed them, and they did not leave any who breathed. ¹⁵ As the LORD had commanded his servant Moses, so Moses commanded Joshua, and so Joshua did; he left nothing undone of all that the LORD had commanded Moses.

Summary of Joshua's Conquests

16 So Joshua took all that land: the hill country and all the Negeb and all the land of Goshen and the lowland and the Arabah and the hill country of Israel and its lowland, ¹⁷ from Mount Halak, which rises toward Seir, as far as Baal-gad in the

---

Mount Hermon.   **11.4** Hazor in the Middle Bronze Age was adjacent to the land of Amurru, which was notable for its export of *horses*. The *chariots*, here mentioned for the first time in Joshua, are probably the lighter two-man variety (carrying a driver and a warrior), which were easily dismantled and transported for assembly in suitable terrain, in contrast to the heavier Hittite chariots which also carried a shieldbearer (and thus a three-man team).   **11.5** *Waters of Merom*, possibly the pond Birket el-Jish roughly four kilometers northeast of Meron. The Wadi Meron is too deep and rugged for a rendezvous involving chariotry.   **11.6** *Do not be afraid of them*, standard Deuteronomic encouragement (8.1; 10.8, 25). As at the "siege" of Jericho (6.3–5) and again at the second battle for Ai (8.18), Yahweh takes direct command to *hamstring their horses* (beginning of the action) *and burn their chariots* (conclusion of the action). Israel would not be in a position to use such newfangled equipment and organization until the imperial days of David and Solomon (2 Sam 8.4; 1 Chr 18.4; 2 Sam 15.1; 1 Kings 1.5; 9.19–22).   **11.8** This verse describes more of a panicked rout than a slaughter. The allied forces seem to have split, some fleeing northwest toward the coastal cities, Sidon and *Misrephoth-maim*. The latter is most likely Khirbet el-Musheirifeh, just

south of Rosh ha-Niqra near the modern Israeli-Lebanese border.   **11.10** As former *head of all those kingdoms*, Hazor had ranked among the most prominent city-state kingdoms of Middle Bronze Age Canaan.   **11.13** The treatment of Hazor was remembered as an exception among towns occupying tells (and thus preferable sites for resettling). Apparently opposition to the Yahwist movement in Galilee was strongest at Hazor.   **11.15** *As the LORD had commanded his servant Moses.* This verse forms a strong inclusion with v. 12 and echoes introductory rhetoric (1.7). There is no indication, however, that Moses had any interest in Galilee. The intervening stories thus serve as examples of how Moses' teaching had been followed.   **11.16–23** Summary of the warfare. This is the second such summary. The first one covers the south (10.40–42). The result is a two-phase presentation of the "conquest," which is now to be followed by a two-phase portrayal of the "settlement" era, described respectively in 13.1–17.18 and 18.1–19.53. The first phase may have been based at Shechem (cf. 8.30–35) or perhaps Gilgal (cf. 10.15, 43). The second phase was based at Shiloh (18.1).   **11.17** *Mount Halak*, "Mount Baldy," lies far to the southeast of Beer-sheba. *Seir* refers to the mountains of Edom. The location of

valley of Lebanon below Mount Hermon. He took all their kings, struck them down, and put them to death. 18 Joshua made war a long time with all those kings. 19 There was not a town that made peace with the Israelites, except the Hivites, the inhabitants of Gibeon; all were taken in battle. 20 For it was the Lord's doing to harden their hearts so that they would come against Israel in battle, in order that they might be utterly destroyed, and might receive no mercy, but be exterminated, just as the Lord had commanded Moses.

21 At that time Joshua came and wiped out the Anakim from the hill country, from Hebron, from Debir, from Anab, and from all the hill country of Judah, and from all the hill country of Israel; Joshua utterly destroyed them with their towns. 22 None of the Anakim was left in the land of the Israelites; some remained only in Gaza, in Gath, and in Ashdod. 23 So Joshua took the whole land, according to all that the Lord had spoken to Moses; and Joshua gave it for an inheritance to Israel according to their tribal allotments. And the land had rest from war.

The Kings Conquered by Moses

12 Now these are the kings of the land, whom the Israelites defeated, whose land they occupied beyond the Jordan toward the east, from the Wadi Arnon to Mount Hermon, with all the Arabah eastward: 2 King Sihon of the Amorites who lived at Heshbon, and ruled from Aroer, which is on the edge of the Wadi Arnon, and from the middle of the valley as far as the river Jabbok, the boundary of the Ammonites, that is, half of Gilead, 3 and the Arabah to the Sea of Chinneroth eastward, and in the direction of Beth-jeshimoth, to the sea of the Arabah, the Dead Sea,^r southward to the foot of the slopes of Pisgah; 4 and King Og^s of Bashan, one of the last of the Rephaim, who lived at Ashtaroth and at

r Heb *Salt Sea*   s Gk: Heb *the boundary of King Og*

Baal-gad is uncertain, possibly Banias near the lower slopes of Mount Hermon. Canaanite Laish (later Israelite Dan) is very near. **11.19** That *all were taken in battle* was the understanding of the historian of the monarchy; it is consistent with the exhortations to faithful service found in Deuteronomy. **11.20** *For it was the Lord's doing . . . be exterminated.* This most extreme statement reflects the nationalistic perspective of the royal historian (Dtr 1; see Introduction). **11.21-22** These verses interrupt the sweeping claim for "all the land." There were areas of continuing resistance, where Israelite constituencies were variously involved. **11.21** *Anakim*, opponents of Israel from the days of Moses (Num 13). They were probably of far northern (Sea Peoples) origin, found in company with Gaza and Ashkelon (both early Philistine settlements) in Jer 47.5. **11.22** *Gaza, Gath, Ashdod*, three Sea People towns. Elimination of the *Anakim* from the southern hills seems to have been overlooked by the royal historian in 10.36-39. The later insertion (Dtr 2; see Introduction) indicates that the actual process was more complex and with more mixed results than previously indicated. **11.23** The summary concludes by emphasizing the obedient chain of command—*Joshua obeys Moses, who obeys the Lord.* The word for *inheritance* had for a long time in ancient feudal society referred to a peasant's plot of land given for promise of services to be rendered. Here *tribal allotments* are to be impartially determined no doubt by use of the sacred

dice called Urim and Thummim. A *land at rest from war* was the goal of the Yahwist reformation/revolution.

12.1-24 A supplemental summary of the former kingdoms based on an older document, probably added by the later editor (Dtr 2; see Introduction), including towns and kings not otherwise mentioned in the book. It also calls attention to the larger Israel which included tribes settled in Transjordan. **12.1-6** Summary of the Transjordanian victories under Moses' leadership. **12.1** *Wadi Arnon*, the immense canyon forming a natural and acknowledged northern border of the kingdom of Moab and the southern limit of Israel's territorial claim in Transjordan prior to the reign of King David. **12.2** The story of *King Sihon* is told in Num 21.21-31. The label *Amorites* here perhaps relates to the great state of Amurru, which early in the thirteenth century B.C.E. became subject to the Hittite king. The exact location of Sihon's capital remains unclear. Occupation at Tell Hesban, which preserves the old name, began in the eleventh century B.C.E. The *Ammonites*, like the Israelites, could not yet be called a "kingdom." *Gilead*, probably a geographical term for the wooded hill country of Transjordan, cut by the deep and winding gorge of the *Jabbok*, the northern limit of Sihon's realm. **12.4** The non-Semitic name of *Og*, who required an exceptionally large bedstead (Deut 3.11), can be explained as Anatolian in origin. *Bashan*, the very productive land centering on the Golan

Edrei 5and ruled over Mount Hermon and Salecah and all Bashan to the boundary of the Geshurites and the Maacathites, and over half of Gilead to the boundary of King Sihon of Heshbon. 6Moses, the servant of the LORD, and the Israelites defeated them; and Moses the servant of the LORD gave their land for a possession to the Reubenites and the Gadites and the half-tribe of Manasseh.

The Kings Conquered by Joshua

7 The following are the kings of the land whom Joshua and the Israelites defeated on the west side of the Jordan, from Baal-gad in the valley of Lebanon to Mount Halak, that rises toward Seir (and Joshua gave their land to the tribes of Israel as a possession according to their allotments, 8in the hill country, in the lowland, in the Arabah, in the slopes, in the wilderness, and in the Negeb, the land of the Hittites, Amorites, Canaanites, Perizzites, Hivites, and Jebusites):

9	the king of Jericho	one
	the king of Ai, which is next to Bethel	one
10	the king of Jerusalem	one
	the king of Hebron	one
11	the king of Jarmuth	one
	the king of Lachish	one
12	the king of Eglon	one
	the king of Gezer	one
13	the king of Debir	one
	the king of Geder	one
14	the king of Hormah	one
	the king of Arad	one
15	the king of Libnah	one
	the king of Adullam	one
16	the king of Makkedah	one
	the king of Bethel	one
17	the king of Tappuah	one
	the king of Hepher	one
18	the king of Aphek	one
	the king of Lasharon	one
19	the king of Madon	one
	the king of Hazor	one
20	the king of Shimron-meron	one
	the king of Achshaph	one
21	the king of Taanach	one
	the king of Megiddo	one
22	the king of Kedesh	one
	the king of Jokneam in Carmel	one
23	the king of Dor in Naphath-dor	one

Heights. *Rephaim* referred originally to an aristocracy of professional chariot warriors, from whose ranks came many of the Canaanite kings. It acquired a secondary sense of "giants," and yet another sense referring to "shades of the dead." **12.5** *Geshurites* and *Maacathites*, two Aramaean (Syrian) groups who were sources of continuing resistance to Israel (13.13) until the time of David, one of whose wives was a Geshurite princess (2 Sam 3.3). **12.7–24** A list of kings dethroned in the era of Joshua making no specific claim to occupation or destruction of towns. **12.9–13a** These verses are closely related to the sequence of stories in 6.1–10.43; every one of these kings has been previously mentioned in those chapters. **12.13b–16a** A passage related in part to ch. 10, but supplying several names in the deep south not previously mentioned—*Geder, Hormah, Arad.* There were no fortified cities in the Negeb, but there were imposing ruins of strong Middle Bronze cities. It is likely that opposing forces, when Israel was based at Kadesh-barnea, were small enough to leave scant artifactual evidence of confrontation. **12.16b–24** Kings from the central and northern regions. **12.16b** *Bethel.* See Judg 1.22–26. **12.17–18** These verses indicate that the takeover of northcentral Canaan did not proceed entirely without violence. **12.17** *Tappuah* was an important town on the border between Ephraim and Manasseh. *Hepher*, a clan of Manasseh situated north of Shechem. **12.18** *Aphek* was never included in any of the tribal claims. *Lasharon*, lit. "to/for the Sharon(-plain)," perhaps intended to cover the entire region which was sparsely settled due to swampy and malarial conditions. **12.19–23** Most of these kings are either mentioned as part of Jabin's coalition (ch. 11) or belong to the coalition's homeland. **12.21** Excavations at *Taanach* suggest a situation in the twelfth-century B.C.E. town where richer Canaanite citizens and poorer Israelite residents were living in distinct residential quarters. Cf. Judg 5.19. *Megiddo* (Hebrew, "Stronghold") controlled the southern flank of the Esdraelon plain and the most heavily traveled route through the Mount Carmel range to the Sharon plain. **12.22** *Kedesh*, probably not the great sanctuary town in the far north (19.37) but a smaller site between Megiddo and Taanach. *Jokneam*, at the tip of Zebulun's southwestern wedge, may have become Israelite at a very early period since there is no mention of it among the unconquered towns in 17.11; Judg 1.27. **12.23** *Goiim in Galilee* suggests the name of Sisera's hometown. "Harosheth-ha-goiim" (Judg

the king of Goiim in
    Galilee,^{t} one
24 the king of Tirzah   one
thirty-one kings in all.

The Parts of Canaan Still Unconquered

13 Now Joshua was old and advanced in years; and the LORD
said to him, "You are old and advanced in
years, and very much of the land still remains to be possessed. 2 This is the land
that still remains: all the regions of the
Philistines, and all those of the Geshurites
3 (from the Shihor, which is east of Egypt,
northward to the boundary of Ekron, it is
reckoned as Canaanite; there are five rulers of the Philistines, those of Gaza, Ashdod, Ashkelon, Gath, and Ekron), and
those of the Avvim 4 in the south; all the
land of the Canaanites, and Mearah that
belongs to the Sidonians, to Aphek, to the
boundary of the Amorites, 5 and the land
of the Gebalites, and all Lebanon, toward
the east, from Baal-gad below Mount
Hermon to Lebo-hamath, 6 all the inhabitants of the hill country from Lebanon to
Misrephoth-maim, even all the Sidonians.
I will myself drive them out from before
the Israelites; only allot the land to Israel
for an inheritance, as I have commanded
you. 7 Now therefore divide this land for
an inheritance to the nine tribes and the
half-tribe of Manasseh."

The Territory East of the Jordan

8 With the other half-tribe of Manas-
seh^u the Reubenites and the Gadites received their inheritance, which Moses
gave them, beyond the Jordan eastward,
as Moses the servant of the LORD gave
them: 9 from Aroer, which is on the edge
of the Wadi Arnon, and the town that is in
the middle of the valley, and all the tableland from^v Medeba as far as Dibon;
10 and all the cities of King Sihon of the
Amorites, who reigned in Heshbon, as far
as the boundary of the Ammonites; 11 and
Gilead, and the region of the Geshurites
and Maacathites, and all Mount Hermon,
and all Bashan to Salecah; 12 all the kingdom of Og in Bashan, who reigned in
Ashtaroth and in Edrei (he alone was left
of the survivors of the Rephaim); these
Moses had defeated and driven out. 13 Yet
the Israelites did not drive out the Geshurites or the Maacathites; but Geshur and
Maacath live within Israel to this day.
14 To the tribe of Levi alone Moses
gave no inheritance; the offerings by fire
to the LORD God of Israel are their inheritance, as he said to them.

The Territory of Reuben

15 Moses gave an inheritance to the
tribe of the Reubenites according to their

t Gk: Heb *Gilgal*   *u* Cn: Heb *With it*
v Compare Gk: Heb lacks *from*

4.2). **12.24** *Tirzah,* probably Tell el-Far'ah (ca.
ten kilometers northeast of Shechem), which was
first favored as capital of the northern throne
(1 Kings 14–16) when it moved the seat of government away from Shechem. *Thirty-one,* the
number of nominally independent "kingdoms" in
an area roughly the size of Vermont.
13.1–19.51 The territorial allotments, with
bits of narrative interspersed. **13.1–7** The territory in western Palestine remaining to be conquered. **13.1** *Now Joshua was old and advanced in
years,* in Hebrew a distinctive idiom, occurring
again in 23.1 (another Dtr 2 chapter; see Introduction). **13.2** *Philistines,* mentioned only here
in the book. Philistia only came under Israelite
control, briefly, during the reigns of David and
Solomon. **13.4–7** This part of the ancient ideal,
control of Phoenicia, was never realized.
13.8–13 This flashback describing the extent
of the Transjordanian conquest and tribal allotments made by Moses, clearly related to 12.1–5
(and Deut 3.8, 10a, more Dtr 2; see Introduction),

begins abruptly. Archaeological evidence and biblical texts combine to indicate that the success of
the Yahwist movement in Transjordan was real
but short-lived. **13.9** *The town . . . in the middle of
the valley* (lit. "of the wadi") perhaps refers to the
general habitable area between two main courses
of the Arnon, which flow together on the west
and also meet twice in the east. **13.13** The first
of a series of explanatory statements faulting various tribes for failure to achieve total "conquest"
(15.63; 16.10; 17.12–13; Judg 1.19, 21, 27–35),
contrary to the summary claims found elsewhere. **13.14** References to Levi here and in
v. 33 frame the description of allotments in
Transjordan. *The tribe of Levi* formed the one exception to all tribes sharing equally in the apportionment of the land. As carriers of the Mosaic
teaching, the Levites were dispersed with residential and grazing rights in designated towns
throughout the land allotted to other tribes
(ch. 21).
13.15–31 Reuben, Gad, and the half-tribe of

clans. 16 Their territory was from Aroer, which is on the edge of the Wadi Arnon, and the town that is in the middle of the valley, and all the tableland by Medeba; 17 with Heshbon, and all its towns that are in the tableland; Dibon, and Bamoth-baal, and Beth-baal-meon, 18 and Jahaz, and Kedemoth, and Mephaath, 19 and Kiria-thaim, and Sibmah, and Zereth-shahar on the hill of the valley, 20 and Beth-peor, and the slopes of Pisgah, and Beth-jeshimoth, 21 that is, all the towns of the tableland, and all the kingdom of King Si-hon of the Amorites, who reigned in Heshbon, whom Moses defeated with the leaders of Midian, Evi and Rekem and Zur and Hur and Reba, as princes of Si-hon, who lived in the land. 22 Along with the rest of those they put to death, the Israelites also put to the sword Balaam son of Beor, who practiced divination. 23 And the border of the Reubenites was the Jordan and its banks. This was the in-heritance of the Reubenites according to their families, with their towns and villages.

The Territory of Gad

24 Moses gave an inheritance also to the tribe of the Gadites, according to their families. 25 Their territory was Jazer, and all the towns of Gilead, and half the land of the Ammonites, to Aroer, which is east of Rabbah, 26 and from Heshbon to Ramath-mizpeh and Betonim, and from Mahanaim to the territory of Debir,*w* 27 and in the valley Beth-haram, Beth-nimrah, Succoth, and Zaphon, the rest of the kingdom of King Sihon of Heshbon, the Jordan and its banks, as far as the lower end of the Sea of Chinnereth, east-ward beyond the Jordan. 28 This is the in-

heritance of the Gadites according to their clans, with their towns and villages.

The Territory of the Half-Tribe of Manasseh (East)

29 Moses gave an inheritance to the half-tribe of Manasseh; it was allotted to the half-tribe of the Manassites according to their families. 30 Their territory ex-tended from Mahanaim, through all Ba-shan, the whole kingdom of King Og of Bashan, and all the settlements of Jair, which are in Bashan, sixty towns, 31 and half of Gilead, and Ashtaroth, and Edrei, the towns of the kingdom of Og in Ba-shan; these were allotted to the people of Machir son of Manasseh according to their clans—for half the Machirites.

32 These are the inheritances that Moses distributed in the plains of Moab, beyond the Jordan east of Jericho. 33 But to the tribe of Levi Moses gave no inheri-tance; the LORD God of Israel is their in-heritance, as he said to them.

The Distribution of Territory West of the Jordan

14 These are the inheritances that the Israelites received in the land of Canaan, which the priest Eleazar, and Joshua son of Nun, and the heads of the families of the tribes of the Israelites dis-tributed to them. 2 Their inheritance was by lot, as the LORD had commanded Mo-ses for the nine and one-half tribes. 3 For Moses had given an inheritance to the two and one-half tribes beyond the Jordan; but to the Levites he gave no inheritance among them. 4 For the people of Joseph were two tribes, Manasseh and Ephraim;

w Gk Syr Vg: Heb Lidebir

Manasseh. **13.15–28** The geographical ar-rangement here (Reuben in the south, Gad in the north) is at odds with the story line in Num 32.34–38. **13.15** The *Reubenites* receive the larger southern segment of Sihon's realm. **13.16** The *Wadi Arnon*, the southern limit of Israel's claim. **13.21** *Tableland*, or "plateau," must refer to an administrative unit that includes major western approaches from the Jordan Val-ley. *Leaders of Midian*, another coalition, evidence that an earlier amity created in the days of Mo-ses and Jethro had collapsed (cf. Judg 7–8). **13.22** *Balaam son of Beor*. Cf. Num 22–24. Texts referring to Balaam were found in 1967 at Tell

Deir Alla in Transjordan. **13.24** To the *Gadites* is allotted the southern half of Gilead, overlap-ping the northern stretch of Sihon's turf while reducing the reach of Ammonite sovereignty by half. **13.30** *Bashan*, the Golan Heights, lies north of the Yarmuk River. *Jair*. See Num 32.41 (Deut 3.14). **13.31** This *half of Gilead* is territory north of the Jabbok.

14.1–5 Introduction to the western allot-ments. **14.1** *Land of Canaan* sounds ironic, oc-curring elsewhere in 21.2; 22.9, 10, 11, 32—all contributions of the later redactor. *Eleazar's* role as keeper of the sacred lot (Urim and Thummim, Deut 33.8) is stipulated at the commissioning of

and no portion was given to the Levites in the land, but only towns to live in, with their pasture lands for their flocks and herds. 5 The Israelites did as the LORD commanded Moses; they allotted the land.

Hebron Allotted to Caleb

6 Then the people of Judah came to Joshua at Gilgal; and Caleb son of Jephunneh the Kenizzite said to him, "You know what the LORD said to Moses the man of God in Kadesh-barnea concerning you and me. 7 I was forty years old when Moses the servant of the LORD sent me from Kadesh-barnea to spy out the land; and I brought him an honest report. 8 But my companions who went up with me made the heart of the people melt; yet I wholeheartedly followed the LORD my God. 9 And Moses swore on that day, saying, 'Surely the land on which your foot has trodden shall be an inheritance for you and your children forever, because you have wholeheartedly followed the LORD my God.' 10 And now, as you see, the LORD has kept me alive, as he said, these forty-five years since the time that the LORD spoke this word to Moses, while Israel was journeying through the wilderness; and here I am today, eighty-five years old. 11 I am still as strong today as I was on the day that Moses sent me; my strength now is as my strength was then, for war, and for going and coming. 12 So now give me this hill country of which the LORD spoke on that day; for you heard on that day how the Anakim were there, with great fortified cities; it may be that the LORD will be with me, and I shall drive them out, as the LORD said."

13 Then Joshua blessed him, and gave Hebron to Caleb son of Jephunneh for an inheritance. 14 So Hebron became the inheritance of Caleb son of Jephunneh the Kenizzite to this day, because he wholeheartedly followed the LORD, the God of Israel. 15 Now the name of Hebron formerly was Kiriath-arba;x this Arba wasy the greatest man among the Anakim. And the land had rest from war.

The Territory of Judah

15 The lot for the tribe of the people of Judah according to their families reached southward to the boundary of Edom, to the wilderness of Zin at the farthest south. 2 And their south boundary ran from the end of the Dead Sea,z from the bay that faces southward; 3 it goes out southward of the ascent of Akrabbim, passes along to Zin, and goes up south of Kadesh-barnea, along by Hezron, up to Addar, makes a turn to Karka, 4 passes along to Azmon, goes out by the Wadi of Egypt, and comes to its end at the sea. This shall be your south boundary. 5 And the east boundary is the Dead Sea,z to the mouth of the Jordan. And the boundary on the north side runs from the bay of the sea at the mouth of the Jordan; 6 and the boundary goes up to Beth-hoglah, and passes along north of Beth-arabah; and the boundary goes up to the Stone of Bohan, Reuben's son; 7 and the boundary goes up to Debir from the Valley of Achor, and so northward, turning toward Gilgal, which is opposite the ascent of Adummim, which is on the south side of the valley; and the boundary passes along to the waters of En-shemesh, and ends at En-rogel; 8 then the boundary goes up by

x That is *the city of Arba*   y Heb lacks *this Arba was*   z Heb *Salt Sea*

Joshua (Num 27.21). **14.4** The *Levites* have no territorial identity, and so *the people of Joseph were two tribes, Manasseh and Ephraim,* to make twelve. **14.6–15** Allotment to Caleb in the south, invoking a promise by Moses, is a special case structurally balanced by the example of Zelophehad's daughters in the north (17.1–6). **14.6** *Came,* or "had come," thus setting the scene at *Gilgal* prior to the hill country warfare. **14.7** *The LORD sent me from Kadesh-barnea to spy.* See Num 13. **14.12** That Joshua has already settled accounts with the *Anakim* (11.21–22) confirms the reading of this chapter as a flashback. Tradition described the Anakim as of awesome stature (Num 13.28;

Deut 2.21; 9.2), descended from a union of divine and human beings (Gen 6.4; Num 13.33). **14.13** *Hebron,* twenty miles south of Jerusalem, figures prominently in stories of the ancestors, especially Sarah and Abraham (see Gen 13.18; 18.1; 23.19). It was the hub of the powerful tribe of Judah, where David first became king (2 Sam 2.1–5). The story of Caleb resumes in 15.13–19. **14.15** *And the land had rest from war* echoes the identical statement at the end of ch. 11, framing the lengthy explanatory additions, chs. 12–14.

15.1–63 Judah gets pride of place in description of the territories in Canaan. **15.1–12** Judah's boundaries. **15.8–9** Description of the

the valley of the son of Hinnom at the southern slope of the Jebusites (that is, Jerusalem); and the boundary goes up to the top of the mountain that lies over against the valley of Hinnom, on the west, at the northern end of the valley of Rephaim; 9 then the boundary extends from the top of the mountain to the spring of the Waters of Nephtoah, and from there to the towns of Mount Ephron; then the boundary bends around to Baalah (that is, Kiriath-jearim); 10 and the boundary circles west of Baalah to Mount Seir, passes along to the northern slope of Mount Jearim (that is, Chesalon), and goes down to Beth-shemesh, and passes along by Timnah; 11 the boundary goes out to the slope of the hill north of Ekron, then the boundary bends around to Shikkeron, and passes along to Mount Baalah, and goes out to Jabneel; then the boundary comes to an end at the sea. 12 And the west boundary was the Mediterranean with its coast. This is the boundary surrounding the people of Judah according to their families.

Caleb Occupies His Portion

13 According to the commandment of the LORD to Joshua, he gave to Caleb son of Jephunneh a portion among the people of Judah, Kiriath-arba,[a] that is, Hebron (Arba was the father of Anak). 14 And Caleb drove out from there the three sons of Anak: Sheshai, Ahiman, and Talmai, the descendants of Anak. 15 From there he went up against the inhabitants of Debir; now the name of Debir formerly was Kiriath-sepher. 16 And Caleb said, "Whoever attacks Kiriath-sepher and takes it, to him I will give my daughter Achsah as wife." 17 Othniel son of Kenaz, the brother of Caleb, took it; and he gave him his daughter Achsah as wife. 18 When she came to him, she urged him to ask her father for a field. As she dismounted from her donkey, Caleb said to her,

"What do you wish?" 19 She said to him, "Give me a present; since you have set me in the land of the Negeb, give me springs of water as well." So Caleb gave her the upper springs and the lower springs.

The Towns of Judah

20 This is the inheritance of the tribe of the people of Judah according to their families. 21 The towns belonging to the tribe of the people of Judah in the extreme south, toward the boundary of Edom, were Kabzeel, Eder, Jagur, 22 Kinah, Dimonah, Adadah, 23 Kedesh, Hazor, Ithnan, 24 Ziph, Telem, Bealoth, 25 Hazor-hadattah, Kerioth-hezron (that is, Hazor), 26 Amam, Shema, Moladah, 27 Hazar-gaddah, Heshmon, Beth-pelet, 28 Hazar-shual, Beer-sheba, Biziothiah, 29 Baalah, Iim, Ezem, 30 Eltolad, Chesil, Hormah, 31 Ziklag, Madmannah, Sansannah, 32 Lebaoth, Shilhim, Ain, and Rimmon: in all, twenty-nine towns, with their villages.

33 And in the lowland, Eshtaol, Zorah, Ashnah, 34 Zanoah, En-gannim, Tappuah, Enam, 35 Jarmuth, Adullam, Socoh, Azekah, 36 Shaaraim, Adithaim, Gederah, Gederothaim: fourteen towns with their villages.

37 Zenan, Hadashah, Migdal-gad, 38 Dilan, Mizpeh, Jokthe-el, 39 Lachish, Bozkath, Eglon, 40 Cabbon, Lahmam, Chitlish, 41 Gederoth, Beth-dagon, Naamah, and Makkedah: sixteen towns with their villages.

42 Libnah, Ether, Ashan, 43 Iphtah, Ashnah, Nezib, 44 Keilah, Achzib, and Mareshah: nine towns with their villages.

45 Ekron, with its dependencies and its villages; 46 from Ekron to the sea, all that were near Ashdod, with their villages.

47 Ashdod, its towns and its villages; Gaza, its towns and its villages; to the

a That is *the city of Arba*

---

northern border carefully skirts *Jerusalem* on the south.
15.13–19 This resumption and partial repetition of Caleb's acquisition of Hebron (14.6–12) and its sequel interrupts the cartographic description. **15.14** *Sheshai, Ahiman, and Talmai*. Not clearly Semitic, these names probably came to Canaan with an early wave of Sea Peoples. **15.15** *Debir*. See note on 10.36–39. **15.16–19** The

story of Othniel and Achsah is repeated nearly verbatim in Judg 1.12–15 (Dtr 2; see Introduction).
15.20–63 This list of towns belonging to Judah, organized into districts, is probably based on later administrative organization in the kingdom of Judah. 1 Kings 4.7–19 has a similar list covering the entire country from the reign of Solomon. **15.63** *Jebusites*. The pre-Israelite name of

Wadi of Egypt, and the Great Sea with its coast.

48 And in the hill country, Shamir, Jattir, Socoh, 49 Dannah, Kiriath-sannah (that is, Debir), 50 Anab, Eshtemoh, Anim, 51 Goshen, Holon, and Giloh: eleven towns with their villages.

52 Arab, Dumah, Eshan, 53 Janim, Beth-tappuah, Aphekah, 54 Humtah, Kiriath-arba (that is, Hebron), and Zior: nine towns with their villages.

55 Maon, Carmel, Ziph, Juttah, 56 Jezreel, Jokdeam, Zanoah, 57 Kain, Gibeah, and Timnah: ten towns with their villages.

58 Halhul, Beth-zur, Gedor, 59 Maarath, Beth-anoth, and Eltekon: six towns with their villages.

60 Kiriath-baal (that is, Kiriathjearim) and Rabbah: two towns with their villages.

61 In the wilderness, Beth-arabah, Middin, Secacah, 62 Nibshan, the City of Salt, and En-gedi: six towns with their villages.

63 But the people of Judah could not drive out the Jebusites, the inhabitants of Jerusalem; so the Jebusites live with the people of Judah in Jerusalem to this day.

The Territory of Ephraim

16 The allotment of the Josephites went from the Jordan by Jericho, east of the waters of Jericho, into the wilderness, going up from Jericho into the hill country to Bethel; 2 then going from Bethel to Luz, it passes along to Ataroth, the territory of the Archites; 3 then it goes down westward to the territory of the Japhletites, as far as the territory of Lower Beth-horon, then to Gezer, and it ends at the sea.

4 The Josephites — Manasseh and Ephraim — received their inheritance.

5 The territory of the Ephraimites by their families was as follows: the boundary of their inheritance on the east was Ataroth-addar as far as Upper Bethhoron, 6 and the boundary goes from there to the sea; on the north is Michmethath; then on the east the boundary makes a turn toward Taanath-shiloh, and passes along beyond it on the east to Janoah, 7 then it goes down from Janoah to Ataroth and to Naarah, and touches Jericho, ending at the Jordan. 8 From Tappuah the boundary goes westward to the Wadi Kanah, and ends at the sea. Such is the inheritance of the tribe of the Ephraimites by their families, 9 together with the towns that were set apart for the Ephraimites within the inheritance of the Manassites, all those towns with their villages. 10 They did not, however, drive out the Canaanites who lived in Gezer: so the Canaanites have lived within Ephraim to this day but have been made to do forced labor.

The Other Half-Tribe of Manasseh (West)

17 Then allotment was made to the tribe of Manasseh, for he was the firstborn of Joseph. To Machir the firstborn of Manasseh, the father of Gilead, were allotted Gilead and Bashan, because he was a warrior. 2 And allotments were made to the rest of the tribe of Manasseh,

---

Jerusalem was "Jebus." See also note on 13.13.
16.1–10 The Ephraimites named after one of the two sons of Joseph who take the place of "Levi" in a roster of twelve territorial units. **16.1–4** Ephraim's border with Benjamin and Dan is given in very general terms. **16.2** *Bethel* and *Luz* are the same place in Judg 1.22–26. The change of name to Bethel was credited to Jacob (Gen 28.19; 35.6; 48.3). *Archites* refers to a clan or village population that became part of Benjamin. One of David's most loyal advisers, Hushai, was recruited from them (2 Sam 15.32; 16.16; 17.5). **16.3** *Gezer.* See 10.33. **16.5–10** The fragmentary description of borders for the great northern tribe contrasts sharply with the description of Judah in ch. 15. **16.10** *Canaanites . . . forced labor.* The chapter concludes on a note of partial failure, which appears sporadically throughout the

description of the northern tribes (cf. note on 13.13).
17.1–13 Western Manasseh. Description of Manasseh west of the Jordan, unlike the preceding tribal descriptions, falls into two parts, one concerned with subgroups (vv. 1–6), one with borders (vv. 7–13). **17.1–2** *Tribe of Manasseh.* The families, or "clans," of Manasseh here constitute a tribe, in contrast to the eastern "half-tribe" in 13.29 and elsewhere. **17.1** *Firstborn of Joseph.* See Gen 41.51; 46.20. *Machir* as "eldest son" of Manasseh appears to have been a constituency that was originally at home in the west (Judg 5.14) and then in part shifted to Transjordan. *Father of Gilead.* Genealogy adjusts to reflect changing socio-political realities (cf. Num 26.28–34; 1 Chr 7.14–19). Gilead was originally a geographical term (12.2, 5; 13.11, 25, 31). **17.2** *The rest of the*

by their families, Abiezer, Helek, Asriel, Shechem, Hepher, and Shemida; these were the male descendants of Manasseh son of Joseph, by their families.

3 Now Zelophehad son of Hepher son of Gilead son of Machir son of Manasseh had no sons, but only daughters; and these are the names of his daughters: Mahlah, Noah, Hoglah, Milcah, and Tirzah. 4 They came before the priest Eleazar and Joshua son of Nun and the leaders, and said, "The LORD commanded Moses to give us an inheritance along with our male kin." So according to the commandment of the LORD he gave them an inheritance among the kinsmen of their father. 5 Thus there fell to Manasseh ten portions, besides the land of Gilead and Bashan, which is on the other side of the Jordan, 6 because the daughters of Manasseh received an inheritance along with his sons. The land of Gilead was allotted to the rest of the Manassites.

7 The territory of Manasseh reached from Asher to Michmethath, which is east of Shechem; then the boundary goes along southward to the inhabitants of Entappuah. 8 The land of Tappuah belonged to Manasseh, but the town of Tappuah on the boundary of Manasseh belonged to the Ephraimites. 9 Then the boundary went down to the Wadi Kanah. The towns here, to the south of the wadi,

among the towns of Manasseh, belong to Ephraim. Then the boundary of Manasseh goes along the north side of the wadi and ends at the sea. 10 The land to the south is Ephraim's and that to the north is Manasseh's, with the sea forming its boundary; on the north Asher is reached, and on the east Issachar. 11 Within Issachar and Asher, Manasseh had Bethshean and its villages, Ibleam and its villages, the inhabitants of Dor and its villages, the inhabitants of En-dor and its villages, the inhabitants of Taanach and its villages, and the inhabitants of Megiddo and its villages (the third is Naphath).b 12 Yet the Manassites could not take possession of those towns; but the Canaanites continued to live in that land. 13 But when the Israelites grew strong, they put the Canaanites to forced labor, but did not utterly drive them out.

The Tribe of Joseph Protests

14 The tribe of Joseph spoke to Joshua, saying, "Why have you given me but one lot and one portion as an inheritance, since we are a numerous people, whom all along the LORD has blessed?" 15 And Joshua said to them, "If you are a

b Meaning of Heb uncertain

---

tribe of Manasseh were those who had not already settled in Transjordan. Abiezer ("Iezer" in Num 26.30), Gideon's hometown (Judg 6.11, 24, 34). Helek is the area to the northwest of Shechem. Asriel (1 Chr 7.14) is located northwest of Helek. Shechem in the perspective of the first edition (Dtr 1; see Introduction) figures merely as one of the clans of Manasseh and is otherwise not mentioned until the end of the era (ch. 24). Hepher is the area north of Shechem, but see also "Epher" in 1 Chr 5.24. Shemida. Shechem is one of his sons in 1 Chr 7.19. 17.3–6 Special provision for the daughters of Zelophehad in the north balances the special treatment of Caleb in the south (14.6–15; 15.13–14). Both are based on appeal to a prior ruling from Moses. Location of the areas identified by the names Mahlah, Noah, Hoglah, and Milcah are unknown. Tirzah is probably the impressive site of Tell el-Far'ah, north of Shechem. 17.4 Eleazar is always mentioned before Joshua when they are found together (14.1; 21.1). The LORD commanded Moses. See Num 27.1–11. 17.5 Six clans, one of which is "grandfather" of the five daughters, account for ten portions for Ma-

nasseh west of the river. 17.7–13 The boundaries of western Manasseh were sketchy and presented questions about the tribal "ownership" of certain towns (v. 9). For the allotments to the northern tribes there was apparently no archival source comparable to that for Judah and Benjamin in the south. 17.11–13 The plain of Esdraelon (or Jezreel), supporting a number of well-fortified city-states, separated Manasseh from the Galilean tribes. With the exception of Dor and En-dor, the same towns mentioned here are listed as Manasseh's responsibility, unfulfilled, in Judg 1.27. 17.11 Beth-shean was a strongly fortified city controlling the southeast corner of Jezreel Valley. Taanach and Megiddo controlled access from the Plain of Sharon to Jezreel Valley.

17.14–18 These verses show Joshua functioning as "judge," dealing with a petition of the tribe of Joseph (lit. "the sons of Joseph," v. 14), presumably as a single constituency. This is another older story inserted here as the last thing to be said about the pre-Shiloh phase of settlement. 17.15 Perizzites. See 3.10; 9.1; 11.3; 12.8; 24.11. Rephaim. See note on 12.4. The hill country of

numerous people, go up to the forest, and clear ground there for yourselves in the land of the Perizzites and the Rephaim, since the hill country of Ephraim is too narrow for you." 16 The tribe of Joseph said, "The hill country is not enough for us; yet all the Canaanites who live in the plain have chariots of iron, both those in Beth-shean and its villages and those in the Valley of Jezreel." 17 Then Joshua said to the house of Joseph, to Ephraim and Manasseh, "You are indeed a numerous people, and have great power; you shall not have one lot only, 18 but the hill country shall be yours, for though it is a forest, you shall clear it and possess it to its farthest borders; for you shall drive out the Canaanites, though they have chariots of iron, and though they are strong."

The Territories of the Remaining Tribes

18 Then the whole congregation of the Israelites assembled at Shiloh, and set up the tent of meeting there. The land lay subdued before them.
2 There remained among the Israelites seven tribes whose inheritance had not yet been apportioned. 3 So Joshua said to the Israelites, "How long will you be slack about going in and taking possession of the land that the LORD, the God of your ancestors, has given you? 4 Provide three men from each tribe, and I will send them out that they may begin to go throughout the land, writing a description of it with a view to their inheritances. Then come back to me. 5 They shall divide it into seven portions, Judah continuing in its territory on the south, and the house of Joseph in their territory on the north. 6 You shall describe the land in seven divisions and bring the description here to me; and I will cast lots for you here before the LORD our God. 7 The Levites have no portion among you, for the priesthood of the LORD is their heritage; and Gad and Reuben and the half-tribe of Manasseh have received their inheritance beyond the Jordan eastward, which Moses the servant of the LORD gave them."
8 So the men started on their way; and Joshua charged those who went to write the description of the land, saying, "Go throughout the land and write a description of it, and come back to me; and I will cast lots for you here before the LORD in Shiloh." 9 So the men went and traversed the land and set down in a book a description of it by towns in seven divisions; then they came back to Joshua in the camp at Shiloh, 10 and Joshua cast lots for them in Shiloh before the LORD; and there Joshua apportioned the land to the Israelites, to each a portion.

The Territory of Benjamin

11 The lot of the tribe of Benjamin according to its families came up, and the territory allotted to it fell between the tribe of Judah and the tribe of Joseph. 12 On the north side their boundary began at the Jordan; then the boundary goes up

---

Ephraim is most likely the region immediately surrounding the town (2 Sam 13.23) that gave its name to the tribe. **17.16** *Not enough.* It was not merely the heavily forested condition of the hill country that posed the problem, but its extent, hemmed in by Canaanite chariotry of the plains. **17.18** *You shall clear it.* Originally forests covered much of the watershed ridge and western slopes of the hill country. The clearing of forest land required enormous amounts of cooperative labor. **18.1–10** A regional survey of western Palestine is the basis for the remaining allotments. **18.1** *Congregation.* See 9.15–21. See note on 9.18. *Shiloh,* twenty miles north of Jerusalem, has succeeded Gilgal and Shechem as a major sanctuary site and rallying point for the tribes of Israel. It may have been the destruction of Shechem by Abimelech (Judg 9) that brought Shiloh to the fore as the place of tribal assembly. The *tent of meeting* was the portable sanctuary of the wilderness period (Ex 33.7; Num 11.16; 12.4; Deut 31.14). **18.6** *I will cast lots.* Readers are totally unprepared to find Joshua (and not Eleazar; Num 27.21) doing this. **18.7** *Levites.* See 13.14, 33; note on 13.14. *Gad and Reuben and the half-tribe of Manasseh.* See 13.8–32.
18.11–28 Benjamin, immediately to the north of Judah, is the first of seven tribes whose land apportionment is determined at Shiloh. This section returns to the pattern displayed in describing Judah (15.1–63): borders (18.11–20) followed by town list (18.21–28). It may be derived from the same source document. The towns are numerous and close together, concentrated in the area that was the center of action in the warfare recounted in chs. 2–9. The towns are listed in two groups, one crowded onto the watershed ridge north and west of Jerusalem (vv. 25–28), the other on the less desirable eastern ridge and falling away to Jericho and the Jordan.

to the slope of Jericho on the north, then up through the hill country westward, and it ends at the wilderness of Beth-aven. 13 From there the boundary passes along southward in the direction of Luz, to the slope of Luz (that is, Bethel), then the boundary goes down to Ataroth-addar, on the mountain that lies south of Lower Beth-horon. 14 Then the boundary goes in another direction, turning on the western side southward from the mountain that lies to the south, opposite Beth-horon, and it ends at Kiriath-baal (that is, Kiriath-jearim), a town belonging to the tribe of Judah. This forms the western side. 15 The southern side begins at the outskirts of Kiriath-jearim; and the boundary goes from there to Ephron, c to the spring of the Waters of Nephtoah; 16 then the boundary goes down to the border of the mountain that overlooks the valley of the son of Hinnom, which is at the north end of the valley of Rephaim; and it then goes down the valley of Hinnom, south of the slope of the Jebusites, and downward to En-rogel; 17 then it bends in a northerly direction going on to En-shemesh, and from there goes to Geliloth, which is opposite the ascent of Adummim; then it goes down to the Stone of Bohan, Reuben's son; 18 and passing on to the north of the slope of Beth-arabah d it goes down to the Arabah; 19 then the boundary passes on to the north of the slope of Beth-hoglah; and the boundary ends at the northern bay of the Dead Sea, e at the south end of the Jordan: this is the southern border. 20 The Jordan forms its boundary on the eastern side. This is the inheritance of the tribe of Benjamin, according to its families, boundary by boundary all around.

21 Now the towns of the tribe of Benjamin according to their families

were Jericho, Beth-hoglah, Emek-keziz, 22 Beth-arabah, Zemaraim, Bethel, 23 Avvim, Parah, Ophrah, 24 Chephar-ammoni, Ophni, and Geba—twelve towns with their villages: 25 Gibeon, Ramah, Beeroth, 26 Mizpeh, Chephirah, Mozah, 27 Rekem, Irpeel, Taralah, 28 Zela, Haeleph, Jebus f (that is, Jerusalem), Gibeah g and Kiriath-jearim h—fourteen towns with their villages. This is the inheritance of the tribe of Benjamin according to its families.

The Territory of Simeon

19 The second lot came out for Simeon, for the tribe of Simeon, according to its families; its inheritance lay within the inheritance of the tribe of Judah. 2 It had for its inheritance Beer-sheba, Sheba, Moladah, 3 Hazar-shual, Balah, Ezem, 4 Eltolad, Bethul, Hormah, 5 Ziklag, Beth-marcaboth, Hazar-susah, 6 Beth-lebaoth, and Sharuhen—thirteen towns with their villages; 7 Ain, Rimmon, Ether, and Ashan—four towns with their villages; 8 together with all the villages all around these towns as far as Baalath-beer, Ramah of the Negeb. This was the inheritance of the tribe of Simeon according to its families. 9 The inheritance of the tribe of Simeon formed part of the territory of Judah; because the portion of the tribe of Judah was too large for them, the tribe of Simeon obtained an inheritance within their inheritance.

The Territory of Zebulun

10 The third lot came up for the tribe of Zebulun, according to its families. The

---

c Cn See 15.9. Heb *westward*   d Gk: Heb *to the slope over against the Arabah*   e Heb *Salt Sea*   f Gk Syr Vg: Heb *the Jebusite*   g Heb *Gibeath*   h Gk: Heb *Kiriath*

19.1–9 In the case of Simeon, situated at the brink of the Negeb desert and entirely surrounded by Judah, there is no trace of boundary descriptions, only a list of towns. The situation is explained in terms of Judah's magnanimity for a near destitute brother (v. 9). Simeon had once ranged much farther north (Gen 34; 49.5–6). **19.2–8a** This list of towns is very closely related to the second part of Judah's first district, the northern Negeb around Beer-sheba (15.26–32), and even more closely related to the Simeonite towns in 1 Chr 4.28–32. Differences between Simeon's area here and Judah's first district re-

flect political and demographic changes that came with consolidation of the large tribe of Judah, as implicitly acknowledged in v. 9. Rapid, if short-lived, development of the region—a pattern of permanent unwalled villages all across the northern Negeb at the beginning of the Iron Age—provides archaeological illustration. The rapid demise of the villages (early tenth century B.C.E.) is readily attributed to Philistine and Amalekite pressures. **19.10–16** Zebulun's territory was the poorer southern flank of the Galilean mountains together with a contiguous wedge out of the Jezreel

boundary of its inheritance reached as far as Sarid; 11then its boundary goes up westward, and on to Maralah, and touches Dabbesheth, then the wadi that is east of Jokneam; 12from Sarid it goes in the other direction eastward toward the sunrise to the boundary of Chisloth-tabor; from there it goes to Daberath, then up to Japhia; 13from there it passes along on the east toward the sunrise to Gath-hepher, to Eth-kazin, and going on to Rimmon it bends toward Neah; 14then on the north the boundary makes a turn to Hannathon, and it ends at the valley of Iphtah-el; 15and Kattath, Nahalal, Shimron, Idalah, and Bethlehem—twelve towns with their villages. 16This is the inheritance of the tribe of Zebulun, according to its families—these towns with their villages.

The Territory of Issachar

17   The fourth lot came out for Issachar, for the tribe of Issachar, according to its families. 18Its territory included Jezreel, Chesulloth, Shunem, 19Hapharaim, Shion, Anaharath, 20Rabbith, Kishion, Ebez, 21Remeth, En-gannim, En-haddah, Beth-pazzez; 22the boundary also touches Tabor, Shahazumah, and Beth-shemesh, and its boundary ends at the Jordan—sixteen towns with their villages. 23This is the inheritance of the tribe of Issachar, according to its families—the towns with their villages.

The Territory of Asher

24   The fifth lot came out for the tribe of Asher according to its families. 25Its boundary included Helkath, Hali, Beten, Achshaph, 26Allammelech, Amad, and Mishal; on the west it touches Carmel and Shihor-libnath, 27then it turns eastward, goes to Beth-dagon, and touches Zebulun and the valley of Iphtah-el northward to Beth-emek and Neiel; then it continues in the north to Cabul, 28Ebron, Rehob, Hammon, Kanah, as far as Great Sidon; 29then the boundary turns to Ramah, reaching to the fortified city of Tyre; then the boundary turns to Hosah, and it ends at the sea; Mahalab,i Achzib, 30Ummah, Aphek, and Rehob—twenty-two towns with their villages. 31This is the inheritance of the tribe of Asher according to its families—these towns with their villages.

The Territory of Naphtali

32   The sixth lot came out for the tribe of Naphtali, for the tribe of Naphtali, according to its families. 33And its boundary ran from Heleph, from the oak in Zaanannim, and Adami-nekeb, and Jabneel, as far as Lakkum; and it ended at the Jordan; 34then the boundary turns westward to Aznoth-tabor, and goes from there to Hukkok, touching Zebulun at the south, and Asher on the west, and Judah

i Cn Compare Gk: Heb *Mehebel*

---

plain. The boundary descriptions in this chapter look like fragments that vary greatly in their state of preservation.
19.17–23   Issachar's territory was the center of a continuing struggle to control the fertile fields and strategic crossroads of the Jezreel Valley. Here there is no effort to describe a border. Instead, three fixed reference points (Jezreel, Tabor, and the Jordan) are given with two segments of a town list intervening. **19.17** *Issachar*, lit. "hired man," which may refer to forced labor at one time supplied by this tribe in the fields and caravans of Jezreel. **19.18** *Jezreel*. The village (modern Zer'in), at the foot of Mount Gilboa, looks out upon the entire fertile plain of Jezreel. **19.22** The isolated round dome of Mount *Tabor*, at the southern limit of the Galilean mountains and five miles east of Nazareth, is the most conspicuous landmark in the entire region.
19.24–31   The tribe of Asher claimed one of the most prosperous areas, the lush plain of Acco

and its narrowing northern extension as far as Rosh ha-Niqra (the ancient Ladder of Tyre). It is not clear that Sidon (v. 28) and Tyre (v. 29) were counted as part of Israelite territory.   **19.25** The king of *Achshaph* was in league with Jabin of Hazor (11.1) and was removed by Israel (12.20). The Mount *Carmel* spur juts to the coast just south of Haifa Bay, presenting steep and precipitous slopes, a decisive natural boundary.   **19.27** *Cabul* lies about fourteen kilometers east-southeast of Acco, the center of a district of twenty towns that Solomon traded to Hiram of Tyre in exchange for building supplies (1 Kings 9.13).
19.32–39   The territory described for Naphtali is the heartland of Galilee. Major trade routes connecting the port of Acco and the coastal plains with all points north and northeast passed through this corridor.   **19.33** For the *boundary* this verse projects a line running for the most part along the eastern crests of Galilee (but including the little plain of Chinnereth). The *oak in Zaanan-*

on the east at the Jordan. 35 The fortified towns are Ziddim, Zer, Hammath,
Rakkath, Chinnereth, 36 Adamah, Ramah, Hazor, 37 Kedesh, Edrei, En-hazor,
38 Iron, Migdal-el, Horem, Beth-anath,
and Beth-shemesh—nineteen towns with
their villages. 39 This is the inheritance of
the tribe of Naphtali according to its
families—the towns with their villages.

The Territory of Dan

40 The seventh lot came out for the
tribe of Dan, according to its families.
41 The territory of its inheritance included
Zorah, Eshtaol, Ir-shemesh, 42 Shaalabbin,
Aijalon, Ithlah, 43 Elon, Timnah, Ekron,
44 Eltekeh, Gibbethon, Baalath, 45 Jehud,
Bene-berak, Gath-rimmon, 46 Me-jarkon,
and Rakkon at the border opposite Joppa.
47 When the territory of the Danites was
lost to them, the Danites went up and
fought against Leshem, and after captur-
ing it and putting it to the sword, they
took possession of it and settled in it, calling Leshem, Dan, after their ancestor
Dan. 48 This is the inheritance of the tribe
of Dan, according to their families—these
towns with their villages.

Joshua's Inheritance

49 When they had finished distribut-
ing the several territories of the land as
inheritances, the Israelites gave an inheritance among them to Joshua son of Nun.
50 By command of the LORD they gave
him the town that he asked for, Timnath-
serah in the hill country of Ephraim; he
rebuilt the town, and settled in it.
51 These are the inheritances that the
priest Eleazar and Joshua son of Nun and
the heads of the families of the tribes of
the Israelites distributed by lot at Shiloh
before the LORD, at the entrance of the
tent of meeting. So they finished dividing
the land.

The Cities of Refuge

20 Then the LORD spoke to Joshua,
saying, 2 "Say to the Israelites,
'Appoint the cities of refuge, of which I
spoke to you through Moses, 3 so that anyone who kills a person without intent or
by mistake may flee there; they shall be
for you a refuge from the avenger of
blood. 4 The slayer shall flee to one of
these cities and shall stand at the entrance

---

nim figures in the story of Deborah (Judg 4.11).
19.35 *Fortified towns.* Naphtali was remembered
as especially formidable.   **19.37** *Kedesh.* Tell
Qades, in the hills approximately eleven kilometers northwest of Hazor, is perhaps the most impressive archaeological site in the entire land.
There was also a Kedesh in Issachar (1 Chr 6.72)
and another one in southern Naphtali (Khirbet
Kedesh near the southwestern tip of the Sea of
Galilee). Despite the presence of walled towns
controlling the valleys, the highlands of Galilee in
the twelfth century B.C.E. saw a rapid multiplication of unwalled villages whose inhabitants practiced a satisfactory subsistence farming, thanks to
the construction of agricultural terraces. These
villages can be plausibly recognized as part of a
withdrawal from Canaanite society and expansion
of the Israelite movement.
19.40–48   While the tradition located Dan
originally in the south, as described here, it also
remembered Dan's relocation in the far north.
19.40–46 These verses resemble the form that
has been used throughout, a combination of border elements and lists. Dan's territory is a wedge
of coastal region bordering Judah on the south,
Ephraim on the north, and Benjamin to the
east.   **19.47–48** See Judg 18 for the story of
Dan's migration. *Leshem* is "Laish" in Judg 18.27.
19.49–51 Conclusion to the redistribution of

the land. Joshua receives a personal inheritance.
19.50 *Timnath-serah in the hill country of Ephraim,*
Khirbet Tibnah, some twenty-four kilometers
southwest of Shechem.   **19.51** This verse and
14.1, especially in the mention of leaders Eleazar
and Joshua, form a strong inclusion. At the same
time, this verse echoes 18.1 at the beginning of
the Shiloh phase. From this point on, *Eleazar* will
be mentioned with surprising frequency (21.1;
22.13, 31, 32; 24.33). Mention of *the heads of the
families* turns back on 14.1. They will appear again
in 21.1.
20.1–9   Introduction of the first of two institutions with high symbolic value in the final edition (Dtr 2; see Introduction), *cities of refuge* (v. 2).
Six towns were so designated as a means of curbing the blood feud. They provided right of asylum for one accused of murder until the case was
properly tried.   **20.2** This setting up of the cities
of refuge completed what God had commanded
Moses (Num 35.9–34), who so designated three
towns in Transjordan (Deut 4.41–43) and commanded Joshua to do the same west of the river
(Deut 19.1–13).   **20.3** The *avenger* (Hebrew, "redeemer") *of blood* was the nearest relative of the
deceased.   **20.4** The *gate of the city* was an elaborate structure, often two stories high with guard-
rooms and bench-lined courts and towers, where
the elders met to hear cases and to conduct other

of the gate of the city, and explain the case to the elders of that city; then the fugitive shall be taken into the city, and given a place, and shall remain with them. 5 And if the avenger of blood is in pursuit, they shall not give up the slayer, because the neighbor was killed by mistake, there having been no enmity between them before. 6 The slayer shall remain in that city until there is a trial before the congregation, until the death of the one who is high priest at the time: then the slayer may return home, to the town in which the deed was done.' "

7 So they set apart Kedesh in Galilee in the hill country of Naphtali, and Shechem in the hill country of Ephraim, and Kiriath-arba (that is, Hebron) in the hill country of Judah. 8 And beyond the Jordan east of Jericho, they appointed Bezer in the wilderness on the tableland, from the tribe of Reuben, and Ramoth in Gilead, from the tribe of Gad, and Golan in Bashan, from the tribe of Manasseh. 9 These were the cities designated for all the Israelites, and for the aliens residing among them, that anyone who killed a person without intent could flee there, so as not to die by the hand of the avenger of blood, until there was a trial before the congregation.

Cities Allotted to the Levites

21 Then the heads of the families of the Levites came to the priest Eleazar and to Joshua son of Nun and to the heads of the families of the tribes of the Israelites; 2 they said to them at Shiloh in the land of Canaan, "The LORD commanded through Moses that we be given towns to live in, along with their pasture lands for our livestock." 3 So by command of the LORD the Israelites gave to the Levites the following towns and pasture lands out of their inheritance.

4 The lot came out for the families of the Kohathites. So those Levites who were descendants of Aaron the priest received by lot thirteen towns from the tribes of Judah, Simeon, and Benjamin.

5 The rest of the Kohathites received by lot ten towns from the families of the tribe of Ephraim, from the tribe of Dan, and the half-tribe of Manasseh.

6 The Gershonites received by lot thirteen towns from the families of the tribe of Issachar, from the tribe of Asher, from the tribe of Naphtali, and from the half-tribe of Manasseh in Bashan.

7 The Merarites according to their families received twelve towns from the tribe of Reuben, the tribe of Gad, and the tribe of Zebulun.

8 These towns and their pasture lands the Israelites gave by lot to the Levites, as the LORD had commanded through Moses.

9 Out of the tribe of Judah and the tribe of Simeon they gave the following towns mentioned by name, 10 which went to the descendants of Aaron, one of the families of the Kohathites who belonged to the Levites, since the lot fell to them first. 11 They gave them Kiriath-arba

---

public business. The elders, infrequently mentioned in the body of the book (7.6; 8.10, 33; 9.11), are especially important in these concluding chapters (23.2; 24.1, 31). **20.6** The *death of the ... high priest* was apparently occasion for a general amnesty (Num 35.25, 28). **20.7** The three towns designated by Joshua were *Kedesh* (probably the great mound of Tell Qades in upper Galilee), *Shechem*, in the north central hill country, and *Kiriath-arba (that is, Hebron)*, in the south. **20.8** The three in Transjordan were *Bezer*, on the southern plateau opposite Hebron, *Ramoth in Gilead*, opposite Shechem, and *Golan in Bashan*, opposite Kedesh. Each of these is also included in the list of Levitical cities (ch. 21). **20.9** There is no trace of the cities of refuge system functioning during the monarchical period, when it was probably displaced by a more elaborate system of law courts. It was revived by the later redactor (Dtr 2;

see Introduction) because of its symbolic value in relation to responsibilities of the *congregation* (cf. 9.15, 18, 19, 21, 27), which survived in the Babylonian exile. **21.1–42** In Num 35.1–8, Moses is commanded to establish a system of Levitical cities, so designated to provide residential and grazing rights for families of this tribe which had no territorial inheritance. The Levites were dispersed throughout Israel as bearers and teachers of the covenant tradition. The roster of towns (mostly paralleled in 1 Chr 6.54–81) must have fluctuated over time. The earliest period in which all of the towns on the list were occupied, judging from the evidence of archaeology, was the eighth century B.C.E. **21.1** *Heads of families, Eleazar, Joshua.* See 14.1; 17.4; 19.51. **21.2** That *Shiloh* is *in the land of Canaan* (see also 22.9; Judg 21.12) provides

(Arba being the father of Anak), that is Hebron, in the hill country of Judah, along with the pasture lands around it. 12 But the fields of the town and its villages had been given to Caleb son of Jephunneh as his holding.

13 To the descendants of Aaron the priest they gave Hebron, the city of refuge for the slayer, with its pasture lands, Libnah with its pasture lands, 14 Jattir with its pasture lands, Eshtemoa with its pasture lands, 15 Holon with its pasture lands, Debir with its pasture lands, 16 Ain with its pasture lands, Juttah with its pasture lands, and Beth-shemesh with its pasture lands—nine towns out of these two tribes. 17 Out of the tribe of Benjamin: Gibeon with its pasture lands, Geba with its pasture lands, 18 Anathoth with its pasture lands, and Almon with its pasture lands—four towns. 19 The towns of the descendants of Aaron—the priests—were thirteen in all, with their pasture lands.

20 As to the rest of the Kohathites belonging to the Kohathite families of the Levites, the towns allotted to them were out of the tribe of Ephraim. 21 To them were given Shechem, the city of refuge for the slayer, with its pasture lands in the hill country of Ephraim, Gezer with its pasture lands, 22 Kibzaim with its pasture lands, and Beth-horon with its pasture lands—four towns. 23 Out of the tribe of Dan: Elteke with its pasture lands, Gibbethon with its pasture lands, 24 Aijalon with its pasture lands, Gath-rimmon with its pasture lands—four towns. 25 Out of the half-tribe of Manasseh: Taanach with its pasture lands, and Gath-rimmon with its pasture lands—two towns. 26 The towns of the families of the rest of the Kohathites were ten in all, with their pasture lands.

27 To the Gershonites, one of the families of the Levites, were given out of the half-tribe of Manasseh, Golan in Bashan with its pasture lands, the city of refuge for the slayer, and Beeshterah with its pasture lands—two towns. 28 Out of the tribe of Issachar: Kishion with its pasture lands, Daberath with its pasture lands,

29 Jarmuth with its pasture lands, En-gannim with its pasture lands—four towns. 30 Out of the tribe of Asher: Mishal with its pasture lands, Abdon with its pasture lands, 31 Helkath with its pasture lands, and Rehob with its pasture lands—four towns. 32 Out of the tribe of Naphtali: Kedesh in Galilee with its pasture lands, the city of refuge for the slayer, Hammoth-dor with its pasture lands, and Kartan with its pasture lands—three towns. 33 The towns of the several families of the Gershonites were in all thirteen, with their pasture lands.

34 To the rest of the Levites—the Merarite families—were given out of the tribe of Zebulun: Jokneam with its pasture lands, Kartah with its pasture lands, 35 Dimnah with its pasture lands, Nahalal with its pasture lands—four towns. 36 Out of the tribe of Reuben: Bezer with its pasture lands, Jahzah with its pasture lands, 37 Kedemoth with its pasture lands, and Mephaath with its pasture lands—four towns. 38 Out of the tribe of Gad: Ramoth in Gilead with its pasture lands, the city of refuge for the slayer, Mahanaim with its pasture lands, 39 Heshbon with its pasture lands, Jazer with its pasture lands—four towns in all. 40 As for the towns of the several Merarite families, that is, the remainder of the families of the Levites, those allotted to them were twelve in all.

41 The towns of the Levites within the holdings of the Israelites were in all forty-eight towns with their pasture lands. 42 Each of these towns had its pasture lands around it; so it was with all these towns.

43 Thus the LORD gave to Israel all the land that he swore to their ancestors that he would give them; and having taken possession of it, they settled there. 44 And the LORD gave them rest on every side just as he had sworn to their ancestors; not one of all their enemies had withstood them, for the LORD had given all their enemies into their hands. 45 Not one of all the good promises that the LORD had made to the house of Israel had failed; all came to pass.

---

a touch of irony in the final edition (Dtr 2; Introduction), where Israel in the next chapter narrowly averts intertribal war. **21.43–45** This summary makes no reference, direct or indirect, to the cities of refuge and Levitical cities, but fol- lows coherently the end of ch. 19. The rhetoric is thoroughly Deuteronomic. This emphasis on the faithfulness of Yahweh casts in comic relief the squabbling over an altar that follows.

The Eastern Tribes Return to Their Territory

22 Then Joshua summoned the Reubenites, the Gadites, and the half-tribe of Manasseh, 2 and said to them, "You have observed all that Moses the servant of the LORD commanded you, and have obeyed me in all that I have commanded you; 3 you have not forsaken your kindred these many days, down to this day, but have been careful to keep the charge of the LORD your God. 4 And now the LORD your God has given rest to your kindred, as he promised them; therefore turn and go to your tents in the land where your possession lies, which Moses the servant of the LORD gave you on the other side of the Jordan. 5 Take good care to observe the commandment and instruction that Moses the servant of the LORD commanded you, to love the LORD your God, to walk in all his ways, to keep his commandments, and to hold fast to him, and to serve him with all your heart and with all your soul." 6 So Joshua blessed them and sent them away, and they went to their tents.

7 Now to the one half of the tribe of Manasseh Moses had given a possession in Bashan; but to the other half Joshua had given a possession beside their fellow Israelites in the land west of the Jordan. And when Joshua sent them away to their tents and blessed them, 8 he said to them, "Go back to your tents with much wealth, and with very much livestock, with silver, gold, bronze, and iron, and with a great quantity of clothing; divide the spoil of your enemies with your kindred." 9 So the Reubenites and the Gadites and the half-tribe

of Manasseh returned home, parting from the Israelites at Shiloh, which is in the land of Canaan, to go to the land of Gilead, their own land of which they had taken possession by command of the LORD through Moses.

10 When they came to the region*j* near the Jordan that lies in the land of Canaan, the Reubenites and the Gadites and the half-tribe of Manasseh built there an altar by the Jordan, an altar of great size. 11 The Israelites heard that the Reubenites and the Gadites and the half-tribe of Manasseh had built an altar at the frontier of the land of Canaan, in the region*k* near the Jordan, on the side that belongs to the Israelites. 12 And when the people of Israel heard of it, the whole assembly of the Israelites gathered at Shiloh, to make war against them.

13 Then the Israelites sent the priest Phinehas son of Eleazar to the Reubenites and the Gadites and the half-tribe of Manasseh, in the land of Gilead, 14 and with him ten chiefs, one from each of the tribal families of Israel, every one of them the head of a family among the clans of Israel. 15 They came to the Reubenites, the Gadites, and the half-tribe of Manasseh, in the land of Gilead, and they said to them, 16 "Thus says the whole congregation of the LORD, 'What is this treachery that you have committed against the God of Israel in turning away today from following the LORD, by building yourselves an altar today in rebellion against the LORD? 17 Have we not had enough of the sin at Peor from which even yet we have

j Or *to Geliloth*   *k* Or *at Geliloth*

22.1–34 This chapter has three parts. Vv. 1–5 are Joshua's farewell exhortation to the Transjordanian militiamen, structurally balancing the introduction to these tribes in 1.12–18. Vv. 6–8 are a redactional transition to the older story about the altar near the Jordan (vv. 9–34). **22.2** *Moses the servant of the LORD*, an inclusion with 1.1 (cf. 1.2, 7). **22.5** The *commandment and instruction*. The singular form can stand for the entire covenant relationship in Dtn/Dtr (see Introduction). To *love the LORD* (again in address to all the tribes, 23.11) evokes the prime covenant stipulation (Deut 6.5 and repeatedly). **22.6–8** This transition indicates that the warriors, richly laden with booty, might look forward to a splendid homecoming. **22.9–34** The story caricatures some major

"priestly" preoccupations. Cf. the story of events at Gilgal (circumcision and Passover) early in the era (ch. 5), which is the introductory counterpart to this altar story. The unilateral action by the Transjordanian tribes of building a Jordan Valley altar poses a problem of "all-Israel" proportions. **22.10** The referent of *the region near the Jordan* is unclear (intentionally so?). **22.11** *On the side that belongs to the Israelites*. Which side was that? **22.12** *The whole assembly . . . gathered* is wording almost identical to 18.1 (peaceful partitioning of the land), but the situation is inverted (as in the story of full-blown civil war that unfolds in Judg 20). **22.13** *Phinehas son of Eleazar*, probably a predecessor of the ranking priest at Bethel whom the Israelites will tardily consult in warfare against Benjamin (Judg 20.27–29). **22.17** *The sin at*

not cleansed ourselves, and for which a plague came upon the congregation of the LORD, [18]that you must turn away today from following the LORD! If you rebel against the LORD today, he will be angry with the whole congregation of Israel tomorrow. [19]But now, if your land is unclean, cross over into the LORD's land where the LORD's tabernacle now stands, and take for yourselves a possession among us; only do not rebel against the LORD, or rebel against us[1] by building yourselves an altar other than the altar of the LORD our God. [20]Did not Achan son of Zerah break faith in the matter of the devoted things, and wrath fell upon all the congregation of Israel? And he did not perish alone for his iniquity!' "

[21] Then the Reubenites, the Gadites, and the half-tribe of Manasseh said in answer to the heads of the families of Israel, [22]"The LORD, God of gods! The LORD, God of gods! He knows; and let Israel itself know! If it was in rebellion or in breach of faith toward the LORD, do not spare us today [23]for building an altar to turn away from following the LORD; or if we did so to offer burnt offerings or grain offerings or offerings of well-being on it, may the LORD himself take vengeance. [24]No! We did it from fear that in time to come your children might say to our children, 'What have you to do with the LORD, the God of Israel? [25]For the LORD has made the Jordan a boundary between us and you, you Reubenites and Gadites; you have no portion in the LORD.' So your children might make our children cease to worship the LORD. [26]Therefore we said, 'Let us now build an altar, not for burnt offering, nor for sacrifice, [27]but to be a witness between us and you, and between the generations after us, that we do perform the service of the LORD in his presence with our burnt offerings and sacrifices and offerings of well-being; so that your children may never say to our

children in time to come, "You have no portion in the LORD." ' [28]And we thought, If this should be said to us or to our descendants in time to come, we could say, 'Look at this copy of the altar of the LORD, which our ancestors made, not for burnt offerings, nor for sacrifice, but to be a witness between us and you.' [29]Far be it from us that we should rebel against the LORD, and turn away this day from following the LORD by building an altar for burnt offering, grain offering, or sacrifice, other than the altar of the LORD our God that stands before his tabernacle!"

[30] When the priest Phinehas and the chiefs of the congregation, the heads of the families of Israel who were with him, heard the words that the Reubenites and the Gadites and the Manassites spoke, they were satisfied. [31]The priest Phinehas son of Eleazar said to the Reubenites and the Gadites and the Manassites, "Today we know that the LORD is among us, because you have not committed this treachery against the LORD; now you have saved the Israelites from the hand of the LORD."

[32] Then the priest Phinehas son of Eleazar and the chiefs returned from the Reubenites and the Gadites in the land of Gilead to the land of Canaan, to the Israelites, and brought back word to them. [33]The report pleased the Israelites; and the Israelites blessed God and spoke no more of making war against them, to destroy the land where the Reubenites and the Gadites were settled. [34]The Reubenites and the Gadites called the altar Witness;[m] "For," said they, "it is a witness between us that the LORD is God."

Joshua's Farewell Address

23 A long time afterward, when the LORD had given rest to Israel from all their enemies all around, and Joshua was old and well advanced in

1 Or *make rebels of us*   m Cn Compare Syr: Heb lacks *Witness*

Peor. See Num 25. **22.20** *Achan* is mentioned only here and in 1 Chr 2.7 outside the story in ch. 7. **22.27** That the altar will *be a witness* anticipates 24.27. The crowning irony is that the location of the one near the Jordan given such expansive legitimation remained entirely unspecified. **22.34** *Witness.* Cf. the struggle and truce between Jacob and Laban, also marked by a stone "Witness" (Gen 31.43–54). The tribes all

agree, at last, that *the LORD is God.*

23.1–16 Joshua's farewell address is another of the edifying discourses made by great leaders that give structure to the historical work Deuteronomy–2 Kings. See speeches by Moses (Deut 29–31), Samuel (1 Sam 12), and David (1 Kings 2.1–9). Here Joshua uses the same Deuteronomic rhetoric as at the outset in ch. 1. **23.1** *A long time afterward* introduces a period, however brief,

years, 2 Joshua summoned all Israel, their elders and heads, their judges and officers, and said to them, "I am now old and well advanced in years; 3 and you have seen all that the LORD your God has done to all these nations for your sake, for it is the LORD your God who has fought for you. 4 I have allotted to you as an inheritance for your tribes those nations that remain, along with all the nations that I have already cut off, from the Jordan to the Great Sea in the west. 5 The LORD your God will push them back before you, and drive them out of your sight; and you shall possess their land, as the LORD your God promised you. 6 Therefore be very steadfast to observe and do all that is written in the book of the law of Moses, turning aside from it neither to the right nor to the left, 7 so that you may not be mixed with these nations left here among you, or make mention of the names of their gods, or swear by them, or serve them, or bow yourselves down to them, 8 but hold fast to the LORD your God, as you have done to this day. 9 For the LORD has driven out before you great and strong nations; and as for you, no one has been able to withstand you to this day. 10 One of you puts to flight a thousand, since it is the LORD your God who fights for you, as he promised you. 11 Be very careful, therefore, to love the LORD your God. 12 For if you turn back, and join the survivors of these nations left here among you, and intermarry

with them, so that you marry their women and they yours, 13 know assuredly that the LORD your God will not continue to drive out these nations before you; but they shall be a snare and a trap for you, a scourge on your sides, and thorns in your eyes, until you perish from this good land that the LORD your God has given you. 14 "And now I am about to go the way of all the earth, and you know in your hearts and souls, all of you, that not one thing has failed of all the good things that the LORD your God promised concerning you; all have come to pass for you, not one of them has failed. 15 But just as all the good things that the LORD your God promised concerning you have been fulfilled for you, so the LORD will bring upon you all the bad things, until he has destroyed you from this good land that the LORD your God has given you. 16 If you transgress the covenant of the LORD your God, which he enjoined on you, and go and serve other gods and bow down to them, then the anger of the LORD will be kindled against you, and you shall perish quickly from the good land that he has given to you."

The Covenant at Shechem

24 Then Joshua gathered all the tribes of Israel to Shechem, and summoned the elders, the heads, the judges, and the officers of Israel; and they presented themselves before God.

---

when Israelite control of the land is far from complete, but hostilities have pretty much ceased, and Joshua has grown old. *The LORD had given rest*, fifth and final occurrence of this idiom in Joshua (1.13, 15; 21.44; 22.4), all of which are recognized on other grounds as belonging to the later edition (Dtr 2; see Introduction). *Joshua . . . advanced in years*, exactly as in 13.1, the introduction to the Transjordanian allotments and the unconquered land. **23.2a** *Joshua summoned*. The location is unclear; presumably the tent-sanctuary, still at Shiloh, is intended. *All Israel*, the larger definition of Israel in former days, tribes on both sides of the river interacting and interdependent, is a special concern of the final redactor. **23.2b–16** Joshua's speech is in two parts (vv. 2b–10, 11–16), each displaying a form of envelope construction. **23.3–10** The first part of the speech is framed by a description of the Divine Warrior (vv. 3, 9–10) focusing on the recent past and emphasizing that Yahweh has indeed kept his promises (vv. 4–5). **23.5** *The LORD your*

God will complete the "conquest," unassisted. With the death of Joshua, Israel's expansionist warfare is all in the past (Judg 2.1–5). **23.6** *Be very steadfast*. The Hebrew echoes the exhortation in 1.6, 9. *The book of the law of Moses*. Cf. 1.7–8. **23.11–16** The second half of the speech turns the envelope inside out, thunderous warnings (vv. 11–13, 15–16) framing a compact echo of the first half (v. 14). **23.16** *You shall perish quickly*. The distinctive concluding emphasis on the threat of national destruction and expulsion from the land as just punishment for failure of covenant suggests a time when the covenantal curses were coming to frightful fulfillment, in the sequel to Josiah's reign. **24.1–28** The major section of ch. 24 describes the Shechem covenant on the basis of an older source document that shows scant signs of editorial revision and that the historian (Dtr 1?; see Introduction) simply placed at the end of the era. It gives a fuller description of events first reported in 8.30–35, which we assigned to the later

2 And Joshua said to all the people, "Thus says the LORD, the God of Israel: Long ago your ancestors — Terah and his sons Abraham and Nahor — lived beyond the Euphrates and served other gods. 3 Then I took your father Abraham from beyond the River and led him through all the land of Canaan and made his offspring many. I gave him Isaac; 4 and to Isaac I gave Jacob and Esau. I gave Esau the hill country of Seir to possess, but Jacob and his children went down to Egypt. 5 Then I sent Moses and Aaron, and I plagued Egypt with what I did in its midst; and afterwards I brought you out. 6 When I brought your ancestors out of Egypt, you came to the sea; and the Egyptians pursued your ancestors with chariots and horsemen to the Red Sea.n 7 When they cried out to the LORD, he put darkness between you and the Egyptians, and made the sea come upon them and cover them; and your eyes saw what I did to Egypt. Afterwards you lived in the wilderness a long time. 8 Then I brought you to the land of the Amorites, who lived on the other side of the Jordan; they fought with you, and I handed them over to you, and you took possession of their land, and I destroyed them before you. 9 Then King Balak son of Zippor of Moab, set out to fight against Israel. He sent and invited Balaam son of Beor to curse you, 10 but I would not listen to Balaam; therefore he blessed you; so I rescued you out of his hand. 11 When you went over the Jordan and came to Jericho, the citizens of Jericho fought against you, and also the Amorites, the Perizzites, the Canaanites, the Hittites, the Girgashites, the Hivites, and the Jebusites; and I handed them over to you. 12 I sent the horneto ahead of you, which drove out before you the two kings of the Amorites; it was not by your sword or by your bow. 13 I gave you a land on which you had not labored, and towns that you had not built, and you live in them; you eat the fruit of vineyards and oliveyards that you did not plant.

14 "Now therefore revere the LORD, and serve him in sincerity and in faithfulness; put away the gods that your ancestors served beyond the River and in Egypt, and serve the LORD. 15 Now if you are unwilling to serve the LORD, choose this day whom you will serve, whether the gods your ancestors served in the region beyond the River or the gods of the Amorites in whose land you are living; but as for me and my household, we will serve the LORD."

16 Then the people answered, "Far be it from us that we should forsake the LORD to serve other gods; 17 for it is the LORD our God who brought us and our ancestors up from the land of Egypt, out of the house of slavery, and who did those great signs in our sight. He protected us

n Or Sea of Reeds   o Meaning of Heb uncertain

editor who wanted to make it clear that the Shechem Valley negotiations came early in the era. **24.2–13** A number of parallel recitals of God's acts are also clearly related to covenant ceremonies (Ex 19.3b–6; Deut 6.20–25; 26.5–9). The covenant is grounded in the prior benevolent acts of the divine Lord and thus there is no mention of Sinai in the recital itself. **24.3** The description *through all the land of Canaan* reflects a wideranging network of effective control — not the life and seasonal movements of pastoral nomads. *Made his offspring many.* This way of fulfilling promises to the ancestors (Gen 12.1–3; 15.4–5) is not stressed in the book of Joshua. **24.6–7** A compact paraphrase of Ex 14. **24.9** *Balak . . . set out to fight.* See also 13.22. The text here seems to be in sharp contradiction to Judg 11.25. Or does it intend to show Balak's belligerence simply exhausted and frustrated in his employment of a famous diviner? **24.11** The Israelite takeover west of the Jordan is here represented entirely by the capture of *Jericho* (a variant tradition from those in chs. 2, 6?). **24.12** The referent of *the hornet* (see also Deut 7.20) is unclear. *Two kings of the Amorites* refers to Sihon (12.2; 13.10, 27) and Og (12.4; 13.12, 30–31). **24.14** *Now therefore revere.* See also 4.14, 24. There was precedent in ancestral tradition for the renunciation of old *gods* at Shechem (Gen 35.2–4). **24.15** *Choose.* The issue is not monotheism in the abstract but allegiance in concrete particularity. *Living.* The same word can mean "sitting." Many Israelites were in fact squatters in the perspective of the local elites. **24.16–18** The people indicate that they have already made up their minds. **24.16** *Forsake the LORD to serve other gods.* The final redactor would not leave anyone with excuse for saying "I told you so." In the Babylonian exile it was time for a new covenant. **24.17–18** The bulk of the people's response is a polished rhetorical piece, the irreducible minimum of Joshua's recital in vv. 2b–13. **24.17** *The LORD our God.* Cf. 22.34; 23.3, 10. An introductory particle in Hebrew gives exclamatory force to the statement.

along all the way that we went, and among all the peoples through whom we passed; 18 and the LORD drove out before us all the peoples, the Amorites who lived in the land. Therefore we also will serve the LORD, for he is our God."

19 But Joshua said to the people, "You cannot serve the LORD, for he is a holy God. He is a jealous God; he will not forgive your transgressions or your sins. 20 If you forsake the LORD and serve foreign gods, then he will turn and do you harm, and consume you, after having done you good." 21 And the people said to Joshua, "No, we will serve the LORD!" 22 Then Joshua said to the people, "You are witnesses against yourselves that you have chosen the LORD, to serve him." And they said, "We are witnesses." 23 He said, "Then put away the foreign gods that are among you, and incline your hearts to the LORD, the God of Israel." 24 The people said to Joshua, "The LORD our God we will serve, and him we will obey." 25 So Joshua made a covenant with the people that day, and made statutes and ordinances for them at Shechem. 26 Joshua

wrote these words in the book of the law of God; and he took a large stone, and set it up there under the oak in the sanctuary of the LORD. 27 Joshua said to all the people, "See, this stone shall be a witness against us; for it has heard all the words of the LORD that he spoke to us; therefore it shall be a witness against you, if you deal falsely with your God." 28 So Joshua sent the people away to their inheritances.

Concluding Notices

29 After these things Joshua son of Nun, the servant of the LORD, died, being one hundred ten years old. 30 They buried him in his own inheritance at Timnath-serah, which is in the hill country of Ephraim, north of Mount Gaash.

31 Israel served the LORD all the days of Joshua, and all the days of the elders who outlived Joshua and had known all the work that the LORD did for Israel.

32 The bones of Joseph, which the Israelites had brought up from Egypt, were buried at Shechem, in the portion of ground that Jacob had bought from the

---

24.19 The word for *jealous* is here better rendered "zealous." The construction may preserve a pre-Yahwist name for God as "El the Zealous," now identified with Yahweh. See "the living God" in 3.10, which may also be rendered as "El the Living One." **24.20, 23** *Foreign gods* seems to assume that the God of Israel has national or tribal identity. The expression continues the caricature of the Yahwist ideal, with which the book now concludes. **24.22** *To serve him.* Joshua rules out any other possible motive for choosing Yahweh. *We are witnesses.* Cf. Ruth 4.9–11. **24.23** *Incline your hearts.* The heart was understood to be the decision-making center, seat of mind and will. **24.25–27** Joshua makes final arrangements for the future of relationships among the people, chief of which is a large stone at Shechem that will betoken the internal surveillance function. The stone in question was perhaps first coated with a plaster into which were carved the covenant stipulations. Excavations at Tell Balata, ancient site of Shechem, have uncovered a cultic tradition of large sacred pillars, in use there for centuries in the pre-Yahwist period. **24.26** The *book of the law of God,* the text of the covenant or digest thereof. Since the Hebrew root of *law* means "to teach," we might better render "text of the covenant-teaching." *The oak in the sanctuary.* Cf. "the oak of the pillar at Shechem" (Judg 9.6). For another sacred tree, cf. "the oak of Moreh" (Gen

12.6). Excavations at Tell Balata have shown that there can scarcely be any location for this other than the temenos (sacred precinct) in front of the old fortress-temple. **24.27** The inscribed stone would be a *witness* to worshipers and pilgrims. **24.28** *Joshua sent the people away.* His work was satisfactorily finished (first edition, Dtr 1) if curiously so (second edition, Dtr 2; see Introduction). In the first edition Joshua provides a model for the two great achievements of King Josiah, military conquest and covenant renewal. In the final edition he offers a perspective indispensable for life in exile.

24.29–33 The book now concludes with a variety of notices. **24.29** Given the frequency of the title *servant of the LORD* in reference to Moses (1.1, 2, 13; 8.31, 33; 11.12, 15; 12.6; 13.8; 14.7; 18.7; 22.2, 4, 5), it is somewhat surprising that it is not applied to Joshua until now. *One hundred ten years* was considered an ideal lifetime. Joseph too lived one hundred and ten years (Gen 50.23). **24.30** *Timnath-serah.* See 19.50. **24.32** Reference to *the bones of Joseph* forms an envelope construction with Gen 50.25, tying the end of the Joshua book to the end of Genesis and showing that the Tetrateuch is presupposed as one long epic preface to the historical work Deuteronomy– 2 Kings. *Jacob had bought.* See Gen 33.18–20. *Hamor, the father of Shechem.* See Gen 34, where he is identified as a "Hivite" (Greek OT "Horite"), i.e.,

children of Hamor, the father of Shechem, for one hundred pieces of
money;*p* it became an inheritance of the
descendants of Joseph.

33 Eleazar son of Aaron died; and

they buried him at Gibeah, the town of his
son Phinehas, which had been given him
in the hill country of Ephraim.

p Heb *one hundred qesitah*

---

not from the indigenous population. *One hundred
pieces of money.* The value (weight) of the unit is
unknown. **24.33** *Eleazar* and his son *Phinehas*

are encountered in Joshua only in contexts supplied by Dtr 2 (17.4; 21.1; 22.13, 30–32; cf. Judg
20.28; see Introduction).

JUDGES

[handwritten: time? death of Joshua to civil war]

Historical Context

THE BOOK OF JUDGES SPANS A CRITICAL PERIOD in Israelite history from the death of Joshua to a tragically costly and unholy civil war (chs. 19–20) in which total liquidation of the tribe of Benjamin is narrowly averted (ch. 21). The period that is the book's background extends from the closing decades of the Late Bronze Age through the Iron I period (ca. 1200–1020 B.C.E.). The 410-year span that results from adding up the periods of oppression, the tenures of the judges, and the periods of "rest" mentioned in the book assumes that the judges governed "all Israel" sequentially. In fact, leadership was more likely local and overlapping.

Despite sweeping claims in the book of Joshua of conquest of all the land, Judges describes continued warfare with Canaanites, plus challenges to Israel's hegemony posed by various tribal groups (Midianites, Amalekites, and other Easterners), by emerging territorial states (Moab and Ammon), and by the arrival of the Philistines on the coast. Equally serious was the threat posed by aspirants to kingship within Israel (e.g., Abimelech, ch. 9). The historical situation described by Judges continues into the narrative of 1 Samuel, named after the prophet who is also remembered as an itinerating "judge" and who legitimated the establishment of the monarchy, anointing first Saul, then David.

Protagonists and Terminology

The book presents twelve leaders: Othniel, Ehud, Shamgar, Deborah, Gideon, Tola, Jair, Jephthah, Ibzan, Elon, Abdon, and Samson. The English title Judges (Latin *Liber Judicum*, Greek *kritai*) reflects the fact that a majority of the book's protagonists are said to have "judged" (Hebrew *shafat*) Israel. The verb is not limited in suggesting a strictly judicial function, however; it connotes a general exercise of legitimate "rule." Though scholars often describe the judges' leadership sociologically as "charismatic," it is with very mixed results that "the spirit of the LORD" activates the various leaders. Scholars distinguish between "major judges," military chiefs whose exploits are recounted in stories, and "minor judges," about whom very little is known apart from their being listed in 10.1–5; 12.7–15. There are two exceptions: Jephthah, who is a "major judge" (11.1–12.6) but is also listed in the group of "minor judges" (12.7), and Samson, who belongs in neither category (he was not a military chief).

Apart from the introduction (2.16–19), the noun "judge" (Hebrew *shofēt*) occurs only once in this book, as a title of the Lord (11.27). As universal Judge, the Lord retains a prerogative that had been attributed to various deities in other ancient Near Eastern societies.

As striking as the absence of the noun "judge" from this book is the presence of the noun "deliverer," or "savior" (Hebrew *moshia‘*), or its related verb (Hebrew *yasha‘*) in reference to four characters (Othniel, Ehud, Tola, and Samson). There are numerous similarities between these judges' stories and the accounts of the birth, enlistment, and diplomatic functioning of Moses in Ex 1–13. Most puzzling, therefore, is the uniform absence of the language of deliverance regarding those leaders about whom popular lore was most prolific (Deborah, Gideon, and Jephthah). In the case of Gideon, neither the "judicial" nor the "deliverance" language is used. What, then, did Gideon do? Perhaps that is precisely the question. The discerning reader will be alert to a sense of irony throughout the depiction of the judges.

Sources and Development

Judges is part of one long historical work extending from Joshua through 2 Kings and prefaced by the farewell addresses of Moses in Deuteronomy, which serve as a theological introduction. It is therefore part of the Deuteronomistic History. (See also the Introduction to Joshua.) Four stages of development may be discerned in the book. First were various stories of local crises and leaders, classic examples of narrative artistry. The stories, rarely involving more than a few tribes, originated in highland villages that comprised immediate and extended families, the so-called fathers' houses and clans. Israel had begun as a lineage system and developed over time to become an agrarian territorial state. An older alignment of tribes worshiping God as "El" ("Israel" is Hebrew for "El governs"), mentioned in the Egyptian pharaoh Merneptah's inscription (ca. 1207 B.C.E.) and probably represented by the tribal roster in Gen 49, had fallen on hard times. But the tribal alignment had then been revived and reformed under the influence of those who brought the Sinai traditions into Canaan. Stories of the judges preserve memories of that tumultuous epoch. Scholars generally think that in the second stage these stories were collected for didactic purposes, perhaps by the mid-eighth century B.C.E., when both Israel and Judah were at a peak of national revival. The stories are arranged so that good examples of leadership (Othniel, Deborah, Jephthah) alternate with not-so-good examples (Ehud, Gideon, Samson), with the whole book centering on Abimelech's abortive reign at Shechem. In the third stage these stories were incorporated into the Deuteronomistic History. The hypothesis of such a history is well established. Stemming probably from the reign of the reforming king Josiah (640–609 B.C.E.), the Deuteronomistic History (Dtr 1) was composed to tell the story of life in the land. It comprises the bulk of the OT from Joshua through 2 Kings 23 and originally used an older form of Deuteronomy (Dtn) as a theological preface. In contrast to Joshua, cast as role model for kings, the judges are depicted with rough edges so as to highlight the instability of Israel without a king (see esp. chs. 17–18). Finally, after the short-lived Judahite reform and revival under Josiah and the destruction of the nation, the historical work was updated for life in exile (Dtr 2). The era of the judges was set finally within a grimly tragicomic framework (see esp. 1.1–2.5; chs. 19–21).   *Robert G. Boling*

Israel's Failure to Complete the Conquest of Canaan

1 After the death of Joshua, the Israelites inquired of the LORD, "Who shall go up first for us against the Canaanites, to fight against them?" 2 The LORD said, "Judah shall go up. I hereby give the land into his hand." 3 Judah said to his brother Simeon, "Come up with me into the territory allotted to me, that we may fight against the Canaanites; then I too will go with you into the territory allotted to you." So Simeon went with him. 4 Then Judah went up and the LORD gave the Canaanites and the Perizzites into their hand; and they defeated ten thousand of them at Bezek. 5 They came upon Adoni-bezek at Bezek, and fought against him, and defeated the Canaanites and the Perizzites. 6 Adoni-bezek fled; but they pursued him, and caught him, and cut off his thumbs and big toes. 7 Adoni-bezek said, "Seventy kings with their thumbs and big toes cut off used to pick up scraps under my table; as I have done, so God has paid me back." They brought him to Jerusalem, and he died there.

8 Then the people of Judah fought against Jerusalem and took it. They put it to the sword and set the city on fire. 9 Afterward the people of Judah went down to fight against the Canaanites who lived in the hill country, in the Negeb, and in the lowland. 10 Judah went against the Canaanites who lived in Hebron (the name

1.1–36 This introduction to the final edition of the Deuteronomistic History (Dtr 2; see Introduction) reviews the performance of the generation that outlived Joshua. It affirms the Lord's preservation of Israel in a tumultuous period. Stories, archival information, and various notices report tribal activities roughly from south to north, beginning with Judah eager for the offensive but ending with Dan at a stalemate and Israel's back against the wall. The chapter complements a telling of the "conquest" in the book of Joshua that gives prominence to northern tribes. Its purpose is to contrast the situation under Joshua's leadership with the subsequent deterioration of tribal and individual achievements. **1.1–2** The context suggests that *inquired* should be read as "had inquired," making 1.1–2.10 a flashback to the generation that outlived Joshua. *Who shall go up first?* That the question and its answer, *Judah*, recur in 20.18 regarding civil warfare suggests editorial irony. **1.3** The tribe of *Simeon* once ranged into the north-central highlands (Gen 34.25, 30–31) but finally settled in the south, entirely surrounded by *Judah*. **1.4** The precise meaning of *Perizzites* is uncertain; it is perhaps related to a word for peasantry. The word for *thousand* may also refer to the clan or village muster unit. The number in each such unit is unspecified here but is said to be five to fourteen men in the "census" lists of Num 1; 26. **1.5** *Adoni-bezek*, or "Lord of Bezek" in Hebrew. *Bezek*, Khirbet Bezka, near Gezer, is on the outskirts of Judah. Another Bezek lies northeast of Shechem (1 Sam 11.8). **1.8** *Jerusalem* came finally under Israelite control in the time of King David (2 Sam 5.6–9). **1.10** *Hebron* lies twenty miles south of Jerusalem. *Kiriath-arba*, Hebrew, "Town of Arba." Arba was the legendary father of Anak, who gave rise to a lineage of giants (Josh 15.13–14). *Sheshai and Ahiman and Talmai, sons of*

of Hebron was formerly Kiriath-arba); and they defeated Sheshai and Ahiman and Talmai.

11 From there they went against the inhabitants of Debir (the name of Debir was formerly Kiriath-sepher). 12 Then Caleb said, "Whoever attacks Kiriath-sepher and takes it, I will give him my daughter Achsah as wife." 13 And Othniel son of Kenaz, Caleb's younger brother, took it; and he gave him his daughter Achsah as wife. 14 When she came to him, she urged him to ask her father for a field. As she dismounted from her donkey, Caleb said to her, "What do you wish?" 15 She said to him, "Give me a present; since you have set me in the land of the Negeb, give me also Gulloth-mayim."*a* So Caleb gave her Upper Gulloth and Lower Gulloth.

16 The descendants of Hobab*b* the Kenite, Moses' father-in-law, went up with the people of Judah from the city of palms into the wilderness of Judah, which lies in the Negeb near Arad. Then they went and settled with the Amalekites,*c* 17 Judah went with his brother Simeon, and they defeated the Canaanites who inhabited Zephath, and devoted it to destruction. So the city was called Hormah. 18 Judah took Gaza with its territory, Ashkelon with its territory, and Ekron with its territory. 19 The LORD was with Judah, and he took possession of the hill country, but could not drive out the inhabitants of the plain, because they had chariots of iron. 20 Hebron was given to Caleb, as Moses had said; and he drove out from it the three sons of Anak. 21 But the Benjaminites did not drive out the Jebusites who lived in Jerusalem; so the Jebusites have lived in Jerusalem among the Benjaminites to this day.

22 The house of Joseph also went up against Bethel; and the LORD was with them. 23 The house of Joseph sent out spies to Bethel (the name of the city was formerly Luz). 24 When the spies saw a man coming out of the city, they said to him, "Show us the way into the city, and we will deal kindly with you." 25 So he showed them the way into the city; and they put the city to the sword, but they let the man and all his family go. 26 So the man went to the land of the Hittites and built a city, and named it Luz; that is its name to this day.

27 Manasseh did not drive out the inhabitants of Beth-shean and its villages, or Taanach and its villages, or the inhabitants of Dor and its villages, or the inhabitants of Ibleam and its villages, or the inhabitants of Megiddo and its villages; but the Canaanites continued to live in that land. 28 When Israel grew strong, they put the Canaanites to forced labor, but did not in fact drive them out.

29 And Ephraim did not drive out the

*a That is Basins of Water   b Gk: Heb lacks Hobab
c See 1 Sam 15.6: Heb people*

Anak defeated by Caleb, according to v. 20; Josh 15.14. **1.11–15** These verses are nearly identical to Josh 15.13–19. **1.11** *Debir*, long identified with Tell Beit Mirsim, is perhaps better located at Tell Rabud, south of Hebron. *Kiriath-sepher*, Hebrew, "Booktown" or "Town of the Treaty-Stele," suggests a covenanting role for the town comparable to that of Shechem (Josh 24; cf. Josh 8.30–35) in the north. **1.12** *Caleb*, Hebrew, "Dog." **1.13** *Othniel*, first and model "savior-judge" in Dtr 1 (see Introduction; 3.7–11). **1.14** *Urged*, "nagged." **1.15** The referent of *Gulloth*, which may mean "basins," is unclear. **1.16** *Hobab*, probably not Moses' *father-in-law* (Hebrew *chotēn*) but his son-in-law (*chatan*). *Kenite* identifies him as a traveling metalworker. The smiths were probably also Midianites in political affiliation. *City of palms*, probably Jericho. Tell Arad was only lightly occupied throughout the second millennium. Late Bronze Age Arad may be at Tell el-Milh, seven miles southwest of Tell Arad. **1.17** *Hormah*, Hebrew, "Bantown" (related to Hebrew *cherem*, the ad hoc decree of total destruction) may be Tell Meshash, four miles west of Tell el-Milh. **1.18–19** These verses, claiming conquest of certain cities but not their surroundings, cannot be harmonized. **1.18** *Gaza . . . Ashkelon . . . and Ekron*, three cities of the Philistine Pentapolis. **1.19** That *the LORD was with Judah* sounds ironic in light of the following disclaimer. *Chariots of iron*. Chariots were made of wood and leather, with iron introduced for assemblage and fittings. **1.22–26** The capture of *Bethel* (Hebrew, "House of God") formerly *Luz* ("Deception") and later a royal sanctuary of the Northern Kingdom, is presented as exemplary of covenant faithfulness and is ironically reminiscent of the story of Rahab at Jericho (Josh 2.1–24; 6.22–25). **1.27–33** The failure of five northern tribes (*Manasseh, Ephraim, Zebulun, Asher,* and *Naphtali*) to drive out the Canaanites results in a complex mix of land tenure and inverted social hierarchy, with Israelites lording it over non-Israelite labor in various neighborhoods.

Canaanites who lived in <u>Gezer</u>; but the Canaanites lived among them in Gezer.

30 Zebulun did not drive out the inhabitants of Kitron, or the inhabitants of Nahalol; but the Canaanites lived among them, and became subject to forced labor.

31 Asher did not drive out the inhabitants of Acco, or the inhabitants of Sidon, or of Ahlab, or of Achzib, or of Helbah, or of Aphik, or of Rehob; 32 but the Asherites lived among the Canaanites, the inhabitants of the land; for they did not drive them out.

33 Naphtali did not drive out the inhabitants of Beth-shemesh, or the inhabitants of Beth-anath, but lived among the Canaanites, the inhabitants of the land; nevertheless the inhabitants of Beth-shemesh and of Beth-anath became subject to forced labor for them.

34 The Amorites pressed the Danites back into the hill country; they did not allow them to come down to the plain. 35 The Amorites continued to live in Har-heres, in Aijalon, and in Shaalbim, but the hand of the house of Joseph rested heavily on them, and they became subject to forced labor. 36 The border of the Amorites ran from the ascent of Akrabbim, from Sela and upward.

Israel's Disobedience

2 Now the angel of the LORD went up from Gilgal to Bochim, and said, "I brought you up from Egypt, and brought you into the land that I had promised to your ancestors. I said, 'I will never break my covenant with you. 2 For your part, do not make a covenant with the inhabitants of this land; tear down their altars.' But you have not obeyed my command. See what you have done! 3 So now I say, I will not drive them out before you; but they shall become adversaries*d* to you, and their gods shall be a snare to you." 4 When the angel of the LORD spoke these words to all the Israelites, the people lifted up their voices and wept. 5 So they named that place Bochim,*e* and there they sacrificed to the LORD.

Death of Joshua

6 When Joshua dismissed the people, the Israelites all went to their own inheritances to take possession of the land. 7 The people worshiped the LORD all the days of Joshua, and all the days of the elders who outlived Joshua, who had seen all the great work that the LORD had done for Israel. 8 Joshua son of Nun, the servant of the LORD, died at the age of one hundred ten years. 9 So they buried him within the bounds of his inheritance in Timnath-heres, in the hill country of Ephraim, north of Mount Gaash. 10 Moreover, that whole generation was gathered to their ancestors, and another generation grew up after them, who did not know the LORD or the work that he had done for Israel.

d OL Vg Compare Gk: Heb *sides*   *e* That is *Weepers*

1.34–35 The *Danites* were the least successful of the tribes, failing in their attempt to control the foothills between the coastal plain and the Judean highlands. This failure led ultimately to their resettlement in the north (chs. 17–18). **2.1–5** Israel's covenantal failure leads to revision of the Lord's strategy. There will be no more expansionist warfare. The polemical story explains how a place of tribal assembly (probably Bethel) acquired a nickname. **2.1** *The angel of the LORD* is a diplomatic envoy from the heavenly court, often preparing the way for God's direct appearance and here speaking in unmistakably Deuteronomistic style. Cf. also the speeches of the anonymous prophet (6.8–10) and of the Lord (10.11–14). *Gilgal*, base camp in Joshua (see esp. Josh 4.19–20; 5.9–10; 9.6). **2.4** The Israelites *wept*, as they would again at Bethel on the eve of the solution to the problem of finding wives for Benjamin (21.2). **2.5** *Bochim*, Hebrew, meaning "weepers." **2.6–10** In another flashback, these verses describe a generation gap, repeating Josh 24.28–31 in a sequence more appropriate to the beginning of an era. **2.6** *Joshua dismissed*, better "Joshua had dismissed," indicates another flashback. **2.8** The title *servant of the LORD* was first borne by Moses (Josh 1.1), then by Joshua, who left no designated successor. Samson applies the title to himself in 15.18. Elsewhere, among figures mentioned from the Judges era, only Caleb is called "servant" (Num 14.24). The title is applied honorifically to patriarchs, kings, and prophets—several in each category. *Died*, better "had died." **2.9** *Timnath-heres*, "Portion of the Sun" in Hebrew lies some fifteen miles southwest of Shechem. A transposition of letters makes the name "Timnath-serah" ("Leftover Portion") in Josh 19.50; 24.30. **2.10** The statement that the generation after Joshua *did not know the LORD* does not

Israel's Unfaithfulness

11 Then the Israelites did what was evil in the sight of the LORD and worshiped the Baals; 12 and they abandoned the LORD, the God of their ancestors, who had brought them out of the land of Egypt; they followed other gods, from among the gods of the peoples who were all around them, and bowed down to them; and they provoked the LORD to anger. 13 They abandoned the LORD, and worshiped Baal and the Astartes. 14 So the anger of the LORD was kindled against Israel, and he gave them over to plunderers who plundered them, and he sold them into the power of their enemies all around, so that they could no longer withstand their enemies. 15 Whenever they marched out, the hand of the LORD was against them to bring misfortune, as the LORD had warned them and sworn to them; and they were in great distress. 16 Then the LORD raised up judges, who delivered them out of the power of those who plundered them. 17 Yet they did not listen even to their judges; for they lusted after other gods and bowed down to them. They soon turned aside from the way in which their ancestors had walked, who had obeyed the commandments of the LORD; they did not follow their example. 18 Whenever the LORD raised up judges for them, the LORD was with the judge, and he delivered them from the hand of their enemies all the days of the judge; for the LORD would be moved to pity by their groaning because of those who persecuted and oppressed them. 19 But whenever the judge died, they would relapse and behave worse than their ancestors, following other gods, worshiping them and bowing down to them. They would not drop any of their practices or their stubborn ways. 20 So the anger of the LORD was kindled against Israel; and he said, "Because this people have transgressed my covenant that I commanded their ancestors, and have not obeyed my voice, 21 I will no longer drive out before them any of the nations that Joshua left when he died." 22 In order to test Israel, whether or not they would take care to walk in the way of the LORD as their ancestors did, 23 the LORD had left those nations, not driving them out at once, and had not handed them over to Joshua.

Nations Remaining in the Land

3 Now these are the nations that the LORD left to test all those in Israel who had no experience of any war in Canaan 2 (it was only that successive generations of Israelites might know war, to teach those who had no experience of it before): 3 the five lords of the Philistines, and all the Canaanites, and the Sidonians,

---

offer an excuse for ignorance. It may report an experiential lack or may fault lack of acknowledgment of the Lord. This observation marks the turn of an era, a basic change in situation and relationships. **2.11–23** These verses set forth a recurring pattern—apostasy, hardship, moaning (crying out to the Lord), and rescue—that provides a framework for the stories of the "major" judges. **2.11–13** *Baal* was the Canaanite storm god, divine warrior, and "king of the city." *Astarte* was the popular fertility goddess, consort of Baal. In scripture these names are used in the plural to refer to the entire pantheon of deities. The Baals and the Astartes, mentioned again in 10.6 provide a rubric of sorts that emphasizes the pattern of apostasy and deliverance. See also 3.7. **2.14** *Enemies all around.* The earliest judges have to deal with threats posed by neighbors in the immediate vicinity: southern highlanders (3.7–11); Moabite invaders from Transjordan (3.12–30); Philistines along the coastal plain (3.31); and a Canaanite coalition (4.1–5.31). Thereafter the enemy comes from farther afield (Midianites in chs. 6–8, Ammonites in ch. 11) or arises within Israel itself (Abimelech in ch. 9). **2.16–19** The *judges* are tribal chiefs whose military victories (presented generally as results of the Lord's gracious intervention) earn them continuing preeminence in local tribal governance. Israel experiences both divine justice and compassion, discipline and deliverance. **2.20–23** These verses, from a Deuteronomistic editor, restate the theme of 2.1–5 and the pattern of the period. Repeated covenantal failure on Israel's part at last brings a change of strategy from the Lord. The remnants of the "nations" formerly occupying Canaan will survive to test the faithfulness of Israel. **3.1–6** Two lists of peoples (vv. 3, 5) in the midst of whom Israel will be tested are introduced by the explanation that Israel has had inadequate experience of warfare. Divine discipline through the experience of warfare is a major theme toward the end of the book (ch. 20). **3.3** *Lords,* better "tyrants," a reference to the political organization newly introduced to the southern coastal

and the Hivites who lived on Mount Leba-non, from Mount Baal-hermon as far as Lebo-hamath. 4 They were for the testing of Israel, to know whether Israel would obey the commandments of the LORD, which he commanded their ancestors by Moses. 5 So the Israelites lived among the Canaanites, the Hittites, the Amorites, the Perizzites, the Hivites, and the Jebusites; 6 and they took their daughters as wives for themselves, and their own daughters they gave to their sons; and they wor-shiped their gods.

Othniel "Judge"

7 The Israelites did what was evil in the sight of the LORD, forgetting the LORD their God, and worshiping the Baals and the Asherahs. 8 Therefore the anger of the LORD was kindled against Israel, and he sold them into the hand of King Cushan-rishathaim of Aram-naharaim; and the Israelites served Cushan-rishathaim eight years. 9 But when the Is-raelites cried out to the LORD, the LORD raised up a deliverer for the Israelites, who delivered them, Othniel son of Ke-naz, Caleb's younger brother. 10 The spirit of the LORD came upon him, and he judged Israel; he went out to war, and the LORD gave King Cushan-rishathaim of Aram into his hand; and his hand pre-vailed over Cushan-rishathaim. 11 So the land had rest forty years. Then Othniel son of Kenaz died.

Ehud

12 The Israelites again did what was evil in the sight of the LORD; and the LORD strengthened King Eglon of Moab against Israel, because they had done what was evil in the sight of the LORD. 13 In alliance with the Ammonites and the Amalekites, he went and defeated Israel; and they took possession of the city of palms. 14 So the Israelites served King Eg-lon of Moab eighteen years.

15 But when the Israelites cried out to the LORD, the LORD raised up for them a deliverer, Ehud son of Gera, the Benja-minite, a left-handed man. The Israelites sent tribute by him to King Eglon of Moab. 16 Ehud made for himself a sword with two edges, a cubit in length; and he

cities by the Philistines. *Hivites*, also relative newcomers, probably from southeastern Asia Minor. **3.4** This verse echoes the note on which the preceding section ends (2.23) and gives the issue of continued resistance by "the nations" a covenantal setting in terms of the command-ments. The presence of these communities makes possible the alternation of times of crisis and peace, depending upon Israel's behavior. **3.5** The list of peoples living among the Israelites includes not only near neighbors (from the geo-graphical perspective of the later nation of Israel) but those living in enclaves in the heart of con-tested territory. The list is related to Deut 7.1, which mentions seven "nations." *Hittites*, descen-dants of small kingdoms left behind by the once-mighty Anatolian empire. *Amorites*, originally "Westerners" (from the Mesopotamian perspec-tive), appear often in scripture as synonymous with *Canaanites. Perizzites*. See note on 1.4. *Hivites*. See note on 3.4. *Jebusites*. "Jebus" was a pre-Israelite name of Jerusalem. **3.6** Intermarriage was frowned upon not because it threatened ge-nealogical purity but because it challenged Israel's covenantal loyalty.
3.7–11 The brief career notice for Othniel, conqueror of Debir (1.13), employs elements of the framework described in the note on 2.11–23. Information about the first judge is minimal; his story is offered as exemplary of the Deutero-nomic ideal. **3.7** *The Baals and the Asherahs.* Asherah was a Canaanite goddess. See note on 2.11–13. **3.8** *Cushan-rishathaim*, in Hebrew "Cu-shan Double-Wickedness," looks like a distorted name. *Aram-naharaim* is presumably Syria-Mesopotamia, an unlikely threat to the Judean highlands. Redivision of the Hebrew consonants would make him king of "a mountain fortress." **3.10** *The spirit of the LORD* in Judges stands for an impersonal power or force in which a person might be so absorbed or enveloped as to become capable of extraordinary deeds. *Judged*, i.e., mobi-lized Israel for successful defensive warfare. **3.11** *Forty years* may mean a generation.
3.12–30 The swashbuckling story of Ehud, a Benjaminite, unfolds within the familiar edito-rial framework (vv. 12–15, 30; see note on 2.11–23). **3.12–13** The agent of the Lord's dis-cipline is *Eglon* ("Young Bull," "Fat Calf" in He-brew), king of *Moab* in Transjordan, with support from his northern neighbors, the *Ammonites*, and from Israel's traditional enemies of the wilderness era, the *Amalekites* (Ex 17.8–16). *City of palms*, Jericho, as in 1.16. **3.15–25** *Ehud*, the *deliv-erer*, is remembered as a *left-handed man.* Left-handedness was unusually common in the tribe of Benjamin (see 20.16). Ehud was also famous for his murderous diplomacy; cf. Jephthah's exem-plary diplomacy in ch. 11. Regarding Ehud, there is no mention of *the spirit of the LORD* (cf. 3.10).

fastened it on his right thigh under his clothes. 17 Then he presented the tribute to King Eglon of Moab. Now Eglon was a very fat man. 18 When Ehud had finished presenting the tribute, he sent the people who carried the tribute on their way. 19 But he himself turned back at the sculptured stones near Gilgal, and said, "I have a secret message for you, O king." So the king said, *f* "Silence!" and all his attendants went out from his presence. 20 Ehud came to him, while he was sitting alone in his cool roof chamber, and said, "I have a message from God for you." So he rose from his seat. 21 Then Ehud reached with his left hand, took the sword from his right thigh, and thrust it into Eglon's*g* belly; 22 the hilt also went in after the blade, and the fat closed over the blade, for he did not draw the sword out of his belly; and the dirt came out.*h* 23 Then Ehud went out into the vestibule,*i* and closed the doors of the roof chamber on him, and locked them.

24 After he had gone, the servants came. When they saw that the doors of the roof chamber were locked, they thought, "He must be relieving himself*j* in the cool chamber." 25 So they waited until they were embarrassed. When he still did not open the doors of the roof chamber, they took the key and opened them. There was their lord lying dead on the floor.

26 Ehud escaped while they delayed, and passed beyond the sculptured stones,

and escaped to Seirah. 27 When he arrived, he sounded the trumpet in the hill country of Ephraim; and the Israelites went down with him from the hill country, having him at their head. 28 He said to them, "Follow after me; for the LORD has given your enemies the Moabites into your hand." So they went down after him, and seized the fords of the Jordan against the Moabites, and allowed no one to cross over. 29 At that time they killed about ten thousand of the Moabites, all strong, able-bodied men; no one escaped. 30 So Moab was subdued that day under the hand of Israel. And the land had rest eighty years.

Shamgar

31 After him came Shamgar son of Anath, who killed six hundred of the Philistines with an oxgoad. He too delivered Israel.

Deborah and Barak

4 The Israelites again did what was evil in the sight of the LORD, after Ehud died. 2 So the LORD sold them into the hand of King Jabin of Canaan, who reigned in Hazor; the commander of his army was Sisera, who lived in Harosheth-ha-goiim. 3 Then the Israelites cried out to

f Heb *he said*   *g* Heb *his*   *h* With Tg Vg: Meaning of Heb uncertain   *i* Meaning of Heb uncertain   *j* Heb *covering his feet*

3.19 *Stones near Gilgal*. The referent is unclear, but cf. Josh 4.20. Ehud acts alone; he is balanced structurally by another "loner," the tragicomic figure of Samson (chs. 13–16). **3.21–22** The assassination is told with obscene humor. **3.26–30** His Samson-like exploits over, Ehud now functions as Deborah does in ch. 4, rallying forces from the *hill country of Ephraim* to expel invaders and take control of the Jordan crossings. **3.26** The location of *Seirah* is unknown. **3.27** The ram's-horn *trumpet* was simultaneously a military and liturgical piece of equipment (Num 10.9; 31.6). When Saul sounded it, the accompanying shout was, "Let the Hebrews [i.e., the Israelite resistance] hear" (1 Sam 13.3). **3.29** *Ten thousand*, more likely "ten (village) muster units." See note on 1.4. **3.30** *Eighty years*. The chronology is an editorial construct.

3.31 *Shamgar* is a non-Semitic (perhaps a Hurrian) name. Lacking editorial framework, this notice was inserted in anticipation of 5.6. In some

Greek manuscripts it occurs instead of 16.31, after the stories of Samson, who also fights *Philistines*. Shamgar may have been a mercenary (perhaps a convert) who engineered a victory against northern Philistines, i.e., early Sea Peoples migrating south from bases along the Syrian-Lebanese coast.

4.1–5.31 Deborah outshines Barak as the Israelites oppose a superior Canaanite force in the north. The memory is told in classical prose (ch. 4) and celebrated in archaic poetry, the "Song of Deborah" (ch. 5). Editorial notices (4.1–3; 5.31b) frame the two chapters.

4.1–24 The exploits of Deborah and Barak. **4.1–3** This editorial notice of events before Deborah's time does not mention Shamgar. **4.2** *King Jabin of Canaan*, an unusual title in an area of many city-states. Jabin is king of Hazor in Josh 11. *Sisera* is a non-Semitic name; he probably belonged to one of the immigrating Sea Peoples. **4.3** *Chariots of iron*. See note on 1.19. The Philis-

the Lord for help; for he had nine hundred chariots of iron, and had oppressed the Israelites cruelly twenty years.

4 At that time Deborah, a prophetess, wife of Lappidoth, was judging Israel. 5 She used to sit under the palm of Deborah between Ramah and Bethel in the hill country of Ephraim; and the Israelites came up to her for judgment. 6 She sent and summoned Barak son of Abinoam from Kedesh in Naphtali, and said to him, "The Lord, the God of Israel, commands you, 'Go, take position at Mount Tabor, bringing ten thousand from the tribe of Naphtali and the tribe of Zebulun. 7 I will draw out Sisera, the general of Jabin's army, to meet you by the Wadi Kishon with his chariots and his troops; and I will give him into your hand.'" 8 Barak said to her, "If you will go with me, I will go; but if you will not go with me, I will not go." 9 And she said, "I will surely go with you; nevertheless, the road on which you are going will not lead to your glory, for the Lord will sell Sisera into the hand of a woman." Then Deborah got up and went with Barak to Kedesh. 10 Barak summoned Zebulun and Naphtali to Kedesh; and ten thousand warriors went up

behind him; and Deborah went up with him.

11 Now Heber the Kenite had separated from the other Kenites,^{k} that is, the descendants of Hobab the father-in-law of Moses, and had encamped as far away as Elon-bezaanannim, which is near Kedesh.

12 When Sisera was told that Barak son of Abinoam had gone up to Mount Tabor, 13 Sisera called out all his chariots, nine hundred chariots of iron, and all the troops who were with him, from Harosheth-ha-goiim to the Wadi Kishon. 14 Then Deborah said to Barak, "Up! For this is the day on which the Lord has given Sisera into your hand. The Lord is indeed going out before you." So Barak went down from Mount Tabor with ten thousand warriors following him. 15 And the Lord threw Sisera and all his chariots and all his army into a panic^l before Barak; Sisera got down from his chariot and fled away on foot, 16 while Barak pursued the chariots and the army to Harosheth-ha-goiim. All the army of Sisera fell by the sword; no one was left.

17 Now Sisera had fled away on foot

k Heb *from the Kain* l Heb adds *to the sword*; compare verse 16

---

tines brought superior knowledge of ironworking to Canaan, enjoying monopolistic control until the time of Saul and David. **4.4–5** *Deborah* ("Bee" in Hebrew) was *a prophetess* at a holy site near Bethel with a *palm* tree named in her honor. *Lappidoth*. The Hebrew can mean "torches," as in 15.4. *Was judging*, i.e., giving oracular response to inquiries on various concerns.
4.6–8 Reluctant *Barak* ("Lightning" in Hebrew), not Deborah, is the recognized military commander, remembered as praiseworthy in Heb 11.32. **4.6** *Kedesh*, "Holy Place," is a common place-name. This Kedesh is probably a site in southern Galilee, not to be confused with the great site of Tell Qades, eleven kilometers northwest of Hazor. *Mount Tabor*, at the northern edge of the Esdraelon plain, was ideally suited for muster of troops from Galilee. *Naphtali and ... Zebulun* are the only tribes mentioned in this account. **4.7** The battleground lies where the pass between Megiddo and Taanach opens into Esdraelon, near the confluence of streams that flow together to form the *Kishon* river. The battle is for control of the rich Esdraelon, Acco, and northern Sharon plains, and it marks the first time that Israelites from the highlands are able successfully to challenge the occupants of the plains. **4.8** There is irony in Barak's conditional acceptance of Deb-

orah's unconditional command. Barak's hesitancy is further developed in the Greek text which adds, "for I never know what day the angel of the Lord will give me success." **4.9** *Into the hand of a woman* sets the audience up for an ironic fulfillment—the woman is not Deborah but Jael. **4.10** *Ten thousand*, more likely ten "muster units." See note on 1.4. **4.11** This verse explains why some *Kenites*, "smiths," descended from *Hobab* in the south (see note on 1.16) are encamped in the far north, on the line of Sisera's flight after the battle. *Elon-bezaanannim* (Hebrew, "Oak in Zaanannim") may have been another sacred tree or perhaps it served to distinguish the northern *Kedesh*, which is different from the Kedesh where the muster took place (vv. 6–10). **4.12–16** *Barak* leads the warriors; there is no mention of *Deborah*, except for her proclamation of the *day* of the Lord's victory (v. 14). **4.15** The account is strikingly similar to that of the victory at the Reed Sea (Ex 14.24). The prose gives no details of how *the Lord* created the *panic*, but no Israelite could take the credit. **4.17–22** The humiliation and assassination of Sisera are told with an ironic twist— *Jael* offers hospitality. **4.17** A *Kenite* clan had migrated and changed sides in the time of *Jabin*. Providentially, the Kenite chief had a wife who remained loyal to the cause of the Lord,

to the tent of Jael wife of Heber the Kenite; for there was peace between King Jabin of Hazor and the clan of Heber the Kenite. 18 Jael came out to meet Sisera, and said to him, "Turn aside, my lord, turn aside to me; have no fear." So he turned aside to her into the tent, and she covered him with a rug. 19 Then he said to her, "Please give me a little water to drink; for I am thirsty." So she opened a skin of milk and gave him a drink and covered him. 20 He said to her, "Stand at the entrance of the tent, and if anybody comes and asks you, 'Is anyone here?' say, 'No.' " 21 But Jael wife of Heber took a tent peg, and took a hammer in her hand, and went softly to him and drove the peg into his temple, until it went down into the ground—he was lying fast asleep from weariness—and he died. 22 Then, as Barak came in pursuit of Sisera, Jael went out to meet him, and said to him, "Come, and I will show you the man whom you are seeking." So he went into her tent; and there was Sisera lying dead, with the tent peg in his temple.

23 So on that day God subdued King Jabin of Canaan before the Israelites. 24 Then the hand of the Israelites bore harder and harder on King Jabin of Canaan, until they destroyed King Jabin of Canaan.

The Song of Deborah

5 Then Deborah and Barak son of Abinoam sang on that day, saying:
2   "When locks are long in Israel,
     when the people offer
       themselves willingly—
     bless m the LORD!

3   "Hear, O kings; give ear,
       O princes;
     to the LORD I will sing,
     I will make melody to the
       LORD, the God of
       Israel.

4   "LORD, when you went out from
       Seir,
     when you marched from the
       region of Edom,
     the earth trembled,
       and the heavens poured,
     the clouds indeed poured
       water.

5   The mountains quaked before
       the LORD, the One of
       Sinai,
     before the LORD, the God of
       Israel.

6   "In the days of Shamgar son of
       Anath,
     in the days of Jael, caravans
       ceased
     and travelers kept to the
       byways.

7   The peasantry prospered in
       Israel,
     they grew fat on plunder,
     because you arose, Deborah,
     arose as a mother in Israel.

8   When new gods were chosen,
       then war was in the gates.
     Was shield or spear to be seen
       among forty thousand in
       Israel?

m Or You who offer yourselves willingly among the people, bless

---

to the point of murderously exploiting the obligation of hospitality. **4.19** Certain goat *milk* products have a strong sleep-inducing effect. **4.23–24** These verses are editorial wrap-up. *King Jabin of Canaan* remains obscure.

5.1–31 The Song of Deborah (and Barak, but the verb in v. 1 is singular) is datable to the twelfth century B.C.E., not far removed from the events being celebrated. There are a number of obscurities in the text. The genre (victory hymn) is well known from Egypt and Assyria in the fifteenth to twelfth centuries B.C.E. The Song exhibits repetitive parallelism familiar from fourteenth-century B.C.E. Ugaritic texts. **5.1** This is the narrator's link, which, prior to insertion of the poem, was probably followed by the exclamation and concluding framework note (v. 31). **5.3** *Hear,*

O kings announces the general theme: praise of the Divine King in Israel as testimony to kings such as those recently defeated by the forces of Deborah and Barak. **5.4–5** The singer describes a theophany of Israel's Divine Warrior, *the One of Sinai*, arriving in Canaan via *Seir, . . . region of Edom*, in southern Transjordan. **5.6–7** The crisis is framed by the exploits of *Shamgar* at its beginning and *Jael* at its end. Mobilization of the hill-country *peasantry* to hijack trade *caravans* brought unprecedented prosperity to Israelites. The title *mother in Israel* recognizes Deborah's prophetic leadership, as does the title "father" for a male prophet (see 2 Kings 2.1–2; 13.14). **5.8** A choice of *new gods* is appropriate mythologically to the collapse of trade-route agreements and general security that brought on the warfare. Deities

9 My heart goes out to the
       commanders of Israel
   who offered themselves
       willingly among the people.
   Bless the LORD.

10 "Tell of it, you who ride on white
       donkeys,
   you who sit on rich carpetsⁿ
   and you who walk by the way.
11 To the sound of musiciansⁿ at
       the watering places,
   there they repeat the triumphs
       of the LORD,
   the triumphs of his peasantry
       in Israel.

   "Then down to the gates
       marched the people of the
       LORD.

12 "Awake, awake, Deborah!
       Awake, awake, utter a song!
   Arise, Barak, lead away your
       captives,
       O son of Abinoam.
13 Then down marched the remnant
       of the noble;
   the people of the LORD
       marched down for him^o
       against the mighty.
14 From Ephraim they set out^p into
       the valley,^q
   following you, Benjamin, with
       your kin;
   from Machir marched down the
       commanders,
   and from Zebulun those who
       bear the marshal's staff;
15 the chiefs of Issachar came with
       Deborah,

and Issachar faithful to Barak;
       into the valley they rushed out
       at his heels.
   Among the clans of Reuben
       there were great searchings of
       heart.
16 Why did you tarry among the
       sheepfolds,
   to hear the piping for the
       flocks?
   Among the clans of Reuben
       there were great searchings of
       heart.
17 Gilead stayed beyond the Jordan;
       and Dan, why did he abide with
       the ships?
   Asher sat still at the coast of
       the sea,
   settling down by his landings.
18 Zebulun is a people that scorned
       death;
   Naphtali too, on the heights of
       the field.

19 "The kings came, they fought;
       then fought the kings of
       Canaan,
   at Taanach, by the waters of
       Megiddo;
   they got no spoils of silver.
20 The stars fought from heaven,
       from their courses they fought
       against Sisera.
21 The torrent Kishon swept them
       away,
   the onrushing torrent, the
       torrent Kishon.
   March on, my soul, with might!

n Meaning of Heb uncertain   o Gk: Heb me
p Cn: Heb From Ephraim their root   q Gk: Heb in
Amalek

were regularly listed as witnesses and guarantors of treaties. *Shield* and *spear* were aristocratic weapons belonging to professional military men. *Forty thousand.* Forty "muster units" (see note on 1.4) would be more in keeping with the description in vv. 6–7. **5.10** Appeal is made to the entire citizenry: the chiefs, *who ride*, and the general populace, *who walk*. **5.11–13** The focus shifts to town and village wells, describing public response to the appeal. **5.14–18** In the setting of the victory celebration, the poet reviews the performance of tribal contingents. Six tribes had responded: *Ephraim, Benjamin, Machir* (western Manasseh), *Zebulun, Issachar,* and *Naphtali.* Four or five are censured for not responding: *Reuben, Gilead* (possibly Gad), *Dan, Asher,* and *Meroz* (v. 23, Meroz may be either a town or a clan). Passed over in silence are Judah, Simeon, and Levi. The former two may already have been under Philistine domination. Levi was a specialist tribe without territorial definition, its families dispersed throughout the territory as carriers of the covenantal lore. **5.15** *At his heels,* idiomatic for "under his command" (the term is translated *behind him* in 4.10). **5.19–23** These verses recount the battle and Israel's victory thanks to a timely maneuver by the Lord—a cloudburst and flash flood—that gave the advantage to foot soldiers. **5.19** The opposition is described as a coalition of *kings of Canaan;* Jabin is not mentioned. **5.20** *The stars fought* as the source of rain. Cf. the performance of the sun and moon at the defense

22 "Then loud beat the horses' hoofs
     with the galloping, galloping of
     his steeds.

23 "Curse Meroz, says the angel of
     the LORD,
   curse bitterly its inhabitants,
   because they did not come to the
     help of the LORD,
   to the help of the LORD against
     the mighty.

24 "Most blessed of women be Jael,
     the wife of Heber the Kenite,
   of tent-dwelling women most
     blessed.

25 He asked water and she gave him
     milk,
   she brought him curds in a
     lordly bowl.

26 She put her hand to the tent peg
     and her right hand to the
     workmen's mallet;
   she struck Sisera a blow,
   she crushed his head,
   she shattered and pierced his
     temple.

27 He sank, he fell,
     he lay still at her feet;
   at her feet he sank, he fell;
   where he sank, there he fell
     dead.

28 "Out of the window she peered,
     the mother of Sisera gazed[r]
     through the lattice:

'Why is his chariot so long in
     coming?
   Why tarry the hoofbeats of his
     chariots?'

29 Her wisest ladies make answer,
     indeed, she answers the
     question herself:

30 'Are they not finding and
     dividing the spoil?—
   A girl or two for every man;
   spoil of dyed stuffs for Sisera,
     spoil of dyed stuffs
     embroidered,
   two pieces of dyed work
     embroidered for my neck
     as spoil?'

31 "So perish all your enemies,
     O LORD!
   But may your friends be like
     the sun as it rises in its
     might."

And the land had rest forty years.

The Midianite Oppression

6 The Israelites did what was evil in
   the sight of the LORD, and the LORD
gave them into the hand of Midian seven
years. 2 The hand of Midian prevailed
over Israel; and because of Midian the Israelites provided for themselves hiding
places in the mountains, caves and strong-
holds. 3 For whenever the Israelites put in
seed, the Midianites and the Amalekites

r Gk Compare Tg: Heb *exclaimed*

---

of Gibeon (Josh 10.11–14). **5.23** *Meroz* is otherwise unknown; see note on 5.14–18. The *angel
of the LORD* may here be a human being, the professional diviner (prophet or prophetess) regularly consulted in the conduct of warfare.
5.24–27 This description of the demise of Sisera
heaps praise upon Jael. **5.25** *Milk.* See note on
4.19. **5.26** A *tent peg and . . . mallet* were handy
because pitching the tent was woman's work, as it
is today among Bedouin. **5.27** *At her feet,* or "under her command," ironically echoes the usage in
v. 15; 4.10. **5.28** The final scene begins with another woman, the *mother of Sisera* (cf. Deborah as a
mother in Israel, v. 7), in a poetically inverted vantage point, awaiting Sisera's triumphant return.
5.30 The final irony attributes to Canaanite warriors a license with captive women that Mosaic
tradition sought to outlaw (Deut 21.10–14).
5.31 *So perish . . . its might.* In the original Hebrew,
v. 31 is strikingly more proselike in style than

vv. 2–30 (cf. note on 5.1). *Your friends,* or "those
who love you." *Forty years,* twice as long as the
oppression (4.3), half as long as the *rest* following
Ehud (3.30).
6.1–8.35 Gideon (also identified in ch. 7 as
Jerubbaal) mobilizes several central hill-country
and Galilean tribes against annual raiding parties
from Transjordan (Midianites, Amalekites, and
other easterners). **6.1–10** This introduction
uses the now-familiar framework (apostasy, oppression, appeal for help; see note on 2.11–23) in
vv. 1–6. Economic exploitation originating from
distant oases was made possible by the recent
domestication of the camel. **6.2** *Midian* was a
desert confederation alternately in alliance (Ex
2.15–4.31; 18.1–27) and at war (Num 25–31)
with Israel. Midian's revival, with newly superior
mobility for annual collection of taxes, crowds
peasant agrarians once again into the highlands.

and the people of the east would come up against them. 4 They would encamp against them and destroy the produce of the land, as far as the neighborhood of Gaza, and leave no sustenance in Israel, and no sheep or ox or donkey. 5 For they and their livestock would come up, and they would even bring their tents, as thick as locusts; neither they nor their camels could be counted; so they wasted the land as they came in. 6 Thus Israel was greatly impoverished because of Midian; and the Israelites cried out to the Lord for help.

7 When the Israelites cried to the Lord on account of the Midianites, 8 the Lord sent a prophet to the Israelites; and he said to them, "Thus says the Lord, the God of Israel: I led you up from Egypt, and brought you out of the house of slavery; 9 and I delivered you from the hand of the Egyptians, and from the hand of all who oppressed you, and drove them out before you, and gave you their land; 10 and I said to you, 'I am the Lord your God; you shall not pay reverence to the gods of the Amorites, in whose land you live.' But you have not given heed to my voice."

The Call of Gideon

11 Now the angel of the Lord came and sat under the oak at Ophrah, which belonged to Joash the Abiezrite, as his son Gideon was beating out wheat in the wine press, to hide it from the Midianites. 12 The angel of the Lord appeared to him and said to him, "The Lord is with you, you mighty warrior." 13 Gideon answered him, "But sir, if the Lord is with us, why then has all this happened to us? And where are all his wonderful deeds that our ancestors recounted to us, saying, 'Did not the Lord bring us up from Egypt?' But now the Lord has cast us off, and given us into the hand of Midian." 14 Then the Lord turned to him and said, "Go in this might of yours and deliver Israel from the hand of Midian; I hereby commission you." 15 He responded, "But sir, how can I deliver Israel? My clan is the weakest in Manasseh, and I am the least in my family." 16 The Lord said to him, "But I will be with you, and you shall strike down the Midianites, every one of them." 17 Then he said to him, "If now I have found favor with you, then show me a sign that it is you who speak with me. 18 Do not depart from here until I come to you, and bring out my present, and set it before you." And he said, "I will stay until you return."

19 So Gideon went into his house and prepared a kid, and unleavened cakes from an ephah of flour; the meat he put in a basket, and the broth he put in a pot, and brought them to him under the oak and presented them. 20 The angel of God said to him, "Take the meat and the

---

6.3 *Amalekites.* See note on 3.13.   6.7–10 This time, when *Israelites cry*, instead of the expected deliverer the Lord sends a *prophet* who delivers an indictment, as the angel of the Lord did in 2.1–5. The warning in 2.3 that other gods would be a *snare* is coming true.
6.11–32   The only early narrative in the book where the Lord speaks directly to a protagonist or to Israel. The Lord receives a new altar (vv. 11–24), and an old altar is destroyed (vv. 25–32). Gideon is slow to recognize the voice of the Lord, foreshadowing Israel's problem in ch. 10.   6.11–24 Gideon (in contrast to Othniel, Ehud, and Deborah) is first approached by an angel, who appears in human form and prepares the way for direct conversation between Gideon and the Lord.   6.11 *Ophrah*, a village of Manasseh not far from Shechem. *Joash*, lit. "the Lord has given," presides over a pagan shrine. *Abiezrite.* See Josh 17.2. *Gideon* means "Hewer" or "Hacker" in Hebrew; it is probably a nickname based on his reforming activities.   6.12–13 The pronoun *you* is singular. Gideon misses the point and replies about the plight of *us*.   6.12 Relatively aristocratic status is suggested by the designation *mighty warrior*, which otherwise does not well describe Gideon in the bulk of chs. 6–7.   6.13 *Did not ... up from Egypt*, an unshakable element in the Israelite credo, might also be a liturgical cliché.   6.14 *The Lord* and the angel are not identical. Gideon is unknowingly involved in a three-way conversation.   6.15 *Family*, lit. "father's house," can also designate the smallest military unit. Saul uses similar overly modest language (1 Sam 9.21; cf. 1 Sam 15.17). Cf. the recruitment of Moses (Ex 3.1–4.23), where vastly disproportionate space is given to eliciting the dutiful response.   6.16–17 *I will be with you* is directly reminiscent of Ex 3, as is the request for *a sign* to certify the Lord's credentials.   6.19 An *ephah of flour*, more than a bushel, seems disproportionately large.   6.20–23 The story has Gideon seeing the Lord's angel face-to-face so that the invisible Lord may enter into direct negotiations with Gideon, as he had with Moses. Gideon's exclamation indicates that his encounter with the envoy was a traumatic

unleavened cakes, and put them on this rock, and pour out the broth." And he did so. 21 Then the angel of the LORD reached out the tip of the staff that was in his hand, and touched the meat and the unleavened cakes; and fire sprang up from the rock and consumed the meat and the unleavened cakes; and the angel of the LORD vanished from his sight. 22 Then Gideon perceived that it was the angel of the LORD; and Gideon said, "Help me, Lord GOD! For I have seen the angel of the LORD face to face." 23 But the LORD said to him, "Peace be to you; do not fear, you shall not die." 24 Then Gideon built an altar there to the LORD, and called it, The LORD is peace. To this day it still stands at Ophrah, which belongs to the Abiezrites.

25 That night the LORD said to him, "Take your father's bull, the second bull seven years old, and pull down the altar of Baal that belongs to your father, and cut down the sacred pole[s] that is beside it; 26 and build an altar to the LORD your God on the top of the stronghold here, in proper order; then take the second bull, and offer it as a burnt offering with the wood of the sacred pole[s] that you shall cut down." 27 So Gideon took ten of his servants, and did as the LORD had told him; but because he was too afraid of his family and the townspeople to do it by day, he did it by night.

Gideon Destroys the Altar of Baal

28 When the townspeople rose early in the morning, the altar of Baal was broken down, and the sacred pole[s] beside it was cut down, and the second bull was offered on the altar that had been built. 29 So they said to one another, "Who has

done this?" After searching and inquiring, they were told, "Gideon son of Joash did it." 30 Then the townspeople said to Joash, "Bring out your son, so that he may die, for he has pulled down the altar of Baal and cut down the sacred pole[s] beside it." 31 But Joash said to all who were arrayed against him, "Will you contend for Baal? Or will you defend his cause? Whoever contends for him shall be put to death by morning. If he is a god, let him contend for himself, because his altar has been pulled down." 32 Therefore on that day Gideon[t] was called Jerubbaal, that is to say, "Let Baal contend against him," because he pulled down his altar.

33 Then all the Midianites and the Amalekites and the people of the east came together, and crossing the Jordan they encamped in the Valley of Jezreel. 34 But the spirit of the LORD took possession of Gideon; and he sounded the trumpet, and the Abiezrites were called out to follow him. 35 He sent messengers throughout all Manasseh, and they too were called out to follow him. He also sent messengers to Asher, Zebulun, and Naphtali, and they went up to meet them.

The Sign of the Fleece

36 Then Gideon said to God, "In order to see whether you will deliver Israel by my hand, as you have said, 37 I am going to lay a fleece of wool on the threshing floor; if there is dew on the fleece alone, and it is dry on all the ground, then I shall know that you will deliver Israel by my hand, as you have said." 38 And it was so. When he rose early next morning and squeezed the fleece, he wrung enough dew from the fleece to fill a bowl with wa-

s Heb *Asherah*　　t Heb *he*

---

experience, but the Lord is shown to be compassionate and gracious, as promised to Moses (Ex 33.19). **6.24** *Peace* (Hebrew *shalom*), comprehensive well-being, individual and communal. **6.25–32** The dismantling of Joash's *altar* and the hacking down of the *sacred pole*, an invariable feature of the fertility cult that supported the feudal hierarchy in Canaanite society, provide ironic legitimacy for the given name *Jerubbaal* (v. 32), Hebrew, "Let Baal Contend" (Hebrew *riv* is the root of the part of name that can be translated "contend"; see note on 11.12–28). **6.25–27** Gideon is prosperous enough to command the assistance of *ten . . . servants* but is only

brave enough to act *by night.* **6.30–32** Apostate Joash, facing the zeal of Jerubbaal, is no longer an avid supporter of Baal. **6.35** Gideon rallies warriors from his own tribe, *Manasseh*, and from three Galilean tribes: *Asher, Zebulun, and Naphtali.* **6.36–40** Gideon demands further proof that *God* (never "the LORD" in these verses) really meant what was said in the recruitment scene (vv. 11–24). Fishermen living on one of the streamless and springless desert islands have obtained sufficient water by spreading out fleece in the evening and wringing dew from it in the morning. The true miracle is the reverse, and that is what Gideon requires.

ter. 39 Then Gideon said to God, "Do not let your anger burn against me, let me speak one more time; let me, please, make trial with the fleece just once more; let it be dry only on the fleece, and on all the ground let there be dew." 40 And God did so that night. It was dry on the fleece only, and on all the ground there was dew.

Gideon Surprises and Routs the Midianites

7 Then Jerubbaal (that is, Gideon) and all the troops that were with him rose early and encamped beside the spring of Harod; and the camp of Midian was north of them, below[u] the hill of Moreh, in the valley. 2 The LORD said to Gideon, "The troops with you are too many for me to give the Midianites into their hand. Israel would only take the credit away from me, saying, 'My own hand has delivered me.' 3 Now therefore proclaim this in the hearing of the troops, 'Whoever is fearful and trembling, let him return home.'" Thus Gideon sifted them out;[v] twenty-two thousand returned, and ten thousand remained. 4 Then the LORD said to Gideon, "The troops are still too many; take them down to the water and I will sift them out for you there. When I say, 'This one shall go with you,' he shall go with you; and when I say, 'This one shall not go with you,' he shall not go." 5 So he brought the troops down to the water; and the LORD said to Gideon, "All those who lap the water with

their tongues, as a dog laps, you shall put to one side; all those who kneel down to drink, putting their hands to their mouths,[w] you shall put to the other side." 6 The number of those that lapped was three hundred; but all the rest of the troops knelt down to drink water. 7 Then the LORD said to Gideon, "With the three hundred that lapped I will deliver you, and give the Midianites into your hand. Let all the others go to their homes." 8 So he took the jars of the troops from their hands,[x] and their trumpets; and he sent all the rest of Israel back to their own tents, but retained the three hundred. The camp of Midian was below him in the valley.

9 That same night the LORD said to him, "Get up, attack the camp; for I have given it into your hand. 10 But if you fear to attack, go down to the camp with your servant Purah; 11 and you shall hear what they say, and afterward your hands shall be strengthened to attack the camp." Then he went down with his servant Purah to the outposts of the armed men that were in the camp. 12 The Midianites and the Amalekites and all the people of the east lay along the valley as thick as locusts; and their camels were without number, countless as the sand on the seashore. 13 When Gideon arrived, there was a man

u Heb *from*   v Cn: Heb *home, and depart from Mount Gilead'*"   w Heb places the words *putting their hands to their mouths* after the word *lapped* in verse 6   x Cn: Heb *So the people took provisions in their hands*

7.1–23 The Lord's rout of the Midianites comprises three scenes: the reduction of the Israelite force (vv. 1–8); an enemy sentry's dream (vv. 9–15); and the rout and retreat of the Midianites (vv. 16–22). **7.1** *Jerubbaal (that is, Gideon)*. It is improbable that memories of two different figures have merged. The name Jerubbaal (Hebrew, "Let Baal Contend") stands for God's accomplishment through one historical savior. The name Gideon ("Hacker") stands for the man in all his fearful, heavy-handed individuality. The *spring of Harod* is near the foot of Mount Gilboa in the southeastern Jezreel Valley. The *hill of Moreh* (Hebrew, "Teacher's Hill") in the Jezreel Valley is presumably another place of oracular inquiry, like Deborah's palm (4.5). **7.3** *Whoever is fearful and trembling*. See list of exemptions in Deut 20.5–8. Instead of *thousand* we should again recognize the local unit for the military muster (see note on 1.4). Num 1; 26 indicate that Manasseh's muster quota

at one time was thirty-two units totaling approximately three hundred men, a sizable army in the premonarchical period. **7.5–7** The text is obscure. It is not clear whether the Lord chooses the more alert or the less cautious. The latter would serve to make it plain that victory is due to God's action, not to human initiative or prowess. If the numbers in the story originate in the muster of Gideon's tribe alone, his force would have been *three hundred* before the reductions in vv. 2, 6, so the final force is much smaller, perhaps fifty or so. **7.8** The abrupt mention of *jars . . . and . . . trumpets* appears to anticipate vv. 16–17. **7.9–14** The story continues to emphasize Gideon's fearful hesitancy and the Lord's providential response, this time via a pagan sentry's dream. **7.10** The *servant* (Hebrew na'ar, generally translated "young man") is Gideon's squire, personal attendant, handyman, and armor bearer (see 9.54; 1 Sam 14.1, 6). **7.13** *The tent*, pre-

telling a dream to his comrade; and he said, "I had a dream, and in it a cake of barley bread tumbled into the camp of Midian, and came to the tent, and struck it so that it fell; it turned upside down, and the tent collapsed." 14 And his comrade answered, "This is no other than the sword of Gideon son of Joash, a man of Israel; into his hand God has given Midian and all the army."

15 When Gideon heard the telling of the dream and its interpretation, he worshiped; and he returned to the camp of Israel, and said, "Get up; for the LORD has given the army of Midian into your hand." 16 After he divided the three hundred men into three companies, and put trumpets into the hands of all of them, and empty jars, with torches inside the jars, 17 he said to them, "Look at me, and do the same; when I come to the outskirts of the camp, do as I do. 18 When I blow the trumpet, I and all who are with me, then you also blow the trumpets around the whole camp, and shout, 'For the LORD and for Gideon!' "

19 So Gideon and the hundred who were with him came to the outskirts of the camp at the beginning of the middle watch, when they had just set the watch; and they blew the trumpets and smashed the jars that were in their hands. 20 So the three companies blew the trumpets and broke the jars, holding in their left hands the torches, and in their right hands the trumpets to blow; and they cried, "A sword for the LORD and for Gideon!" 21 Every man stood in his place all around the camp, and all the men in camp ran; they cried out and fled. 22 When they blew the three hundred trumpets, the LORD set every man's sword against his fellow and against all the army; and the army fled as far as Beth-shittah toward Zererah,y as far as the border of Abel-meholah, by Tabbath. 23 And the men of Israel were called out from Naphtali and from Asher and from all Manasseh, and they pursued after the Midianites.

24 Then Gideon sent messengers throughout all the hill country of Ephraim, saying, "Come down against the Midianites and seize the waters against them, as far as Beth-barah, and also the Jordan." So all the men of Ephraim were called out, and they seized the waters as far as Beth-barah, and also the Jordan. 25 They captured the two captains of Midian, Oreb and Zeeb; they killed Oreb at the rock of Oreb, and Zeeb they killed at the wine press of Zeeb, as they pursued the Midianites. They brought the heads of Oreb and Zeeb to Gideon beyond the Jordan.

Gideon's Triumph and Vengeance

8 Then the Ephraimites said to him, "What have you done to us, not to call us when you went to fight against the Midianites?" And they upbraided him violently. 2 So he said to them, "What have I done now in comparison with you? Is not the gleaning of the grapes of Ephraim better than the vintage of Abiezer? 3 God has given into your hands the captains of Midian, Oreb and Zeeb; what have I been able to do in comparison with you?" When he said this, their anger against him subsided.

4 Then Gideon came to the Jordan

y Another reading is *Zeredah*

---

sumably the sheik's tent, the command center. **7.15** Gideon *worshipped*, i.e., fell prostrate. **7.16** With *trumpets, empty jars,* and *torches,* the Israelites are heavily laden for a spectacular demonstration. There is no mention of weapons. **7.22** The verse describes a splintered force in leaderless retreat to Transjordan. **7.23** This verse harks back to 6.35, where *Manasseh* was mobilized and *Asher,* Zebulun, and *Naphtali* were placed on alert. All except Zebulun now take the field.

7.24–8.3 These verses are transitional. Gideon advocates total mobilization against the desert confederation, whereas the Lord, it appears, had intended a noncombative stampede of the superstitious nomads (7.18–21). Gideon will now take the militia into the field, east of the Jordan, pursuing private vengeance (as becomes clear in 8.19). **7.24** Troops from *Ephraim* arrive uninvited in 12.1. **7.25** *Oreb and Zeeb,* Hebrew, "Raven" and "Wolf." See Ps 83.9–12; Isa 10.26. **8.1** *Ephraimites* complain about not having been included in the original summons. **8.2** *Is not the gleaning . . . of Abiezer?* Gideon is either coining a proverb or adapting one. The story may preserve the memory of an attempt by Manasseh's southern neighbor to put a stop to Gideon's retaliatory raiding. The Ephraimites are talked out of their resentment of Gideon's preferential treatment of other tribes. **8.4–21** The focus shifts from the somewhat miraculous recruitment of Gideon to scenes of Gideon in action. The Lord does not

and crossed over, he and the three hundred who were with him, exhausted and famished.^z 5 So he said to the people of Succoth, "Please give some loaves of bread to my followers, for they are exhausted, and I am pursuing Zebah and Zalmunna, the kings of Midian." 6 But the officials of Succoth said, "Do you already have in your possession the hands of Zebah and Zalmunna, that we should give bread to your army?" 7 Gideon replied, "Well then, when the Lord has given Zebah and Zalmunna into my hand, I will trample your flesh on the thorns of the wilderness and on briers." 8 From there he went up to Penuel, and made the same request of them; and the people of Penuel answered him as the people of Succoth had answered. 9 So he said to the people of Penuel, "When I come back victorious, I will break down this tower."

10 Now Zebah and Zalmunna were in Karkor with their army, about fifteen thousand men, all who were left of all the army of the people of the east; for one hundred twenty thousand men bearing arms had fallen. 11 So Gideon went up by the caravan route east of Nobah and Jogbehah, and attacked the army; for the army was off its guard. 12 Zebah and Zalmunna fled; and he pursued them and took the two kings of Midian, Zebah and Zalmunna, and threw all the army into a panic.

13 When Gideon son of Joash returned from the battle by the ascent of Heres, 14 he caught a young man, one of the people of Succoth, and questioned him; and he listed for him the officials and elders of Succoth, seventy-seven people. 15 Then he came to the people of Succoth, and said, "Here are Zebah and Zalmunna, about whom you taunted me, saying, 'Do you already have in your possession the hands of Zebah and Zalmunna, that we should give bread to your troops who are exhausted?' " 16 So he took the elders of the city and he took thorns of the wilderness and briers and with them he trampled^a the people of Succoth. 17 He also broke down the tower of Penuel, and killed the men of the city.

18 Then he said to Zebah and Zalmunna, "What about the men whom you killed at Tabor?" They answered, "As you are, so were they, every one of them; they resembled the sons of a king." 19 And he replied, "They were my brothers, the sons of my mother; as the Lord lives, if you had saved them alive, I would not kill you." 20 So he said to Jether his firstborn, "Go kill them!" But the boy did not draw his sword, for he was afraid, because he was still a boy. 21 Then Zebah and Zalmunna said, "You come and kill us; for as the man is, so is his strength." So Gideon proceeded to kill Zebah and Zalmunna; and he took the crescents that were on the necks of their camels.

Gideon's Idolatry

22 Then the Israelites said to Gideon, "Rule over us, you and your son and your

z Gk: Heb *pursuing*   a With verse 7, Compare Gk: Heb *he taught*

---

participate apart from being referred to by Gideon (vv. 7, 19). The purpose of this section is to show what becomes of the young reformer who has become a commander. **8.4** *Three hundred* may mean the full strength of Manasseh's militia. See notes on 7.3; 7.5–7. **8.5** *Succoth* ("huts"), probably Tell Deir ʿAlla in the Jordan Valley, a sanctuary site that continued in use as such after the settlement there was destroyed by earthquake ca. 1180 B.C.E. (plus or minus sixty years). **8.6** The commandeering of provisions is frustrated by distrust of Gideon's capability, despite his threats. *Hands* refers to mutilation of prisoners, a gruesome reality (1.6–7). *Zebah* (Hebrew, "Victim") and *Zalmunna* ("Protection Refused") were *kings* (v. 5), in contrast to *captains* Oreb and Zeeb (v. 3). **8.7** *Thorns* and *briars* recall treaty curses involving weeds and various domestic plants. Is Gideon taking the law into his own hands? **8.8** *Penuel*, Hebrew, "Face of God" (Gen 32.24–32; Hos 12.4), perhaps Tulūl edh-Dhahab, not far from Succoth. **8.10** *Karkor* lay in Wadi Sirhan, east of the Dead Sea. *Fifteen thousand*, is an improbable number for the oasis setting; "tribal units" may be more accurate (cf. note on 7.3). **8.12** The Midianite army is stampeded in the desert terrain by the loss of two kings. **8.13–17** Gideon is as good as his word. **8.18–21** These verses would follow well after v. 12. **8.18** *Tabor*. Nothing has prepared for this reference. **8.19** Gideon is pursuing a blood feud. Private vengeance usurps a prerogative of the Lord (Deut 32.35; cf. Rom 12.19). *As the Lord lives*, or "By the life of the Lord." Gideon rides roughshod over a basic covenant stipulation (Ex 20.7; Deut 5.11). **8.20** *Jether . . . a boy*. Similar narrative sympathy is accorded Jotham, the youngest son of Gideon, in 9.7–21.

grandson also; for you have delivered us out of the hand of Midian." 23 Gideon said to them, "I will not rule over you, and my son will not rule over you; the LORD will rule over you." 24 Then Gideon said to them, "Let me make a request of you; each of you give me an earring he has taken as booty." (For the enemy[b] had golden earrings, because they were Ishmaelites.) 25 "We will willingly give them," they answered. So they spread a garment, and each threw into it an earring he had taken as booty. 26 The weight of the golden earrings that he requested was one thousand seven hundred shekels of gold (apart from the crescents and the pendants and the purple garments worn by the kings of Midian, and the collars that were on the necks of their camels). 27 Gideon made an ephod of it and put it in his town, in Ophrah; and all Israel prostituted themselves to it there, and it became a snare to Gideon and to his family. 28 So Midian was subdued before the Israelites, and they lifted up their heads no more. So the land had rest forty years in the days of Gideon.

Death of Gideon

29　Jerubbaal son of Joash went to live in his own house. 30 Now Gideon had seventy sons, his own offspring, for he had many wives. 31 His concubine who was in Shechem also bore him a son, and he named him Abimelech. 32 Then Gideon son of Joash died at a good old age, and was buried in the tomb of his father Joash at Ophrah of the Abiezrites.

33　As soon as Gideon died, the Israelites relapsed and prostituted themselves with the Baals, making Baal-berith their god. 34 The Israelites did not remember the LORD their God, who had rescued them from the hand of all their enemies on every side; 35 and they did not exhibit loyalty to the house of Jerubbaal (that is, Gideon) in return for all the good that he had done to Israel.

Abimelech Attempts to Establish a Monarchy

9 Now Abimelech son of Jerubbaal went to Shechem to his mother's kinsfolk and said to them and to the whole clan of his mother's family, 2 "Say in the hearing of all the lords of Shechem, 'Which is better for you, that all seventy of the sons of Jerubbaal rule over you, or that one rule over you?' Remember also that I am your bone and your flesh." 3 So his mother's kinsfolk spoke all these

b Heb they

8.22–28　Declining an offer to rule the Israelites, Gideon requests contributions of booty to make an elaborate divinatory device. **8.22** *Rule over us*, Hebrew *mashal* (not *malak*, "be king"). The rule was to be dynastic: *you and your son and your grandson*. **8.24** *Ishmaelites* were "related" to Israel through Abraham's son by Hagar (Gen 16). Midianites were related to Israel through Abraham's second wife, Keturah (Gen 25.1–4). **8.27** *Ephod*, an elaborate vestment worn only by the chief priest. It had a "breastpiece of judgment" with a pocket for the sacred dice, Urim and Thummim (Ex 28; 39). Gideon's ephod may have cloaked an idol (cf. 17.4–5) used in oracle seeking (1 Sam 23.9–12; 30.7–8). *Israel prostituted themselves* echoes 2.17; *snare* echoes 2.3. In contrast with preceding judges, Gideon is still alive when apostasy resumes and is faulted for it. Allegedly rejecting the idea of dynastic rule, he covets the means of religiopolitical control over Israel. **8.28** The *rest* formula (3.11, 30; 5.31) occurs here for the last time. **8.29–32** Transition describing the political "family" of Gideon, *seventy sons* and *many wives*. **8.31** *Concubine*, a legitimate wife of secondary rank. **8.33–35** Compiler's introduction to the story of Abimelech's reign at Shechem,

which interrupts the familiar framework pattern (apostasy; punishment; crying out; deliverance; see note on 2.11–23). **8.33** *Baal-berith*, Hebrew, "Lord of the Covenant," more likely "Covenant Baal," standing for the exploitative misuse of religion at Shechem, where the deity also has the name El-berith ("Covenant God") in 9.46.

9.1–57　Abimelech becomes commander in Israel, king of the Shechem city-state, and agent of Shechem's destruction. This story is the centerpiece of the Josian edition of the Deuteronomistic History (Dtr 1; see Introduction), which begins with polemic against Bethel (2.1–5) and ends with polemic against Dan (chs. 17–18), thus eliminating all strong contenders with Jerusalem for domination of Israel. **9.1** *Abimelech*, in Hebrew means "My Father is King," perhaps referring to God as Father. The name occurs thirty-one times in the chapter, strongly implying the narrator's contempt for its bearer. **9.2** *Lords of Shechem*, local elite, evoking a political system common to the Bronze Age. *Seventy* is a politically symbolic number; cf. Abdon's seventy sons and grandsons (12.14). Many of Gideon's *sons* would be brothers or half brothers. Appeal to *bone and ... flesh* manipulates a covenantal metaphor (Gen 2.23).

words on his behalf in the hearing of all
the lords of Shechem; and their hearts inclined to follow Abimelech, for they said,
"He is our brother." 4They gave him seventy pieces of silver out of the temple of
Baal-berith with which Abimelech hired
worthless and reckless fellows, who followed him. 5He went to his father's house
at Ophrah, and killed his brothers the
sons of Jerubbaal, seventy men, on one
stone; but Jotham, the youngest son of
Jerubbaal, survived, for he hid himself.
6Then all the lords of Shechem and all
Beth-millo came together, and they went
and made Abimelech king, by the oak of
the pillarᶜ at Shechem.

The Parable of the Trees

7 When it was told to Jotham, he went
and stood on the top of Mount Gerizim,
and cried aloud and said to them, "Listen
to me, you lords of Shechem, so that God
may listen to you.
8   The trees once went out
         to anoint a king over
         themselves.
     So they said to the olive tree,
         'Reign over us.'
9   The olive tree answered them,
         'Shall I stop producing my
         rich oil
         by which gods and mortals
         are honored,
         and go to sway over the
         trees?'
10   Then the trees said to the fig
         tree,
         'You come and reign over us.'
11   But the fig tree answered them,
         'Shall I stop producing my
         sweetness
         and my delicious fruit,
         and go to sway over the
         trees?'
12   Then the trees said to the vine,

'You come and reign over us.'
13   But the vine said to them,
         'Shall I stop producing my wine
         that cheers gods and mortals,
         and go to sway over the
         trees?'
14   So all the trees said to the
         bramble,
         'You come and reign over us.'
15   And the bramble said to the
         trees,
         'If in good faith you are
         anointing me king
         over you,
         then come and take refuge in
         my shade;
         but if not, let fire come out of
         the bramble
         and devour the cedars of
         Lebanon.'
16 "Now therefore, if you acted in
good faith and honor when you made
Abimelech king, and if you have dealt
well with Jerubbaal and his house, and
have done to him as his actions deserved
— 17for my father fought for you, and
risked his life, and rescued you from the
hand of Midian; 18but you have risen up
against my father's house this day, and
have killed his sons, seventy men on one
stone, and have made Abimelech, the son
of his slave woman, king over the lords of
Shechem, because he is your kinsman—
19if, I say, you have acted in good faith
and honor with Jerubbaal and with his
house this day, then rejoice in Abimelech,
and let him also rejoice in you; 20but if
not, let fire come out from Abimelech,
and devour the lords of Shechem, and
Beth-millo; and let fire come out from the
lords of Shechem, and from Beth-millo,
and devour Abimelech." 21Then Jotham
ran away and fled, going to Beer, where

c Cn: Meaning of Heb uncertain

9.4 The massive *temple* at Shechem would double
as a fortress. **9.5** Jotham survived in hiding, like
the young Gideon (6.11). **9.6** *Beth-millo*, Hebrew, possibly "House of the Fill," may be named
for a huge earthen platform supporting Shechem's fortress-temple. Jerusalem also had a
"Millo" (2 Sam 5.9; 1 Kings 9.15). *The oak of the
pillar*. The Hebrew text is problematic. Cf. Gen
35.4; Josh 24.26.
9.7–21 From a promontory on Mount Gerizim, Jotham denounces the deal with a scathing

antimonarchical allegory or parable (vv. 8–15)
and a curse (vv. 16–20). **9.8–15** Cf. the imagery
and literary form of 2 Kings 14.9; 2 Chr 25.18.
The *olive, fig,* and *vine* are all content to be themselves, for the benefit and enjoyment of humankind. Only the worthless *bramble*, good only for
burning, aspires to power. **9.16–20** It is perhaps not monarchy in principle, but monarchy
founded on theft and murder, that Jotham denounces. **9.21** *Beer*, Hebrew "well," a common
place-name.

he remained for fear of his brother
Abimelech.

The Downfall of Abimelech

22 Abimelech ruled over Israel three
years. 23 But God sent an evil spirit between Abimelech and the lords of Shechem; and the lords of Shechem dealt
treacherously with Abimelech. 24 This
happened so that the violence done to the
seventy sons of Jerubbaal might be
avenged[d] and their blood be laid on their
brother Abimelech, who killed them, and
on the lords of Shechem, who strengthened his hands to kill his brothers. 25 So,
out of hostility to him, the lords of Shechem set ambushes on the mountain tops.
They robbed all who passed by them
along that way; and it was reported to
Abimelech.
26 When Gaal son of Ebed moved into
Shechem with his kinsfolk, the lords of
Shechem put confidence in him. 27 They
went out into the field and gathered the
grapes from their vineyards, trod them,
and celebrated. Then they went into the
temple of their god, ate and drank, and
ridiculed Abimelech. 28 Gaal son of Ebed
said, "Who is Abimelech, and who are we
of Shechem, that we should serve him?
Did not the son of Jerubbaal and Zebul
his officer serve the men of Hamor father
of Shechem? Why then should we serve
him? 29 If only this people were under my
command! Then I would remove Abimelech; I would say[e] to him, 'Increase your
army, and come out.' "

30 When Zebul the ruler of the city
heard the words of Gaal son of Ebed, his
anger was kindled. 31 He sent messengers
to Abimelech at Arumah,[f] saying, "Look,
Gaal son of Ebed and his kinsfolk have
come to Shechem, and they are stirring
up[g] the city against you. 32 Now therefore, go by night, you and the troops that
are with you, and lie in wait in the fields.
33 Then early in the morning, as soon as
the sun rises, get up and rush on the city;
and when he and the troops that are with
him come out against you, you may deal
with them as best you can."
34 So Abimelech and all the troops
with him got up by night and lay in wait
against Shechem in four companies.
35 When Gaal son of Ebed went out and
stood in the entrance of the gate of the
city, Abimelech and the troops with him
rose from the ambush. 36 And when Gaal
saw them, he said to Zebul, "Look, people
are coming down from the mountain
tops!" And Zebul said to him, "The shad-
ows on the mountains look like people to
you." 37 Gaal spoke again and said, "Look,
people are coming down from Tabbur-
erez, and one company is coming from
the direction of Elon-meonenim."[h]
38 Then Zebul said to him, "Where is your
boast[i] now, you who said, 'Who is Abimelech, that we should serve him?' Are not
these the troops you made light of?
Go out now and fight with them." 39 So
Gaal went out at the head of the lords of

d Heb *might come*   e Gk: Heb *and he said*
f Cn See 9.41. Heb *Tormah*   g Cn: Heb *are
besieging*   h That is *Diviners' Oak*   i Heb *mouth*

9.22–33 Abimelech's downfall begins with
dissension in the city, God's way of bringing
Abimelech and his collaborators to justice
(vv. 22–25), followed by the return of Gaal, a
native Shechemite, who arouses the citizenry
to an older loyalty to the city-state (vv. 26–33).
9.22 *Abimelech ruled*, as military commander (the
Hebrew verb *sarar* is used rather than one based
on the root *mlk*, "rule-as-king"), *over Israel*. Israel
and Israelites are mentioned elsewhere in connection with Abimelech only in 8.33–35; 9.55. Abimelech's rule is a local affair, lasting *three years*.
9.23 Split loyalty is Abimelech's undoing. *Evil
spirits* from God, rare in scripture, stand generally
for the unexplainable, such as Saul's mental
breakdown (1 Sam 16.14). **9.24** God's purpose
is to bring the appropriate consequences upon
both parties to the crime. **9.25** With lookouts
for Abimelech posted, the Shechem elite take to

plundering the caravans in a striking inversion of
the situation in the Song of Deborah (5.6–8).
9.26–33 Conspiracy in the city during the vintage
festival centers in the temple. **9.26** *Gaal son of
Ebed*, in Hebrew possibly "loathsome son of a
slave," an obviously distorted name. **9.28** The
NRSV obscures the particulars of Gaal's speech,
which objects to Abimelech's half-breed Shechemite status and appears to base its appeal on genealogical purity. The Shechemites are urged to
serve the men of Hamor father of Shechem (see Gen
33.19; 34.6). **9.30** *Zebul*, Hebrew "Exalted
(One)," or "Big Shot." **9.34–41** A surprise attack puts Gaal to flight. **9.37** *Tabbur-erez*, Hebrew, "The Navel of the Land," is a mythic
designation for the temple location, a narrow
east-west pass between Mounts Gerizim and Ebal
emptying into the broader north-south plain.
Elon-meonenim, Hebrew, "Diviner's Oak," possibly

Shechem, and fought with Abimelech.
40 Abimelech chased him, and he fled before him. Many fell wounded, up to the entrance of the gate. 41 So Abimelech resided at Arumah; and Zebul drove out Gaal and his kinsfolk, so that they could not live on at Shechem.

42 On the following day the people went out into the fields. When Abimelech was told, 43 he took his troops and divided them into three companies, and lay in wait in the fields. When he looked and saw the people coming out of the city, he rose against them and killed them. 44 Abimelech and the company that was *j* with him rushed forward and stood at the entrance of the gate of the city, while the two companies rushed on all who were in the fields and killed them. 45 Abimelech fought against the city all that day; he took the city, and killed the people that were in it; and he razed the city and sowed it with salt.

46 When all the lords of the Tower of Shechem heard of it, they entered the stronghold of the temple of El-berith. 47 Abimelech was told that all the lords of the Tower of Shechem were gathered together. 48 So Abimelech went up to Mount Zalmon, he and all the troops that were with him. Abimelech took an ax in his hand, cut down a bundle of brushwood, and took it up and laid it on his shoulder. Then he said to the troops with him, "What you have seen me do, do quickly, as I have done." 49 So every one of the troops cut down a bundle and following Abimelech put it against the stronghold,

and they set the stronghold on fire over them, so that all the people of the Tower of Shechem also died, about a thousand men and women.

50 Then Abimelech went to Thebez, and encamped against Thebez, and took it. 51 But there was a strong tower within the city, and all the men and women and all the lords of the city fled to it and shut themselves in; and they went to the roof of the tower. 52 Abimelech came to the tower, and fought against it, and came near to the entrance of the tower to burn it with fire. 53 But a certain woman threw an upper millstone on Abimelech's head, and crushed his skull. 54 Immediately he called to the young man who carried his armor and said to him, "Draw your sword and kill me, so people will not say about me, 'A woman killed him.' " So the young man thrust him through, and he died. 55 When the Israelites saw that Abimelech was dead, they all went home. 56 Thus God repaid Abimelech for the crime he committed against his father in killing his seventy brothers; 57 and God also made all the wickedness of the people of Shechem fall back on their heads, and on them came the curse of Jotham son of Jerubbaal.

Tola and Jair

10 After Abimelech, Tola son of Puah son of Dodo, a man of Issachar, who lived at Shamir in the hill country of Ephraim, rose to deliver Israel. 2 He

j Vg and some Gk Mss: Heb *companies that were*

---

the *oak of the pillar* in v. 6.   **9.42–45** An ambush of farm families at work and Shechem's demise. Excavations have uncovered a massive destruction of the city dating from the early to mid-twelfth century B.C.E.   **9.45** *Sowed it with salt*, perhaps put it under a curse.   **9.46–49** Another account emphasizes the destruction of the temple and conspirators.   **9.46** The *Tower of Shechem*, probably an alternative designation for *Beth-millo* (v. 6) and *temple of El-berith*.   **9.48** *Zalmon*, Hebrew, "Dark One," probably Ebal, mountain of the covenantal curses (Deut 27.11–26; Josh 8.30–35). **9.49** *Stronghold*, some part of the temple, perhaps a tower.   **9.50–57** Abimelech's demise. **9.50** No offense of *Thebez* is specified.   **9.51** *A strong tower*, apparently another fortress-temple, like the one at Shechem destroyed by Abimelech and the one at Penuel destroyed by Gideon (8.9, 17).   **9.53** The tactic that worked at Shechem is

foiled at Thebez by an anonymous woman, whose achievement is ironically in light of v. 54, the one thing elsewhere remembered about Abimelech (see 2 Sam 11.21).   **9.54** *Draw your sword . . . killed him.* Cf. Saul's orders to his armor bearer (1 Sam 31.4).   **9.56–57** Editor's confessional conclusion, corresponding to the theological introduction to Abimelech in 8.33–35.   **9.57** *Curse of Jotham*, i.e., the covenantal curse as expounded by Jotham.

10.1–5 These verses describe two "minor" judges. Like those in 12.7–15 (with the exception of Jephthah), they are said to have *judged Israel*, but no narratives survive about them. **10.1–2** *Tola*, possibly meaning "Worm" in Hebrew. *Shamir*, a reference to Samaria? In what sense Tola *delivered Israel* is unclear. Perhaps, *after Abimelech*, what was needed was *twenty-three years* of continuously effective intertribal leadership.

judged Israel twenty-three years. Then he died, and was buried at Shamir.

3 After him came Jair the Gileadite, who judged Israel twenty-two years. ⁴He had thirty sons who rode on thirty donkeys; and they had thirty towns, which are in the land of Gilead, and are called Havvoth-jair to this day. ⁵Jair died, and was buried in Kamon.

Oppression by the Ammonites

6 The Israelites again did what was evil in the sight of the LORD, worshiping the Baals and the Astartes, the gods of Aram, the gods of Sidon, the gods of Moab, the gods of the Ammonites, and the gods of the Philistines. Thus they abandoned the LORD, and did not worship him. ⁷So the anger of the LORD was kindled against Israel, and he sold them into the hand of the Philistines and into the hand of the Ammonites, ⁸and they crushed and oppressed the Israelites that year. For eighteen years they oppressed all the Israelites that were beyond the Jordan in the land of the Amorites, which is in Gilead. ⁹The Ammonites also crossed the Jordan to fight against Judah and against Benjamin and against the house of Ephraim; so that Israel was greatly distressed.

10 So the Israelites cried to the LORD, saying, "We have sinned against you, because we have abandoned our God and have worshiped the Baals." ¹¹And the LORD said to the Israelites, "Did I not deliver youᵏ from the Egyptians and from the Amorites, from the Ammonites and from the Philistines? ¹²The Sidonians also, and the Amalekites, and the Maonites, oppressed you; and you cried to me, and I delivered you out of their hand. ¹³Yet you have abandoned me and worshiped other gods; therefore I will deliver you no more. ¹⁴Go and cry to the gods whom you have chosen; let them deliver you in the time of your distress." ¹⁵And the Israelites said to the LORD, "We have sinned; do to us whatever seems good to you; but deliver us this day!" ¹⁶So they put away the foreign gods from among them and worshiped the LORD; and he could no longer bear to see Israel suffer.

17 Then the Ammonites were called to arms, and they encamped in Gilead; and the Israelites came together, and they encamped at Mizpah. ¹⁸The commanders of the people of Gilead said to one another, "Who will begin the fight against the Ammonites? He shall be head over all the inhabitants of Gilead."

k Heb lacks *Did I not deliver you*

The years of service of the "minor judges" are stated precisely, not in round numbers as in the preceding chronological notices. **10.3–5** *Jair*, in Hebrew "He Enlightens," was a powerful chief in *Gilead* (north-central Transjordan). Kinship language, *thirty sons*, denotes subtribal alignments, which fluctuated over time. The Greek text credits Jair with thirty-two sons, while 1 Chr 2.22 credits him with twenty-three towns. Elsewhere the *Havvoth-jair*, "Villages of Jair," are located with reference to either Gilead (1 Kings 4.13) or Bashan (Josh 13.30).

10.6–18 These verses resume the framework cycle (see note on 2.11–23). Oppression by the Ammonites in Transjordan is the setting for Jephthah's career, here given an elaborate and ironic introduction by a Deuteronomistic narrator (see Introduction). **10.6** *The Baals and the Astartes.* See note on 2.11–13. Among the states and peoples named, only *Sidon* has not already been mentioned, unless it is a parallel for *Canaan* in 4.2. *Ammonites.* See 3.13. **10.7** *Philistines* recalls Shamgar (3.31) and the probable opposition of Sea Peoples to Deborah and Barak (chs. 4–5).

The link between the two groups is probably political; archaeological evidence indicates that Philistines extended their influence into Transjordan. **10.8** Oppression centers in contested territory that Israel had acquired from Sihon of the *Amorites* (11.8–22; cf. Deut 2.24–37; Num 21.21–30). **10.9** *Ammonites* also invaded the western highlands of *Judah, Benjamin,* and *Ephraim.* **10.10–14** The pattern described by 2.11–23 is here interrupted for a third dramatic confrontation between Israel and the deity; see *the angel of the LORD* (2.1–5) and *a prophet* (6.7–10). Israel's appeal has become a conditioned reflex. Now *the LORD* deals directly. The response, *let them deliver you,* ironically recalls the urging of Joash that Baal be allowed to fend for himself (6.31). **10.15–16** Genuine repentance, nowhere else explicit in Judges, evokes the Lord's compassion for Israel's suffering. **10.17–18** *Ammonites were called to arms,* technical language, as in Barak's muster (4.10) and Gideon's muster (6.35; 7.23–24). The *Israelites* merely *came together.* **10.18** The *commanders* offer a new title, *head over all,* to whoever will assume leadership.

Jephthah

11 Now Jephthah the Gileadite, the son of a prostitute, was a mighty warrior. Gilead was the father of Jephthah. ²Gilead's wife also bore him sons; and when his wife's sons grew up, they drove Jephthah away, saying to him, "You shall not inherit anything in our father's house; for you are the son of another woman." ³Then Jephthah fled from his brothers and lived in the land of Tob. Outlaws collected around Jephthah and went raiding with him.

4 After a time the Ammonites made war against Israel. ⁵And when the Ammonites made war against Israel, the elders of Gilead went to bring Jephthah from the land of Tob. ⁶They said to Jephthah, "Come and be our commander, so that we may fight with the Ammonites." ⁷But Jephthah said to the elders of Gilead, "Are you not the very ones who rejected me and drove me out of my father's house? So why do you come to me now when you are in trouble?" ⁸The elders of Gilead said to Jephthah, "Nevertheless, we have now turned back to you, so that you may go with us and fight with the Ammonites, and become head over us, over all the inhabitants of Gilead." ⁹Jephthah said to the elders of Gilead, "If you bring me home again to fight with the Ammonites, and the LORD gives them over to me, I will be your head." ¹⁰And the elders of Gilead said to Jephthah, "The LORD will be witness between us; we will surely do as you say." ¹¹So Jephthah went with the elders of Gilead, and the people made him head and commander over them; and Jephthah spoke all his words before the LORD at Mizpah.

12 Then Jephthah sent messengers to the king of the Ammonites and said, "What is there between you and me, that you have come to me to fight against my land?" ¹³The king of the Ammonites answered the messengers of Jephthah, "Because Israel, on coming from Egypt, took away my land from the Arnon to the Jabbok and to the Jordan; now therefore restore it peaceably." ¹⁴Once again Jephthah sent messengers to the king of the Ammonites ¹⁵and said to him: "Thus says Jephthah: Israel did not take away the land of Moab or the land of the Ammonites, ¹⁶but when they came up from Egypt, Israel went through the wilderness to the Red Sea*¹* and came to Kadesh. ¹⁷Israel then sent messengers to the king of Edom, saying, 'Let us pass through your land'; but the king of Edom would not listen. They also sent to the king of Moab, but he would not consent. So Israel remained at Kadesh. ¹⁸Then they

1 Or Sea of Reeds

11.1–11 Jephthah is presented in contrast to Gideon and Abimelech by the circumstances of his birth, his expulsion by his half brothers, and his mercenary associates. Kinship language is used literally in vv. 1–3 but reflects political and military reality in the old story that follows (vv. 4–11). **11.1** *Jephthah is a mighty warrior*, like Gideon (6.11–12); but Jephthah's wealth is uninherited. **11.3** *Tob*, a Syrian town (2 Sam 10.6–8). *Outlaws* echoes 9.4. **11.6** *Commander*, not Hebrew *sar* (10.18) but *gasin*, a ranking officer (Josh 10.24). **11.7–8** Elders increase the ante by using the term *head* (Hebrew *ro'sh*). Perhaps *gasin* (see note on 11.6) refers to a temporary role, field commander, while *ro'sh* refers to a permanent post, tribal chief. **11.9–11** To conclude the negotiations, Jephthah speaks *words before the LORD*. Effective bestowal of the office awaits the Lord's ratification of the proceedings. *The LORD will be witness* echoes the Hebrew of the opening to Jotham's parable concerning Abimelech's leadership (9.7). The *Mizpah* (Hebrew, "Lookout," or "Watchtower") of Transjordan lay somewhere not far south of the Jabbok. **11.12–28** This is the only narrative of Israelite diplomacy in Judges and is one of the clearest examples of the genre of the sovereign's indictment (Hebrew *riv*, a root meaning "strive," "contend," or more technically "to conduct a lawsuit," as in the name "J*erubbaal*," lit. "Let Baal Contend"). Two delegations are sent. The first (vv. 12–13) addresses a brief, direct question, receives an equally brief, direct answer, and goes home. The second (vv. 14–27) makes elaborate appeal to historical precedent in response to the answer given to the first delegation and receives no reply. **11.12** *Ammon* was a small territorial state at the desert fringe; it first emerged in the twelfth century B.C.E. and expanded westward into territory in which Moab on the south and Sihon on the north had also vied for control. **11.15–27** For the epic tradition of Israel's journey from Egypt, see Num 21. **11.15** *The land of Moab* and *the land of the Ammonites*, land once occupied by Moab and here claimed by Ammon. The king of Ammon apparently makes his claim in the name of Moabite sovereignty, since Israelite claims would antedate his own. **11.18** Texts referring to the

journeyed through the wilderness, went around the land of Edom and the land of Moab, arrived on the east side of the land of Moab, and camped on the other side of the Arnon. They did not enter the territory of Moab, for the Arnon was the boundary of Moab. 19 Israel then sent messengers to King Sihon of the Amorites, king of Heshbon; and Israel said to him, 'Let us pass through your land to our country.' 20 But Sihon did not trust Israel to pass through his territory; so Sihon gathered all his people together, and encamped at Jahaz, and fought with Israel. 21 Then the LORD, the God of Israel, gave Sihon and all his people into the hand of Israel, and they defeated them; so Israel occupied all the land of the Amorites, who inhabited that country. 22 They occupied all the territory of the Amorites from the Arnon to the Jabbok and from the wilderness to the Jordan. 23 So now the LORD, the God of Israel, has conquered the Amorites for the benefit of his people Israel. Do you intend to take their place? 24 Should you not possess what your god Chemosh gives you to possess? And should we not be the ones to possess everything that the LORD our God has conquered for our benefit? 25 Now are you any better than King Balak son of Zippor of Moab? Did he ever enter into conflict with Israel, or did he ever go to war with them? 26 While Israel lived in Heshbon and its villages, and in Aroer and its villages, and in all the towns that are along

the Arnon, three hundred years, why did you not recover them within that time? 27 It is not I who have sinned against you, but you are the one who does me wrong by making war on me. Let the LORD, who is judge, decide today for the Israelites or for the Ammonites." 28 But the king of the Ammonites did not heed the message that Jephthah sent him.

Jephthah's Vow

29 Then the spirit of the LORD came upon Jephthah, and he passed through Gilead and Manasseh. He passed on to Mizpah of Gilead, and from Mizpah of Gilead he passed on to the Ammonites. 30 And Jephthah made a vow to the LORD, and said, "If you will give the Ammonites into my hand, 31 then whoever comes out of the doors of my house to meet me, when I return victorious from the Ammonites, shall be the LORD's, to be offered up by me as a burnt offering." 32 So Jephthah crossed over to the Ammonites to fight against them; and the LORD gave them into his hand. 33 He inflicted a massive defeat on them from Aroer to the neighborhood of Minnith, twenty towns, and as far as Abel-keramim. So the Ammonites were subdued before the people of Israel.

Jephthah's Daughter

34 Then Jephthah came to his home at Mizpah; and there was his daughter

---

premonarchical period agree that *the Arnon was the boundary of Moab*; contested territory lay north of the Arnon. **11.19–21** See Num 21.21–24. **11.19** *Heshbon.* Excavations at Tell Hesban found no evidence for a town of the thirteenth to twelfth century B.C.E. *Sihon*'s capital may have been elsewhere. **11.20** Jephthah cites how, in connection with another area, Israel fought only when negotiations failed. **11.24** *Chemosh* was god of Moab, not Ammon, suggesting to some scholars that an account of a conflict against Moab has been clumsily redrafted as one against Ammon. **11.25** In Num 22–24 a major theme is the great labor exerted to communicate with *King Balak son of Zippor of Moab. Enter into conflict,* i.e., "contend" through diplomacy (Hebrew *riv;* cf. note on 11.12–28). **11.26** *Three hundred years* may reflect the book's chronology. The years of oppression and successive judges thus far, excluding eighteen Ammonite and Philistine years (10.8), total 301.

11.27 Both the noun *judge* (used only here in Judges) and the verb *decide* share the Hebrew root *shpt.* Cf. 1 Sam 24.15. **11.29** The influence of *the spirit of the LORD* here, as in 3.10, contrasts with its influence in 6.34, where Gideon overreacts. **11.30–31** Though Jephthah is respected as one who exhausted all diplomatic channels before taking the field, he has a tragic flaw: a penchant for making deals, even with the Lord. Is his vow hastily worded? Instead of *whoever,* Jephthah may have intended "whatever." Standard plans of Iron Age houses accommodated livestock as well as family. **11.33** *Aroer, Minnith,* and *Abel-keramim* were all located in the district west of Rabbah Ammon. **11.34–40** Human sacrifice was known but not condoned in Israel (2 Kings 16.3; Ezek 20.25–26.31; cf. Gen 22). **11.34** This verse describes a traditional role of women, singing after victory (Ex 15.20–21) to welcome the victors home (1 Sam 18.6–7). Cf. the Song of Deborah,

coming out to meet him with timbrels and with dancing. She was his only child; he had no son or daughter except her. 35 When he saw her, he tore his clothes, and said, "Alas, my daughter! You have brought me very low; you have become the cause of great trouble to me. For I have opened my mouth to the LORD, and I cannot take back my vow." 36 She said to him, "My father, if you have opened your mouth to the LORD, do to me according to what has gone out of your mouth, now that the LORD has given you vengeance against your enemies, the Ammonites." 37 And she said to her father, "Let this thing be done for me: Grant me two months, so that I may go and wander[m] on the mountains, and bewail my virginity, my companions and I." 38 "Go," he said and sent her away for two months. So she departed, she and her companions, and bewailed her virginity on the mountains. 39 At the end of two months, she returned to her father, who did with her according to the vow he had made. She had never slept with a man. So there arose an Israelite custom that 40 for four days every year the daughters of Israel would go out to lament the daughter of Jephthah the Gileadite.

Intertribal Dissension

12 The men of Ephraim were called to arms, and they crossed to Zaphon and said to Jephthah, "Why did you cross over to fight against the Ammonites,

and did not call us to go with you? We will burn your house down over you!" 2 Jephthah said to them, "My people and I were engaged in conflict with the Ammonites who oppressed us[n] severely. But when I called you, you did not deliver me from their hand. 3 When I saw that you would not deliver me, I took my life in my hand, and crossed over against the Ammonites, and the LORD gave them into my hand. Why then have you come up to me this day, to fight against me?" 4 Then Jephthah gathered all the men of Gilead and fought with Ephraim; and the men of Gilead defeated Ephraim, because they said, "You are fugitives from Ephraim, you Gileadites—in the heart of Ephraim and Manasseh."[o] 5 Then the Gileadites took the fords of the Jordan against the Ephraimites. Whenever one of the fugitives of Ephraim said, "Let me go over," the men of Gilead would say to him, "Are you an Ephraimite?" When he said, "No," 6 they said to him, "Then say Shibboleth," and he said, "Sibboleth," for he could not pronounce it right. Then they seized him and killed him at the fords of the Jordan. Forty-two thousand of the Ephraimites fell at that time.

7 Jephthah judged Israel six years.

m Cn: Heb go down   n Gk OL, Syr H: Heb lacks who oppressed us   o Meaning of Heb uncertain: Gk omits because . . . Manasseh

---

especially 5.28–30.   **11.36** The vow once made is irrevocable. Jephthah's daughter speaks wisdom.   **11.37–40** To die a virgin was to die childless. Women friends grieve with Jephthah's daughter, establishing precedent for an annual ritual of remembrance, otherwise unknown.

12.1–7   Final episodes from the career of Jephthah were added as a sequel, loosely joined to the preceding sections.   **12.1–4** The powerful West Bank tribe of *Ephraim* initiates hostilities with Gilead. Jephthah reacts vigorously. **12.1** The editor understood the Ephraimites to have raised their objection at least two months after Jephthah's victory (see 11.37–39). The Ephraimites claim to have been excluded from the muster of forces against the Ammonites; this is essentially the same complaint they made to Gideon in the Midianite crisis (8.1).   **12.2** Jephthah more literally responds, "I was a *riv* man," i.e., one using diplomacy (Hebrew *riv*; see note on

11.12–28). The translation *engaged in conflict* obscures the referent. *I called you.* The stories offer no clear support for Jephthah's counterclaim. **12.3** The argument ends with a question, *Why . . . fight against me?*, as did the unsuccessful negotiations with the Ammonite king (11.26).   **12.4** The taunt presented as the cause of war is unclear. **12.5–6** Jephthah is not mentioned in this puzzling conclusion to his story.   **12.5** The *fugitives* were presumably escapees from the battle in v. 4.   **12.6** The test does not turn on the uncertain meaning of the word *Shibboleth* but on regional differences in pronunciation. *Forty-two thousand* is better understood as forty-two "military units" (see note on 1.4).

12.7 This information links Jephthah with the list of "minor judges" (10.1–5; 12.7–15) into which the stories of the Ammonite crisis were inserted.

Then Jephthah the Gileadite died, and was buried in his town in Gilead.p

Ibzan, Elon, and Abdon

8 After him Ibzan of Bethlehem judged Israel. 9 He had thirty sons. He gave his thirty daughters in marriage outside his clan and brought in thirty young women from outside for his sons. He judged Israel seven years. 10 Then Ibzan died, and was buried at Bethlehem.

11 After him Elon the Zebulunite judged Israel; and he judged Israel ten years. 12 Then Elon the Zebulunite died, and was buried at Aijalon in the land of Zebulun.

13 After him Abdon son of Hillel the Pirathonite judged Israel. 14 He had forty sons and thirty grandsons, who rode on seventy donkeys; he judged Israel eight years. 15 Then Abdon son of Hillel the Pirathonite died, and was buried at Pirathon In the land of Ephraim, in the hill country of the Amalekites.

The Birth of Samson

13 The Israelites again did what was evil in the sight of the LORD, and the LORD gave them into the hand of the Philistines forty years.

2 There was a certain man of Zorah, of the tribe of the Danites, whose name was Manoah. His wife was barren, having borne no children. 3 And the angel of the LORD appeared to the woman and said to her, "Although you are barren, having borne no children, you shall conceive and bear a son. 4 Now be careful not to drink wine or strong drink, or to eat anything unclean, 5 for you shall conceive and bear a son. No razor is to come on his head, for the boy shall be a naziriteq to God from birth. It is he who shall begin to deliver Israel from the hand of the Philistines." 6 Then the woman came and told her husband, "A man of God came to me, and his appearance was like that of an angelr of God, most awe-inspiring; I did not ask

p Gk: Heb *in the towns of Gilead*   q That is *one separated* or *one consecrated*   r Or *the angel*

12.8 *Ibzan*, Hebrew, "Swift." The name is otherwise unknown. If the book is organized around twelve judges (one per tribe), *Bethlehem* may be not the famous little town south of Jerusalem but one located in Lower Galilee, about seven miles northwest of Nazareth, near Zebulun's border with Asher (Josh 19.15). **12.9** *Thirty* is a political number, as in 10.4. Numerous "progeny" stand for effective, wide-ranging control as tribal chief. **12.11–12** *Elon*, "Oak" or "Terebinth," a "son" of Zebulun in epic tradition (Gen 46.14; Num 26.26). These verses may be etymological, explaining Elon's name as derived from that of the town where he resided, *Aijalon* (spelled identically to Elon in the early Hebrew script). **12.13** *Abdon* is otherwise unknown. **12.14** *Forty sons and thirty grandsons* is a surprising regression, unless the numbers stand for declining political effectiveness, thus anticipating the need for another deliverer-judge. *Pirathon in . . . Ephraim* is probably modern Far´ata, about five miles westsouthwest of Shechem, near the border with Manasseh.

13.1–16.31 The Samson stories have no close parallel in Judges. They are rowdy tales from the old frontier with Philistia, reflecting Dan's inability to take control of the coastal plain (see 1.34; ch. 18). Samson's primary pursuits, however, are amorous. For injuries to his vanity he kills many Philistines, but he is not a deliverer of Israel or any Israelite tribe. He is presented as a tragicomic

example of selfishly wasted brute strength and, ironically, as an unwitting instrument of God. **13.1–25** The birth story focuses on Samson's unnamed mother's perceptiveness and her collaboration with the Lord. **13.1** *Philistines* were Sea Peoples from the Aegean and Asia Minor who settled the southern coast of Canaan in the twelfth century B.C.E., not long after the reconstitution of Israel in the highlands. **13.2** *Zorah* is in the Shephelah, the foothills near Dan's border with Judah. The *Danites* here are a "clan" (Hebrew *mishpacha*), not yet (or perhaps no longer) having the dimensions of a *tribe*. *Manoah*, "Rest," a root also found in the name Noah, is head of his village sodality. **13.3** *The angel of the LORD* was last met in 6.11–24, engaged in another recruitment mission. There are many echoes of the Gideon and Jephthah materials in the Samson stories. **13.4–5** *Nazirite*, any Israelite man or woman taking special vows of consecration to God according to rules such as those in Num 6.1–21. The highly militant Nazirites were known in later years as tenaciously conservative proponents of the early Israelite life-style. Here the rule of the Nazirite volunteer is delightfully adapted and urged as prenatal care for Samson, who would begin the liberation of Israel from the Philistines. Cf. 1 Sam 1.11, where Hannah initiates the proposal and promises that her son will be both priest and Nazirite. **13.6** *A man of God . . . angel of God.* As repeatedly happens in 6.11–24, participants speak

him where he came from, and he did not tell me his name; 7but he said to me, 'You shall conceive and bear a son. So then drink no wine or strong drink, and eat nothing unclean, for the boy shall be a nazirite[s] to God from birth to the day of his death.'"

8 Then Manoah entreated the LORD, and said, "O LORD, I pray, let the man of God whom you sent come to us again and teach us what we are to do concerning the boy who will be born." 9God listened to Manoah, and the angel of God came again to the woman as she sat in the field; but her husband Manoah was not with her. 10So the woman ran quickly and told her husband, "The man who came to me the other day has appeared to me." 11Manoah got up and followed his wife, and came to the man and said to him, "Are you the man who spoke to this woman?" And he said, "I am." 12Then Manoah said, "Now when your words come true, what is to be the boy's rule of life; what is he to do?" 13The angel of the LORD said to Manoah, "Let the woman give heed to all that I said to her. 14She may not eat of anything that comes from the vine. She is not to drink wine or strong drink, or eat any unclean thing. She is to observe everything that I commanded her."

15 Manoah said to the angel of the LORD, "Allow us to detain you, and prepare a kid for you." 16The angel of the LORD said to Manoah, "If you detain me, I will not eat your food; but if you want to prepare a burnt offering, then offer it to the LORD." (For Manoah did not know that he was the angel of the LORD.) 17Then Manoah said to the angel of the

LORD, "What is your name, so that we may honor you when your words come true?" 18But the angel of the LORD said to him, "Why do you ask my name? It is too wonderful."

19 So Manoah took the kid with the grain offering, and offered it on the rock to the LORD, to him who works[t] wonders.[u] 20When the flame went up toward heaven from the altar, the angel of the LORD ascended in the flame of the altar while Manoah and his wife looked on; and they fell on their faces to the ground. 21The angel of the LORD did not appear again to Manoah and his wife. Then Manoah realized that it was the angel of the LORD. 22And Manoah said to his wife, "We shall surely die, for we have seen God." 23But his wife said to him, "If the LORD had meant to kill us, he would not have accepted a burnt offering and a grain offering at our hands, or shown us all these things, or now announced to us such things as these."

24 The woman bore a son, and named him Samson. The boy grew, and the LORD blessed him. 25The spirit of the LORD began to stir him in Mahaneh-dan, between Zorah and Eshtaol.

Samson's Marriage

14 Once Samson went down to Timnah, and at Timnah he saw a Philistine woman. 2Then he came up, and told his father and mother, "I saw a Philistine woman at Timnah; now get her for

s That is one separated or one consecrated
t Gk Vg: Heb and working   u Heb wonders, while Manoah and his wife looked on

---

more truly than they know. **13.7** The mother's breathless recounting of the interview makes no mention of the prohibition of haircuts. A Nazirite's hair was cut when the consecration was complete and the Nazirite returned to secular life. **13.8–14** Manoah requires a second visit from God's envoy but learns nothing more. **13.15–23** See Gideon's similar hospitality to God's envoy (6.19–21). Like Gideon (6.36–40), Manoah requires a sign. **13.18** Too wonderful, i.e., beyond comprehension. **13.19** Works wonders. The Lord is known for "doing wonders" (Ex 15.11). **13.22** We shall surely die. Cf. Gideon's exclamation in 6.22. **13.23** Again, not the panicky Manoah but the unnamed wife speaks common sense. **13.24** Samson's name is related to the Hebrew shemesh ("sun"), meaning something like

"man of Shamash." The ending may be diminutive: "Little Sun," or "Sunny." The boy grew, and the Lord blessed him. Cf. 1 Sam 2.26; Lk 2.52. **13.25** Mention of the spirit of the LORD is anticipatory. It will be substantiated by the incidents in ch. 14 displaying Samson's physical prowess. Mahaneh-dan, Hebrew, "Camp of Dan." **14.1–20** These verses tell the story of Samson's first love. **14.1–3** These verses come to a peak with Samson's point-blank directive: get her for me. **14.1** Timnah, Hebrew, "Allotted Portion," is probably Tell el-Batashi, four miles north of Beth-shemesh, "House/Temple of the Sun-god." The Alexandrian Greek text continues: "and she was the right one in his eyes." The concept of acting rightly in one's own eyes is reiterated in 17.6 and 21.25 as the book draws to a

me as my wife." 3 But his father and mother said to him, "Is there not a woman among your kin, or among all our*v* people, that you must go to take a wife from the uncircumcised Philistines?" But Samson said to his father, "Get her for me, because she pleases me." 4 His father and mother did not know that this was from the LORD; for he was seeking a pretext to act against the Philistines. At that time the Philistines had dominion over Israel.

5 Then Samson went down with his father and mother to Timnah. When he came to the vineyards of Timnah, suddenly a young lion roared at him. 6 The spirit of the LORD rushed on him, and he tore the lion apart barehanded as one might tear apart a kid. But he did not tell his father or his mother what he had done. 7 Then he went down and talked with the woman, and she pleased Samson. 8 After a while he returned to marry her, and he turned aside to see the carcass of the lion, and there was a swarm of bees in the body of the lion, and honey. 9 He scraped it out into his hands, and went on, eating as he went. When he came to his father and mother, he gave some to them, and they ate it. But he did not tell them that he had taken the honey from the carcass of the lion.

10 His father went down to the woman, and Samson made a feast there as the young men were accustomed to do. 11 When the people saw him, they brought thirty companions to be with him. 12 Samson said to them, "Let me now put a riddle to you. If you can explain it to me within the seven days of the feast, and find it out, then I will give you thirty linen garments and thirty festal garments. 13 But if you cannot explain it to me, then you shall give me thirty linen garments and thirty festal garments." So they said to him, "Ask your riddle; let us hear it." 14 He said to them,

"Out of the eater came something
              to eat.
Out of the strong came
              something sweet."

But for three days they could not explain the riddle.

15 On the fourth*w* day they said to Samson's wife, "Coax your husband to explain the riddle to us, or we will burn you and your father's house with fire. Have you invited us here to impoverish us?" 16 So Samson's wife wept before him, saying, "You hate me; you do not really love me. You have asked a riddle of my people, but you have not explained it to me." He said to her, "Look, I have not told my father or my mother. Why should I tell you?" 17 She wept before him the seven days that their feast lasted; and because she nagged him, on the seventh day he told her. Then she explained the riddle to her people. 18 The men of the town said to him on the seventh day before the sun went down,

"What is sweeter than honey?

v Cn: Heb *my*   *w* Gk Syr: Heb *seventh*

close.   **14.3** Philistines, so far as we know, were the only *uncircumcised* people in Israel's near vicinity. The reason for disapproval here is not simply the absence of the rite but the dual loyalty portended.   **14.4** This verse is an explanation inserted between story segments. In this case, an action contrary to basic Israelite standards is actually part of the divine plan.   **14.5–10a** These verses are framed by an *inclusio* (a repetition signaling the beginning and end of a unit): first Samson and later his father *went down*.   **14.6** *The spirit of the LORD* could equip Samson to face any physical threat.   **14.8–9** *Bees*, Hebrew *deborim*, evokes comparison with Deborah. *Honey* was regarded as having the potential to enlighten and to give courage (1 Sam 14.24–30).   **14.10a** *His father went down*, presumably to negotiate the marriage agreement. Ancient Near Eastern evidence describes a type of marriage in which the bride continued to live with her parents rather than join her husband at his family or clan location. Perhaps the tale of Samson suggests such a marital arrangement.   **14.10b–20** These verses show how the marriage is providentially annulled. **14.10b–14** Samson's lavish style of entertainment was not characteristic of all Israelite *young men* (Hebrew *bachurim*, "chosen" or "choice" ones who composed a military elite). Few families could afford it.   **14.11** The combination of Samson's social position and physical stature was apparently enough to arouse suspicion and to recommend surveillance.   **14.15** *Wife*. Hebrew makes no distinction between "wife" and "woman." It was a legal marriage, for when Samson abandoned the woman they were legally divorced, as becomes clear in the next scene. At this point, however, the divine plan for Samson to defeat the Philistines (13.5) is nearly foiled by the liberal allowance in Israelite law for exemptions from military service for the newly betrothed (Deut 20.7) or newly married (Deut 24.5).   **14.18** The text uses a rare word for *sun*, Hebrew *charsah*, apparently to avoid

What is stronger than a lion?"
And he said to them,
    "If you had not plowed with my
        heifer,
    you would not have found out
        my riddle."
19 Then the spirit of the LORD rushed on
him, and he went down to Ashkelon. He
killed thirty men of the town, took their
spoil, and gave the festal garments to
those who had explained the riddle. In
hot anger he went back to his father's
house. 20 And Samson's wife was given
to his companion, who had been his
best man.

Samson Defeats the Philistines

15 After a while, at the time of the
wheat harvest, Samson went to
visit his wife, bringing along a kid. He
said, "I want to go into my wife's room."
But her father would not allow him to go
in. 2 Her father said, "I was sure that you
had rejected her; so I gave her to your
companion. Is not her younger sister
prettier than she? Why not take her instead?" 3 Samson said to them, "This time,
when I do mischief to the Philistines, I will
be without blame." 4 So Samson went and
caught three hundred foxes, and took
some torches; and he turned the foxes*x*
tail to tail, and put a torch between each
pair of tails. 5 When he had set fire to the

torches, he let the foxes go into the standing grain of the Philistines, and burned
up the shocks and the standing grain, as
well as the vineyards and*y* olive groves.
6 Then the Philistines asked, "Who has
done this?" And they said, "Samson, the
son-in-law of the Timnite, because he has
taken Samson's wife and given her to his
companion." So the Philistines came up,
and burned her and her father. 7 Samson
said to them, "If this is what you do, I
swear I will not stop until I have taken
revenge on you." 8 He struck them down
hip and thigh with great slaughter; and
he went down and stayed in the cleft of
the rock of Etam.

9 Then the Philistines came up and
encamped in Judah, and made a raid on
Lehi. 10 The men of Judah said, "Why
have you come up against us?" They said,
"We have come up to bind Samson, to do
to him as he did to us." 11 Then three
thousand men of Judah went down to the
cleft of the rock of Etam, and they said to
Samson, "Do you not know that the Philistines are rulers over us? What then have
you done to us?" He replied, "As they did
to me, so I have done to them." 12 They
said to him, "We have come down to bind
you, so that we may give you into the
hands of the Philistines." Samson answered them, "Swear to me that you yourselves will not attack me." 13 They said to

---

x Heb *them*   *y* Gk Tg Vg: Heb lacks *and*

---

confusion with the common word *shemesh* in Samson's name (see note on 13.24). **14.20** The *best
man*, Samson's *companion*, was presumably another
Timnite, but not one of the thirty who had been
chosen for him.

15.1–8 Some time later, Samson is in Timnah
once again. The outraged father of the young
woman explains that it had looked like divorce to
him, but he tries to make the best of a bad situation by suggesting that the younger sister is better
anyway. **15.1** A *kid* is a prostitute's negotiated
fee in Gen 38.17. **15.2** The father has performed an irreparable act in giving his daughter
to another; she cannot return to Samson under
any conditions (Deut 24.1–4). For Samson to
deny that he has divorced her would only compound the hopelessness of the situation by making her an adulteress. **15.7** Samson will have
revenge. The Hebrew root used here, *nqm*, long
stood exclusively for divine prerogative (Deut
32.35), the idea being to remove vengeance (self-
help, taking the law into one's own hands) from

the human scene. **15.8** *Hip and thigh* may be a
wrestler's term. There were probably feats of
strength to be witnessed when the people gathered to be entertained and edified by such material as the Samson cycle. *Etam*, in Hebrew possibly
"Place of Birds of Prey." The meaning of the
name may be more important than the location of
the place, which is uncertain.

15.9–20 Samson's single-handed victory
against an entire Philistine military unit and his
extreme thirst afterwards precipitate a direct confrontation with the Lord. **15.9** *Lehi*, Hebrew,
"Jawbone," was probably in the vicinity of Beth-
shemesh. **15.10** *Men of Judah*. This is the first
hint given in the exploits of Samson that more is
at stake than the situation of one man's family.
Samson has left home, plundered Philistines, and
found a hideout in territory controlled by the
tribe of Judah, which must handle the extradition. **15.11–13** At last Samson is the man in the
middle, contending with Philistine belligerence
and Judahite servility. He is willing to take his

him, "No, we will only bind you and give you into their hands; we will not kill you." So they bound him with two new ropes, and brought him up from the rock.

14 When he came to Lehi, the Philistines came shouting to meet him; and the spirit of the LORD rushed on him, and the ropes that were on his arms became like flax that has caught fire, and his bonds melted off his hands. 15 Then he found a fresh jawbone of a donkey, reached down and took it, and with it he killed a thousand men. 16 And Samson said,

"With the jawbone of a donkey,
    heaps upon heaps,
with the jawbone of a donkey
    I have slain a thousand men."

17 When he had finished speaking, he threw away the jawbone; and that place was called Ramath-lehi.[z]

18 By then he was very thirsty, and he called on the LORD, saying, "You have granted this great victory by the hand of your servant. Am I now to die of thirst, and fall into the hands of the uncircumcised?" 19 So God split open the hollow place that is at Lehi, and water came from it. When he drank, his spirit returned, and he revived. Therefore it was named En-hakkore,[a] which is at Lehi to this day.

20 And he judged Israel in the days of the Philistines twenty years.

Samson and Delilah

16 Once Samson went to Gaza, where he saw a prostitute and went in to her. 2 The Gazites were told,[b] "Samson has come here." So they circled around and lay in wait for him all night at the city gate. They kept quiet all night, thinking, "Let us wait until the light of the morning; then we will kill him." 3 But Samson lay only until midnight. Then at midnight he rose up, took hold of the doors of the city gate and the two posts, pulled them up, bar and all, put them on his shoulders, and carried them to the top of the hill that is in front of Hebron.

4 After this he fell in love with a woman in the valley of Sorek, whose name was Delilah. 5 The lords of the Philistines came to her and said to her, "Coax him, and find out what makes his strength so great, and how we may overpower him,

z That is The Hill of the Jawbone   a That is The Spring of the One who Called   b Gk: Heb lacks were told

chances with the Philistines rather than exercise his great strength against his Israelite brothers. **15.14** We are to picture Samson with his hands tied, walking straight into a pack of Philistines clamoring for revenge and suddenly manifesting *the spirit of the LORD*, as in 14.6. There the demonstration of the spirit was providential; here it is salvific, to keep Samson alive. **15.15** A sickle made of an animal *jawbone* fitted with flint teeth might double as a formidable weapon, enabling Samson to disable an entire posse. A *thousand* is most implausible (see note on 1.4). **15.16** This Song of Samson is an archaic poetic fragment, with repetitive parallelism, and is much older than the prose story. **15.17** *Ramath-lehi*, Hebrew, "Jawbone's Height." Samson's story explains the name of the Lehi area, where the fight occurred. **15.18** *He called on the LORD*. The verb is not the recurring technical one of the framework (Hebrew root *tz/z'q*, translated *cried out/cried* in 3.9, 15; 4.3; 6.7; 10.10), but *qr'*, the ordinary word for "called." It is, at last, a direct address to the deity, and it has impressive results. *Your servant* is not merely a polite form of address; see note on 2.8. Samson is the only one in the book to speak this way. *Uncircumcised* echoes the usage of his father and mother (14.3), as he repays the

Philistines, insult for insult (15.6). But here he is, in a way, pleading for life. That is what he gets. **15.19** *The hollow place*, apparently a rocky spring. *Revived*, better translated "came alive." En-hakkore, lit. "Spring of the Caller," thus receives a new etymology. **15.20** Having shown Samson at last in direct communication with the LORD, the narrator can now say that he *judged Israel . . . twenty years* (possibly a round number for a generation). The repetition of this formula in 16.31 suggests that an early rendition of the Samson cycle (pre-Deuteronomistic; see Introduction) probably ended here.

16.1–31 Three stories answer the question: What became of Samson the Israelite judge? **16.1–3** Another tale of lusty Samson's enormous strength. **16.1** *Gaza*, one of five major Philistine cities on the southern coastal plain. **16.3** Exaggeration underscores Samson's brute strength. It is forty miles uphill from Gaza to *Hebron*, where David was later elevated as king. **16.4–22** These verses show many similarities with the story of Samson's first love (ch. 14). **16.4** The *valley of Sorek*, Hebrew, "Vineyard Valley," begins about thirteen miles southwest of Jerusalem. We are not told whether *Delilah* (possibly "Flirtatious" in Hebrew) is Philistine or Israelite. **16.5** *The lords*

so that we may bind him in order to subdue him; and we will each give you eleven hundred pieces of silver." 6 So Delilah said to Samson, "Please tell me what makes your strength so great, and how you could be bound, so that one could subdue you." 7 Samson said to her, "If they bind me with seven fresh bowstrings that are not dried out, then I shall become weak, and be like anyone else." 8 Then the lords of the Philistines brought her seven fresh bowstrings that had not dried out, and she bound him with them. 9 While men were lying in wait in an inner chamber, she said to him, "The Philistines are upon you, Samson!" But he snapped the bowstrings, as a strand of fiber snaps when it touches the fire. So the secret of his strength was not known.

10 Then Delilah said to Samson, "You have mocked me and told me lies; please tell me how you could be bound." 11 He said to her, "If they bind me with new ropes that have not been used, then I shall become weak, and be like anyone else." 12 So Delilah took new ropes and bound him with them, and said to him, "The Philistines are upon you, Samson!" (The men lying in wait were in an inner chamber.) But he snapped the ropes off his arms like a thread.

13 Then Delilah said to Samson, "Until now you have mocked me and told me lies; tell me how you could be bound." He said to her, "If you weave the seven locks of my head with the web and make it tight with the pin, then I shall become weak, and be like anyone else." 14 So while he slept, Delilah took the seven locks of his head and wove them into the web,c and made them tight with the pin. Then she said to him, "The Philistines are upon you, Samson!" But he awoke from his

sleep, and pulled away the pin, the loom, and the web.

15 Then she said to him, "How can you say, 'I love you,' when your heart is not with me? You have mocked me three times now and have not told me what makes your strength so great." 16 Finally, after she had nagged him with her words day after day, and pestered him, he was tired to death. 17 So he told her his whole secret, and said to her, "A razor has never come upon my head; for I have been a nazirited to God from my mother's womb. If my head were shaved, then my strength would leave me; I would become weak, and be like anyone else."

18 When Delilah realized that he had told her his whole secret, she sent and called the lords of the Philistines, saying, "This time come up, for he has told his whole secret to me." Then the lords of the Philistines came up to her, and brought the money in their hands. 19 She let him fall asleep on her lap; and she called a man, and had him shave off the seven locks of his head. He began to weaken,e and his strength left him. 20 Then she said, "The Philistines are upon you, Samson!" When he awoke from his sleep, he thought, "I will go out as at other times, and shake myself free." But he did not know that the LORD had left him. 21 So the Philistines seized him and gouged out his eyes. They brought him down to Gaza and bound him with bronze shackles; and he ground at the mill in the prison. 22 But the hair of his head began to grow again after it had been shaved.

c Compare Gk: in verses 13-14, Heb lacks *and make it tight . . . into the web*   d That is *one separated* or *one consecrated*   e Gk: Heb *She began to torment him*

(better "tyrants") *of the Philistines*, a title imported from their Aegean homeland. **16.6–17** While Samson teases, Delilah pouts and pesters. Samson is trapped into squandering his great strength, unable to believe that she would betray him. Samson's "explanation" of his strength is not always clear. **16.7** Naming *fresh bowstrings*, i.e., inferior unprocessed gut, may be an appeal to belief in the efficacy of magic. **16.11** *New ropes* is anticipated by the extradition scene (15.13). **16.13–14** In the most curious of the efforts to destroy Samson's strength, Delilah weaves his hair into the warp on her loom. This may represent a resort to stronger magic. **16.15–17** Return to the truth.

16.15 The *heart*, very important for emotional matters, was also the seat of mind and will. Delilah accuses Samson of not trusting her. **16.16** *He was tired to death*. Cf. the feelings of Elijah (1 Kings 19.4) and Jonah (Jon 4.8); those prophets were so exasperated with God that each requested death, using the same idiom. **16.17** Cf. 13.5, 7. The plot revolves around a vow that had never been taken seriously. Nazirite status was voluntary, but the Nazirite rule means so little to Samson that he can put it in the same category with the other superstitions. The cutting of the Nazirite's hair symbolized discharge from the duties of the vow (Num 6.13–20). **16.22** With a new head of hair,

Samson's Death

23 Now the lords of the Philistines gathered to offer a great sacrifice to their god Dagon, and to rejoice; for they said, "Our god has given Samson our enemy into our hand." 24 When the people saw him, they praised their god; for they said, "Our god has given our enemy into our hand, the ravager of our country, who has killed many of us." 25 And when their hearts were merry, they said, "Call Samson, and let him entertain us." So they called Samson out of the prison, and he performed for them. They made him stand between the pillars; 26 and Samson said to the attendant who held him by the hand, "Let me feel the pillars on which the house rests, so that I may lean against them." 27 Now the house was full of men and women; all the lords of the Philistines were there, and on the roof there were about three thousand men and women, who looked on while Samson performed. 28 Then Samson called to the LORD and said, "Lord GOD, remember me and strengthen me only this once, O God, so that with this one act of revenge I may pay back the Philistines for my two eyes."f 29 And Samson grasped the two middle pillars on which the house rested, and he leaned his weight against them, his right hand on the one and his left hand on the other. 30 Then Samson said, "Let me die with the Philistines." He strained with all his might; and the house fell on the lords and all the people who were in it. So those he killed at his death were more than those he had killed during his life. 31 Then his brothers and all his family came down and took him and brought him up and buried him between Zorah and Eshtaol in the tomb of his father Manoah. He had judged Israel twenty years.

Micah and the Levite

17 There was a man in the hill country of Ephraim whose name was Micah. 2 He said to his mother, "The eleven hundred pieces of silver that were taken from you, about which you uttered a curse, and even spoke it in my hearing, — that silver is in my possession; I took it; but now I will return it to you."g And his mother said, "May my son be blessed by the LORD!" 3 Then he returned the eleven hundred pieces of silver to his mother; and his mother said, "I consecrate the silver to the LORD from my hand for my son, to make an idol of cast metal." 4 So when he returned the money to his

f Or *so that I may be avenged upon the Philistines for one of my two eyes*   g The words *but now I will return it to you* are transposed from the end of verse 3 in Heb

---

Samson might reenlist.   **16.23–31** The final Samson story centers on his last-minute reenlistment and momentary settling of accounts during festival time at a Philistine temple.   **16.23** *Dagon*, sometimes known as the father of Baal, was a Canaanite god of rain and fertility, especially of grain, with temples at two Philistine cities, Gaza and Ashdod (see 1 Sam 5.1–5).   **16.26** *Attendant* (Hebrew *na'ar*, "young man") evokes an image of the elite warrior's squire who appeared in the stories of Gideon (7.10) and Abimelech (9.54) and who, upon the latter's request, assisted him to an honorable death.   **16.27** The *roof* may refer to some neighboring structure, or even a nearby hill, from which most of the spectators watched the proceedings.   **16.28** *Lord GOD.* See 6.22. *O God.* Samson pleads with God, in contrast to his sarcastic outburst at Ramath-lehi (15.18). He seeks retribution, which he will achieve in his death. **16.29** The main hall of a Philistine temple excavated at Tell Qasile was a long room with two wooden *pillars* set on round stone bases along the center axis.   **16.31** *He had judged*, perfect tense, in contrast to the past tense in 15.20, is the mark of an ancient editor's insertion of material. King Josiah's historian (Dtr 1; see Introduction) doubtless drew a moral from the story: Israel would be safe as long as Israel's leaders truly turned to the Lord.

17.1–18.31   These chapters resume the polemic against northern sanctuaries; see note on 9.1–57. Ch. 17 preserves two background stories about the migration of Dan and the origin of its priesthood.   **17.1–5** Ironic portrayal of *Micah*, a maker of images whose name means "Who Is Like Yahweh?"   **17.1** The *hill country of Ephraim*, the north-central highlands.   **17.2** *Eleven hundred pieces of silver*, the same amount that each individual gave Delilah to betray Samson (16.5). Micah's mother forgets the crime in her response to the confession. The narrative style here is complex, because the narrator begins well past the midpoint in the action in order to highlight a discrepancy between the mother's pledge and her payment.   **17.3** Images of any sort were outlawed by covenant stipulation (Ex 20.4–6; Deut

mother, his mother took two hundred pieces of silver, and gave it to the silversmith, who made it into an idol of cast metal; and it was in the house of Micah. 5 This man Micah had a shrine, and he made an ephod and teraphim, and installed one of his sons, who became his priest. 6 In those days there was no king in Israel; all the people did what was right in their own eyes.

7 Now there was a young man of Bethlehem in Judah, of the clan of Judah. He was a Levite residing there. 8 This man left the town of Bethlehem in Judah, to live wherever he could find a place. He came to the house of Micah in the hill country of Ephraim to carry on his work.*h* 9 Micah said to him, "From where do you come?" He replied, "I am a Levite of Bethlehem in Judah, and I am going to live wherever I can find a place." 10 Then Micah said to him, "Stay with me, and be to me a father and a priest, and I will give you ten pieces of silver a year, a set of clothes, and your living."*i* 11 The Levite agreed to stay with the man; and the young man became to him like one of his sons. 12 So Micah installed the Levite, and the young man became his priest, and was in the house of Micah. 13 Then Micah said, "Now I know that the LORD will prosper me, because the Levite has become my priest."

The Migration of Dan

18 In those days there was no king in Israel. And in those days the tribe of the Danites was seeking for itself a territory to live in; for until then no territory among the tribes of Israel had been allotted to them. 2 So the Danites sent five valiant men from the whole number of their clan, from Zorah and from Eshtaol, to spy out the land and to explore it; and they said to them, "Go, explore the land." When they came to the hill country of Ephraim, to the house of Micah, they stayed there. 3 While they were at Micah's house, they recognized the voice of the young Levite; so they went over and asked him, "Who brought you here? What are you doing in this place? What is your business here?" 4 He said to them, "Micah did such and such for me, and he hired me, and I have become his priest." 5 Then they said to him, "Inquire of God that we may know whether the mission we are undertaking will succeed." 6 The priest replied, "Go in peace. The mission you are on is under the eye of the LORD."

7 The five men went on, and when they came to Laish, they observed the people who were there living securely, after the manner of the Sidonians, quiet

h Or *Ephraim, continuing his journey*   *i* Heb *living, and the Levite went*

5.8–10).   **17.5** *Ephod,* a priestly vestment. See 8.27. *Teraphim,* plural (see note on Gen 31.19), were used in divination, but here they are apparently identified with the *idol of cast metal* (v. 3). *One of his sons* looks ahead to the next unit, where a Levite becomes *like one of his sons* (v. 11) by contractual arrangement.   **17.6** This transitional verse is repeated twice in part (18.1; 19.1) and once in its entirety, as the last word on the era (21.25). Here it describes an ominous situation involving a cultic opportunist and an exploitable careerist.   **17.7–13** Dissatisfied with prospects at Bethlehem in Judah, a young Levite finds employment in the north as Micah's priest.   **17.7** *Clan of Judah.* That Judah is a clan, not a "tribe," suggests a very early period, prior to Judah's consolidation. Though any Israelite male might exercise priestly functions, *Levites* were members of the priestly tribe, which had no territorial definition (see note on 5.14–18). Only much later did "Levite" become a designation for lower-ranking clergy.   **17.10** The title *father* implies a priestly role as diviner (see 18.4–6).

17.13 *Now I know.* Micah clinches the deal, believing that he has, in effect, hired the Lord.

18.1–31 Resuming the subject of the final introductory note (1.34), this polemical story of Dan's northern migration and rival temple is much older than the Deuteronomistic framework.   **18.1** A connectional verse implies how providential it was, in the premonarchical era, that the tribe of *Dan* (whose name in Hebrew means "He Judged") was ready to relocate.   **18.2–10** The reconnaissance of the north is reminiscent of the Jericho spy story (Josh 2).   **18.2** *Valiant men,* elite warriors.   **18.3** The *voice* has a recognizable southern accent.   **18.5** To *inquire of God* was to seek an oracle by consulting a diviner.   **18.6** The answer assures a successful mission.   **18.7** The people of *Laish* ("Lion") are *living securely,* i.e., "without defenses." Excavations have shown that the early Iron Age site of Dan was unwalled. Far from the *Sidonians* on the Phoenician coast, nonaligned with *Aram* on the north, the Laishans are minding their own business (v. 10). Laish looks like the ideal community Israel

and unsuspecting, lacking[j] nothing on earth, and possessing wealth.[k] Furthermore, they were far from the Sidonians and had no dealings with Aram.[l] 8 When they came to their kinsfolk at Zorah and Eshtaol, they said to them, "What do you report?" 9 They said, "Come, let us go up against them; for we have seen the land, and it is very good. Will you do nothing? Do not be slow to go, but enter in and possess the land. 10 When you go, you will come to an unsuspecting people. The land is broad—God has indeed given it into your hands—a place where there is no lack of anything on earth."

11 Six hundred men of the Danite clan, armed with weapons of war, set out from Zorah and Eshtaol, 12 and went up and encamped at Kiriath-jearim in Judah. On this account that place is called Mahaneh-dan[m] to this day; it is west of Kiriath-jearim. 13 From there they passed on to the hill country of Ephraim, and came to the house of Micah.

14 Then the five men who had gone to spy out the land (that is, Laish) said to their comrades, "Do you know that in these buildings there are an ephod, teraphim, and an idol of cast metal? Now therefore consider what you will do." 15 So they turned in that direction and came to the house of the young Levite, at the home of Micah, and greeted him. 16 While the six hundred men of the Danites, armed with their weapons of war, stood by the entrance of the gate, 17 the five men who had gone to spy out the land proceeded to enter and take the idol of cast metal, the ephod, and the teraphim.[n] The priest was standing by the entrance of the gate with the six hundred men armed with weapons of war. 18 When the men went into Micah's house and took the idol of cast metal, the ephod, and the teraphim, the priest said to them, "What are you doing?" 19 They said to him, "Keep quiet! Put your hand over your mouth, and come with us, and be to us a father and a priest. Is it better for you to be priest to the house of one person, or to be priest to a tribe and clan in Israel?" 20 Then the priest accepted the offer. He took the ephod, the teraphim, and the idol, and went along with the people.

21 So they resumed their journey, putting the little ones, the livestock, and the goods in front of them. 22 When they were some distance from the home of Micah, the men who were in the houses near Micah's house were called out, and they overtook the Danites. 23 They shouted to the Danites, who turned around and said to Micah, "What is the matter that you come with such a company?" 24 He replied, "You take my gods that I made, and the priest, and go away, and what have I left? How then can you ask me, 'What is the matter?'" 25 And the Danites said to him, "You had better not let your voice be heard among us or else hot-tempered fellows will attack you, and you will lose your life and the lives of your household." 26 Then the Danites went their way. When Micah saw that they were too strong for him, he turned and went back to his home.

j Cn Compare 18.10: Meaning of Heb uncertain k Meaning of Heb uncertain l Symmachus: Heb with anyone m That is Camp of Dan n Compare 17.4, 5; 18.14: Heb teraphim and the cast metal

was meant to be. 18.9–10 The Danite assembly is spurred on by the report of the spies, so that what began as the prospect of peaceful resettlement in the north becomes the Lord's conquest of Micah's place (without bloodshed), followed by the Danites' unnecessary slaughter of the peaceable folk of Laish. 18.11–13 These verses explain the existence and location of Mahaneh-dan. Six hundred reads like an exaggeration, given that Dan is regarded as a clan (as is Judah in 17.7). 18.12 Kiriath-jearim, Hebrew, "Forestville," was a border town of the tribes of Judah, Benjamin, and Dan, lying northeast of Zorah and Eshtaol, and about eight miles northwest of Jerusalem. On this account, a late etymological note, perhaps meant to distinguish this "Camp of Dan" from the one in 13.25. 18.14–26 The Danites steal Micah's cult objects and entice away the priest. 18.14 The teraphim and idol are here distinct objects (cf. note on 17.5). 18.15 They greeted him, i.e., "asked about his well-being" (Hebrew shalom). 18.19 A father and a priest. See note on 17.10. In Num 26.42 the tribe of Dan consists of a single clan, which might consist of a town and its satellite villages. 18.25 Danites are caricatured as hot-tempered, lit. "bitter of soul," like a bear robbed of her cubs (2 Sam 17.8). 18.26 Micah went back to his home, like the Israelites after the "providential" demise of Abimelech (9.55).

The Danites Settle in Laish

27 The Danites, having taken what
Micah had made, and the priest who belonged to him, came to Laish, to a people
quiet and unsuspecting, put them to the
sword, and burned down the city.
28 There was no deliverer, because it was
far from Sidon and they had no dealings
with Aram.[o] It was in the valley that belongs to Beth-rehob. They rebuilt the city,
and lived in it. 29 They named the city
Dan, after their ancestor Dan, who was
born to Israel; but the name of the city
was formerly Laish. 30 Then the Danites
set up the idol for themselves. Jonathan
son of Gershom, son of Moses,[p] and his
sons were priests to the tribe of the Danites until the time the land went into captivity. 31 So they maintained as their own
Micah's idol that he had made, as long as
the house of God was at Shiloh.

The Levite's Concubine

19 In those days, when there was no
king in Israel, a certain Levite, residing in the remote parts of the hill country of Ephraim, took to himself a
concubine from Bethlehem in Judah.
2 But his concubine became angry with[q]
him, and she went away from him to her
father's house at Bethlehem in Judah, and
was there some four months. 3 Then her
husband set out after her, to speak tenderly to her and bring her back. He had
with him his servant and a couple of donkeys. When he reached[r] her father's
house, the girl's father saw him and came
with joy to meet him. 4 His father-in-law,
the girl's father, made him stay, and he
remained with him three days; so they ate
and drank, and he[s] stayed there. 5 On
the fourth day they got up early in the
morning, and he prepared to go; but the
girl's father said to his son-in-law, "Fortify
yourself with a bit of food, and after that
you may go." 6 So the two men sat and ate
and drank together; and the girl's father
said to the man, "Why not spend the night
and enjoy yourself?" 7 When the man got
up to go, his father-in-law kept urging
him until he spent the night there again.
8 On the fifth day he got up early in the
morning to leave; and the girl's father
said, "Fortify yourself." So they lingered[t]
until the day declined, and the two of
them ate and drank.[u] 9 When the man
with his concubine and his servant got up
to leave, his father-in-law, the girl's father,

o Cn Compare verse 7: Heb *with anyone* *p* Another reading is *son of Manasseh* *q* Gk OL: Heb *prostituted herself against* *r* Gk: Heb *she brought him* *s* Compare verse 7 and Gk: Heb *they* *t* Cn: Heb *Linger* *u* Gk: Heb lacks *and drank*

18.27–31 Dan's atrocious conquest of Laish and establishment of the notorious cult center. Micah's unholy cult was dismantled and intentionally exploited by the Danites on their way to the massacre of Laish's inhabitants. **18.28** *Far from Sidon . . . no dealings with Aram* echoes v. 7 for emphasis. **18.30** *Jonathan . . . Moses.* At last the priestly family is identified. In the Hebrew text a letter has been inserted to spell "Manasseh," avoiding the reference to Moses that implies idol worship on the part of his descendants. *Captivity* probably refers to the end of the Northern Kingdom and the removal of the Danites from that location after 721 B.C.E. **18.31** The Danite sanctuary is ironically devalued by reference to *Shiloh,* some ten miles north of Bethel, east of the main highway, regarded by King Josiah's historians as the one legitimate sanctuary in the premonarchical period. The Josian edition of Judges (Dtr 1; see Introduction) perhaps ended here.

19.1–21.25 Tragically misled, Israel reacts to the unspeakable outrage of gang rape and murder (ch. 19) in such a way as to compound the tragedy many times over. Civil war nearly obliterates the tribe of Benjamin (ch. 20). The final scenes, an ancient counterpart to modern theater of the absurd, show Israel maneuvering to recover from disastrous consequences of slavish reliance upon archaic institutions (ch. 21). These were old and painful memories, reworked by editors in exile (Dtr 2; see Introduction) when, once again, it was time for Israel to make a new start. **19.1** *No king in Israel* laments the lack of human kingship (17.6; 18.1) but also, by implication, Israel's dysfunctional confession of the Lord's sovereignty and governance by covenantal ethic. The story of a *Levite* from the *hill country of Ephraim* is a narrative inversion of the preceding story of a Levite from Bethlehem in the south (17.7). This northern Levite appears to be well established. He has a *concubine,* or wife of secondary rank, from Bethlehem. **19.2** Israelite law did not allow for divorce by the wife. She became an adulteress by walking out. **19.3** The husband seeks reconciliation, suggesting that she is the offended party. A *servant and a couple of donkeys* give the appearance of prosperous self-sufficiency, in contrast to the circumstances of the young Levite in ch. 17. **19.4–9** The father-in-law will be pleased to see his daughter return with her husband, but his

said to him, "Look, the day has worn on until it is almost evening. Spend the night. See, the day has drawn to a close. Spend the night here and enjoy yourself. Tomorrow you can get up early in the morning for your journey, and go home."

10 But the man would not spend the night; he got up and departed, and arrived opposite Jebus (that is, Jerusalem). He had with him a couple of saddled donkeys, and his concubine was with him. 11 When they were near Jebus, the day was far spent, and the servant said to his master, "Come now, let us turn aside to this city of the Jebusites, and spend the night in it." 12 But his master said to him, "We will not turn aside into a city of foreigners, who do not belong to the people of Israel; but we will continue on to Gibeah." 13 Then he said to his servant, "Come, let us try to reach one of these places, and spend the night at Gibeah or at Ramah." 14 So they passed on and went their way; and the sun went down on them near Gibeah, which belongs to Benjamin. 15 They turned aside there, to go in and spend the night at Gibeah. He went in and sat down in the open square of the city, but no one took them in to spend the night.

16 Then at evening there was an old man coming from his work in the field. The man was from the hill country of Ephraim, and he was residing in Gibeah. (The people of the place were Benjaminites.) 17 When the old man looked up and saw the wayfarer in the open square of the city, he said, "Where are you going and where do you come from?" 18 He answered him, "We are passing from Bethlehem in Judah to the remote parts of the hill country of Ephraim, from which I come. I went to Bethlehem in Judah; and I am going to my home.ᵛ Nobody has offered to take me in. 19 We your servants have straw and fodder for our donkeys, with bread and wine for me and the woman and the young man along with us. We need nothing more." 20 The old man said, "Peace be to you. I will care for all your wants; only do not spend the night in the square." 21 So he brought him into his house, and fed the donkeys; they washed their feet, and ate and drank.

Gibeah's Crime

22 While they were enjoying themselves, the men of the city, a perverse lot, surrounded the house, and started pounding on the door. They said to the old man, the master of the house, "Bring out the man who came into your house, so that we may have intercourse with him." 23 And the man, the master of the house, went out to them and said to them, "No, my brothers, do not act so wickedly. Since this man is my guest, do not do this vile thing. 24 Here are my virgin daughter and his concubine; let me bring them out now. Ravish them and do whatever you want to them; but against this man do not do such a vile thing." 25 But the men would not listen to him. So the man seized his concubine, and put her out to them. They wantonly raped her, and abused her all through the night until the morning. And

v Gk Compare 19.29. Heb *to the house of the LORD*

---

hospitality will create a new crisis. **19.9** *Go home,* lit. "go to your tent." This term perhaps explains the Levite's reluctance to leave the lavish setting. **19.10** The narrator implies that they might have been safe and atrocity avoided at Canaanite *Jebus* (the pre-Israelite name for Jerusalem; see 1.21). **19.12** *Gibeah,* King Saul's hometown, a few miles north of Jerusalem. **19.16–21** The only resident of Gibeah to take up the obligation of hospitality is likewise from the Ephraimite hill country. The Levite meets with the same hospitality from the elderly Levite as he had received from his father-in-law in Bethlehem. **19.18** *Home,* possibly not a "tent" (see note on 19.9). **19.19** The Levite has feed for his donkeys and food and wine for his entire party. All he needs is a roof. **19.21** The traveler lets the old man do the foddering. **19.22–30** This story has striking similarities to that of Sodom and Gomorrah (Gen 19.4–11). Both stories hinge on a breakdown or misuse of the obligation of hospitality. Also, the locals complain of Lot, "This fellow came here as an alien, and he would play the judge!" (Gen 19.9). Here the Levite will self-righteously elevate himself to the leadership role. **19.22** *They were enjoying themselves* verbally echoes 16.25, where the Philistine crowd demands that Samson entertain them. *Perverse lot,* hell-raisers, lit. "sons of Belial," a malicious character of the mythic underworld ("perdition" in Ps 18.4; 2 Sam 22.5–6). *Have intercourse.* The Hebrew root is *yd',* "to know." With the offer of the young women (v. 24), the ambiguity disappears. **19.23–25** Here the obligation of hospitality is grotesquely acted out by the men for their own protection. **19.25** It is not clear which

as the dawn began to break, they let her go. 26 As morning appeared, the woman came and fell down at the door of the man's house where her master was, until it was light.

27 In the morning her master got up, opened the doors of the house, and when he went out to go on his way, there was his concubine lying at the door of the house, with her hands on the threshold. 28 "Get up," he said to her, "we are going." But there was no answer. Then he put her on the donkey; and the man set out for his home. 29 When he had entered his house, he took a knife, and grasping his concubine he cut her into twelve pieces, limb by limb, and sent her throughout all the territory of Israel. 30 Then he commanded the men whom he sent, saying, "Thus shall you say to all the Israelites, 'Has such a thing ever happened w since the day that the Israelites came up from the land of Egypt until this day? Consider it, take counsel, and speak out.'"

The Other Tribes Attack Benjamin

20 Then all the Israelites came out, from Dan to Beer-sheba, including the land of Gilead, and the congregation assembled in one body before the LORD at Mizpah. 2 The chiefs of all the people, of all the tribes of Israel, presented themselves in the assembly of the people of God, four hundred thousand foot-soldiers bearing arms. 3 (Now the Benjaminites heard that the people of Israel had gone up to Mizpah.) And the Is-raelites said, "Tell us, how did this criminal act come about?" 4 The Levite, the husband of the woman who was mur-dered, answered, "I came to Gibeah that belongs to Benjamin, I and my concubine, to spend the night. 5 The lords of Gibeah rose up against me, and surrounded the house at night. They intended to kill me, and they raped my concubine until she died. 6 Then I took my concubine and cut her into pieces, and sent her throughout the whole extent of Israel's territory; for they have committed a vile outrage in Is-rael. 7 So now, you Israelites, all of you, give your advice and counsel here."

8 All the people got up as one, saying, "We will not any of us go to our tents, nor will any of us return to our houses. 9 But now this is what we will do to Gibeah: we will go up x against it by lot. 10 We will take ten men of a hundred throughout all the tribes of Israel, and a hundred of a thousand, and a thousand of ten thou-sand, to bring provisions for the troops, who are going to repay y Gibeah of Benja-min for all the disgrace that they have done in Israel." 11 So all the men of Israel gathered against the city, united as one.

12 The tribes of Israel sent men through all the tribe of Benjamin, saying, "What crime is this that has been commit-ted among you? 13 Now then, hand over those scoundrels in Gibeah, so that we may put them to death, and purge the evil

w Compare Gk: Heb 30And all who saw it said, "Such a thing has not happened or been seen   x Gk: Heb lacks we will go up   y Compare Gk: Meaning of Heb uncertain

---

man *seized his concubine, and put her out.* **19.28** *No answer.* The Greek text continues, "for she was dead," resolving the ambiguity. **19.29** *House* may be used sarcastically, to judge from the father-in-law's usage in v. 9, "tent"; see note on 19.9. The man's actions are a gross caricature of practices for raising an emergency force that ap-pear elsewhere in the OT and other texts of the ancient Near East. Cf. Saul summoning the militia (with twelve parts of an ox; 1 Sam 11.7) and the prophet Ahijah dramatically announcing division of the kingdom (with twelve pieces of a garment; 1 Kings 11.30–39). This story will get worse be-fore it gets better.

20.1–48 Cf. the assembly at Shechem (Josh 24) and the promissory oath of the tribes there. Here the assembly is stampeded into wrathful in-dignation by one man telling half of the truth. **20.1** *All the Israelites.* This phrase is used in the indictment at the outset (2.1–5) but nowhere else in Judges. In 8.27, after Gideon had likewise used the militia to pursue private vengeance, *all Israel* prostituted itself at his ephod. *From Dan to Beer-sheba,* from the northern to the southern limits of Israel. *Mizpah,* Hebrew, "Lookout" or "Watch-tower," probably Tell en-Nasbeh, eight miles north of Jerusalem. **20.5** The Levite's testi-mony, enlarging the threat to himself, passes over his own culpability in surrendering the concu-bine. **20.10** *Ten men . . . the troops.* A 10 percent quota of eligible men, anticipating that one-tenth will be needed as a quartermaster corps, is plausi-ble. In Num 1.36–37 Benjamin counted thirty-five units totaling four hundred. On another occasion Benjamin's quota was forty-five units to-taling six hundred (Num 26.38–41). **20.11** *All the men of Israel* are *united* as never before in the book, except at Gideon's ephod (8.27).

from Israel." But the Benjaminites would not listen to their kinsfolk, the Israelites. 14 The Benjaminites came together out of the towns to Gibeah, to go out to battle against the Israelites. 15 On that day the Benjaminites mustered twenty-six thousand armed men from their towns, besides the inhabitants of Gibeah. 16 Of all this force, there were seven hundred picked men who were left-handed; every one could sling a stone at a hair, and not miss. 17 And the Israelites, apart from Benjamin, mustered four hundred thousand armed men, all of them warriors.

18   The Israelites proceeded to go up to Bethel, where they inquired of God, "Which of us shall go up first to battle against the Benjaminites?" And the LORD answered, "Judah shall go up first."

19   Then the Israelites got up in the morning, and encamped against Gibeah. 20 The Israelites went out to battle against Benjamin; and the Israelites drew up the battle line against them at Gibeah. 21 The Benjaminites came out of Gibeah, and struck down on that day twenty-two thousand of the Israelites. 23 z The Israelites went up and wept before the LORD until the evening; and they inquired of the LORD, "Shall we again draw near to battle against our kinsfolk the Benjaminites?" And the LORD said, "Go up against them." 22 The Israelites took courage, and again formed the battle line in the same place where they had formed it on the first day.

24   So the Israelites advanced against the Benjaminites the second day. 25 Benjamin moved out against them from Gibeah

the second day, and struck down eighteen thousand of the Israelites, all of them armed men. 26 Then all the Israelites, the whole army, went back to Bethel and wept, sitting there before the LORD; they fasted that day until evening. Then they offered burnt offerings and sacrifices of well-being before the LORD. 27 And the Israelites inquired of the LORD (for the ark of the covenant of God was there in those days, 28 and Phinehas son of Eleazar, son of Aaron, ministered before it in those days), saying, "Shall we go out once more to battle against our kinsfolk the Benjaminites, or shall we desist?" The LORD answered, "Go up, for tomorrow I will give them into your hand."

29   So Israel stationed men in ambush around Gibeah. 30 Then the Israelites went up against the Benjaminites on the third day, and set themselves in array against Gibeah, as before. 31 When the Benjaminites went out against the army, they were drawn away from the city. As before they began to inflict casualties on the troops, along the main roads, one of which goes up to Bethel and the other to Gibeah, as well as in the open country, killing about thirty men of Israel. 32 The Benjaminites thought, "They are being routed before us, as previously." But the Israelites said, "Let us retreat and draw them away from the city toward the roads." 33 The main body of the Israelites drew back its battle line to Baal-tamar, while those Israelites who were in ambush

z Verses 22 and 23 are transposed

20.15–16 Considering the odds against Benjamin, we should probably understand *twenty-six thousand* as twenty-six military units, totaling *seven hundred* individuals (see notes on 1.4; 20.10), who were able to hold out against the entire militia because they were all superb marksmen. 20.18 *Bethel*, Hebrew, "House of God," may refer instead to a sanctuary at Mizpah (see v. 23). *Which of us . . . first* is the same question as in 1.1. *Judah* is chosen, as in 1.2, but here it is chosen for civil war. 20.21 *Struck down*, lit., "ruined on the ground," "made ineffective." The same idiom describes Onan's action (Gen 38.9). It does not describe the total loss of *twenty-two* units but indicates enough damage to force their retreat. 20.22–23 If the location is a sanctuary at Mizpah, these verses should not be transposed as the NRSV suggests (see text note z). 20.22 *Place*, or "holy place," as in 2.5. 20.25 The collapse of another

eighteen units (a total of forty in two battles) appears nearly catastrophic. Like Gideon's force against the Midianites (7.2–8), the Israelite army is reduced to a decimated level so that victory can only be attributed to the Lord. 20.26–28 *Bethel* is the proper place of inquiry because *the ark of the covenant of God was there*, ironically in the keeping of a northern *Aaronite* priest. *Phinehas* is an Egyptian name meaning "The Black Man." Only here do the Israelites ask the prior question, *Shall we go*, and only here is the response reliable: *tomorrow I will give them into your hand.* 20.29–43 Two accounts of the victory are given (vv. 29–36; 37–43). There are strong resemblances to the takeover of Ai (Josh 8), where ambush was the Lord's strategy. 20.31 *About thirty men*. This figure, the actual casualties on one occasion, is important for perspective on the numbers elsewhere in the chapter. 20.33 *Baal-tamar*, somewhere

rushed out of their place west[a] of Geba.
34 There came against Gibeah ten thousand picked men out of all Israel, and the battle was fierce. But the Benjaminites did not realize that disaster was close upon them.

35 The LORD defeated Benjamin before Israel; and the Israelites destroyed twenty-five thousand one hundred men of Benjamin that day, all of them armed.

36 Then the Benjaminites saw that they were defeated.[b]

The Israelites gave ground to Benjamin, because they trusted to the troops in ambush that they had stationed against Gibeah. 37 The troops in ambush rushed quickly upon Gibeah. Then they put the whole city to the sword. 38 Now the agreement between the main body of Israel and the men in ambush was that when they sent up a cloud of smoke out of the city 39 the main body of Israel should turn in battle. But Benjamin had begun to inflict casualties on the Israelites, killing about thirty of them; so they thought, "Surely they are defeated before us, as in the first battle." 40 But when the cloud, a column of smoke, began to rise out of the city, the Benjaminites looked behind them—and there was the whole city going up in smoke toward the sky! 41 Then the main body of Israel turned, and the Benjaminites were dismayed, for they saw that disaster was close upon them. 42 Therefore they turned away from the Israelites in the direction of the wilderness; but the battle overtook them, and those who came out of the city[c] were slaughtering them in between.[d] 43 Cutting down[e] the Benjaminites, they pursued them from Nohah[f] and trod them down as far as a place east of Gibeah. 44 Eighteen thousand Benjaminites fell, all of them courageous fighters. 45 When they turned and fled toward the wilderness to the rock of Rimmon, five thousand of them were cut down on the main roads, and they were pursued as far as Gidom, and two thousand of them were slain. 46 So all who fell that day of Benjamin were twenty-five thousand arms-bearing men, all of them courageous fighters. 47 But six hundred turned and fled toward the wilderness to the rock of Rimmon, and remained at the rock of Rimmon for four months. 48 Meanwhile, the Israelites turned back against the Benjaminites, and put them to the sword—the city, the people, the animals, and all that remained. Also the remaining towns they set on fire.

The Benjaminites Saved from Extinction

21 Now the Israelites had sworn at Mizpah, "No one of us shall give his daughter in marriage to Benjamin." 2 And the people came to Bethel, and sat there until evening before God, and they lifted up their voices and wept bitterly. 3 They said, "O LORD, the God of Israel, why has it come to pass that today there should be one tribe lacking in Israel?" 4 On the next day, the people got up early, and built an altar there, and offered burnt offerings and sacrifices of well-being. 5 Then the Israelites said, "Which

---

a Gk Vg: Heb *in the plain*   b This sentence is continued by verse 45.   c Compare Vg and some Gk Mss: Heb *cities*   d Compare Syr: Meaning of Heb uncertain   e Gk: Heb *Surrounding*   f Gk: Heb *pursued them at their resting place*

---

near Gibeah, is otherwise unknown. **20.35** *The LORD* was not explicitly credited with Benjamin's earlier victories. *Twenty-five thousand one hundred*, more likely "twenty-five military units, one hundred men." See note on 1.4. If the total of Benjamin's force is seven hundred (see note on 20.15–16), a loss of 14 percent would be extremely costly. **20.43** *Nohah* is elsewhere a "son" of Benjamin (1 Chr 8.2). **20.46** *Courageous fighters* is an *inclusio* (see note on 14.5–10a) with *valiant men* (18.2). **20.47–48** The bulk of the force, *six hundred*, fled and went into hiding, to become the only Benjaminite survivors in the story.

21.1–25 This concluding chapter brings together two distinct stories: one concerning a punitive expedition against Jabesh-gilead, the other a most obscure abduction of young women during a vintage festival at Shiloh. **21.1–5** The problem of finding wives for the Benjaminites is emphasized in the *inclusio* (see note on 14.5–10a) formed by references to the oath (vv. 1, 5). **21.1** The prohibition of marriage with Benjaminites is previously unmentioned. **21.2** The Israelites *wept*, as in 2.4, but now *bitterly*. **21.3** *Lacking*, lit. "counted out." The Hebrew root *pqd* has to do with setting quotas for military service. **21.4** *Got up early*, better "busied themselves." Receiving no oracular response to their *offerings*, however, they must rely on their own wits. **21.5** One more small-scale civil war will be necessary.

of all the tribes of Israel did not come up in the assembly to the LORD?" For a solemn oath had been taken concerning whoever did not come up to the LORD to Mizpah, saying, "That one shall be put to death." 6 But the Israelites had compassion for Benjamin their kin, and said, "One tribe is cut off from Israel this day. 7 What shall we do for wives for those who are left, since we have sworn by the LORD that we will not give them any of our daughters as wives?"

8 Then they said, "Is there anyone from the tribes of Israel who did not come up to the LORD to Mizpah?" It turned out that no one from Jabesh-gilead had come to the camp, to the assembly. 9 For when the roll was called among the people, not one of the inhabitants of Jabesh-gilead was there. 10 So the congregation sent twelve thousand soldiers there and commanded them, "Go, put the inhabitants of Jabesh-gilead to the sword, including the women and the little ones. 11 This is what you shall do; every male and every woman that has lain with a male you shall devote to destruction." 12 And they found among the inhabitants of Jabesh-gilead four hundred young virgins who had never slept with a man and brought them to the camp at Shiloh, which is in the land of Canaan.

13 Then the whole congregation sent word to the Benjaminites who were at the rock of Rimmon, and proclaimed peace to them. 14 Benjamin returned at that time; and they gave them the women whom they had saved alive of the women of Jabesh-gilead; but they did not suffice for them.

15 The people had compassion on Benjamin because the LORD had made a breach in the tribes of Israel. 16 So the elders of the congregation said, "What shall we do for wives for those who are left, since there are no women left in Benjamin?" 17 And they said, "There must be heirs for the survivors of Benjamin, in order that a tribe may not be blotted out from Israel. 18 Yet we cannot give any of our daughters to them as wives." For the Israelites had sworn, "Cursed be anyone who gives a wife to Benjamin." 19 So they said, "Look, the yearly festival of the LORD is taking place at Shiloh, which is north of Bethel, on the east of the highway that goes up from Bethel to Shechem, and south of Lebonah." 20 And they instructed the Benjaminites, saying, "Go and lie in wait in the vineyards, 21 and watch; when the young women of Shiloh come out to dance in the dances, then come out of the vineyards and each of you carry off a wife for himself from the young women of Shiloh, and go to the land of Benjamin. 22 Then if their fathers or their brothers come to complain to us, we will say to them, 'Be generous and allow us to have them; because we did not capture in battle a wife for each man. But neither did you incur guilt by giving your daughters to them.' " 23 The Benjaminites did so; they took wives for each of them from the dancers whom they abducted. Then they went and returned to their territory, and rebuilt the towns, and lived in

---

21.6–12 These verses restate the problem and describe the proposal and implementation of a solution. **21.6** *Cut off.* The Hebrew root, *gd´*, is otherwise not used in the book, except in the name Gideon, "Hacker." **21.8** *Jabesh-gilead* lay in Transjordan. It is probably either Tell Abu Kharaz or Tell el-Meqbereh. The narrative elicits sympathy for a city later friendly and faithful to Saul. **21.11** *Devote to destruction,* or put under the ban (Hebrew *cherem*). After their tragic use of the ban against the Benjaminites (strongly suggested by 20.48), the Israelites now exercise compassion for the survivors by condemning another constituency. **21.12** *Shiloh,* situated at a respectable distance from both Mizpah and Bethel, is *in the land of Canaan,* a curious designation, signaling the irony of the situation. Conditions in the land, as the next scene will show, had not changed very

much under Israelite control. **21.14–15** That there are not enough captive women to go around reinforces the ironic truth that *the LORD had made a breach in the tribes of Israel.* **21.16–23** The story assumes that the venerable covenant sanctuary at Shiloh had reverted to pre-Israelite patterns of cultic revelry. The theme of the rape of maidens in comparable circumstances recurs in Greek poetry. **21.16** *Elders of the congregation* suggests exilic editing. **21.19** The elders seem to be thinking out loud, recalling the yearly festival at Shiloh (1 Sam 1.3) and struggling to fix its location precisely. **21.22** *To complain,* or "contend," Hebrew *riv,* as in Gideon's name Jerubbaal (see note on 6.25–32) and in Jephthah's negotiations (see note on 11.12–28). The rationalization here makes acceding to the abduction appear as a matter of do-it-yourself grace. **21.25** The cliché that

them. 24So the Israelites departed from there at that time by tribes and families, and they went out from there to their own territories.

25 In those days there was no king in Israel; all the people did what was right in their own eyes.

---

first appears in 17.6, where it definitely delivers a negative judgment in the era of King Josiah, sounds a bit different at the end of the book. Far from approving of the atrocious behaviors in these stories, it commends a manner of decision making, in fact encouraging survivors in exile to "do what is right in their own eyes," i.e., be governed by internal ethical control, as the people were in the presettlement era of Moses (Deut 12.8).

RUTH

THE BOOK OF RUTH, a short narrative with a pastoral tone, is one of the most beautiful pieces of literature in the Bible. The few characters in the story, with the exception of Boaz, are unmentioned elsewhere in the Hebrew Bible, and, in contrast to most other biblical narratives, the concern seems to be with a private family rather than national or international affairs. The plot revolves around family relationships—between husbands, wives, children, in-laws, and kinsmen—and the role each member plays in filling the needs of other members and hence the family as a whole. The characters' names seem highly symbolic of their roles. Elimelech, "My God is King," suggests the period before human kings ruled Israel—the time of the judges in which the story is set. The epilogue ends with the human king *par excellence*, King David. Mahlon and Chilion mean "Sickness" and "Spent"; Orpah, "Back of the Neck," turns her back to Naomi. Naomi, whose name means "Pleasant," calls herself Mara, "Bitter," when she returns bereaved and impoverished to Bethlehem. Ruth has been interpreted as deriving from the word meaning "Friend, Companion," and Boaz from two words meaning "In Him is Strength." But the apparent simplicity of the plot and characters belie the seriousness of the book's themes.

Major Themes

According to rabbinic tradition, the main theme is *chesed* (Hebrew), loyalty or faithfulness arising from commitment. *Chesed* may pertain between God and a human community and between members of a family or community. The main characters, Naomi, Ruth, and Boaz, all manifest acts of *chesed*. Naomi shows concern for the welfare of her widowed daughters-in-law, especially Ruth, although technically she has no obligation toward them. Ruth's *chesed* in cleaving to Naomi goes beyond all expectation, and her seeking marriage with Boaz, the family protector, underlines her loyalty to the family. Boaz, too, acts with *chesed* when he accepts the double responsibility of land purchase and marriage, thereby preserving the lineage and inheritance of a family that were almost lost.